McDougal Littell

THE LANGUAGE OF
LITERATURE

STUDENT GUIDE TO THE CALIFORNIA STANDARDS

At the beginning of every lesson in this book, you will see a listing of Key Standards covered in the lesson. You will often see Other Standards as well that relate to the lesson. The standards are identified by combinations of letters and numbers (like R1.1). These combinations are codes that refer to standards from the Reading and Language Arts Framework for California Public Schools. The standards define the skills that you are expected to develop during 7th grade.

The following chart contains a simplified version of those standards. When you see a list of codes, you can use this chart to find out which skills you will be studying as you work through the selection. In this way, you will be able to keep track of what you learn throughout the year.

READING (R)

1.0 Word Study, Fluency, and Vocabulary Development

Use word origins, word relationships, and context clues to figure out the meaning of unfamiliar words.

Vocabulary and Concept Development

1.1 Identify idioms, analogies, metaphors, and similes in prose and poetry.

1.2 Use knowledge of roots and affixes to understand vocabulary in different content areas.

1.3 Use context clues (definition, example, restatement, contrast) to determine the meaning of unknown words.

2.0 Reading Comprehension (Informational Materials)

Read and understand purposes of and different types of reading materials. Restate and connect key ideas, arguments, and points of view. Use the structure and organization of a piece for help in understanding it.

Structural Features of Informational Materials

2.1 Understand differences between various categories of informational materials (such as textbooks, newspapers, and manuals).

2.2 Locate information by using different types of consumer, workplace, and public documents.

2.3 Analyze text that uses cause-and-effect organization.

Comprehension and Analysis of Text

2.4 Identify an author's argument and point of view in a text.

2.5 Understand and explain the use of a simple device by following technical directions.

Expository Critique

2.6 Evaluate the strength and accuracy of the evidence an author uses to support a claim. Recognize bias and stereotyping.

3.0 Literary Response and Analysis

Read and respond to important works of literature. Understand the meaning of the ideas presented and connect them to other pieces of literature.

Structural Features of Literature

3.1 Be able to describe the purposes and characteristics of different forms of prose, such as the short story, novel, or essay.

Analysis of Narrative Text

3.2 Identify events that advance the plot and describe how they explain the past, present, and future.

3.3 Analyze characters by examining what they think, say, and do, and by studying the words of the narrator and the reactions of other characters.

3.4 Identify and analyze themes that appear across works.

3.5 Contrast points of view (first and third person, limited and omniscient) and explain how they affect the narrative.

Literary Criticism

3.6 Analyze several responses to a literary work. Decide how different literary elements may have affected those responses.

WRITING (W)

1.0 Writing Strategies

Use the writing process to write clear, coherent, and focused essays. The writing should show an understanding of audience and purpose and contain an introduction, supporting details, and a conclusion.

Organization and Focus

1.1 Choose an appropriate type of organization, and use transitions to connect ideas effectively.

1.2 Support statements with such evidence as facts, statistics, examples, and anecdotes.

1.3 Use such strategies as notetaking, outlining, and summarizing to help determine a structure for composition drafts.

Research and Technology

1.4 Identify research topics, and develop questions and ideas to help guide investigation of the topic.

1.5 Use citations and a properly formatted bibliography to give credit to all sources used.

1.6 Create effective documents by using word-processing skills and publishing programs.

Evaluation and Revision

1.7 Revise writing to improve organization, word choice, and logic.

2.0 Types of Writing

Write narrative, expository, persuasive, and descriptive texts that show correct grammar, usage, punctuation, and spelling. Writing should also demonstrate understanding of all the skills mentioned in Writing Standard 1.0.

2.1 Write fictional or autobiographical narratives that contain a standard plot line, complex major and minor characters, and a definite setting.

2.2 Write responses to literature that present interpretations that show careful reading and understanding of the text, and that support the interpretation with evidence from the selection.

2.3 Write research reports that contain a clear focus, include evidence gathered through a formal research process, and demonstrate documentation of sources.

2.4 Write a persuasive composition that presents a clear proposition or proposal, supports that position with evidence, and addresses a reader's possible arguments.

2.5 Write summaries of reading materials that include the main idea and key supporting details, and that are written in the student's own words.

WRITTEN AND ORAL ENGLISH LANGUAGE CONVENTIONS (LC)

Show an understanding of sentence structure, grammar, punctuation, capitalization, and spelling.

1.0 English Language Conventions

1.1 Place modifiers correctly; use the active voice.

1.2 Identify and properly use infinitives and participles; have clear pronoun/antecedent references.

1.3 Identify all parts of speech and types of sentences.

1.4 Use the mechanics of writing correctly; demonstrate correct language usage.

1.5 Use hyphens, dashes, brackets, and semicolons correctly.

1.6 Use correct capitalization.

1.7 Correctly spell words when adding affixes to base words.

LISTENING AND SPEAKING (LS)

1.0 Listening and Speaking Strategies

Deliver oral presentations that present ideas clearly and show an awareness of audience. Evaluate the content of oral presentations.

Comprehension

1.1 Ask the speaker questions to gather information or evidence that supports the speaker's statements.

1.2 Determine the speaker's attitude.

1.3 Respond to persuasive messages by questioning, challenging, or agreeing with the statements.

Organization and Delivery of Oral Communication

1.4 Organize information to achieve a particular purpose, and to appeal to the audience.

1.5 Arrange supporting details, reasons, etc, in a way that will be most effective for the audience.

1.6 Use voice, gestures, and eye contact effectively to keep audience interested.

Evaluation of Oral and Media Communications

1.7 Provide helpful feedback to the speaker about both content and the effect on the listener.

1.8 Analyze the effect on the viewer of images, text, and sound in electronic journalism.

2.0 Types of Presentations and Their Characteristics

Deliver different types of well-organized formal presentations that show a command of standard American English and display the skills and strategies listed in Listening and Speaking Standard 1.0.

2.1 Deliver narrative presentations that contain a standard plot line, complex major and minor characters, and a definite setting.

2.2 Deliver oral summaries of articles and books that include the main idea and key supporting details, and that are written in the student's own words.

2.3 Deliver research presentations that contain a clear focus, include evidence gathered through a formal research process, and demonstrate documentation of sources.

2.4 Deliver persuasive presentations that present a clear proposition or proposal, support that position with evidence, and address a reader's possible arguments.

McDougal Littell

THE LANGUAGE OF
LITERATURE

McDougal Littell
A HOUGHTON MIFFLIN COMPANY
Evanston, Illinois • Boston • Dallas

Acknowledgments

Front Matter

    Grolier: "Arthur, King" reviewed by Carolyn W. Field, from *The New Book of Knowledge*. Copyright © 2000 by Grolier Incorporated. Reprinted by permission of Grolier, Inc.

    Chicago Tribune: "King Arthur leads patrons to Middle Ages" by Bob Goldsborough, from the *Chicago Tribune*, January 15, 1999. Copyright © 1999, Chicago Tribune Company. All rights reserved. Used with permission.

Unit One

    Simon & Schuster: "A Day's Wait," from *The Short Stories of Ernest Hemingway* by Ernest Hemingway. Copyright © 1933 by Charles Scribner's Sons. Copyright renewed © 1961 by Mary Hemingway. Reprinted with permission of Simon & Schuster, Inc.

    Harcourt Brace & Company: "Seventh Grade," from *Baseball in April and Other Stories* by Gary Soto. Copyright © 1990 by Gary Soto. Reprinted by permission of Harcourt Brace & Company.

    Hill and Wang: "Thank You, M'am," from *Short Stories* by Langston Hughes. Copyright © 1996 by Ramona Bass and Arnold Rampersad. Reprinted by permission of Hill and Wang, a division of Farrar, Straus & Giroux, Inc.

Continued on page R171

ISBN 0-618-11572-2

Senior Advisers

Cathy Barkett California Curriculum Consultant for McDougal Littell; formerly Administrator of the Curriculum Frameworks and Instructional Resources Office for the California Department of Education. Ms. Barkett reviewed the program for adherence to the guidelines set forth in the Reading Language Arts Framework for California Public Schools; she also worked as part of the development team for McDougal Littell's *California Standards Manager* and its support components.

Olga Bautista Reading Facilitator, Will C. Wood Middle School, Sacramento, California. Ms. Bautista served as a consultant on the *Bridges to Literature* component of the program, providing advice on reading and EL instruction during the development phase and reviewing final prototypes of both the Pupil Edition and the Teacher's Edition.

Linda Diamond Executive Vice-President, Consortium on Reading Excellence (CORE); co-author of *Building a Powerful Reading Program*. Ms. Diamond reviewed program components as part of the development of a teacher-training program designed to accompany those materials. She also reviewed and contributed to McDougal Littell's *Reading Toolkit*, the professional-development component of the program.

Jane Greene Literacy Intervention Specialist; Reading, Writing, Language, and Evaluation Consultant to schools nationwide; author of *LANGUAGE! A Literacy Intervention Curriculum*. Dr. Greene served as primary consultant and author on the *Bridges to Literature* component of the program, establishing the underlying goals and philosophy, advising on the tables of contents, reviewing prototypes, and supervising the development of the assessment strand.

Judy Lewis Director, state and federal programs for reading proficiency and high-risk populations, Folsom, California; Editor, *Context*, a newsletter for teachers with English learners in their classes. Ms. Lewis reviewed selections for the program and provided special guidance on the development of EL notes and support materials.

Sharon Sicinski-Skeans Assistant Professor of Reading, University of Houston-Clear Lake; former K-12 Language Arts Program Director, Spring Independent School District, Houston, Texas. Dr. Sicinski-Skeans served as primary consultant on the *InterActive Reader* component, providing guidance on prototype development and reviewing final manuscript.

Touchstone Applied Science, Inc. Developer of literacy and assessment tools, including the DRP reading formula. Created the placement and progress tests found in the *Reading Toolkit* and the *Bridges to Literature* component.

Multicultural Advisory Board

Dr. Joyce M. Bell Chairperson, English Department, Townview Magnet Center, Dallas, Texas

Dr. Eugenia W. Collier author; lecturer; Chairperson, Department of English and Language Arts and teacher of creative writing and American literature, Morgan State University, Maryland

Kathleen S. Fowler President, Palm Beach County Council of Teachers of English, Boca Raton Middle School, Boca Raton, Florida

Corey Lay ESL Department Chairperson, Chester Nimitz Middle School, Los Angeles Unified School District, Los Angeles, California

Noreen M. Rodriguez Trainer for Hillsborough County School District's Staff Development Division; independent consultant, Gaither High School, Tampa, Florida

Michelle Dixon Thompson Seabreeze High School, Daytona Beach, Florida

Teacher Review Panels

The following educators provided ongoing review during the development of the tables of contents, lesson design, and key components of the program.

CALIFORNIA

Steve Bass Eighth-Grade Team Leader, Meadowbrook Middle School, Poway Unified School District

Cynthia Brickey Eighth-Grade Academic Block Teacher, Kastner Intermediate School, Clovis Unified School District

Karen Buxton English Department Chairperson, Winston Churchill Middle School, San Juan School District

Sharon Cook Independent consultant, Fresno Unified School District

continued on pages R183

Manuscript Reviewers

The following educators reviewed prototype lessons and tables of contents during the development of *The Language of Literature* program

William A. Battaglia Herman Intermediate School, San Jose, California

Hugh Delle Broadway McCullough High School, The Woodlands, Texas

Robert M. Bucan National Mine Middle School, Ishpeming, Michigan

Ann E. Clayton Department Chairperson for Language Arts, Rockway Middle School, Miami, Florida

Hillary Crain Diegueño Middle School, Encinitas, California

Linda C. Dahl National Mine Middle School, Ishpeming, Michigan

Mary Jo Eustis Language Arts Coordinator, Lodi Unified School District, Lodi, California

Anita Graham Muirlands Middle School, La Jolla, California

Carol Hammons English Department Chair, Washington Middle School, Salinas, California

continued on page R184

Student Panel

LITERATURE REVIEWERS

The following students read and evaluated selections to assess their appeal for the seventh grade.

Tommy Bartsch, Schimelpfenig Middle School, Plano, Texas

Tai-Ling Bloomfield, Mears Jr. High/Alyeska Central School, Anchorage, Alaska

Gabriel Bonilla, George Washington Carver Middle School, Coconut Grove, Florida

Christopher Bradrick, Theodore Schor Middle School, Piscataway, New Jersey

Eric de Armas, George Washington Carver Middle School, Coconut Grove, Florida

Christel Fowler, W. I. Stevenson Middle School, Houston, Texas

Ashley Barnett Green, Cooper Intermediate School, Fairfax County, Virginia

Stephanie Hicks, Grant Sawyer School, Las Vegas, Nevada

David C. Hsu, Foothill Middle School, Walnut Creek, California

Chrissy Kennedy, Foothill Middle School, Walnut Creek, California

Tony Liberati, Hampton Middle School, Allison Park, Pennsylvania

Danae Lowe, Kenilworth Jr. High School, Petaluma, California

Leslie Michelle Martinez, Sam Houston Jr. High School, Irving, Texas

Michael F. Regula, Old Trail School, Bath, Ohio

Scott Stanley Terrill, Swartz Creek Middle School, Swartz Creek, Michigan

ACTIVE READERS

The following students participated in the development of The Active Reader: Skills and Strategies pages in this book:

Matt Catanzano

Sophia Durbano

Elvia Lopes

Steve Mtunis

Leah Jaffe

Chase Abreu

Angeli Forber-Pratt

Rafael Moses

Erlin Guillen

Lindsay Sheah

STUDENT MODEL WRITERS

The following students wrote the student models for Writing Workshop pages that appear in this book:

Shoshannah Seed

Kristin Richardson

Sabrina Probasco

Steve Hernandez

Stephen Shimshock

Rachel Lee Granzow

M. De los Santos

Andrea Martinez

Weston Sager

The Language of Literature
Overview

Table of Contents

Student Resource Bank

Reading Handbook
Vocabulary Handbook
Spelling Handbook
Writing Handbook
Grammar Handbook
Speaking and Listening Handbook
Research and Technology Handbook
Glossary of Literary and Reading Terms
Glossary of Words to Know in English and Spanish

Literature Connections

Each of the books in the *Literature Connections* series combines a novel or play with related readings—poems, stories, plays, personal essays, articles—that add new perspectives on the theme or subject matter of the longer work.

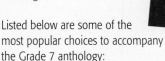

Listed below are some of the most popular choices to accompany the Grade 7 anthology:

The Call of the Wild* by Jack London

Across Five Aprils by Irene Hunt

The Clay Marble by Minfong Ho

The Diary of Anne Frank by Frances Goodrich and Albert Hackett

Dogsong by Gary Paulsen

The Glory Field by Walter Dean Myers

I, Juan de Pareja* by Elizabeth Borton de Treviño

Island of the Blue Dolphins by Scott O'Dell

Maniac Magee by Jerry Spinelli

Roll of Thunder, Hear My Cry* by Mildred D. Taylor

Taking Sides by Gary Soto

A Wrinkle in Time by Madeleine L'Engle

*A Spanish version is also available.

THE LANGUAGE OF LITERATURE

Reading Strategies Unit

Unit One

Learning from Experience

CALIFORNIA SOCIAL STUDIES CONNECTION
See Unit Six, "The Oral Tradition: Tales from Around the World" for links to Unit One.

Unit Two

Relationships

**CALIFORNIA
SOCIAL STUDIES
CONNECTION**

See Unit Six, "The Oral
Tradition: Tales from
Around the World"
for links to Unit Two.

READING AND WRITING SKILLS

Unit Three

Flights of Imagination

**CALIFORNIA
SOCIAL STUDIES
CONNECTION**
See Unit Six, "The Oral
Tradition: Tales from
Around the World"
for links to Unit Three.

Nothing Stays the Same

**CALIFORNIA
SOCIAL STUDIES
CONNECTION**

See Unit Six, "The Oral
Tradition: Tales from
Around the World"
for links to Unit Four.

Unit Five

Personal Challenges

CALIFORNIA SOCIAL STUDIES CONNECTION
See Unit Six, "The Oral Tradition: Tales from Around the World" for links to Unit Five.

Unit Six

THE ORAL TRADITION:
Tales from Around the World

The Language of Literature
Student Resource Bank

The Language of Literature
Teaching by Genre

Fiction

Nonfiction

The Language of Literature
Teaching by Genre

The Language of Literature
Special Features

Author Study

Comparing Literature

Learning the Language of Literature

Reading for Information

The Active Reader: Skills and Strategies

Writing Workshops

Communication Workshops

Building Vocabulary

Standardized Test Practice

Becoming an Active Reader

Active readers comprehend what they read and connect it to their own lives. An active reader asks questions, forms opinions, and visualizes scenes. The strategies in this special unit and throughout the book will help you become an active reader of all kinds of materials.

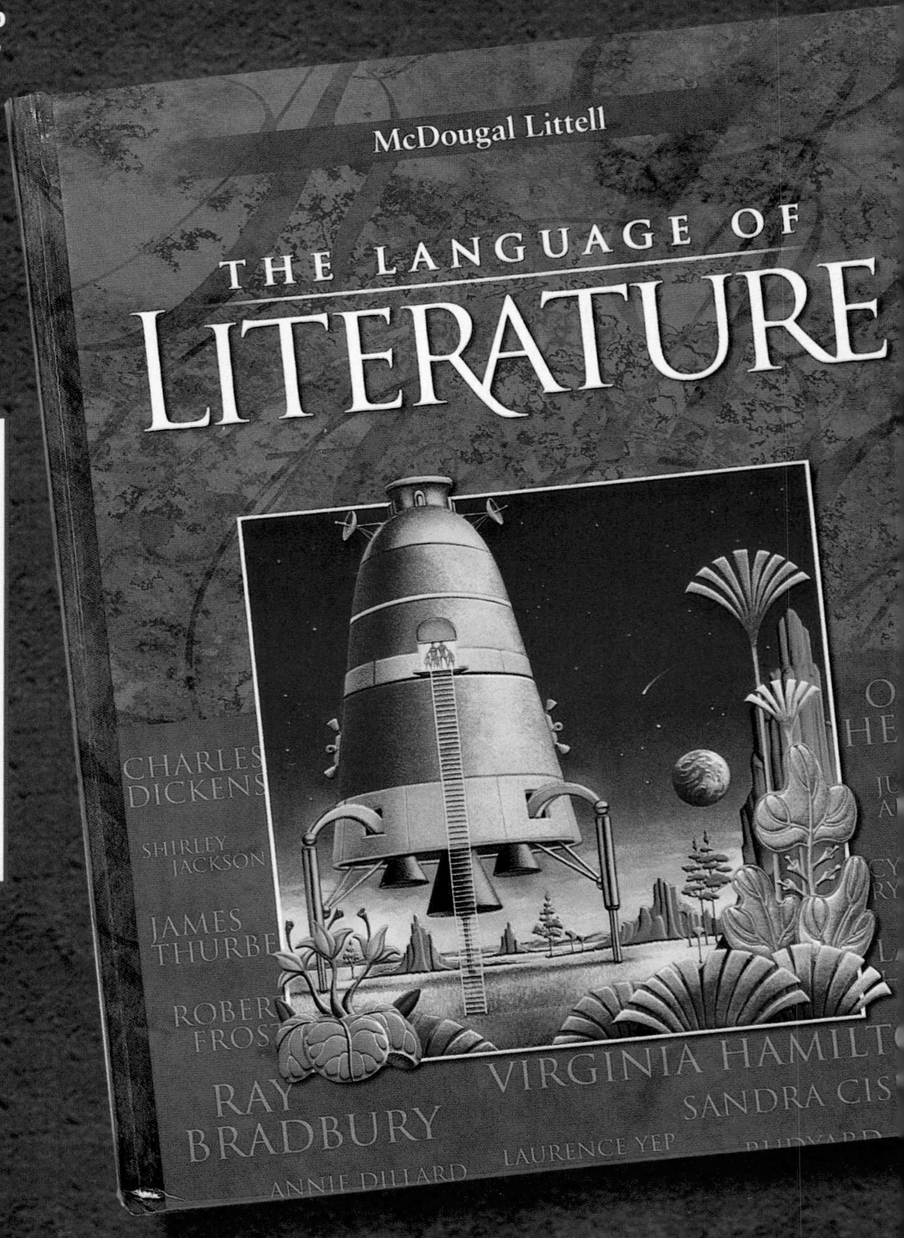

McDougal Littell

THE LANGUAGE OF

LITERATURE

CHARLES
DICKENS

SHIRLEY
JACKSON

JAMES
THURBE

ROBER
FROST

RAY
BRADBURY

VIRGINIA HAMILT

SANDRA CIS

ANNIE DILLARD   LAURENCE YEP

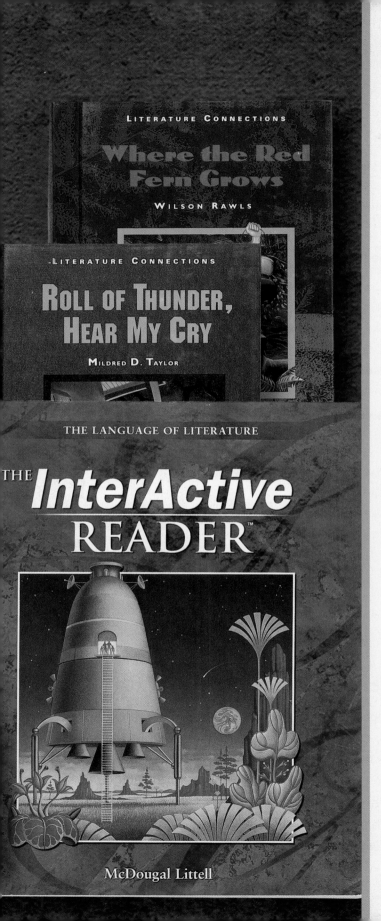

STRATEGIES FOR READING

Active readers learn and apply reading strategies to get the most out of what they read. Whether you are reading for information or for enjoyment, pause from time to time and **monitor** your understanding of the material. Reread if necessary and **reflect** on what you have read. As you reflect, use one or more of these techniques.

PREDICT

Try to figure out what might happen next. Then read on to see how accurate your guesses were.

VISUALIZE

Picture the people, places, and events being described to help you understand what's happening.

CONNECT

Connect personally with what you're reading. Think of similarities between what is being described and what you have experienced, heard about, or read about.

QUESTION

Ask questions about events in the material you're reading. What happened? Why? How do the people involved feel about the events? Searching for reasons can help you feel closer to what you are reading.

CLARIFY

From time to time, review your understanding of what you read. You can do this by **summarizing** what you have read, identifying the **main idea,** and **making inferences—** drawing conclusions from the information you are given. Reread passages you don't understand. If you need to, consult a dictionary, glossary, or other source.

EVALUATE

Form opinions about what you read, both while you're reading and after you've finished. Develop your own ideas about people, places, and events.

READER'S NOTEBOOK

Putting your thoughts on paper can help you understand and connect with literature. Many readers record their ideas in a Reader's Notebook. You can use almost any kind of notebook for this purpose. This page describes two ways you can use your notebook.

1 PREPARE TO READ

Complete the 📖 **READER'S NOTEBOOK** activity on the Preparing to Read page of each literature lesson. This activity will help you apply an important skill as you read the literature selection.

> ## "Young Arthur"
> retold by Robert D. San Souci
>
> | Text | Response |
> |---|---|
> | p. 58 "Soon rebellion divided the kingdom." | In social studies class, we read about how knights took an oath to protect their king. |

2 RECORD YOUR THOUGHTS

In your Reader's Notebook, record responses, connections, questions, sketches, and charts. Use your notebook before and after reading a selection, as well as while you read. Jot down notes that might later be a springboard to your own writing.

Watch for reminders about your Reader's Notebook throughout this textbook.

Tim Rieber
PORTFOLIO

Date	Project	Comments
10/6	Essay on "Rikki-tikki-tavi"	Finished
11/19	Report on author Ray Bradbury	Needs more work
11/22	Research report on medieval England	Outline and notes only

Personal Word List

Word: melancholy
Selection: Young Arthur
Page: S8 ("Merlin was unable to rouse him from his melancholy")
Definition: sadness, misery

Word: grievous
Selection: Young Arthur
Page: S9 ("ready to bear even grievous wounds")
Definition: serious

Reading Log

Name: **Gabrielle Davis**

Date	Title / Author	Genre / Type	Time/Number of Pages
10/15	_Tuck Everlasting_ by Natalie Babbitt	Novel	40 minutes/ 22 pages
10/16	_Soccer Player_	Magazine	10 minutes/8 pages

WORKING PORTFOLIO

Artists and writers keep portfolios in which they store works in progress. Your portfolio can be a folder, a box, or a notebook. Add drafts of your writing experiments and notes on your goals as a reader and writer.

PERSONAL WORD LISTS

Vocabulary In your Reader's Notebook you can add words you learn to a personal word list—a list of words you want to use.

Spelling Add words that you are having difficulty spelling to a separate spelling list in your Reader's Notebook.

READING LOG

Keep track of how much you read and how often. You may be surprised at how many books and other materials you read in a year! Keep your reading log in your Reader's Notebook or on a worksheet your teacher provides for you.

Integrated Technology

Your involvement doesn't stop with the last line of the text. Use these technology products to further your study and understanding:

- **Literature in Performance videos**
- **NetActivities CD-ROM**
- **Audio Library**
- **INTERNET ClassZone, McDougal Littell's companion Web site, at www.mcdougallittell.com**

Reading Literature

When you read short stories, literary nonfiction, poems, plays, or myths, you are interacting with the literature in many ways. You may be enjoying the power of storytelling. You could be finding connections with your own life. You may even be encountering new ideas and experiences. The tips on these pages will help you become an active reader of literature.

NONFICTION

POETRY

STRATEGIES FOR READING

BEFORE READING

- Set a purpose for reading. What do you want to learn? Are you reading as part of an assignment or for fun? Establishing a purpose will help you focus.
- Preview the text by looking at the title and any images and captions. Try to **predict** what the literature will be about.
- Ask yourself if you can **connect** what you are reading with what you already know.

DURING READING

- Check your understanding of what you read. Can you restate the text in your own words?
- Try to **connect** what you're reading to your own life. Have you experienced similar events or emotions?
- **Question** what's happening. You may wonder about events and characters' feelings.
- **Visualize,** or create a mental picture of, what the author is describing.
- Pause from time to time to **predict** what will happen next.

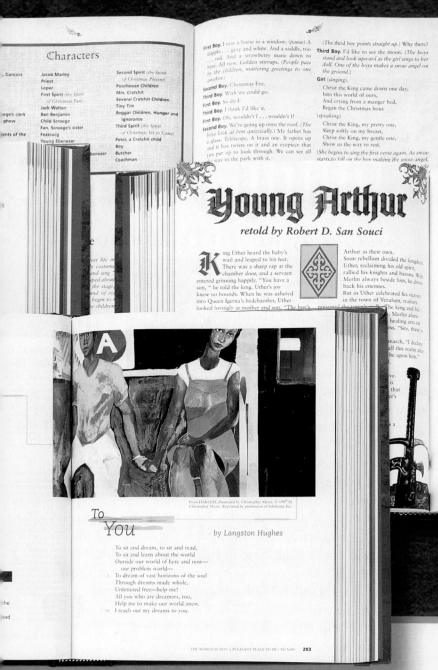

Characters

Dancers	Jacob Marley
	Priest
	Leper
	First Spirit (the Spirit of Christmas Past)
...oge's clerk	Jack Walton
...phew	Ben Benjamin
	Child Scrooge
	Fan, Scrooge's sister
...ents of the	Fezziwig
	Young Ebenezer
...benezer	Peter, a Cratchit child

	Second Spirit (the Spirit of Christmas Present)
	Poorhouse Children
	Mrs. Cratchit
	Several Cratchit Children
	Tiny Tim
	Beggar Children, Hunger and Ignorance
	Third Spirit (the Spirit of Christmas Yet to Come)
	Boy
	Butcher
	Coachman

First Boy. I saw a horse in a window. (pause) A dapple . . . gray and white. And a saddle, too . . . red. And a strawberry mane down to here. All new. Golden stirrups. (People pass by the children, muttering greetings to one another.)

Second Boy. Christmas Eve.

Third Boy. Wish we could go.

First Boy. So do I.

Third Boy. I think I'd like it.

First Boy. Oh, wouldn't I . . . wouldn't I!

Second Boy. We're going up onto the roof. (The boys look at him quizzically.) My father has a glass. Telescope. A brass one. It opens up and it has twists on it and an eyepiece that you put up to look through. We can see all the way to the park with it.

(The third boy points straight up.) Why there?

Third Boy. I'd like to see the moon. (The boys stand and look upward as the girl sings to her doll. One of the boys makes a snow angel on the ground.)

Girl (singing).
Christ the King came down one day,
Into this world of ours,
And crying from a manger bed,
Began the Christmas hour.

(speaking)

Christ the King, my pretty one,
Sleep softly on my breast,
Christ the King, my gentle one,
Show us the way to rest.

(She begins to sing the first verse again. As snow starts to fall on the boy making the snow angel...

Young Arthur

retold by Robert D. San Souci

King Uther heard the baby's wail and leaped to his feet. There was a sharp rap at the chamber door, and a servant entered grinning happily. "You have a son, " he told the king. Uther's joy knew no bounds. When he was ushered into Queen Igerna's bedchamber, Uther looked lovingly at mother and son. "The boy's...

Arthur as their own. Soon rebellion divided the kingdom. Uther, reclaiming his old spirit, rallied his knights and barons. With Merlin always beside him, he drove back his enemies.

But as Uther celebrated his victory in the town of Verulum, traitors poisoned the town's wells. The king and his ... Merlin alone ... healing arts on ... ess, "Sire, there is ...

...onarch, "I declare ... ll this realm after ... be upon him," ...

...ve.
...that
...er's

...s
...

alongside his foster brother, Kay, who was four years older. By the time he was fifteen, Arthur was a tall, handsome, quick-witted lad. Though he had great strength, he also had a gentle manner.

Kay, who had recently been knighted, decided to train Arthur in the knightly arts himself. But Kay was vain and jealous of the favor Arthur found with their father, so he was a harsh taskmaster. Arthur came away from his lessons in swordsmanship with many bruises and cuts. When he complained, Kay replied, "A knight must be thick-skinned and ready to bear even grievous wounds without flinching." Yet if Arthur so much as pricked his brother, Kay would bellow loudly for the physician.

Eventually Kay appointed Arthur his apprentice. This was an honor the younger boy would happily have forgone. However, seeing that Sir Ector wished it so, Arthur sighed and agreed. But he felt in his heart that he already was a knight, though no lord had dubbed him such.

Both Arthur and Kay knew it was vital to learn the arts of war. The kingdom was still at the mercy of upstart lords who ruled by fire and sword.

The story of Uther's lost son, the true heir to the throne, would have been forgotten but for Merlin. One Christmas Eve, the long-absent magician reappeared and summoned the bishops, lords, and common folk to London's square. There he drove a broadsword halfway into a huge stone. Written on the blade in blazing gold letters were the words: "Whoso pulleth out the sword from this stone is born the rightful King of England."

In the days that followed, knights and barons, cowherds and bakers, an endless parade of would-be kings eagerly pulled at the sword. But none could loosen it, let alone draw it forth.

When they accused Merlin of trickery, he said, "The rightful king has not yet come. God will make him known at the proper time."

Now it happened that a great tournament was held in London. Among those who came were Sir Ector, Sir Kay, and young Arthur, who served Kay. So eager was the boy to see the jousts that he forgot to pack Kay's sword. There was great upset when the mistake was discovered.

"Woe to you, boy," snarled Kay, "if your error costs me the victory I would otherwise win today!"

YOUNG ARTHUR **829**

To You

by Langston Hughes

From HARLEM, illustrated by Christopher Myers. © 1997 by Christopher Myers. Reprinted by permission of Scholastic Inc.

To sit and dream, to sit and read,
To sit and learn about the world
Outside our world of here and now—
our problem world—
To dream of vast horizons of the soul
Through dreams made whole,
Unfettered free—help me!
All you who are dreamers, too,
Help me to make our world anew.
I reach out my dreams to you.

THE WORLD IS NOT A PLEASANT PLACE TO BE / TO YOU. **203**

DRAMA

MYTHS AND LEGENDS

AFTER READING

- Review your predictions. Were they correct?
- Try to **summarize** the text. Give the main idea or the basic plot.
- Reflect on and **evaluate** what you have read. Did the reading fulfill your purpose?
- To **clarify** your understanding, write down opinions or thoughts about the piece, or discuss it with someone.

The story on these pages is part of a legend that appears in Unit Six. Read the excerpt and record your responses in your 📖 READER'S NOTEBOOK. Then read the Strategies in Action columns to find out how two students applied the strategies for reading.

Tim: *From the title and the pictures, I think this story is about King Arthur.*
PREDICTING

Gabrielle: *We read about medieval times in social studies class. I wonder if this story will tell me more about what it was like to live during the Middle Ages?*
CONNECTING, QUESTIONING

Young Arthur

retold by Robert D. San Souci

King Uther heard the baby's wail and leaped to his feet. There was a sharp rap at the chamber door, and a servant entered grinning happily. "You have a son," he told the king. Uther's joy knew no bounds. When he was ushered into Queen Igerna's bedchamber, Uther looked lovingly at mother and son. "The boy's name shall be Arthur," he declared, "and he shall be a great king. For Merlin [the magician] has foretold that he will one day rule the greatest kingdom under heaven."

But Uther's happiness did not last. His beloved queen died soon after Arthur's birth, and sadness sapped the king's spirit. He lost interest in ruling, and Merlin was unable to rouse him from his melancholy. "Unrest grows throughout the land," Merlin warned. "Your old foes are rising in rebellion. Give the babe into my keeping, for you have enemies even at court."

Anxious for his son's safety, Uther agreed. So Merlin, disguised as a beggar, took the infant Arthur to Sir Ector and his lady, who lived some distance from the court and all its dangers. He told them nothing about the child, save that his name was Arthur. The couple had recently lost their infant son and welcomed Arthur as their own.

Soon rebellion divided the kingdom. Uther, reclaiming his old spirit, rallied his knights and barons. With Merlin always beside him, he drove back his enemies.

But as Uther celebrated his victory in the town of Verulum, traitors poisoned the town's wells. The king and his loyal followers were stricken. Merlin alone escaped. Though he tried his healing arts on Uther, he was forced to confess, "Sire, there is no remedy."

"Then," said the dying monarch, "I declare that my son shall be king of all this realm after me. God's blessing and mine be upon him." With these words, Uther died.

When the rebels entered Verulum, only Merlin was alive.

"Tell us where Uther's son is hidden," they demanded, "so that we can slay him and end Uther's line."

But Merlin vanished before their eyes.

Young Arthur was raised as a son in Sir Ector's house. He learned to read and write alongside his foster brother, Kay, who was four years older. By the time he was fifteen, Arthur was a tall, handsome, quick-witted lad. Though he had great strength, he also had a gentle manner.

Kay, who had recently been knighted, decided to train Arthur in the knightly arts himself. But Kay was vain and jealous of the favor Arthur found with their father, so he was a harsh taskmaster. Arthur came away from his lessons in swordsmanship with many bruises and cuts. When he complained, Kay replied, "A knight must be thick-skinned and ready to bear even grievous wounds without flinching." Yet if Arthur so much as pricked his brother, Kay would bellow loudly for the physician.

Eventually Kay appointed Arthur his apprentice. This was an honor the younger boy would happily have forgone.

Gabrielle: *What does* stricken *mean? I think it must mean* sick, *since the paragraph talks about poison and only one person escaping.*
CLARIFYING: MAKING INFERENCES

Tim: *I can picture Merlin disappearing in a cloud of smoke!*
VISUALIZING

Tim: *Kay seems like a jerk. I think there will be trouble from him later in the story.*
EVALUATING, PREDICTING

The entire story can be found on pages 828–831. To practice reading strategies, go to "Your Turn" on pages S18–S23.

Reading for Information

Reading literature often leads to other kinds of reading experiences. For example, you may read about a historical event in this book and then do research on that event for social studies class. When you read encyclopedia articles, newspapers, magazines, Web pages, and textbooks, you are reading for information. This kind of reading requires you to use a different set of skills. The strategies below will help you.

REFERENCE BOOK

652   King Arthur

ARTHUR, KING
In romance and legend, in music and art, King Arthur and his Knights of the Round Table are among the world's best-known heroes. For centuries they have been favorites of storytellers in many different countries.

The tales, as they are most often told today, are set in Arthur's court at Camelot, in a castle with noble towers and a great hall. In the great hall stood the Round Table, where only the best and most valiant knights could sit. Because the table had no head and no foot, all the knights seated around it were of equal rank. Each knight had his own seat with his own name carved on it. The knights were bound by oath to help one another in time of danger and never to fight among themselves.

The tales tell of the wise and courteous Sir Gawaine; the brave Sir Percival; Sir Lancelot, who loved King Arthur's wife, Guinevere; the traitor Sir Modred, who seized the throne and tried to wed Queen Guinevere; the noble Sir Bedivere, who received Arthur's last commands before he died; and Sir Tristram, the knight of many skills. One seat at the Round Table had no name on it. It was reserved for the knight who found the Holy Grail, the cup supposedly used by Christ at the Last Supper. The seat was finally won by Sir Galahad, the purest and noblest of all the knights.

Religion and magic run through all the stories about Arthur and his knights. On the side of good was the mighty magician Merlin, who was Arthur's adviser. On the side of evil was the wicked sorceress Morgan le Fay. . . .

SOURCES OF THE ARTHURIAN LEGENDS
The book that is the chief source today for all the legends about Arthur and his knights was written by an Englishman, Sir Thomas Malory. It was printed in 1485 and was one of the first books to come from the press of the first English printer, William Caxton. Although the tales were written in English, the title of the book, *Le Morte Darthur* ("The Death of Arthur") is French and most of the tales were adapted from various French versions of the legends.

Tales about Arthur were particularly popular in France during

Here is one artist's idea of what Arthur looked like.

STRATEGIES FOR READING

SET A PURPOSE FOR READING

- Decide why you are reading the material—to study for a test, to do research, or simply to find out more about a topic that interests you.

- Use your purpose to determine how detailed your notes will be.

LOOK FOR DESIGN FEATURES

- Look at the title, any subheads, boldfaced words or phrases, boxed text, and any other text that is highlighted in some way.

- Use these text organizers to help you preview the text and identify the main ideas.

- Study photographs, maps, charts, graphs, and captions.

NOTICE TEXT STRUCTURES AND PATTERNS

- Does the text make comparisons? Does it describe causes and effects? Is there a sequence of events?

- Look for signal words such as *same, different, because, first,* and *then* to help you see the organizational pattern.

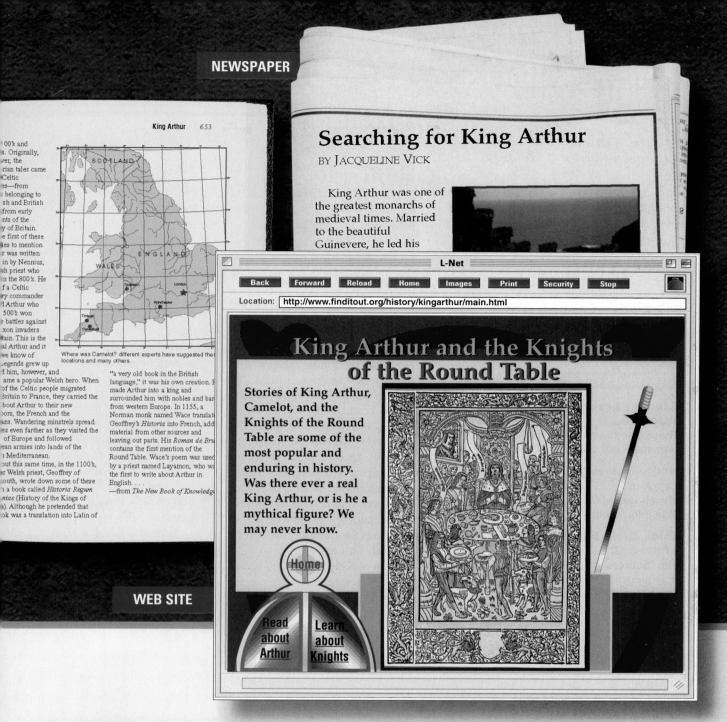

King Arthur   653

SCOTLAND

ENGLAND

WALES

London

Winchester

Tintagel

Camelot

Where was Camelot? different experts have suggested these locations and many others.

00's and
s. Originally,
ver, the
rian tales came
Celtic
es—from
belonging to
sh and British
from early
nts of the
y of Britain.
e first of these
ies to mention
r was written
in by Nennius,
sh priest who
in the 800's. He
f a Celtic
ry commander
d Arthur who
500's won
battles against
xon invaders
tain. This is the
al Arthur and it
we know of
egends grew up
d him, however, and
ame a popular Welsh hero. When
of the Celtic people migrated
Britain to France, they carried the
bout Arthur to their new
bors, the French and the
ans. Wandering minstrels spread
es even farther as they visited the
of Europe and followed
ean armies into lands of the
n Mediterranean.
ut this same time, in the 1100's,
r Welsh priest, Geoffrey of
outh, wrote down some of these
n a book called *Historia Regum*
ntae (History of the Kings of
a). Although he pretended that
ok was a translation into Latin of

"a very old book in the British
language," it was his own creation.
made Arthur into a king and
surrounded him with nobles and bar
from western Europe. In 1155, a
Norman monk named Wace translate
Geoffrey's *Historia* into French, add
material from other sources and
leaving out parts. His *Roman de Bru*
contains the first mention of the
Round Table. Wace's poem was used
by a priest named Layamon, who wa
the first to write about Arthur in
English. . . .
—from *The New Book of Knowledge*

Searching for King Arthur

BY JACQUELINE VICK

King Arthur was one of
the greatest monarchs of
medieval times. Married
to the beautiful
Guinevere, he led his

L-Net

Back   Forward   Reload   Home   Images   Print   Security   Stop

Location: http://www.finditout.org/history/kingarthur/main.html

King Arthur and the Knights of the Round Table

Stories of King Arthur,
Camelot, and the
Knights of the Round
Table are some of the
most popular and
enduring in history.
Was there ever a real
King Arthur, or is he a
mythical figure? We
may never know.

Home

Read about Arthur

Learn about Knights

READ SLOWLY AND CAREFULLY

- Take notes on the main ideas. Try to paraphrase, or state the information in your own words.
- Map the information by using a concept web or other graphic organizer.
- Notice unfamiliar words. These are sometimes defined in the text.
- If there are questions with the text, be sure you can answer them.

EVALUATE THE INFORMATION

- Think about what you have read. Does the text make sense? Is it complete?
- Summarize the information—give the main points in just a few words.

Reading for Information
Reference Books

For useful and reliable information, try encyclopedias, textbooks, and other reference books. Use the strategies from the previous pages and the tips below to read the encyclopedia article. Then read how Tim and Gabrielle applied the strategies as they did research for a social studies project.

STRATEGIES FOR READING

Ⓐ Read the heading and subheads.
These give the main idea and organizational structure.

Ⓑ Notice images and their captions.
Visuals are interesting and provide information.

Ⓒ Think about the structure of the text.
The "Sources" section describes a sequence of events—how stories about a real person may have changed into legends. For more on text organization, see pages R6–R11 in the Reading Handbook.

Ⓓ Look for clues to difficult words.
You can sometimes figure out the meaning of words like *valiant* by thinking about the context—the words and sentences around the word.

Ⓔ Evaluate the article.
Did you find the information you need? Decide whether you need to consult other sources.

---

652   **King Arthur**

Ⓐ ARTHUR, KING

In romance and legend, in music and art, King Arthur and his Knights of the Round Table are among the world's best-known heroes. For centuries they have been favorites of storytellers in many different countries.

The tales, as they are most often told today, are set in Arthur's court at Camelot, in a castle with noble towers and a great hall. In the great hall stood the Round Table, where only the best and most valiant Ⓓ knights could sit. Because the table had no head and no foot, all the knights seated around it were of equal rank. Each knight had his own seat with his own name carved on it. The knights were bound by oath to help one another in time of danger and never to fight among themselves.

The tales tell of the wise and courteous Sir Gawaine; the brave Sir Percival; Sir Lancelot, who loved King Arthur's wife, Guinevere; the traitor Sir Modred, who seized the throne and tried to wed Queen Guinevere; the noble Sir Bedivere, who received Arthur's last commands before he died; and Sir Tristram, the knight of many skills. One seat at the Round Table had no name on it. It was reserved for the knight who found the Holy Grail, the cup supposedly used by Christ at the Last Supper. The seat was finally won by Sir Galahad, the purest and noblest of all the knights.

Religion and magic run through all the stories about Arthur and his knights. On the side of good was the mighty magician Merlin, who was Arthur's adviser. On the side of evil was the wicked sorceress Morgan le Fay. . . .

Ⓒ SOURCES OF THE ARTHURIAN LEGENDS

The book that is the chief source today for all the legends about Arthur and his knights was written by an Englishman, Sir Thomas Malory. It was printed in 1485 and was one of the first books to come from the press of the first English printer, William Caxton. Although the tales were written in English, the title of the book, *Le Morte Darthur* ("The Death of Arthur") is French and most of the tales were adapted from various French versions of the legends.

Tales about Arthur were particularly popular in France during

Ⓑ Here is one artist's idea of what Arthur looked like.

the 1100's and 1200's. Originally, however, the Arthurian tales came from Celtic sources—from myths belonging to the Irish and British races from early accounts of the history of Britain.

The first of these histories to mention Arthur was written in Latin by Nennius, a Welsh priest who lived in the 800's. He tells of a Celtic military commander named Arthur who in the 500's won twelve battles against the Saxon invaders of Britain. This is the original Arthur and it is all we know of him. Legends grew up around him, however, and he became a popular Welsh hero. When some of the Celtic people migrated from Britain to France, they carried the tales about Arthur to their new neighbors, the French and the Normans. Wandering minstrels spread the tales even farther as they visited the courts of Europe and followed European armies into lands of the eastern Mediterranean.

About this same time, in the 1100's, another Welsh priest, Geoffrey of Monmouth, wrote down some of these tales in a book called *Historia Regum Britanniae* (History of the Kings of Britain). Although he pretended that the book was a translation into Latin of "a very old book in the British

King Arthur   653

Where was Camelot? Different experts have suggested these locations and many others.

language," it was his own creation. He made Arthur into a king and surrounded him with nobles and barons from western Europe. In 1155, a Norman monk named Wace translated Geoffrey's *Historia* into French, adding material from other sources and leaving out parts. His *Roman de Brut* contains the first mention of the Round Table. Wace's poem was used by a priest named Layamon, who was the first to write about Arthur in English. . . .
—from *The New Book of Knowledge*

E

STRATEGIES IN ACTION

Gabrielle: I can tell from the title and subhead that this article has information on how the legend developed.

Tim: I want to do my social studies project on what the real Arthur was like, so the "Sources of the Arthurian Legends" section is especially helpful.

Tim: I don't know what valiant means, but the article mentions "the best and most valiant knights," so it must be something positive. The dictionary says it means "brave."

Gabrielle: I want to read more about Sir Percival and Sir Galahad. I'll see if the library has more information on them.

Newspapers and magazines inform you about your community and the world. Read the tips below. Then practice your skills by reading the article.

STRATEGIES FOR READING

(A) Read the headline and subheads.
These will tell you what the article is about and how it is organized.

(B) Notice visuals and captions.
Photographs, maps, and graphics draw your attention and provide information.

(C) Think about the structure of the text.
This article first gives the main idea—that many towns claim ties to King Arthur. Then it gives details about the different claims. For more on text organization, see pages R6–R11 in the Reading Handbook.

(D) Watch for difficult words and phrases.
The article includes the words *slate* and *crypt*. If you can't find an explanation or definition in the text, consult a dictionary.

(E) Notice any quotations.
Think about whether the people quoted are likely to be reliable. Then decide whether you need to do more research on the topic.

(A) # Searching for King Arthur

BY JACQUELINE VICK

King Arthur was one of the greatest monarchs of medieval times. Married to the beautiful Guinevere, he led his Knights of the Round Table in battle and upheld the highest ideals of courage and honor. Or did he?

(C) We think we know King Arthur from books, movies, plays, video games, and comic books. However, the real King Arthur, if he existed at all, was probably a tribal chieftain. The legends that have developed around Arthur are so powerful, though, that more than 160 towns and villages in four countries claim connections with Arthur. Local pride and huge sums of tourists' money are at stake.

(B) According to local legend, King Arthur lived on this site, Tintagel Castle.

The Mysteries of Tintagel

The tiny English village of Tintagel (pronounced tin-TA-jull) is overwhelmed with more than one million tourists a year, most of them Americans. They stay at the King Arthur Castle Hotel, buy Guinevere souvenirs, and eat Excaliburgers.

(E) "Everyone knows Arthur came from Tintagel," explains Bob Flower, the chairman of the local district council. Brochures from the area's tourist board are full of information about Arthur, and an expensive new visitors' center describes the history and the legends.

Tintagel Castle is a majestic ruin, a pile of weathered stones on the edge of the ocean. Anyone who walks under the ancient stone archway can imagine Arthur and his knights living, fighting, and feasting here. The stones, however, date from the 1100s—about 600 years after Arthur's time. The Earl of Cornwall built the structure and claimed it had been Arthur's castle to attract visitors and their money to his land.

Archaeologists have found fragments of pottery from the 400s or 500s at Tintagel, as well as a slate reading PATER COLI-AVI FICIT ARTOGNOV, or "Artognou, father of a descendant of Coll, has had this made." Many people believe that Artognou was Arthur, but archaeologist Kevin Brady does not. "One, to connect King Arthur to Tintagel takes quite a leap of imagination," Brady explains. "And two, the name doesn't say Arthur."

The prefix *Art-* means "bear" or "bearlike," and there are many medieval British names that share it: Arthun, Arthwys, Arcturus, Artorius, and Arviragus, to name a few. Victories won by later chieftains and kings with similar names may have been added to the Arthur legend.

The Graves at Glastonbury

Other English towns have centuries-old claims to Arthur. In 1190 or 1191, a group of monks told of uncovering the bodies of a nobleman and noble-woman buried together. The monks said the man wore a cross that read "Here lies the renowned King Arthur, buried in the isle of Avalon." They reburied the man and woman in a crypt, which has disappeared. The monastery was destroyed in 1539 and only ruins remain. Some historians believe that the monks never found Arthur and Guinevere—that the tomb was created to bring visitors and their money to the area.

Other Towns Make Claims

About 55 towns and villages in western England claim that Arthur was born or died or fought there. Roughly 110 sites elsewhere in England and in Wales, Scotland, and France also claim Arthur connections. A gigantic King Arthur theme park is being built in Wales.

Why is Arthur so well remembered? One reason is that everyone loves a good story, and the stories of Arthur are some of the best. Even one of the earliest translators of the Arthur stories urged readers to remember that the tales were "not all a lie, nor all truth, nor all fable, nor all known."

Another reason is tourist income. As one hotel manager put it, "King Arthur, I suppose, is our Loch Ness Monster." In other words, Arthur is a source of mystery and tourist income even if he didn't exist as we picture him.

The most important reason may be that the Arthur legends describe one of the greatest heroes in literature. The British leader Winston Churchill put it best: "If King Arthur didn't live, he should have."

Reading for Information
Web Sites

World Wide Web pages that are created by museums, libraries, universities, and government agencies can be good sources of information. The strategies below will help you read a Web page and evaluate what you find.

STRATEGIES FOR READING

A Find the page's Web address.
This is usually in a box at the top of the screen. Write down or bookmark the address in case you get lost while Web surfing.

B Read the page's title.
The title usually gives the main idea of the page.

C Look for links to other parts of the site.
Scan the menu options and decide which are most likely to have the information you need. Don't get lost following link after link. Use the Back button to retrace your steps when necessary.

D Notice source citations.
Some sites tell you where their information is from so you can judge its reliability.

E Write down important ideas and details.
Try to paraphrase the text, or restate it in your own words. Then decide whether you need to check other sources.

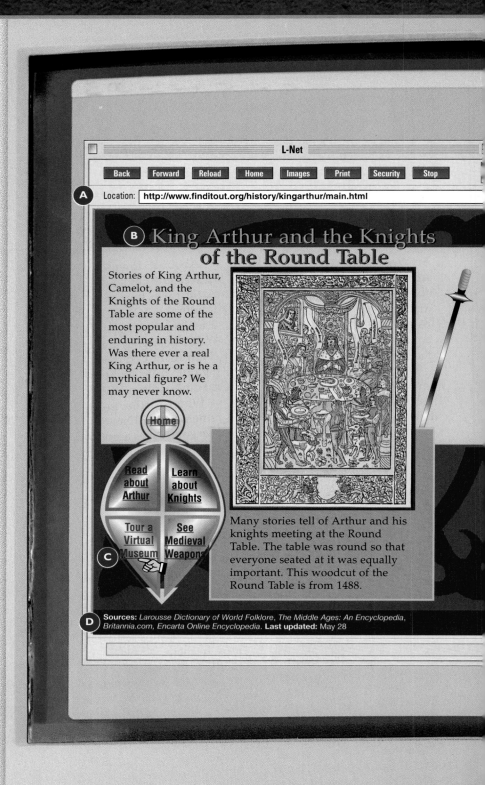

L-Net

Back Forward Reload Home Images Print Security Stop

A Location: http://www.finditout.org/history/kingarthur/main.html

B **King Arthur and the Knights of the Round Table**

Stories of King Arthur, Camelot, and the Knights of the Round Table are some of the most popular and enduring in history. Was there ever a real King Arthur, or is he a mythical figure? We may never know.

Home

Read about Arthur

Learn about Knights

Tour a Virtual Museum

See Medieval Weapons

Many stories tell of Arthur and his knights meeting at the Round Table. The table was round so that everyone seated at it was equally important. This woodcut of the Round Table is from 1488.

D **Sources:** *Larousse Dictionary of World Folklore, The Middle Ages: An Encyclopedia, Britannia.com, Encarta Online Encyclopedia.* **Last updated:** May 28

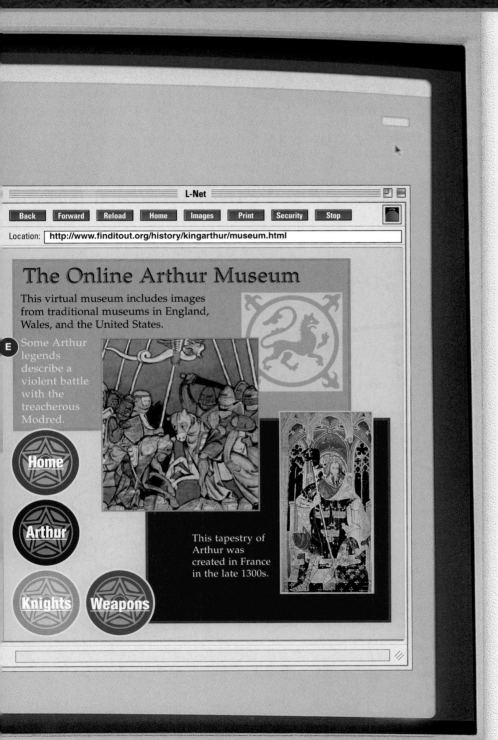

The Online Arthur Museum

This virtual museum includes images from traditional museums in England, Wales, and the United States.

E Some Arthur legends describe a violent battle with the treacherous Modred.

Home

Arthur

Knights   Weapons

This tapestry of Arthur was created in France in the late 1300s.

L-Net

Back   Forward   Reload   Home   Images   Print   Security   Stop

Location: http://www.finditout.org/history/kingarthur/museum.html

STRATEGIES IN ACTION

Gabrielle: I can tell from the title that this site probably has information I need. There are some reference books listed as sources, which is a good sign that the site is reliable.

Gabrielle: I'm interested in finding out what Arthur and his knights might have looked like, so I'll click on the Virtual Museum link.

Tim: I might use the information about Modred in my report, so I'll write it down.

Tim: I'll see if the library has any articles or books about Modred.

Your Turn
Applying the Strategies

As you read the following story, create a **Reader's Notebook** to help you understand and reflect on what you read. Prompts and questions in the margins will help you. For instructions on how to create a Reader's Notebook, see page S4.

Here are sample pages from the notebooks Gabrielle and Tim created as they read "A Day's Wait." For strategies to use before, during, and after reading, see "Reading Literature" on pages S6–S7.

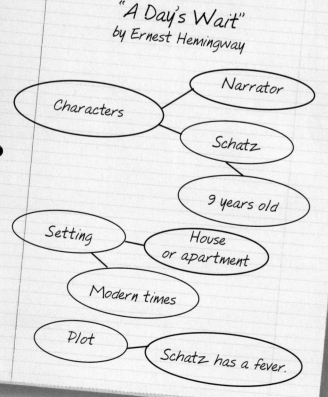

"A Day's Wait"
by Ernest Hemingway

Text	Response
title	What are they waiting for?
	The dialogue sounds like real people talking.
p. S20 "What's the matter, Schatz?"	

"A Day's Wait"
by Ernest Hemingway

Characters — Narrator
Characters — Schatz — 9 years old
Setting — House or apartment
Setting — Modern times
Plot — Schatz has a fever.

A Day's Wait

by Ernest Hemingway

He came into the room to shut the windows
while we were still in bed and I saw he looked ill. He was shivering,
his face was white, and he walked slowly as though it ached to
move.

"What's the matter, Schatz?"

"I've got a headache."

"You better go back to bed."

"No. I'm all right."

"You go to bed. I'll see you when I'm dressed."

But when I came downstairs he was dressed, sitting by the fire,
looking a very sick and miserable boy of nine years. When I put my
hand on his forehead I knew he had a fever.

"You go up to bed," I said, "you're sick."

"I'm all right," he said.

◄ CONNECT
*Is Schatz's behavior similar to
how you act when you are
sick?*

When the doctor came he took the boy's temperature.
"What is it?" I asked him.
"One hundred and two."

Downstairs, the doctor left three different medicines in different-colored capsules with instructions for giving them. One was to bring down the fever, another a purgative, the third to overcome an acid condition. The germs of influenza can only exist in an acid condition, he explained. He seemed to know all about influenza and said there was nothing to worry about if the fever did not go above one hundred and four degrees. This was a light epidemic of flu and there was no danger if you avoided pneumonia.

Back in the room I wrote the boy's temperature down and made a note of the time to give the various capsules.
"Do you want me to read to you?"
"All right. If you want to," said the boy. His face was very white and there were dark areas under his eyes. He lay still in the bed and seemed very detached from what was going on.

I read aloud from Howard Pyle's *Book of Pirates;* but I could see he was not following what I was reading.
"How do you feel, Schatz?" I asked him.
"Just the same, so far," he said.

I sat at the foot of the bed and read to myself while I waited for it to be time to give another capsule. It would have been natural for him to go to sleep, but when I looked up he was looking at the foot of the bed, looking very strangely.
"Why don't you try to go to sleep? I'll wake you up for the medicine."
"I'd rather stay awake."

After a while he said to me, "You don't have to stay in here with me, Papa, if it bothers you."
"It doesn't bother me."
"No, I mean you don't have to stay if it's going to bother you."

I thought perhaps he was a little lightheaded and after giving him the prescribed capsules at eleven o'clock I went out for a while.

CLARIFY: SUMMARIZE ▶
In your own words, describe what has happened in the story so far.

QUESTION ▶
What is strange about how Schatz is acting? Write down any details that seems unusual.

PREDICT ▶
What do you think will happen to Schatz?

January's Shadows, Robert Frank.

It was a bright, cold day, the ground covered with a sleet that had frozen so that it seemed as if all the bare trees, the bushes, the cut brush, and all the grass and the bare ground had been varnished with ice. I took the young Irish setter for a little walk up the road and along a frozen creek, but it was difficult to stand or walk on the glassy surface and the red dog slipped and slithered and I fell twice, hard, once dropping my gun and having it slide away over the ice.

We flushed a covey of quail under a high clay bank with overhanging brush and I killed two as they went out of sight over the top of the bank. Some of the covey lit in trees, but most of them scattered into brush piles and it was necessary to jump on the ice-coated mounds of brush several times before they would flush. Coming out while you were poised unsteadily on the icy,

◀ *VISUALIZE*
How does the art fit the story?

CLARIFY: MAKE INFERENCES ▶
*What clues can you find that
tell you the emotions Schatz
is experiencing?*

springy brush, they made difficult shooting and I killed two, missed five, and started back pleased to have found a covey close to the house and happy there were so many left to find on another day.

At the house they said the boy had refused to let anyone come into the room.

"You can't come in," he said. "You mustn't get what I have."

I went up to him and found him in exactly the position I had left him, white-faced, but with the tops of his cheeks flushed by the fever, staring still, as he had stared, at the foot of the bed.

I took his temperature.

"What is it?"

"Something like a hundred," I said. It was one hundred and two and four tenths.

"It was a hundred and two," he said.

"Who said so?"

"The doctor."

"Your temperature is all right," I said. "It's nothing to worry about."

"I don't worry," he said, "but I can't keep from thinking."

"Don't think," I said. "Just take it easy."

"I'm taking it easy," he said and looked straight ahead. He was evidently holding tight onto himself about something.

"Take this with water."

"Do you think it will do any good?"

"Of course it will."

I sat down and opened the *Pirate* book and commenced to read, but I could see he was not following, so I stopped.

"About what time do you think I'm going to die?" he asked.

"What?"

"About how long will it be before I die?"

"You aren't going to die. What's the matter with you?"

"Oh, yes, I am. I heard him say a hundred and two."

"People don't die with a fever of one hundred and two. That's a silly way to talk."

"I know they do. At school in France the boys told me you can't live with forty-four degrees. I've got a hundred and two."

He had been waiting to die all day, ever since nine o'clock in

Mexican Morning (1942), Private Collection/G. G. Kopilak/SuperStock.

the morning.

"You poor Schatz," I said. "Poor old Schatz. It's like miles and kilometers. You aren't going to die. That's a different thermometer. On that thermometer thirty-seven is normal. On this kind it's ninety-eight."

"Are you sure?"

"Absolutely," I said. "It's like miles and kilometers. You know, like how many kilometers we make when we do seventy miles in the car?"

"Oh," he said.

But his gaze at the foot of the bed relaxed slowly. The hold over himself relaxed too, finally, and the next day it was very slack and he cried very easily at little things that were of no importance. ❖

◀ QUESTION
Why do you think Schatz waited a whole day to tell his father his fear?

◀ EVALUATE
Why do you think Schatz cried easily the next day?

Learning from

Experience

"I think success has no rules, but you can learn a lot from failures."

Jean Kerr
American humorist and dramatist

13

The Literature You'll Read

The Concepts You'll Study

Vocabulary and Reading Comprehension
Vocabulary Focus: Understanding Context Clues
Connecting
Cause and Effect
Identifying Author's Purpose
Making Inferences

Literary Analysis
Genre Focus: Fiction
Setting
Conflict
Personal Essay
Character

Writing and Language Conventions
Writing Workshop: Response to Literature
Complete Subjects and Predicates
Compound Verbs
Combining Complete Sentences
Sentence Fragments

Speaking and Listening
Write and Perform a Skit
Film Review
Interview a Writer
Persuasive Speech

LEARNING the Language of Literature

Fiction

Key Standard
R3.1 Be able to describe the purposes and characteristics of different forms of prose, such as the short story, novel, or essay.
Other Standards **R3.2, R3.3, R3.4**

> *Great stories give us [images] which flash upon the mind the way lightning flashes upon the earth . . .*
> —Paula Fox

Where do stories come from? Some are whispered in the glow of a campfire. Others are discovered in a book. Wherever you find them, all stories begin in someone's imagination. Stories that come from a writer's imagination are called **fiction.** Two forms of fiction are **short stories** and **novels.** Both contain the elements of **plot, character, setting,** and **theme.**

Sometimes a writer bases a fictional story on actual events or on real people, adding invented elements such as additional characters or dialogue. The purpose of fiction is to entertain, but it can also provide the reader with a deeper understanding of life.

Characteristics of Forms of Fiction

short story
- usually revolves around a single idea
- is short enough to be read at one sitting

novel
- involves a more complicated plot
- is a longer work

15

Plot

The sequence of events in a story is called the **plot**. A plot is usually built around a central **conflict**—a problem or struggle between opposing forces. Although the development of every plot is different, most plots develop in four stages:

- **Exposition** sets the stage for the story. Characters are introduced, and the setting is described.
- **Rising action** occurs as the story continues. The central conflict unfolds as the plot becomes more complex and problems and complications arise. Suspense builds as the characters struggle to find solutions to the conflict.
- **Climax** is the turning point of the story. The action reaches a peak, and the outcome of the conflict is decided. The climax usually results in a change in the characters or a solution to the problem.
- **Falling action** (sometimes called **resolution** or **denouement**) occurs at the conclusion of the story. Loose ends are tied up, and the story ends.

PLOT

"About what time do you think I'm going to die?" he asked.

"What?"

"About how long will it be before I die?"

"You aren't going to die. What's the matter with you?"

"Oh, yes, I am. I heard him say a hundred and two."

"People don't die with a fever of one hundred and two. That's a silly way to talk."

"I know they do. At school in France the boys told me you can't live with forty-four degrees. I've got a hundred and two."

—Ernest Hemingway, "A Day's Wait"

YOUR TURN Read the passage above. What conflict is introduced? What do you think could happen to resolve the conflict?

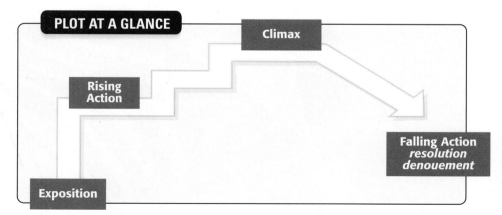

PLOT AT A GLANCE

Climax

Rising Action

Exposition

Falling Action
resolution
denouement

Character

The **characters** in a story are the people, animals, or imaginary creatures who take part in the action. Usually a story focuses on the events surrounding one character—the main character. Other characters—minor characters—interact with the main character and help move the story along. Characters are defined by their **traits,** or the more permanent qualities in their personalities. Characters are revealed by their **motives,** or the reasons they act the way they do.

YOUR TURN In the passage at the right, what words and details give you clues about what the boy is like?

CHARACTER

I went up to him and found him in exactly the position I had left him, white-faced, but with the tops of this cheeks flushed by the fever, staring still, as he had stared, at the foot of the bed.

I took his temperature.

"What is it?"

"Something like a hundred," I said. It was one hundred and two and four tenths.

"It was a hundred and two," he said.

"Who said so?"

"The doctor."

"Your temperature is all right," I said. "It's nothing to worry about."

"I don't worry," he said, "but I can't keep from thinking."

"Don't think," I said. "Just take it easy."

"I'm taking it easy," he said and looked straight ahead. He was evidently holding tight onto himself about something.

—Ernest Hemingway, "A Day's Wait"

They shook hands *raza*-style and jerked their heads at one another in a *saludo de vato*.
—Gary Soto, "Seventh Grade"

"I don't worry," he said, "but I can't keep from thinking."
—Ernest Hemingway, "A Day's Wait"

Willie started to ask another question, but decided he would not get an answer.
—Avi, "What Do Fish Have to Do with Anything?"

Setting

The **setting** of a story is the time and place in which the action of the story happens. The time may be the past, present, or future; daytime or nighttime; or any season of the year. The events of the story may unfold in any place, real or imaginary. The writer's descriptions help readers picture the setting in their minds. Setting can help determine what happens to the characters and how they resolve their problems.

YOUR TURN In the paragraph on the right, what words and phrases describe the setting of the story?

SETTING

It was a bright, cold day, the ground covered with a sleet that had frozen so that it seemed as if all the bare trees, the bushes, the cut brush, and all the grass and the bare ground had been varnished with ice. I took the young Irish setter for a little walk up the road and along a frozen creek, but it was difficult to stand or walk on the glassy surface and the red dog slipped and slithered and I fell twice, hard, once dropping my gun and having it slide away over the ice.

—Ernest Hemingway, "A Day's Wait"

From "A Day's Wait"

Theme

The **theme** of a story is the meaning, moral, or main message the writer wishes to share with the reader. This message or moral might be a lesson about life or an insight into human nature. Most themes are not stated directly; the reader must infer them from the details and events of the story. Different readers may find different themes in the same story. Themes can be revealed by

- thinking about the meaning of the title of the story
- skimming the story for key phrases and sentences about big ideas such as courage, freedom, or honesty
- examining how the main character changes or noting what he or she learns about life

In this passage from "A Day's Wait," the statement "You aren't going to die" is a clue to the theme of the story. This may be that a brush with death (whether it be real or imagined) can make us appreciate life.

THEME

"You poor Schatz," I said. ". . . You aren't going to die. That's a different thermometer. On that thermometer thirty-seven is normal. On this kind it's ninety-eight." . . .

"Oh," he said.

But his gaze at the foot of the bed relaxed slowly. The hold over himself relaxed too, finally, and the next day it was very slack and he cried very easily at little things that were of no importance.

—Ernest Hemingway, "A Day's Wait"

Reading Fiction

Great stories capture our imaginations. They create a world of interesting characters, faraway places, and exciting events. While many stories entertain, they may also inform us about ourselves and our circumstances. Try using the **strategies** explained here to get the most from a work of fiction.

How to Apply the Strategies

Preview the story and set a purpose for reading. Look at the title and illustrations. Then skim through the selection's pages to see what the story is about. Use the strategies below as you read. **Monitor** how well the strategies are working for you and modify if necessary.

CONNECT Think about experiences and feelings that you share with the characters or the narrator. Can you connect any of their feelings, ideas, and values to your own?

QUESTION Ask questions about the story's events, characters, and ideas. As you read, look for the answers to your questions. Asking good questions is at the heart of good reading.

PREDICT Stop occasionally to predict what might happen next or how the story might end. To find out whether your predictions are correct, read on.

VISUALIZE Can you picture a similar setting in your mind? Is the action easy to imagine? Can you "see" the characters?

EVALUATE Do your feelings toward the characters and their actions change as you read? How well does the author tell the story?

CLARIFY Remember to pause now and then. Reread when necessary. It may also help to take notes or to discuss the story with a friend. Expect your thoughts to change as the story unfolds.

Here's how Matt uses some of the strategies:

*"I like mysteries the best. When I read, it's almost like being a detective. I become involved in the story and **visualize** how each character looks, where the story takes place, and how the events occur. I make **connections** to some parts of the story where I've had similar experiences. Above all I like to **predict** what will happen. My favorite books have twists in the plot. It keeps reading interesting."*

Seventh Grade

by GARY SOTO

Key Standard
R3.2 Identify events that advance the plot and describe how they explain the past, present, and future.
Other Standards **R1.3, R2.2, W2.1, LS1.6, LS2.1**

Connect to Your Life

Being Yourself How do seventh graders try to impress each other? Think about what you and your friends do to make others admire you. Do you behave differently with boys than with girls? Discuss your ideas with your classmates.

Build Background

GEOGRAPHY

The story "Seventh Grade" takes place in Fresno, California. Fresno is located in the San Joaquin Valley, southeast of San Francisco. Fresno's dry, hot summers and cool, humid winters are excellent for growing grapes. A large number of Hispanics whose families are originally from Spanish-speaking countries are employed in Fresno's vineyards.

California

San Francisco
• Fresno

CALIFORNIA

Pacific Ocean

Miles
0 100 200

WORDS TO KNOW	**Vocabulary Preview**		
bluff	ferocity	quiver	sheepishly
conviction	linger	scowl	trudge
elective	portly		

Focus Your Reading

LITERARY ANALYSIS **SETTING**

A story's **setting** is the time and the place in which events in the story occur. "Seventh Grade" takes place on the first day of class in a middle school in Fresno, California. The author provides several details to help you picture the school in your imagination. See how a small detail about Victor's first day helps establish the time and the place on the first day of school.

> *On the first day of school, Victor stood in the line half an hour before he came to a wobbly card table.*

As you read, find the details that best help you picture the setting.

ACTIVE READING **CONNECTING**

When you read a story, **connect** the characters, the setting, and the plot to information you already know and to your own experience. Pay special attention to

- details about the setting and the characters
- statements the characters make
- events that happen in the plot

READER'S NOTEBOOK As you read, use a chart to help you find connections between Victor's experiences and your own.

What Victor and I have in common	How Victor and I are different
We both had summer jobs.	Victor took French; I took Spanish.

Seventh Grade

by Gary Soto

Illustration by Hugh Harrison.

On the first day of school, Victor stood in line half an hour before he came to a wobbly card table. He was handed a packet of papers and a computer card on which he listed his one <u>elective</u>, French. He already spoke Spanish and English, but he thought some day he might travel to France, where it was cool; not like Fresno, where summer days reached 110 degrees in the shade. There were rivers in France, and huge churches, and fair-skinned people everywhere, the way there were brown people all around Victor.

Besides, Teresa, a girl he had liked since they were in catechism classes[1] at Saint Theresa's, was taking French, too. With any luck they would be in the same class. Teresa is going to be my girl this year, he promised himself as he left the gym full of students in their new fall clothes. She was cute. And good in math, too, Victor thought as he walked down the hall to his homeroom. He ran into his friend, Michael Torres, by the water fountain that never turned off.

---

1. **catechism classes** (kăt′ĭ-kĭz′əm): formal classes in religious instruction.

Illustration by Pamela Daly.

They shook hands, *raza*-style,[2] and jerked their heads at one another in a *saludo de vato*.[3] "How come you're making a face?" asked Victor.

ACTIVE READER

CONNECT Do you and your friends have a special way of greeting each other? What is it?

"I ain't making a face, *ese*.[4] This *is* my face." Michael said his face had changed during the summer. He had read a *GQ* magazine that his older brother had borrowed from the Book Mobile and noticed that the male models all had the same look on their faces. They would stand, one arm around a beautiful woman, and <u>scowl</u>. They would sit at a pool, their rippled stomachs dark with shadow, and *scowl*. They would sit at dinner tables, cool drinks in their hands, and *scowl*.

"I think it works," Michael said. He scowled and let his upper lip <u>quiver</u>. His teeth showed along with the <u>ferocity</u> of his soul. "Belinda Reyes walked by a while ago and looked at me," he said.

Victor didn't say anything, though he thought his friend looked pretty strange. They talked about recent movies, baseball, their parents, and the horrors of picking grapes in order to buy their fall clothes. Picking grapes was like living in Siberia, except hot and more boring.

---

2. *raza*-style (rä′sä) *Spanish:* in the familiar manner that local Chicanos greet each other.

3. *saludo de vato* (sä-lo͞o′dō dě bä′tō) *Spanish:* greeting between Chicano buddies.

4. *ese* (ě′sě) *Spanish:* a slang term used when addressing someone, as in "Hey, man."

WORDS TO KNOW
scowl (skoul) *v.* to look angry by drawing the eyebrows together and frowning
quiver (kwĭv′ər) *v.* to shake with a slight, rapid movement
ferocity (fə-rŏs′ĭ-tē) *n.* extreme fierceness; intensity

He felt himself blushing again.

"What classes are you taking?" Michael said, scowling.

"French. How 'bout you?"

"Spanish. I ain't so good at it, even if I'm Mexican."

"I'm not either, but I'm better at it than math, that's for sure."

A tinny, three-beat bell propelled students to their homerooms. The two friends socked each other in the arm and went their ways, Victor thinking, man, that's weird. Michael thinks making a face makes him handsome.

On the way to his homeroom, Victor tried a scowl. He felt foolish, until out of the corner of his eye he saw a girl looking at him. Umm, he thought, maybe it does work. He scowled with greater <u>conviction</u>.

In homeroom, roll was taken, emergency cards were passed out, and they were given a bulletin to take home to their parents. The principal, Mr. Belton, spoke over the crackling loudspeaker, welcoming the students to a new year, new experiences, and new friendships. The students squirmed in their chairs and ignored him. They were anxious to go to first period. Victor sat calmly, thinking of Teresa, who sat two rows away, reading a paperback novel. This would be his lucky year. She was in his homeroom, and would probably be in his English and math classes. And, of course, French.

The bell rang for first period, and the students herded noisily through the door. Only Teresa <u>lingered</u>, talking with the homeroom teacher.

"So you think I should talk to Mrs. Gaines?" she asked the teacher. "She would know about ballet?"

"She would be a good bet," the teacher said. Then added, "Or the gym teacher, Mrs. Garza."

Victor lingered, keeping his head down and staring at his desk. He wanted to leave when she did so he could bump into her and say something clever.

He watched her on the sly. As she turned to leave, he stood up and hurried to the door, where he managed to catch her eye. She smiled and said, "Hi, Victor."

He smiled back and said, "Yeah, that's me."

ACTIVE READER

QUESTION Why do you think Victor answers Teresa so rudely?

His brown face blushed. Why hadn't he said, "Hi, Teresa," or "How was your summer?" or something nice?

As Teresa walked down the hall, Victor walked the other way, looking back, admiring how gracefully she walked, one foot in front of the other. So much for being in the same class, he thought. As he <u>trudged</u> to English, he practiced scowling.

In English they reviewed the parts of speech. Mr. Lucas, a <u>portly</u> man, waddled down the aisle, asking, "What is a noun?"

"A person, place, or thing," said the class in unison.

"Yes, now somebody give me an example of a person—you, Victor Rodriguez."

"Teresa," Victor said automatically. Some of the girls giggled. They knew he had a crush on Teresa. He felt himself blushing again.

"Correct," Mr. Lucas said. "Now provide me with a place."

Mr. Lucas called on a freckled kid who answered, "Teresa's house with a kitchen full of big brothers."

WORDS TO KNOW	
conviction (kən-vĭk'shən) *n.* a strong belief; assuredness
linger (lĭng'gər) *v.* to continue to stay; delay leaving
trudge (trŭj) *v.* to walk heavily; plod
portly (pôrt'lē) *adj.* stout or overweight

After English, Victor had math, his weakest subject. He sat in the back by the window, hoping he would not be called on. Victor understood most of the problems, but some of the stuff looked like the teacher made it up as she went along. It was confusing, like the inside of a watch.

After math he had a fifteen-minute break, then social studies, and, finally, lunch. He bought a tuna casserole with buttered rolls, some fruit cocktail, and milk. He sat with Michael, who practiced scowling between bites.

Girls walked by and looked at him.

"See what I mean, Vic?" Michael scowled. "They love it."

"Yeah, I guess so."

They ate slowly, Victor scanning the horizon for a glimpse of Teresa. He didn't see her. She must have brought lunch, he thought, and is eating outside. Victor scraped his plate and left Michael, who was busy scowling at a girl two tables away.

The small, triangle-shaped campus bustled with students talking about their new classes. Everyone was in a sunny mood. Victor hurried to the bag lunch area, where he sat down and opened his math book. He moved his lips as if he were reading, but his mind was somewhere else. He raised his eyes slowly and looked around. No Teresa.

He lowered his eyes, pretending to study, then looked slowly to the left. No Teresa. He turned a page in the book and stared at some math problems that scared him because he knew he would have to do them eventually. He looked to the right. Still no sign of her. He stretched out lazily in an attempt to disguise his snooping.

Then he saw her. She was sitting with a girlfriend under a plum tree. Victor moved to a table near her and daydreamed about taking her to a movie. When the bell sounded, Teresa looked up, and their eyes met. She smiled sweetly and gathered her books. Her next class was French, same as Victor's.

They were among the last students to arrive in class, so all the good desks in the back had already been taken. Victor was forced to sit near the front, a few desks away from Teresa, while Mr. Bueller wrote French words on the chalkboard. The bell rang, and Mr. Bueller wiped his hands, turned to the class, and said, *"Bonjour."*[5]

"Bonjour," braved a few students.

"Bonjour," Victor whispered. He wondered if Teresa heard him.

Mr. Bueller said that if the students studied hard, at the end of the year they could go to France and be understood by the populace.

One kid raised his hand and asked, "What's 'populace'?"

"The people, the people of France."

Mr. Bueller asked if anyone knew French. Victor raised his hand, wanting to impress Teresa. The teacher beamed and said, *"Très bien. Parlez-vous français?"*[6]

Victor didn't know what to say. The teacher wet his lips and asked something else in French. The room grew silent. Victor felt all eyes staring at him. He tried to <u>bluff</u> his way out by making noises that sounded French.

"La me vave me con le grandma," he said uncertainly.

Mr. Bueller, wrinkling his face in curiosity, asked him to speak up.

Great rosebushes of red bloomed on Victor's cheeks. A river of nervous sweat ran down his

---

5. *Bonjour* (bôn´zhōōr) *French:* Good day.
6. *Très bien. Parlez-vous français?* (trĕ byăn pär´lā vōō frän´sĕ) *French:* Very good. Do you speak French?

bluff (blŭf) *v.* to mislead or deceive; to fake

palms. He felt awful. Teresa sat a few desks away, no doubt thinking he was a fool. Without looking at Mr. Bueller, Victor mumbled, "Frenchie oh wewe gee in September."

ACTIVE READER

CONNECT Have you ever done or said something to impress somebody that you later felt foolish about? What was it?

Mr. Bueller asked Victor to repeat what he said.

"Frenchie oh wewe gee in September," Victor repeated.

Mr. Bueller understood that the boy didn't know French and turned away. He walked to the blackboard and pointed to the words on the board with his steel-edged ruler.

"*Le bateau,*" he sang.

"*Le bateau,*" the students repeated.

"*Le bateau est sur l'eau,*"[7] he sang.

"*Le bateau est sur l'eau.*"

Victor was too weak from failure to join the class. He stared at the board and wished he had taken Spanish, not French. Better yet, he wished he could start his life over. He had never been so embarrassed. He bit his thumb until he tore off a sliver of skin.

The bell sounded for fifth period, and Victor shot out of the room, avoiding the stares of the other kids, but had to return for his math book. He looked sheepishly at the teacher, who was erasing the board, then widened his eyes in terror at Teresa who stood in front of him. "I didn't know you knew French," she said. "That was good."

Mr. Bueller looked at Victor, and Victor looked back. Oh please, don't say anything, Victor pleaded with his eyes. I'll wash your car, mow your lawn, walk your dog—anything! I'll be your best student, and I'll clean your erasers after school.

Mr. Bueller shuffled through the papers on his desk. He smiled and hummed as he sat down to work. He remembered his college years when he dated a girlfriend in borrowed cars. She thought he was rich because each time he picked her up he had a different car. It was fun until he had spent all his money on her and had to write home to his parents because he was broke.

Victor couldn't stand to look at Teresa. He was sweaty with shame. "Yeah, well, I picked up a few things from movies and books and stuff like that." They left the class together. Teresa asked him if he would help her with her French.

"Sure, anytime," Victor said.

"I won't be bothering you, will I?"

"Oh no, I like being bothered."

"*Bonjour,*" Teresa said, leaving him outside her next class. She smiled and pushed wisps of hair from her face.

"Yeah, right, *bonjour,*" Victor said. He turned and headed to his class. The rosebushes of shame on his face became bouquets of love. Teresa is a great girl, he thought. And Mr. Bueller is a good guy.

He raced to metal shop. After metal shop there was biology, and after biology a long sprint to the public library, where he checked out three French textbooks.

He was going to like seventh grade. ❖

---

7. *Le bateau est sur l'eau.* (lə bä′tō ĕ sür lō) *French:* The boat is on the water.

WORDS TO KNOW   **sheepishly** (shē′pĭsh-lē) *adv.* with a bashful or embarrassed look

Connect to the Literature

1. **What Do You Think?** What was your reaction to Victor's lie? Explain.

Comprehension Check
- What was the main reason that Victor wanted to take French?
- What happened when Victor told Mr. Bueller that he spoke French?
- Why does Victor go to the library? What is he going to do and why?

Think Critically

2. Do you feel Victor should feel proud of or ashamed of his actions? Why or why not?

   Think About:
   - why he claimed to know French
   - what happens, or might happen, as a result of his claim

3. **ACTIVE READING** **CONNECTING**
   Look at the chart that you made in your **READER'S NOTEBOOK**. In what ways did you connect to Victor's experience? Discuss this with a classmate.

4. The French teacher, Mr. Bueller, realizes that Victor is faking his knowledge of French. Why do you think he keeps the truth to himself?

5. It seems that Victor succeeds in impressing Teresa. What is your opinion of her? Support your answer with evidence from the story.

Extend Interpretations

6. **Different Perspectives** How do you think this story would be different if it were told from Teresa's perspective instead of Victor's?

7. **Connect to Life** Why do people feel the need to create false impressions of themselves? Has anyone ever tried to impress you by saying or doing something you knew was dishonest? What happened? Discuss your experiences with a classmate.

Literary Analysis

SETTING A story's **setting**—the time and the place of its action—may include the geographical location, the historical period, the time of day, and the beliefs, customs, and standards of a society. In some stories, such as "Seventh Grade," the setting is simple and straightforward. For example " . . . he thought some day he might travel to France, where it was cool: not like Fresno, where summer days reached 110 degrees in the shade."

Activity Make a list of at least three details in "Seventh Grade" that are examples of setting.

Setting
Fresno
1st day of school
autumn

DIALECT A **dialect** is a form of language that is spoken in a certain place by a certain group of people. In "Seventh Grade" the author makes his characters more realistic by including dialogue that might be used by young people.

"What classes are you taking?". . .
"French. How 'bout you?"
"Spanish. I ain't so good at it, even if I'm Mexican."

Writing

Write a Letter Put yourself in Victor's shoes. Write a letter that Victor might send to a good friend about his experience in French class. Remember that he "was too weak from failure," "had never been so embarrassed," "looked sheepishly." What did Victor learn about himself from those feelings? Address the one-page letter to someone you know, and use the first-person point of view ("I was so embarrassed today because . . ."). Place your draft in your **Working Portfolio.**

Speaking & Listening

Comedy from Tragedy Watching someone try to impress someone else can sometimes be pretty funny. Imagine that a character gets to meet a famous person he or she really admires. With a partner, write a short skit about what the character does to be impressive, only to end up doing something embarrassing instead. Include in your skit lots of specific gestures, actions, and dialogue. Then act it out for the class. Be sure you enunciate your words and vary the tone of your voice so the audience understands what's happening.

Art Connection

Look at Hugh Harrison's illustration on page 21. What does the posture of the boys tell you? Who do you think they are? What are they doing? Do you think this is a good illustration for "Seventh Grade"?

Research & Technology

Mexican Americans Consult history books, encyclopedias, and other resources to find out about one of the contributions Mexican Americans have made to the culture of the United States, or to an individual state, such as California.

Research and Technology Handbook See p. R110.

Vocabulary

EXERCISE: ANTONYMS For each group of words below, write the letter of the word that is most nearly opposite in meaning to the boldfaced Word to Know.

1. **elective:**
   (a) chosen (b) required (c) optional
2. **scowl:**
   (a) frown (b) grimace (c) smile
3. **quiver:**
   (a) tremble (b) vibrate (c) hold
4. **ferocity:**
   (a) aggressiveness
   (b) bravery
   (c) gentleness
5. **conviction:**
   (a) uncertainty (b) force (c) belief
6. **linger:**
   (a) struggle (b) hasten (c) prolong
7. **trudge:**
   (a) sprint (b) jump (c) amble
8. **portly:**
   (a) fluid (b) overweight (c) lean
9. **bluff:**
   (a) lie (b) admit (c) know
10. **sheepishly:**
    (a) shyly (b) boldly (c) easily

Vocabulary Handbook
See p. R26: Synonyms and Antonyms.

Grammar in Context: Complete Subjects and Predicates

Notice how Gary Soto uses a series of short sentences to create a feeling of Victor's anxiety.

> Victor didn't <u>know</u> what to say. The teacher <u>wet</u> his lips and <u>asked</u> something else in French. The room <u>grew</u> silent. Victor <u>felt</u> all eyes staring at him.

A sentence consists of a subject and a predicate. The **complete subject** includes all the words that tell whom or what the sentence is about. The **complete predicate** includes all the words that tell what the subject is or does. The predicate contains the <u>**verb**</u> and any words that modify the verb.

The verb expresses an action, a condition, or a state of being. Sometimes the verb is a complete predicate. In other cases the verb is part of a longer predicate.

WRITING EXERCISE Read these incomplete sentences. Write a predicate for each subject. Underline the verbs.

Example: *Original* **Mr. Bueller,** the French teacher,

Rewritten **Mr. Bueller,** the French teacher, **kept** Victor's secret.

1. **Talking** to Teresa
2. At lunch **Victor**
3. The **students**
4. **Mr. Bueller**

Connect to the Literature Imagine a study session during which Victor tutors Teresa. Write complete sentences for their dialogue. Circle your subjects and underline your verbs.

Grammar Handbook
See p. R71: Writing Complete Sentences.

Gary Soto
born 1952

"I do get many of my ideas from remembering my own childhood in Fresno."

Mexican-American Roots Gary Soto grew up in a Mexican-American community in Fresno, California. His father worked for a raisin company, and his mother peeled potatoes at a food-processing company. At various times during his childhood, Soto wanted to be a priest, a hobo, and a paleontologist (a scientist who studies fossils).

Geography or Poetry? In college, Soto planned to study geography, until he discovered poetry. "I don't think I had any literary aspirations when I was a kid," says Soto. "In fact, we didn't have books, and no one encouraged us to read. So my wanting to write poetry was a sort of fluke."

Award-Winning Writer and Filmmaker Today Soto is a celebrated poet, essayist, novelist, and filmmaker. He taught at the University of California at Berkeley, and now devotes his time to writing for young people. He has won numerous awards, including the American Book Award for *Living Up the Street.*

Thank You, M'am

by LANGSTON HUGHES

Key Standard
R3.2 Identify events that advance the plot and describe how they explain the past, present, and future.
Other Standards **R1.3, R2.3, W2.2, LC1.3, LC1.4, LC1.7**

Connect to Your Life

Good Neighbors An African proverb says, "It takes two parents to produce a child, but it takes an entire village to raise the child." What values do you associate with community spirit?

Build Background

GEOGRAPHY

The action of "Thank You, M'am" takes place in the late 1950s in Harlem, a section of New York City. In the early 1900s, Harlem attracted a community of African-American musicians, artists, and writers, including Langston Hughes. The vibrant and stimulating life of Harlem had a deep influence on the work of these creative people.

Historic photo of Harlem, showing 122nd Street between 7th and 8th Avenues. Copyright © Archive Photos.

Focus Your Reading

LITERARY ANALYSIS   CONFLICT

The action of a **plot** is usually set in motion by a **central conflict,** or struggle between opposing forces. A character's struggle against an outside force—another character, a physical obstacle, nature, or society—is called an **external conflict.** A struggle within a character is an **internal conflict.** As you read "Thank You, M'am," look for examples of both types of conflict.

ACTIVE READING   CAUSE AND EFFECT

Events in stories are often related as **cause and effect**—that is, one event brings about another. Cause-and-effect relationships are often signaled by words such as *because, since, thus, therefore, so,* and *as a result.* Such a series of cause-and-effect events helps advance the plot.

READER'S NOTEBOOK As you read this story, try to connect the major events in a series of causes and effects. Make a diagram, including as many events as necessary.

WORDS TO KNOW
Vocabulary Preview

barren   presentable
frail   suede
mistrust

Reverie (1989), Frank Webb. Pastel, 12″ × 8″, collection of Barbara Webb.

Thank You, M'am

BY LANGSTON HUGHES

She was a large woman with a large purse that had everything in it but hammer and nails. It had a long strap, and she carried it slung across her shoulder. It was about eleven o'clock at night, and she was walking alone, when a boy ran up behind her and tried to snatch her purse. The strap broke with the single tug the boy gave it from behind. But the boy's weight and the weight of the purse combined caused him to lose his balance so, instead of taking off full blast as he had hoped, the boy fell on his back on the sidewalk, and his legs flew up. The large woman simply turned around and kicked him right square in his blue-jeaned sitter. Then she reached down, picked the boy up by his shirt front, and shook him until his teeth rattled.

After that the woman said, "Pick up my pocketbook, boy, and give it here."

She still held him. But she bent down enough to permit him to stoop and pick up her purse. Then she said, "Now ain't you ashamed of yourself?"

Firmly gripped by his shirt front, the boy said, "Yes'm."

The woman said, "What did you want to do it for?"

The boy said, "I didn't aim to."

She said, "You a lie!"

By that time two or three people passed, stopped, turned to look, and some stood watching.

"If I turn you loose, will you run?" asked the woman.

"Yes'm," said the boy.

"Then I won't turn you loose," said the woman. She did not release him.

"I'm very sorry, lady, I'm sorry," whispered the boy.

"Um-hum! And your face is dirty. I got a great mind to wash your face for you. Ain't you got nobody home to tell you to wash your face?"

"No'm," said the boy.

"Then it will get washed this evening," said the large woman starting up the street, dragging the frightened boy behind her.

He looked as if he were fourteen or fifteen, <u>frail</u> and willow-wild, in tennis shoes and blue jeans.

The woman said, "You ought to be my son. I would teach you right from wrong. Least I can do right now is to wash your face. Are you hungry?"

"No'm," said the being-dragged boy. "I just want you to turn me loose."

"Was I bothering *you* when I turned that corner?" asked the woman.

"No'm."

"But you put yourself in contact with *me*," said the woman. "If you think that that contact is not going to last awhile, you got another thought coming. When I get through with you, sir, you are going to remember Mrs. Luella Bates Washington Jones."

Sweat popped out on the boy's face and he began to struggle. Mrs. Jones stopped, jerked him around in front of her, put a half nelson[1] about his neck, and continued to drag him up the street. When she got to her door, she dragged the boy inside, down a hall, and into a large kitchenette-furnished room at the rear of the house. She switched on the light and left the door open.

---

1. **half nelson:** a wrestling hold with one arm under the opponent's arm from behind to the back of the neck.

The boy could hear other roomers laughing and talking in the large house. Some of their doors were open, too, so he knew he and the woman were not alone. The woman still had him by the neck in the middle of her room.

She said, "What is your name?"

"Roger," answered the boy.

"Then, Roger, you go to that sink and wash your face," said the woman, whereupon she turned him loose—at last. Roger looked at the door—looked at the woman—looked at the door—*and went to the sink.*

"Let the water run until it gets warm," she said. "Here's a clean towel."

"You gonna take me to jail?" asked the boy, bending over the sink.

"Not with that face, I would not take you nowhere," said the woman. "Here I am trying to get home to cook me a bite to eat and you snatch my pocketbook! Maybe you ain't been to your supper either, late as it be. Have you?"

"There's nobody home at my house," said the boy.

"Then we'll eat," said the woman. "I believe you're hungry—or been hungry—to try to snatch my pocketbook."

"I wanted a pair of blue <u>suede</u> shoes," said the boy.

"Well, you didn't have to snatch *my* pocketbook to get some suede shoes," said Mrs. Luella Bates Washington Jones. "You could of asked me."

"M'am?"

The water dripping from his face, the boy looked at her. There was a long pause. A very long pause. After he had dried his face and not knowing what else to do dried it again, the boy turned around, wondering what next. The door was open. He could make a dash for it down the hall. He could run, run, run, run, *run!*

The woman was sitting on the day-bed. After a while she said, "I were young once and I wanted things I could not get."

There was another long pause. The boy's mouth opened. Then he frowned, but not knowing he frowned.

The woman said, "Um-hum! You thought I was going to say *but,* didn't you? You thought I was going to say, *but I didn't snatch people's pocketbooks.* Well, I wasn't going to say that." Pause. Silence. "I have done things, too, which I would not tell you, son—neither tell God, if he didn't already know. So you set down while I fix us something to eat. You might run that comb through your hair so you will look <u>presentable</u>."

In another corner of the room behind a screen was a gas plate and an icebox. Mrs. Jones got up and went behind the screen. The woman did not watch the boy to see if he was going to run now, nor did she watch her purse which she left behind her on the day-bed. But the boy took care to sit on the far side of the room where he thought she could easily see him out of the corner of her eye, if she wanted to. He did not trust the woman *not* to trust him. And he did not want to be <u>mistrusted</u> now.

"Do you need somebody to go to the store," asked the boy, "maybe to get some milk or something?"

WORDS TO KNOW

suede (swād) *n.* leather with a soft, fuzzy surface
presentable (prĭ-zĕn′tə-bəl) *adj.* fit to be seen by people
mistrust (mĭs-trŭst′) *v.* to have no confidence in

"Don't believe I do," said the woman, "unless you just want sweet milk yourself. I was going to make cocoa out of this canned milk I got here."

"That will be fine," said the boy.

She heated some lima beans and ham she had in the icebox, made the cocoa, and set the table. The woman did not ask the boy anything about where he lived, or his folks, or anything else that would embarrass him. Instead, as they ate, she told him about her job in a hotel beauty-shop that stayed open late, what the work was like, and how all kinds of women came in and out, blondes, red-heads, and Spanish. Then she cut him a half of her ten-cent cake.

"Eat some more, son," she said.

When they were finished eating she got up and said, "Now, here, take this ten dollars and buy yourself some blue suede shoes. And next time, do not make the mistake of latching onto *my* pocketbook *nor nobody else's*—because shoes come by devilish like that will burn your feet. I got to get my rest now. But I wish you would behave yourself, son, from here on in."

She led him down the hall to the front door and opened it. "Goodnight! Behave yourself, boy!" she said, looking out into the street.

The boy wanted to say something else other than "Thank you, m'am" to Mrs. Luella Bates Washington Jones, but he couldn't do so as he turned at the <u>barren</u> stoop and looked back at the large woman in the door. He barely managed to say "Thank you" before she shut the door. And he never saw her again. ❖

If I Can Stop One Heart from Breaking
by Emily Dickinson

If I can stop one Heart from breaking
I shall not live in vain
If I can ease one Life the Aching
Or cool one Pain

Or help one fainting Robin
Unto his Nest again
I shall not live in Vain.

WORDS
TO
KNOW

barren (băr′ən) *adj.* empty; deserted

Connect to the Literature

1. **What Do You Think?** How did you feel about the last sentence in the story ("And he never saw her again")? Explain your reaction.

   Comprehension Check
   • What happens when Roger tries to steal Mrs. Jones's purse?
   • Why does Roger want to steal money from Mrs. Jones?
   • What happens when Mrs. Jones gets Roger to her house?

Think Critically

2. Why do you think Mrs. Jones treats Roger the way she does?

   Think About:
   • what she reveals about her past
   • what she seems to understand about Roger's life
   • how Roger answers her questions

3. Do you think Roger will steal again? Why or why not?

4. **ACTIVE READING** **CAUSE AND EFFECT**
   Compare the **cause-and-effect** diagram you made in your ▯ **READER'S NOTEBOOK** with a classmate's. How are the events and details in the two series of causes and effects similar? How do they differ?

Extend Interpretations

5. **COMPARING TEXTS** Reread the poem on page 33. Which lines remind you of the way Mrs. Jones thinks?

6. **Connect to Life** In this story, Roger is willing to go to extreme lengths to get blue suede shoes. Most people would not approve of his actions. Can you think of other ways he could have tried to get the shoes? Discuss your ideas with a classmate.

Literary Analysis

CONFLICT A story's plot usually centers on a **central conflict**—a struggle between opposing forces. An **external conflict** is a character's struggle against a force outside himself or herself. An **internal conflict** takes place inside a character. For example, a character may struggle against his or her fears or may experience a conflict between wanting something and knowing that taking it is wrong. While some stories, like "Thank You M'am," can have both kinds of conflict occurring at the same time, only one is the central conflict.

Paired Activity Go through the story with a partner, looking for examples of conflict. Determine which are external and which are internal. Record your findings in a chart like the one shown here. After you finish, discuss these questions:

• Which conflict is the central conflict?

• Which conflicts convey important information about the characters?

• Which conflicts add the most excitement to the story?

Conflict	Internal	External
Roger tries to steal Mrs. Jones's purse.		✔
Mrs. Jones grabs Roger.		✔
Mrs. Jones must decide what to do with Roger.	✔	

CHOICES and CHALLENGES

Writing

Response to Literature Do you think Mrs. Jones treated Roger fairly after he tried to steal her purse? How would you have reacted to Mrs. Jones if you were Roger? Choose one of these questions and write your response in paragraph form. Include at least three examples from the story, including dialogue and specific action. Place your draft in your **Working Portfolio.**

Writing Handbook
See p. R39: Paragraphs.

Speaking & Listening

Film Review View the video version of "Thank You, M'am." Pay special attention to how the actors portray the characters through voice and action. Then, with classmates, discuss whether the video portrays the characters as you visualized them.

VIDEO: Literature in Performance

"Thank You, M'am"

Art Connection

Look at Frank Webb's drawing *Reverie* on page 30. What are your impressions of the subject of the drawing?

Research & Technology

Life in Harlem With a group of classmates, read about the history of Harlem in reference books or on the Internet. Select a two-year time period to investigate further. Develop questions to help you focus your research.

Research and Technology Handbook See p. R110.

Vocabulary and Spelling

STANDARDIZED TEST PRACTICE

Choose the word or group of words that means the same, or nearly the same, as the underlined Word to Know.

1. <u>Presentable</u> clothing
   A old-fashioned **B** tattered
   C proper **D** sturdy

2. A pair of <u>suede</u> shoes
   J canvas **K** leather
   L rubber **M** silk

3. A <u>barren</u> playground
   A deserted **B** dark
   C private **D** beloved

4. <u>Frail</u> patients
   J unconscious **K** friendly
   L nervous **M** weak

5. To <u>mistrust</u> someone's advice
   A accept **B** doubt
   C seek **D** mistake

Vocabulary Handbook
See p. R26: Synonyms and Antonyms.

SPELLING STRATEGY: PREFIXES When a prefix is added to a root word, as in *mistrust,* do not drop a letter from either the prefix or the root word.

1. Write out the following words with prefixes.
   mis + trust = _____
   mis + spell = _____
   de + part = _____
   de + serve = _____
   ex + act = _____
   ex + claim = _____

Spelling Handbook
See p. R30.

THANK YOU, M'AM **35**

Grammar in Context: Compound Verbs

Langston Hughes shows how quickly Mrs. Jones reacts when Roger tries to take her purse:

> Mrs. Jones **stopped, jerked** him around in front of her, **put** a half nelson about his neck, and **continued** to drag him up the street.

The words in green are main verbs. They tell what the single subject, Mrs. Jones, does. When a sentence has two or more main verbs that have the same subject, it has a **compound verb**.

Punctuation Tip: When a compound verb has more than two parts, use **commas** to separate the parts.

> She **reached** down, **picked** the boy up by his shirt front, and **shook** him until his teeth rattled.

WRITING EXERCISE Streamline each pair of sentences by writing one complete sentence with a compound predicate.

Example: ***Original*** Roger, go to that sink. Wash your face at that sink.

Rewritten Roger, go to that sink and wash your face.

1. Roger ran up behind Mrs. Jones. Roger tried to snatch her purse.
2. Mrs. Jones switched on the light. She left the door open.
3. Take this ten dollars. Buy yourself some blue suede shoes.
4. She led him down the hall to the front door. She opened the front door.

Langston Hughes
1902–1967

"Books began to happen to me, and I began to believe in nothing but books. . . ."

Early Years Langston Hughes is one of the most renowned and influential of African-American writers. His poems have been widely translated and appear in poetry anthologies all over the world. Here's how he recalls his youth in Lawrence, Kansas: "Books began to happen to me, and I began to believe in nothing but books and the wonderful world in books—where if people suffered, they suffered in beautiful language, not in monosyllables, as we did in Kansas."

One of the First Hughes was one of the first African Americans to earn his living solely from writing. His first recognition came when, while working as a busboy, he left three of his poems at a table where the poet Vachel Lindsay was dining. Lindsay presented some of the young poet's works at one of his own poetry readings, and Hughes's career was launched.

Hughes went on to write novels, short stories, plays, song lyrics, and radio scripts as well as poetry. To portray the African-American experience, he often focused on the ordinary people whose vitality contributed to the special atmosphere of life in Harlem.

Names/Nombres

by JULIA ALVAREZ

 Key Standard
R3.1 Be able to describe the purposes and characteristics of different forms of prose, such as the short story, novel, or essay.
Other Standards **R1.3, R3.2, W2.1, LC1.4, LC1.7**

Connect to Your Life

Fitting In Think about a time when someone new joined your class. How did the newcomer try to fit in? If you were in a situation where you were a newcomer, how might you try to fit in? Discuss this with your class.

Ways to Fit In

Join a club.

Build Background

SOCIAL STUDIES

In Spanish tradition, a child normally has two last names—the father's family name and the mother's maiden name. Often, a child's full name can include four generations of family names.

Although Julia Alvarez was born in New York City, she spent ten years of her childhood in the Dominican Republic, a country located on the island of Hispaniola in the Caribbean Sea.

WORDS TO KNOW	Vocabulary Preview	
chaotic	inevitably	merge
convoluted	initial	specify
ethnicity	ironically	usher
exotic		

Focus Your Reading

LITERARY ANALYSIS PERSONAL ESSAY

"Names/Nombres" is a **personal essay,** a short form of nonfiction that expresses the author's thoughts and feelings about one subject. Often personal essays include anecdotes in which authors use elements of **character, setting,** and **plot.** Notice how Alvarez uses an anecdote to establish setting and character in the very first sentence of this essay.

> *When we arrived in New York City, our names changed almost immediately. At Immigration, the officer asked my father,* Mister Elbures, *if he had anything to declare.*

ACTIVE READING IDENTIFYING AUTHOR'S PURPOSE

An author can have various **purposes** in a single piece of writing. Usually these purposes include one or more of the following:

- to express an opinion
- to persuade
- to inform or to explain
- to entertain

As you read, think about the purpose or purposes that Julia Alvarez had for writing this essay.

📖 **READER'S NOTEBOOK** As a writer, Julia Alvarez certainly wanted to write an entertaining essay. As you read "Names/Nombres," think about what other purposes she may have had in mind, and jot them down.

NAMES
Nombres
by Julia Alvarez

When we arrived in New York City, our names changed almost immediately.

At Immigration, the officer asked my father, *Mister Elbures,* if he had anything to declare. My father shook his head no, and we were waved through. I was too afraid we wouldn't be let in if I corrected the man's pronunciation, but I said our name to myself, opening my mouth wide for the organ blast of the *a,* trilling my tongue[1] for the drumroll of the *r, All-vah-rrr-es!* How could anyone get *Elbures* out of that orchestra of sound?

At the hotel my mother was *Missus Alburest,* and I was *little girl,* as in, "Hey, little girl, stop riding the elevator up and down. It's *not* a toy."

When we moved into our new apartment building, the super called my father *Mister Alberase,* and the neighbors who became mother's friends pronounced her name *Jew-lee-ah* instead of *Hoo-lee-ah.* I, her namesake, was known as *Hoo-lee-tah* at home. But at school I was *Judy* or *Judith,*

---

1. **trilling my tongue:** rapid vibration of the tongue against the roof of the mouth, as in pronouncing a Spanish *r.*

Illustration by Rosanne Kaloustian.

and once an English teacher mistook me for *Juliet*.

It took a while to get used to my new names. I wondered if I shouldn't correct my teachers and new friends. But my mother argued that it didn't matter. "You know what your friend Shakespeare said, 'A rose by any other name would smell as sweet.'" My family had gotten into the habit of calling any literary figure "my friend" because I had begun to write poems and stories in English class.

By the time I was in high school, I was a popular kid, and it showed in my name. Friends called me *Jules* or *Hey Jude,* and once a group of troublemaking friends my mother forbade me to hang out with called me *Alcatraz.* I was *Hoo-lee-tah* only to Mami and Papi and uncles and aunts who came over to eat *sancocho*[2] on Sunday afternoons—old world folk whom I would just as soon go back to where they came from and leave me to pursue whatever mischief I wanted to in America. JUDY ALCATRAZ: the name on the wanted poster would read. Who would ever trace her to me?

My older sister had the hardest time getting an American name for herself because *Mauricia* did not translate into English. Ironically, although she had the most foreign-sounding name, she and I were the Americans in the family. We had been born in New York

---

2. *sancocho* (säng-kō'chō) *Spanish*: traditional Caribbean stew of meat and vegetables.

WORDS TO KNOW **ironically** (ī-rŏn'ĭk-lē) *adv.* in a way that is contrary to what is expected or intended

Julia Altagracia María Teresa Álvarez Tavares

City when our parents had first tried immigration and then gone back "home," too homesick to stay. My mother often told the story of how she had almost changed my sister's name in the hospital.

After the delivery, Mami and some other new mothers were cooing over their new baby sons and daughters and exchanging names and weights and delivery stories. My mother was embarrassed among the Sallys and Janes and Georges and Johns to reveal the rich, noisy name of *Mauricia,* so when her turn came to brag, she gave her baby's name as *Maureen.*

"Why'd ya give her an Irish name with so many pretty Spanish names to choose from?" one of the women asked her.

My mother blushed and admitted her baby's real name to the group. Her mother-in-law had recently died, she apologized, and her husband had insisted that the first daughter be named after his mother, *Mauran.* My mother thought it the ugliest name she had ever heard, and she talked my father into what she believed was an improvement, a combination of *Mauran* and her own mother's name, *Felicia.*

"Her name is Mao-ree-shee-ah," my mother said to the group.

"Why, that's a beautiful name," the new mothers cried. *"Moor-ee-sha, Moor-ee-sha,"* they cooed into the pink blanket. *Moor-ee-sha* it was when we returned to the States eleven years later. Sometimes, American tongues found even that mispronunciation tough to say and called her *Maria* or *Marsha* or *Maudy* from her nickname *Maury.* I pitied her. What

an awful name to have to transport across borders!

My little sister, Ana, had the easiest time of all. She was plain *Anne*—that is, only her name was plain, for she turned out to be the pale, blond "American beauty" in the family. The only Hispanic-seeming thing about her was the affectionate nicknames her boyfriends sometimes gave her. *Anita,* or as one goofy guy used to sing to her to the tune of the banana advertisement, *Anita Banana.*

Later, during her college years in the late 60's, there was a push to pronounce Third World[3] names correctly. I remember calling her long distance at her group house and a roommate answering.

"Can I speak to Ana?" I asked, pronouncing her name the American way.

"Ana?" The man's voice hesitated. "Oh! You must mean *Ah-nah!*"

Our first few years in the States, though, ethnicity was not yet "in." Those were the blond, blue-eyed, bobby-sock years of junior high and high school before the 60's ushered in peasant blouses, hoop earrings, *sarapes.*[4] My initial desire to be known by my correct Dominican name faded. I just wanted to be Judy and merge with the Sallys and Janes in

---

3. **Third World:** the developing nations of Latin America, Africa, and Asia.

4. *sarapes* (sä-rä'pĕs) *Spanish*: a long, blanket-like shawl.

WORDS TO KNOW	**ethnicity** (ĕth-nĭs'ĭ-tē) *n.* a racial, national, or cultural heritage
	usher (ŭsh'ər) *v.* to make known the presence or arrival of; to introduce
	initial (ĭ-nĭsh'əl) *adj.* first
	merge (mûrj) *v.* to blend together

Perello Espaillat Julia Pérez Rochet González

my class. But, inevitably, my accent and coloring gave me away. "So where are you from, Judy?"

"New York," I told my classmates. After all, I had been born blocks away at Columbia Presbyterian Hospital.

"I mean, *originally.*"

"From the Caribbean," I answered vaguely, for if I specified, no one was quite sure what continent our island was located on.

"Really? I've been to Bermuda. We went last April for spring vacation. I got the worst sunburn! So, are you from Portoriko?"

"No," I shook my head. "From the Dominican Republic."

"Where's that?"

"South of Bermuda."

They were just being curious, I knew, but I burned with shame whenever they singled me out as a "foreigner," a rare, exotic friend.

"Say your name in Spanish, oh, please say it!" I had made mouths drop one day by rattling off my full name, which, according to Dominican custom, included my middle names, Mother's and Father's surnames for four generations back.

"Julia Altagracia María Teresa Álvarez Tavares Perello Espaillat Julia Pérez Rochet González." I pronounced it slowly, a name as chaotic with sounds as a Middle Eastern bazaar or market day in a South American village.

I suffered most whenever my extended family attended school occasions. For my graduation, they all came, the whole noisy, foreign-looking lot of fat aunts in their dark mourning dresses and hair nets, uncles with full, droopy mustaches and baby-blue or salmon-colored suits and white pointy shoes and fedora hats,[5] the many little cousins who snuck in without tickets. They sat in the first row in order to better understand the Americans' fast-spoken English. But how could they listen when they were constantly speaking among themselves in florid-sounding[6] phrases, rococo[7] consonants, rich, rhyming vowels? Their loud voices carried.

Introducing them to my friends was a further trial to me. These relatives had such complicated names and there were so many of them, and their relationships to myself were so convoluted. There was my Tía[8] Josefina, who was not really an aunt but a much older cousin. And her daughter, Aída Margarita, who was adopted, *una hija de crianza.*[9] My uncle of affection, Tío José, brought my *madrina*[10] Tía Amelia and her *comadre*[11] Tía Pilar. My friends rarely had more than their

---

5. **fedora hats** (fĭ-dôr′ə): soft felt hats with low crowns.
6. **florid-sounding:** flowery; very ornate.
7. **rococo** (rə-kō′kō): elaborate; flamboyant.
8. ***Tía/Tío*** (tē′ä, tē′ō) *Spanish:* Aunt/Uncle.
9. ***una hija de crianza*** (oō′nä ē′hä dĕ kryän′sä) *Spanish:* a child raised as if one's own.
10. ***madrina*** (mä-drē′nä) *Spanish:* godmother.
11. ***comadre*** (kō-mä′drĕ) *Spanish:* close friend.

WORDS TO KNOW	
inevitably (ĭn-ĕv′ĭ-tə-blē) *adv.* impossible to avoid or prevent
specify (spĕs′ə-fī) *v.* to make known or identify
exotic (ĭg-zŏt′ĭk) *adj.* unusual or different
chaotic (kā-ŏt′ĭk) *adj.* confused; disordered
convoluted (kŏn′və-loō′tĭd) *adj.* difficult to understand; complicated

nuclear family[12] to introduce, youthful, glamorous-looking couples ("Mom and Dad") who skied and played tennis and took their kids for spring vacations to Bermuda.

After the commencement ceremony, my family waited outside in the parking lot while my friends and I signed yearbooks with nicknames which recalled our high school good times: "Beans" and "Pepperoni" and "Alcatraz." We hugged and cried and promised to keep in touch.

Sometimes if our goodbyes went on too long, I heard my father's voice calling out across the parking lot. *"Hoo-lee-tah! Vámonos!"*[13]

Back home, my tíos and tías and primas,[14] Mami and Papi, and *mis hermanas*[15] had a party for me with *sancocho* and a store-bought *pudín,*[16] inscribed with *Happy Graduation, Julie.* There were many gifts—that was a plus to a large family! I got several wallets and a suitcase with my initials and a graduation charm from my godmother and money from my uncles. The biggest gift was a portable typewriter from my parents for writing my stories and poems.

Someday, the family predicted, my name would be well-known throughout the United States. I laughed to myself, wondering which one I would go by. ❖

Cover Illustration by German Perez.

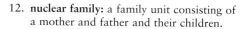

---

12. **nuclear family:** a family unit consisting of a mother and father and their children.

13. *Vámonos* (bä′mō-nōs) *Spanish:* Let's go.

14. *primas* (prē′mäs) *Spanish:* cousins.

15. *mis hermanas* (mēs ĕr-mä′näs) *Spanish:* my sisters.

16. *pudín* (pōō-thēn′) *Spanish:* pudding.

Connect to the Literature

1. What Do You Think?
If you were in Alvarez's position as a newcomer, do you think you might fit in as well as she did? Explain.

Comprehension Check
- Where is the Alvarez family from?
- Why did Mrs. Alvarez first tell the ladies at the hospital that her oldest daughter's name was Maureen?
- Why did Alvarez find it difficult to introduce her relatives to her friends?

Think Critically

2. ACTIVE READING | IDENTIFYING AUTHOR'S PURPOSE
Look at what you wrote about writer's purpose in your 📖 READER'S NOTEBOOK. Besides wanting to tell an interesting story, what do you think Alvarez's purpose might be? Give evidence for your answer.

Think About:
- Alvarez's high-school days
- the experiences of her sisters
- her feelings toward her extended family

3. Why do you think some people permanently change their names when they come to the United States, while others don't?

4. How would you describe Mrs. Alvarez?

Think About:
- the scene in the hospital
- her quoting of Shakespeare
- what she calls her daughter

Extend Interpretations

5. The Writer's Style In this essay Alvarez uses humor to deal with otherwise serious topics. Why do you think she does that? How does humor help get her ideas across?

Literary Analysis

PERSONAL ESSAY One form of nonfiction is the **personal essay.** These essays are often **autobiographical,** focusing on a writer's own experiences. "Names/Nombres," like most personal essays, is centered around one main issue. In this essay, Alvarez shares her thoughts about her Dominican name and culture and the way they were interpreted by Americans when she and her family moved to the United States.

Group Activity Review Alvarez's essay. Then answer the following questions:
- What is the author's attitude toward her subject matter?
- What lessons did the author learn from her experiences?
- What is the author's purpose for writing this essay?

Compare your answers with those of some of your classmates.

REVIEW: SETTING The **setting** of a literary work is the time when the events described happen and the place where they happen. Setting plays an important role in what happens and why. In this essay Alvarez writes of trying to bring into harmony aspects of her Dominican background and her new American home.

Writing

Personal Narrative Write a short narrative about a first-time meeting with someone you later got to know. If possible, use elements of fiction such as character and setting to establish the scene. Then write about ways your first impression was accurate and ways it was not.

Writing Handbook
See p. R45: Narrative Writing.

Speaking & Listening

Interview Questions Suppose you are a talk show host, and your audience is made up of your classmates. You are interviewing writers who write about their childhood experiences. Julia Alvarez is one of your guests. How would you introduce her to your audience? What questions would you ask? Identify topics and develop questions that would be of interest to your audience.

Speaking and Listening Handbook
See p. R100.

Research & Technology

Life in the U.S.A. The United States is home to many immigrants. Do you have a relative, a friend, or a neighbor who moved to the United States from another country? Ask about his or her adjustment to American life. Tape your conversation. Use your tape to create a short essay or oral report.

INTERNET Research Starter
www.mcdougallittell.com

Vocabulary and Spelling

Choose the word or group of words that means the same, or nearly the same, as the underlined Word to Know.

1. Exotic means—
   A unusual   **B** bashful
   C respectful   **D** colorful

2. To specify something is to—
   F conceal it   **G** correct it
   H identify it   **J** strengthen it

3. Initial is another word for—
   A independent   **B** first
   C partial   **D** meaningful

4. To merge is to—
   F balance   **G** complete
   H search   **J** blend

5. Convoluted means—
   A crucial   **B** complicated
   C clear   **D** concise

Vocabulary Handbook
See p. R26: Synonyms and Antonyms.

SPELLING STRATEGY: SUFFIXES Add -ly to adjectives to form adverbs. When the suffix -ly is added to a word ending in l, as in initially, both l's are retained. Add -ally to adjectives that end in -c, as in chaotically. For words ending in -ble, just replace the -e with -y, as in inevitably.

1. Add the suffix -ly to the following words.

ironic	exotic
chaotic	initial
national	gradual
inevitable	historic
regrettable	capable

2. Use each of the spelling words in a complete sentence.

Spelling Handbook
See p. R30.

Grammar in Context: Combining Complete Sentences

In the compound sentence shown below, Julia Alvarez describes her family's experience with an immigration officer.

> **My father shook his head no, and we were waved through.**

When complete sentences are combined into one sentence, they become a **compound sentence.**

Here are three ways to join sentences.

1. Use *and, or,* or *but* preceded by a comma: **I was known as *Hoo-lee-tah* at home, but at school I was *Judy* or *Judith*.**

2. Use words like *however* or *therefore* preceded by a semicolon and followed by a comma: **I was known as *Hoo-lee-tah* at home; however, at school I was *Judy* or *Judith*.**

3. If there are no joining words, just use a semicolon: **I was known as *Hoo-lee-tah* at home; at school I was *Judy* or *Judith*.**

WRITING EXERCISE Combine each pair of sentences using one of the three methods listed.

Example: *Original* I was afraid to correct the man's pronunciation. I said our name to myself.

Rewritten I was afraid to correct the man's pronunciation, <u>but</u> I said our name to myself.

1. Some friends called me *Jules* or *Hey Jude.* Other friends called me *Alcatraz.*

2. My friends had only their parents to introduce. My whole extended family attended school occasions.

3. I wanted to ask my new friends to say my name correctly. My mother said it didn't matter.

Grammar Handbook

See p. R71: Writing Complete Sentences.

Julia Alvarez
born 1950

"Mine was an American childhood."

New in New York Although Julia Alvarez was born in New York City, she lived in the Dominican Republic until she was ten. When Alvarez returned, she felt out of place—a foreigner with a different language, name, and way of life.

Young Writer Alvarez's first years back in New York were tough, but she soon found a way to cope. She started to write stories and poetry.

"I could save what I didn't want to lose— memories and smells and sounds, things too precious to put anywhere else." Alvarez's writings continue to draw on her early memories and immigrant experiences. Her best-selling novel, *How the Garcia Girls Lost Their Accents,* tells the story of an immigrant Dominican family and how they adjust to American life and become, like Alvarez, at home in two cultures.

AUTHOR ACTIVITY
Dominican Heritage Find out more about the Dominican Republic and the harsh government under which Alvarez and her family lived until returning to the United States in the early 1960s. Discuss your findings with your classmates.

Zebra

by CHAIM POTOK (khī′ĭm pō′täk)

Key Standard
R3.3 Analyze characters by examining what they think, say, and do, and by studying the words of the narrator and the reactions of other characters.
Other Standards **R1.3, W2.3, LC1.3, LS1.5, LS2.4**

In 1982, the Vietnam Veterans Memorial was unveiled in Washington, D.C., to honor the men and women who served in Vietnam.

Connect to Your Life

What do you know about the Vietnam War?

Build Background

Approximately 58,000 Americans died and over 300,000 were wounded in the Vietnam War. After the war, many veterans, like John Wilson in "Zebra," struggled to piece their lives back together.

Focus Your Reading

Characters are the people, animals, or imaginary creatures who appear in stories. Usually, a short story focuses on one or two **main characters** (also called major characters). Less important characters are called **minor characters.** As you read "Zebra," identify the main characters.

WORDS TO KNOW **Vocabulary Preview**

disciplinarian	gaunt	menacing	tensing
encrusted	intricate	poised	wince
exuberantly	jauntily		

An **inference** is a logical conclusion based on evidence. Whenever you read a story, look for **details** that help you understand what is going on. Using these details and what you know from your own experience, you can figure out more than just what the words say.

In your ▢ **READER'S NOTEBOOK** create a chart to help you keep track of the inferences you make about Zebra and his experiences.

ZEBRA

by
Chaim
Potok

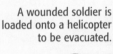

A wounded soldier is loaded onto a helicopter to be evacuated.

Silent Fall, Nicholas Wilton. Acrylic on wood, 24" × 14 1/2"

His name was Adam Martin Zebrin, but everyone in his neighborhood knew him as Zebra.

He couldn't remember when he began to be called by that name. Perhaps they started to call him Zebra when he first began running. Or maybe he began running when they started to call him Zebra.

He loved the name and he loved to run.

When he was very young, his parents took him to a zoo, where he saw zebras for the first time. They were odd-looking creatures, like stubby horses, short-legged, thick-necked, with dark and white stripes.

Then one day he went with his parents to a movie about Africa, and he saw zebras, hundreds of them, thundering across a grassy plain, dust rising in boiling brown clouds.

Was he already running before he saw that movie, or did he begin to run afterward? No one seemed able to remember.

He would go running through the neighborhood for the sheer joy of feeling the wind on his face. People said that when he ran he arched his head up and back, and his face kind of flattened out. One of his teachers told him it was clever to run that way, his balance was better. But the truth was he ran that way, his head thrown back, because he loved to feel the wind rushing across his neck.

Each time, after only a few minutes of running, his legs would begin to feel wondrously light. He would run past the school and the homes on the street beyond the church. All the neighbors knew him and would wave and call out, "Go, Zebra!" And sometimes one or two of their dogs would run with him awhile, barking.

He would imagine himself a zebra on the African plain. Running.

There was a hill on Franklin Avenue, a steep hill. By the time he reached that hill, he would feel his legs so light it was as if he had no legs at all and was flying. He would begin to descend the hill, certain as he ran that he needed only to give himself the slightest push

and off he would go, and instead of a zebra he would become the bird he had once seen in a movie about Alaska, he would swiftly change into an eagle, soaring higher and higher, as light as the gentlest breeze, the cool wind caressing his arms and legs and neck.

Then, a year ago, racing down Franklin Avenue, he had given himself that push and had begun to turn into an eagle, when a huge rushing shadow appeared in his line of vision and crashed into him and plunged him into a darkness from which he emerged very, very slowly. . . .

"Never, never, *never* run down that hill so fast that you can't stop at the corner," his mother had warned him again and again.

His schoolmates and friends kept calling him Zebra even after they all knew that the doctors had told him he would never be able to run like that again.

His leg would heal in time, the doctors said, and perhaps in a year or so the brace would come off. But they were not at all certain about his hand. From time to time his injured hand, which he still wore in a sling, would begin to hurt. The doctors said they could find no cause for the pain.

One morning, during Mr. Morgan's geography class, Zebra's hand began to hurt badly. He sat staring out the window at the sky. Mr. Morgan, a stiff-mannered person in his early fifties, given to smart suits and dapper[1] bow ties, called on him to respond to a question. Zebra stumbled about in vain for the answer. Mr. Morgan told him to pay attention to the geography inside the classroom and not to the geography outside.

"In this class, young man, you will concentrate your attention upon the earth, not upon the sky," Mr. Morgan said.

---

1. **dapper:** neatly dressed; stylish.

Later, in the schoolyard during the midmorning recess, Zebra stood near the tall fence, looking out at the street and listening to the noises behind him.

His schoolmates were racing about, playing <u>exuberantly</u>, shouting and laughing with full voices. Their joyous sounds went ringing through the quiet street.

Most times Zebra would stand alongside the basketball court or behind the wire screen at home plate and watch the games. That day, because his hand hurt so badly, he stood alone behind the chain-link fence of the schoolyard.

That's how he happened to see the man. And that's how the man happened to see him.

One minute the side street on which the school stood was strangely empty, without people or traffic, without even any of the dogs that often roamed about the neighborhood—vacant and silent, as if it were already in the full heat of summer. The red-brick ranch house that belonged to Mr. Morgan, and the white clapboard two-story house in which Mrs. English lived, and the other homes on the street, with their columned front porches and their back patios, and the tall oaks—all stood curiously still in the warm golden light of the mid-morning sun.

Then a man emerged from wide and busy Franklin Avenue at the far end of the street.

Zebra saw the man stop at the corner and stand looking at a public trash can. He watched as the man poked his hand into the can and fished about but seemed to find nothing he wanted. He withdrew the hand

That's how he happened

to see the man.

and, raising it to shield his eyes from the sunlight, glanced at the street sign on the lamppost.

He started to walk up the street in the direction of the school.

He was tall and wiry, and looked to be about forty years old. In his right hand he carried a bulging brown plastic bag. He wore a khaki army jacket, a blue denim shirt, blue jeans, and brown cowboy boots. His <u>gaunt</u> face and muscular neck were reddened by exposure to the sun. Long brown hair spilled out below his dark-blue farmer's cap. On the front of the cap, in large orange letters, were the words LAND ROVER.[2]

He walked with his eyes on the sidewalk and the curb, as if looking for something, and he went right past Zebra without noticing him.

Zebra's hand hurt very much. He was about to turn away when he saw the man stop and look around and peer up at the red-brick wall of the school. The man set down the bag and took off his cap and stuffed it into a pocket of his jacket. From one of his jeans pockets he removed a handkerchief, with which he then wiped his face. He shoved the handkerchief back into the pocket and put the cap back on his head.

Then he turned and saw Zebra.

He picked up the bag and started down the street to where Zebra was standing. When the man was about ten feet away, Zebra noticed that the left sleeve of his jacket was empty.

---

2. **Land Rover:** a type of sport utility vehicle.

The man came up to Zebra and said in a low, friendly, shy voice, "Hello."

Zebra answered with a cautious "Hello," trying not to look at the empty sleeve, which had been tucked into the man's jacket pocket.

The man asked, with a distinct Southern accent, "What's your name, son?"

Zebra said, "Adam."

"What kind of school is this here school, Adam?"

"It's a good school," Zebra answered.

"How long before you-all begin your summer vacation?"

"Three days," Zebra said.

"Anything special happen here during the summer?"

"During the summer? Nothing goes on here. There are no classes."

"What do you-all do during the summer?"

"Some of us go to camp. Some of us hang around. We find things to do."

Zebra's hand had begun to tingle and throb. Why was the man asking all those questions? Zebra thought maybe he shouldn't be talking to him at all. He seemed vaguely <u>menacing</u> in that army jacket, the dark-blue cap with the words LAND ROVER on it in orange letters, and the empty sleeve. Yet there was kindness in his gray eyes and ruddy features.

The man gazed past Zebra at the students playing in the yard. "Adam, do you think your school would be interested in having someone teach an art class during the summer?"

That took Zebra by surprise. "An *art* class?"

"Drawing, sculpting, things like that."

Zebra was trying *very hard* not to look at the man's empty sleeve. "I don't know. . . ."

"Where's the school office, Adam?"

"On Washington Avenue. Go to the end of the street and turn right."

"Thanks," the man said. He hesitated a moment. Then he asked, in a quiet voice, "What happened to you, Adam?"

"A car hit me," Zebra said. "It was my fault."

The man seemed to <u>wince</u>.

For a flash of a second, Zebra thought to ask the man what had happened to *him*. The words were on his tongue. But he kept himself from saying anything.

The man started back up the street, carrying the brown plastic bag.

Zebra suddenly called, "Hey, mister."

The man stopped and turned. "My name is John Wilson," he said softly.

"Mr. Wilson, when you go into the school office, you'll see signs on two doors. One says 'Dr. Winter,' and the other says 'Mrs. English.' Ask for Mrs. English."

Dr. Winter, the principal, was a <u>disciplinarian</u> and a grump. Mrs. English, the assistant principal, was generous and kind. Dr. Winter would probably tell the man to call his secretary for an appointment. Mrs. English might invite him into her office and offer him a cup of coffee and listen to what he had to say.

The man hesitated, looking at Zebra.

"Appreciate the advice," he said.

Zebra watched him walk to the corner.

Under the lamppost was a trash can. Zebra saw the man set down the plastic bag and stick his hand into the can and haul out a battered umbrella.

The man tried to open the umbrella, but its metal ribs were broken. The black fabric dangled flat and limp from the pole. He put the umbrella into the plastic bag and headed for the entrance to the school.

A moment later, Zebra heard the whistle

that signaled the end of recess. He followed his classmates at a distance, careful to avoid anyone's bumping against his hand.

He sat through his algebra class, copying the problems on the blackboard while holding down his notebook with his left elbow. The sling chafed[3] his neck and felt warm and clumsy on his bare arm. There were sharp pains now in the two curled fingers of his hand.

Right after the class he went downstairs to the office of Mrs. Walsh, a cheerful, gray-haired woman in a white nurse's uniform.

She said, "I'm sorry I can't do very much for you, Adam, except give you two Tylenols."

He swallowed the Tylenols down with water.

On his way back up to the second floor, he saw the man with the dark-blue cap emerge from the school office with Mrs. English. He stopped on the stairs and watched as the man and Mrs. English stood talking together. Mrs. English nodded and smiled and shook the man's hand.

The man walked down the corridor, carrying the plastic bag, and left the school building.

Zebra went slowly to his next class.

The class was taught by Mrs. English, who came hurrying into the room some minutes after the bell had rung.

"I apologize for being late," she said, sounding a little out of breath. "There was an important matter I had to attend to."

Mrs. English was a tall, gracious woman in her forties. It was common knowledge that early in her life she had been a journalist on a Chicago newspaper and had written short stories, which she could not get published. Soon after her marriage to a doctor, she had become a teacher.

This was the only class Mrs. English taught.

Ten students from the upper school—seventh and eighth grades—were chosen every year for this class. They met for an hour three times a week and told one another stories. Each story would be discussed and analyzed by Mrs. English and the class.

Mrs. English called it a class in the *imagination.*

Zebra was grateful he did not have to take notes in this class. He had only to listen to the stories.

That day, Andrea, the freckle-faced, redheaded girl with very thick glasses who sat next to Zebra, told about a woman scientist who discovered a method of healing trees that had been blasted apart by lightning.

Mark, who had something wrong with his upper lip, told in his quavery[4] voice about a selfish space cadet who stepped into a time machine and met his future self, who turned out to be a hateful person, and how the cadet then returned to the present and changed himself.

Kevin talked in blurred, high-pitched tones and often related parts of his stories with his hands. Mrs. English would quietly repeat many of his sentences. Today he told about an explorer who set out on a journey through a valley filled with yellow stones and surrounded by red mountains, where he encountered an army of green shadows that had been at war for hundreds of years with an army of purple shadows. The explorer showed them how to make peace.

When it was Zebra's turn, he told a story about a bird that one day crashed against a closed windowpane and broke a wing. A boy tried to heal the wing but couldn't. The bird died, and the boy buried it under a tree on his lawn.

---

3. **chafed** (chāfd): irritated by rubbing.
4. **quavery** (kwā′vər-ē): quivering or trembling.

When he had finished, there was silence. Everyone in the class was looking at him.

"You always tell such sad stories," Andrea said.

The bell rang. Mrs. English dismissed the class.

In the hallway, Andrea said to Zebra, "You know, you are a very gloomy life form."

"Andrea, get off my case," Zebra said.

He went out to the schoolyard for the midafternoon recess. On the other side of the chain-link fence was the man in the dark-blue cap.

Zebra went over to him.

"Hello again, Adam," the man said. "I've been waiting for you."

"Hello," said Zebra.

"Thanks much for suggesting I talk to Mrs. English."

"You're welcome."

"Adam, you at all interested in art?"

"No."

"You ever try your hand at it?"

"I've made drawings for class. I don't like it."

"Well, just in case you change your mind, I'm giving an art class in your school during the summer."

"I'm going to camp in August," Zebra said.

"There's the big long month of July."

"I don't think so," Zebra said.

"Well, okay, suit yourself. I'd like to give you something, a little thank-you gift."

He reached into an inside pocket and drew out a small pad and a pen. He placed the pad against the fence.

"Adam, you want to help me out a little bit here? Put your fingers through the fence and grab hold of the pad."

Extending the fingers of his right hand, Zebra held the pad to the fence and watched as the man began to work with the pen. He felt the pad move slightly.

"I need you to hold it real still," the man said.

He was standing bent over, very close to Zebra. The words LAND ROVER on his cap shone in the afternoon sunlight. As he worked, he glanced often at Zebra. His tongue kept pushing up against the insides of his cheeks, making tiny hills rise and fall on his face. Wrinkles formed <u>intricate</u> spidery webs in the skin below his gray eyes. On his smooth forehead, in the blue and purple shadows beneath the peak of his cap, lay glistening beads of sweat. And his hand—how dirty it was, the fingers and palm smudged with black ink and <u>encrusted</u> with colors.

Then Zebra glanced down and noticed the plastic bag near the man's feet. It lay partly open. Zebra was able to see a large pink armless doll, a dull metallic object that looked like a dented frying pan, old newspapers, strings of cord, crumpled pieces of red and blue cloth, and the broken umbrella.

"One more minute is all I need," the man said.

He stepped back, looked at the pad, and nodded slowly. He put the pen back into his pocket and tore the top page from the pad. He rolled up the page and pushed it through the fence. Then he took the pad from Zebra.

"See you around, Adam," the man said, picking up the plastic bag.

Zebra unrolled the sheet of paper and saw a line drawing, a perfect image of his face.

He was looking at himself as if in a mirror. His long straight nose and thin lips and sad eyes and gaunt face; his dark hair and smallish ears and the scar on his forehead where he had hurt himself years before while roller skating.

In the lower right-hand corner of the page

WORDS TO KNOW

intricate (ĭn′trĭ-kĭt) *adj.* arranged in a complex way
encrusted (ĕn-krŭst′əd) *adj.* covered with crusts

Jarvis (1996), Elizabeth Peyton. Oil on masonite, 11″ × 14″. Courtesy of Gavin Brown's enterprise, Corp., New York. Collection of Susan and Michael Hort.

the man had written: "To Adam, with thanks. John Wilson."

Zebra raised his eyes from the drawing. The man was walking away.

Zebra called out, "Mr. Wilson, all my friends call me Zebra."

The man turned, looking surprised.

"From my last name," Adam said. "Zebrin. Adam Martin Zebrin. They call me Zebra."

"Is that right?" the man said, starting back toward the fence. "Well, in that case you want to give me back that piece of paper."

He took the pad and pen from his pocket, placed the page on the pad, and, with Zebra holding the pad to the fence, did something to the page and then handed it back.

"You take real good care of yourself, Zebra," the man said.

He went off toward Franklin Avenue.

Zebra looked at the drawing. The man had crossed out Adam and over it had drawn an animal with a stubby neck and short legs and a striped body.

A zebra!

Its legs were in full gallop. It seemed as if it would gallop right off the page.

A strong breeze rippled across the drawing, causing it to flutter like a flag in Zebra's hand. He looked out at the street.

The man was walking slowly in the shadows of the tall oaks. Zebra had the odd sensation that all the houses on the street had turned toward the man and were watching him as he walked along. How strange that was: the windows and porches and columns and front doors following intently the slow walk of that tall, one-armed man—until he turned into Franklin Avenue and was gone.

The whistle blew, and Zebra went inside. Seated at his desk, he slipped the drawing carefully into one of his notebooks.

From time to time he glanced at it.

Just before the bell signaled the end of the school day, he looked at it again.

Now *that* was strange!

He thought he remembered that the zebra had been drawn directly over his name: the head over the A and the tail over the M. Didn't it seem now to have moved a little beyond the A?

Probably he was running a fever again. He would run mysterious fevers off and on for about three weeks after each operation on his hand. Fevers sometimes did that to him: excited his imagination.

He lived four blocks from the school. The school bus dropped him off at his corner. In his schoolbag he carried his books and the notebook with the drawing.

His mother offered him a snack, but he said he wasn't hungry. Up in his room, he looked again at the drawing and was astonished to discover that the zebra had reached the edge of his name and appeared <u>poised</u> to leap off.

It *had* to be a fever that was causing him to see the zebra that way. And sure enough, when his mother took his temperature, the thermometer registered 102.6 degrees.

She gave him his medicine, but it didn't seem to have much effect, because when he woke at night and switched on his desk light and peered at the drawing, he saw the little zebra galloping across the page, along the contours of his face, over the hills and valleys of his eyes and nose and mouth, and he heard the tiny clickings of its hooves as cloudlets of dust rose in its wake.

He knew he was asleep. He knew it was the fever working upon his imagination.

But it was so real.

The little zebra running . . .

When he woke in the morning the fever was

WORDS
TO
KNOW
poised (poizd) *adj.* balanced or held in suspension

gone, and the zebra was quietly in its place over ADAM.

Later, as he entered the school, he noticed a large sign on the bulletin board in the hallway:

SUMMER ART CLASS

The well-known American artist Mr. John Wilson will conduct an art class during the summer for students in 7th and 8th grades. For details, speak to Mrs. English. There will be no tuition fee for this class.

During the morning, between classes, Zebra ran into Mrs. English in the second-floor hallway.

"Mrs. English, about the summer art class . . . is it okay to ask where—um—where Mr. Wilson is from?"

"He is from a small town in Virginia. Are you thinking of signing up for his class?"

"I can't draw," Zebra said.

"Drawing is something you can learn."

"Mrs. English, is it okay to ask how did Mr. Wilson—um—get hurt?"

The school corridors were always crowded between classes. Zebra and Mrs. English formed a little island in the bustling, student-jammed hallway.

"Mr. Wilson was wounded in the war in Vietnam," Mrs. English said. "I would urge you to join his class. You will get to use your imagination."

For the next hour, Zebra sat impatiently through Mr. Morgan's geography class, and afterward he went up to the teacher.

"Mr. Morgan, could I—um—ask where is Vietnam?"

Mr. Morgan smoothed down the jacket of his beige summer suit, touched his bow tie,

But it was so real. The little zebra running...

rolled down a wall map, picked up his pointer, and cleared his throat.

"Vietnam is this long, narrow country in southeast Asia, bordered by China, Laos, and Cambodia. It is a land of valleys in the north, coastal plains in the center, and marshes in the south. There are barren mountains and tropical rain forests. Its chief crops are rice, rubber, fruits, and vegetables. The population numbers close to seventy million people. Between 1962 and 1973, America fought a terrible war there to prevent the south from falling into the hands of the communist north. We lost the war."

"Thank you."

"I am impressed by your suddenly awakened interest in geography, young man, though I must remind you that your class is studying the Mediterranean," said Mr. Morgan.

During the afternoon recess, Zebra was watching a heated basketball game, when he looked across the yard and saw John Wilson walk by, carrying a laden plastic bag. Some while later, he came back along the street, empty-handed.

Over supper that evening, Zebra told his parents he was thinking of taking a summer art class offered by the school.

His father said, "Well, I think that's a fine idea."

"Wait a minute. I'm not so sure," his mother said.

"It'll get him off the streets," his father said. "He'll become a Matisse[5] instead of a lawyer like his dad. Right, Adam?"

---

5. **Matisse** (mə-tēs′) (1869–1954): a French painter who was one of the most well-known artists of the 20th century.

"Just you be very careful," his mother said to Adam. "Don't do anything that might injure your hand."

"How can drawing hurt his left hand, for heaven's sake?" said his father.

That night, Zebra lay in bed looking at his hand. It was a dread and a mystery to him, his own hand. The fingers were all there, but like dead leaves that never fell, the ring and little fingers were rigid and curled, the others barely moved. The doctors said it would take time to bring them back to life. So many broken bones. So many torn muscles and tendons. So many injured nerves. The dark shadow had sprung upon him so suddenly. How stupid, stupid, *stupid* he had been!

He couldn't sleep. He went over to his desk and looked at John Wilson's drawing. The galloping little zebra stood very still over ADAM.

Early the following afternoon, on the last day of school, Zebra went to Mrs. English's office and signed up for John Wilson's summer art class.

"The class will meet every weekday from ten in the morning until one," said Mrs. English. "Starting Monday."

Zebra noticed the three plastic bags in a corner of the office.

"Mrs. English, is it okay to ask what Mr. Wilson—um—did in Vietnam?"

"He told me he was a helicopter pilot," Mrs. English said. "Oh, I neglected to mention that you are to bring an unlined notebook and a pencil to the class."

"That's all? A notebook and a pencil?"

He told me he was a helicopter pilot...

Mrs. English smiled. "And your imagination."

When Zebra entered the art class the next Monday morning, he found about fifteen students there—including Andrea from his class with Mrs. English.

The walls of the room were bare. Everything had been removed for the summer. Zebra noticed two plastic bags on the floor beneath the blackboard.

He sat down at the desk next to Andrea's.

She wore blue jeans and a yellow summer blouse with blue stripes. Her long red hair was tied behind her head with a dark-blue ribbon. She gazed at Zebra through her thick glasses, leaned over, and said, "Are you going to make gloomy drawings, too?"

Just then John Wilson walked in, carrying a plastic bag, which he put down on the floor next to the two others.

He stood alongside the front desk, wearing a light-blue long-sleeved shirt and jeans. The left shirtsleeve had been folded back and pinned to the shirt. The dark-blue cap with the words LAND ROVER sat jauntily on his head.

"Good morning to you-all," he said, with a shy smile. "Mighty glad you're here. We're going to do two things this summer. We're going to make paper into faces and garbage into people. I can see by your expressions that you don't know what I'm talking about, right? Well, I'm about to show you."

He asked everyone to draw the face of someone sitting nearby.

WORDS TO KNOW **jauntily** (jôn′tĭ-lē) *adv.* in a light and carefree way

Zebra hesitated, looked around, then made a drawing of Andrea. Andrea carefully drew Zebra.

He showed Andrea his drawing.

"It's awful." She grimaced. "I look like a mouse."

Her drawing of him was good. But was his face really so sad?

John Wilson went from desk to desk, peering intently at the drawings. He paused a long moment over Zebra's drawing. Then he spent more than an hour demonstrating with chalk on the blackboard how they should not be thinking *eyes* or *lips* or *hands* while drawing, but should think only *lines* and *curves* and *shapes*; how they should be looking at where everything was situated in relation to the edge of the paper; and how they should not be looking *directly* at the edges of what they were drawing but at the space *outside* the edges.

Zebra stared in wonder at how fast John Wilson's hand raced across the blackboard, and at the empty sleeve rising and falling lightly against the shirt.

"You-all are going to learn how to *see* in a new way," John Wilson said.

They made another drawing of the same face.

"Now I look like a horse," Andrea said. "Are you going to add stripes?"

"You are one big pain, Andrea," Zebra said.

Shortly before noon, John Wilson laid out on his desk the contents of the plastic bags: a clutter of junked broken objects, including the doll and the umbrella.

Using strips of cloth, some lengths of string, crumpled newspaper, his pen, and his one hand, he swiftly transformed the battered doll into a red-nosed, umbrella-carrying clown, with baggy pants, a tattered coat, a derby hat, and a somber smile. Turning over the battered frying pan, he made it into a pedestal, on which he placed the clown.

"That's a sculpture," John Wilson said, with his shy smile. "Garbage into people."

The class burst into applause. The clown on the frying pan looked as if it might take a bow.

"You-all will be doing that, too, before we're done," John Wilson said. "Now I would like you to sign and date your drawings and give them to me."

When they returned the next morning the drawings were on a wall.

Gradually, in the days that followed, the walls began to fill with drawings. Sculptures made by the students were looked at with care, discussed by John Wilson and the class, and then placed on shelves along the walls: a miniature bicycle made of wire; a parrot made of an old sofa cushion; a cowboy made of rope and string; a fat lady made of a dented metal pitcher; a zebra made of glued-together scraps of cardboard.

"I like your zebra," Andrea said.

"Thanks," Zebra said. "I like your parrot."

One morning John Wilson asked the class members to make a contour drawing of their right or left hand. Zebra felt himself sweating and trembling as he worked.

"That's real nice," John Wilson said, when he saw Andrea's drawing.

He gazed at the drawing made by Zebra.

"You-all were looking at your hand," he said. "You ought to have been looking at the edge of your hand and at the space outside."

Zebra drew his hand again. Strange and ugly, the two fingers lay rigid and curled. But astonishingly, it looked like a hand this time.

One day, a few minutes before the end of class, John Wilson gave everyone an assignment: draw or make something at home, something very special that each person *felt deeply* about. And bring it to class.

Zebra remembered seeing a book titled *Incredible Cross-Sections* on a shelf in the family room at home. He found the book and took it into his room.

There was a color drawing of a rescue helicopter on one of the Contents pages. On pages 30 and 31, the helicopter was shown in pieces, its complicated insides displayed in detailed drawings. Rotor blades, control rods, electronics equipment, radar scanner, tail rotor, engine, lifeline, winch—all its many parts.

Zebra sat at his desk, gazing intently at the space outside the edges of the helicopter on the Contents page.

He made an outline drawing and brought it to class the next morning.

John Wilson looked at it. Was there a stiffening of his muscular neck, a sudden tensing of the hand that held the drawing?

He took the drawing and tacked it to the wall.

The next day he gave them all the same home assignment: draw or make something they *felt very deeply* about.

That afternoon, Zebra went rummaging through the trash bin in his kitchen and the garbage cans that stood near the back door of his home. He found some sardine cans, a broken eggbeater, pieces of cardboard, chipped buttons, bent bobby pins, and other odds and ends.

With the help of epoxy glue, he began to make of those bits of garbage a kind of helicopter. For support, he used his desktop, the floor, his knees, the elbow of his left arm, at one point even his chin. Struggling with the last piece—a button he wanted to position as a wheel—he realized that without thinking he had been using his left hand, and the two curled fingers had straightened slightly to his needs.

His heart beat thunderously. There had been so many hope-filled moments before, all of them ending in bitter disappointment. He would say nothing. Let the therapist or the doctors tell him. . . .

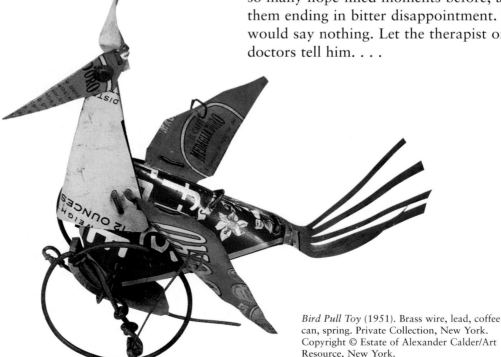

Bird Pull Toy (1951). Brass wire, lead, coffee can, spring. Private Collection, New York. Copyright © Estate of Alexander Calder/Art Resource, New York.

WORDS
TO
KNOW

tensing (tĕns′ĭng) *n.* a tightening or becoming taut **tense** *v.*

58

The following morning, he brought the helicopter to the class.

"Eeewwww, what is *that*?" Andrea grimaced.

"Something to eat you with," Zebra said.

"Get human, Zebra. Mr. Wilson will have a laughing fit over that."

But John Wilson didn't laugh. He held the helicopter in his hand a long moment, turning it this way and that, nodded at Zebra, and placed it on a windowsill, where it shimmered in the summer sunlight.

The next day, John Wilson informed everyone that three students would be leaving the class at the end of July. He asked each of those students to make a drawing for him that he would get to keep. Something to remember them by. All their other drawings and sculptures they could take home.

Zebra lay awake a long time that night, staring into the darkness of his room. He could think of nothing to draw for John Wilson.

In the morning, he sat gazing out the classroom window at the sky and at the helicopter on the sill.

"What are you going to draw for him?" Andrea asked.

Zebra shrugged and said he didn't know.

"Use your imagination," she said. Then she said, "Wait, what am I seeing here? Are you able to move those fingers?"

"I think so."

"You *think* so?"

"The doctors said there was some improvement."

Her eyes glistened behind the thick lenses. She seemed genuinely happy.

He sat looking out the window. Dark birds wheeled and soared. There was the sound of traffic. The helicopter sat on the windowsill,

its eggbeater rotor blades ready to move to full throttle.

Later that day, Zebra sat at his desk at home, working on a drawing. He held the large sheet of paper in place by pressing down on it with the palm and fingers of his left hand. He drew a landscape: hills and valleys, forests and flatlands, rivers and plateaus. Oddly, it all seemed to resemble a face.

Racing together over that landscape were a helicopter and a zebra.

It was all he could think to draw. It was not a very good drawing. He signed it: "To JOHN WILSON, with thanks. Zebra."

The next morning, John Wilson looked at the drawing and asked Zebra to write on top of the name "John Wilson" the name "Leon."

"He was an old buddy of mine, an artist. We were in Vietnam together. Would've been a much better artist than I'll ever be."

Zebra wrote in the new name.

"Thank you kindly," John Wilson said, taking the drawing. "Zebra, you have yourself a good time in camp and a good life. It was real nice knowing you."

He shook Zebra's hand. How strong his fingers felt!

"I think I'm going to miss you a little," Andrea said to Zebra after the class.

"I'll only be away a month."

"Can I help you carry some of those drawings?"

"Sure. I'll carry the helicopter."

Zebra went off to a camp in the Adirondack Mountains. He hiked and read and watched others playing ball. In the arts and crafts program he made some good drawings and even got to learn a little bit about watercolors. He put together clowns and airplanes and helicopters out of discarded cardboard and wood and clothing. From time to time his hand hurt, but the fingers seemed slowly to be coming back to life.

"Patience, young man," the doctors told him when he returned to the city. "You're getting there."

One or two additional operations were still necessary. But there was no urgency. And he no longer needed the leg brace.

On the first day of school, one of the secretaries found him in the hallway and told him to report to Mrs. English.

"Did you have a good summer?" Mrs. English asked.

"It was okay," Zebra said.

"This came for you in the mail."

She handed him a large brown envelope. It was addressed to Adam Zebrin, Eighth Grade, at the school. The sender was John Wilson, with a return address in Virginia.

"Adam, I admit I'm very curious to see what's inside," Mrs. English said.

She helped Zebra open the envelope.

Between two pieces of cardboard were a letter and a large color photograph.

The photograph showed John Wilson down on his right knee before a glistening dark wall. He wore his army jacket and blue jeans and boots, and the cap with the words LAND ROVER. Leaning against the wall to his right was Zebra's drawing of the helicopter and the zebra racing together across a facelike landscape. The drawing was enclosed in a narrow frame.

The wall behind John Wilson seemed to glitter with a strange black light.

Zebra read the letter and showed it to Mrs. English.

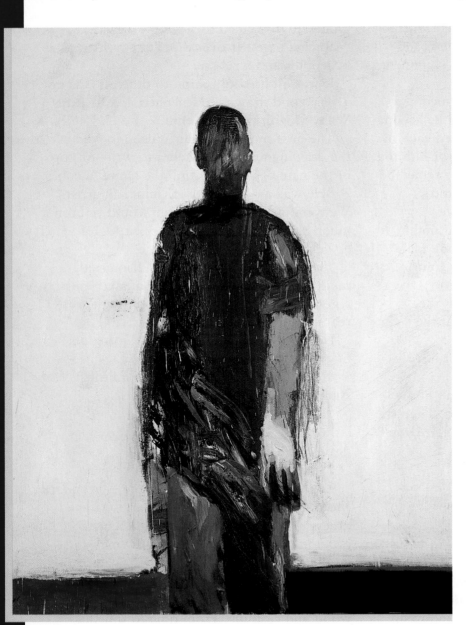

Man Walking (1958), Nathan Oliveira. Oil on canvas, 60 1/8″ × 48 1/8″, courtesy of Hirshhorn Museum and Sculpture Garden, Smithsonian Institution. Gift of Joseph H. Hirshhorn, 1966. Photo by Lee Stalsworth.

Dear Zebra,

One of the people whose names are on this wall was among my very closest friends. He was an artist named Leon Kellner. Each year I visit him and leave a gift—something very special that someone creates and gives me. I leave it near his name for a few hours, and then I take it to my studio in Virginia, where I keep a collection of those gifts. All year long I work in my studio, but come summer I go looking for another gift to give him.

Thank you for your gift.

Your friend,

John Wilson

P.S. I hope your hand is healing.

Mrs. English stood staring awhile at the letter. She turned away and touched her eyes. Then she went to a shelf on the wall behind her, took down a large book, leafed through it quickly, found what she was searching for, and held it out for Zebra to see.

Zebra found himself looking at the glistening black wall of the Vietnam Memorial in Washington, D.C. And at the names on it, the thousands of names. . . .

Later, in the schoolyard during recess, Zebra stood alone at the chain-link fence and gazed down the street toward Franklin Avenue. He thought how strange it was that all the houses on this street had seemed to turn toward John Wilson that day, the windows and porches and columns and doors, as if saluting him.

Had that been only his imagination?

Maybe, Zebra thought, just maybe he could go for a walk to Franklin Avenue on Saturday or Sunday. He had not walked along Franklin Avenue since the accident; had not gone down that steep hill. Yes, he would walk carefully down that hill to the corner and walk back up

and past the school and then the four blocks home.

Andrea came over to him.

"We didn't get picked for the story class with Mrs. English," she said. "I won't have to listen to any more of your gloomy stories."

Zebra said nothing.

"You know, I think I'll walk home today instead of taking the school bus," Andrea said.

"Actually, I think I'll walk, too," Zebra said. "I was thinking maybe I could pick up some really neat stuff in the street."

"You are becoming a pleasant life form," Andrea said. ❖

RELATED READING

The Rider

by Naomi Shihab Nye

A boy told me
if he rollerskated fast enough
his loneliness couldn't catch up
    to him,

5   the best reason I ever heard
for trying to be a champ.

What I wonder tonight
pedaling hard down King William
    Street
10 is if it translates to bicycles.

A victory! To leave your loneness
panting behind you on some
    street corner
while you float free into a cloud
15   of sudden azaleas,
luminous pink petals that have
    never felt loneliness,
no matter how slowly they fell

Connect to the Literature

1. What Do You Think?
What was your reaction to the letter that John Wilson writes to Zebra?

Comprehension Check
- How does Zebra get hurt?
- What is John Wilson's injury?
- What does John Wilson do with Zebra's gift?

Think Critically

2. ACTIVE READING MAKING INFERENCES
Why do you think Zebra spends a lot of time alone? Refer to the chart you made in your 📖READER'S NOTEBOOK. Discuss with a classmate the **details** in the story that helped you make your **inferences.** How do your inferences compare with your partner's?

3. Why do you think Zebra chooses to take John Wilson's art class?

4. What role does art play in the story?

> **Think About**
> - Zebra's discussion with his parents about taking an art class
> - Zebra's first class with John Wilson
> - John Wilson's reaction to Zebra's helicopter sculpture
> - Zebra's last conversation with Andrea

5. Would you describe John Wilson as a **main character** or a **minor character**? Give reasons for your answer.

6. Think about the characteristics of a zebra. Do you think Zebra is a good name for the main character? Why or why not?

Extend Interpretations

7. COMPARING TEXTS Consider the main character in "Zebra" and the boy in the poem "The Rider" on page 61. How are they alike and how do they differ? Support your answer with examples from the story and the poem.

8. Connect to Life In this story, John Wilson visits the Vietnam Veterans Memorial in Washington, D.C., as a way of healing. What are some other ways in which a person might attempt to heal emotional wounds?

Literary Analysis

CHARACTER **Main characters** (also called major characters) are the most important characters in stories. The events of the stories' plots are based on what they think, feel, say, and do. A main character often grows or changes in some way, as Zebra does in this story. **Minor characters,** like Mrs. English, are less important. They usually do not grow or change.

Authors want their characters to act in such a way that readers can understand their traits and motives. **Traits** are consistent qualities of the character's personality. **Motives** are the emotions, wants, or needs that cause a character to act or react.

Activity Working with a partner, go back through the story, using a chart like the one below to note what you learn about Zebra. When you are done, discuss the following questions with a larger group:

- How would you describe Zebra's traits? Did you get most of your knowledge from what he says, from what he does, or from what others say about him?
- What do you think motivates Zebra to act as he does?

CHARACTER	
Traits	**Motives**
kindness	loneliness

CHOICES and CHALLENGES

Writing

Personal Letter Imagining that you are Zebra, write a letter to John Wilson. You may want to write a response to the letter in the story, or you may want to write a letter in which Zebra shares his thoughts about what he learned in the art class. Place the letter in your **Working Portfolio**. 📁

Speaking & Listening

Persuasive Speech Think of a class that you would like to attend in summer school. Present your idea to your classmates as if they were a panel deciding which classes to offer. Be sure to do the following:

• describe clearly the class you wish to take

• tell the reasons why you think you and others would benefit

• support each reason with facts or specific examples.

Speaking and Listening Handbook
See p. R100.

Research & Technology

SOCIAL STUDIES

The Vietnam Veterans Memorial honors those who died in the Vietnam War. There are many other war memorials in the United States, especially in Washington, D.C. There may be a memorial in your hometown. Find out who designed it, when it was built, and what it memorializes. Create a brochure describing the memorial.

Reading for INFORMATION
Read the magazine article on p. 65 to help you begin your research.

Vocabulary

EXERCISE: WORD MEANING On a sheet of paper, write the letter of the word, or words, that is most different in meaning from the other words. Use a dictionary if you need help.

1. (a) joyously (b) glumly (c) enthusiastically (d) exuberantly
2. (a) thick (b) fat (c) gaunt (d) full
3. (a) dangerous (b) menacing (c) threatening (d) harmless
4. (a) recoil (b) flinch (c) approach (d) wince
5. (a) disciplinarian (b) weakling (c) drill sergeant (d) football coach
6. (a) elaborate (b) ornate (c) intricate (d) plain
7. (a) clean (b) dirt (c) grim (d) encrusted
8. (a) ready (b) poised (c) waiting (d) late
9. (a) jauntily (b) slowly (c) lively (d) sprightly
10. (a) easing (b) loosening (c) relaxing (d) tensing

Vocabulary Handbook
See p. R26: Synonyms and Antonyms.

Grammar in Context: Sentence Fragments

Potok uses a series of fragments to reflect the intense feelings of the "broken" boy, Zebra, in this description.

> The doctors said it would take time to bring [his fingers] back to life. So many broken bones. So many torn muscles and tendons. So many injured nerves. . . . How stupid, stupid, *stupid* he had been!

A sentence expresses a complete thought. A **sentence fragment** expresses an incomplete thought. It is incomplete because it is missing a subject, a predicate, or both. Potok uses fragments to create a special effect, but writers usually avoid them. They can be distracting to readers.

Apply to Your Writing Use sentence fragments as sparingly as possible.

WRITING EXERCISE Rewrite the following fragments as complete sentences. You may add or delete words.

Example: *Original* The darkness from which he emerged very slowly.

Rewritten He emerged very slowly from the darkness.

1. He imagined that he was a zebra. Running.
2. In the world of his memories.
3. Because he had broken something that could never be repaired.
4. Asking questions and wanting to understand.
5. Buildings on the street that seemed to salute him.

Grammar Handbook

See p. R71: Writing Complete Sentences.

Chaim Potok
born 1929

"Each of these characters . . . is really, I suppose, a different aspect of myself and a reflection of my fundamental interests."

Early Days While growing up in the Bronx (a part of New York City), Chaim Potok lived the strict life of a Hasidic Jew. His parents, both Polish immigrants, wanted him to grow up to be a religious scholar. Potok himself wasn't so sure. By the time he was 16, he had started reading literature other than traditional Jewish texts. The more he read, the more he was struck by a contradiction between religious learning and the calling of a creative artist.

Coming to Terms Potok eventually left the Hasidic community for the Conservative movement of Judaism. He became a rabbi and served as a U.S. chaplain in Korea in the mid-1950s. Much of Potok's writing centers on characters who try to live both in the spiritual world and in the nonreligious world of everyday life. When asked whether his novels are autobiographical, Potok has said, "My characters tend to be loners. . . . They are extensions of my own being, because I grew up very much involved in the world of the mind, and in the worlds of art and literature."

AUTHOR ACTIVITY

Growing Up The short story you have read appears in Potok's book *Zebra and Other Stories.* All six stories in this collection feature young people facing challenges. Read one of the other stories in the book. Compare and contrast the main character with Zebra. Discuss your observations with your classmates.

Source: *Smithsonian*

Offerings at The Wall

by Don Moser

Key Standard

W1.4 Identify research topics, and develop questions and ideas to help guide investigation of the topic.
Other Standards R1.3, R2.2

"In the fall of 1982, a U.S. Navy officer walked up to the trench where the concrete for the foundation of The Wall was being poured. He stood over the trench for a moment, then tossed something into it and saluted. A workman asked him what he was doing. He said he was giving his dead brother's Purple Heart to The Wall. That was the first offering."

The story is told in a new book about the Vietnam Veterans Memorial, *Offerings at The Wall*, released by Turner Publishing Inc. The photographs in the book record some of the 30,000 objects and letters that have been placed at The Wall, as if at a shrine, by relatives and comrades of the men and women there memorialized.

These gifts of remembrance are collected each day by volunteers and preserved by the National Park Service in the Vietnam Veterans Memorial Collection, housed in a climate-controlled repository where the mementos lie

Reading for Information

In some classes you will be asked to write research reports. Before you write such a report, you'll need to identify a topic, pose research questions, and find answers to those questions in informative articles.

Forming and Evaluating Research Questions
To formulate a **research question,** find a subject that interests you and turn it into a question. For example, if you are interested in the Purple Heart medal, you might ask, For what reasons were Purple Hearts awarded in Vietnam? This question is a guide for your research into the topic. The answer you give to your research question will become the **thesis statement** of your finished research report.

Reading for Information *continued*

YOUR TURN *Use the questions and activities below to help you practice formulating, evaluating, and revising research questions.*

1 It is important to evaluate your research questions to be sure they are not too broad. For example, you would have to do a lot of research to answer a question like, "What is the origin of the Smithsonian National Museum of American History?" Based on the information in the article, how might you revise this question to give it a narrower focus?

2 There are some topics for which research sources do not exist. Consider the question, "Why did someone leave a royal flush at the wall?" Would you be able to research an answer to this question? Why or why not?

After you read the article, it may help to quickly brainstorm all the ideas that occurred to you as you read.

Research & Technology
Activity Link: "Zebra," p. 63. Formulate your own research question about the Vietnam Veterans Memorial or another memorial. Evaluate your questions and revise them if necessary. Write a short report about the memorial and share it with the class.

near such historic artifacts as the life mask of Abraham Lincoln. (Five hundred of the objects are on view in an exhibition at the Smithsonian's National Museum of American History.) **1**

Some of the offerings were left with poems or letters (letters that were sealed will always remain so), but others bear meanings known only to those who offered them: a Bible, a fishing float, service ribbons, a sock for an amputee's stump, a popsicle stick, four mortarboard tassels, a foil wrapper from a chocolate candy. In his eloquent introduction to the book, Thomas B. Allen writes that The Wall "became a place for wishes, for futures that could not be. Tucked into a wreath are the things of an imagined life: new baby shoes for a baby who never would be, the pencils and crayons for a first day of kindergarten that never would be, champagne glasses to toast a wedding anniversary that never would be, ornaments for a Christmas tree that never would be." Someone left five cards, a royal flush for a poker game that never would be played. And **2** a soldier left a photograph of a North Vietnamese man with a young girl, along with a note: "Dear Sir: For twenty-two years I have carried your picture in my wallet. I was only eighteen years old that day that we faced one another on that trail in Chu Lai, Vietnam. Why you did not take my life I'll never know. You stared at me for so long. . . . Forgive me for taking your life."

And the boots. So intimately shaped by those who wore them, yet so universal—the familiar black leather and tough green fabric, the lugged soles bearing the memory of the earth of the Delta or Con Thien—that they seem a symbol for the whole.

Building Vocabulary
Understanding Context Clues

When you come across an unfamiliar word in your reading, you can figure out its meaning by looking at its **context**—the words and phrases around it. These words can provide clues to the word's meaning.

> But the boy took care to sit on the far side of the room where he thought she could easily see him out of the corner of her eye, if she wanted to. He did not trust the woman *not* to trust him. And he did not want to be mistrusted now.
>
> —Langston Hughes, "Thank You, M'am"

To figure out the meaning of mistrusted, look at the details that describe Roger's thoughts and actions.

Strategies for Building Vocabulary

In the example above, the context clues in the passage are known as **description clues.** The description of Roger's thoughts and actions shows that he does not want Mrs. Jones to doubt him. The word *mistrusted,* therefore, means "looked on without trust." Here are some other types of context clues.

❶ **Definition and Restatement Clues** Words that restate unfamiliar words' meanings are **definition clues** and **restatement clues.** In the second sentence of the following example, the meaning of the word *frail* is restated in simpler language:

> Roger looked as though he were frail. In other words, he looked weak and thin in his tennis shoes and jeans.

Restatement clues may be signaled by commas or by words like *as, or, that is, in other words,* and *also.*

❷ **Example Clues** An **example clue** illustrates another word's meaning by providing examples. Words like *including* and *such as* often signal example clues. In the following sentence, the examples after *such as* are clues to the meaning of *presentable:*

> Mrs. Jones wanted Roger to do things to make himself presentable for dinner, such as washing his face and running a comb through his hair.

❸ **Comparison and Contrast Clues** A **comparison clue** illustrates a word's meaning with a comparison to a more familiar word or idea.

> Mr. Lucas was as portly as a large bear.

A **contrast clue** involves a writer's pointing out differences between words or ideas. Contrast clues may be signaled by *although, but, however, yet,* and *in contrast.*

> Zebra at first thought the stranger seemed menacing, but Wilson turned out to be kind and friendly.

The contrast with "kind and friendly" shows that *menacing* means "possibly dangerous."

EXERCISE Use a context clue to define each underlined word. Then identify the kind of context clue that you used.

1. Roger wanted blue <u>suede</u> shoes. He thought about how the soft, fuzzy leather would feel on his feet.
2. Wilson was <u>gaunt</u>, a thin, bony shadow of a man.
3. Mrs. Jones's front stoop was as <u>barren</u> as the stoop of an abandoned home.
4. Several things reminded Julia of her <u>ethnicity</u>, including her long Spanish name.
5. The children played <u>exuberantly.</u> Zebra, on the other hand, stood sad and motionless.

A Crush

by Cynthia Rylant

When the windows of Stan's Hardware started filling up with flowers, everyone in town knew something had happened. Excess flowers usually mean death, but since these were all real flowers bearing the aroma of nature instead of floral preservative, and since they stood bunched in clear Mason jars instead of impaled on Styrofoam crosses, everyone knew nobody had died. So they all figured somebody had a crush and kept quiet.

There wasn't really a Stan of Stan's Hardware. Dick Wilcox was the owner, and since he'd never liked his own name, he gave his store half the name of his childhood hero, Stan Laurel in the movies. Dick had been married for twenty-seven years. Once, his wife, Helen, had dropped a German chocolate cake on his head at a Lion's Club dance, so Dick and Helen were not likely candidates for the honest expression of the flowers in those clear Mason jars lining the windows of Stan's Hardware, and speculation had to move on to Dolores.

Dolores was the assistant manager at Stan's and had worked there for twenty years, since high school. She knew the store like a mother knows her baby, so Dick—who had trouble keeping up with things like prices and new brands of drywall compound—tried to keep himself busy in the back and give Dolores the run of the floor. This worked fine because the carpenters and plumbers and painters in town trusted Dolores and took her advice to heart. They also liked her tattoo.

Dolores was the only woman in town with a tattoo. On the days she went sleeveless, one could see it on the taut brown skin of her upper arm: "Howl at the Moon." The picture was of a baying coyote, which must have been a dark gray in its early days but which had faded to the color of the spackling paste Dolores stocked in the third aisle. Nobody had gotten out of Dolores the true story behind the tattoo. Some of the men who came in liked to show off their own, and they'd roll up their sleeves or pull open their shirts, exhibiting bald eagles and rattlesnakes and Confederate flags, and they'd try to coax out of Dolores the history of her coyote. All of the men had gotten their tattoos when they were in the service, drunk on weekend leave and full of the spitfire of young soldiers. Dolores had never been in the service, and she'd never seen weekend leave, and there wasn't a tattoo parlor anywhere near. They couldn't figure why or where any half-sober woman would have a howling coyote ground into the soft skin of her upper arm. But Dolores wasn't telling.

That the flowers in Stan's front window had anything to do with Dolores seemed completely improbable. As far as anyone knew, Dolores had never been in love, nor had anyone ever been in love with her. Some believed it was the tattoo, of course, or the fine dark hair coating Dolores's upper lip which kept suitors away. Some felt it was because Dolores was just more of a man than most of the men in town, and fellows couldn't figure out how to court someone who knew more about the carburetor of a car or the back side of a washing machine than they did. Others thought Dolores simply didn't want love. This was a popular theory among the women in town who sold Avon and Mary Kay cosmetics. Whenever one of them ran into the hardware for a package of light bulbs or some batteries, she would mentally pluck every one of the black hairs above Dolores's lip. Then she'd wash that grease out of Dolores's hair, give her a good blunt cut, dress her in a decent silk-blend blouse with a nice Liz

> That the flowers in Stan's front window had anything to do with Dolores seemed completely improbable.

Claiborne skirt from the Sports line, and, finally, tone down that swarthy, longshoreman look of Dolores's with a concealing beige foundation,[1] some frosted peach lipstick, and a good gray liner for the eyes.

Dolores simply didn't want love, the Avon lady would think as she walked back to her car carrying her little bag of batteries. If she did, she'd fix herself up.

The man who was in love with Dolores and who brought her zinnias and cornflowers and nasturtiums and marigolds and asters and four-o'clocks in clear Mason jars did not know any of this. He did not know that men showed Dolores their tattoos. He did not know that Dolores understood how to use and to sell a belt sander. He did not know that Dolores needed some concealing beige foundation so she could get someone to love her. The man who brought flowers to Dolores on Wednesdays when the hardware opened its doors at 7:00 A.M. didn't care who Dolores had ever been or what anyone had ever thought of her. He loved her, and he wanted to bring her flowers.

Ernie had lived in this town all of his life and had never before met Dolores. He was thirty-three years old, and for thirty-one of those years he had lived at home with his mother in a small dark house on the edge of town near Beckwith's Orchards. Ernie had been a beautiful baby, with a shock of shining black hair and large blue eyes and a round, wise face. But as he had grown, it had become clearer and clearer

---

1. **concealing beige foundation:** a cosmetic that covers skin flaws.

that though he was indeed a perfectly beautiful child, his mind had not developed with the same perfection. Ernie would not be able to speak in sentences until he was six years old. He would not be able to count the apples in a bowl until he was eight. By the time he was ten, he could sing a simple song. At age twelve, he understood what a joke was. And when he was twenty, something he saw on television made him cry.

Ernie's mother kept him in the house with her because it was easier, so Ernie knew nothing of the world except this house. They lived, the two of them, in tiny dark rooms always illuminated by the glow of a television set, Ernie's bags of Oreos and Nutter Butters littering the floor, his baseball cards scattered across the sofa, his heavy winter coat thrown over the arm of a chair so he could wear it whenever he wanted, and his box of Burpee seed packages sitting in the middle of the kitchen table.

These Ernie cherished. The seeds had been delivered to his home by mistake. One day a woman wearing a brown uniform had pulled up in a brown truck, walked quickly to the front porch of Ernie's house, set a box down, and with a couple of toots of her horn, driven off again. Ernie had watched her through the curtains and, when she was gone, had ventured onto the porch and shyly, cautiously, picked up the box. His mother checked it when he carried it inside. The box didn't have their name on it, but the brown truck was gone, so whatever was in the box was theirs to keep. Ernie pulled off the heavy tape, his fingers trembling, and found inside the box more little packages of seeds than he could count. He lifted them out, one by one, and examined the beautiful photographs of flowers on each. His mother was not interested, had returned to the television, but Ernie sat down at the kitchen table and quietly looked at each package for a long time, his fingers running across the slick paper and outlining the shapes of zinnias and cornflowers and nasturtiums and marigolds and asters and four-o'clocks, his eyes drawing up their colors.

Two months later Ernie's mother died. A neighbor found her at the mailbox beside the road. People from the county courthouse came out to get Ernie, and as they ushered him from the home he would never see again, he picked up the box of seed packages from his kitchen table and passed through the doorway.

Eventually Ernie was moved to a large white house near the main street of town. This house was called a group home, because in it lived a group of people who, like Ernie, could not live on their own. There were six of them. Each had his own room. When Ernie was shown the room that would be his, he put the box of Burpee seeds—which he had kept with him since his mother's death—on the little table beside the bed, and then he sat down on the bed and cried.

Ernie cried every day for nearly a month. And then he stopped. He dried his tears, and he learned how to bake refrigerator biscuits and how to dust mop and what to do if the indoor plants looked brown.

Ernie loved watering the indoor plants, and it was this pleasure which finally drew him outside. One of the young men who worked at the group home—a college student named Jack—grew a large garden in the back of the house. It was full of tomato vines and the large yellow blossoms of healthy squash. During his first summer at the house, Ernie would stand at the kitchen window, watching Jack and sometimes a resident of the home move among the vegetables. Ernie was curious but too afraid to go into the garden.

Illustration by Patty Dryden. Copyright © Patty Dryden.

Then one day when Ernie was watching through the window, he noticed that Jack was ripping open several slick little packages and emptying them into the ground. Ernie panicked and ran to his room. But the box of Burpee seeds was still there on his table, untouched. He grabbed it, slid it under his bed, then went back through the house and out into the garden as if he had done this every day of his life.

He stood beside Jack, watching him empty seed packages into the soft black soil, and as the packages were emptied, Ernie asked for them, holding out his hand, his eyes on the photographs of red radishes and purple eggplant. Jack handed the empty packages over with a smile and with that gesture became Ernie's first friend.

Jack tried to explain to Ernie that the seeds would grow into vegetables, but Ernie could not believe this until he saw it come true. And when it did, he looked all the more intently at the packages of zinnias and cornflowers and the rest hidden beneath his bed. He thought more deeply about them, but he could not carry them to the garden. He could not let the garden have his seeds.

That was the first year in the large white house.

The second year, Ernie saw Dolores, and after that he thought of nothing else but her and of the photographs of flowers beneath his bed.

Jack had decided to take Ernie downtown for breakfast every Wednesday morning to ease him into the world outside that of the group home. They left very early, at 5:45 A.M., so there would be few people and almost no traffic to frighten Ernie and make him beg for his room. Jack and Ernie drove to the Big Boy restaurant which sat across the street from Stan's Hardware. There they ate eggs and bacon and French toast among those whose work demanded rising before the sun: bus drivers, policemen, nurses, mill workers. Their first time in the Big Boy, Ernie was too nervous to eat. The second time, he could eat, but he couldn't look up. The third time, he not only ate everything on his plate, but he lifted his head and he looked out the window of the Big Boy restaurant toward Stan's Hardware across the street. There he saw a dark-haired woman in jeans and a black T-shirt unlocking the front door of the building, and that was the moment Ernie started loving Dolores and thinking about giving up his seeds to the soft black soil of Jack's garden.

Love is such a mystery.

Love is such a mystery, and when it strikes the heart of one as mysterious as Ernie himself, it can hardly be spoken of. Ernie could not explain to Jack why he went directly to his room later that morning, pulled the box of Burpee seeds from under his bed, then grabbed Jack's hand in the kitchen and walked with him to the garden, where Ernie had come to believe things would grow. Ernie handed the packets of seeds one by one to Jack, who stood in silent admiration of the lovely photographs before asking Ernie several times, "Are you sure you want to plant these?" Ernie was sure. It didn't take him very long, and when the seeds all lay under the moist black earth, Ernie carried his empty packages inside the house and spent the rest of the day spreading them across his bed in different arrangements.

That was in June. For the next several Wednesdays at 7:00 A.M. Ernie watched every movement of the dark-haired woman behind the lighted windows of Stan's

Sweetpeas (1992), Julia Jordan. Acrylic on paper, private collection. Photo by James Hart.

Hardware. Jack watched Ernie watch Dolores and discreetly said nothing.

When Ernie's flowers began growing in July, Ernie spent most of his time in the garden. He would watch the garden for hours, as if he expected it suddenly to move or to impress him with a quick trick. The fragile green stems of his flowers stood uncertainly in the soil, like baby colts on their first legs, but the young plants performed no magic for Ernie's eyes. They saved their shows for the middle of the night and next day surprised Ernie with tender small blooms in all the colors the photographs had promised.

The flowers grew fast and hardy, and one early Wednesday morning when they looked as big and bright as their pictures on the empty packages, Ernie pulled a glass canning jar off a dusty shelf in the basement of his house. He washed the jar, half filled it with water, then carried it to the garden, where he placed in it one of every kind of flower he had grown. He met Jack at the car and rode off to the Big Boy with the jar of flowers held tight between his small hands. Jack told him it was a beautiful bouquet.

When they reached the door of the Big Boy, Ernie stopped and pulled at Jack's arm, pointing to the building across the street. "OK," Jack said, and he led Ernie to the front door of Stan's Hardware. It was 6:00 A.M., and the building was still dark. Ernie set the clear Mason jar full of flowers under the sign that read "Closed," then he smiled at Jack and followed him back across the street to get breakfast.

When Dolores arrived at seven and picked up the jar of zinnias and cornflowers and nasturtiums and marigolds and asters and four-o'clocks, Ernie and Jack were watching her from a booth in the Big Boy. Each had a wide smile on his face as Dolores put her nose to the flowers. Ernie giggled. They watched the lights of the hardware store come up and saw Dolores place the clear Mason jar on the ledge of the front window. They drove home still smiling.

All the rest of that summer Ernie left a jar of flowers every Wednesday morning at the front door of Stan's Hardware. Neither Dick Wilcox nor Dolores could figure out why the flowers kept coming, and each of them assumed somebody had a crush on the other. But the flowers had an effect on them anyway. Dick started spending more time out on the floor making conversation with the customers, while Dolores stopped wearing T-shirts to work and instead wore crisp white blouses with the sleeves rolled back off her wrists. Occasionally she put on a bracelet.

By summer's end Jack and Ernie had become very good friends, and when the flowers in the garden behind their house began to wither, and Ernie's face began to grow gray as he watched them, Jack brought home one bright day in late September a great long box. Ernie followed Jack as he carried it down to the basement and watched as Jack pulled a long glass tube from the box and attached this tube to the wall above a table. When Jack plugged in the tube's electric cord, a soft lavender light washed the room.

"Sunshine," said Jack.

Then he went back to his car for a smaller box. He carried this down to the basement, where Ernie still stood staring at the strange light. Jack handed Ernie the small box, and when Ernie opened it, he found more little packages of seeds than he could count, with new kinds of photographs on the slick paper.

"Violets," Jack said, pointing to one of them.

Then he and Ernie went outside to get some dirt. ❖

Cynthia Rylant
born 1954

"It took me about seven years to feel like a writer."

Inspiration In Kent, Ohio, where Cynthia Rylant lives, a strange man sometimes brings flowers to waitresses at a little diner. He became the inspiration for Ernie. Beside the diner is a hardware store. "That's where my imagination found Dolores," said Rylant, who claims that she enjoys taking "people who don't get any attention in the world and making them really valuable in my fiction—making them absolutely shine with their beauty."

Success Rylant has achieved success in many forms of writing. Her book *Missing May* (1992) was awarded the Newbery Medal in 1993.

Writing Workshop

Response to Literature

Sharing responses to a story . . .

From Reading to Writing Stories touch people in different ways. Some readers might like "Seventh Grade" by Gary Soto because they recognize themselves in Victor. Others might like "Zebra" by Chaim Potok because they admire Zebra's strength. In a **response to literature,** you can share your interpretation of a piece of literature. You may include your thoughts about how an author goes about communicating scenes and images in his or her writing.

For Your Portfolio

WRITING PROMPT Write a personal response to a short story or poem.

Purpose: To share your interpretation of a piece of literature
Audience: Your classmates, teacher, friends, or family

Basics in a Box

Response to Literature at a Glance

Introduction
Introduces the title and author and a clear statement of your response

Body
Supports the response with evidence from the work

Evidence

examples from the story

quotations

connections to your own life

Conclusion
Summarizes the response

RUBRIC STANDARDS FOR WRITING

A successful response to literature should

- include an introduction that names the literary work and clearly states your overall response to it
- tell enough about the literature so that readers can understand your response
- contain clearly described, specific reactions and responses to the literary work
- support your statements with quotations and details from the story
- summarize the response in the conclusion

Analyzing a Student Model

SPEAKING OPPORTUNITY

See the Speaking and Listening Handbook, p. R100 for oral presentation tips.

**Shoshannah Seed
Edna Thomas Middle School**

RUBRIC
IN ACTION

Personal Response to "Seventh Grade"

Life in seventh grade can be confusing. That's what Gary Soto shows us in the story "Seventh Grade." At the beginning of the story, Victor, the main character, starts seventh grade with a big crush on a girl named Teresa. This sets in motion a number of realistic scenes in which he struggles to get her attention. I liked how well the story shows the real-life struggles of searching for yourself in seventh grade. I was also surprised by how much I had in common with Victor. I, too, once had a crush and felt very unsure of myself.

In the story, Victor does many things to get Teresa's attention. It all starts with scowling, a trick he learns from his friend Michael. When Victor asks Michael why he is making a face, Michael answers, "I ain't making a face, *ese*. This *is* my face." Michael is imitating some scowling male models he saw in a magazine. He thinks they look really cool and that scowling is a good way to get girls to look at him. "Belinda Reyes walked by a while ago and looked at me," he tells Victor. I think Victor wonders if it would make Teresa look at him because later he tries scowling. When a girl notices him, he decides it works. In truth, the girl probably notices Michael and Victor because they look foolish, not handsome. From my experiences in seventh grade, I can say that everyone is trying to be noticed—to be seen as special in some way. However, not everyone knows how to handle it yet. Therefore, people go to drastic measures. I can relate to Victor and Michael because I, too, have tried doing something outrageous to get attention—wearing weird clothes or hairstyles.

In the story, Victor thinks of Teresa constantly and can't wait to see her in French class. One day at lunch, Victor wants to see if Teresa is around, but he doesn't want anyone to know he is looking for her. He acts like a spy. He pretends he is reading or stretching. I know just how Victor feels because I often find myself trying to hide my feelings by pretending in a similar way.

❶ Names title, author, and main character of the work in the introduction

❷ States a response to the story and the major reasons for the response

❸ Supports response with textual evidence from the story, exhibiting careful reading

❹ Includes dialogue to bring the story to life for readers

❺ Brings in personal experiences as examples to support the response

❻ Exhibits understanding of and insight into Victor's character

Victor also tries to impress Teresa, but ends up really embarrassing himself. This is because he pretends to know something he doesn't. When Mr. Bueller, the French teacher, asks if anyone knows French, Victor raises his hand to impress Teresa. Mr. Bueller says to Victor in French, *"Très bien. Parlez-vous français?"* Victor doesn't know what that means because he only knows English and Spanish! A lot of people in seventh grade try to impress others. I think it is because they feel unsure of themselves and they don't think they're good enough as they are. In order to be liked and to feel secure, they try and make themselves into something they're not. Like Victor, I, too, have tried to be something different to impress someone I liked, only to find out the person thought I was okay just the way I was.

In conclusion, I really liked this story because I could relate to the struggles of the main character, Victor. I think the story's message is that everyone does embarrassing things when trying to impress others. In the end, though, you're better off being yourself. In my opinion, the story captures what really happens in the seventh grade. It describes the highs and lows, the stress of wanting so much for other people to like you, and the good feeling you get when they do.

❼ Writer organizes composition by interpreting Victor's behavior and relating the story to her own life.

Other Option
• Interpret the story first. Then use personal experiences as evidence.

❽ Concludes essay with a general observation about life in the seventh grade

Other Option
• States a lesson that was learned from the story that could be applied to life

1. Your Working Portfolio
Look for ideas in the **Writing** sections that you completed earlier.

2. Literary Journal
Keep a journal of your responses to literature that you read both in and out of school. Choose a piece to which you responded strongly.

3. Wishful Thinking
Find a story that is the kind of story that you wish you could write. Decide which part of the story you most admire and why.

Have a question?

See the **Writing Handbook**, Writing Introductions, p. R38.

See **Language Network**
    Prewriting, p. 310
    Drafting, p. 315

Writing Your Response to Literature

❶ Prewriting

Writing and reading decrease our sense of isolation.
            —Anne Lamott, contemporary American writer

To select a short story for your response, **write down** your reactions to some of the short stories you have read. Jot down the names of **characters** that most affected you. Think about whether you have had similar experiences to the ones described in the story. See the **Idea Bank** in the margin for more suggestions. After you have chosen a short story, follow the steps below.

Planning Your Response to Literature

▶ 1. **Carefully reread the short story.** As you read, write down insights you might have.

▶ 2. **Freewrite about your responses.** Spend five minutes writing down your overall response to the story. Identify your reactions, such as sadness, anger, excitement, or curiosity.

▶ 3. **Focus your response.** Decide whether you will respond to the entire story, to a character, to a particular event, or to the author's style. Think about the scene that most impressed you. How did the author communicate the scene? Was it through description? dialogue? an action or an image?

▶ 4. **Identify your audience.** How familiar is your audience with the story you are discussing? What will they need to know in order to understand your response?

❷ Drafting

Remember that you get to express your own opinion in a response to literature. As long as you explain your understanding of the story and support your statements with **examples,** you'll be on the right track.

Ask Your Peer Reader

• What would make my essay more interesting to you?

• Did I use effective examples?

• What ideas came through most clearly in my writing?

• Use your **introductory paragraph** to tell your readers what they need to know about the story and to introduce your response.

• Give reasons for your response and examples in the **body** of your essay. Explain why you responded the way you did.

- Include **quotations** and **descriptions** of scenes, among other things. Describe how these examples relate to your own life.
- **Summarize** your response in the conclusion of the essay.

❸ Revising

TARGET SKILL ▶ SUPPORTING YOUR RESPONSE WITH QUOTATIONS Using the actual words spoken by a character can help readers understand a character's personality and shows that you know the work well. Dialogue can also support your own thoughts about the story. Notice how the added quotations below give a glimpse of Michael's personality. Find a place in your own writing where such a revision would make an improvement.

> When Victor asks Michael why he is making a face, Michael
> *"I ain't making a face, ese. This is my face."*
> says ~~it happened over the summer.~~ Michael is imitating some
>
> scowling male models he saw in a magazine. He thinks they
>
> look really cool and that scowling is a good way to get girls to
>
> look at him. *He tells Victor, "Belinda Reyes walked by a while ago and looked at me."*

❹ Editing and Proofreading

TARGET SKILL ▶ CORRECTING RUN-ON SENTENCES A sentence expresses one complete thought. A run-on sentence is two or more sentences written as though they were one. Correct run-ons by rewriting long sentences as two separate sentences.

> Life in the seventh grade can be confusing that's what
> Gary Soto shows us in the story "Seventh Grade."

❺ Reflecting

FOR YOUR WORKING PORTFOLIO How did writing about the short story help you to understand it? Did your ideas about the story change as you wrote your personal response essay? Attach your thoughts to your finished work. Save your personal response essay in your **Working Portfolio.**

Need revising help?

Review the **Rubric,** p. 75.

Consider **peer reader** comments.

Check **Revising, Editing, and Proofreading,** p. R35.

See **Language Network,** Punctuating Quotations, p. 258.

Puzzled about how to get nouns to behave properly?

See the **Grammar Handbook,** p. R75.

SPELLING From Writing

As you revise your work, look back at the words you misspelled and determine why you made the errors you did. For additional help, refer to the strategies and generalizations in the **Spelling Handbook** on page R30.

SPEAKING Opportunity

Turn your written response into an oral presentation.

Publishing IDEAS

- Meet with a classmate who had a different response to the same story. Debate for the class and ask them to discuss why they agree with one response or the other.
- Each month look back at the stories you have read and choose a "Story of the Month." Generate a class newsletter on the computer featuring that story.

INTERNET

Publishing Options www.mcdougallittell.com

Standardized Test Practice

Mixed Review

Zebra is the first person to see <u>john Wilson at the school</u>. He finds
₍₁₎
out that Wilson is planning to teach an art class. <u>His Teacher, Mrs.</u>
₍₂₎
<u>english</u>, urges Zebra to join the class. Zebra says, "I can't draw." Then
the fact that Wilson has only one arm inspires him. Zebra decides to try.
He <u>will learn</u> that his own <u>injurys</u> do not have to hold him back. He
₍₃₎ ₍₄₎
helps Wilson when he gives him the drawing. Along the way he <u>helped</u>
₍₅₎
himself. Ultimately, his hopes for his own life change. By the end of the
story, his <u>freind</u> Andrea says, "You are becoming a pleasant life form."
₍₆₎

1. What is the correct capitalization in sentence 1?

  A. john Wilson at the School.

  B. John Wilson at the school.

  C. John Wilson at the School.

  D. Correct as is

2. What is the correct capitalization in sentence 2?

  A. His teacher, Mrs. English,

  B. His Teacher, Mrs. English,

  C. His teacher, mrs. English,

  D. Correct as is

3. What is the correct verb tense in item 3?

  A. learns

  B. will have learned

  C. learning

  D. Correct as is

4. What is the correct spelling in item 4?

  A. injuiries

  B. injuries

  C. injuiryes

  D. Correct as is

5. What is the correct verb tense in sentence 5?

  A. will help

  B. had helped

  C. helps

  D. Correct as is

6. What is the correct spelling in sentence 6?

  A. frend

  B. friend

  C. friende

  D. Correct as is

Key Standard
LC1.4 Use the mechanics of writing correctly; demonstrate correct language usage.
Other Standards **LC1.6, LC1.7**

Review Your Skills

Use the passage and the questions that follow it to check how well you remember the language conventions you've learned in previous grades.

Self-Assessment

Check your own answers in the **Grammar Handbook**

Quick Reference: Capitalization, p. R70

Quick Reference: Punctuation, p. R68

Run-on Sentences, p. R71

PART 2
Moments of Discovery
Meeting Standards

The Literature You'll Read

The Concepts You'll Study

Vocabulary and Reading Comprehension
Vocabulary Focus: Idioms and Slang
Chronological Order
Identifying Author's Purpose
Cause and Effect
Predicting
Monitoring
Comparing Across Texts

Writing and Language Conventions
Writing Workshop: Personal Narrative
Predicate Adjectives
Direct Objects
Pronoun Agreement
Varying Sentence Length
Subjects in Unusual Order
Kinds of Sentences

Literary Analysis
Genre Focus: Nonfiction
Biography
First-Person Point of View
Climax
Personification
Surprise Ending
Falling Action

Speaking and Listening
Conduct an Interview
Dedication Speech
Radio Drama
Compare and Contrast Film and Short Story

*N*onfiction

Key Standard
R3.1 Be able to describe the purposes and characteristics of different forms of prose, such as the short story, novel, or essay.

If I write about sharks or rattlesnakes, I want the reader to come away from my book with a greater appreciation of these remarkable living creatures. . . . If I write about frontier children, . . . I want to leave the reader with a . . . feeling of kinship with people of another era.

— Russell Freedman

When you read a movie review, a science textbook, or almost any article in a magazine like *Sports Illustrated for Kids,* you are reading nonfiction prose. **Nonfiction** is a type of writing that deals with real people, places, and events. A newspaper article, a set of instructions, and an encyclopedia article are also forms of nonfiction prose. Nonfiction contains factual information; however, the writer can select and organize the information to suit his or her purpose.

Forms of Nonfiction

- autobiography
- biography
- essay
- informative article
- interview

Autobiography

An **autobiography** is the story of a person's life told by that person. It is written from the **first-person point of view,** using pronouns like *I* and *me.* An autobiography is usually book length because it covers a long period of the writer's life. Shorter forms of autobiographical writing include **journals, diaries, letters,** and **memoirs.** Autobiographies can be written to entertain, persuade, inform, or express an opinion.

YOUR TURN What details in the paragraph help you understand what Eleanor Roosevelt felt and experienced?

AUTOBIOGRAPHY

In the beginning, because I felt, as only a young girl can feel it, all the pain of being an ugly duckling, I was not only timid, I was afraid. Afraid of almost everything, I think: of mice, of the dark, of imaginary dangers, of my own inadequacy. My chief objective, as a girl, was to do my duty. This had been drilled into me as far back as I could remember. Not my duty as I saw it, but my duty as laid down for me by other people. It never occurred to me to revolt. Anyhow, my one overwhelming need in those days was to be approved, to be loved, and I did whatever was required of me, hoping it would bring me nearer to the approval and love I so much wanted.

—Eleanor Roosevelt,
The Autobiography of Eleanor Roosevelt

Biography

A **biography** is the story of a person's life as told by someone else. It is written in the **third-person point of view,** using pronouns like *her* and *she.* The writer, or **biographer,** gets information by conducting interviews and by reading letters, diaries, and documents. Biographies contain some of the same elements as fiction, such as **characters** and **setting.** Unlike fiction, the purpose of biographies is to present an accurate account of the subject's life.

YOUR TURN What do the details in the paragraph tell you about Eleanor Roosevelt's life and background?

BIOGRAPHY

Eleanor was born in a fine townhouse in Manhattan. Her family also owned an elegant mansion along the Hudson River, where they spent weekends and summers. As a child Eleanor went to fashionable parties. A servant took care of her and taught her to speak French.

Her mother, the beautiful Anna Hall Roosevelt, wore magnificent jewels and fine clothing. Her father, Elliott Roosevelt, had his own hunting lodge and liked to sail and to play tennis and polo. Elliott, who loved Eleanor dearly, was the younger brother of Theodore Roosevelt, who in 1901 became president of the United States. The Roosevelt family, one of America's oldest, wealthiest families, was respected and admired.

—William Jay Jacobs, "Eleanor Roosevelt"

Essay

An **essay** is a short piece of writing on a single subject. Essays are often found in newspapers and magazines. The purpose of an essay might be to share an opinion, try to entertain or persuade, or simply describe a topic or incident that has special meaning for the writer. Three common types of essays are expository (formal), personal (informal), and persuasive. Formal essays tend to have a scholarly tone, while informal essays tend to have a conversational tone.

ESSAY

expository

- is tightly structured
- has impersonal style
- presents or explains information and ideas

The story of the *Titan* predicted exactly what would happen to the *Titanic* fourteen years later. It was an eerie prophecy of terrible things to come.

In 1907, nearly ten years after *The Wreck of the Titan* was written, two men began making plans to build a real titanic ship.

—Robert D. Ballard, *Exploring the* Titanic

personal

- has looser structure
- has personal style
- expresses writer's thoughts and feelings

Sometimes I think we would be better off if we forgot about the broad strokes and concentrated on the details. Here is a woman without a bureau. There is a man with no mirror, no wall to hang it on. They are not the homeless. They are people who have no homes. No drawer that holds the spoons. No window to look out upon the world.

—Anna Quindlen, "Homeless"

persuasive

- develops arguments
- tries to convince readers to adopt a point of view, or perspective

The only thing that can help [Native Americans] is genuine love. You must truly love us, be patient with us and share with us. And we must love you—with a genuine love that forgives and forgets. . . . This is brotherhood. . . . Anything less is not worthy of the name.

—Chief Dan George as told to Helmut Hirnschall, "I Am a Native of North America"

Informative Article

Informative articles provide facts about a subject. **Newspaper** and **magazine articles** and **feature stories** are examples of informative nonfiction. Other types of informational materials include textbooks, pamphlets, history books, gardening books, and how-to books.

YOUR TURN What is the subject of this informative article?

INFORMATIVE ARTICLE

Men, women, and children were packed into dark, foul-smelling compartments. They slept in narrow bunks stacked three high. They had no showers, no lounges, and no dining rooms. Food served from huge kettles was dished into dinner pails provided by the steamship company. Because steerage conditions were crowded and uncomfortable, passengers spent as much time as possible up on deck.

—Russell Freedman,
Immigrant Kids

Interview

An **interview** is a conversation in which one person asks questions of another for the purpose of obtaining information. The interviewer takes notes on, tape-records, or films the conversation in order to keep an accurate record. Interviews with Ray Bradbury and Virginia Hamilton are included on pages 500 and 749.

YOUR TURN What information is the interviewer trying to obtain?

INTERVIEW

Q: I know you never have trouble coming up with ideas. Walk me through your daily inspiration and writing process.

A: I just wake up with ideas every morning from my subconscious percolating. At 7 in the morning I lie in bed and I watch all the fragments of ideas swarming around in my head and these voices talk to me. And when they get to a certain point, I jump out of bed and run to the typewriter. So I'm not in control. Two hours later I have a new short story or an essay or part of a play.

—"An Interview with Ray Bradbury," 1997

Reading Nonfiction

Key Standard
R2.6 Evaluate the strength and accuracy of the evidence an author uses to support a claim. Recognize bias and stereotyping.

Nonfiction writing connects us to a world of information. **Autobiographies, biographies, essays, informative articles,** and **interviews** teach us about real people, places, and events. The reading strategies explained below can help you to enjoy many types of nonfiction.

How to Apply the Strategies

Preview the selection. Look at the title, the pictures or diagrams, and any subtitles or terms in boldface or italic type. All of these will give you an idea of what the selection is about. As you read, stop now and then to **predict** what will come next.

Clarify the organization. If the work is a biography or an autobiography, the organization is probably **chronological**—events presented in the order in which they happened. Other selections may be organized around ideas the author wants to discuss. As you read, look for dates and signal words that clarify the sequence of events, such as *before, during, after, first, next,* and *last.*

Summarize the main idea. Think about the main idea and details. Are there enough details to support the main points? Can you summarize them?

Separate facts and opinions. Facts are statements that can be proved. Opinions are statements that cannot be proved. Opinions simply express a person's beliefs. Be aware that writers of nonfiction sometimes present opinions as if they were facts.

Evaluate what you read. Evaluating means forming your own opinions about people, events, and ideas. You can also evaluate the author's purpose. Did the author write this work to inform, to influence, or to express an opinion or bias?

Here's how Sophia uses the strategies:

*"My hobby is ancient shipwrecks. When I read a ship's history, the events are told in **chronological order.** Knowing this helps me keep the facts straight. As I read, I think about the author's purpose and **evaluate** the information—to do this I need to know which of the writer's statements are **facts** and which are **opinions.** Then I come to my own conclusion."*

Across the
Curriculum
Social Studies

**ACTIVE READER
GUIDE**

Eleanor Roosevelt

by WILLIAM JAY JACOBS

Key Standard
R3.1 Be able to describe the purposes and characteristics of different forms of prose, such as the short story, novel, or essay.
***Other Standards* R1.3, R2.1, W1.2, W2.1, LC1.4, LC1.7**

Connect to Your Life

What women who have made significant social change do you know about?

Build Background

Eleanor Roosevelt, wife of President Franklin Roosevelt, lived through a period of dramatic changes.

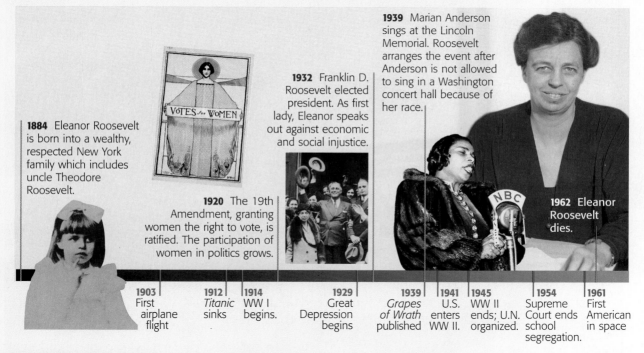

1939 Marian Anderson sings at the Lincoln Memorial. Roosevelt arranges the event after Anderson is not allowed to sing in a Washington concert hall because of her race.

1932 Franklin D. Roosevelt elected president. As first lady, Eleanor speaks out against economic and social injustice.

1884 Eleanor Roosevelt is born into a wealthy, respected New York family which includes uncle Theodore Roosevelt.

1920 The 19th Amendment, granting women the right to vote, is ratified. The participation of women in politics grows.

1962 Eleanor Roosevelt dies.

1903	1912	1914	1929	1939	1941	1945	1954	1961
First airplane flight	*Titanic* sinks	WW I begins.	Great Depression begins	*Grapes of Wrath* published	U.S. enters WW II.	WW II ends; U.N. organized.	Supreme Court ends school segregation.	First American in space

Focus Your Reading

LITERARY ANALYSIS **BIOGRAPHY**

A **biography** is the story of a person's life, written by another person. Biographers take information from many sources—letters, journals, interviews—with the purpose of bringing it together to present accurate accounts of their subjects' lives.

WORDS TO KNOW Vocabulary Preview

brooding   migrant   prominent
combatant   priority

ACTIVE READING **CHRONOLOGICAL ORDER**

Chronological order is the order in which events happen in time. Signal words such as *before, during, after, first, next, while,* and *later* indicate the order of events. As you read, create a chart in your 📖 **READER'S NOTEBOOK** to keep track of the chronological order of key events in Eleanor Roosevelt's life.

Eleanor Roosevelt

by William Jay Jacobs

President Franklin Delano Roosevelt and First Lady Eleanor Roosevelt. UPI/Bettmann.

Eleanor Roosevelt was the wife of President Franklin Delano Roosevelt. But Eleanor was much more than just a president's wife, an echo of her husband's career.

Sad and lonely as a child, Eleanor was called "Granny" by her mother because of her seriousness. People teased her about her looks and called her the "ugly duckling.". . .

Yet despite all of the disappointments, the bitterness, the misery she experienced, Eleanor Roosevelt refused to give up. Instead she turned her unhappiness and pain to strength. She devoted her life to helping others. Today she is remembered as one of America's greatest women.

Eleanor was born in a fine townhouse in Manhattan. Her family also owned an elegant mansion along the Hudson River, where they spent weekends and summers. As a child Eleanor went to fashionable parties. A servant took care of her and taught her to speak French. Her mother, the beautiful Anna Hall Roosevelt, wore magnificent jewels and fine clothing. Her father, Elliott Roosevelt, had his own hunting lodge and liked to sail and to play tennis and polo. Elliott, who loved Eleanor dearly, was the younger brother of Theodore Roosevelt, who in 1901 became president of the United States. The Roosevelt family, one of America's oldest, wealthiest families, was respected and admired.

To the outside world it might have seemed that Eleanor had everything that any child could want—everything that could make her happy. But she was not happy. Instead her childhood was very sad.

Almost from the day of her birth, October 11, 1884, people noticed that she was an unattractive child. As she grew older, she could not help but notice her mother's extraordinary beauty, as well as the beauty of her aunts and cousins. Eleanor was plain looking, ordinary, even, as some called her, homely. For a time she had to wear a bulky brace on her back to straighten her crooked spine.

When Eleanor was born, her parents had wanted a boy. They were scarcely able to hide their disappointment. Later, with the arrival of two boys, Elliott and Hall, Eleanor watched her mother hold the boys on her lap and lovingly stroke their hair, while for Eleanor there seemed only coolness, distance.

Feeling unwanted, Eleanor became shy and withdrawn. She also developed many fears. She was afraid of the dark, afraid of animals, afraid of other children, afraid of being scolded, afraid of strangers, afraid that people would not like her. She was a frightened, lonely little girl.

The one joy in the early years of her life was her father, who always seemed to care for her, love her. He used to dance with her, to pick her up and throw her into the air while she laughed and laughed. He called her "little golden hair" or "darling little Nell."

Then, when she was six, her father left. An alcoholic, he went to live in a sanitarium[1] in

ACTIVE READER

CHRONOLOGICAL ORDER
What are some of the transition words the author uses here and in the next 4 paragraphs to indicate the order in which events happened?

---

1. **sanitarium** (săn´ĭ-târ´ē-əm): an institution for the care of people with a specific disease or other health problem.

Virginia in an attempt to deal with his drinking problem. Eleanor missed him greatly.

Next her mother became ill with painful headaches. Sometimes for hours at a time Eleanor would sit holding her mother's head in her lap and stroking her forehead. Nothing else seemed to relieve the pain. At those times Eleanor often remembered how her mother had teased her about her looks and called her "Granny." But even at the age of seven Eleanor was glad to be helping someone, glad to be needed — and noticed.

The next year, when Eleanor was eight, her mother, the beautiful Anna, died. Afterward her brother Elliott suddenly caught diphtheria[2] and he, too, died. Eleanor and her baby brother, Hall, were taken to live with their grandmother in Manhattan.

A few months later another tragedy struck. Elliott Roosevelt, Eleanor's father, also died. Within eighteen months Eleanor had lost her mother, a brother, and her dear father.

For the rest of her life Eleanor carried with her the letters that her father had written to her from the sanitarium. In them he had told her to be brave, to become well educated, and to grow up into a woman he could be proud of, a woman who helped people who were suffering.

Only ten years old when her father died, Eleanor decided even then to live the kind of life he had described—a life that would have made him proud of her.

Few things in life came easily for Eleanor, but the first few years after her father's death proved exceptionally hard. Grandmother Hall's dark and gloomy townhouse had no place for children to play. The family ate meals in silence. Every morning Eleanor and Hall were expected to take cold baths for their health. Eleanor had to work at better posture by walking with her arms behind her back, clamped over a walking stick.

Instead of making new friends, Eleanor often sat alone in her room and read. For many months after her father's death she pretended that he was still alive. She made him the hero of stories she wrote for school. Sometimes, alone and unhappy, she just cried.

Some of her few moments of happiness came from visiting her uncle, Theodore Roosevelt, in Oyster Bay, Long Island. A visit with Uncle Ted meant playing games and romping outdoors with the many Roosevelt children.

Once Uncle Ted threw her into the water to teach her how to swim, but when she started to sink, he had to rescue her. Often he would read to the children old Norse tales and poetry. It was at Sagamore Hill, Uncle Ted's home, that Eleanor first learned how much fun it could be to read books aloud.

For most of the time Eleanor's life was grim. Although her parents had left plenty of money for her upbringing, she had only two dresses to wear to school. Once she spilled ink on one of them, and since the other was in the wash, she had to wear the dress with large ink stains on it to school the next day. It was not that Grandmother Hall was stingy. Rather, she was old and often confused.

> The one joy in the early years of her life was her father, who always seemed to care for her, love her.

---

2. **diphtheria** (dĭf-thîr′ē-ə): a serious infectious disease.

Nor did she show much warmth or love for Eleanor and her brother. Usually she just neglected them.

Just before Eleanor turned fifteen, Grandmother Hall decided to send her to boarding school in England. The school she chose was Allenswood, a private academy for girls located on the outskirts of London.

It was at Allenswood that Eleanor, still thinking of herself as an "ugly duckling," first dared to believe that one day she might be able to become a swan.

At Allenswood she worked to toughen herself physically. Every day she did exercises in the morning and took a cold shower. Although she did not like competitive team sports, as a matter of self-discipline she tried out for field hockey. Not only did she make the team but, because she played so hard, also won the respect of her teammates.

They called her by her family nickname, "Totty," and showed their affection for her by putting books and flowers in her room, as was the custom at Allenswood. Never before had she experienced the pleasure of having schoolmates actually admire her rather than tease her.

At Allenswood, too, she began to look after her health. She finally broke the habit of chewing her fingernails. She learned to eat nutritious foods, to get plenty of sleep, and to take a brisk walk every morning, no matter

Elliott Roosevelt and his daughter, Eleanor, aged six. Eleanor adored her father, who called her "little golden hair" or "darling little Nell." UPI/Bettmann.

how miserable the weather.

Under the guidance of the school's headmistress, Mademoiselle Souvestre (or "Sou"), she learned to ask searching questions and think for herself instead of just giving back on tests what teachers had said.

She also learned to speak French fluently, a skill she polished by traveling in France, living for a time with a French family. Mademoiselle Souvestre arranged for her to have a new red dress. Wearing it, after all of the old, worn dresses Grandmother Hall had given her, made her feel very proud.

Eleanor was growing up, and the joy of young womanhood had begun to transform her personality.

In 1902, nearly eighteen years old, she left Allenswood, not returning for her fourth year there. Grandmother Hall insisted that, instead, she must be introduced to society as a debutante—to go to dances and parties and begin to take her place in the social world with other wealthy young women.

Away from Allenswood, Eleanor's old uncertainty about her looks came back again. She saw herself as too tall, too thin, too plain. She worried about her buckteeth, which she thought made her look horselike. The old teasing began again, especially on the part of Uncle Ted's daughter, "Princess" Alice Roosevelt, who seemed to take pleasure in making Eleanor feel uncomfortable.

Eleanor, as always, did as she was told. She went to all of the parties and dances. But she also began working with poor children at the Rivington Street Settlement House on New York's Lower East Side. She taught the girls gymnastic exercises. She took children to museums and to musical performances. She tried to get the parents interested in politics in order to get better schools and cleaner, safer streets.

Meanwhile Eleanor's life reached a turning point. She fell in love! The young man was her fifth cousin, Franklin Delano Roosevelt.

Eleanor and Franklin had known each other since childhood. Franklin recalled how once he had carried her piggyback in the nursery. When she was fourteen, he had danced with her at a party. Then, shortly after her return from Allenswood, they had met by chance on a train. They talked and almost at once realized how much they liked each other.

For a time they met secretly. Then they attended parties together. Franklin—tall, strong, handsome—saw her as a person he could trust. He knew that she would not try to dominate him.

But did he really love her? Would he always? She wrote to him, quoting a poem she knew: "Unless you can swear, 'For life, for death!' . . . Oh, never call it loving!"

Franklin promised that his love was indeed "for life," and Eleanor agreed to marry him. It was the autumn of 1903. He was twenty-one. She was nineteen.

On March 17, 1905, Eleanor and Franklin were married. "Uncle Ted," by then president of the United States, was there to "give the bride away." It was sometimes said that the dynamic, energetic Theodore Roosevelt had to be "the bride at every wedding and the corpse at every funeral." And it was certainly true that day. Wherever the president went, the guests followed at his heels.

Before long Eleanor and Franklin found themselves standing all alone, deserted. Franklin seemed annoyed, but Eleanor didn't mind. She had found the ceremony deeply moving. And she stood next to her husband in a glow of idealism—very serious, very grave, very much in love.

In May 1906 the couple's first child was born. During the next nine years Eleanor gave birth to five more babies, one of whom died in infancy. Still timid, shy, afraid of making mistakes, she found herself so busy that there was little time to think of her own drawbacks.

Still, looking back later on the early years of her marriage, Eleanor knew that she should have been a stronger person, especially in the handling of Franklin's mother, or, as they both called her, "Mammá." Too often Mammá made the decisions about such things as where they would live, how their home would be furnished, how the children would be disciplined. Eleanor and Franklin let her pay for things they could not afford—extra servants, vacations, doctor bills, clothing. She offered, and they accepted.

Before long, trouble developed in the relationship between Eleanor and Franklin. Serious, shy, easily embarrassed, Eleanor could not share Franklin's interests in golf and tennis. He enjoyed light talk and flirting with women. She could not

> Eleanor threw herself into the war effort. Sometimes she worked fifteen and sixteen hours a day.

be lighthearted. So she stayed on the sidelines. Instead of losing her temper, she bottled up her anger and did not talk to him at all. As he used to say, she "clammed up." Her silence only made things worse, because it puzzled him. Faced with her coldness, her brooding silence, he only grew angrier and more distant.

Meanwhile Franklin's career in politics advanced rapidly. In 1910 he was elected to the New York State Senate. In 1913 President Wilson appointed him Assistant Secretary of the Navy—a powerful position in the national government, which required the Roosevelts to move to Washington, D.C.

In 1917 the United States entered World War I as an active combatant. Like many socially prominent women, Eleanor threw herself into the war effort. Sometimes she worked fifteen and sixteen hours a day. She made sandwiches for soldiers passing through the nation's capital. She knitted sweaters. She used Franklin's influence to get the Red Cross to build a recreation room for soldiers who had been shell-shocked in combat. . . .

In 1920 the Democratic Party chose Franklin as its candidate for vice-president of the United States. Even though the Republicans won the election, Roosevelt became a well-known figure in national politics. All the time, Eleanor stood by his side, smiling, doing what was expected of her as a candidate's wife.

She did what was expected—and much more—in the summer of 1921 when disaster struck the Roosevelt family. While on vacation Franklin suddenly fell ill with infantile paralysis—polio—the horrible disease that each year used to kill or cripple thousands of children, and many adults as well. When Franklin became a victim of polio, nobody knew what caused the disease or how to cure it.

Franklin lived, but the lower part of his body remained paralyzed. For the rest of his life he never again had the use of his legs. He had to be lifted and carried from place to place. He had to wear heavy steel braces from his waist to the heels of his shoes.

His mother, as well as many of his advisers, urged him to give up politics, to live the life of a country gentleman on the Roosevelt estate at Hyde Park, New York. This time, Eleanor, calm and strong, stood up for her ideas. She argued that he should not be treated like a sick person, tucked away in the country, inactive, just waiting for death to come.

ACTIVE READER

EVALUATE What effect do you think Franklin's illness had in changing Eleanor's attitude toward her own role?

Franklin agreed. Slowly he recovered his health. His energy returned. In 1928 he was elected governor of New York. Then, just four years later, he was elected president of the United States.

Meanwhile Eleanor had changed. To keep Franklin in the public eye while he was recovering, she had gotten involved in politics herself. It was, she thought, her "duty." From childhood she had been taught "to do the thing that has to be done, the way it has to be done, when it has to be done."

With the help of Franklin's adviser Louis Howe, she made fund-raising speeches for the Democratic Party all around New York State. She helped in the work of the League of Women Voters, the Consumer's League, and the Foreign Policy Association. After becoming interested in the problems of working women, she gave time to the Women's Trade Union League (WTUL).

It was through the WTUL that she met a

WORDS
TO
KNOW
brooding (brōo′dĭng) *adj.* full of worry; troubled **brood** *v.*
combatant (kəm-băt′nt) *n.* fighter
prominent (prŏm′ə-nənt) *adj.* well-known; widely recognized

group of remarkable women—women doing exciting work that made a difference in the world. They taught Eleanor about life in the slums. They awakened her hopes that something could be done to improve the condition of the poor. She dropped out of the "fashionable" society of her wealthy friends and joined the world of reform—social change.

For hours at a time Eleanor and her reformer friends talked with Franklin. They showed him the need for new laws: laws to get children out of the factories and into schools; laws to cut down the long hours that women worked; laws to get fair wages for all workers.

By the time that Franklin was sworn in as president, the nation was facing its deepest depression. One out of every four Americans was out of work, out of hope. At mealtimes people stood in lines in front of soup kitchens for something to eat. Mrs. Roosevelt herself knew of once-prosperous families who found themselves reduced to eating stale bread from thrift shops or traveling to parts of town where they were not known to beg for money from house to house.

Eleanor worked in the charity kitchens, ladling out soup. She visited slums. She crisscrossed the country learning about the suffering of coal miners, shipyard workers, migrant farm workers, students, housewives— Americans caught up in the paralysis of the Great Depression. Since Franklin himself remained crippled, she became his eyes and ears, informing him of what the American people were really thinking and feeling.

Eleanor also was the president's conscience, personally urging on him some of the most compassionate, forward-looking laws of his presidency, including, for example, the National Youth Administration (NYA), which provided money to allow impoverished young people to stay in school.

She lectured widely, wrote a regularly syndicated[3] newspaper column, "My Day," and spoke frequently on the radio. She fought for equal pay for women in industry. Like no other First Lady up to that time, she became a link between the president and the American public.

Above all she fought against racial and religious prejudice. When Eleanor learned that the DAR (Daughters of the American Revolution) would not allow the great black singer Marian Anderson to perform in their auditorium in Washington, D.C., she resigned from the organization. Then she arranged to have Miss Anderson sing in front of the Lincoln Memorial.

Similarly, when she entered a hall where, as often happened in those days, blacks and whites were seated in separate sections, she made it a point to sit with the blacks. Her example marked an important step in making the rights of blacks a matter of national priority.

On December 7, 1941, Japanese forces launched a surprise attack on the American naval base at Pearl Harbor, Hawaii, as well as on other American installations in the Pacific. The United States entered World War II, fighting not only against Japan but against the brutal dictators who then controlled Germany and Italy.

Eleanor helped the Red Cross raise money. She gave blood, sold war bonds. But she also did the unexpected. In 1943, for example, she visited barracks and hospitals on islands throughout the South Pacific. When she visited a hospital, she stopped at every bed. To each soldier she said

---

3. **syndicated:** sold to many newspapers for publication.

Nobody else had done so much to help raise the spirits of the men.

Eleanor Roosevelt talks animatedly as she has lunch with American soldiers in their mess hall, September 26, 1943. AP/Wide World Photos.

something special, something that a mother might say. Often, after she left, even battle-hardened men had tears in their eyes. Admiral Nimitz, who originally thought such visits would be a nuisance, became one of her strongest admirers. Nobody else, he said, had done so much to help raise the spirits of the men.

By spring 1945 the end of the war in Europe seemed near. Then, on April 12, a phone call brought Eleanor the news that Franklin Roosevelt, who had gone to Warm Springs, Georgia, for a rest, was dead.

As Eleanor later declared, "I think that sometimes I acted as his conscience. I urged him to take the harder path when he would have preferred the easier way. In that sense, I acted on occasion as a spur, even though the spurring was not always wanted or welcome.

"Of course," said Eleanor, "I loved him, and I miss him."

After Franklin's funeral, every day that Eleanor was home at Hyde Park, without fail, she placed flowers on his grave. Then she would stand very still beside him there.

With Franklin dead, Eleanor Roosevelt might have dropped out of the public eye, might have been remembered in the history books only as a footnote to the president's program of social reforms. Instead she found new strengths within herself, new ways to live a useful, interesting life—and to help others. Now, moreover, her successes were her own, not the result of being the president's wife.

In December 1945 President Harry S Truman invited her to be one of the American delegates going to London to begin the work of the United

Nations. Eleanor hesitated, but the president insisted. He said that the nation needed her; it was her duty. After that, Eleanor agreed.

In the beginning some of her fellow delegates from the United States considered her unqualified for the position, but after seeing her in action, they changed their minds.

It was Eleanor Roosevelt who, almost single-handedly, pushed through the United Nations General Assembly a resolution giving refugees from World War II the right *not* to return to their native lands if they did not wish to. The Russians angrily objected, but Eleanor's reasoning convinced wavering delegates. In a passionate speech defending the rights of the refugees she declared, "We [must] consider first the rights of man and what makes men more free— not governments, but man!"

Next Mrs. Roosevelt helped draft the United Nations Declaration of Human Rights. The Soviets wanted the declaration to list the duties people owed to their countries. Again Eleanor insisted that the United Nations should stand for individual freedom—the rights of people to free speech, freedom of religion, and such human needs as health care and education. In December 1948, with the Soviet Union and its allies refusing to vote, the Declaration of Human Rights won approval of the UN General Assembly by a vote of forty-eight to zero.

Even after retiring from her post at the UN, Mrs. Roosevelt continued to travel. In places around the world she dined with presidents and kings. But she also visited tenement slums[4] in Bombay, India; factories in Yugoslavia; farms in Lebanon and Israel.

Everywhere she met people who were eager to greet her. Although as a child she had been brought up to be formal and distant, she had grown to feel at ease with people. They wanted to touch her, to hug her, to kiss her.

Eleanor's doctor had been telling her to slow down, but that was hard for her. She continued to write her newspaper column, "My Day," and to appear on television. She still began working at seven-thirty in the morning and often continued until well past midnight. Not only did she write and speak, she taught retarded children and raised money for health care of the poor.

As author Clare Boothe Luce put it, "Mrs. Roosevelt has done more good deeds on a bigger scale for a longer time than any woman who ever appeared on our public scene. No woman has ever so comforted the distressed or so distressed the comfortable."

Gradually, however, she was forced to withdraw from some of her activities, to spend more time at home.

On November 7, 1962, at the age of seventy-eight, Eleanor died in her sleep. She was buried in the rose garden at Hyde Park, alongside her husband.

Adlai Stevenson, the American ambassador to the United Nations, remembered her as "the First Lady of the World," as the person—male or female—most effective in working for the cause of human rights. As Stevenson declared, "She would rather light a candle than curse the darkness."

And perhaps, in sum, that is what the struggle for human rights is all about. ❖

> She would rather light a candle than curse the darkness.

---

4. **tenement slums:** parts of a city where poor people live in crowded, shabby buildings.

from

The Autobiography of Eleanor Roosevelt
by Eleanor Roosevelt

In the beginning, because I felt, as only a young girl can feel it, all the pain of being an ugly duckling, I was not only timid, I was afraid. Afraid of almost everything, I think: of mice, of the dark, of imaginary dangers, of my own inadequacy. My chief objective, as a girl, was to do my duty. This had been drilled into me as far back as I could remember. Not my duty as I saw it, but my duty as laid down for me by other people. It never occurred to me to revolt. Anyhow, my one overwhelming need in those days was to be approved, to be loved, and I did whatever was required of me, hoping it would bring me nearer to the approval and love I so much wanted.

As a young woman, my sense of duty remained as strict and rigid as it had been when I was a girl, but it had changed its focus. My husband and my children became the center of my life, and their needs were my new duty. I am afraid now that I approached this new obligation much as I had my childhood duties. I was still timid, still afraid of doing something wrong, of making mistakes, of not living up to the standards required by my mother-in-law, of failing to do what was expected of me.

As a result, I was so hidebound by duty that I became too critical, too much of a disciplinarian. I was so concerned with bringing up my children properly that I was not wise enough just to love them. Now, looking back, I think I would rather spoil a child a little and have more fun out of it.

from

No Ordinary Time
by Doris Kearns Goodwin

It was said jokingly in Washington during the war years that Roosevelt had a nightly prayer: "Dear God, please make Eleanor a little tired." But in the end, he often came around to her way of thinking. Labor adviser Anna Rosenberg had been one of those who criticized Eleanor's unceasing pressure on the president, but years later she changed her mind. "I remember him saying, 'We're not going to do that now. Tell Eleanor to keep away; I don't want to hear about that anymore.'

And then 2–3 weeks later he would say, 'Do you remember that thing Eleanor brought up? Better look into it, maybe there's something to it—I heard something to indicate that maybe she's right.' I'm not sure she would have had the opportunity to bring things to his attention unless she pressured him—I mean he was so involved and in retrospect it was never anything for herself. . . He would never have become the kind of president he was without her."

THINKING through the LITERATURE

Connect to the Literature

1. **What Do You Think?**
   What words and phrases would you use to describe Eleanor Roosevelt?

   Comprehension Check
   - When did Roosevelt learn to be strong and think for herself?
   - How did she help out during World War I?
   - What was her role in the United Nations?

Think Critically

2. Which of Mrs. Roosevelt's accomplishments do you find most impressive? Why?

3. How do you think Eleanor's childhood experiences affected the choices she made later in life?

   Think About:
   - how she felt about herself
   - her goals and values
   - what she says in the excerpt from her autobiography on page 97

4. Adlai Stevenson said that Mrs. Roosevelt "would rather light a candle than curse the darkness." What do you think he meant? Explain.

5. **ACTIVE READING** | **CHRONOLOGICAL ORDER**
   How well were you able to record the **chronological order** of the events of Mrs. Roosevelt's life in your **READER'S NOTEBOOK**? Compare your chart with a classmate's. Were there details that you missed? If so, add them to your chart in the chronologically correct places.

Extend Interpretations

6. **COMPARING TEXTS** Contrast the excerpt from *The Autobiography of Eleanor Roosevelt* (page 97) with William Jay Jacobs's biography. Does reading a first-person account of Eleanor Roosevelt's girlhood influence you differently than the biographer's third-person account? Why or why not?

7. **Connect to Life** If Eleanor Roosevelt were alive today, which national and world issues do you think would concern her? To what person living today would you compare her?

Literary Analysis

BIOGRAPHY A **biography** is the story of a person's life told by someone else. A **biographer's** purpose may be to inform or explain, to entertain, to portray accurately the life of his or her subject, or all of these. In a good biography, the presentation of the subject's life is comprehensive and accurate.

Biographers often focus on remarkable aspects of their subjects' lives, such as Eleanor Roosevelt's way of caring for others, but they also strive to balance their opinion of the person with the facts.

Paired Activity With a partner, go back through the selection and make a list of some of the signal words William Jay Jacobs uses to indicate the chronological order of the events of Eleanor Roosevelt's life. Discuss how these signal words help you understand the order in which events happened.

Signal Words
1. today
2. as
3. for a time
4. later
5.

Writing

Helping Hand Have you made an impact on someone else's life? Maybe you were part of a large volunteer effort, or did a small favor for someone in need. Write an autobiographical paragraph describing the time and place, the people involved, and the event. Place the paragraph in your **Working Portfolio.**

Writing Handbook
See p. R39: Paragraphs.

Research & Technology

Time Line With a partner, make a list of important events in Mrs. Roosevelt's life. Then make a time line, including important details from the Across the Curriculum time line as well as details from your list. When you finish, discuss the following questions with a larger group:

• Which event best reveals Mrs. Roosevelt's character? How does it do so?

• Why do you think Jacobs chose to include the other events he presents?

SOCIAL STUDIES

In 1968 the United Nations gave out its first awards in human rights to honor individuals who have taken a stand against oppression. Mrs. Roosevelt was among the first group of people chosen to receive the award. Identify another person who has received a human rights award. Look for information about the awards on the Internet, and then do some additional research to find out about that person.

INTERNET Research Starter
www.mcdougallittell.com

Vocabulary and Spelling

STANDARDIZED TEST PRACTICE

Choose the word or group of words that means the same, or nearly the same, as the underlined Word to Know.

1. A <u>priority</u> means a—
   A difficult problem   **B** final answer
   C top concern   **D** sudden crisis

2. <u>Prominent</u> is another word for—
   F mysterious   **G** enormous
   H previous   **J** famous

3. A <u>combatant</u> is a—
   A fighter   **B** negotiator
   C governor   **D** researcher

4. <u>Brooding</u> is another word for—
   F bored   **G** troubled
   H enraged   **J** battered

5. <u>Migrant</u> means—
   A struggling   **B** thriving
   C moving   **D** working

Vocabulary Handbook
See p. R26: Synonyms and Antonyms.

SPELLING STRATEGY: THE SUFFIXES -ANT/-ENT
It is important to distinguish the spelling of the the suffixes -*ant* and -*ent.* They sound alike.

combat<u>ant</u>   effici<u>ent</u>
contest<u>ant</u>   defend<u>ant</u>
promin<u>ent</u>   suffici<u>ent</u>
adolesc<u>ent</u>   attend<u>ant</u>
inhabit<u>ant</u>   anci<u>ent</u>

1. Which prefix is added to complete words?
2. Which prefix is added to roots?
3. Which words have *ci* before -*ent*?
4. Write seven sentences, each of which uses one of the spelling words.

Spelling Handbook
See p. R30.

Grammar in Context: Predicate Adjectives

Jacobs states Eleanor Roosevelt's childhood fears through a series of **predicate adjectives.**

> Feeling unwanted, Eleanor became shy and withdrawn. She was afraid of the dark, afraid of animals, afraid of other children, afraid of being scolded, afraid of strangers, afraid that people would not like her.

A **predicate adjective** follows a **linking verb,** such as *be, seem, become,* or *feel,* and describes the subject.

Punctuation Tip: When you use a series of predicate adjectives, with or without a coordinating conjunction *(and, or, but),* separate them with commas: *Eleanor felt* ***plain looking, ordinary,*** *and* ***homely.***

WRITING EXERCISE Complete each sentence with a linking verb and a predicate adjective. Underline the predicate adjective.

Example: ***Original*** As a child, Eleanor
Rewritten As a child, Eleanor felt <u>uncomfortable</u> about her appearance.

1. Eleanor Roosevelt
2. Eleanor's friends
3. During the depression, many families

Connect to the Literature Turn to page 90. Reread the paragraph beginning, "For most of the time Eleanor's life was grim." What linking verbs followed by predicate adjectives do you find in the paragraph?

William Jay Jacobs
born 1933

"I saw [Eleanor Roosevelt] as a woman of courage."

Strong Role Model William Jay Jacobs admires Eleanor Roosevelt for her strength of character: "The more I learned about Eleanor Roosevelt, the more I saw her as a woman of courage. She turned her pain to strength." Jacobs believes that young people need role models like Eleanor Roosevelt—historical figures who faced tests and persisted. He says that by writing biographies he is "able to reach a very special audience: young people searching for models, trying to understand themselves."

Biography as Inspiration Jacobs has written many biographies for young people, including biographies of Hernando Cortés, Edgar Allan Poe, Abraham Lincoln, and Winston Churchill. Jacobs says that perhaps his primary task in writing biographies for young people "is to introduce them to that great reservoir of recorded history from which our civilization has drawn inspiration."

AUTHOR ACTIVITY
History for Today Read another biography by Jacobs, keeping in mind his claim that the lives of historical figures can inspire people today. Think about how the subject of the biography might serve as a role model to others. Share your ideas with classmates.

Homeless

by ANNA QUINDLEN

Key Standard
R3.5 Contrast points of view (first and third person, limited and omniscient) and explain how they affect the narrative.
***Other Standards* R2.2, R2.4, W2.1, W2.2, W2.3, LC1.3, LS2.2**

Connect to Your Life

This selection tells you about homelessness in America. What do you know about homelessness? What do you want to know? With your classmates, make a chart like this one and fill in the first two columns. Complete the third after you read the selection.

What We Know About Homelessness	What We Want to Know	What We Learned

Build Background

CURRENT EVENTS

Every night in cities across the United States, people without homes sleep on sidewalks, in bus stations, or in cardboard boxes. It is hard to get an exact count, but estimates of the nation's homeless population range from 250,000 to 3 million.

People become homeless for a variety of reasons. A commonly held image of the homeless is that they are mainly older men. In the late 1990s, however, it was determined that about 40 percent of the people without homes were women, children, and families.

WORDS TO KNOW **Vocabulary Preview**		
compassionate	enfeebled	rummage
crux	legacy	

Focus Your Reading

LITERARY ANALYSIS **FIRST-PERSON POINT OF VIEW**

A personal essay is often told from the **first-person point of view** with first-person pronouns: *I, me, we, us.* The writer of the essay is therefore also a participant in the action. Notice the first-person pronoun in this sentence from "Homeless":

> *I'm not simply talking about shelter from the elements, or three square meals a day. . . . I'm talking about a home.*

By using a first-person point of view in this personal essay, Quindlen shows her emotional closeness to the people and events she describes.

ACTIVE READING **IDENTIFYING AUTHOR'S PURPOSE**

Authors write for many reasons, including the following:

- to express an opinion
- to inform or explain
- to persuade
- to entertain

READER'S NOTEBOOK As you read this essay, jot down the purposes Quindlen may have had for writing it.

Detail	Purpose
Quindlen describes Ann, whom she met in the Port Authority Bus Terminal.	to inform
Quindlen says: "Home is where the heart is."	to express an opinion

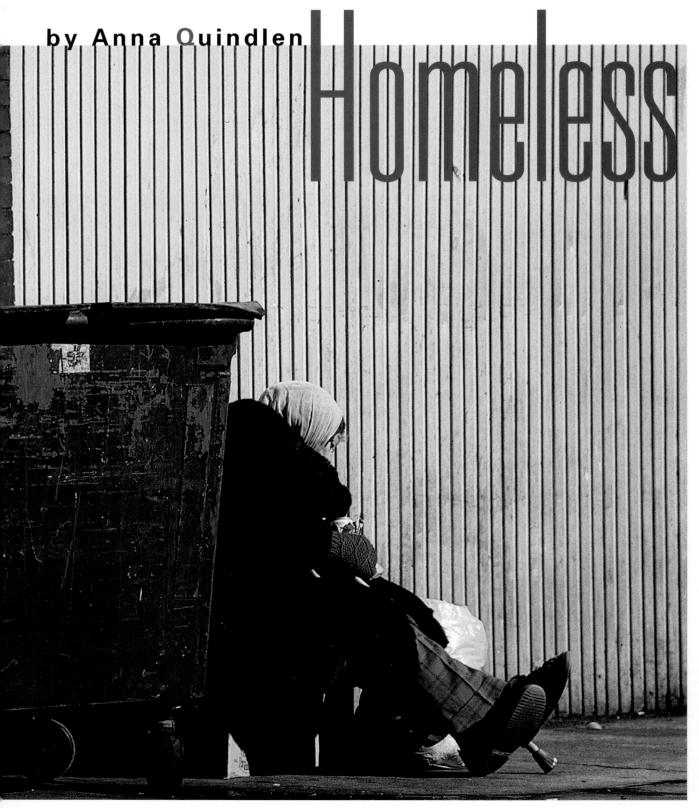

by Anna Quindlen

Homeless

Woman in New York City.
Copyright © 1982 Christopher Morris/Black Star.

Her name was Ann, and we met in the Port Authority Bus Terminal several Januarys ago. I was doing a story on homeless people. She said I was wasting my time talking to her; she was just passing through, although she'd been passing through for more than two weeks. To prove to me that this was true, she rummaged through a tote bag and a manila envelope and finally unfolded a sheet of typing paper and brought out her photographs.

They were not pictures of family, or friends, or even a dog or cat, its eyes brown-red in the flashbulb's light. They were pictures of a house. It was like a thousand houses in a hundred towns, not suburb, not city, but somewhere in between, with aluminum siding and a chainlink fence, a narrow driveway running up to a one-car garage and a patch of backyard. The house was yellow. I looked on the back for a date or a name, but neither was there. There was no need for discussion. I knew what she was trying to tell me, for it was something I had often felt. She was not adrift, alone, anonymous, although her bags and her raincoat with the grime shadowing its creases had made me believe she was. She had a house, or at least once upon a time had had one. Inside were curtains, a couch, a stove, potholders. You are where you live. She was somebody.

I've never been very good at looking at the big picture, taking the global view, and I've always been a person with an overactive sense of place, the legacy of an Irish grandfather. So it is natural that the thing that seems most wrong with the world to me right now is that

She had a house, or at least once upon a time had had one.

there are so many people with no homes. I'm not simply talking about shelter from the elements, or three square meals a day or a mailing address to which the welfare[1] people can send the check—although I know that all these are important for survival. I'm talking about a home, about precisely those kinds of feelings that have wound up in cross-stitch and French knots on samplers[2] over the years.

Home is where the heart is. There's no place like it. I love my home with a ferocity totally out of proportion to its appearance or location. I love dumb things about it: the hot-water heater, the plastic rack you drain dishes in, the roof over my head, which occasionally leaks. And yet it is precisely those dumb things that make it what it is—a place of certainty, stability, predictability, privacy, for me and for my family. It is where I live. What more can you say about a place than that? That is everything.

Yet it is something that we have been edging away from gradually during my lifetime and the lifetimes of my parents and grandparents. There was a time when where you lived often was where you worked and where you grew the food you ate and even where you were buried. When that era passed, where you lived at least was where your parents had lived and where you would live with your children

---

1. **welfare:** program of financial aid provided to people in need by the government.
2. **in cross-stitch and French knots on samplers:** spelled out in fancy stitching on embroidered decorations.

when you became <u>enfeebled</u>. Then, suddenly, where you lived was where you lived for three years, until you could move on to something else and something else again.

And so we have come to something else again, to children who do not understand what it means to go to their rooms because they have never had a room, to men and women whose fantasy is a wall they can paint a color of their own choosing, to old people reduced to sitting on molded plastic chairs, their skin blue-white in the lights of a bus station, who pull pictures of houses out of their bags. Homes have stopped being homes. Now they are real estate.

People find it curious that those without homes would rather sleep sitting up on benches or huddled in doorways than go to shelters. Certainly some prefer to do so because they are emotionally ill, because they have been locked in before and they are damned if they will be locked in again. Others are afraid of the violence and trouble they may find there. But some seem to want something that is not available in shelters, and they will not compromise, not for a cot, or oatmeal, or a shower with special soap that kills the bugs. "One room," a woman with a baby who was sleeping on her sister's floor, once told me, "painted blue." That was the <u>crux</u> of it; not size or location, but pride of ownership. Painted blue.

This is a difficult problem, and some wise and <u>compassionate</u> people are working hard at it. But in the main I think we work around it, just as we walk around it when it is lying on the sidewalk or sitting in the bus terminal— the problem, that is. It has been customary to take people's pain and lessen our own participation in it by turning it into an issue, not a collection of human beings. We turn an adjective into a noun: the poor, not poor people; the homeless, not Ann or the man who lives in the box or the woman who sleeps on the subway grate.

Sometimes I think we would be better off if we forgot about the broad strokes and concentrated on the details. Here is a woman without a bureau. There is a man with no mirror, no wall to hang it on. They are not the homeless. They are people who have no homes. No drawer that holds the spoons. No window to look out upon the world. My God. That is everything. ❖

They are not the homeless. They are people who have no homes.

BUMS IN THE ATTIC
from THE HOUSE ON MANGO STREET
by Sandra Cisneros

I want a house on a hill like the ones with the gardens where Papa works. We go on Sundays, Papa's day off. I used to go. I don't anymore. You don't like to go out with us, Papa says. Getting too old? Getting too stuck-up, says Nenny. I don't tell them I am ashamed—all of us staring out the window like the hungry. I am tired of looking at what we can't have. When we win the lottery . . . Mama begins, and then I stop listening.

People who live on hills sleep so close to the stars they forget those of us who live too much on earth. They don't look down at all except to be content to live on hills. They have nothing to do with last week's garbage or fear of rats. Night comes. Nothing wakes them but the wind.

One day I'll own my own house, but I won't forget who I am or where I came from. Passing bums will ask, Can I come in? I'll offer them the attic, ask them to stay, because I know how it is to be without a house.

Some days after dinner, guests and I will sit in front of a fire. Floorboards will squeak upstairs. The attic grumble.

Rats? they'll ask.

Bums, I'll say, and I'll be happy.

Friedensreich Hundert-wasser, #763A *River Under the Roof.* Japanese woodcut, Tokyo, 1985. Copyright © 2000 Harel, Vienna, Austria.

Connect to the Literature

1. What Do You Think? What is the main concern you had when you finished reading "Homeless"?

Comprehension Check
- What was Ann trying to tell Quindlen by showing her photographs of a house?
- What does Quindlen's home mean to her?
- Why do many homeless people prefer not to live in shelters?

Think Critically

2. Did reading this selection change any of your thoughts or opinions about homelessness? Explain your answer.

3. **ACTIVE READING** **AUTHOR'S PURPOSE** Look over the chart you made in your **READER'S NOTEBOOK.** What were Quindlen's purposes for writing this essay? Which do you think was her main purpose?

4. In your opinion, did Quindlen accomplish her main purpose for writing the essay? Why or why not?

Think About:
- why Quindlen focused on only one homeless person
- why she described her own home and her feelings about it
- the last sentence of the essay

5. What is your reaction to Quindlen's opinion that "home is where the heart is"? Explain your response.

Extend Interpretations

6. **COMPARING TEXTS** Reread Sandra Cisneros's anecdote on page 105. How do Cisneros's views on owning a home compare with Ann's?

7. Connect to Life Review the chart you created for Connect to Your Life on page 101. Do you have any questions the selection didn't answer? Discuss them with your classmates.

Literary Analysis

FIRST-PERSON POINT OF VIEW
"Homeless" is a personal essay told from a **first-person point of view**—that is, the writer uses the first-person pronouns *I, me, we,* and *us* and is a participant in the events described. An essay told from a first-person point of view usually gives the reader a strong sense of the writer's personality and opinions. In "Homeless," the reader sees Ann through the writer's eyes and learns the writer's opinions about the plight of homeless people.

Activity Working with a partner, go back through the essay and locate four or five consecutive sentences that contain first-person pronouns. List these sentences. Then change all the first-person pronouns to third-person pronouns. For example, change "I" to "she." Reread the sentences. When you are done, discuss the following questions with a larger group:

- Discuss how you feel about this excerpt being written in the third-person point of view.
- If "Homeless" were written entirely in the third-person, could it still be called a personal essay?
- Would reading this essay in the third-person point of view affect your understanding of its message? Why or why not?

Writing

Personal Narrative Think of a time when your opinion about an issue, a situation, or a person changed unexpectedly. Like the narrator of "Homeless," write a short personal narrative about what happened, and how your mind was changed. Be sure to include the people (characters) and the place (setting) involved. Remember, even a short narrative needs a beginning, a middle, and an end. Place the story in your **Working Portfolio.**

Writing Handbook
See p. R45: Narrative Writing.

Speaking & Listening

Interview As part of your research assignment on this page, you might want to interview someone who works in a homeless shelter. Find out how many people use the shelter and what services are available to them. Ask what is being done to help them find homes of their own. Share your findings with your classmates.

Speaking and Listening Handbook
See p. R100.

Research & Technology

Homelessness Research what the state and local governments are doing to help the homeless in your area, or in a city near you. Develop a list of research questions before you begin. You might want to find out what percentage of the population in your region is homeless. What type of assistance is available? What is planned for the future? Use the Internet and your local library to find public documents that might contain this information. As you research, evaluate your list of questions, and revise as necessary.

Vocabulary

STANDARDIZED TEST PRACTICE

Choose the word or group of words that means the same, or nearly the same, as the underlined Word to Know.

1. The crux of a problem
  A discovery **B** end
  C correction **D** core

2. Enfeebled hands
  J folded **K** wrinkled
  L weakened **M** empty

3. To rummage through a closet
  A sweep **B** search
  C walk **D** run

4. A compassionate friend
  J dishonest **K** constant
  L sympathetic **M** lively

5. A family legacy
  A tradition **B** reunion
  C outing **D** photograph

Vocabulary Handbook
See p. R26: Synonyms and Antonyms.

Grammar in Context: Direct Objects

Notice how the **direct objects** in these sentences from "Homeless" communicate important information about the subject of the sentence.

> She had a house, or at least once upon a time she had one. You are where you live. She was somebody. . . . Home is where the heart is. I love my home with a ferocity totally out of proportion to its appearance or location.

All sentences need a **subject** and a **verb.** Some sentences need a **direct object** that names the receiver of the verb's action:

> She had a dream.

WRITING EXERCISE Read these incomplete sentences. Underline the verb once. Then complete each sentence by writing a logical direct object. Underline the direct object twice.

Example: *Original* Some homeless people fear

Rewritten Some homeless people <u>fear</u> <u>violence</u>.

1. I really appreciate
2. The author wrote
3. Her tote bag held
4. Her house had

Grammar Handbook

See p. R67: The Sentence and Its Parts.

Anna Quindlen
born 1953

"Real life is in the dishes."

Cub Reporter After graduating from Barnard College in 1974, Anna Quindlen published her first story and started working as a newspaper reporter. In 1981 she was offered the "About New York" column in the *New York Times.* She has called writing that column her dream job, because she "got to write about anything": "I'd go to a cop's funeral or I'd go to Coney Island and talk to the homeless people. . . . I developed a voice of my own . . . and I developed the ability to come up with column ideas."

Prize-Winning Columnist After the birth of her first child, Quindlen began writing a column about her own family, called "Life in the 30s." In her next column, "Public & Private," she tackled public and political issues on the opinion-editorial page. In 1992 she won a Pulitzer prize for commentary. Quindlen has also published a children's book and three novels about families. According to her, families mirror society. "Real life is in the dishes," she says.

AUTHOR ACTIVITY

Something in Common To readers of her newspaper columns and novels, Anna Quindlen is known for her personal concern about social issues. Find and read one of the columns in her collection *Thinking Out Loud* or *Living Out Loud.* Present an oral summary of the column to your classmates.

The War of the Wall

by TONI CADE BAMBARA

Key Standard
R3.2 Identify events that advance the plot and describe how they explain the past, present, and future.
Other Standards **R1.3, R2.3, W2.1, W2.3, LC1.2, LC1.4, LC1.7**

Connect to Your Life

Hanging Out Is there a place in your neighborhood that seems to belong to young people? Perhaps it is a park or a schoolyard or a theater. What's special about the place? Why is it important to young people? What does the place mean to the rest of the community?

Build Background

ART

Murals are large pictures or scenes painted on or applied to a wall. In the United States, during the hard times of the 1930s and the 1940s, a murals program was launched by the federal government. Artists in need were commissioned to paint murals in hundreds of new post offices.

At the same time in Mexico, artists such as Diego Rivera, José Clemente Orozco, and David Siqueiros were representing Mexican life and history on the walls of public buildings.

In the 1960s, African-American artists began a "wall of respect" movement. These artists painted murals on walls in their communities as symbols of their respect for the neighborhoods.

> **WORDS TO KNOW Vocabulary Preview**
> beckon   drawl   inscription   liberation   scheme

Focus Your Reading

LITERARY ANALYSIS CLIMAX

The turning point in a **plot,** the moment of greatest intensity and interest, is called the **climax.** Usually, a series of events leads to the climax of a story, which occurs near the end of the plot. The climax often involves an important decision or discovery that affects the outcome of the story. As you read "The War of the Wall," look for an event that marks the climax.

ACTIVE READING CAUSE AND EFFECT

Two events have a **cause-and-effect** relationship when one event brings about the other. The event that happens first in time is the **cause**; the event that comes afterward is the **effect.** However, the effect may sometimes be *stated* before the cause.

READER'S NOTEBOOK As you read, jot down some causes and their effects.

Cause	Effect
A stranger was painting the wall.	Lou and the narrator were angry because they felt that the wall was *their* wall.

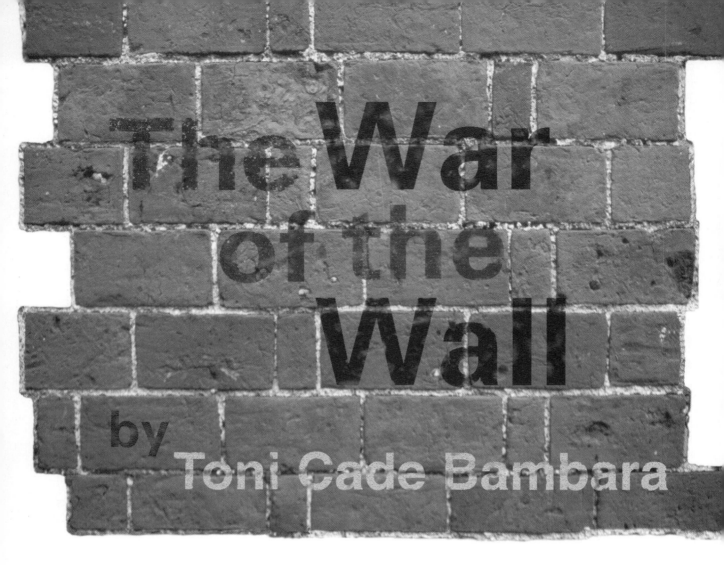

The War of the Wall

by Toni Cade Bambara

Me and Lou had no time for courtesies. We were late for school. So we just flat out told the painter lady to quit messing with the wall. It was our wall, and she had no right coming into our neighborhood painting on it. Stirring in the paint bucket and not even looking at us, she mumbled something about Mr. Eubanks, the barber, giving her permission. That had nothing to do with it as far as we were concerned. We've been pitching pennies against that wall since we were little kids. Old folks have been dragging their chairs out to sit in the shade of the wall for years. Big kids have been playing handball against the wall since so-called integration[1] when the crazies 'cross town poured cement in our pool so we couldn't use it. I'd sprained my neck one time boosting my cousin Lou up to chisel Jimmy Lyons's name into the wall when we found out he was never coming home from the war in Vietnam to take us fishing.

"If you lean close," Lou said, leaning hipshot against her beat-up car, "you'll get a

---

1. **since so-called integration:** from the time in the 1960s when segregation, the separation of the races in public places, was outlawed. The narrator is being sarcastic, suggesting that integration has not been successful.

whiff of bubble gum and kids' sweat. And that'll tell you something—that this wall belongs to the kids of Taliaferro Street." I thought Lou sounded very convincing. But the painter lady paid us no mind. She just snapped the brim of her straw hat down and hauled her bucket up the ladder.

"You're not even from around here," I hollered up after her. The license plates on her old piece of car said "New York." Lou dragged me away because I was about to grab hold of that ladder and shake it. And then we'd really be late for school.

When we came from school, the wall was slick with white. The painter lady was running string across the wall and taping it here and there. Me and Lou leaned against the gumball machine outside the pool hall and watched. She had strings up and down and back and forth. Then she began chalking them with a hunk of blue chalk.

The Morris twins crossed the street, hanging back at the curb next to the beat-up car. The twin with the red ribbons was hugging a jug of cloudy lemonade. The one with yellow ribbons was holding a plate of dinner away from her dress. The painter lady began snapping the strings. The blue chalk dust measured off halves and quarters up and down and sideways too. Lou was about to say how hip it all was, but I dropped my book satchel on his toes to remind him we were at war.

Some good aromas were drifting our way from the plate leaking pot likker onto the Morris girl's white socks. I could tell from where I stood that under the tinfoil was baked ham, collard greens, and candied yams. And knowing Mrs. Morris, who sometimes bakes for my mama's restaurant, a slab of buttered cornbread was probably up under there too, sopping up some of the pot likker. Me and

Lou rolled our eyes, wishing somebody would send us some dinner. But the painter lady didn't even turn around. She was pulling the strings down and prying bits of tape loose.

Side Pocket came strolling out of the pool hall to see what Lou and me were studying so hard. He gave the painter lady the once-over, checking out her paint-spattered jeans, her chalky T-shirt, her floppy-brimmed straw hat. He hitched up his pants and glided over toward the painter lady, who kept right on with what she was doing.

"Whatcha got there, sweetheart?" he asked the twin with the plate.

"Suppah," she said all soft and countrylike.

"For her," the one with the jug added, jerking her chin toward the painter lady's back.

Still she didn't turn around. She was rearing back on her heels, her hands jammed into her back pockets, her face squinched up like the masterpiece she had in mind was taking shape on the wall by magic. We could have been gophers crawled up into a rotten hollow for all

> She was rearing back on her heels, her hands jammed into her back pockets, her face squinched up like the masterpiece she had in mind was taking shape on the wall by magic.

she cared. She didn't even say hello to anybody. Lou was muttering something about how great her concentration was. I butt him with my hip, and his elbow slid off the gum machine.

"Good evening," Side Pocket said in his best ain't-I-fine voice. But the painter lady was moving from the milk crate to the step stool to the ladder, moving up and down fast, scribbling all over the wall like a crazy person. We looked at Side Pocket. He looked at the twins. The twins looked at us. The painter lady was giving a show. It was like those old-timey music movies where the dancer taps on the tabletop and then starts jumping all over the furniture, kicking chairs over and not skipping a beat. She didn't even look where she was stepping. And for a minute there, hanging on the ladder to reach a far spot, she looked like she was going to tip right over.

"Ahh," Side Pocket cleared his throat and moved fast to catch the ladder. "These young ladies here have brought you some supper."

"Ma'am?" The twins stepped forward. Finally the painter turned around, her eyes "full of sky," as my grandmama would say. Then she stepped down like she was in a trance. She wiped her hands on her jeans as the Morris twins offered up the plate and the jug. She rolled back the tinfoil, then wagged her head as though something terrible was on the plate.

"Thank your mother very much," she said, sounding like her mouth was full of sky too. "I've brought my own dinner along." And then, without even excusing herself, she went back up the ladder, drawing on the wall in a wild way. Side Pocket whistled one of those oh-brother breathy whistles and went back into the pool hall. The Morris twins shifted their weight from one foot to the other, then crossed the street and went home. Lou had to drag me away, I was so mad. We couldn't wait to get to the firehouse to tell my daddy all about this rude woman who'd stolen our wall.

All the way back to the block to help my mama out at the restaurant, me and Lou kept asking my daddy for ways to run the painter lady out of town. But my daddy was busy talking about the trip to the country and telling Lou he could come too because Grandmama can always use an extra pair of hands on the farm.

Later that night, while me and Lou were in the back doing our chores, we found out that the painter lady was a liar. She came into the restaurant and leaned against the glass of the steam table, talking about how starved she was. I was scrubbing pots and Lou was chopping onions, but we could hear her through the service window. She was asking Mama was that a ham hock in the greens, and was that a neck bone in the pole beans, and were there any vegetables cooked without meat, especially pork.

"I don't care who your spiritual leader is," Mama said in that way of hers. "If you eat in the community, sistuh, you gonna eat pig by-and-by, one way or t'other."

Me and Lou were cracking up in the kitchen, and several customers at the counter were clearing their throats, waiting for Mama to really fix her wagon for not speaking to the elders when she came in. The painter lady

All the way back to the block to help my mama out at the restaurant, me and Lou kept asking my daddy for ways to run the painter lady out of town.

took a stool at the counter and went right on with her questions. Was there cheese in the baked macaroni, she wanted to know? Were there eggs in the salad? Was it honey or sugar in the iced tea? Mama was fixing Pop Johnson's plate. And every time the painter lady asked a fool question, Mama would dump another spoonful of rice on the pile. She was tapping her foot and heating up in a dangerous way. But Pop Johnson was happy as he could be. Me and Lou peeked through the service window, wondering what planet the painter lady came from. Who ever heard of baked macaroni without cheese, or potato salad without eggs?

Sibling Rivals (1989), Phoebe Beasley. Collage, 32″ × 40″, courtesy of the artist.

"Do you have any bread made with unbleached flour?" the painter lady asked Mama. There was a long pause, as though everybody in the restaurant was holding their breath, wondering if Mama would dump the next spoonful on the painter lady's head. She didn't. But when she set Pop Johnson's plate down, it came down with a bang.

When Mama finally took her order, the starving lady all of a sudden couldn't make up her mind whether she wanted a vegetable plate or fish and a salad. She finally settled on the broiled trout and a tossed salad. But just when Mama reached for a plate to serve her, the painter lady leaned over the counter with her finger all up in the air.

"Excuse me," she said. "One more thing." Mama was holding the plate like a Frisbee, tapping that foot, one hand on her hip. "Can I get raw beets in that tossed salad?"

"You will get," Mama said, leaning her face close to the painter lady's, "whatever Lou back there tossed. Now sit down." And the painter lady sat back down on her stool and shut right up.

All the way to the country, me and Lou tried to get Mama to open fire on the painter lady. But Mama said that seeing as how she was from the North, you couldn't expect her to have any manners. Then Mama said she was sorry she'd been so impatient with the woman because she seemed like a decent person and was simply trying to stick to a very strict diet. Me and Lou didn't want to hear that. Who did that lady think she was, coming into our neighborhood and taking over our wall?

"Welllll," Mama <u>drawled</u>, pulling into the filling station so Daddy could take the wheel,

"it's hard on an artist, ya know. They can't always get people to look at their work. So she's just doing her work in the open, that's all."

Me and Lou definitely did not want to hear that. Why couldn't she set up an easel downtown or draw on the sidewalk in her own

All weekend long me and Lou tried to scheme up ways to recapture our wall.

neighborhood? Mama told us to quit fussing so much; she was tired and wanted to rest. She climbed into the back seat and dropped down into the warm hollow Daddy had made in the pillow.

All weekend long, me and Lou tried to <u>scheme</u> up ways to recapture our wall. Daddy and Mama said they were sick of hearing about it. Grandmama turned up the TV to drown us out. On the late news was a story about the New York subways. When a train came roaring into the station all covered from top to bottom, windows too, with writings and drawings done with spray paint, me and Lou slapped five. Mama said it was too bad kids in New York had nothing better to do than spray paint all over the trains. Daddy said that in the cities, even grown-ups wrote all over the trains and buildings too. Daddy called it "graffiti." Grandmama called it a shame.

We couldn't wait to get out of school on Monday. We couldn't find any black spray paint anywhere. But in a junky hardware store downtown we found a can of white epoxy[2] paint, the kind you touch up old refrigerators with when they get splotchy and peely. We spent our whole allowance on it. And because it was

_____
2. **epoxy** (ĭ-pŏk′sē): a plastic used in glues and paints.

WORDS TO KNOW	**drawl** (drôl) *v.* to speak slowly, stretching the vowel sound **scheme** (skēm) *v.* to plot or plan in a secretive way

too late to use our bus passes, we had to walk all the way home lugging our book satchels and gym shoes, and the bag with the epoxy.

When we reached the corner of Taliaferro and Fifth, it looked like a block party or something. Half the neighborhood was gathered on the sidewalk in front of the wall. I looked at Lou, he looked at me. We both looked at the bag with the epoxy and wondered how we were going to work our scheme. The painter lady's car was nowhere in sight. But there were too many people standing around to do anything. Side Pocket and his buddies were leaning on their cue sticks, hunching each other. Daddy was there with a lineman he catches a ride with on Mondays. Mrs. Morris had her arms flung around the shoulders of the twins on either side of her. Mama was talking with some of her customers, many of them with napkins still at the throat. Mr. Eubanks came out of the barbershop, followed by a man in a striped poncho, half his face shaved, the other half full of foam.

"She really did it, didn't she?" Mr. Eubanks huffed out his chest. Lots of folks answered right quick that she surely did when they saw the straight razor in his hand.

Mama <u>beckoned</u> us over. And then we saw it. The wall. Reds, greens, figures outlined in black. Swirls of purple and orange. Storms of blues and yellows. It was something. I recognized some of the faces right off. There was Martin Luther King, Jr. And there was a man with glasses on and his mouth open like he was laying down a heavy rap. Daddy came up alongside and reminded us that that was Minister Malcolm X. The serious woman with a rifle I knew was Harriet Tubman because my grandmama has pictures of her all over the house. And I knew Mrs. Fannie Lou Hamer 'cause a signed photograph of her hangs in the restaurant next to the calendar.

Then I let my eyes follow what looked like a vine. It trailed past a man with a horn, a woman with a big white flower in her hair, a handsome dude in a tuxedo seated at a piano, and a man with a goatee holding a book. When I looked more closely, I realized that what had looked like flowers were really faces. One face with yellow petals looked just like Frieda Morris. One with red petals looked just like Hattie Morris. I could hardly believe my eyes.

"Notice," Side Pocket said, stepping close to the wall with his cue stick like a classroom pointer. "These are the flags of <u>liberation</u>," he

I recognized some of the faces right off. There was Martin Luther King, Jr. And there was a man with glasses on and his mouth open like he was laying down a heavy rap.

said in a voice I'd never heard him use before. We all stepped closer while he pointed and spoke. "Red, black and green," he said, his pointer falling on the leaflike flags of the vine. "Our liberation flag. And here Ghana, there Tanzania. Guinea-Bissau, Angola, Mozambique." Side Pocket sounded very tall, as though he'd been waiting all his life to give this lesson.

Mama tapped us on the shoulder and pointed to a high section of the wall. There was a fierce-looking man with his arms crossed against his chest guarding a bunch of children. His muscles bulged, and he looked a lot like my daddy. One

Another Time's Voice Remembers My Passion's Humanity (1979), Calvin B. Jones and Mitchell Caton. Outdoor mural, 22′ × 48′, Elliott Donnelley Youth Center, Chicago. Restored in 1993 by Bernard Williams and Paige Hinson, Chicago Mural Project.

kid was looking at a row of books. Lou hunched me 'cause the kid looked like me. The one that looked like Lou was spinning a globe on the tip of his finger like a basketball. There were other kids there with microscopes and compasses. And the more I looked, the more it looked like the fierce man was not so much guarding the kids as defending their right to do what they were doing.

Then Lou gasped and dropped the paint bag and ran forward, running his hands over a rainbow. He had to tiptoe and stretch to do it, it was so high. I couldn't breathe either. The painter lady had found the chisel marks and had painted Jimmy Lyons's name in a rainbow.

"Read the inscription, honey," Mrs. Morris said, urging little Frieda forward. She didn't have to urge much. Frieda marched right up, bent down, and in a loud voice that made everybody quit oohing and ahhing and listen, she read,

To the People of Taliaferro Street
I Dedicate This Wall of Respect
Painted in Memory of My Cousin
Jimmy Lyons

WORDS TO KNOW **inscription** (ĭn-skrĭp'shən) *n.* something written, carved, or engraved on a surface

from
Song of Myself

BY WALT WHITMAN

I exist as I am, that is enough,
If no other in the world be aware
    I sit content,
And if each and all be aware I sit
    content.

One world is aware and by far the
    largest to me, and that is myself,
And whether I come to my own
    today or in ten thousand or ten
    million years,
I can cheerfully take it now, or with
    equal cheerfulness I can wait.

Closed Windows, Hessam Abrishami. Giclee on paper.
Copyright © Collectors Editions.

Connect to the Literature

1. What Do You Think? What do you think of the ending of the story?

Comprehension Check
- What do Lou and the narrator think of the painter lady at the beginning of the story?
- Why is Mama irritated by the painter lady?
- How do Lou and the narrator feel about the painter lady when they see her mural?

Think Critically

2. Why do you think the painter lady doesn't speak to the young people or tell them what her plans for the wall are?

3. What do you think the painter lady accomplishes by creating the mural?

4. **ACTIVE READING** **CAUSE AND EFFECT**
Look over the chart with examples of **cause and effect** that you made in your **READER'S NOTEBOOK**. Why didn't Lou and the narrator use the can of white epoxy paint?

5. Do you think the mural will make a difference in the lives of the neighborhood kids? Explain your answer.

   Think About:
   - Lou and the narrator's first meeting with the painter lady
   - how Mama's opinion of the painter lady changes over time
   - the people and the images depicted in the mural
   - the last four lines of the story

Extend Interpretations

6. **COMPARING TEXTS** Do you think the narrator of "The War of the Wall" would agree with the feelings expressed in the poem "Song of Myself" on page 117? Why or why not?

7. Connect to Life If an artist painted a mural in your neighborhood, what heroes do you think your neighbors would want represented? Explain.

Literary Analysis

CLIMAX A **climax,** or turning point of a story, is the moment when the **plot** has reached its greatest intensity. The climax usually occurs near the end, after the reader understands the conflict and knows the characters. Writers use a series of events to advance the plot, moving the story toward the climax. The climax of "The War of the Wall" occurs when the painter lady's inscription to Jimmy Lyons is unveiled.

REVIEW: CONFLICT When struggle occurs between characters or between a character and another force, it is called **external conflict,** as in the struggle between the narrator and the painter lady. When the struggle occurs within a character, it is called **internal conflict,** such as Mama's conflicting feelings of irritation and respect for the painter lady. In this story, the **central conflict** is external.

Paired Activity Working with a partner, go back through the story and jot down examples of internal and external conflict. When you are done, discuss the following questions with a larger group.

- Which conflicts add the most excitement to the story?
- Which conflicts tell something important about one of the characters? Explain.

Writing

Personal Narrative Write a short narrative about a conflict you have had with someone you know. Tell how you resolved the conflict. Find a beginning, middle, and end for your story. Share your writing with the class. Place your writing in your **Working Portfolio.** 📁

Writing Handbook
See p. R45: Narrative Writing.

Speaking & Listening

Dedication Speech Write a speech that the painter lady might deliver to the community if she were to return for the dedication of the mural. Try to see the neighborhood through the painter lady's eyes, from her point of view. What do you think she would want to tell the community about why she painted the mural? Would she have any special message for the narrator and Lou? Present your speech to the class.

Research & Technology

Mural Subjects Research the "wall of respect" movement or one of the four African-American heroes—Martin Luther King, Jr., Malcolm X, Harriet Tubman, Fannie Lou Hamer—that the narrator recognizes in the painter lady's mural. Think of at least three things you would like to know about your subject. Write these as questions and research to find the answers. Prepare a report about the subject you researched.

Vocabulary and Spelling

EXERCISE: MEANING CLUES On a sheet of paper, write the letter of the situation that best demonstrates the meaning of the Word to Know.

1. beckon
   a. you are hailing a taxicab
   b. you are passing a test
   c. you are eating lunch

2. inscription
   a. the end of a game
   b. the words on a tombstone
   c. the parts of a vehicle

3. drawl
   a. speak very slowly
   b. paddle a canoe
   c. make a sketch

4. scheme
   a. write a play
   b. go on a trip
   c. plan a surprise party

5. liberation
   a. end slavery
   b. go on a picnic
   c. attend a rally

Vocabulary Handbook
See p. R24: Context Clues.

SPELLING STRATEGY: SUFFIXES The word ending pronounced *shun* is usually spelled *-tion.* Many verbs ending in *-ate* can be changed to nouns by adding the suffix *-ion,* as in *liberate/liberation.* The hard *t* in *-ate* becomes the soft *t* in *-tion.*

1. Drop the final *e* and add the suffix *-ion* to the following verbs to make them nouns.
   vacate   calculate
   educate   graduate
   celebrate   migrate
   liberate   complicate
   regulate   eliminate

2. Write a complete sentence using each of the spelling words.

Spelling Handbook
See p. R30.

Grammar in Context: Pronoun Agreement

In this description, Bambara captures the astonishment of the narrator when he first sees the mural the painter lady has created.

> **And then we saw it. The wall. Reds, greens, figures outlined in black. Swirls of purple and orange. Storms of blues and yellows. It was something.**

A **pronoun** is a word that replaces a noun. Using pronouns allows writers to avoid monotonous repetition of nouns, but for pronouns to be effective a reader needs to know exactly which noun they refer to, which is called the **pronoun antecedent.** In the first sentence of the passage, Bambara shows the narrator's amazement by leaving the antecedent of "it" momentarily unclear. What "it" refers to becomes clear in the next sentence. "It" is the wall.

WRITING EXERCISE Rewrite the sentences so they have no unclear pronoun antecedents.

Example: *Original* Although the boys were annoyed at first, <u>it</u> disappeared after they saw the mural.

Rewritten The annoyance the boys felt at first disappeared after they saw the mural.

1. The boys wanted the painter to stop painting the wall, <u>which</u> made them angry.
2. Side Pocket came out of the pool hall to see what the boys were up to. <u>It</u> had sparked his curiosity.
3. The Morris girls brought a covered plate with baked ham, greens, and yams, but the painter lady wouldn't eat <u>them</u>.
4. The boys considered the wall theirs. <u>It</u> is why they wanted the painter lady to leave it alone.

Grammar Handbook
See p. R75: Using Nouns and Pronouns.

Toni Cade Bambara
1939–1995

"I move toward the short story because I'm a sprinter."

City Life Toni Cade Bambara believed that writers "are everyday people who write stories that come out of their neighborhoods." "The War of the Wall" was inspired by her memories of growing up in New York City. As a child, she and her companions created a park in a vacant city lot. One day they found a large advertisement there. "We were incensed," she recalled. "We went to city hall and got the billboard removed."

A Variety of Interests After college, Bambara studied theater and mime in Europe and dance and film in the United States. She also worked in a welfare department, planned recreation for mentally ill patients, held community-action workshops, and taught college English and African-American studies. During her later years, Bambara led a writers' workshop and remained intensely involved in her community. Her writing won many major awards, including the American Book Award in 1981.

Author Activity

Growing Up in the City Bambara once said, "Temperamentally, I move toward the short story because I'm a sprinter rather than a long-distance runner. I cannot sustain characters over a long period of time." Many of her short stories are about young people facing the challenges of inner-city life. Read another short story by Bambara. Compare it with "The War of the Wall." Discuss your comparison with your classmates.

PREPARING to Read

ACTIVE READER GUIDE

Rikki-tikki-tavi

by RUDYARD KIPLING

Key Standard
R3.5 Contrast points of view (first and third person, limited and omniscient) and explain how they affect the narrative.
Other Standards **R1.3, R3.1, W2.1, W2.3, LC1.5, LS2.1**

Connect to Your Life

Natural Enemies In nature some animals instinctually prey on other animals. These animals are called natural enemies. What natural enemies in the animal kingdom can you name? With a partner, brainstorm a list of natural enemies, both common and exotic. Share your list with your classmates.

Build Background

SOCIAL STUDIES

If you lived in India, you certainly would know the mongoose and the cobra as a pair of natural enemies—a pair that will fight to the death. The mongoose, growing only to a length of 16 inches, seems hardly a match for the poisonous cobra, a snake that averages 6 feet in length and 6 inches around.

This story is set in India during the late 1800s. At that time, Great Britain ruled India. British families lived in open, airy houses called **bungalows.**

WORDS TO KNOW
Vocabulary Preview

consolation	cunningly	scuttle
cower	revive	

Focus Your Reading

LITERARY ANALYSIS **PERSONIFICATION**

When a writer gives human qualities to an animal, object, or idea, the technique is called **personification.** Kipling uses personification in "Rikki-tikki-tavi." Personification allows readers to imagine what the animals think, feel, and say about each other.

> *"Well," said Rikki-tikki, and his tail began to fluff up again, "marks or no marks, do you think it is right for you to eat fledgelings out of a nest?"*

As you read, look for examples of personification, especially in the character of Rikki-tikki-tavi and of his cobra enemies.

ACTIVE READING **PREDICTING**

A **prediction** is an attempt to answer the question "What will happen next?" To make predictions, pay attention to the following:

• interesting details about character, **plot,** and setting
• unusual statements by the main characters

READER'S NOTEBOOK As you read this story, jot down at least three predictions, as well as a good reason for each guess. Record your predictions on a chart.

My Predictions		
Who?	**Why?**	**What Next?**
Rikki-tikki	Teddy's mother takes him home.	Rikki-tikki will live with Teddy's family.

Rikki-tikki-tavi

by Rudyard Kipling

This is the story of the great war that Rikki-tikki-tavi fought single-handed, through the bathrooms of the big bungalow[1] in Segowlee cantonment.[2] Darzee, the tailorbird, helped him, and Chuchundra, the muskrat, who never comes out into the middle of the floor but always creeps round by the wall, gave him advice; but Rikki-tikki did the real fighting.

He was a mongoose, rather like a little cat in his fur and his tail but quite like a weasel in his head and his habits. His eyes and the end of his restless nose were pink; he could scratch himself anywhere he pleased with any leg, front or back, that he chose to use; he could fluff up his tail till it looked like a bottle-brush, and his war cry as he scuttled through the long grass was:

Rikk-
    tikk-
        tikki-
            tikki-
                tchk!

---

1. **bungalow** (bŭng′gə-lō′): in India, a house surrounded by a large outer porch.
2. **cantonment** (kăn-tōn′mənt): a military base.

One day, a high summer flood washed him out of the burrow where he lived with his father and mother and carried him, kicking and clucking, down a roadside ditch. He found a little wisp of grass floating there and clung to it till he lost his senses. When he <u>revived</u>, he was lying in the hot sun on the middle of a garden path, very draggled indeed, and a small boy was saying, "Here's a dead mongoose. Let's have a funeral."

"No," said his mother, "let's take him in and dry him. Perhaps he isn't really dead."

They took him into the house, and a big man picked him up between his finger and thumb and said he was not dead but half choked; so they wrapped him in cotton wool and warmed him over a little fire, and he opened his eyes and sneezed. "Now," said the big man (he was an Englishman who had just moved into the bungalow), "don't frighten him, and we'll see what he'll do."

It is the hardest thing in the world to frighten a mongoose, because he is eaten up from nose to tail with curiosity. The motto of all the mongoose family is "Run and Find Out"; and Rikki-tikki was a true mongoose. He looked at the cotton wool, decided that it was not good to eat, ran all round the table, sat up and put his fur in order, scratched himself, and jumped on the small boy's shoulder.

"Don't be frightened, Teddy," said his father. "That's his way of making friends."

"Ouch! He's tickling under my chin," said Teddy.

Rikki-tikki looked down between the boy's collar and neck, snuffed at his ear, and climbed down to the floor, where he sat rubbing his nose.

"Good gracious," said Teddy's mother, "and that's a wild creature! I suppose he's so tame because we've been kind to him."

"All mongooses are like that," said her husband. "If Teddy doesn't pick him up by the tail or try to put him in a cage, he'll run in and out of the house all day long. Let's give him something to eat."

They gave him a little piece of raw meat. Rikki-tikki liked it immensely; and when it was finished, he went out into the veranda[3] and sat in the sunshine and fluffed up his fur to make it dry to the roots. Then he felt better.

"There are more things to find out about in this house," he said to himself, "than all my family could find out in all their lives. I shall certainly stay and find out."

He spent all that day roaming over the house. He nearly drowned himself in the bathtubs, put his nose into the ink on a writing table, and burnt it on the end of the big man's cigar, for he climbed up in the big man's lap to see how writing was done. At nightfall he ran into Teddy's nursery to watch how kerosene lamps were lighted, and when Teddy went to bed, Rikki-tikki climbed up too; but he was a restless companion, because he had to get up and attend to every noise all through the night and find out what made it. Teddy's mother and father came in, the last thing, to look at their boy, and Rikki-tikki was awake on the pillow.

"I don't like that," said Teddy's mother; "he may bite the child."

"He'll do no such thing," said the father. "Teddy is safer with that little beast than if he had a bloodhound to watch him. If a snake came into the nursery now—"

But Teddy's mother wouldn't think of anything so awful.

---

3. **veranda** (və-răn′də): a long open porch.

Early in the morning Rikki-tikki came to early breakfast in the veranda, riding on Teddy's shoulder, and they gave him banana and some boiled egg; and he sat on all their laps one after the other, because every well-brought-up mongoose always hopes to be a house mongoose some day and have rooms to run about in; and Rikki-tikki's mother (she used to live in the general's house at Segowlee) had carefully told Rikki what to do if ever he came across white men.

Then Rikki-tikki went out into the garden to see what was to be seen. It was a large garden, only half-cultivated,[4] with bushes, as big as summerhouses, of Marshal Niel roses, lime and orange trees, clumps of bamboos, and thickets of high grass. Rikki-tikki licked his lips. "This is a splendid hunting ground," he said, and his tail grew bottlebrushy at the thought of it; and he scuttled up and down the garden, snuffing here and there till he heard very sorrowful voices in a thorn bush. It was Darzee, the tailorbird, and his wife. They had made a beautiful nest by pulling two big leaves together and stitching them up the edges with fibers and had filled the hollow with cotton and downy fluff. The nest swayed to and fro, as they sat on the rim and cried.

"What is the matter?" asked Rikki-tikki.

"We are very miserable," said Darzee. "One of our babies fell out of the nest yesterday, and Nag ate him."

"H'm!" said Rikki-tikki, "that is very sad—but I am a stranger here. Who is Nag?"

Darzee and his wife only <u>cowered</u> down in the nest without answering, for from the thick grass at the foot of the bush there came a low hiss—a horrid, cold sound that made Rikki-tikki jump back two clear feet. Then inch by inch out of the grass rose up the head and spread hood of Nag, the big black cobra, and he was five feet long from tongue to tail. When he had lifted one-third of himself clear of the ground, he stayed, balancing to and fro exactly as a dandelion tuft balances in the wind; and he looked at Rikki-tikki with the wicked snake's eyes that never change their expression, whatever the snake may be thinking of.

"Who is Nag?" said he. "*I* am Nag. The great god Brahm[5] put his mark upon all our people when the first cobra spread his hood to keep the sun off Brahm as he slept. Look, and be afraid!"

---

4. **cultivated:** cleared for the growing of garden plants.
5. **Brahm:** another name for Brahma, creator of the universe in the Hindu religion.

He spread out his hood more than ever, and Rikki-tikki saw the spectacle mark on the back of it that looks exactly like the eye part of a hook-and-eye fastening. He was afraid for the minute, but it is impossible for a mongoose to stay frightened for any length of time; and though Rikki-tikki had never met a live cobra before, his mother had fed him on dead ones, and he knew that all a grown mongoose's business in life was to fight and eat snakes. Nag knew that too, and at the bottom of his cold heart, he was afraid.

"Well," said Rikki-tikki, and his tail began to fluff up again, "marks or no marks, do you think it is right for you to eat fledgelings out of a nest?"

Nag was thinking to himself and watching the least little movement in the grass behind Rikki-tikki. He knew that mongooses in the garden meant death sooner or later for him and his family; but he wanted to get Rikki-tikki off his guard. So he dropped his head a little, and put it on one side.

"Let us talk," he said. "You eat eggs. Why should not I eat birds?"

"Behind you! Look behind you!" sang Darzee.

Rikki-tikki knew better than to waste time in staring. He jumped up in the air as high as he could go, and just under him whizzed by the head of Nagaina, Nag's wicked wife. She had crept up behind him as he was talking, to make an end of him; and he heard her savage hiss as the stroke missed. He came down almost across her back, and if he had been an old mongoose, he would have known that then was the time to break her back with one bite; but he was afraid of the terrible lashing return stroke of the cobra. He bit, indeed, but did not bite long enough; and he jumped clear of the whisking tail, leaving Nagaina torn and angry.

"Wicked, wicked Darzee!" said Nag, lashing up as high as he could reach toward the nest in the thorn bush; but Darzee had built it out of reach of snakes, and it only swayed to and fro.

Rikki-tikki felt his eyes growing red and hot (when a mongoose's eyes grow red, he is angry), and he sat back on his tail and hind legs like a little kangaroo and looked all around him and chattered with rage. But Nag and Nagaina had disappeared into the grass. When a snake misses its stroke, it never says anything or gives any sign of what it means to do next. Rikki-tikki did not care to follow them, for he did not feel sure that he could manage two snakes at once. So he trotted off to the gravel path near the house and sat down to think. It was a serious matter for him.

If you read the old books of natural history, you will find they say that when the mongoose fights the snake and happens to get bitten, he runs off and eats some herb that cures him. That is not true. The victory is only a matter of quickness of eye and quickness of foot—

snake's blow against mongoose's jump—and as no eye can follow the motion of a snake's head when it strikes, this makes things much more wonderful than any magic herb. Rikki-tikki knew he was a young mongoose, and it made him all the more pleased to think that he had managed to escape a blow from behind.

It gave him confidence in himself, and when Teddy came running down the path, Rikki-tikki was ready to be petted. But just as Teddy was stooping, something wriggled a little in the dust, and a tiny voice said, "Be careful. I am Death!" It was Karait, the dusty brown snakeling that lies for choice on the dusty earth; and his bite is as dangerous as the cobra's. But he is so small that nobody thinks of him, and so he does the more harm to people.

Rikki-tikki's eyes grew red again, and he danced up to Karait with the peculiar rocking, swaying motion that he had inherited from his family. It looks very funny, but it is so perfectly balanced a gait that you can fly off from it at any angle you please; and in dealing with snakes this is an advantage.

If Rikki-tikki had only known, he was doing a much more dangerous thing than fighting Nag; for Karait is so small and can turn so quickly, that unless Rikki bit him close to the back of the head, he would get the return stroke in his eye or his lip. But Rikki did not know: his eyes were all red, and he rocked back and forth, looking for a good place to hold. Karait struck out. Rikki jumped

ACTIVE READER

PREDICT What do you think Rikki-tikki is planning to do next?

sideways and tried to run in, but the wicked little dusty gray head lashed within a fraction of his shoulder, and he had to jump over the body, and the head followed his heels close.

Teddy shouted to the house, "Oh, look here! Our mongoose is killing a snake"; and Rikki-tikki heard a scream from Teddy's mother. His father ran out with a stick, but by the time he came up, Karait had lunged out once too far, and Rikki-tikki had sprung, jumped on the snake's back, dropped his head far between his forelegs, bitten as high up the back as he could get hold, and rolled away.

That bite paralyzed Karait, and Rikki-tikki was just going to eat him up from the tail, after the custom of his family at dinner, when he remembered that a full meal makes a slow mongoose; and if he wanted all his strength and quickness ready, he must keep himself thin. He went away for a dust bath under the castor-oil bushes, while Teddy's father beat the dead Karait. "What is the use of that?" thought Rikki-tikki; "I have settled it all."

And then Teddy's mother picked him up from the dust and hugged him, crying that he had saved Teddy from death; and Teddy's father said that he was a providence,[6] and Teddy looked on with big scared eyes. Rikki-tikki was rather amused at all the fuss, which, of course, he did not understand. Teddy's mother might just as well have petted Teddy for playing in the dust. Rikki was thoroughly enjoying himself.

That night at dinner, walking to and fro among the wineglasses on the table, he might have stuffed himself three times over with nice things; but he remembered Nag and Nagaina,

---

6. **providence:** blessing; something good given by God.

and though it was very pleasant to be patted and petted by Teddy's mother and to sit on Teddy's shoulder, his eyes would get red from time to time, and he would go off into his long war cry of *"Rikk-tikk-tikki-tikki-tchk!"*

Teddy carried him off to bed and insisted on Rikki-tikki sleeping under his chin. Rikki-tikki was too well-bred to bite or scratch, but as soon as Teddy was asleep, he went off for his nightly walk around the house; and in the dark he ran up against Chuchundra, the muskrat, creeping around by the wall. Chuchundra is a brokenhearted little beast. He whimpers and cheeps all the night, trying to make up his mind to run into the middle of the room; but he never gets there.

"Don't kill me," said Chuchundra, almost weeping. "Rikki-tikki, don't kill me!"

"Do you think a snake killer kills muskrats?" said Rikki-tikki scornfully.

"Those who kill snakes get killed by snakes," said Chuchundra, more sorrowfully than ever. "And how am I to be sure that Nag won't mistake me for you some dark night?"

"There's not the least danger," said Rikki-tikki; "but Nag is in the garden, and I know you don't go there."

"My cousin Chua, the rat, told me—" said Chuchundra, and then he stopped.

"Told you what?"

"H'sh! Nag is everywhere, Rikki-tikki. You should have talked to Chua in the garden."

"I didn't—so you must tell me. Quick, Chuchundra, or I'll bite you!"

So long as the bungalow is empty, we are king and queen of the garden.

Chuchundra sat down and cried till the tears rolled off his whiskers. "I am a very poor man," he sobbed. "I never had spirit enough to run out into the middle of the room. H'sh! I mustn't tell you anything. Can't you *hear*, Rikki-tikki?"

Rikki-tikki listened. The house was as still as still, but he thought he could just catch the faintest *scratch-scratch* in the world—a noise as faint as that of a wasp walking on a windowpane—the dry scratch of a snake's scales on brickwork.

"That's Nag or Nagaina," he said to himself, "and he is crawling into the bathroom sluice.[7] You're right, Chuchundra; I should have talked to Chua."

He stole off to Teddy's bathroom, but there was nothing there, and then to Teddy's mother's bathroom. At the bottom of the smooth plaster wall, there was a brick pulled out to make a sluice for the bath water, and as Rikki-tikki stole in by the masonry curb where the bath is put, he heard Nag and Nagaina whispering together outside in the moonlight.

"When the house is emptied of people," said Nagaina to her husband, "*he* will have to go away, and then the garden will be our own again. Go in quietly, and remember that the big man who killed Karait is the first one to bite. Then come out and tell me, and we will hunt for Rikki-tikki together."

---

7. **bathroom sluice** (slo͞os): a channel and opening in a wall through which the water in a bathtub can be drained outdoors.

"But are you sure that there is anything to be gained by killing the people?" said Nag.

"Everything. When there were no people in the bungalow, did we have any mongoose in the garden? So long as the bungalow is empty, we are king and queen of the garden; and remember that as soon as our eggs in the melon bed hatch (as they may tomorrow), our children will need room and quiet."

"I had not thought of that," said Nag. "I will go, but there is no need that we should hunt for Rikki-tikki afterward. I will kill the big man and his wife, and the child if I can, and come away quietly. Then the bungalow will be empty, and Rikki-tikki will go."

Rikki-tikki tingled all over with rage and hatred at this, and then Nag's head came through the sluice, and his five feet of cold body followed it. Angry as he was, Rikki-tikki was very frightened as he saw the size of the big cobra. Nag coiled himself up, raised his head, and looked into the bathroom in the dark, and Rikki could see his eyes glitter.

"Now, if I kill him here, Nagaina will know; and if I fight him on the open floor, the odds are in his favor. What am I to do?" said Rikki-tikki-tavi.

Nag waved to and fro, and then Rikki-tikki heard him drinking from the biggest water jar that was used to fill the bath. "That is good," said the snake. "Now, when Karait was killed, the big man had a stick. He may have that stick still, but when he comes in to bathe in the morning, he will not have a stick. I shall wait here till he comes. Nagaina— do you hear me?—I shall wait here in the cool till daytime."

There was no answer from outside, so Rikki-tikki knew Nagaina had gone away. Nag coiled himself down, coil by coil, around the bulge at the bottom of the water jar, and Rikki-tikki stayed still as death. After an hour he began to move, muscle by muscle, toward the jar. Nag was asleep, and Rikki-tikki looked at his big back, wondering which would be the best place for a good hold. "If I don't break his back at the first jump," said Rikki, "he can still fight; and if he fights—O Rikki!" He looked at the thickness of the neck below the hood, but that was too much for him; and a bite near the tail would only make Nag savage.

"It must be the head," he said at last; "the head above the hood. And, when I am once there, I must not let go."

Then he jumped. The head was lying a little clear of the water jar, under the curve of it; and, as his teeth met, Rikki braced his back against the bulge of the red earthenware to hold down the head. This gave him just one second's purchase,[8] and he made the most of it. Then he was battered to and fro as a rat is shaken by a dog—to and fro on the floor, up and down, and round in great circles; but his eyes were red, and he held on as the body cart-whipped over the floor, upsetting the tin dipper and the soap dish and the flesh brush, and banged against the tin side of the bath.

ACTIVE READER

CLARIFY What happened in the fight?

As he held, he closed his jaws tighter and tighter, for he made sure he would be banged to death; and, for the honor of his family, he preferred to be found with his teeth locked. He was dizzy, aching, and felt shaken to pieces when something went off like a thunderclap just behind him; a hot wind knocked him senseless, and red fire singed his fur. The big man had been awakened by the noise and had fired both barrels of a shotgun into Nag just behind the hood.

Rikki-tikki held on with his eyes shut, for now he was quite sure he was dead; but the head did not move, and the big man picked him up and said, "It's the mongoose again, Alice; the little chap has saved *our* lives now."

Then Teddy's mother came in with a very white face and saw what was left of Nag, and Rikki-tikki dragged himself to Teddy's bedroom and spent half the rest of the night shaking himself tenderly to find out whether he really was broken into forty pieces, as he fancied.

When morning came, he was very stiff but well pleased with his doings. "Now I have Nagaina to settle with, and she will be worse than five Nags, and there's no knowing when the eggs she spoke of will hatch. Goodness! I must go and see Darzee," he said.

Without waiting for breakfast, Rikki-tikki ran to the thorn bush where Darzee was singing a song of triumph at the top of his voice. The news of Nag's death was all over the garden, for the sweeper had thrown the body on the rubbish heap.

"Oh, you stupid tuft of feathers!" said Rikki-tikki angrily. "Is this the time to sing?"

"Nag is dead—is dead—is dead!" sang Darzee. "The valiant Rikki-tikki caught him by the head and held fast. The big man brought the bang stick, and Nag fell in two pieces! He will never eat my babies again."

"All that's true enough; but where's Nagaina?" said Rikki-tikki, looking carefully round him.

"Nagaina came to the bathroom sluice and called for Nag," Darzee went on; "and Nag came out on the end of a stick—the sweeper picked him up on the end of a stick and threw him upon the rubbish heap. Let us sing about the great, the red-eyed Rikki-tikki!" And Darzee filled his throat and sang.

ACTIVE READER

QUESTION What danger does Rikki still face?

"If I could get up to your nest, I'd roll your babies out!" said Rikki-tikki. "You don't know when to do the right thing at the right time. You're safe enough in your nest there, but it's war for me down here. Stop singing a minute, Darzee."

"For the great, the beautiful Rikki-tikki's sake I will stop," said Darzee. "What is it, O Killer of the terrible Nag?"

---

8. **purchase:** secure grasp or hold.

"Where is Nagaina, for the third time?"

"On the rubbish heap by the stables, mourning for Nag. Great is Rikki-tikki with the white teeth."

"Bother my white teeth! Have you ever heard where she keeps her eggs?"

"In the melon bed, on the end nearest the wall, where the sun strikes nearly all day. She hid them there weeks ago."

"And you never thought it worthwhile to tell me? The end nearest the wall, you said?"

"Rikki-tikki, you are not going to eat her eggs?"

"Not eat exactly, no. Darzee, if you have a grain of sense, you will fly off to the stables and pretend that your wing is broken and let Nagaina chase you away to this bush. I must get to the melon bed, and if I went there now, she'd see me."

Darzee was a featherbrained little fellow who could never hold more than one idea at a time in his head; and just because he knew that Nagaina's children were born in eggs like his own, he didn't think at first that it was fair to kill them. But his wife was a sensible bird, and she knew that cobra's eggs meant young cobras later on; so she flew off from the nest and left Darzee to keep the babies warm and continue his song about the death of Nag. Darzee was very like a man in some ways.

She fluttered in front of Nagaina by the rubbish heap and cried out, "Oh, my wing is broken! The boy in the house threw a stone at me and broke it." Then she fluttered more desperately than ever.

Nagaina lifted up her head and hissed, "You warned Rikki-tikki when I would have killed him. Indeed and truly, you've chosen a bad place to be lame in." And she moved toward Darzee's wife, slipping along over the dust.

"The boy broke it with a stone!" shrieked Darzee's wife.

"Well! It may be some <u>consolation</u> to you when you're dead to know that I shall settle accounts with the boy. My husband lies on the rubbish heap this morning, but before night the boy in the house will lie very still. What is the use of running away? I am sure to catch you. Little fool, look at me!"

Darzee's wife knew better than to do *that,* for a bird who looks at a snake's eyes gets so frightened that she cannot move. Darzee's wife fluttered on, piping sorrowfully, and never leaving the ground, and Nagaina quickened her pace.

Rikki-tikki heard them going up the path from the stables, and he raced for the end of the melon patch near the wall. There, in the warm litter above the melons, very <u>cunningly</u> hidden, he found twenty-five eggs, about the size of a bantam's eggs[9] but with whitish skins instead of shells.

"I was not a day too soon," he said, for he could see the baby cobras curled up inside the

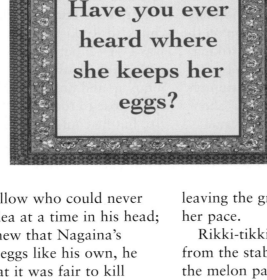

Bother my white teeth! Have you ever heard where she keeps her eggs?

---

9. **bantam's eggs:** the eggs of a small hen.

WORDS
TO
KNOW

consolation (kŏn′sə-lā′shən) *n.* something that comforts
cunningly (kŭn′ĭng-lē) *adv.* in a clever way that is meant to trick or deceive

131

skin, and he knew that the minute they were hatched they could each kill a man or a mongoose. He bit off the tops of the eggs as fast as he could, taking care to crush the young cobras, and turned over the litter from time to time to see whether he had missed any. At last there were only three eggs left, and Rikki-tikki began to chuckle to himself when he heard Darzee's wife screaming.

"Rikki-tikki, I led Nagaina toward the house, and she has gone into the veranda and—oh, come quickly—she means killing!"

Rikki-tikki smashed two eggs and tumbled backward down the melon bed with the third egg in his mouth and <u>scuttled</u> to the veranda as hard as he could put foot to the ground. Teddy and his mother and father were there at early breakfast; but Rikki-tikki saw that they were not eating anything. They sat stone still, and their faces were white. Nagaina was coiled up on the matting by Teddy's chair, within easy striking distance of Teddy's bare leg; and she was swaying to and fro, singing a song of triumph.

"Son of the big man that killed Nag," she hissed, "stay still. I am not ready yet. Wait a little. Keep very still, all you three! If you move, I strike, and if you do not move, I strike. Oh, foolish people who killed my Nag!"

Teddy's eyes were fixed on his father, and all his father could do was to whisper, "Sit still, Teddy. You mustn't move. Teddy, keep still."

Then Rikki-tikki came up and cried, "Turn round, Nagaina; turn and fight!"

"All in good time," said she, without moving her eyes. "I will settle my account with you presently. Look at your friends, Rikki-tikki. They are still and white. They are afraid. They dare not move, and if you come a step nearer, I strike."

"Look at your eggs," said Rikki-tikki, "in the melon bed near the wall. Go and look, Nagaina!"

The big snake turned half round and saw the egg on the veranda. "Ah-h! Give it to me," she said.

Rikki-tikki put his paws one on each side of the egg, and his eyes were blood-red. "What price for a snake's egg? For a young cobra? For a young king cobra? For the last—the very last of the brood? The ants are eating all the others down by the melon bed."

Nagaina spun clear round, forgetting everything for the sake of the one egg; and Rikki-tikki saw Teddy's father shoot out a big hand, catch Teddy by the shoulder, and drag him across the little table with the teacups, safe and out of reach of Nagaina.

"Tricked! Tricked! Tricked! *Rikk-tck-tck!*" chuckled Rikki-tikki. "The boy is safe, and it was I—I—I that caught Nag by the hood last night in the bathroom." Then he began to jump up and down, all four feet together, his head close to the floor. "He threw me to and fro, but he could not shake me off. He was dead before the big man blew him in two. I did it! *Rikki-tikki-tck-tck!* Come then, Nagaina. Come and fight with me. You shall not be a widow long."

Nagaina saw that she had lost her chance of killing Teddy, and the egg lay between Rikki-tikki's paws. "Give me the egg, Rikki-tikki. Give me the last of my eggs, and I will go away and never come back," she said, lowering her hood.

"Yes, you will go away, and you will never come back, for you will go to the rubbish heap with Nag. Fight, widow! The big man has gone for his gun! Fight!"

Rikki-tikki was bounding all round Nagaina, keeping just out of reach of her

stroke, his little eyes like hot coals. Nagaina gathered herself together and flung out at him. Rikki-tikki jumped up and backwards. Again and again and again she struck, and each time her head came with a whack on the matting of the veranda, and she gathered herself together like a watch spring. Then Rikki-tikki danced in a circle to get behind her, and Nagaina spun round to keep her head to his head, so that the rustle of her tail on the matting sounded like dry leaves blown along by the wind.

He had forgotten the egg. It still lay on the veranda, and Nagaina came nearer and nearer to it, till at last, while Rikki-tikki was drawing breath, she caught it in her mouth, turned to the veranda steps, and flew like an arrow down the path, with Rikki-tikki behind her. When the cobra runs for her life, she goes like a

whiplash flicked across a horse's neck. Rikki-tikki knew that he must catch her, or all the trouble would begin again.

She headed straight for the long grass by the thorn bush, and as he was running, Rikki-tikki heard Darzee still singing his foolish little song of triumph. But Darzee's wife was wiser. She flew off her nest as Nagaina came along and flapped her wings about Nagaina's head. If Darzee had helped, they might have turned her; but Nagaina only lowered her hood and went on. Still, the instant's delay brought Rikki-tikki up to her, and as she plunged into the rat hole where she and Nag used to live, his little white teeth were clenched on her tail, and he went down with her—and very few mongooses, however wise and old they may be, care to follow a cobra into its hole.

It was dark in the hole; and Rikki-tikki never knew when it might open out and give Nagaina room to turn and strike at him. He held on savagely and stuck out his feet to act as brakes on the dark slope of the hot, moist earth.

Then the grass by the mouth of the hole stopped waving, and Darzee said, "It is all over with Rikki-tikki! We must sing his death song. Valiant Rikki-tikki is dead! For Nagaina will surely kill him underground."

So he sang a very mournful song that he made up on the spur of the minute; and just as he got to the most touching part, the grass quivered again, and Rikki-tikki, covered with dirt, dragged himself out of the hole leg by leg, licking his whiskers. Darzee stopped with a little shout. Rikki-tikki shook some of the dust out of his fur and sneezed. "It is all over," he said. "The widow will never come out again." And the red ants that live between the grass stems heard him and began to troop down one after another to see if he had spoken the truth.

Very few mongooses, however wise and old they may be, care to follow a cobra into its hole.

Rikki-tikki curled himself up in the grass and slept where he was—slept and slept till it was late in the afternoon, for he had done a hard day's work.

"Now," he said, when he awoke, "I will go back to the house. Tell the coppersmith, Darzee, and he will tell the garden that Nagaina is dead."

The coppersmith is a bird who makes a noise exactly like the beating of a little hammer on a copper pot; and the reason he is always making it is because he is the town crier to every Indian garden and tells all the news to everybody who cares to listen. As Rikki-tikki went up the path, he heard his "attention" notes like a tiny dinner gong, and then the steady *"Ding-dong-tock! Nag is dead—dong! Nagaina is dead! Ding-dong-tock!"* That set all the birds in the garden singing and the frogs croaking, for Nag and Nagaina used to eat frogs as well as little birds.

When Rikki got to the house, Teddy and Teddy's mother (she looked very white still, for she had been fainting) and Teddy's father came out and almost cried over him; and that night he ate all that was given him till he could eat no more and went to bed on Teddy's shoulder, where Teddy's mother saw him when she came to look late at night.

"He saved our lives and Teddy's life," she said to her husband. "Just think, he saved all our lives."

Rikki-tikki woke up with a jump, for the mongooses are light sleepers.

"Oh, it's you," said he. "What are you bothering for? All the cobras are dead; and if they weren't, I'm here."

Rikki-tikki had a right to be proud of himself; but he did not grow too proud, and he kept that garden as a mongoose should keep it, with tooth and jump and spring and bite, till never a cobra dared show its head inside the walls. ❖

Connect to the Literature

1. **What Do You Think?**
   What did you think about Rikki-tikki by the end of the story?

   Comprehension Check
   • Why was Rikki-tikki grateful to Teddy's family?
   • Why did Rikki-tikki destroy Nagaina's eggs?
   • Why did Teddy's mother change her mind about Rikki-tikki?

Think Critically

2. What qualities or abilities enable Rikki-tikki to fight the cobras to the finish? Explain.

3. Which of Rikki-tikki's battles do you think takes the greatest courage? Explain your choice.

4. What do you think the use of personification adds to the story? Explain.

   Think About:
   • Nagaina's threatened attack on the family at breakfast
   • the battle with Nag in the bathroom
   • Darzee's warnings to Rikki-tikki

5. **ACTIVE READING** | **PREDICTING**
   Look back at the chart you made in your
   READER'S NOTEBOOK. How accurate were the **predictions** you made as you read the story? Discuss with a classmate the details in the story that either helped or misled you.

Extend Interpretations

6. **Critic's Corner** "Rikki-tikki-tavi" is considered by many to be a classic story—a story that has been enjoyed by many generations of readers. How would you explain what gives this story its lasting appeal?

7. **Connect to Life** Have you ever helped to take care of an unusual pet, or would you like to have one? Share your thoughts with a partner.

Literary Analysis

PERSONIFICATION When a writer gives human qualities to an animal, object, or idea, this is called **personification.** In "Rikki-tikki-tavi," the animals in the garden are personified, conversing as if they were human.

Group Activity With a small group, make a list of animals in this story and brainstorm the "human" qualities that each shows. Rank the qualities on a scale from 1 to 10, with 10 being the most admirable. Then share your list with the rest of the class and give reasons for your rankings.

Animal	Rating	Qualities
Rikki-tikki-tavi	10	brave, loyal
Nag		

REVIEW: POINT OF VIEW The **third-person omniscient** (all-knowing) point of view allows the narrator to relate the thoughts and feelings of several, if not all, of the story's characters. "Rikki-tikki liked it immensely; and when it was finished . . . he felt better," is an example of the omniscient narrator telling the reader what Rikki-tikki thinks and how he feels.

Writing

Different Perspectives Most, but not all, of the characters in the story consider Rikki-tikki to be a hero. Write a paragraph or two of the story from Nagaina's perspective. Use the third-person omniscient point of view. What is Nagaina thinking and feeling about Rikki-tikki in the scene after Nag's death? Place your work in your **Working Portfolio.**

Writing Handbook
See p. R45: Narrative Writing.

Speaking & Listening

Radio Script Stage a radio reading of a scene from the story. Some students can perform the parts of the characters and the narrator, while other students provide sound effects. Rehearse your performance, then tape-record it for other classes.

Research & Technology

Just Like People? Many people think that animals don't have important human qualities—such as kindness and sympathy. The fictional character Rikki-tikki-tavi has these qualities in the story, but do real animals have them? Check an encyclopedia, other books, a computer database, or the Internet for information about an animal's instincts and behavior. To focus your research, choose one type of animal and determine what, specifically, you would like to know about. Write down your inquiry. For example, "I would like to find three unusual acts of bravery by dogs." Type or write the results of your findings and share them with the class.

> **Reading for INFORMATION**
> To begin your research, read "Primal Compassion" on p. 138.

Vocabulary

STANDARDIZED TEST PRACTICE

Choose the word or group of words that means the same, or nearly the same, as the underlined Word to Know in each sentence.

1. The warmth of the fire <u>revived</u> the wet little mongoose. <u>Revived</u> means—
   A fascinated   **B** burned
   C scared   **D** woke

2. When he saw the cobra, Darzee, the tailorbird, <u>cowered</u> in his nest. <u>Cowered</u> means—
   F chirped   **G** attacked
   H cringed   **J** fluttered

3. It was a <u>consolation</u> to the family to have Rikki-tikki-tavi as a pet. <u>Consolation</u> means—
   A chore   **B** comfort
   C prize   **D** punishment

4. Rikki-tikki-tavi <u>cunningly</u> found the cobra eggs among the melons. <u>Cunningly</u> means—
   F quickly   **G** carefully
   H cleverly   **J** bravely

5. The muskrat <u>scuttled</u> away when the cobra came near. <u>Scuttled</u> means—
   A hurried   **B** shuffled
   C rolled   **D** sneaked

Vocabulary Handbook
See p. R24: Context Clues.

Grammar in Context: Varying Sentence Length

Notice how Rudyard Kipling sandwiches one long sentence between two shorter ones:

> Then Rikki-tikki went out into the garden to see what was to be seen. It was a large garden, only half-cultivated, with bushes, as big as summerhouses, of Marshal Niel roses, lime and orange trees, clumps of bamboos, and thickets of high grass. Rikki-tikki licked his lips.

Using sentences of different lengths adds variety to your writing. Using only short sentences can make your writing sound choppy.

Punctuation Tip: Notice how Kipling uses the **semicolon** to join three sentences:

> His eyes and the end of his restless nose were pink; he could scratch himself anywhere he pleased with any leg, front or back, that he chose to use; he could fluff up his tail till it looked like a bottlebrush. . . .

WRITING EXERCISE Choose two sentences from each group of three. Rewrite the two simple sentences as one longer sentence.

Example: *Original* Rikki-tikki's eyes grew red. He rocked back and forth. He looked for a good place to bite the snake.

Rewritten Rikki-tikki's eyes grew red. He rocked back and forth, looking for a good place to bite the snake.

1. Rikki-tikki ran all around the room. Rikki-tikki jumped up onto the table. Then he sneezed.
2. At night the mongoose slept with Teddy. The mongoose slept in the nursery. Rikki protected him.
3. No one liked cobras. Nag and Nagaina ate frogs for dinner. Nag and Nagaina ate small birds, too.

Rudyard Kipling
1865–1936

"I always prefer to believe the best of everybody—it saves so much trouble."

Childhood in India Rudyard Kipling was born in Bombay, India, but educated in England. His father was an architect and artist, and his mother was devoted to the arts. As a child, Kipling loved to read and he wrote verse. After his schooling, he returned to India in 1882 and worked as a writer for a daily newspaper in Lahore. Kipling's stories about his Indian travels made him extremely popular in India. He returned to London in 1889, and wrote poems and new stories about India that made him famous.

Animal Storyteller When he had children of his own, Kipling turned to writing children's stories. Early collections, *The Jungle Book* and *The Second Jungle Book,* include animal stories set in India about an Indian boy raised by wolves.

Nobel Prize Kipling received numerous honors and awards. In 1907 he received the Nobel Prize in literature. He is buried in London in the Poets' Corner of Westminster Abbey.

Source: *Life*

Primal *Compassion*

By Charles Hirshberg and Robert Allison

Key Standard
R2.6 Evaluate the strength and accuracy of the evidence an author uses to support a claim. Recognize bias and stereotyping. **Other Standards R2.3, R2.4, R3.5**

*I*t was gut-wrenching, seeing that little guy smack onto the concrete floor," says Robert Allison, who saw it, heard it and then started photographing it. He was there when Binti Jua (Swahili for "Daughter of Sunshine"), a western lowland gorilla in Illinois's Brookfield Zoo, came to the rescue of a three-year-old boy who had fallen 18 feet to the floor of her enclosure.

By now, thanks in no small part to Bob Allison, almost everyone knows of Binti, and it is common knowledge in Illinois that the boy—whose identity is being shielded by his parents—has made a complete recovery. Brookfield visitors can see that Binti has returned to the calm, dull life of a zoo animal, snacking on sweet potatoes and grooming Koola, her one-and-a-half-year-old baby. But

"We never made it to the aquarium"

there is much that remains unknown, as people around the world continue to ponder the lessons of the remarkable story. None ponder more deeply than the Allisons, a Bettendorf, Iowa, family changed forever by the emotional force of what they witnessed.

❶ It started when Bob, a 51-year-old carpenter, and his wife, Vicki, 50, a bookstore manager, decided to take a weekend in Chicago with their daughter-in-law Johnna, the 31-year-old wife of their son Randy, and the grandkids—Charli, 10, and Ryan, five. Also along for the adventure was Randy's brother, Eric, 31. The plan was to visit the zoo and the aquarium, but, says Bob wryly, "we never made it to the aquarium."

At Brookfield's Tropic World exhibit, Bob, who has been an animal lover since his Kentucky boyhood, was enthusiastically taking pictures of the gorillas with his point-and-shoot camera, even though the apes were having "a pretty boring day, staring at their feet." Eric was enjoying his niece and nephew almost as much as they were enjoying the animals. Little Ryan was having the time of his life, darting around in excitement.

Then, for reasons he can't explain, Eric

began watching a three-year-old boy as rambunctious as Ryan, climbing the rocks in front of a faux bamboo fence that surrounds the exhibit. "I know it sounds weird, but something kept telling me to look over there," Eric recalls. He watched the boy lifting himself toward the top of the fence and wondered with growing anxiety, "Is he going to go higher?" The boy's upper body teetered above the fence. And then, suddenly, his momentum carried him over.

Eric gasped as he watched the boy tumble wide-eyed through the air, caroming off a ledge that jutted from the cliff. A second later, Eric heard "a huge thud. Even people who had no idea what had happened knew it was something horrible."

Vicki began to tremble and reeled as though she might faint. Eric seized her and buried her face in his chest. "Don't look," he whispered. Five-year-old Ryan grew suddenly hysterical, springing into Johnna's arms wailing, "Don't let me fall! Don't let me fall!"

Bob, too, was upset, "but I also knew something incredible was about to happen." He moved along the rail, photographing the drama in the pit below. Though Eric, enraged, roared at him to stop, Bob went on shooting.

Binti had hopped off her perch without hesitation, and now she made her way toward the boy, little Koola still at her breast. "She moved with such deliberateness," says Bob,

still amazed several weeks later. When she reached the boy, "she lifted his arm as if she were looking for signs of life. She did that twice." To Eric, "it seemed like she was asking, 'Are you O.K.?'" Then, says Bob, "she lifted the boy and put him to her chest, just exactly the way she was holding her own baby."

"What's happening?" Vicki asked. "A gorilla's got him," Eric told her. It may seem like a strange thing to have said by way of comfort, but Eric swears that "you could tell, you could just feel she was going to help the boy."

At first Binti seemed to want to take him in the direction of the crowd, but, looking up, she appeared to sense panic from that direction. "You could definitely see her making decisions," Bob says. "You could see her look up and concentrate." Still carrying the child as though he were her own, she started off in the other direction. When Alpha, another female gorilla, much larger than Binti, approached, Binti stopped and challenged her with a guttural noise. "I don't think Alpha would have hurt the child," says Eric, "but that's the way a mom is."

Finally, to the amazement of everyone, Binti gently laid the boy by the door of the enclosure. Moments later, keepers came with fire hoses to hold the gorillas at bay while they collected the injured boy. The hoses bothered Eric. "She's gonna have a weird

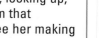

night tonight, trying to figure that out," he thought to himself. "She saves him, and then sees the hose."

Once the boy was removed, the Allisons spoke to authorities and left the zoo. At first, says Eric, "we could hardly look at each other." They returned to their motel room and, unable to sleep, began to open up. Though he admitted the event had been truly extraordinary, Eric was still angry that his father had taken pictures. "We came to a decision about the photographs as a family," says Bob. "If the boy didn't recover, we wouldn't show them."

Of course, the boy did recover. In a matter of days he was up and around and acting like a normal three-year-old, despite a broken hand and a vicious gash on the left side of his face. Doctors said he remembered nothing about what had happened.

In the wake of the good news about the boy, the Allisons began to pore over the pictures. "I can't begin to explain the thoughts, the feelings they've caused us to have," says Bob. He has read that some scientists have expressed skepticism about Binti's actions. ("Would Binti have acted any differently if it had been handling, say, a sack of flour?" a researcher asked in the *San Francisco Examiner*.) Bob agrees that "we can't know for sure what was going on in her mind." But there is not a glimmer of doubt in his mind about what her intentions were. And whenever he reexamines his pictures, he experiences a new sense of exhilaration. "I keep studying them, studying her face and her posture," he says. "I can't help but think there's a message in this. She didn't hesitate to help. If this animal that's supposed to be below us can be this way, why can't we?"

Which of the following statements are facts, and which are opinions?

- The Allisons were a "family changed forever by the emotional force of what they witnessed."
- Bob Allison was taking pictures of the apes with his camera.
- ". . . She [Binti] lifted his arm as if she were looking for signs of life. She did that twice."

"Primal Compassion" is based on an eyewitness account. Quotes and conversations of the Allison family are used to tell the the way they experienced it. However, the author may also have a certain **bias** about the subject, and may organize the information to suit his or her purpose.

Identifying Bias
Which statement about "Primal Compassion" best expresses the author's bias?

a. Binti was acting out of the human-like emotions of love, compassion, and concern for the boy's safety.

b. Binti was acting from instinct and prior training, and could just as easily have hurt the child.

Trace the author's perspective through the article, finding evidence to support your answer.

Research & Technology
Activity Link: "Rikki-tikki-tavi," p. 136. Do you think animals are able to show human qualities? Search for other articles on the subject, preferably ones that present opposing views. Include this in your report, using facts from your readings or experience to support your claim.

Building Vocabulary
Informal Language: Idioms and Slang

Most people use casual expressions when they are speaking in a relaxed atmosphere.

This expression has a definite meaning but does not make sense when considered word by word. This is an example of an **idiom**—an expression that cannot be understood by simply putting together the meanings of the individual words. Many idioms are part of informal English.

> When Mama finally took her order, the starving lady all of a sudden couldn't **make up her mind** whether she wanted a vegetable plate or fish and a salad.
>
> —Toni Cade Bambara, "The War of the Wall"

This phrase means **"come to a definite decision"**

Strategies for Building Vocabulary

Informal English also includes **slang**—words and phrases that are specially made up or adapted for use in casual speech. The word *freaky* and the use of *cool* in the sentence "That's a cool car" are examples of slang. You can use the following strategies to help you understand unfamiliar slang and idioms.

❶ Find Context Clues English idioms and slang can sometimes be hard to understand, especially for people whose first language is not English. You can often figure out what an idiom or slang expression means by looking at its context—the surrounding words and phrases. Consider the following example:

> The rice, beans, and vegetables at the restaurant really **stick to the diners' ribs,** so they never leave hungry.

Here, *stick to the diners' ribs* means "are substantial or filling." You can understand the

idiom if you understand the situation: the diners are never hungry after eating the food.

The following passage contains slang:

> He gave the painter lady the once-over, **checking out** her paint-spattered jeans, her chalky T-shirt, her floppy-brimmed straw hat.
>
> —Toni Cade Bambara, "The War of the Wall"

Checking out means "examining." You can use the context to help you recognize that Side Pocket is examining the painter lady's clothes.

❷ Use Reference Materials Many dictionaries give the meanings of idioms and slang terms of the past and present. Look in a library or on the World Wide Web for dictionaries of slang terms and idioms.

Key Standard
R1.1 Identify idioms, analogies, metaphors, and similes in prose and poetry.
Other Standard **R1.3**

EXERCISE Use context clues to define the underlined examples of informal language. Check your definitions in a dictionary.

1. After our fight, we decided to <u>bury the hatchet</u> and become friends.
2. I decided to <u>hang out</u> after school.
3. The boys <u>kicked around</u> a few ideas about how to save their wall from the painter.
4. The boys realized that they had only enough <u>dough</u> to buy one can of paint.
5. They <u>changed their tune</u> when they saw the amazing and wonderful mural.

Dirk the Protector

by Gary Paulsen

Illustration by Murray Kimber

For a time in my life I became a street kid. It would be nice to put it another way but what with the drinking at home and the difficulties it caused with my parents I couldn't live in the house.

I made a place for myself in the basement by the furnace and hunted and fished in the woods around the small town. But I had other needs as well—clothes, food, school supplies—and they required money.

I was not afraid of work and spent most of my summers working on farms for two, three and finally five dollars a day. This gave me enough for school clothes, though never for enough clothes or the right kind; I was never cool or in. But during the school year I couldn't leave town to work the farms. I looked for odd jobs but most of them were taken by the boys who stayed in town through the summer. All the conventional[1] jobs like working in the markets or at the drugstore were gone and all I could find was setting pins in the small bowling alley over the Four Clover Bar.

It had just six alleys and they were busy all the time—there were leagues each night from seven to eleven—but the pay for truly brutal work was only seven cents a line. There weren't many boys willing to do the work but with so few alleys, it was still very hard to earn much money. A dollar a night was not uncommon and three was outstanding.

To make up the difference I started selling newspapers in the bars at night. This kept me up and out late, and I often came home at midnight. But it added to my income so that I could stay above water.[2]

Unfortunately it also put me in the streets at a time when there was what might be called a rough element. There weren't gangs then, not exactly, but there were groups of boys who more or less hung out together and got into trouble. They were the forerunners of the gangs we have now, but with some singular differences. They did not have firearms—but many carried switchblade knives.

These groups were predatory,[3] and they hunted the streets at night.

I became their favorite target in this dark world. Had the town been larger I might have hidden from them, or found different routes. But there was only a small uptown section and it was impossible for me to avoid them. They would catch me walking a dark street and surround me and with threats and blows steal what money I had earned that night.

I tried fighting back but there were usually several of them. I couldn't win. Because I was from "the wrong side of the tracks" I didn't think I could go to the authorities. It all seemed hopeless.

And then I met Dirk.

The bowling alley was on a second floor and had a window in back of the pit area. When all the lanes were going, the heat from the pin lights made the temperature close to a hundred degrees. Outside the window a ladder led to the roof. One fall evening, instead of leaving work through the front door, I made my way out the window and up the ladder onto the roof. I hoped to find a new way home to escape the boys who waited for me. That night one of the league bowlers had bowled a perfect game—300—and in celebration had bought the pit boys hamburgers and Cokes. I had put the burger and Coke in a bag to take back to my basement. The bag had grease stains and smelled of toasted buns, and my mouth watered as I moved from the roof of the bowling alley to the flat roof over the hardware store, then down a fire escape that led to a dark alcove off an alley.

---

1. **conventional** (kən-vĕn′shə-nəl): usual, traditional.
2. **stay above water**: survive.
3. **predatory** (prĕd′ə-tôr′ē): stealing from or hurting others.

There was a black space beneath the stairs and as I reached the bottom and my foot hit the ground I heard a low growl. It was not loud, more a rumble that seemed to come from the earth and so full of menace that it stopped me cold, my foot frozen in midair.

I raised my foot and the growl stopped.

I lowered my foot and the growl came again. My foot went up and it stopped.

I stood there, trying to peer through the steps of the fire escape. For a time I couldn't see more than a dark shape crouched back in the gloom. There was a head and a back, and as my eyes became accustomed to the dark I could see that it had scraggly, scruffy hair and two eyes that glowed yellow.

We were at an impasse.[4] I didn't want to climb up the ladder again but if I stepped to the ground it seemed likely I would be bitten. I hung there for a full minute before I thought of the hamburger. I could use it as a decoy and get away.

The problem was the hamburger smelled so good and I was so hungry.

I decided to give the beast under the stairs half a burger. I opened the sack, unwrapped the tinfoil and threw half the sandwich under the steps, then jumped down and ran for the end of the alley. I was just getting my stride, legs and arms pumping, pulling air with a heaving chest, when I rounded the corner and ran smack into the latest group of boys who were terrorizing me.

There were four of them, led by a thug—he and two of the others would ultimately land in prison—named, absurdly, "Happy" Santun.

Happy was built like an upright freezer and had just about half the intelligence but this time it was easy. I'd run right into him.

"Well—lookit here. He came to us this time. . . ."

Over the months I had developed a policy of flee or die—run as fast as I could to avoid the pain, and to hang on to my hard-earned money. Sometimes it worked, but most often they caught me.

This time, they already had me. I could have handed over the money, taken a few hits and been done with it, but something in me snapped and I hit Happy in the face with every ounce of strength in my puny body.

He brushed off the blow easily and I went down in a welter of blows and kicks from all four of them. I curled into a ball to protect what I could. I'd done this before, many times, and knew that they would stop sometime—although I suspected that because I'd hit Happy it might take longer than usual for them to get bored hitting me.

Instead there was some commotion that I didn't understand and the kicks stopped coming. There was a snarling growl that seemed to come from the bowels of the earth, followed by the sound of ripping cloth, screams, and then the fading slap of footsteps running away.

For another minute I remained curled up, then opened my eyes to find that I was alone.

But when I rolled over I saw the dog.

It was the one that had been beneath the stairs. Brindled,[5] patches of hair gone, one ear folded over and the other standing straight and notched from fighting. He didn't seem to be any particular breed. Just big and rangy, right on the edge of ugly, though I would come to think of him as beautiful. He was Airedale crossed with hound crossed with alligator.

---

4. **impasse** (ĭm′păs′): a situation in which no progress can be made; a deadlock.

5. **brindled** (brĭn′dld): light brownish yellow or grayish with streaks or spots of a darker color.

He was

Airedale

crossed with

hound

crossed with

alligator.

Dog (1955), Derrick Greaves. Oil on canvas. Arts Council Collection, Hayward Gallery, London, UK/Bridgeman Art Library, London/New York.

Alley dog. Big, tough, mean alley dog. As I watched he spit cloth—it looked like blue jeans—out of his mouth.

"You bit Happy, and sent them running?" I asked.

He growled, and I wasn't sure if it was with menace, but he didn't bare his teeth and didn't seem to want to attack me. Indeed, he had saved me.

"Why?" I asked. "What did I do to deserve . . . oh, the hamburger."

I swear, he pointedly looked at the bag with the second half of hamburger in it.

"You want more?"

He kept staring at the bag and I thought, Well, he sure as heck deserves it. I opened the sack and gave him the rest of it, which disappeared down his throat as if a hole had opened into the universe.

He looked at the bag.

"That's it," I said, brushing my hands together. "The whole thing."

A low growl.

"You can rip my head off—there still isn't any more hamburger." I removed the Coke and handed him the bag, which he took, held on the ground with one foot and deftly ripped open with his teeth.

"See? Nothing." I was up by this time and I started to walk away. "Thanks for the help . . ."

He followed me. Not close, perhaps eight feet back, but matching my speed. It was now nearly midnight and I was tired and sore from setting pins and from the kicks that had landed on my back and sides.

"I don't have anything to eat at home but crackers and peanut butter and jelly," I told him. I kept some food in the basement of the apartment building, where I slept near the furnace.

He kept following and, truth be known, I didn't mind. I was still half scared of him but the memory of him spitting out bits of Happy's pants and the sound of the boys running off made me smile. When I arrived at the apartment house I held the main door open and he walked right in. I opened the basement door and he followed me down the steps into the furnace room.

I turned the light on and could see that my earlier judgment had been correct. He was scarred from fighting, skinny and flat sided and with patches of hair gone. His nails were worn down from scratching concrete.

"Dirk," I said. "I'll call you Dirk." I had been trying to read a detective novel and there was a tough guy in it named Dirk. "You look like somebody named Dirk."

And so we sat that first night. I had two boxes of Ritz crackers I'd hustled somewhere, a jar of peanut butter and another one of grape jelly, and a knife from the kitchen upstairs. I would smear a cracker, hand it to him—he took each one with great care and gentleness—and then eat one myself. We did this, back and forth, until both boxes were empty and my stomach was bulging; then I fell asleep on the old outdoor lounge I used for furniture.

The next day was a school day. I woke up and found Dirk under the basement stairs, watching me. When I opened the door he trotted up the steps and outside—growling at me as he went past—and I started off to school.

He followed me at a distance, then stopped across the street when I went into the front of the school building. I thought I'd probably never see him again.

But he was waiting when I came out that afternoon, sitting across the street by a mailbox. I walked up to him.

He likes to guard things, doesn't he?

Dog in Field (1967), Richard Crozier. Courtesy of Tatistcheff Gallery, New York. Collection of Brooke L. Larson. Photo by Glenn Rudolph.

"Hi, Dirk." I thought of petting him but when I reached a hand out he growled. "All right—no touching."

I turned and made my way toward the bowling alley. It was Friday and sometimes on Friday afternoon there were people who wanted to bowl early and I could pick up a dollar or two setting pins.

Dirk followed about four feet back—closer than before—and as I made my way along Second Street and came around the corner by Ecker's Drugstore I ran into Happy. He had only two of his cohorts[6] with him and I don't think they had intended to do me harm, but I surprised them and Happy took a swing at me.

Dirk took him right in the middle. I mean bit him in the center of his stomach, hard, before Happy's fist could get to me. Happy screamed and doubled over and Dirk went around and ripped into his rear and kept tearing at it even as Happy and his two companions fled down the street.

It was absolutely great. Maybe one of the great moments in my life.

I had a bodyguard.

It was as close to having a live nuclear weapon as you can get. I cannot say we became friends. I touched him only once, when he wasn't looking—I petted him on the head and received a growl and a lifted lip for it. But we became constant companions. Dirk moved into the basement with me, and I gave him a hamburger every day and hustled up dog food for him and many nights we sat down there eating Ritz crackers and he watched me working on stick model airplanes.

---

6. **cohorts** (kō′hôrts′): companions or associates.

He followed me to school, waited for me, followed me to the bowling alley, waited for me. He was with me everywhere I went, always back three or four feet, always with a soft growl, and to my great satisfaction every time he saw Happy—every time—Dirk would try to remove some part of his body with as much violence as possible.

He caused Happy and his mob to change their habits. They not only stopped hunting me but went out of their way to avoid me, or more specifically, Dirk. In fact after that winter and spring they never bothered me again, even after Dirk was gone.

Dirk came to a wonderful end. I always thought of him as a street dog—surely nobody owned him—and in the summer when I was hired to work on a farm four miles east of town I took him with me. We walked all the way out to the farm, Dirk four feet in back of me, and he would trot along beside the tractor when I plowed, now and then chasing the hundreds of seagulls that came for the worms the plow turned up.

The farmer, whose name was Olaf, was a bachelor and did not have a dog. I looked over once to see Dirk sitting next to Olaf while we ate some sandwiches and when Olaf reached out to pet him Dirk actually—this was the first time I'd seen it—wagged his tail.

He'd found a home.

I worked the whole summer there and when it came time to leave, Dirk remained sitting in the yard as I walked down the driveway. The next summer I had bought an old Dodge for twenty-five dollars and I drove out to Olaf's to say hello and saw Dirk out in a field with perhaps two hundred sheep. He wasn't herding them, or chasing them, but was just standing there, watching the flock.

"You have him with the sheep?" I asked Olaf.

He nodded. "Last year I lost forty-three to coyotes," he said. "This year not a one. He likes to guard things, doesn't he?"

I thought of Dirk chasing Happy down the street, and later spitting out bits of his pants, and I smiled. "Yeah, he sure does." ❖

Gary Paulsen
born 1939

"I still read like . . . a wolf eats. I read myself to sleep every night."

Precious Gift Because Gary Paulsen's father was an army officer, his family moved frequently when he was a boy. "School was a nightmare because I was unbelievably shy, and terrible at sports," he recalls. One cold winter night when he was living in a small town in northern Minnesota, Paulsen went into a library to get warm. The librarian offered him a library card and the chance to take out books. Paulsen read the books he took out "as though I had been dying of thirst and the librarian had handed me a five gallon bucket of water."

Outdoor Adventures Besides being a writer, Paulsen has been, among other things, a soldier, a trapper, and a rancher. His experiences in the outdoors have been the inspiration for more than forty books, among them the Newbery Honor Books *Dogsong, Hatchet,* and *The Winter Room.*

Author Study O. HENRY

1862–1910

CONTENTS

A Writer by Profession

"It was never intended that I should write novels. . . . I was designed, created, and set going to write short stories, and as long as I stick to that I will have my measure of success. . . ."

YOUNG READER

O. Henry is the pen name of William Sydney Porter, who was born in Greensboro, North Carolina. Will's mother died when he was three years old, leaving him to be raised by his aunt Lina, who ran a small private school. Under her guidance, Will developed a taste for literature and a talent for humorous drawing. He began by devouring dime novels but eventually moved on to one of his lifetime favorites, *The Arabian Nights,* as well as other classics.

Will left school at 15 and trained to be a pharmacist. The teenager spent many hours at his uncle's drugstore and gained a reputation as a

O. Henry's uncle's drugstore

His LIFE and TIMES

1860 — 1870 — 1880

1862 Born September 11 Greensboro, North Carolina

1865 Mother dies; family moves in with aunt and grandmother.

1877 Works in uncle's drugstore

1882 Moves to Texas

1861–1865 Lincoln presidency; Civil War

1869 U.S. transcontinental railroad completed; joins East and West

1876 Alexander Graham Bell invents the telephone.

prankster. Will would amuse the regular customers with his skillful caricature drawings of them or of the town elders.

A ROLLING STONE

By the age of 19, Porter was a licensed pharmacist, but a racking cough caused him concern. Both his mother and grandmother had died of tuberculosis, and Porter was terrified that he, too, might have the disease. In 1882, he moved to Texas—a state noted for its dry, healthy climate—where he lived on a cattle ranch. But Porter turned out to be an unusual cowboy, sometimes carrying a small dictionary in one pocket and a book of poems in the other.

Later, Porter moved to Austin. In his free time, he would stroll the sidewalks absorbing the atmosphere and noting the colorful characters he met. Many of the short stories he would later write contain vivid profiles of Texas Rangers, cattle rustlers, train robbers, and other Westerners.

In 1887 Porter married a local girl, Athol Estes, whose connections helped him find work as a bank teller in Austin. To earn extra money, he submitted sketches to newspapers and magazines. In 1894, while still working at the bank, he started *The Rolling Stone*, a humorous weekly newspaper.

While working in Austin, Texas, O. Henry started a weekly humor newspaper.

| 1887 Marries Athol Estes | 1894 Publishes *The Rolling Stone* | 1898–1901 In prison | 1902 Moves to New York City | 1907 Marries Sara L. Coleman | 1910 Dies June 5 in New York City |

1890 — **1900** — **1910**

| 1886 Statue of Liberty is erected in New York Harbor. | 1898 Spanish-American-Cuban War | 1908 Henry Ford introduces the Model T. |

The paper lasted barely a year. Rumors were that Porter had used some of the money from the bank where he was working to finance his failing paper.

A NEW IDENTITY

In 1896, Porter was arrested and charged with stealing funds. He fled to Honduras, although his family and friends believed he was merely an innocent victim. Porter returned to Texas several months later to keep watch at the bedside of his wife, who was to die, at 29, of tuberculosis.

It was while awaiting trial that Porter had his first short story published. In 1898 he was convicted and sentenced to five years in a federal prison. While serving his time, he supported his daughter, Margaret, by working as a pharmacist and writing stories about life in Central America and the Southwest. On his early release after only three years, Porter left behind his shameful identity as a convict. He changed his name to O. Henry, a name that soon would be known throughout America.

In 1902 O. Henry moved to New York City, where he was to live until his death writing weekly stories for newspapers and magazines. The vibrant city with its variety of inhabitants became the setting for O. Henry's most famous stories, including "After Twenty Years." (page 155) In 1904 O. Henry published his first book of stories, *Cabbages and Kings*. With his next collection, *The Four Million* (1906), O. Henry became famous worldwide.

Portrait of O. Henry

In 1907 O. Henry remarried. Unhappily, his health was failing, and, as was true for most of his life, he had no money. He continued to write at a furious pace, however, producing seven collections of short stories in the last three years of his life. When he died in 1910, O. Henry steadfastly refused to admit to his birth name.

FACT OR FICTION?

Because O. Henry guarded the secret of his past so carefully, biographers have drawn heavily on his stories to explain the author himself. Certainly, he lived as colorful a life as many of his characters, and his stories show a unique understanding of people on both sides of the law.

Most of O. Henry's famous "Westerns" were inspired by his years in Texas, and one of his most popular characters— Jimmy Valentine of "A Retrieved Reformation" (page 164)—was based on a safe-cracker he met while in prison. His tales are famous for their surprise endings, and the later stories are based on O. Henry's life in New York City.

 **Author Link**
www.mcdougallittell.com

NetActivities: Author Exploration

THE TEXAS CATTLE BOOM

O. Henry lived on a cattle ranch in Texas in the 1880s. Cattle ranching had begun in Texas when settlers from Mexico arrived in the 1700s. After the Civil War, a new demand for beef turned ranching into big business. Cattle "kingdoms" spread over Texas.

The largest of these covered more then three million acres! Ranchers didn't fence their property but relied on cowboys to watch the cattle and drive them to market. Cowboys could be on a cattle drive for several months, depending on where they took the cattle.

More than 35,000 cowboys rode herd along the Texas cattle trails. Although folklore and picture postcards depicted the cowboy as Anglo-American, about 25 percent were African American and another 12 percent were Mexican *vaqueros*—cowboys who had worked in Texas since the days before Texas's independence. There were Native American cowboys, too, and a few women. O. Henry did not actually stray far from the ranch where he lived, but the forty-or-so stories he set in Texas are rich in the details and characters of frontier life.

After Twenty Years

by O. HENRY

Me-Twenty Years From Now
- I will be 32 years old.

Connect to Your Life

Into the Future In this story, two friends meet again after twenty years. They discover that their lives have taken different paths. Have you ever wondered what your life might be like in twenty years? In a small group, describe how you see yourself twenty years from now. How will you be different? What choices might you have made in order to achieve your goals?

Build Background

HISTORY

The main character in "After Twenty Years" has just returned to New York from the West, where he made his fortune. After gold was discovered in California in 1848, adventure seekers poured into the American West hoping to get rich.

WORDS TO KNOW
Vocabulary Preview

dismally	staunchest
habitual	vicinity
simultaneously	

Key Standards

R3.2 Identify events that advance the plot and describe how they explain the past, present, and future.
R3.3 Analyze characters by examining what they think, say, and do, and by studying the words of the narrator and the reactions of other characters.
Other Standards **R1.3, LC1.3**

Focus Your Reading

LITERARY ANALYSIS **SURPRISE ENDING**

Surprise endings may be a sudden turn in the action or offer a new realization about the story. Usually there are events in the story that hint at, or **foreshadow,** future action. As you read "After Twenty Years," look for events that foreshadow the surprise ending.

ACTIVE READING **MONITORING**

When you read a story or other literary work, it helps to pause occasionally and **monitor,** or check your understanding. Keep in mind the reading strategies you have learned and apply a different one if you are having difficulty. Stopping and rereading descriptive passages or dialogue will help you understand twists in the plot.

READER'S NOTEBOOK As you read "After Twenty Years," make notes of points in the story that help you monitor, or keep track of, how the main characters are described by the author and by other characters in the story.

AFTER TWENTY YEARS

Illustration by
Stephen Peringer

by O. Henry

Rainy Night (1929-30), Charles Ephraim Burchfield. Watercolor over pencil on paper, 30″ × 42″, San Diego Museum of Art. Gift of Anne R. and Amy Putnam.

The policeman on the beat moved up the avenue impressively. The impressiveness was <u>habitual</u> and not for show, for spectators were few. The time was barely ten o'clock at night, but chilly gusts of wind with a taste of rain in them had well nigh depeopled the streets.

Trying doors as he went, twirling his club with many intricate and artful movements, turning now and then to cast his watchful eye down the pacific[1] thoroughfare, the officer, with his stalwart form and slight swagger, made a fine picture of a guardian of the peace. The <u>vicinity</u> was one that kept early hours. Now and then you might see the lights of a cigar store or of an all-night lunch counter, but the majority of the doors belonged to business places that had long since been closed.

When about midway of a certain block, the policeman suddenly slowed his walk. In the doorway of a darkened hardware store a man leaned, with an unlighted cigar in his mouth. As the policeman walked up to him, the man spoke up quickly.

"It's all right, officer," he said reassuringly. "I'm just waiting for a friend. It's an appointment made twenty years ago. Sounds a little funny to you, doesn't it? Well, I'll explain if you'd like to make certain it's all straight. About that long ago there used to be a restaurant where this store stands—'Big Joe' Brady's restaurant."

"Until five years ago," said the policeman. "It was torn down then."

The man in the doorway struck a match and lit his cigar. The light showed a pale, square-jawed face with keen eyes and a little white

---

1. **pacific:** calm and peaceful.

scar near his right eyebrow. His scarf pin was a large diamond, oddly set.

"Twenty years ago tonight," said the man, "I dined here at 'Big Joe' Brady's with Jimmy Wells, my best chum and the finest chap in the world. He and I were raised here in New York, just like two brothers, together. I was eighteen and Jimmy was twenty. The next morning I was to start for the West to make my fortune. You couldn't have dragged Jimmy out of New York; he thought it was the only place on earth. Well, we agreed that night that we would meet here again exactly twenty years from that date and time, no matter what our conditions might be or from what distance we might have to come. We figured that in twenty years each of us ought to have our destiny[2] worked out and our fortunes made, whatever they were going to be."

"It sounds pretty interesting," said the policeman. "Rather a long time between meets, though, it seems to me. Haven't you heard from your friend since you left?"

"Well, yes, for a time we corresponded," said the other. "But after a year or two we lost track of each other. You see, the West is a pretty big proposition, and I kept hustling[3] around over it pretty lively. But I know Jimmy will meet me here if he's alive, for he always was the truest, <u>staunchest</u> old chap in the world. He'll never forget. I came a thousand miles to stand in this door tonight, and it's worth it if my old partner turns up."

The waiting man pulled out a handsome watch, the lids of it set with small diamonds.

"Three minutes to ten," he announced. "It was exactly ten o'clock when we parted here at the restaurant door."

"Did pretty well out West, didn't you?" asked the policeman.

"You bet! I hope Jimmy has done half as well. He was a kind of plodder, though, good fellow as he was. I've had to compete with some of the sharpest wits going to get my pile. A man gets in a groove[4] in New York. It takes the West to put a razor edge on him."

The policeman twirled his club and took a step or two.

"I'll be on my way. Hope your friend comes around all right. Going to call time on him sharp?"

"I should say not!" said the other. "I'll give him half an hour at least. If Jimmy is alive on earth, he'll be here by that time. So long, officer."

"Good night, sir," said the policeman, passing on along his beat, trying doors as he went.

There was now a fine, cold drizzle falling, and the wind had risen from its uncertain puffs into a steady blow. The few foot passengers astir in that quarter hurried <u>dismally</u> and silently along with coat collars turned high and pocketed hands. And in the door of the hardware store the man who had come a thousand miles to fill an appointment,

---

2. **destiny:** the fate or outcome of a person's life.

3. **hustling** (hŭs′əl-ĭng): moving or working energetically and rapidly.

4. **groove:** a long funnel or narrow channel; slang for a settled routine.

*Unfinished Portrait of
Tadeusz Lempicki* (about
1928), Tamara de Lempicka.
Oil on canvas,
126 cm × 82 cm, Musée
National d'Art Moderne,
Centre National d'Art et de
Culture Georges Pompidou,
Paris. Copyright © 1999
Estate of Tamara de
Lempicka/Artists Rights
Society (ARS), New York.

uncertain almost to absurdity, with the friend of his youth, smoked his cigar and waited.

About twenty minutes he waited, and then a tall man in a long overcoat, with collar turned up to his ears, hurried across from the opposite side of the street. He went directly to the waiting man.

"Is that you, Bob?" he asked, doubtfully.

"Is that you, Jimmy Wells?" cried the man in the door.

"Bless my heart!" exclaimed the new arrival, grasping both the other's hands with his own. "Yes Bob, sure as fate. I was certain I'd find you here if you were still in existence. Well, well, well!—twenty years is a long time. The old restaurant's gone, Bob; I wish it had lasted, so we could have had another dinner there. How has the West treated you, old man?"

"Bully;[5] it has given me everything I asked it for. You've changed lots, Jimmy. I never thought you were so tall by two or three inches."

"Oh, I grew a bit after I was twenty."

"Doing well in New York, Jimmy?"

"Moderately, I have a position in one of the city departments. Come on, Bob; we'll go around to a place I know of and have a good long talk about old times."

The two men started up the street, arm in arm. The man from the West, his egotism[6] enlarged by success, was beginning to outline the history of his character. The other, submerged in his overcoat, listened with interest.

At the corner stood a drugstore, brilliant with electric lights. When they came into this glare, each of them turned simultaneously to gaze upon the other's face.

The man from the West stopped suddenly and released his arm.

"You're not Jimmy Wells," he snapped. "Twenty years is a long time, but not long enough to change a man's nose from a Roman to a pug."[7]

"It sometimes changes a good man into a bad one," said the tall man. "You've been under arrest for ten minutes, 'Silky' Bob. Chicago thinks you may have dropped over our way and wires us she wants to have a chat with you. Going quietly, are you? That's sensible. Now, before we go to the station, here's a note I was asked to hand to you. You may read it here at the window. It's from Patrolman Wells."

The man from the West unfolded the little piece of paper handed him. His hand was steady when he began to read, but it trembled a little by the time he had finished. The note was rather short.

> Bob: I was at the appointed place on time. When you struck the match to light your cigar, I saw it was the face of the man wanted in Chicago. Somehow I couldn't do it myself, so I went around and got a plainclothes man to do the job.
>
> Jimmy

---

5. **bully:** excellent; great.

6. **egotism** (ē′gə-tĭz′əm): a sense of one's own great importance; conceit.

7. **"change a man's nose from a Roman to a pug":** a Roman nose has a high, prominent, bony ridge, whereas a pug nose is short and turned up at the end.

Connect to the Literature

1. **What Do You Think?** What are your feelings about the ending of this story? Explain.

Comprehension Check
- How does "Silky" Bob describe his friend Jimmy to the policeman?
- How has "Silky" Bob made his fortune?
- Why doesn't Jimmy identify himself to "Silky" Bob right away?

Think Critically

2. Why do you think Jimmy turned his friend in?

   Think About:
   - the arrangement Jimmy made with "Silky" Bob twenty years earlier
   - his loyalties as a police officer
   - his loyalty as a friend

3. Jimmy and "Silky" Bob promise to meet after twenty years. What does that say about their friendship twenty years earlier?

4. **ACTIVE READING** **MONITORING**
   Review the notes you made in your **READER'S NOTEBOOK.** Compare the descriptions of the two main characters—Jimmy Wells and "Silky" Bob. How do they differ? How are they alike?

Extend Interpretations

5. **Different Perspectives** What if the story had been told from Jimmy Wells's perspective? Explain how the story would have been different.

6. **Connect to Life** What would you do if you were faced with the decision Jimmy had to make? Use details from the story when you respond.

Literary Analysis

SURPRISE ENDING A **surprise ending** is an unexpected outcome in the plot of a story. In "After Twenty Years," the moment when "Silky" Bob is arrested comes as a surprise.

The revelation that Jimmy Wells has become a police officer gives a new meaning to many details in the story. "Silky" Bob's description of Jimmy as the "truest, staunchest old chap," as a "kind of plodder," and as a "good fellow" are seen to mean something different from what "Silky" Bob meant when he first spoke the words.

Paired Activity With a partner, go back through the story and identify events in the plot that foreshadow the future outcome. What clues were there to Jimmy Wells's character? to "Silky" Bob's?

REVIEW: CHARACTER The people who appear in stories are called **characters.** Both major and minor characters have traits and motives. **Traits** are qualities of the character's personality that are consistent, or aren't easily changed. **Motives** are emotions, wants, or needs that cause characters to act the way they do. Name some of Jimmy's and "Silky" Bob's traits and motives.

Grammar in Context: Subjects in Unusual Order

O. Henry surprises the reader with twists and turns in plot in "After Twenty Years." Similarly, he writes sentences with **subjects** that do not always come at the beginning of the sentence.

> Twirling his club with many intricate and artful movements, the officer, with his stalwart form and slight swagger, made a fine picture of a guardian of the peace. . . .
> When about midway of a certain block, the policeman suddenly slowed his walk. In the doorway of a darkened hardware store, a man leaned with an unlighted cigar in his mouth.

Many sentences use the basic **subject-verb** pattern.

> I was eighteen. Jimmy was twenty. The officer spoke. The man stopped suddenly.

Placing the subject somewhere other than at the beginning of the sentence is one way to make your writing more interesting. Here are some suggestions:

1. Begin with an **introduction.**
   Twenty years ago, I dined here with Jimmy Wells.
   If Jimmy is alive on earth, he'll be here.

2. Another way to add variety to your writing is to invert the traditional **subject-verb** order.
   At the corner **stood** a **drug store.**

3. Sentences that start with **here** or **there** always invert the **subject-verb** order.
   Here **is** a **note.**
   There **were** two **strangers** by the hardware store.

WRITING EXERCISE "After Twenty Years" ends with a note from Jimmy to Bob. Compose a reply (four sentences) from Bob to Jimmy. Use two of the methods discussed above to add variety to your writing.

Vocabulary

Choose the word or group of words that means the opposite, or nearly the opposite, of the underlined Word to Know in each sentence.

1. Bob's clothing showed his wealth and <u>habitual</u> elegance.
   A typical   **B** spontaneous
   C unusual   **D** uncomfortable

2. Bob thought Jim the <u>staunchest</u> friend anybody could have.
   F smartest   **G** most disloyal
   H most honest   **J** strongest

3. Bob stood waiting in the <u>vicinity</u> of the darkened hardware store.
   A doorway   **B** shadow
   C block opposite   **D** neighborhood

4. Under the bright light of the electric streetlamps, the policeman and Bob turned <u>simultaneously</u> to see each other.
   F separately   **G** instinctively
   H quickly   **J** at the same time

5. Bob stood on the dark street, <u>dismally</u> reading Jim's letter.
   A happily   **B** calmly
   C slowly   **D** gloomily

Vocabulary Handbook
See p. R24: Context Clues.

A Retrieved Reformation

by O. HENRY

Key Standard
R3.4 Identify and analyze themes that appear across works.
Other Standards **R1.3, R3.2, R3.5, LC1.3**

Connect to Your Life

Making Friends In small groups, think up a list of characters in stories, books, and movies—or of people that you know—who change for the better or for the worse. How do you explain the reasons for the change in each of these characters? What do you think some of the most powerful motives for change are?

Build Background

HISTORY

Banks played an important role in the economy of small towns in the late 19th and early 20th centuries. The National Banking Act of 1863 helped establish a system of federally chartered banks. In the late 1800s, Will Porter, who would later take the pen name O. Henry, worked as a teller for the First National Bank in Austin, Texas.

Will Porter (O. Henry) working as a bank teller in Austin, Texas.

Focus Your Reading

LITERARY ANALYSIS | **FALLING ACTION**

The plot of a story is usually set in motion by a **conflict** between opposing forces or characters. As the story moves ahead, the conflict increases until the moment of greatest intensity—the **climax**, or turning point. After the climax, the central conflict of the story is usually resolved in a part of the plot called the **falling action.** As you read, note how the conflict in "A Retrieved Reformation" is resolved.

ACTIVE READING | **COMPARING ACROSS TEXTS**

Drawing connections between the different literary works you read will help you understand them better and enjoy them more. All of the important aspects of stories may be compared, including plot, characters, setting, point of view, and theme.

READER'S NOTEBOOK As you read "A Retrieved Reformation," note similarities and differences between the main characters of the story and those of "After Twenty Years." Also think about point of view in the two stories. Is the point of view the same in each? How does the point of view affect the way each story is told?

WORDS TO KNOW **Vocabulary Preview**

assiduously	compulsory	eminent	retribution	unperceived
balk	elusive	rehabilitate	unobtrusively	virtuous

Portrait of Prince Eristoff (1925), Tamara de Lempicka. Courtesy of Barry Frideman Ltd., New York. Copyright © 1996 Artists Rights Society (ARS), New York/SPADEM, Paris.

A Retrieved Reformation

by O. Henry

A guard came to the prison shoe shop, where Jimmy Valentine was <u>assiduously</u> stitching uppers, and escorted him to the front office. There the warden handed Jimmy his pardon, which had been signed that morning by the governor. Jimmy took it in a tired kind of way. He had served nearly ten months of a four-year sentence. He had expected to stay only about three months, at the longest. When a man with as many friends on the outside as Jimmy Valentine had is received in the "stir" it is hardly worthwhile to cut his hair.

"Now, Valentine," said the warden, "you'll go out in the morning. Brace up, and make a man of yourself. You're not a bad fellow at heart. Stop cracking safes, and live straight."

"Me?" said Jimmy, in surprise. "Why, I never cracked a safe in my life."

"Oh, no," laughed the warden. "Of course not. Let's see, now. How was it you happened to get sent up on that Springfield job? Was it because you wouldn't prove an alibi for fear of compromising somebody in extremely high-toned society? Or was it simply a case of a mean old jury that had it in for you? It's always one or the other with you innocent victims."

"Me?" said Jimmy, still blankly <u>virtuous</u>. "Why, warden, I never was in Springfield in my life!"

"Take him back, Cronin," smiled the warden, "and fix him up with outgoing clothes. Unlock him at seven in the morning, and let him come to the bull-pen. Better think over my advice, Valentine."

At a quarter past seven on the next morning Jimmy stood in the warden's outer office. He had on a suit of the villainously fitting, ready-made clothes and a pair of the stiff, squeaky shoes that the state furnishes to its discharged <u>compulsory</u> guests.

The clerk handed him a railroad ticket and the five-dollar bill with which the law expected him to <u>rehabilitate</u> himself into good citizen-ship and prosperity. The warden gave him a cigar, and shook hands. Valentine, 9762, was chronicled on the books "Pardoned by Governor," and Mr. James Valentine walked out into the sunshine.

Disregarding the song of the birds, the waving green trees, and the smell of the flowers, Jimmy headed straight for a restaurant. There he tasted the first sweet joys of liberty in the shape of a broiled chicken and a bottle of white wine—followed by a cigar a grade better than the one the warden had given him. From there he proceeded leisurely to the depot. He tossed a quarter into the hat of a blind man sitting by the door, and boarded his train. Three hours set him down in a little town near the state line. He went to the café of one Mike Dolan and shook hands with Mike, who was alone behind the bar.

"Sorry we couldn't make it sooner, Jimmy, me boy," said Mike. "But we had that protest from Springfield to buck against, and the governor nearly <u>balked</u>. Feeling all right?"

"Fine," said Jimmy. "Got my key?"

He got his key and went upstairs, unlocking the door of a room at the rear. Everything was just as he had left it. There on the floor was still Ben Price's collar-button that had been torn from that <u>eminent</u> detective's shirt-band when

WORDS
TO
KNOW

assiduously (ə-sĭj′o͞o-əs-lē) *adv.* in a steady and hard-working way
virtuous (vûr′cho͞o-əs) *adj.* morally good; honorable
compulsory (kəm-pŭl′sə-rē) *adj.* that which must be done; required
rehabilitate (rē′hə-bĭl′ĭ-tāt′) *v.* to restore to useful life, as through therapy and education
balk (bôk) *v.* to refuse to move or act
eminent (ĕm′ə-nənt) *adj.* better than most others; very famous

they had overpowered Jimmy to arrest him.

Pulling out from the wall a folding-bed, Jimmy slid back a panel in the wall and dragged out a dust-covered suitcase. He opened this and gazed fondly at the finest set of burglar's tools in the East. It was a complete set, made of specially tempered steel, the latest designs in drills, punches, braces and bits, jimmies, clamps, and augers, with two or three novelties invented by Jimmy himself, in which he took pride. Over nine hundred dollars they had cost him to have made at _____, a place where they make such things for the profession.

In half an hour Jimmy went downstairs and through the café. He was now dressed in tasteful and well-fitting clothes, and carried his dusted and cleaned suitcase in his hand.

"Got anything on?" asked Mike Dolan, genially.

"Me?" said Jimmy, in a puzzled tone. "I don't understand. I'm representing the New York Amalgamated Short Snap Biscuit Cracker and Frazzled Wheat Company."

This statement delighted Mike to such an extent that Jimmy had to take a seltzer-and-milk on the spot. He never touched "hard" drinks.

A week after the release of Valentine, 9762, there was a neat job of safe-burglary done in Richmond, Indiana, with no clue to the author. A scant eight hundred dollars was all that was secured. Two weeks after that a patented, improved, burglar-proof safe in Logansport was opened like a cheese to the tune of fifteen hundred dollars, currency; securities and silver untouched. That began to interest the rogue catchers. Then an old-fashioned bank safe in Jefferson City became active and threw out of its crater an eruption of banknotes amounting to five thousand dollars. The losses were now high enough to bring the matter up into Ben Price's class of work. By comparing notes, a remarkable similarity in the methods of the burglaries was noticed. Ben Price investigated the scenes of the robberies, and was heard to remark: "That's Dandy Jim Valentine's autograph. He's resumed business. Look at that combination knob—jerked out as easy as pulling up a radish in wet weather. He's got the only clamps that can do it. And look how clean those tumblers were punched out! Jimmy never has to drill but one hole. Yes, I guess I want Mr. Valentine. He'll do his bit next time without any short-time or clemency foolishness."

Ben Price knew Jimmy's habits. He had learned them while working up the Springfield case. Long jumps, quick get-aways, no confederates,[1] and a taste for good society—these ways had helped Mr. Valentine to become noted as a successful dodger of <u>retribution</u>. It was given out that Ben Price had taken up the trail of the <u>elusive</u> cracksman, and other people with burglar-proof safes felt more at ease.

---

1. **confederates** (kən-fĕd′ər-ĭts): accomplices or associates in crime.

WORDS TO KNOW

retribution (rĕt′rə-byoo′shən) *n.* punishment for bad behavior
elusive (ĭ-loo′sĭv) *adj.* escaping from capture as by daring, cleverness, or skill

166

One afternoon Jimmy Valentine and his suitcase climbed out of the mailhack in Elmore, a little town five miles off the railroad down in the blackjack country of Arkansas. Jimmy, looking like an athletic young senior just home from college, went down the board sidewalk toward the hotel.

A young lady crossed the street, passed him at the corner, and entered a door over which was the sign "The Elmore Bank." Jimmy Valentine looked into her eyes, forgot what he was, and became another man. She lowered her eyes and colored slightly. Young men of Jimmy's style and looks were scarce in Elmore.

Jimmy collared a boy that was loafing on the steps of the bank as if he were one of the stockholders, and began to ask him questions about the town, feeding him dimes at intervals. By and by the young lady came out, looking royally unconscious of the young man with the suitcase, and went her way.

"Isn't that young lady Miss Polly Simpson?" asked Jimmy, with specious guile.[2]

"Naw," said the boy. "She's Annabel Adams. Her pa owns this bank. What'd you come to Elmore for? Is that a gold watch-chain? I'm going to get a bulldog. Got any more dimes?"

Jimmy went to the Planters' Hotel, registered as Ralph D. Spencer, and engaged a room. He leaned on the desk and declared his platform to the clerk. He said he had come to Elmore to look for a location to go into business. How was the shoe business, now, in the town? He had thought of the shoe business. Was there an opening?

The clerk was impressed by the clothes and manner of Jimmy. He, himself, was something of a pattern of fashion to the thinly gilded youth of Elmore, but he now perceived his shortcomings. While trying to figure out Jimmy's manner of tying his four-in-hand[3] he cordially gave information.

Yes, there ought to be a good opening in the shoe line. There wasn't an exclusive shoe store in the place. The dry-goods and general stores handled them. Business in all lines was fairly good. Hoped Mr. Spencer would decide to locate in Elmore. He would find it a pleasant town to live in, and the people very sociable.

Mr. Spencer thought he would stop over in the town a few days and look over the situation. No, the clerk needn't call the boy. He would carry up his suitcase, himself; it was rather heavy.

Mr. Ralph Spencer, the phoenix[4] that arose from Jimmy Valentine's ashes—ashes left by the flame of a sudden and alterative attack of love—remained in Elmore, and prospered. He opened a shoe store and secured a good run of trade.

Socially he was also a success and made many friends. And he accomplished the wish of his heart. He met Miss Annabel Adams, and became more and more captivated by her charms.

At the end of a year the situation of Mr. Ralph Spencer was this: he had won the respect of the community, his shoe store was flourishing, and he and Annabel were engaged to be married in two weeks. Mr. Adams, the typical, plodding, country banker, approved of Spencer. Annabel's pride in him almost equaled her affection. He was as much at home in the family of Mr. Adams and that of Annabel's married sister as if he were already a member.

2. **specious guile** (spē′shəs gīl): innocent charm masking real slyness.

3. **four-in-hand:** a necktie tied in the usual way, that is, in a slipknot with the ends left hanging.

4. **phoenix** (fē′nĭks): a mythological bird that lived for over 500 years and then burned itself to death, only to rise out of its own ashes to live another long life. The phoenix is a symbol of immortality.

One day Jimmy sat down in his room and wrote this letter, which he mailed to the safe address of one of his old friends in St. Louis:

DEAR OLD PAL:

I want you to be at Sullivan's place, in Little Rock, next Wednesday night, at nine o'clock.
I want you to wind up some little matters for me. And, also, I want to make you a present of my kit of tools. I know you'll be glad to get them—you couldn't duplicate the lot for a thousand dollars. Say, Billy, I've quit the old business—a year ago. I've got a nice store. I'm making an honest living, and I'm going to marry the finest girl on earth two weeks from now. It's the only life, Billy—the straight one. I wouldn't touch a dollar of another man's money now for a million. After I get married I'm going to sell out and go West, where there won't be so much danger of having old scores brought up against me. I tell you, Billy, she's an angel. She believes in me; and I wouldn't do another crooked thing for the whole world. Be sure to be at Sully's, for I must see you. I'll bring along the tools with me.

Your old friend,
JIMMY

On the Monday night after Jimmy wrote this letter, Ben Price jogged <u>unobtrusively</u> into Elmore in a livery buggy. He lounged about town in his quiet way until he found out what he wanted to know. From the drugstore across the street from Spencer's shoe store he got a good look at Ralph D. Spencer.

"Going to marry the banker's daughter are you, Jimmy?" said Ben to himself, softly. "Well, I don't know!"

The next morning Jimmy took breakfast at the Adamses. He was going to Little Rock that day to order his wedding suit and buy something nice for Annabel. That would be the first time he had left town since he came to Elmore. It had been more than a year now since those last professional "jobs," and he thought he could safely venture out.

After breakfast quite a family party went down together—Mr. Adams, Annabel, Jimmy, and Annabel's married sister with her two little girls, aged five and nine. They came by the hotel where Jimmy still boarded, and he ran up to his room and brought along his suitcase. Then they went on to the bank. There stood Jimmy's horse and buggy and Dolph Gibson, who was going to drive him over to the railroad station.

All went inside the high, carved oak railings into the banking room—Jimmy included, for Mr. Adams's future son-in-law was welcome anywhere. The clerks were pleased to be greeted by the good-looking, agreeable young man who was going to marry Miss Annabel. Jimmy set his suitcase down. Annabel, whose heart was bubbling with happiness and lively youth, put on Jimmy's hat and picked up the suitcase. "Wouldn't I make a nice drummer?" said Annabel. "My! Ralph, how heavy it is. Feels

I wouldn't do another crooked thing for the whole world.

unobtrusively (ŭn′əb-trōō′sĭv-lē) *adv.* in a way that attracts little or no attention

like it was full of gold bricks."

"Lot of nickel-plated shoehorns in there," said Jimmy, coolly, "that I'm going to return. Thought I'd save express charges by taking them up. I'm getting awfully economical."

The Elmore Bank had just put in a new safe and vault. Mr. Adams was very proud of it, and insisted on an inspection by everyone. The vault was a small one, but it had a new patented door. It fastened with three solid steel bolts thrown simultaneously with a single handle, and had a time lock. Mr. Adams beamingly explained its workings to Mr. Spencer, who showed a courteous but not too intelligent interest. The two children, May and Agatha, were delighted by the shining metal and funny clock and knobs.

While they were thus engaged Ben Price sauntered in and leaned on his elbow, looking casually inside between the railings. He told the teller that he didn't want anything; he was just waiting for a man he knew.

Suddenly there was a scream or two from the women, and a commotion. Unperceived by the elders, May, the nine-year-old girl, in a spirit of play, had shut Agatha in the vault. She had then shot the bolts and turned the knob of the combination as she had seen Mr. Adams do.

The old banker sprang to the handle and tugged at it for a moment. "The door can't be opened," he groaned. "The clock hasn't been wound nor the combination set."

Copyright © Gary Kelley.

Agatha's mother screamed again, hysterically.

"Hush!" said Mr. Adams, raising his trembling hand. "All be quiet for a moment. Agatha!" he called as loudly as he could. "Listen to me." During the following silence they could just hear the faint sound of the child wildly shrieking in the dark vault in a panic of terror.

"My precious darling!" wailed the mother. "She will die of fright! Open the door! Oh, break it open! Can't you men do something?"

"There isn't a man nearer than Little Rock who can open that door," said Mr. Adams, in a shaky voice. "My God! Spencer, what shall we do? That child—she can't stand it long in there. There isn't enough air, and, besides, she'll go into convulsions from fright."

Agatha's mother, frantic now, beat the door of the vault with her hands. Somebody wildly suggested dynamite. Annabel turned to Jimmy, her large eyes full of anguish, but not yet despairing. To a woman nothing seems quite impossible to the powers of the man she worships.

"Can't you do something, Ralph—try, won't you?"

He looked at her with a queer, soft smile on his lips and in his keen eyes.

"Annabel," he said, "give me that rose you are wearing, will you?"

Hardly believing that she had heard him aright, she unpinned the bud from the bosom of her dress, and placed it in his hand. Jimmy stuffed it into his vest pocket, threw off his coat and pulled up his shirt sleeves. With that act Ralph D. Spencer passed away and Jimmy Valentine took his place.

"Get away from the door, all of you," he commanded, shortly.

He set his suitcase on the table, and opened it out flat. From that time on he seemed to be unconscious of the presence of anyone else. He laid out the shining, queer implements swiftly and orderly, whistling softly to himself as he always did when at work. In a deep silence and immovable, the others watched him as if under a spell.

In a minute Jimmy's pet drill was biting smoothly into the steel door. In ten minutes—breaking his own burglarious record— he threw back the bolts and opened the door.

Agatha, almost collapsed, but safe, was gathered into her mother's arms.

Jimmy Valentine put on his coat, and walked outside the railings toward the front door. As he went he thought he heard a faraway voice that he once knew call "Ralph!" But he never hesitated. At the door a big man stood somewhat in his way.

"Hello, Ben!" said Jimmy, still with his strange smile. "Got around at last, have you? Well, let's go. I don't know that it makes much difference, now."

And then Ben Price acted rather strangely.

"Guess you're mistaken, Mr. Spencer," he said. "Don't believe I recognize you. Your buggy's waiting for you, ain't it?"

And Ben Price turned and strolled down the street. ❖

Connect to the Literature

1. What Do You Think? How did you react to Jimmy's decision to crack the safe? Explain.

Comprehension Check
- Why was Jimmy sent to prison?
- What successes does Jimmy have in Elmore?
- How does Ben Price react when Jimmy cracks the safe?

Think Critically

2. Why do you think Ben Price lets Jimmy go free?

3. What is your opinion of Jimmy Valentine?

   Think About:
   - Jimmy's history and what the warden says about his character
   - Jimmy's motives for changing
   - what Jimmy risks in opening the vault

4. How do you think Jimmy will explain his actions to Annabel?

5. Both Jimmy Valentine and Ben Price make important decisions. Who showed more courage? Explain.

Extend Interpretations

6. What If? Suppose Agatha had not been locked in the safe. Do you think Jimmy ever would have confessed his past to Annabel?

7. **ACTIVE READING** | **COMPARING ACROSS TEXTS**
Review the notes you made in your
READER'S NOTEBOOK. How would you describe the similarities and differences between the main characters in "A Retrieved Reformation" and "After Twenty Years"? Explain your response.

8. Connect to Life In both "After Twenty Years" and "A Retrieved Reformation," police officers have to make difficult decisions about turning someone in. If you were in the same situation as Ben Price, what would you do? Use details from the story to support your response.

Literary Analysis

FALLING ACTION The series of events that make up a story is its **plot.** The part of the plot in which the conflict intensifies is called the **rising action.** The point of highest tension is called the **climax**, or turning point. In "A Retrieved Reformation" the climax comes when Jimmy decides to crack the safe and free Agatha.

Jimmy's decision affects the resolution, or **falling action,** of the story. Because Jimmy has decided to sacrifice his own reputation to save Agatha, Ben makes the decision not to arrest Jimmy. In this way, the conflict that has moved the action of the story forward is resolved.

Group Activity Working with a small group, go back through the story and create a plot diagram. Identify events that advance the plot of "A Retrieved Reformation." Include events in the rising action, the climax, and the falling action (also called denouement).

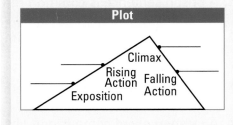
Plot

Climax
Rising Action   Falling Action
Exposition

Grammar in Context: Kinds of Sentences

Notice how O. Henry uses four types of sentences in "A Retrieved Reformation."

> "Did the mean old jury have it in for you?"
> The warden handed Jimmy his pardon.
> "Stop cracking safes, and live straight."
> "I never cracked a safe in my life!"

There are four types of sentences.

1. **Declarative sentences** make a statement. They end with a **period (.)**:
   The warden handed Jimmy his pardon.

2. **Exclamatory sentences** express strong emotion. They end with an **exclamation point (!)**:
   I never cracked a safe in my life!

3. **Interrogative sentences** ask a question. They are punctuated with a **question mark (?)**:
   Did the mean old jury have it in for you?

4. **Imperative sentences** issue a command. They end with a **period (.)**:
   Stop cracking safes, and live straight.

Connect to the Literature Reread the third paragraph on page 170. The mother whose daughter is trapped in the bank vault speaks almost entirely in exclamatory sentences. This series of exclamations expresses her intense anxiety for her daughter's well-being.

Usage Tip Use exclamation points sparingly in your writing unless you want to convey intense emotion.

WRITING EXERCISE Remember when you were five years old. Imagine how you would feel if, like Agatha in the story, you had been trapped in a bank vault. Write a short paragraph about your imagined experience. Use each sentence type—declarative, exclamatory, interrogative, and imperative. Be careful to use end punctuation correctly.

Connect to the Literature Look at page 165 of "A Retrieved Reformation." Find an example of the four types of sentences.

Vocabulary

EXERCISE: WORD MEANING On your paper, write *True* if the statement is true. Write *False* if the statement is false.

1. A prison sentence is common **retribution** for a serious crime.

2. A police officer may refuse a **compulsory** assignment and not suffer any consequences.

3. A **virtuous** person shows concern for others.

4. An **unperceived** crime is one observed by several eyewitnesses.

5. Lazy people work **assiduously**.

6. An **eminent** detective is likely to be new to the job.

7. To **rehabilitate** a criminal means to restore the person to honest ways.

8. You will attract much attention by entering a room **unobtrusively**.

9. Most thieves would not **balk** at stealing jewels.

10. An **elusive** criminal is easy to catch.

Vocabulary Handbook
See p. R24: Context Clues.

O. HENRY

FROM SHORT STORY to the BIG SCREEN

Standards W1.7, W2.1,
W2.3, LC1.3, LS1.6, LS2.1

Although O. Henry would not live to see a movie himself, his story "A Retrieved Reformation" (page 164) played an important part in launching a popular type of American film, the gangster movie. In 1909, the year before O. Henry's death, playwright Paul Armstrong dramatized O. Henry's story of the reformed bank robber and gave it the title *Alias Jimmy Valentine*. The play was one of the biggest hits on Broadway in the years before World War I. O. Henry was delighted with the play's early popularity, but died without ever suspecting how truly successful the play would become.

Poster for *Alias Jimmy Valentine* (1928).

The popularity of *Alias Jimmy Valentine* sparked a fashion for plays about the lives of criminals and the detectives who pursued them. This fashion occurred just as a new kind of artistic expression, motion pictures, was coming into being. In 1905 the first movie theater opened in the United States. Soon there were theaters across the nation.

By 1913 a number of studios producing motion pictures had established themselves in a suburb of Los Angeles, California, named Hollywood. Audiences were eager to see motion pictures, and Hollywood was on the lookout for screen plays to film. *Alias Jimmy Valentine* was filmed a total of three times. In 1915 Maurice Touneur directed the first silent version. Audiences were fascinated with the reformed safe cracker and the detective who showed him mercy. Within five years, another silent version of the play was filmed. In 1927 the first "talkie," or movie with sound effects and dialogue, *The Jazz Singer*, was shown to the public. The next year *Alias Jimmy Valentine* made its third appearance, this time with spoken dialogue.

The demand for crime and detective films only grew during the "Roaring" Twenties and on into the 1930s, the years of the Great Depression. Certain actors, such as Edward G. Robinson, James Cagney, and Paul Muni became famous for their portrayal of "underworld" figures. Three of the most famous of these early films are *Little Caesar* (1930), *The Public Enemy* (1931), and *Scarface: The Shame of the Nation* (1932).

As popular as movies about gangsters were movies that told of the detectives who hunted the gangsters down. Two masterpieces of the

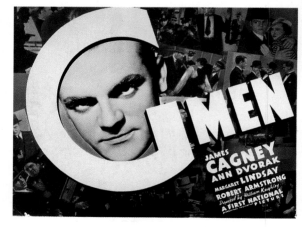

Poster for *"G"-Men* (1935).

detective movie are *The Maltese Falcon* (1941) and *Key Largo* (1948).

The popularity of crime and detective films has not diminished since the time when *Alias Jimmy Valentine* made its first appearance as a silent film about a hundred years ago. This type of film remains a staple of the movie industry today. What movies have you seen that fit the crime and detective genre?

Posters for two popular gangster films, *Key Largo* (1948) and *The Maltese Falcon* (1941).

THINKING *through the* LITERATURE

1. What insights into O. Henry did you gain from reading this expository essay?

2. *Alias Jimmy Valentine* became very popular as a play and three films. Do you think that O. Henry's original title, "A Retrieved Reformation," would have had the same appeal? Why or why not?

3. **Connect to Life** Have you watched a movie or video version of a story you read first as a book? Or has a favorite movie or video sent you looking for the the book it was based on? Talk about your experiences with your classmates.

The Author's Style

O. Henry's Lively Description

O. Henry said he wrote his stories for the busy, ordinary people who wanted a quick, interesting story to distract them now and then. O. Henry's lively descriptions helped him accomplish his goal.

Key Style Points

Well-Chosen Modifiers O. Henry uses adjectives and adverbs to create vivid, interesting images in his writing. In the passage from "A Retrieved Reformation," look for the adjectives and adverbs and the words they modify.

Simple Sentences O. Henry sometimes uses a series of simple sentences, one following the other, to give a feeling of rapid movement or urgency. Remember that simple sentences contain one independent clause and no dependent clauses. Identify the simple sentences in this passage from "After Twenty Years."

Specific Details Part of O. Henry's talent for description lies in his use of specific details in his writing. What specific details stand out in the passage below from "After Twenty Years"?

Well-Chosen Modifiers

. . . Jimmy stood in the warden's outer office. He had on a suit of the villainously fitting, ready-made clothes and a pair of the stiff, squeaky shoes that the state furnishes to its discharged compulsory guests.

—"A Retrieved Reformation"

Simple Sentences

"You bet! I hope Jimmy has done half as well. He was a kind of a plodder, though, good fellow as he was. I've had to compete with some of the sharpest wits going to get my pile. A man gets in a groove in New York. It takes the West to put a razor-edge on him."

—"After Twenty Years"

Specific Details

Trying doors as he went, twirling his club with many intricate and artful movements, turning now and then to cast his watchful eye down the pacific thoroughfare, the officer, with his stalwart form and slight swagger, made a fine picture . . .

—"After Twenty Years"

Applications

1. **Active Reading** With a partner, look back at the O. Henry stories. Identify well-chosen modifiers, simple sentences, and specific details. Find three examples of each element of description.

2. **Writing** Write a letter describing a typical day in summer. Use the three elements of O. Henry's style listed above. Underline vivid adjectives and adverbs, simple sentences, and specific details.

3. **Speaking and Listening** Choose one of the passages above that has plenty of vivid adjectives and adverbs. Rewrite it, substituting weak, less vivid adjectives and adverbs. Then, read it to a partner and discuss how the feeling of the passage has changed.

Writing

Supervisor's Report Suppose you are Ben Price. Write a report to your supervisor explaining why you have closed the case on Jimmy Valentine. Save the report in your **Working Portfolio.**

Speaking & Listening

Short Story and Video View the video "Alias Jimmy Valentine." How does the video differ from "The Retrieved Reformation" on which it was based?

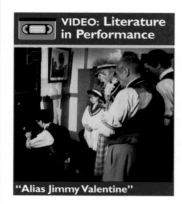

VIDEO: Literature in Performance

"Alias Jimmy Valentine"

Research & Technology

Back in Time Using informational materials like history books, the Internet, and other factual media, find out what life was like in New York City at the beginning of the 20th century. Choose three things to focus your research on. You might want to find information about the population, landmarks, social customs, economy, politics, the arts, or other aspects of city life about which you are curious.

Research and Technology Handbook
See p. R110: Getting Information.

Author Study Project

Creating a Scene

Working with a small group, retell one of the stories, or parts of it, in dialogue form.

❶ Choose a Dramatic Scene With your group, decide which scene you will act out. Think about which scenes can best be adapted to dialogue; then narrow your choice to one.

TOOLS

❷ Write a Script Write the script for your scene. You may want to include dialogue from the story.

❸ Revise the Script Read through the script, checking for ways to tighten the organization or make better word choices. Make changes that members of your group agree will improve the script.

❹ Rehearse the Skit Once you have completed the script, have members of your group decide which of the roles they will play—the director, characters in the scene, members of the stage crew, and so on.

❺ Perform the Skit Performers should practice speaking clearly, making eye contact with the audience, and pacing the performance according to the dialogue of the script.

Other Works by O. HENRY

O. Henry is an acknowledged master of the surprise story ending. His stories remain popular today, however, not just for their plot twists, but because O. Henry was such a keen observer of ordinary human beings—rich and poor, winners and losers, con artists and cops. In his stories, O. Henry described in stark simplicity the tragedies, comedies, conflicts, and motives of ordinary men and women.

The Gift of the Magi

This story, O. Henry's most famous, tells the tale of a poor young husband and wife, each of whom sacrifices a treasured possession in order to buy a Christmas gift for the other. This beloved story has been dramatized for the stage and made into a movie and several television dramas.

The Ransom of Red Chief

Two dim-witted hoodlums carry out a kidnapping, planning to collect a large ransom from their victim's father. Hilariously, the boy they kidnap is so troublesome the two end up paying the boy's father to take his son off their hands.

One Thousand Dollars

A spendthrift nephew inherits a thousand dollars from a rich uncle. The inheritance is merely a small part of the uncle's great wealth, and it comes with a stipulation: the nephew must account for how he spends every cent of the inheritance. This story tells of the nephew's secret act of generosity.

You may find the three stories mentioned above, as well as many others, in various collections of the stories of O. Henry.

Writing Workshop | Personal Narrative

Describing an important experience . . .

From Reading to Writing Many people love to tell stories about their lives. That may be why life stories are the subject of much great writing. For example, in "Eleanor Roosevelt," William Jay Jacobs describes the life of the First Lady. In "Homeless" two women reveal their beliefs about what it means to have a home. Both of these selections describe events that taught people lessons about life. Writing a **personal narrative** is a chance to share your own point of view. It is one way to explore what your experience has taught you.

For Your Portfolio

WRITING PROMPT Write a narrative about something that actually happened to you.
Purpose: To describe your behavior in a particular setting
Audience: Your classmates, family members, and friends

Basics in a Box

Personal Narrative at a Glance

Middle
• Describes the incident using descriptive details and dialogue
• Makes the importance clear

Beginning
Introduces the incident including the people and place involved

End
• Tells the outcome or result of the event
• Presents the writer's feelings about the experience

RUBRIC **STANDARDS FOR WRITING**

A successful personal narrative should

• focus on one well-defined experience
• begin with an image or idea that makes readers want to find out more
• make the importance of the event clear
• show clearly the order in which events occurred

• use details that appeal to the senses to describe characters and setting
• use dialogue to develop characters
• provide a strong conclusion

Analyzing a Student Model

**Kristin Richardson
Whipple Middle School**

SPEAKING
See the Speaking and Listening Handbook, p. R100, for oral presentation tips.
OPPORTUNITY

A View from the Outside

"We're moving, but I'm not sure where," my father said one night at the dinner table. I sat there, staring at him. Then I dropped my fork.

"What did you say?" I managed.

"I'm taking a sabbatical."

"What's a sabbatical?" I looked at my mother.

She explained that this meant Dad would be taking a leave of absence from his job. It would last for one year. Then Dad said the family would be spending the year in Germany. Germany? I thought to myself. But what would happen to my spot on the volleyball team?

He explained that a friend of his from Marburg had invited us to spend a year there and live in his apartment. I had to really think twice about this. Since I had made such good friends last year, I did not want to leave. I also didn't want to leave because I would be starting the seventh grade. Still, I really did want to see Europe. How bad could it be? Little did I know there would be many more challenges than I had imagined.

Our trip started off badly. When we arrived in Germany, we were presented with a broken-down car, probably made in the early 1980s. It was so old that when we drove, exhaust would shoot out of the car! Next, the apartment we were to live in, which was very big and located in the center of the historic district, had electrical problems. Sometimes the lights would go out for no reason at all. But that was only the beginning.

I came to Germany not knowing a word of German. Because I was expected to go to a German school, I had to prepare myself before school started. I had a tutor for three months, and she came twice a week. But I only learned some of the basics, like "How are you?" and "Where is the bathroom?" I was unprepared on the first day of school. It seemed to last forever. No one spoke a word to me. In my old school I had been popular. Now I had to adjust to being on the outside of everything.

Eventually, one of my teachers introduced himself. His name was Herr Shauermann. He was the English teacher and was very nice to me. He brought me to meet my classmates. The kids in my grade were learning English, but they could hardly say much.

RUBRIC IN ACTION

1 Introduces essay with dialogue and specific narrative actions to capture readers' attention and develop characters' personalities

Other Option:
• Begin with a question to the reader.

2 The writer uses details to develop the main characters and set up the conflict.

3 Makes the order of events clear

4 Vivid details create a sense of a definite setting and help readers relate to the writer's feelings.

5 Stays focused on one experience: adjusting to school in Germany

That first week I stayed by myself during lunch. I tried hanging around with the other kids, hoping they would notice me. They never did. It made me think about kids who were outsiders at my old school. Did I ever invite them to play? Had I tried to include them or did I make them feel worse? Now I was in their shoes. Finally one day, I gathered my courage and walked up to some girls who were sitting on the steps, listening to music. I smiled at one of them. In broken English, she told me her name was Anja. She spoke English well enough because her father was American. She asked if I wanted to be shown around. We laughed and joked the whole day. We became the best of friends.

Though school continued to be challenging, everything else was marvelous. The town I lived in was very charming and had very pretty shops. On weekends and vacations, my family took trips to other nearby countries, and I enjoyed that a lot.

By the end of the year I had learned a little German. I was able to make my way around town by myself. But I rarely had to. Anja was with me often and together we shared many memories. Many days after school we'd sit in the park teaching each other our native languages. It was particularly fun trying to teach her English idioms like "It's raining cats and dogs" and "Play it by ear." Some things don't translate well into another language.

But friendship does.

Now I am home in the United States and am happy once again. Still, I haven't forgotten the lessons I learned in Germany. How could I? Anja and I keep our friendship alive by e-mailing almost every day. These days, when I see someone in school who looks as though he or she doesn't fit in, I go up and talk to that person because I know how it feels to be an outsider. I have even met some new friends this way. My experience in Germany taught me that everyone wants to fit in. Most people just need to be given a chance.

> **❻ Transitional words** help establish chronological order and contribute to plot development.

> **❼ Conclusion** explores the importance of the experience and tells the lessons that were learned from the point of view of the writer.
>
> **Other Option:**
> • End with a recommendation or suggestion to readers.

Writing Your Personal Narrative

❶ Prewriting

Stories sometimes begin with memory. . . .

—Gary Soto, fiction writer, essayist, and poet

Brainstorming is a good way to begin working on your essay. Think about the recent past. What happened last summer? What experiences in your life have taught you a lesson? To get ideas, you might look in a box of souvenirs, or make a time line of your life. See the **Idea Bank** in the margin for other ways to get started. After you select an incident, follow the steps below.

Planning Your Personal Narrative

1. **Freewrite about the incident.** Describe the emotions you felt. What sights, smells, and sounds do you remember? Who else was involved? What did they say? Recall gestures, movements, and expressions. Note when and where the events took place. If you can't remember every detail, try looking at family albums or talking to friends, family members, or neighbors.

2. **Describe the importance of the event.** Think about why the incident was significant in your life. Did you learn an important lesson? Are you different than you were before the incident?

3. **Make a time line.** List all the parts of the event in time order to help you develop the plot line of your narrative. Decide which parts to include and which parts are not necessary.

4. **Tell your story aloud.** Try telling the incident to friends or family members. Use chronological order for this exercise. Which parts of your story make your audience react? Which parts seem confusing to them?

❷ Drafting

Begin exploring your ideas by writing them down. Try writing as if you are telling the story aloud. At this stage, don't worry about missing information, the flow of your ideas, or spelling and grammar. Just figure out what you really think and go wherever your draft takes you. Use dialogue and plenty of descriptive details. Build in suspense if you can.

IDEA Bank

1. Your Working Portfolio
Look for ideas in the **Writing** sections that you completed earlier.

2. On Location
Use a web to brainstorm important places in your life, such as houses or apartments you've lived in, school or neighborhood playgrounds, etc. What important events have taken place there?

3. Good Neighbors
Talk to the neighbors who have known your family for a while and have seen you grow up. Ask them what they remember about your life. Write about one event that appeals to you.

Have a question?

See the **Writing Handbook**
Writing Tip, p. R45
Show, Don't Tell, p. R43
See **Language Network**
   Prewriting, p. 310
   Drafting, p. 315

Ask Your Peer Reader

- Did you understand the order of events?
- Which details made you feel a part of my experience?
- What parts confused you?
- How did you feel after reading the piece? Why?

Need revising help?

Review the **Rubric**, p. 178.

Consider **peer reader** comments.

Check **Revising, Editing, and Proofreading,** p. R35.

SPELLING From Writing

 As you revise your work, look back at the words you misspelled and determine why you made the errors you did. For additional help, refer to the strategies and generalizations in the **Spelling Handbook** on page R30.

SPEAKING Opportunity

Turn your narrative into an oral presentation.

Publishing IDEAS

- To go along with your personal narrative, create a collage of images that symbolically tells your story.
- Separate the personal narratives written by your classmates into categories such as humorous or challenging. Have your classmates record their narratives on audiotape and compare experiences that fall into the same category.

Publishing Options
www.mcdougallittell.com

❸ Revising

TARGET SKILL ▶ USING SENSORY DETAILS Sensory details help your reader hear, see, and feel the experience you are writing about. For example, instead of writing, "I ran quickly," Gary Paulsen wrote, *"I was just getting my stride, legs and arms pumping, pulling air with a heaving chest, when I rounded the corner and ran smack into the latest group of boys who were terrorizing me."*

When we arrived, we were ~~given an old~~ *presented with a broken-down* car, probably made in the early 1980s. It was so old that ~~it didn't drive very well.~~ *when we drove, exhaust would shoot out of the car!*

❹ Editing and Proofreading

TARGET SKILL ▶ PARALLELISM Keeping similar ideas parallel will help your writing flow more smoothly. Balance nouns with nouns, prepositional phrases with prepositional phrases, and so on.

When I was in seventh grade, I moved to Germany, started at a new school, and ~~was learning~~ *learned* German.

❺ Reflecting

FOR YOUR WORKING PORTFOLIO What was easiest about writing your narrative? What was hardest? What did you learn about the importance of the experience? Attach your reflections to your finished work. Save your personal narrative in your **Working Portfolio.**

Standardized Test Practice

Mixed Review

My performance ended with a roar of laughter, <u>witch</u> filled the
⁽¹⁾
auditorium. My face <u>turned red and, hot tears</u> formed in my eyes. I
⁽²⁾
looked for <u>someone to rescue me but</u> only open mouths greeted my
⁽³⁾
stare. Every person in the audience was laughing, waving playbills, <u>and</u>
⁽⁴⁾
<u>talked.</u> Not even my older brothers could stop <u>themselfes</u> from laughing.
⁽⁵⁾
However, <u>one single glimmer of hope lit up the darkness perhaps I could</u>
⁽⁶⁾
<u>turn my talents to comedy.</u>

Review Your Skills

Use the passage and the questions that follow it to check how well you remember the language conventions you've learned in previous grades.

1. What is the correct spelling in sentence 1?

   A. which

   B. whitch

   C. wich

   D. Correct as is

2. What is the correct punctuation in sentence 2?

   A. turned red, and, hot, tears

   B. turned red, and hot tears

   C. turned red; and hot tears

   D. Correct as is

3. What is the correct punctuation in sentence 3?

   A. someone to rescue me, but

   B. someone to rescue me but,

   C. someone to rescue me; but

   D. Correct as is

4. How is sentence 4 best written?

   A. and they talked

   B. and talking.

   C. and would talk.

   D. Correct as is

5. What is the correct spelling in sentence 5?

   A. themselfs

   B. themselves

   C. themselvs

   D. Correct as is

6. How is sentence 6 best written?

   A. one single glimmer of hope lit up the darkness, perhaps I could turn my talents to comedy.

   B. one single glimmer of hope lit up the darkness. Perhaps I could turn my talents to comedy.

   C. one single glimmer of hope lit up the darkness; Perhaps I could turn my talents to comedy.

   D. Correct as is

Self-Assessment

Check your own answers in the **Grammar Handbook**

Quick Reference: Capitalization, p. R70

Quick Reference: Punctuation, p. R68

Commas with Coordinating Conjunctions, p. R68

Run-on Sentences, p. R71

Key Standard
LC1.4 Use the mechanics of writing correctly; demonstrate correct language usage.
Other Standard **LC1.7**

Learning from Experience

Key Standard
R3.3 Analyze characters by examining what they think, say, and do, and by studying the words of the narrator and the reactions of other characters.
***Other Standards* R3.1, R3.2, R3.4, R3.5, R3.6**

In this unit, new experiences lead characters to make discoveries about themselves, about other people, and about the world around them. Often the lessons they learn make them stronger. Did you recognize yourself in any of the characters? What did you learn from the characters? Explore these questions by completing some of the options in each of the following sections.

Painting Copyright © 1999 Brad Holland

Reflecting on Theme

OPTION 1

Connecting Literature and Life The characters in this unit make many discoveries. Choose two of these discoveries that you think are especially important for young people to apply in their own lives. Explain your choices in a paragraph or two. Consider the parallels between the characters' situations and the situations of other young people.

OPTION 2

Creating Dialogue Select a character in Part 1 and a character in Part 2 who gain new insights from their experiences. With a partner, stage a dialogue between the characters, in which they comment on what they know about themselves and what they have learned.

OPTION 3

Discussing With a small group of classmates, discuss the different ways in which a person might learn that things are not as he or she believed them to be. Recall instances from your own experiences and from the selections. Think about the following factors:

friends	society	family
parents	human nature	the world

Self ASSESSMENT

READER'S NOTEBOOK

Make a before-and-after chart. In it, show how one or more of your ideas about experience and discovery developed as you read the selections in this unit.

REVIEWING YOUR PERSONAL
WORD LIST

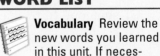
Vocabulary Review the new words you learned in this unit. If necessary, use a dictionary to check the meaning of each word.

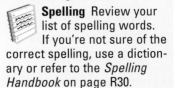
Spelling Review your list of spelling words. If you're not sure of the correct spelling, use a dictionary or refer to the *Spelling Handbook* on page R30.

Reviewing Literary Concepts

OPTION 1

Comparing Characters A character may be classified as main or minor, depending on his or her importance to the plot of a story. Make a chart in which you list and classify the characters in the selections you have read. After you complete your chart, circle the name of the main character who you think changes the most. Explain your reasons for choosing that character.

Selection	Name of Character	Main or Minor?	Description of Change (If Dynamic)
"A Crush"	Ernie	Main	Overcomes his fear of getting involved

OPTION 2

Exploring Plot A plot is the sequence of events in a story. During the rising action, the conflicts in the story build in intensity until a climax, or turning point, is reached. The climax may involve an important revelation. The falling action follows the climax. In this part of the plot, the conflicts are often resolved. With a partner, choose three stories from this unit and identify the major events that advance the plot. Discuss whether the stories could have turned out differently.

Portfolio Building

- **Choices and Challenges—Writing** Several of the writing assignments in this unit asked you to expand upon situations in stories. Choose the response that you feel best captures the spirit of the story that it is based on. Write a note explaining the reasons for your choice. Place it in your **Presentation Portfolio.**

- **Writing Workshops** In this unit you wrote a personal response and about an autobiographical incident. Which do you think does a better job of communicating your personal perspective? Explain your choice on a cover page and place it in your **Presentation Portfolio.**

- **Additional Activities** Think about the assignments you completed for **Speaking & Listening** and **Research & Technology.** Keep a record in your portfolio of any assignments that you especially enjoyed, found helpful, or would like to explore further.

Self ASSESSMENT

READER'S NOTEBOOK

On a sheet of paper, copy the following literary terms introduced in this unit. Next to each term, jot down a brief definition. If you have trouble explaining a particular concept, refer to the **Glossary of Literary and Reading Terms** on p. R120.

setting	main characters
theme	autobiography
climax	external conflict
biography	point of view
essay	personification
internal conflict	surprise ending
personal essay	rising action
character	falling action
minor characters	

Self ASSESSMENT

At this point, you may just be beginning your **Presentation Portfolio.** Think about the pieces that you have selected to include in your portfolio. Do you think that you will keep these pieces as the year goes on?

Setting GOALS

Look back through your **READER'S NOTEBOOK.** What kinds of writing would you like to become more skilled at? What kinds of writing would you like to try for the first time?

LITERATURE CONNECTIONS
Taking Sides

By Gary Soto

Lincoln Mendoza is a Mexican-American youth struggling to find himself. He has recently moved from the inner city to the suburbs. As Lincoln tries to adjust, he fears that he may lose an important part of himself—the barrio and its Mexican culture. His skills at basketball make him the star of his new school's team. As his new school plays his old one, Lincoln must decide where his loyalties lie.

These thematically related readings are provided along with *Taking Sides*:

Endless Search
By Alonso Lopez

from **Barrio Boy**
By Ernesto Galarza

In the Inner City
By Lucille Clifton

I Yearn
By Ricardo Sanchez

Two Worlds
By Jim Yoshida, with Bill Hosokawa

Granny Ed and the Lewisville Raiders
By Rae Rainey

A Game of Catch
By Richard Wilbur

More Choices

Children of the Wild West
By Russell Freedman
Documentary photographs show what life on the frontier was really like for pioneer children.

Rikki-Tikki-Tavi
By Rudyard Kipling
Rikki-Tikki-Tavi is a mongoose living with an English family in the Indian jungle. He faces dangerous cobras who are trying to kill both him and his human family.

The Jungle Book
By Rudyard Kipling
In this classic collection of tales, Mowgli, a boy raised by wolves, has many adventures while discovering more about himself.

The Summer of the Swans
By Betsy C. Byars
When fourteen-year-old Sara's retarded younger brother Charlie gets lost, she discovers something important about herself as she searches for him.

Permanent Connections
By Sue Ellen Bridgers
When seventeen-year-old Rob goes to live with relatives in a small town in North Carolina, he begins to feel new bonds with family and friends.

Red Badge of Courage
By Stephen Crane
In this Civil War story, a young soldier must decide for himself what true courage is.

The True Confessions of Charlotte Doyle

BY AVI

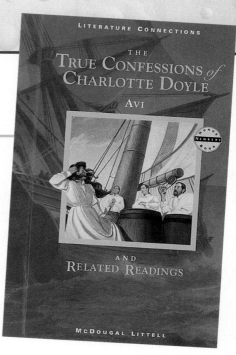

It is 1832. Thirteen-year-old Charlotte Doyle is booked on the Seahawk for a trans-Atlantic voyage, to join her family in America. From the beginning, things go wrong. During the dramatic two-month voyage, she learns more than she dreamed possible about seafaring, about command, and about herself.

These thematically related readings are provided along with *The True Confessions of Charlotte Doyle*:

Mary Patten *from* Seafaring Women
BY LINDA GRANT DE PAUW

***from* Two Years Before the Mast**
BY RICHARD HENRY DANA

Walking the Trestle
BY JAY PARINI

The Princess and the Admiral
BY CHARLOTTE POMERANTZ

This Morning There Were Rainbows in the Sprinklers
BY LORNA DEE CERVANTES

Social Studies Connection

The Christians as the Romans Saw Them
BY ROBERT WILKIN
The author describes the lives of several famous Greek and Roman philosophers while explaining their views of early Christianity.

The Rotten Romans
BY TERRY DEARY
A collection of trivia regarding daily life in ancient Rome.

The Fall of the Roman Empire
BY DON NARDO
Many causes led to the fall of the Roman Empire. This book includes lively discussions of the people, the conflicts, and the economic issues.

Discovering Our Past
BY PETER SEYMOUR
The author uses pop-up and movable illustrations to explain how archaeologists use the clues they discover to find out about past civilizations.

"The People of Rome" in Rome: Its People, Life and Customs
BY ENRICO PAOLI UGO
A realistic description of the city of Rome, with all its noise, confusion, and crowds during the decline of the Roman Empire.

Medieval People
BY SARAH HOWARTH
An overview of the culture and geography of medieval Europe.

Relationships

"The easiest kind
of relationship
is with ten
thousand people;
the hardest is
with one."

Joan Baez
American Folksinger

Illustration by
Bernie Fuchs

The Literature You'll Read

The Concepts You'll Study

Vocabulary and Reading Comprehension
Vocabulary Focus: Root Words and Word Families
Read Aloud
Making Inferences
Drawing Conclusions
Main Idea and Details

Writing and Language Conventions
Writing Workshop: Interpretive Essay
Choosing the Right Verb
Abstract and Concrete Nouns

Literary Analysis
Genre Focus: Poetry
Rhyme
Speaker
Dynamic and Static Characters
Informative Nonfiction

Speaking and Listening
Poetry Reading
Evaluation of a Speech
Characterization Sketch
Conduct an Interview

LEARNING the Language of *Literature*

*P*oetry

Key Standard
R1.1 Identify idioms, analogies, metaphors, and similes in prose and poetry.
Other Standard R3.1

> *A man doesn't go in search of a poem—
> the poem must come to him.*
> —Yang Wan-Li, "Written on a Cold Evening"

Like other forms of fiction, poems can be written about anything. A poem packs all kinds of ideas, feelings, and sounds into a few carefully chosen words. Poetry is compact, imaginative, and rhythmic. Learning the key elements of poetry can unlock some of its mystery, and help interpret the meaning of different types of poems.

Key Elements of Poetry
- form
- speaker
- sound
- imagery
- figurative language

Form

The way a poem looks on the page is called its **form.** Poems are written in **lines,** which may or may not be complete sentences. In some forms of poetry, lines are grouped into **stanzas.** If lines in a stanza have a regular, repeated pattern, the poem has a **structured form.** Poems that have no regular pattern are called **free verse** poems.

YOUR TURN What are the main differences between these two poems? Which is structured, and which is free verse?

Speaker

The **speaker** of a poem is the **voice** that relates the story or ideas of the poem. The speaker may be the poet, speaking directly to the reader, or the speaker may be a character or voice created by the poet.

The voice may include the use of **dialect,** a form of language spoken in a certain place by a certain group of people. The poet may also use idioms to make the speaker's voice more realistic. An **idiom** is a descriptive expression that means something different than the combination of the words that make it up. For example, *hold on a minute* means *be patient.* It isn't a request for someone to physically hold something, such as a minute, in one's hands. Idioms are used in all forms of literature.

If I Can Stop One Heart from Breaking
by Emily Dickinson

If I can stop one Heart from breaking
I shall not live in vain
If I can ease one Life the Aching
Or cool one Pain

Or help one fainting Robin
Unto his Nest again
I shall not live in Vain.

The Rider
by Naomi Shihab Nye

A boy told me
if he rollerskated fast enough
his loneliness couldn't catch up
to him,

the best reason I ever heard
for trying to be a champion.

What I wonder tonight
pedaling hard down King William Street
is if it translates to bicycles.

A victory! To leave your loneliness
panting behind you on some
street corner
while you float free into a cloud
of sudden azaleas,
luminous pink petals that have
never felt loneliness,
no matter how slowly they fell.

Sound

Because most poems are meant to be read aloud, poets choose and arrange words to create **sounds** that appeal to the listener. Four techniques that poets use to create sound are **rhyme, rhythm, repetition,** and **onomatopoeia.**

- **Rhyme** is the repetition of similar sounds at the ends of words, for example, *place* and *face*. Many poems with a structured form contain rhyming words at the end of lines, such as in "Casey at the Bat." Free verse poems do not usually contain rhymes.

- **Rhythm** is the pattern of stressed and unstressed syllables in each line. Stressed syllables (´) are read with more emphasis, and unstressed syllables (˘) are read with less emphasis. Some poems have a regular, repeated arrangement of stressed and unstressed syllables. This is called **meter.**

- **Repetition** of sounds, words, phrases, or whole lines is a device poets use to emphasize an idea or create a certain feeling. **Alliteration** is the repetition of consonant sounds at the beginning of words, such as the "w" in the line "And wait to watch the water clear, I may."

- **Onomatopoeia** is the use of words whose sounds suggest their meanings, such as *crack, boom,* and *bang.*

RHYME

To dream of vast horizons of the soul
through dreams made whole,
Unfettered free—help me!

—Langston Hughes, "To You"

RHYTHM

Thĕre wăs éase ĭn Cásĕy's mánnĕr ăs hĕ
stépped ĭntŏ hĭs pláce,
Thĕre wăs príde ĭn Cásĕy's béarĭng ănd ă
smíle ŏn Cásĕy's fáce;
Ănd whĕn rĕspóndĭng tŏ thĕ chéers, hĕ
líghtlў dóffĕd hĭs hát,
Nŏ strángĕr ĭn thĕ crówd cŏuld dóubt
'twăs Cásĕy ăt thĕ bát.

—Ernest Lawrence Thayer,
"Casey at the Bat"

YOUR TURN Write a list of the rhyming words in these excerpts from "To You" and "Casey at the Bat." Where are they placed in the lines?

Imagery and Figurative Language

Imagery is language that appeals to the reader's five senses—sight, hearing, smell, taste, and touch. Writers often use imagery to draw readers into a scene. Think about the phrases "blistering sands" and "feather clouds." Do the images remind you of places you've been or experiences you've had?

Writers may use **figurative language** when they choose words and phrases that help readers picture ordinary things in new ways. There are three main types of figurative language.

- A **simile** is a comparison that uses the signal word *like* or *as.* An example is "her eyes shone like stars."

- A **metaphor** is a direct comparison, with no signal words. "Into the sea of death" is a metaphor that compares death to a sea.

- An **analogy** is a comparison between two things that seem dissimilar, in order to show the ways in which they might be similar.

- When a poet describes an animal or object as if it were human or had human qualities, that is called **personification.** "The warm smile of the sun" is one example of personification.

YOUR TURN What metaphor is used to describe what the moose in the poem looks like? How does that comparison help you "see" the moose?

FIGURATIVE LANGUAGE

The goofy Moose, the walking house-frame,
Is lost
In the forest. He bumps, he blunders,
he stands.

—Ted Hughes, "Mooses"

From "A Time to Talk"

The Active Reader: Skills and Strategies

Reading Poetry

Reading poetry can move us from laughter to tears. Why? Because many poems are written to express emotion. To understand the effect of a poem, pay attention to the elements of **form, sound, imagery, figurative language,** and **speaker.** To get the most from every poem, follow the reading strategies listed below.

How to Apply the Strategies

Preview the poem and read it aloud a few times. Notice the poem's form—what shape it has on the page, how long it is, how long the lines are, and whether or not it has stanzas. Look for end punctuation to help you find where each thought ends. As you read, listen for rhymes and rhythm and for the overall sound of the words.

Visualize the images. Create a mental picture of the images and comparisons you find in the poem. Do the images give you clues about the deeper meaning or message of the poem?

Clarify the words and phrases. Allow yourself to wonder about any phrases or words that seem to stand out. Think about what the choice of those words adds to the poem. Also think about the poem's speaker. What is his or her particular view of life? Look for clues that will help you make **inferences,** logical conclusions based on evidence about the speaker's experiences, attitudes, and perspectives.

Evaluate the poem's theme. Ask, what's the point of this poem? What message is the poet trying to send or help me to understand?

Let your understanding grow. Think about what the poem is saying to you. Does it relate to anything in your own life? Does it give you a new way of looking at something? Over time, your rereading of the poem, your discussions in class, and the other poetry you read will add to your understanding.

Here's how Elvia uses the strategies:

*"With some poems, you really know what the poet means. I like to read a poem aloud first, listening to how it sounds. I **visualize** the images. It's interesting to think about the speaker of the poem and look for details that help interpret his or her unique way of looking at life."*

The Pasture
by ROBERT FROST

A Time to Talk
by ROBERT FROST

Connect to Your Life

Slow Down! Setting aside time for people who are important to you is essential to a healthy and happy life. Think of ways people benefit when they interrupt their busy lives to share time with friends, family, and neighbors. Create a word web and share your ideas with your classmates.

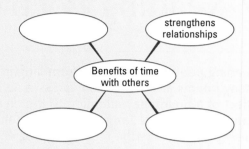

Build Background

GEOGRAPHY

By the 1600s, when the first European immigrants arrived, New England was covered with thick forests. The immigrants established communities and turned this sometimes harsh environment into farmland.

Many of Robert Frost's poems are set on the rugged farms of New England, where he spent much of his adult life. His poems give the reader a vivid sense of the landscape with its rough-hewn character, changing seasons, farm animals, trees, and stone walls.

Key Standard
LS1.6 Use voice, gestures, and eye contact effectively to keep audience interested.
Other Standards **R2.2, R3.1, W2.2**

Focus Your Reading

LITERARY ANALYSIS **RHYME**

Rhyme is a repetition of identical or similar sounds. The most common form is **end rhyme,** where the rhymes occur at the ends of lines. Notice the end rhymes in "The Pasture":

> *I'm going out to clean the pasture spring;*
> *I'll only stop to rake the leaves away*
> *(And wait to watch the water clear, I may):*
> *I shan't be gone long. —You come too.*

ACTIVE READING **READ ALOUD**

Reading a poem aloud helps you enjoy the sound and understand the meaning. Try following these steps:

- Read the poem to yourself to get a sense of the meaning.
- Try to picture the images or scenes that the poet creates.
- Try to imagine how the voice of the speaker might sound.

READER'S NOTEBOOK Copy "The Pasture." Circle the punctuation that indicates where you should pause, draw an arrow at the end of lines where you should not pause, and draw a wavy line under words you want to emphasize.

> I'm going out to clean the pasture spring;
>
> I'll only stop to rake the leaves away
>
> (And wait to watch the water clear, I may):
>
> I shan't be gone long. You come too.

Silverstrim's Farm (1989),
David Bareford. Quester Gallery,
Stonington, Connecticut.

The Pasture

by Robert Frost

I'm going out to clean the pasture spring;
I'll only stop to rake the leaves away
(And wait to watch the water clear, I may):
I shan't be gone long.—You come too.

5   I'm going out to fetch the little calf
That's standing by the mother. It's so young
It totters when she licks it with her tongue.
I shan't be gone long.—You come too.

THINKING *through the* LITERATURE

1. Would you like to share the speaker's experiences? Why or why not?

2. Why might the speaker want a companion?

    Think About:
    • what a companion might add to the experience
    • the tasks the speaker describes

3. How would you describe the speaker's attitude toward nature?

A Time to Talk

by Robert Frost

Galena (1988), Robert L. Barnum.
Watercolor, private collection.

When a friend calls to me from the road
And slows his horse to a meaning walk,
I don't stand still and look around
On all the hills I haven't hoed,
5   And shout from where I am, "What is it?"
No, not as there is a time to talk.
I thrust my hoe in the mellow ground,
Blade-end up and five feet tall,
And plod: I go up to the stone wall
10   For a friendly visit.

Connect to the Literature

1. **What Do You Think?** What do you think about the speaker of "A Time to Talk"? What do you imagine he is like?

Comprehension Check
- What does the speaker mean by the phrase, "And slows his horse to a meaning walk"?
- According to the speaker, is it more important to get work done or to visit with a friend?

Think Critically

2. Why do you think the speaker in "A Time to Talk" chooses to stop and talk rather than to keep working?

   Think About:
   - the solitary nature of farm work
   - how a farmer decides when his work must be finished

3. What phrases or words in each poem provide you with images of life in the country?

4. How are the speakers of the two poems alike, and how are they different? How does each speaker "let others in"?

5. **ACTIVE READING** **READ ALOUD**
   Copy and mark up "A Time to Talk" in your
   READER'S NOTEBOOK as you did with "The Pasture." Then read both poems aloud to a small group. As you read, vary the modulation—the tone and intensity of your voice—as well as making regular eye contact. By using these speaking techniques, you will help the audience understand the meaning of these poems.

Extend Interpretations

6. **The Writer's Style** In both poems, Frost uses everyday language to write about ordinary experiences. What effect does this have as you read?

7. **Connect to Life** What advice might the speaker of these poems have for people living in today's fast-paced world?

Literary Analysis

RHYME **Rhyme** is a repetition of sounds at the end of words. Words rhyme when their accented vowels and all the letters that follow have identical sounds. For example, in "A Time to Talk," *road* and *hoed* rhyme, as do *walk* and *talk*. There are several other pairs of words that rhyme in this poem as well. Notice that the kind of rhyme in this poem is **end rhyme,** or rhyming that occurs at the end of lines. This end rhyme forms a pattern, or **rhyme scheme,** which can be charted.

Paired Activity Working with a partner, chart the rhyme schemes of "The Pasture" and "A Time to Talk." You can chart the pattern of the rhyme by assigning a letter of the alphabet to each line. Begin with the letter *a,* then *b,* and so forth. Lines that rhyme are given the same letter. The first four lines of "The Pasture" are done for you.

"The Pasture"		"A Time to Talk"
spring	a	
away	b	
may	b	
too	c	

Writing

Response to Literature Do a second careful reading of "The Pasture" and "A Time to Talk." What do you think is the message or moral of each of these poems? What is the speaker emphasizing as important in each? In two paragraphs or more, write your interpretation of each poem. Save your draft in your **Working Portfolio**.

Writing Workshop
See p. 238: Basics in a Box.

Speaking & Listening

Poetry Reading Read more of Robert Frost's poetry. With a small group of classmates, choose poems you think would make good oral interpretations. Present a reading of these poems to the whole class. Practice good voice inflection and eye contact for an effective presentation.

Research & Technology

The Vacation of a Lifetime! Frost is often called a regional writer because his poems focus on the landscape and people of New England, especially New Hampshire. Use the Internet to find out more about the region and the interesting places to visit in New England.

Research and Technology Handbook
See p. R110: Getting Information Electronically.

Robert Frost
1874–1963

"Something there is that doesn't love a wall, and wants it down."

A Late Start The man who became one of America's most popular poets did not publish a book of poetry until he was 39 years old. By the end of Frost's life, his name had become known to most Americans.

A New Hampshire Farmer Frost spent his early years in San Francisco. At 11, he and his widowed mother moved East, where he attended Dartmouth College and Harvard University, married and raised a family, and began to write poetry.

An American Literary Hero Frost moved his family to England for a period, but ties to his native land eventually brought him back to New Hampshire. Frost won the Pulitzer Prize for poetry four times. Congress voted him a gold medal "in recognition of his poetry, which has enriched the culture of the United States and the philosophy of the world." In 1961 he recited one of his poems at the inauguration of President John F. Kennedy.

AUTHOR ACTIVITY
Poet for a Nation The poem Robert Frost recited at President Kennedy's inauguration was "The Gift Outright." Find a copy of this poem and read it. Then, with your classmates, discuss the reasons why Frost might have chosen this poem to read at the inauguration.

The World Is Not a Pleasant Place to Be

by NIKKI GIOVANNI

To You

by LANGSTON HUGHES

Standards R3.1, W1.4

Connect to Your Life

Care to Join Me? Think about times when you like to be alone, as well as times when you like to be with friends or family members. Write down three examples of each. Discuss them with a partner.

Things I Like to Do Alone	Things I Like to Do with Others
1.	1.
2.	2.
3.	3.

Build Background

African-American Voices
Langston Hughes was a leading figure of the Harlem Renaissance, the period during the 1920s when many gifted African-American artists came to New York City. In his poetry Hughes celebrated ordinary people and their everyday struggles.

Nikki Giovanni began writing in the 1960s, a time of great social upheaval. Giovanni's somewhat bitter poems attracted wide audiences. In later years her poetry became more gentle. "The World Is Not a Pleasant Place to Be" comes from a book of poems entitled *My House*.

Focus Your Reading

LITERARY ANALYSIS SPEAKER

In a poem, the **speaker** is the voice that "talks" to the reader. A speaker may be a distant observer, or he or she may play a key role in the poem. The poet may have created the speaker with a distinct identity in order to achieve a particular effect. As you read these two poems, pay attention to the emotions and thoughts that the speakers express.

ACTIVE READING MAKING INFERENCES

An **inference** is a logical guess you make based on evidence or your own knowledge. Making inferences is important when you read poetry. Because a poem usually does not tell a story directly, you must learn to "read between the lines" to decide who the speaker is and why he or she feels a certain way.

READER'S NOTEBOOK As you read "The World Is Not a Pleasant Place to Be" and "To You," try to **infer** what the speakers are like on the basis of what they say. In a chart like the one shown here, record the inferences you make about the speakers.

"The World Is Not ..." | "To You"
• The speaker seems to be lonely.

The World Is Not a Pleasant Place to Be

by Nikki Giovanni

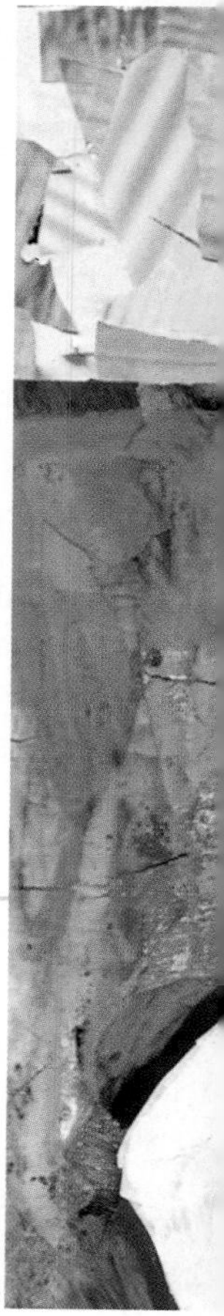

the world is not a pleasant place
to be without
someone to hold and be held by

a river would stop
5   its flow if only
a stream were there
to receive it

an ocean would never laugh
if clouds weren't there
10   to kiss her tears

the world is not
a pleasant place to be without
someone

THINKING *through the* LITERATURE

1. How would you describe the feelings that the speaker expresses in the first stanza?
2. How do the examples from nature help you understand the speaker's feelings?
3. Why do you think the poet chose the word *pleasant* instead of another word?

Illustration by Christopher Myers, from *Harlem: A Poem* by Walter Dean Myers. Published by Scholastic Press, a division of Scholastic Inc. Illustration copyright © 1997 by Christopher Myers. Reprinted by permission.

To You

by Langston Hughes

To sit and dream, to sit and read,
To sit and learn about the world
Outside our world of here and now—
    our problem world—
5 To dream of vast horizons of the soul
Through dreams made whole,
Unfettered free—help me!
All you who are dreamers, too,
Help me to make our world anew.
10 I reach out my dreams to you.

Connect to the Literature

1. What Do You Think? How do you feel about the speaker of "To You"?

Comprehension Check
- What does the speaker say about dreaming?
- What help does the speaker want from the reader?

Think Critically

2. What does the speaker mean by "our problem world"? Infer the meaning from the lines just before and after that line.

3. Why is dreaming important to the speaker?

> **Think About:**
> - the phrase "vast horizons of the soul"
> - the help that the speaker wants from other dreamers
> - the last line

4. | ACTIVE READING | MAKING INFERENCES |
Review the **inferences** you recorded in your ▥ READER'S NOTEBOOK. What did you infer about each speaker? What details or images helped you to make your inferences?

Extend Interpretations

5. Critic's Corner Robert Frost once said that a poem should "begin in delight and end in wisdom" (page 199). In your opinion, do these poems do that? How would you describe the ways that they begin and end?

6. Connect to Life In "To You," the speaker asks dreamers for help. Do you think dreams are useful, or are they a waste of time? Explain your opinion.

Literary Analysis

SPEAKER A poem's **speaker** is the voice that "talks" to the reader. Some speakers show little or no emotion and seem detached from what they describe. Others express strong feelings about the ideas and experiences they present. Read these lines from "To You" aloud:

> *All you who are dreamers, too,*
> *Help me to make our world*
> *anew.*

Is there emotion in this speaker's voice? What kind? How would you describe it?

Group Activity Get together with a small group of classmates and choose one of the two poems. Compare your ▥ READER'S NOTEBOOK inferences about the speaker of that poem. Make a chart that includes the inferences of all the group members. Then, with a group that chose the other poem, discuss the similarities and differences between the two speakers.

FREE VERSE Poetry with no regular pattern of rhyme, rhythm, or line length is called **free verse.** Free verse often sounds like conversation. Read "The World Is Not a Pleasant Place to Be" aloud as naturally as you can. Do you think free verse is a good way of presenting the ideas in the poem? Explain.

CHOICES and CHALLENGES

Writing

Personal Poem Try your hand at writing a poem about a thought or feeling you have had. The poem can be based on something that frustrates you or something you are grateful for. It could be funny or surprising. Share your finished poem with classmates, then save it in your **Working Portfolio.**

Writing Handbook
See p. R34: Prewriting.

Speaking & Listening

Listening Strategies Find a recording of the "I Have a Dream" speech by Dr. Martin Luther King, Jr. Play the recording and listen for the following speaking techniques:

- rhythm and repetition
- tempo, inflection, modulation (tone and intensity)
- enunciation of words

Make notes as you listen. Then, evaluate the speech. Determine:

- the speaker's attitude toward the subject
- the persuasiveness of his message
- overall impact on the listener

Write down your findings and share them with a small group. Compare your answers.

Research & Technology

Times of Change Both Langston Hughes and Nikki Giovanni wrote during times of change for African Americans. Do some research about the Harlem Renaissance of the 1920s or about the Black Power movement of the 1960s. Some questions to consider while researching are, What ideas came out of these movements? What aspect of your findings do you want to know more about? Develop questions that could lead to further investigation.

INTERNET Research Starter
www.mcdougallittell.com

Nikki Giovanni
born 1943

"I write out of my own experiences."

Childhood Nikki Giovanni was born Yolande Cornelia Giovanni, Jr., in Knoxville, Tennessee. She spent her early years with her parents and sister in Cincinnati, Ohio. At 14, she went to live with her grandparents in Tennessee.

Early Success Giovanni graduated with honors from Fisk University and soon achieved national recognition for her poetry. An album of her readings, *Truth Is on Its Way*, was produced when she was 28 years old. It brought her huge popular success. She is the author of some 15 books of poetry and holds 14 honorary degrees. In addition to teaching, she lectures and reads her poetry all over the United States.

Poetry from Experience Many of Giovanni's poems reflect her childhood and her experience as an African-American woman. "I write," she says, "out of my own experiences—which also happen to be the experiences of my people. Human beings fascinate me. I just keep trying to dissect them poetically to see what's there."

Langston Hughes

See the biography on page 36.

What Do Fish Have to Do with Anything?

by AVI

Connect to Your Life

Important Lessons Have you ever had an experience in which someone unexpected taught you an important lesson about life? Perhaps it was a person you knew well, like a sister. Perhaps it was someone you had never seen before. What was the lesson that you learned? Share your experience with a classmate.

Key Standard
R3.3 Analyze characters by examining what they think, say, and do, and by studying the words of the narrator and the reactions of other characters.
Other Standards **R1.3, W1.7, W2.2, LC1.3, LS1.6**

Build Background

CURRENT EVENTS

In recent years, a growing number of children in the United States have had to take care of themselves while their parents were away at work.

While parents try to prepare their children to be responsible and to know what to do in case of emergency, for many children being on their own brings loneliness and worry. In the following story Willie must stay home by himself while his mother works. As you read, think about how this might contribute to the overall story.

WORDS TO KNOW **Vocabulary Preview**
contemplated   interval   urgency
intently   nuisance

Focus Your Reading

LITERARY ANALYSIS **DYNAMIC AND STATIC CHARACTERS**

Static characters are relatively simple characters who do not change throughout a story. **Dynamic characters** are more complex characters who undergo change as the result of events in a story's plot. Both main and minor characters can be dynamic or static.

ACTIVE READING **DRAWING CONCLUSIONS**

To understand a story, you need to **draw conclusions** about the **characters** based on information in the story and what you know from your own experience. What characters do, say, think, and what others say and think about them is called **characterization.** You get to know characters in a story through characterization.

READER'S NOTEBOOK
As you read this story, choose a character and jot down the way in which he or she is characterized. Then write conclusions you can draw from the details.

Mrs. Markham	
Characterization	Conclusion
She gives Willie a glass of milk, a piece of cake she measures with her thumb, and a folded napkin every day.	She likes order and routine.
She cuts off Willie's questions about his father.	Willie's father is a painful subject for her.

What Do Fish Have to Do with Anything?

by Avi

E very day at three o'clock Mrs. Markham waited for her son, Willie, to come out of school. They walked home together. If asked why she did it, Mrs. Markham would say, "Parents need to watch their children."

As they left the schoolyard, Mrs. Markham inevitably asked, "How was school?"

Willie would begin to talk, then stop. He was never sure his mother was listening. She seemed preoccupied with her own thoughts. She had been like that ever since his dad had abandoned them six months ago. No one knew where he'd gone. Willie had the feeling that his mother was lost too. It made him feel lonely.

One Monday afternoon, as they approached the apartment building where they lived, she suddenly tugged at him. "Don't look that way," she said.

"Where?"

"At that man over there."

Willie stole a look over his shoulder. A man, whom Willie had never seen before, was sitting on a red plastic milk crate near

Aquarium Green/Red (Two Small Scenes . . .) (1921), Paul Klee. Norton Simon Museum, Pasadena, CA, The Blue Four Galka Scheyer Collection, 1953.

the curb. His matted, streaky gray hair hung like a ragged curtain over his dirty face. His shoes were torn. Rough hands lay upon his knees. One hand was palm up. No one seemed to pay him any mind. Willie was certain he had never seen a man so utterly alone. It was as if he were some spat-out piece of chewing gum on the pavement.

"What's the matter with him?" Willie asked his mother in a hushed voice.

> ## Is unhappiness a sickness you can cure?

Keeping her eyes straight ahead, Mrs. Markham said, "He's sick." She pulled Willie around. "Don't stare. It's rude."

"What kind of sick?"

As Mrs. Markham searched for an answer, she began to walk faster. "He's unhappy," she said.

"What's he doing?"

"Come on, Willie, you know perfectly well. He's begging."

"Do you think anyone gave him anything?"

"I don't know. Now, come on, don't look."

"Why don't you give him anything?"

"We have nothing to spare."

When they got home, Mrs. Markham removed a white cardboard box from the refrigerator. It contained pound cake. Using her thumb as a measure, she carefully cut a half-inch piece of cake and gave it to Willie on a clean plate. The plate lay on a plastic mat decorated with images of roses with diamondlike dewdrops. She also gave him a glass of milk and a folded napkin. She moved slowly.

Willie said, "Can I have a bigger piece of cake?"

Mrs. Markham picked up the cake box and ran a manicured pink fingernail along the nutrition information panel. "A half-inch piece is a portion, and a portion contains the following health requirements. Do you want to hear them?"

"No."

"It's on the box, so you can believe what it says. Scientists study people, then write these things. If you're smart enough you could become a scientist. Like this." Mrs. Markham tapped the box. "It pays well." Willie ate his cake and drank the milk. When he was done he took care to wipe the crumbs off his face as well as to blot his milk mustache with the napkin. His mother liked him to be neat.

His mother said, "Now go on and do your homework. Carefully. You're in sixth grade. It's important."

Willie gathered up his books that lay on the empty third chair. At the kitchen entrance he paused and looked back at his mother. She was staring sadly at the cake box, but he didn't think she was seeing it. Her unhappiness made him think of the man on the street.

"What *kind* of unhappiness do you think he has?" he suddenly asked.

"Who's that?"

"That man."

Mrs. Markham looked puzzled.

"The begging man. The one on the street."

"Oh, could be anything," his mother said, vaguely. "A person can be unhappy for many reasons." She turned to stare out the window, as if an answer might be there.

"Is unhappiness a sickness you can cure?"

"I wish you wouldn't ask such questions."

"Why?"

After a moment she said, "Questions that have no answers shouldn't be asked."

"Can I go out?"

"Homework first."

Ada & Vincent (1967), Alex Katz. Oil on canvas, 94 1/2" x 71 1/2", © Alex Katz/ Licensed by VAGA, New York, NY/ Marlborough Gallery, NY.

Willie turned to go again.

"Money," Mrs. Markham suddenly said. "Money will cure a lot of unhappiness. That's why that man was begging. A salesman once said to me, 'Maybe you can't buy happiness, but you can rent a lot of it.' You should remember that."

"How much money do we have?"

"Not enough."

"Is that why you're unhappy?"

"Willie, do your homework."

Willie started to ask another question, but decided he would not get an answer. He left the kitchen.

The apartment had three rooms. The walls were painted mint green. Willie walked down the hallway to his room, which was at the front of the building. By climbing up on the windowsill and pressing against the glass he could see the sidewalk five stories below. The man was still there.

It was almost five when he went to tell his mother he had finished his school assignments. He found her in her dim bedroom, sleeping. Since she had begun working the night shift at a convenience store—two weeks now—she took naps in the late afternoon.

For a while Willie stood on the threshold,[1] hoping his mother would wake up. When she didn't, he went to the front room and looked down on the street again. The begging man had not moved.

Willie returned to his mother's room.

"I'm going out," he announced—softly.

Willie waited a decent <u>interval</u> for his mother to waken. When she did not, he made sure his keys were in his pocket. Then he left the apartment.

By standing just outside the building door, he could keep his eyes on the man. It appeared as if he had still not moved. Willie wondered how anyone could go without moving for so long in the chill October air. Was staying still part of the man's sickness?

During the twenty minutes that Willie watched, no one who passed looked in the beggar's direction. Willie wondered if they even saw the man. Certainly no one put any money into his open hand.

A lady leading a dog by a leash went by. The dog strained in the direction of the man sitting on the crate. His tail wagged. The lady pulled the dog away. "Heel!" she commanded.

The dog—tail between his legs—scampered to the lady's side. Even so, the dog twisted around to look back at the beggar.

Willie grinned. The dog had done exactly what Willie had done when his mother told him not to stare.

Pressing deep into his pocket, Willie found a nickel. It was warm and slippery. He wondered how much happiness you could rent for a nickel.

Squeezing the nickel between his fingers, Willie walked slowly toward the man. When he came before him, he stopped, suddenly nervous. The man, who appeared to be looking at the ground, did not move his eyes. He smelled bad.

"Here." Willie stretched forward and dropped the coin into the man's open right hand.

"God bless you," the man said hoarsely as he folded his fingers over the coin. His eyes, like high beams on a car, flashed up at Willie, then dropped.

Willie waited for a moment, then went back up to his room. From his window he looked down on the street. He thought he saw the coin in the man's hand, but was not sure.

---

1. **threshold:** a doorway or entrance.

After supper Mrs. Markham readied herself to go to work, then kissed Willie good night. As she did every night, she said, "If you have regular problems, call Mrs. Murphy downstairs. What's her number?"

"274-8676," Willie said.

"Extra bad problems, call Grandma."

"369-6754."

"Super special problems, you can call me."

"962-6743."

"Emergency, the police."

"911."

"Lay out your morning clothing."

"I will."

"Don't let anyone in the door."

"I won't."

"No television past nine."

"I know."

"But you can read late."

"You're the one who's going to be late," Willie reminded her.

"I'm leaving," Mrs. Markham said.

After she went, Willie stood for a long while in the hallway. The empty apartment felt like a cave that lay deep below the earth. That day in school Willie's teacher had told the class about a kind of fish that lived in caves. These fish could not see. They had no eyes. The teacher had said it was living in the dark cave that made them like that.

Willie had raised his hand and asked, "If they want to get out of the cave, can they?"

"I suppose."

"Would their eyes come back?"

"Good question," she said, but did not give an answer.

Before he went to bed, Willie took another look out the window. In the pool of light cast by the street lamp, Willie saw the man.

On Tuesday morning when Willie went to school, the man was gone. But when he came home from school with his mother, he was there again.

"*Please* don't look at him," his mother whispered with some urgency.

During his snack, Willie said, "Why shouldn't I look?"

"What are you talking about?"

"That man. On the street. Begging."

"I told you. He's sick. It's better to act as if you never saw him. When people are that way they don't wish to be looked at."

"Why not?"

Mrs. Markham pondered for a little while. "People are ashamed of being unhappy."

Willie looked thoughtfully at his mother. "Are you sure he's unhappy?"

"You don't have to ask if people are unhappy. They tell you all the time."

"How?"

"The way they look."

"Is that part of the sickness?"

"Oh, Willie, I don't know. It's just the way they are."

Willie contemplated the half-inch slice of cake his mother had just given him. A year ago his parents seemed to be perfectly happy. For Willie, the world seemed easy, full of light. Then his father lost his job. He tried to get another but could not. For long hours he sat in dark rooms. Sometimes he drank. His parents began to argue a lot. One day, his father was gone.

For two weeks his mother kept to the dark. And wept.

Willie looked at his mother. "You're unhappy," he said. "Are *you* ashamed?"

Mrs. Markham sighed and closed her eyes. "I wish you wouldn't ask that."

"Why?"

"It hurts me."

"But are you ashamed?" Willie persisted.

WORDS TO KNOW	**urgency** (ûr′jən-sē) *n.* insistence; a condition of pressing importance **contemplate** (kŏn′təm-plāt′) *v.* to look at attentively and thoughtfully

He felt it was urgent that he know. So that he could do something.

She only shook her head.

Willie said, "Do you think Dad might come back?"

She hesitated before saying, "Yes, I think so."

Willie wondered if that was what she really thought.

"Do you think Dad is unhappy?" Willie asked.

"Where do you get such questions?"

"They're in my mind."

"There's much in the mind that need not be paid attention to."

"Fish who live in caves have no eyes."

"What are you talking about?"

"My teacher said it's all that darkness. The fish forget how to see. So they lose their eyes."

"I doubt she said that."

"She did."

"Willie, you have too much imagination."

After his mother went to work, Willie gazed down onto the street. The man was there. Willie thought of going down, but he knew he was not supposed to leave the building when his mother worked at night. He decided to speak to the man the next day.

Fish who live in caves have no eyes.

That afternoon—Wednesday—Willie stood before the man. "I don't have any money," Willie said. "Can I still talk to you?"

The man lifted his face. It was a dirty face with very tired eyes. He needed a shave.

"My mother," Willie began, "said you were unhappy. Is that true?"

"Could be," the man said.

"What are you unhappy about?"

The man's eyes narrowed as he studied Willie intently. He said, "How come you want to know?"

Willie shrugged.

"I think you should go home, kid."

"I am home." Willie gestured toward the apartment. "I live right here. Fifth floor. Where do you live?"

"Around."

"*Are* you unhappy?" Willie persisted.

The man ran a tongue over his lips. His Adam's apple bobbed. "A man has the right to remain silent," he said, and closed his eyes.

Willie remained standing on the pavement for a while before retreating back to his apartment. Once inside he looked down from the window. The man was still there. For a moment Willie was certain the man was looking at the apartment building and the floor where Willie lived.

The next day, Thursday—after dropping a nickel in the man's palm—Willie said, "I've never seen anyone look so unhappy as you do. So I figure you must know a lot about it."

The man took a deep breath. "Well, yeah, maybe."

Willie said, "And I need to find a cure for it."

"A *what*?"

"A cure for unhappiness."

The man pursed his cracked lips and blew a silent whistle. Then he said, "Why?"

"My mother is unhappy."

"Why's that?"

"My dad went away."

"How come?"

"I think because he was unhappy. Now my mother's unhappy too—all the time. So if I

Idle Hands (1935), Will Barnet. Oil on canvas, 36" x 26". Licensed by VAGA, New York, NY.

found a cure for unhappiness, it would be a good thing, wouldn't it?"

"I suppose. Hey, you don't have anything to eat on you, do you?"

Willie shook his head, then said, "Would you like some cake?"

"What kind?"

"I don't know. Cake."

"Depends on the cake."

On Friday Willie said to the man, "I found out what kind of cake it is."

"Yeah?"

"Pound cake. But I don't know why it's called that."

"Long as it's cake it probably don't matter."

Neither spoke. Then Willie said, "In school my teacher said there are fish who live in caves and the caves are so dark the fish don't have eyes. What do you think? Do you believe that?"

"Sure."

"You do? How come?"

"Because you said so."

"You mean, just because someone *said* it you believe it?"

"Not someone. You."

Willie was puzzled. "But, well, maybe it *isn't* true."

The man grunted. "Hey, do you believe it?"

Willie nodded.

"Well, you're not just anyone. You got eyes. You see. You ain't no fish."

"Oh." Willie was pleased.

"What's your name?" the man asked.

"Willie."

"That's a boy's name. What's your grown-up name?"

"William."

"And that means another thing."

"What?"

"I'll take some of that cake."

Willie started. "You will?" he asked, surprised.

"Just said it, didn't I?"

Willie suddenly felt excited. It was as if the man had given him a gift. Willie wasn't sure what it was except that it was important and he was glad to have it. For a moment he just gazed at the man. He saw the lines on the man's face, the way his lips curved, the small scar on the side of his chin, the shape of his eyes, which he now saw were blue.

"I'll get the cake," Willie cried and ran back to the apartment. He snatched the box from the refrigerator as well as a knife, then hurried back down to the street. "I'll cut you a piece," he said, and he opened the box.

"Hey, that don't look like a pound of cake," the man said.

Willie, alarmed, looked up.

"But like I told you, it don't matter."

Willie held his thumb against the cake to make sure the portion was the right size. With a poke of the knife he made a small mark for the proper width.

Just as he was about to cut, the man said, "Hold it!"

Willie looked up. "What?"

"What were you doing there with your thumb?"

"I was measuring the size. The right portion. A person is supposed to get only one portion."

"Where'd you learn that?"

"It says so on the box. You can see for yourself." He held out the box.

The man studied the box then handed it back to Willie. "That's just lies," he said.

"How do you know?"

"William, how can a box say how much a person needs?"

"But it does. The scientists say so. They measured, so they know. Then they put it there."

"Lies," the man repeated.

Willie began to feel that this man knew many things. "Well, then, how much should I cut?" he asked.

The man said, "You have to look at me, then at the cake, and then you're going to have to decide for yourself."

"Oh." Willie looked at the cake. The piece was about three inches wide. Willie looked up at the man. After a moment he cut the cake into two pieces, each an inch and a half wide. He gave one piece to the man and kept the other in the box.

"God bless you," the man said as he took the piece and laid it in his left hand. He began to break off pieces with his right hand and put them in his mouth one by one. Each piece was chewed thoughtfully. Willie watched him eat.

When the man was done, he licked the crumbs on his fingers.

"Now I'll give you something," the man said.

"What?" Willie said, surprised.

"The cure for unhappiness."

"You know it?" Willie asked, eyes wide.

The man nodded.

"What is it?"

"It's this: What a person needs is always more than they say."

"Who's *they*?" Willie asked.

The man pointed to the cake box. "The people on the box," he said.

In his mind Willie repeated what he had been told, then he gave the man the second piece of cake.

The man took it, saying, "Good man," and he ate it.

Willie grinned.

The next day was Saturday. Willie did not go to school. All morning he kept looking down from his window for the man, but it was raining and he did not appear. Willie wondered where he was, but could not imagine it.

Willie's mother woke about noon. Willie sat with her while she ate her breakfast. "I found the cure for unhappiness," he announced.

"Did you?" his mother said. She was reading a memo from the convenience store's owner.

"It's 'What a person needs is always more than they say.'"

His mother put her papers down. "That's nonsense. Where did you hear that?"

"That man."

"What man?"

"On the street. The one who was begging. You said he was unhappy. So I asked him."

"Willie, I told you I didn't want you to even look at that man."

"He's a nice man. . . ."

"How do you know?"

"I've talked to him."

"When? How much?"

Willie shrank down. "I did, that's all."

"Willie, I forbid you to talk to him. Do you understand me? Do you? Answer me!" She was shrill.

"Yes," Willie said, but he'd already decided he would talk to the man one more time. He needed to explain why he could not talk to him anymore.

On Sunday, however, the man was not there. Nor was he there on Monday.

"That man is gone," Willie said to his mother as they walked home from school.

"I saw. I'm not blind."

"Where do you think he went?"

"I couldn't care less. But you might as well know, I arranged for him to be gone."

Willie stopped short. "What do you mean?"

"I called the police. We don't need a <u>nuisance</u> like that around here. Pestering kids."

"He wasn't pestering me."

"Of course he was."

"How do you know?"

"Willie, I have eyes. I can see."

Willie glared at his mother. "No, you can't. You're a fish. You live in a cave."

"Fish?" retorted Mrs. Markham. "What do fish have to do with anything? Willie, don't talk nonsense."

"My name isn't Willie. It's William. And I know how to keep from being unhappy. I do!" He was yelling now. "What a person needs is always more than they say! *Always!*"

He turned on his heel and walked back toward the school. At the corner he glanced back. His mother was following. He kept going. She kept following. ❖

THINKING through the LITERATURE

Connect to the Literature

1. **What Do You Think?** How did you feel when you learned that Willie's mother had called the police about the homeless man?

Comprehension Check
- What does Willie's mother say is wrong with the homeless man?
- What does Willie say is wrong with his mother?

Think Critically

2. Willie's mother says, "Parents need to watch their children." Does she succeed in protecting Willie? Explain.

3. When the homeless man accepts Willie's offer of pound cake, Willie feels as if the man has given him a gift. What does he give Willie? Explain.

   Think About:
   - Mrs. Markham's statement, "Questions that have no answers shouldn't be asked"
   - the way the man who has no name calls Willie "William"
   - "What a person needs is always more than they say"

4. At the end of the story Willie tells his mother, "You're a fish. You live in a cave." What does he mean? What other references to "not seeing" are in the story?

5. **ACTIVE READING** **DRAWING CONCLUSIONS**
   Find a classmate who took notes on the same character you did in his or her 📖 READER'S NOTEBOOK. Talk about how you reached your **conclusions.**

Extend Interpretations

6. **What If?** Imagine that Willie had explained to his mother how he felt about her calling the police instead of walking away from her. How would this have changed the meaning of the story for you?

7. **Connect to Life** Do you think that children sometimes have things to teach their parents? Describe a situation where this might happen.

Literary Analysis

DYNAMIC AND STATIC CHARACTERS

A **dynamic character** is one who changes as the result of events in the story. A character may think, act, even speak differently because he or she has come to understand something in a new way. A **static character** does not change or gain deeper understanding as the plot unfolds.

Paired Activity Working with a partner, choose a dynamic or static character from the story and make a chart. Go back through the story together and record details that show change or lack of change in your character.

Willie		
Monday	Tuesday	Wednesday
asks mother questions about the homeless man	decides to talk to the homeless man	

CHARACTERIZATION

Characterization is the way an author presents details that give you clues about a character's personality. A character's thoughts, words, speech patterns, actions, and the reaction of other characters are some tools an author uses to make the character seem believable. Was the homeless man described in a way that made him seem believable? If so, how?

Writing

Characterization Suppose Willie had kept a journal to record details and descriptions of the homeless man. How do the kinds of things Willie notices change as he gets to know the man better? Write some journal entries as you think Willie would have written them. Note the way the homeless man is characterized. You might start your entry, "Monday I saw a man outside our building. . . ." and build from there.

Speaking & Listening

How would you characterize someone you know? Picture that person's gestures, facial expressions, mannerisms, ways of speaking and acting. Write a characterization of that person, and then read it to your classmates. If you like, choose a volunteer to act out the characterization as you've written it. Was he or she accurate? Ask for feedback about how you could make your written characterization more specific and effective.

Art Connection

Take another look at the painting on page 209. Do you think Alex Katz's *Ada & Vincent* captures the mood of the story? What might the woman and boy be looking at?

Research & Technology

Getting Involved Go to your school or local library and locate information about volunteer programs in your community. Look for groups or organizations such as hospitals, shelters, soup kitchens, libraries, or social service agencies. Find specific names of these groups, then call or write and request publications like newsletters and pamphlets. Compile and organize results of your inquiry from three or four such groups, and share your findings with the class.

> **Reading *for* INFORMATION**
> Read "The Difference a City Year Makes" on p. 219 to begin your research. Find out how young people can get involved in community service.

Vocabulary

STANDARDIZED TEST PRACTICE

Choose the word or group of words that means the same, or nearly the same, as the underlined Word to Know in each sentence.

1. A decent <u>interval</u> passed before Willie went outside to talk to the man sitting on the sidewalk. <u>Interval</u> means—
   A storm   **B** period
   C truck   **D** thought

2. His mother tried, with some <u>urgency,</u> to convince him to ignore the man. <u>Urgency</u> means—
   F decency   **G** cruelty
   H insistence   **J** annoyance

3. Sometimes, Willie sat quietly for a long time and <u>contemplated</u> his father's empty chair. <u>Contemplated</u> means—
   A ignored   **B** abandoned
   C contested   **D** considered

4. The man in the street stared <u>intently</u> at Willie and wouldn't tell him anything at first. <u>Intently</u> means—
   F attentively **G** spitefully
   H ignorantly   **J** cheerfully

5. Willie's mother thought the man was a <u>nuisance,</u> but Willie disagreed. <u>Nuisance</u> means—
   A neighbor   **B** pest
   C guardian   **D** newcomer

Vocabulary Handbook
See p. R24: Context Clues.

Grammar in Context: Choosing the Right Verb

Avi uses **vivid, precise verbs** to create strong and accurate descriptions.

> The dog strained in the direction of the man sitting on the crate. His tail wagged. The lady pulled the dog away. "Heel!" she commanded.
> The dog—tail between his legs—scampered to the lady's side. Even so, the dog twisted around to look back at the beggar.

Compare the same passage with overused general verbs: *The dog* <u>pulled</u> *in the direction of the man sitting on the crate. His tail* <u>moved</u>. *The lady pulled the dog away. "Heel!" she* <u>said</u>. *The dog—tail between his legs—*<u>went</u> *to the lady's side. Even so, the dog* <u>turned</u> *around to look back at the beggar.*

Apply to Your Writing Choosing a precise verb instead of an overused, more general one will strengthen your writing. If necessary, consult a dictionary or a thesaurus for ideas.

WRITING EXERCISE Replace the overused, <u>general verbs</u> in these sentences with vivid, precise verbs.

Example: *Original* Mrs. Markham <u>thought about</u> Willie's question.

Rewritten Mrs. Markham pondered Willie's question.

1. Willie <u>ran</u> toward the school.
2. He <u>put</u> his books down on his desk.
3. The man on the street <u>spoke</u> quietly.
4. From a distance, children <u>looked</u> at him.
5. Willie <u>walked</u> across the street with the pound cake.
6. The man <u>ate</u> the cake, even the crumbs.

Connect to the Literature Reread page 210. Find other examples of vivid, precise verbs. Explain your choices.

Avi
born 1937

"Ideas do not come to me whole; they are created slowly by looking at things and people and situations in terms of stories."

School Years Avi Wortis was born in New York City and grew up in Brooklyn. His twin sister Emily gave him the name Avi when they were a year old, and that is the name he has used since. As a boy, he had trouble writing and spelling in school. He later discovered he had a learning disability called *dysgraphia* that affected his ability to write.

All Kinds of Jobs After graduating from the University of Wisconsin, Avi worked as a sign painter (sometimes making spelling mistakes), a carpenter, a theater coach, and a library clerk. He became a librarian because he loved books.

Writing and Rewriting Avi has published more than 35 novels, 2 of them Newbery Honor Books. He revises some books 40 to 50 times. He says the most important thing for a writer is to read deeply.

AUTHOR ACTIVITY
On Your Own Avi says, "Don't assume that because everyone believes a thing it is right or wrong. Reason things out for yourself. Work to get answers on your own. Understand why you believe things." Read one or more of Avi's works. Do his main characters do this? What does it take to get answers on your own?

①  TEEN RAP

by Lauren Beckham

Source: *The Boston Herald*

② The Difference a City Year Makes

What kind of person gets up at the break of dawn, spends all day tutoring teenagers, cleaning up former crack houses, or teaching kids to read and write—all in the name of community service?

The kind who joins City Year. Hundreds of young adults come together in Boston for CYZYGY, City Year's Annual Convention of Idealism, to show community leaders, business people and—most importantly—other young adults that community service, though difficult, is rewarding to both those who give and those who receive.

Reading for Information

Have you wondered how you could help your community? In this article you will find out how several teenagers answered that question.

Text Organizers

Newspaper articles often use **text organizers** such as headlines and photo captions to present information clearly. Skimming text organizers can help you preview an article.

YOUR TURN *Use the questions and activities below with the article to learn about text organizers.*

❶ "Teen Rap" is the name of a column. A **column** is a type of article that appears regularly in a newspaper and is usually written by the same writer, the columnist. What kind of topics would you infer a column called "Teen Rap" would deal with?

❷ The title of a newspaper article is called a **headline.** What is the headline of this article? How does it help you preview the article?

Another important part of a newspaper article is the byline. The **byline** tells who wrote the article. Find the byline in this article.

Key Standard
R2.1 Understand differences between various categories of informational materials (such as textbooks, newspapers, and manuals).
***Other Standards* R2.2, R3.1**

City Year members participate in the Thomson Island Clean-Up.

Young Heroes
Martin Luther King Day
1998

3 Opening day for Young Heroes, City Year's program for middle school students, on Martin Luther King Day.

"Young people are coming together and giving back"

When Anthony Samuels of Dorchester graduated from Melrose High School last year, he had a specific plan.

"I was ready to give back to my community," Samuels, 19, said. "When I learned about City Year, I jumped right in."

Samuels spends his days at the Umana Barnes Middle School in East Boston, mentoring and tutoring at-risk boys in a remedial class.

"I could say that it was a challenge but that's what I needed," said the Dorchester teen. "And they needed me. I'm proud to be part of their accomplishments."

Samuels plans to attend Bunker Hill Community College next year and then pursue a bachelor's degree in child psychology. Meanwhile, he is looking forward to the CYZYGY conference.

"Hopefully in the next five years we'll have, instead of eight City Year sites, 15 to 20," he said. "CYZYGY will show Boston that young people are coming together and giving back."

"I kind of wish I had done it sooner"

Julie Xifaras' day is a little different than that of most 21-year-olds.

"I play a lot of kickball at recess," said the City Year volunteer from Marion, MA.

For the past 10 months, Xifaras has been volunteering as an education aide in the Chelsea Early Childhood Education Center with other members of Boston's City Year team.

"It's been awesome," she said. "I had never worked with kids, so I was a bit nervous at first. I have gained such an appreciation for children and in the process learned how to be a kid myself."

Xifaras took a break from her studies at Boston College last year after questioning

Members help out at the Special Olympics at the Massachusetts Institute of Technology.

She followed in her footsteps.

St. Jean and members of her City Year team run Young Heroes, a Saturday service corps for eighth graders. She also tutors Mission Pride children at the housing development's after-school program in Roxbury.

"It makes me feel real good to be with these kids," said St. Jean, 20. "Once I was in their shoes. I know what it feels like to live in the projects. I talk to them, I support them and tell them they can do anything they want to. That's what my sister told me."

St. Jean, who dropped out of high school in the 11th grade, is also working for her G.E.D. in City Year's education program.

"All we ever talk about is our diploma," she said. "Before I wasn't motivated enough. I got here and I got so much support, it makes me want to get it."

4

"You get out of City Year what you put into it"

Attending college part-time and working full-time wasn't enough for 21-year-old Desiree Escajeda of San Jose, NM.

what she was doing with her life.

"I didn't think I was being productive. I had enjoyed BC, but I still needed to gain some focus," she said.

Xifaras suggested everybody take a year off after high school to volunteer because "it's a perfect time because you're in transition anyway."

"I've been exposed to so many different types of people and opportunities, anything from helping a kid tie a shoe to doing a presentation for corporate people," she said. "I have really grown. I kind of wish I had done it sooner."

"Every day you are helping someone"

Call it sibling rivalry.

Ludmia St. Jean of Boston was sick of listening to her older sister brag about how much fun she was having as a corps member of Boston's City Year. So she did what most sisters do.

Reading for Information *continued*

3 Photographs or other visuals often accompany informative articles. A **caption** can tell you a lot about how the visual relates to the article. What information does this caption provide? What does each photo add to the article?

4 Titles in boldface type within the article are called subheadings. **Subheadings** introduce the beginning of a new topic. What does the writer use as a subheading here, and throughout the article?

"I wasn't being challenged," she said. "I wasn't into school, I wasn't into work. I really wanted to make a difference."

She does—by working with third- through sixth-graders at the Santee Elementary School's vacation day camp in San Jose.

"I think you get out of City Year what you put into it," she said. "What I am doing turned out to be more than I ever expected. I have developed skills I never thought I could and discovered more of who I want to be."

Escajeda will attend West Valley Junior College in the fall and transfer to a four-year

college within a year, which she admitted wasn't in her plans before she started volunteering.

"I feel like now I know where I want to go," she said. "I have more direction, more confidence and a better outlook on what I can do with my life."

And she's happy she was able to pass her positive attitude on to her students.

"City Year has given me a lot of opportunities to help kids," she said. "The fact that I can go into a school system and make kids feel good about themselves and their future is really amazing."

Reading for Information *continued*

❺ Feature articles are special reports, unlike regular news stories that report the day's events. The subheadings in a feature article try to catch the readers' interest. How does this subheading catch your interest? How is it better than a one-line summary of the information contained in the section?

Research & Technology
Activity Link: "What Do Fish Have to Do with Anything?" p. 217. Create a database like the one below to record the different types of community service in your area. List the name of the service, such as a hospital or animal shelter, and include information about whom you should contact, what times they need help, and what type of work is involved. Use headings to organize the information in your database.

Service	Contact	Times	Type of Work

❺ **"These kids need people to take the time to teach them"**

Michael Ketcham wasn't out to change the world when he joined City Year.

The 20-year-old criminal-justice major simply wanted to work with his friend.

"I wasn't really ready for college when I graduated from high school," said the Columbia, S.C. native. "I stopped school and started a job. My friend was going to apply to City Year, so I figured we could do it together."

Ketcham works as a teacher's aide and tutor at Bradley Elementary School in Columbia.

"It's a challenge," Ketcham said. "But I really saw the difference I was making right from the start. These kids need people to take the time to teach them."

After he completes his year of service, Ketcham plans to spend the $4,725 City Year post-graduate award at Midland Technical College to continue his studies in criminal justice.

Ketcham said everyone should experience helping a child.

"When you see these kids walk away from you, knowing they learned something from you, the feeling is indescribable," he said. "One thing's for sure, I have a new respect for teachers."

PREPARING to *Read*

Across the Curriculum
Social Studies

from **Immigrant Kids**

by RUSSELL FREEDMAN

Key Standard
R3.1 Be able to describe the purposes and characteristics of different forms of prose, such as the short story, novel, or essay.
***Other Standards* R1.3, R2.3, LC1.3**

Connect to Your Life

What would it be like to move with your family to a different country?

A Nation of Immigrants
The United States is called a nation of immigrants because most Americans' ancestors came from other countries.

Until the middle of the 20th century, the majority of immigrants came from Europe.

Today the majority of immigrants come not from Europe, but from Mexico, Central America, Asia, and the Caribbean.

Arrows indicate points of origin of immigrants to the United States.

Focus Your Reading

LITERARY ANALYSIS | **INFORMATIVE NONFICTION**

Informative nonfiction provides factual information about real people, places, and events. Writers of informative works get their information from both primary and secondary sources. **Primary sources** are original, firsthand accounts or information. **Secondary sources** are descriptions based on primary sources.

WORDS TO KNOW **Vocabulary Preview**

din   impoverished   teeming
fervent   indomitable

ACTIVE READING | **MAIN IDEA AND DETAILS**

A **main idea** is a central message that a writer tries to get across. It may be the central message of an entire work or the thought expressed in the topic sentence of a paragraph. Nonfiction writers back up, or support, their main ideas with **details.** As you read, try to identify the main idea of this selection. Choose a paragraph in the selection and make a rough outline of it in your **READER'S NOTEBOOK**.

IMMIGRANT KIDS   **223**

from
IMMIGRANT
KIDS

by Russell Freedman

I n the years around the turn of the century,

immigration to America reached an all-time

high. Between 1880 and 1920, 23 million immigrants

arrived in the United States. They came mainly

from the countries of Europe, especially from

Italian girl at Ellis Island, 1926. Lewis
W. Hine. Lewis W. Hine collection;
United States History, Local History,
and Genealogy Division; The New
York Public Library; Astor, Lenox,
and Tilden Foundations.

The luggage of Irish immigrants sits on
the dock at Ellis Island. Brown Brothers.

impoverished towns and villages in southern and eastern Europe. The one thing they had in common was a fervent belief that in America, life would be better.

Most of these immigrants were poor. Somehow they managed to scrape together enough money to pay for their passage to America. Many immigrant families arrived penniless. Others had to make the journey in stages. Often the father came first, found work, and sent for his family later.

Immigrants usually crossed the Atlantic as steerage passengers. Reached by steep, slippery stairways, the steerage lay deep down in the hold of the ship. It was occupied by passengers paying the lowest fare.

Men, women, and children were packed into dark, foul-smelling compartments. They slept in narrow bunks stacked three high. They had no showers, no lounges, and no dining rooms. Food served from huge kettles was dished into dinner pails provided by the steamship company. Because steerage conditions were crowded and uncomfortable, passengers spent as much time as possible up on deck.

The voyage was an ordeal, but it was worth it. They were on their way to America.

The great majority of immigrants landed in New York City, at America's busiest port. They never forgot their first glimpse of the Statue of Liberty.

⟖⊰◆⊱⟕

The voyage was an ordeal,

but it was worth it.

They were on their way to America.

⟖⊰◆⊱⟕

Edward Corsi, who later became United States Commissioner of Immigration, was a ten-year-old Italian immigrant when he sailed into New York harbor in 1907:

My first impressions of the New World will always remain etched in my memory, particularly that hazy October morning when I first saw Ellis Island. The steamer *Florida,* fourteen days out of Naples, filled to capacity

WORDS TO KNOW

impoverished (ĭm-pŏv′ər-ĭsht) *adj.* poor
fervent (fûr′vənt) *adj.* having or expressing great warmth or depth of feeling

225

with 1,600 natives of Italy, had weathered one of the worst storms in our captain's memory; and glad we were, both children and grown-ups, to leave the open sea and come at last through the Narrows into the Bay.

My mother, my stepfather, my brother Giuseppe, and my two sisters, Liberta and Helvetia, all of us together, happy that we had come through the storm safely, clustered on the foredeck for fear of separation and looked with wonder on this miraculous land of our dreams.

Giuseppe and I held tightly to Stepfather's hands, while Liberta and Helvetia clung to Mother. Passengers all about us were crowding against the rail. Jabbered conversation, sharp cries, laughs and cheers—a steadily rising <u>din</u> filled the air. Mothers and fathers lifted up babies so that they too could see, off to the left, the Statue of Liberty. . . .

Finally the *Florida* veered to the left, turning northward into the Hudson River, and now the incredible buildings of lower Manhattan came very close to us.

A mother and her children arrive at Ellis Island. Brown Brothers.

WORDS
TO
KNOW   **din** (dĭn) *n.* a loud, confused mixture of noises

Jewish war orphans arriving from eastern Europe, 1921. American Jewish Joint Distribution Committee, Inc., New York.

The officers of the ship . . . went striding up and down the decks shouting orders and directions and driving the immigrants before them. Scowling and gesturing, they pushed and pulled the passengers, herding us into separate groups as though we were animals. A few moments later we came to our dock, and the long journey was over.

Giuseppe and I held tightly to Stepfather's hands, while Liberta and Helvetia clung to Mother.

But the journey was not yet over. Before they could be admitted to the United States, immigrants had to pass through Ellis Island, which became the nation's chief immigrant processing center in 1892. There they would be questioned and examined. Those who could not pass all the exams would be detained; some would be sent back to Europe. And so their arrival in America was filled with great anxiety. Among the immigrants, Ellis Island was known as "Heartbreak Island."

When their ship docked at a Hudson River pier, the immigrants had numbered identity tags pinned to their clothing. Then they were herded onto special ferryboats that carried them to Ellis Island. Officials hurried them along, shouting "Quick! Run! Hurry!" in half a dozen languages.

Filing into an enormous inspection hall, the immigrants formed long lines separated by iron railings that made the hall look like a great maze.

Now the examinations began. First the immigrants were examined by two doctors of the United States Health Service. One doctor looked for physical and mental abnormalities. When a case aroused suspicion, the immigrant received a chalk mark on the right shoulder for further inspection: L for lameness, H for heart, X for mental defects, and so on.

The second doctor watched for contagious and infectious diseases. He looked especially for infections of the scalp and at the eyelids for symptoms of trachoma, a blinding disease. Since trachoma caused more than half of all medical detentions, this doctor was greatly feared. He stood directly in the immigrant's path. With a swift movement, he would grab the immigrant's eyelid, pull it up, and peer beneath it. If all was well, the immigrant was passed on.

Those who failed to get past both doctors had to undergo a more thorough medical exam. The others moved on to the registration clerk, who questioned them with the aid of an interpreter: What is your name? Your nationality? Your occupation? Can you read and write? Have you ever been in prison? How much money do you have with you? Where are you going?

Some immigrants were so flustered that they could not answer. They were allowed to sit and rest and try again.

About one immigrant out of every five or six was detained for additional examinations or questioning.

The writer Angelo Pellegrini has recalled his own family's detention at Ellis Island:

We lived there for three days—Mother and we five children, the youngest of whom was three years old. Because of the rigorous physical examination that we had to submit to, particularly of the eyes, there was this terrible anxiety that one of us might be rejected. And if one of us was, what would the rest of the family do? My sister was indeed momentarily rejected; she had been so ill and had cried so much that her eyes were absolutely bloodshot, and Mother was told, "Well, we can't let her in." But fortunately, Mother was an <u>indomitable</u> spirit and finally made them understand that if her child had a few hours' rest and a little bite to eat she would be all right. In the end we did get through.

Most immigrants passed through Ellis Island in about one day. Carrying all their worldly possessions, they left the examination hall and waited on the dock for the ferry that would take them to Manhattan, a mile away. Some of them still faced long journeys overland before they reached their final destination. Others would head directly for the <u>teeming</u> immigrant neighborhoods of New York City. . . .

Immigrants still come to America. Since World War II, more than 8 million immigrants have entered the country. While this is a small number compared to the mass migrations at the turn of the century, the United States continues to admit more immigrants than any other nation.

Many of today's immigrants come from countries within the Western Hemisphere, and from Asia and Africa as well as Europe. When they reach the United States, they face many of the same problems and hardships that have always confronted newcomers. And they come here for the same reason that immigrants have always come: to seek a better life for themselves and their children. ❖

WORDS TO KNOW

indomitable (ĭn-dŏm′ĭ-tə-bəl) *adj.* unconquerable
teeming (tē′mĭng) *adj.* full of people or things **teem** *v.*

THE NEW COLOSSUS
by Emma Lazarus 1849–1887

Joseph Sohm/ChromoSohm Inc./Corbis.

Not like the brazen giant of Greek fame,[1]
With conquering limbs astride from land to land;
Here at our sea-washed, sunset gates shall stand
A mighty woman with a torch, whose flame
5 Is the imprisoned lightning, and her name
Mother of Exiles. From her beacon-hand
Glows world-wide welcome; her mild eyes command
The air-bridged harbor that twin cities frame.
"Keep, ancient lands, your storied pomp!"[2] cries she
10 With silent lips. "Give me your tired, your poor,
Your huddled masses yearning to breathe free,
The wretched refuse of your teeming shore.
Send these, the homeless, tempest-tost[3] to me,
I lift my lamp beside the golden door!"

---

1. **giant of Greek fame:** The original colossus was a huge Greek statue of the sun god Helios, considered to be one of the Seven Wonders of the World.

2. **storied pomp:** the splendor of your history.

3. **tempest-tost:** tossed by violent windstorms.

Connect to the Literature

1. **What Do You Think?**
   What are your reactions to the immigrants' experiences?

   Comprehension Check
   • Which passengers traveled in the steerage part of the ship?
   • Why were some immigrants not admitted into the country?
   • How many immigrants have come to the United States since World War II?

Think Critically

2. Which of the hardships that the immigrants faced seem most difficult to you?

   Think About:
   • the voyage across the sea
   • the procedures at Ellis Island
   • the challenges after leaving Ellis Island

3. Do you think all of the immigration procedures at Ellis Island were necessary? Why or why not?

4. The final lines of "The New Colossus" (page 229) are engraved on the base of the Statue of Liberty. Read this poem. What does it suggest about people's attitude toward immigrants at the time it was written?

5. **ACTIVE READING** **MAIN IDEA AND DETAILS**
   Look again at the outline you made in your
   READER'S NOTEBOOK. Compare your outline with a classmate's. Would you have outlined the paragraph that your classmate chose the way he or she did? Discuss your ideas with your classmate.

Extend Interpretations

6. **What If?** Imagine how the Pellegrini family felt when immigration officials said that Angelo's sister couldn't be let into the country. What decision do you think Mrs. Pellegrini would have made if the officials hadn't changed their minds?

7. **Connect to Life** Edward Corsi recorded the joy of immigrants arriving in New York Harbor: "Mothers and fathers lifted up babies so that they too could see . . . the Statue of Liberty. . . ." What does the Statue of Liberty mean to you?

Literary Analysis

INFORMATIVE NONFICTION
The type of nonfiction that provides factual information is called **informative nonfiction**. It is the type of nonfiction found in science and history books, encyclopedias, pamphlets, and many magazine and newspaper articles.

In this excerpt from *Immigrant Kids,* Russell Freedman draws on **primary sources** and **secondary sources** to support his descriptions. Among the primary sources are lively firsthand accounts from Edward Corsi and Angelo Pellegrini.

Paired Activity Think about Freedman's description of the challenges that faced children immigrating to the United States in the early 1900s. With a partner, discuss how the quotations from immigrants' own accounts added to the effectiveness of the selection. What did you learn from the primary sources that you wouldn't have learned any other way?

BIBLIOGRAPHY
When writing informative nonfiction, writers must keep track of primary and secondary sources used for their research. A **bibliography** is a list of those sources (articles, books, encyclopedias) that document what the author has included in his or her work. Bibliographies can also recommend further study on the subject.

CHOICES and CHALLENGES

Writing

Bibliography Try your hand at writing a bibliography. Choose a historical event or topic that interests you. Find a few books or articles that provide information on it, or use your Ellis Island research from the exercise on this page. Write a short synopsis, a paragraph or so, on one aspect of the topic. Then write a list of at least three sources used.

Writing Handbook
See p. R56: Works Cited.

Speaking & Listening

Interview Interview someone who has immigrated to the United States. Ask questions like these: Where did you emigrate from? What was the most difficult part of immigrating? What did you expect your life in the United States to be like? Did anything about the United States surprise you? Remember to use good listening skills as an interviewer.

Speaking and Listening Handbook
See p. R109: Conducting Interviews

Research & Technology

SOCIAL STUDIES

Samuel Ellis owned Ellis Island in the 18th century. Later it was named for him. Research the island's interesting past, especially how it came to be a major reception center for immigrants. Search a library for books and articles about Ellis Island, and look for helpful sites on the Internet.

INTERNET **Research Starter**
www.mcdougallittell.com

Vocabulary

EXERCISE A: DENOTATION On your paper, match each vocabulary word in the left column with its dictionary meaning, or denotation, in the right column.

1. **din**   a. crowded
2. **fervent**   b. marked by intense emotion
3. **impoverished**   c. jumble of loud, conflicting sounds
4. **indomitable**   d. poor
5. **teeming**   e. unconquerable

EXERCISE B: CONNOTATION On your paper, write the letter of the phrase that best captures the connotation, or associated meaning, of each vocabulary word.

1. **din:** (a) steady rain falling on the roof (b) an orchestra playing loudly (c) the crowd during overtime at a basketball game, shouting encouragement for the teams

2. **fervent:** (a) the single-minded pursuit of a goal (b) the graduation of an older brother or sister (c) a lingering feeling of resentment

3. **impoverished:** (a) buying products with a credit card (b) leading a simple life with few possessions (c) lacking basic necessities of life

4. **indomitable:** (a) someone who overcomes great personal challenges through willpower (b) an especially talented athlete (c) a clever child who can talk his or her way out of any situation

5. **teeming:** (a) an overstuffed suitcase (b) thousands of tropical fish swimming around a coral reef (c) an apple tree with 20 ripe apples

Vocabulary Handbook
See p. R27: Connotative and Denotative Meaning.

Grammar in Context: Abstract and Concrete Nouns

Russell Freedman uses both abstract and concrete nouns to describe modern-day immigrants to the United States.

> When they reach the United States, they face many of the same problems and hardships that have always confronted newcomers. And they come here for the same reason that immigrants have always come: to seek a better life for themselves and their children.

Abstract nouns name ideas, qualities, or feelings. **Concrete nouns** name persons, places, or things that can be perceived by the senses.

Apply to Your Writing While both abstract and concrete nouns are necessary, do not use an abstract noun when you can use a concrete one.

WRITING EXERCISE Provide an abstract and a concrete noun to complete each sentence.

Example: *Original* Their greatest _____ was that a family member might be rejected by one of the _____.

Rewritten Their greatest fear was that a family member might be rejected by one of the doctors.

1. Many families nurtured a _____ that _____ would be a land of promise.
2. _____ and their parents showed remarkable _____ on the perilous journey.
3. The woman's _____ was an example for her daughters and _____.
4. The immigrants felt tremendous _____ on arriving at _____.
5. Doctors questioned the _____ with the _____ of an interpreter.

Connect to the Literature Reread page 228. Find five abstract nouns and five concrete nouns.

Russell Freedman
born 1929

". . . I always feel that I have a story to tell that is worth telling."

Learning to Write Even as a young boy, Russell Freedman wanted to be a writer. His first job was as a reporter. "That's where I really learned to write," he says. "I learned to organize my thoughts, respect facts, and meet deadlines." A newspaper article about a 16-year-old blind boy who invented a Braille typewriter inspired his first book, *Teenagers Who Made History*. His career as a writer of nonfiction books had been launched.

Telling a Story In 1980, Freedman attended an exhibit featuring photos of children in 19th- and 20th-century America. He was deeply moved by the faces of the children, and he wrote *Immigrant Kids* to tell the story behind the pictures. "Like every writer," Freedman says, "a nonfiction writer is essentially a storyteller. Whatever my subject, I always feel that I have a story to tell that is worth telling."

AUTHOR ACTIVITY
Photographs Find out more about Freedman's storytelling by reading his book *Lincoln: A Photobiography*. Discuss with classmates how the many photographs in the book help Freedman to tell the story of Abraham Lincoln's life.

Building Vocabulary
Analyzing Word Parts: Base Words and Word Families

Many of the words that you use every day belong to groups of related words called word families.

All members of a word family share the same base word.

Prefixes and suffixes can be added to the base words to form words with new meanings.

Key Standard
R1.2 Use knowledge of roots and affixes to understand vocabulary in different content areas.

> She was staring sadly at the cake box, but he didn't think she was seeing it. Her **unhappiness** made him think of the man on the street. . . .
> "Oh, could be anything," his mother said, vaguely. "A person can be **unhappy** for many reasons."
> —Avi, "What Do Fish Have to Do with Anything?"

The **base word** can stand by itself.

Prefixes can be added to the beginning of base words and suffixes can be added to the end of base words.

Strategies for Building Vocabulary

In the example above, you can see how a single base word—*happy*—can be the source of more than one related word. Notice how the prefix and the suffix add to the base word's meaning.

❶ **Recognize Base Words** When you encounter a long word that is unfamiliar to you, see if you can recognize a **base word** in it. In the word *unhappiness*, for example, you probably recognized the base word *happy*. Identifying a base word can help you to figure out the meaning of a word in which other parts are added to it.

❷ **Recognize Other Word Parts** Once you have identified a base word, you can try to figure out the meanings of **prefixes** and **suffixes** attached to it. Think about how they change the base word's meaning. Look at the chart on this page to find the meanings of *un-* and *-ness*. Consider how they combine with the base word *happy* to produce the word *unhappiness*, meaning "a state of not being happy."

Base Word	Prefix or Suffix	Related Word
manage	*mis-* (wrong)	**mis**manage ("to manage badly")
	-ment (an act or state of)	manage**ment** ("an act of managing")
satisfy	*dis-* (the opposite of)	**dis**satisfy ("to do the opposite of satisfying")
	-ing (causing, engaged in)	satisfy**ing** ("causing to be satisfied")
safe	*un-* (not)	**un**safe ("not safe")
	-ly (in a certain way)	safe**ly** ("in a safe way")
perfect	*im-* (not)	**im**perfect ("not perfect")
	-ion (an act or state of)	perfect**ion** ("a state of being perfect")
build	*re-* (again)	**re**build ("to build again")
	-er (one who)	build**er** ("one who builds")
sad	*-ness* (a state of)	sad**ness** ("a state of being sad")
tolerate	*in-* (not)	**in**toler**able** ("not capable of being tolerated")
	-able (capable of being)	

EXERCISE Add prefixes and suffixes to these base words to make as many related words as you can.

1. contain   **2.** interpret   **3.** complain   **4.** polite   **5.** honor

GOOD HOT DOGS

by Sandra Cisneros

for Kiki

Fifty cents apiece
To eat our lunch
We'd run
Straight from school
5 Instead of home
Two blocks
Then the store
That smelled like steam
You ordered
10 Because you had the money
Two hot dogs and two pops for here
Everything on the hot dogs
Except pickle lily
Dash those hot dogs
15 Into buns and splash on
All that good stuff
Yellow mustard and onions
And french fries piled on top all
Rolled up in a piece of wax
20 Paper for us to hold hot
In our hands
Quarters on the counter
Sit down
Good hot dogs
25 We'd eat
Fast till there was nothing left
But salt and poppy seeds even
The little burnt tips
Of french fries
30 We'd eat
You humming
And me swinging my legs

BUENOS HOT DOGS

**Translated from English
by Lori M. Carlson**

para Kiki

Cincuenta centavos cada uno
Para comer nuestro lonche
Corríamos
Derecho desde la escuela
5 En vez de a casa
Dos cuadras
Después la tienda
Que olía a vapor
Tú pedías
10 Porque tenías el dinero
Dos hot dogs y dos refrescos para comer aquí
Los hot dogs con todo
Menos pepinos
Echa esos hot dogs
15 En sus panes y salpícalos
Con todas esas cosas buenas
Mostaza amarilla y cebollas
Y papas fritas amontonadas encima
Envueltos en papel de cera
20 Para llevarlos calientitos
En las manos
Monedas encima del mostrador
Siéntate
Buenos hot dogs
25 Comíamos
Rápido hasta que no quedaba nada
Menos sal y semillas de amapola hasta
Las puntitas quemadas
De las papas fritas
30 Comíamos
Tú canturreando
Y yo columpiando mis piernas

SCAFFOLDING

Seamus Heaney

Masons when they start upon a building,
Are careful to test out the scaffolding;

Make sure that planks won't slip at busy points,
Secure all ladders, tighten bolted joints.

5 And yet all this comes down when the job's done
Showing off walls of sure and solid stone.

So if, my dear, there sometimes seem to be
Old bridges breaking between you and me

Never fear. We may let the scaffolds fall
10 Confident that we have built our wall.

Sandra Cisneros
born 1954

"I am the only daughter in a family of six sons. That explains everything."

Seamus Heaney
born 1939

"I think literature is there to open the spaces, not to erect tariff barriers."

Moving Days Sandra Cisneros was born in Chicago, Illinois, and grew up as the only daughter in a family with seven children. Her father was Mexican, and her mother was Mexican American. The family moved frequently between Chicago and Mexico City. "I didn't like school because we moved so much, and I was always new and funny looking," she says.

Reading and Writing Despite her awkwardness in class, Cisneros read a great deal on her own. Reading led her to develop an interest in writing. While working for a master's degree, Cisneros began her novel *The House on Mango Street.* It is the story of Esperanza Cordero, a young girl who moves from house to house while growing up in Chicago.

Working with Youth After graduation, Cisneros completed her novel while teaching and counseling high school dropouts at Chicago's Latino Youth Alternative High School. The stories that her students told her about their lives influenced her writing. Later, she became a poet-in-residence at several schools.

Success as a Writer In 1986 Cisneros moved to San Antonio, Texas, where she currently lives. She continues to teach, and this once shy student has received numerous awards and other recognition for her writing.

Childhood Seamus Heaney's life, like his poetry, has been influenced by both the past and the present. Heaney loves the ancient Ireland of myth and legend, but he is also part of the modern Ireland of cities and factories. Born in Northern Ireland, he is the oldest of nine children. His parents owned a small farm, and his memories of working there appear in many of his poems.

Poetry When Heaney was 12, he won a scholarship to a boarding school 40 miles from home. At school he studied Latin and Irish, languages that opened new horizons for him and would later become important in his poetry. He went on to attend Queen's University in Belfast. There he met Marie Devlin, his future wife. Though Belfast was torn by the violence of civil conflict, it was during this time that Heaney began publishing poems expressing his love for his wife and memories of his boyhood.

Creativity Heaney's response to the growing violence in his native Northern Ireland was to encourage creativity and study. He began to translate ancient Irish myths. He also made translations of ancient Greek tragedies, which were performed by a theater company that he helped to found.

Recognition Today, Heaney lectures and conducts writing workshops in both Ireland and the United States. In 1995 he was awarded the Nobel Prize in literature.

Writing Workshop — Interpretive Essay

Interpreting a poem . . .

From Reading to Writing Some people say that reading a poem is like peeling an onion—with every layer you peel away, there is another underneath. At first, "The Pasture" by Robert Frost seems like a simple poem about chores on a farm. However, if you read it again, you may discover new meanings. Writing an **interpretive essay** means going beyond the surface to discover the deeper messages of a work. Great literature always reveals something new. Now is your chance to find it.

For Your Portfolio

WRITING PROMPT Write an essay exploring your understanding of a poem.

Purpose: To explain your interpretation
Audience: Your teacher, classmates, and anyone else familiar with the work

---

Basics in a Box

Interpretive Essay at a Glance

Introduction
Introduces the literary work and includes a clear thesis statement introducing the interpretation

Body
Supports the interpretation with evidence from the literary work

> Evidence
>
> Example
>
> Example
>
> Example

Conclusion
Summarizes the interpretation

RUBRIC STANDARDS FOR WRITING

A successful interpretive essay should

- identify the title and author of the work
- give a clearly stated interpretation of the work's message at or near the beginning of the essay
- present examples from the work to support the interpretation
- use transitions to guide the reader
- summarize the interpretation in the conclusion

Analyzing a Student Model

Sabrina Probasco
Parkland Middle School

SPEAKING
OPPORTUNITY
See the
Speaking and
Listening Handbook,
p. R100 for oral
presentation
tips.

Interpretation of "The World Is Not a Pleasant Place to Be"

"The World Is Not a Pleasant Place to Be" by Nikki Giovanni is a poem that captures the many deep emotions of its author. Although the poem is built on the feeling of loneliness, it is actually hopeful and inspiring. Giovanni's message is that people need one another to be happy.

In the first stanza of the poem, Giovanni creates an atmosphere of loneliness. The line "the world is not a pleasant place/to be without/someone to hold and be held by" says a lot about her feelings. As I read this, I pictured the poet living in a big, empty apartment. She is alone in the world around her, and also in the world of feelings inside her. However, in the lines "without/someone to hold and be held by," she seems to be saying that there is hope. People don't need to feel this way. Each living creature can find comfort by feeling connected to others.

In the second stanza, Giovanni writes, "a river would stop/its flow if only/a stream were there/to receive it." The speaker is expressing the feeling of longing. She uses a metaphor from nature. The river is a symbol of a person with no direction or purpose in life. The river has no goals to follow or boundaries to hold it in. Without boundaries, it can flow on and on forever. In other words, a person without someone to care for, to hold, and to be held by may search forever in many different directions. I also think she is saying that the person who breaks away from his or her loved ones or tries to be free will find only loneliness. It seems to me that the thing that person is running from is the thing he or she is searching for—love and a connection to others. Like the river, the person will only stop running when another is there waiting. There is another meaning also. That is that people might stop searching so hard if they knew there was someone who was devoted to them.

The third stanza of the poem says that "an ocean would never laugh/if clouds weren't there/to kiss her tears." I think Giovanni's message here is that not only are all human beings connected but we also need each other to bring joy into our lives. Together, we can get past the pain, disappointments, and sorrows of life. Here,

---

RUBRIC
IN ACTION

❶ Introduction states the title and author and briefly summarizes the main message of the poem.

❷ Transitions guide the reader through the interpretation and reveal the stanza-by-stanza organization of the poem.

❸ Essay can be built around interpretation of specific images, like this river metaphor.

❹ Direct quotations from the poem support the writer's interpretation.
Other Options:
• Paraphrase lines to support interpretation.
• Take images from the poem as support.

once again, the cycle of life is shown. The ocean is connected to the sky just as we are connected to each other. Ocean water evaporates into the clouds, which give off rain, filling the ocean again. I think the message here is that what we give comes back to us. All things come full circle.

The poem's final stanza, "the world is not/a pleasant place to be without/someone" repeats the first stanza. This gives the poem a feeling of completion. Once more, Giovanni presents her view of life. While many writers and poets try to entertain, Giovanni inspires us with her words. In my opinion, both the young and old will be able to relate to this poem. It is a short poem with a very big point: that all people are connected and need each other to be happy.

> **❺** Offers a clear statement of writer's insights into the meaning of the poem

> **❻** Conclusion summarizes and expands upon the writer's interpretation.

Writing Your Interpretive Essay

❶ Prewriting

> *To read a poem is to hear with our eyes; to hear it is to see it with our ears.*
>
> —Octavio Paz, poet

Go back to the poems you have studied and **read** each one aloud. Which sparks an idea or reminds you of something? Which has the most interesting sound devices or imagery? Also **list** the poems with unusual structures, powerful themes, or confusing lines. See the **Idea Bank** in the margin for more ideas. After you select a poem, follow the steps on the next page.

Planning Your Interpretive Essay

▸ 1. **Carefully read the poem several times.** Read it both aloud and silently to understand the full meaning.

▸ 2. **Look at elements in the poem.** To help you see how the poet communicates meaning, try making a chart that shows the sound devices, the figurative language, and the words or phrases that convey the meaning.

Sound Devices	Figurative Language	Words or Phrases	Represents

▸ 3. **Discuss your reactions to the poem.** In a small group, ask each other questions and exchange ideas on reactions to the poem and ideas about different interpretations.

▸ 4. **Decide on your focus.** Look back at your chart and decide on the main message or theme of the poem. Which of the poem's elements or images contribute most to the message?

❷ Drafting

Now it is time to put your thoughts down on paper. Include all of the observations and examples you gathered that help make the poem effective. You can eliminate less important details later. For help, try filling in the blanks:

The main message of (name of poem) by (name of author) is _____.

Organize Your Essay. Use your **introductory** paragraph to identify the poem and the author and to briefly state your interpretation. For the **body** of your essay, decide which idea you want to present first. Then use examples and evidence in the text to support your main points. **Conclude** with a summary of the meaning of the poem.

IDEA Bank

1. Your Working Portfolio
Look for ideas in the **Writing** sections that you completed earlier.

2. Many Meanings
With a partner, choose a poem you both like. Discuss your interpretations. Do you agree on the message and/or theme? Use examples to support your points.

3. Meet the Challenge
Look over the poetry selections in your textbook. Interpret the one that is the most difficult for you to understand.

Have a question?

See the **Writing Handbook**
Paragraph Unity, p. R39
Elaboration with Examples, p. R42
See **Language Network**
   Prewriting, p. 310
   Drafting, p. 315

Ask Your Peer Reader

- What is my main point about the author's message or theme(s)?
- What examples best support my point?
- What do you disagree with or want to know more about?
- How could my conclusion be strengthened?

Need revising help?

Review the **Rubric**, p. 238.

Consider **peer reader** comments.

Check **Revising, Editing, and Proofreading**, p. R35.

See **Language Network**, Elaboration, p. 375.

Confused about complete sentences?

See the **Grammar Handbook,** p. R71.

SPELLING From Writing

As you revise your work, look back at the words you misspelled and determine why you made the errors you did. For additional help, refer to the strategies and generalizations in the **Spelling Handbook,** p. R30.

SPEAKING Opportunity

Turn your interpretation into an oral presentation.

Publishing IDEAS

• Create a poetry Web site and publish your interpretation as well as those of your classmates.

• Work with classmates who interpreted the same poem to prepare a lesson for the class.

Publishing Options
www.mcdougallittell.com

❸ Revising

TARGET SKILL ▶ SUPPORTING YOUR RESPONSE WITH EXAMPLES In your interpretation, it is not enough to simply state your point. You must tell your reader how you reached that point. You can do this by supporting your point with direct quotes and other examples from the text itself. To help your readers understand, you might need to explain your thought process.

> The speaker is expressing the feeling of longing. She uses a metaphor from nature. *The river is a symbol of a person with no direction or purpose in life. The river has no goals to follow or boundaries to hold it in.*

❹ Editing and Proofreading

TARGET SKILL ▶ SUBJECT-VERB AGREEMENT Verbs should always agree with their subjects in number. A singular subject takes a singular verb. A plural subject takes a plural verb.

> The speaker ~~are~~ *is* expressing the feeling of longing. She use *s* a metaphor from nature. The river ~~are~~ *is* a symbol of a person with no direction or purpose in life. The river ~~have~~ *has* no goals to follow or boundaries to hold it in.

❺ Reflecting

FOR YOUR WORKING PORTFOLIO What did you learn about the poem as a result of writing this interpretation? Which step of the process gave you the most difficulty? What will you do differently the next time you write an interpretation? Attach your answers to your finished essay. Save your **interpretive essay** in your Working Portfolio.

Standardized Test Practice

Mixed Review

> "The Pasture" by Robert Frost is a poem <u>rich in imagery and meaning and the poet uses</u> ₍₁₎ sound devices and symbols to get across his theme. The first task of the speaker <u>are to clean the spring</u>, ₍₂₎ and he invites the listener to join him. He says, "I'll only stop to rake the leaves away/(And wait to watch the water clear, I may)." <u>The symbol of water is introduced in these lines, water</u> ₍₃₎ represents life. It is necessary for <u>existence</u>. ₍₄₎ Later in the poem, <u>the young calf, to,</u> ₍₅₎ becomes a symbol of rebirth. <u>Both symbols reinforces</u> ₍₆₎ the importance of nature.

Review Your Skills

Use the passage and the questions that follow it to check how well you remember the language conventions you've learned in previous grades.

1. How is sentence 1 best written?

A. rich in imagery and meaning, and the poet uses

B. rich in imagery and meaning; and the poet uses

C. rich in imagery and meaning. The poet uses

D. Correct as is

2. How is sentence 2 best written?

A. were to clean the spring,

B. is to clean the spring,

C. are being to clean the spring,

D. Correct as is

3. How is sentence 3 best written?

A. The symbol of water is introduced in these lines water

B. The symbol of water is introduced in these lines. Water

C. The symbol of water is introduced in these lines; and water

D. Correct as is

4. What is the correct spelling in sentence 4?

A. existanse

B. existense

C. existince

D. Correct as is

5. What is the correct spelling in sentence 5?

A. the young calf, too,

B. the young calf, two,

C. the young calf, tow,

D. Correct as is

6. How is sentence 6 best written?

A. Both symbols reinforce

B. Both symbols reinforcing

C. Both symbols has reinforced

D. Correct as is

Key Standard

LC1.4 Use the mechanics of writing correctly; demonstrate correct language usage.
Other Standard **LC1.6**

Self-Assessment

Check your own answers in the **Grammar Handbook**
Quick Reference: Capitalization, p. R70
Quick Reference: Punctuation, p. R68
Subject-Verb Agreement, p. R72

The Literature You'll Read

The Concepts You'll Study

Vocabulary and Reading Comprehension
Vocabulary Focus: Affixes
Visualizing
Connecting
Summarizing
Questioning
Setting Purposes

Writing and Language Conventions
Writing Workshop: Character Sketch
Action Verbs
Consistent Verb Tense
Active Voice and Passive Voice

Literary Analysis
Genre Focus: Drama
Stage Directions
Theme
Autobiography
Sound Devices
Fable and Moral
Modern Fable

Speaking and Listening
Oral Summary
Interview and Response
Evaluation of Video Portrayal
Speech and Interview

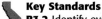

*D*rama

> *All the world's a stage,*
> *And all the men and women merely players . . .*
> *—Shakespeare, As You Like It*

Drama is one of the major forms of literature. In drama, characters and plot are developed through dialogue and action. Drama can be thought of as literature in play form.

Drama is intended to be performed for an audience, either on stage or before a camera. For this reason, dramas are written in a special form called a **script**, which includes stage directions and dialogue between characters. You see drama on television, in movies, in videos, and on stage.

Key Elements of Drama

- stage direction
- plot
- character
- dialogue

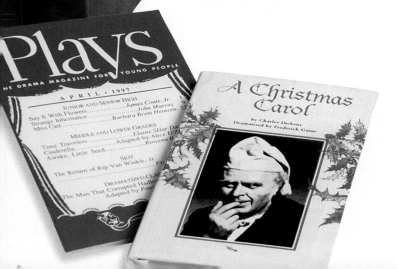

Stage Directions

A play's script includes instructions for the director, the actors, and the stage crew. These are called **stage directions.** They are often printed in italic type and enclosed in parentheses. In addition to telling the actors how to speak and move, the stage directions describe the **scenery**—the items that are on stage to help create the setting. Stage directions also describe the **props,** which are the objects the actors use during the play. Many scripts also include suggestions for lighting and sound.

YOUR TURN What scenery and props would be necessary to create the setting for this scene in the play *A Christmas Carol,* which is based on Charles Dickens's story?

STAGE DIRECTION

(The percussion thunders. Scrooge hurls himself through the descending snowflakes and sends the children scattering. They retreat, watching. Cratchit comes in. He takes some coal from the mound and puts it into a small bucket; as he carries it to a corner of the stage, the stage area is transformed from street to office. Scrooge's nephew Fred enters, talks with the children, gives them coins, and sends them away with a "Merry Christmas.")

—Charles Dickens, *A Christmas Carol,* Dramatization by Frederick Gaines

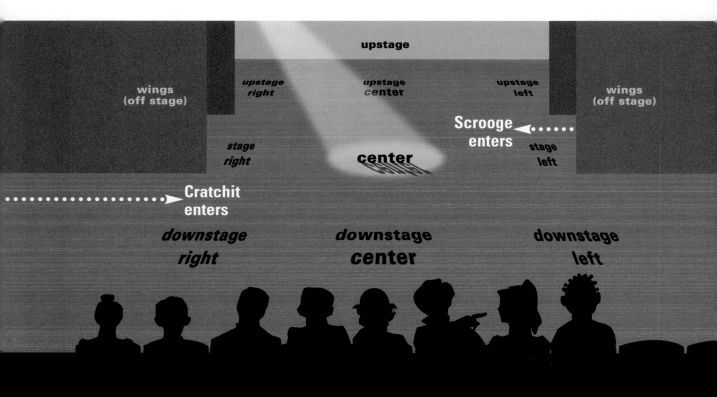

upstage

wings (off stage)

upstage right

upstage center

upstage left

wings (off stage)

Scrooge enters

stage right

center

stage left

Cratchit enters

downstage right

downstage center

downstage left

downstage audience

Plot

As in fiction, the **plot** of a drama is the sequence of related events that happen in the work. The plot begins with an **exposition,** which introduces the characters and setting and presents any necessary background. In the **rising action,** the central conflict is developed, and dramatic tension builds. The moment of highest tension is called the **climax.** After the climax comes the **falling action** (also called the **denouement**), in which the conflict is often resolved and the loose ends of the plot may be tied up. (For more on plot, see pages 343–346.)

In drama, the action is often divided into **scenes.** The scene changes whenever the setting (the time and the place of the story) changes. Sometimes two or more scenes are grouped into an **act.**

Character

In a play the **main** (also called major) and **minor characters** are often listed in the cast of characters at the beginning of the script. This list often includes a short description next to each character's name.

Occasionally one of the characters is a **narrator,** who sets the scene for the drama and may comment on what happens. Some characters, acting as **foils,** provide a sharp contrast to the qualities of the main characters. For instance, if the main character is lighthearted, the foil character might be serious.

YOUR TURN Read the dialogue between Scrooge and his nephew Fred in the beginning of Scene 1 of *A Christmas Carol.* How is Fred a foil for Scrooge?

From *A Christmas Carol*

CHARACTER

Fred. A Merry Christmas, Uncle! God save you!

Scrooge. Bah! Humbug!

Fred. Christmas a humbug, Uncle? I hope that's meant as a joke.

Scrooge. Well, it's not. Come, come, what is it you want? Don't waste all the day, Nephew.

Fred. I only want to wish you a Merry Christmas, Uncle. Don't be cross.

Scrooge. What else can I be when I live in such a world of fools as this? Merry Christmas! Out with Merry Christmas!

—Charles Dickens, *A Christmas Carol,* Dramatization by Frederick Gaines

Dialogue

A play is composed almost entirely of **dialogue,** that is, conversation between the characters. Throughout the course of the play, the dialogue reveals the plot as well as the characters' personalities.

YOUR TURN How does the playwright use dialogue and stage directions to reveal character and guide the actors in this excerpt from *The Monsters Are Due on Maple Street?*

DIALOGUE

Steve. Go ahead, Tommy, We'll be right back. And you'll see. That wasn't any ship or anything like it. That was just a . . . meteor or something. Likely as not — (*He turns to the group, now trying very hard to sound more optimistic than he feels.*) No doubt it did have something to do with all this power failure and the rest of it. Meteors can do some crazy things. Like sunspots.

Don. (*picking up the cue*) Sure. That's the kind of thing—like sunspots. They raise Cain with radio reception all over the world. And this thing being so close—why there's no telling the sort of stuff it can do. (*He wets his lips and smiles nervously.*) Go ahead, Charlie. You and Steve go into town and see if that isn't what's causing it all.

—Rod Serling,
The Monsters Are Due on Maple Street

From *The Monsters Are
Due on Maple Street*

$\mathcal{R}$eading Drama

Key Standard
R3.2 Identify events that advance the plot and describe how they explain the past, present, and future.
***Other Standard* R3.3**

You can bring a drama to life just by reading the script—if you know how to visualize. Interesting **characters** and **dialogue,** powerful **themes, plots,** and detailed **stage directions** can all work together to produce an exciting dramatic story. To get the most from every play, follow the reading strategies suggested here.

How to Apply the Strategies

Read the play silently. Before you read the play aloud with others, read it to yourself. You should know the entire plot and the characters before you perform. You may have to reread the play a few times to fully understand what is happening.

Read the stage directions carefully. Stage directions tell you where and when each scene is happening. If you skip over them, you miss out on much of the play.

Get to know the characters. In drama, you get to know the characters through dialogue—the characters' own words. You can also **visualize** the characters as you read, picturing the set and props as the characters are moving about, speaking their lines.

Keep track of the plot. As in fiction, the plot of a drama centers on a main conflict that the characters try to resolve. Look for the conflict and let yourself become involved in the story. Watch for the action to build to a climax and then notice how that conflict is resolved.

Read the play aloud with others. As you read the part of a character, be ready with your character's lines and read only the words your character says. Do not read the stage directions aloud. Be sure to listen to other actors as they read their lines. In acting, listening is just as important as speaking.

Here's how Steve uses the strategies:

"I love being in plays. When I'm reading a script, I read all the stage directions and **visualize** *how a character looks and acts. Sometimes I write down phrases that describe how my character might feel when he says his lines. I enjoy playing the part of someone who is different than me."*

A Christmas Carol

by CHARLES DICKENS   *Dramatized by* FREDERICK GAINES

Key Standard
R3.2 Identify events that advance the plot and describe how they explain the past, present, and future.
Other Standards **R1.3, R1.7, W1.7, W2.3, W2.5, LC1.3**

Connect to Your Life

How people lead their lives depends partly on the choices they make. In a small group, discuss characters you've read about in this book. How do their choices affect them? How do their choices affect the people around them? Do any of their choices change their attitudes and behavior? Why or why not?

Build Background

HISTORY

When Charles Dickens published *A Christmas Carol* in 1843, about one-third of the people in London, England, lived in poverty.

Factories had changed the face of London, with people flooding the city from rural areas. The city quickly became dirty and overcrowded. Wages were low and children were hungry. Jobs and housing were in short supply. The Poor Law of 1834 forced the homeless into workhouses that were little more than prisons.

By exposing the suffering of the poor in a vivid and sympathetic manner, Dickens convinced many readers that conditions had to be corrected.

WORDS TO KNOW **Vocabulary Preview**

abundance	emerge	mortal	solitude
anonymous	endeavor	odious	summon
charitable	finale	pledge	surplus
currency	incoherent	provision	transform
destitute	macabre	reassurance	welfare

Focus Your Reading

LITERARY ANALYSIS **STAGE DIRECTIONS**

In adapting Dickens's novel into a play, Frederick Gaines chose to depict some of the poor people and conditions of London in his stage directions. **Stage directions** are notes in the scripts of plays. These directions are frequently in italics, and guide actors and readers by explaining the settings of scenes, the movements of actors, the rate and tone of the dialogue, and the sound effects. When you read a play, don't skip the stage directions. They give you information that you won't get any other way.

ACTIVE READING **VISUALIZING**

When you read the script of a play rather than see the play performed on a stage, use the stage directions to help you **visualize** the play's **setting, characters,** and **action.** Try to imagine what you would see if you were watching the play performed on a stage.

READER'S NOTEBOOK As you read the stage directions in this play, pause to visualize the scenes that are being described. In your mind, try to position the characters in the correct places on the stage. Then draw or sketch the scenes.

A Christmas Carol

by Charles Dickens
Dramatized by Frederick Gaines

Characters

Carolers, Families, Dancers
First Boy
Second Boy
Third Boy
Girl with a doll
Ebenezer Scrooge
Bob Cratchit, Scrooge's clerk
Fred, Scrooge's nephew
Gentleman Visitor
Warder and Residents of the
    Poorhouse
Sparsit, Scrooge's servant
Cook
Charwoman

Jacob Marley
Priest
Leper
First Spirit (*the Spirit*
   of Christmas Past)
Jack Walton
Ben Benjamin
Child Scrooge
Fan, Scrooge's sister
Fezziwig
Young Ebenezer
Dick Wilkins
Sweetheart of Young Ebenezer

Second Spirit (*the Spirit*
   of Christmas Present)
Poorhouse Children
Mrs. Cratchit
Several Cratchit Children
Tiny Tim
Beggar Children, Hunger and
   Ignorance
Third Spirit (*the Spirit*
   of Christmas Yet to Come)
Peter, a Cratchit child
Boy
Butcher
Coachman

Prologue

The play begins amid a swirl of street life in Victorian London. Happy groups pass; brightly costumed carolers and families call out to one another and sing "Joy to the World." Three boys and a girl are grouped about a glowing mound of coal. As the carolers leave the stage, the lights dim and the focus shifts to the mound of coals, bright against the dark. Slowly, the children begin to respond to the warmth. A piano plays softly as the children talk.

First Boy. I saw a horse in a window. (*pause*) A dapple . . . gray and white. And a saddle, too . . . red. And a strawberry mane down to here. All new. Golden stirrups. (*People pass by the children, muttering greetings to one another.*)

Second Boy. Christmas Eve.

Third Boy. Wish we could go.

First Boy. So do I.

Third Boy. I think I'd like it.

First Boy. Oh, wouldn't I . . . wouldn't I!

Second Boy. We're going up onto the roof. (*The boys look at him quizzically.*) My father has a glass. Telescope. A brass one. It opens up and it has twists on it and an eyepiece that you put up to look through. We can see all the way to the park with it.

Third Boy. Could I look through it?

Second Boy. Maybe . . . where would you look?

(*The third boy points straight up.*) Why there?

Third Boy. I'd like to see the moon. (*The boys stand and look upward as the girl sings to her doll. One of the boys makes a snow angel on the ground.*)

Girl (*singing*).

Christ the King came down one day,
Into this world of ours,
And crying from a manger bed,
Began the Christmas hour.

(*speaking*)

Christ the King, my pretty one,
Sleep softly on my breast,
Christ the King, my gentle one,
Show us the way to rest.

(*She begins to sing the first verse again. As snow starts to fall on the boy making the snow angel, he stands up and reaches out to catch a single flake.*)

Scene 1

SCROOGE IN HIS SHOP

The percussion thunders. Scrooge hurls himself through the descending snowflakes and sends the children scattering. They retreat, watching. Cratchit comes in. He takes some coal from the mound and puts it into a small bucket; as he carries it to a corner of the stage, the stage area is <u>transformed</u> *from street to office. Scrooge's nephew Fred enters, talks with the children, gives them coins, and sends them away with a "Merry Christmas."*

Fred. A Merry Christmas, Uncle! God save you!

Scrooge. Bah! Humbug!

Fred. Christmas a humbug, Uncle? I hope that's meant as a joke.

Scrooge. Well, it's not. Come, come, what is it you want? Don't waste all the day, Nephew.

Fred. I only want to wish you a Merry Christmas, Uncle. Don't be cross.

Scrooge. What else can I be when I live in such a world of fools as this? Merry Christmas! Out with Merry Christmas! What's Christmas to you but a time for paying bills without money, a time for finding yourself a year older and not an hour richer. If I could work my will, every idiot who goes about with "Merry Christmas" on his lips should be boiled with his own pudding and buried with a stake of holly through his heart.

Fred. Uncle!

Scrooge. Nephew, keep Christmas in your own way and let me keep it in mine.

Fred. But you don't keep it.

Scrooge. Let me leave it alone then. Much good may it do you. Much good it has ever done you.

Fred. There are many things from which I might have derived good by which I have not profited, I daresay, Christmas among the rest. And though it has never put a scrap of gold in my pocket, I believe it has done me good and will do me good, and I say, God bless it!

Scrooge. Bah!

Fred. Don't be angry, Uncle. Come! Dine with us tomorrow.

Scrooge. I'll dine alone, thank you.

Fred. But why?

Scrooge. Why? Why did you get married?

Fred. Why, because I fell in love with a wonderful girl.

Scrooge. And I with <u>solitude</u>. Good afternoon.

Fred. Nay, Uncle, but you never came to see me before I was married. Why give it as a reason for not coming now?

Scrooge. Good afternoon.

Fred. I am sorry with all my heart to find you so determined; but I have made the attempt in homage to[1] Christmas, and I'll keep that good spirit to the last. So, a Merry Christmas, Uncle.

Scrooge. Good afternoon!

Fred. And a Happy New Year!

Scrooge. Good afternoon! (*Fred hesitates as if to say something more. He sees that Scrooge has gone to get a volume down from the shelf, and so he starts to leave. As he leaves, the doorbell rings.*) Bells. Is it necessary to always have bells? (*The gentleman visitor enters, causing the doorbell to ring again.*) Cratchit!

ACTIVE READER

VISUALIZE Close your eyes and imagine the scene in Scrooge's shop. What do you see?

Cratchit. Yes, sir?

Scrooge. The bell, fool! See to it!

Cratchit. Yes, sir. (*He goes to the entrance.*)

Scrooge (*muttering*). Merry Christmas . . . Wolves howling and a Merry Christmas . . .

Cratchit. It's for you, sir.

Scrooge. Of course it's for me. You're not receiving callers, are you? Show them in.

Cratchit. Right this way, sir. (*The gentleman visitor approaches Scrooge.*)

Scrooge. Yes, yes?

Gentleman Visitor. Scrooge and Marley's, I believe. Have I the pleasure of addressing Mr. Scrooge or Mr. Marley?

Scrooge. Marley's dead. Seven years tonight. What is it you want?

Gentleman Visitor. I have no doubt that his liberality[2] is well represented by his surviving partner. Here, sir, my card. (*He hands Scrooge his business card.*)

Scrooge. Liberality? No doubt of it? All right, all right, I can read. What is it you want? (*He returns to his work.*)

Gentleman Visitor. At this festive season of the year . . .

---

1. **in homage to** (hŏm´ĭj): in honor of.
2. **liberality** (lĭb´ə-răl´ĭ-tē): generousness.

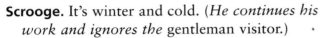

Scrooge. It's winter and cold. (*He continues his work and ignores the* gentleman visitor.)

Gentleman Visitor. Yes . . . yes, it is, and the more reason for my visit. At this time of the year it is more than usually desirable to make some slight <u>provision</u> for the poor and <u>destitute</u> who suffer greatly from the cold. Many thousands are in want of common necessaries; hundreds of thousands are in want of common comforts, sir.

Scrooge. Are there no prisons?

Gentleman Visitor. Many, sir.

Scrooge. And the workhouse?[3] Is it still in operation?

Gentleman Visitor. It is; still, I wish I could say it was not.

Scrooge. The poor law is still in full vigor then?

Gentleman Visitor. Yes, sir.

Scrooge. I'm glad to hear it. From what you said, I was afraid someone had stopped its operation.

Gentleman Visitor. Under the impression that they scarcely furnish Christian cheer of mind or body to the multitude, a few of us are <u>endeavoring</u> to raise a fund to buy the poor some meat and drink and means of warmth. We choose this time because it is the time, of all others, when want is keenly felt and <u>abundance</u> rejoices. May I put you down for something, sir?

Scrooge (*retreating into the darkness temporarily*). Nothing.

Gentleman Visitor. You wish to be <u>anonymous</u>?

Scrooge. I wish to be left alone. Since you ask me what I wish, sir, that is my answer. I don't make merry myself at Christmas, and I can't afford to make idle people merry. I help support the establishments I have mentioned . . . they cost enough . . . and those who are poorly off must go there.

Gentleman Visitor. Many can't go there, and many would rather die.

Scrooge. If they would rather die, they had better do it and decrease the <u>surplus</u> population. That is not my affair. My business is. It occupies me constantly. (*He talks both to the* gentleman visitor *and to himself while he thumbs through his books.*) Ask a man to give up life and means . . . fine thing. What is it, I want to know? Charity? . . . (*His nose deep in his books, he vaguely hears the dinner bell being rung in the workhouse; he looks up as if he has heard it but never focuses on the actual scene. The warder of the poorhouse stands in a pool of light at the far left, slowly ringing a bell.*)

ACTIVE READER

EVALUATE What do you think the author wants you to feel about Scrooge?

Warder. Dinner. All right. Line up. (*The poorly clad, dirty residents of the poorhouse line up and file by to get their evening dish of gruel,[4] wordlessly accepting it and going back to eat listlessly in the gloom. Scrooge returns to the business of his office. The procession continues for a moment, then the image of the poorhouse is obscured by darkness. The dejected* gentleman visitor *exits.*)

Scrooge. Latch the door, Cratchit. Firmly, firmly. Draft as cold as Christmas blowing in here. Charity! (*Cratchit goes to the door, starts to close it, then sees the little* girl *with the doll. She seems to beckon to him; he*

---

3. **workhouse:** prison where prisoners are required to work.

4. **gruel** (grōō′əl): a thin, watery food made by boiling ground grain in water or milk.

WORDS
TO
KNOW

provision (prə-vĭzh′ən) *n.* a supplying of needs
destitute (dĕs′tĭ-tōōt′) *n.* people lacking the necessities of life
endeavor (ĕn-dĕv′ər) *v.* to try
abundance (ə-bŭn′dəns) *n.* wealth
anonymous (ə-nŏn′ə-məs) *adj.* not having one's name known
surplus (sûr′pləs) *adj.* extra; more than is needed

moves slowly toward her, and they dance together for a moment. Scrooge continues to work. Suddenly carolers appear on the platform, and a few phrases of their carol, "Angels We Have Heard on High," are heard. Scrooge looks up.) Cratchit! *(As soon as Scrooge shouts, the girl and the carolers vanish and Cratchit begins to close up the shop.)* Cratchit!

Cratchit. Yes, sir.

Scrooge. Well, to work then!

Cratchit. It's evening, sir.

Scrooge. Is it?

Cratchit. Christmas evening, sir.

Scrooge. Oh, you'll want all day tomorrow off, I suppose.

Cratchit. If it's quite convenient, sir.

Scrooge. It's not convenient, and it's not fair. If I was to deduct half a crown[5] from your salary for it, you'd think yourself ill-used, wouldn't you? Still you expect me to pay a day's wage for a day of no work.

Cratchit. It's only once a year, sir.

Scrooge. Be here all the earlier the next morning.

Cratchit. I will, sir.

Scrooge. Then off, off.

Cratchit. Yes, sir! Merry Christmas, sir!

Scrooge. Bah! *(As soon as Cratchit opens the door, the sounds of the street begin, very bright and loud. Cratchit is caught up in a swell of people hurrying through the street. Children pull him along to the top of an ice slide, and he runs and slides down it, disappearing in darkness as the stage suddenly is left almost empty. Scrooge goes around the room blowing out the candles, talking to himself.)* Christmas Eve. Carolers! Bah! There. Another day. *(He opens his door and peers out.)* Black, very black. Now where are they? *(The children are heard singing carols for a moment.)* Begging pennies for their songs, are they? Oh, boy! Here, boy! *(The little girl emerges from the shadows. Scrooge hands her a dark lantern, and she holds it while he lights it with an ember from the pile of coals.)*

---

5. **half a crown:** until 1971, an amount of British money equal to 2½ shillings or one-eighth of a pound.

THINKING through the LITERATURE

1. What was your response to the meeting between Ebenezer Scrooge and his nephew, Fred?

2. Skim the stage directions. How is the **mood**—the feeling conveyed to the reader—outside Scrooge's office different from the mood within the office?

WORDS
TO
KNOW

emerge (ĭ-mûrj′) *v.* to come into sight

Scene 2

SCROOGE GOES HOME

Scrooge (*talking to the little girl*). Hold it quiet! There. Off now. That's it. High. Black as pitch. Light the street, that's it. You're a bright lad! Good to see that. Earn your supper, boy. You'll not go hungry this night. Home. You know the way, do you? Yes, that's the way. The house of Ebenezer Scrooge. (*As the two find their way to Scrooge's house, the audience sees and hears a brief image of a cathedral interior with a living crèche and a large choir singing "Amen!"; the image ends in a blackout. The lights come up immediately, and* Scrooge *is at his door.*) Hold the light up, boy, up. (*The* girl *with the lantern disappears.*) Where did he go? Boy? No matter. There's a penny saved. Lantern's gone out. No matter. A candle saved. Yes, here's the key. (*He turns with the key toward the door, and* Marley's *face swims out of the darkness.* Scrooge *watches, unable to speak. He fumbles for a match, lights the lantern, and swings it toward the figure, which melts away. Pause.* Scrooge *fits the key in the lock and turns it as the door suddenly is opened from the inside by the porter,* Sparsit. Scrooge *is startled, then recovers.*) Sparsit?

Sparsit. Yes, sir?

Scrooge. Hurry, hurry. The door . . . close it.

Sparsit. Did you knock, sir?

Scrooge. Knock? What matter? Here, light me up the stairs.

Sparsit. Yes, sir. (*He leads* Scrooge *up the stairs. They pass the cook on the way.* Scrooge *brushes by her, stops, looks back, and she leans toward him.*)

Cook. Something to warm you, sir? Porridge?

Scrooge. Wha . . . ? No. No, nothing.

Cook (*waiting for her Christmas coin*). Merry Christmas, sir. (Scrooge *ignores the request and the* cook *disappears. Mumbling,* Scrooge *follows* Sparsit.)

Scrooge (*looking back after the* cook *is gone*). Fright a man nearly out of his life . . . Merry Christmas . . . bah!

Sparsit. Your room, sir.

Scrooge. Hmmm? Oh, yes, yes. And good night.

Sparsit (*extending his hand for his coin*). Merry Christmas, sir.

Scrooge. Yes, yes . . . (*He sees the outstretched hand; he knows what* Sparsit *wants and is infuriated.*) Out! Out! (*He closes the door after* Sparsit, *turns toward his chamber, and discovers the* charwoman *directly behind him.*)

Charwoman. Warm your bed for you, sir?

Scrooge. What? Out! Out!

Charwoman. Aye, sir. (*She starts for the door.* Marley's *voice is heard mumbling something unintelligible.*)

Scrooge. What's that?

Charwoman. Me, sir? Not a thing, sir.

Scrooge. Then, good night.

Charwoman. Good night. (*She exits, and* Scrooge *pantomimes shutting the door behind her. The voice of* Marley *over an offstage microphone whispers and reverberates: "Merry Christmas, Scrooge!" Silence.* Scrooge *hears the voice but cannot account for it. He climbs up to open a window and looks down. A cathedral choir singing "O Come, All Ye Faithful" is heard in the distance.* Scrooge *listens a moment, shuts the window, and prepares for bed. As soon as* *he has shut the sound out of his room, figures appear; they seem to be coming down the main aisle of a church, bearing gifts to the living crèche. The orchestra plays "O Come, All Ye Faithful" as the procession files out. Scrooge, ready for bed, warms himself before the heap of coals. As he pulls his nightcap from a chair, a small hand-bell tumbles off onto the floor. Startled, he picks it up and rings it for* <u>reassurance</u>*; an echo answers it. He turns and sees the little girl on the street; she is swinging her doll, which produces the echo of his bell. Scrooge escapes to his bed; the girl is swallowed up in the darkness. The bell sounds grow to a din,* <u>incoherent</u> *as in a dream, then suddenly fall silent. Scrooge sits up in bed, listens, and hears the chains of* Marley *coming up the stairs. Scrooge reaches for the bell pull to* <u>summon</u> Sparsit. *The bell responds with a gong, and* Marley *appears. He and* Scrooge *face one another.*)

Scrooge. What do you want with me?

Marley (*in a ghostly, unreal voice*). Much.

Scrooge. Who are you?

Marley. Ask who I was.

Scrooge. Who were you?

Marley. In life, I was your partner, Jacob Marley.

Scrooge. He's dead.

Marley. Seven years this night, Ebenezer Scrooge.

Scrooge. Why do you come here?

Marley. I must. It is commanded me. I must wander the world and see what I can no longer share, what I would not share when I walked where you do.

Scrooge. And must go thus?

Marley. The chain? Look at it, Ebenezer, study it.

Locks and vaults and golden coins. I forged it, each link, each day when I sat in these chairs, commanded these rooms. Greed, Ebenezer Scrooge, wealth. Feel them, know them. Yours was as heavy as this I wear seven years ago, and you have labored to build it since.

Scrooge. If you're here to lecture, I have no time for it. It is late; the night is cold. I want comfort now.

Marley. I have none to give. I know not how you see me this night. I did not ask it. I have sat invisible beside you many and many a day. I am commanded to bring you a chance, Ebenezer. Heed it!

Scrooge. Quickly then, quickly.

Marley. You will be haunted by three spirits.

Scrooge (*scoffing*). Is that the chance?

Marley. Mark it.

Scrooge. I do not choose to.

Marley (*ominously*). Then you will walk where I do, burdened by your riches, your greed.

Scrooge. Spirits mean nothing to me.

Marley (*slowly leaving*). Expect the first tomorrow, when the bell tolls one, the second on the next night at the same hour, the third upon the next night when the last stroke of twelve has ended. Look to see me no more. I must wander. Look that, for your own sake, you remember what has passed between us.

Scrooge. Jacob . . . Don't leave me! . . . Jacob! Jacob!

Marley. Adieu,[6] Ebenezer. (*At Marley's last words a funeral procession begins to move across the stage. A boy walks in front; a priest follows, swinging a censer;[7] sounds of*

---

6. **adieu** (ə-dyo͞o′): farewell.

7. **censer:** incense burner.

WORDS TO KNOW	**reassurance** (rē′ə-sho͝or′əns) *n.* a restoring of confidence **incoherent** (ĭn′kō-hîr′ənt) *adj.* without connection or harmony **summon** (sŭm′ən) *v.* to call for or send for with authority or urgency; to order to come or appear

259

mourning and the suggestion of church music are heard. Scrooge calls out, "Jacob, don't leave me!" as if talking in the midst of a bad dream. At the end of the procession is the little girl, swinging her doll and singing softly.)

Girl.

Hushabye, don't you cry,
Go to sleep, little baby.
When you wake, you shall have
All the pretty little horses,
Blacks and bays, dapples and grays,
All the pretty little horses.

(*She stops singing and looks up at Scrooge; their eyes meet, and she solemnly rings the doll in greeting. Scrooge pulls shut the bed curtains, and the girl exits. The bell sounds are picked up by the bells of a* leper[8] *who enters, dragging himself along.*)

Leper (*calling out*). Leper! Leper! Stay the way! Leper! Leper! Keep away! (*He exits and the* clock begins to chime, ringing the hours. Scrooge *sits up in bed and begins to count the chimes.*)

Scrooge. Eight . . . nine . . . ten . . . eleven . . . it can't be . . . twelve. Midnight? No. Not twelve. It can't be. I haven't slept the whole day through. Twelve? Yes, yes, twelve noon. (*He hurries to the window and looks out.*) Black. Twelve midnight. (*pause*) I must get up. A day wasted. I must get down to the office. (*Two small chimes are heard.*) Quarter past. But it just rang twelve. Fifteen minutes haven't gone past, not so quickly. (*Again two small chimes are heard.*) A quarter to one. The spirit . . . It's to come at one. (*He hurries to his bed as the chimes ring again.*) One.

---

8. **leper** (lĕp'ər): a person who has leprosy, a skin disease once believed to be highly contagious.

Scene 3

THE SPIRIT OF CHRISTMAS PAST

The hour is struck again by a large street clock, and the first spirit *appears. It is a figure dressed to look like the little* girl's doll.

Scrooge. Are you the spirit whose coming was foretold to me?

First Spirit. I am.

Scrooge. Who and what are you?

First Spirit. I am the Ghost of Christmas Past.

Scrooge. Long past?

First Spirit. Your past.

Scrooge. Why are you here?

First Spirit. Your <u>welfare</u>. Rise. Walk with me.

Scrooge. I am <u>mortal</u> still. I cannot pass through air.

First Spirit. My hand. (Scrooge *grasps the spirit's hand tightly, and the doll's bell rings softly.* Scrooge *remembers a scene from his past in which two boys greet each other in the street.*)

First Voice. Halloo, Jack!

Second Voice. Ben! Merry Christmas, Ben!

Scrooge. Jack Walton. Young Jack Walton. Spirits . . . ?

First Voice. Have a good holiday, Jack

Scrooge. Yes, yes, I remember him. Both of them. Little Ben Benjamin. He used to . . .

WORDS TO KNOW

welfare (wĕl'fâr') *n.* well-being
mortal (môr'tl) *adj.* of the earth; not a spirit

260

VIEW AND COMPARE

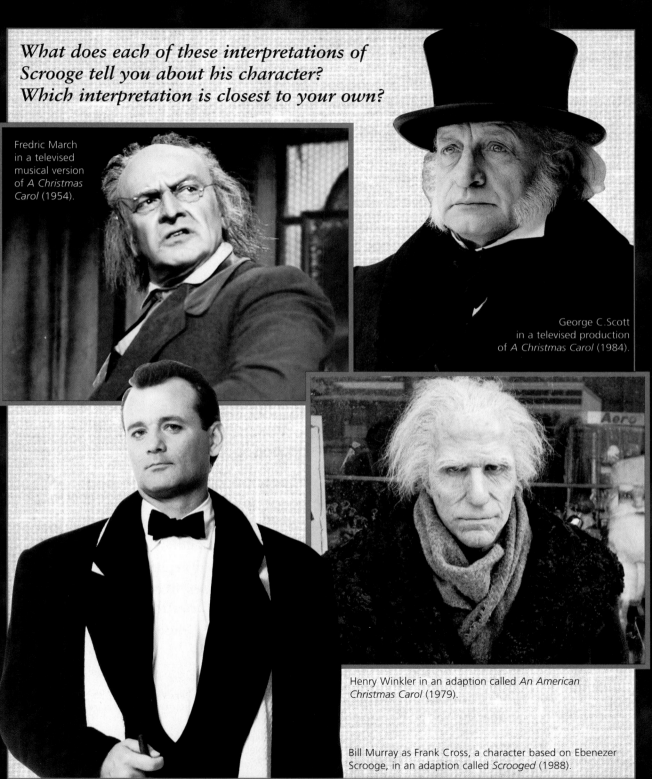

What does each of these interpretations of Scrooge tell you about his character? Which interpretation is closest to your own?

Fredric March in a televised musical version of *A Christmas Carol* (1954).

George C. Scott in a televised production of *A Christmas Carol* (1984).

Henry Winkler in an adaption called *An American Christmas Carol* (1979).

Bill Murray as Frank Cross, a character based on Ebenezer Scrooge, in an adaption called *Scrooged* (1988).

First Voice. See you next term, Jack. Next . . . term . . .

Scrooge. They . . . they're off for the holidays and going home from school. It's Christmas time . . . all of the children off home now . . . No . . . no, not all . . . there was one . . . (*The spirit motions for* Scrooge *to turn, and he sees a young* boy *playing with a teddy bear and talking to it.*) Yes . . . reading . . . poor boy.

First Spirit. What, I wonder?

Scrooge. Reading? Oh, it was nothing. Fancy,[9] all fancy and make-believe and take-me-away. All of it. Yes, nonsense.

Child Scrooge. Ali Baba.[10]

Scrooge. Yes . . . that was it . . .

Child Scrooge. Yes, and remember . . . and remember . . . remember Robinson Crusoe?[11]

Scrooge. And the parrot!

Child Scrooge. Yes, the parrot! I love him best.

Scrooge (*imitating the parrot*). With his stripy green body and yellow tail drooping along and couldn't sing—awk—but could talk, and a thing like a lettuce growing out the top of his head . . . and he used to sit on the very top of the tree—up there.

Child Scrooge. And Robinson Crusoe sailed around the island, and he thought he had escaped the island, and the parrot said, the parrot said . . .

Scrooge (*imitating the parrot*). Robinson Crusoe, where you been? Awk! Robinson Crusoe, where you been?

Child Scrooge. And Robinson Crusoe looked up in the tree and saw the parrot and knew he hadn't escaped and he was still there, still all alone there.

Scrooge. Poor Robinson Crusoe.

Child Scrooge (*sadly replacing the teddy bear*). Poor Robinson Crusoe.

Scrooge. Poor child. Poor child.

First Spirit. Why poor?

Scrooge. Fancy . . . fancy . . . (*He tries to mask his feelings by being brusque.*) It's his way, a child's way to . . . to lose being alone in . . . in dreams, dreams . . . Never matter if they are all nonsense, yes, nonsense. But he'll be all right, grow out of it. Yes. Yes, he did outgrow it, the nonsense. Became a man and left there, and he became, yes, he became a man and . . . yes, successful . . . rich! (*The sadness returns.*) Never matter . . . never matter. (Fan *runs in and goes to* Child Scrooge.) Fan!

Fan. Brother, dear brother! (*She kisses Child Scrooge.*)

Child Scrooge. Dear, dear Fan.

Fan. I've come to bring you home, home for good and ever. Come with me, come now. (*She takes his hand, and they start to run off, but the* spirit *stops them and signals for the light on them to fade. They look at the* spirit, *aware of their role in the* spirit's "education" *of* Scrooge.)

Scrooge. Let me watch them go? Let them be happy for a moment! (*The* spirit *says nothing.* Scrooge *turns away from them, and the light goes out.*) A delicate, delicate child. A breath might have withered her.

First Spirit. She died a woman and had, as I remember, children.

Scrooge. One child.

First Spirit. Your nephew.

Scrooge. Yes, yes, Fred, my nephew. (Scrooge *pauses, then tries to bluster through.*) Well? Well, all of us have that, haven't we?

---

9. **fancy:** illusion.

10. **Ali Baba** (ä′lē bä′bə): in the *Arabian Nights*, a poor woodcutter who discovers the treasure-filled cave of 40 thieves.

11. **Robinson Crusoe:** in the novel *Robinson Crusoe* by Daniel Defoe, a shipwrecked sailor who survives for years on a small island.

Childhoods? Sadnesses? But we grow and we become men, masters of ourselves. (*The spirit gestures for music to begin. It is heard first as from a great distance, then* Scrooge *becomes aware of it.*) I've no time for it, Spirit. Music and all of your Christmas folderol.[12] Yes, yes, I've learnt what you have to show me. (Fezziwig, Young Ebenezer, *and* Dick *appear, busily preparing for a party.*)

Fezziwig. Yo ho, there! Ebenezer! Dick!

Scrooge. Fezziwig! It's old Fezziwig that I 'prenticed[13] under.

First Spirit. Your master?

Scrooge. Oh, aye, and the best that any boy could have. There's Dick Wilkins! Bless me. He was very much attached to me was Dick. Poor Dick. Dear, dear.

Fezziwig. Yo ho, my boys! No more work tonight. Christmas Eve, Dick! Christmas, Ebenezer! Let's have the shutters up before a man can say Jack Robinson! (*The music continues. Chandeliers are pulled into position, and mistletoe, holly, and ivy are draped over everything by bustling servants. Dancers fill the stage for* Fezziwig's *wonderful Christmas party. In the midst of the dancing and the gaiety servants pass back and forth through the crowd with huge platters of food. At a pause in the music,* Young Ebenezer, *who is dancing, calls out.*)

Young Ebenezer. Mr. Fezziwig, sir, you're a wonderful master!

Scrooge and Young Ebenezer. A wonderful master!

Scrooge (*echoing the phrase*). A wonderful master! (*The music changes suddenly, and the dancers jerk into distorted postures and then begin to move in slow motion. The celebrants slowly exit, performing a* <u>macabre</u> *dance to discordant sounds.*)

First Spirit. Just because he gave a party? It was very small.

ACTIVE READER

QUESTION Why does the author show Scrooge's happy days with his first master?

Scrooge. Small!

First Spirit. He spent a few pounds[14] of your "mortal" money, three, four at the most. Is that so much that he deserves this praise?

Scrooge. But it wasn't the money. He had the power to make us happy, to make our service light or burdensome. The happiness he gives is quite as great as if it cost a fortune. That's what . . . a good master is.

First Spirit. Yes?

Scrooge. No, no, nothing.

First Spirit. Something, I think.

Scrooge. I should like to be able to say a word or two to my clerk just now, that's all.

First Spirit. But this is all past. Your clerk, Cratchit, couldn't be here.

Scrooge. No, no, of course not, an idle thought. Are we done?

First Spirit (*motioning for the waltz music to begin*). Nearly.

Scrooge (*hearing the waltz and remembering it*). Surely it's enough. Haven't you tormented me enough? (Young Ebenezer *is seen waltzing with his* Sweetheart.)

First Spirit. I only show the past, what it promised you. Look. Another promise.

Scrooge. Oh. Oh, yes. I had forgotten . . . her.

---

12. **folderol** (fŏl′də-rŏl′): foolishness, nonsense.

13. **'prenticed:** short for apprenticed, here meaning "learned a trade while working."

14. **pounds:** basic British units of money, each equal to 20 shillings.

WORDS TO KNOW   **macabre** (mə-kä′brə) *adj.* suggesting the horror of death and decay

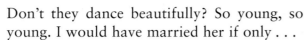

Don't they dance beautifully? So young, so young. I would have married her if only . . .

Sweetheart. Can you love me, Ebenezer? I bring no dowry[15] to my marriage, only me, only love. It is no <u>currency</u> that you can buy and sell with, but we can live with it. Can you? (*She pauses, then returns the ring* Scrooge *gave her as his* <u>pledge</u>.) I release you, Ebenezer, for the love of the man you once were. Will that man win me again, now that he is free?

Scrooge (*trying to speak to her*). If only you had held me to it. You should not have let me go. I was young; I did love you.

Sweetheart (*speaking to* Young Ebenezer). We have never lied to one another. May you be happy in the life you have chosen. Good-bye. (*She runs out.* Young Ebenezer *slowly leaves.*)

Scrooge. No, no, it was not meant that way . . . !

First Spirit. You cannot change now what you would not change then. I am your mistakes, Ebenezer Scrooge, all of the things you could have done and did not.

Scrooge. Then leave me! I have done them. I shall live with them. As I have, as I do; as I will.

First Spirit. There is another Christmas, seven years ago, when Marley died.

Scrooge. No! I will not see it. I will not! He died. I could not prevent it. I did not choose for him to die on Christmas Day.

First Spirit. And when his day was chosen, what did you do then?

Scrooge. I looked after his affairs.

First Spirit. His business.

Scrooge. Yes! His business! Mine! It was all that I had, all that I could do in this world. I have nothing to do with the world to come after.

First Spirit. Then I will leave you.

Scrooge. Not yet! Don't leave me here! Tell me what I must do! What of the other spirits?

First Spirit. They will come.

Scrooge. And you? What of you?

First Spirit. I am always with you. (*The little* girl *appears with her doll; she takes* Scrooge's *hand and gently leads him to bed. Numbed, he follows her. She leans against the foot of the bed, ringing the doll and singing. The* first spirit *exits as she sings.*)

Girl.
When you wake, you shall have
All the pretty little horses,
Blacks and bays, dapples and grays,
All the pretty little horses.

(*She rings the doll, and the ringing becomes the chiming of* Scrooge's *bell. The girl exits.* Scrooge *sits upright in bed as he hears the chimes.*)

Scrooge. A minute until one. No one here. No one's coming. (*A larger clock strikes one o'clock.*)

---

15. **dowry:** the property a bride brings to her husband when they marry.

WORDS
TO
KNOW

currency (kûr′ən-sē) *n.* money
pledge (plĕj) *n.* something given to guarantee fulfillment of a promise

Scene 4

THE SPIRIT OF CHRISTMAS PRESENT

A light comes on. Scrooge *becomes aware of it and goes slowly to it. He sees the* second spirit, *the Spirit of Christmas Present, who looks like* Fezziwig.

Scrooge. Fezziwig!

Second Spirit. Hello, Scrooge.

Scrooge. But you can't be . . . not Fezziwig.

Second Spirit. Do you see me as him?

Scrooge. I do.

Second Spirit. And hear me as him?

Scrooge. I do.

Second Spirit. I wish I were the gentleman, so as not to disappoint you.

Scrooge. But you're not . . . ?

Second Spirit. No, Mr. Scrooge. You have never seen the like of me before. I am the Ghost of Christmas Present.

Scrooge. But . . .

Second Spirit. You see what you will see, Scrooge, no more. Will you walk out with me this Christmas Eve?

Scrooge. But I am not yet dressed.

Second Spirit. Take my tails, dear boy, we're leaving.

Scrooge. Wait!

Second Spirit. What is it now?

Scrooge. Christmas Present, did you say?

Second Spirit. I did.

Scrooge. Then we are traveling here? In this town? London? Just down there?

Second Spirit. Yes, yes, of course.

Scrooge. Then we could walk? Your flying is . . . well, too sudden for an old man. Well?

Second Spirit. It's your Christmas, Scrooge; I am only the guide.

Scrooge (*puzzled*). Then we can walk? (*The* spirit *nods.*) Where are you guiding me to?

Second Spirit. Bob Cratchit's.

Scrooge. My clerk?

Second Spirit. You did want to talk to him? (Scrooge *pauses, uncertain how to answer.*) Don't worry, Scrooge, you won't have to.

Scrooge (*trying to change the subject, to cover his error*). Shouldn't be much of a trip. With fifteen bob[16] a week, how far off can it be?

Second Spirit. A world away, Scrooge, at least that far. (Scrooge *and the* spirit *start to step off a curb when a funeral procession enters with a child's coffin, followed by the* poorhouse children, *who are singing. Seated on top of the coffin is the little* girl. *She and* Scrooge *look at one another.*) That is the way to it, Scrooge. (*The procession follows the coffin offstage;* Scrooge *and the* spirit *exit after the procession. As they leave, the lights focus on* Mrs. Cratchit *and her* children. Mrs. Cratchit *sings as she puts* Tiny Tim *and the other* children *to bed, all in one bed. She pulls a dark blanket over them.*)

Mrs. Cratchit (*singing*).
When you wake, you shall have
All the pretty little horses,
Blacks and bays, dapples and grays,
All the pretty little horses.

---

16. **bob:** a British slang term for shilling.

To sleep now, all of you. Christmas tomorrow. (*She kisses them and goes to* Bob Cratchit, *who is by the hearth.*) How did our little Tiny Tim behave?

Bob Cratchit. As good as gold and better. He told me, coming home, that he hoped the people saw him in church because he was a cripple and it might be pleasant to them to remember upon Christmas Day who made the lame to walk and the blind to see.

Mrs. Cratchit. He's a good boy. (*The second spirit and* Scrooge *enter.* Mrs. Cratchit *feels a sudden draft.*) Oh, the wind. (*She gets up to shut the door.*)

Second Spirit. Hurry. (*He nudges* Scrooge *in before* Mrs. Cratchit *shuts the door.*)

Scrooge. Hardly hospitable is what I'd say.

Second Spirit. Oh, they'd say a great deal more, Scrooge, if they could see you.

Scrooge. Oh, they should, should they?

Second Spirit. Oh yes, I'd think they might.

Scrooge. Well, I might have a word for them . . .

Second Spirit. You're here to listen.

Scrooge. Oh. Oh yes, all right. By the fire?

Second Spirit. But not a word.

Bob Cratchit (*raising his glass*). My dear, to Mr. Scrooge. I give you Mr. Scrooge, the founder of the feast.

Mrs. Cratchit. The founder of the feast indeed! I wish I had him here! I'd give him a piece of my mind to feast upon, and I hope he'd have a good appetite for it.

Bob Cratchit. My dear, Christmas Eve.

Mrs. Cratchit. It should be Christmas Eve, I'm sure, when one drinks the health of such an <u>odious</u>, stingy, hard, unfeeling man as Mr. Scrooge. You know he is, Robert! Nobody knows it better than you do, poor dear.

Bob Cratchit. I only know one thing on Christmas: that one must be <u>charitable</u>.

Mrs. Cratchit. I'll drink to his health for your sake and the day's, not for his. Long life to him! A Merry Christmas and a Happy New Year. He'll be very merry and very happy, I have no doubt.

Bob Cratchit. If he cannot be, we must be happy for him. A song is what is needed. Tim!

Mrs. Cratchit. Shush! I've just gotten him down, and he needs all the sleep he can get.

Bob Cratchit. If he's asleep on Christmas Eve, I'll be much mistaken. Tim! He must sing, dear; there is nothing else that might make him well.

Tiny Tim. Yes, Father?

Bob Cratchit. Are you awake?

Tiny Tim. Just a little.

Bob Cratchit. A song then! (*The* children *awaken and, led by* Tiny Tim, *sit up to sing "What Child Is This?" As they sing,* Scrooge *speaks.*)

Scrooge. (*He holds up his hand; all stop singing and look at him.*) I . . . I have seen enough. (*When the spirit signals to the children, they leave the stage, singing the carol quietly.* Tiny Tim *remains, covered completely by the dark blanket, disappearing against the black.*) Tiny Tim . . . will he live?

Second Spirit. He is very ill. Even song cannot keep him whole through a cold winter.

Scrooge. But you haven't told me!

Second Spirit (*imitating* Scrooge). If he be like to die, he had better do it and decrease the surplus population. (Scrooge *turns away.*) Erase, Scrooge, those words from your thoughts. You are not the judge. Do not judge, then. It may be that in the sight of heaven you are more worthless and less fit to live than millions like this poor man's child. Oh God! To hear an insect on a leaf pronouncing that there is too

much life among his hungry brothers in the dust. Good-bye, Scrooge.

Scrooge. But is there no happiness in Christmas Present?

Second Spirit. There is.

Scrooge. Take me there.

Second Spirit. It is at the home of your nephew . . .

Scrooge. No!

Second Spirit (*disgusted with* Scrooge). Then there is none.

Scrooge. But that isn't enough . . . You must teach me!

Second Spirit. Would you have a teacher, Scrooge? Look at your own words.

Scrooge. But the first spirit gave me more . . . !

Second Spirit. He was Christmas Past. There was a lifetime he could choose from. I have only this day, one day, and you, Scrooge. I have nearly lived my fill of both. Christmas Present must be gone at midnight. That is near now. (*He speaks to two* beggar children *who pause shyly at the far side of the stage. The* children *are thin and wan; they are barefoot and wear filthy rags.*) Come. (*They go to him.*)

Scrooge. Is this the last spirit who is to come to me?

Second Spirit. They are no spirits. They are real. Hunger, Ignorance. Not spirits, Scrooge, passing dreams. They are real. They walk your streets, look to you for comfort. And you deny them. Deny them not too long, Scrooge. They will grow and multiply, and they will not remain children.

Scrooge. Have they no refuge, no resource?

Second Spirit (*again imitating* Scrooge). Are there no prisons? Are there no workhouses? (*tenderly to the* children) Come. It's Christmas Eve. (*He leads them offstage.*)

Scene 5

THE SPIRIT OF CHRISTMAS YET TO COME

Scrooge *is entirely alone for a long moment. He is frightened by the darkness and feels it approaching him. Suddenly he stops, senses the presence of the* third spirit, *turns toward him, and sees him. The* spirit *is bent and cloaked. No physical features are distinguishable.*

Scrooge. You are the third. (*The* spirit *says nothing.*) The Ghost of Christmas Yet to Come. (*The* spirit *says nothing.*) Speak to me. Tell me what is to happen—to me, to all of us. (*The* spirit *says nothing.*) Then show me what I must see. (*The* spirit *points. Light illumines the shadowy recesses of* Scrooge's *house.*) I know it. I know it too well, cold and cheerless. It is mine. (*The* cook *and the* charwoman *are dimly visible in* Scrooge's *house.*) What is . . . ? There are . . . thieves! There are thieves in my rooms! (*He starts forward to accost them, but the* spirit *beckons for him to stop.*) I cannot. You cannot tell me that I must watch them and do nothing. I will not. It is mine still. (*He rushes into the house to claim his belongings and to protect them. The two women do not notice his presence.*)

Cook. He ain't about, is he? (*The* charwoman *laughs.*) Poor ol' Scrooge 'as met 'is end.[17] (*She laughs with the* charwoman.)

Charwoman. An' time for it, too; ain't been alive in deed for half his life.

Cook. But the Sparsit's nowhere, is he . . . ?

Sparsit (*emerging from the blackness*). Lookin' for someone, ladies? (*The* cook *shrieks, but the* charwoman *treats the matter more practically, anticipating competition from* Sparsit.)

Charwoman. There ain't enough but for the two of us!

Sparsit. More 'an enough . . . if you know where to look.

Cook. Hardly decent is what I'd say, hardly decent, the poor old fella hardly cold and you're thievin' his wardrobe.

Sparsit. You're here out of love, are ya?

Charwoman. There's no time for that. (Sparsit *acknowledges* Scrooge *for the first time, gesturing toward him as if the living* Scrooge *were the corpse.* Scrooge *stands as if rooted to the spot, held there by the power of the* spirit.)

ACTIVE READER

VISUALIZE Close your eyes and imagine the scene. What do you see? How does what you see make you feel?

Sparsit. He ain't about to bother us, is he?

Charwoman. Ain't he a picture?

Cook. If he is, it ain't a happy one. (*They laugh.*)

Sparsit. Ladies, shall we start? (*The three of them grin and advance on* Scrooge.) Cook?

Cook (*snatching the cuff links from the shirt* Scrooge *wears*). They're gold, ain't they?

Sparsit. The purest, madam.

Charwoman. I always had a fancy for that nightcap of his. My old man could use it. (*She takes the nightcap from* Scrooge's *head.* Sparsit *playfully removes* Scrooge's *outer garment, the coat or cloak that he has worn in the previous scenes.*)

Sparsit. Bein' a man of more practical tastes, I'll go for the worsted[18] and hope the smell ain't permanent. (*The three laugh.*) Cook, we go round again.

Cook. Do you think that little bell he's always ringing at me is silver enough to sell? (*The three of them move toward the nightstand, and* Scrooge *cries out.*)

Scrooge. No more! No more! (*As the* spirit *directs* Scrooge's *attention to the tableau[19] of the three thieves standing poised over the silver bell,* Scrooge *bursts out of the house, clad only in his nightshirt.*) I cannot. I cannot. The room is . . . too like a cheerless place that is familiar. I won't see it. Let us go from here. Anywhere. (*The* spirit *directs his attention to the* Cratchit *house; the* children *are sitting together near* Mrs. Cratchit, *who is sewing a coat.* Peter *reads by the light of the coals.*)

Peter. "And he took a child and set him in the midst of them."

Mrs. Cratchit (*putting her hand to her face*). The light tires my eyes so. (*pause*) They're better now. It makes them tired to try to see by firelight, and I wouldn't show reddened eyes to your father when he comes home for the world. It must be near his time now.

Peter. Past it, I think, but he walks slower than he used to, these last few days, Mother.

Mrs. Cratchit. I have known him to walk with . . . I have known him to walk with Tiny Tim upon his shoulder very fast indeed. (*She catches herself, then hurries on.*) But he was

---

17. **'as met 'is end:** Cockney dialect for "has met his end." Cockneys (residents of the East End of London) drop the letter *h* when pronouncing words.

18. **worsted:** a smooth woolen fabric.

19. **tableau** (tăb′lō′): a portion of a play in which the actors momentarily freeze in their positions for dramatic effect.

very light to carry and his father loved him, so that it was no trouble, no trouble. (*She hears* Bob Cratchit *approaching.*) Smiles, everyone, smiles.

Bob Cratchit (*entering*). My dear, Peter . . . (*He greets the other* children *by their real names.*) How is it coming?

Mrs. Cratchit (*handing him the coat*). Nearly done.

Bob Cratchit. Yes, good, I'm sure that it will be done long before Sunday.

Mrs. Cratchit. Sunday! You went today then, Robert?

Bob Cratchit. Yes. It's . . . it's all ready. Two o'clock. And a nice place. It would have done you good to see how green it is. But you'll see it often. I promised him that, that I would walk there on Sunday . . . often.

Mrs. Cratchit. We mustn't hurt ourselves for it, Robert.

Bob Cratchit. No. No, he wouldn't have wanted that. Come now. You won't guess who I've seen. Scrooge's nephew, Fred. And he asked after us and said he was heartily sorry and to give his respect to my good wife. How he ever knew that, I don't know.

Mrs. Cratchit. Knew what, my dear?

Bob Cratchit. Why, that you were a good wife.

Peter. Everybody knows that.

Bob Cratchit. I hope that they do. "Heartily sorry," he said, "for your good wife, and if I can be of service to you in any way—" and he gave me his card—"that's where I live"—and Peter, I shouldn't be at all surprised if he got you a position.

Mrs. Cratchit. Only hear that, Peter!

Bob Cratchit. And then you'll be keeping company with some young girl and setting up for yourself.

Peter. Oh, go on.

Bob Cratchit. Well, it will happen, one day, but remember, when that day does come—as it must—we must none of us forget poor Tiny Tim and this first parting in our family.

Scrooge. He died! No, no! (*He steps back and the scene disappears; he moves away from the* spirit.)

THINKING *through the* LITERATURE

1. What do you think Scrooge felt when he saw Sparsit, the charwoman, and the cook laughing over his corpse and dividing his belongings? Explain.

2. What thoughts came to mind when you read Scrooge's reaction to news of Tiny Tim's death?

3. Why do you think Tiny Tim's death affects Scrooge so deeply?

Observe three of the spirits who visited Scrooge. Which has a more powerful impact on the viewer?

The Spirit of Christmas Present from *A Christmas Carol* (1938).

The ghost of Jacob Marley from *A Christmas Carol* (1938).

The Spirit of Christmas Yet to Come from *A Christmas Carol* (1938).

Scene 6

THE SPIRIT OF CHRISTMAS PRESENT

Scrooge. Because he would not . . . no! You cannot tell me that he has died, for that Christmas has not come! I will not let it come! I will be there . . . It was me. Yes, yes, and I knew it and couldn't look. I won't be able to help. I won't. (*pause*) Spirit, hear me. I am not the man I was. I will not be that man that I have been for so many years. Why show me all of this if I am past all hope? Assure me that I yet may change these shadows you have shown me. Let the boy live! I will honor Christmas in my heart and try to keep it all the year. I will live in the Past, the Present, and the Future. The spirits of all three shall strive within me. I will not shut out the lessons that they teach. Oh, tell me that I am not too late! (*A single light focuses on the little* girl, *dressed in a blue cloak like that of the Virgin Mary. She looks up, and from above a dove is slowly lowered in silence to her; she takes it and encloses it within her cloak, covering it. As soon as she does this, a large choir is heard singing "Gloria!" and the bells begin to ring. Blackout. When the lights come up again,* Scrooge *is in bed. The* third spirit *and the figures in the church have disappeared.* Scrooge *awakens and looks around his room.*) The curtains! They are mine and they are real. They are not sold. They are here. I am here; the shadows to come may be dispelled. They will be. I know they will be. (*He dresses himself hurriedly.*) I don't know what to do. I'm as light as a feather, merry as a boy again. Merry Christmas! Merry Christmas! A Happy New Year to all the world! Hello there! Whoop! Hallo! What day of the month is it? How long did the spirits keep me? Never mind. I don't care. (*He opens the window and calls to a* boy *in the street below.*) What's today?

Boy. Eh?

Scrooge. What's the day, my fine fellow?

Boy. Today? Why, Christmas Day!

Scrooge. It's Christmas Day! I haven't missed it! The spirits have done it all in one night. They can do anything they like. Of course they can. Of course they can save Tim. Hallo, my fine fellow!

Boy. Hallo!

Scrooge. Do you know the poulterers[20] in the next street at the corner?

Boy. I should hope I do.

Scrooge. An intelligent boy. A remarkable boy. Do you know whether they've sold the prize turkey that was hanging up there? Not the little prize; the big one.

Boy. What, the one as big as me?

Scrooge. What a delightful boy! Yes, my bucko!

Boy. It's hanging there now.

Scrooge. It is? Go and buy it.

Boy. G'wan!

Scrooge. I'm in earnest! Go and buy it and tell 'em to bring it here that I may give them the direction where to take it. Come back with the butcher and I'll give you a shilling.[21] Come back in less than two minutes and I'll give you half a crown!

Boy. Right, guv! (*He exits.*)

Scrooge. I'll send it to Bob Cratchit's. He shan't know who sends it. It's twice the size of Tiny Tim and such a Christmas dinner it will make. (Carolers *suddenly appear singing "Hark! The Herald Angels Sing."* Scrooge *leans out the window and joins them in the song.*) I must dress, I must. It's Christmas

---

20. **poulterers** (pōl′tər-ərz): people who sell poultry.
21. **shilling:** a British coin. Five shillings equal a crown.

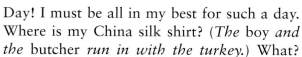

Day! I must be all in my best for such a day. Where is my China silk shirt? (*The boy and the butcher run in with the turkey.*) What? Back already? And such a turkey. Why, you can't carry that all the way to Cratchit's. Here, boy, here is your half a crown and here an address in Camden Town. See that it gets there. Here, money for the cab, for the turkey, and for you, good man! (*The boy and the butcher, delighted, catch the money and run out. Scrooge sees the gentleman visitor walking by the window.*) Halloo, sir!

ACTIVE READER

CONNECT How is this holiday celebration like ones you have attended? How is it different?

Gentleman Visitor (*looking up sadly, less than festive*). Hello, sir.

Scrooge. My dear sir, how do you do? I hope you succeeded yesterday. It was very kind of you to stop by to see me.

Gentleman Visitor (*in disbelief*). Mr. Scrooge?

Scrooge. Yes, that is my name, and I fear it may not be pleasant to you. Allow me to ask your pardon, and will you have the goodness to add this (*throwing him a purse*) to your good work!

Gentleman Visitor. Lord bless me! My dear Mr. Scrooge, are you serious?

Scrooge. If you please, not a penny less. A great many back payments are included in it, I assure you. Will you do me that favor?

Gentleman Visitor. My dear sir, I don't know what I can say to such generosity . . .

Scrooge. Say nothing! Accept it. Come and see me. Will you come and see me?

Gentleman Visitor. I will.

Scrooge. Thank 'ee. I am much obliged to you. I thank you fifty times. God bless you and Merry Christmas!

Gentleman Visitor. Merry Christmas to you, sir!

Scrooge (*running downstairs, out of his house, and onto the street*). Now which is the way to that nephew's house. Girl! Girl!

Girl (*appearing immediately*). Yes, sir?

Scrooge. Can you find me a taxi, miss?

Girl. I can, sir. (*She rings her doll, and a coachman appears.*)

Scrooge (*handing the coachman a card*). Can you show me the way to this home?

Coachman. I can, sir.

Scrooge. Good man. Come up, girl. (*They mount to the top of the taxi. This action may be stylistically suggested.*) Would you be an old man's guide to a Christmas dinner?

Girl. I would, sir, and God bless you!

Scrooge. Yes, God bless us every one! (*raising his voice almost in song*) Driver, to Christmas! (*They exit, all three singing "Joy to the World." Blackout. The lights come up for the <u>finale</u> at Fred's house. The Cratchits are there with Tiny Tim. All stop moving and talking when they see Scrooge standing in the center, embarrassed and humble.*) Well, I'm very glad to be here at my nephew's house! (*He starts to cry.*) Merry Christmas! Merry Christmas!

All (*softly*). Merry Christmas. (*They sing "Deck the Halls," greeting one another and exchanging gifts. Scrooge puts Tiny Tim on his shoulders.*)

Tiny Tim (*shouting as the carol ends*). God bless us every one!

Scrooge (*to the audience*). Oh, yes! God bless us every one!

WORDS TO KNOW
finale (fə-năl′ē) *n.* the concluding part

Connect to the Literature

1. **What Do You Think?** After reading this play, what is the first thing you would say to a friend about it?

   Comprehension Check
   • What kind of person is Scrooge in the first scene?
   • What event most changed Scrooge during the visits of the three spirits?
   • What does Scrooge do for Bob Cratchit's family at the end of the play?

Think Critically

2. **ACTIVE READING** **VISUALIZING**
   Review the sketches of scenes you made in your **READER'S NOTEBOOK**. What details in the stage directions most influenced your visualization of each scene?

3. Why do you think the Spirit of Christmas Present appeared to Scrooge as his old master Fezziwig?

   Think About:
   • how Fezziwig treated Scrooge
   • Scrooge's feelings toward Fezziwig
   • how Scrooge treated Bob Cratchit

4. Bob Cratchit and his wife differ on their attitudes toward Scrooge. What does this tell you about each character?

5. Which spirit do you think has the greatest influence in motivating Scrooge to change his life? Explain.

6. How did you react to Scrooge's change of heart in the final scene? Do you think it will be a lasting change? Why or why not?

Extend Interpretations

7. **What If** Imagine that Scrooge had not had such a sad, lonely childhood. How do you think his story would have been different?

8. **Connect to Life** Charles Dickens wrote about many serious problems of his time. How would you compare the problems of poor people today with the problems of poor people in Dickens's time? Explain.

Literary Analysis

STAGE DIRECTIONS All plays have **stage directions**—instructions included in the script to help performers, directors, and stage crew put on the play, and to help readers visualize the action. Stage directions can suggest setting, lighting, music, sound effects, movement of actors, and how dialogue is spoken.

Activity Make a chart like the one below. Use it to record the major points you learned from the stage directions about aspects of the play, such as Scrooge's character, Scrooge's past, Scrooge's shop, Bob Cratchit's character, and the Cratchit family.

What I learned about . . .	Through stage directions
Scrooge's character	Scrooge hurls himself through the descending snowflakes and sends the children scattering.
Scrooge's past	

REVIEW: PLOT **Plot** is the series of events that move a story forward. An **event** might be an action, reaction, or decision. A typical plot structure has four stages—**exposition, rising action, climax,** and **falling action.** Which key events in *A Christmas Carol* help advance the plot?

CHOICES and CHALLENGES

Writing

Plotting Drama Using the four stages of a typical plot structure, write a plot summary for *A Christmas Carol*. Remember, the **exposition** introduces characters and setting. Identifying the central conflict will help you find the **rising action,** which continues until the **climax. Falling action** is the part of the story where conflicts are often resolved. You may want to begin by making a plot chart, like the one on page 16, and then fill in key events that advance the plot. Place your Summary in your **Working Portfolio.**

Writing Handbook
See p. R58: Summary.

Speaking & Listening

Oral Summary Further develop the plot summary you prepared for the "Writing" option on this page. Use it as the basis for an oral summary that you'll present to the class. Write the summary in your own words, and include quotes from the play when effective. Be sure that your summary is clear so the audience can follow along.

Speaking and Listening Handbook
See p. R103: Oral Summaries.

Research & Technology

Research the history of carols and caroling. Try to find recordings of some of the carols mentioned in *A Christmas Carol*. Extend your inquiry to include the holiday customs of other countries or religions. Is singing or caroling an important part of celebrations in other cultures? If so, how?

Vocabulary and Spelling

EXERCISE: SYNONYMS/ANTONYMS On your paper, write *S* if the words are synonyms and *A* if they are antonyms.

1. **finale**–ending
2. **pledge**–promise
3. **surplus**–lack
4. **destitute**–wealthy
5. **transform**–change
6. **solitude**–isolation
7. **summon**–dismiss
8. **provision**–arrangement
9. **mortal**–human
10. **charitable**–stingy
11. **welfare**–well-being
12. **reassurance**–discouragement
13. **abundance**–plenty
14. **currency**–money
15. **emerge**–disappear
16. **endeavor**–try
17. **anonymous**–known
18. **incoherent**–understandable
19. **macabre**–pleasant
20. **odious**–hateful

SPELLING STRATEGY: WORDS ENDING IN A SILENT *e*
When a suffix beginning with a vowel is added to a word ending in a silent *e,* the *e* is usually dropped, as in *reassurance.*

1. Add the suffixes to these words.
   reassure + ance = _____
   relate + ion = _____
   fame + ous = _____
   create + ive = _____
   amaze + ing = _____
2. Use each of the spelling words in a complete sentence.

Spelling Handbook
See p. 30.

Grammar in Context: Action Verbs

Playwright Frederick Gaines uses **action verbs** in his vivid adaption of Dickens's *A Christmas Carol:*

> The percussion **thunders**. Scrooge **hurls** himself through the descending snowflakes and **sends** the children scattering. They **retreat, watching**.

Compare these sentences: *The percussion sounds like thunder* and *The percussion thunders.* The second sentence, which uses an action verb, has fewer words and is more forceful than the first.

Apply to Your Writing Choosing action verbs to express your ideas will make your writing more concise and effective.

WRITING EXERCISE Rewrite each sentence using an action verb.

Example: *Original* In bed at night, Scrooge is afraid of the darkness.

Rewritten Afraid of the darkness, Scrooge trembled under the bed sheets.

1. Bob Cratchit was a devoted clerk.
2. Nevertheless, his family was poor.
3. At Christmas, many children are hungry.
4. This is the Spirit of Christmas Past.

Connect to the Literature Reread the accompanying stage directions at the beginning of Scene 2 on page 258. Starting with "As the two find . . . ," make a list of action verbs.

Grammar Handbook
See p. R80: Using Verbs Correctly.

Charles Dickens
1812-1870

"Dickens's own childhood provided material for a number of his works."

Social Crusader Charles Dickens had intended to write a pamphlet called "An Appeal to the People of England, on Behalf of the Poor Man's Child," but instead he decided to get his idea across by using the form of a story. When *A Christmas Carol* came out in December 1843, about 6,000 copies were sold in just a few days. Since then, *A Christmas Carol* has become a classic holiday tradition.

Unhappy Childhood Dickens's own childhood provided material for a number of his works.

When Dickens was 12, his father was imprisoned for debt, and Dickens had to leave school and go to work in a rat-infested factory. The hopelessness and the shame he experienced there affected him deeply. One of his novels, *David Copperfield,* was based partly on his experiences in that factory. In such other novels as *Oliver Twist* and *Little Dorrit,* Dickens draws on childhood memories to depict the plight of the poor in a society that values wealth.

AUTHOR ACTIVITY
From Novel to Play You have read an adaptation of a novel by one of England's favorite authors. Read Dickens's novel *A Christmas Carol,* and then compare and contrast it with Frederick Gaines's dramatized version. What is lost in the dramatized version? What is gained? Which did you enjoy more?

The Scholarship Jacket

by MARTA SALINAS

Connect to Your Life

It's Not Right! Have you ever been treated unfairly? Have you ever had to stand up for your beliefs against someone who seemed more powerful than you? With two or three classmates, discuss an example of prejudice you have experienced, or know about.

Key Standard
R3.4 Identify and analyze themes that appear across works.
Other Standards **R1.3, W1.5, W2.1, LC1.3, LC1.4**

Build Background

SOCIAL STUDIES

Hispanic Americans are an important segment of the U.S. population. Many have family ties to Mexico, Puerto Rico, Cuba, or the Spanish-speaking countries of Central America. Others are members of families that have lived in the United States for hundreds of years.

The more than 27 million Hispanic Americans have made many contributions to American history and culture. "The Scholarship Jacket" is about a Mexican-American girl who lives in Texas. The story tells how she deals with the possibility of losing an award she deserves.

WORDS TO KNOW	Vocabulary Preview	
agile	falsify	resign
coincidence	fidget	valedictorian
despair	gaunt	vile
dismay	muster	

Focus Your Reading

LITERARY ANALYSIS   THEME

A story's **theme** is the message or moral it expresses about human nature or life in general. Usually, a theme is not directly stated. The reader must figure it out by making logical inferences based on details in the story. As you read the story, think about how the theme of "The Scholarship Jacket" is revealed through Martha's experiences.

ACTIVE READING   CONNECTING

When you use the strategy of **connecting** in reading a story, you look for elements that you can relate to your own knowledge and experience. While reading "The Scholarship Jacket," take note of things that you can connect with your own life. Do any of the **characters** resemble people you know? Which details, events, and emotions seem familiar? Which are unfamiliar?

📖 READER'S NOTEBOOK

As you read the story, jot down details that remind you of your own life, as well as details that seem unfamiliar.

Martha studied hard.

The Scholarship Jacket

by Marta Salinas

The small Texas school that I went to had a tradition carried out every year during the eighth-grade graduation: a beautiful gold and green jacket (the school colors) was awarded to the class valedictorian, the student who had maintained the highest grades for eight years. The scholarship jacket had a big gold S on the left front side and your name written in gold letters on the pocket.

My oldest sister, Rosie, had won the jacket a few years back, and I fully expected to also. I was fourteen and in the eighth grade. I had been a straight A student since the first grade and this last year had looked forward very much to owning that jacket. My father was a farm laborer who couldn't earn enough money to feed eight children, so when I was six I was given to my grandparents to raise. We couldn't participate in sports at school because there were registration fees, uniform costs, and trips out of town; so, even though our family was quite agile and athletic there would never be a school sports jacket for us. This one, the scholarship jacket, was our only chance.

In May, close to graduation, spring fever had struck as usual with a vengeance.[1] No one paid any attention in class; instead we stared out the

windows and at each other, wanting to speed up the last few weeks of school. I despaired every time I looked in the mirror. Pencil thin, not a curve anywhere. I was called "beanpole" and "string bean," and I knew that's what I looked like. A flat chest, no hips, and a brain; that's what I had. That really wasn't much for a fourteen-year-old to work with, I thought, as I absent-mindedly wandered from my history class to the gym. Another hour of sweating in basketball and displaying my toothpick legs was coming up. Then I remembered my P.E. shorts were still in a bag under my desk where I'd forgotten them. I had to walk all the way back and get them. Coach Thompson was a real bear if someone wasn't dressed for P.E. She had said I was a good forward and even tried to talk Grandma into letting me join the team once. Of course Grandma said no.

I was almost back at my classroom door when I heard voices raised in anger as if in some sort of argument. I stopped. I didn't mean to eavesdrop,[2] I just hesitated, not knowing

---

1. **with a vengeance** (věn′jəns): to an extreme degree.
2. **eavesdrop** (ēvz′drŏp′): to listen secretly to a private conversation of others.

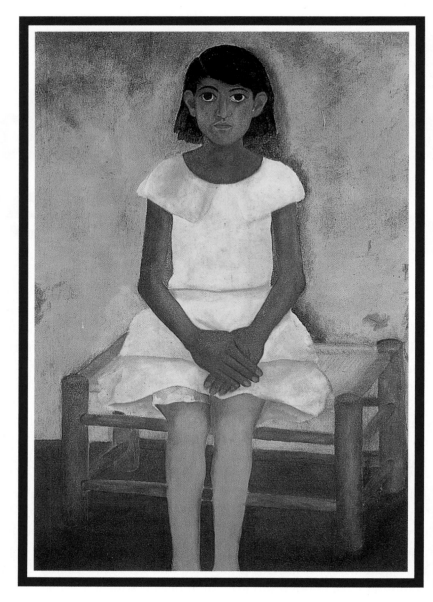

Retrato de muchacha
[Portrait of a girl]
(1929), Frida Kahlo.
Oil on canvas, 46½″ ×
31½″, collection of
the Dolores Olmedo
Patiño Foundation,
Museo Frida Kahlo,
Mexico City.

what to do. I needed those shorts and I was going to be late, but I didn't want to interrupt an argument between my teachers. I recognized the voices: Mr. Schmidt, my history teacher, and Mr. Boone, my math teacher. They seemed to be arguing about me. I couldn't believe it. I still remember the feeling of shock that rooted me flat against the wall as if I were trying to blend in with the graffiti written there.

"I refuse to do it! I don't care who her father is, her grades don't even begin to compare to Martha's. I won't lie or <u>falsify</u> records. Martha has a straight A-plus average and you know it." That was Mr. Schmidt and he sounded very angry. Mr. Boone's voice sounded calm and quiet.

"Look. Joann's father is not only on the Board, he owns the only store in town: we could say it was a close tie and—"

The pounding in my ears drowned out the rest of the words, only a word here and there filtered through. " . . . Martha is Mexican . . . <u>resign</u> . . . won't do it . . . . " Mr. Schmidt came

WORDS
TO
KNOW
falsify (fôl′sə-fī′) *v.* to make false by adding to or changing
resign (rĭ-zīn′) *v.* to give up (a job or an award, for instance)

rushing out and luckily for me went down the opposite way toward the auditorium, so he didn't see me. Shaking, I waited a few minutes and then went in and grabbed my bag and fled from the room. Mr. Boone looked up when I came in but didn't say anything. To this day I don't remember if I got in trouble in P.E. for being late or how I made it through the rest of the afternoon. I went home very sad and cried into my pillow that night so Grandmother wouldn't hear me. It seemed a cruel <u>coincidence</u> that I had overheard that conversation.

The next day when the principal called me into his office I knew what it would be about. He looked uncomfortable and unhappy. I decided I wasn't going to make it any easier for him, so I looked him straight in the eyes. He looked away and <u>fidgeted</u> with the papers on his desk.

"Martha," he said, "there's been a change in policy this year regarding the scholarship jacket. As you know, it has always been free." He cleared his throat and continued. "This year the Board has decided to charge fifteen dollars, which still won't cover the complete cost of the jacket."

I stared at him in shock, and a small sound of <u>dismay</u> escaped my throat. I hadn't expected this. He still avoided looking in my eyes.

"So if you are unable to pay the fifteen dollars for the jacket it will be given to the next one in line." I didn't need to ask who that was.

Standing with all the dignity I could <u>muster</u>, I said, "I'll speak to my grandfather about it, sir, and let you know tomorrow." I cried on the walk home from the bus stop. The dirt road was a quarter mile from the highway, so by the time I got home, my eyes were red and puffy.

"Where's Grandpa?" I asked Grandma, looking down at the floor so she wouldn't ask me why I'd been crying. She was sewing on a quilt as usual and didn't look up.

"I think he's out back working in the bean field."

I went outside and looked out at the fields. There he was. I could see him walking between the rows, his body bent over the little plants, hoe in hand. I walked slowly out to him, trying to think how I could best ask him for the money. There was a cool breeze blowing and a sweet smell of mesquite[3] fruit in the air, but I didn't appreciate it. I kicked at a dirt clod. I wanted that jacket so much. It was more than just being a valedictorian and giving a little thank you speech for the jacket on graduation night. It represented eight years of hard work and expectation. I knew I had to be honest with Grandpa; it was my only chance. He saw my shadow and looked up.

He waited for me to speak. I cleared my throat nervously and clasped my hands behind my back so he wouldn't see them shaking. "Grandpa, I have a big favor to ask you," I said in Spanish, the only language he knew. He still waited silently. I tried again. "Grandpa, this year the principal said the scholarship jacket is not going to be free. It's going to cost fifteen dollars, and I have to take the money in tomorrow, otherwise it'll be given to someone else." The last words came out in an eager rush. Grandpa straightened up tiredly and leaned his chin on the hoe handle. He looked out over the field that was filled with the tiny green bean plants. I waited, desperately hoping he'd say I could have the money.

He turned to me and asked quietly, "What does a scholarship jacket mean?"

---

3. **mesquite** (mĕ-skēt′): small spiny tree native to hot, dry regions of North America.

WORDS TO KNOW

coincidence (kō-ĭn′sĭ-dəns) n. accidental sequence of events that seems planned
fidget (fĭj′ĭt) v. to behave nervously or restlessly
dismay (dĭs-mā′) n. loss of courage in the face of trouble
muster (mŭs′tər) v. to call forth, to summon up

I answered quickly; maybe there was a chance. "It means you've earned it by having the highest grades for eight years and that's why they're giving it to you." Too late I realized the significance of my words. Grandpa knew that I understood it was not a matter of money. It wasn't that. He went back to hoeing the weeds that sprang up between the delicate little bean plants. It was a time-consuming job; sometimes the small shoots were right next to each other. Finally he spoke again as I turned to leave, crying.

"Then if you pay for it, Marta, it's not a scholarship jacket, is it? Tell your principal I will not pay the fifteen dollars."

I walked back to the house and locked myself in the bathroom for a long time. I was angry with Grandfather even though I knew he was right, and I was angry with the Board, whoever they were. Why did they have to change the rules just when it was my turn to win the jacket? Those were the days of belief and innocence.

It was a very sad and withdrawn girl who dragged into the principal's office the next day. This time he did look me in the eyes.

"What did your grandfather say?"

I sat very straight in my chair.

"He said to tell you he won't pay the fifteen dollars."

The principal muttered something I couldn't understand under his breath and walked over to the window. He stood looking out at something outside. He looked bigger than usual when he stood up; he was a tall, gaunt man with gray hair, and I watched the back of his head while I waited for him to speak.

"Why?" he finally asked. "Your grandfather has the money. He owns a two-hundred acre ranch."

I looked at him, forcing my eyes to stay dry. "I know, sir, but he said if I had to pay for it, then it wouldn't be a scholarship jacket." I stood up to leave. "I guess you'll just have to give it to Joann." I hadn't meant to say that, it had just slipped out. I was almost to the door when he stopped me.

"Martha—wait."

I turned and looked at him, waiting. What did he want now? I could feel my heart pounding loudly in my chest and see my blouse fluttering where my breasts should have been. Something bitter and <u>vile</u> tasting was coming up in my mouth; I was afraid I was going to be sick. I didn't need any sympathy speeches. He sighed loudly and went back to his big desk. He watched me, biting his lip.

"Okay. We'll make an exception in your case. I'll tell the Board, you'll get your jacket."

I could hardly believe my ears. I spoke in a trembling rush. "Oh, thank you, sir!" Suddenly I felt great. I didn't know about adrenalin in those days, but I knew something was pumping through me, making me feel as tall as the sky. I wanted to yell, jump, run the mile, do something. I ran out so I could cry in the hall where there was no one to see me.

At the end of the day, Mr. Schmidt winked at me and said, "I hear you're getting the scholarship jacket this year."

His face looked as happy and innocent as a baby's, but I knew better. Without answering I gave him a quick hug and ran to the bus. I cried on the walk home again, but this time because I was so happy. I couldn't wait to tell Grandpa and ran straight to the field. I joined him in the row where he was working, and without saying anything I crouched down and started pulling up the weeds with my hands. Grandpa worked alongside me for a few minutes, and he didn't ask what had

WORDS TO KNOW **vile** (vīl) *adj.* disgusting, unpleasant

happened. After I had a little pile of weeds between the rows, I stood up and faced him.

"The principal said he's making an exception for me, Grandpa, and I'm getting the jacket after all. That's after I told him what you said."

Grandpa didn't say anything; he just gave me a pat on the shoulder and a smile. He pulled out the crumpled red handkerchief that he always carried in his back pocket and wiped the sweat off his forehead.

"Better go see if your grandmother needs any help with supper."

I gave him a big grin. He didn't fool me. I skipped and ran back to the house whistling some silly tune. ❖

RELATED READING

GRADUATION MORNING

by Pat Mora

for Anthony

She called him *Lucero*,[1] morning star,
snared him with sweet coffee, pennies,
Mexican milk candy, brown bony hugs.

Through the years she'd cross the Rio
5 Grande to clean his mother's home. *"Lucero,
mi*[2] *lucero,"* she'd cry, when she'd see him
running toward her in the morning,
when she pulled stubborn cactus thorns
from his small hands, when she found him
10 hiding in the creosote.[3]

Though she's small and thin,
black sweater, black scarf,
the boy in the white graduation robe
easily finds her at the back of the cathedral,
15 finds her amid the swirl of sparkling clothes,
finds her eyes.

Tears slide down her wrinkled cheeks.
Her eyes, *luceros*, stroke his face.

Copyright © The Stock Illustration Source, Inc.

1. **lucero** (lōō-sĕ′rō) *Spanish:* bright star.
2. **mi** (mē) *Spanish:* my.
3. **creosote** (krē′ə-sōt′): creosote bushes, shrubs found in Mexico and the southwestern United States.

Connect to the Literature

1. **What Do You Think?** How did you feel when you came to the end of the story? If this had happened to you, would you feel like Martha felt?

Comprehension Check
- What are Mr. Boone and Mr. Schmidt arguing about?
- Why does Martha's grandfather refuse to pay for the jacket?
- How does the principal respond when Martha will not pay the 15 dollars?

Think Critically

2. How do Mr. Schmidt and Mr. Boone differ? What does Martha mean to each of them as a person?

3. Why do you think the principal changes his mind?

4. When at last Martha knows that she will get the jacket, what else has she won?

   Think About:
   - Martha's conflicting feelings in the principal's office
   - the ways different adults act toward her
   - the amount of control she has over the decisions being made

5. Martha's grandfather says very little, but his words are very important. What does he teach Martha? How? Support your answers with examples or quotes from the story.

6. **ACTIVE READING** **CONNECTING**
   Look over the notes you took in your
   📖 **READER'S NOTEBOOK** and compare them with a classmate's notes. Then discuss how the details in the story helped you relate to Martha's experience.

Extend Interpretations

7. **The Writer's Style** Consider the kinds of words and sentences Marta Salinas uses in this passage: "There was a cool breeze blowing and a sweet smell of mesquite fruit in the air, but I didn't appreciate it. I kicked at a dirt clod. I wanted that jacket so much." How does Salinas's style help you get to know her main character better?

Literary Analysis

THEME A **theme** is a message or moral about life or human nature expressed in a literary work. In most cases, readers must infer themes. (Remember, inferring consists of making logical guesses based on evidence.)

One way to infer a story's theme is to decide what general statement could be supported by the experiences of the main character. Look for clues to the theme of "The Scholarship Jacket" in key words and phrases, in dialogue, and in the ways that characters change as a result of the events in the story.

Paired Activity Working with a partner, identify an important **theme** in "The Scholarship Jacket." Look back at the text together, and jot down details of Martha's experiences that support the theme you've chosen. Compare your ideas with those of another pair of classmates.

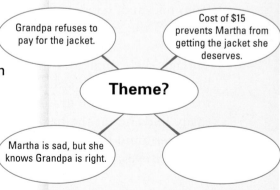

Grandpa refuses to pay for the jacket.

Cost of $15 prevents Martha from getting the jacket she deserves.

Martha is sad, but she knows Grandpa is right.

Theme?

Writing

Theme What other stories have you read in this book that share a similar theme with "The Scholarship Jacket"? Think of other characters who faced a difficult choice or situation, maybe one that they thought was unfair. Write down the names of the characters and the stories they appear in. Identify the theme of each story, and analyze the ways in which each theme is similar to that of "The Scholarship Jacket."

Research & Technology

¡La Causa! Cesar Chavez was a Mexican-American leader who worked to improve the lives of migrant workers. Find out about his life and about the United Farm Workers of America, the union that he helped found. Then write a brief biography of Chavez. Include any photographs you come across in your study. Keep a list of your sources, and write a bibliography to go with your biography. Exchange your completed work with a classmate. Share opinions of Cesar Chavez based on what you've read.

Writing Handbook
See p. R56: Works Cited.

Art Connection

Look at Frida Kahlo's painting *Retrato de muchacha* on page 280. What are your impressions of the girl in the painting? How do they compare with your impressions of Martha in the story?

Vocabulary

EXERCISE: MEANING CLUES On a separate sheet of paper, write the answer that best demonstrates the meaning of each vocabulary word.

1. **coincidence**
   a. setting a date for a party
   b. running into a friend far from home
   c. learning about a solar eclipse

2. **agile**
   a. learning a difficult song
   b. climbing a rock face easily
   c. finishing a job early

3. **despair**
   a. playing with the dog
   b. painting a brightly colored mural
   c. staring silently at a wall

4. **falsify**
   a. make a fake ID
   b. correct what someone else says
   c. speak in another language

5. **resign**
   a. put up a new sign
   b. change your mind
   c. quit a job or leave a position

Vocabulary Handbook
See p. R24: Context Clues.

Grammar in Context: Consistent Verb Tense

In this excerpt Martha, the narrator of "The Scholarship Jacket," describes her meeting with the principal of her school about the jacket.

> The next day when the principal called me into his office I knew what it would be about. He looked uncomfortable and unhappy. I decided I wasn't going to make it any easier for him, so I looked him straight in the eyes. He looked away and fidgeted with the papers on his desk.

Because Martha is describing an incident from the past, she uses **verbs** in the **past tense.** The past tense is the basic time of the story. Martha uses other tenses only where they are logical, for example, when reporting the dialogue spoken by the characters. Otherwise, she uses the past tense consistently.

Apply to Your Writing Student writers sometimes shift tenses illogically without being aware of it. When you revise your writing, check to be sure that you have not made any illogical shifts in tense.

WRITING EXERCISE Rewrite the following sentences to make the verb tenses consistent.

Example: *Original* I couldn't wait to tell Grandpa, so I run straight to the field.

Rewritten I couldn't wait to tell Grandpa, so I <u>ran</u> straight to the field.

1. I joined him, and without saying anything, I crouch down and started pulling up the weeds.
2. Grandpa worked alongside me for a few minutes, and he doesn't ask what happened.
3. After I have a little pile of weeds between the rows, I stood up and face him.
4. Grandpa doesn't say anything; he just gave me a pat on the shoulder and a smile.
5. I skipped and run back to the house, whistling some silly tune.

Connect to the Literature Martha encountered prejudice. Recall a time when you believe that you were treated unfairly. Write five sentences about what you remember. Be careful to use past-tense verbs consistently.

Grammar Handbook
See p. R80: Using Verbs Correctly.

Marta Salinas
born 1949

"What does a scholarship jacket mean?"

Young Author Born in Coalinga, California, Marta Salinas received an M.F.A. in creative writing from the University of California at Irvine. She has published several short stories in journals and anthologies. "The Scholarship Jacket" originally appeared in *Nosotras: Latina Literature Today.*

AUTHOR ACTIVITY
Interview Imagine that you are going to interview Marta Salinas about the story you have read. Make a list of questions you would like to ask her.

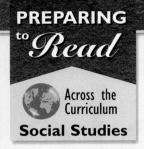
The Noble Experiment

from **I Never Had It Made**

by JACKIE ROBINSON   *as told to* ALFRED DUCKETT

Connect to Your Life

What do you think causes people to feel prejudice?

Build Background

In the 1940s, African Americans faced many barriers created by prejudice. Segregation kept blacks from using schools, restaurants, and hospitals used by whites. In baseball, the Negro League was completely separate from the white league. Jackie Robinson would help change that.

The All Stars, in the Negro League, 1939.

Antidiscrimination poster, 1949.

SUNDAY GAMES IN JEOPARDY

Boston. City Councilman Isidore Muchneck has proposed a ban on Sunday ballgames at Fenway

attitude in baseball is that white business would suffer if blacks were hired. Most fans think baseball

Focus Your Reading

LITERARY ANALYSIS **AUTOBIOGRAPHY**

An **autobiography** is the story of a person's life, written by that person. In this excerpt, Jackie Robinson tells of Branch Rickey's plan to hire Robinson as a player.

WORDS TO KNOW **Vocabulary Preview**

cynical	insinuation	shrewdly	taunt
eloquence	integrated	speculating	ultimate
incredulous	retaliate		

ACTIVE READING **SUMMARIZING**

When you **summarize**, you restate in your own words the **main ideas** and important **details** of something you've read. A summary should be shorter than the original work. Jot down important details in your 📖 **READER'S NOTEBOOK**. These will help you summarize the selection later on.

Key Standard
R3.1 Be able to describe the purposes and characteristics of different forms of prose, such as the short story, novel, or essay. *Other Standards* **R1.3, W1.3, W1.6, W2.3, W2.5, W3.1, LC1.1, LC1.4**

287

The Noble

Jackie Robinson steals home during a Braves-Dodgers game at Ebbets Field in Brooklyn, August 22, 1948.
UPI/Bettmann.

from *I Never Had It Made*

Experiment

by Jackie Robinson as told to Alfred Duckett

In 1910 Branch Rickey was a coach for Ohio Wesleyan. The team went to South Bend, Indiana, for a game. The hotel management registered the coach and team but refused to assign a room to a black player named Charley Thomas. In those days college ball had a few black players. Mr. Rickey took the manager aside and said he would move the entire team to another hotel unless the black athlete was accepted. The threat was a bluff because he knew the other hotels also would have refused accommodations to a black man. While the hotel manager was thinking about the threat, Mr. Rickey came up with a compromise. He suggested a cot be put in his own room, which he would share with the unwanted guest. The hotel manager wasn't happy about the idea, but he gave in.

Years later Branch Rickey told the story of the misery of that black player to whom he had given a place to sleep. He remembered that Thomas couldn't sleep.

"He sat on that cot," Mr. Rickey said, "and was silent for a long time. Then he began to cry, tears he couldn't hold back. His whole body shook with emotion. I sat and watched him, not knowing what to do until he began tearing at one hand with the other—just as if

he were trying to scratch the skin off his hands with his fingernails. I was alarmed. I asked him what he was trying to do to himself.

"'It's my hands,' he sobbed. 'They're black. If only they were white, I'd be as good as anybody then, wouldn't I, Mr. Rickey? If only they were white.'"

"Charley," Mr. Rickey said, "the day will come when they won't have to be white."

Thirty-five years later, while I was lying awake nights, frustrated, unable to see a future, Mr. Rickey, by now the president of the Dodgers, was also lying awake at night, trying to make up his mind about a new experiment.

He had never forgotten the agony of that black athlete. When he became a front-office executive in St. Louis, he had fought, behind the scenes, against the custom that consigned black spectators to the Jim Crow section of the Sportsman's Park, later to become Busch Memorial Stadium. His pleas to change the rules were in vain. Those in power argued that if blacks were allowed a free choice of seating, white business would suffer.

Branch Rickey lost that fight, but when he became the boss of the Brooklyn Dodgers in 1943, he felt the time for equality in baseball had come. He knew that achieving it would be terribly difficult. There would be deep resentment, determined opposition, and perhaps even racial violence. He was convinced he was morally right, and he <u>shrewdly</u> sensed that making the game a truly national one would have healthy financial results. He took his case before the startled directors of the club, and using persuasive <u>eloquence</u>, he won the first battle in what would be a long and bitter campaign. He was voted permission to make the Brooklyn club the pioneer in bringing blacks into baseball.

Winning his directors' approval was almost insignificant in contrast to the task which now lay ahead of the Dodger president. He made certain that word of his plans did not leak out, particularly to the press. Next, he had to find the ideal player for his project, which came to be called "Rickey's noble experiment." This player had to be one who could take abuse, name-calling, rejection by fans and sportswriters and by fellow players not only on opposing teams but on his own. He had to be able to stand up in the face of merciless persecution and not <u>retaliate</u>. On the other hand, he had to be a contradiction in human terms; he still had to have spirit. He could not be an "Uncle Tom."[1]

Jackie Robinson after he signed a contract with the Brooklyn Dodgers, April 10, 1947. AP/Wide World Photos.

His ability to turn the other cheek had to be predicated[2] on his determination to gain acceptance. Once having proven his ability as player, teammate, and man, he had to be able to cast off humbleness and stand up as a full-fledged participant whose triumph did not carry the poison of bitterness.

Unknown to most people and certainly to me, after launching a major scouting program, Branch Rickey had picked me as that player. The Rickey talent hunt went beyond national borders. Cuba, Mexico, Puerto Rico, Venezuela, and other countries where dark-skinned people lived had been checked out. Mr. Rickey had learned that there were a number of black players, war veterans mainly, who had gone to these countries, despairing of finding an opportunity in their own country. The manhunt had to be camouflaged. If it became known he was looking for a black recruit for the Dodgers, all hell would have broken loose. The gimmick he used as a cover-up was to make the world believe that he was about to establish a new Negro league. In the spring of 1945 he called a press conference and announced that the Dodgers were organizing the United States League, composed of all black teams. This, of course, made blacks and prointegration whites indignant. He was accused of trying to uphold the existing segregation and, at the same time, capitalize on black players. Cleverly, Mr. Rickey replied that his league would be better organized than the current ones. He said its main purpose, eventually, was to be absorbed

---

1. **Uncle Tom:** an offensive term for a black person who is regarded as trying overly hard to please white people; originally from the novel *Uncle Tom's Cabin*, written by Harriet Beecher Stowe in 1851.
2. **predicated** (prĕd′ĭ-kā′tĭd): based.

WORDS
TO
KNOW

shrewdly (shrōōd′lē) *adv.* wisely; in a clever way
eloquence (ĕl′ə-kwəns) *n.* forceful, convincing speech
retaliate (rĭ-tăl′ē-āt′) *v.* to get revenge; get even

into the majors. It is ironic that by coming very close to telling the truth, he was able to conceal that truth from the enemies of integrated baseball. Most people assumed that when he spoke of some distant goal of integration, Mr. Rickey was being a hypocrite on this issue as so many of baseball's leaders had been.

Black players were familiar with this kind of hypocrisy. When I was with the Monarchs, shortly before I met Mr. Rickey, Wendell Smith, then sports editor of the black weekly Pittsburgh *Courier*, had arranged for me and two other players from the Negro league to go to a tryout with the Boston Red Sox. The tryout had been brought about because a Boston city councilman had frightened the Red Sox management. Councilman Isadore Muchneck threatened to push a bill through banning Sunday baseball unless the Red Sox hired black players. Sam Jethroe of the Cleveland Buckeyes, Marvin Williams of the Philadelphia Stars, and I had been grateful to Wendell for getting us a chance in the Red Sox tryout, and we put our best efforts into it. However, not for one minute did we believe the tryout was sincere. The Boston club officials praised our performance, let us fill out application cards, and said, "So long." We were fairly certain they wouldn't call us, and we had no intention of calling them.

Incidents like this made Wendell Smith as cynical as we were. He didn't accept Branch Rickey's new league as a genuine project, and he frankly told him so. During this conversation, the Dodger boss asked Wendell whether any of the three of us who had gone to Boston was really good major league material. Wendell said I was. I will be forever indebted to Wendell because, without his even knowing it, his recommendation was in the end partly responsible for my career. At the time, it started a thorough investigation of my background.

In August 1945, at Comiskey Park in Chicago, I was approached by Clyde Sukeforth, the Dodger scout. Blacks have had to learn to protect themselves by being cynical but not cynical enough to slam the door on potential

> Unknown to most people and certainly to me, after launching a major scouting program, Branch Rickey had picked me as that player.

opportunities. We go through life walking a tightrope to prevent too much disillusionment. I was out on the field when Sukeforth called my name and beckoned. He told me the Brown Dodgers were looking for top ballplayers, that Branch Rickey had heard about me and sent him to watch me throw from the hole.[3] He had come at an unfortunate time. I had hurt my shoulder a couple of days before that, and I wouldn't be doing any throwing for at least a week.

Sukeforth said he'd like to talk with me anyhow. He asked me to come to see him after the game at the Stevens Hotel.

Here we go again, I thought. Another time-wasting experience. But Sukeforth looked like a sincere person, and I thought I might as well listen. I agreed to meet him that night. When we met, Sukeforth got right to the point. Mr. Rickey wanted to talk to me about the

---

3. **throw from the hole:** to throw from deep in the infield to first base.

WORDS
TO
KNOW

integrated (ĭn′tĭ-grā′tĭd) *adj.* open to people of all races or ethnic groups without restriction; desegregated

cynical (sĭn′ĭ-kəl) *adj.* mistrustful of others' sincerity

possibility of becoming a Brown Dodger. If I could get a few days off and go to Brooklyn, my fare and expenses would be paid. At first I said that I couldn't leave my team and go to Brooklyn just like that. Sukeforth wouldn't take no for an answer. He pointed out that I couldn't play for a few days anyhow because of my bum arm. Why should my team object?

I continued to hold out and demanded to know what would happen if the Monarchs fired me. The Dodger scout replied quietly that he didn't believe that would happen.

I shrugged and said I'd make the trip. I figured I had nothing to lose.

Branch Rickey was an impressive-looking man. He had a classic face, an air of command, a deep, booming voice, and a way of cutting through red tape and getting down to basics. He shook my hand vigorously and, after a brief conversation, sprang the first question.

"You got a girl?" he demanded.

It was a hell of a question. I had two reactions: why should he be concerned about my relationship with a girl; and, second, while I thought, hoped, and prayed I had a girl, the way things had been going, I was afraid she might have begun to consider me a hopeless case. I explained this to Mr. Rickey and Clyde.

Mr. Rickey wanted to know all about Rachel. I told him of our hopes and plans.

"You know, you _have_ a girl," he said heartily. "When we get through today, you may want to call her up because there are times when a man needs a woman by his side."

My heart began racing a little faster again as I sat there <u>speculating</u>. First he asked me if I really understood why he had sent for me. I told him what Clyde Sukeforth had told me.

"That's what he was supposed to tell you," Mr. Rickey said. "The truth is you are not a candidate for the Brooklyn Brown Dodgers. I've sent for you because I'm interested in you as a candidate for the Brooklyn National League Club. I think you can play in the major leagues. How do you feel about it?"

My reactions seemed like some kind of weird mixture churning in a blender. I was thrilled, scared, and excited. I was <u>incredulous.</u> Most of all, I was speechless.

"You think you can play for Montreal?" he demanded.

> Here was a guy questioning my courage. That virtually amounted to him asking me if I was a coward.

I got my tongue back. "Yes," I answered.

Montreal was the Brooklyn Dodgers' top farm club. The players who went there and made it had an excellent chance at the big time.

I was busy reorganizing my thoughts while Mr. Rickey and Clyde Sukeforth discussed me briefly, almost as if I weren't there. Mr. Rickey was questioning Clyde. Could I make the grade?

Abruptly, Mr. Rickey swung his swivel chair in my direction. He was a man who conducted himself with great drama. He pointed a finger at me.

"I know you're a good ballplayer," he barked. "What I don't know is whether you have the guts."

I knew it was all too good to be true. Here was a guy questioning my courage. That virtually amounted to him asking me if I was a coward. Mr. Rickey or no Mr. Rickey, that was an <u>insinuation</u> hard to take. I felt the heat coming up into my cheeks.

WORDS TO KNOW

speculating (spĕk′yə-lā′-tĭng) *adj.* thinking about different possibilities; guessing what might happen **speculate** *v.*

incredulous (ĭn-krĕj′ə-ləs) *adj.* unable or unwilling to believe something

insinuation (ĭn-sĭn′yōō-ā′shən) *n.* a suggestion or hint intended to insult

Before I could react to what he had said, he leaned forward in his chair and explained.

I wasn't just another athlete being hired by a ball club. We were playing for big stakes. This was the reason Branch Rickey's search had been so exhaustive. The search had spanned the globe and narrowed down to a few candidates, then finally to me. When it looked as though I might be the number-one choice, the investigation of my life, my habits, my reputation, and my character had become an intensified study.

"I've investigated you thoroughly, Robinson," Mr. Rickey said.

One of the results of this thorough screening were reports from California athletic circles that I had been a "racial agitator"[4] at UCLA. Mr. Rickey had not accepted these criticisms on face value. He had demanded and received more information and came to the conclusion that if I had been white, people would have said, "Here's a guy who's a contender, a competitor."

(From left) Gil Hodges, Gene Hermanski, Branch Rickey, and Jackie Robinson at Yankee Stadium during the World Series, October 4, 1949. The Bettmann Archive.

After that he had some grim words of warning. "We can't fight our way through this, Robinson. We've got no army. There's virtually nobody on our side. No owners, no umpires, very few newspapermen. And I'm afraid that many fans will be hostile. We'll be in a tough position. We can win only if we can convince the world that I'm doing this because you're a great ballplayer and a fine gentleman."

He had me transfixed as he spoke. I could feel his sincerity, and I began to get a sense of how much this major step meant to him. Because of his nature and his passion for justice, he had to do what he was doing. He continued. The rumbling voice, the theatrical gestures were gone. He was speaking from a deep, quiet strength.

---

4. **racial agitator** (ăj´ĭ-tā´tər): a negative term used for someone who tries to stir up trouble between the races.

"So there's more than just playing," he said. "I wish it meant only hits, runs, and errors—only the things they put in the box score. Because you know—yes, you would know, Robinson, that a baseball box score is a democratic thing. It doesn't tell how big you are, what church you attend, what color you are, or how your father voted in the last election. It just tells what kind of baseball player you were on that particular day."

I interrupted. "But it's the box score that really counts—that and that alone, isn't it?"

"It's all that *ought* to count," he replied. "But it isn't. Maybe one of these days it *will* be all that counts. That is one of the reasons I've got you here, Robinson. If you're a good enough man, we can make this a start in the right direction. But let me tell you, it's going to take an awful lot of courage."

He was back to the crossroads question that made me start to get angry minutes earlier. He asked it slowly and with great care.

"Have you got the guts to play the game no matter what happens?"

"I think I can play the game, Mr. Rickey," I said.

The next few minutes were tough. Branch Rickey had to make absolutely sure that I knew what I would face. Beanballs[5] would be thrown at me. I would be called the kind of names which would hurt and infuriate any man. I would be physically attacked. Could I take all of this and control my temper, remain steadfastly loyal to our <u>ultimate</u> aim?

He knew I would have terrible problems and wanted me to know the extent of them before I agreed to the plan. I was twenty-six years old, and all my life—back to the age of eight when a little neighbor girl called me a nigger—I had believed in payback, retaliation.

> Beanballs would be thrown at me. I would be called the kind of names which would hurt and infuriate any man. I would be physically attacked.

The most luxurious possession, the richest treasure anybody has, is his personal dignity. I looked at Mr. Rickey guardedly, and in that second I was looking at him not as a partner in a great experiment, but as the enemy—a white man. I had a question, and it was the age-old one about whether or not you sell your birthright.

"Mr. Rickey," I asked, "are you looking for a Negro who is afraid to fight back?"

I never will forget the way he exploded.

"Robinson," he said, "I'm looking for a ballplayer with guts enough not to fight back."

After that, Mr. Rickey continued his lecture on the kind of thing I'd be facing.

He not only told me about it, but he acted out the part of a white player charging into me, blaming me for the "accident" and calling me all kinds of foul racial names. He talked about my race, my parents, in language that was almost unendurable.

"They'll <u>taunt</u> and goad you," Mr. Rickey said. "They'll do anything to make you react. They'll try to provoke a race riot in the ballpark. This is the way to prove to the public that a Negro should not be allowed in the major league. This is the way to frighten the fans and make them afraid to attend the games."

---

5. **beanballs:** pitches thrown purposefully at a batter's head.

WORDS
TO
KNOW

ultimate (ŭl'tə-mĭt) *adj.* final; most important
taunt (tônt) *v.* to make fun of; jeer

If hundreds of black people wanted to come to the ballpark to watch me play and Mr. Rickey tried to discourage them, would I understand that he was doing it because the emotional enthusiasm of my people could harm the experiment? That kind of enthusiasm would be as bad as the emotional opposition of prejudiced white fans.

Suppose I was at shortstop. Another player comes down from first, stealing, flying in with spikes high, and cuts me on the leg. As I feel the blood running down my leg, the white player laughs in my face.

"How do you like that, nigger boy?" he sneers.

Could I turn the other cheek? I didn't know how I would do it. Yet I knew that I must. I had to do it for so many reasons. For black youth, for my mother, for Rae, for myself. I had already begun to feel I had to do it for Branch Rickey.

I was offered, and agreed to sign later, a contract with a $3,500 bonus and $600-a-month salary. I was officially a Montreal Royal. I must not tell anyone except Rae and my mother. ❖

The pennant-winning 1949 Brooklyn Dodgers team. Jackie Robinson is second from the right in the third row. UPI/Bettmann.

Connect to the Literature

1. **What Do You Think?**
   What is your impression of Jackie Robinson? What kind of a person was he?

   Comprehension Check
   • What was Rickey's intention when he recruited Jackie Robinson?
   • What challenges would Robinson face if he became a major-league player?

Think Critically

2. **ACTIVE READING** **SUMMARIZING**
   Review the notes you made in your ▯READER'S NOTEBOOK. Then summarize Branch Rickey's plan to integrate major-league baseball.

3. What is your opinion of Rickey's plan?

   Think About:
   • his reasons for wanting to carry out the plan
   • how and why he kept it secret
   • the final results of the plan

4. What does Robinson mean when he says of African Americans, "We go through life walking a tightrope to prevent too much disillusionment"?

5. Rickey interpreted reports that Robinson had been a "racial agitator" at UCLA to mean that Robinson was "a contender, a competitor." What made him think that?

6. Consider the difficulties both Rickey and Robinson faced. Who showed the greater courage? Give reasons for your answer.

Extend Interpretations

7. **What If?** Imagine that Jackie Robinson had not been such a strong, self-controlled person or such an exceptional athlete. How might Rickey's plan have turned out differently?

8. **Connect to Life** Many saw Jackie Robinson as a role model for young people. Should we expect professional athletes to be role models, or should we judge them only on their athletic performance?

Literary Analysis

AUTOBIOGRAPHY

An **autobiography** is a form of **nonfiction** in which a person tells the story of his or her own life. An autobiography is usually written from the **first-person point of view.** The writer tells about past events from the perspective of being older and wiser. Therefore, autobiographies often provide revealing insights into the writer's attitudes toward the events that shaped and changed his or her life. Autobiographies also help the reader understand the society in which the writer lived.

Group Activity With a small group, discuss one of the following two points. When you have finished, gather with a group that has chosen the other point and discuss how both points together contribute to the autobiography.
• Point 1: Robinson's attitude toward the important event in his life described in "The Noble Experiment"
• Point 2: The society in which Robinson's and Rickey's integration of major-league baseball took place

Discussion Results	
Our Group	Other Group

Writing

Summarize Take notes on the key events and main ideas in "The Noble Experiment." Then, turn those notes into a summary. Your summary should be about 500 words in length. It should include the main idea and significant details of the piece. Express the ideas and details in your own words, showing that you understand the story's meaning. Type up your summary using a word processing program, and bring it to class. Place your summary in your **Working Portfolio.**

Writing Handbook
See p. R58: Summary.

Speaking & Listening

Interview If you had an opportunity to interview Jackie Robinson and Branch Rickey, what questions would you ask them? Identify topics you think they would want to talk about, based on their background. Work with two other students to develop thoughtful interview questions and responses. Practice and then stage an interview with Robinson and Rickey for your class.

Speaking and Listening Handbook
See p. R109: Conducting Interviews.

Research & Technology

SOCIAL STUDIES

Jackie Robinson experienced prejudice and discrimination in breaking the "color barrier" in major-league baseball. Find out more about segregation policies, such as the Jim Crow laws, that existed during Robinson's lifetime. How did these policies affect African-American athletes in the 1940s and 1950s? How were major-league sports affected after these laws changed?

INTERNET Research Starter
www.mcdougallittell.com

Vocabulary

EXERCISE: SYNONYMS On your paper, write the Word to Know that is the best substitute for each italicized word or phrase below.

1. Branch Rickey *cleverly* devised a cover story for the press.
2. Robinson was *disbelieving* when Rickey said he wanted him to play for the Brooklyn National League Club.
3. The majority of newspapermen *guessing* about Rickey's plans had been wrong.
4. Many blacks felt very *mistrustful* of the sincerity of the promises made by whites.
5. Some ballplayers on other teams would *make fun of* Robinson and try to anger him.
6. Robinson was not allowed to *get even.*

7. The goal of the experiment was to have *desegregated* major leagues.
8. Sometimes a sportswriter would make a *suggestion* in his column intended to insult Robinson's character.
9. Several ministers spoke with *forceful verbal skill* about the evils of prejudice.
10. The *final* result of Rickey's "noble experiment" was highly successful.

Vocabulary Handbook
See p. R26: Synonyms and Antonyms.

WORDS TO KNOW				
cynical	incredulous	integrated	shrewdly	taunt
eloquence	insinuation	retaliate	speculating	ultimate

Grammar in Context: Active Voice and Passive Voice

Notice the use of verbs in the **active voice** to express Mr. Rickey's fear that the fans will harass Jackie Robinson.

> They'll taunt and goad you. . . . They'll do anything to make you react. They'll try to provoke a race riot in the ballpark.

Compare this sentence written in the **passive voice** with the original sentence above: *You will be taunted and goaded by them.* Verbs in the **active voice** emphasize the doer of the action. Verbs in the passive voice take emphasis away from the doer of an action and make sentences wordy.

Apply to Your Writing Generally use verbs in the active voice to make your writing stronger and more concise.

WRITING EXERCISE Rewrite each sentence, changing the verbs from the passive voice to the active voice.

Example: *Original* The Boston Red Sox were threatened by a councilman.

Rewritten A councilman threatened the Boston Red Sox.

1. A passion for justice was shown by Branch Rickey.
2. Robinson's performance was praised by Boston club officials.
3. Robinson was approached by Clyde Sukeforth, the Dodger scout.
4. Many black athletes had been discouraged by years of lies and disappointments.

Alfred Duckett
1917–1984

"I wasn't just another athlete being hired by a ball club. We were playing for big stakes."
—Jackie Robinson

Fan and Writer It seems natural that Alfred Duckett would want to tell Jackie Robinson's story, since Duckett was born in Brooklyn, New York, and was a baseball fan as well as a journalist. Robinson and Duckett worked together to write *I Never Had It Made: An Autobiography.* Besides writing books, Duckett also wrote poetry, magazine articles, and speeches.

Full Life Duckett cofounded *Equal Opportunities* magazine and served as director of Associated Negro Press International. He appeared on national television programs and lectured in many schools, churches, and universities. He also cowrote some of the speeches of Dr. Martin Luther King, Jr. Until his death in 1984, Duckett ran a public relations firm in Chicago, Illinois.

AUTHOR ACTIVITY
Read the rest of Jackie Robinson's autobiography, *I Never Had It Made.* Create a time line of Robinson's accomplishments and give a report on his experiences in baseball and his other achievements.

PREPARING to Read   POETRY

Casey at the Bat

by ERNEST LAWRENCE THAYER

Key Standard
R3.2 Identify events that advance the plot and describe how they explain the past, present, and future.
Other Standards **R3.1, R3.6, W2.2, W2.3, LS1.8**

Connect to Your Life

Answer these questions, then discuss your answers with the class.
- My favorite athlete is _____.
- What I admire most about him or her is _____.
- When a game is "on the line," I expect him or her to _____.
- I was disappointed in him or her when _____.

Build Background

SOCIAL STUDIES

Baseball began in the United States in the mid-1800s. By the early 1900s the sport was so popular that people began calling it America's national pastime.

In the light of the nation's continuing enthusiasm for baseball, it is small wonder that "mighty Casey" has remained a popular figure for more than 100 years. As you read this poem, think about what has changed in baseball since 1888, when the poem was written, and what has remained the same.

A cartoon showing baseball players and fans reacting to an umpire's call. Culver Pictures.

Focus Your Reading

LITERARY ANALYSIS   SOUND DEVICES

Poets often use **sound devices,** such as repetition, rhyme, and rhythm, in their poems.

- **Repetition** of a sound, word, phrase, or line can be used for emphasis.
- **Rhyme** is a repetition of sounds at the end of words.
- **Rhythm** is a pattern of stressed and unstressed syllables in the lines of a poem.

ACTIVE READING   QUESTIONING

Good readers ask questions both before they read a work and while they are reading it. "Casey at the Bat" is a **narrative poem**—poetry that tells a story. Before you read the poem, look at it to get an idea of what it's about. What is the **setting?** Who are the **characters?** What is the **conflict** that gets the **plot** moving?

READER'S NOTEBOOK

As you read "Casey at the Bat," think about the setting, the conflict, and the characters. Jot down details that help you identify these elements. Also note any questions that occur to you.

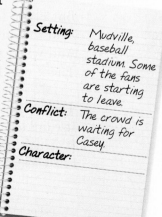

Setting: Mudville, baseball stadium. Some of the fans are starting to leave.

Conflict: The crowd is waiting for Casey.

Character:

Casey at the Bat

by Ernest Lawrence Thayer

It looked extremely rocky for the Mudville nine that day;
The score stood two to four, with but an inning left to play.
So, when Cooney died at second, and Burrows did the same,
A pallor[1] wreathed the features of the patrons of the game.

5 A straggling few got up to go, leaving there the rest,
With that hope which springs eternal within the human breast.
For they thought: "If only Casey could get a whack at that,"
They'd put even money now, with Casey at the bat.

But Flynn preceded Casey, and likewise so did Blake,
10 And the former was a pudd'n, and the latter was a fake.
So on that stricken multitude a deathlike silence sat;
For there seemed but little chance of Casey's getting to the bat.

But Flynn let drive a "single," to the wonderment of all.
And the much-despised Blakey "tore the cover off the ball."
15 And when the dust had lifted, and they saw what had occurred,
There was Blakey safe at second, and Flynn a-huggin' third.

Then from the gladdened multitude went up a joyous yell—
It rumbled in the mountaintops, it rattled in the dell;[2]
It struck upon the hillside and rebounded on the flat;
20 For Casey, mighty Casey, was advancing to the bat.

---

1. **pallor** (păl'ər): extreme paleness.
2. **dell:** valley.

Baseball Scene of Batter, Catcher, and Umpire (1915), Joseph Christian Leyendecker. Photo courtesy of the Archives of the American Illustrators Gallery, New York City. Copyright © 1995 by ARTShows and Products of Holderness, NH 03245.

There was ease in Casey's manner as he stepped into his place,
There was pride in Casey's bearing and a smile on Casey's face;
And when responding to the cheers he lightly doffed his hat,
No stranger in the crowd could doubt 'twas Casey at the bat.

25 Ten thousand eyes were on him as he rubbed his hands with dirt,
Five thousand tongues applauded when he wiped them on his shirt;
Then when the writing[3] pitcher ground the ball into his hip,
Defiance glanced in Casey's eye, a sneer curled Casey's lip.

And now the leather-covered sphere came hurtling through the air,
30 And Casey stood a-watching it in haughty grandeur there.
Close by the sturdy batsman the ball unheeded sped;
"That ain't my style," said Casey. "Strike one," the umpire said.

From the benches, filled with people, there went up a muffled roar,
Like the beating of the storm waves on the stern and distant shore.
35 "Kill him! Kill the umpire!" shouted someone on the stand;
And it's likely they'd have killed him had not Casey raised his hand.

With a smile of honest charity great Casey's visage[4] shone;
He stilled the rising tumult,[5] he made the game go on;
He signaled to the pitcher, and once more the spheroid flew;
40 But Casey still ignored it, and the umpire said, "Strike two."

"Fraud!" cried the maddened thousands, and the echo answered "Fraud!"
But one scornful look from Casey and the audience was awed;
They saw his face grow stern and cold, they saw his muscles strain,
And they knew that Casey wouldn't let the ball go by again.

45 The sneer is gone from Casey's lips, his teeth are clenched in hate,
He pounds with cruel vengeance his bat upon the plate;
And now the pitcher holds the ball, and now he lets it go,
And now the air is shattered by the force of Casey's blow.

Oh, somewhere in this favored land the sun is shining bright,
50 The band is playing somewhere, and somewhere hearts are light;
And somewhere men are laughing, and somewhere children shout,
But there is no joy in Mudville: Mighty Casey has struck out.

---

3. **writing** (rīth′ĭng): twisting, as in pain or embarrassment.
4. **visage** (vĭz′ĭj): face.
5. **tumult** (tōō′mŭlt′): a disorderly disturbance.

Connect to the Literature

1. **What Do You Think?** When you reached the end of the poem, how did you feel about Casey? How did you feel about the crowd?

   Comprehension Check
   - At the beginning of the poem, how many runs does the Mudville team have? What inning is it?
   - How does Casey react to the first two pitches thrown to him?

Think Critically

2. What is your impression of Casey as he steps up to the plate? How might he have impressed the crowd?

3. How do you feel about Casey's response to his team's situation in the game?

   Think About:
   - his attitude as he steps up to the plate
   - his "smile of honest charity" after the first strike is called
   - his attitude after the second strike is called

4. **ACTIVE READING** **QUESTIONING**
   Look over the notes you took in your 📖 **READER'S NOTEBOOK**. With two other classmates, review the details and questions you wrote down. Answer any questions that are not answered in your notes.

Extend Interpretations

5. **The Writer's Style** A writer's use of exaggeration or overstatement for emphasis is called **hyperbole.** One example of hyperbole in this poem occurs in the description of the crowd's yell: "It rumbled in the mountaintops, it rattled in the dell." What does hyperbole add to "Casey at the Bat"?

6. **Connect to Life** Think of a real-life situation in which success or failure has depended upon the performance of a single person. What goes through a person's mind at a moment like that?

Literary Analysis

SOUND DEVICES Repetition, rhyme, and rhythm are three of the **sound devices** used in poetry. **Repetition** is a repeating sound, word, phrase, or line. **Rhyme** is a repetition of sounds at the end of words. (In many poems, lines end with rhyming words.) **Rhythm** is a pattern of stressed (ˊ) and unstressed (˘) syllables in a poem's lines.

These sound devices can intensify the emotional effect of a poem. All three can be heard in the following lines from "Casey at the Bat":

> *"Kill him! Kill the umpire!"*
> *shouted someone on the stand;*
> *And it's likely they'd have killed him*
> *had not Casey raised his hand.*

Activity Much of the energy and excitement of "Casey at the Bat" comes from the poet's use of repetition, rhyme, and rhythm. With a partner, copy the poem on a sheet of paper. On the copy, mark the rhythm, identify the rhyme scheme, and note any repetitions. Then, using your marked-up copy as a script, read the poem to your classmates.

CHOICES *and* CHALLENGES

Writing

Response to Literature
Imagine that you work for a literary magazine and have just been asked to write an interpretation of "Casey at the Bat." Because this is a narrative poem (a poem that tells a story), you can read the poem like a story, noting the sequence of events that move it along. What do these events tell you about Casey's character and his relationship with his fans? Use examples from the poem in your interpretation. Place your response in your **Working Portfolio.**

Writing Workshop
See p. 506: Basics in a Box.

Speaking & Listening

Film Review View the film version of "Casey at the Bat." Then discuss how the images, dialogue, and sound work together to tell the story, and explain how they affect the viewer.

VIDEO: Literature in Performance

"Casey at the Bat"

Research & Technology

Record-Setters Consult a sports records book, almanac, or encyclopedia to find the names of baseball players whose accomplishments have made history. Choose one player to research in-depth. What team did he play for? What do his fellow players say about him? What are his stats? Who previously held the record he broke?

Reading for INFORMATION
Before you begin, read "Out of the Ballpark" on p. 305.

Ernest Lawrence Thayer
1863–1940

"I evolved 'Casey' from the situation I had seen so often in baseball . . ."

Early Years Although Ernest Lawrence Thayer wrote many poems for newspapers, he is remembered for just one: "Casey at the Bat." Thayer was educated at Harvard University, where he served as editor of its humor magazine, the *Lampoon.* After graduation, he joined the staff of the *San Francisco Examiner,* where in 1887 he began writing a poem for each Sunday issue. "Casey at the Bat" was first printed in the paper in 1888.

Origin of "Casey" Thayer said, "I evolved 'Casey' from the situation I had seen so often in baseball—a crack batsman coming to the bat with the bases filled, and then fallen down." Although he insisted that no particular person was the model for Casey, many ballplayers claimed to be the unfortunate hero of the poem. By the time of Thayer's death in 1940, "Casey at the Bat" had become an American favorite.

Sports

Out of the Ballpark

by Avery Foster

In the summer of 1998, Mark McGwire and Sammy Sosa raced to break the single season home run record set by Roger Maris in 1961. The two sluggers found themselves caught up in a surge of publicity. Thousands of cameras flashed each time they swung the bat. The nightly news never missed reporting a game. Suddenly, baseball was the subject everyone was talking about. Had one of them hit one out today? Did you hear that it smashed through a billboard? At times the media frenzy seemed to overwhelm Sosa and McGwire. Often, however, they coped with their success by drawing attention away from themselves. The skill it took to smash the ball out of the park day after day was extraordinary, but the ability to homer was not the most extraordinary thing about these two power hitters.

Key Standard
R2.4 Identify an author's argument and point of view in a text.
Other Standards R2.2, R2.3, R2.6

❶ Fans surround Sosa and McGwire in Orlando.

Reading for Information

Making Generalizations & Drawing Conclusions
When writers make broad general statements based on several pieces of specific information, they are making **generalizations.** "Elephants are large" and "Anita gets up early" are examples of generalizations. An **overgeneralization** is a statement too broad to be true, for example, "It never rains in California."

YOUR TURN *Use the questions below to learn more about making generalizations.*

❶ Words such as *everyone, no one, always,* and *never* often tell you that a statement is an overgeneralization. In these two sentences, what words reveal that these statements are overgeneralizations?

Better Than Babe Ruth

2 If McGwire wanted to brag about himself, he certainly could. In 1998, he towered over the rest of the league in both stats and stature. His powerful bat would have put him in the history books even if he hadn't surpassed Roger Maris's 61 home runs. For three seasons in a row he hit at least 50 homers (1996, 1997, and 1998), and his home run ratio was an astonishing one homer per 11.2 at bats. That means that if you chose to spend a beautiful summer afternoon watching McGwire at bat, you would have a better chance of seeing him smash one out than you would if you were watching any other player in history, including Babe Ruth.

3 When he signed with the Cardinals in the fall of 1997, McGwire was already making a name for himself away from the ballpark. At the televised press conference announcing the deal, he pledged to donate $1 million per year of his Cardinals salary to help abused children. More impressive than that pledge was what happened to the big guy when he tried to talk about his reasons for setting up the Mark McGwire Charitable Foundation. He couldn't. There was only silence. And then he started to cry. The sight instantly endeared him to the public. Here was a giant of a man who broke into tears when he thought about what was happening to defenseless children. It was a theme to which McGwire would return again and again throughout 1998. Breaking the record for the most home runs in a season was exhilarating, but the chance to help children affected McGwire more profoundly.

Right fielder Sammy Sosa trailed McGwire in total home runs for most of the season, but he too could rocket the ball out of the park. At 6′0″ and 200 lbs., Sosa is not small by any means, but his performance in 1998 emphasized that smashing the ball out of the stadium also required excellent skill and timing. People were amazed when Sosa hit homer number 66 and pulled ahead of McGwire for only the second time during the season.

McGwire reacts to his 61st home run of the 1998 season.

McGwire follows through to hit a single against the Milwaukee Brewers.

Not only had the two sluggers battled to break the record of 61 home runs in a single season, they were continuing the battle.

Strength of Character

Besides a place in the record books, the home run race offered Sosa an opportunity to reveal his strength of character. Out of the batting box, he demonstrated the respect and humility that were the very model of sportsmanship. If he finished the season with the most home runs, Sammy said, he would be happy. If McGwire finished with more, he added, he still would be happy! It astonished everyone that Sosa and McGwire seemed to get along so well together. Again and again Sosa maintained that McGwire was a great player and he wished him the best. In an age when many sports superstars couldn't care less about being an example for others, the conduct of the Cubs right fielder was refreshing.

Reading for Information *continued*

After writers gather information and combine it with their own ideas and prior knowledge, they make decisions about what they've learned. This is called **drawing conclusions.** Readers draw conclusions by making inferences about the details in the works they read.

YOUR TURN *Use the questions below to learn more about drawing conclusions.*

2 The writer begins this paragraph with a conclusion drawn from his research. What specific information does he provide in the rest of the paragraph to support the conclusion? Does the conclusion make sense?

3 What conclusion can you draw about McGwire, based on the specific information in this paragraph?

Growing up in the Dominican Republic, Sosa's first job as a kid was shining shoes, and he has never forgotten where he came from. By founding the Sammy Sosa Charitable Foundation, Sosa began helping his country, with the goal of providing aid for children's healthcare in his hometown of San Pedro. His country needed him most, however, when tragedy struck in September of 1998. Hurricane Georges swept quickly through the Caribbean, wreaking havoc on the Dominican Republic and leaving thousands homeless. Rising to the occasion, Sosa turned the constant publicity from the home run race into a daily opportunity for raising disaster relief funds. In the process, he sent three planeloads of food and medical supplies to the Dominican Republic and joined other Dominican baseball players in a pledge to help out any way possible.

④

Reading for Information *continued*

④ Writers may state their conclusion as a topic sentence *before* the information that supports it or as a summing up *after* the information. Read this paragraph. Where is the conclusion? Restate it in your own words.

⑤ There are three overgeneralizations in this paragraph. Rewrite them to make them valid generalizations.

Research & Technology
Activity Link: "Casey at the Bat," p. 304.
Find out more about Roger Maris, a previous holder of the single season home run record. What characterized him as a player? What was he known for outside the ballpark? What controversy is associated with his record? Write a paragraph in which you make a generalization about Maris's accomplishments and draw a conclusion based on a group of facts.

Sosa takes a big swing.

⑤ Sosa may not have set the final home run record, but he proved himself an excellent ballplayer and an excellent human being. The entire nation watched with excitement as two legendary players chased one of the most glorious records in baseball. There will never be another season like it. Sosa and McGwire, by reaching out to help others, drew everyone into their success. With equal parts skill and heart, they propelled themselves into sports history. ∎

Building Vocabulary
Analyzing Word Parts: Affixes

The words *mistrust* and *excitable* each have an affix—a word part that can be attached to base words to make new words. Affixes added to the beginning of words are called **prefixes**; those added to the end are called **suffixes**.

mistrust

| prefix **mis-** means "not" | base word: **trust** |

excitable

| base word: **excite** | suffix **-able** means "capable of being" |

> The next day when the principal called me into his office I knew what it would be about. He looked **uncomfortable** and **unhappy**. I decided I wasn't going to make it any easier for him, so I looked him straight in the eyes. He looked away and fidgeted with the papers on his desk.
>
> —Marta Salinas, "The Scholarship Jacket"

Both words share the prefix **un-**, which means "not." Can you figure out their meaning?

Strategies for Building Vocabulary

Below are some common prefixes and suffixes used in forming English words.

❶ Recognize Common Affixes Knowing the meanings of some of the most common affixes can help you understand the meanings of unfamiliar words. Some of the most common prefixes and suffixes are listed in the charts below, along with their meanings.

❷ Analyze Words You can use your knowledge of prefixes, suffixes, and base words to analyze the meanings of words you don't know. Think about the word *resealable*, for example. The prefix *re-* means "again." The base word *seal* means "to close tightly." The suffix *-able* means "capable of." Therefore, *resealable* means "capable of being closed tightly again."

Prefix	Meaning	Examples
co-, com-, con-	with, together	costar, compress, conjunction
dis-	the absence of	disagree
e-, ex-	opposite of, out, away from	emigrate, exchange
em-, en-	to provide with, to cause to be	empower, enrich
im-, in-, il-, ir-	not	inoperable, imperfect, illogical, irresponsible
re-	again, back	recharge, review
trans-	across, change	transact, transcontinental
un-	not, opposite	unbearable, unhook, unnoticed

Suffix	Meaning	Examples
-able, -ible	likely to be, capable of being	adorable, flexible
-ance	an act or state of	appearance
-ate	characterized by, to cause to become	passionate, activate
-er, -or	one who	driver, visitor
-ion	an act or state of	creation, eruption
-ive	tending to, performing an act of	reflective, selective
-ous	full of, characterized by	joyous, poisonous

Key Standard
R1.2 Use knowledge of roots and affixes to understand vocabulary in different content areas.

EXERCISE Divide each word into a base word and a prefix or suffix. Then define the word.

1. transform   **2.** destitution   **3.** enable   **4.** inefficient   **5.** endurance

Comparing Literature

Key Standard

R3.1 Be able to describe the purposes and characteristics of different forms of prose, such as the short story, novel, or essay.

Fables

You are about to read two versions of the **fable** "Ant and Grasshopper" by the ancient Greek storyteller Aesop. The fable teaches a simple lesson, or **moral,** about the importance of work. Then you will read "The Richer, the Poorer," a modern story based on Aesop's fable. The **characters** in "The Richer, the Poorer" have much in common with the ant and the grasshopper of the original fable, but the modern characters have a more complex view of the role of work in a happy life.

ANT and GRASSHOPPER

The classic fable retold in prose by JAMES REEVES and in verse by ENNIS REES

The Richer, the Poorer

A short story by DOROTHY WEST

Connect to Your Life

Hard Work and No Play Why is work such an important part of life? How do you feel about your work? Do you put your best effort into it? Do you sometimes try to avoid it? What do you get in return for the work you do? Think about your attitudes toward work.

- How important is work for a happy life?

- Which is more important, work or play?

In a small group, discuss your views on the role of work in life.

POINTS OF COMPARISON

Fables are brief tales written in prose or verse that are told to illustrate a **moral**, or lesson. Traditional fables often have animal characters, and the moral appears in a statement at the end. **Modern fables** are often more subtle and complex. In the pages that follow you will compare and contrast a traditional and a modern fable. To help you note similarities and differences, keep these questions in mind as you read.

- When was the **fable** written?
- Who are the **characters**? What do they represent?
- What happens in the **fable**?
- What is the **moral**?

	Ant and Grasshopper	The Richer, the Poorer
When was the fable written?		
Who are the characters? What do they represent?		
What happens in the fable?		
What is the moral?		

Use a diagram like the one at the right to take notes as you read.

Assessment Option: Comparison-and-Contrast Essay

After you have finished reading both versions of "Ant and Grasshopper" and "The Richer, the Poorer," you will have the option of writing a comparison-and-contrast essay. Your notes will help you plan and write the essay.

Ant and Grasshopper

Aesop's fable retold in prose by JAMES REEVES

Aesop's fable retold in verse by ENNIS REES

Build Background

`BIOLOGY`

Both ants and grasshoppers are insects, but their habits are different. Ants live in organized communities called colonies, and are divided into queens, males, and workers. Most ants are workers, whose main job is to gather food. Ants eat both vegetable matter and other insects.

Grasshoppers, on the other hand, don't live in communities. Most grasshoppers eat vegetable matter, but some eat animal remains and other insects. Grasshoppers spend most of their time searching for food and eating.

Focus Your Reading

`LITERARY ANALYSIS` `FABLE AND MORAL`

A **fable** is a brief story that teaches a lesson. The lesson can be expressed in a short, clear statement, or **moral**. The **characters** in fables are often animals who represent ideas such as "patience" or "cleverness." As you read the two retellings of Aesop's "Ant and Grasshopper," notice that one is told in verse and the other in prose.

`ACTIVE READING` `SETTING PURPOSES`

When you **set a purpose for reading,** you choose specific reasons for reading a work. Here you will read to compare and contrast two versions of the same fable. As you read, notice the difference between reading for fun and reading in order to prepare for writing an essay.

READER'S NOTEBOOK As you read, try to answer the Points of Comparison questions from page 311.

Key Standard
R3.1 Be able to describe the purposes and characteristics of different forms of prose, such as the short story, novel, or essay.

ANT and GRASSHOPPER

Aesop's fable retold in prose by JAMES REEVES

The Grasshopper and the Ant, Charles Henry Bennett (1828–1867). Pen and ink drawing. The Granger Collection, New York.

All summer the ant had been working hard, gathering a store of corn for the winter. Grain by grain she had taken it from the fields and stowed it away in a hole in the bank, under a hawthorn bush.

One bright, frosty day in winter Grasshopper saw her. She was dragging out a grain of corn to dry it in the sun. The wind was keen, and poor Grasshopper was cold.

"Good morning, Ant," said he. "What a terrible winter it is! I'm half dead with hunger. Please give me just one of your corn grains to eat. I can find nothing, although I've hopped all over the farmyard. There isn't a seed to be found. Spare me a grain, I beg."

"Why haven't you saved anything up?" asked Ant. "I worked hard all through the summer, storing food for the winter. Very glad I am too, for as you say, it's bitterly cold."

"I wasn't idle last summer, either," said Grasshopper.

"And what did you do, pray?"

"Why, I spent the time singing," answered Grasshopper. "Every day from dawn till sunset I jumped about or sat in the sun, chirruping to my heart's content."

"Oh you did, did you?" replied Ant. "Well, since you've sung all summer to keep yourself cheerful, you may dance all winter to keep yourself warm. Not a grain will I give you!"

And she scuttled off into her hole in the bank, while Grasshopper was left cold and hungry.

IN GOOD TIMES PREPARE FOR WHEN THE BAD TIMES COME.

The ANT and the GRASSHOPPER

Aesop's fable retold in verse by ENNIS REES

A mean grasshopper,
Green as a lime,
Noticed an ant
In the summertime
Climbing a plant,
Gathering food
To eat in the winter.
And since she was rude,
The grasshopper said:

"To work in the summer
You must be dumber
Than almost anyone.
Don't you have any fun?
Even though you're an ant,
Surely you can't
Be quite so absurd!"

To this the ant
Didn't answer a word,
But she took the chance
To give her a glance

As sharp as a splinter,
Then worked right on
Getting ready for winter,
When there's little to light on
And little to eat
And even less heat
Than that. And soon

Winter came. And the grasshopper,
Green as a lime,
Felt stiff and lame
In the wintertime.

"I'm old and I'm twice
As cold as lime ice,"
She said with a jerk.
And she started to lurk
Round the ant's house—to eat!
Which shows that hard work
Isn't easy to beat.

ESOPO

Aesop
620–560 B.C.

"In good times prepare for when the bad times come."

A Mysterious Life Little is known about Aesop, the world's most famous creator of fables. Some historians think he may have been a slave who worked on Samos, a Greek island in the Aegean Sea, near Turkey.

Fast Talker One account of Aesop's life is as eventful as one of his fables. According to this story, Aesop's second master granted him his freedom in appreciation of his wit. After telling stories throughout Greece and Egypt, Aesop was appointed ambassador by King Croesus. On diplomatic missions, Aesop told fables to advise, instruct, or win an argument. Most of the time, his skill with words enabled him to wriggle out of trouble. His luck, however, ran out in Delphi, where he was sent to distribute money to the citizens. Aesop found them so greedy that he returned the money to Croesus. As Aesop prepared to leave Delphi, someone hid a golden bowl in his baggage. He was arrested for theft, condemned by the court, and executed by being pushed off a cliff.

Connect to the Literature

1. **What Do You Think?**
   How did you feel about the ant's treatment of the grasshopper? Did you have the same reaction to both versions of the fable? Explain.

   Comprehension Check
   • How had the ant prepared for winter?
   • What did the grasshopper want from the ant?
   • How did the ant respond?

Think Critically

2. **ACTIVE READING** **SETTING PURPOSES**
   Review the notes you made in your **READER'S NOTEBOOK** while reading. With a partner, identify details both versions of "Ant and Grasshopper" share. Then discuss how looking for information changed the way you read the fables.

3. Connect to Life Think about how much time most Americans spend working. In a small group, discuss whether the ant or the grasshopper is the better symbol for Americans' attitudes toward work.

Literary Analysis

FABLE AND MORAL A **fable** is a short tale told to teach a lesson. The characters in fables are usually animals that represent ideas. The lesson of the fable, called the **moral,** is sometimes directly stated at the end of the fable, as in James Reeves's retelling of "Ant and Grasshopper." Other times, as with Ennis Rees's version in verse, the reader must infer the moral from the characters' behavior. In either case, the same moral applies to both.

POINTS OF COMPARISON

Paired Activity With a partner, study both versions of the fable and answer the Points of Comparison questions from page 311. Together, complete the diagram you began earlier.

	Ant and Grasshopper	The Richer, the Poorer
When was the fable written?	in ancient Greece	
Who are the characters? What do they represent?	grasshopper = play ant = work	
What happens in the fable?		
What is the moral?		

The Richer, the Poorer

by DOROTHY WEST

Key Standard
R3.1 Be able to describe the purposes and characteristics of different forms of prose, such as the short story, novel, or essay.
Other Standards R3.2, R3.4, W2.2, W2.3, LS2.4

Build Background

SCIENCE

Have you wondered why some people are adventurous while others are more cautious? Experts who study human behavior disagree about the factors that make people who they are. Some believe that it is nature—the genes inherited from a person's parents—that has the most important influence on personality. Others believe that nurture—the influence of other people and the environment on a person's life—has the most impact.

Focus Your Reading

LITERARY ANALYSIS   **MODERN FABLE**

Modern fables differ in some ways from traditional fables. The **characters** are not usually animals, and they are more complicated; they don't just represent an idea. The **moral** in a modern fable is seldom stated. The reader is left to infer it from what the characters do and say, and what is said about them. As you read, notice how the character Lottie changes.

ACTIVE READING   **SETTING PURPOSES**

When reading stories in order to **compare** and **contrast** them, your purpose is to find similarities and differences between them. As you read "The Richer, the Poorer," pay careful attention to the characters and the plot. Notice the lessons each character learns. Think about the title. Then think how these story elements relate to those in "Ant and Grasshopper."

READER'S NOTEBOOK As you read, refer again to the Points of Comparison questions from page 311. Record your findings in your Reader's Notebook for later use in completing your Points of Comparison diagram.

WORDS TO KNOW **Vocabulary Preview**
enhanced   self-denial   whim
frugally   sentimental

The Richer, the Poorer

by DOROTHY WEST

Victorian Parlor II (1945), Horace Pippin. Oil on canvas, 25 1/4" x 30". The Metropolitan Museum of Art, Arthur Hoppock Hearn Fund, 1958. (58.26)

Over the years Lottie had urged Bess to prepare for her old age. Over the years Bess had lived each day as if there were no other. Now they were both past sixty, the time for summing up. Lottie had a bank account that had never grown lean. Bess had the clothes on her back and the rest of her worldly possessions in a battered suitcase.

Lottie had hated being a child, hearing her parents' skimping and scraping. Bess had never seemed to notice. All she ever wanted was to go outside and play. She learned to skate on borrowed skates. She rode a borrowed bicycle. Lottie couldn't wait to grow up and buy herself the best of everything.

As soon as anyone would hire her, Lottie put herself to work. She minded babies; she ran errands for the old.

She never touched a penny of her money, though her child's mouth watered for ice cream and candy. But she could not bear to share with Bess, who never had anything to share with her. When the dimes began to add up to dollars, she lost her taste for sweets.

By the time she was twelve, she was clerking after school in a small variety store. Saturdays she worked as long as she was wanted. She decided to keep her money for clothes. When she entered high school, she would wear a wardrobe that neither she nor anyone else would be able to match.

But her freshman year found her unable to indulge so frivolous a <u>whim</u>, particularly when her admiring instructors advised her to think seriously of college. No one in her family had ever gone to college, and certainly Bess would never get there.

She would show them all what she could do, if she put her mind to it. She began to bank her money, and her bank became her most private and precious possession.

In her third year in high school, she found a job in a small but expanding restaurant, where she cashiered from the busy hour until closing. In her last year in high school, the business increased so rapidly that Lottie was faced with the choice of staying in school or working full time. She made her choice easily. A job in hand was worth two in the future.

Bess had a beau[1] in the school band, who had no other ambition except to play a horn. Lottie expected to be settled with a home and family while Bess was still waiting for Harry to earn enough to buy a marriage license.

That Bess married Harry straight out of high school was not surprising. That Lottie never married at all was not really surprising either. Two or three times she was halfway persuaded, but to give up a job that paid well for a homemaking job that paid nothing was a risk she was incapable of taking.

Bess's married life was nothing for Lottie to envy. She and Harry lived like gypsies, Harry playing in second-rate bands all over the country, even getting himself and Bess stranded in Europe. They were often in rags and never in riches.

Bess grieved because she had no child, not having sense enough to know she was better off without one. Lottie was certainly better off without nieces and nephews to feel sorry for. Very likely Bess would have dumped them on her doorstep.

That Lottie had a doorstep they might have been left on was only because her boss, having bought a second house, offered Lottie his first house at a price so low and terms so reasonable that it would have been like losing money to refuse.

She shut off the rooms she didn't use, letting them go to rack and ruin.[2] Since she ate her meals out, she had no food at home and did not encourage callers, who always expected a cup of tea.

Her way of life was mean and miserly, but she did not know it. She thought she lived <u>frugally</u> in her middle years so that she could live in comfort and ease when she most needed peace of mind.

The years, after forty, began to race. Suddenly Lottie was sixty and retired from her job by her boss's son, who had no <u>sentimental</u> feeling about keeping her on until she was ready to quit.

She made several attempts to find other

> **To know how much there is to know is the beginning of learning to live.**

---

1. **beau:** boyfriend.
2. **go to rack and ruin:** become rundown; deteriorate.

WORDS
TO
KNOW

whim (hwĭm) *n.* a fanciful notion or impulse
frugally (froo'gə-lē) *adv.* in a thrifty way; economically
sentimental (sĕn'tə-mĕn'tl) *adj.* showing or characterized by tender emotions

employment, but her dowdy[3] appearance made her look old and inefficient. For the first time in her life Lottie would gladly have worked for nothing, to have some place to go, something to do with her day.

Harry died abroad, in a third-rate hotel, with Bess weeping as hard as if he had left her a fortune. He had left her nothing but his horn. There wasn't even money for her passage home.

Lottie, trapped by the blood tie, knew she would not only have to send for her sister but take her in when she returned. It didn't seem fair that Bess should reap the harvest of Lottie's lifetime of <u>self-denial</u>.

Carmen and Hilda (1941), Alice Neel. Watercolor on paper, 29″ x 22″. Schomburg Center for Research in Black Culture, Art & Artifacts Division, The New York Public Library, Astor, Lenox and Tilden Foundations. Copyright © The Estate of Alice Neel. Courtesy Robert Miller Gallery

It took Lottie a week to get a bedroom ready, a week of hard work and hard cash. There was everything to do, everything to replace or paint. When she was through, the room looked so fresh and new that Lottie felt she deserved it more than Bess.

She would let Bess have her room, but the mattress was so lumpy, the carpet so worn, the curtains so threadbare that Lottie's conscience pricked her. She supposed she would have to redo that room, too, and went about doing it

with an eagerness that she mistook for haste. When she was through upstairs, she was shocked to see how dismal[4] downstairs looked by comparison. She tried to ignore it, but with nowhere to go to escape it, the contrast grew more intolerable.

She worked her way from kitchen to parlor, persuading herself she was only putting the rooms to right to give herself something to do. At night she slept like a child after a long and happy day of playing house. She was having more fun than she had ever had in her life. She was living each hour for itself.

There was only a day now before Bess would arrive. Passing her gleaming mirrors, at first with vague awareness, then with painful clarity, Lottie saw herself as others saw her and could not stand the sight. She went on a spending spree from specialty shops to beauty salon, emerging transformed into a woman who believed in miracles.

She was in the kitchen basting a turkey when Bess rang the bell. Her heart raced, and she wondered if the heat from the oven was responsible. She went to the door, and Bess stood before her. Stiffly she suffered Bess's

---

3. **dowdy:** dull and unfashionable.
4. **dismal:** dreary; gloomy.

embrace, her heart racing harder, her eyes suddenly smarting from the onrush of cold air.

"Oh, Lottie, it's good to see you," Bess said, but saying nothing about Lottie's splendid appearance. Upstairs, Bess, putting down her shabby suitcase, said, "I'll sleep like a rock tonight," without a word of praise for her lovely room. At the lavish table, top-heavy with turkey, Bess said, "I'll take light and dark both," with no marveling at the size of the bird or that there was turkey for two elderly women, one of them too poor to buy her own bread.

With the glow of good food in her stomach, Bess began to spin stories. They were rich with places and people, most of them lowly, all of them magnificent. Her face reflected her telling, the joys and sorrows of her remembering, and above all, the love she lived by that <u>enhanced</u> the poorest place, the humblest person.

Then it was that Lottie knew why Bess had made no mention of her finery, or the shining room, or the twelve-pound turkey. She had not even seen them. Tomorrow she would see the room as it really looked and Lottie as she really looked and the warmed-over turkey in its second-day glory. Tonight she saw only what she had come seeking, a place in her sister's home and heart.

She said, "That's enough about me. How have the years used you?"

"It was me who didn't use them," said Lottie wistfully. "I saved for them. I forgot the best of them would go without my ever spending a day or a dollar enjoying them. That's my life story in those few words, a life never lived. Now it's too near the end to try."

Bess said, "To know how much there is to know is the beginning of learning to live. Don't count the years that are left us. At our time of life it's the days that count. You've too much catching up to do to waste a minute of a waking hour feeling sorry for yourself."

Lottie grinned, a real wide-open grin, "Well, to tell the truth I felt sorry for you. Maybe, if I had any sense, I'd feel sorry for myself, after all. I know I'm too old to kick up my heels, but I'm going to let you show me how. If I land on my head, I guess it won't matter. I feel giddy[5] already, and I like it." ❖

---

5. **giddy:** lightheaded; frivolous.

Dorothy West
1907–1998

"I knew I wanted to be a writer."

Early Years Dorothy West was known to her fellow writers of the Harlem Renaissance—a literary movement of African-American artists during the 1920s—as the "kid," a name that fit because she started writing at age 7 and published her first article at 14. In the collections of stories and essays she called *The Richer, the Poorer,* West writes about the middle-class African-American family in which she grew up. "I knew I wanted to be a writer," West said. "Living with [my family] was like living inside a story." Later, friends such as Langston Hughes and Zora Neale Hurston became another family for her.

Unique Personal View West encouraged African-American writers. However, she also believed that "color is not important," that people should be understood as individuals influenced as much by class and values as by race. In this she disagreed with many activists of the 1960s. Today, West's work is well received. Her 1995 novel *The Wedding* became a bestseller and successful TV miniseries.

WORDS
TO
KNOW

enhance (ĕn-hăns′) *v.* to increase the attractiveness of

Connect to the Literature

1. What Do You Think? Did you think the ancient fable or the modern fable was more effective in getting across its moral? Explain.

Comprehension Check
- What was Lottie's main concern through most of her life?
- How did Bess spend her life?
- How did Lottie feel when she learned Bess was coming to stay with her?

Think Critically

2. ACTIVE READING SETTING PURPOSES
Review the notes you made in your READER'S NOTEBOOK. How do they help you compare and contrast the two works?

3. What lessons do Lottie and Bess learn? How do they differ from those learned by Ant and Grasshopper?

4. Which sister has lived the more fulfilling life? Why? What do you think Lottie would do differently if she could live her life over again?

5. Connect to Life Think of a family member. In what ways are you similar to that person? How are you different? How can family members use their differences to help one another grow?

Literary Analysis

MODERN FABLE Unlike traditional fables, **modern fables** often contain complex characters. Instead of being character types, who represent single ideas, Lottie and Bess represent several ideas.

Most modern fables have a **theme,** which includes a moral, and is a broader statement about life.

REVIEW: THEME In a work of literature, the **theme** is the message or moral about life or human nature that the writer presents to the reader. Sometimes the title of the work can give you an important clue to the theme. What does the title, "The Richer, the Poorer," suggest about the theme?

POINTS OF COMPARISON

Paired Activity Now that you've read both traditional and modern versions of this fable, talk with a partner about the similarities and differences you found. Respond to the Points of Comparison questions from page 311. Use your discussion to help you complete your diagram. Once you've completed it, identify the theme of each, and compare the two.

	Ant and Grasshopper	The Richer, the Poorer
When was the fable written?	in ancient Greece	1920s
Who are the characters? What do they represent?	grasshopper = play ant = work	Bess = joy of living each day fully Lottie = at first the need to prepare for bad times; then, the wisdom of Bess's view
What happens in the fable?		
What is the moral?		

CHOICES and CHALLENGES

Writing

Recurring Themes Consider again the moral of "Ant and Grasshopper" and "The Ant and the Grasshopper." What do you think are the themes of these fables? Next, consider "The Richer, the Poorer." Are any themes from "Ant and Grasshopper" or "The Ant and the Grasshopper" repeated here? Write down a possible theme for each, and choose one that might apply to all three. Include evidence from each story to support your theme choice.

Speaking & Listening

Speech Decide which fable's moral you most agree with. Write a speech you could give to younger students about the relative value of work and play. Use examples from the fables to support your position.

Planning Options People in real life prepare for bad times in many ways. Talk with adults, such as parents, teachers, or business owners. Find out what measures they take against "a stormy day". What plans have they made in case of lean or difficult times?

Decide which are more common and which are less common.

Research & Technology

Insect Profiles Using nature books and magazines, direct observation, and other resources, compare and contrast the way ants and grasshoppers behave. Do ants seem more focused on work? Do grasshoppers look like they don't work as hard? Use a Venn Diagram to chart your findings.

Standardized Test Practice

Comparing Literature

Key Standard
W1.1 Choose an appropriate type of organization, and use transitions to connect ideas effectively.
Other Standard **W2.2**

PART 1 **Reading the Prompt**

When you are asked to create a written response to a prompt like the one below, first read the entire prompt carefully. Then read it again, looking for key words that suggest the purpose of the essay.

Write a Comparison-and-Contrast Essay

Write a five- or six-paragraph essay comparing and contrasting the traditional ❶ fable "Ant and Grasshopper" and the modern fable "The Richer, the Poorer." Show similarities and differences between the ❷ characters and morals of the two fables. Support your ideas using quotations and examples from the fables. ❸

STRATEGIES
IN ACTION

❶ I have to **compare and contrast** a traditional and a modern fable.

❷ I have to show **similarities and differences** between the characters and the morals of the two versions.

❸ I need to use **quotations and examples** from the fables.

PART 2 **Planning a Comparison-and-Contrast Essay**

- Review the Points of Comparison diagram (p. 311) you began and completed.

- Create an outline with the headings "Introduction," "Body," and "Conclusion."

- Using your diagram, find examples of similarities and differences to use in the body of your essay.

For more help in planning a comparison-and-contrast essay, see **Writing Workshop**, p. 636.

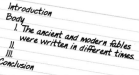

PART 3 **Drafting Your Essay**

Introduction Clearly state your essay's main purpose—to explain the similarities and differences you found when comparing a traditional and a modern fable. Briefly define the characteristics of a fable.

Body Decide the best way to organize your comparison-and-contrast essay. One way is to compare and contrast each important aspect of the ancient and modern fables one at a time. Use your Points of Comparison diagram for details and examples.

Conclusion End your essay with a strong statement about the most important difference between the traditional and modern fables. If you're having trouble identifying this difference, look again at your Points of Comparison chart.

Revising Make sure you always clearly indicate which fable you are discussing. Also, add signal words like *also* and *in contrast* to show the relationship you see between the fables.

Key Standard
W1.7 Revise writing to improve organization, word choice, and logic.
Other Standards W1.1, W1.2, W1.4, W2.1, W2.3, LC1.2, LC1.7

Writing Workshop | Character Sketch

Describing a character . . .

From Reading to Writing Drawing isn't the only way to create a portrait. You can also create a portrait using words—in a **character sketch.** For example, in *A Christmas Carol,* the reader forms an image of Scrooge's personality based on what he looks like, what he says, what he does, and how others behave toward him. Character sketches appear in many genres, from poetry to fiction to drama to news stories. They can help your audience feel like they truly know your character.

For Your Portfolio

WRITING PROMPT Write a character sketch about someone who interests you.

Purpose: To reveal the key elements of an individual's personality
Audience: Anyone interested in your sketch

Basics in a Box

Character Sketch at a Glance

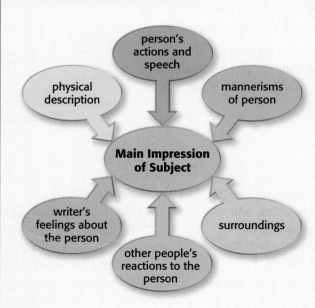

person's actions and speech

physical description

mannerisms of person

Main Impression of Subject

writer's feelings about the person

surroundings

other people's reactions to the person

RUBRIC STANDARDS FOR WRITING

A successful character sketch should

• present a vivid picture of the personality and physical appearance of the person

• give a main impression of the person

• include dialogue, mannerisms, descriptions and other devices that show, rather than tell, what the character is like

• reveal the writer's response to the person

• place the person in natural surroundings to help readers understand him or her

• have a clear structure, a strong beginning, and a strong conclusion

Analyzing a Student Model

SPEAKING
OPPORTUNITY

See the Speaking and Listening Handbook, p. R100 for oral presentation tips.

**Steve Hernandez
Parkland Middle School**

Grandma Andrea

You could say I had three mothers, my real mom and my two grandmas, Rosa and Andrea. My grandmas took care of me because my mom needed a lot of help when I was little. Both of my grandmothers spoke Spanish, but only Grandma Andrea knew English, too. Because of this, we spent a good deal of time together. I thought there was something special about her because she was the only older lady I knew who could speak two languages. Ours was not a typical relationship between a boy and his grandma.

Grandma Andrea was not much taller than most of her grandchildren, but I looked up to her. She taught me things like discipline, manners, and respect. Whenever I was alone in the house with her, she'd speak to me in English and in Spanish. Once, I remember that she asked me in Spanish if I wanted a glass of milk and a snack. *"¿Te gustaría un vaso de leche y una merienda?"* I didn't answer her in Spanish, only in English. But she refused to give me my milk and snack until I answered her in Spanish. She didn't want me to be lazy about learning both English and Spanish.

Her brown eyes always looked gentle but I saw strength in them. She didn't give up when her husband died in 1979. Instead, she continued to work and raise ten kids, including my father, Raul Hernandez. No matter what her troubles were, she always made everyone feel at home. Every holiday was an excuse to celebrate and have family and friends together at her place. She was friendly with all her neighbors and was always ready to give a helping hand. When a neighbor was sick, she would bring food or medicine. She would also pray for them in church.

On Sundays, she dressed formally to go to church. She always wore her gray suit, and her curly dark hair framed her round face. I remember how she looked one Sunday morning. The front door had been left open to let the sun in. Activity filled the house. Everybody was talking, making breakfast, watching TV, or getting ready for church. Grandma Andrea stood in the doorway, and the sunlight acted like a spotlight. Her cheeks were flushed and she wore a proud smile as she looked out at her family. I'll

RUBRIC
IN ACTION

❶ Introduction describes why the subject is important to the writer.

Other options:
- Begin with a strong visual image of the subject, including movement, gestures, and expressions.
- Tell an anecdote or open with a quotation about or from the subject.

❷ Dialogue shows what the character is like.

❸ Background information helps to establish a main impression of the person as strong and compassionate.

❹ Concrete details create a physical portrait of the subject.

❺ The writer places the person in her natural surroundings to help readers understand her.

always remember this moment when she looked like a very dignified, elegant, and sophisticated lady.

Grandma Andrea was very strict about how I behaved in public. She encouraged me not to get in trouble in the neighborhood. "Don't hang around with nothing to do," she'd say. "I have plenty of things at home that will keep you out of trouble." She didn't stand for any nonsense. But she never tried to stop me from exploring and being a kid. If I wanted to go by myself to the store a few blocks away, she'd let me. She'd only say, "Watch for cars," or "Be on time for dinner." She made me feel safe. I respected her because she respected me.

> **❻** Dialogue and details present a vivid picture of the person's personality.

Grandma Andrea was not only sweet, she was a good friend and teacher. She died in 1995 after a very full life. There is nothing I can do to bring her back but remember her. When my memories of her seem to be fading, I look at old photographs. If I shut my eyes and concentrate, I can hear her voice in Spanish. *"Trabaja mucho y vive bien."* "Work hard and live well." This is the way I will honor her.

> **❼** The writer uses a quote to create a powerful conclusion that reinforces the meaning of the subject in the writer's life.

Writing Your Character Sketch

❶ Prewriting

Whom do you want to write about? Start by thinking about your favorite people—teachers, neighbors, coaches, or relatives you know and admire. **Jot down** as many details about these people as you can. See the **Idea Bank** in the margin for more suggestions. Once you've chosen your subject, follow the steps at the top of the next page.

Planning Your Character Sketch

1. **Explore your feelings.** Why is this person significant to you? What details or incidents can you describe that show why he or she is important?

2. **Create mental images of the person.** Try picturing your subject in his or her usual surroundings. How does your subject act, speak, and look? Make a chart like this one to record details.

Personality Characteristics			
Physical	What subject says	What subject does	How others react

3. **Place your character in a definite setting.** Describe the person in a time and place that will reveal his or her personality. If your subject is a famous figure, do research using library resources or the Internet. To get information about someone you don't know well, you may choose to interview the person.

4. **Decide on your main impression.** What impression do you want your readers to have about the person? Which details from your chart best create this impression?

❷ Drafting

As you write your first draft, try to visualize the person. Focus on the main impression you want to create. Get your ideas down on paper. You can go back and revise your work later.

Show, Don't Tell

Good character sketches include plenty of details that help readers visualize. Instead of telling readers everything about your subject, use examples and dialogue that show what your subject is like. For example, in *A Christmas Carol* Scrooge refuses to give Christmas tips to his servants or his employee. Readers can see for themselves that Scrooge is stingy.

Organizing Your Draft

However you choose to organize your draft, you'll want to have an attention-getting **introduction,** a **body** that develops your subject's personality, and an **ending** that reveals how you feel about your subject. All of these parts should be balanced and connected by effective transitions that unify important ideas.

IDEA Bank

1. Your Working Portfolio
Look for ideas in the **Writing** sections that you completed earlier.

2. Celebrity Sketch
Look for character sketches in magazines. Notice how they create vivid portraits of subjects. Choose to write a sketch of a leader in your school, town, or city.

3. Word Play
Jot down descriptive words like *brave, funny, serious,* and *athletic.* Then think of a person you know who has one of those qualities.

Have a question?

See the **Writing Handbook**
Sensory Details, p. R42
Elaboration with Incidents, p. R42

See **Language Network**
Prewriting, p. 310
Drafting, p. 315

Ask Your Peer Reader

- How do you think I feel about my subject?
- How would you describe my subject's personality?
- What details help you picture my subject?
- What more would you like to know about my subject?

Need revising help?

Review the **Rubric**, p. 324.

Consider **peer reader** comments.

Check **Revising, Editing, and Proofreading**, p. R35.

See **Language Network,** Choosing Precise Words, p. 404.

Perplexed by pronoun-antecedent agreement?

See the **Grammar Handbook,** p. R78.

SPELLING
From Writing

As you revise your work, look back at the words you misspelled and determine why you made the errors you did. For additional help, refer to the strategies and generalizations in the **Spelling Handbook** on page R30.

SPEAKING
Opportunity

Turn your sketch into an oral presentation.

Publishing
IDEAS

• Exchange character sketches with a classmate. Draw a sketch of the person described. Display your sketch and the essay in class.

• Prepare a biography talk show. The host will interview you about the subject of your character sketch. Videotape the interviews so that they can be played back for the class.

Publishing Options
www.mcdougallittell.com

---

❸ Revising

TARGET SKILL ▶ **WORD CHOICE** Carefully chosen verbs and adjectives can bring a character to life. For example, instead of saying *Scrooge walked through the streets,* choose more specific words, as in: *Scrooge shuffled through the crowded streets.* Specific words help to create vivid writing.

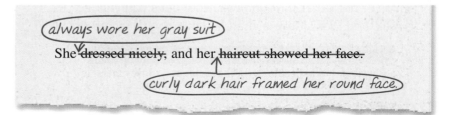

❹ Editing and Proofreading

TARGET SKILL ▶ **PRONOUN-ANTECEDENT AGREEMENT** An antecedent usually comes before the pronoun. The antecedent is the noun or pronoun to which the pronoun refers. Pronouns must agree with their antecedents in number, person, and gender. For example, in the sentence *Jane ate because she was hungry,* the pronoun *she* refers back to the antecedent *Jane.* Proofread your character sketch to make sure you catch errors in pronoun-antecedent agreement.

> they d
> My grandmothers took care of me because ~~she~~ wanted to
>
> help my mother.

❺ Reflecting

FOR YOUR WORKING PORTFOLIO What did you learn while doing this assignment? How did writing this character sketch change the way you look at people? Attach your reflections to your finished profile. Save your character sketch in your **Working Portfolio.**

Standardized Test Practice

Mixed Review

> "Waaaaa!" My baby sister's yell shatters the silence of the sleeping house. <u>She is not hurt or scared she is just awake</u> and ready to begin
> (1)
> her active day. Sophie is like a factory whistle: <u>he</u> begins the day
> (2)
> shrieking and ends it the same way. After she <u>leap</u> out of bed, she
> (3)
> demands hugs from everyone. Then she <u>has gone</u> down to the kitchen
> (4)
> for breakfast. Bath time comes after almost everyone has fled to go to school or to work. My mother often says that <u>they</u> might as well take
> (5)
> her bath at the same time because of <u>Sophie's splashing.</u>
> (6)

1. How is sentence 1 best written?

  A. She is not hurt or scared: she is just awake

  B. She is not hurt or scared; she is just awake

  C. She is not hurt, or scared, she is just awake

  D. Correct as is

2. What is the correct pronoun in sentence 2?

  A. she

  B. they

  C. we

  D. Correct as is

3. What is the correct verb tense in sentence 3?

  A. leaped

  B. leaps

  C. leaping

  D. Correct as is

4. What is the correct verb tense in sentence 4?

  A. going

  B. goes

  C. went

  D. Correct as is

5. What is the correct pronoun in item 5?

  A. we

  B. she

  C. he

  D. Correct as is

6. What is the correct possessive form in item 6?

  A. Sophies' splashing

  B. Sophies splashing

  C. Sophies's splashing

  D. Correct as is

Review Your Skills

Use the passage and the questions that follow it to check how well you remember the language conventions you've learned in previous grades.

Self-Assessment

Check your own answers in the **Grammar Handbook**

Plural and Possessive Nouns, p. R75

Pronoun-Antecedent Agreement, p. R78

Run-On Sentences, p. R71

Possessives, p. R76

Key Standard
LC1.4 Use the mechanics of writing correctly; demonstrate correct language usage.
***Other Standard* LC1.3**

Relationships

How have your ideas about reaching out to others developed as you read the selections in this unit? Are you more willing now to face obstacles? Choose one or more of the options in each of the following sections to help you explore what you've learned.

Key Standard
R3.4 Identify and analyze themes that appear across works.
Other Standards R3.1, R3.3, R3.6

Reflecting on Theme

OPTION 1

Making Connections Jot down themes about reaching out that you discovered from the selections you read in this unit. Then choose a recurring theme that you think young people should take to heart. Write a paragraph or two, explaining your choice.

OPTION 2

Discussing Which of the characters in Unit Two do you think develops the most as a result of his or her choices? Which characters develop little or not at all? Discuss these questions with a small group of classmates. Support your views with examples from the selections and insights from your own experience.

OPTION 3

Role-Playing Imagine that a friend needs more self-confidence to meet a new challenge. With a partner, role-play a conversation in which you attempt to inspire your friend with the will to overcome the obstacle. To support your points, use examples from several of this unit's selections. Which characters have you found the most inspiring? What qualities help them meet their challenges?

Self ASSESSMENT

READER'S NOTEBOOK

Think about the quotation at the beginning of this unit: page 188. Write a paragraph explaining how reading the selections in the unit has given you a better understanding of the quotation's meaning.

REVIEWING YOUR PERSONAL
WORD List

Vocabulary Review the new words you learned in this unit. If necessary, use a dictionary to check the meaning of each word.

Spelling Review your list of spelling words. If you're not sure of the correct spelling, use a dictionary or refer to the *Spelling Handbook* on page R30.

Reviewing Literary Concepts

OPTION 1

Rhyme and Rhythm Rhyme and rhythm are elements of many poems. Rhyme is a similarity of ending sounds in words. Rhythm is the pattern of stressed and unstressed syllables in a poem's lines. Some poems have regular rhythms. Others have irregular rhythms that are more like speech. Look back at the poems in this unit. In which is rhyme used? Which have regular rhythms and which do not? Record your findings in a chart.

Selection	Rhyme?	Regular Rhythm	Rhythm of Spoken Language?

OPTION 2

Visualizing Scenes Stage directions are instructions in a play's script about the settings of scenes and the actions of characters. When reading a play, you can use the stage directions to help you visualize the appearance of the stage and the characters. With a small group of classmates, choose a scene from "The Noble Experiment" and discuss how you would turn it into a play. Write the stage directions for one scene of your proposed play.

📁 Portfolio Building

- **Choices and Challenges—Writing** In this unit, you were asked to write a plot summary, identify themes, and interpret a poem. Which of these represents your strongest writing? Use a word processing program to write a cover letter explaining your choice. Place it in your **Presentation Portfolio.** 📁

- **Writing Workshops** In this unit you wrote an interpretation of a poem and a character sketch. Reread the two pieces and decide which is a stronger piece of writing. Explain your choice and place it in your **Presentation Portfolio.** 📁

- **Additional Activities** Think back to any of the assignments you completed for **Speaking & Listening** and **Research & Technology.** Keep a record in your portfolio of any assignments that you especially enjoyed, found helpful, or would like to do further work on in the future.

Self ASSESSMENT

📖 READER'S NOTEBOOK

On a sheet of paper, copy the following literary terms introduced in this unit. Next to each term, jot down a brief definition. If you don't understand a particular concept very well, refer to the **Glossary of Literary and Reading Terms** on page R120.

rhyme scheme

end rhyme

imagery

figurative language

simile

metaphor

static and dynamic characters

stanza

dialogue

acts and scenes

speaker

informative nonfiction

fable

moral

modern fable

Self ASSESSMENT

Review all the writing samples in your **Presentation Portfolio.** Which reflect your strengths as a writer? What skills would you like to improve?

Setting GOALS

Look back through your portfolio, worksheets, and **📖 READER'S NOTEBOOK.** What did you learn from this unit that might help you in your own life? Make a list of ideas that you would like to learn more about.

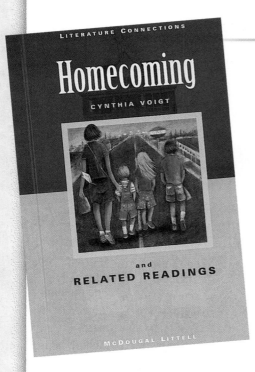

LITERATURE CONNECTIONS
Homecoming

BY CYNTHIA VOIGT

In this moving novel by Cynthia Voigt, 13-year-old Dicey is left to care for her two brothers and sister when the Tillerman children are abandoned by their mother in a parking lot. Determined to keep her siblings together, Dicey leads them on a hike across Connecticut to Aunt Cilla's, where the fight for her family begins.

These thematically related readings are provided along with *Homecoming*:

Shells
BY CYNTHIA RYLANT

Little Sister
BY NIKKI GRIMES

A Christmas Tree for Lydia
BY ELIZABETH ENRIGHT

The Journey
BY HU FENG

from **The Resilient Child**
BY KEVIN BUSHWELLER

Train Time
BY D'ARCY MCNICKLE

A Celebration of Grandfathers
BY RUDOLFO A. ANAYA

More Choices

The Big Wave
BY PEARL S. BUCK
When Jiya's family is swept away in a tidal wave, Kino and his family reach out and provide Jiya with a new family and a loving home.

Summer of My German Soldier
BY BETTE GREENE
As twelve-year-old Patty befriends Anton, who escaped from a camp for German prisoners, she is faced with a difficult choice: will she risk her family and life to help him?

Bridge to Terabithia
BY KATHERINE PATERSON
Leslie and her best friend, Jess, reach out and grow close by escaping to Terabithia, an imaginary land.

One-Eyed Cat
BY PAULA FOX
One night, eleven-year-old Ned climbs into the attic and accidentally shoots a cat with his air rifle. Afterwards, he feels terribly guilty. Will he choose to admit his guilt?

Dragonwings
BY LAURENCE YEP
Moonshadow had never seen his father before he joined him in California. Although the two face prejudice and danger in Chinatown, they choose all the while to keep pursuing their dream of making a flying machine.
A McDougal Littell *Literature Connection*

So Far from the Bamboo Grove

BY YOKO KAWASHIMA WATKINS

Yoko Kawashima, though Japanese, spent most of her childhood in Nanam, Korea, where she attended Japanese schools. Yoko was only seven when Japan entered World War II in 1941. Four years later, Kawashima's family had to flee from its home and begin a trek to Seoul, Korea. In *So Far from the Bamboo Grove,* Kawashima retells her family's struggle to survive.

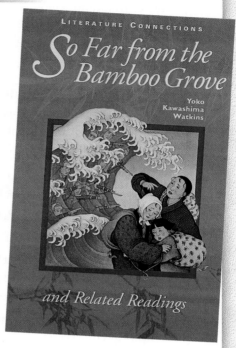

These thematically related readings are provided along with *So Far from the Bamboo Grove:*

Refugee Mother and Child
BY CHINUA ACHEBE

Old Man at the Bridge
BY ERNEST HEMINGWAY

from **The Endless Steppe: Growing Up in Siberia**
BY ESTHER HAUTZIG

The First Day of the War
BY MAIA WOJCIECHOWSKA

The Key
BY VÕ PHIÊN

Please Don't Leave
BY MR. LUE LEE

Generations
BY AMY LOWELL

Social Studies Connection

African Myths and Legends
BY KATHLEEN ARNOTT
These stories of flying horses, greedy spiders, and magic drums are from all parts of Africa.

From Slave Ship to Freedom Road
BY JULIUS LESTER
This award-winning author gives a painful portrayal of life on a slave ship.

The Arabian Nights Entertainments
EDITED BY ANDREW LANG
Faced with death, the young bride Shahrazad calms a cruel sultan by entertaining him with these 26 tales.

My Little African King
BY KATHERINE ROUNDTREE
This is the story of Mansa Musa, the great ruler of Mali who is known as the "Black Moses" of western Africa.

Antar and Abla: A Bedouin Romance
REWRITTEN AND ARRANGED BY DIANE RICHMOND
Antar is the Arabic hero, and Abla is his bride. This collection of tales recounts their adventures in sixth-century pre-Islamic Arabia.

Standardized Test Practice

Reading and Writing for Assessment

Throughout middle school, you will be tested on your ability to read and understand many different kinds of reading selections. The following pages will give you helpful test-taking strategies. Practice applying these strategies by working through the following models.

PART 1   How to Read the Test Selection

In many tests, you will read a passage and then answer multiple-choice questions about it. Applying the basic test-taking strategies that follow can help you focus on the right information.

STRATEGIES FOR READING A TEST SELECTION

▹ **Before you begin reading, skim the questions that follow the passage.** These can help focus your reading.

▹ **Use active reading strategies such as analyzing, predicting, and questioning.** Make notes in the margin only if the test directions allow you to mark on the test itself.

▹ **Think about the title, the message, and the theme.** What does the title suggest about the overall selection? What larger lesson can you draw from the passage?

▹ **Look for main ideas.** These are often stated at the beginning or end of paragraphs. Sometimes they are implied, not stated. After reading each paragraph, ask, "What was this passage about?"

▹ **Examine the sequence of ideas.** Are the ideas developed in chronological order, order of importance, or organized in some other way?

▹ **Evaluate the literary elements and techniques used by the writer.** How does the writer use tone (writer's attitude toward the subject), point of view, figurative language, or other elements to create a certain effect or get the message across?

▹ **Unlock word meanings.** Use context clues and word parts to help you unlock the meaning of unfamiliar words.

Key Standard
R2.4 Identify an author's argument and point of view in a text.
Other Standards **R1.3, R3.4, R3.6, LC1.2, LC1.3, LC1.6, LC1.7**

Reading Selection

❶ The Power of a Voice

by Danna Ruby

1   "You've got too much going against you. You're black, you're a woman, and you're large." In 1964 a political analyst spoke these words to a young African-American lawyer from Texas after she had lost her first political race. ❷ However, Barbara Charline Jordan refused to give up. She had a mission—to stamp out discrimination and make a difference in people's lives. Eventually she would fulfill this mission and more.

2   Barbara Jordan was born in 1936 in Houston, Texas, the youngest of three daughters. Her family was not well-off, and she grew up in a world of ❸ segregation. The separation of blacks and whites in all areas of life, including in the schools, was enforced by law.

3   Despite ongoing discrimination, Jordan excelled in school and honed her speaking skills on her high school speech team. In the 1954 case of *Brown v. Board of Education of Topeka,* the Supreme Court ruled that segregation kept African-Americans from receiving an education equal to that received by whites. Two years later Jordan graduated with honors from Texas Southern University, where she had been an award-winning member of the previously all-male debate team. In 1959, she received a law degree from Boston University. Although she passed the bar examination in Massachusetts and
4   Texas, politics pulled her away from practicing law.

     ❹ The door to a political career opened by accident. In 1960 she was inspired by the civil-rights platform of Democrat John F. Kennedy, a United States senator running for president. Jordan stuffed envelopes at the headquarters of the Harris County, Texas, Democratic Committee until a twist of fate pushed her into the spotlight. One evening a speaker called in sick. Jordan was asked to fill in and speak to the congregation of a local African-American church. Her deep, booming voice and powerful message impressed her listeners. Before long she began lecturing, asking African Americans to register and vote as Democrats. Soon, the voter turnout was the largest Harris County had ever seen. This, along with Kennedy's presidential victory, propelled Jordan into politics.

STRATEGIES
IN ACTION

❶ **Think about the title.**
One Student's Thoughts
"I wonder what the writer means by *power.*"

❷ **Skim the questions that follow the passage.**
One Student's Thoughts
"One question asks how Jordan's upbringing influenced her success. She grew up with segregation, so how could this help her in politics?"

❸ **Use context clues to understand vocabulary.**
One Student's Thoughts
"It seems that *segregation* means blacks and whites were forced to be separated."

❹ **Look for main ideas.**
One Student's Thoughts
"It's amazing that her speaking skills led her into politics."
YOUR TURN
Find one or two other key ideas in this selection.

Jordan ran for the Texas House of Representatives in 1962 but was defeated. She lost again in 1964, the same year ❺ Congress passed the Civil Rights Act, banning segregation in public facilities and guaranteeing equal employment. Jordan relied on her family's support. They wished she would get married and have a family, but Jordan chose to devote her life to politics.

In 1966, she finally won a seat in the Texas House of Representatives. She became the first African-American state senator since 1883. Six years later, she won a congressional seat in the U.S. House of Representatives, becoming the first African-American woman from the Deep South to be elected to that body.

Soon after, the ❻ Watergate scandal erupted. The nation learned that President Richard Nixon was involved in the cover-up of the 1972 burglary of the headquarters of the Democratic National Committee. Jordan was asked to state her feelings on the issue. On July 25, 1974, she spoke during a televised hearing and asked that President Nixon be impeached for his crime. ❼ "My faith in the Constitution is whole, it is complete, it is total." Her speaking skills were praised all over the world, and she rose in the spotlight. Nixon resigned his office soon after, and Jordan was reelected to another term.

In 1976, Jordan was selected by the Democratic Party to deliver the keynote address for the party's national convention. She again impressed the nation with her inspirational words in support of Jimmy Carter, the Democratic presidential candidate. Carter was elected and Jordan served a third term in Congress before retiring from politics. She became a professor at the University of Texas at Austin.

In 1990, Barbara Jordan was inducted into the National Women's Hall of Fame. She was awarded the Spingarn Medal by the NAACP for outstanding achievement by an African American in 1992, and in 1994 the Presidential Medal of Freedom, the highest civilian award in the nation. She died of complications of leukemia in 1996. Her life is an example of how neither poverty, racial discrimination, nor gender bias should stop us from reaching our goals.

STRATEGIES
IN ACTION

❺ **Read actively by asking questions.**

"The Civil Rights Act must have changed things for African Americans as well as whites. I wonder how people's lives were affected."

❻ **Note literary elements like use of figurative language.**

"The writer uses the word *erupted* to describe the Watergate scandal. Sounds like it was like a volcano, and that people were unprepared for it.

YOUR TURN
Determine the writer's purpose.

❼ **Look for examples of tone.**

"The writer chooses an interesting quote. It really shows what Barbara Jordan was like."

YOUR TURN
How else does the writer show Jordan's character?

How to Answer Multiple-Choice Questions

Use the strategies and notes in the side column to help you answer the questions below and on the following pages.

Based on the selection you have just read, choose the best answer for each of the following questions.

1. Why does the writer begin by quoting a person who had tried to discourage Jordan?
   A. because research papers must include quotes
   B. to show how cut-throat political candidates can be
   C. to show the obstacles that Jordan faced
   D. to prove that Jordan really was a Democrat

2. In paragraph 9, what did Jordan mean when she said, "My faith in the Constitution is whole"?
   A. The Constitution should apply to everyone, including the president.
   B. She has lost faith in the Constitution.
   C. She should not be blamed for the president's crimes.
   D. Watergate shook her faith in the Constitution.

3. How did Jordan's upbringing influence her success?
   A. After growing up poor, she was determined to make money through politics.
   B. Because her family did not support her, she did not want her own family.
   C. She had felt the effects of discrimination and was determined to do something about it.
   D. She became suspicious of politicians and therefore never ran for president.

4. How does the title of the article relate to its theme?
   A. It doesn't relate to the theme.
   B. Jordan used her voice to make changes in the world.
   C. Using your voice is the only way to gain power.
   D. One voice is stronger than many voices.

5. What is the writer's tone toward Barbara Jordan?
   A. She believes that Jordan should have listened to her critics and gotten out of politics.
   B. She admires Jordan for her achievements.
   C. She judges Jordan poorly for not getting married.
   D. She pities Jordan for having had a tough life.

STRATEGIES FOR ANSWERING MULTIPLE-CHOICE QUESTIONS

▸ **Ask questions** that help you eliminate some of the choices.
▸ **Pay attention to choices** such as "all of the above" or "none of the above." To eliminate them, all you need to find is one answer that doesn't fit.
▸ **Skim your notes.** Details you noticed as you read may provide answers.

STRATEGIES IN ACTION

Skim your notes.

One Student's Thoughts
"The writer doesn't mention Jordan ever wanting to run for president. *So I can eliminate choice D.*"

YOUR TURN
What other choices can you eliminate?

Ask questions. What makes sense in the real world?

"The writer wouldn't use a title that doesn't relate to the theme. Also, using your voice is one way to gain power, but it is not the only way. *So, I can eliminate choices A and C.*"

YOUR TURN
Which other choice doesn't make sense?

PART 3   How to Respond in Writing

You may be asked to write answers to questions about a reading passage. **Short-answer questions** often ask you to answer in a sentence or two. **Essay questions** require a fully developed piece of writing.

Short-Answer Questions

STRATEGIES FOR RESPONDING TO SHORT-ANSWER QUESTIONS

▸ **Identify key words** in the writing prompt that tell you the ideas to discuss.
▸ **State your response directly** and to the point.
▸ **Support your ideas** by using evidence from the selection.
▸ **Use correct grammar.**

> **Sample Question**
> Answer the following question in one or two sentences.
>
> Explain what you think the writer's purpose was in researching and reporting on Barbara Jordan's life.

Essay Question

STRATEGIES FOR ANSWERING ESSAY QUESTIONS

▸ **Look for direction words** in the writing prompt such as *essay, analyze, describe,* or *compare and contrast.*
▸ **List the points** you want to make before beginning to write.
▸ **Writing an interesting introduction** that presents your main point.
▸ **Develop your ideas** by using evidence from the selection that supports the statements you make. Present the ideas in a logical order.
▸ **Write a conclusion** that summarizes your points.
▸ **Check your work** for correct grammar.

> **Sample Prompt**
> Write an essay in which you analyze how early obstacles may have actually contributed to Barbara Jordan's desire to succeed.

STRATEGIES
IN ACTION

Identify key words.
One Student's Thoughts
"The key words are *explain* and *purpose*. This means that I'll have to decide why the writer wrote the article and tell why I think that way."

YOUR TURN
What clues to the writer's purpose can you find in the selection?

Look for direction words.
One Student's Thoughts
"The important words are *essay* and *analyze*. This means that I'll have to create a fully developed piece of writing that explains the connections between things."

YOUR TURN
What are the main points you will need to cover?

PART 4

How to Revise, Edit, and Proofread a Test Response

Here is a student's first draft in response to the writing prompt at the bottom of page 338. Read it and answer the multiple-choice questions that follow.

1	Some people are spurred on by challenges. Barbara
2	Jordan was one such person. She faced many challenges.
3	She was determined to make changes in the world.
4	Being raised in an era of discrimination; she felt the
5	effects on a daily basis. Her early experiences may have
6	left her with powerful feelings about fairness and equality.
7	She developed a strong desire and to become a powerful
8	speaker in order to voice her views.

> **STRATEGIES** FOR REVISING, EDITING, AND PROOFREADING
>
> ▸ **Read the passage carefully.**
> ▸ **Note the parts that are confusing** or don't make sense. What kinds of errors would that signal?
> ▸ **Look for errors** in grammar, usage, spelling, and capitalization. Common errors include:
> - run-on sentences
> - sentence fragments
> - lack of subject-verb agreement
> - unclear pronoun antecedents
> - lack of transition words

1. What is the BEST way, if any, to combine the sentences in lines 2 and 3 ("She faced . . . in the world.")?

   A. Because she faced many challenges, she was determined to make changes in the world.

   B. She was determined to make changes in the world, but she faced many challenges.

   C. Because she made changes in the world, she faced many challenges.

   D. Make no change.

2. What is the BEST change, if any, to make to the sentence in lines 4 and 5 ("Being raised . . . daily basis.")?

   A. Remove the semicolon after *discrimination*.

   B. Replace the semicolon after *discrimination* with a colon.

   C. Replace the semicolon after *discrimination* with a comma.

   D. Make no change.

3. What is the BEST way, if any, to change the sentence in lines 7 and 8 ("She developed . . . voice her views")?

   A. She developed a strong desire to become a powerful speaker in order to voice her views.

   B. She developed a strong desire but became a powerful speaker in order to voice her views.

   C. She developed a strong desire to become a powerful speaker but to voice her views.

   D. Make no change.

Flights of Imagination

"The man who has no imagination has no wings."

Muhammad Ali   American prizefighter and world heavyweight title holder

© Kamil Vojnar/Photonica

340

The Literature You'll Read

The Concepts You'll Study

Vocabulary and Reading Comprehension
Vocabulary Focus: Interpreting Analogies
Making Inferences
Predicting
Visualizing
Cause and Effect
Clarifying

Literary Analysis
Literary Focus: Plot
Irony
Suspense
Metaphor
Narrative Nonfiction
Symbol

Writing and Language Conventions
Writing Workshop: Cause-and-Effect Essay
Using Vivid and Precise Adjectives
Coordinate Adjectives
Avoiding Too Many Adjectives

Speaking and Listening
Scripted Dialogue
Writing and Presenting a Speech
Reading and Interpreting Poetry

LEARNING *the Language of* *Literature*

*P*lot

Key Standard
R3.2 Identify events that advance the plot and describe how they explain the past, present, and future.
Other Standard R2.3

> *A story to me means a plot where there is some surprise. . . . Because that is how life is—full of surprises.*
>
> —Isaac Bashevis Singer

When someone comes to join you as you are watching a television show, what's the first thing he or she asks you? "What happened?" In response, you might give a brief description of the show's **plot.** Plot refers to the **sequence of events** in a story. In literature, every piece of fiction and drama has a plot, as does some nonfiction and poetry. In most cases, a plot moves forward because of some sort of **conflict.** The reader wants to find out what will happen to the **characters** next, how they will resolve the conflict, and how they might **change** as a result. In a good, tight plot, there will be plenty of suspense to keep the reader interested. There may also be a surprise ending. A typical plot structure contains an **exposition, rising action,** a **climax,** and **falling action** (sometimes called the **denouement**).

PLOT STRUCTURE AT A GLANCE

Climax
- is the turning point of story
- is the moment when suspense reaches its peak
- results in some kind of change for main character
- sometimes ends the story

Rising Action
- is where main conflict unfolds
- builds suspense and raises questions
- is when plot develops

Exposition
- introduces characters and setting
- sets mood and tone of story

Falling Action (Denouement)
- occurs after climax
- ties up loose ends
- may provide a resolution to main conflict

Sequence of Events

An **event** in a story is an action or reaction that moves the story forward, or advances the plot. Not all things that happen in a story are considered events. Thoughts, feelings, details, and descriptions make a story interesting and fun to read, but may not be necessary to the plot. In the story "The Scholarship Jacket," Martha overhears Mr. Boone and Mr. Schmidt arguing about the jacket. This is considered an event because the rest of the story could not have taken place without it.

Two techniques that authors use to build suspense in a story are flashbacks and foreshadowing. **Flashbacks** occur when there is a break in sequence of events, and the reader is shown a scene from the past. **Foreshadowing** happens when an author gives readers hints that suggest what might happen later in the story.

When following a sequence of events, it is useful to identify those events that help explain past or present action in the story. For example, when the reader knows that Martha's sister Rosie won the Scholarship Jacket a few years back, it helps explain part of the reason Martha was so disappointed with the thought of not winning it.

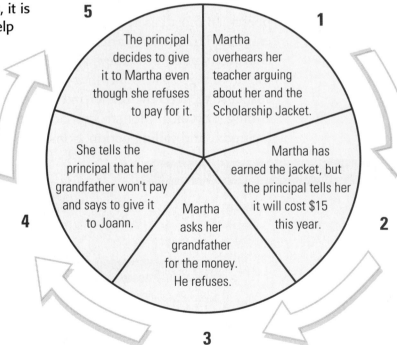

5 — The principal decides to give it to Martha even though she refuses to pay for it.

1 — Martha overhears her teacher arguing about her and the Scholarship Jacket.

2 — Martha has earned the jacket, but the principal tells her it will cost $15 this year.

3 — Martha asks her grandfather for the money. He refuses.

4 — She tells the principal that her grandfather won't pay and says to give it to Joann.

Cause-and-Effect

When discussing sequence of events, it is also important to consider cause and effect. A **cause-and-effect** relationship occurs when one event brings about, or causes, another. The story wheel on page 344 shows the sequence of events in "The Scholarship Jacket."

YOUR TURN Which events in the story wheel on the previous page have a cause-and-effect relationship?

From "The Scholarship Jacket"

Conflict

The conflict in a plot generally has to do with what a character wants and what is stopping him or her from getting it. When a character struggles against another character or an outside force, the conflict is **external**. When the struggle is within the character, the conflict is **internal**.

YOUR TURN What does the boy in this excerpt from "Thank You, M'am" want at this point? What is standing in his way?

CONFLICT

The water dripping from his face, the boy looked at her. There was a long pause. A very long pause. After he had dried his face and not knowing what else to do dried it again, the boy turned around, wondering what next. The door was open. He could make a dash for it down the hall. He could run, run, run, run, *run!*

—Langston Hughes,
"Thank You, M'am"

Change

Sometimes what happens to a **character** in a story causes him or her to **change.** In "Thank You, M'am," it seems very likely that, as a result of his meeting with Mrs. Jones, Roger will never try to steal another purse. A story of personal change can be just as powerful and absorbing as a story with lots of exciting events.

Wrapping Up the Plot . . .

Endings are an important part of a story. A good ending may leave us with a strong image, feeling, or realization. Some endings are open-ended, sparking more questions, while others tie all the loose ends together with an action or event. Many people like **surprise endings,** in which an unexpected event or realization changes the outcome of the story.

YOUR TURN Read the ending from "What Do Fish Have to Do with Anything," by Avi. Willie has just found out his mother has had his homeless friend "removed." Think about whether you would have ended the story differently.

Avi's story is open-ended. The reader wonders whether Willie will ever forgive his mother. Two seventh-graders wrote their own endings to this story. Ending 1 uses a surprise ending—the police have been looking for the man. In Ending 2, Willie and his mother look for the man. Think about how these different endings affect your interpretation of the story and characters.

Willie glared at his mother. "No, you can't [see]. You're a fish. You live in a cave."

"Fish?" retorted Mrs. Markham. "What do fish have to do with anything? Willie, don't talk nonsense."

"My name isn't Willie. It's William. And I know how to keep from being unhappy. I do!" He was yelling now. "What a person needs is always more than they say! Always!"

He turned on his heel and walked back toward the school. At the corner he glanced back. His mother was following. He kept going. She kept following.

—Avi, "What Do Fish Have to Do with Anything?"

From "What Do Fish Have to Do with Anything?"

ENDING 1

"I called the police, and they told me that they've been looking for that man for some time now."

Willie looked at his mother. "It's not true!"

"People like that want to fool you. You shouldn't be so trusting."

Willie thought for a moment and stared off into the distance.

"I've been blind, just like the fish." With that, Willie went into the house and shut off the lights. He would sit in his cave and he didn't know for how long.

ENDING 2

"I want to go and look for him," said Willie.

"Don't be ridiculous," his mother replied.

"Please," Willie said. "He is my friend. He is a kind man."

His mother watched the tear rolling down Willie's cheek just before he brushed it away.

"Okay," she whispered. "We'll go look, but only for a short while."

*M*aking Inferences

Have you ever heard the phrase "read between the lines"? It means coming to a logical conclusion or **inference** about something based on evidence. As you read, look for clues in the text and read between the lines. The deeper meaning may not be as hidden as you think!

How to Apply the Skill

To **make inferences**, an active reader will
- Pay attention to details and clues
- **Evaluate** based on what he or she knows
- **Visualize** descriptions
- **Connect** personally to the selection

Try It Now!

Read and make inferences about the excerpt below.

Outside [Mr. Johnson] found a beggar staring into the windows of the restaurant he had left and, carefully looking through the money in his pocket, Mr. Johnson approached the beggar and pressed some coins and a couple of bills into his hand.

—Shirley Jackson, "One Ordinary Day, with Peanuts"

Here's how Leah uses the skill:

*"To **make inferences** I use details and clues from the selection. As I read, I **evaluate** the information and develop my own opinions about Mr. Johnson's character. From the way the author describes his actions, and the way other characters react to him, my first response is to infer that Mr. Johnson is a generous man."*

One Ordinary Day, with Peanuts

by SHIRLEY JACKSON

Key Standard
R3.2 Identify events that advance the plot and describe how they explain the past, present, and future.
Other Standards **R1.3, W2.1, W2.3, LC1.3, LC1.4**

Connect to Your Life

Random Acts of Kindness What acts of kindness have you done in the past few days for people you know? for strangers? Or, have you done something that hurt somebody's feelings? Think of some positive and negative experiences that seem to take place on a typical day. Fill in a diagram like the one on the right.

Build Background

Shirley Jackson has a distinctive writing style, and readers who have not read her stories can benefit from knowing a little about her style. Jackson's writing seems matter-of-fact and unemotional. Her stories often appear to be about normal events, but the reader discovers that behind these apparently ordinary events may hide a twisted reality.

WORDS TO KNOW **Vocabulary Preview**

ambiguous	impertinent	repress
genial	insatiable	

Focus Your Reading

LITERARY ANALYSIS | **IRONY**

Irony occurs in a literary work when there is a difference between what a reader expects to happen and what actually happens. This type of irony is called **situational irony,** and authors often use it to deliver a **surprise ending** to the **plot.** Shirley Jackson is known for writing stories with ironic surprises. "One Ordinary Day, with Peanuts" is no exception.

ACTIVE READING | **MAKING INFERENCES**

While you read a story, you learn details that help you understand what is happening. Using these details and what you know from your own experience, you can figure out more than what the words actually say. This is called making an **inference.** Every time you use evidence to figure something out, you are making inferences.

READER'S NOTEBOOK As you read "One Ordinary Day, with Peanuts," record details that help you make inferences. Then record the inferences you make.

Detail from Story	What I Can Infer
Mr. Johnson smiled at people he passed on the street.	Mr. Johnson is in a good mood; he likes people.

one ordinary day, with peanuts

shirley jackson

Mr. John Philip Johnson shut his front door behind him and went down his front steps into the bright morning with a feeling that all was well with the world on this best of all days, and wasn't the sun warm and good, and didn't his shoes feel comfortable after the resoling, and he knew that he had undoubtedly chosen the very precise tie that belonged with the day and the sun and his comfortable feet, and, after all, wasn't the world just a wonderful place? In spite of the fact that he was a small man, and though the tie was perhaps a shade vivid, Mr. Johnson radiated a feeling of well-being as he went down the steps and onto the dirty sidewalk, and he smiled at people who passed him, and some of them even smiled back. He stopped at the newsstand on the corner and bought his paper, saying, "*Good* morning" with real conviction to the man who sold him the paper and the two or three other people who were lucky enough to be buying papers when Mr. Johnson skipped up.

84 Madison (1982), Philip Reisman. Oil on canvas, 48¼″ × 22″, Edwin A. Ulrich Museum of Art, Wichita (Kansas) State University, Endowment Association Art Collection (84.7.3).

349

He remembered to fill his pockets with candy and peanuts, and then he set out to get himself uptown. He stopped in a flower shop and bought a carnation for his buttonhole, and stopped almost immediately afterward to give the carnation to a small child in a carriage, who looked at him dumbly, and then smiled, and Mr. Johnson smiled, and the child's mother looked at Mr. Johnson for a minute and then smiled, too.

When he had gone several blocks uptown, Mr. Johnson cut across the avenue and went along a side street, chosen at random; he did not follow the same route every morning, but preferred to pursue his eventful way in wide detours, more like a puppy than a man intent upon business. It happened this morning that halfway down the block a moving van was parked, and the furniture from an upstairs apartment stood half on the sidewalk, half on the steps, while an amused group of people loitered, examining the scratches on the tables and the worn spots on the chairs, and a harassed woman, trying to watch a young child and the movers and the furniture all at the same time, gave the clear impression of endeavoring to shelter her private life from the people staring at her belongings. Mr. Johnson stopped, and for a moment joined the crowd, then he came forward and, touching his hat civilly, said, "Perhaps I can keep an eye on your little boy for you?"

The woman turned and glared at him distrustfully, and Mr. Johnson added hastily, "We'll sit right here on the steps." He beckoned to the little boy, who hesitated and then responded agreeably to Mr. Johnson's genial smile. Mr. Johnson took out a handful of peanuts from his pocket and sat on the steps with the boy, who at first refused the peanuts on the grounds that his mother did not allow him to accept food from strangers; Mr. Johnson said that probably his mother had not intended peanuts to be included, since elephants at the circus ate them, and the boy considered, and then agreed solemnly. They sat on the steps cracking peanuts in a comradely fashion, and Mr. Johnson said, "So you're moving?"

"Yep," said the boy.

"Where you going?"

"Vermont."

"Nice place. Plenty of snow there. Maple sugar, too; you like maple sugar?"

"Sure."

"Plenty of maple sugar in Vermont. You going to live on a farm?"

"Going to live with Grandpa."

"Grandpa like peanuts?"

"Sure."

"Ought to take him some," said Mr. Johnson, reaching into his pocket. "Just you and Mommy going?"

"Yep."

"Tell you what," Mr. Johnson said. "You take some peanuts to eat on the train."

The boy's mother, after glancing at them frequently, had seemingly decided that Mr. Johnson was trustworthy, because she had devoted herself wholeheartedly to seeing that the movers did not—what movers rarely do, but every housewife believes they will—crack a leg from her good table, or set a kitchen chair down on a lamp. Most of the furniture was loaded by now, and she was deep in that nervous stage when she knew there was something she had forgotten to pack—hidden away in the back of a closet somewhere, or left at a neighbor's and forgotten, or on the clothesline—and was trying to remember under stress what it was.

"This all, lady?" the chief mover said, completing her dismay.

Uncertainly, she nodded.

"Want to go on the truck with the furniture,

WORDS TO KNOW **genial** (jēn′yəl) *adj.* pleasant; friendly

sonny?" the mover asked the boy, and laughed. The boy laughed, too, and said to Mr. Johnson, "I guess I'll have a good time at Vermont."

"Fine time," said Mr. Johnson, and stood up. "Have one more peanut before you go," he said to the boy.

The boy's mother said to Mr. Johnson, "Thank you so much; it was a great help to me."

"Nothing at all," said Mr. Johnson gallantly. "Where in Vermont are you going?"

The mother looked at the little boy accusingly, as though he had given away a secret of some importance, and said unwillingly, "Greenwich."

"Lovely town," said Mr. Johnson. He took out a card, and wrote a name on the back. "Very good friend of mine lives in Greenwich," he said. "Call on him for anything you need. His wife makes the best doughnuts in town," he added soberly to the little boy.

"Swell," said the little boy.

"Goodbye," said Mr. Johnson.

He went on, stepping happily with his new-shod[1] feet, feeling the warm sun on his back and on the top of his head. Halfway down the block he met a stray dog and fed him a peanut.

At the corner, where another wide avenue faced him, Mr. Johnson decided to go on uptown again. Moving with comparative laziness, he was passed on either side by people hurrying and frowning, and people brushed past him going the other way, clattering along to get somewhere quickly. Mr. Johnson stopped on every corner and waited patiently for the light to change, and he stepped out of the way of anyone who seemed to be in any particular hurry, but one young lady came too fast for him, and crashed wildly into him when he stooped to pat a kitten, which had run out onto the sidewalk from an apartment house and was now unable to get back through the rushing feet.

"Excuse me," said the young lady, trying frantically to pick up Mr. Johnson and hurry on at the same time, "terribly sorry."

The kitten, regardless now of danger, raced back to its home. "Perfectly all right," said Mr. Johnson, adjusting himself carefully. "You seem to be in a hurry."

"Of course I'm in a hurry," said the young lady. "I'm late."

She was extremely cross, and the frown between her eyes seemed well on its way to becoming permanent. She had obviously awakened late, because she had not spent any extra time in making herself look pretty, and her dress was plain and unadorned with collar or brooch, and her lipstick was noticeably crooked. She tried to brush past Mr. Johnson, but, risking her suspicious displeasure, he took her arm and said, "Please wait."

"Look," she said ominously, "I ran into you, and your lawyer can see my lawyer and I will gladly pay all damages and all inconveniences suffered therefrom, but please this minute let me go because *I am late*."

ACTIVE READER

VISUALIZE If you close your eyes, can you form a picture of the young lady in your mind?

"Late for what?" said Mr. Johnson; he tried his winning smile on her but it did no more than keep her, he suspected, from knocking him down again.

"Late for work," she said between her teeth. "Late for my employment. I have a job, and if I am late I lose exactly so much an hour and I cannot really afford what your pleasant conversation is costing me, be it *ever* so pleasant."

---

1. **new-shod:** wearing new shoes.

"I'll pay for it," said Mr. Johnson. Now, these were magic words, not necessarily because they were true, or because she seriously expected Mr. Johnson to pay for anything, but because Mr. Johnson's flat statement, obviously innocent of irony, could not be, coming from Mr. Johnson, anything but the statement of a responsible and truthful and respectable man.

"What *do* you mean?" she asked.

"I said that since I am obviously responsible for your being late, I shall certainly pay for it."

"Don't be silly," she said, and for the first time the frown disappeared. "*I* wouldn't expect you to pay for anything—a few minutes ago I was offering to pay *you*. Anyway," she added, almost smiling, "it *was* my fault."

"What happens if you don't go to work?"

She stared. "I don't get paid."

"Precisely," said Mr. Johnson.

"What do you mean, precisely? If I don't show up at the office exactly twenty minutes ago I lose a dollar and twenty cents an hour, or two cents a minute or"—she thought—"almost a dime for the time I've spent talking to you."

Mr. Johnson laughed, and finally she laughed, too. "You're late already," he pointed out. "Will you give me another four cents' worth?"

"I don't understand why."

"You'll see," Mr. Johnson promised. He led her over to the side of the walk, next to the buildings, and said, "Stand here," and went out into the rush of people going both ways. Selecting and considering, as one who must make a choice involving perhaps whole years of lives, he estimated the people going by. Once he almost moved, and then at the last minute thought better of it and drew back. Finally, from half a block away, he saw what he wanted, and moved out into the center of the traffic to intercept a young man, who was hurrying, and dressed as though he had awakened late, and frowning.

"Oof," said the young man, because Mr. Johnson had thought of no better way to

Detail of *Autobiographical* (1954), Moses Soyer. Courtesy of ACA Gallerie New York. Copyright © Estate of Moses Soyer/Licensed by VAGA, New Yo

intercept anyone than the one the young woman had unwittingly used upon him. "Where do you think you're going?" the young man demanded from the sidewalk.

"I want to speak to you," said Mr. Johnson ominously.

The young man got up nervously, dusting himself and eyeing Mr. Johnson. "What for?" he said. "What'd *I* do?"

"That's what bothers me most about people nowadays," Mr. Johnson complained broadly to the people passing. "No matter whether they've done anything or not, they always figure someone's after them. About what you're going to do," he told the young man.

"Listen," said the young man, trying to brush past him, "I'm late, and I don't have any time to listen. Here's a dime, now get going."

"Thank you," said Mr. Johnson, pocketing the dime. "Look," he said, "what happens if you stop running?"

"I'm late," said the young man, still trying to get past Mr. Johnson, who was unexpectedly clinging.

"How much you make an hour?" Mr. Johnson demanded.

"A Communist,[2] are you?" said the young man. "Now will you please let me—"

"No," said Mr. Johnson insistently, "*how much?*"

"Dollar fifty," said the young man. "And *now* will you—"

"You like adventure?"

The young man stared, and, staring, found himself caught and held by Mr. Johnson's genial smile; he almost smiled back and then <u>repressed</u> it and made an effort to tear away. "I got to *hurry*," he said.

"Mystery? You like surprises? Unusual and exciting events?"

"You selling something?"

"Sure," said Mr. Johnson. "You want to take a chance?"

The young man hesitated, looking longingly up the avenue toward what might have been his destination and then, when Mr. Johnson said, "I'll pay for it" with his own peculiar convincing emphasis, turned and said, "Well, okay. But I got to *see* it first, what I'm buying."

Mr. Johnson, breathing hard, led the young man over to the side, where the girl was standing; she had been watching with interest Mr. Johnson's capture of the young man and now, smiling timidly, she looked at Mr. Johnson as though prepared to be surprised at nothing.

Mr. Johnson reached into his pocket and took out his wallet. "Here," he said, and handed a bill to the girl. "This about equals your day's pay."

"But no," she said, surprised in spite of herself. "I mean, I *couldn't.*"

"Please do not interrupt," Mr. Johnson told her. "And *here,*" he said to the young man, "this will take care of *you.*" The young man accepted the bill dazedly, but said, "Probably counterfeit" to the young woman out of the side of his mouth.

"Now," Mr. Johnson went on, disregarding the young man, "what is your name, miss?"

"Kent," she said helplessly. "Mildred Kent."

"Fine," said Mr. Johnson. "And you, sir?"

"Arthur Adams," said the young man stiffly.

"Splendid," said Mr. Johnson. "Now, Miss Kent, I would like you to meet Mr. Adams.

ACTIVE READER

QUESTION Why are most people wary of Mr. Johnson?

---

2. **Communist:** At the time the story was written (1951), Communists—people who believed that workers should own all businesses—were thought to be everywhere, trying to bring down the United States by convincing workers that they were underpaid, oppressed, and should control the government.

WORDS TO KNOW
repress (rĭ-prĕs′) *v.* to hold something back

Mr. Adams, Miss Kent."

Miss Kent stared, wet her lips nervously, made a gesture as though she might run, and said, "How do you do?"

Mr. Adams straightened his shoulders, scowled at Mr. Johnson, made a gesture as though *he* might run, and said, "How do you do?"

"Now, *this*," said Mr. Johnson, taking several bills from his wallet, "should be enough for the day for both of you. I would suggest, perhaps, Coney Island—although I personally am not fond of the place—or perhaps a nice lunch somewhere, and dancing, or a matinee, or even a movie, although take care to choose a really *good* one; there are *so* many bad movies these days. You might," he said, struck with an inspiration, "visit the Bronx Zoo, or the Planetarium. Anywhere, as a matter of fact," he concluded, "that you would like to go. Have a nice time."

As he started to move away, Arthur Adams, breaking from his dumbfounded stare, said, "But see here, mister, you *can't* do this. Why—how do you know—I mean, *we* don't even know—I mean, how do you know we won't just take the money and not do what you said?"

"You've taken the money," Mr. Johnson said. "You don't have to follow any of my suggestions. You may know something you prefer to do—perhaps a museum, or something."

"But suppose I just run away with it and leave her here?"

"I know you won't," said Mr. Johnson gently, "because you remembered to ask *me* that. Goodbye," he added, and went on.

As he stepped up the street, conscious of the sun on his head and his good shoes, he heard from somewhere behind him the young man saying, "Look, you know you don't *have* to if you don't want to," and the girl saying, "But unless *you* don't want to. . ." Mr. Johnson smiled to himself and then thought that he had better hurry along; when he wanted to he could move very quickly, and before the young woman had gotten around to saying, "Well, *I* will if *you* will," Mr. Johnson was several blocks away and had already stopped twice, once to help a lady lift several large packages into a taxi, and once to hand a peanut to a sea gull. By this time he was in an area of large stores and many more people, and he was buffeted constantly from either side by people hurrying and cross and late and sullen. Once he offered a peanut to a man who asked him for a dime, and once he offered a peanut to a bus driver who had stopped his bus at an intersection and had opened the window next to his seat and put out his head as though longing for fresh air and the comparative quiet of the traffic. The man wanting a dime took the peanut because Mr. Johnson had wrapped a dollar bill around it, but the bus driver took the peanut and asked ironically, "You want a transfer, Jack?"

On a busy corner Mr. Johnson encountered two young people—for one minute he thought they might be Mildred Kent and Arthur Adams—who were eagerly scanning a newspaper, their backs pressed against a storefront to avoid the people passing, their heads bent together. Mr. Johnson, whose curiosity was <u>insatiable</u>, leaned onto the storefront next to them and peeked over the

ONCE HE OFFERED A PEANUT TO A MAN WHO ASKED HIM FOR A DIME.

man's shoulder; they were scanning the Apartments Vacant columns.

Mr. Johnson remembered the street where the woman and her little boy were going to Vermont and he tapped the man on the shoulder and said amiably, "Try down on West Seventeen. About the middle of the block people moved out this morning."

"Say, what do you—" said the man, and then, seeing Mr. Johnson clearly, "Well, thanks. Where did you say?"

"West Seventeen," said Mr. Johnson. "About the middle of the block." He smiled again and said, "Good luck."

"Thanks," said the man.

"Thanks," said the girl as they moved off.

"Goodbye," said Mr. Johnson.

He lunched alone in a pleasant restaurant, where the food was rich, and only Mr. Johnson's excellent digestion could encompass two of their whipped-cream-and-chocolate-and-rum-cake pastries for dessert. He had three cups of coffee, tipped the waiter largely, and went out into the street again into the wonderful sunlight, his shoes still comfortable and fresh on his feet. Outside he found a beggar staring into the windows of the restaurant he had left and, carefully looking through the money in his pocket, Mr. Johnson approached the beggar and pressed some coins and a couple of bills into his hand. "It's the price of the veal cutlet lunch plus tip," said Mr. Johnson. "Goodbye."

After his lunch he rested; he walked into the nearest park and fed peanuts to the pigeons. It was late afternoon by the time he was ready to start back downtown, and he had refereed two checker games, and watched a small boy and girl whose mother had fallen asleep and awakened with surprise and fear that turned to amusement when she saw Mr. Johnson. He had given away almost all of his candy, and

had fed all the rest of his peanuts to the pigeons, and it was time to go home. Although the late afternoon sun was pleasant, and his shoes were still entirely comfortable, he decided to take a taxi downtown.

He had a difficult time catching a taxi, because he gave up the first three or four empty ones to people who seemed to need them more; finally, however, he stood alone on the corner and—almost like netting a frisky fish—he hailed desperately until he succeeded in catching a cab that had been proceeding with haste uptown, and seemed to draw in toward Mr. Johnson against its own will.

"Mister," the cabdriver said as Mr. Johnson climbed in, "I figured you was an omen, like. I wasn't going to pick you up at all."

"Kind of you," said Mr. Johnson ambiguously.

ACTIVE READER

MAKE INFERENCES

What inferences can you make about Mr. Johnson's character?

"If I'd of let you go it would of cost me ten bucks," said the driver. "Really?" said Mr. Johnson.

"Yeah," said the driver. "Guy just got out of the cab, he turned around and give me ten bucks, said take this and bet it in a hurry on a horse named Vulcan,[3] right away."

"Vulcan?" said Mr. Johnson, horrified. "A fire sign on a Wednesday?"

"What?" said the driver. "Anyway, I said to myself, if I got no fare between here and there I'd bet the ten, but if anyone looked like they needed a cab I'd take it as an omen and I'd take the ten home to the wife."

---

3. **Vulcan:** the god of fire in Roman mythology.

WORDS TO KNOW **insatiable** (ĭn-sā'shə-bəl) *adj.* impossible to satisfy (p. 354)
ambiguous (ăm-bĭg'yōō-əs) *adj.* can be understood in more than one way

"You were very right," said Mr. Johnson heartily. "This is Wednesday, you would have lost your money. Monday, yes, or even Saturday. But never never never a fire sign on a Wednesday. Sunday would have been good, now."

"Vulcan don't run on Sunday," said the driver.

"You wait till another day," said Mr. Johnson. "Down this street, please, driver. I'll get off on the next corner."

"He *told* me Vulcan, though," said the driver.

"I'll tell you," said Mr. Johnson, hesitating with the door of the cab half open. "You take that ten dollars and I'll give you another ten dollars to go with it, and you go right ahead and bet that money on any Thursday on any horse that has a name indicating . . . let me see, Thursday . . . well, grain. Or any growing food."

"Grain?" said the driver. "You mean a horse named, like, Wheat or something?"

"Certainly," said Mr. Johnson. "Or, as a matter of fact, to make it even easier, any horse whose name includes the letters C, R, L. Perfectly simple."

"Tall Corn?" said the driver, a light in his eye. "You mean a horse named, like, Tall Corn?"

"Absolutely," said Mr. Johnson. "Here's your money."

"Tall Corn," said the driver. "Thank *you*, mister."

"Goodbye," said Mr. Johnson.

He was on his own corner, and went straight up to his apartment. He let himself in and called, "Hello?" and Mrs. Johnson answered from the kitchen, "Hello, dear, aren't you early?"

"Took a taxi home," Mr. Johnson said. "I remembered the cheesecake, too. What's for dinner?"

Mrs. Johnson came out of the kitchen and kissed him; she was a comfortable woman, and smiling as Mr. Johnson smiled. "Hard day?" she asked.

"Not very," said Mr. Johnson, hanging his coat in the closet. "How about you?"

"So-so," she said. She stood in the kitchen doorway while he settled into his easy chair and took off his good shoes and took out the paper he had bought that morning. "Here and there," she said.

ACTIVE READER

PREDICTING How will the story end?

"I didn't do so badly," Mr. Johnson said. "Couple young people."

"Fine," she said. "I had a little nap this afternoon, took it easy most of the day. Went into a department store this morning and accused the woman next to me of shoplifting, and had the store detective pick her up. Sent three dogs to the pound—*you* know, the usual thing. Oh, and listen," she added, remembering.

"What?" asked Mr. Johnson.

"Well," she said, "I got onto a bus and asked the driver for a transfer, and when he helped someone else first I said that he was <u>impertinent</u>, and quarreled with him. And then I said why wasn't he in the army,[4] and I said it loud enough for everyone to hear, and I took his number and I turned in a complaint. Probably got him fired."

"Fine," said Mr. Johnson. "But you do look tired. Want to change over tomorrow?"

"I *would* like to," she said. "I could do with a change."

"Right," said Mr. Johnson. "What's for dinner?"

"Veal cutlet."

"Had it for lunch," said Mr. Johnson. ❖

---

4. **"why wasn't he in the army . . .":** In 1951 the United States was in the middle of the Korean War, and thousands of males volunteered or were drafted for army duty.

Autobiographical (1954), Moses Soyer. Courtesy of ACA Galleries, New York.
Copyright © Estate of Moses Soyer/Licensed by VAGA, New York.

Connect to the Literature

1. What Do You Think? What was your reaction to the ending of the story? Explain.

Comprehension Check
- How does Mr. Johnson help the woman who is moving?
- What is Mr. Johnson's attitude toward the young couple?
- Why do Mr. and Mrs. Johnson seem to spend most days separately?

Think Critically

2. ACTIVE READING MAKING INFERENCES
Review the chart you made in your 📖 READER'S NOTEBOOK. Why do you think Mr. and Mrs. Johnson spend their days the way they do?

> **Think About:**
> - the mood each is in at the end of the day
> - what values you think they have
> - what they may gain from their deceptive behavior

3. Would you describe the story as serious or humorous? Explain your answer.

4. Did its ending change your understanding of the story? Why or why not?

Extend Interpretations

5. Critic's Corner One of the members of our student advisory board wrote that the story "seemed like a fairy tale until almost the end. Then I thought the irony was great." Do you agree or disagree with this observation? Explain your reasoning.

6. Connect to Life Do you feel kind and friendly toward people on certain days? On other days do you feel less sociable and prefer to be alone?

Literary Analysis

IRONY One type of irony is **situational irony,** or the contrast between what a reader or character expects and what actually exists or happens. For example, in "One Ordinary Day, with Peanuts," Mr. Johnson performs acts of kindness for strangers throughout the story, but at the end the reader sees him as he really is: a dishonest person who was just pretending to be nice. This example of situational irony, an unexpected twist at the end of a story, is also an example of a **surprise ending.**

Paired Activity Working with a partner, make a chart to explain examples of situational irony in "One Ordinary Day, with Peanuts." For each character, identify what the reader expects to happen and what actually happens.

Situational Irony	
What I expect to happen	**What actually happens**
Mr. Johnson will repeat his day's kindnesses the next day.	
Mrs. Johnson will describe her day's kindnesses to Mr. Johnson.	

Writing

Narrative Description Think of a situation you witnessed, were involved in, or heard about, in which someone helped someone else. What was the problem? How did the person help? What was the outcome? Reconstruct the event the best you can in a short piece of narrative writing. As you write, refer to the plot structure chart on page 343 and include a short exposition, rising action, climax and resolution in your narrative. Place your piece in your **Working Portfolio.**

Writing Handbook
See p. R45: Narrative Writing.

Speaking & Listening

Next Day Dialogue Suppose it is now the end of the next day in the story *An Ordinary Day, with Peanuts,* a day during which Mr. and Mrs. Johnson have switched their behaviors. With a partner, write a dialogue the two might have had, in which they tell one another what they did that day. Write the dialogue in script form, in which Mr. and Mrs. Johnson take turns speaking. Read your dialogue out loud for the class.

Speaking and Listening Handbook
See p. R102: Present.

Research & Technology

What's in a Word? Intangible traits are often difficult to define. What does it mean to be *trustworthy,* or to be *deceitful*? Using a dictionary, look up the definitions of these words. Does the dictionary explain these words differently than you thought it might? Based on prior knowledge and your research, write your own definition of these words. Take an informal poll, asking others in your school what these words mean to them. Discuss the results with a group of classmates.

Vocabulary

STANDARDIZED TEST PRACTICE

Choose the word or group of words that means the same, or nearly the same, as the underlined Word to Know in each sentence.

1. Mr. Johnson had a <u>genial</u> smile on his face as he left the house. Genial means—
   A friendly   **B** joking
   C sly   **D** sarcastic

2. The young man couldn't <u>repress</u> a smile in response to Mr. Johnson. Repress means—
   F release   **G** resist
   H recall   **J** reconsider

3. Wishing to seem sincere, Mr. Johnson gave the cab driver an <u>ambiguous</u> answer. Ambiguous means—
   A lengthy   **B** honest
   C ambitious   **D** unclear

4. Mr. Johnson always wanted to know things; his curiosity was <u>insatiable</u>. Insatiable means—
   F unending   **G** unstable
   H unusual   **J** unreliable

5. Mrs. Johnson accused the bus driver of having bad manners and being <u>impertinent</u>. Impertinent means—
   A important   **B** temporary
   C unclear   **D** responsible

EXERCISE In small groups, tell a "round robin" story. One person starts a story and keeps talking until he or she has spoken one Word to Know. The next person continues the story, and so on, until all Words to Know have been used.

Vocabulary Handbook
See p. R24: Context Clues.

WORDS TO KNOW	ambiguous	genial	impertinent	insatiable	repress

Grammar in Context: Using Vivid and Precise Adjectives

Shirley Jackson vividly sets the scene for "One Ordinary Day, with Peanuts" in the first sentence.

> Mr. John Philip Johnson shut his front door behind him and went down his front steps into the bright morning with a feeling that all was well with the world on this best of all days, and wasn't the sun warm and good, and didn't his shoes feel comfortable after the resoling. . . .

An **adjective** is a word that modifies a noun or pronoun; that is, an adjective adds information about the noun or pronoun that makes it more specific and precise. In this excerpt the adjectives not only describe what kind of day it was, they make clear that the main character, Mr. Johnson, is in a very good mood.

WRITING EXERCISE Replace the underlined phrase with one or two precise, vivid adjectives.

Example: *Original* The boy's mother decided Mr. Johnson was <u>somebody she could trust.</u>

Rewritten The boy's mother decided Mr. Johnson was trustworthy.

1. The girl gave Mr. Johnson a look <u>that said she thought she couldn't trust him.</u>
2. The girl carried a purse <u>into which she could fit lots of things.</u>
3. Her scowl looked <u>like it was going to last forever.</u>
4. The taxidriver <u>who was in a hurry</u> wanted a horse <u>that could run fast.</u>

Connect to the Literature Suppose that the young couple take Mr. Johnson's advice and visit a zoo. Using precise, vivid adjectives, write three or four sentences describing the animals they might see. Circle your nouns and underline your adjectives.

Grammar Handbook
See p. R82: Using Modifiers Correctly.

Shirley Jackson
1919–1965

"I will not tolerate having these other worlds called imaginary."

Rebel with a Cause Shirley Jackson was born to a wealthy San Francisco family. From an early age, she rebelled against what she considered her family's selfish lifestyle. Instead of taking part in social events, she would disappear into her journals. Here, she would strike out against the snobbish attitudes she witnessed among the wealthy.

Home in Vermont After she married, Jackson moved to a small town in Vermont, where she raised her family. She continued to write essays, novels, and short stories. She almost never gave interviews but was generous in advising young writers about how to turn experience into writing.

An Early Death For much of her life, Jackson suffered from stress and anxiety. In her later years, her physical and mental health declined. Jackson was only 45 years old when she died.

Author Activity
Edgar Allan Poe Award In 1961 Jackson was honored with the Edgar Allan Poe Award for her short story "Louisa, Please." Use an encyclopedia or the Internet to find out more about this award—what it is, why it is significant, and how recipients are chosen.

Amigo Brothers

by PIRI THOMAS

Key Standard
R3.2 Analyze characters by examining what they think, say, and do, and by studying the words of the narrator and the reactions of other characters.
Other Standards **R1.3, W2.2, W2.3, LC1.3, LC1.4, LS1.6, LS2.3**

Connect to Your Life

Suppose that you have to compete against a good friend in order to win something you really want. Maybe you and your friend are competing on opposing teams for a championship trophy or are running against each other in a class election. What would it be like to be your friend's rival?

Build Background

HISTORY

Boxing is one of the oldest forms of athletic competition. For most of the history of the sport, boxers fought without gloves. Then, in the mid-1860s, the marquis of Queensberry, an English nobleman, helped to establish rules to protect boxers from serious injury. The Queensberry Rules called for the use of padded gloves, three-minute rounds separated by one-minute rest periods, and a ten-second count for a knockout.

Today, boxers are classified and matched in different divisions according to their weights. Amateur boxers are not paid for their bouts and compete in tournaments sponsored by local and national organizations. Of all the amateur tournaments, none is more famous than the annual Golden Gloves tournament.

WORDS TO KNOW	**Vocabulary Preview**		
barrage	evading	improvise	perpetual
bedlam	feint	pensively	unbridled
dispel	game		

Focus Your Reading

LITERARY ANALYSIS SUSPENSE

Writers create **suspense** by raising questions in readers' minds about what might happen next in the **plot.** Tension grows and suspense builds in the part of the plot called the "rising action." In "Amigo Brothers" the event that sparks the rising action is when the two friends, both amateur boxers, learn they will have to fight each other.

ACTIVE READING PREDICTING

A **prediction** is an attempt to answer the question "What will happen next?" Predictions are based on both what you read and your prior knowledge. When reading a suspenseful story, active readers pay attention to details about character, plot, and setting in order to make predictions. These details may also tell readers how events in the story foreshadow the future or help explain past events in the story.

READER'S NOTEBOOK As you read, look for events that will help you predict the answers to the two questions in the chart below. Log your findings as you read.

Question	Events from the Plot	Your Prediction
Will they not fight hard?		
Will they remain friends after the fight?		

AMIGO BROTHERS

by Piri Thomas

Antonio Cruz and **Felix Vargas** were both seventeen years old. They were so together in friendship that they felt themselves to be brothers. They had known each other since childhood, growing up on the lower east side of Manhattan in the same tenement building on Fifth Street between Avenue A and Avenue B.

Antonio was fair, lean, and lanky, while Felix was dark, short, and husky. Antonio's hair was always falling over his eyes, while Felix wore his black hair in a natural Afro style.

Each youngster had a dream of someday becoming lightweight champion of the world. Every chance they had the boys worked out, sometimes at the Boys Club on 10th Street and Avenue A and sometimes at the pro's gym on 14th Street. Early morning sunrises would find them running along the East River Drive, wrapped in sweatshirts, short towels around their necks, and handkerchiefs Apache style around their foreheads.

While some youngsters were into street negatives, Antonio and Felix slept, ate, rapped, and dreamt positive. Between them, they had a collection of *Fight* magazines second to none, plus a scrapbook filled with torn tickets to every boxing match they had ever attended and some

Flight (1988), Douglas Safranek. Egg tempera on panel, 40″ × 32″, courtesy of Schmidt Bingham Gallery, New York.

clippings of their own. If asked a question about any given fighter, they would immediately zip out from their memory banks divisions,[1] weights, records of fights, knockouts, technical knockouts, and draws or losses.

Each had fought many bouts representing their community and had won two gold-plated medals plus a silver and bronze medallion. The

---

1. **divisions:** weight groups into which boxers are separated.

difference was in their style. Antonio's lean form and long reach made him the better boxer, while Felix's short and muscular frame made him the better slugger. Whenever they had met in the ring for sparring sessions, it had always been hot and heavy.

Now, after a series of elimination bouts,[2] they had been informed that they were to meet each other in the division finals that were scheduled for the seventh of August, two weeks away— the winner to represent the Boys Club in the Golden Gloves Championship Tournament.

The two boys continued to run together along the East River Drive. But even when joking with each other, they both sensed a wall rising between them.

One morning less than a week before their bout, they met as usual for their daily workout. They fooled around with a few jabs at the air, slapped skin, and then took off, running lightly along the dirty East River's edge.

Antonio glanced at Felix, who kept his eyes purposely straight ahead, pausing from time to time to do some fancy leg work while throwing one-twos followed by upper cuts to an imaginary jaw. Antonio then beat the air with a <u>barrage</u> of body blows and short devastating lefts with an overhand, jawbreaking right.

After a mile or so, Felix puffed and said, "Let's stop for awhile, bro. I think we both got something to say to each other."

Antonio nodded. It was not natural to be acting as though nothing unusual was happening when two ace boon buddies were going to be blasting . . . each other within a few short days.

They rested their elbows on the railing separating them from the river. Antonio wiped his face with his short towel. The sunrise was now creating day.

Felix leaned heavily on the river's railing and stared across to the shores of Brooklyn. Finally, he broke the silence.

". . . , man. I don't know how to come out with it."

Antonio helped. "It's about our fight, right?"

"Yeah, right." Felix's eyes squinted at the rising orange sun.

"I've been thinking about it too, *panin*.[3] In fact, since we found out it was going to be me and you, I've been awake at night, pulling punches[4] on you, trying not to hurt you."

"Same here. It ain't natural not to think about the fight. I mean, we both are *cheverote*[5] fighters, and we both want to win. But only one of us can win. There ain't no draws in the eliminations."

Felix tapped Antonio gently on the shoulder. "I don't mean to sound like I'm bragging, bro. But I wanna win, fair and square."

Antonio nodded quietly. "Yeah. We both know that in the ring the better man wins. Friend or no friend, brother or no . . ."

Felix finished it for him. "Brother. Tony, let's promise something right here. Okay?"

"If it's fair, *hermano*,[6] I'm for it." Antonio admired the courage of a tugboat pulling a barge five times its welterweight[7] size.

"It's fair, Tony. When we get into the ring, it's gotta be like we never met. We gotta be like two heavy strangers that want the same

2. **elimination bouts:** matches to determine which boxers advance in a competition.
3. *panin* (pä′nēn) *American Spanish:* pal; buddy.
4. **pulling punches:** holding back in delivering blows.
5. *cheverote* (chĕ-vĕ-rō′tĕ) *American Spanish:* really cool.
6. *hermano* (ĕr-mä′nō) *Spanish:* brother.
7. **welterweight:** one of boxing's weight divisions, with a maximum weight of 147 pounds.

WORDS
TO
KNOW   **barrage** (bə-räzh′) *n.* a rapid, heavy attack

thing, and only one can have it. You understand, don'tcha?"

"*Sí*, I know." Tony smiled. "No pulling punches. We go all the way."

"Yeah, that's right. Listen, Tony. Don't you think it's a good idea if we don't see each other until the day of the fight? I'm going to stay with my Aunt Lucy in the Bronx. I can use Gleason's Gym for working out. My manager says he got some sparring partners with more or less your style."

Tony scratched his nose <u>pensively</u>. "Yeah, it would be better for our heads." He held out his hand, palm upward. "Deal?"

"Deal." Felix lightly slapped open skin.

"Ready for some more running?" Tony asked lamely.

"Naw, bro. Let's cut it here. You go on. I kinda like to get things together in my head."

"You ain't worried, are you?" Tony asked.

El abrazo [The Hug] (1966), Fletcher Martin. Acrylic on paper, 22″ × 17″, private collection.

WORDS
TO
KNOW

pensively (pĕn'sĭv-lē) *adv.* in a way that suggests deep thought

"No way, man." Felix laughed out loud. "I got too much smarts for that. I just think it's cooler if we split right here. After the fight, we can get it together again like nothing ever happened."

The amigo brothers were not ashamed to hug each other tightly.

"Guess you're right. Watch yourself, Felix. I hear there's some pretty heavy dudes up in the Bronx. *Suavecito*,[8] okay?"

"Okay. You watch yourself too, *sabe*[9]?"

Tony jogged away. Felix watched his friend disappear from view, throwing rights and lefts. Both fighters had a lot of psyching up to do before the big fight.

The days in training passed much too slowly. Although they kept out of each other's way, they were aware of each other's progress via the ghetto grapevine.

The evening before the big fight, Tony made his way to the roof of his tenement. In the quiet early dark, he peered over the ledge. Six stories below, the lights of the city blinked, and the sounds of cars mingled with the curses and the laughter of children in the street. He tried not to think of Felix, feeling he had succeeded in psyching his mind. But only in the ring would he really know. To spare Felix hurt, he would have to knock him out, early and quick.

Up in the South Bronx, Felix decided to take in a movie in an effort to keep Antonio's face away from his fists. The flick was *The Champion* with Kirk Douglas, the third time Felix was seeing it.

The champion was getting . . . beat . . . , his face being pounded into raw, wet hamburger. His eyes were cut, jagged, bleeding, one eye swollen, the other almost shut. He was saved only by the sound of the bell.

Felix became the champ and Tony the challenger.

The movie audience was going out of its head, roaring in blood lust at the butchery going on. The champ hunched his shoulders, grunting and sniffing red blood back into his broken nose. The challenger, confident that he had the championship in the bag, threw a left. The champ countered with a dynamite right that exploded into the challenger's brains.

Felix's right arm felt the shock. Antonio's face, superimposed on the screen, was shattered and split apart by the awesome force of the killer blow. Felix saw himself in the ring, blasting Antonio against the ropes. The champ had to be forcibly restrained. The challenger was allowed to crumble slowly to the canvas, a broken, bloody mess.

When Felix finally left the theatre, he had figured out how to psyche himself for tomorrow's fight. It was Felix the Champion vs. Antonio the Challenger.

He walked up some dark streets, deserted except for small pockets of wary-looking kids wearing gang colors. Despite the fact that he was Puerto Rican like them, they eyed him as a stranger to their turf. Felix did a last shuffle, bobbing and weaving, while letting loose a torrent of blows that would demolish whatever got in its way. It seemed to impress the brothers, who went about their own business.

Finding no takers, Felix decided to split to his aunt's. Walking the streets had not relaxed him, neither had the fight flick. All it had done was to stir him up. He let himself quietly into his Aunt Lucy's apartment and went straight to bed, falling into a fitful sleep with sounds of the gong for Round One.

Antonio was passing some heavy time on his rooftop. How would the fight tomorrow affect his relationship with Felix? After all, fighting was like any other profession. Friendship had nothing to do with it. A gnawing doubt crept

---

8. *Suavecito* (swä-vĕ-sē′tō) *American Spanish:* Take it easy.

9. *sabe?* (sä′bĕ) *Spanish:* you know?

in. He cut negative thinking real quick by doing some speedy fancy dance steps, bobbing and weaving like mercury. The night air was blurred with <u>perpetual</u> motions of left hooks and right crosses. Felix, his *amigo* brother, was not going to be Felix at all in the ring. Just an opponent with another face. Antonio went to sleep, hearing the opening bell for the first round. Like his friend in the South Bronx, he prayed for victory via a quick, clean knockout in the first round.

Large posters plastered all over the walls of local shops announced the fight between Antonio Cruz and Felix Vargas as the main bout.

The fight had created great interest in the neighborhood. Antonio and Felix were well liked and respected. Each had his own loyal following. Betting fever was high and ranged from a bottle of Coke to cold, hard cash on the line.

Antonio's fans bet with <u>unbridled</u> faith in his boxing skills. On the other side, Felix's admirers bet on his dynamite-packed fists.

Felix had returned to his apartment early in the morning of August 7th and stayed there, hoping to avoid seeing Antonio. He turned the radio on to salsa music sounds and then tried to read while waiting for word from his manager.

The fight was scheduled to take place in Tompkins Square Park. It had been decided that the gymnasium of the Boys Club was not large enough to hold all the people who were sure to attend. In Tompkins Square Park, everyone who wanted could view the fight, whether from ringside or window fire escapes or tenement rooftops.

The morning of the fight, Tompkins Square was a beehive of activity with numerous workers setting up the ring, the seats, and the guest speakers' stand. The scheduled bouts began shortly after noon, and the park had begun filling up even earlier.

The local junior high school across from Tompkins Square Park served as the dressing room for all the fighters. Each was given a separate classroom, with desktops, covered with mats, serving as resting tables. Antonio thought he caught a glimpse of Felix waving to him from a room at the far end of the corridor. He waved back just in case it had been him.

The fighters changed from their street clothes into fighting gear. Antonio wore white trunks, black socks, and black shoes. Felix wore sky blue trunks, red socks, and white boxing shoes. Each had dressing gowns to match their fighting trunks with their names neatly stitched on the back.

The loudspeakers blared into the open window of the school. There were speeches by dignitaries, community leaders, and great boxers of yesteryear. Some were well prepared, some <u>improvised</u> on the spot. They all carried the same message of great pleasure and honor at being part of such a historic event. This great day was in the tradition of champions emerging from the streets of the lower east side.

Interwoven with the speeches were the sounds of the other boxing events. After the sixth bout, Felix was much relieved when his trainer, Charlie, said, "Time change. Quick knockout. This is it. We're on."

Waiting time was over. Felix was escorted from the classroom by a dozen fans in white T-shirts with the word FELIX across their fronts.

Antonio was escorted down a different stairwell and guided through a roped-off path.

WORDS	**perpetual** (pər-pĕch'o͞o-əl) *adj.* continual; unending
TO	**unbridled** (ŭn-brīd'ld) *adj.* lacking in restraint or control
KNOW	**improvise** (ĭm'prə-vīz') *v.* to speak or perform without preparation

As the two climbed into the ring, the crowd exploded with a roar. Antonio and Felix both bowed gracefully and then raised their arms in acknowledgment.

Antonio tried to be cool, but even as the roar was in its first birth, he turned slowly to meet Felix's eyes looking directly into his. Felix nodded his head and Antonio responded. And both as one, just as quickly, turned away to face his own corner.

Bong, bong, bong. The roar turned to stillness.

"Ladies and Gentlemen, *Señores y Señoras.*"

The announcer spoke slowly, pleased at his bilingual efforts.

"Now the moment we have all been waiting for—the main event between two fine young Puerto Rican fighters, products of our lower east side."

"Loisaida,"[10] called out a member of the audience.

"In this corner, weighing 131 pounds, Felix Vargas. And in this corner, weighing 133 pounds, Antonio Cruz. The winner will represent the Boys Club in the tournament of champions, the Golden Gloves. There will be no draw. May the best man win."

The cheering of the crowd shook the windowpanes of the old buildings surrounding

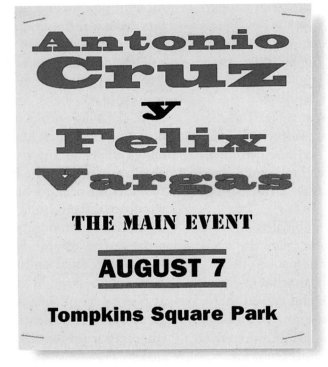

Antonio **Cruz** y **Felix** **Vargas**

THE MAIN EVENT

AUGUST 7

Tompkins Square Park

Tompkins Square Park. At the center of the ring, the referee was giving instructions to the youngsters.

"Keep your punches up. No low blows. No punching on the back of the head. Keep your heads up. Understand. Let's have a clean fight. Now shake hands and come out fighting."

Both youngsters touched gloves and nodded. They turned and danced quickly to their corners. Their head towels and dressing gowns were lifted neatly from their shoulders by their trainers' nimble fingers. Antonio crossed himself. Felix did the same. BONG! BONG! ROUND ONE. Felix and Antonio turned and faced each other squarely in a fighting pose. Felix wasted no time. He came in fast, head low, half hunched toward his right shoulder, and lashed out with a straight left. He missed a right cross as Antonio slipped the punch and countered with one-two-three lefts that snapped Felix's head back, sending a mild shock coursing through him. If Felix had any small doubt about their friendship affecting their fight, it was being neatly <u>dispelled</u>.

---

10. **Loisaida** (lō´-ē-sī´dä): a Hispanic slang pronunciation of *Lower East Side.*

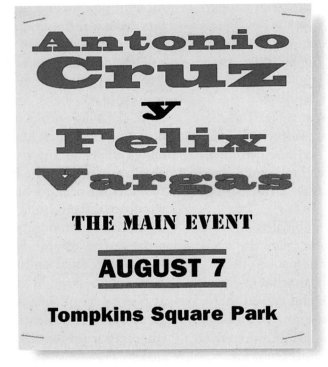

WORDS
TO
KNOW

dispel (dǐ-spěl´) *v.* to scatter; get rid of

Right to the Jaw (about 1926), Mahonri Mackintosh Young. Bronze, courtesy of Wood River Gallery, Mill Valley, California.

Antonio danced, a joy to behold. His left hand was like a piston pumping jabs one right after another with seeming ease. Felix bobbed and weaved and never stopped boring in. He knew that at long range he was at a disadvantage. Antonio had too much reach on him. Only by coming in close could Felix hope to achieve the dreamed-of knockout.

Antonio knew the dynamite that was stored in his amigo brother's fist. He ducked a short right and missed a left hook. Felix trapped him against the ropes just long enough to pour some punishing rights and lefts to Antonio's hard midsection. Antonio slipped away from Felix, crashing two lefts to his head, which set Felix's right ear to ringing.

Bong! Both *amigos* froze a punch well on its way, sending up a roar of approval for good sportsmanship.

Felix walked briskly back to his corner. His right ear had not stopped ringing. Antonio gracefully danced his way toward his stool none the worse, except for glowing glove burns, showing angry red against the whiteness of his midribs.

"Watch that right, Tony." His trainer talked into his ear. "Remember Felix always goes to the body. He'll want you to drop your hands for his overhand left or right. Got it?"

Antonio nodded, spraying water out between his teeth. He felt better as his sore midsection was being firmly rubbed.

Felix's corner was also busy.

"You gotta get in there, fella." Felix's trainer poured water over his curly Afro locks. "Get in there or he's gonna chop you up from way back."

Bong! Bong! Round two. Felix was off his stool and rushed Antonio like a bull, sending a hard right to his head. Beads of water exploded from Antonio's long hair.

Antonio, hurt, sent back a blurring barrage of lefts and rights that only meant pain to Felix, who returned with a short left to the head followed by a looping right to the body. Antonio countered with his own flurry, forcing Felix to give ground. But not for long.

Felix bobbed and weaved, bobbed and weaved, occasionally punching his two gloves together.

Antonio waited for the rush that was sure to come. Felix closed in and <u>feinted</u> with his left shoulder and threw his right instead. Lights suddenly exploded inside Felix's head as Antonio slipped the blow and hit him with a pistonlike left, catching him flush on the point of his chin.

<u>Bedlam</u> broke loose as Felix's legs momentarily buckled. He fought off a series of rights and lefts and came back with a strong right that taught Antonio respect.

Antonio danced in carefully. He knew Felix had the habit of playing possum when hurt, to sucker an opponent within reach of the powerful bombs he carried in each fist.

A right to the head slowed Antonio's pretty dancing. He answered with his own left at Felix's right eye that began puffing up within three seconds.

Antonio, a bit too eager, moved in too close, and Felix had him entangled into a rip-roaring, punching toe-to-toe slugfest that brought the whole Tompkins Square Park screaming to its feet.

Rights to the body. Lefts to the head. Neither fighter was giving an inch. Suddenly a short right caught Antonio squarely on the chin. His long legs turned to jelly, and his arms flailed out desperately. Felix, grunting like a bull, threw wild punches from every direction. Antonio, groggy, bobbed and weaved, <u>evading</u> most of the blows. Suddenly his head cleared. His left flashed out hard and straight catching Felix on the bridge of his nose.

Felix lashed back with a haymaker, right off the ghetto streets. At the same instant, his eye caught another left hook from Antonio. Felix swung out, trying to clear the pain. Only the frenzied screaming of those along ringside let him know that he had dropped Antonio. Fighting off the growing haze, Antonio struggled to his feet, got up, ducked, and threw a smashing right that dropped Felix flat on his back.

Felix got up as fast as he could in his own corner, groggy but still <u>game</u>. He didn't even hear the count. In a fog, he heard the roaring of the crowd, who seemed to have gone insane. His head cleared to hear the bell sound at the end of the round. He was damned glad. His trainer sat him down on the stool.

In his corner, Antonio was doing what all fighters do when they are hurt. They sit and smile at everyone.

The referee signaled the ring doctor to check the fighters out. He did so and then gave his okay. The cold-water sponges brought clarity to both *amigo* brothers. They were rubbed until their circulation ran free.

Bong! Round three—the final round. Up to

WORDS TO KNOW	**feint** (fānt) *v.* to make a pretended attack in order to draw attention away from one's real purpose or target
	bedlam (bĕd′ləm) *n.* a noisy confusion
	evading (ĭ-vā′dĭng) *adj.* avoiding; escaping **evade** *v.*
	game (gām) *adj.* ready and willing to proceed

now it had been tick-tack-toe, pretty much even. But everyone knew there could be no draw and that this round would decide the winner.

This time, to Felix's surprise, it was Antonio who came out fast, charging across the ring. Felix braced himself but couldn't ward off the barrage of punches. Antonio drove Felix hard against the ropes.

The crowd ate it up. Thus far the two had fought with *mucho corazón*.[11] Felix tapped his gloves and commenced his attack anew. Antonio, throwing boxer's caution to the winds, jumped in to meet him.

Both pounded away. Neither gave an inch, and neither fell to the canvas. Felix's left eye was tightly closed. Claret red blood poured from Antonio's nose. They fought toe-to-toe.

The sounds of their blows were loud in contrast to the silence of a crowd gone completely mute. The referee was stunned by their savagery.

Bong! Bong! Bong! The bell sounded over and over again. Felix and Antonio were past hearing. Their blows continued to pound on each other like hailstones.

Finally the referee and the two trainers pried Felix and Antonio apart. Cold water was poured over them to bring them back to their senses.

They looked around and then rushed toward each other. A cry of alarm surged through Tompkins Square Park. Was this a fight to the death instead of a boxing match?

The fear soon gave way to wave upon wave of cheering as the two amigos embraced.

No matter what the decision, they knew they would always be champions to each other.

Bong! Bong! Bong! "Ladies and Gentlemen. *Señores* and *Señoras*. The winner and representative to the Golden Gloves Tournament of Champions is . . ."

The announcer turned to point to the winner and found himself alone. Arm in arm, the champions had already left the ring.

---

11. *mucho corazón* (mōō′chô kō-rä-sōn′) *Spanish:* a lot of heart; great courage.

Connect to the Literature

1. **What Do You Think?** What do you think about the ending of the story?

Comprehension Check
- How long have the two friends known each other?
- Why do they have to fight each other?
- What happens at the end of the fight?

Think Critically

2. Why do you think the two boys leave the ring together before the victor is announced? Why might the author have ended the story this way?

3. What is your opinion of the way Antonio and Felix handle their inner conflicts as two good friends competing for the same prize?

    Think About:
    - the promise they exchange while training for the fight
    - how each of them gets psyched up for the fight
    - their conduct in the ring

4. How do Antonio's and Felix's fighting styles differ? What does this tell you about each boy?

5. How do you think the community will regard Antonio and Felix after the fight? Explain.

Extend Interpretations

6. **What If?** Imagine that one of the boys had won the boxing match by a knockout. What effect do you think that might have had on their friendship?

7. **Connect to Life** How would you compare your ideas about friendship and competition with those expressed in this story?

Literary Analysis

SUSPENSE The tension or excitement that readers feel as they are drawn into a story is called **suspense.** A writer creates suspense when he or she purposely leaves readers uncertain about what will happen. Sometimes a story builds suspense and then has a **surprise ending.** A surprise ending is an outcome that is different from what readers expect. Did the ending of "Amigo Brothers" surprise you?

Paired Activity Compare the chart you created in your 📖 **READER'S NOTEBOOK** with that of a classmate who also made predictions. Discuss with each other the reasons and events you used for your predictions. Did you find clues to the ending you didn't notice when you read the story for the first time? In what ways does Piri Thomas create suspense in the story?

Question	Events from the Plot	Your Prediction
Will they not fight hard?	• Each dreamed of becoming lightweight champion of the world.	They will fight hard.
Will they remain friends after the fight?	• They had each already won several medals.	

CHOICES and CHALLENGES

Writing

Editorial Although many people are opposed to boxing because of its violence, some people—like the writer Joyce Carol Oates—are boxing fans. According to Oates, "Boxing, like any sport, or art, or vocation in life, is about character." Write an editorial in favor of or opposed to boxing. Support your opinion with details from the story, and comment on Oates's opinion.

Writing Handbook
See p. R51: Persuasive Writing.

Speaking & Listening

Victory Speech Imagine that you know who won the boxing match in this story. Write a victory speech for the winner. Think about what he would want to say to the crowd, the community, and his friend and opponent. Summarize what you want to say before writing, and then complete a draft of the speech. Present the speech to the class.

Speaking and Listening Handbook
See p. R100: Writing Your Speech.

Art Connection

Look at Fletcher Martin's painting *El abrazo* on page 365. Do you think it catches  the spirit of Felix and Antonio's friendship? Support your answer with descriptions from the story.

Research & Technology

A Physical Education Research the conditioning programs that boxers must follow to prepare for their matches. If possible, interview a boxer or a physical education instructor as part of your research. Then present your findings to the rest of the class.

Speaking and Listening Handbook
See p. R109: Conducting Interviews.

Vocabulary

EXERCISE: MEANING CLUES Match each vocabulary word on the left with the italicized word or phrase on the right that suggests its meaning.

1. unbridled
2. pensively
3. bedlam
4. perpetual
5. game
6. barrage
7. improvise
8. dispel
9. evading
10. feint

a. Felix was in *continual* motion on his feet.
b. Antonio's fans had an *uncontrolled* belief in him.
c. Antonio and Felix were *ready* for the match to begin.
d. *The crowd was so loud,* Felix couldn't hear himself think.
e. The trainer sat *deep in thought*.
f. Felix *pretended to make* a left jab.
g. Antonio was *dodging* Felix's punches.
h. Felix threw a *series* of rapid punches.
i. The community leaders *made up* speeches *on the spot*.
j. Felix and Antonio *got rid of* any doubts about their friendship.

Vocabulary Handbook
See p. R24: Context Clues.

AMIGO BROTHERS **373**

Grammar in Context: Coordinate Adjectives

Piri Thomas uses several adjectives to contrast the appearances of Antonio and Felix in the first sentence of "Amigo Brothers."

> **Antonio was fair, lean, and lanky, while Felix was dark, short, and husky.**

Sometimes, to make their descriptions clear and effective, writers need to use more than one adjective to modify a noun or pronoun. When this happens, the adjectives are called **coordinate adjectives.**

Punctuation Tip: When more than one adjective modifies a noun or pronoun, the adjectives are separated by a comma. "Felix walked the **dark, quiet** streets." But, when the first adjective modifies the second adjective and not the noun or pronoun, the two adjectives are not separated. "Felix wore **dark red** socks."

WRITING EXERCISE Insert coordinate adjectives to modify the underlined nouns. Choose adjectives that would fit the descriptions in "Amigo Brothers."

Example: Original Antonio and Felix were <u>friends</u>.

Rewritten Antonio and Felix were good, close friends.

1. In the ring, they acted like <u>opponents</u>.
2. The day before the <u>fight</u>, both boys were tense.
3. Felix let fly a series of <u>jabs</u>.
4. Antonio displayed his <u>footwork</u>.

Connect to the Literature Look on page 366 for two or three examples of coordinate adjectives. How do these help create the mood of the story?

Grammar Handbook
See p. R91: Elements in a Series.

Piri Thomas
born 1928

"I believe every child is born a poet and every poet is born a child."

An About-Face While serving a prison sentence, Piri Thomas decided to turn his life around. He began writing his autobiography as a step toward accomplishing this goal. For him, writing became a tool to discover his real nature and to depict honestly his Puerto Rican and African-American heritage. After his release from prison, Thomas suffered a severe setback—the manuscript he had labored over for four years was accidentally destroyed. Choosing to begin writing his autobiography anew, he spent more

than five years in completing the work. When *Down These Mean Streets* was finally published in 1967, critics praised its power and honesty as well as its creative use of language and imagery.

Spanish Harlem Thomas's autobiography and his stories are all set in "El Barrio," the Puerto Rican community in New York City where Thomas grew up. His writing, which draws upon his memories of his experiences in Spanish Harlem, celebrates the vitality, strength, and determination of the people in his community.

AUTHOR ACTIVITY
Fiction and Real Life Find out more about the arts in the Puerto Rican community of New York City by researching El Museo del Barrio. What other artists have been inspired by Spanish Harlem?

Ode to an Artichoke

by PABLO NERUDA

Key Standard
R1.1 Identify idioms, analogies, metaphors, and similes in prose and poetry.
Other Standards **R3.1, W2.3, LS1.6**

Connect to Your Life

Your Dream Job Did you know that it's good to daydream about what you want to do in life? There are many interesting and challenging occupations available to you. What do you dream of becoming one day? Discuss with your classmates what it would take to get the job of your dreams.

Build Background

GEOGRAPHY

In "Ode to an Artichoke," Chilean poet Pablo Neruda celebrates the characteristics of a rugged artichoke plant. While artichokes are growing, they look anything but edible. In fact, the artichoke is a kind of thistle with hard green petals whose tips end in sharp stickers. When people from Spain, Italy, and Portugal settled in the New World, they brought the artichoke with them. Now artichokes are grown in many parts of the world, such as California and Chile.

Chile is a long, narrow country on the Pacific Ocean coast of South America. Like California, it has a long coastline and sandy, fertile valleys inland that provide a long, cool growing season.

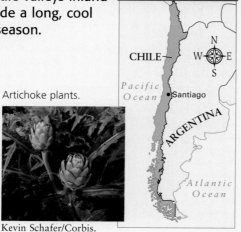

Artichoke plants.

Kevin Schafer/Corbis.

Chile

CHILE

Pacific Ocean • Santiago

N W E S

ARGENTINA

Atlantic Ocean

Focus Your Reading

LITERARY ANALYSIS   METAPHOR

A **metaphor** compares two things that seem dissimilar but have at least one thing in common. Writers make this comparison by saying one thing is another thing without using the words *like* or *as.* For example, instead of "The wind sounds like a song," a writer might use a metaphor— "The wind is a song." The poem "Ode to an Artichoke" is an **extended metaphor**, a longer comparison. Throughout this poem, the extended metaphor compares vegetables to an army. As you read, identify the comparisons you find.

ACTIVE READING   VISUALIZING

When you form mental pictures of things you read about, you are **visualizing.** Good readers use the details supplied by writers to visualize characters, settings, and events in their minds.

📖 **READER'S NOTEBOOK** As you read, visualize something that Neruda describes. Sketch your mental picture in your notebook. Above the sketch, write the key words or phrase that helped you visualize the picture.

Ode to an Artichoke

Oda a la alcachofa

BY

PABLO NERUDA

The soft-hearted	La alcachofa
artichoke	de tierno corazón
put on armor,	se vistió de guerrero,
stood at attention, raised	erecta, construyó
a small turret[1]	una pequeña cúpula,
and kept itself	se mantuvo
watertight	impermeable
under	bajo
its scales.	sus escamas,
Beside it,	a su lado
the fertile plants	los vegetales locos
tangled,	se encresparon,
turned into	se hicieron
tendrils, cattails,	zarcillos, espadañas,
moving bulbs.	bulbos conmovedores,
In the subsoil	en el subsuelo
the red-whiskered	durmió la zanahoria
carrot slept,	de bigotes rojos
the grapevine	la viña
parched[2] the shoots	resecó los sarmientos
that wine climbs up,	por donde sube el vino,
the cabbage	la col
busied itself	se dedicó
with trying on skirts,	a probarse faldas,
the marjoram[3]	el orégano
with making the world smell sweet,	a perfumar el mundo,
and the gentle	y la dulce
artichoke	alcachofa
in the kitchen garden,	allí en el huerto,

1. **turret:** a small tower.
2. **parched:** dried out.
3. **marjoram:** a sweet herb used in cooking.

equipped like a soldier,	vestida de guerrero,
burnished[4]	bruñida
like a grenade,	como una granada,
was full of itself.	orgullosa,
And one day,	y un día
packed with others,	una con otra
in big willow	en grandes cestos
baskets, it marched	de mimbre, caminó
through the market	por el mercado
to act out its dream—	a realizar su sueño:
the militia.[5]	la milicia.
It was never as martial[6]	En hileras
in rows	nunca fue tan marcial
as at the fair.	como en la feria,
Among the vegetables,	los hombres
men in white shirts	entre las legumbres
were	con sus camisas blancas
the artichokes'	eran
marshals,	mariscales
closed ranks,	de las alcachofas,
commands,	las filas apretadas,
the explosion	las voces de comando,
	y la detonación

4. **burnished:** polished.
5. **militia:** an irregular military force.
6. **martial:** relating to the armed forces.

of a falling crate;
but
then
Maria
shows up
with her basket,
fearlessly
chooses
an artichoke,
studies it, squints at it
against the light like an egg,
buys it,
dumps it
into her bag
with a pair of shoes,
a white cabbage and
a bottle
of vinegar
till
she enters the kitchen
and drowns it
in the pot.
And so
this armored vegetable
men call an artichoke
ends its career
in peace.
Later,
scale by scale,
we strip
this delight
and dine on
the peaceful pulp
of its green heart.

Translation by Cheli Durán

de una caja que cae,
pero
entonces
viene
María
con su cesto,
escoge
una alcachofa,
no le teme,
la examina, la observa
contra la luz como si fuera un huevo,
la compra,
la confunde
en su bolsa
con un par de zapatos,
con un repollo y una
botella
de vinagre
hasta
que entrando a la cocina
la sumerge en la olla.
Así termina
en paz
esta carrera
del vegetal armado
que se llama alcachofa,
luego
escama por escama
desvestimos
la delicia
y comemos
la pacífica pasta
de su corazón verde.

THINKING through the LITERATURE

Connect to the Literature

1. **What Do You Think?** What is your impression of the poem? Did you find it funny? serious? difficult? Explain.

Comprehension Check
- Why does the artichoke dream of becoming a warrior?
- Who buys the artichoke at the fair?
- What eventually happens to the artichoke?

Think Critically

2. Neruda wrote odes to many everyday things, such as salt, tomatoes, and onions. Why do you think he chose to write this particular one?

   Think About:
   - the artichoke's dream
   - how he describes the vegetables
   - the artichoke's fate

3. What details does Neruda use to describe the garden? What is it like?

4. How is the artichoke different from the other vegetables?

5. **ACTIVE READING** **VISUALIZING** In small groups, share the drawings in your **READER'S NOTEBOOK**. Invite each group's members to explain why they drew the picture as they did. Did anybody choose the same words or phrase to sketch?

6. Does the artichoke end "its career in peace"? Explain.

Extend Interpretations

7. **Critic's Corner** A traditional ode is a complex poem that develops a serious, dignified theme and often celebrates an element of nature. How is "Ode to an Artichoke" like a traditional ode? How is it different? What do you think the poet's intent was in writing an ode to a garden vegetable?

Literary Analysis

METAPHOR The most frequent figure of speech in "Ode to an Artichoke" is the **metaphor.** Remember that a metaphor compares two things that are basically unlike each other but that have something in common. When the two things are compared at some length and in several ways, the figure of speech is called an **extended metaphor.** The description of the artichoke plant as an armored warrior is an extended metaphor.

Paired Activity Working with a partner, reread "Ode to an Artichoke" and write down as many metaphors as you can find. When you are done, discuss these questions with a group of your classmates.
- Which metaphor do you think is the most vivid? Why?
- What is the effect of the metaphors? Are they serious? humorous?

ANALOGY An **analogy** is a comparison between things that seem dissimilar but share at least one thing in common. Writers use analogies to make a point about one of the things being compared. For example, in "Ode to an Artichoke" Pablo Neruda makes point-by-point comparisons between a basket of vegetables and the armed forces. One reason for this comparison might be to help readers see common vegetables in a new way. Can you think of another?

Writing

Everyday Ode An ode is usually a ceremonious poem full of personal emotion and reflection. Neruda's odes are unusual in that they celebrate everyday, ordinary objects, like onions, tomatoes, and salt. Write your own ode celebrating an everyday object. Include metaphors and similes, and one extended metaphor. Before beginning, you may want to do the research suggested in the Research & Technology section of this page.

Speaking & Listening

Poetry Reading "Ode to an Artichoke" was written in Spanish and then translated into English. If you know Spanish, read the original version of the poem aloud for the class. Afterward, identify any differences between the original Spanish version and the English translation. Do the metaphors and similes you've identified come across differently in the translation? Discuss as a class.

Research & Technology

What is an Ode? Originally, odes were songs performed along with a musical instrument. There are two kinds of odes—classical and modern. Using resources in your school or public library, define the difference between classical and modern odes. Try to find one example of each kind. Then, list the characteristics and purposes of each. Bring your findings to class and compare notes with a classmate.

> **Research and Technology Handbook** See p. R110: Getting Information Electronically.

Pablo Neruda
1904–1973

"The soft-hearted artichoke put on armor, . . ."

A Young Chilean Poet When Pablo Neruda was ten, his family moved to the southern part of Chile, a region where it rains much of the year, and vegetation is green and lush. Neruda was immediately inspired. "Nature there went to my head," he said. "I was barely ten at the time, but already a poet." By the time Neruda was 20, he had published his first book of poetry.

World Traveler Neruda was appointed to the Chilean diplomatic service and spent time in Burma, Ceylon, the Dutch East Indies, Argentina, Mexico, Spain, and France. His travels influenced his poetry, but nothing was more influential to him than the landscape and culture of Latin America. Neruda received many awards for his poetry, including the Nobel Prize in literature.

AUTHOR ACTIVITY
Neruda's Life Abroad Neruda spent much of his life living in places other than his native Chile. Find out more about Neruda's life abroad. In small groups, create a map that shows places Neruda lived. Be sure to list the years he spent at each location.

from **An American Childhood**

by ANNIE DILLARD

> **Key Standard**
> **R2.3** Analyze text that uses cause-and-effect organization.
> *Other Standards* **R1.2, R1.3, R3.1, R3.2, W1.6, W1.7, W2.1, W2.3, LC1.3, LC1.4**

Connect to Your Life

Harmless Pranks Have you ever been involved in an innocent prank or a prank that *seemed* innocent to you but that caused a different reaction in someone else? What happened? Did you change your mind when you heard the other person's point of view? Share your experiences with the class.

Build Background

SOCIAL STUDIES

The selection you are about to read takes place in a suburban neighborhood of Pittsburgh, Pennsylvania. Pittsburgh is the largest city in western Pennsylvania. It sprawls over the hilly area where the Allegheny and Monongahela rivers come together to form the Ohio River.

A residential neighborhood of Pittsburgh, Pennsylvania.

> WORDS TO KNOW **Vocabulary Preview**
> redundant   righteous   translucent
> revert   spherical

Focus Your Reading

LITERARY ANALYSIS **NARRATIVE NONFICTION**

The selection you are about to read is a work of **narrative nonfiction.** Like other nonfiction, it describes people, places, and events that are real, not fictional. As a narrative, however, it shares many of the characteristics of fiction, such as **character, setting, dialogue,** and some elements of **plot.** Writers of narrative nonfiction often use these characteristics to present factual matter in a lively way that draws readers into the action. As you read, notice how the author draws the reader into the story.

ACTIVE READING **CAUSE AND EFFECT**

Good readers try to understand relationships of cause and effect when they read. Two events are related as **cause and effect** when one event brings about the other. The event that happens first in time is the cause; the one that follows is the effect. Often an event that is the effect of one cause in turn becomes the cause of the next effect, forming a chain of cause and effect. As you read, jot down in your ▢ **READER'S NOTEBOOK** any examples of cause and effect you find in the narrative.

Heavy snow covers the ground.

↓

It's not possible to play baseball or football.

↓

Boys and girls look for other things to do outdoors.

from

An American Childhood

BY ANNIE DILLARD

Backyards, Greenwich Village (1914), John Sloan. Oil on canvas, 26″ x 32″.
Photograph by Geoffrey Clements. © 2000: Whitney Museum of American Art.

Some boys taught me to play football.
This was fine sport. You thought up a new strategy for every play and whispered it to the others. You went out for a pass, fooling everyone. Best, you got to throw yourself mightily at someone's running legs. Either you brought him down or you hit the ground flat out on your chin, with your arms empty before you. It was all or nothing. If you hesitated in fear, you would miss and get hurt: you would take a hard fall while the kid got away, or you would get kicked in the face while the kid got away. But if you flung yourself wholeheartedly at the back of his knees—if you gathered and joined body and soul and pointed them diving fearlessly—then you likely wouldn't get hurt, and you'd stop the ball. Your fate, and your team's score, depended on your concentration and courage. Nothing girls did could compare with it.

Boys welcomed me at baseball, too, for I had, through enthusiastic practice, what was weirdly known as a boy's arm. In winter, in the snow, there was neither baseball nor football, so the boys and I threw snowballs at passing cars. I got in trouble throwing snowballs, and have seldom been happier since.

On one weekday morning after Christmas, six inches of new snow had just fallen. We were standing up to our boot tops in snow on a front yard on trafficked Reynolds Street, waiting for cars. The cars traveled Reynolds Street slowly and evenly; they were targets all but wrapped in red ribbons, cream puffs. We couldn't miss.

I was seven; the boys were eight, nine, and ten. The oldest two Fahey boys were there—Mikey and Peter—polite blond boys who lived near me on Lloyd Street, and who already had four brothers and sisters. My parents approved Mikey and Peter Fahey. Chickie McBride was there, a tough kid, and Billy Paul and Mackie Kean, too, from across Reynolds, where the boys grew up dark and furious, grew up skinny, knowing, and skilled. We had all drifted from our houses that morning looking for action, and had found it here on Reynolds Street.

It was cloudy but cold. The cars' tires laid behind them on the snowy street a complex trail of beige chunks like crenellated castle walls. I had stepped on some earlier; they squeaked. We could have wished for more traffic. When a car came, we all popped it one. In the intervals between cars we <u>reverted</u> to the natural solitude of children.

I started making an iceball—a perfect iceball, from perfectly white snow, perfectly <u>spherical</u>, and squeezed perfectly <u>translucent</u> so no snow remained all the way through. (The Fahey boys and I considered it unfair actually to throw an iceball at somebody, but it had been known to happen.)

I had just embarked on the iceball project when we heard tire chains come clanking from afar. A black Buick was moving toward us down the street. We all spread out, banged together some regular snowballs, took aim, and, when the Buick drew nigh, fired.

A soft snowball hit the driver's windshield right before the driver's face. It made a smashed star with a hump in the middle.

Often, of course, we hit our target, but this time, the only time in all of life, the car pulled over and stopped. Its wide black door opened; a man got out of it, running. He didn't even close the car door.

He ran after us, and we ran away from him, up the snowy Reynolds sidewalk. At the corner, I looked back; incredibly, he was still after us. He was in city clothes: a suit and tie,

WORDS	**revert** (rĭ-vûrt') *v.* to return to a former condition
TO	**spherical** (sfîr'ĭ-kəl) *adj.* having the shape of a round ball
KNOW	**translucent** (trăns-lōō'sənt) *adj.* allowing light to pass through

street shoes. Any normal adult would have quit, having sprung us into flight and made his point. This man was gaining on us. He was a thin man, all action. All of a sudden, we were running for our lives.

Wordless, we split up. We were on our turf; we could lose ourselves in the neighborhood backyards, everyone for himself. I paused and considered. Everyone had vanished except Mikey Fahey, who was just rounding the corner of a yellow brick house. Poor Mikey—I trailed him. The driver of the Buick sensibly picked the two of us to follow. The man apparently had all day.

He chased Mikey and me around the yellow house and up a backyard path we knew by heart: under a low tree, up a bank, through a hedge, down some snowy steps, and across the grocery store's delivery driveway. We smashed through a gap in another hedge, entered a scruffy backyard, and ran around its back porch and tight between houses to Edgerton Avenue; we ran across Edgerton to an alley and up our own sliding woodpile to the Halls' front yard; he kept coming. We ran up Lloyd Street and wound through mazy backyards toward the steep hilltop at Willard and Lang.

He chased us silently, block after block. He chased us silently over picket fences, through thorny hedges, between houses, around garbage cans, and across streets. Every time I glanced back, choking for breath, I expected he would have quit. He must have been as breathless as we were. His jacket strained over his body. It was an immense discovery, pounding into my hot head with every sliding, joyous step, that this ordinary adult evidently knew what I thought only children who trained at football knew: that you have to fling yourself at what you're doing, you have to point yourself, forget yourself, aim, dive.

Mikey and I had nowhere to go, in our own neighborhood or out of it, but away from this man who was chasing us. He impelled us forward; we compelled him to follow our route. The air was cold; every breath tore my throat. We kept running, block after block; we kept improvising, backyard after backyard, running a frantic course and choosing it simultaneously, failing always to find small places or hard places to slow him down, and discovering always, exhilarated, dismayed, that only bare speed could save us—for he would never give up, this man—and we were losing speed.

He chased us through the backyard labyrinths of ten blocks before he caught us by our jackets. He caught us and we all stopped.

We three stood staggering, half blinded, coughing, in an obscure hilltop backyard: a man in his twenties, a boy, a girl. He had released our jackets, our pursuer, our captor, our hero: he knew we weren't going anywhere. We all played by the rules. Mikey and I un-zipped our jackets. I pulled off my sopping mittens. Our tracks multiplied in the backyard's new snow. We had been breaking new snow all morning. We didn't look at each other. I was cherishing my excitement. The man's lower pant legs were wet; his cuffs were full of snow, and there was a prow of snow beneath them on his shoes and socks. Some trees bordered the little flat backyard, some messy winter trees. There was no one around: a clearing in a grove, and we the only players.

Snow (1967), Alice Neel. Oil on canvas, 80″ × 60″, © The Estate of Alice Neel, courtesy of Robert Miller Gallery, New York, NY. Collection Katherine Cole. (page 384)

It was a long time before he could speak. I had some difficulty at first recalling why we were there. My lips felt swollen; I couldn't see out of the sides of my eyes; I kept coughing.

"You stupid kids," he began perfunctorily.

We listened perfunctorily indeed, if we listened at all, for the chewing out was <u>redundant</u>, a mere formality, and beside the point. The point was that he had chased us passionately without giving up, and so he had caught us. Now he came down to earth. I wanted the glory to last forever.

But how could the glory have lasted forever?
We could have run through every backyard in North America until we got to Panama. But when he trapped us at the lip of the Panama Canal, what precisely could he have done to prolong the drama of the chase and cap its glory? I brooded about this for the next few years. He could only have fried Mikey Fahey and me in boiling oil, say, or dismembered us piecemeal, or staked us to anthills. None of which I really wanted, and none of which any adult was likely to do, even in the spirit of fun. He could only chew us out there in the Panamanian jungle, after months or years of exalting pursuit. He could only begin, "You stupid kids," and continue in his ordinary Pittsburgh accent with his normal <u>righteous</u> anger and the usual common sense.

If in that snowy backyard the driver of the black Buick had cut off our heads, Mikey's and mine, I would have died happy, for nothing has required so much of me since as being chased all over Pittsburgh in the middle of winter—running terrified, exhausted—by this sainted, skinny, furious redheaded man who wished to have a word with us. I don't know how he found his way back to his car. ❖

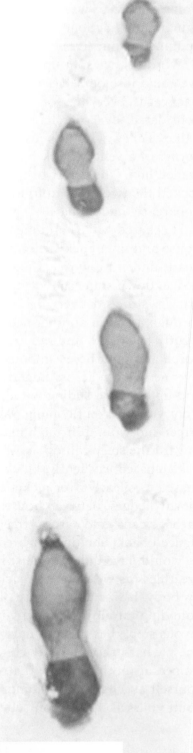

WORDS
TO
KNOW

redundant (rĭ-dŭn′dənt) *adj.* more than what is necessary
righteous (rī′chəs) *adj.* caused by an insult to one's sense of right

Winter Poem

BY NIKKI GIOVANNI

once a snowflake fell
on my brow and i loved
it so much and i kissed
it and it was happy and called its cousins
and brothers and a web
of snow engulfed me then
i reached to love them all
and i squeezed them and they became
a spring rain and i stood perfectly
still and was a flower

Snowflakes Photomicrographs by Wilson A. Bentley (1865–1931). Courtesy Jericho
(Vermont) Historical Society.

Connect to the Literature

1. **What Do You Think?** Do you think Dillard would make an interesting friend? Explain your response.

Comprehension Check
- Why did the man chase Dillard and her friends?
- What was he like?
- What happened when he caught up to them?

Think Critically

2. Why do you think Dillard chose to write about this particular childhood memory?

   Think About:
   - her reaction when she got caught
   - the chase scene
   - what the man said

3. How well does Dillard describe the man in the story? Find a passage that helps you imagine what kind of person he was.

4. **ACTIVE READING** **CAUSE AND EFFECT** Look over the list you made in your **READER'S NOTEBOOK.** Using your notes, discuss with classmates what you think are the major cause-and-effect events in the story.

Extend Interpretations

5. **COMPARING TEXTS** Read "Winter Poem" on page 387. Compare and contrast how Nikki Giovanni and Annie Dillard describe winter.

6. **What If?** How do you think the telling of the story would have changed if the man had given up before he caught Dillard and her friend?

7. **Connect to Life** Dillard says that when she was growing up, nothing girls did could compare to playing football. Do you think there is still a difference between girls' and boys' athletic activities? Explain your answer.

Literary Analysis

NARRATIVE NONFICTION Writing that deals with real people, places, and events is called nonfiction. *An American Childhood* is an example of **narrative nonfiction.** It uses elements usually found in fiction, such as **character, setting, dialogue,** and elements of **plot** to present factual information and bring the events to life for the reader.

Dillard's fast-paced description of the chase reads like one you might find in a short story:

Under a low tree, up a bank, through a hedge, down some snowy steps, and across the grocery store's delivery driveway.

Paired Activity Suspense, conflict, and climax are three elements of plot that you can find in this nonfiction narrative from *An American Childhood.* With a partner, go back through the story and find examples of each. Do you think Dillard was successful in creating these three elements of plot? Discuss your opinion with your partner.

Suspense	Conflict	Climax
A black car moves forward as the group with snowballs waits.	The group throws snowballs and the driver stops his car and chases them.	

Writing

Adventure Narrative Write about a real-life adventure you have experienced or heard about. Use elements of narrative nonfiction, such as plot, characters, dialogue, and setting, to bring your story to life. Place the narrative in your **Working Portfolio.**

Writing Handbook
See p. R45: Narrative.

Art Connection

Look at the painting by John Sloan on page 382. How do you interpret this piece? How does it affect you? Do you think it captures the mood of the selection? Why or why not?

Detail of *Backyards, Greenwich Village* (1914), John Sloan. Oil on canvas, 26" x 32". Copyright © 2000: Whitney Museum of American Art.

Research & Technology

Winter Games Using the Internet, an encyclopedia, or other resources, find out more about winter activities and sports. With a partner, brainstorm a list of winter sports, Olympic winter events, and activities that can only take place in cold climates. Choose two items from your list. Find out in what part of the world the games or activities originated. Also find out in what part of the country or world they are popular today. Using a word processor, write a report about your findings.

Research and Technology Handbook
See page R110: Getting Information Electronically.

Vocabulary and Spelling

EXERCISE: SYNONYMS AND ANTONYMS On a separate sheet of paper, write *S* if the word pairs are synonyms and *A* if they are antonyms. You may use a dictionary to help you.

1. **revert**—return
2. **spherical**—round
3. **translucent**—opaque
4. **redundant**—superfluous
5. **righteous**—immoral

SPELLING STRATEGY: COMBINING FORMS Many English words contain elements derived from Greek words. Recognizing these elements and knowing their meanings can help you spell and understand English words that contain them. Some common Greek combining forms are *astro* (star); *bio* (life); *geo* (earth); *hemi* (half, partial); *logy* (study of); *physio*

(nature); *psych, psycho* (spirit); *therapy* (medical treatment); *spher, sphere* (sphere).

sphere	spherical	hemisphere
biohazard	antibiotic	biosphere
astrology	biology	geology
psychic	psychology	psychotherapy
physics	physician	astrophysics

1. Which Greek word elements make up the word *psychology*?
2. Which spelling words in the list above contain the Greek word element meaning "life"?
3. Write three complete sentences using three or more of the spelling words from the list above.

Spelling Handbook See p. R30.

Grammar in Context: Avoiding Too Many Adjectives

Annie Dillard uses carefully chosen **adjectives** to make her writing lively and effective.

> **We . . . entered a scruffy backyard . . .**

> **I pulled off my sopping mittens.**

A less careful writer might try to make his or her writing vivid by using several adjectives where one well-chosen adjective would do the job better. What if Dillard had written, "We entered a messy, untidy, and cluttered backyard" or "I pulled off my sopping, wet mittens"? Would that give you a clearer idea of the condition of the yard or the mittens? Do these adjectives add more information than Dillard's original words?

WRITING EXERCISE Replace the underlined adjectives with a single, more precise adjective. You may keep one of the original adjectives if it seems adequate.

Example: *Original* I had, through <u>long</u>, <u>eager</u> practice, developed a <u>mighty</u> <u>strong</u> pitching arm.

Rewritten I had, through <u>enthusiastic</u> practice, developed a <u>strong</u> pitching arm.

1. The owner of the <u>dark</u>, <u>black</u> car was a <u>slender</u>, <u>thin</u>, <u>agile</u> man who seemed to have time on his hands.
2. He was wearing a <u>heavy</u>, <u>warm</u>, <u>lined</u> jacket.
3. Mikey and I ran through the <u>old</u>, <u>familiar</u>, local playground.
4. When he finally caught us, Mikey and I were panting, <u>tired</u> and <u>weary</u> from the chase.

Grammar Handbook
See p. R82: Using Modifiers Effectively.

Annie Dillard
born 1945

"I'll go anywhere that beauty leads me."

Nature Lover Annie Doak Dillard, the eldest of three daughters, was born in Pittsburgh. Her parents encouraged her love of reading and the outdoors. One of Dillard's favorite books while she was growing up was *The Field Book of Ponds and Streams.* With a microscope and a jar of pond water, she would spend many hours observing daphnia, planaria, and other small pond creatures. While in high school, Dillard rebelled against her privileged upbringing and began reading and writing poetry. She particularly admired Ralph Waldo Emerson, who spoke to her love of the natural world.

Inspirational Writer Dillard's 1968 master's thesis, on Henry David Thoreau's *Walden,* pointed to her continued interest in nature. Then frail health led her to spend a year in meditation and closer observation of the natural world. The result was the 1975 Pulitzer Prize–winning *Pilgrim at Tinker Creek.* This work earned Dillard a reputation as an inspirational writer who worked religious teachings and the role of the artist in society into her celebrations of the natural world.

AUTHOR ACTIVITY
Tales of Childhood The story you just read is a chapter from Dillard's book *An American Childhood.* Read one of the other chapters in the book. How is it similar to and how does it differ from the selection you just read? Present an oral report on your chosen selection to your classmates.

The Bat
by THEODORE ROETHKE

Mooses
by TED HUGHES

Connect to Your Life

Creature Features Has anyone ever told you that you are as wise as an owl? stubborn as a mule? fast as a rabbit? With your classmates, brainstorm a list of the human features or characteristics that are sometimes applied to animals.

Human characteristic	Animal
loyal, happy	dog
clumsy	hippopotamus
humorous	monkey
	bat
	moose

Build Background

BIOLOGY

The poems in this lesson feature two mammals—bats and moose. Bats and moose are very different from each other. The bat is small and agile. It is the only mammal capable of flying. The moose, on the other hand, is the largest member of the deer family and lumbers along on the ground, bearing antlers that can weigh up to 85 pounds.

Although many frightening myths have been invented about them, bats are actually helpful to humans. They eat enormous quantities of insect pests. A bat can eat up to 600 mosquitoes in an hour. Today, many bat species are endangered.

Moose have been more fortunate. Though they have disappeared from large portions of their former range because of hunting and destruction of the forests where they lived, moose are now making a significant comeback in protected areas and are in no danger of extinction.

Key Standard
W2.2 Write responses to literature that present interpretations that show careful reading and understanding of the text, and that support the interpretation with evidence from the selection.
Other Standards **R3.1, W2.3**

Focus Your Reading

LITERARY ANALYSIS **SYMBOL**

A person, place, object, or action that stands for something beyond itself is a **symbol.** The bald eagle, for example, is a symbol of the United States. Some symbols, such as the dove, which represents peace, are traditional. As you read "The Bat" and "Mooses," look for clues that tell you what the bat and the moose in these poems might symbolize.

ACTIVE READING **CLARIFY**

The process of pausing while reading to check your understanding is called **clarifying.** Good readers stop to reflect on what they know in order to better understand what they are reading. One good way to clarify poetry is to read it aloud. After you read the two poems silently to yourself, practice reading them aloud.

📖 **READER'S NOTEBOOK** As you read each poem silently, write down details, images, and ideas that you notice. Then read the poems aloud and jot down anything interesting that you missed while you read silently.

The Bat

by Theodore Roethke

By day the bat is cousin to the mouse.
He likes the attic of an aging house.

His fingers make a hat about his head.
His pulse beat is so slow we think him dead.

5 He loops in crazy figures half the night
Among the trees that face the corner light.

But when he brushes up against a screen,
We are afraid of what our eyes have seen:

For something is amiss or out of place
10 When mice with wings can wear a human face.

THINKING *through the* LITERATURE

1. **What Do You Think?** Did the poem change your opinion about bats? Support your answer.

2. In your opinion, what is it about bats that many people are afraid of? Explain.

Mooses

by Ted Hughes

Moose Horn State Park (1975), Alex Katz. Oil on canvas, 78″ × 144″. © Alex Katz/Licensed by VAGA, New York, NY./Marlborough Gallery, NY.

The goofy Moose, the walking house-frame,
Is lost
In the forest. He bumps, he blunders, he stands.

With massy bony thoughts sticking out near his ears—
5   Reaching out palm upwards, to catch whatever might be
       falling from heaven—
He tries to think,
Leaning their huge weight
On the lectern of his front legs.

He can't find the world!
10 Where did it go? What does a world look like?
The Moose
Crashes on, and crashes into a lake, and stares at the
       mountain, and cries
"Where do I belong? This is no place!"

He turns and drags half the lake out after him
15 And charges the cackling underbrush—

He meets another Moose.
He stares, he thinks "It's only a mirror!"

"Where is the world?" he groans, "O my lost world!
And why am I so ugly?
20 And why am I so far away from my feet?"

He weeps.
Hopeless drops drip from his droopy lips.

The other Moose just stands there doing the same.

Two dopes of the deep woods.

Connect to the Literature

1. What Do You Think?
What was your reaction to the moose in this poem? Did you find it humorous? sad? Explain.

Comprehension Check
- What does the moose look like?
- What is the moose's problem?
- What questions does the moose ask in the third stanza? in the sixth stanza?

Think Critically

2. What is happening to the moose in this poem? Explain your answer.

3. **ACTIVE READING** **CLARIFY**
Review the notes you made for "The Bat" and "Mooses" in your 📖 **READER'S NOTEBOOK.** How did reading the poems aloud help clarify the things that you missed when you read them silently the first time?

Think About:
- what the moose is looking for
- what the moose mistakes the other moose for
- what the two moose are called at the end of the poem

4. What do you think the moose symbolizes? Give examples to support your answer.

Extend Interpretations

5. **COMPARING TEXTS** How do the poets differ in their attitude toward the animal each describes in his poem? Do you think the bat and the moose are presented accurately? Give examples to support your answer.

6. Connect to Life Do you think it is important that animals are protected? Discuss with classmates.

Literary Analysis

SYMBOL A person, place, object, or action that stands for something beyond itself is called a **symbol.** Some symbols are traditional. A dark forest, for example, has often been used as a symbol of being lost and confused in life. What might the large, awkward moose described by Ted Hughes symbolize? You may find an answer by looking for the ways in which the moose feels lost and confused.

Paired Activity With a partner, reread "Mooses" to look for clues to symbols in the poems. Use the lists you made in your 📖 **READER'S NOTEBOOK.**

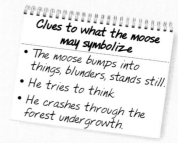

Clues to what the moose may symbolize
- The moose bumps into things, blunders, stands still.
- He tries to think.
- He crashes through the forest undergrowth.

HUMOR What makes readers laugh or smile is difficult to define. Often they find **humor** in descriptions of things that are surprising or very out of place. Think of the moose who discovers another moose in the forest. "He stares, he thinks 'It's only a mirror!'" What other examples of humor can you find in "The Bat" and "Mooses"?

CHOICES *and* CHALLENGES

Writing

Response to Literature Choose one of the poems and discuss your response to it. Organize your response around an idea or image from the poem. Your essay should show that you understand the poem, and include examples from the selection. After interpreting the poem, discuss what you did and did not like about it.

Writing Workshop
See p. 238: Basics in a Box.

Research & Technology

Animal Behavior Each of these poems describes an animal that is not well understood by most humans. In an effort to learn more about moose, for example, some scientists have created and worn moose costumes. Find out more about how scientists go about studying animal behavior. To locate information, use an encyclopedia, a science textbook, a nature guide, or the World Wide Web. Report back to your class.

Reading *for* INFORMATION
Before you begin your project, read "They're Well-Suited for Studying Moose" on page 396 to find out about scientists who dressed in moose disguises.

Theodore Roethke
1908–1963

"Deep in their roots, all flowers keep the light."

Roots Theodore Roethke was raised in a German immigrant family in Saginaw, Michigan, and helped in a family-run greenhouse and market garden. In high school, he began a lifelong interest in writing.

Work and Play Roethke's early experiences in the family business had a major effect on the developing poet. Through poetry, Roethke explored his love of nature and the challenges of growing up a very shy young man. Although haunted by bouts of depression, he was a popular teacher at a number of universities. Roethke won many awards for his verse, including the Pulitzer Prize.

Ted Hughes
1930–1998

"We think we're writing something to amuse, but we're actually saying something we desperately need to share."

Early Fame Ted Hughes was born in Yorkshire, England. He graduated from Cambridge University in 1954. In 1956, he married the American poet and novelist Sylvia Plath. Both Hughes and Plath became well-known writers in their twenties.

Love of Nature From the beginning, Ted Hughes included the natural world in his poetry. Many of the voices in his first book of poems, *The Hawk in the Rain* (1957), are animals. Ten years later, Hughes introduced the character Crow, a keen observer of human nature. Crow appears in several volumes of Hughes's poetry, including *Crow Wakes* and *Eat Crow*.

Source: *National Wildlife*

They're Well-Suited for Studying Moose

by **Steve Mirsky**

If you can't beat 'em, join 'em. That was the conclusion wildlife biologist Joel Berger came to before starting fieldwork studying moose—*Alces alces*—in Wyoming's Grand Teton National Park and in parts of Alaska.

Along with wife and colleague Carol Cunningham, Berger is interested in learning how moose behavior may have been altered by humanity's century-old experiment of removing grizzlies, wolves and other predators from the habitat. "Our research is concerned with what happens to prey in systems where large carnivores[1] are absent," Berger explains. "We feel this is an important issue because in most of the world more systems are going to be losing large carnivores, rather than gaining them. What are the direct consequences of such losses?"

In the course of doing this research, Berger realized that the only way to get the information he was looking for was to perform a variation of the old "wolf in sheep's clothing" routine. He decided to become a "scientist in moose clothing."

He was aware of a wildlife photographer who wore a zebra skin like a poncho to wander among herds in Africa. He has also seen paintings of Native Americans wearing wolf heads and capes to sneak up on bison. He thus enlisted Debra Markert, who was a designer for the *Star Wars* movies, to create a moose suit.

"I thought he was kind of loony to be considering it, to be frank, until I saw the suit in action," recalls Steve Cain, a senior wildlife biologist. "It became clear that the thing might actually have some utility, that it would probably let him approach moose closer than he would be able to on foot."

A big part of the success of the suit, according to Cain, is that Berger and Cunningham do a pretty good moose impression. "They've got their movement to mimic[2] that of a feeding moose," he notes, "one that's calm and basically going about its business. So I don't think the costume drew as much attention, or perhaps fright, from other moose as it would have had less experienced people been in it."

---

1. **carnivore**: a meat-eating animal.
2. **mimic**: to imitate.

Even given their talent for mimicry, traipsing around in the moose suit can be a risky enterprise. A large moose in the lower 48 states weighs as much as 1,000 pounds, so getting charged by one would be highly dangerous.

Berger carries a whistle and pepper spray, but he found a far better defense when a moose suddenly took umbrage as he and Cunningham came too close. "Carol and I were in deep snow and a moose lowered its ears, dropped its head and the hair on its nape stood up," Berger recalls. "Think of a dog, when it gets nervous and its hackles stand up. That's basically what a moose does. And we were only about 15 yards away from it. And because we were in deep snow, it was like, uh oh. So we took the suit off. And the moose was very confused. Its demeanor changed. We went in opposite directions."

Berger will again attempt to approach moose, while trying to put more distance between himself and park visitors. "The typical tourist response when they see us," Berger says, "is they just roar and they want to get pictures." Clearly, some scientists must go to great lengths to get into the animals they study.

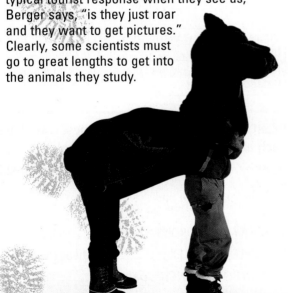

Reading for Information

Sometimes as you research a specific topic, you will be asked to present to the class what you have found. To do this, you will want to provide a **summary** of an article.

Summarizing

To summarize you need to provide a shortened version of a text in your own words. First find the **main idea** of the whole article. Then include other important **supporting details** and ideas.

YOUR TURN *Use the questions below to help you learn how to summarize.*

1 As you read, watch for facts and information that might express, or help you find, the main idea of the article. Which of the details in this paragraph do you think are important to the main idea?

2 Sometimes you have to leave interesting details out of a summary if they are not part of the main idea. What details in these paragraphs are interesting but not necessary for a summary of the article?

Summarizing Now write a summary of the article. Remember not to copy information directly. Use your own words when writing about the main idea and supporting details.

Research & Technology
Activity Link: "Mooses," p. 395 Find out more about the moose's feeding habits and environment by consulting reference sources and the Internet. How accurate is the portrayal of the moose's habitat in Ted Hughes's poem?

Building Vocabulary
Interpreting Analogies

Analogies can be expressed in different ways. In "Amigo Brothers," an analogy occurs to Felix as he watches the fight film *The Champion* the night before he must fight Antonio. The challenger puts up a good fight, but the champion wins.

You can express the analogy like this:

Felix is to a champion as Antonio is to a challenger.

In abbreviated form, this analogy is:

FELIX : CHAMPION :: Antonio : challenger

> When Felix finally left the theatre, he had figured out how to psyche himself for tomorrow's fight. It was Felix the Champion vs. Antonio the Challenger.
>
> —Piri Thomas, "Amigo Brothers"

| Felix compares himself to the champion in the film. | He compares Antonio to the challenger. |

 Key Standard
R1.1 Identify idioms, analogies, metaphors, and similes in prose and poetry.

Strategies for Building Vocabulary

You may find analogies in tests as well as in literature. Test analogies involve relationships between pairs of words and ideas. Some analogy problems are expressed like this:

> Determine the relationship between the capitalized words. Then decide which of the choices best completes the analogy.
>
> LOVE : HATE :: war : _____
>
> **a.** soldier **b.** peace **c.** battle **d.** argument

You might express this problem as *Love* is to *hate* as *war* is to _____. Here are some strategies for solving analogy problems.

❶ **Determine Word Relationships** To complete an analogy, you need to figure out the relationship between the first pair of words. In this example *love* and *hate* are antonyms—words with opposite meanings. Therefore, you must find a word that is an antonym to *war*. The best answer is *peace*.

❷ **Learn Relationship Types** The word pairs in analogy problems express various kinds of relationships. Learning these relationships will help you solve analogy problems. The chart above contains some common types.

Common Types of Analogies		
Type	**Example**	**Relationship**
Part to Whole	letter : alphabet	is a part of
Synonyms	serene : calm	same meaning
Antonyms	loud : quiet	opposite meaning
Cause-Effect	fire : smoke	results in or leads to
Worker to Tool	farmer : plow	works with
Grammar	run : ran	grammatically related to
Degree of Intensity	warm : hot	is less or more intense than
Item to Category	Mars : planet	is a type or example of

EXERCISE Choose the word that best completes each analogy. Identify the type of analogy.

book	contorted	genial	optimistic
brush	dispel	legitimate	serious
chaos	famished	pensive	

1. FUNNY : HUMOROUS :: bedlam : _____

2. SIMPLE : COMPLEX :: _____ : disagreeable

3. PLUMBER : WRENCH :: painter : _____

4. HOUSE : NEIGHBORHOOD :: page : _____

5. WORRIED : TERRIFIED :: _____ : thoughtful

The Night the Bed Fell

by James Thurber

I suppose that the high-water mark of my youth in Columbus, Ohio, was the night the bed fell on my father. It makes a better recitation (unless, as some friends of mine have said, one has heard it five or six times) than it does a piece of writing, for it is almost necessary to throw furniture around, shake doors, and bark like a dog, to lend the proper atmosphere and verisimilitude[1] to what is admittedly a somewhat incredible tale. Still, it did take place.

It happened, then, that my father had decided to sleep in the attic one night, to be away where he could think. My mother opposed the notion strongly because, she said, the old wooden bed up there was unsafe; it was wobbly, and the heavy headboard would crash down on father's head in case the bed fell, and kill him. There was no dissuading him, however, and at a quarter past ten he closed the attic door behind him and went up the narrow twisting stairs. We later heard ominous creakings as he crawled into bed. Grandfather, who usually slept in the attic bed when he was with us, had disappeared some days before. (On these occasions he was usually gone six or eight days and returned growling and out of temper, with the news that the federal Union was run by a passel of blockheads and that the Army of the Potomac[2] didn't have any more chance than a fiddler's dog.)

We had visiting us at this time a nervous first cousin of mine named Briggs Beall, who believed that he was likely to cease breathing when he was asleep. It was his feeling that if he were not awakened every hour during the night, he might die of suffocation. He had been accustomed to setting an alarm clock to ring at intervals until morning, but I persuaded him to abandon this. He slept in my room,

---

1. **verisimilitude** (věr′ə-sĭ-mĭl′ĭ-tood′): appearance of truth.
2. **federal Union . . . Army of the Potomac** (pə-tō′mək): references to the government and army of the North during the Civil War.

and I told him that I was such a light sleeper that if anybody quit breathing in the same room with me, I would wake instantly. He tested me the first night—which I had suspected he would—by holding his breath after my regular breathing had convinced him I was asleep. I was not asleep, however, and called to him. This seemed to allay his fears a little, but he took the precaution of putting a glass of spirits of camphor[3] on a little table at the head of his bed. In case I didn't arouse him until he was almost gone, he said, he would sniff the camphor, a powerful reviver. Briggs was not the only member of his family who had his crotchets.[4] Old Aunt Melissa Beall (who could whistle like a man, with two fingers in her mouth) suffered under the premonition that she was destined to die on South High Street, because she had been born on South High Street and married on South High Street. Then there was Aunt Sarah Shoaf, who never went to bed at night without the fear that a burglar was going to get in and blow chloroform[5] under her door through a tube. To avert this calamity—for she was in greater dread of anesthetics than of losing her household goods—she always piled her money, silverware, and other valuables in a neat stack just outside her bedroom, with a note reading, "This is all I have. Please take it and do not use your chloroform, as this is all I have." Aunt Gracie Shoaf also had a burglar phobia, but she met it with more fortitude. She was confident that burglars had been getting into her house every night for forty years. The fact that she never missed anything was to her no proof to the contrary. She always claimed that she scared them off before they could take anything, by throwing shoes down the hallway. When she went to bed she piled, where she could get at them handily, all the shoes there were about her house. Five minutes after she had turned off the light, she would sit up in bed and say "Hark!" Her husband, who had learned to ignore the whole situation as long ago as 1903 would either be sound asleep or pretend to be sound asleep. In either case he would not respond to her tugging and pulling, so that presently she would arise, tiptoe to the door, open it slightly and heave a shoe down the hall in one direction, and its mate down the hall in the other direction. Some nights she threw them all, some nights only a couple of pairs.

But I am straying from the remarkable incidents that took place during the night that the bed fell on father. By midnight we were all in bed. The layout of the rooms and the disposition[6] of their occupants is important to an understanding of what later occurred. In the front room upstairs (just under father's attic bedroom) were my mother and my brother Herman, who sometimes sang in his sleep, usually "Marching Through Georgia" or "Onward, Christian Soldiers." Briggs Beall and myself were in a room adjoining this one. My brother Roy was in a room across the hall from ours. Our bull terrier, Rex, slept in the hall.

My bed was an army cot, one of those affairs that are made wide enough to sleep on comfortably only by putting up, flat with the middle section, the two sides which ordinarily hang down like the sideboards of a drop-leaf table. When these sides are up, it is perilous to roll too far toward the edge, for then the cot is likely to tip completely over, bringing the whole bed down on top of one, with a tremendous banging crash. This, in fact, is precisely what happened, about two o'clock

---

3. **spirits of camphor** (kăm′fər): a liquid with a sharp odor, formerly used to relieve faintness.
4. **crotchets**: peculiar notions.
5. **chloroform** (klôr′ə-fôrm′): a liquid formerly used to put patients into a deep sleep while surgery was performed on them.
6. **disposition**: arrangement.

in the morning. (It was my mother who, in recalling the scene later, first referred to it as "the night the bed fell on your father.")

Always a deep sleeper, slow to arouse (I had lied to Briggs), I was at first unconscious of what had happened when the iron cot rolled me onto the floor and toppled over on me. It left me still warmly bundled up and unhurt, for the bed rested above me like a canopy. Hence I did not wake up, only reached the edge of consciousness and went back. The racket, however, instantly awakened my mother, in the next room, who came to the immediate conclusion that her worst dread was realized: the big wooden bed upstairs had fallen on father. She therefore screamed, "Let's go to your poor father!" It was this shout, rather than the noise of my cot falling, that awakened Herman, in the same room with her. He thought that mother had become, for no apparent reason, hysterical. "You're all right, Mamma!" he shouted, trying to calm her. They exchanged shout for shout for perhaps ten seconds: "Let's go to your poor father!" and "You're all right!" That woke up Briggs. By this time I was conscious of what was going on, in a vague way, but did not yet realize that I was under my bed instead of on it. Briggs, awakening in the midst of loud shouts of fear and apprehension, came to the quick conclusion that he was suffocating and that we were all trying to "bring him out."

© 1999 James Thurber from the cartoonbank.com. All Rights Reserved.

With a low moan, he grasped the glass of camphor at the head of his bed and instead of sniffing it, poured it over himself. The room reeked of camphor. "Ugf, ahfg," choked Briggs, like a drowning man, for he had almost succeeded in stopping his breath under the deluge of pungent spirits. He leaped out of bed and groped toward the open window, but he came up against one that was closed. With his hand, he beat out the glass, and I could hear it crash and tinkle on the alleyway below. It was at this juncture that I, in trying to get up, had the uncanny sensation of feeling my bed above me! Foggy with sleep, I now suspected, in my turn, that the whole uproar was being made in a frantic endeavor to extricate me from what must be an unheard-of and perilous[7] situation. "Get me out of this!" I bawled. "Get me out!" I think I had the nightmarish belief that I was entombed in a mine. "Gugh," gasped Briggs, floundering in his camphor.

By this time my mother, still shouting, pursued by Herman, still shouting, was trying to open the door to the attic, in order to go up and get my father's body out of the wreckage. The door was stuck, however, and wouldn't yield. Her frantic pulls on it only added to the general banging and confusion. Roy and the dog were now up, the one shouting questions, the other barking.

---

7. **perilous:** dangerous.

© 1999 James Thurber from the cartoonbank.com.
All Rights Reserved.

Father, farthest away and soundest sleeper of all, had by this time been awakened by the battering on the attic door. He decided that the house was on fire. "I'm coming, I'm coming!" he wailed in a slow, sleepy voice—it took him many minutes to regain full consciousness. My mother, still believing he was caught under the bed, detected in his "I'm coming!" the mournful, resigned note of one who is preparing to meet his Maker. "He's dying!" she shouted.

"I'm all right!" Briggs yelled to reassure her. "I'm all right!" He still believed that it was his own closeness to death that was worrying mother. I found at last the light switch in my room, unlocked the door, and Briggs and I joined the others at the attic door. The dog, who never did like Briggs, jumped for him—assuming that he was the culprit in whatever was going on—and Roy had to throw Rex and hold him. We could hear father crawling out of bed upstairs. Roy pulled the attic door open, with a mighty jerk, and father came down the stairs, sleepy and irritable but safe and sound. My mother began to weep when she saw him. Rex began to howl. "What in the name of Pete is going on here?" asked father.

The situation was finally put together like a gigantic jig-saw puzzle. Father caught a cold from prowling around in his bare feet, but there were no other bad results. "I'm glad," said mother, who always looked on the bright side of things, "that your grandfather wasn't here." ❖

James Thurber
1894–1961

"I suppose the high-water mark of my youth . . . was the night the bed fell on my father."

Early Years When James Thurber was a child, he was hit in the eye with an arrow. He lost his sight in that eye, and was troubled with vision problems the rest of his life. Despite this setback, Thurber attended Ohio State University for five years. From 1918 to 1920, Thurber worked as a code clerk at the State Department in Washington and later in Paris. He then turned to journalism, working for the *Chicago Tribune* in Paris.

The *New Yorker* Years In 1927 the *New Yorker* magazine published one of Thurber's stories. Shortly thereafter, Thurber was given a full-time job as managing editor and staff writer. Although Thurber left the *New Yorker* after six years, he continued to contribute stories, essays, poems, and cartoons to the magazine for the rest of his life. In addition to writings, Thurber also provided illustrations for many of his works, and, although he did not consider himself an artist, his cartoons had a distinctive style and became as popular as his stories.

Near Blindness By the age of 57, Thurber's childhood eye injury had resulted in almost total blindness. When his vision began to fail completely, Thurber started dictating his stories to a secretary. His memory was so sharp that he could easily compose a 2,000-word story in his mind, remember it overnight, and dictate it to his secretary the next day.

Key Standard
W1.2 Support statements with such evidence as facts, statistics, examples, and anecdotes.
Other Standards **R2.3, W1.1, W1.3, W1.4, W1.7, LC1.3**

Writing Workshop — Cause-and-Effect Essay

Tracing causes and effects

From Reading to Writing Did you ever notice that everything you say and do has an effect? This is true in fiction and nonfiction as well. In "Amigo Brothers," an upcoming boxing match causes two friends to separate for a while. In "An American Childhood," kids throwing snowballs cause a driver to chase after the culprits. Writing a **cause-and-effect essay** can help you explore how certain actions can cause specific effects.

For Your Portfolio

WRITING PROMPT Write a cause-and-effect essay about how a behavior or situation led to a certain effect.

Purpose: To inform and explain
Audience: Your classmates or anyone interested in your subject

---

Basics in a Box

Cause-and-Effect Essay at a Glance

Introduction
introduces the subject

↓

Body
describes the cause and its effects*

> cause

↓ ↓ ↓

> effect   effect   effect

↓

Conclusion
summary

* or may present an effect
and then analyze the causes

RUBRIC **STANDARDS FOR WRITING**

A successful cause-and-effect essay should

- clearly state the cause-and-effect relationship
- provide any necessary background information
- make clear the relationship between causes and effects
- arrange details logically and include transitions to show relationships between causes and effects
- summarize the cause-and-effect relationship in the conclusion

Analyzing a Student Model

SPEAKING OPPORTUNITY

See the Speaking and Listening Handbook, p. R100 for oral presentation tips.

**Stephen Shimshock
Sunnyvale Middle School**

A Day at Tiptoe Falls

Trust me—every experience can be worthwhile. Sometimes even the most annoying incident can turn out well. I know this because of an adventure I had while hiking with my family. On one of our favorite paths, we found that a bridge we needed to cross had been broken. This changed the course of our hike. Little did I know it would also change my life at school.

Our hike took place on an ordinary spring Sunday in our state park. After walking for a few minutes, I began running ahead. I almost always do this because I like to be the leader. Soon the trouble began. As I came upon the river I saw cold water rushing by. I saw that the bridge was broken and that park rangers hadn't realized it yet. We were all annoyed. We didn't want to turn back without reaching our goal—seeing the beautiful Tiptoe Falls. We decided to try to walk across the slippery stones. I stepped into the ice-cold water, and then ran to reach the other side as quickly as possible. However, I slipped and fell just a step away from the riverbank. Not only did my sneakers get soaking wet but I also twisted my ankle. "This is going to be a long day," I moaned as I limped away from the river, my feet squishing in my sneakers.

The day wasn't that bad. Because I had to move slowly, I could no longer be the leader. Trailing at the back of the line, I was able to notice things about the woods I had never seen before. I saw interesting trees, different kinds of plants, and oddly colored birds. I asked my mother if I could use the camera to take some pictures. I promised myself that from now on I would try to notice more on our hikes.

We made it to Tiptoe Falls, had lunch, and rested. When it was time to leave, we decided to take another path because my ankle was sore and it would be hard for me to cross the river again. After only a short distance, we came upon five huge trees that had fallen over in a mudslide and were blocking this path. Everyone had to climb over the trees. My father had to carry me on his back to reach the other side. Once everyone was finally across, I stopped to rub my sore ankle. I felt grouchy, cold, and tired. Then I

RUBRIC
IN ACTION

❶ The writer's conversational tone captures the reader's attention in the introduction.

The writer presents the first cause of a series of events.

❷ Explains the most immediate effects at the beginning of the essay

Another Option:
- Present the effects in order of importance.

❸ Supports statement with a specific example

remembered the promise I had made to myself earlier—about being more observant. I didn't want the hike to be a waste, so I looked around. There on the muddy ground, I noticed an interesting-looking slug. My mother said it was a banana slug. It was at least 6 inches long and had a huge brown spot on its back. My attitude melted away as I grabbed the camera and took a picture of the slug. I realized that if I had been running ahead as I usually do, I would never have noticed it.

After we returned home, I found that my day of being "thrown off course" in the woods had more effects. First, the doctor said that I should stop playing baseball for three weeks in order to give my ankle a rest. I've always played baseball, so this was terrible news. One afternoon, while I was feeling sorry for myself, my mother showed me the photos from the hike. I saw all the trees, plants, and animals that had caught my eye that day. I was especially interested in the photograph of the funny-looking banana slug. I had an idea. My science project was due in two weeks. Usually during baseball season, I don't give much time to a project. I often do it quickly and get an average grade. This year I had a lot of time and an interest in learning more about the banana slug I had discovered. I also wanted to learn about other creatures like it. So, I did research, created models and charts, and wrote the report. I received my first A on a project! This made me feel good about myself as a student, especially as a science student. This project, along with the photographs from my day in the woods, made me realize I'm interested in environmental science. Who knows? One day I may actually become a scientist who works to save the natural environment. Knowing I have a goal, and knowing I can do well in school, makes me want to work harder.

So, some ordinary hiking problems had a positive effect on my life. Who would have thought that a missing bridge could have caused so much trouble and, at the same time, so much good? My injury helped me notice something about myself I won't forget— that when I slow down and pay attention, I am able to discover a world of amazing things.

❹ The writer cites other effects and explains the connections between all the events and the first cause.

❺ Provides background information

❻ Mentions possible future effects of the cause

❼ The writer concludes by restating the cause-and-effect relationship. He ends by describing an important and permanent effect.

Writing Your Cause-and-Effect Essay

IDEABank

1. Your Working Portfolio
Look for ideas in the projects you completed earlier.

2. Surprising Consequences
Watch the news for stories in which a certain cause had surprising or unexpected effects.

3. Root of the Problem
Pick a problem in your community or school and investigate the causes.

Have a question?

See the **Writing Handbook**
Cause-and-Effect Writing, p. R48
Conclusions, p. R41

See **Language Network**
Prewriting, p. 312
Drafting, p. 315

❶ Prewriting

Do not write merely to be understood; write so that you cannot possibly be misunderstood.
—Robert Louis Stevenson, 19th-century British writer

Brainstorm a list of causes and effects you see in your school or community. List good deeds you have done that have had a positive result. Write down instances when something you did had a negative result. See the **Idea Bank** in the margin for more suggestions. After you have decided on a topic, follow the steps below.

Planning Your Cause-and-Effect Essay

▷ **1. Determine all possible causes and effects.** Does the cause have just one effect? Does the effect have more than one cause? Use a web diagram, an outline, or a flow chart to help you discover all connections.

▷ **2. Identify your audience.** What background information or explanation would your audience need in order to understand the cause-and-effect relationship?

▷ **3. List specific details.** Take notes on what additional details you need to help you examine the cause-and-effect relationship. Collect facts or note personal experiences or observations.

❷ Drafting

As you write your draft, don't worry about explaining everything perfectly. Just stay focused on fleshing out a cause-and-effect relationship. You will revise to improve your organization later.

• First, identify the cause and effect and state them clearly in the **introduction.**

• In the **body paragraphs,** develop the cause-and-effect relationship with specific details and examples. Also, provide any necessary background information here. Use **transitions**—such as *before, after, therefore, consequently, because,* and *since*—to signal the connections between events and to unify important ideas.

• **Conclude** by summing up the cause-and-effect relationship.

Ask Your Peer Reader: EVALUATING

• What would make my essay more interesting to you?

• Why do you think I responded as I did?

• What feelings came through strongly in my writing?

❸ Revising

TARGET SKILL ▶ A STRONG CONCLUSION Your concluding paragraph must make a strong final impression on your reader. You could restate the cause-and-effect relationship so the reader is left with no unanswered questions. Or, you could make an observation about the significance of the events or make a prediction. Reread your essay to improve its organization by making sure the introduction and the body lead to the conclusion.

> Who would have thought that a missing bridge could have caused so much trouble and, at the same time, so much good? *My injury helped me notice something about myself I won't forget—that when I slow down and pay attention, I am able to discover a world of amazing things.*

❹ Editing and Proofreading

TARGET SKILL ▶ COMBINING SENTENCES Combining some of your short sentences into longer sentences can create writing that flows smoothly and is interesting to read. You might put two or more short sentences together to form compound or complex sentences.

> I received my first A on a project! This made me feel good about myself as a student*, especially* ~~It made me feel good about myself~~ as a science student.

❺ Reflecting

FOR YOUR WORKING PORTFOLIO What additional causes or effects did you find as you wrote your essay? Which steps were most helpful in writing your essay? Attach your answers to your finished essay. Save your cause-and-effect essay in your **Working Portfolio.**

Need revising help?

Review the **Rubric,** p. 403.

Consider **peer reader** comments.

Check **Revising, Editing, and Proofreading,** p. R35.

SPELLING From Writing

As you revise your work, look back at the words you misspelled and determine why you made the errors you did. For additional help, refer to the strategies and generalizations in the **Spelling Handbook** on page R30.

SPEAKING Opportunity

Turn your essay into an oral presentation.

Publishing IDEAS

- Represent your cause-and-effect relationship graphically and display both your essay and your graph on the bulletin board.

- Create a dramatic reading of your essay. Have your classmates act out the different parts.

▶ INTERNET

Publishing Options
www.mcdougallittell.com

Standardized Test Practice

Mixed Review

> She won the marathon! <u>Neither her trainer nor her friends were ever in doubt,</u> but she was. <u>She won because of her training. She had begun</u> (1)
> <u>training sixteen months ago.</u> At first, <u>she only was able to run a mile</u> and (2) (3)
> had to stop frequently. <u>Then she were able</u> to increase her distance to (4)
> several miles and added an aerobics workout. A diet high in protein and
> vitamins <u>reinforced her exercise program the foods she ate</u> made her more (5)
> resistant to sickness and injury. <u>During the race, she gave up almost once.</u> (6)

Review Your Skills

Use the passage and the questions that follow it to check how well you remember the language conventions you've learned in previous grades.

1. How is sentence 1 best written?

  A. Neither her trainer nor her friends was ever in doubt

  B. Neither her trainer nor her friends are ever in doubt

  C. Both her friends and her trainer was never in doubt

  D. Correct as is

2. How is sentence 2 best written?

  A. She won because of her training, which she had begun sixteen months ago.

  B. She won because of her training, and she had begun it sixteen months ago.

  C. She won because of her training, began sixteen months ago.

  D. Correct as is

3. How is sentence 3 best written?

  A. At first, only she was able to run a mile

  B. At first, she was able to run only a mile

  C. Only, at first, she was able to run a mile

  D. Correct as is

4. What is the correct verb tense in sentence 4?

  A. Then she are able

  B. Then she is able

  C. Then she was able

  D. Correct as is

5. How is sentence 5 best written?

  A. reinforced her exercise program; the foods she ate

  B. reinforced her exercise program; and the foods she ate

  C. reinforced her exercise program, the foods she ate

  D. Correct as is

6. How is sentence 6 best written?

  A. Almost during the race, she gave up once.

  B. During the race, she gave up once almost.

  C. During the race, she almost gave up.

  D. Correct as is

 Key Standard
LC1.4 Use the mechanics of writing correctly; demonstrate correct language usage.
Other Standards **LC1.3, LC1.6**

Self-Assessment

Check your own answers in the **Grammar Handbook**

Quick Reference: Capitalization, p. R70

Quick Reference: Punctuation, p. R68

Run-on Sentences, p. R71

Modifiers, p. R82

Making Subjects and Verbs Agree, p. R72

The Literature You'll Read

The Concepts You'll Study

Vocabulary and Reading Comprehension
Vocabulary Focus: Learning and Remembering New Words
Author's Purpose
Predicting
Clarifying
Evaluating
Visualizing
Connecting with Other Stories

Writing and Language Conventions
Writing Workshop: Short Story
Participles
Placement of Adverbs
Precise Adverbs
Essential and Nonessential Modifiers

Literary Analysis
Genre Focus: Science Fiction and Fantasy
Teleplay
Science Fiction
Fantasy
Sound Devices
Persuasive Essay
Circular Plot Structure
Theme

Speaking and Listening
Stage a Teleplay
Imaginative Dialogue
Write a Monologue
Persuasive Presentation
Film Review

LEARNING the Language of Literature

Key Standard
R3.1 Be able to describe the purposes and characteristics of different forms of prose, such as the short story, novel, or essay.
Other Standard R3.4

Science Fiction and Fantasy

". . . Science fiction is the art of the possible, not the art of the impossible. As soon as you deal with things that can't happen, you are writing fantasy."
—Ray Bradbury

What if the cure for all of earth's diseases was found in the DNA of an insect? How would it be to live on the moon? What if trees talked and walked and people grew into the earth? Answers to these questions may be found in **science fiction** and **fantasy.** Both types of literature can carry you to new worlds, introduce you to imaginary creatures, and tell you about strange events. In science fiction, imaginary objects and events are based on real or possible science or technology. While **science fiction** is usually set in the future, the characters may face problems similar to those people face today.

Fantasy, on the other hand, is literature that includes at least one completely unreal or fantastic element. A fantasy story may include imaginary creatures—such as elves or talking plants and animals—strange settings, and impossible events. Writers of both of these types of fiction create fantastic characters, settings, and events not only to entertain but also to comment on the present-day real world.

From "Dark They Were, and Golden-Eyed"

Science Fiction

Science fiction is a type of writing that involves scientific data, theories, and technology. Science fiction writers like to imagine what effects scientific theories will have when they are carried out, so they often set their stories in the future. In most science fiction stories, vivid details describe futuristic settings, characters, and events.

Sometimes the ideas of science fiction writers come true. For example, when writer Jules Verne wrote *Twenty-thousand Leagues Under the Sea* in 1870, submarines were very crude vessels that could stay under water only for short periods of time. In his story, Verne described a submarine that was practically a small city. Today, submarines can stay below the water for months, sustaining large crews.

YOUR TURN Read the text above on the right. Which details show things that happen in everyday life? Which details describe things that don't normally happen, or technology that belongs in the future?

SCIENCE FICTION

(*The crowd starts to converge around the mother, who grabs* Tommy *and starts to run with him. The crowd starts to follow, at first walking fast, and then running after him. Suddenly* Charlie's *lights go off and the lights in other houses go on, then off.*)

Man One (*shouting*). It isn't the kid . . . it's Bob Weaver's house.

Woman. It isn't Bob Weaver's house, it's Don Martin's place.

Charlie. I tell you it's the kid.

Don. It's Charlie. He's the one.

(*People shout, accuse, and scream as the lights go on and off. . . .*)

(. . . *We see the metal side of a spacecraft that sits shrouded in darkness. An open door throws out a beam of light from the illuminated interior. Two figures appear, silhouetted against the bright lights. We get only a vague feeling of form.*)

Figure One. Understand the procedure now? Just stop a few of their machines and radios and telephones and lawn mowers. . . . Throw them into darkness for a few hours, and then just sit back and watch the pattern.

—Rod Serling, *The Monsters Are Due on Maple Street*

From *The Monsters Are Due on Maple Street*

Fantasy

Writers of **fantasy** often create worlds and characters that can exist only in the imagination. These worlds may be totally whimsical and unreal, like the one described in Lewis Carroll's *Alice's Adventures in Wonderland,* where there are talking rabbits and croquet mallets that are actually flamingos. Other writers of fantasy, such as Joan Aiken in "The Serial Garden," create realistic settings and characters along with impossible events. All fantasy includes at least one fantastic or unreal element. To help you believe in the impossible, a writer might include imaginative settings, fantastic details, imaginary creatures, or impossible events.

YOUR TURN In the passage from "The Serial Garden," notice how the author makes the unbelievable seem believable.

FANTASY

"Hullo. That's funny," said Mark.

It was funny. The openwork iron gate he had just stuck in position now suddenly towered above him. On either side, to right and left, ran the high stone wall, stretching away into foggy distance. . . .

"I wonder if the gate will open."

He chuckled as he tried it. . . . The gate did open, and he went through into the garden.

—Joan Aiken, "The Serial Garden"

From "The Serial Garden"

Theme

The **theme** is the central idea, message, or moral the writer wants to communicate with the reader through his or her writing. In a story, the theme should not be confused with the subject. The subject is what the story is about. For instance, the subject of a story might be about humans living in outer space, while the theme of that story might deal with how people adapt to new and strange environments. The theme is often a thought about life or human nature that the writer wants to share.

Clues to a story's theme are sometimes found in the **title,** the **setting,** the **plot,** and the way **characters** are shown and how they change. For example, the title *The Monsters Are Due on Maple Street* suggests the subject of the teleplay. The theme is revealed when we find out who the real monsters are. Careful readers often notice similar themes occurring from one story to the next.

As you read the science fiction and fantasy selections, use a chart like this one to find and analyze the theme of each story. Which stories have similar themes?

IDENTIFYING THEMES

Where to look	Questions to answer
Title	• What idea does the title emphasize? *unusual characters ("monsters") in a real setting (Maple Street)*
Setting	• What is the setting? *a quiet, tree-lined street in small-town America* • How does it affect characters? *characters are regular people, not used to anything out of the ordinary* • How does it affect plot? *the action is drawn out, people become fearful and suspicious of their neighbors, their hidden prejudices come to light*
Plot	• How do problems arise? • How are they resolved?
Characters	• How do characters act alone? • How do they act with each other? • What do the characters learn? • What does the narrator say about the characters?

From *The Monsters Are Due on Maple Street*

$\mathcal{A}$uthor's Purpose

Key Standard
R2.4 Identify an author's argument and point of view in a text.

You and your friend watch the same movie. You think it's a comedy, but your friend thinks the movie has a serious message about society. Who is right? It's possible you both are. The movie's writer may have had more than one purpose—to entertain and to express an opinion. An active reader can also recognize the author's purpose in literature by carefully evaluating the language, tone, and the way information is presented. There are four basic author's purposes: **to entertain, to inform, to express an opinion,** and **to persuade.**

How to Apply the Skill

To determine an **author's purpose**, an active reader will
- Look for direct or inferred statements of purpose
- Analyze how the author presents the information
- **Clarify** the language and tone of the work
- **Monitor** his or her reaction
- **Evaluate** how well the purpose is achieved

Try It Now!

Read the excerpt below and state the author's purpose.

Narrator. The tools of conquest do not necessarily come with bombs and explosions and fallout. There are weapons that are simply thoughts, attitudes, prejudices—to be found only in the minds of men. For the record, prejudices can kill and suspicion can destroy. A thoughtless, frightened search for a scapegoat has a fallout all its own for the children . . . and the children yet unborn, (*a pause*) and the pity of it is . . . that these things cannot be confined to . . . The Twilight Zone!
—Rod Serling, *The Monsters Are Due on Maple Street*

Here's how Chase uses the strategies:

*"To better understand the **author's purpose,** I look for clues. For example, in* The Monsters Are Due on Maple Street, *I analyze the author's strong language—his serious tone. I **monitor** my reaction to the play and agree with the author that people can become ruled by their prejudices. Finally, I **evaluate** how well the author achieved his purposes—to entertain and to express an opinion. I feel that the author made his point very well. I get the message."*

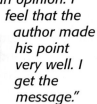

The Monsters Are Due on Maple Street

by ROD SERLING

Standards R1.1, R2.4, R3.1, W2.3,
W2.4, W2.5, LC1.2, LC1.4, LS1.6

Connect to Your Life

Facing the Unknown What happens to you when you think that danger is near? With a classmate, brainstorm ways in which you and other people might react to fear. List your ideas in a chart. Then watch as the characters in this selection deal with their fear of the unknown.

Individual	Groups
heart races	cling together

Build Background

HISTORY

On March 4, 1960, *The Monsters Are Due on Maple Street* was aired as an episode of *The Twilight Zone*, a television series created by Rod Serling. Eerie and very suspenseful, the series became one of the most popular shows in television history during its 1959–1964 run. Its stories often involved ordinary people in suburban settings typical of the late 1950s. The events in the stories were far from ordinary, however; they were a window into an imaginary world beyond ours—the twilight zone.

Rod Serling. Culver Pictures.

WORDS TO KNOW **Vocabulary Preview**

antagonism	idiosyncrasy	legitimate
contorted	incriminate	optimistic
defiant	intense	persistent
flustered		

Focus Your Reading

LITERARY ANALYSIS   TELEPLAY

A play written for television is called a **teleplay.** Like all drama scripts, a teleplay includes **stage directions.** Stage directions explain the setting, provide suggestions for the actors and the director, and describe props, lighting, sound effects, and camera directions. As you read, visualize what a performance of the drama might look like.

ACTIVE READING   AUTHOR'S PURPOSE

An **author's purpose** is his or her reason for creating a particular work. The purpose may be to entertain, to explain or inform, to express an opinion, or to persuade readers to do or believe something. Often, understanding the **theme** (the moral or message) of a work can help you identify the author's purpose.

📖READER'S NOTEBOOK As you read, record details that help you identify Rod Serling's purpose or purposes for writing this drama.

The Monsters Are Due on Maple Street

BY ROD SERLING

Rush Hour (1983), George Segal. Courtesy Sidney Janis Gallery, New York. Copyright © George Segal/VAGA, New York.

CAST OF CHARACTERS

Narrator	**Voice One**	**Man One**
Tommy	**Voice Two**	**Les Goodman**
Steve Brand	**Voice Three**	**Ethel Goodman,** *Les's wife*
Don Martin	**Voice Four**	**Man Two**
Myra Brand, *Steve's wife*	**Voice Five**	**Figure One**
Woman	**Pete Van Horn**	**Figure Two**
	Charlie	
	Sally, *Tommy's mother*	

Act One

(*Fade in on a shot of the night sky. The various heavenly bodies stand out in sharp, sparkling relief. The camera moves slowly across the heavens until it passes the horizon and stops on a sign that reads "Maple Street." It is daytime. Then we see the street below. It is a quiet, tree-lined, small-town American street. The houses have front porches on which people sit and swing on gliders, talking across from house to house. Steve Brand is polishing his car, which is parked in front of his house. His neighbor,* Don Martin, *leans against the fender watching him. An ice-cream vendor riding a bicycle is just in the process of stopping to sell some ice cream to a couple of kids. Two women gossip on the front lawn. Another man is watering his lawn with a garden hose. As we see these various activities, we hear the* Narrator's *voice.*)

Narrator. Maple Street, U.S.A., late summer. A tree-lined little world of front-porch gliders, hopscotch, the laughter of children, and the bell of an ice-cream vendor.

(*There is a pause, and the camera moves over to a shot of the ice-cream vendor and two small boys who are standing alongside just buying ice cream.*)

Narrator. At the sound of the roar and the flash of the light, it will be precisely six-forty-three p.m. on Maple Street.

(*At this moment* Tommy, *one of the two boys buying ice cream from the vendor, looks up to listen to a tremendous screeching roar from overhead. A flash of light plays on the faces of both boys and then moves down the street and disappears. Various people leave their porches or stop what they are doing to stare up at the sky.* Steve Brand, *the man who has been polishing his car, stands there transfixed, staring upwards. He looks at* Don Martin, *his neighbor from across the street.*)

Steve. What was that? A meteor?

Don. That's what it looked like. I didn't hear any crash though, did you?

Steve. Nope. I didn't hear anything except a roar.

Myra (*from her porch*). What was that?

Steve (*raising his voice and looking toward the porch*). Guess it was a meteor, honey. Came awful close, didn't it?

Myra. Too close for my money! Much too close.

(*The camera moves slowly across the various porches to people who stand there watching and talking in low conversing tones.*)

Narrator. Maple Street. Six-forty-four p.m. on a late September evening. (*He pauses.*) Maple Street in the last calm and reflective moment (*pause*) before the monsters came!

(*The camera takes us across the porches again. A man is replacing a light bulb on a front porch. He gets off his stool to flick the switch and finds that nothing happens. Another man is working on an electric power mower. He plugs in the plug, flicks the switch of the mower off and on, but nothing happens. Through a window we see a woman pushing her finger up and down on the dial hook of a telephone. Her voice sounds far away.*)

Woman. Operator, operator, something's wrong on the phone, operator! (Myra Brand *comes out on the porch and calls to* Steve.)

Myra (*calling*). Steve, the power's off. I had the soup on the stove, and the stove just stopped working.

Woman. Same thing over here. I can't get anybody on the phone either. The phone seems to be dead.

(*We look down again on the street. Small, mildly disturbed voices are heard coming from below.*)

Voice One. Electricity's off.

Voice Two. Phone won't work.

Voice Three. Can't get a thing on the radio.

Voice Four. My power mower won't move, won't work at all.

Voice Five. Radio's gone dead!

(Pete Van Horn, *a tall, thin man, is seen standing in front of his house.*)

Pete. I'll cut through the back yard to see if the power's still on, on Floral Street. I'll be right back!

(*He walks past the side of his house and disappears into the back yard. The camera pans down slowly until we are looking at ten or eleven people standing around the street and overflowing to the curb and sidewalk. In the background is* Steve Brand's *car.*)

Steve. Doesn't make sense. Why should the power go off all of a sudden and the phone line?

Don. Maybe some kind of an electrical storm or something.

Charlie. That don't seem likely. Sky's just as blue as anything. Not a cloud. No lightning. No thunder. No nothing. How could it be a storm?

Woman. I can't get a thing on the radio. Not even the portable.

(*The people again begin to murmur softly in wonderment.*)

Charlie. Well, why don't you go downtown and check with the police, though they'll probably think we're crazy or something. A little power failure and right away we get all <u>flustered</u> and everything—

Steve. It isn't just the power failure, Charlie. If it was, we'd still be able to get a broadcast on the portable.

(*There is a murmur of reaction to this. Steve looks from face to face and then at his car.*)

Steve. I'll run downtown. We'll get this all straightened out.

(*He gets in the car and turns the key. Looking through the open car door, we see the crowd watching* Steve *from the other side. He starts the engine. It turns over sluggishly and then stops dead. He tries it again, and this time he can't get it to turn over. Then very slowly he turns the key back to "off" and gets out of the car. The people stare at* Steve. *He stands for a moment by the car and then walks toward them.*)

Steve. I don't understand it. It was working fine before—

Don. Out of gas?

Steve (*shakes his head*). I just had it filled.

Woman. What's it mean?

Charlie. It's just as if (*pause*) as if everything had stopped. (*Then he turns toward* Steve.) We'd better walk downtown.

(*Another murmur of assent to this.*)

Steve. The two of us can go, Charlie. (*He turns to look back at the car.*) It couldn't be the meteor. A meteor couldn't do this.

(*He and* Charlie *exchange a look. Then they start to walk away from the group.* Tommy

Alice Listening to Her Poetry and Music (1970), George Segal. Bayer Staatsgemäldesammlungen–Staatsgalerie Moderner Kunst, Munich, Germany. Copyright © George Segal/VAGA, New York.

comes into view. He is a serious-faced young boy in spectacles. He stands halfway between the group and the two men, who start to walk down the sidewalk.)

Tommy. Mr. Brand—you'd better not!

Steve. Why not?

Tommy. They don't want you to.

(Steve *and* Charlie *exchange a grin, and* Steve *looks back toward the boy.*)

Steve. *Who* doesn't want us to?

Tommy (*jerks his head in the general direction of the distant horizon*). Them!

Steve. Them?

Charlie. Who are them?

Tommy (*intently*). Whoever was in that thing that came by overhead.

ACTIVE READER

CLARIFY Why are the people of Maple Street so frightened?

(Steve *knits his brows for a moment, cocking his head questioningly. His voice is* <u>*intense*</u>.)

Steve. What?

Tommy. Whoever was in that thing that came over. I don't think they want us to leave here.

(Steve *leaves* Charlie, *walks over to the boy, and puts his hand on the boy's shoulder. He forces his voice to remain gentle.*)

Steve. What do you mean? What are you talking about?

Tommy. They don't want us to leave. That's why they shut everything off.

Steve. What makes you

Detail of *Rush Hour* (1983), George Segal.

say that? Whatever gave you that idea?

Woman (*from the crowd*). Now isn't that the craziest thing you ever heard?

Tommy (<u>*persistent*</u> *but a little frightened*). It's always that way, in every story I ever read about a ship landing from outer space.

Woman (*to the boy's mother,* Sally, *who stands on the fringe of the crowd*). From outer space yet! Sally, you better get that boy of yours up to bed. He's been reading too many comic books or seeing too many movies or something!

Sally. Tommy, come over here and stop that kind of talk.

Steve. Go ahead, Tommy. We'll be right back. And you'll see. That wasn't any ship or anything like it. That was just a . . . a meteor or something. Likely as not— (*He turns to the group, now trying very hard to sound more* <u>*optimistic*</u> *than he feels.*) No doubt it did have something to do with all this power failure and the rest of it. Meteors can do some crazy things. Like sunspots.

Don (*picking up the cue*). Sure. That's the kind of thing—like sunspots. They raise Cain[1] with radio reception all over the world. And this thing being so close—why, there's no telling the sort of stuff it can do. (*He wets his lips and smiles nervously.*) Go ahead, Charlie. You and Steve go into town and see if that isn't what's causing it all.

(Steve *and* Charlie *walk away from the group down the sidewalk as the people watch silently.* Tommy *stares at them, biting his lips, and finally calls out again.*)

---

1. **raise Cain:** cause trouble; create a disturbance. (In the Bible, Adam and Eve's son Cain becomes the first murderer when he kills his brother Abel.)

WORDS TO KNOW
intense (ĭn-tĕns′) *adj.* showing great concentration or determination
persistent (pər-sĭs′tənt) *adj.* refusing to give up; continuing stubbornly
optimistic (ŏp′tə-mĭs′tĭk) *adj.* hopeful about the future; confident

Tommy. Mr. Brand!

(*The two men stop.* Tommy *takes a step toward them.*)

Tommy. Mr. Brand . . . please don't leave here.

(Steve *and* Charlie *stop once again and turn toward the boy. In the crowd there is a murmur of irritation and concern, as if the boy's words—even though they didn't make sense— were bringing up fears that shouldn't be brought up.* Tommy *is both frightened and* defiant.)

Tommy. You might not even be able to get to town. It was that way in the story. Nobody could leave. Nobody except—

Steve. Except who?

Tommy. Except the people they sent down ahead of them. They looked just like humans. And it wasn't until the ship landed that— (*The boy suddenly stops, conscious of the people staring at him and his mother and of the sudden hush of the crowd.*)

Sally. (*in a whisper, sensing the* antagonism *of the crowd*). Tommy, please son . . . honey, don't talk that way—

Man One. That kid shouldn't talk that way . . . and we shouldn't stand here listening to him. Why this is the craziest thing I ever heard of. The kid tells us a comic book plot, and here we stand listening—

(Steve *walks toward the camera and stops beside the boy.*)

Steve. Go ahead, Tommy. What kind of story was this? What about the people they sent out ahead?

Tommy. That was the way they prepared things for the landing. They sent four people. A mother and a father and two kids who looked just like humans . . . but they weren't.

(*There is another silence as* Steve *looks toward the crowd and then toward* Tommy. *He wears a tight grin.*)

Steve. Well, I guess what we'd better do then is to run a check on the neighborhood and see which ones of us are really human.

(*There is laughter at this, but it's a laughter that comes from a desperate attempt to lighten the atmosphere. The people look at one another in the middle of their laughter.*)

Charlie (*rubs his jaw nervously*). I wonder if Floral Street's got the same deal we got. (*He looks past the houses.*) Where is Pete Van Horn anyway? Isn't he back yet?

(*Suddenly there is the sound of a car's engine starting to turn over. We look across the street toward the driveway of* Les Goodman's *house. He is at the wheel trying to start the car.*)

Sally. Can you get started, Les?

(Les Goodman *gets out of the car, shaking his head.*)

Les. No dice.

(*He walks toward the group. He stops suddenly as, behind him, the car engine starts up all by itself.* Les *whirls around to stare at the car. The car idles roughly, smoke coming from the exhaust, the frame shaking gently.* Les's *eyes go wide, and he runs over to his car. The people stare at the car.*)

Man One. He got the car started somehow. He got *his* car started!

(*The people continue to stare, caught up by this revelation and wildly frightened.*)

Woman. How come his car just up and started like that?

Sally. All by itself. He wasn't anywheres near it.

421

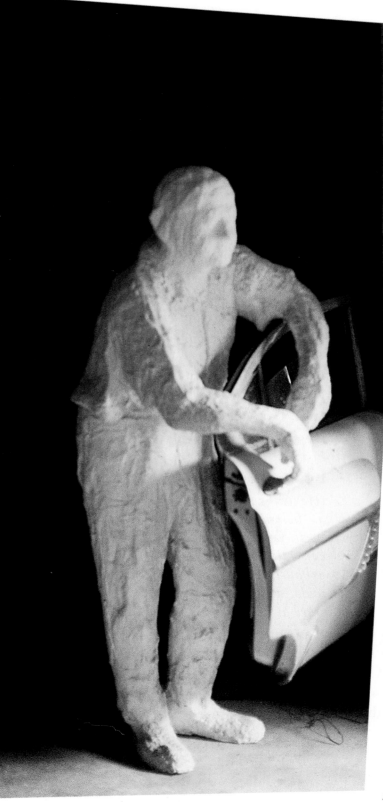

Man Leaning on a Car Door (1963), George Segal. Courtesy Sidney Janis Gallery, New York. Copyright © George Segal/VAGA, New York.

It started all by itself.

(Don Martin *approaches the group and stops a few feet away to look toward* Les's *car.*)

Don. And he never did come out to look at that thing that flew overhead. He wasn't even interested. (*He turns to the group, his face taut and serious.*) Why? Why didn't he come out with the rest of us to look?

Charlie. He always was an oddball. Him and his whole family. Real odd-ball.

Don. What do you say we ask him?

(*The group starts toward the house. In this brief fraction of a moment,*

ACTIVE READER

MAKE INFERENCES

What does this dialogue tell you about Charlie and Don?

it takes the first step toward changing from a group into a mob. The group members begin to head purposefully across the street toward the house. Steve *stands in front of them. For a moment their fear almost turns their walk into a wild stampede, but* Steve's *voice, loud, incisive, and commanding, makes them stop.*)

Steve. Wait a minute . . . wait a minute! Let's not be a mob!

(*The people stop, pause for a moment, and then, much more quietly and slowly, start to walk across the street.* Les *stands alone facing the people.*)

Les. I just don't understand it. I tried to start it, and it wouldn't start. You saw me. All of you saw me.

(*And now, just as suddenly as the engine started, it stops, and there is a long silence that is gradually intruded upon by the frightened murmuring of the people.*)

Les. I don't understand. I swear . . . I don't understand. What's happening?

Don. Maybe you better tell us. Nothing's working on this street. Nothing. No lights, no power, no radio, (*then meaningfully*) nothing except one car—yours!

(*The people's murmuring becomes a loud chant filling the air with accusations and demands for action. Two of the men pass* Don *and head toward* Les, *who backs away from them against his car. He is cornered.*)

Les. Wait a minute now. You keep your distance—all of you. So I've got a car that starts by itself—well, that's a freak thing—I admit it. But does that make me a criminal or something? I don't know why the car works— it just does!

(*This stops the crowd momentarily, and* Les, *still backing away, goes toward his front porch. He goes up the steps and then stops, facing the mob.*)

Les. What's it all about, Steve?

Steve (*quietly*). We're all on a monster kick, Les. Seems that the general impression holds that maybe one family isn't what we think they are. Monsters from outer space or something. Different from us. Aliens from the vast beyond. (*He chuckles.*) You know anybody that might fit that description around here on Maple Street?

Les. What is this, a gag? (*He looks around the group again.*) This a practical joke or something?

(*Suddenly the car engine starts all by itself, runs for a moment, and stops. One woman begins to cry. The eyes of the crowd are cold and accusing.*)

Les. Now that's supposed to <u>incriminate</u> me, huh? The car engine goes on and off, and that really does it, doesn't it? (*He looks around at the faces of the people.*) I just don't understand it . . . any more than any of you do! (*He wets his lips, looking from face to face.*) Look, you all know me. We've lived here five years. Right in this house. We're no different from any of the rest of you! We're no different at all. . . . Really . . . this whole thing is just . . . just weird—

Woman. Well, if that's the case, Les Goodman, explain why— (*She stops suddenly, clamping her mouth shut.*)

Les (*softly*). Explain what?

Steve (*interjecting*). Look, let's forget this—

Charlie (*overlapping him*). Go ahead, let her talk. What about it? Explain what?

Woman (*a little reluctantly*). Well . . . sometimes I go to bed late at night. A couple of times . . . a couple of times I'd come out here on the porch, and I'd see Mr. Goodman here in the wee hours of the morning standing out in front of his house . . . looking up at the sky. (*She looks around the circle of faces.*) That's right, looking up at the sky as if . . . as if he were waiting for something, (*pauses*) as if he were looking for something.

(*There's a murmur of reaction from the crowd again as* Les *backs away.*)

Les. She's crazy. Look, I can explain that. Please . . . I can really explain that. . . . She's making it up anyway. (*Then he shouts.*) I tell you she's making it up!

(*He takes a step toward the crowd, and they back away from him. He walks down the steps after them, and they continue to back away. Suddenly he is left completely alone, and he looks like a man caught in the middle of a menacing circle as the scene slowly fades to black.*)

WORDS
TO
KNOW

incriminate (ĭn-krĭm′ə-nāt′) *v.* to cause to appear guilty

Act Two

Scene One

(*Fade in on Maple Street at night. On the sidewalk, little knots of people stand around talking in low voices. At the end of each conversation they look toward* Les Goodman's *house. From the various houses, we can see candlelight but no electricity. The quiet that blankets the whole area is disturbed only by the almost whispered voices of the people standing around. In one group* Charlie *stands staring across at the Goodmans' house. Two men stand across the street from it in almost sentrylike poses.*)

Sally (*in a small, hesitant voice*). It just doesn't seem right, though, keeping watch on them. Why . . . he was right when he said he was one of our neighbors. Why, I've known Ethel Goodman ever since they moved in. We've been good friends—

Charlie. That don't prove a thing. Any guy who'd spend his time lookin' up at the sky early in the morning—well, there's something wrong with that kind of person. There's something that ain't <u>legitimate</u>. Maybe under normal circumstances we could let it go by, but these aren't normal circumstances. Why, look at this street! Nothin' but candles. Why, it's like goin' back into the Dark Ages or somethin'!

(Steve *walks down the steps of his porch, down the street to the Goodmans' house, and then stops at the foot of the steps.* Les *is standing there;* Ethel Goodman *behind him is very frightened.*)

Les. Just stay right where you are, Steve. We don't want any trouble, but this time if anybody sets foot on my porch—that's what they're going to get—trouble!

Steve. Look, Les—

Les. I've already explained to you people. I don't sleep very well at night sometimes. I get up and I take a walk and I look up at the sky. I look at the stars!

Ethel. That's exactly what he does. Why, this whole thing, it's . . . it's some kind of madness or something.

Steve (*nods grimly*). That's exactly what it is—some kind of madness.

Charlie's Voice (*shrill, from across the street*). You best watch who you're seen with, Steve! Until we get this all straightened out, you ain't exactly above suspicion yourself.

Steve (*whirling around toward him*). Or you, Charlie. Or any of us, it seems. From age eight on up!

Woman. What I'd like to know is—what are we gonna do? Just stand around here all night?

Charlie. There's nothin' else we *can* do! (*He turns back, looking toward* Steve *and* Les *again.*) One of 'em'll tip their hand. They got to.

Steve (*raising his voice*). There's something you can do, Charlie. You can go home and keep your mouth shut. You can quit strutting around like a self-appointed judge and climb into bed and forget it.

ACTIVE READER

AUTHOR'S PURPOSE
How do you think the author wants you to feel toward the people of Maple Street?

Charlie. You sound real anxious to have that happen, Steve. I think we better keep our eye on you, too!

WORDS
TO
KNOW

legitimate (lə-jĭt'ə-mĭt) *adj.* in accordance with accepted practices; reasonable

424

Don (*as if he were taking the bit in his teeth, takes a hesitant step to the front*). I think everything might as well come out now. (*He turns toward Steve.*) Your wife's done plenty of talking, Steve, about how odd you are!

Charlie (*picking this up, his eyes widening*). Go ahead, tell us what she's said.

(Steve *walks toward them from across the street.*)

Steve. Go ahead, what's my wife said? Let's get it all out. Let's pick out every idiosyncrasy of every single man, woman, and child on the street. And then we might as well set up some kind of citizens' court. How about a firing squad at dawn, Charlie, so we can get rid of all the suspects. Narrow them down. Make it easier for you.

Don. There's no need gettin' so upset, Steve. It's just that . . . well . . . Myra's talked about how there's been plenty of nights you spent hours down in your basement workin' on some kind of radio or something. Well, none of us have ever seen that radio—

(*By this time* Steve *has reached the group. He stands there defiantly.*)

Charlie. Go ahead, Steve. What kind of "radio set" you workin' on? I never seen it. Neither has anyone else. Who do you talk to on that radio set? And who talks to you?

Steve. I'm surprised at you, Charlie. How come you're so dense all of a sudden? (*He pauses.*) Who do I talk to? I talk to monsters from outer space. I talk to three-headed green men who fly over here in what look like meteors.

(Myra Brand *steps down from the porch, bites her lip, calls out.*)

Myra. Steve! Steve, please. (*Then looking around, frightened, she walks toward the group.*) It's just a ham radio set, that's all. I bought him a book on it myself. It's just a ham radio set. A lot of people have them. I can show it to you. It's right down in the basement.

Steve (*whirls around toward her*). Show them nothing! If they want to look inside our house—let them go and get a search warrant.

Charlie. Look, buddy, you can't afford to—

Steve (*interrupting him*). Charlie, don't start telling me who's dangerous and who isn't and who's safe and who's a menace. (*He turns to the group and shouts.*) And you're with him, too—all of you! You're standing here all set to crucify—all set to find a scapegoat—all desperate to point some kind of a finger at a neighbor! Well now, look, friends, the only thing that's gonna happen is that we'll eat each other up alive—

(*He stops abruptly as* Charlie *suddenly grabs his arm.*)

Charlie (*in a hushed voice*). That's not the only thing that can happen to us.

(*Down the street, a figure has suddenly materialized in the gloom. In the silence we hear the clickety-clack of slow, measured footsteps on concrete as the figure walks slowly toward them. One of the women lets out a stifled cry. Sally grabs her boy, as do a couple of other mothers.*)

Tommy (*shouting, frightened*). It's the monster! It's the monster!

(*Another woman lets out a wail, and the people fall back in a group staring toward the darkness and the approaching figure. The people stand in the shadows watching.* Don Martin *joins them, carrying a shotgun. He holds it up.*)

Don. We may need this.

Steve. A shotgun? (*He pulls it out of* Don's *hand.*) No! Will anybody think a thought around here! Will you people wise up. What good would a shotgun do against—

(*The dark figure continues to walk toward them*

WORDS TO KNOW

idiosyncrasy (ĭd'ē-ō-sĭng'krə-sē) *n.* a personal way of acting; odd mannerism

425

as the people stand there, fearful, mothers clutching children, men standing in front of their wives.)

Charlie (*pulling the gun from* Steve's *hands*). No more talk, Steve. You're going to talk us into a grave! You'd let whatever's out there walk right over us, wouldn't yuh? Well, some of us won't!

(Charlie *swings around, raises the gun, and suddenly pulls the trigger. The sound of the shot explodes in the stillness. The figure suddenly lets out a small cry, stumbles forward onto his knees, and then falls forward on his face. Don, Charlie, and Steve race forward to him. Steve is there first and turns the man over. The crowd gathers around them.*)

Steve (*slowly looks up*). It's Pete Van Horn.

Don (*in a hushed voice*). Pete Van Horn! He was just gonna go over to the next block to see if the power was on—

ACTIVE READER

PREDICT What do you think the neighbors will do now?

Woman. You killed him, Charlie. You shot him dead!

Charlie (*looks around at the circle of faces, his eyes frightened, his face contorted*). But . . . but I didn't know who he was. I certainly didn't know who he was. He comes walkin' out of the darkness—how am I supposed to know who he was? (*He grabs* Steve.) Steve—you know why I shot! How was I supposed to know he wasn't a monster or something? (*He grabs* Don.) We're all scared of the same thing. I was just tryin' to . . . tryin' to protect my home, that's all! Look, all of you, that's all I was tryin' to do. (*He looks down wildly at the body.*) I didn't know it was somebody we knew! I didn't know—

(*There's a sudden hush and then an intake of breath in the group. Across the street all the lights go on in one of the houses.*)

Woman (*in a hushed voice*). Charlie . . . Charlie . . . the lights just went on in your house. Why did the lights just go on?

Don. What about it, Charlie? How come you're the only one with lights now?

Les. That's what I'd like to know.

(*Pausing, they all stare toward* Charlie.)

Les. You were so quick to kill, Charlie, and you were so quick to tell us who we had to be careful of. Well, maybe you had to kill. Maybe Pete there was trying to tell us something. Maybe he'd found out something and came back to tell us who there was amongst us we should watch out for—

(Charlie *backs away from the group, his eyes wide with fright.*)

Charlie. No . . . no . . . it's nothing of the sort! I don't know why the lights are on. I swear I don't. Somebody's pulling a gag or something.

(*He bumps against* Steve, *who grabs him and whirls him around.*)

Steve. A gag? A gag? Charlie, there's a dead man on the sidewalk, and you killed him! Does this thing look like a gag to you?

(Charlie *breaks away and screams as he runs toward his house.*)

Charlie. No! No! Please!

(*A man breaks away from the crowd to chase* Charlie. *As the man tackles him and lands on top of him, the other people start to run toward them.* Charlie *gets up, breaks away from the other man's grasp, and lands a couple of desperate punches that push the man aside. Then he forces his way, fighting, through the crowd and jumps up on his front porch.* Charlie *is on his porch as a rock thrown from the group smashes a window beside him, the broken glass*

WORDS
TO
KNOW
contorted (kən-tôr′tĭd) *adj.* twisted or pulled out of shape **contort** v.

flying past him. A couple of pieces cut him. He stands there perspiring, rumpled, blood running down from a cut on the cheek. His wife breaks away from the group to throw herself into his arms. He buries his face against her. We can see the crowd converging on the porch.)

Voice One. It must have been him.

Voice Two. He's the one.

Voice Three. We got to get Charlie.

(Another rock lands on the porch. Charlie pushes his wife behind him, facing the group.)

Charlie. Look, look I swear to you. . . . it isn't me . . . but I do know who it is . . . I swear to you, I do know who it is. I know who the monster is here. I know who it is that doesn't belong. I swear to you I know.

Don *(pushing his way to the front of the crowd).* All right, Charlie, let's hear it!

(Charlie's eyes dart around wildly.)

Charlie. It's . . . it's . . .

Man Two *(screaming).* Go ahead, Charlie.

Charlie. It's . . . it's the kid. It's Tommy. He's the one!

(There's a gasp from the crowd as we see Sally *holding the boy.* Tommy *at first doesn't understand and then, realizing the eyes are all*

Detail of *Man Leaning on a Car Door* (1963), George Segal.

on him, buries his face against his mother.)

Sally *(backs away).* That's crazy! He's only a boy.

Woman. But he knew! He was the only one! He told us all about it. Well, how did he know? How could he have known?

(Various people take this up and repeat the question.)

Voice One. How could he know?

Voice Two. Who told him?

Voice Three. Make the kid answer.

(The crowd starts to converge around the mother, who grabs Tommy *and starts to run with him. The crowd starts to follow, at first walking fast, and then running after him. Suddenly* Charlie's *lights go off and the lights in other houses go on, then off.)*

Man One *(shouting).* It isn't the kid . . . it's Bob Weaver's house.

Woman. It isn't Bob Weaver's house, it's Don Martin's place.

Charlie. I tell you it's the kid.

Don. It's Charlie. He's the one.

(People shout, accuse, and scream as the lights go on and off. Then, slowly, in the middle of this nightmarish confusion of sight and sound, the camera starts to pull away until, once again, we have reached the opening shot looking at the Maple Street sign from high above.)

Scene Two

(The camera continues to move away while gradually bringing into focus a field. We see the metal side of a spacecraft that sits shrouded in darkness. An open door throws out a beam of light from the illuminated interior. Two figures appear, silhouetted against the bright lights. We get only a vague feeling of form.)

Figure One. Understand the procedure now? Just stop a few of their machines and radios and telephones and lawn mowers. . . . Throw them into darkness for a few hours, and then just sit back and watch the pattern.

Figure Two. And this pattern is always the same?

Figure One. With few variations. They pick the most dangerous enemy they can find . . . and it's themselves. And all we need do is sit back . . . and watch.

ACTIVE READER

VISUALIZE Close your eyes and picture the spacecraft. How does its appearance make you feel?

Figure Two. Then I take it this place . . . this Maple Street . . . is not unique.

Figure One (*shaking his head*). By no means. Their world is full of Maple Streets. And we'll go from one to the other and let them destroy themselves. One to the other . . . one to the other . . . one to the other—

Scene Three

(*The camera slowly moves up for a shot of the starry sky, and over this we hear the* Narrator's *voice.*)

Narrator. The tools of conquest do not necessarily come with bombs and explosions and fallout.[2] There are weapons that are simply thoughts, attitudes, prejudices—to be found only in the minds of men. For the record, prejudices can kill and suspicion can destroy. A thoughtless, frightened search for a scapegoat has a fallout all its own for the children . . . and the children yet unborn, (a pause) and the pity of it is . . . that these things cannot be confined to . . . The Twilight Zone!

(*Fade to black.*)

---

2. **fallout:** radioactive particles that fall to earth after a nuclear explosion.

Detail of *Rush Hour* (1983), George Segal.

Connect to the Literature

1. **What Do You Think?** What is your reaction to the fear and confusion on Maple Street?

Comprehension Check
- When do people first sense something is wrong?
- Why is Pete Van Horn killed?
- Who are the most dangerous enemies of human beings?

Think Critically

2. In your opinion, who are the monsters on Maple Street referred to in the title? Give reasons for your answer.

3. Do you think the aliens are correct in their judgment of human behavior? Explain your answer.

4. After the crowd turns on him, why does Charlie accuse someone else of being the monster? What evidence does he have?

5. Why do you think the author chose Maple Street as the setting of this teleplay?

   Think About:
   - the children playing along the street
   - the peacefulness of the street
   - the fact that the houses all look alike

6. **ACTIVE READING** **AUTHOR'S PURPOSE** Have you identified the author's purpose? Compare the list of details in your **READER'S NOTEBOOK** with a classmate's list. Discuss what some possible themes might be, and the different purposes Serling might have had as he wrote.

Extend Interpretations

7. **What If?** What if the story, instead of being told by someone offstage, were told from the point of view of Charlie? How would Charlie defend his actions?

8. **Connect to Life** This teleplay shows what can happen when a crowd becomes a mob. How does being in a crowd change the way people act? What other examples of "mob mentality" have you heard about?

Literary Analysis

TELEPLAY A play written for television is called a **teleplay.** The **stage directions** in a teleplay are often written in italics, and they include directions for the camera to fade in or out on a shot or to focus on a certain character. Camera directions help readers visualize what the drama might look like on television. They also help the producer of the television program know what details the author wants to emphasize or focus on.

Paired Activity With a partner, go back over the stage directions and find the camera directions. Discuss what the different camera directions lead you to visualize. Would you have shot the scenes differently? If so, how?

THEME The **theme** of a story is the main message or moral an author wishes to communicate to the reader. Theme should not be confused with subject, or what the story is about. The subject of a story might be "aliens landing on earth," while the theme might be "how people react to fear in a crisis." A theme tells the reader something about life. What does this drama tell you about life?

Writing

Draft a Proposal Think about how you would revise *The Monsters Are Due on Maple Street* to present a more positive perspective on human behavior. Write a proposal for changing the script, describing the reason for each of your changes and the way it would affect the theme of the teleplay. Place the proposal in your **Working Portfolio.**
Writing Handbook
See p. R51: Persuasive Writing.

Speaking & Listening

Read It Aloud Dramas are meant to be read aloud. Have volunteer groups read a scene from the teleplay. Cast readers for each part, including a narrator to read the stage directions. Have the actors pay attention to stage directions for movement, gestures, and expressions. As a class, vote for a favorite.

Art Connection

Human Sculpture Do you think pictures of George Segal's sculptures capture an important aspect of the teleplay? What effect do these images have on you? Explain your response.

Research & Technology

Suspicion and Fear How have fear and suspicions served to hurt and destroy people throughout history? Find out by looking through books about American and world history. Write a short summary of a tragic situation that was caused by irrational fear and prejudice, such as the Salem witch trials or the "Red scare." Then explain how you think people could avoid repeating the same mistakes if that event were to occur again.

Vocabulary

An analogy contains two pairs of words that are related in the same way, as in the example TALL : HIGH :: wild : untamed. The analogy is read *"Tall is to high as wild is to untamed."* In this example, the words are synonyms; that is, they have similar meanings. An analogy may also use antonyms to express a relationship between words. For each item below, decide which Word to Know best completes the second pair of the analogy.

1. QUICK : FAST :: _____ : stubborn
2. DIFFICULT : HARD :: confused : _____
3. SOAKED : DRENCHED :: _____ : peculiarity
4. HIGH : LOW :: _____ : friendship
5. ANGER : RAGE :: twisted : _____
6. CHEERFUL : GENIAL :: accuse : _____
7. FAR : DISTANT :: _____ : lawful
8. ANNOYANCE : PLEASURE :: _____ : gloomy
9. RUNNING : STROLLING :: _____ : weak
10. BORED : INTERESTED :: agreeable : _____

Vocabulary Handbook
See p. R28: Analogies.

| WORDS TO KNOW | antagonism | defiant | idiosyncrasy | intense | optimistic |
| | contorted | flustered | incriminate | legitimate | persistent |

Grammar in Context: Participles

Rod Serling uses **participles** in his stage directions to set the scene in *The Monsters Are Due on Maple Street.*

Tommy stares at them, biting his lips.

Tommy is both frightened and defiant.

Participles are verb forms that function as modifiers. Present participles end in *-ing* and past participles of regular verbs end in *-d* or *-ed.*

Apply to Your Writing A participle has some of the characteristics of a verb, but a participle can never be the main verb in a sentence. A sentence without a main verb is a fragment. Always review your writing to make sure you haven't inadvertently written a sentence with a participle instead of a main verb.

WRITING EXERCISE Rewrite the following sentences to avoid any fragments.

Example: *Original* Small knots of people were watching the sky. Talking in low voices.

Rewritten Small knots of people talking in low voices were watching the sky.

1. Sally stood there. Watching him as he mowed.
2. Walking down the street. A figure suddenly materialized in the gloom.
3. The car idled roughly. Smoke coming from the exhaust.
4. Rumpled and perspiring. Charlie sits there with blood running down his cheek.

Connect to the Literature Look at the stage directions on page 419 that begin *"He gets in the car . . ."* How many participles do you find in that paragraph?

Grammar Handbook See p. 80: Using Verbs Correctly.

Rod Serling
1924–1975

". . . I felt a need to write, a kind of compulsion to get some of my thoughts down. . . ."

Social Issues Rod Serling began his career by writing for radio and television in Cincinnati, Ohio. In 1955, he scored his first big hit with his television drama *Patterns,* which won an Emmy Award. Though the public knew Serling as a creator of exciting television shows, those in the entertainment business knew him as "the angry young man of television." Although Serling wanted to write meaningful plays about important social issues, television sponsors and

executives often found his topics too controversial. Thus began his long battle with those who controlled the networks.

Science Fiction Serling turned to writing science fiction and fantasy in series such as *The Twilight Zone* and *Night Gallery.* Because these shows were not realistic, he had more freedom to deal with issues such as prejudice and intolerance. Serling eventually won six Emmy Awards and many other honors for the extraordinary quality of his work.

AUTHOR ACTIVITY
The Twilight Zone Find and watch other episodes of *The Twilight Zone.* Besides the paranoia portrayed in *The Monsters Are Due on Maple Street,* what other social issues did Serling deal with?

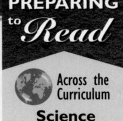

Across the Curriculum

Science

Key Item

by ISAAC ASIMOV

 Key Standard
R3.1 Be able to describe the purposes and characteristics of different forms of prose, such as the short story, novel, or essay.
Other Standard **W2.1**

Connect to Your Life

What do you like most about computers?

Build Background

Scientists in the field of Artificial Intelligence build machines that perform activities requiring intelligence, such as learning, interacting with human beings, and making decisions. Cog (*below*) is a robot in human form developed in the Artificial Intelligence Laboratory at the Massachusetts Institute of Technology (MIT). Cog represents many of the latest advancements in the field.

The Whole Arm Manipulator (*right*), also developed at MIT, has been designed with complex sensory and motor skills. It is shown here catching a ball.

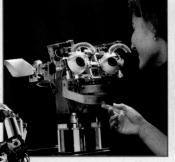

An MIT researcher plays with Kismet (*above*), a robot capable of a range of expressions and gestures. In Kismet, scientists hope to develop a robot that can interact socially with human beings.

Focus Your Reading

LITERARY ANALYSIS **SCIENCE FICTION**

Science fiction is a type of fiction based on real or imagined scientific and technological developments. A science fiction writer generally uses realistic characters but almost always places them in a futuristic setting. Science fiction helps readers imagine what the future might be like.

WORDS TO KNOW **Vocabulary Preview**
accede   circuit   complex   diffidently   neurotic

ACTIVE READING **PREDICTING**

Active readers use information from the work they are reading and from what they already know to make logical **predictions** about plot, character, and setting. As you read the selection, jot down in your [📖]**READER'S NOTEBOOK** details that may help you predict what the key item mentioned in the title might be.

Key Item

by
Isaac Asimov

Illustration by Franco Accornero

Jack Weaver came out of the vitals of Multivac looking utterly worn and disgusted.

From the stool, where the other maintained his own stolid watch, Todd Nemerson said, "Nothing?"

"Nothing," said Weaver. "Nothing, nothing, nothing. No one can find anything wrong with it."

"Except that it won't work, you mean."

"You're no help sitting there!"

"I'm thinking."

"Thinking!" Weaver showed a canine at one side of his mouth.

Nemerson stirred impatiently on his stool. "Why not? There are six teams of computer technologists roaming around in the corridors of

Multivac. They haven't come up with anything in three days. Can't you spare one person to think?"

"It's not a matter of thinking. We've got to look. Somewhere a relay[1] is stuck."

"It's not that simple, Jack!"

"Who says it's simple? You know how many million relays we have there?"

"That doesn't matter. If it were just a relay, Multivac would have alternate circuits, devices for locating the flaw, and facilities to repair or replace the ailing part. The trouble is, Multivac won't only not answer the original question, it won't tell us what's wrong with it. —And meanwhile, there'll be panic in every city if we don't do something. The world's economy depends on Multivac, and everyone knows that."

"I know it, too. But what's there to do?"

"I told you, *think*. There must be something we're missing completely. Look, Jack, there isn't a computer bigwig in a hundred years who hasn't devoted himself to making Multivac more complicated. It can do so much

"Next you'll be saying Multivac is human."

now—it can even talk and listen. It's practically as complex as the human brain. We can't understand the human brain, so why should we understand Multivac?"

"Aw, come on. Next you'll be saying Multivac is human."

"Why not?" Nemerson grew absorbed and seemed to sink into himself. "Now that you mention it, why not? Could we tell if Multivac passed the thin dividing line where it stopped being a machine and started being human? *Is* there a dividing line, for that matter? If the

brain is just more complex than Multivac, and we keep making Multivac more complex, isn't there a point where . . ." He mumbled down into silence.

Weaver said impatiently, "What are you driving at? Suppose Multivac were human. How would that help us find out why it isn't working?"

"For a human reason, maybe. Suppose *you* were asked the most probable price of wheat next summer and didn't answer. Why wouldn't you answer?"

"Because I wouldn't know. But Multivac would know! We've given it all the factors. It can analyze futures in weather, politics, and economics. We know it can. It's done it before."

"All right. Suppose I asked the question and you knew the answer but didn't tell me. Why not?"

Weaver snarled, "Because I had a brain tumor. Because I had been knocked out. Because my machinery was out of order. That's just what we're trying to find out about Multivac. We're looking for the place where its machinery is out of order, for the key item."

"Only you haven't found it."

Nemerson got off his stool.

"Listen, ask me the question Multivac stalled on."

"How? Shall I run the tape through you?"

"Come on, Jack. Give me the talk that goes along with it. You do talk to Multivac, don't you?"

"I've got to. Therapy."

Nemerson nodded. "Yes, that's the story. Therapy. That's the official story. We talk to it in order to pretend it's a human being so that

---

1. **relay:** a device that responds to a small current or voltage charge by activating switches on an electric circuit.

we don't get <u>neurotic</u> over having a machine know so much more than we do. We turn a frightening metal monster into a protective father image."

"If you want to put it that way."

"Well, it's wrong and you know it. A computer as complex as Multivac *must* talk and listen to be efficient. Just putting in and taking out coded dots[2] isn't sufficient. At a certain level of complexity, Multivac must be made to seem human because, it *is* human. Come on, Jack, ask me the question. I want to see my reaction to it."

Jack Weaver flushed. "This is silly."

"Come on, will you?"

It was a measure of Weaver's depression and desperation that he <u>acceded</u>. Half sullenly, he pretended to be feeding the program into Multivac, speaking as he did so in his usual manner. He commented on the latest information concerning farm unrest, talked about the new equations describing jet-stream[3] contortions, lectured on the solar constant.[4]

He began stiffly enough, but warmed to this task out of long habit, and when the last of the program was slammed home, he almost closed contact with a physical snap at Todd Nemerson's waist.

He ended briskly, "All right, now. Work that out and give us the answer pronto."

For a moment, having done, Jack Weaver stood there, nostrils flaring, as though he was feeling once more the excitement of throwing into action the most gigantic and glorious machine ever put together by the mind and hands of man.

Then he remembered and muttered, "All right. That's it."

Nemerson said, "At least I know now why *I* wouldn't answer, so let's try that on Multivac. Look, clear Multivac; make sure the investigators have their paws off it. Then run the program into it and let me do the talking. Just once."

Weaver shrugged and turned to Multivac's control wall, filled with its somber, unwinking dials and lights. Slowly he cleared it. One by one he ordered the teams away.

Then, with a deep breath, he began once more feeding the program into Multivac. It was the twelfth time all told, the dozenth time.

He paused and added the key item.

Somewhere a distant news commentator would spread the word that they were trying again. All over the world a Multivac-dependent people would be holding its collective breath.

Nemerson talked as Weaver fed the data silently. He talked <u>diffidently</u>, trying to remember what it was that Weaver had said, but waiting for the moment when the key item might be added.

Weaver was done and now a note of tension was in Nemerson's voice. He said, "All right, now, Multivac. Work that out and give us the answer." He paused and added the key item. He said *"Please!"*

And all over Multivac, the valves and relays went joyously to work. After all, a machine has feelings—when it isn't a machine anymore. ❖

---

2. **coded dots:** a reference to an older method of giving a computer directions by inserting a coded instruction card.

3. **jet-stream:** a long, wandering current of high-speed winds, generally blowing from a westerly direction. The winds often exceed 250 miles per hour at altitudes of 10 to 15 miles above Earth.

4. **solar constant:** the average density of solar radiation, measured outside of Earth's atmosphere.

WORDS TO KNOW

accede (ăk-sēd′) *v.* to consent due to outside influences
diffidently (dĭf′ĭ-dənt-lē) *adv.* reserved or restrained in manner
neurotic (noŏ-rŏt′ĭk) *adj.* having excessive anxiety and emotional upset

Connect to the Literature

1. What Do You Think? Does it seem possible to you that a computer could have feelings? Share your thoughts with a classmate.

Comprehension Check
- What problem is Multivac having as the story begins?
- Why do the programmers talk to Multivac and pretend it is human?
- What does the "key item" turn out to be?

Think Critically

2. What do you think the dividing line between being a machine and becoming human might be? Do you think Multivac crossed the line?

3. | ACTIVE READING | PREDICTING |
Review the notes you took in your 📖 READER'S NOTEBOOK. Did the details you selected help you predict accurately what the key item was? Explain.

4. Do you think the people in the story have become too dependent on the computer? Why or why not?

5. Why do you think Weaver doesn't want to hear Nemerson's ideas about solving the computer problem?

> **Think About:**
> - the pressure of the situation
> - all of the people already working on Multivac
> - Nemerson's different way of thinking

Extend Interpretations

6. | COMPARING TEXTS | In both "Key Item" and "An Ordinary Day, with Peanuts" (page 348), there is a surprise ending. In your opinion, which is the better surprise ending? Why?

7. Connect to Life Think about other machines, besides computers, that we sometimes give human characteristics. Have you ever talked to or become angry with a machine? Discuss in small groups.

Literary Analysis

SCIENCE FICTION Fiction based on real or imagined scientific and technological advances is called **science fiction.** The characters of science fiction may be either realistic or imaginary, but the plot of a work of science fiction is usually set in the future. Science fiction allows writers and readers to imagine what the unforeseen results of scientific and technological developments might be in the distant future.

In "Key Item," Isaac Asimov suggests that some day computers will be able to think and feel like human beings. Do you think that will happen? What changes would such an occurrence bring about in the the world?

Paired Activity With a partner, reread "Key Item" and look for details that identify it as a work of science fiction. Jot down your findings. Then discuss these questions with your partner:

- What details suggested that this story was written several decades ago?
- What did you find most surprising about Asimov's prediction of the future?

Setting	Scientific Language
• computer of the "future"	• Multivac
	• million relays

Writing

Science Fiction Do you have any ideas about technology in the future? Try your hand at science fiction. Write your own story about an important scientific advance that might take place in the future. How might it affect people's daily lives? Place your story in your **Working Portfolio.**

Writing Handbook
See p. R45: Narrative Writing.

Speaking & Listening

Talking Computer Imagine that the computer you were working on suddenly began talking to you. What would it say? What would you say back? Write such a dialogue and then read it to the class. If you wish, have a classmate read the lines with you. Use appropriate vocal inflection to distinguish the computer voice from the human voice.

Research & Technology

SCIENCE

Have you ever wished that you could tell the computer what to write, instead of typing the words in yourself? Scientists have developed technology so you can do just that. Voice-recognition software allows people to instruct their computer simply by speaking to it. Find out more about voice-recognition programs by searching science and computer magazines and the Internet.

Research and Technology Handbook
See p. R110: Getting Information Electronically.

Isaac Asimov
1920–1992

"I do not fear computers. I fear the lack of them."

Love at First Sight Isaac Asimov was born in the Soviet Union but left at age three when his parents immigrated to the United States. Once here, his parents opened several candy stores. It was at one of these stores that Asimov first saw a science fiction magazine. He was hooked from the beginning. Soon, Asimov was writing his own science fiction stories. He submitted his first manuscript to the magazine *Astounding Science* when he was 18.

Popular Writer Although his first stories were rejected by publishers, Asimov was not discouraged and went on to publish hundreds of stories, articles, and books. He has been called "the world's most prolific science writer." In his books, Asimov was able to popularize difficult scientific concepts and introduce new ones. The term *robotics,* for example, is his invention. Asimov wrote not only science fiction but fantasy, mystery, and nonfiction on such topics as astronomy, mathematics, history, and the Bible.

The Serial Garden

by JOAN AIKEN

Key Standard
R3.1 Be able to describe the purposes and characteristics of different forms of prose, such as the short story, novel, or essay.
***Other Standards* R1.3, R3.6, W1.2, W2.1, W2.3, LC1.1**

Connect to Your Life

Fantasies The story you are about to read is a fantasy. Lewis Carroll's *Alice's Adventures in Wonderland* is an example of a well-known fantasy. What other fantasies have you read or seen? Do you have any favorites? Compare your favorites with those of your classmates.

Build Background

SOCIAL STUDIES

"The Serial Garden" is part of a collection of short stories titled *Armitage, Armitage, Fly Away Home,* by Joan Aiken, published in 1968. The story, probably set in the late 1940s or early 1950s in England, portrays the English love of beautiful gardens. Even the smallest English cottage is likely to be adorned with colorful, carefully tended flower gardens.

Focus Your Reading

LITERARY CONCEPT **FANTASY**

The type of fiction in which impossible and often wondrous events occur is called **fantasy.** Unlike science fiction, which usually involves a future world that is explainable in terms of scientific or technological advances, fantasy involves magic, which cannot be explained. Fantasies can take place in realistic settings or in make-believe ones.

ACTIVE READING **PREDICTING**

Below are ten terms that relate to "The Serial Garden." Use the terms, the story's title, and your knowledge of fantasy to help you predict what might happen in the story.

1. boy
2. corner store
3. cereal box
4. cereal
5. garden
6. princess
7. magic spell
8. teacher
9. shaggy dog
10. spring cleaning

READER'S NOTEBOOK Jot your prediction down in your notebook. As you read, compare your prediction with the actual events. Change your prediction if you uncover new clues. Include the clues that help you change your mind.

WORDS TO KNOW **Vocabulary Preview**				
aggrievedly	convalescing	gaudy	susceptible	vigil
chaos	forage	incalculable	tantalizing	wan

The Serial Garden

BY JOAN AIKEN

"Cold rice pudding for breakfast?" said Mark, looking at it with disfavor.

"Don't be fussy," said his mother. "You're the only one who's complaining." This was unfair, for she and Mark were the only members of the family at table, Harriet having developed measles while staying with a school friend, while Mr. Armitage had somehow managed to lock himself in the larder.[1] Mrs. Armitage never had anything but toast and marmalade for breakfast anyway.

Mark went on scowling at the chilly-looking pudding. It had come straight out of the fridge, which was not in the larder.

"If you don't like it," said Mrs. Armitage, "unless you want Daddy to pass your corn flakes through the larder ventilator, flake by flake, you'd better run down to Miss Pride and get a small packet of cereal. She opens at eight; Hickmans doesn't open till nine. It's no use waiting till the blacksmith comes to let your father out; I'm sure he won't be here for hours yet."

There came a gloomy banging from the direction of the larder, just to remind them that Mr. Armitage was alive and suffering in there.

"*You're* all right," shouted Mark heartlessly as he passed the larder door. "There's nothing to stop you having corn flakes. Oh, I forgot, the milk's in the fridge. Well, have cheese and pickles then. Or treacle tart."[2]

Even through the zinc grating on the door he could hear his father shudder at the thought of treacle tart and pickles for breakfast. Mr. Armitage's imprisonment was his own fault, though; he had sworn that he was going to find out where the mouse got into the larder if it took him all night, watching and waiting. He had shut himself in, so that no member of the family should come bursting in and disturb his vigil. The larder door had a spring catch which sometimes jammed; it was bad luck that this turned out to be one of the times.

Mark ran across the fields to Miss Pride's shop at Sticks Corner and asked if she had any corn flakes.

"Oh, I don't think I have any left, dear," Miss Pride said woefully. "I'll have a look. . . . I think I sold the last packet a week ago Tuesday."

"What about the one in the window?"

"That's a dummy, dear."

Miss Pride's shop window was full of nasty, dingy old cardboard cartons with nothing inside them, and several empty display stands which had fallen down and never been propped up again. Inside the shop were a few small, tired-looking tins and jars, which had a worn and scratched appearance as if mice had tried them and given up. Miss Pride herself was small and wan, with yellowish gray hair; she rooted rather hopelessly in a pile of empty boxes. Mark's mother never bought any groceries from Miss Pride's if she could help it, since the day when she had found a label inside the foil wrapping of a cream cheese saying, "This cheese should be eaten before May 11, 1899."

"No corn flakes I'm afraid, dear."

"Any wheat crispies? Puffed corn? Rice nuts?"

"No, dear. Nothing left, only Brekkfast Brikks."

"Never heard of *them*," said Mark doubtfully.

"Or I've a jar of Ovo here. You spread it on bread. That's nice for breakfast," said Miss

---

1. larder: pantry.
2. treacle (trē′kəl) tart: a small pastry made with molasses.

Pride, with a sudden burst of salesmanship. Mark thought the Ovo looked beastly, like yellow paint, so he took the packet of Brekkfast Brikks. At least it wasn't very big. . . . On the front of the box was a picture of a fat, repulsive, fair-haired boy, rather like the chubby Augustus, banging on his plate with his spoon.

"They look like tiny door-mats," said Mrs. Armitage, as Mark shoveled some Brikks into the bowl.

"They taste like them too. Gosh," said Mark, "I must hurry or I'll be late for school. There's rather a nice cutout garden on the back of the packet though; don't throw it away when it's empty, Mother. Good-by, Daddy," he shouted through the larder door; "hope Mr. Ellis comes soon to let you out." And he dashed off to catch the school bus.

At breakfast next morning Mark had a huge helping of Brekkfast Brikks and persuaded his father to try them.

"They taste just like esparto grass,"[3] said Mr. Armitage fretfully.

"Yes I know, but do take some more, Daddy. I want to cut out the model garden; it's so lovely."

"Rather pleasant, I must say. It looks like an eighteenth-century German engraving," his father agreed. "It certainly was a stroke of genius putting it on the packet. No one would ever buy these things to eat for pleasure. Pass me the sugar, please. And the cream. And the strawberries."

It was the half-term holiday, so after breakfast Mark was able to take the empty packet

"THEY LOOK LIKE TINY DOORMATS"

. . .

"THEY TASTE LIKE THEM TOO."

away to the playroom and get on with the job of cutting out the stone walls, the row of little trees, the fountain, the yew arch, the two green lawns, and the tiny clumps of brilliant flowers. He knew better than to "stick tabs in slots and secure with paste," as the directions suggested; he had made models from packets before and knew they always fell to pieces unless they were firmly bound together with transparent sticky tape.

It was a long, fiddling, pleasurable job.

Nobody interrupted him. Mrs. Armitage only cleaned the playroom once every six months or so, when she made a ferocious descent on it and tidied up the tape recorders, roller skates, meteorological sets, and dismantled railway engines, and threw away countless old magazines, stringless tennis rackets, abandoned paintings, and unsuccessful models. There were always bitter complaints from Mark and Harriet; then they forgot, and things piled up again till next time.

As Mark worked, his eye was caught by a verse on the outside of the packet:

"Brekkfast Brikks to start the day
Make you fit in every way.
Children bang their plates with glee
At Brekkfast Brikks for lunch and tea!
Brekkfast Brikks for supper too
Give peaceful sleep the whole night through."

---

3. **esparto** (ĭ-spär′tō) **grass**: long, coarse grass used in making rope, shoes, and paper.

Portrait of Ari Redon (about 1898), Odilon Redon. Pastel on paper, 44.8 × 30.8 cm, The Art Institute of Chicago, gift of Kate L. Brewster (1950.130). Photo Copyright © 1994 The Art Institute of Chicago, all rights reserved.

"Blimey," thought Mark, sticking a cedar tree into the middle of the lawn and then bending a stone wall round at dotted lines A, B, C, and D. "I wouldn't want anything for breakfast, lunch, tea, and supper, not even Christmas pudding. Certainly not Brekkfast Brikks."

He propped a clump of gaudy scarlet flowers against the wall and stuck them in place.

The words of the rhyme kept coming into his head as he worked, and presently he found that they went rather well to a tune that was running through his mind, and he began to hum, and then to sing; Mark often did this when he was alone and busy.

"Brekkfast Brikks to sta-art the day,
Ma-ake you fi-it in every way—

"Blow, where did I put that little bit of sticky tape? Oh, there it is.

"Children bang their pla-ates with glee
At Brekkfast Brikks for lunch and tea

"Slit gate with razor blade, it says, but it'll have to be a penknife.

"Brekkfast Brikks for supper toohoo
Give peaceful sleep the whole night throughoo. . . .

"Hullo. That's funny," said Mark.

It was funny. The openwork iron gate he had just stuck in position now suddenly towered above him. On either side, to right and left, ran the high stone wall, stretching away into foggy distance. Over the top of the wall he could see tall trees, yews and cypresses and others he didn't know.

"Well, that's the neatest trick I ever saw," said Mark. "I wonder if the gate will open."

He chuckled as he tried it, thinking of the larder door. The gate did open, and he went through into the garden.

One of the things that had already struck him as he cut them out was that the flowers were not at all in the right proportions. But they were all the nicer for that. There were huge velvety violets and pansies the size of saucers; the hollyhocks were as big as dinner plates, and the turf was sprinkled with enormous daisies. The roses, on the other hand, were miniature, no bigger than cuff buttons. There were real fish in the fountain, bright pink.

"I made all this," thought Mark, strolling along the mossy path to the yew arch. "Won't Harriet be surprised when she sees it. I wish she could see it now. I wonder what made it come alive like that."

He passed through the yew arch as he said this and discovered that on the other side there was nothing but gray, foggy blankness. This, of course, was where his cardboard garden had ended. He turned back through the archway and gazed with pride at a border of huge scarlet tropical flowers which were perhaps supposed to be geraniums but certainly hadn't turned out that way. "I know! Of course, it was the rhyme, the rhyme on the packet."

He recited it. Nothing happened. "Perhaps you have to sing it," he thought, and (feeling a little foolish) he sang it through to the tune that fitted so well. At once, faster than blowing out a match, the garden drew itself together and shrank into its cardboard again, leaving Mark outside.

"What a marvelous hiding place it'll make when I don't want people to come bothering,"

WORDS
TO
KNOW   **gaudy** (gô′dē) *adj.* excessively bright and showy

443

he thought. He sang the spell once more, just to make sure that it worked, and there was the high mossy wall, the stately iron gate, and the treetops. He stepped in and looked back. No playroom to be seen, only gray blankness.

At that moment he was startled by a tremendous clanging, the sort of sound the Trump of Doom[4] would make if it was a dinner bell. "Blow," he thought, "I suppose that's lunch." He sang the spell for the fourth time; immediately he was in the playroom, and the garden was on the floor beside him, and Agnes was still ringing the dinner bell outside the door.

"All right, I heard," he shouted. "Just coming."

He glanced hurriedly over the remains of the packet to see if it bore any mention of the fact that the cutout garden had magic properties. It did not. He did, however, learn that this was Section Three of the Beautiful Brekkfast Brikk Garden Series, and that Sections One, Two, Four, Five, and Six would be found on other packets. In case of difficulty in obtaining supplies, please write to Fruhstucksgeschirr-ziegelsteinindustrie (Great Britain), Lily Road, Shepherds Bush.

"Elevenpence a packet," Mark murmured to himself, going to lunch with unwashed hands. "Five elevens are thirty-five. Thirty-five pennies are—no, that's wrong. Fifty-five pence are four-and-sevenpence. Father, if I mow the lawn and carry coal every day for a month, can I have four shillings and sevenpence?"

"You don't want to buy another space gun, do you?" said Mr. Armitage looking at him suspiciously. "Because one is quite enough in this family."

"No, it's not for a space gun, I swear."

"Oh, very well."

"And can I have the four-and-seven now?"

Mr. Armitage gave it reluctantly. "But that lawn has to be like velvet, mind," he said. "And if there's any falling off in the coal supply, I shall demand my money back."

"No, no, there won't be," Mark promised in reply. As soon as lunch was over, he dashed down to Miss Pride's. Was there a chance that she would have Sections One, Two, Four, Five, and Six? He felt certain that no other shop had even heard of Brekkfast Brikks, so she was his only hope, apart from the address in Shepherds Bush.

"Oh, I don't know, I'm sure," Miss Pride said, sounding very doubtful—and more than a little surprised. "There might just be a couple on the bottom shelf—yes, here we are."

They were Sections Four and Five, bent and dusty, but intact, Mark saw with relief. "Don't you suppose you have any more anywhere?" he pleaded.

"I'll look in the cellar, but I can't promise. I haven't had deliveries of any of these for a long time. Made by some foreign firm they were; people didn't seem very keen on them," Miss Pride said aggrievedly. She opened a door revealing a flight of damp stone stairs. Mark followed her down them like a bloodhound on the trail.

*T*he cellar was a fearful confusion of mildewed, tattered, and toppling cartons, some full, some empty. Mark was nearly knocked cold by a shower of pilchards

---

4. **Trump of Doom:** the trumpet that, according to the Bible, will be blown to signal the end of the world.

in tins,[5] which he dislodged onto himself from the top of a heap of boxes. At last Miss Pride, with a cry of triumph, unearthed a little cache of Brekkfast Brikks, three packets which turned out to be the remaining sections, Six, One, and Two.

"There, isn't that a piece of luck now!" she said, looking quite faint with all the excitement. It was indeed rare for Miss Pride to sell as many as five packets of the same thing at one time.

Mark galloped home with his booty and met his father on the porch. Mr. Armitage let out a groan of dismay.

"I'd almost rather you'd bought a space gun," he said. Mark chanted in reply:

"Brekkfast Brikks for supper too
Give peaceful sleep the whole
    night through."

"I don't want peaceful sleep," Mr. Armitage said. "I intend to spend tonight mouse watching again. I'm tired of finding footprints in the Stilton."[6]

During the next few days Mark's parents watched anxiously to see, Mr. Armitage said, whether Mark would start to sprout esparto grass instead of hair. For he doggedly ate Brekkfast Brikks for lunch, with soup, or sprinkled over his pudding; for tea, with jam; and for supper lightly fried in dripping, not to mention, of course, the immense helpings he had for breakfast with sugar and milk.

BREKKFAST BRIKKS FOR SUPPER TOO GIVE PEACEFUL SLEEP THE WHOLE NIGHT THROUGH.

Mr. Armitage for his part soon gave out; he said he wouldn't taste another Brekkfast Brikk even if it were wrapped in an inch-thick layer of *pâté de foie gras*.[7] Mark regretted that Harriet, who was a handy and uncritical eater, was still away, convalescing from her measles with an aunt.

In two days the second packet was finished (sundial, paved garden, and espaliers[8]). Mark cut it out, fastened it together, and joined it onto Section Three with trembling hands. Would the spell work for this section, too? He sang the rhyme in rather a quavering voice, but luckily the playroom door was shut and there was no one to hear him. Yes! The gate grew again above him, and when he opened it and ran across the lawn through the yew arch, he found himself in a flagged garden full of flowers like huge blue cabbages.

Mark stood hugging himself with satisfaction and then began to wander about smelling the flowers, which had a spicy perfume most unlike any flower he could think

---

5. **pilchards** (pĭl'chərdz) **in tins:** cans of sardines.

6. **Stilton:** a rich, crumbly cheese.

7. *pâté de foie gras* (pä-tā' də fwä grä') *French:* a food made of chopped goose livers, often eaten spread on crackers.

8. **espaliers** (ĭ-spăl'yərz): trees or shrubs trained to grow flat against a wall.

of. Suddenly he pricked up his ears. Had he caught a sound? There! It was like somebody crying and seemed to come from the other side of the hedge. He ran to the next opening and looked through. Nothing: only gray mist and emptiness. But, unless he had imagined it, just before he got there, he thought his eye had caught the flash of white-and-gold draperies swishing past the gateway.

"Do you think Mark's all right?" Mrs. Armitage said to her husband next day. "He seems to be in such a dream all the time."

"Boy's gone clean off his rocker if you ask me," grumbled Mr. Armitage. "It's all these doormats he's eating. Can't be good to stuff your insides with moldy jute.[9] Still I'm bound to say he's cut the lawn very decently and seems to be remembering the coal. I'd better take a day off from the office and drive you over to the shore for a picnic; sea air will do him good."

Mrs. Armitage suggested to Mark that he should slack off on the Brekkfast Brikks, but he was so horrified that she had to abandon the idea. But, she said, he was to run four times round the garden every morning before breakfast. Mark almost said, "Which garden?" but stopped just in time. He had cut out and completed another large lawn, with a lake and weeping willows, and on the far side of the lake had a <u>tantalizing</u> glimpse of a figure dressed in white and gold who moved away and was lost before he could get there.

After munching his way through the fourth packet, he was able to add on a broad grass walk bordered by curiously clipped trees. At the end of the walk he could see the white-and-gold person, but when he ran to the spot, no one was there—the walk ended in the usual gray mist.

When he had finished and had cut out the fifth packet (an orchard), a terrible thing happened to him. For two days he could not remember the tune that worked the spell. He tried other tunes, but they were no use. He sat in the playroom singing till he was hoarse or silent with despair. Suppose he never remembered it again?

His mother shook her head at him that evening and said he looked as if he needed a dose. "It's lucky we're going to Shinglemud Bay for the day tomorrow," she said. "That ought to do you good."

"Oh, *blow*. I'd forgotten about that," Mark said. "Need I go?"

His mother stared at him in utter astonishment.

But in the middle of the night he remembered the right tune, leaped out of bed in a tremendous hurry, and ran down to the playroom without even waiting to put on his dressing gown and slippers.

The orchard was most wonderful, for instead of mere apples its trees bore oranges, lemons, limes and all sorts of tropical fruits whose names he did not know, and there were melons and pineapples growing, and plantains and avocados. Better still, he saw the lady in her white and gold waiting at the end of an alley and was able to draw near enough to speak to her.

"Who are you?" she asked. She seemed very much astonished at the sight of him.

"My name's Mark Armitage," he said politely. "Is this your garden?"

---

9. **jute:** a strong fiber used for making mats, rope, and sacks.

446

Illustration by Ruth Sanderson.

Close to, he saw that she was really very grand indeed. Her dress was white satin, embroidered with pearls, and swept the ground; she had a gold scarf, and her hair, dressed high and powdered, was confined in a small gold-and-pearl tiara. Her face was rather plain, pink with a long nose, but she had a kind expression and beautiful gray eyes.

"Indeed it is," she announced with hauteur. "I am Princess Sophia Maria Louisa of Saxe-Hoffenpoffen-und-Hamster. What are you doing here, pray?"

"Well," Mark explained cautiously, "it seemed to come about through singing a tune."

"Indeed. That is most interesting. Did the tune, perhaps, go like this?"

The princess hummed a few bars.

"That's it! How did you know?"

"Why, you foolish boy, it was I who put the spell on the garden, to make it come alive when the tune is played or sung."

"I say!" Mark was full of admiration. "Can you do spells as well as being a princess?"

She drew herself up. "Naturally! At the court of Saxe-Hoffenpoffen, where I was educated, all princesses were taught a little magic, not so much as to be vulgar, just enough to get out of social difficulties."

"Jolly useful," Mark said. "How did you work the spell for the garden, then?"

"Why, you see," (the princess was obviously delighted to have somebody to talk to; she sat on a stone seat and patted it, inviting Mark to do likewise) "I had the misfortune to fall in love with Herr Rudolf, the court Kapellmeister,[10] who taught me music. Oh, he was so kind and handsome! And he was most talented, but my father, of course, would not hear of my marrying him because he was only a common person."

"So what did you do?"

"I arranged to vanish, of course. Rudi had given me a beautiful book with many pictures of gardens. My father kept strict watch to see I did not run away, so I used to slip between the pages of the book when I wanted to be alone. Then, when we decided to marry, I asked my maid to take the book to Rudi. And I sent him a note telling him to play the tune when he received the book. But I believe that spiteful Gertrud must have played me false and never taken the book, for more than fifty years have now passed and I have been here all alone, waiting in the garden, and Rudi has never come. Oh, Rudi, Rudi," she exclaimed, wringing her hands and crying a little, "where can you be? It is so long—so long!"

"Fifty years," Mark said kindly, reckoning that must make her nearly seventy. "I must say you don't look it."

"Of course I do not, dumbhead. For me, I make it that time does not touch me. But tell me, how did you know the tune that works the spell? It was taught me by my dear Rudi."

"I'm not sure where I picked it up," Mark confessed. "For all I know it may be one of the Top Ten. I'll ask my music teacher; he's sure to know. Perhaps he'll have heard of your Rudolf too."

Privately Mark feared that Rudolf might very well have died by now, but he did not like to depress Princess Sophia Maria by such a suggestion, so he bade her a polite good night, promising to come back as soon as he could with another section of the garden and any news he could pick up.

---

10. **Kapellmeister** (kə-pĕl′mī′stər): the leader of a choir or orchestra.

He planned to go and see Mr. Johansen, his music teacher, next morning, but he had forgotten the family trip to the beach. There was just time to scribble a hasty post card to the British office of Fruhstucksgeschirrziegelsteinindustrie, asking them if they could inform him from what source they had obtained the pictures used on the packets of Brekkfast Brikks. Then Mr. Armitage drove his wife and son to Shinglemud Bay, gloomily prophesying wet weather.

In fact, the weather turned out fine, and Mark found it quite restful to swim and play beach cricket and eat ham sandwiches and lie in the sun. For he had been struck by a horrid thought: suppose he should forget the tune again when he was inside the garden—would he be stuck there, like Father in the larder? It was a lovely place to go and wander at will, but somehow he didn't fancy spending the next fifty years there with Princess Sophia Maria. Would she oblige him by singing the spell if he forgot it, or would she be too keen on company to let him go? He was not inclined to take any chances.

It was late when they arrived home, too late, Mark thought, to disturb Mr. Johansen, who was elderly and kept early hours. Mark ate a huge helping of sardines on Brekkfast Brikks for supper—he was dying to finish Section Six—but did not visit the garden that night.

Next morning's breakfast (Brikks with hot milk, for a change) finished the last packet—and just as well, for the larder mouse, which Mr. Armitage still had not caught, was discovered to have nibbled the bottom left-hand corner of the packet, slightly damaging an ornamental grotto[11] in a grove of lime trees. Rather worried about this, Mark decided to make up the last section straightaway, in case the magic had been affected. By now he was becoming very skillful at the tiny fiddling task of cutting out the little tabs and slipping them into the little slots; the job did not take long to finish. Mark attached Section Six to Section Five and then, drawing a deep breath, sang the incantation[12] once more. With immense relief he watched the mossy wall and rusty gate grow out of the playroom floor; all was well.

He raced across the lawn, round the lake, along the avenue, through the orchard, and into the lime grove. The scent of the lime flowers was sweeter than a cake baking.

Princess Sophia Maria came towards him from the grotto, looking slightly put out.

"Good morning!" she greeted Mark. "Do you bring me any news?"

"I haven't been to see my music teacher yet," Mark confessed. "I was a bit anxious because there was a hole—"

"Ach, yes, a hole in the grotto! I have just been looking. Some wild beast must have made its way in, and I am afraid it may come again. See, it has made tracks like those of a big bear." She showed him some enormous footprints in the soft sand of the grotto floor. Mark stopped up the hole with prickly branches and promised to bring a dog when he next came, though he felt fairly sure the mouse would not return.

"I can borrow a dog from my teacher—he has plenty. I'll be back in an hour or so—see you then," he said.

"*Auf Wiedersehen,*[13] my dear young friend." Mark ran along the village street to Mr.

---

11. **grotto:** a structure made to look like a small cave.

12. **incantation** (ĭn′kăn-tā′shən): magic spell.

13. *auf Wiedersehen* (ouf vē′dər-zā′ən) *German:* goodbye.

Johansen's house, Houndshaven Cottage. He knew better than to knock at the door because Mr. Johansen would be either practicing his violin or out in the barn at the back, and in any case the sound of barking was generally loud enough to drown any noise short of gunfire.

*B*esides giving music lessons at Mark's school, Mr. Johansen kept a guest house for dogs whose owners were abroad or on holiday. He was extremely kind to the guests and did his best to make them feel at home in every way, finding out from their owners what were their favorite foods, and letting them sleep on his own bed, turn about. He spent all his spare time with them, talking to them and playing either his violin or long-playing records of domestic sounds likely to appeal to the canine fancy—such as knives being sharpened, cars starting up, and children playing ball games.

Mark could hear Mr. Johansen playing Brahms's lullaby in the barn, so he went out there; the music was making some of the more susceptible inmates feel homesick: howls, sympathetic moans, and long shuddering sighs came from the numerous comfortably carpeted cubicles all the way down the barn.

Mr. Johansen reached the end of the piece as Mark entered. He put down his fiddle and smiled welcomingly.

"Ach, how *gut!* It is the young Mark."

"Hullo, sir."

"You know," confided Mr. Johansen, "I play to many audiences in my life all over the world, but never anywhere do I get such a response as from zese dear doggies—it is really remarkable. But come in; come into ze house and have some coffee cake."

Mr. Johansen was a gentle, white-haired elderly man; he walked slowly with a slight stoop and had a kindly, sad face with large dark eyes. He looked rather like some sort of dog himself, Mark always thought, perhaps a collie or a long-haired dachshund.

"Sir," Mark said, "if I whistle a tune to you, can you write it down for me?"

"Why, yes, I shall be most happy," Mr. Johansen said, pouring coffee for both of them.

So Mark whistled his tune once more; as he came to the end, he was surprised to see the music master's eyes fill with tears, which slowly began to trickle down his thin cheeks.

"It recalls my youth, zat piece," he explained, wiping the tears away and rapidly scribbling crotchets and minims on a piece of music paper. "Many times I am whistling it myself—it is wissout doubt from me you learn it—but always it is reminding me of how happy I was long ago when I wrote it."

"You *wrote* that tune?" Mark said, much excited.

"Why yes. What is so strange in zat? Many, many tunes haf I written."

"Well—" Mark said, "I won't tell you just yet in case I'm mistaken—I'll have to see somebody else first. Do you mind if I dash off right away? Oh, and might I borrow a dog—preferably a good ratter?"

"In zat case, better have my dear Lotta—alzough she is so old she is ze best of zem all," Mr. Johansen said proudly. Lotta was his own dog, an enormous shaggy lumbering animal with a tail like a palm tree and feet the size of electric polishers; she was reputed to be of incalculable age; Mr. Johansen called her his

WORDS TO KNOW

susceptible (sə-sĕp′tə-bəl) *adj.* easily affected or influenced
incalculable (ĭn-kăl′kyə-lə-bəl) *adj.* too great to be measured or counted

Le jardin potager, Yerres [The kitchen garden, Yerres] (1875–77), Gustave Caillebotte. Private collection.

strudel-hound. She knew Mark well and came along with him quite biddably, though it was rather like leading a mammoth.

Luckily his mother, refreshed by her day at the sea, was heavily engaged with Agnes the maid in spring cleaning. Furniture was being shoved about, and everyone was too busy to notice Mark and Lotta slip into the playroom.

A letter addressed to Mark lay among the clutter on the table; he opened and read it while Lotta <u>foraged</u> happily among the piles of magazines and tennis nets and cricket bats and rusting electronic equipment, managing to upset several things and increase the general state of huggermugger in the room.

Dear Sir, (the letter said—it was from Messrs. Digit, Digit, & Rule, a firm of chartered accountants)—We are in receipt of your inquiry as to the source of pictures on packets of Brekkfast Brikks. We are pleased to inform you that these were reproduced from the illustrations of a little-known 18th-century German work, *Steinbergen's Gartenbuch.* Unfortunately the only known remaining copy of this book was burnt in the disastrous fire which destroyed the factory and premises of Mssrs.Fruhstucksgeschirrziegelsteinindustrie two months ago. The firm has now gone into liquidation and we are winding up their effects. Yours faithfully, P. J. Zero, Gen. Sec.

"Steinbergen's Gartenbuch," Mark thought. "That must have been the book that Princess Sophia Maria used for the spell—probably the same copy. Oh, well, since it's burned, it's lucky the pictures were reproduced on the Brekkfast Brikks packets. Come on, Lotta, let's go and find a nice princess then. Good girl! Rats! Chase 'em!"

He sang the spell, and Lotta, all enthusiasm, followed him into the garden.

They did not have to go far before they saw the princess—she was sitting sunning herself on the rim of the fountain. But what happened then was unexpected. Lotta let out the most extraordinary cry—whine, bark, and howl all in one—and hurled herself towards the princess like a rocket.

"Hey! Look out! Lotta! *Heel!*" Mark shouted in alarm. But Lotta, with her great paws on the princess's shoulders, had about a yard of salmon-pink tongue out, and was washing the princess's face all over with frantic affection.

The princess was just as excited. "Lotta, Lotta! She knows me; it's dear Lotta; it must be! Where did you get her?" she cried to Mark, hugging the enormous dog, whose tail was going round faster than a turboprop.

"Why, she belongs to my music master, Mr. Johansen, and it's he who made up the tune," Mark said.

The princess turned quite white and had to sit down on the fountain's rim again.

IT'S LUCKY THE PICTURES WERE REPRODUCED ON THE BREKKFAST BRIKKS PACKETS.

"*Johansen?* Rudolf Johansen? My Rudi! At last! After all these years! Oh, run, run, and fetch him immediately, please! Immediately!"

Mark hesitated a moment.

"Please make haste!" she besought him. "Why do you wait?"

"It's only—well, you won't be surprised if he's quite *old*, will you? Remember he hasn't been in a garden keeping young like you."

"All that will change," the princess said confidently. "He has only to eat the fruit of the garden. Why, look at Lotta—when she was a puppy, for a joke I gave her a fig from this tree, and you can see she is a puppy still, though she must be older than any other dog in the world! Oh, please hurry to bring Rudi here."

"Why don't you come with me to his house?"

"That would not be correct etiquette," she said with dignity. "After all, I *am* royal."

"Okay," said Mark. "I'll fetch him. Hope he doesn't think I'm crackers."

"Give him this." The princess took off a locket on a gold chain. It had a miniature of a romantically handsome young man with dark curling hair. "My Rudi," she explained fondly. Mark could just trace a faint resemblance to Mr. Johansen.

He took the locket and hurried away. At the gate something made him look back: the princess and Lotta were sitting at the edge of the fountain, side by side. The princess had an arm round Lotta's neck; with the other hand she waved to him, just a little.

"Hurry!" she called again.

Mark made his way out of the house, through the spring-cleaning <u>chaos</u>, and flew down the village to Houndshaven Cottage. Mr. Johansen was in the house this time, boiling up a noisome mass of meat and bones for the dogs' dinner. Mark said nothing at all, just handed him the locket. He took one look at it and staggered, putting his hand to his heart; anxiously, Mark led him to a chair.

"Are you all right, sir?"

"Yes, yes! It was only ze shock. Where did you get ziss, my boy?"

So Mark told him.

Surprisingly, Mr. Johansen did not find anything odd about the story; he nodded his head several times as Mark related the various points.

"Yes, yes, her letter, I have it still—" he pulled out a worn little scrap of paper, "but ze *Gartenbuch* it reached me never. Zat wicked Gertrud must haf sold it to some bookseller who sold it to Fruhstucksgeschirrziegelsteinindustrie. And so she has been waiting all ziss time! My poor little Sophie!"

"Are you strong enough to come to her now?" Mark asked.

"*Natürlich!* But first we must give ze dogs zeir dinner; zey must not go hungry."

So they fed the dogs, which was a long job as there were at least sixty and each had a different diet, including some very odd preferences like Swiss roll spread with Marmite and yeast pills wrapped in slices of caramel. Privately, Mark thought the dogs were a bit spoiled, but Mr. Johansen was very careful to see that each visitor had just what it fancied.

"After all, zey are not mine! Must I not take good care of zem?"

At least two hours had gone by before the last willow-pattern plate was licked clean, and they were free to go. Mark made rings round Mr. Johansen all the way up the village; the music master limped quietly along, smiling a little; from time to time he said, "Gently, my friend. We do not run a race. Remember I am an old man."

That was just what Mark did remember. He longed to see Mr. Johansen young and happy once more.

The chaos in the Armitage house had changed its location: the front hall was now clean, tidy, and damp; the rumpus of vacuuming had shifted to the playroom. With a black hollow of apprehension in his middle, Mark ran through the open door and stopped, aghast. All the toys, tools, weapons, boxes, magazines, and bits of machinery had been rammed into the cupboards; the floor where his garden had been laid out was bare. Mrs. Armitage was in the playroom taking down the curtains.

"*Mother!* Where's my Brekkfast Brikks garden?"

"Oh, darling, you didn't want it, did you? It was all dusty; I thought you'd finished with it. I'm afraid I've burned it in the furnace. Really you *must* try not to let this room get into such a clutter; it's perfectly disgraceful. Why, hullo, Mr. Johansen," she added in embarrassment. "I didn't see you; I'm afraid you've called at the worst possible moment. But I'm sure you'll understand how it is at spring-cleaning time."

She rolled up her bundle of curtains, glancing worriedly at Mr. Johansen; he looked rather odd, she thought. But he gave her his tired, gentle smile and said, "Why, yes, Mrs. Armitage, I understand; I understand very well. Come, Mark. We have no business here, you can see."

Speechlessly, Mark followed him. What was there to say?

"Never mind," Mrs. Armitage called after Mark. "The Rice Nuts pack has a helicopter on it."

Every week in The Times newspaper you will see this advertisement:

BREKKFAST BRIKKS PACKETS. £100
offered for any in good condition,
whether empty or full.

So, if you have any, you know where to send them.

But Mark is growing anxious; none have come in yet, and every day Mr. Johansen seems a little thinner and more elderly. Besides, what will the princess be thinking? ❖

Connect to the Literature

1. **What Do You Think?**
   What were your thoughts as you finished reading this story?

   Comprehension Check
   • How does Mark get into the magic garden?
   • Whom does Mark meet in the garden?
   • How does Mr. Johansen know the Brekkfast Brikks song?

Think Critically

2. What are some of the things Mark might have done to bring about a different ending to this story? Explain your answer.

3. Do you think Mr. Johansen and Princess Sophia will ever be reunited? Why or why not?

   Think About:
   • the princess's knowledge of magic
   • Mr. Johansen's age and physical condition
   • the advertisement that appears in *The Times* every week

4. If you were in Mark's place, would you go back and forth into the magic garden? Explain your answer.

5. **ACTIVE READING** **PREDICTING**
   Look back at the notes you made in your **READER'S NOTEBOOK**. How do the predictions you made compare to the actual events in the story? If you changed any of your predictions as you were reading, what clues led you to do so?

Extend Interpretations

6. **COMPARING TEXTS** You listed three of your favorite fantasy stories for the Connect to Your Life on page 438. Identify possible themes for each story. How would you compare the theme of "The Serial Garden" with these other stories? Are the themes similar? identical? dissimilar? Explain.

Literary Analysis

FANTASY A **fantasy** is a story that takes place in an unreal, imaginary world, such as the garden in "The Serial Garden." Fantasies often involve magic, characters with superhuman powers, and impossible events. Sometimes the boundary between fantasy and the real world becomes blurred or hard to recognize, as in this passage from the story:

My father kept strict watch to see I did not run away, so I used to slip between the pages of the book when I wanted to be alone.

Paired Activity With a partner, find three other examples of fantasy in "The Serial Garden."

REVIEW: HUMOR Writers often create humor by means of amusing descriptions, witty dialogue, and other devices. What do you find humorous in this story?

CHOICES and CHALLENGES

Writing

Escape Plan At one point, Mark fears that he might forget the magic tune and that Princess Sophia might keep him in the garden for company. If that happened, how could Mark get back home? Write a description of an escape plan he might design. Place your plan in your **Working Portfolio.**

Writing Handbook
See p. R43: Descriptive Writing.

Speaking & Listening

Monologue Write a monologue that shows how Princess Sophia might react when she finds out that Mark and Mr. Johansen have failed to return. Or, with a partner, compose the dialogue between the princess and Mr. Johansen, had they met. Present your monologue or dialogue to a group of classmates.

Speaking and Listening Handbook
See p. R102: Present.

Research & Technology

How many authors of science fiction and fantasy are you familiar with? Choose a time period of ten years anywhere between 1940 and the present, and compile a list of the most famous science fiction or fantasy authors during that time period. Or, you might choose two or three authors you already know and compile a list of their life's work. Were any of the stories made into films? Which ones? You may want to use your lists for further exploration into the genre. List the sources you used in your search.

Research and Technology Handbook
See p. R110: Getting Information Electronically.

Vocabulary

STANDARDIZED TEST PRACTICE

For each sentence below, write the letter of the word that is most nearly opposite in meaning to the underlined Word to Know.

1. Mr. Johansen's music made those dogs that were susceptible howl.
   A sympathetic   C friendly
   B unaffected   D influenced

2. Miss Pride was a small, wan woman with yellowish hair.
   A thin   C unhealthy
   B pale   D depressed

3. Mark had a tantalizing glimpse of someone on the far side of the lake.
   A pleasing   C boring
   B panting   D interesting

4. Mrs. Pride said aggrievedly that not many people liked Brekkfast Brikks.
   A resentfully   C slowly
   B loudly   D merrily

5. The house was in spring-cleaning chaos when Mark left.
   A activity   C order
   B rest   D confusion

EXERCISE Answer the following questions.

1. Is a person who is foraging likely to be arguing, relaxing, or searching?

2. Would a person who has been keeping a vigil be sleepy, happy, or careless?

3. Are the convalescing people in a hospital the doctors, the visitors, or the patients?

4. Would a person be most likely to wear a gaudy outfit to a funeral, a costume party, or a job interview?

5. On a lonely beach, which might you find in incalculable numbers—seals, swimmers, or grains of sand?

Vocabulary Handbook
See p. R26: Synonyms and Antonyms.

Grammar in Context: Placement of Adverbs

Through careful placement of adverbs, writers can emphasize certain words. Notice where Joan Aiken places the **adverbs** in the following sentences.

> Mrs. Armitage only cleaned the playroom once every six months or so, . . .

> Speechlessly, Mark followed him. What was there to say?

In the first sentence, how would the meaning change if *only* appeared before *Mrs. Armitage*? In the second sentence, how would the emphasis change if *speechlessly* were to appear at the end of the sentence rather than the beginning of the sentence?

Apply to Your Writing Changing the position of an adverb in a sentence can vary the meaning and emphasis of the sentence.

WRITING EXERCISE Change the placement of the underlined adverbs. Briefly describe how the change affects the meaning of the sentence.

Example: *Original* The larder door opened and creaked <u>suddenly</u>.

Rewritten Suddenly the larder door opened and and creaked. [Emphasis shifts from the <u>larder door</u> to <u>suddenly</u>.]

1. <u>Surprisingly</u> Mrs. Pride entered the cellar and found some Brikks.
2. Mark <u>slowly</u> tried to remember the tune.
3. The princess smiled <u>nervously</u> as Mark sneaked into her garden.
4. The princess <u>fondly</u> opened the locket.

Grammar Handbook
See p. R82: Using Modifiers Effectively.

Joan Aiken
born 1924

"I find short fantasy much easier to manage than long fantasy. . . . And characters can be much simpler in a short fantasy."

Literary Family Joan Aiken, the daughter of American poet Conrad Aiken, was born and raised in England where she still lives. She spent much of her childhood reading and making up stories to amuse herself and her younger stepbrother. She knew at an early age that she wanted to become a writer, having filled notebooks with poems and stories from the time she was five.

Popular Writer Aiken's husband died when their children were young, and she had to work as an editor at a magazine to support her family, supplementing her income by publishing short stories. In 1960 she revised a novel that she had written when she was 17. It became her first published novel, *The Kingdom and the Cave*. Her first big success came soon after, with *The Wolves of Willoughby Chase*. Marketed as a children's book, it was praised and read by adults as well.

AUTHOR ACTIVITY
The Fate of the Armitages Read more about the Armitages in Aiken's book *Armitage, Armitage, Fly Away Home* and present a short report to the class.

Jabberwocky

by LEWIS CARROLL

Sarah Cynthia Sylvia Stout Would Not Take the Garbage Out

by SHEL SILVERSTEIN

 Key Standard
LS1.6 Use voice, gestures, and eye contact effectively to keep audience interested.
Other Standards **R3.6, W2.3, W2.5**

Connect to Your Life

Challenges Life has many challenges. Some are simple, like making your bed, while others are more risky. Think about a challenge you have had that was either hard to do or that you just didn't want to do. Why was it so hard for you? How did you finally get motivated to do it? Share your experience with your classmates.

Build Background

HISTORY

The two humorous poems you are about to read were written especially for young people. They have fun-to-read language and elements of fantasy. In "Sarah Cynthia Sylvia Stout Would Not Take the Garbage Out," a pile of garbage grows so high it touches the sky.

"Jabberwocky" tells the story of a boy who slays a dragon. Lewis Carroll wrote the poem to go in his book *Through the Looking Glass.* Carroll's books transformed literature for young adults. Before his work, most people felt that children's books should instruct children in more serious matters. Although some of Carroll's work is serious, most historians agree that his playful attitude toward language and his imaginative settings changed writing for young people.

Focus Your Reading

LITERARY ANALYSIS   SOUND DEVICES

Poets use **sound devices** such as **rhyme, rhythm,** and **repetition** to enliven their poems. In **humorous poetry** these devices often are exaggerated for comic effect. Two other sound devices used in the poems you are about to read are alliteration and onomatopoeia. **Alliteration** is the repetition of consonant sounds at the beginnings of words or syllables. *Ten tame tigers* is an example of alliteration. **Onomatopoeia** is the use of sounds that suggest their meaning. *Buzz, crack,* and *gargle* are common onomatopoetic words. Read a poem aloud to best appreciate its sound devices.

ACTIVE READING   CLARIFY

Stopping now and then to reread a difficult passage can help you **clarify** a poem's meaning. You can also clarify the meaning of a poem by reading it aloud.

📖 **READER'S NOTEBOOK** As you read each of the poems aloud, jot down notes about aspects of them that you stop to clarify.

"Jabberwocky"	
A father is telling his son to beware.	The Jabberwock must be dangerous.
The Jabberwock has claws and jaws.	It must be some kind of animal.

Jabberwocky

by Lewis Carroll

'Twas brillig, and the slithy toves
    Did gyre and gimble in the wabe:
All mimsy were the borogoves,
    And the mome raths outgrabe.

5 "Beware the Jabberwock, my son!
    The jaws that bite, the claws that catch!
Beware the Jubjub bird, and shun
    The frumious Bandersnatch!"

He took his vorpal sword in hand:
10   Long time the manxome foe he sought—
So rested he by the Tumtum tree,
    And stood awhile in thought.

And, as in uffish thought he stood,
    The Jabberwock, with eyes of flame,
15 Came whiffling through the tulgey wood,
    And burbled as it came!

One, two! One, two! And through and through
    The vorpal blade went snicker-snack!
He left it dead, and with its head
20   He went galumphing back.

Culver Pictures

"And hast thou slain the Jabberwock?
    Come to my arms, my beamish boy!
O frabjous day! Callooh! Callay!"
    He chortled in his joy.

25 'Twas brillig, and the slithy toves
    Did gyre and gimble in the wabe:
All mimsy were the borogoves,
    And the mome raths outgrabe.

THINKING *through the* LITERATURE

1. How would you describe the Jabberwock? The boy?

2. What do you think "O frabjous day! Callooh! Callay!" means?

Sarah Cynthia Sylvia Stout Would Not Take the Garbage Out

by Shel Silverstein

Sarah Cynthia Sylvia Stout
Would not take the garbage out!
She'd scour the pots and scrape the pans,
Candy the yams and spice the hams,
5   And though her daddy would scream
        and shout,
She simply would not take the garbage
        out.
And so it piled up to the ceilings:
Coffee grounds, potato peelings,
Brown bananas, rotten peas,
10   Chunks of sour cottage cheese.
It filled the can, it covered the floor,
It cracked the window and blocked
        the door
With bacon rinds and chicken bones,
Drippy ends of ice cream cones,
15   Prune pits, peach pits, orange peel,
Gloppy glumps of cold oatmeal,
Pizza crusts and withered greens,
Soggy beans and tangerines,
Crusts of black burned buttered toast,
20   Gristly bits of beefy roasts . . .
The garbage rolled on down the hall,
It raised the roof, it broke the wall . . .
Greasy napkins, cookie crumbs,
Globs of gooey bubble gum,

25   Cellophane from green baloney,
Rubbery blubbery macaroni,
Peanut butter, caked and dry,
Curdled milk and crusts of pie,
Moldy melons, dried-up mustard,
30   Eggshells mixed with lemon custard,
Cold french fries and rancid meat,
Yellow lumps of Cream of Wheat.
At last the garbage reached so high
That finally it touched the sky.
35   And all the neighbors moved away,
And none of her friends would come
        to play.
And finally Sarah Cynthia Stout said,
"OK, I'll take the garbage out!"
But then, of course, it was too late . . .
40   The garbage reached across the state,
From New York to the Golden Gate.
And there, in the garbage she did hate,
Poor Sarah met an awful fate,
That I cannot right now relate
45   Because the hour is much too late.
But children, remember Sarah Stout
And always take the garbage out!

Connect to the Literature

1. **What Do You Think?**
   What is your reaction to Sarah's predicament?

Comprehension Check
- What does the garbage do to Sarah's house?
- How do the neighbors and her friends react?
- How much garbage is there?

Think Critically

2. How does Silverstein make the garbage so vivid?

3. What do you think Sarah Stout's "awful fate" was?

4. What can you infer about Sarah's parents based on this poem? Explain.

   Think About:
   - the chores she had to do
   - her stubbornness
   - the fact that they refused to do Sarah's job for her

5. **ACTIVE READING** **CLARIFY**
   Review the notes you took in your
   READER'S NOTEBOOK. How did reading the poems aloud help you **clarify** their meaning? Compare your notes with those of classmates and discuss differences.

Extend Interpretations

6. **COMPARING TEXTS** How are "Jabberwocky" and "Sarah Cynthia Sylvia Stout Would Not Take the Garbage Out" similar? How are they different? Compare the theme, the writers' purposes, the subjects of the poems, and the sound devices the poets use. A Venn diagram may help you organize your ideas.

7. **Connect to Life** How do you react to a challenge? Are you more like Sarah Stout or the boy in "Jabberwocky"? Explain.

Literary Analysis

SOUND DEVICES Poets use **sound devices,** such as alliteration, onomatopoeia, and rhyme to create a unified effect in their poems.

Alliteration is the repetition of consonant sounds at the beginnings of the words and syllables, as in "Tumtum tree" or "moldy melons."

Onomatopoeia is the use of words whose sounds suggest their meaning. The "snicker-snack" of the "vorpal blade," for example, is an onomatopoeia that suggests the blade's rapid movement.

Another important sound device is **rhyme,** the repetition of sounds at the ends of words. Both poems use rhymes at the ends of lines.

Paired Activity With a partner, go through the poems and create a chart to list examples of **sound devices** you find.

"Jabberwocky"		
alliteration	onomatopoeia	rhyme
Callooh! Callay!	Bandersnatch	toves/borogoves
Tumtum tree		wabe/outgrabe

When you finish, take turns reading the poems aloud to one another. Which poem do you think uses sound devices more effectively?

Writing

Nonsense Poem Both "Jabberwocky" and "Sarah Cynthia Sylvia Stout Would Not Take the Garbage Out" are humorous poems. Write your own rhymed humorous poem, or if you prefer, write a sequel to either of the selected poems, starting where the poet left off.

Summarizing Sarah Stout Imagine that you are a newspaper reporter sent to cover the Sarah Stout story. Write an article summarizing what happened. Be sure your story includes the main idea and most important details of the story. Use quotes from the poem, and be sure there's a beginning, middle, and end. Conclude with a lesson your readers might learn from Sarah Stout's misfortune.

Research & Technology

Poetry Project Find an anthology of humorous poetry and choose a poem you like. Use an encyclopedia or other resource to learn a little about the author. Memorize the poem and perform it for the class. After you recite the poem, tell the class where you found it and provide information about the author.

Speaking and Listening Handbook

See p. R102: Present.

Lewis Carroll
1832–1898

"Oh frabjous day! Callooh! Callay!"

Reading, Writing, and Nonsense Lewis Carroll, whose real name was Charles Lutwidge Dodgson, grew up in a family with ten brothers and sisters in rural England. As a child, he read voraciously and made up nonsense stories. At 12, Carroll left for boarding school. His letters home often included sketches and cartoons in the margins.

Mathematician and Children's Writer After Carroll finished school, he became a mathematician at Oxford University. Many of the stories and poems he wrote grew out of tales he told to the children of friends at Oxford. *Alice's Adventures in Wonderland* and *Through the Looking Glass* have become classics.

Shel Silverstein
1932–1999

"Poor Sarah met an awful fate."

City Kid Shel Silverstein was known for his ability to understand and express young people's fears and silliness. It was during his own childhood that Silverstein turned to writing and drawing. Silverstein grew up in Chicago, where he said he "couldn't play ball, couldn't dance. . . . So I started to draw and write." Silverstein himself created all the drawings for his poetry.

Cartoonist, Composer, Poet Silverstein had many books of poetry and prose to his credit, including the very popular *Where the Sidewalk Ends.* He wrote hundreds of poems. Most are silly or comic, though some are more serious. Silverstein was also a distinguished music composer and song writer.

The Eternal Frontier
by LOUIS L'AMOUR

Connect to Your Life

What frontiers would you like to explore?

Build Background

Sixteen nations are working together to build the International Space Station. One of the project's goals is the promise of conducting valuable scientific research. Another is to encourage international cooperation.

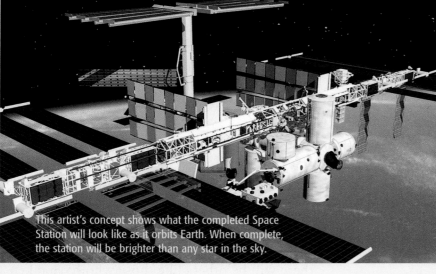

This artist's concept shows what the completed Space Station will look like as it orbits Earth. When complete, the station will be brighter than any star in the sky.

Two astronauts check a module connection during the first stages of construction, December 1998.

Focus Your Reading

LITERARY ANALYSIS PERSUASIVE ESSAY

A **persuasive essay** is a type of nonfiction work that offers an opinion on a subject and tries to sway readers to accept that opinion. A persuasive essay appeals not only to the mind but also to the heart of the reader.

WORDS TO KNOW **Vocabulary Preview**

antidote   impetus   multitude
devastating incorporate

Key Standard
R2.6 Evaluate the strength and accuracy of the evidence an author uses to support a claim. Recognize bias and stereotyping.
Other Standards **R1.3, W2.3, W2.4, LC1.1, LC1.3, LC1.4, LS1.1, LS2.4**

ACTIVE READING EVALUATING

A persuasive essay may be **evaluated** in terms of how well the author supports his or her opinions. Writers use evidence to help convince the reader that their **claims** (opinions) are correct. **Evidence** could be in the form of facts, statistics, examples, or quotations. Questions you might ask when evaluating include: Is the evidence used adequate? accurate? appropriate? What are the writer's biases?

As you read "The Eternal Frontier," evaluate the essay carefully. Record in your
📖 READER'S NOTEBOOK the questions you ask and the opinions you form.

THE ETERNAL FRONTIER

by Louis L'Amour

The question I am most often asked is, "Where is the frontier now?"

The answer should be obvious. Our frontier lies in outer space.

The moon, the asteroids, the planets, these are mere stepping stones, where we will test ourselves, learn needful lessons, and grow in knowledge before we attempt those frontiers beyond our solar system. Outer space is a frontier without end, the eternal frontier, an everlasting challenge to explorers not alone of other planets and other solar systems but also of the mind of man.

All that has gone before was preliminary. We have been preparing ourselves mentally for what lies ahead. Many problems remain, but if we can avoid a <u>devastating</u> war we shall move with a rapidity scarcely to be believed. In the past seventy years we have developed the automobile, radio, television, transcontinental and transoceanic flight, and the electrification of the country, among a <u>multitude</u> of other such developments. In 1900 there were 144 miles of surfaced road in the United States. Now there are over 3,000,000. Paved roads and the development of the automobile have gone hand in hand, the automobile being civilized man's <u>antidote</u> to overpopulation.

What is needed now is leaders with perspective; we need leadership on a thousand fronts, but they must be men and women who can take the long view and help to shape the outlines of our future. There will always be the nay-sayers,[1] those who cling to our lovely green planet as a baby clings to its mother, but there will be others like those who have taken us this far along the path to a limitless future.

We are a people born to the frontier. It has been a part of our thinking, waking, and sleeping since men first landed on this continent. The frontier is the line that separates the known from the unknown wherever it may be, and we have a driving

---

1. **nay-sayers:** people who disagree or have negative attitudes.

need to see what lies beyond. It was this that brought people to America, no matter what excuses they may have given themselves or others.

Freedom of religion, some said, and the need for land, a better future for their children, the lust for gold, or the desire to escape class restrictions—all these reasons were given. The fact remains that many, suffering from the same needs and restrictions, did not come.

Why then did some cross the ocean to America and not others? Of course, all who felt that urge did not come to America; some went to India, Africa, Australia, New Zealand, or elsewhere. Those who did come to America began almost at once to push inland, challenging the unknown, daring to go beyond the thin line that divides the known and the unknown. Many had, after landing from the old country, developed good farms or successful businesses; they had become people

of standing in their communities. Why then did they move on, leaving all behind?

I believe it to be something buried in their genes, some inherited trait,[2] perhaps something essential to the survival of the species.

They went to the edge of the mountains; then they crossed the mountains and found their way through impassable forests to the Mississippi. After that the Great Plains, the Rocky Mountains, and on to Oregon and California. They trapped fur, traded with Indians, hunted buffalo, ranched with cattle or sheep, built towns, and farmed. Yet the genes lay buried within them, and after a few months, a few years, they moved on.

Each science has its own frontiers, and the future of our nation and the world lies in research and development, in probing what lies beyond.

---

2. **something buried . . . inherited trait:** a characteristic passed on from ancestors, such as eye color or height.

A few years ago we moved into outer space. We landed men on the moon; we sent a vehicle beyond the limits of the solar system, a vehicle still moving farther and farther into that limitless distance. If our world were to die tomorrow, that tiny vehicle would go on and on forever, carrying its mighty message to the stars. Out there, someone, sometime, would know that once we existed, that we had the vision and we made the effort. Mankind is not bound by its atmospheric envelope or by its gravitational field, nor is the mind of man bound by any limits at all.

One might ask—why outer space, when so much remains to be done here? If that had been the spirit of man we would still be hunters and food gatherers, growling over the bones of carrion[3] in a cave somewhere. It is our destiny to move out, to accept the challenge, to dare the unknown. It is our destiny to achieve.

Yet we must not forget that along the way to outer space whole industries are springing into being that did not exist before. The computer age has arisen in part from the space effort, which gave great <u>impetus</u> to the development of computing devices. Transistors, chips, integrated circuits, Teflon, new medicines, new ways of treating diseases, new ways of performing operations, all these and a multitude of other developments that enable man to live and to live better are linked to the space effort. Most of these developments have been so <u>incorporated</u> into our day-to-day life that they are taken for granted, their origin not considered.

If we are content to live in the past, we have no future. And today is the past. ❖

---

3. **carrion** (kăr′ē-ən): the flesh of dead animals.

Connect to the Literature

1. **What Do You Think?** In what way does the essay make you think about the future? Explain your response.

Comprehension Check
- According to L'Amour, what is needed now?
- In L'Amour's opinion, why did Europeans come to America?

Think Critically

2. L'Amour mentions several achievements of 20th-century technology. Which achievement do you consider the most important? Give reasons for your choice.

3. **ACTIVE READING** **EVALUATING**
   What is your evaluation of L'Amour's persuasiveness? Is the essay convincing? Use the details you recorded in your **READER'S NOTEBOOK** to explain why you agree or disagree with him.

4. In what ways are modern space explorers and the early settlers similar? How are they different?

   Think About:
   - transportation in the 19th century
   - desire for new lands
   - human curiosity

5. What does L'Amour mean when he says, "If we are content to live in the past, we have no future. And today is the past"? What is the effect of closing the essay this way?

6. What does *eternal* mean? How can space be an "eternal" frontier?

Extend Interpretations

7. **Connect to Life** What do you think might be the greatest benefit of space exploration to human beings? Support your opinion with reasons.

Literary Analysis

PERSUASIVE ESSAY A **persuasive essay** is a type of writing that presents the writer's opinion on a subject and attempts to convince the reader to accept that opinion.

The **title** of a persuasive essay is important because it often tells what the writer is trying to persuade the reader of. L'Amour, for example, wants to convince readers that there is an "Eternal Frontier" in space.

Paired Activity With a partner, reread the essay, looking for evidence the author uses to support his opinion. A fact is a statement that can be proved; a statistic is a fact that is stated in numbers; examples are specific instances that explain the point; a quotation is a direct quote from an expert in the field. Evaluate the essay for its persuasiveness. Are L'Amour's arguments convincing? Explain your response.

Author's Opinion: Our next frontier is outer space			
Facts	Statistics	Examples	Quotations
1. In the past 70 years automobiles, radio, television, flight, electrification of the country have occurred.	1.	1.	1.
2.	2.	2.	2.

Writing

A Different Response At the beginning of the essay, L'Amour poses the question "Where is the frontier now?" Write a draft of a persuasive essay that provides an answer to this question that is different from L'Amour's answer. Place it in your **Working Portfolio.**

Writing Handbook
See p. R51: Persuasive.

Speaking & Listening

Present Your Argument Present the essay you wrote for the writing activity on the left. Be sure that your essay states your position clearly and describes each point you use as evidence. Include any books, resources, or visual aids. After your presentation, answer questions from your audience about the evidence you've provided, and your attitude toward the subject. The audience could also pose challenges to your argument, or affirm your position.

Speaking and Listening Handbook
See p. R104: Persuasive Presentations.

Research & Technology

SCIENCE

Search for information about what scientists have learned and are learning currently from space exploration. What new inventions or technologies have resulted from our journeys to space? Organize your research and make a presentation to the class.

Reading *for* INFORMATION
As part of your research, read "Four Decades in Space" on p. 470.

Vocabulary

EXERCISE A: WORD MEANING For each phrase in the first column, write the letter of the rhyming phrase in the second column that matches its meaning.

1. add a new quality
2. a guaranteed antidote
3. a multitude of fish
4. an impetus to add salt
5. pausing before putting out a forest fire

a. reason to season
b. masses of bass
c. devastating hesitating
d. sure cure
e. incorporate a trait

EXERCISE B Write a sentence using as many of the Words to Know as possible. Describe a humorous or unlikely situation if you wish, but be sure to use the words correctly.

WORDS TO KNOW	antidote	devastating	impetus	incorporate	multitude

Grammar in Context: Precise Adverbs

Notice how the **adverbs** affect the meaning of the first sentence of "The Eternal Frontier."

> The question I am **most often** asked is, "**Where** is the frontier now?"

An **adverb** is a word that modifes a verb, an adjective, or another adverb. Adverbs supply additional information about *when, where, how,* or *how much/to what degree* something happens or is done. They help readers visualize or more clearly understand a scene or character.

Usage Tip: To avoid confusing your readers, place each adverb close to the word that it modifies.

WRITING EXERCISE For each sentence, supply an adverb that gives the reader more detail about *where, how, how much/to what degree,* or *when* each action is performed.

Example: *Original* There will <u>be</u> nay-sayers.

Rewritten There will <u>always</u> be nay-sayers.

1. They will cling to our <u>green</u> planet.
2. Those who came to America <u>began</u> to push inward.
3. What we <u>need</u> is leaders with perspective.
4. There is a vehicle <u>moving</u> into space.

Connect to the Literature Look for the adverbs used to prepare the argument that space is the "eternal" frontier at the beginning of the fourth paragraph of the essay on page 464. What additional information do the adverbs supply?

Grammar Handbook
See p. 82: Using Modifiers Effectively.

Louis L'Amour
1908–1988

"I don't have to imagine what happened in the old West—I know what happened."

Jack of All Trades When Louis L'Amour left Jamestown, North Dakota, at the age of 15, few would have predicted that he would become one of the most popular writers of the 20th century. L'Amour wandered from place to place, working as a hay shocker, a longshoreman, a lumberjack, a fruit picker, a miner, an elephant handler, an amateur archaeologist, and a professional boxer.

Witness of the West L'Amour was a descendant of pioneers. During his travels, he got to know people who told him stories about the frontier. L'Amour drew on these experiences to make his stories of the frontier seem true to life. Over the years, he wrote some 95 novels and more than 400 short stories. L'Amour received two of the country's highest honors, a Congressional National Gold Medal and the Presidential Medal of Freedom.

AUTHOR ACTIVITY
Read some of L'Amour's western stories, such as "The Gift of Cochise," to find out more about the western frontier.

Source: *The Boston Globe*

Four Decades in Space

By Richard Sanchez and Sean McNaughton / GLOBE STAFF

John Glenn made history in 1962 by becoming the first American to orbit the Earth. In 1998, he made history again, returning to space at the age of 77. This graphic provides a detailed look at Glenn's second trip, mission STS-95. The text that follows the graphic compares the space program at its beginning with developments almost four decades later.

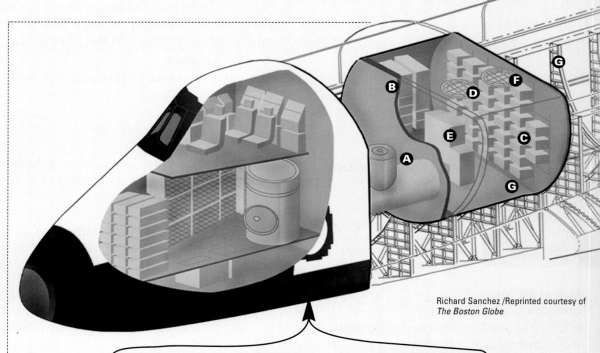

Richard Sanchez /Reprinted courtesy of *The Boston Globe*

❶

FLIGHT DECK
Flight controls for launch, orbit, and landing; holds the commander, pilot, a mission specialist, and payload specialist during launch.

MID-DECK
Three avionics[1] bays, galley, airlock to access tunnel, waste collection system, sleep accommodations, and storage.

EQUIPMENT DECK
Parts of life support systems and waste disposal.

1. **avionics:** aviation electronics; the science and technology of electronic devices used in air- and spacecrafts.

Key Standard

R2.1 Understand differences between various categories of informational materials (such as textbooks, newspapers, and manuals).
Other Standards **R2.2, R2.3**

The Mission

STS-95 marked the 92nd shuttle flight, and the 25th flight for the Discovery. Payloads[2] allowed astronauts to conduct more than three dozen experiments on subjects ranging from solar radiation to the effects of microgravity and equipment tests.

SPACEHAB

10-foot by 13.5-foot removable laboratory module connects to the orbiter mid-deck, and allows the crew to conduct experiments in the cargo bay.

Ⓐ Access tunnel

Ⓑ Forward and aft bulkheads

Ⓒ Lockers and trays: 56-liter volume, 27-kilogram capacity

Ⓓ Viewport—two windows available

Ⓔ Racks up to 740 liters volume, 300 kilograms capacity

Ⓕ External payloads up to 454 kilogram total

Ⓖ Interior payload 2,177–4,082 kilograms total

Payloads

CRYOTSU
CRYOGENIC THERMAL STORAGE UNIT
Test four thermal control devices for use in future missions.

BRIC
BIOLOGICAL RESEARCH IN CANNISTERS
Spacehab experiments will examine low gravity's effects on plant growth and cell division.

SEM-4
SPACE EXPERIMENT MODULE 4
Microgravity experiments from eight schools in the U.S., Italy, and Argentina.

E-NOSE
ELECTRONIC NOSE
Test new air quality monitor's ability to identify ten airborne toxic chemicals.

2. **payload:** the part of a load that is carried for scientific or commercial purposes.

Reading for Information

Learn how to skim and scan as you view the graphic of mission STS-95 and learn about the history of the space program.

Skimming, Scanning, and Understanding Graphics

To **skim**, you read a passage quickly to get an overview of it. To **scan**, you search through writing and headings for a particular fact or piece of information.

YOUR TURN *Use the questions below to help you learn how to skim and scan.*

❶ Skimming The picture of the shuttle shows the three decks in the spacecraft's nose. *Skim* the information provided about the three decks. Does the nose contain everything the astronauts need? How would you evaluate the arrangement? **Understanding Graphics** Read and study the graphic closely to answer the following questions:

❷ The payloads are the items in the shuttle's cargo that will be tested while in orbit. The results of the experiments will help scientists develop new technology. In the shuttle, where do the astronauts conduct the tests? Which of the payloads involves testing plant growth and cell division?

❸ Mercury *There and back*

The primary goals of the Mercury mission, which made six manned flights between 1961 and 1963, were to orbit the earth, test man's ability to work in space, and recover man and capsule safely.

Shuttles *Working in orbit*

The shuttle program's goal was to create a reusable orbiter for scientific research and commercial payloads, and for satellite deployment, retrieval, and repair.

The Suit

Mercury-era space suits were modified versions of Navy high-altitude jet pilot pressure suits.

An outer layer of aluminized nylon protected an inner layer of Neoprene-coated nylon. Its purpose was to keep the astronaut alive if the spacecraft lost pressure.

Despite fabric breaks at the joints, it was hard to bend the knees and elbows.

Better suits let Gemini astronauts make the first U.S. space walks, but Apollo's lunar missions required much greater mobility, comfort, and protection.

Onboard the shuttle, today's astronauts wear cotton T-shirts and pants like you might wear on the street. The suits they use on space walks let astronauts work in the vacuum for hours at a time and maneuver free of the shuttle while protecting them from temperature, radiation, and micro-meteoroids. ■

John Glenn walks to the Mercury capsule *Friendship 7* before his history-making flight Feb. 20, 1962.

NASA Photo

An astronaut on an untethered space walk in 1994.

NASA Photo

Reading for Information

❸ **Scanning** *Scan* the text above to find the answers to these questions: What is the difference between the left and right columns of text? Why did Mercury-era space suits have a layer of aluminized nylon?

Research & Technology

Activity Link: "The Eternal Frontier," p. 468
Can human beings handle living in space? Research for information that scientists have gathered about humanity's ability to live in space. What experiments have they conducted? What were the results? Present a one-page, cause-and-effect report to the class.

Writing Handbook
See p. R48: Cause and Effect.

Building Vocabulary
Learning and Remembering New Words

How do you figure out the meanings of unfamiliar words you come across in your reading?

Think about words you already know that are related or have similar affixes. You can also look for context clues in the other words around it. These are two good ways of determining the meaning of an unfamiliar word.

> Paved roads and the development of the automobile have gone hand in hand, the automobile being civilized man's **antidote** to overpopulation.
>
> —Louis L'Amour, "The Eternal Frontier"

Related words: **Antidote** might make you think of words like **antibiotic** or **anticlimax,** which share the prefix *anti-*, meaning "against."

Context: The words around **antidote** describe technological advances.

An antidote is a remedy against something.

Strategies for Building Vocabulary

Consider the following strategies for learning new words. The last strategy suggests a way for you to remember the words you learn.

❶ Use Context Clues You can use context clues to help you understand unfamiliar words like *indomitable.* Read the sentence in box 1. What does the context clue "didn't rest until" suggest about the meaning of the word *indomitable?*

❷ Think of Related Words When you come across a new word, think of words you know that have a similar root or base word. For example, *dominate* ("to rule, to control") is related to *indomitable.* If you know the meanings of related words, you can often figure out the meaning of the new word.

❸ Analyze Word Parts The parts of a word can sometimes reveal its meaning. *Indomitable* has three parts: *in-, domit,* and *-able.* If you find out that the Latin prefix *in-* means "not," *domit* is the root of the Latin word *domitare,* which means "to tame," and the suffix *-able* means "capable of being," then you can guess a meaning for *indomitable*—"not capable of being tamed."

❹ Use a Dictionary A dictionary lists a word's most common meaning first. When you look up a word, read all the definitions and decide which one best fits the context in which the word appears. Check the **etymology,** or word origin, to help you remember the root and connect it to words with similar origins.

❺ Record and Use New Words When you encounter a new word, record the word, its definition, its root, and related words in your 📖 READER'S NOTEBOOK. Say it aloud and use it in your writing.

INDOMITABLE	
1 Context Clues	**2 Related Words**
My mother was an <u>indomitable</u> spirit who didn't rest until she made them understand.	dominate, dominant
3 Word Parts	**4 Dictionary**
in- ("not") + *domitare* ("to tame") + *-able* ("capable of being")	**in•dom•i•ta•ble:** incapable of being subdued [from Latin *indomitabilis,* untamable]

ACTIVITY Choose three Words to Know from the selections you have read in this unit. For each word, provide a definition and synonyms for the word.

Key Standard
R1.3 Use context clues (definition, example, restatement, contrast) to determine the meaning of unknown words.
***Other Standard* R1.2**

Author Study: RAY BRADBURY

CONTENTS

Master of Fantasy

"What better way is there to become immortal than to write every day of your life?"

born 1920

"IN LOVE WITH THE FUTURE"

Who is Ray Bradbury? Steven Spielberg, director of *Close Encounters of the Third Kind* and *E.T.: The Extra-Terrestrial*, calls him "Papa." Filmmaker Gary Kurtz claims he may never have produced *Star Wars* and *The Empire Strikes Back* if he had not heard Bradbury speak in the 1960s. Who is Ray Bradbury? Perhaps the most influential writer of science fiction and fantasy in generations.

Not only has Bradbury influenced filmmakers, he himself has been deeply influenced by the adventure movies he saw and adored as a child.

Bradbury and Steven Spielberg on the set of *Jurassic Park*.

His LIFE and TIMES

1920 Born August 22 in Waukegan, Illinois

1932 Writes first Martian stories

1950 Publishes *The Martian Chronicles*

1920 — 1930 — 1940 — 1950

1920 Treaty of Versailles takes effect; WWI ends.

1929 Stock market crash

1939 Germany invades Poland; WWII begins.

1945 U.S. drops atomic bombs on Japan; WWII ends.

474

While living in Waukegan, Illinois, his mother took him to his first silent picture—*The Hunchback of Notre Dame*—when he was just three. By the time he was eight, Bradbury had discovered science fiction. "I was in love . . . with monsters and skeletons and circuses and carnivals and dinosaurs and, at last, the red planet Mars," he fondly remembers. At 9, Bradbury started collecting the comic strip *Buck Rogers*, which he said made him fall "completely in love with the future." Bradbury wrote his first Martian stories when he was 12.

In 1934 Bradbury's family moved to Los Angeles, California. There Bradbury was able to indulge the passion he had felt for movies since early childhood. He would sneak into the film studios and beg the stars for signed photographs—souvenirs that hang in his office today.

"WHEN I WAS 19, I SOLD NEWSPAPERS."
The world had fallen upon hard times in 1938, the year Bradbury graduated from high school. His family had no money to spare. Bradbury sold newspapers on Los Angeles street corners by day and spent hours reading and writing in the public library at night. Just before his 21st birthday, he sold a story. Soon he was selling about one story a

Bradbury, age 14, with comedian George Burns.

1953 Publishes *Fahrenheit 451*	1963 Nominated for an Academy Award	1977 Receives World Fantasy Award for Lifetime Achievement	1985 *The Ray Bradbury Theater* debuts on TV 	1995 Named Los Angeles Citizen of the Year
1960	**1970**	**1980**	**1990**	**2000**
1957 Soviets launch *Sputnik* satellite.	1965–1973 U.S. ground troops in Vietnam War	1969 U.S. astronauts walk on moon.	1975 U.S. *Viking* spacecraft lands on Mars.	1989 Berlin Wall is torn down; German reunification begins.	1998 Construction begins on International Space Station.

month to popular science-fiction and horror magazines. Bradbury quit selling papers and was instead selling his own stories to national magazines, such as *The Saturday Evening Post*. Bradbury's career was off the launchpad.

In 1947, Bradbury, an admirer of Edgar Allan Poe and other masters of fantasy and horror, published a collection of horror tales called *Dark Carnival*. Then came *The Martian Chronicles*, tales of Earth people trying to conquer and settle Mars. These Martian stories reflected fears that many Americans felt during the 1950s—nuclear war, racism, censorship, and a longing to maintain a simpler life against an increasingly technological age.

"I WAS LITERALLY WRITING A DIME NOVEL."

In the early 1950s Bradbury wrote the first draft of the novel that became *Fahrenheit 451* on a coin-operated typewriter in the basement of the library of the University of California, Los Angeles. The typewriters rented for a dime each half hour. Working feverishly, Bradbury spent a total of $9.80 in dimes as he cranked out his novel.

Fahrenheit 451—the temperature at which book paper catches fire—is a novel set in a future when the written word is seen as subversive and forbidden by the authorities. In this world firemen have the job of destroying libraries and burning books. The novel has its roots in Bradbury's revulsion at the Nazi book burnings

that took place before and during World War II, but it is a protest against censorship in general. Bradbury describes a small group of rebels who risk their lives by memorizing entire works of literature in the hope of preserving the accomplishments of the human spirit. In 1967, François Truffaut directed a motion-picture version of *Fahrenheit 451* that was extremely popular, and a new film version was being planned in 2001.

"Firemen" burning books in *Fahrenheit 451*.

Besides the numerous collections of short stories, poems, and essays Bradbury has authored, he has also written screenplays and scripts for television, including *The Twilight Zone* and *The Ray Bradbury Theater*. And he has shown his creativity not only in his writing. The futuristic U.S. Pavilion at the 1964 New York World's Fair was Bradbury's brainchild. He also designed the Spaceship Earth exhibit at the Epcot Center in Florida. Ray Bradbury's rich imagination has made him a powerful creative force on the American literary scene for more than half a century.

Bradbury in his office, standing behind a desk covered with futuristic toys.

 **Author Link**
www.mcdougallittell.com

 NetActivities: Author Exploration

FUTURE WORLDS, PRESENT REALITY

Science-fiction writers often comment on society and its problems in their works. Even though they may set their stories in the future, these works comment on the real world in which their authors live.

In science fiction, writers are free to imagine worlds in which current trends whose final consequences are still unknown can be seen fully developed. During the Cold War, the period that followed World War II and ended in 1989, many science-fiction writers wrote works that explored the consequences of authoritarian philosophies such as Fascism and Communism. For example, classics such as *Brave New World* (1932), by Aldous Huxley, *Nineteen Eighty-Four* (1949), by George Orwell, *Fahrenheit 451* (1953), by Ray Bradbury, and *Cat's Cradle* (1963), by Kurt Vonnegut, explore worlds in which governments have near total control over the lives, minds, and emotions of ordinary people. These writers were reacting to events of their own day.

When you read science fiction, you should enjoy the fantasy, but you should also pay attention to what the writer may be saying about the world in which you live.

Dark They Were, and Golden-Eyed

by RAY BRADBURY

Key Standard
R3.2 Identify events that advance the plot and describe how they explain the past, present, and future.
Other Standard **R3.1**

Connect to Your Life

Starting a New Life Have you ever been in a situation where you had to adapt to a very different environment from what you were used to? How did you react? What things about yourself did you have to change? Share your thoughts with a small group.

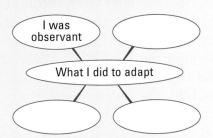

I was observant

What I did to adapt

Build Background

The Red Planet Named for the Roman god of war because of its "warlike" reddish color, Mars is the fourth planet from the Sun. The first "modern" map of Mars, drawn by astronomer Giovanni Schiaparelli in 1877, showed a planet crisscrossed by channels or canals. Inspired by Schiaparelli's work, astronomer Percival Lowell, in the 1890s, speculated that the "canals" might have been constructed by intelligent beings. This theory is now known to be untrue. Yet, Mars has been the setting for numerous science-fiction stories, most of which rarely depict the planet realistically.

WORDS TO KNOW
Vocabulary Preview
amiss   flimsy   recede
dwindle   forlorn

Focus Your Reading

LITERARY ANALYSIS   CIRCULAR PLOT STRUCTURE

Plot development is often explained in terms of a triangle, in which the rising action is one side of the triangle, the climax is the apex, and the falling action is the other side (see page 171). Some plots can be explained in terms of a circle because important details and events are repeated at the beginning and end of the story. As you read this story, pay careful attention to the beginning and ending of the story to see what elements make the plot "circular."

ACTIVE READING   VISUALIZE

Forming a mental picture based on a written description is called **visualizing.** Visualizing involves all the senses, not just sight. When you read, try to "see" the settings and characters described, but also try to hear, feel, smell, and taste what the writer describes.

READER'S NOTEBOOK As you read "Dark They Were, and Golden-Eyed," jot down a few descriptions that help you visualize the setting, characters, or action.

DARK THEY WERE, AND GOLDEN-EYED

BY RAY BRADBURY

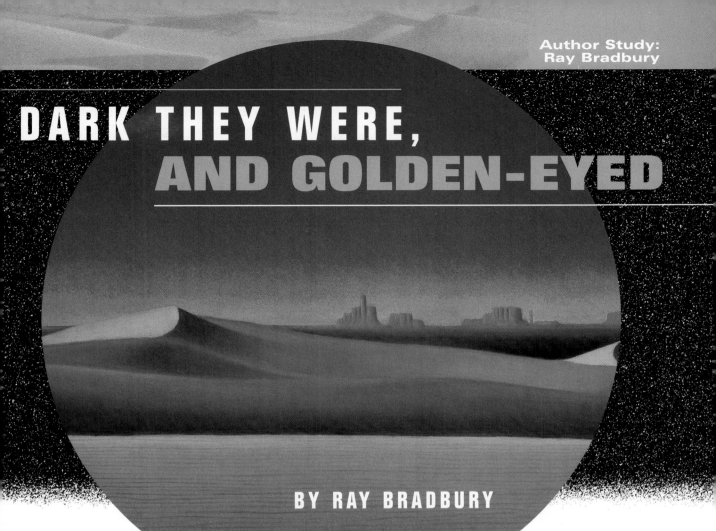

The rocket metal cooled in the meadow winds. Its lid gave a bulging *pop*. From its clock interior stepped a man, a woman, and three children. The other passengers whispered away across the Martian meadow, leaving the man alone among his family.

The man felt his hair flutter and the tissues of his body draw tight as if he were standing at the center of a vacuum. His wife, before him, seemed almost to whirl away in smoke. The children, small seeds, might at any instant be sown to all the Martian climes.

The children looked up at him, as people look to the sun to tell what time of their life it is. His face was cold.

Illustration by Kam Mak (detail).

479

"What's wrong?" asked his wife.

"Let's get back on the rocket."

"Go back to Earth?"

"Yes! Listen!"

The wind blew as if to flake away their identities. At any moment the Martian air might draw his soul from him, as marrow comes from a white bone. He felt submerged in a chemical that could dissolve his intellect and burn away his past.

They looked at Martian hills that time had worn with a crushing pressure of years. They saw the old cities, lost in their meadows, lying like children's delicate bones among the blowing lakes of grass.

"Chin up, Harry," said his wife. "It's too late. We've come over sixty million miles."

The children with their yellow hair hollered at the deep dome of Martian sky. There was no answer but the racing hiss of wind through the stiff grass.

He picked up the luggage in his cold hands. "Here we go," he said—a man standing on the edge of a sea, ready to wade in and be drowned.

They walked into town.

Their name was Bittering. Harry and his wife Cora; Dan, Laura, and David. They built a small white cottage and ate good breakfasts there, but the fear was never gone. It lay with Mr. Bittering and Mrs. Bittering, a third unbidden partner at every midnight talk, at every dawn awakening.

"I feel like a salt crystal," he said, "in a mountain stream, being washed away. We don't belong here. We're Earth people. This is

> **At any moment the Martian air might draw his soul from him, as marrow comes from a white bone.**

Mars. It was meant for Martians. For heaven's sake, Cora, let's buy tickets for home!"

But she only shook her head. "One day the atom bomb will fix Earth. Then we'll be safe here."

"Safe and insane!"

Tick-tock, seven o'clock sang the voice-clock; *time to get up.* And they did.

Something made him check everything each morning—warm hearth, potted blood-geraniums—precisely as if he expected something to be <u>amiss</u>. The morning paper was toast-warm from the 6 A.M. Earth rocket. He broke its seal and tilted it at his breakfast place. He forced himself to be convivial.

"Colonial days all over again," he declared. "Why, in ten years there'll be a million Earthmen on Mars. Big cities, everything! They said we'd fail. Said the Martians would resent our invasion. But did we find any Martians? Not a living soul! Oh, we found their empty cities, but no one in them. Right?"

A river of wind submerged the house. When the windows ceased rattling Mr. Bittering swallowed and looked at the children.

"I don't know," said David. "Maybe there're Martians around we don't see. Sometimes nights I think I hear 'em. I hear the wind. The sand hits my window. I get scared. And I see those towns way up in the mountains where the Martians lived a long time ago. And I think I see things moving around those towns, Papa. And I wonder if those Martians *mind* us living here. I wonder if they won't do something to us for coming here."

WORDS
TO
KNOW

amiss (ə-mĭs′) *adj.* out of proper order; wrong

"Nonsense!" Mr. Bittering looked out the windows. "We're clean, decent people." He looked at his children. "All dead cities have some kind of ghosts in them. Memories, I mean." He stared at the hills. "You see a staircase and you wonder what Martians looked like climbing it. You see Martian paintings and you wonder what the painter was like. You make a little ghost in your mind, a memory. It's quite natural. Imagination." He stopped. "You haven't been prowling up in those ruins, have you?"

"No, Papa." David looked at his shoes.

"See that you stay away from them. Pass the jam."

"Just the same," said little David, "I bet something happens."

Something happened that afternoon.

Laura stumbled through the settlement, crying. She dashed blindly onto the porch.

"Mother, Father—the war, Earth!" she sobbed. "A radio flash just came. Atom bombs hit New York! All the space rockets blown up. No more rockets to Mars, ever!"

"Oh, Harry!" The mother held onto her husband and daughter.

"Are you sure, Laura?" asked the father quietly.

Laura wept. "We're stranded on Mars, forever and ever!"

For a long time there was only the sound of the wind in the late afternoon.

Alone, thought Bittering. Only a thousand of us here. No way back. No way. No way. Sweat poured from his face and his hands and his body; he was drenched in the hotness of his fear. He wanted to strike Laura, cry, "No, you're lying! The rockets will come back!" Instead, he stroked Laura's head against him and said, "The rockets will get through someday."

"Father, what will we do?"

"Go about our business, of course. Raise crops and children. Wait. Keep things going until the war ends and the rockets come again."

The two boys stepped out onto the porch.

"Children," he said, sitting there, looking beyond them, "I've something to tell you."

"We know," they said.

In the following days, Bittering wandered often through the garden to stand alone in his fear. As long as the rockets had spun a silver web across space, he had been able to accept Mars. For he had always told himself: Tomorrow, if I want, I can buy a ticket and go back to Earth.

But now: The web gone, the rockets lying in jigsaw heaps of molten girder and unsnaked wire. Earth people left to the strangeness of Mars, the cinnamon dusts and wine airs, to be baked like gingerbread shapes in Martian summers, put into harvested storage by Martian winters. What would happen to him, the others? This was the moment Mars had waited for. Now it would eat them.

He got down on his knees in the flower bed, a spade in his nervous hands. Work, he thought, work and forget.

He glanced up from the garden to the Martian mountains. He thought of the proud old Martian names that had once been on those peaks. Earthmen, dropping from the sky, had gazed upon hills, rivers, Martian seats left nameless in spite of names. Once Martians had built cities, named cities; climbed mountains, named mountains; sailed seas, named seas. Mountains melted, seas drained, cities tumbled. In spite of this, the Earthmen had felt a silent guilt at putting new names to these ancient hills and valleys.

Nevertheless, man lives by symbol and label. The names were given.

The Body of a House #1 of 8 (1993), Robert Beckmann. Oil on canvas, 69" × 96½". Copyright © 1993 Robert Beckmann. Permanent collection: Nevada Museum of Art. Photograph by Tony Scodwell.

Mr. Bittering felt very alone in his garden under the Martian sun, anachronism bent here, planting Earth flowers in a wild soil.

Think. Keep thinking. Different things. Keep your mind free of Earth, the atom war, the lost rockets.

He perspired. He glanced about. No one watching. He removed his tie. Pretty bold, he thought. First your coat off, now your tie. He hung it neatly on a peach tree he had imported as a sapling from Massachusetts.

He returned to his philosophy of names and mountains. The Earthmen had changed names. Now there were Hormel Valleys, Roosevelt Seas, Ford Hills, Vanderbilt Plateaus, Rockefeller Rivers, on Mars. It wasn't right. The American settlers had shown wisdom, using old Indian prairie names: Wisconsin, Minnesota, Idaho, Ohio, Utah, Milwaukee, Waukegan, Osseo. The old names, the old meanings.

Staring at the mountains wildly, he thought: Are you up there? All the dead ones, you Martians? Well, here we are, alone, cut off! Come down, move us out! We're helpless!

The wind blew a shower of peach blossoms.

He put out his sun-browned hand and gave a small cry. He touched the blossoms and picked them up. He turned them, he touched them again and again. Then he shouted for his wife.

"Cora!"

She appeared at a window. He ran to her.

"Cora, these blossoms!"

She handled them.

"Do you see? They're different. They've changed! They're not peach blossoms any more!"

"Look all right to me," she said.

"They're not. They're wrong! I can't tell how. An extra petal, a leaf, something, the color, the smell!"

The children ran out in time to see their father hurrying about the garden, pulling up radishes, onions, and carrots from their beds.

"Cora, come look!"

They handled the onions, the radishes, the carrots among them.

"Do they look like carrots?"

"Yes . . . no." She hesitated. "I don't know."

"They're changed."

"Perhaps."

"You know they have! Onions but not onions, carrots but not carrots. Taste: the same but different. Smell: not like it used to be." He felt his heart pounding, and he was afraid. He dug his fingers into the earth. "Cora, what's happening? What is it? We've got to get away from this." He ran across the garden. Each tree felt his touch. "The roses. The roses. They're turning green!"

And they stood looking at the green roses.

And two days later Dan came running. "Come see the cow. I was milking her and I saw it. Come on!"

They stood in the shed and looked at their one cow.

It was growing a third horn.

And the lawn in front of their house very quietly and slowly was coloring itself like spring violets. Seed from Earth but growing up a soft purple.

"We must get away," said Bittering. "We'll eat this stuff and then we'll change—who knows to what? I can't let it happen. There's only one thing to do. Burn this food!"

"It's not poisoned."

"But it is. Subtly, very subtly. A little bit. A very little bit. We mustn't touch it."

He looked with dismay at their house. "Even the house. The wind's done something to it. The air's burned it. The fog at night. The boards, all warped out of shape. It's not an Earthman's house any more."

"Oh, your imagination!"

He put on his coat and tie. "I'm going into town. We've got to do something now. I'll be back."

"Wait, Harry!" his wife cried. But he was gone.

In town, on the shadowy step of the grocery store, the men sat with their hands on their knees, conversing with great leisure and ease. Mr. Bittering wanted to fire a pistol in the air.

What are you doing, you fools! he thought. Sitting here! You've heard the news—we're stranded on this planet. Well, move! Aren't you frightened? Aren't you afraid? What are you going to do?

"Hello, Harry," said everyone.

"Look," he said to them. "You did hear the news, the other day, didn't you?"

They nodded and laughed. "Sure. Sure, Harry."

"What are you going to do about it?"

"Do, Harry, do? What *can* we do?"

"Build a rocket, that's what!"

"A rocket, Harry? To go back to all that trouble? Oh, Harry!"

"But you *must* want to go back. Have you

noticed the peach blossoms, the onions, the grass?"

"Why, yes, Harry, seems we did," said one of the men.

"Doesn't it scare you?"

"Can't recall that it did much, Harry."

"Idiots!"

"Now, Harry."

Bittering wanted to cry. "You've got to work with me. If we stay here, we'll all change. The air. Don't you smell it? Something in the air. A Martian virus, maybe; some seed, or a pollen. Listen to me!"

They stared at him.

"Sam," he said to one of them.

"Yes, Harry?"

"Will you help me build a rocket?"

"Harry, I got a whole load of metal and some blueprints. You want to work in my metal shop on a rocket, you're welcome. I'll sell you that metal for five hundred dollars. You should be able to construct a right pretty rocket, if you work alone, in about thirty years."

Everyone laughed.

"Don't laugh."

Sam looked at him with quiet good humor.

"Sam," Bittering said. "Your eyes—"

"What about them, Harry?"

"Didn't they used to be gray?"

"Well now, I don't remember."

"They were, weren't they?"

"Why do you ask, Harry?"

"Because now they're kind of yellow-colored."

"Is that so, Harry?" Sam said, casually.

"And you're taller and thinner—"

"You might be right, Harry."

"Sam, you shouldn't have yellow eyes."

"Harry, what color eyes have *you* got?" Sam said.

"My eyes? They're blue, of course."

"Here you are, Harry." Sam handed him a pocket mirror. "Take a look at yourself."

Mr. Bittering hesitated, and then raised the mirror to his face.

There were little, very dim flecks of new gold captured in the blue of his eyes.

"Now look what you've done," said Sam a moment later. "You've broken my mirror."

Harry Bittering moved into the metal shop and began to build the rocket. Men stood in the open door and talked and joked without raising their voices. Once in a while they gave him a hand on lifting something. But mostly they just idled and watched him with their yellowing eyes.

"It's suppertime, Harry," they said.

His wife appeared with his supper in a wicker basket.

"I won't touch it," he said. "I'll eat only food from our Deepfreeze. Food that came from Earth. Nothing from our garden."

His wife stood watching him. "You can't build a rocket."

"I worked in a shop once, when I was twenty. I know metal. Once I get it started, the others will help," he said, not looking at her, laying out the blueprints.

"Harry, Harry," she said, helplessly.

"We've *got* to get away, Cora. We've got to!"

The nights were full of wind that blew down the empty moonlit sea meadows past the little white chess cities lying for their twelve-thousandth year in the shallows. In the Earthmen's settlement, the Bittering house shook with a feeling of change.

Lying abed, Mr. Bittering felt his bones shifted, shaped, melted like gold. His wife, lying beside him, was dark from many sunny afternoons. Dark she was, and golden-eyed, burnt almost black by the sun, sleeping, and the children metallic in their beds, and the wind roaring <u>forlorn</u> and changing through the old peach trees, the violet grass, shaking out green rose petals.

The fear would not be stopped. It had his throat and heart. It dripped in a wetness of the arm and the temple and the trembling palm.

A green star rose in the east.

A strange word emerged from Mr. Bittering's lips.

"*Iorrt. Iorrt.*" He repeated it.

It was a Martian word. He knew no Martian.

In the middle of the night he arose and dialed a call through to Simpson, the archaeologist.

"Simpson, what does the word *Iorrt* mean?"

"Why that's the old Martian word for our planet Earth. Why?"

"No special reason."

The telephone slipped from his hand.

"Hello, hello, hello, hello," it kept saying while he sat gazing out at the green star. "Bittering? Harry, are you there?"

The days were full of metal sound. He laid the frame of the rocket with the reluctant help of three indifferent men. He grew very tired in an hour or so and had to sit down.

"The altitude," laughed a man.

"Are you *eating*, Harry?" asked another.

"I'm eating," he said, angrily.

"From your Deepfreeze?"

"Yes!"

"You're getting thinner, Harry."

"I'm not!"

"And taller."

"Liar!"

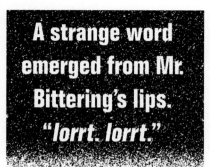

A strange word emerged from Mr. Bittering's lips. "*Iorrt. Iorrt.*"

His wife took him aside a few days later. "Harry, I've used up all the food in the Deepfreeze. There's nothing left. I'll have to make sandwiches using food grown on Mars."

He sat down heavily.

"You must eat," she said. "You're weak."

"Yes," he said.

He took a sandwich, opened it, looked at it, and began to nibble at it.

"And take the rest of the day off," she said. "It's hot. The children want to swim in the canals and hike. Please come along."

"I can't waste time. This is a crisis!"

"Just for an hour," she urged. "A swim'll do you good."

He rose, sweating. "All right, all right. Leave me alone. I'll come."

"Good for you, Harry."

The sun was hot, the day quiet. There was only an immense staring burn upon the land. They moved along the canal, the father, the mother, the racing children in their swimsuits. They stopped and ate meat sandwiches. He saw their skin baking brown. And he saw the yellow eyes of his wife and his children, their eyes that were never yellow before. A few tremblings shook him, but were carried off in waves of pleasant heat as he lay in the sun. He was too tired to be afraid.

"Cora, how long have your eyes been yellow?"

She was bewildered. "Always, I guess."

"They didn't change from brown in the last three months?"

She bit her lips. "No. Why do you ask?"

"Never mind."

They sat there.

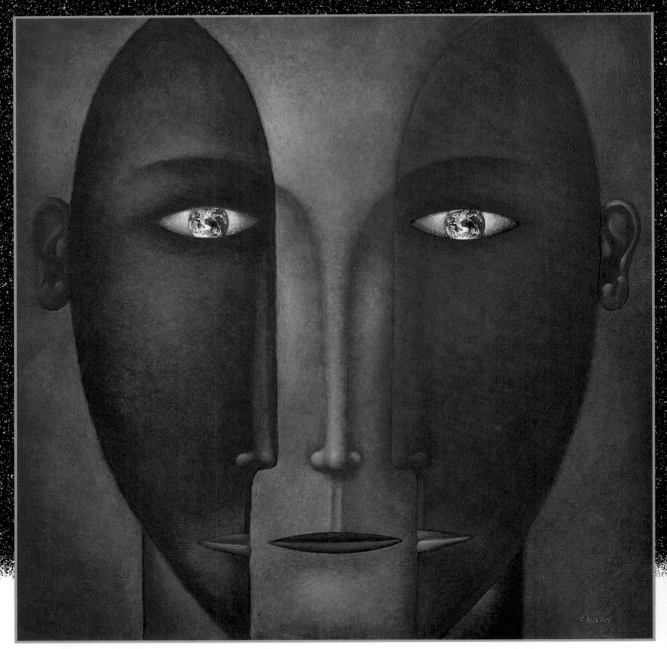

Illustration by Tom Curry.

"The children's eyes," he said. "They're yellow, too."

"Sometimes growing children's eyes change color."

"Maybe *we're* children, too. At least to Mars. That's a thought." He laughed. "Think I'll swim."

They leaped into the canal water, and he let himself sink down and down to the bottom like a golden statue and lie there in green silence. All was water-quiet and deep, all was peace. He felt the steady, slow current drift him easily.

If I lie here long enough, he thought, the

water will work and eat away my flesh until the bones show like coral. Just my skeleton left. And then the water can build on that skeleton—green things, deep water things, red things, yellow things. Change. Change. Slow, deep, silent change. And isn't that what it is up *there?*

He saw the sky submerged above him, the sun made Martian by atmosphere and time and space.

Up there, a big river, he thought, a Martian river; all of us lying deep in it, in our pebble houses, in our sunken boulder houses, like crayfish hidden, and the water washing away our old bodies and lengthening the bones and—

He let himself drift up through the soft light.

Dan sat on the edge of the canal, regarding his father seriously.

"*Utha*," he said.

"What?" asked his father.

The boy smiled. "You know. *Utha's* the Martian word for 'father.'"

"Where did you learn it?"

"I don't know. Around. *Utha!*"

"What do you want?"

The boy hesitated. "I—I want to change my name."

"Change it?"

"Yes."

His mother swam over. "What's wrong with Dan for a name?"

Dan fidgeted. "The other day you called Dan, Dan, Dan. I didn't even hear. I said to myself, That's not my name. I've a new name I want to use."

Mr. Bittering held to the side of the canal, his body cold and his heart pounding slowly. "What is this new name?"

"Linnl. Isn't that a good name? Can I use it? Can't I, please?"

Mr. Bittering put his hand to his head. He thought of the silly rocket, himself working alone, himself alone even among his family, so alone.

He heard his wife say, "Why not?"

He heard himself say, "Yes, you can use it."

"Yaaa!" screamed the boy. "I'm Linnl, Linnl!"

Racing down the meadowlands, he danced and shouted.

Mr. Bittering looked at his wife. "Why did we do that?"

"I don't know," she said. "It just seemed like a good idea."

They walked into the hills. They strolled on old mosaic paths, beside still pumping fountains. The paths were covered with a thin film of cool water all summer long. You kept your bare feet cool all the day, splashing as in a creek, wading.

They came to a small deserted Martian villa with a good view of the valley. It was on top of a hill. Blue marble halls, large murals, a swimming pool. It was refreshing in this hot summertime. The Martians hadn't believed in large cities.

"How nice," said Mrs. Bittering, "if we could move up here to this villa for the summer."

"Come on," he said. "We're going back to town. There's work to be done on the rocket."

But as he worked that night, the thought of the cool blue marble villa entered his mind. As the hours passed, the rocket seemed less important.

In the flow of days and weeks, the rocket <u>receded</u> and <u>dwindled</u>. The old fever was gone. It frightened him to think he had let it slip this way. But somehow the heat, the air, the working conditions—

WORDS TO KNOW	**recede** (rĭ-sēd') *v.* to become fainter and more distant **dwindle** (dwĭn'dl) *v.* to become less, until little remains

Skater (1956), Giacomo Manzu. Bronze, 80″ × 17⅛″. Hirshhorn Museum and Sculpture Garden, Smithsonian Institution, gift of Joseph H. Hirshhorn, 1966. Photography by Lee Stalsworth.

He heard the men murmuring on the porch of his metal shop.

"Everyone's going. You heard?"

"All going. That's right."

Bittering came out. "Going where?" He saw a couple of trucks, loaded with children and furniture, drive down the dusty street.

"Up to the villas," said the man.

"Yeah, Harry. I'm going. So is Sam. Aren't you Sam?"

"That's right, Harry. What about you?"

"I've got work to do here."

"Work! You can finish that rocket in the autumn, when it's cooler."

He took a breath. "I got the frame all set up."

"In the autumn is better." Their voices were lazy in the heat.

"Got to work," he said.

"Autumn," they reasoned. And they sounded so sensible, so right.

"Autumn would be best," he thought. "Plenty of time, then."

No! cried part of himself, deep down, put away, locked tight, suffocating. No! No!

"In the autumn," he said.

"Come on, Harry," they all said.

"Yes," he said, feeling his flesh melt in the hot liquid air. "Yes, in the autumn. I'll begin work again then."

"I got a villa near the Tirra Canal," said someone.

"You mean the Roosevelt Canal, don't you?"

"Tirra. The old Martian name."

"But on the map—"

"Forget the map. It's Tirra now. Now I found a place in the Pillan Mountains—"

"You mean the Rockefeller Range," said Bittering.

"I mean the Pillan Mountains," said Sam.

"Yes," said Bittering, buried in the hot, swarming air. "The Pillan Mountains."

Everyone worked at loading the truck in the hot, still afternoon of the next day.

Laura, Dan, and David carried packages. Or, as they preferred to be known, Ttil, Linnl, and Werr carried packages.

The furniture was abandoned in the little white cottage.

"It looked just fine in Boston," said the mother. "And here in the cottage. But up at the villa? No. We'll get it when we come back in the autumn."

Bittering himself was quiet.

"I've some ideas on furniture for the villa," he said after a time. "Big, lazy furniture."

"What about your encyclopedia? You're taking it along, surely?"

Mr. Bittering glanced away. "I'll come and get it next week."

They turned to their daughter. "What about your New York dresses?"

The bewildered girl stared. "Why, I don't want them any more."

They shut off the gas, the water, they locked the doors and walked away. Father peered into the truck.

"Gosh, we're not taking much," he said. "Considering all we brought to Mars, this is only a handful!"

He started the truck.

Looking at the small white cottage for a long moment, he was filled with a desire to rush to it, touch it, say good-bye to it, for he felt as if he were going away on a long journey, leaving something to which he could never quite return, never understand again.

Just then Sam and his family drove by in another truck.

"Hi, Bittering! Here we go!"

The truck swung down the ancient highway out of town. There were sixty others traveling in the same direction. The town filled with a silent, heavy dust from their passage. The canal waters lay blue in the sun, and a quiet wind moved in the strange trees.

"Good-bye, town!" said Mr. Bittering.

"Good-bye, good-bye," said the family, waving to it.

They did not look back again.

Summer burned the canals dry. Summer moved like flame upon the meadows. In the empty Earth settlement, the painted houses flaked and peeled. Rubber tires upon which children had swung in back yards hung suspended like stopped clock pendulums in the blazing air.

At the metal shop, the rocket frame began to rust.

In the quiet autumn Mr. Bittering stood, very dark now, very golden-eyed, upon the slope above his villa, looking at the valley.

"It's time to go back," said Cora.

"Yes, but we're not going," he said quietly. "There's nothing there any more."

"Your books," she said. "Your fine clothes."

"Your *llles* and your fine *ior uele rre*," she said.

"The town's empty. No one's going back," he said. "There's no reason to, none at all."

The daughter wove tapestries and the sons played songs on ancient flutes and pipes, their laughter echoing in the marble villa.

Mr. Bittering gazed at the Earth settlement far away in the low valley. "Such odd, such ridiculous houses the Earth people built."

"They didn't know any better," his wife mused. "Such ugly people. I'm glad they've gone."

They both looked at each other, startled by all they had just finished saying. They laughed.

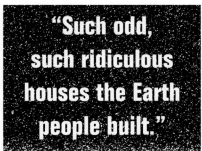

"Such odd, such ridiculous houses the Earth people built."

"Where did they go?" he wondered. He glanced at his wife. She was golden and slender as his daughter. She looked at him, and he seemed almost as young as their eldest son.

"I don't know," she said.

"We'll go back to town maybe next year, or the year after, or the year after that," he said, calmly. "Now—I'm warm. How about taking a swim?"

They turned their backs to the valley. Arm in arm they walked silently down a path of clear-running spring water.

Five years later a rocket fell out of the sky. It lay steaming in the valley. Men leaped out of it, shouting.

"We won the war on Earth! We're here to rescue you! Hey!"

But the American-built town of cottages, peach trees, and theaters was silent. They found a <u>flimsy</u> rocket frame rusting in an empty shop.

The rocket men searched the hills. The captain established headquarters in an abandoned bar. His lieutenant came back to report.

"The town's empty, but we found native life in the hills, sir. Dark people. Yellow eyes. Martians. Very friendly. We talked a bit, not much. They learn English fast. I'm sure our relations will be most friendly with them, sir."

"Dark, eh?" mused the captain. "How many?"

"Six, eight hundred, I'd say, living in those marble ruins in the hills, sir. Tall, healthy. Beautiful women."

"Did they tell you what became of the men and women who built this Earth settlement, Lieutenant?"

"They hadn't the foggiest notion of what happened to this town or its people."

"Strange. You think those Martians killed them?"

"They look surprisingly peaceful. Chances are a plague did this town in, sir."

"Perhaps. I suppose this is one of those mysteries we'll never solve. One of those mysteries you read about."

The captain looked at the room, the dusty windows, the blue mountains rising beyond, the canals moving in the light, and he heard the soft wind in the air. He shivered. Then, recovering, he tapped a large fresh map he had thumbtacked to the top of an empty table.

"Lots to be done, Lieutenant." His voice droned on and quietly on as the sun sank behind the blue hills. "New settlements. Mining sites, minerals to be looked for. Bacteriological specimens taken. The work, all the work. And the old records were lost. We'll have a job of remapping to do, renaming the mountains and rivers and such. Calls for a little imagination.

"What do you think of naming those mountains the Lincoln Mountains, this canal the Washington Canal, those hills—we can name those hills for you, Lieutenant. Diplomacy. And you, for a favor, might name a town for me. Polishing the apple. And why not make this the Einstein Valley, and farther over . . . are you *listening*, Lieutenant?"

The lieutenant snapped his gaze from the blue color and the quiet mist of the hills far beyond the town.

"What? Oh, *yes*, sir!" ❖

WORDS TO KNOW   **flimsy** (flĭm′zē) *adj.* not solid or strong

Connect to the Literature

1. **What Do You Think?** What was your reaction to the changes that took place in the colonists from Earth?

   Comprehension Check
   - Why did the Bitterings settle on Mars?
   - Why did the rockets from Earth stop coming to Mars?
   - What details tell you that the Bitterings have become more Martian than human?

Think Critically

2. In your opinion, what is the significance of the physical and psychological changes that take place in the Bitterings?

3. What do you think happened to the original inhabitants of Mars? What do you think will happen to the Bitterings?

4. Does the character of Harry Bittering make the story more or less believable?

   Think About:
   - how he deals with his own fears in comparison to Cora's fear of nuclear war
   - how he reacts to the children's new names
   - how he copes with the changes within himself

5. **ACTIVE READING VISUALIZING**
   Look back at your 📖 READER'S NOTEBOOK. Which of the descriptions you recorded creates the most vivid picture in your mind? What phrases help you to visualize that scene?

6. The lieutenant likes the Martian landscape. What could you predict from that information?

7. What do you think the relationship between the Bitterings and the newcomers will be? Explain.

Extend Interpretations

8. **Critic's Corner** One critic said that Bradbury's stories are "of people, real and honest and true in their understanding of human nature. . . ." Do you agree? Cite details from the story to support your answer.

9. **Connect to Life** How do you think you would react if you were in the Bittering's situation? Explain your answer.

Literary Analysis

CIRCULAR PLOT STRUCTURE
Some story plots can be called circular because their endings repeat details and events from their beginnings. At the beginning of this selection, the new colonists from Earth, the Bitterings, find themselves in a place they think has been deserted. At the end of the story, they retreat to the mountains, and a new set of colonists from Earth arrives, believing that *they* are the only inhabitants. Events at the end of the story repeat events at the beginning.

Paired Activity Reread the story, paying attention to the changes that the colonists go through. With a partner, create a circular **story map** to plot the major events. Include as many **events** as you think important. How are the beginning and the ending of the story similar? What do you predict will happen to the second group of colonists? Why?

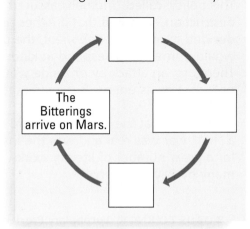

The Bitterings arrive on Mars.

The Golden Kite, the Silver Wind

by RAY BRADBURY

Key Standard
R3.4 Identify and analyze themes that appear across works.
Other Standards **R3.1, R3.2, LC1.1, LC1.4**

Connect to Your Life

Deadlock Have you ever found yourself facing a problem for which there seemed to be no good solution? How did you resolve the problem? Did someone give you helpful advice? With a small group of classmates, discuss your experiences.

Build Background

HISTORY

The Cold War was a period of strained relations between the Western powers and the communist bloc, following the end of World War II and lasting until 1989.

One aspect of the Cold War was the arms race. Each side tried to protect itself by creating weapons that could match or surpass in destructiveness the weapons created by the other side. The result was that both sides possessed an arsenal of weapons capable of destroying life on Earth several times over. This policy, called "mutually assured destruction," ensured that if either side decided to attack its opponent, the opponent would immediately respond in kind. Therefore, an attack by one side would not only destroy its enemy but guarantee its own destruction.

The fear that the Cold War would turn into a "hot" war was real and was the inspiration for a great number of literary works, including many by Ray Bradbury.

WORDS TO KNOW **Vocabulary Preview**

acclaimed	quench	spurn
pandemonium	ravenous	

Focus Your Reading

LITERARY ANALYSIS THEME

A **theme** is a central idea, message, or moral in a work of literature. "The Golden Kite, the Silver Wind" is a **modern fable,** a type of fiction that usually has a message. One way to discover the theme of a work is to think about what happens to the central characters. The importance of these events, stated in terms that apply to all human beings, is the theme.

ACTIVE READING CONNECT WITH OTHER STORIES

Active readers seek to **connect** the themes in the work they are reading with others they have already read. This enriches their reading and helps them to better understand the message in what they are reading. Think of Dorothy West's modern fable "The Richer, the Poorer" (page 316). What theme or themes does it have in common with "The Golden Kite, the Silver Wind"?

READER'S NOTEBOOK As you read, jot down similarities that you find between "The Golden Kite, the Silver Wind" and "The Richer, the Poorer." Similarities between works can often give you clues to the characters and the themes.

The Golden Kite, the Silver Wind

by Ray Bradbury

The Yueh-Yang Tower, Hsia Yung (Yuan Dynasty). Courtesy of the Freer Gallery of Art, Smithsonian Institution, Washington, D.C. (F1915.36i)

"In the shape of a pig?" cried the Mandarin.

"In the shape of a pig," said the messenger, and departed.

"Oh, what an evil day in an evil year," cried the Mandarin. "The town of Kwan-Si, beyond the hill, was very small in my childhood. Now it has grown so large that at last they are building a wall."

"But why should a wall two miles away make my good father sad and angry all within the hour?" asked his daughter quietly.

"They build their wall," said the Mandarin, "in the

shape of a pig! Do you see? Our own city wall is built in the shape of an orange. That pig will devour us, greedily!"

"Ah."

They both sat thinking.

Life was full of symbols and omens. Demons lurked everywhere, Death swam in the wetness of an eye, the turn of a gull's wing meant rain, a fan held *so*, the tilt of a roof, and, yes, even a city wall was of immense importance. Travelers and tourists, caravans, musicians, artists, coming upon these two towns, equally judging the portents, would say, "The city shaped like an orange? No! I will enter the city shaped like a pig and prosper, eating all, growing fat with good luck and prosperity!"

The Mandarin wept. "All is lost! These symbols and signs terrify. Our city will come on evil days."

"Then," said the daughter, "call in your stonemasons and temple builders. I will whisper from behind the silken screen and you will know the words."

The old man clapped his hands despairingly. "Ho, stonemasons! Ho, builders of towns and palaces!"

The men who knew marble and granite and onyx and quartz came quickly. The Mandarin faced them most uneasily, himself waiting for a whisper from the silken screen behind his throne. At last the whisper came.

"I have called you here," said the whisper.

"I have called you here," said the Mandarin aloud, "because our city is shaped like an orange, and the vile city of Kwan-Si has this day shaped theirs like a <u>ravenous</u> pig—"

Here the stonemasons groaned and wept.

Death rattled his cane in the outer courtyard. Poverty made a sound like a wet cough in the shadows of the room.

"And so," said the whisper, said the Mandarin, "you raisers of walls must go bearing trowels and rocks and change the shape of *our* city!"

The architects and masons gasped. The Mandarin himself gasped at what he had said. The whisper whispered. The Mandarin went on: "And you will change our walls into a club which may beat the pig and drive it off!"

The stonemasons rose up, shouting. Even the Mandarin, delighted at the words from his mouth, applauded, stood down from his throne. "Quick!" he cried. "To work!"

When his men had gone, smiling and bustling, the Mandarin turned with great love to the silken screen. "Daughter," he whispered, "I will embrace you." There was no reply. He stepped around the screen, and she was gone.

Such modesty, he thought. She has slipped away and left me with a triumph, as if it were mine.

The news spread through the city; the Mandarin was <u>acclaimed</u>. Everyone carried stone to the walls. Fireworks were set off and the demons of death and poverty did not linger, as all worked together. At the end of the month the wall had been changed. It was now a mighty bludgeon with which to drive pigs, boars, even lions, far away. The Mandarin slept like a happy fox every night.

"I would like to see the Mandarin of Kwan-Si when the news is learned. Such <u>pandemonium</u> and hysteria; he will likely throw himself from a mountain! A little more of that wine, oh Daughter-who-thinks-like-a-son."

WORDS	**ravenous** (răv′ə-nəs) *adj.* extremely hungry; greedy
TO	**acclaimed** (ə-klāmd′) *adj.* welcomed publicly with praise **acclaim** *v.*
KNOW	**pandemonium** (păn′də-mō′nē-əm) *n.* a noisy upset; a wild uproar

But the pleasure was like a winter flower; it died swiftly. That very afternoon the messenger rushed into the courtroom. "Oh, Mandarin, disease, early sorrow, avalanches, grasshopper plagues, and poisoned well water!"

The Mandarin trembled.

"The town of Kwan-Si," said the messenger, "which was built like a pig and which animal we drove away by changing our walls to a mighty stick, has now turned triumph to winter ashes. They have built their city's walls like a great bonfire to burn our stick!"

The Mandarin's heart sickened within him, like an autumn fruit upon an ancient tree. "Oh, gods! Travelers will <u>spurn</u> us. Tradesmen, reading the symbols, will turn from the stick, so easily destroyed, to the fire, which conquers all!"

"No," said a whisper like a snowflake from behind the silken screen.

"No," said the startled Mandarin.

"Tell my stonemasons," said the whisper that was a falling drop of rain, "to build our walls in the shape of a shining lake."

The Mandarin said this aloud, his heart warmed.

"And with this lake of water," said the whisper and the old man, "we will <u>quench</u> the fire and put it out forever!"

The city turned out in joy to learn that once again they had been saved by the magnificent Emperor of ideas. They ran to the walls and built them nearer to this new vision, singing, not as loudly as before, of course, for they were tired, and not as quickly, for since it had taken a month to build the wall the first time, they had had to neglect business and crops and therefore were somewhat weaker and poorer.

There then followed a succession of horrible and wonderful days, one in another like a nest of frightening boxes.

"Oh, Emperor," cried the messenger, "Kwan-Si has rebuilt their walls to resemble a mouth with which to drink all our lake!"

"Then," said the Emperor, standing very close to his silken screen, "build our walls like a needle to sew up that mouth!"

"Emperor!" screamed the messenger. "They make their walls like a sword to break your needle!"

The Emperor held, trembling, to the silken screen. "Then shift the stones to form a scabbard to sheathe that sword!"

"Mercy," wept the messenger the following morn, "they have worked all night and shaped the walls like lightning which will explode and destroy that sheath!"

Sickness spread in the city like a pack of evil dogs. Shops closed. The population, working now steadily for endless months upon the changing of the walls, resembled Death himself, clattering his white bones like musical instruments in the wind. Funerals began to appear in the streets, though it was the middle of summer, a time when all should be tending and harvesting. The Mandarin fell so ill that he had his bed drawn up by the silken screen and there he lay, miserably giving his architectural orders. The voice behind the screen was weak now, too, and faint, like the wind in the eaves.

"Kwan-Si is an eagle. Then our walls must be a net for that eagle. They are a sun to burn our net. Then we build a moon to eclipse their sun!"

Like a rusted machine, the city ground to a halt.

WORDS
TO
KNOW

spurn (spûrn) *v.* to reject or turn down scornfully
quench (kwĕnch) *v.* to put out; to extinguish

At last the whisper behind the screen
cried out:

"In the name of the gods, send for Kwan-Si!"

Upon the last day of summer the Mandarin
Kwan-Si, very ill and withered away, was
carried into our Mandarin's courtroom by four
starving footmen. The two mandarins were
propped up, facing each other. Their breaths
fluttered like winter winds in their mouths.
A voice said:

"Let us put an end to this."

The old men nodded.

"This cannot go on," said the faint voice.
"Our people do nothing but rebuild our cities
to a different shape every day, every hour.
They have no time to hunt, to fish, to love, to
be good to their ancestors and their ancestors'
children."

"This I admit," said the mandarins of the
towns of the Cage, the Moon, the Spear, the
Fire, the Sword and this, that, and other things.

"Carry us into the sunlight," said the voice.

The old men were borne out under the sun
and up a little hill. In the late summer breeze
a few very thin children were flying dragon
kites in all the colors of the sun, and frogs and
grass, the color of the sea and the color of
coins and wheat.

The first Mandarin's daughter stood by
his bed.

"See," she said.

"Those are nothing but kites," said the two
old men.

"But what is a kite on the ground?" she said.
"It is nothing. What does it need to sustain it
and make it beautiful and truly spiritual?"

"The wind, of course!" said the others.

"And what do the sky and the wind need to
make *them* beautiful?"

"A kite, of course—many kites, to break the
monotony, the sameness of the sky. Colored
kites, flying!"

"So," said the Mandarin's daughter. "You,
Kwan-Si, will make a last rebuilding of your
town to resemble nothing more nor less than
the wind. And we shall build like a golden kite.
The wind will beautify the kite and carry it
to wondrous heights. And the kite will break
the sameness of the wind's existence and give
it purpose and meaning. One without the other
is nothing. Together, all will be beauty and cooperation and a long and enduring life."

Whereupon the two mandarins were so
overjoyed that they took their first
nourishment in days, momentarily were given
strength, embraced, and lavished praise upon
each other, called the Mandarin's daughter a
boy, a man, a stone pillar, a warrior, and a true
and unforgettable son. Almost immediately
they parted and hurried to their towns, calling
out and singing, weakly but happily.

And so, in time, the towns became the Town
of the Golden Kite and the Town of the Silver
Wind. And harvestings were harvested and
business tended again, and the flesh returned,
and disease ran off like a frightened jackal.
And on every night of the year the inhabitants
in the Town of the Kite could hear the good
clear wind sustaining them. And those in the
Town of the Wind could hear the kite singing,
whispering, rising, and beautifying them.

"So be it," said the Mandarin in front of his
silken screen. ❖

THE GOLDEN KITE, THE SILVER WIND   **497**

THINKING through
the **LITERATURE**

Connect to the Literature

1. What Do You Think?
What was your
impression of the
solution to the two
towns' rivalry?
Explain.

Comprehension Check
- Why are both towns
surrounded by walls?
- Why do the two towns keep
rebuilding these walls?
- How was the towns' rivalry
resolved?

Think Critically

2. Why do you think the Mandarin was willing to listen to
his daughter's advice?

> **Think About:**
> - her first question to her father about his anger
> - the consequences of her advice
> - the compliments of the two mandarins after she
> solved their problem

3. The characters in this story are described only as the
Mandarin, the daughter, the messenger, and so forth.
Why do you think none of the characters has a name?

4. Do you think that this story portrays an accurate
picture of human behavior? Explain your response.

5. What theme, or lesson about human nature, do you
think the author is trying to get across in this tale?

6. ACTIVE READING | CONNECT WITH OTHER STORIES |
Look back at the notes you made in your
📖 READER'S NOTEBOOK. What thematic **connections**
did you make between "The Golden Kite, the Silver
Wind" and "The Richer, the Poorer"? Share your
ideas with your classmates.

Extend Interpretations

7. What If? What if the two towns had not been able to
resolve their rivalry? What might have happened?

8. Connect to Life The Mandarin's daughter is praised as
"a boy, a man, a stone pillar, a warrior, and a true and
unforgettable son." What do you think is meant by
this? How would you describe the daughter?

Literary Analysis

THEME A **fable** is a brief story
that teaches a lesson about
human nature. The lesson, or
moral, of the fable appears in
a statement at the end. Modern
fables seldom have stated
morals. Instead, they have a
theme, or message about life or
human nature, that the reader
must infer. To determine the
theme of a work you read, look
at the events that happen to
the main characters. Restate the
significance of these events in
terms that apply to all human
beings. That is the theme.

Paired Activity With a partner,
look at the main events of "The
Golden Kite, the Silver Wind."
What is their significance to the
main characters of the selection?
Using your own words, restate
this message in more general
terms. Share your statement
of the theme with other pairs.

REVIEW: EVENT An **event** in a
story is an occurrence that is
necessary to the plot. You can
tell whether or not something is
an event by asking, "How would
the plot change without this
event?" If the plot would not
change significantly, it is not
considered an event. For
example, in "The Golden Kite,
the Silver Wind," if the town of
Kwan-Si had not built a wall, the
rest of the story could not be
told in the same way.

Grammar in Context: Essential and Nonessential Modifiers

In "The Golden Kite, the Silver Wind," Bradbury uses two kinds of modifiers to add important information to his sentences.

> Travelers . . . would say, "The city shaped like an orange? No! I will enter the city shaped like a pig **and prosper! . . .**"

An **essential modifier** is one that is necessary to the meaning of a sentence. In the excerpt above, "shaped like an orange" and "shaped like a pig" are essential for identifying which city is referred to. The sentences would not be clear without these modifiers.

> "The town of Kwan-Si, beyond the hill, was very small in my childhood. . . ."

A **nonessential modifier** is one that adds more information to a sentence that is already clear without the addition. In the sentence above it is clear which town is referred to without the extra information "beyond the hill."

Punctuation Tip: A nonessential modifier is set off from the rest of the sentence with commas.

WRITING EXERCISE Rewrite each sentence, adding an essential or nonessential modifier to provide more information about the underlined noun or pronoun.

Example: **Original** The Mandarin feared that the city would devour the city with walls shaped like an orange.

Rewritten The Mandarin feared that the city with walls shaped like a pig would devour the city with walls shaped like an orange.

1. The town of Kwan-Si now had a wall.
2. A voice from behind the screen whispered advice.
3. The Mandarin thought his walls would extinguish the walls built like a fire.
4. The two mandarins decided to stop competing.

Vocabulary

Choose the word or group of words that means the same, or nearly the same, as the underlined Word to Know.

1. Acclaimed is another word for—
   A humbled   **B** mocked
   C praised   **D** ignored
2. To quench something is to—
   F guide it   **G** protect it
   H examine it   **J** extinguish it
3. Pandemonium refers to an—
   A animal   **B** uproar
   C adventure   **D** athlete
4. To spurn something is to—
   F reject it   **G** release it
   H embrace it   **J** enlarge it

5. Ravenous means—
   A generous   **B** hungry
   C sleepy   **D** dangerous

EXERCISE: WORD MEANING For each phrase in the first column, write the letter of the phrase in the second that matches its meaning.

1. hungry streets   a. renowned clown
2. acclaimed jester   b. spurn a turn
3. great pandemonium   c. quench a stench
4. refuse a chance   d. ravenous avenues
5. get rid of an odor   e. colossal chaos

Vocabulary Handbook
See p. R24: Context Clues.

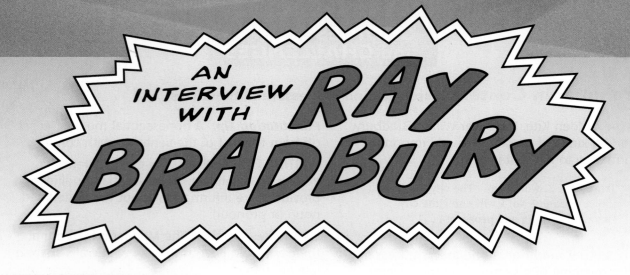

AN INTERVIEW WITH RAY BRADBURY

PREPARING to *Read*

Focus Your Reading

LITERARY ANALYSIS **INTERVIEW**

An **interview** is a source of firsthand information about the subject of the interview. Interviews, like letters, stories, essays, poems, and speeches by a writer, are known as **primary sources.**

Illustration by Steve Vance.

Key Standard
W2.5 Write summaries of reading materials that include the main idea and key supporting details, and that are written in the student's own words.
***Other Standards* R3.1, W1.2, W2.3, LS2.2**

Q: YOU DON'T CONSIDER YOURSELF A SCIENCE FICTION WRITER, EVEN THOUGH OTHERS CALL YOU THAT. HOW DO YOU SEE YOURSELF?

A: I am a collector of metaphors. Any idea that strikes me I run with. I've published in the last seven years two murder mysteries, *Death Is a Lonely Business* and *Graveyard for a Lunatic*. I have published two books of essays, *Zen and the Art of Writing*, which I like to think is one of the better books on writing, then *Yestermorrow*, on how to cure current problems and make our society work.

I wrote *The October Country*, which is weird fantasy. There is no science fiction there. And *Halloween Tree*, which is a history of Halloween. And *Dandelion Wine*, which is my childhood in Illinois. *Something Wicked This Way Comes*, which is also my childhood plus fantasy. So when you look at the spread of things, there is only one novel that is science fiction. And that's *Fahrenheit 451*. In other words, science fiction is the art of the possible, not the art of the impossible. As soon as you deal with things that can't happen you are writing fantasy.

Q: I KNOW YOU NEVER HAVE TROUBLE COMING UP WITH IDEAS. WALK ME THROUGH YOUR DAILY INSPIRATION AND WRITING PROCESS.

A: I just wake up with ideas every morning from my subconscious percolating. At 7 in the morning I lie in bed and I watch all the fragments of ideas swarming around in

my head and these voices talk to me. And when they get to a certain point, I jump out of bed and run to the typewriter. So I'm not in control. Two hours later I have a new short story or an essay or part of a play.

Q: WHEN YOU'VE FINISHED TYPING YOUR SHORT STORIES, DO YOU REVISE?

A: No. Never. A few words, but that's not revision. That's just cleaning up.

Q: WHAT ARE YOU PASSIONATE ABOUT?

A: Everything. If you're in love, you're in love.

Q: YOU SAID ONCE THAT "THE GREAT THING ABOUT MY LIFE IS THAT EVERYTHING I'VE DONE IS A RESULT OF WHAT I WAS WHEN I WAS 12 OR 13." WHAT DOES THAT MEAN TO YOU?

A: Or even younger, when I was 3, when I was 5, when I was 9. All the things that I loved have been part of my writing. *The Hunchback of Notre Dame* when I was 3 years old; *The Phantom of the Opera* with Lon Chaney when I was 5 in 1925. . . . When I was 9, I collected all the Buck Rogers comic strips. Edgar Rice Burroughs, the "Tarzan" books, *Warlord of Mars*, I memorized those books. The "Oz" books when I was 9, 10, 11. . . . *King Kong* in 1933 when I was 13, H. G. Wells, Jules Verne. All those things. My childhood was packed with metaphors. Plus the Bible. Plus the hundreds of other

films during that time. [*In 1934, the family moved to Los Angeles.*] I was a real freak. I hung around the studios when I was 14 so I could see famous people. I intruded on the life of George Burns when he and Gracie Allen were doing their radio show. I wrote scripts for the show every week and gave them to George. They used one routine. I did radio acting. I read the comic strips to the kiddies when I was 12 years old. Out of all those images and metaphors, I became a good screenwriter, because a good screenwriter is making storyboards like comic strips. So I am a natural outgrowth of the impact of all these wonderful art forms.

Q: WHAT KIND OF ADVICE WOULD YOU GIVE BEGINNING WRITERS?

A: Explode. Don't intellectualize. Get passionate about ideas. Cram your head full of images. Stay in the library. Stay off the Internet. Read all the great books. Read all the great poetry. See all the great films. Fill your life with metaphors. And then explode. And you're bound to do something good.

THINKING *through the* LITERATURE

1. What impression do you have of Ray Bradbury from this interview?
2. Were you surprised at Bradbury's method of writing? Explain.

The Author's Style

Ray Bradbury's Poetic Prose

The use of striking images, loosely structured sentences, and long passages of dialogue are important elements of Ray Bradbury's style.

Key Style Points

Dialogue Bradbury often uses dialogue rather than descriptive or explanatory passages to get across his points. What important idea is revealed in the passage to the right?

Imagery Images help readers imagine how things look, feel, sound, smell, and taste. What images does Bradbury use here to create an impression of Mr. Bittering's helplessness and sense of an important change about to happen?

Loosely Structured Sentences Bradbury's prose is characterized by loosely structured poetic sentences connected by coordinating conjunctions. What coordinating conjunction is repeated in the bottom passage at the right?

Dialogue

"Sam," Bittering said. "Your eyes—"

"What about them, Harry?"

"Didn't they used to be gray?"

"Well now, I don't remember."

"They were, weren't they?"

"Why do you ask, Harry?"

"Because now they're kind of yellow-colored."

"Is that so, Harry?" Sam said, casually. . . .

"Harry, what color eyes have *you* got?" Sam said.

"My eyes? They're blue, of course."

"Here you are, Harry," Sam handed him a pocket mirror. "Take a look at yourself."

—"Dark They Were, and Golden-Eyed"

Imagery

The wind blew as if to flake away their identities. At any moment the Martian air might draw [Mr. Bittering's] soul from him, as marrow comes from a white bone. He felt submerged in a chemical that could dissolve his intellect and burn away his past.

—"Dark They Were, and Golden-Eyed"

Applications

1. **Active Reading** Working with a small group, look back at the stories and find examples of passages or dialogue that reveal important points of style. Compare your examples with those of other groups.

2. **Writing** Think of an event that has impressed you. Using elements of Bradbury's style, write a description of the event.

3. **Speaking and Listening** With a partner, discuss imagery in one of the selections. Choose a particularly strong passage and write a paragraph about the images that the passage creates in your mind. Point out details that help you imagine how things look, feel, sound, smell, or taste. Read the paragraph to your partner.

Loosely Structured Sentences

And so, in time, the towns became the Town of the Golden Kite and the Town of the Silver Wind. And harvestings were harvested and business tended again, and the flesh returned, and disease ran off like a frightened jackal. And on every night of the year the inhabitants in the Town of the Kite could hear the good clear wind sustaining them. And those in the Town of the Wind could hear the kite singing, whispering, rising, and beautifying them.

—"The Golden Kite, the Silver Wind"

Writing

Time Capsule Imagine that you are the last person to leave Earth for Mars. What items would you leave in a time capsule for future scientists and scholars to discover? Make a list. What would the items tell the discoverers about you? Give specific reasons and examples for your choices. Compare your list with that of a classmate.

Speaking & Listening

Film Review View "The Long Years," an episode from *The Ray Bradbury Theater*. Then discuss with classmates similarities and differences between the film's presentation of Mars and the way you visualized it while reading "Dark They Were, and Golden-Eyed."

VIDEO: Literature in Performance

"The Long Years"

Courtesy of Alliance Atlantis Communications, Inc.

Research & Technology

To Mars! Use nonfiction books, the Internet, and other sources to gather information about travel to Mars. Include in your report:

- the distance between Mars and Earth
- the average time a spaceship would take to reach Mars
- the problems of sustaining life on Mars
- the research about Mars that is currently being conducted by NASA or other agencies

Compare your findings with a small group of classmates.

Research and Technology Handbook See p. R110: Getting Information Electronically.

Author Study Project

Summary of Literature

Working with a partner, choose one of the two short stories from the Bradbury Author Study. Summarize the work in writing, and then present your summary to the class.

1 Identify the theme of the story, as well as examples and significant details that support the theme (see page 413).

2 Summarize the story in your own words, using quotations when helpful.

3 Your summary should reflect the deeper meaning of the story, not just the sequence of events.

4 Present your summary to the class.

Ray Bradbury is commonly given credit for bringing respectability to science fiction and making it a legitimate form of literature. He calls himself a "lover of the whole experience of life" and his sense of expectancy and joy shows in his writing. His stories celebrate the human imagination while exploring serious issues such as racism, censorship, and the impact of technology on morality and values.

The Martian Chronicles 1950

This book tells the story of the first attempts of Earth men and women to colonize Mars during the years 1999–2026 and their encounters with telepathic Martians.

Fahrenheit 451 1953

Awarded the Prometheus Hall of Fame Award for Best Classic Libertarian Science Fiction Novel, 1984

This novel is set in a future in which the written word is forbidden. Firemen do not put out fires. Rather, they are in charge of burning books. Individuals in a group of rebels memorize entire works of literature and philosophy in order to preserve civilization.

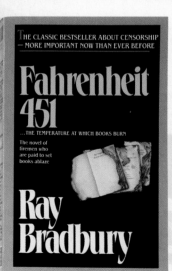

Something Wicked This Way Comes 1962

This novel tells the tale of two boys who discover the terrifying mystery behind the carnival that arrives in town during the dark of night.

A Medicine for Melancholy 1960

This fine collection of Bradbury stories contains works of science fiction, fantasy, and realism. Along with "Dark They Were, and Golden-Eyed," it contains favorites such as "All Summer in a Day," "The Pedestrian," and "The Day It Rained Forever."

The Vintage Bradbury 1965

Bradbury's own selection of his best stories, this collection contains "The Veldt" and "The Fog Horn," as well as excerpts from *The Martian Chronicles* and *Dandelion Wine*.

The Toynbee Convector 1988

Awarded the Bram Stoker Award for Superior Achievement in a Fiction Collection

This book, set in the year 2084, tells the story of Craig Bennett Stiles. He is the inventor of the Toynbee Convector, a time machine he last used one hundred years ago in 1984.

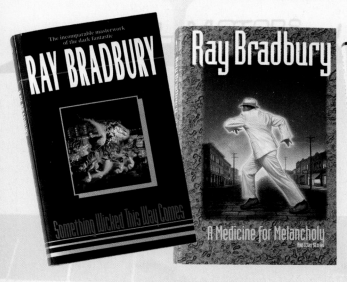

Key Standard
W2.1 Write fictional or autobiographical narratives that contain a standard plot line, complex major and minor characters, and a definite setting.
Other Standards R3.5, W1.1, W1.2, W1.4, W1.7, LC1.4, LC1.7

Writing Workshop | Short Story

Developing a plot . . .

From Reading to Writing Have you ever held your breath in suspense as you read a story? A good suspenseful plot keeps you wondering but also gives enough clues about what *might* happen. For instance, in "The Serial Garden" you may have noticed clues that foreshadowed the fact that Mark's mother would clean the playroom and throw away the magic garden. Writing a suspenseful **short story** will help you learn how to keep your readers guessing.

For Your Portfolio

WRITING PROMPT Write a short story with a suspenseful plot.

Purpose: To entertain
Audience: Your classmates, family, or general readers

Basics in a Box

Short Story at a Glance

Introduction

Sets the stage by
• introducing the **characters**
• describing the **setting**

Body

Develops the plot by
• introducing the conflict
• telling a sequence of **events**
• developing **characters** through words and actions
• building toward a **climax**

Conclusion

Finishes the story by
• possibly resolving the **conflict**
• telling the **last event**

RUBRIC STANDARDS FOR WRITING

A successful short story should

• have a strong beginning and ending
• use the elements of character, setting, and plot to create a convincing world
• use techniques such as vivid sensory language, concrete details, and dialogue to create believable characters and setting
• have a main conflict, which may or may not be resolved
• present a clear sequence of events
• maintain a consistent point of view

Analyzing a Student Model

SPEAKING

See the Speaking and Listening Handbook, p. R100 for oral presentation tips.

OPPORTUNITY

**Rachel Leah Granzow
Campbell Junior High**

RUBRIC
IN ACTION

Plan Bee

In the year 3021, Kali trudged down the purple sidewalk on her home planet, Yein. She wiped her tear-stained cheeks and gripped the letter in her shaking hands. What's wrong with me? she thought. Is it the way I look? my clothes? my personality? She yanked a mirror out of her bag and stared at her reflection. Purple hair, military apparel, grunge boots. . . . She looked like all the other girls on the planet. Then why did her best friend Jareka send a letter stating that their lifelong friendship was over? Kali shoved the mirror back into her bag and read the letter again. "I don't want you to take this the wrong way, but we can't be friends any longer. I'm practically dying when I write this. . . ." Kali read that last sentence over again. Practically dying? That didn't make sense. Kali paused a minute and stared off into the distance. From out of nowhere, a group of gray figures surrounded her. "Lanx," she whispered, before a strong blow to the head knocked her out.

"Ow. Oh, nikum." Kali's eyes fluttered open. She found herself in a dark room surrounded by Lanx, the alien species that threatened to take over Yein.

"So, you've awakened," the Lanx said. The smooth, deep voice sent chills up Kali's spine. "You have been brought here to supply us with information we need. You will cooperate. After all, you don't want to end up like your friend over there." It gestured to a bench in the corner of the room. There lay Jareka.

"Why am I here?" Kali stared defiantly at the metal links on their jackets.

"I have not gone to all this trouble to play games. Jareka was the leader of the CDB-99 spy mission. She stole our map with the location of our most powerful missile. We want it back. You are her best friend, so you know where it is. Now, <u>we have a virtual reality recording</u> of a message to you from Jareka."

The Lanx flipped a switch, and a 3D image of Jareka appeared.

"Kali, if you hear this, tell them about the *buzz,* and Plan Bee. The image faded. Kali understood. Jareka had used their special code. It reminded her of the difference between them.

❶ The writer begins the narration with specific details about the setting.

❷ Includes movements and gestures of the main character

❸ The conflict captures readers' attention.

❹ The central conflict is introduced.

❺ Gives concrete technological details

Jareka had alien blood, not Lanx but another species called Drone. She was able to turn into a deadly bee in an emergency situation. But the transformation could only take place in the presence of another person who knew the code word "Buzz." Kali was that person. If she could recite the words by Jareka's side, the transformation could take place. However, first she had to make up a story to distract the Lanx.

Kali cleared her throat and began. "Well, since I have no choice, I'll confess."

The creatures smiled.

"What Jareka meant by 'buzz' was the code word to the secret place where your map is hidden. The Yein government headquarters are disguised as bee farms on the far east side of the planet. If you have the code word, they'll let you in."

The leader smiled. "We'll see if you're lying. We'll be back soon. Then you'll be terminated." The Lanx marched out and locked the door behind them.

Kali carefully picked up Jareka's hand and recited the code, "Yuma Kachine Leotie Xanthus Lomasi Cadell Tallulah Niabi Sibyl!"

Slowly, Jareka's chest began to rise and fall. Her eyes flew open. She looked at Kali and smiled quickly. Jareka's human features disappeared as she shrank, turning into a bee. She would remain this way until Kali uttered the code again.

The hours of the night passed slowly. Shortly after daybreak, Kali heard heavy footsteps rushing towards the door. The Lanx burst in, armed with lasers. Unseen, Jareka flew over their heads as they blocked Kali's escape. Suddenly, one Lanx warrior fell. Another thudded to the ground. The rest toppled like dominoes. Soon every Lanx lay on the floor. Kali saw Jareka hovering near her. She recited the code backwards. "Sibyl Niabi Tallulah Cadell Lomasi Xanthus Leotie Kachine Yuma!" Jareka rested on the ground and quickly resumed her human shape. Kali and Jareka smiled at each other in relief.

There would now be peace on Yein, at least for the time being. Kali felt at peace, too. She knew that Jareka had tried to end their friendship to protect her. She also knew that true friendship could conquer all.

6 Third-person point of view allows the writer to reveal thoughts and feelings of the main character as well as the actions and words of other minor characters.

Another Option:
- Use first-person point of view to narrate the action from the main character's perspective.

7 Dialogue fits the characters and advances the rising action.

8 Events are ordered chronologically. Transitions make order of events clear.

9 Uses figurative language to bring the scene to life

10 The climax is reached and the central conflict is resolved.

Another Option:
- Don't resolve the conflict; instead let readers imagine how it might be resolved.

11 The conclusion ties up loose ends of the plot and settles the initial conflict of the story.

Writing Your Short Story

❶ Prewriting

> *Imagination is the highest kite one can fly.*
> —Lauren Bacall, actress

To find an idea for your short story, **list** possible settings, characters, and plots. Write down mysterious settings in your neighborhood, like abandoned warehouses or houses with creaking shutters and ivy over the windows. **Skim** newspapers for bizarre incidents or unexplained events. See the **Idea Bank** in the margin for more suggestions. After you have an idea for your short story, follow the steps below.

Planning Your Short Story

1. **Consider the elements of character, setting, and point of view.** Who will be your major character? What does he or she look like? Who else is in the story? Where and when will your story take place? Who will tell your story? Bring your characters to life by making them complex personalities.

2. **Develop the plot.** What is your central conflict? Try to imagine how your main character will react to the conflict. What events might his or her reaction lead to? How do you want the conflict to be resolved?

3. **Share ideas with other writers.** In a small group, take turns outlining your story line and describing your characters. Take note of suggestions or reactions to your plot or characters. Ask group members to take the part of your major character and speak as they imagine the character would.

❷ Drafting

Set aside a block of time to write your first draft. Try to get all the ideas that are floating in your mind down on paper. You will polish your draft later.

- Write **dialogue** that sounds natural and moves the story along.

- Include **foreshadowing**, or hints of what is to happen, which will increase suspense and keep your readers interested.

- Give your readers **concrete and descriptive details** so that the characters, setting, and action seem real.

IDEA Bank

1. For Your Working Portfolio
Look for ideas in the **Writing** sections you completed earlier.

2. Center Stage
Choose three ordinary places that might make interesting story settings, such as a baseball field, a classroom, or a busy supermarket. Imagine what stories could take place in each setting.

3. Strange Matters
Focus on a small but puzzling incident, such as answering the phone and finding no one there or driving into a town that seems completely empty. Brainstorm a list of such incidents with a partner.

Have a question?

See the **Writing Handbook**
Descriptive Writing, p. R43
See **Language Network**
Prewriting, p. 312
Drama, p. 315

Ask Your Peer Reader

- Where can I add details to make the characters and events more real?
- Did the structure of the story make sense?
- Did the ending seem realistic and satisfying?

Need revising help?

Review the **Rubric**, p. 506.

Consider **peer reader** comments.

Check **Revising, Editing, and Proofreading,** p. R35.

SPELLING From Writing

 As you revise your work, look back at the words you misspelled and determine why you made the errors you did. For additional help, refer to the strategies and generalizations in the **Spelling Handbook** on page R30.

SPEAKING Opportunity

Turn your narrative into an oral presentation.

Publishing IDEAS

- Record your short story on audiotape. Enlist classmates to take the parts of different characters. Plan and create sound effects to go along with the reading.

- Adapt your story for a younger audience. Read it aloud to a group of younger students.

Publishing Options
www.mcdougallittell.com

❸ Revising

TARGET SKILL ▶ USING CONCRETE DETAILS A concrete detail gives a precise and specific image that appeals to the senses. For example, instead of saying that the flowers in a garden were beautiful, which can mean different things to different people, Joan Aiken provides concrete details about the flowers: *"There were huge velvety violets and pansies the size of saucers; the hollyhocks were as big as dinner plates, and the turf was sprinkled with enormous daisies."* Choose precise and specific words to involve your readers.

> *heavy footsteps rushing toward the door*
> Shortly after daybreak, Kali heard ~~them return.~~

❹ Editing and Proofreading

TARGET SKILL ▶ PARALLELISM One way to avoid awkwardness in your sentences is to make sure they are written in parallel structure. For instance, if you have a compound verb, where appropriate, make sure all of the verbs are in the same tense and form. For example, the verbs in this sentence are not parallel: *Mark sang and was dancing in the garden.* Instead you should write, *Mark sang and danced in the garden.*

> *locked*
> The Lanx marched out and ~~were locking~~ the door
> securely behind them.

❺ Reflecting

FOR YOUR WORKING PORTFOLIO What part of writing the story did you most enjoy? What have you learned about writing a short story? What ideas would you like to remember for your next story? Attach these reflections to your finished story. Save your short story in your **Working Portfolio.**

Standardized Test Practice

Mixed Review

> Kali pushed slowly the door open. She had not never seen such thick cobwebs as those that formed a gauzy curtain in front of her face. She brushed they aside and stepped into the dark attic. She turned on the light and immediately was seeing the object they're on the windowsill. A crash from the stairs warned her of danger. She decided to leave go of the bottle and lie it on the nearest piece of furniture so she would not be caught with it.
>
> (1) Kali pushed slowly the door open.
> (2) She had not never seen such thick
> (3) She brushed they aside
> (4) was seeing
> (5) they're
> (6) She decided to leave go of the bottle and lie it

Review Your Skills

Use the passage and the questions that follow it to check how well you remember the language conventions you've learned in previous grades.

1. How is sentence 1 best written?
- **A.** Kali pushed slowly the open door.
- **B.** Kali pushed the slowly door open.
- **C.** Slowly, Kali pushed the door open.
- **D.** Correct as is

2. How is sentence 2 best written?
- **A.** She hadn't never seen such thick cobwebs
- **B.** She didn't never see such thick cobwebs
- **C.** She had never seen such thick cobwebs
- **D.** Correct as is

3. What is the correct pronoun usage in sentence 3?
- **A.** She brushed them aside
- **B.** She brushed it aside
- **C.** She brushed their aside
- **D.** Correct as is

4. What is the correct verb tense in item 4?
- **A.** saw
- **B.** sight
- **C.** will see
- **D.** Correct as is

5. What is the correct spelling in item 5?
- **A.** their
- **B.** there
- **C.** thier
- **D.** Correct as is

6. How is sentence 6 best written?
- **A.** She decided to let go of the bottle and lay it
- **B.** She decided to leave go of the bottle lie it
- **C.** She decided to let go of the bottle and lie it
- **D.** Correct as is

Self-Assessment

Check your own answers in the **Grammar Handbook**

Quick Reference: Pronoun Forms, p. R77

Quick Reference: Double Negatives, p. R83

Using Verbs Correctly, p. R81

Parallelism, p. R91

Key Standard
LC1.4 Use the mechanics of writing correctly; demonstrate correct language usage.
Other Standards LC1.1, LC1.3, LC1.6, LC1.7

Flights of Imagination

Through the imagination, we can experience new sights, have adventures, and visit places we have never dreamed of. Whether we seek to experience a distant place or a distant time, stories can take us there. The selections in this unit involve several flights of imagination. Complete one or more of the options below to explore what you have learned.

Key Standard
R3.4 Identify and analyze themes that appear across works.
Other Standards **R3.1, R3.2, R3.6, W2.1**

Reflecting on Theme

More Than Meets the Eye When you think about the saying "appearances are deceiving," which characters from this unit come to mind? Which people from your own experience do you think of? Write an essay exploring the meaning of this saying. Use characters from this unit and from real life as examples.

OPTION 2

Close to Home In which of this unit's selections do the characters face situations that remind you of experiences from your own life? For each instance, write two to four paragraphs explaining the similarities and differences between the situation in the story and what happened to you.

OPTION 3

Guess My Name This unit contains a number of memorable characters. With a small group, play a game in which each of you pantomimes a character from the unit for the others to identify. You can use gestures or pantomime emotions to portray the character. Keep playing until each group member has had a chance to pantomime.

Self ASSESSMENT

READER'S NOTEBOOK

Think again about the quotation you read at the beginning of the unit: "The man who has no imagination has no wings." Write a paragraph explaining how reading the selections in this unit has helped you to better understand the quotation.

REVIEWING YOUR PERSONAL
WORDList

Vocabulary Review the new words you learned in this unit. If necessary, use a dictionary to check the meaning of each word.

Spelling Review your list of spelling words. If you're not sure of the correct spelling, use a dictionary or refer to the **Spelling Handbook** on page R30.

Reviewing Literary Concepts

OPTION 1

Experiencing Suspense Suspense is the excitement or tension that readers feel as they get involved in a story and become eager to learn the outcome. In this unit, which of the selections do you think generates the most suspense? Which generates the least? Consider the selection that you regard as least suspenseful. How might you change the plot to heighten the suspense?

OPTION 2

Exploring Themes The theme, or message, of a story may be stated directly or only implied. Summarize in a phrase or two the theme of five selections you have read in this unit. Record the themes you have summarized in a chart. Analyze the themes and identify which ones are similar.

Title	Theme
The Monsters Are Due on Maple Street	
Key Item	

Self ASSESSMENT

READER'S NOTEBOOK

On a sheet of paper, copy the following literary terms introduced in this unit. Next to each term, jot down a brief definition. If you have trouble explaining a particular concept, refer to the **Glossary of Literary and Reading Terms** on page R120.

science fiction	conflict
fantasy	humor
persuasive essay	surprise ending
meter	onomatopoeia
scanning	stanza
metaphor	resolution
narrative	teleplay
suspense	irony
symbol	alliteration

Portfolio Building

- **Choices and Challenges—Writing** Several of the writing assignments in this unit asked you to respond by writing poems, stories, essays, editorials, and personal narratives. Choose the two you think are best—one fiction and one nonfiction. Write a cover note explaining the reasons for your choice. Then attach the note to the assignment and place it in your **Presentation Portfolio**.

- **Writing Workshops** In this unit you wrote an essay in which you explored the relationship between actions and their effect. Reread your essay. How will these skills help you recognize cause and effect relationships in texts you read? Answer this question in a note and attach the note to the front of your essay and place it in your **Presentation Portfolio**.

- **Additional Activities** Think back to any assignments you completed under **Speaking & Listening** and **Research & Technology.** Keep a record in your portfolio of any assignments that you especially enjoyed, found helpful, or would like to do further work on in the future.

Self ASSESSMENT

Now that your **Presentation Portfolio** contains several pieces, determine which kinds of writing show your strongest work. What other kinds of writing do you think you would like to try as the year goes on?

Setting GOALS

As you completed the reading and writing activities in this unit, you might have noticed that you have strengths in certain skills but not in others. Look back through your **READER'S NOTEBOOK.** List one or two skills that you intend to develop in the next unit.

LITERATURE CONNECTIONS

Tuck Everlasting

BY NATALIE BABBITT

This fantasy is about an encounter between a young girl and a family that never ages, near the spring that makes them immortal. A confrontation with a man who plans to market the spring water results in an accident, difficulty with the law, and an exciting rescue.

These thematically related readings are provided along with *Tuck Everlasting*:

Remember
BY CHRISTINA ROSSETTI

Why There Is Death
BY JOHN BIERHORST

from **The Population Explosion**
BY JOHN AND SUE BECKLAKE

The Search for the Magic Lake
BY GENEVIEVE BARLOW

Eastside Chic with Drive
BY ALBERT SPECTOR

Hail and Farewell
BY RAY BRADBURY

Guardian Neighbor
BY LYNDA BARRY

More Choices

Behind the Attic Wall
BY SYLVIA CASSEDY
Maggie's life takes a new turn when she finds a secret room in her great-aunts' house.

The Legend of Sleepy Hollow
BY WASHINGTON IRVING
In this dark and fantastic tale, Ichabod Crane, a schoolmaster, is scared away from courting the young Katrina Van Tassel by the headless horseman.

The Hobbit
BY J. R. R. TOLKIEN
Bilbo Baggins leaves his quiet life behind when he joins a band of dwarves on their quest to recover stolen gold.

Peter Pan
BY JAMES BARRIE
Peter Pan, a boy who doesn't want to grow up, takes his friends on adventures to Never Never Land.

The Snow Queen
BY HANS CHRISTIAN ANDERSEN
In this classic fairy tale, Gerda struggles to save her kidnapped friend Kay from the evil Snow Queen.

Yeh-Shen: A Cinderella Story from China
BY AI-LING LOUIE
In this Chinese fairy tale, the young Yeh-Shen ends up marrying a handsome prince.

A Wrinkle in Time

BY MADELEINE L'ENGLE

A science fiction novel about the struggle between good and evil, this absorbing story involves supernatural beings, a distant planet, and a daring rescue.

These thematically related readings are provided along with *A Wrinkle in Time*:

Odd Jobs
BY JUDITH GOROG

Reversible
BY OCTAVIO PAZ

Behind Bars
BY FADWA TUQAN

from **World of the Brain**
BY ALVIN AND VIRGINIA SILVERSTEIN

from **It's Our World, Too!**
BY PHILIP HOOSE

The Dark Princess
BY RICHARD KENNEDY

The Sparrow
BY IVAN TURGENEV

Colony
BY RICK WERNLI

Social Studies Connection

Suho and the White Horse
BY YUZO OTSUKA
A retelling of a Mongolian fairy tale.

Of Nightingales That Weep
BY KATHERINE PATERSON
Takiko, a samurai's daughter living in feudal Japan, learns to face war and death.

The Crane Wife
BY SUMIKO YAGAWA
This is the tale of a Japanese farmer. His life takes a turn for the worse when, against his wife's wishes, he decides to watch her while she is weaving.

The Sign of the Chrysanthemum
BY KATHERINE PATERSON
The award-winning author tells the story of a boy's search for his samurai father in feudal Japan.

UNIT FOUR

516

NOTHING STAYS
the SAME

Time
ripens
all
things;
no
one
is
born
wise.

MIGUEL DE CERVANTES SAAVEDRA
Spanish writer,
author of *Don Quixote*

The Literature You'll Read

The Concepts You'll Study

Vocabulary and Reading Comprehension
Vocabulary Focus: Understanding Denotation and
    Connotation
Predicting
Connecting
Visualizing
Responding to the Writer's Style

Writing and Language Conventions
Prepositional Phrases
Adjective Phrases
Adverb Phrases

Literary Analysis
Literary Focus: Mood and Tone
Mood and Tone
Dialect
Farce
Simile and Metaphor

Speaking and Listening
Communication Workshop: Staging a Scene
Narrative or Persuasive Presentation
Write a Dialogue
Play Performance
Choral Reading

*M*ood and Tone

Key Standard
R2.4 Identify an author's argument and point of view in a text.
Other Standards **R3.2, R3.6**

Fit your figures of speech to the characters and action and to the mood and setting of your story. A city setting could have someone slinking like an alley cat around trash cans, and a country story might have the character moving like a barn cat stalking a field mouse.
—*Kathleen C. Phillips*

Mood is the feeling that the writer creates for the reader. A writer uses details in his or her writing to create this feeling. The **setting,** or time and place of a story, can affect the mood dramatically. For instance, a story that takes place in the jungles of India will have a very different mood from a story that is set on the American frontier in the 1800s.

Tone describes a writer's attitude toward his or her subject. A writer might use a serious tone to write about a subject that he or she feels is very important but a humorous tone to write about a subject that he or she does not take so seriously. Mood and tone differ in that mood is determined by the response of the reader to a piece of writing. Tone, on the other hand, is the writer's attitude about a subject as that attitude comes through in the writing.

From "After Twenty Years"

Mood

A writer has many tools to shape the mood of a piece of writing. He or she carefully selects **details, descriptive words, dialogue, imagery,** and **setting** to create a certain mood and to affect the reader in a particular way. A writer can also use the technique of **foreshadowing**—giving hints about what might happen later in order to create suspense and make the reader wonder what is coming next.

The mood of a work can be anything from silly to terrifying. In the excerpt from *The Monsters Are Due on Maple Street,* notice how the stage directions, setting, and dialogue work together to create a mood. The author uses the ordinary details and frustrations of daily life to help create an extraordinary atmosphere.

YOUR TURN Read the text on the right. What is the mood of the teleplay? Which details help create the mood?

MOOD

Les. I just don't understand it. I tried to start it, and it wouldn't start. You saw me. All of you saw me.

(*And now, just as suddenly as the engine started, it stops, and there is a long silence that is gradually intruded upon by the frightened murmuring of the people.*)

Les. I don't understand. I swear . . . I don't understand. What's happening?

Don. Maybe you better tell us. Nothing's working on this street. Nothing. No lights, no power, no radio, (*then meaningfully*) nothing except one car—yours!

(*The people's murmuring becomes a loud chant filling the air with accusations and demands for action. Two of the men pass Don and head toward Les, who backs away from them against his car. He is cornered.*)

—Rod Serling,
The Monsters Are Due on Maple Street

Tone

The **tone** of a piece of writing can reflect the author's attitude toward his or her subject. This reflects the **author's purpose.** So, if the author's purpose is to entertain, the tone may be playful. If the author's purpose is to inform, the tone may be serious.

The tone of the passage from "Amigo Brothers" might be described as serious and respectful.

YOUR TURN In the excerpt at the right, which details convey the writer's attitude toward the topic?

TONE

Each youngster had a dream of someday becoming lightweight champion of the world. Every chance they had the boys worked out, sometimes at the Boys Club on 10th Street and Avenue A and sometimes at the pro's gym on 14th Street. Early morning sunrises would find them running along the East River Drive, wrapped in sweatshirts, short towels around their necks, and handkerchiefs Apache style around their foreheads.

—Piri Thomas, "Amigo Brothers"

Predicting

Key Standard
R3.2 Identify events that advance the plot and describe how they explain the past, present, and future.

Have you ever chosen a video just by looking at the cover? Were you able to guess what would happen in the plot? Whenever you use clues to logically infer how something will turn out, it is called **predicting.** An active reader can also predict when reading a story. A book with a good plot will have you using clues to predict what happens next almost without your thinking about it.

> **Here's how Angeli uses the strategy:**
>
> *"By 'adding up' clues from story events, character clues, illustrations, and my own personal experience, I can **predict** outcomes. From this example, I predict the narrator will be getting an umbrella. At the end of the story, I **evaluate** my predictions to see if I was correct."*

How to Apply the Strategies

To **PREDICT**, an active reader will
- Note clues and details
- Think about outcomes
- **Connect** new information to prior knowledge
- **Evaluate** and revise the prediction
- Use a chart like this one to help make predictions

clues + prior experience → prediction → new details → revised prediction

Try It Now!

Read the excerpt below. Predict what will happen next.

> [Narrator] "This is the most beautiful umbrella I have ever seen," I said. "Ever, in my whole life."
> [Miss Crosman] "Do you have an umbrella?"
> [Narrator] "No. But my mother's going to get me one just like this for Christmas."
> [Miss Crosman] "Is she? I tell you what. You don't have to wait until Christmas."
>
> —Gish Jen, "The White Umbrella"

The White Umbrella

by GISH JEN

Key Standard
R3.2 Identify events that advance the plot and describe how they explain the past, present, and future.
Other Standards **R2.4, W2.1, W2.3, W2.4, LC1.3, LC1.4, LS2.1, LS2.3, LS2.4**

Connect to Your Life

Keeping Up Appearances With a small group, discuss the idea of "keeping up appearances." What does the expression mean? How important is keeping up appearances to you? In what ways do you and people you've observed keep up appearances? Share your group's ideas with the class.

Build Background

Like most writers, Gish Jen, the author of "The White Umbrella," draws on many sources for her stories. In any story, she says, there are "lots of different ingredients: some of the ingredients come from your life; some come from things you've read, or from other people's lives; many, many things you've just made up."

The narrator of "The White Umbrella" is a character who tries to "fit in" with American society while holding on to her Chinese heritage.

WORDS TO KNOW
Vocabulary Preview

audible	illuminate
confirm	maneuver
credibility	resume
discreet	revelation
diverted	stupendous

Focus Your Reading

LITERARY ANALYSIS | **MOOD AND TONE**

Mood and tone are related but different concepts. **Mood** is the feeling, or atmosphere, that a work conveys to readers. It can be expressed by words such as *peaceful, frightening, despairing*. **Tone** refers to a writer's attitude and feelings toward a subject. A writer may use humor to make light of a subject, or take the subject very seriously. As you read, note details that help establish mood and tone in "The White Umbrella."

ACTIVE READING | **PREDICTING**

A logical guess based on information in a story and what you already know is a **prediction.** Active readers make predictions about plot and character as they read. To be able to predict change or development in a character, you need to pay attention to what that character thinks, feels, and says. Ask yourself how a character may react when a new event occurs in the plot. As you read "The White Umbrella," pay attention to the thoughts and feelings of the narrator and then try to predict how she will change.

READER'S NOTEBOOK Make a chart with three columns. Jot down the narrator's thoughts and feelings in the first column, important events in the second column, and your own predictions as to how the narrator will respond to these events in the third.

Narrator's Thoughts and Feelings	Events in Story	Predictions
The narrator feels jealous of Eugenie Roberts and wants the white umbrella.	Eugenie does not take the umbrella after her piano lesson.	The narrator will try to keep the umbrella for herself.

The White Umbrella

by Gish Jen

When I was twelve, my mother went to work without telling me or my little sister.

"Not that we need the second income." The lilt of her accent drifted from the kitchen up to the top of the stairs, where Mona and I were listening.

"No," said my father, in a barely <u>audible</u> voice. "Not like the Lee family."

The Lees were the only other Chinese family in town. I remembered how sorry my parents had felt for Mrs. Lee when she started waitressing downtown the year before; and so when my mother began coming home late, I didn't say anything and tried to keep Mona from saying anything either.

"But why shouldn't I?" she argued. "Lots of people's mothers work."

"Those are American people," I said.

"So what do you think we are? I can do the pledge of allegiance with my eyes closed."

Nevertheless, she tried to be <u>discreet</u>; and if my mother wasn't home by 5:30, we would start cooking by ourselves, to make sure dinner would be on time. Mona would wash the vegetables and put on the rice; I would chop.

For weeks we wondered what kind of work she was doing. I imagined that she was selling perfume, testing dessert recipes for the local newspaper. Or maybe she was working for the florist. Now that she had learned to drive, she might be delivering boxes of roses to people.

"I don't think so," said Mona as we walked to our piano lesson after school. "She would've hit something by now."

A gust of wind littered the street with leaves.

"Maybe we better hurry up," she went on, looking at the sky. "It's going to pour."

"But we're too early." Her lesson didn't begin until 4:00, mine until 4:30, so we usually tried to walk as slowly as we could. "And anyway, those aren't the kind of clouds that rain. Those are cumulus clouds."[1]

We arrived out of breath and wet.

"Oh, you poor, poor dears," said old Miss Crosman. "Why don't you call me the next time it's like this out? If your mother won't drive you, I can come pick you up."

"No, that's okay," I answered. Mona wrung her hair out on Miss Crosman's rug. "We just couldn't get the roof of our car to close, is all. We took it to the beach last summer and got sand in the mechanism." I pronounced this last word carefully, as if the <u>credibility</u> of my lie depended on its middle syllable. "It's never been the same." I thought for a second. "It's a convertible."

"Well then make yourselves at home." She exchanged looks with Eugenie Roberts, whose lesson we were interrupting. Eugenie smiled good-naturedly. "The towels are in the closet across from the bathroom."

Huddling at the end of Miss Crosman's nine-foot leatherette couch, Mona and I watched Eugenie play. She was a grade ahead of me and, according to school rumor, had a boyfriend in high school. I believed it. . . . She had auburn hair, blue eyes, and, I noted with a particular pang,[2] a pure white folding umbrella.

"I can't see," whispered Mona.

"So clean your glasses."

"My glasses *are* clean. You're in the way."

I looked at her. "They look dirty to me."

"That's because *your* glasses are dirty."

Eugenie came bouncing to the end of her piece.

"Oh! Just <u>stupendous</u>!" Miss Crosman hugged her, then looked up as Eugenie's mother walked in. "Stupendous!" she said again. "Oh! Mrs. Roberts! Your daughter has a gift, a real gift. It's an honor to teach her."

Mrs. Roberts, radiant with pride, swept her daughter out of the room as if she were royalty, born to the piano bench. Watching the way Eugenie carried herself, I sat up and concentrated so hard on sucking in my stomach that I did not realize until the Robertses were gone that Eugenie had left her umbrella. As Mona began to play, I jumped up and ran to the window, meaning to call to them—only to see their brake lights flash then fade at the stop sign at the corner. As if to allow them passage, the rain had let up; a quivering sun lit their way.

---

1. **cumulus** (kyo͞om′yə-ləs) **clouds:** clouds with flat bottoms and fluffy, rounded tops.

2. **pang:** a sudden feeling of longing or distress.

Girl at Piano (1966), Will Barnet. Oil on canvas, 64″ × 39″, private collection. Copyright © 1995 Will Barnet/Licensed by VAGA, New York.

The umbrella glowed like a scepter[3] on the blue carpet while Mona, slumping over the keyboard, managed to eke out[4] a fair rendition of a cat fight. At the end of the piece, Miss Crosman asked her to stand up.

"Stay right there," she said, then came back a minute later with a towel to cover the bench. "You must be cold," she continued. "Shall I call your mother and have her bring over some dry clothes?"

"No," answered Mona. "She won't come because she . . ."

"She's too busy," I broke in from the back of the room.

"I see." Miss Crosman sighed and shook her head a little. "Your glasses are filthy, honey," she said to Mona. "Shall I clean them for you?"

Sisterly embarrassment seized me. Why hadn't Mona wiped her lenses when I told her to? As she <u>resumed</u> abuse of the piano, I stared at the umbrella. I wanted to open it, twirl it around by its slender silver handle; I wanted to dangle it from my wrist on the way to school the way the other girls did. I wondered what Miss Crosman would say if I offered to bring it to Eugenie at school tomorrow. She would be impressed with my consideration for others; Eugenie would be pleased to have it back; and I would have possession of the umbrella for an entire night. I looked at it again, toying with the idea of asking for one for Christmas. I knew, however, how my mother would react.

"Things," she would say. "What's the matter with a raincoat? All you want is things, just like an American."

Sitting down for my lesson, I was careful to keep the towel under me and sit up straight.

"I'll bet you can't see a thing either," said Miss Crosman, reaching for my glasses. "And you can relax, you poor dear. . . . This isn't a boot camp."[5]

When Miss Crosman finally allowed me to start playing, I played extra well, as well as I possibly could. See, I told her with my fingers. You don't have to feel sorry for me.

---

3. **scepter** (sĕp'tər): the rod or baton a ruler holds as a sign of authority.

4. **eke out:** to get or produce with great struggle.

5. **boot camp:** a military base where new members of the armed forces receive basic training.

"That was wonderful," said Miss Crosman. "Oh! Just wonderful."

An entire constellation rose in my heart.

"And guess what," I announced proudly. "I have a surprise for you."

Then I played a second piece for her, a much more difficult one that she had not assigned.

"Oh! That was stupendous," she said without hugging me. "Stupendous! You are a genius, young lady. If your mother had started you younger, you'd be playing like Eugenie Roberts by now!"

I looked at the keyboard, wishing that I had still a third, even more difficult piece to play for her. I wanted to tell her that I was the school spelling bee champion, that I wasn't ticklish, that I could do karate.

"My mother is a concert pianist," I said.

She looked at me for a long moment, then finally, without saying anything, hugged me. I didn't say anything about bringing the umbrella to Eugenie at school.

The steps were dry when Mona and I sat down to wait for my mother.

"Do you want to wait inside?" Miss Crosman looked anxiously at the sky.

"No," I said. "Our mother will be here any minute."

"In a while," said Mona.

"Any minute," I said again, even though my mother had been at least twenty minutes late every week since she started working.

According to the church clock across the street we had been waiting twenty-five minutes when Miss Crosman came out again.

"Shall I give you ladies a ride home?"

"No," I said. "Our mother is coming any minute."

I could not believe that I was actually holding the umbrella.

"Shall I at least give her a call and remind her you're here? Maybe she forgot about you."

"I don't think she *forgot*," said Mona.

"Shall I give her a call anyway? Just to be safe?"

"I bet she already left," I said. "How could she forget about us?"

Miss Crosman went in to call.

"There's no answer," she said, coming back out.

"See, she's on her way," I said.

"Are you sure you wouldn't like to come in?"

"No," said Mona.

"Yes," I said. I pointed at my sister. "She meant yes too. She meant no, she wouldn't like to go in."

Miss Crosman looked at her watch. "It's 5:30 now, ladies. My pot roast will be coming out in fifteen minutes. Maybe you'd like to come in and have some then?"

"My mother's almost here," I said. "She's on her way."

We watched and watched the street. I tried to imagine what my mother was doing; I tried to imagine her writing messages in the sky, even though I knew she was afraid of planes. I watched as the branches of Miss Crosman's big willow tree started to sway; they had all been trimmed to exactly the same height off the ground, so that they looked beautiful, like hair in the wind.

It started to rain.

"Miss Crosman is coming out again," said Mona.

"Don't let her talk you into going inside," I whispered.

"Why not?"

"Because that would mean Mom isn't really coming any minute."

"But she isn't," said Mona. "She's *working.*"

"Shhh! Miss Crosman is going to hear you."

"She's working! She's working! She's working!"

I put my hand over her mouth, but she licked it, and so I was wiping my hand on my wet dress when the front door opened.

"We're getting even *wetter,*" said Mona right away. "Wetter and wetter."

"Shall we all go in?" Miss Crosman pulled Mona to her feet. "Before you young ladies catch pneumonia? You've been out here an hour already."

"We're *freezing.*" Mona looked up at Miss Crosman. "Do you have any hot chocolate? We're going to catch *pneumonia.*"

"I'm not going in," I said. "My mother's coming any minute."

"Come on," said Mona. "Use your *noggin.*"[6]

"Any minute."

"Come on, Mona," Miss Crosman opened the door. "Shall we get you inside first?"

"See you in the hospital," said Mona as she went in. "See you in the hospital with *pneumonia.*"

I stared out into the empty street. The rain was pricking me all over; I was cold; I wanted to go inside. I wanted to be able to let myself go inside. If Miss Crosman came out again, I decided, I would go in.

She came out with a blanket and the white umbrella.

I could not believe that I was actually holding the umbrella, opening it. It sprang up by itself as if it were alive, as if that were what it wanted to do—as if it belonged in my hands, above my head. I stared up at the network of silver spokes, then spun the umbrella around and around and around. It was so clean and white that it seemed to glow, to <u>illuminate</u> everything around it. "It's beautiful," I said.

Miss Crosman sat down next to me, on one end of the blanket. I moved the umbrella over so that it covered that too. I could feel the rain on my left shoulder and shivered. She put her arm around me.

"You poor, poor dear."

I knew that I was in store for another bolt of sympathy, and braced myself by staring up into the umbrella.

"You know, I very much wanted to have children when I was younger," she continued.

"You did?"

She stared at me a minute. Her face looked dry and crusty, like day-old frosting.

"I did. But then I never got married."

I twirled the umbrella around again.

"This is the most beautiful umbrella I have ever seen," I said. "Ever, in my whole life."

"Do you have an umbrella?"

"No. But my mother's going to get me one just like this for Christmas."

"Is she? I tell you what. You don't have to wait until Christmas. You can have this one."

"But this one belongs to Eugenie Roberts," I protested. "I have to give it back to her tomorrow in school."

"Who told you it belongs to Eugenie? It's not Eugenie's. It's mine. And now I'm giving it to you, so it's yours."

"It is?"

She hugged me tighter. "That's right. It's all yours."

"It's mine?" I didn't know what to say. "Mine?" Suddenly I was jumping up and down in the rain. "It's beautiful! Oh! It's beautiful!" I laughed.

Miss Crosman laughed too, even though she was getting all wet.

---

6. **noggin:** head.

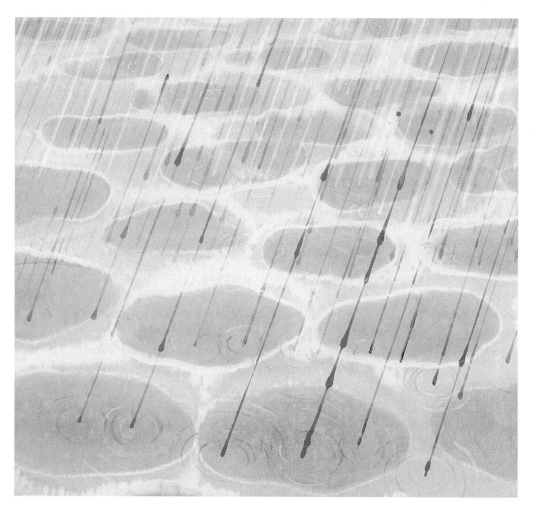

Japanese Rain on Canvas (1972), David Hockney. Acrylic on canvas, 48″ × 48″. Copyright © David Hockney.

"Thank you, Miss Crosman. Thank you very much. Thanks a zillion. It's beautiful. It's *stupendous!*"

"You're quite welcome," she said.

"Thank you," I said again, but that didn't seem like enough. Suddenly I knew just what she wanted to hear. "I wish you were my mother."

Right away I felt bad.

"You shouldn't say that," she said, but her face was opening into a huge smile as the lights of my mother's car cautiously turned the corner. I quickly collapsed the umbrella and put it up my skirt, holding onto it from the outside, through the material.

"Mona!" I shouted into the house. "Mona! Hurry up! Mom's here! I told you she was coming!"

Then I ran away from Miss Crosman, down to the curb. Mona came tearing up to my side as my mother neared the house. We both backed up a few feet so that in case she went onto the curb, she wouldn't run us over.

"But why didn't you go inside with Mona?" my mother asked on the way home. She had taken off her own coat to put over me and had the heat on high.

"She wasn't using her noggin," said Mona, next to me in the back seat.

I should call next time," said my mother. "I just don't like to say where I am."

That was when she finally told us that she was working as a check-out clerk in the A&P. She was supposed to be on the day shift, but the other employees were unreliable, and her boss had promised her a promotion if she would stay until the evening shift filled in.

For a moment no one said anything. Even Mona seemed to find the <u>revelation</u> disappointing.

"A promotion already!" she said, finally.

I listened to the windshield wipers.

"You're so quiet." My mother looked at me in the rear view mirror. "What's the matter?"

"I wish you would quit," I said after a moment.

She sighed. "The Chinese have a saying: one beam cannot hold the roof up."

"But Eugenie Roberts's father supports their family."

She sighed once more. "Eugenie Roberts's father is Eugenie Roberts's father," she said.

As we entered the downtown area, Mona started leaning hard against me every time the car turned right, trying to push me over. Remembering what I had said to Miss Crosman, I tried to <u>maneuver</u> the umbrella under my leg so she wouldn't feel it.

"What's under your skirt?" Mona wanted to know as we came to a traffic light. My mother, watching us in the rear view mirror again, rolled slowly to a stop.

"What's the matter?" she asked.

"There's something under her skirt," said Mona, pulling at me. "Under her skirt."

Meanwhile, a man crossing the street started to yell at us. "Who do you think you are, lady?" he said. "You're blocking the whole crosswalk."

We all froze. Other people walking by stopped to watch.

"Didn't you hear me?" he went on, starting to thump on the hood with his fist. "Don't you speak English?"

My mother began to back up, but the car behind us honked. Luckily, the light turned green right after that. She sighed in relief.

"What were you saying, Mona?" she asked.

We wouldn't have hit the car behind us that hard if he hadn't been moving too but as it was, our car bucked violently, throwing us all first back and then forward.

"Uh oh," said Mona when we stopped. "Another accident."

I was relieved to have attention <u>diverted</u> from the umbrella. Then I noticed my mother's head, tilted back onto the seat. Her eyes were closed.

"Mom!" I screamed. "Mom! Wake up!"

She opened her eyes. "Please don't yell," she said. "Enough people are going to yell already."

"I thought you were dead," I said, starting to cry. "I thought you were dead."

She turned around, looked at me intently, then put her hand to my forehead.

"Sick," she <u>confirmed</u>. "Some kind of sick is giving you crazy ideas."

As the man from the car behind us started tapping on the window, I moved the umbrella away from my leg. Then Mona and my mother were getting out of the car. I got out after them; and while everyone else was inspecting the damage we'd done, I threw the umbrella down a sewer. ❖

Connect to the Literature

1. **What Do You Think?**
   How did you react to the narrator's behavior at the end of the story? Explain.

   Comprehension Check
   • What do the sisters promise not to tell at the beginning of the story? Why?
   • What does the narrator do with the white umbrella at the end of the story?

Think Critically

2. What does the umbrella really mean to the narrator?

   Think About:
   • why she first wants the umbrella
   • her reaction to being given the umbrella
   • her reaction to the car accident

3. How important is keeping up appearances to each of the sisters? Explain.

4. When the narrator says to her mother, "I thought you were dead," how would you describe her feelings toward her mother at that moment? How have those feelings changed throughout the story?

5. **ACTIVE READING** **PREDICTING**
   With a classmate, compare the predictions you made in your **READER'S NOTEBOOK** with what actually happened.

Extend Interpretations

6. **Critic's Corner** A member of the student board that reviewed the stories in this book said, "I liked how the story was told by the main character. When a story is written like this, I think it makes it more interesting, because you see how the main character feels." How might a first-person narrator affect the reader differently than a third-person narrator? How does point of view affect the theme of the story? Explain.

7. **Connect to Life** The narrator assumes that Eugenie Roberts "has everything"—looks, talent, and the white umbrella. What assumptions do people make about others based on appearances? When are looks deceptive?

Literary Analysis

MOOD AND TONE **Mood** is the atmosphere that a literary work conveys by various means, including description, setting, and dialogue. The mood of "The White Umbrella," for example, is one of being trapped between conflicting demands—the narrator's desire to keep up appearances and her love of her mother.

Tone, on the other hand, is the author's attitude toward his or her subject. In this story, Gish Jen seems both critical and sympathetic toward the narrator.

Activity As a class, consider examples from the story that helped set the **mood** at key moments. List them on a chart and discuss the mood they created. Then, look for details that reveal the author's attitude toward her subject—that is, the **tone** of the story. Try to express the tone in words.

REVIEW: SYMBOL A **symbol** is a person, place, or object that stands for something beyond itself. In literature, objects and images are used to symbolize things that cannot actually be seen, such as an idea or feeling. What do you think the white umbrella symbolizes?

Writing

Short Story What do you think finally caused the girls' mother to tell them about her job? Write a story in which you trace the series of events that lead up to her conversation with them in the car. Use details from the story, such as the mother's conversation with the father, but make up details of your own as well, such as what the mother and the store manager might have said to each other. Be sure your story follows a plot structure, includes a setting, and major and minor characters. Build suspense and include dialogue in your story. Place the story in your **Working Portfolio.**

Writing Handbook
See p. R45: Narrative Writing.

Opinion Essay At the beginning of the story, the narrator worries that her family is becoming like "American people." Yet, as the story unfolds, she herself wants to be like Eugenie Roberts. How much should someone change in order to fit in? Write an essay that responds to this question.

Writing Handbook
See p. R51: Persuasive Writing.

Speaking & Listening

Presentations Make revisions to your short story or opinion essay to make it ready to read aloud. Present your work to a small group of classmates. Be sure to speak clearly, but also with inflection in your voice to keep the audience interested. Make eye contact when possible. When you are finished, ask for feedback. If you read the opinion essay, ask questions like, Was my attitude toward the subject clear? Do you agree with my point? Why or why not? If you read your story, ask questions like, Was the story well-organized? Did it impact the listener in any way? If so, how?

Speaking and Listening Handbook
See p. R106: Critical Listening.

Research & Technology

In ancient China, the umbrella represented privilege and authority. Search your school or public library's card catalog for books on ancient Chinese culture. Research how and by whom the umbrella was used. Bring notes and sources to class. Share your findings.

Vocabulary

EXERCISE: WORD MEANING On a sheet of paper, write the word or phrase that best answers each of the following riddles.

1. A <u>revelation</u> has made me disappear. Was I a city, a secret, or a circle?

2. I <u>confirm</u> the spelling of words. Am I a pen, an eraser, or a dictionary?

3. I <u>illuminate</u> a house. Am I a lamp, a roof, or a sheet of plastic?

4. Rain is <u>diverted</u> by me. Am I a well, an umbrella, or a flower garden?

5. I am very <u>discreet</u>. Do people think me rude, cautious, or bold?

6. I make a very <u>audible</u> sound when eaten. Am I celery, a cupcake, or a hamburger?

7. I am about to <u>resume</u> work. Have I just finished, paused, or kept on working?

8. I am truly a <u>stupendous</u> sight. Do people yawn, giggle, or gasp when they see me?

9. I am well known for my <u>credibility</u>. Am I honest, brave, or sassy?

10. I am trying to <u>maneuver</u> a go-cart. Am I stopping it, steering it, or trying to buy it?

Building Vocabulary
See p. R24: Context Clues.

Grammar in Context: Prepositional Phrases

In "The White Umbrella," Gish Jen uses **prepositional phrases** to add details to her writing.

> The umbrella glowed . . . on the blue carpet . . .

The word *on* is a **preposition.** A preposition shows the relationship between a noun or pronoun—the **object of the preposition**—and some other words in a sentence. A **prepositional phrase** includes the preposition, the noun or pronoun that is the object of the preposition, and all of the words that modify the object.

Common prepositions are *above, across, after, against, at, before, beside, by, for, from, in, inside, into, of, off, on, onto, over, through, to,* and *with.*

WRITING EXERCISE Rewrite the sentences, adding a prepositional phrase to give each sentence more detail.

Example: *Original* Mona continued her abuse.

Rewritten Mona continued her abuse <u>of the piano.</u>

1. I waited uncomfortably.
2. Miss Crosman took my glasses.
3. My pot roast is cooking.
4. Finally my mother arrived.
5. My mother's head was resting.

Connect to the Literature Find three prepositional phrases in the last paragraph of "The White Umbrella."

Grammar Handbook
See p. R84: Prepositional Phrases.

Gish Jen
born 1956

"If there is one thing I hope readers come away with, it's to see Asian Americans as 'us' rather than 'other.'"

Growing Up A daughter of immigrant Chinese parents, Gish Jen grew up just north of New York City. "We were almost the only Asian-American family in town," she recalls. "People threw things at us and called us names. We thought it was normal. It was only much later that I realized it had been hard." Jen says these experiences did not make her childhood unhappy. In fact, her writing contains a great deal of humor.

Artistic Beginning Jen's first name is really Lillian. She adopted the name Gish, the last name of the silent-picture actress Lillian Gish, just for fun in high school. After Jen graduated from college, she went to China to teach English and later enrolled at the Writer's Workshop at the University of Iowa. About her writing, Jen says, "If there is one thing I hope readers come away with, it's to see Asian Americans as 'us' rather than 'other.'"

AUTHOR ACTIVITY
Mona and Callie The narrator in "The White Umbrella," along with her sister Mona and their parents, appears in several of Gish Jen's later works. Jen named the narrator Callie and uses her as the narrator for her short story "In the American Society." Read this story and compare it with "The White Umbrella." How have the characters changed, and how have they remained the same?

from **Boy: Tales of Childhood**

by ROALD DAHL (roo'əl däl')

> Standards R1.3, R3.6, W2.1, W2.3, W2.4, LC1.3, LC1.4, LC1.7

Connect to Your Life

Just for Fun Pranks can take many forms—funny or not so funny, harmless or harmful. They may also have unforeseen consequences. Get together with a small group of classmates. Describe some pranks you have played or that have been played on you. What were their consequences?

Build Background

SOCIAL STUDIES

Roald Dahl, a well-known British author of books for young people, played his share of pranks when he was a schoolboy. In this excerpt from his autobiography, he describes a prank he played as a nine-year-old at Llandaff Cathedral School in Wales. This school was what the British call a preparatory school—an elementary school for students planning to attend a private secondary school. Preparatory schools are known for high standards and challenging academic training.

Schoolchildren in Great Britain. Archive Photos.

Focus Your Reading

LITERARY ANALYSIS | DIALECT

One of the ways that an author makes a character come alive for the reader is through **dialect**—a type of language spoken by people of a particular class or region. A dialect may differ from standard language in grammar, pronunciation, and vocabulary. As you read the excerpt from *Boy: Tales of Childhood,* pay attention to the dialect of Mrs. Pratchett—not only what she says but how she says it.

ACTIVE READING | CONNECTING

A reader's process of relating the content of a literary work to his or her own knowledge and experience is called **connecting.** In *Boy: Tales of Childhood* the narrator's description of his schoolboy adventures may lead readers to recall similar events from their own background. Pay attention to how the narrator describes events and characters as well as his own feelings.

📖 **READER'S NOTEBOOK** As you read the selection, note details about actions, characters, thoughts, and emotions from the story that you recognize from your own experience.

The description of the candy sold in the candy store reminds me of my favorite candy as a kid.

> WORDS TO KNOW **Vocabulary Preview**
> elaborate   loathsome   saturated
> flourishing malignant

from

B

Y

Tales of Childhood

by Roald Dahl

The Bicycle and the Sweetshop

When I was seven, my mother decided I should leave kindergarten and go to a proper boys' school. By good fortune, there existed a well-known preparatory school for boys about a mile from our house. It was called Llandaff Cathedral School, and it stood right under the shadow of Llandaff cathedral. Like the cathedral, the school is still there and still <u>flourishing</u>.

But here again, I can remember very little about the two years I attended Llandaff Cathedral School, between the age of seven and nine. Only two moments remain clearly in my mind. The first lasted not more than five seconds, but I will never forget it.

WORDS
TO
KNOW

flourishing (flûr'ĭ-shĭng) *adj.* getting along well and successfully; thriving **flourish** *v.*

535

It was my first term, and I was walking home alone across the village green after school when suddenly one of the senior twelve-year-old boys came riding full speed down the road on his bicycle about twenty yards away from me. The road was on a hill, and the boy was going down the slope, and as he flashed by he started backpedaling very quickly so that the free-wheeling mechanism of his bike made a loud whirring sound. At the same time, he took his hands off the handlebars and folded them casually across his chest. I stopped dead and stared after him. How wonderful he was! How swift and brave and graceful in his long trousers with bicycle clips around them and his scarlet school cap at a jaunty angle on his head! One day, I told myself, one glorious day I will have a bike like that, and I will wear long trousers with bicycle clips, and my school cap will sit jaunty on my head, and I will go whizzing down the hill pedaling backwards with no hands on the handlebars!

I promise you that if somebody had caught me by the shoulder at that moment and said to me, "What is your greatest wish in life, little boy? What is your absolute ambition? To be a doctor? A fine musician? A painter? A writer? Or the Lord Chancellor?"[1] I would have answered without hesitation that my only ambition, my hope, my longing was to have a bike like that and to go whizzing down the hill with no hands on the handlebars. It would be fabulous. It made me

Llandaff Cathedral Green (1986), Hildred Falcon. Courtesy National Library of Wales.

tremble just to think about it.

My second and only other memory of Llandaff Cathedral School is extremely bizarre. It happened a little over a year later, when I was just nine. By then I had made some friends, and when I walked to school in the mornings I would start out alone but would pick up four other boys of my own age along the way. After school was over, the same four boys and I would set out together across the village green and through the village itself, heading for home. On the way to school and on the way back we always passed the sweetshop.

No we didn't; we never passed it. We always stopped. We lingered outside its rather small window, gazing in at the big glass jars full of bull's-eyes and old-fashioned humbugs and strawberry bonbons and glacier mints and acid drops and pear drops and lemon drops and all the rest of them. Each of us received sixpence[2] a week for pocket money, and whenever there was any money in our pockets, we would all troop in together to buy a pennyworth of this or that. My own favorites were sherbet suckers and licorice bootlaces.

One of the other boys, whose name was Thwaites, told me I should never eat licorice

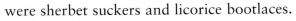

1. **Lord Chancellor:** a high-ranking British government official who presides over the House of Lords.

2. **sixpence:** in Great Britain, six pennies.

bootlaces. Thwaites's father, who was a doctor, had said that they were made from rats' blood. The father had given his young son a lecture about licorice bootlaces when he had caught him eating one in bed. "Every rat catcher in the country," the father had said, "takes his rats to the Licorice Bootlace Factory, and the manager pays tuppence[3] for each rat. Many a rat catcher has become a millionaire by selling his dead rats to the factory."

"But how do they turn the rats into licorice?" the young Thwaites had asked his father.

"They wait until they've got ten thousand rats," the father had answered, "then they dump them all into a huge, shiny steel cauldron[4] and boil them up for several hours. Two men stir the bubbling cauldron with long poles, and in the end they have a thick, steaming rat stew. After that, a cruncher is lowered into the cauldron to crunch the bones, and what's left is a pulpy substance called rat mash."

"Yes, but how do they turn that into licorice bootlaces, Daddy?" the young Thwaites had asked, and this question, according to Thwaites, had caused his father to pause and think for a few moments before he answered it. At last he had said, "The two men who were doing the stirring with the long poles now put on their Wellington boots[5] and climb into the cauldron and shovel the hot rat mash out onto a concrete floor. Then they run a steamroller over it several times to flatten it out. What is left looks rather like a gigantic black pancake, and all they have to do after that is to wait for it to cool and to harden so they can cut it up into strips to make the bootlaces. Don't ever eat them," the father had said. "If you do, you'll get ratitis."

"What is ratitis, Daddy?" young Thwaites had asked.

"All the rats that the rat catchers catch are poisoned with rat poison," the father had said. "It's the rat poison that gives you ratitis."

"Yes, but what happens to you when you catch it?" young Thwaites had asked.

"Your teeth become very sharp and pointed," the father had answered. "And a short, stumpy tail grows out of your back just above your bottom. There is no cure for ratitis. I ought to know. I'm a doctor."

We all enjoyed Thwaites's story, and we made him tell it to us many times on our walks to and from school. But it didn't stop any of us except Thwaites from buying licorice bootlaces. At two for a penny they were the best value in the shop. A bootlace, in case you haven't had the pleasure of handling one, is not round. It's like a flat black tape about half an inch wide. You buy it rolled up in a coil, and in those days it used to be so long that when you unrolled it and held one end at arm's length above your head, the other end touched the ground.

Sherbet suckers were also two a penny. Each sucker consisted of a yellow cardboard tube filled with sherbet powder, and there was a hollow licorice straw sticking out of it. (Rat's blood again, young Thwaites would warn us, pointing at the licorice straw.) You sucked the sherbet up through the straw, and when it was finished you ate the licorice. They were delicious, those

---

3. **tuppence** (tŭp′əns): in Great Britain, two pennies.

4. **cauldron**: a large kettle.

5. **Wellington boots**: high rubber boots.

sherbet suckers. The sherbet fizzed in your mouth, and if you knew how to do it, you could make white froth come out of your nostrils and pretend you were throwing a fit.

Gobstoppers, costing a penny each, were enormous, hard round balls the size of small tomatoes. One gobstopper would provide about an hour's worth of nonstop sucking, and if you took it out of your mouth and inspected it every five minutes or so, you would find it had changed color. There was something fascinating about the way it went from pink to blue to green to yellow. We used to wonder how in the world the Gobstopper Factory managed to achieve this magic. "How *does* it happen?" we would ask each other. "How *can* they make it keep changing color?"

"It's your spit that does it," young Thwaites proclaimed. As the son of a doctor, he considered himself to be an authority on all things that had to do with the body. He could tell us about scabs and when they were ready to be picked off. He knew why a black eye was blue and why blood was red. "It's your spit that makes a gobstopper change color," he kept insisting. When we asked him to <u>elaborate</u> on this theory, he answered, "You wouldn't understand it if I did tell you."

Pear drops were exciting because they had a dangerous taste. They smelled of nail varnish, and they froze the back of your throat. All of us were warned against eating them, and the result was that we ate them more than ever.

The sweetshop in Llandaff in the year 1923 was the very center of our lives.

Then there was a hard brown lozenge called the tonsil tickler. The tonsil tickler tasted and smelled very strongly of chloroform. We had not the slightest doubt that these things were <u>saturated</u> in the dreaded anesthetic which, as Thwaites had many times pointed out to us, could put you to sleep for hours at a stretch.

"If my father has to saw off somebody's leg," he said, "he pours chloroform onto a pad, and the person sniffs it and goes to sleep, and my father saws his leg off without him even feeling it."

"But why do they put it into sweets and sell them to us?" we asked him.

You might think a question like this would have baffled Thwaites. But Thwaites was never baffled. "My father says tonsil ticklers were invented for dangerous prisoners in jail," he said. "They give them one with each meal, and the chloroform makes them sleepy and stops them rioting."

"Yes," we said, "but why sell them to children?"

"It's a plot," Thwaites said. "A grown-up plot to keep us quiet."

The sweetshop in Llandaff in the year 1923 was the very center of our lives. To us, it was what a bar is to a drunk or a church is to a bishop. Without it, there would have been little to live for. But it had one terrible drawback, this sweetshop. The woman who owned it was a horror. We hated her, and we had good reason for doing so.

| WORDS TO KNOW | **elaborate** (ĭ-lăb′ə-rāt′) *v.* to state at greater length or in greater detail |
| | **saturated** (săch′ə-rā′tĭd) *adj.* soaked with moisture; drenched |

538

Her name was Mrs. Pratchett. She was a small, skinny old hag with a moustache on her upper lip and a mouth as sour as a green gooseberry. She never smiled. She never welcomed us when we went in, and the only times she spoke were when she said things like, "I'm watchin' you, so keep yer thievin' fingers off them chocolates!" Or "I don't want you in 'ere just to look around! Either you *forks* out or you *gets* out!"

But by far the most <u>loathsome</u> thing about Mrs. Pratchett was the filth that clung around her. Her apron was grey and greasy. Her blouse had bits of breakfast all over it, toast crumbs and tea stains and splotches of dried egg yolk. It was her hands, however, that disturbed us most. They were disgusting. They were black with dirt and grime. They looked as though they had been putting lumps of coal on the fire all day long. And do not forget, please, that it was these very hands and fingers that she plunged into the sweet jars when we asked for a pennyworth of treacle toffee[6] or wine gums or nut clusters or whatever. There were precious few health laws in those days, and nobody, least of all Mrs. Pratchett, ever thought of using a little shovel for getting out the sweets as they do today. The mere sight of her grimy right hand with its black fingernails digging an ounce of chocolate fudge out of a jar would have caused a starving tramp to go running from the shop. But not us.

Sweets were our lifeblood. We would have put up with far worse than that to get them. So we simply stood and watched in sullen silence while this disgusting old woman stirred around inside the jars with her foul fingers.

The other thing we hated Mrs. Pratchett for was her meanness. Unless you spent a whole sixpence all in one go, she wouldn't give you a bag. Instead you got your sweets twisted up in a small piece of newspaper which she tore off a pile of old *Daily Mirrors* lying on the counter.

So you can well understand that we had it in for Mrs. Pratchett in a big way, but we didn't quite know what to do about it. Many schemes were put forward, but none of them was any good. None of them, that is, until suddenly, one memorable afternoon, we found the dead mouse.

The Great Mouse Plot

My four friends and I had come across a loose floorboard at the back of the classroom, and when we prised it up with the blade of a pocketknife, we discovered a big hollow space underneath. This, we decided, would be our secret hiding place for sweets and other small treasures such as conkers[7] and monkey nuts and birds' eggs. Every afternoon, when the last lesson was over, the five of us would wait until the classroom had emptied; then we would lift up the floorboard and examine our secret hoard, perhaps adding to it or taking something away.

6. **treacle toffee:** a hard, chewy candy made from molasses.
7. **conkers:** large brown nuts threaded on strings for use in a children's game.

WORDS
TO
KNOW

loathsome (lōth′səm) *adj.* disgusting

Three Boys with a Mouse (1981), Terry Mimnaugh. Bronze, 10½″ × 9″ × 7″, from the series *What Little Boys Are Made Of.*

One day, when we lifted it up, we found a dead mouse lying among our treasures. It was an exciting discovery. Thwaites took it out by its tail and waved it in front of our faces. "What shall we do with it?" he cried.

"It stinks!" someone shouted. "Throw it out of the window quick!"

"Hold on a tick," I said. "Don't throw it away."

Thwaites hesitated. They all looked at me.

When writing about oneself, one must strive to be truthful. Truth is more important than modesty. I must tell you, therefore, that it was I and I alone who had the idea for the great and daring Mouse Plot. We all have our moments of brilliance and glory, and this was mine.

"Why don't we," I said, "slip it into one of Mrs. Pratchett's jars of sweets? Then when she puts her dirty hand in to grab a handful, she'll grab a stinky dead mouse instead."

The other four stared at me in wonder. Then, as the sheer genius of the plot began to sink in, they all started grinning. They slapped me on the back. They cheered me and danced around the classroom. "We'll do it today!" they cried. "We'll do it on the way home! *You* had the idea," they said to me, "so *you* can be the one to put the mouse in the jar."

Thwaites handed me the mouse. I put it into my trouser pocket. Then the five of us left the school, crossed the village green, and headed for the sweetshop. We were tremendously jazzed up. We felt like a gang of desperados setting out to rob a train or blow up the sheriff's office.

"Make sure you put it into a jar which is used often," somebody said.

"I'm putting it in gobstoppers," I said. "The gobstopper jar is never behind the counter."

"I've got a penny," Thwaites said, "so I'll ask for one sherbet sucker and one bootlace. And while she turns away to get them, you slip the mouse in quickly with the gobstoppers."

Thus everything was arranged. We were strutting a little as we entered the shop. We were the victors now, and Mrs. Pratchett was the victim. She stood behind the counter, and her small, <u>malignant</u> pig-eyes watched us suspiciously as we came forward.

"One sherbet sucker, please," Thwaites said to her, holding out his penny.

I kept to the rear of the group, and when I saw Mrs. Pratchett turn her head away for a couple of seconds to fish a sherbet sucker out of the box, I lifted the heavy glass lid of the gobstopper jar and dropped the mouse in. Then I replaced the lid as silently as possible. My heart was thumping like mad, and my hands had gone all sweaty.

"And one bootlace, please," I heard Thwaites saying. When I turned around, I saw Mrs. Pratchett holding out the bootlace in her filthy fingers.

"I don't want all the lot of you troopin' in 'ere if only one of you is buyin'," she screamed at us. "Now beat it! Go on, get out!"

As soon as we were outside, we broke into a run. "Did you do it?" they shouted at me.

"Of course I did!" I said.

"Well done, you!" they cried. "What a super show!"

I felt like a hero. I *was* a hero. It was marvelous to be so popular.

Mr. Coombes

The flush of triumph over the dead mouse was carried forward to the next morning as we all met again to walk to school.

"Let's go in and see if it's still in the jar," somebody said as we approached the sweetshop.

"Don't," Thwaites said firmly. "It's too dangerous. Walk past as though nothing has happened."

As we came level with the shop we saw a cardboard notice hanging on the door.

We stopped and stared. We had never known the sweetshop to be closed at this time in the morning, even on Sundays.

"What's happened?" we asked each other. "What's going on?"

We pressed our faces against the window and looked inside. Mrs. Pratchett was nowhere to be seen.

"Look!" I cried. "The gobstopper jar's gone! It's not on the shelf! There's a gap where it used to be!"

"It's on the floor!" someone said. "It's smashed to bits, and there's gobstoppers everywhere!"

"There's the mouse!" someone else shouted.

We could see it all, the huge glass jar smashed to smithereens with the dead mouse lying in the wreckage and hundreds of many-colored gobstoppers littering the floor.

"She got such a shock when she grabbed hold of the mouse that she dropped everything," somebody was saying.

"But why didn't she sweep it all up and open the shop?" I asked.

Nobody answered me.

We turned away and walked towards the school. All of a sudden we had begun to feel slightly uncomfortable. There was something not quite right about the shop being closed. Even Thwaites was unable to offer a reasonable explanation. We became silent. There was a faint scent of danger in the air now. Each one of us had caught a whiff of it. Alarm bells were beginning to ring faintly in our ears.

After a while, Thwaites broke the silence. "She must have got one heck of a shock," he said. He paused. We all looked at him, wondering what wisdom the great medical authority was going to come out with next.

"After all," he went on, "to catch hold of a dead mouse when you're expecting to catch hold of a gobstopper must be a pretty frightening experience. Don't you agree?"

Nobody answered him.

"Well now," Thwaites went on, "when an old person like Mrs. Pratchett suddenly gets a very big shock, I suppose you know what happens next?"

"What?" we said. "What happens?"

"You ask my father," Thwaites said. "He'll tell you."

"You tell us," we said.

"It gives her a heart attack," Thwaites announced. "Her heart stops beating, and she's dead in five seconds."

For a moment or two my own heart stopped beating. Thwaites pointed a finger at me and said darkly, "I'm afraid you've killed her."

"*Me?*" I cried. "Why just *me?*"

"It was *your* idea," he said. "And what's more, *you* put the mouse in."

All of a sudden, I was a murderer.

At exactly that point, we heard the school bell ringing in the distance, and we had to gallop the rest of the way so as not to be late for prayers.

Prayers were held in the Assembly Hall. We all perched in rows on wooden benches while the teachers sat up on the platform in armchairs, facing us. The five of us scrambled into our places just as the Headmaster marched in, followed by the rest of the staff.

The Headmaster is the only teacher at Llandaff Cathedral School that I can remember, and for a reason you will soon discover, I can remember him very clearly indeed. His name was Mr. Coombes, and I have a picture in my mind of a giant of a man with a face like a ham and a mass of rusty-colored hair that sprouted in a tangle all over the top of his head. All grown-ups appear as giants to small children. But Headmasters (and policemen) are the biggest giants of all and acquire a marvelously exaggerated stature. It is possible that Mr. Coombes was a perfectly normal being, but in my memory he was a giant, a tweed-suited giant who always wore a black gown over his tweeds and a waistcoat under his jacket.

Mr. Coombes now proceeded to mumble through the same old prayers we had every day; but this morning, when the last amen had been spoken, he did not turn and lead his group rapidly out of the hall as usual. He remained standing before us, and it was clear he had an announcement to make.

"The whole school is to go out and line up around the playground immediately," he said. "Leave your books behind. And no talking."

Mr. Coombes was looking grim. His hammy pink face had taken on that dangerous scowl which only appeared when he was extremely cross and somebody was for the high jump. I

sat there small and frightened among the rows and rows of other boys; and to me at that moment the Headmaster, with his black gown draped over his shoulders, was like a judge at a murder trial.

"He's after the killer," Thwaites whispered to me.

I began to shiver.

"I'll bet the police are here already," Thwaites went on. "And the Black Maria's[8] waiting outside."

As we made our way out to the playground, my whole stomach began to feel as though it was slowly filling up with swirling water. *I am only eight years old*, I told myself. *No little boy of eight has ever murdered anyone. It's not possible.*

Out in the playground on this warm, cloudy September morning, the Deputy Headmaster was shouting, "Line up in forms! Sixth Form over there! Fifth Form next to them! Spread out! Spread out! Get on with it! Stop talking all of you!"

Thwaites and I and my other three friends were in the Second Form, the lowest but one, and we lined up against the red-brick wall of the playground shoulder to shoulder. I can remember that when every boy in the school was in his place, the line stretched right around the four sides of the playground— about one hundred small boys altogether, aged between six and twelve, all of us wearing identical grey shorts and grey blazers and grey stockings and black shoes.

We stopped and stared. We had never known the sweetshop to be closed at this time.

8. **Black Maria** (mə-rī′ə): a police patrol wagon.

"Stop that *talking!*" shouted the Deputy Head. "I want absolute silence!"

But why for heaven's sake were we in the playground at all? I wondered. And why were we lined up like this? It had never happened before.

I half expected to see two policemen come bounding out of the school to grab me by the arms and put handcuffs on my wrists.

A single door led out from the school onto the playground. Suddenly it swung open, and through it, like the angel of death, strode Mr. Coombes, huge and bulky in his tweed suit and black gown; and beside him, believe it or not, right beside him trotted the tiny figure of Mrs. Pratchett herself!

Mrs. Pratchett was alive!

The relief was tremendous.

"She's alive!" I whispered to Thwaites standing next to me. "I didn't kill her!" Thwaites ignored me.

"We'll start over here," Mr. Coombes was saying to Mrs. Pratchett. He grasped her by one of her skinny arms and led her over to where the Sixth Form was standing. Then, still keeping hold of her arm, he proceeded to lead her at a brisk walk down the line of boys. It was like someone inspecting the troops.

"What on earth are they doing?" I whispered.

Thwaites didn't answer me. I glanced at him. He had gone rather pale.

"Too big," I heard Mrs. Pratchett saying.

Wanted Poster from "Mr. Coombes" from *Boy: Tales of Childhood* by Roald Dahl. Copyright © 1984 by Roald Dahl. Reprinted by permission of Farrar, Straus and Giroux, LLC.

"Much too big. It's none of this lot. Let's 'ave a look at some of them titchy ones."

Mr. Coombes increased his pace. "We'd better go all the way round," he said. He seemed in a hurry to get it over with now, and I could see Mrs. Pratchett's skinny goat's legs trotting to keep up with him. They had already inspected one side of the playground where the Sixth Form and half the Fifth Form were standing. We watched them moving down the second side . . . then the third side. "Still too big," I heard Mrs. Pratchett croaking. "Much too big! Smaller than these! Much smaller! Where's them nasty little ones?"

They were coming closer to us now . . . closer and closer.

They were starting on the fourth side . . .

Every boy in our form was watching Mr. Coombes and Mrs. Pratchett as they came walking down the line towards us.

"Nasty, cheeky lot, these little 'uns!" I heard Mrs. Pratchett muttering. "They comes into my shop, and they thinks they can do what they damn well likes!"

Mr. Coombes made no reply to this.

"They nick things when I ain't lookin'," she went on. "They put their grubby 'ands all over everything, and they've got no manners. I don't mind girls. I never 'ave no trouble with girls, but boys is 'ideous and 'orrible! I don't 'ave to tell *you* that, 'Eadmaster, do I?"

"These are the smaller ones," Mr. Coombes said.

I could see Mrs. Pratchett's piggy little eyes staring hard at the face of each boy she passed.

Suddenly she let out a high-pitched yell and pointed a dirty finger straight at Thwaites. "That's 'im!" she yelled. "That's one of 'em! I'd know 'im a mile away, the scummy little bounder!"

The entire school turned to look at Thwaites. "W-what have *I* done?" he stuttered, appealing to Mr. Coombes.

"Shut up," Mr. Coombes said.

Mrs. Pratchett's eyes flicked over and settled on my own face. I looked down and studied the black asphalt surface of the playground.

"'Ere's another of 'em!" I heard her yelling. "That one there!" She was pointing at me now.

"You're quite sure?" Mr. Coombes said.

"Of course I'm sure!" she cried. "I never forgets a face, least of all when it's as sly as that! 'Ee's one of 'em all right! There was five altogether! Now where's them other three?"

The other three, as I knew very well, were coming up next.

Mrs. Pratchett's face was glimmering with venom as her eyes traveled beyond me down the line.

"There they are!" she cried out, stabbing the air with her finger. "'*Im* . . . and '*im* . . . and '*im*! That's the five of 'em all right!

We don't need to look no farther than this, 'Eadmaster! They're all 'ere, the nasty, dirty little pigs! You've got their names, 'ave you?"

"I've got their names, Mrs. Pratchett," Mr. Coombes told her. "I'm much obliged to you."

"And I'm much obliged to *you*, 'Eadmaster," she answered.

As Mr. Coombes led her away across the playground, we heard her saying, "Right in the jar of gobstoppers it was! A stinkin' dead mouse which I will never forget as long as I live!"

"You have my deepest sympathy," Mr. Coombes was muttering.

"Talk about shocks!" she went on. "When my fingers caught 'old of that nasty, soggy, stinkin' dead mouse . . ." Her voice trailed away as Mr. Coombes led her quickly through the door into the school building. ❖

Editor's Note: After being identified by Mrs. Pratchett in the schoolyard lineup, Roald and his friends were ordered into the Headmaster's office. There they received a caning (beating) from Mr. Coombes, while Mrs. Pratchett watched. When Roald's mother saw her son's bruises, she promised to send him to school in England. The following year, Roald went to boarding school.

Connect to the Literature

1. What Do You Think? Which part of the selection did you enjoy the most? Share your response with a classmate.

Comprehension Check
- At the beginning of the story, what does the narrator say is his "absolute ambition" in life?
- When the entire school is lined up in the schoolyard, what does the narrator assume has happened? How does he feel?

Think Critically

2. Why do you think the narrator is so proud of "The Great Mouse Plot"?

> **Think About:**
> - riding a bike with no hands on the handlebars
> - his relationship with Thwaites
> - his feelings about Mrs. Pratchett

3. How would you describe Thwaites's role in "The Great Mouse Plot"? Do you think he deserved to be punished for that role?

4. How did you feel about the way the headmaster treated the narrator and his friends?

5. Did you feel any differently about the story after you read the Editor's Note at the end? Explain.

6. **ACTIVE READING** **CONNECTING**
Read back over your notes in your **READER'S NOTEBOOK**. What details of the story could you relate to the most? Share your reaction with a classmate.

Extend Interpretations

7. What If? What if the story had been told from Mrs. Pratchett's point of view? How might she have described the narrator and his friends? Would this affect the overall theme? If so, how?

8. Connect to Life In your opinion, when does a prank go too far to be acceptable? Explain.

Literary Analysis

DIALECT A **dialect** is a form of language that is spoken in a certain place or by a certain group of people. Dialects of a language may differ from one another in pronunciation, vocabulary, and grammar. Look at this excerpt from *Boy: Tales of Childhood.* The narrator is describing how Mrs. Pratchett speaks to the boys when they come into her shop.

> *I don't want you in 'ere just to look around! Either you* **forks** *out or you* **gets** *out!*

One way Dahl re-creates Mrs. Pratchett's British working-class dialect is by dropping the *h* at the beginning of words. What other devices does he use to re-create her dialect?

Activity As a class, make a chart that lists the lines of dialogue spoken by Mrs. Pratchett in either of the scenes in which the boys enter her shop. In a column beside this list, take turns rewriting each sentence from her dialect into standard English.

Mrs. Pratchett's English	Standard English
I don't want you in 'ere just to look around! Either you *forks* out, or you *gets* out!	I don't want you in here just to look around! Either buy something or leave!

CHOICES and CHALLENGES

Writing

Opinion Essay Do you think that the boys were justified or irresponsible in playing their prank on Mrs. Pratchett? Write an essay that defends one or the other viewpoint. Give reasons to support your defense. Place the essay in your **Working Portfolio.**

Writing Handbook
See p. R51: Persuasive Writing.

Speaking & Listening

Dialogue With a partner, write a dialogue between the narrator and Thwaites that might have taken place right after their punishment in the headmaster's office for "The Great Mouse Plot." Have them discuss the prank, its

consequences, their feelings about whether the prank was worth doing, and whether or not they'll go into the sweetshop again. Read the dialogue out loud for a small group. Choose one dialogue from each group and read it for the class.

Art Connection

Look at the photograph of Terry Mimnaugh's sculpture *Three Boys with a Mouse* on page 540. How well do you think the sculpture captures the feelings of the boys as they carry out "The Great Mouse Plot"?

Research & Technology

The Origin of Candy Find out about the beginnings of candy. When was it invented? How is today's candy different from candy in the past? in other countries? Has it always been as widely available as it is now? Which candies have been around the longest? Research with a partner to find the answers to these questions.

> **Reading for INFORMATION**
> Before you begin, read "The History of Chocolate" on page 549.

Vocabulary and Spelling

EXERCISE: ANTONYMS Match each Word to Know on the left with the word or phrase that is most nearly its opposite.

1. _____ elaborate   **a.** attractive
2. _____ flourishing   **b.** dry
3. _____ loathsome   **c.** simplify
4. _____ malignant   **d.** in decline
5. _____ saturated   **e.** well-meaning

SPELLING STRATEGY: SILENT/SOUNDED CONSONANTS To spell a word with a silent consonant, think of a similar word in which the consonant is sounded.

mali**gn**	malignant	de**si**gn	designate
dou**bt**	dubious	de**bt**	debit
colu**mn**	columnist	autu**mn**	autumnal

| ha**st**en | haste | fa**st**en | fast |
| mu**sc**le | muscular | bo**mb** | bombard |

Look at the boldfaced letters in the words above. Which letter is silent in each combination?

1. gn _____   3. mn _____   5. st _____
2. bt _____   4. mb _____   6. sc _____

Write the spelling word that fits each group.

7. winter, summer, spring, _____
8. plan, draw, lay out, _____
9. hurry, rush, run, _____
10. editorial, feature, advice, _____

Spelling Handbook
See p. R30.

BOY: TALES OF CHILDHOOD   **547**

Grammar in Context: Adjective Phrases

Notice how **prepositional phrases** add specific details in *Boy: Tales of Childhood.*

> . . . I will wear long trousers with bicycle clips. . . .

> ". . . only one of you is buyin'."

The **prepositional phrases** in the sentences above are used as adjectives. **Adjective phrases** are prepositional phrases that modify **nouns** or **pronouns**.

Usage Tip: Adjective phrases nearly always follow the word they modify.

> . . . I lifted the heavy glass lid of the gobstopper jar and dropped the mouse in.

WRITING EXERCISE Rewrite the following sentences, adding a prepositional phrase to modify the underlined words.

Example: *Original* We passed the sweetshop on our <u>walks</u>.

Rewritten We passed the sweetshop on our walks <u>from school</u>.

1. Thwaites was an <u>authority</u>.
2. Tonsil ticklers were invented for dangerous <u>prisoners</u>.
3. We had a hiding <u>place</u>.
4. Mrs. Pratchett did not die when she found the <u>mouse</u>.
5. The shopkeeper inspected the <u>boys</u>.

Grammar Handbook See p. R84: Prepositional Phrases.

Roald Dahl
1916–1990

"I never get any protests from children. All you get are giggles of mirth and squirms of delight."

School Days As a schoolboy, Roald Dahl apparently showed little promise. One report about him included the comments "I have never met a boy who so persistently writes the exact opposite of what he means. He seems incapable of marshaling his thoughts on paper" and "vocabulary negligible, sentences malconstructed. He reminds me of a camel."

Children's Writer Dahl, however, went on to become a writer of best-selling children's books—some of which deal with unpleasant subjects and feature obnoxious characters. For example, in *The Gremlins,* his first book for children, tiny creatures cause mysterious malfunctions in airplanes. In defense of his books, Dahl remarked, "I never get any protests from children. All you get are giggles of mirth and squirms of delight. I know what children like." Dahl also credited his being a parent for his inspiration as a writer. "Had I not had children of my own," he said, "I would have never written books for children, nor would I have been capable of doing so." His other works include *Matilda, James and the Giant Peach,* and *Charlie and the Chocolate Factory.*

AUTHOR ACTIVITY
Explore Another Genre Read one of Roald Dahl's works of fiction. Prepare an oral book report to share with the class.

Source: *Diner's Digest*

Back Forward Reload Home Search Images Print Security Stop

The History of Chocolate

Key Standard
R2.3 Analyze text that uses cause-and-effect organization.
***Other Standards* R2.1, R2.2**

I t's almost impossible to believe it now, but for most of its very long history, chocolate was not something people ate. It was a beverage, and not only was that beverage rarely hot, it was usually not sweet. Read this chronology to see how chocolate developed into its many delicious forms and came to be enjoyed by people all over the world.

1500 B.C. to 400 B.C.
The Olmec Civilization

Colossal stone Olmec head.

Many scholars think that the Olmecs, an ancient civilization that flourished in southern Mexico, were the first to use the cacao bean to make chocolate. But it is not known how they prepared the chocolate. There were great Olmec settlements in the prime cacao-growing areas in the present-day Mexican states of Chiapas and Yucatán and in Guatemala.

Reading for Information

Text Organizers
Magazine articles often use text organizers to guide readers through the material. This article makes use of a title, subheads, and captions. The introductory paragraph sets up the rest of the article so readers know what to expect.

YOUR TURN *As you read, identify the text organizers, and describe how they help explain the information presented.*

A.D. 250 to 900

Classic Maya Civilization

The Maya, an ancient Central American civilization, used chocolate mainly as a drink. They mixed the roasted, ground cacao beans with water, flavoring it with herbs or spices (chile was common). Then they poured the mixture back and forth from one container to another to make it foamy.

Mayan drinking cup.

14th Century to 1521

The Aztec Empire

The Aztecs used the same methods as the Maya to mix their chocolate drink. They, too, used many different flavorings. The Aztecs thought that the beverage was beneficial to warriors. Cacao wafers, intended to be dissolved as needed, were issued to soldiers, in order to fortify them during marches and in battle.The words _cacao_ and _chocolate_ show traces of Nahuatl, the Aztec language.

1502

Cacao as Currency

The Aztecs used cacao beans as money. An Aztec document containing a list of price equivalents reported that a tomato was worth one cacao bean, an avocado was worth three, and a "good turkey hen" was worth 100 "full" or 120 "shrunken" cacao beans.

1544

First Documented Evidence of Chocolate in Europe

Dominican friars, living in a region of Guatemala occupied by the Maya, accompanied a delegation of Kekchi Maya people to Spain. Among the many gifts they presented to Prince Philip were containers of chocolate, frothed and ready to drink. The Spanish and Portuguese consumed chocolate for nearly a century before the rest of Europe discovered the drink.

European chocolate drinkers in the 18th century.

1753

Food of the Gods

The Swedish botanist Carolus Linnaeus developed a system for classifying living organisms. He

Cacao ready to harvest.

assigned the botanical name _Theobroma cacao_ to the chocolate tree. _Theobroma_, in Greek, means "food of the gods," while _cacao_ is the original word for the plant.

1828

Invention of Dutch Cocoa

3 Coenraad Van Houten, in Amsterdam, devised a process for making chocolate powder by using hydraulic pressure to remove almost half of the cocoa butter—the cacao bean's natural fat—from the chocolate. The process produced a hard cake that could be reduced to a powder. The powder could then be mixed with water to make a chocolate drink or added to other foods.

prenez du Cacao
Van Houten

Van Houten cocoa product label.

1847

First Modern Chocolate Bar

Joseph Fry & Son, British chocolate manufacturers, was founded by a Quaker who had been a doctor before opening the business. In 1847, the firm discovered a way to mix the melted cocoa butter back into "Dutched" cocoa powder (along with sugar) to create a paste that could be pressed into a mold. The resulting bar was a huge hit.

Reading for Information *continued*

When reading informational material, it helps to be familiar with different methods of organization. In this article, the writer uses sequential order, main idea and details, and cause-and-effect order.

YOUR TURN

❶ Sequential order is used to show how events follow one another in a certain order. In the first paragraph, a three-step process is explained. What is the process? Name the three steps.

❷ Good paragraphs have a stated main idea followed by details to support the main idea. What is the main idea of this paragraph? List the supporting details.

❸ Based on the paragraph, what was Van Houten's process for making chocolate into powder? Name the steps in sequential order.

Fry's Chocolate advertisement.

Back　Forward　Reload　Home　Search　Images　Print　Security　Stop

1875

Invention of Milk Chocolate

During the 1860s, a Swiss chocolate manufacturer, Daniel Peter, tried repeatedly but unsuccessfully to create a chocolate bar flavored with milk. As it happened, in 1867, the chemist Henri Nestlé was working on a concentrated infant food formula and needed to find a way to treat milk so that it would not spoil while in storage. Eventually he developed sweetened condensed milk, which turned out to be perfect for Peter's purposes. The milk's low water content made it possible to mix it with the chocolate into a bar that did not spoil.

Reading for Information *continued*

❹ When one event brings about another, the two events have a cause-and-effect relationship. In this paragraph what causes chocolate bars to be associated with peace? Explain the cause-effect relationship. (See pages 708–709 for more help with cause and effect.)

Research & Technology

Activity Link: *Boy: Tales of Childhood*, p. 547 Now that you have learned about the development of chocolate, what can you predict about the history of other kinds of candy? Choose one and research its past. Write a chronology like the one you have just read. Include a time line with your chronology.

1929

Chocolate-Covered Cherries

Celia's Confections (est. 1864) began manufacturing chocolate-covered cherries at their candy factory on West Broadway at Canal Street in New York. In the 19th century this was New York's confectionery district.

WW II

Nourishing the Army

In a move reminiscent of the Aztec practice, the American military decided to include three four-ounce chocolate bars, each with 600 calories, in a soldier's "D-Ration." Although meant to sustain the soldiers, the bars also came to be associated with the return of peace, when long-malnourished victims of the Germans found themselves approached by American G.I.'s offering them chocolate. The chocolate is still a standard issue in the military.

❹

Today

Chocolate is a major industry that requires 40% of the world's almonds, 20% of the world's peanuts, and 8% of the world's sugar. About 3.5 million pounds of whole milk are used to make milk chocolate each day. In the United States, Americans consume over 3.1 billion pounds of chocolate a year, or 11.7 pounds per person!

A Defenseless Creature
from **The Good Doctor**

by NEIL SIMON

based on a story by ANTON CHEKHOV

Connect to Your Life

Some people have a knack for talking other people into doing things for them. Maybe you have even done this yourself! With a classmate, share stories about a time you were either on the giving or receiving end of this.

Key Standard
R3.3 Analyze characters by examining what they think, say, and do, and by studying the words of the narrator and the reactions of other characters. *Other Standards* **R1.3, R3.1, R3.2, R3.6, W2.1, LC1.3, LC1.4, LS1.8**

Build Background

The play you are about to read is one scene from a longer play, *The Good Doctor*, by Neil Simon. In *The Good Doctor* Simon takes several early stories by Anton Chekhov and turns them into separate scenes, each of which is complete in itself.

Chekhov was a late-19th-century Russian playwright and short-story writer whom Simon admires. Chekhov wrote particularly about ordinary people who have failed or been disappointed in life. His mature stories are considered masterpieces. In them the reader's attention is drawn to the characters and what they learn about themselves and about life.

Anton Chekhov, 1860–1904

WORDS TO KNOW **Vocabulary Preview**

clench	incapacitated	provocation
composure	petition	

Focus Your Reading

LITERARY ANALYSIS **FARCE**

A **farce** is an exaggerated comedy with an absurd **plot**, ridiculous situations, and humorous **dialogue**. The main purpose of a farce is to make an audience laugh. Often the characters in a farce are stereotypes with just one exaggerated **character trait**. As you read *A Defenseless Creature*, look for examples of these characteristics.

ACTIVE READING **VISUALIZING**

When you read the script of a play, as opposed to watching it being performed on the stage, you should try to **visualize** the characters, set, and action in your imagination. You should also try to hear the dialogue in your head. Visualizing can heighten your understanding and enjoyment of a play that you read.

READER'S NOTEBOOK
Choose one of the characters in *A Defenseless Creature*. As you read, jot down some clues that help you visualize that character.

Mrs. Schukin

Detail from Play:	How I Visualize Her:
Poorly dressed, forlorn look (stage direction)	She wears an old hat and a coat with patches on it.
Lets out scream (action)	Her eyes get wide and her face gets red.

A Defenseless Creature

by Neil Simon

❧◦❧

BASED ON A STORY BY

Anton Chekhov

The Reader (1840–1862), Honoré Daumier. Bronze, 6¾″ × 2½″ × 3¾″. Hirshhorn Museum and Sculpture Garden, Smithsonian Institution, gift of Joseph H. Hirshhorn, 1966. Photograph by Lee Stalsworth.

The lights come up on the office of a bank official, Kistunov. *He enters on a crutch; his right foot is heavily encased in bandages, swelling it to three times its normal size. He suffers from the gout[1] and is very careful of any mishap which would only intensify his pain. He makes it to his desk and sits. An* Assistant, *rather harried, enters.*

Assistant. (*With volume*) Good morning, Mr. Kistunov!

Kistunov. Shhh! Please. . . . Please lower your voice.

Assistant. (*Whispers*) I'm sorry, sir.

Kistunov. It's just that my gout is acting up again and my nerves are like little firecrackers. The least little friction can set them off.

The Representative Knotting His Tie (1840–1862), Honoré Daumier. Bronze, 7″ × 2¾″ × 2⅛″. Hirshhorn Museum and Sculpture Garden, Smithsonian Institution, gift of Joseph H. Hirshhorn, 1966. Photograph by Lee Stalsworth.

---

1. **gout:** a condition that causes painful swelling of the joints, especially of the feet and hands.

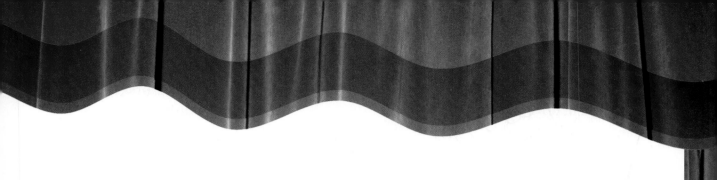

Assistant. It must be very painful, sir.

Kistunov. Combing my hair this morning was agony.

Assistant. Mr. Kistunov. . . .

Kistunov. What is it, Pochatkin?

Assistant. There's a woman who insists on seeing you. We can't make head or tail out of her story, but she insists on seeing the directing manager. Perhaps if you're not well—

Kistunov. No, no. The business of the bank comes before my minor physical ailments. Show her in, please . . . quietly. (*The* Assistant *tiptoes out. A* Woman *enters. She is in her late forties, poorly dressed. She is of the working class. She crosses to the desk, a forlorn look on her face. She twists her bag nervously*) Good morning, madame. Forgive me for not standing, but I am somewhat <u>incapacitated</u>. Please sit down.

Woman. Thank you.

(*She sits*)

Kistunov. Now, what can I do for you?

Woman. You can help me, sir. I pray to God you can help. No one else in this world seems to care. . . .

(*And she begins to cry, which in turn becomes a wail—the kind of wail that melts the spine of strong men.* Kistunov *winces and grits his teeth in pain as he grips the arms of his chair.*)

Kistunov. Calm yourself, madame. I *beg* of you. Please calm yourself.

Woman. I'm sorry.

(*She tries to calm down.*)

Kistunov. I'm sure we can sort it all out if we approach the problem sensibly and quietly. . . . Now, what exactly is the trouble?

Woman. Well, sir. . . . It's my husband. Collegiate Assessor Schukin. He's been sick for five months. . . . Five agonizing months.

Kistunov. I know the horrors of illness and can sympathize with you, madame. What's the nature of his illness?

Woman. It's a nervous disorder. Everything grates on his nerves. If you so much as touch him he'll scream out—

(*And without warning, she screams a loud bloodcurdling scream that sends* Kistunov *almost out of his seat.*)

How or why he got it, nobody knows.

Kistunov. (*Trying to regain his <u>composure</u>*) I have an inkling. . . . Please go on, a little less descriptively, if possible.

Woman. Well, while the poor man was lying in bed—

Kistunov. (*Braces himself*) You're not going to scream again, are you?

Woman. Not that I don't have cause. . . . While he was lying in bed these five months, recuperating, he was dismissed from his job—for no reason at all.

Kistunov. That's a pity, certainly, but I don't quite see the connection with our bank, madame.

Woman. You don't know how I suffered during his illness. I nursed him from morning till night. Doctored him from night till morning. Besides cleaning my house, taking care of my children, feeding our dog, our cat, our goat, my sister's bird, who was sick. . . .

Kistunov. The bird was sick?

Woman. My *sister*! She gets dizzy spells. She's been dizzy a month now. And she's getting dizzier every day. . . .

Kistunov. Extraordinary. However—

Woman. I had to take care of *her* children and *her* house and *her* cat and *her* goat, and then her bird bit one of my children, and so our cat bit her bird, so my oldest daughter, the one with the broken arm, drowned my sister's cat, and now my sister wants my goat in exchange, or else she says she'll either drown my cat or break my oldest daughter's other arm—

Kistunov. Yes, well, you've certainly had your pack of troubles, haven't you? But I don't quite see—

Lithograph with hand coloring (detail), Honoré Daumier. Courtesy of the Boston Public Library, Print Department.

Woman. And then, when I went to get my husband's pay, they deducted twenty-four rubles[2] and thirty-six kopecks.[3] For what? I asked. Because, they said, he borrowed it from the employees' fund. But that's impossible. He could never borrow without my approval. I'd break his arm. . . . Not while he was sick, of course. . . . I don't have the strength. I'm not well myself, sir. I have this racking cough that's a terrible thing to hear—

(*She coughs rackingly*[4]*—so rackingly that* Kistunov *is about to crack.*)

Kistunov. I can well understand why your husband took five months to recuperate. . . . But what is it you want from me, madame?

Woman. What rightfully belongs to my husband—his twenty-four rubles and thirty-six kopecks. They won't give it to me because I'm a woman, weak and defenseless. Some of them have laughed in my face, sir. . . . *Laughed!* (*She laughs loud and painfully.* Kistunov <u>clenches</u> *everything.*) Where's the humor, I wonder, in a poor, defenseless creature like myself?

(*She sobs.*)

Kistunov. None. . . . I see none at all. However, madame, I don't wish to be

---

2. **rubles** (rōō′bəl): units of Russian money.

3. **kopecks** (kō′pĕk): hundredths of a ruble.

4. **rackingly:** with heaves of painful effort.

unkind, but I'm afraid you've come to the wrong place. Your petition, no matter how justified, has nothing to do with us. You'll have to go to the agency where your husband was employed.

Woman. *What do you mean?* I've been to *five* agencies already and none of them will even *listen* to my petition. I'm about to lose my mind. The hair is coming out of my head. (*She pulls out a handful.*) Look at my hair. By the fistful. (*She throws a fistful on his desk.*) *Don't tell me to go to another agency!*

Kistunov. (*Delicately and disgustedly, he picks up her fistful of hair and hands it back to her. She sticks it back in her hair.*) Please, madame, keep your hair in its proper place. Now listen to me carefully. This-is-a-bank. A bank! We're in the banking business. We bank money. Funds that are brought here are banked by us. Do you understand what I'm saying?

Woman. What are you saying?

Kistunov. I'm saying that I can't help you.

Woman. Are you saying you can't help me?

Kistunov. (*Sighs deeply*) I'm trying. I don't think I'm making headway.

Woman. Are you saying you won't believe my husband is sick? Here! Here is a doctor's certificate. (*She puts it on the desk and pounds it.*) There's the proof. Do you still

Lithograph (detail), Honoré Daumier. Snark/Art Resource, NY.

doubt that my husband is suffering from a nervous disorder?

Kistunov. Not only do I not doubt it, I would *swear* to it.

Woman. *Look at it!* You didn't look at it!

Kistunov. It's really not necessary. I know *full well* how your husband must be suffering.

Woman. *What's the point in a doctor's certificate if you don't look at it?!* LOOK AT IT!

Kistunov. (*Frightened, quickly looks at it*) Oh, yes. . . . I see your husband is sick. It's right here on the doctor's certificate. Well, you certainly have a good case, madame, but I'm afraid *you've still come to the wrong place.* (*Getting perplexed*) I'm getting excited.

Woman. (*Stares at him*) You lied to me. I took you as a man of your word and you lied to me.

Kistunov. I? LIE? WHEN?

Woman. (*Snatches the certificate*) When you said you read the doctor's certificate. You couldn't have. You couldn't have read the description of my husband's illness without seeing he was fired unjustly. (*She puts the certificate back on the desk.*) Don't take advantage of me just because I'm a weak, defenseless woman. Do me the simple courtesy of reading the doctor's certificate. That's all I ask. Read it, and then I'll go.

Kistunov. But I *read* it! What's the point in reading something twice when I've already *read it once?*

Woman. You didn't read it carefully.

Kistunov. I read it *in detail!*

Woman. Then you read it too fast. Read it slower.

Kistunov. *I don't have to read it slower. I'm a fast reader.*

Woman. Maybe you didn't absorb it. Let it sink in this time.

Kistunov. (*Almost apoplectic[5]*) I *absorbed* it! It *sank* in! I could pass a *test* on what's written here, *but it doesn't make any difference because it has nothing to do with our bank!*

Woman. (*She throws herself on him from behind.*) Did you read the part where it says he has a nervous disorder? Read that part again and see if I'm wrong.

Kistunov. THAT PART? OH, YES! I SEE YOUR HUSBAND HAS A NERVOUS DISORDER. MY, MY, HOW TERRIBLE! *ONLY I CAN'T HELP YOU! NOW PLEASE GO!*

(*He falls back into his chair, exhausted.*)

Woman. (*Crosses to where his foot is resting*) I'm sorry, Excellency. I hope I haven't caused you any pain.

Kistunov. (*Trying to stop her*) Please, don't kiss my foot. (*He is too late—she has given his foot a most ardent embrace. He screams in pain.*) Aggghhh! Can't you get this into your balding head? If you would just realize that to come to us with this kind of claim is as strange as your trying to get a haircut in a butcher shop.

Woman. You can't get a haircut in a butcher shop. Why would anyone go to a butcher shop for a haircut? Are you laughing at me?

Kistunov. *Laughing!* I'm lucky I'm breathing. . . . Pochatkin!

Woman. Did I tell you I'm fasting? I haven't eaten in three days. I want to eat, but nothing stays down. I had the same cup of coffee three times today.

Kistunov. (*With his last burst of energy, screams*) POCHATKIN!

Woman. I'm skin and bones. I faint at the least <u>provocation</u> . . . . Watch. (*She swoons[6] to the floor*) Did you see? You saw how I just fainted? Eight times a day that happens.

(*The* Assistant *finally rushes in*)

Assistant. What is it, Mr. Kistunov? What's wrong?

Kistunov. (*Screams*) GET HER OUT OF HERE! Who let her in my office?

Assistant. You did, sir. I asked you and you said, "Show her in."

Kistunov. I thought you meant a human being, not a lunatic with a doctor's certificate.

Woman. (*To Pochatkin*) He wouldn't even read it. I gave it to him, he threw it back in my face. . . . You look like a kind person. Have pity on me. *You* read it and see if my husband is sick or not.

(*She forces the certificate on Pochatkin.*)

Assistant. I *read* it, madame. Twice!

Kistunov. Me too. I had to read it twice too.

Assistant. You just showed it to me outside. You showed it to *everyone.* We *all* read it. Even the doorman.

---

5. **apoplectic** (ăp′ə-plĕk′tĭk): bursting with anger.

6. **swoons:** falls in a faint.

WORDS TO KNOW	**provocation** (prŏv′ə-kā′shən) *n.* something that produces an emotional or physical reaction

558

Lithograph with hand coloring, Honoré Daumier. Courtesy of the Boston Public Library, Print Department.

Woman. You just looked at it. You didn't read it.

Kistunov. Don't argue. Read it, Pochatkin. For God's sake, read it so we can get her out of here.

Assistant. (*Quickly scans it*) Oh, yes. It says your husband is sick. (*He looks up; gives it back to her.*) Now will you please leave, madame, or I will have to get someone to remove you.

Kistunov. Yes! Yes! Good! Remove her! Get the doorman and two of the guards. Be careful, she's strong as an ox.

Woman. (*To* Kistunov) If you touch me, I'll scream so loud they'll hear it all over the city. You'll lose all your depositors. No one will come to a bank where they beat weak, defenseless women. . . . I think I'm going to faint again. . . .

Kistunov. (*Rising*) WEAK? DEFENSELESS? You are as defenseless as a charging rhinoceros! You are as weak as the King of the Jungle! You are a plague, madame! A plague that wipes out all that crosses your path! You are a raging river that washes out bridges and stately homes! You are a wind that blows villages over mountains! It is women like you who drive men like me to the condition of husbands like yours!

Woman. Are you saying you're not going to help me?

Kistunov. Hit her, Pochatkin! Strike her! I give you permission to knock her down. Beat some sense into her!

Woman. (*To Pochatkin*) You hear? You hear how I'm abused? He would have you hit an orphaned mother. Did you hear me cough? Listen to this cough.

(*She "racks" up another coughing spell.*)

Assistant. Madame, if we can discuss this in my office—

(*He takes her arm.*)

Woman. Get your hands off me. . . . Help! Help! I'm being beaten! Oh, merciful God, they're beating me!

Assistant. I am not beating you. I am just holding your arm.

Kistunov. Beat her, you fool. Kick her while you've got the chance. We'll never get her out of here. Knock her senseless!

(*He tries to kick her, misses and falls to the floor.*)

Woman. (*Pointing an evil finger at* Kistunov, *she jumps on the desk and punctuates each sentence by stepping on his desk bell.*) A curse! A curse on your bank! I put on a curse on you and your depositors! May the money in your vaults turn to potatoes! May the gold in your cellars turn to onions! May your rubles turn to radishes, and your kopecks to pickles. . . .

Kistunov. STOP! Stop it, I beg of you! . . . Pochatkin, give her the money. Give her what she wants. Give her anything—only get her out of here!

Woman. (*To Pochatkin*) Twenty-four rubles and thirty-six kopecks. . . . Not a penny more. That's all that's due me and that's all I want.

Assistant. Come with me, I'll get you your money.

Woman. And another ruble to get me home. I'd walk but I have very weak ankles.

Kistunov. Give her enough for a taxi, anything, only get her out.

Woman. God bless you, sir. You're a kind man. I remove the curse. (*With a gesture*) Curse be gone! Onions to money, potatoes to gold—

Kistunov. (*Pulls on his hair*) REMOVE HERRRR! Oh, God, my hair is falling out!

(*He pulls some hair out.*)

Woman. Oh, there's one other thing, sir. I'll need a letter of recommendation so my husband can get another job. Don't bother yourself about it today. I'll be back in the morning. God, bless you, sir. . . .

(*She leaves.*)

Kistunov. She's coming back. . . . She's coming back. . . . (*He slowly begins to go mad and takes his cane and begins to beat his bandaged leg*) She's coming back. . . . She's coming back. . . .

(*Dim-out*)

Connect to the Literature

1. **What Do You Think?** What were your feelings about the characters at the end of the play? Explain.

Comprehension Check
- What is the matter with Kistunov's foot?
- What does Mrs. Schukin do when she jumps up on Kistunov's desk?
- What does Mrs. Schukin ask for as she leaves?

Think Critically

2. How do you think Kistunov first perceives Mrs. Schukin? How do you think he plans on controlling her?

3. Do you think that the banker should have responded differently in any way to Mrs. Schukin? Explain.

4. By the end of the play, who turns out to be powerful and who is the defenseless creature?

   Think About:
   - ASSISTANT: "Come with me, I'll get your money."
   - KISTUNOV: "You are as defenseless as a charging rhinoceros!"
   - WOMAN: "I'll be back in the morning."

5. **ACTIVE READING** **VISUALIZING** Get together with a small group of classmates and compare the notes you took in your **READER'S NOTEBOOK.** Did the members of your group visualize characters and events similarly? Discuss, using examples of dialogue to support your interpretations.

Extend Interpretations

6. **Critic's Corner** One critic writes, "The pain the woman inflicts on Kistunov might be funny if Kistunov were presented as a figure deserving discomfort." What is your opinion? Does Kistunov "deserve" the treatment the woman gives him? Explain your answer.

Literary Analysis

FARCE A **farce** is a comedy that exaggerates plot, dialogue, and situation to amuse an audience. For example, the situation of *A Defenseless Creature* centers on Mrs. Schukin's efforts to force Kistunov to pay her money he doesn't owe her. Within that situation, what kind of wild twists and turns do the plot and dialogue take?

Paired Activity What elements of *A Defenseless Creature* fit the characteristics of a farce? Working with a partner, look over the script of *A Defenseless Creature* and jot down aspects of the play that seem exaggerated to really make you laugh.

Twists in the Plot	Lines of Dialogue	Absurd Situations
Mrs. Schukin pulls out a fistful of hair.	After Mrs. Schukin screams and Kistunov says: "You're not going to scream again, are you?"	Mrs. Schukin's relationship with her sister.

REVIEW: MOOD **Mood** is the feeling, or atmosphere, that a writer creates for the reader. Word choice, dialogue, description, and plot complications are some of the techniques writers use to convey mood. How would you characterize the mood of *A Defenseless Creature*?

CHOICES and CHALLENGES

Writing

Sequel to the Play Continue the play by writing a scene in which Mrs. Schukin returns to the bank the next day. Before you write, plan the arguments Mrs. Schukin will use and how Kistunov will respond. When you have written a draft, ask a classmate to review it. Put your sequel in your **Working Portfolio.**

Writing Handbook
See p. R36: Using Peer Response.

Speaking & Listening

Production of the Play Perform *A Defenseless Creature* with a group of classmates. In addition to the actors, you might have a director and a prop manager.

Art Connection

A Defenseless Creature is illustrated with engravings by the 19th-century caricaturist, Honoré Daumier. Do you think the engravings capture the spirit of the play? Explain your interpretation.

Research & Technology

Classic Comedy Rent a video of one of the films of Charlie Chaplin, Buster Keaton, or W. C. Fields. As you watch, look for ways in which *A Defenseless Creature* is similar to these classic comedies. Do they use techniques like exaggeration, absurd situations, plot complications? What is the effect of these techniques on the viewer? Write a short essay on your observations.

Vocabulary

STANDARDIZED TEST PRACTICE

Choose the word or group of words that means the same, or nearly the same, as the underlined Word to Know in each sentence.

1. The banker is <u>incapacitated</u> by gout, which swells his right leg. Incapacitated means—
   A saddened   **B** distracted
   C surprised   **D** disabled

2. The banker tries hard to keep his <u>composure</u> even though the woman drives him crazy. Composure means—
   F calmness   **G** interest
   H position   **J** honesty

3. The woman visits the banker to make a <u>petition</u> on behalf of her husband. Petition means—
   A payment   **B** demand
   C request   **D** delivery

4. Whenever the woman shrieked, the banker would <u>clench</u> the arms of the chair. Clench means—
   F strike   **G** grip
   H rub   **J** crack

5. The woman claims that she will faint from the slightest <u>provocation</u>. Provocation means—
   A lie   **B** compliment
   C production   **D** annoyance

Vocabulary Handbook
See p. R24: Context Clues.

Grammar in Context: Adverb Phrases

Prepositional phrases add important information in these sentences from *A Defenseless Creature.*

> The business of the bank comes before my minor physical ailments.

> He's been sick for five months.

The **prepositional phrases** above are used as adverbs. Adverb phrases modify verbs, adjectives, or adverbs.

Usage Tip: Adverb phrases usually follow the word they modify. However, they also often appear at the beginning of a sentence: ***For five months** he's been sick.* Notice that in this position the phrase gets more emphasis.

WRITING EXERCISE Rewrite the following sentences. Add a prepositional phrase to modify each underlined word or words.

Example: *Original* The woman is still waiting.

Rewritten The woman is still waiting outside your office.

1. I sympathize.
2. He could never borrow.
3. The woman is offended.
4. Are you laughing?

Connect to the Literature Reread the woman's words beginning "May the money . . ." on page 560. What prepositional phrases do you find? Which are used as adjectives and which as adverbs?

Grammar Handbook See p. R84: Phrases and Clauses.

Neil Simon
born 1927

"To sit in a room alone for six or seven or ten hours, sharing the time with characters that you created, is sheer heaven."

Childhood Marvin Neil Simon was born in the Bronx, New York. During his childhood, Simon's father was frequently absent, so "Do it yourself, Neil" became the future playwright's motto. After graduating from public high school, Simon enlisted in the army and soon began writing for an army camp newspaper. After he was discharged from the service, Simon worked as a mailroom clerk but soon began writing comedy routines with his brother Danny. Before long, Simon was writing for radio and television.

Theater Success Simon's first play, *Come Blow Your Horn,* opened on Broadway in 1961. He has written almost 30 plays and has more hits in the American theater than any other playwright. Most of Simon's plays deal with life in New York City. He is the only living playwright to have a theater on Broadway named for him.

On Playwriting Of his profession Simon says, "For a man who wants to be his own master, to depend on no one else, to make life conform to his own visions rather than to follow the blueprints of others, playwriting is the perfect occupation. To sit in a room alone for six or seven or ten hours, sharing the time with characters that you created, is sheer heaven."

AUTHOR ACTIVITY
Screenwriter Several of Neil Simon's plays have been adapted for film, and he has written a dozen original film comedies. Try to find one of these movies, such as *The Odd Couple,* and watch it. Do you see any resemblances to *A Defenseless Creature*?

Across the Curriculum
Social Studies

The Highwayman

by ALFRED NOYES

Key Standard
R1.1 Identify idioms, analogies, metaphors, and similes in prose and poetry.
***Other Standards* R3.6, W2.2, W2.3, LS1.6**

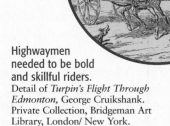

Connect to Your Life

Can you name a legendary figure from your state, city, or local community?

Build Background

With the cry "Stand and Deliver!" highwaymen halted and robbed the carriages of the upper classes in 17th- and 18th-century England. Highwaymen became legendary in the tradition of such figures as Robin Hood. They were celebrated in song and story by the poor who, exploited by the rich and powerful, felt avenged by the exploits of the highwaymen.

Highwaymen needed to be bold and skillful riders.
Detail of *Turpin's Flight Through Edmonton*, George Cruikshank. Private Collection, Bridgeman Art Library, London/ New York.

The Escort, Robert Alexander Hillingford. John Noott Galleries, Broadway, Worcestershire, U.K./Bridgeman Art Library, London/New York

Though highwaymen came from all social classes, they often dressed and spoke like their upper-class victims.
From a collection of paste jewelry (18th century), French and English. Cameo Corner, London/ Bridgeman Art Library, London/New York.

Focus Your Reading

LITERARY ANALYSIS SIMILE AND METAPHOR

Alfred Noyes uses striking similes and metaphors to create memorable descriptions. A **simile** is a comparison that uses *like* or *as*. A **metaphor** is a comparison that suggests one thing *is* another thing, for example, "the road was a gypsy's ribbon." By comparing the road to a ribbon, Noyes gives the reader an unusual way of "seeing" a road winding through the moor. As you read, identify the similes and metaphors.

ACTIVE READING RESPONDING TO THE WRITER'S STYLE

An active reader pays attention to the **writer's style.** You can determine a writer's style by noticing his or her **word choice.** Writers choose vivid verbs to give their readers a colorful image of what is being described. For example, "Over the cobbles he clattered and clashed . . ." offers something vivid for the imagination. As you read, jot down in your 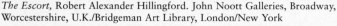READER'S NOTEBOOK these aspects of the writer's style that you notice.

The Highwayman

BY ALFRED NOYES

Illustrations by Charles Mikolaycak. Copyright © 1995 Carole Kismaric Mikolaycak.

*art One

The wind was a torrent of darkness among the gusty trees.
The moon was a ghostly galleon[1] tossed upon cloudy seas.
The road was a ribbon of moonlight over the purple moor,[2]
And the highwayman came riding—
5   Riding—riding—
The highwayman came riding, up to the old inn-door.

He'd a French cocked-hat on his forehead, a bunch of lace at his chin,
A coat of the claret[3] velvet, and breeches of brown doeskin.
They fitted with never a wrinkle. His boots were up to the thigh.
10   And he rode with a jeweled twinkle,
       His pistol butts a-twinkle.
His rapier hilt[4] a-twinkle, under the jeweled sky.

Over the cobbles[5] he clattered and clashed in the dark inn-yard.
He tapped with his whip on the shutters, but all was locked and barred.
15   He whistled a tune to the window, and who should be waiting there
But the landlord's black-eyed daughter,
       Bess, the landlord's daughter,
Plaiting[6] a dark red love-knot into her long black hair.

And dark in the dark old inn-yard a stable wicket[7] creaked
20   Where Tim the ostler[8] listened. His face was white and peaked.
His eyes were hollows of madness, his hair like moldy hay,
But he loved the landlord's daughter,
       The landlord's red-lipped daughter.
Dumb as a dog he listened, and he heard the robber say—

25   "One kiss, my bonny sweetheart, I'm after a prize tonight,
But I shall be back with the yellow gold before the morning light;
Yet, if they press me sharply, and harry me through the day,

---

1. **galleon** (găl'ē-ən): a large sailing ship.
2. **moor:** an open, rolling wasteland, usually covered with low-growing shrubs.
3. **claret:** dark red, like red wine.
4. **rapier** (rā'pē-ər) **hilt:** sword handle.
5. **cobbles:** rounded stones used for paving roads.
6. **plaiting:** braiding.
7. **wicket:** a small door or gate.
8. **ostler** (ŏs'lər): a worker who takes care of horses at an inn.

Then look for me by moonlight,
   Watch for me by moonlight,
30 I'll come to thee by moonlight, though hell should bar the way."

He rose upright in the stirrups. He scarce could reach her hand,
But she loosened her hair in the casement.[9] His face burnt like a brand
As the black cascade of perfume came tumbling over his breast;
And he kissed its waves in the moonlight,
35   (O, sweet black waves in the moonlight!)
Then he tugged at his rein in the moonlight, and galloped away to the west.

He did not come in the dawning. He did not come at noon;
And out of the tawny sunset, before the rise of the moon,
When the road was a gypsy's ribbon, looping the purple moor,
40 A redcoat troop came marching—
   Marching—marching—
King George's men came marching, up to the old inn-door.

They said no word to the landlord. They drank his ale instead.
But they gagged his daughter, and bound her, to the foot of her narrow bed.
45 Two of them knelt at her casement, with muskets at their side!

---

9. **casement:** a window that opens outward on side hinges.

There was death at every window;
    And hell at one dark window;
For Bess could see, through her casement, the road that *he* would ride.

They had tied her up to attention, with many a sniggering jest.
50 They had bound a musket beside her, with the muzzle beneath her breast!
"Now, keep good watch!" and they kissed her. She heard the doomed man say—
Look for me by moonlight;
    Watch for me by moonlight;
I'll come to thee by moonlight, though hell should bar the way!

55 She twisted her hands behind her; but all the knots held good!
She writhed her hands till her fingers were wet with sweat or blood!
They stretched and strained in the darkness, and the hours crawled by like years,
Till, now, on the stroke of midnight,
    Cold, on the stroke of midnight,
60 The tip of one finger touched it! The trigger at least was hers!

The tip of one finger touched it. She strove no more for the rest.
Up, she stood up to attention, with the muzzle beneath her breast.
She would not risk their hearing; she would not strive again;
For the road lay bare in the moonlight;
65   Blank and bare in the moonlight;
And the blood of her veins, in the moonlight, throbbed to her love's refrain.

Tlot-tlot; tlot-tlot! Had they heard it? The horse hoofs ringing clear;
Tlot-tlot, tlot-tlot, in the distance? Were they deaf that they did not hear?
Down the ribbon of moonlight, over the brow of the hill,
70 The highwayman came riding—
    Riding—riding—
The redcoats looked to their priming![10] She stood up, straight and still.

Tlot-tlot, in the frosty silence! *Tlot-tlot,* in the echoing night!
Nearer he came and nearer. Her face was like a light.
75 Her eyes grew wide for a moment; she drew one last deep breath,
Then her finger moved in the moonlight,
    Her musket shattered the moonlight,
Shattered her breast in the moonlight and warned him—with her death.

---

10. **looked to their priming:** prepared their muskets by pouring in the
    explosive used to fire them.

He turned. He spurred to the west; he did not know who stood
80 Bowed, with her head o'er the musket, drenched with her own blood!
Not till the dawn he heard it, his face grew grey to hear
How Bess, the landlord's daughter,
   The landlord's black-eyed daughter,
Had watched for her love in the moonlight, and died in the darkness there.

85 Back, he spurred like a madman, shouting a curse to the sky,
With the white road smoking behind him and his rapier brandished high.
Blood-red were his spurs in the golden noon; wine-red was his velvet coat;
When they shot him down on the highway,
   Down like a dog on the highway,
90 And he lay in his blood on the highway, with a bunch of lace at his throat.

And still of a winter's night, they say, when the wind is in the trees,
When the moon is a ghostly galleon tossed upon cloudy seas,
When the road is a ribbon of moonlight over the purple moor,
A highwayman comes riding—
95   *Riding—riding—*
A highwayman comes riding, up to the old inn-door.

Over the cobbles he clatters and clangs in the dark inn-yard.
He taps with his whip on the shutters, but all is locked and barred.
He whistles a tune to the window, and who should be waiting there
100 *But the landlord's black-eyed daughter,*
   Bess, the landlord's daughter,
Plaiting a dark red love-knot into her long black hair.

Connect to the Literature

1. What Do You Think?
What images stayed in your mind after you finished reading the poem? Describe them.

Comprehension Check
- In Part One, where does Bess wait for the highwayman?
- As Bess and the highwayman talk, who is secretly listening?
- How does Bess warn the highwayman about the redcoats?

Think Critically

2. Think about how the poet describes Tim the ostler. How is he different from the highwayman? What do they have in common?

3. How do you feel about the conduct of the redcoats?

> **Think About:**
> - their duty to uphold the law
> - their treatment of Bess
> - how they shoot the highwayman

4. Both Bess and the highwayman make great sacrifices for love. In your opinion, whose sacrifice shows greater courage? Explain your choice.

5. Would you have liked the poem better if the last two stanzas had not been included? Why or why not?

6. **ACTIVE READING** | **RESPONDING TO THE WRITER'S STYLE**
With a partner, review the notes you took in your 📖 READER'S NOTEBOOK. What images and metaphors, key aspects of the **writer's style,** stood out for you? Explain your choices.

Extend Interpretations

7. Different Perspectives What if the poem had been told from the point of view of Tim the ostler? What might have been his reaction to the events of the poem? Would this have changed the theme? If so, how?

8. Connect to Life Do you know of a case where someone sacrificed something valuable or meaningful for someone he or she loved? Explain.

Literary Analysis

WORD CHOICE Poets choose their words carefully for the effect they have on the reader. Alfred Noyes quickly establishes the mood of mystery and foreboding in "The Highwayman" with a few carefully chosen images that describe the wind and the moon.

The wind was a torrent of darkness among the gusty trees. The moon was a ghostly galleon tossed upon cloudy seas.

Similarly, the poet's description of Tim the ostler as pale with hair "like moldy hay" establishes his appearance in a much more vivid and memorable way than calling him a *blond* would have. Throughout "The Highwayman," the poet's **word choice** helps create vivid characters and settings and heightens the drama of the poem.

Activity As a class, create a sequence diagram that lists the major events in the poem and who is involved in them. Alongside each event, list key words and phrases that made that event come alive for you. As a class, discuss how the language of the poem intensified its sense of drama.

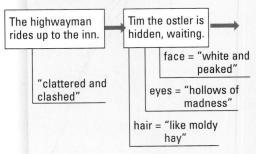

The highwayman rides up to the inn. → Tim the ostler is hidden, waiting. →

"clattered and clashed"

face = "white and peaked"

eyes = "hollows of madness"

hair = "like moldy hay"

CHOICES and CHALLENGES

Writing

Response to Literature Let's say you've just been hired by a literary publication. Your first assignment is to write a response to the poem "The Highwayman." Before you write, you need a clear understanding of what you've read. What is the poem about? List the major events in order. What do you learn about the highwayman, Bess, Tim the ostler? How is each character important to the story? Be sure to use examples and quotes from the poem. Place your response in your **Working Portfolio.**

Writing Workshop
See p. 238: Basics in a Box.

Speaking & Listening

Choral Reading In two groups of four students, read the poem chorally, taking alternating stanzas of the poem. Practice your reading before you present it to the class. Make sure to vary the pitch and volume of your voice, as well as the pace of your reading, to reflect changes in mood. Make a tape of your reading and keep it in your classroom library/listening center.

Art Connection

Review Charles Mikolaycak's illustrations that accompany the poem. Do they match the pictures of Bess and the highwayman that you visualized as you read the poem? Explain your interpretation.

Research & Technology

SOCIAL STUDIES

Most highwaymen were considered thieves and common "thugs." However, a few were mannered, refined, and actually charmed their victims. Using encyclopedias and other reference books, find stories of specific highwaymen in England during the 17th and 18th centuries. Where did they do their work? What happened to highwaymen when they were caught? Write up your findings, and a list of sources, and share with the class.

Alfred Noyes
1880–1958

He loved to read and daydream in a "mountain nook."

Early Success Alfred Noyes was born in England and spent much of his childhood on the Welsh coast, where he loved to read and daydream in a "mountain nook" overlooking the sea. Educated at Oxford University, Noyes wrote most of his poetry before 1942, when glaucoma cost him his eyesight. Noyes's best-known work is "The Highwayman." Generations of students have loved this poem for its driving rhythm and haunting refrain. Noyes wrote the poem in only two days when he was 24 years old.

THE HIGHWAYMAN   **571**

Building Vocabulary
Understanding Denotation and Connotation

Good writers choose their words carefully. They take into consideration the positive or negative associations and the implied meanings of words.

In the excerpt to the right, Roald Dahl could have used the word *plan* instead of *scheme*, but his choice of *scheme* makes this passage more interesting and dramatic.

> Many schemes were put forward, but none of them was any good.
>
> —Roald Dahl,
> from *Boy: Tales of Childhood*

The word **scheme** means "plan" but implies secrecy, dishonesty, or impracticality.

Standard R1.3

Strategies for Building Vocabulary

A word's **denotation** is its dictionary definition, or literal meaning. A word may also have an implied meaning, an association that suggests a particular emotion. This is its **connotation.** Knowing the connotations of words can help you improve your understanding of literature and enhance your writing.

❶ **Look Beyond the Literal Definition** Writers use words to bring out positive or negative connotations. Consider this sentence, noting Dahl's use of the word *plot:*

> "It's a plot," Thwaites said. "A grown-up plot to keep us quiet."

The word *plot*'s negative association with suspicion and distrust fits the situation perfectly.

❷ **Consider Synonyms** Consider the use of the word *loathsome* in the following sentence:

> But by far the most loathsome thing about Mrs. Pratchett was the filth that clung around her.

Dahl might have used such synonyms as *unpleasant, disgusting,* and *foul.* Substitute each of these words for *loathsome* and notice how your impression changes. *Loathsome* conveys the strongest feeling of repulsion.

❸ **Consider Connotations** Think about the connotations of the words you use in your writing. Consider whether particular words have positive associations or negative associations.

Positive Connotations	Negative Connotations
laugh	snicker
multitude	mob

The verbs *laugh* and *snicker* both mean "to express amusement." *Laugh,* however, has a positive connotation of shared enjoyment, whereas *snicker* often connotes making fun of someone or something in an unkind way. In a similar way, *multitude* means a large number of people gathered together, while *mob* has a negative connotation, implying possible danger and disorder.

If you are unsure about a word's connotations, refer to a standard dictionary or thesaurus.

EXERCISE Expand the chart under **Consider Connotations** above with three or four examples of positive and negative connotations. Then write a sentence using each pair of words.

from

KNOTS IN MY YO-YO STRING

by Jerry Spinelli

I was neat.

How neat was I? Say I had to cut a rectangle out of a piece of paper. First I would measure a perfect shape with my ruler, then draw it with a sharp pencil. Then with my scissors I would cut it out. But not just cut it out. I would cut precisely along the right edge of the pencil line, or precisely along the left edge, or I would split

Jerry, age 12

the line in half and cut precisely right down the middle. Consistently, all the way around the rectangle.

In seventh grade at Stewart Junior High, I astonished my shop teacher, Mr. Rohn, with the precision of my mechanical drawings and the perfection of my hand-lettering.

That same year I won numerous Palmer Method penmanship certificates and was declared the outstanding boy penmeister.

Every Eastertime the merchants of the West End shopping district—three blocks on Marshall Street—sponsored a coloring contest. Every day for two weeks line drawings— coloring-book-type pictures—were printed in the *Times Herald*. Each business had its own picture. Kids were invited to cut out the pictures, color them, and deposit their entries in boxes in the stores.

Unlike most kids, I did not use crayons. I used colored pencils. My frequently sharpened points never—never—strayed outside the lines. And my colors were right, too. No green sky or red grass for me.

For me, staying inside the lines was more than a color-the-picture matter.

Give me a direction, I followed it. Put a rule in front of me, I obeyed it. In twelve years I never stayed after school for detention. Once, though, I came close. It happened in the spring of ninth grade. Our homeroom teacher, Miss Busch, announced that our lockers would be reviewed for neatness. Since I kept my locker neat at all times, there was nothing for me to tidy up.

The next morning as the students entered Homeroom 213, we looked to the blackboard for the names of those whose lockers failed to pass muster. Shockingly, my name was among them. The punishment, besides cleaning up the offending locker, was detention.

I told Miss Busch there must be a mistake. She said there wasn't. I said I wouldn't be there for detention. It was the only time I ever talked back to a teacher. She said I'd be sorry.

After school that day, as usual, I went to baseball practice. When I arrived at school the next morning, I discovered I was no longer on the team. Nor was I homeroom president. I was stripped of every office and association.

My locker may have been tidy, but suddenly my life was a mess. One day of watching my backup shortstop was enough. I couldn't stand it. I apologized to Miss Busch, and the picture of my life fell back into place.

I loved routine, repeatedness. To do the same thing twice was to establish a personal tradition. In other words, where there were no lines, I drew my own. I stepped inside and stayed there—cozy, safe.

Summer Saturdays, for example. In the morning I walked a mile from George Street to the YMCA. There I played Ping-Pong in the game room with Lee Holmes, Ralph Cottman, and others. Then a screen and projector were brought out, the lights turned off, and we all settled in to watch a black and white movie, usually a Tarzan adventure.

After the movie I walked down to Main Street, past Block's department store, past the Norris Theater, to Texas Hot Wieners. The best hot dogs in town were sizzling right

> My locker may have been tidy, but suddenly my life was a mess.

there in the front window, daring each passerby not to come in. I sat at the counter and placed my order, always the same: hot dog with mustard and chopped onions, and chocolate milk. I've had a lot of wimpy hot dogs since then, hot dogs so soft you can't feel your teeth go through them, so mushy with fat and cereal you could almost drink them with a straw. Not Texas Hot Wieners. They had spunk. They fought back.

By now it was one o'clock. Across the street I went to the Garrick Theater and the Saturday matinee double feature—cowboy movies plus a Flash Gordon or Captain Midnight serial.

Hours later I emerged blinking in the late-afternoon sun. I walked home along Markley Street, past the sweet-smelling Wonder Bread plant, the sidewalk dusty with flour, past the *Times Herald*, over the Markley Street bridge that spanned Stony Creek. I always stopped at the bridge railing to look for sunfish in the sparkling water below. Only when I spotted one would I continue my journey homeward.

Every summer Saturday. The same thing.

Needless to say, I was well acquainted with perfect attendance in school. Most years went by without my missing a day.

When I walked, I trained myself to keep my feet pointed straight ahead, not pigeon-toed or splayed outward.

I even fantasized about neatness. I imagined our house had been selected for a visit by President Eisenhower. I saw myself going from room to room putting everything precisely in its place. On the racks in the bathroom the corners of the towels came together perfectly.

In another fantasy I set out to tidy up the world. Anything I couldn't fix with hedge trimmers and lawn mower I paved over with asphalt. By the time I was finished, the Amazon jungle looked like the flower beds and crewcut lawns of the North End of Norristown.

I spread my peanut butter evenly over my bread.

I never said bad words (unless you count "poop").

I hardly ever laughed out loud.

As I said, I was neat. And though I did not think of it this way, I believe that what I was actually trying to do was to become perfect.

I set out to tidy up the world.

Funny thing: For all my neatness, my sharp pencil points, my devotion to the right side of the line, I never won the West End shopping district coloring contest. Every year I tried harder than before, tried to be even neater, and still I lost. I couldn't figure out why.

Wasn't neatness enough? Wasn't perfection possible?

No, said my yo-yo. Often I had what seemed to be a perfect day—100 on a spelling test, winning touchdown in a pickup game, a new haircut—only to come home and find knots in my yo-yo string. I began to think the string had a mind of its own. I imagined it waiting until I wasn't looking, then rising up like a cobra and looping itself into knots. My paranoia seemed confirmed one morning when I awoke to find knots that I could have sworn

were not there when I went to bed.

When I was eleven and twelve, I played Biddy basketball, the equivalent of Little League baseball. In my final year I made the all-star team, but not because I was a great scorer. The most points I ever scored in a game was twelve, and usually it was half that. I think I made the all-stars as much for what I did not do as for what I did. That is to say, I did not make mistakes.

Playing the guard position, I dribbled a lot and passed a lot. But these were relatively risk-free ventures. Shooting was where the risk was, and I rarely took more than five shots in a game. I wasn't a bad shooter, but each shot I missed discouraged me from taking more. At home after each game, I neatly entered into a

notebook my statistics: assists, shots taken, shots made, fouls. Of course I hardly ever committed a foul. And because I played the game so carefully, I never found out how good a basketball player I might have become. Too late I learned that neatness does not serve all endeavors equally well, that what is good for penmanship is not necessarily good for basketball.

A willingness to take risks, to color outside the lines, was slow in coming to me. Some stubborn idea of perfection deterred me from fully extending myself in simple, pure participation. I was too afraid to fail. I did not appreciate the value of a mess.

Not that I wasn't given the chance. Looking back, I can see now that that's what the

school-locker incident was: an opportunity to grow beyond my own self-imposed limits. And for one day, I did. Falsely accused of having a disorderly locker, I was properly outraged. I defied my teacher. I refused to submit to injustice. I turned my back on detention. I charged across the line. I became a new me.

Then came the consequences—banishment from the baseball team, from all offices. Did I rise up and cry, "Punish me if you will! I don't care! I will never capitulate to this injustice"? Did I finish out the year in noble exile, stripped of all honors? Did I stand up for what I knew was right?

No.

I caved in. I apologized for protesting an unjust verdict. My life was reinstated. Order was restored, the mess was cleaned up. I was back inside the lines. Once again I was the old familiar me.

Yet even as I publicly conformed in word and deed, a contrary tendency was forming within me. It showed briefly in sixth grade when I wrote the unassigned poem on Mexico. It showed in my neatness fantasies— not in the subject matter but in the mere act of fantasizing. It showed in my swooning wonderment over the endlessness of the sky at night.

And it showed most commonly in my own version of the Garrick Theater's double features. When an event in my life—say, a baseball game—was over, it was not really over. For that night in bed I would relive it in my head. I would again see the vivid colors and hear the voices and feel the feelings, and the reliving would be, in its own way, as real to me as the first time around. Sometimes it was even better. Sometimes I couldn't wait for the event to be over and bedtime to arrive so that I could play it back.

As I have said, if you had asked me what I would grow up to be, I would have answered, "A baseball player." But even as I oiled the deep, fragrant pocket of my Marty Marion glove and taped the hickory handle of my thirty-three-ounce bat, I was unknowingly developing the tool of another trade. The urge to write a poem, to daydream, to ruminate, to wonder, even my tolerance of solitude—all became components of a bearing that I would never have guessed would fit me so well, an aptitude that thrives on disorder, that welcomes green sky and red grass, that serves neither master nor homeroom teacher, that

respects no line or limit. I speak, of course, of imagination—a gift that, like my Roadmaster on that Christmas morning, waited in another room for my discovery. ❖

Jerry Spinelli
born 1941

"If you had asked me what I would grow up to be, I would have answered, 'A baseball player.'"

Baseball Player Jerry Spinelli never set out to be a writer. During his first 16 years he wanted to be, among other things, a rock skipper, a yo-yo tangler, and above all a baseball player. When he was 12 years old, Spinelli played shortstop in the Connie Mack Knee-Hi League, and his team won the state championship. His favorite book at the time was *The Baseball Encyclopedia*.

Finds Writing In high school, however, things changed. Spinelli's family moved, and he no longer did well in school or in sports. Then, when he was in the tenth grade, he saw his high school's football team score an upset victory. He went home and wrote a poem about the game, which was published by the local newspaper. After that, he was determined to become a writer. He attended Gettysburg College and, later, writing seminars at the Johns Hopkins University. Spinelli published his first novel, *Space Station Seventh Grade,* in 1982. Since then, he has written 19 books, including *Maniac Magee,* a Newbery Medal winner in 1991, and *Wringer,* a Newbery Honor Book in 1998.

Communication Workshop

Staging a Scene

Presenting a dramatic scene . . .

From Reading to Staging Have you ever wondered what it would be like to work in a theater or on a movie set? The first step in creating a dramatic production is choosing a script. Neil Simon wrote many scripts for screen and stage. His play *The Good Doctor* is based on short stories by Anton Chekhov. Now you and your classmates can try **staging a scene** from this work. Working together can give you a chance to bring a playwright's words to life.

For Your Portfolio

WRITING PROMPT Create a staged presentation of "A Defenseless Creature" from *The Good Doctor* by Neil Simon.

Purpose: To interpret and perform a scene
Audience: Your classmates and other interested students and adults

---

Basics in a Box

GUIDELINES AND STANDARDS   STAGING A SCENE

A successful script should

- include an overall description of the set, props, lighting, and costumes
- include specific stage directions about the gestures, movements, and tones of voice the performers should use
- include notes about pacing and stage location

A successful performance should

- show an awareness of the audience—actors' voices must be loud enough, and the audience should have an unblocked view of the actors and actions
- maintain audience interest through strong acting, good pacing, and effective staging
- follow the script

Analyzing a Model Script

SPEAKING OPPORTUNITY

See the Speaking and Listening Handbook, p. R100 for oral presentation tips.

Excerpts from Director's Script
The Good Doctor, Scene 3, "A Defenseless Creature"

Set, Costumes, Lighting, and Sound
Set is the inside of an office. Costumes are business attire for Kistunov and his assistant and a dress for the woman. Stage is lit brightly. Woman's sound effects are on cassette tape, to be played at maximum volume off-stage.

Characters
Assistant to Kistunov, Kistunov, Woman

Props
Desk; two chairs; footstool; crutch; bandages; woman's handbag

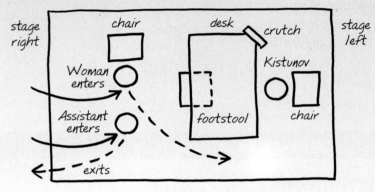

> **GUIDELINES IN ACTION**
>
> - Director describes set, costumes, lighting, and sound at the beginning of the script.
> - A list of performers is given as well as the inventory of props.
> - A sketch shows the set-up of the stage and the actors' places.
> - Handwritten notes show the pacing, gestures, tones, and movements that the actors should use.

Assistant enters stage right, bounces energetically into office.

Assistant. (*With volume*) Good morning, Mr. Kistunov!

Kistunov. Shhh! Please . . . Please lower your voice.

Assistant. (*Whispers*) I'm sorry, sir.

Kistunov cringes, moving his hands as if to cover his ears.

Kistunov. It's just that my gout is acting up again and my nerves are like little firecrackers. The least little friction can set them off.

Assistant. It must be very painful, sir.

Kistunov. Combing my hair this morning was agony.

Assistant has a sympathetic look on his face.

Assistant. Mr. Kistunov. . . .

Kistunov. What is it, Pochatkin?

Assistant. There's a woman who insists on seeing you. We can't make head or tail out of her story, but she insists on seeing the directing manager. Perhaps if you're not well—

He smiles, is friendly and polite.

Kistunov. No, no. The business of the bank comes before my minor physical ailments. Show her in, please . . . quietly. (*The* Assistant *tiptoes out. A* Woman *enters. She is in her late forties, poorly dressed. She is of the working class. She crosses*

to the desk, a forlorn look on her face. She twists her bag nervously.) Good morning, madame. Forgive me for not standing, but I am somewhat incapacitated. Please sit down.

Woman. Thank you. (*She sits*)

Kistunov. Now, what can I do for you?

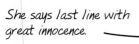
Woman immediately loses her shyness, speaks melodramatically. Soundtrack of wail echoes loudly with actor's voice.

Woman. You can help me, sir. I pray to God you can help. No one else in this world seems to care. . . . (*And she begins to cry, which in turn becomes a wail—the kind of wail that melts the spine of strong men.* Kistunov *winces and grits his teeth in pain as he grips the arms of his chair.*)

Kistunov. Calm yourself, madame. I *beg* of you. Please calm yourself.

Woman. I'm sorry. (*She tries to calm down.*)

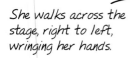
She opens her mouth wide and looks to the sky while soundtrack of scream is played. He jumps and clutches his leg; his crutch crashes to the ground.

Kistunov. I'm sure we can sort it all out if we approach the problem sensibly and quietly. . . . Now, what exactly is the trouble?

Woman. Well, sir. . . . It's my husband. Collegiate Assessor Schukin. He's been sick for five months. . . . Five agonizing months.

Kistunov. I know the horrors of illness and can sympathize with you, madame. What's the nature of his illness?

Woman. It's a nervous disorder. Everything grates on his nerves. If you so much as touch him he'll scream out— (*And without warning, she screams a loud bloodcurdling scream that sends* Kistunov *almost out of his seat.*) How or why he got it, nobody knows.

She says last line with great innocence.

Kistunov. (*Trying to regain his composure*) I have an inkling. . . . Please go on, a little less descriptively, if possible.

He pats his head and loosens his collar.

Woman. Well, while the poor man was lying in bed—

Kistunov. (*Braces himself*) You're not going to scream again, are you?

Woman. Not that I don't have cause. . . . While he was lying in bed these five months, recuperating, he was dismissed from his job—for no reason at all.

She walks across the stage, right to left, wringing her hands.

Kistunov. That's a pity, certainly, but I don't quite see the connection with our bank, madame.

Woman. You don't know how I suffered during his illness. I nursed him from morning till night. Doctored him from night till morning. Besides cleaning my house, taking care of my children, feeding our dog, our cat, our goat, my sister's bird, who was sick. . . .

She leans forward and nearly screams her line. He jumps back. Actors hold these positions for several seconds to end the scene.

Kistunov. The bird was sick?

Woman. My *sister!*

IDEA Bank

1. Your Working Portfolio ▢
Look for ideas in the **Writing** sections that you completed earlier in this unit.

2. Emotional Impact
Choose the scene that is the most humorous or most dramatic.

3. Special Effects
Choose the scene that will allow you to use the most imaginative props, scenery, lighting, and costumes.

See **Language Network**

Speak for Yourself: Drama, p. 471

Performing an Oral Interpretation, p. 548

Staging Your Scene

❶ Planning Your Scene

With your classmates, choose a part of the scene from "A Defenseless Creature" to present. First **divide** the scene into parts by looking for changes in action or dialogue. If you start in the middle, you could use a narrator to set the scene. See the **Idea Bank** in the margin for more ideas. After selecting a scene, follow the steps below.

Steps for Planning Your Scene

▶ **1. List all cast and crew members.** List the characters in your scene and all the other roles involved in a stage production:

- director
- prop manager
- costumer
- prompter
- sound crew
- acting coach
- lighting manager
- set designer

▶ **2. Assign responsibilities.** Do you want group members to try out for acting roles or to volunteer as stage hands? What other tasks need to be assigned?

▶ **3. Decide on an interpretation.** Will you try to recreate the playwright's vision, or do you have your own? Think about presenting the scene as a musical or comedy; or creating unusual costumes or backdrops for a desired effect.

▶ **4. Prepare a director's script.** As a group, mark notes on the script about positions of the actors, their gestures and movements, the tones of their voices for certain lines, the type of scenery required, and the lighting, props, and sound effects.

▶ **5. Locate costumes, props, and other items you will need.** Check out attics, basements, and school resources for costumes and props. The simpler your materials, the more smoothly your staging will go. Think about what you will need to create sound effects or background music.

❷ Developing Your Stage Presentation

Discuss the scene in your group to make sure everyone understands it. Then cast members should read through the scene. They should look up any unfamiliar words and make sure they can pronounce them.

Get interpretations on paper. Cast members should mark their scripts with notes on facial expressions, tones of voice, movements, gestures, and stage positions.

Get everyone involved. Stage personnel should mark their scripts with notes on the lighting, sound, props, scenery, and costume requirements. Try to involve everyone in some phase of the production.

❸ Practicing and Presenting

The entire cast should practice the scene several times before presenting it.

- **Do a read-through.** Have the actors read their parts aloud several times to make sure they can say them with the appropriate expression.

- **Have actors do a walk-through.** Reading from their scripts, actors should perform their movements, gestures, and facial expressions.

- **Add the extras.** Set up the stage, have the actors wear costumes and use props, and try out the lighting and sound. Has the setting been established?

- **Stage a final rehearsal.** Run through the entire scene without stopping. Ask some people to watch the rehearsal and give feedback. Try video-taping the rehearsal for viewing before the performance.

❹ Refining Your Performance

TARGET SKILL ▶ **EVALUATING THE STAGING OF YOUR SCENE** After your final rehearsal, think about the decisions you and your classmates made in interpreting your scene. Consider your choices in the following areas:

- **Awareness of audience** Could your audience clearly see all of the action on the stage? Was everyone able to hear the actors?

- **Following the script** Did the actors remember their lines? Did the performance stay true to the playwright's script?

- **Creating mood and character** Do all parts of the performance work together to show the emotions of the characters, both main and minor? Did your staging show the action and drama of the scene?

❺ Reflecting

FOR YOUR WORKING PORTFOLIO What did you learn about staging a scene? How did performing your role in the production help you learn more about the scene? Attach your reflections to your script. Save the script in your **Working Portfolio.**

Practicing TIP

Before rehearsing the entire scene, pair up students who have speaking parts with students who are involved backstage. Have the actors practice with their partners in different parts of the room until they feel confident about their pronunciation, volume, and tone and have started to memorize their lines.

Ask Your Peer Reviewers

- What did you like best about the performance?
- What parts were hard to follow? Why?
- How can the acting and staging be improved?
- What actions and emotions seemed most real to you?

Standardized Test Practice

Mixed Review

Review Your Skills

Use the passage and the questions that follow it to check how well you remember the language conventions you've learned in previous grades.

> Six students and a teacher was the leading force behind the school's
> (1)
> spring production, senes from *The Good Doctor* by Neil Simon. Earlier
> (2)
> in the year, the students had asked of the teacher about staging a play.
> (3)
> She was open with enthusiasm to the idea and greeted it. The students
> (4)
> put in a great deal of their time. On opening night, the crowd gave us
> (5)
> two standing ovations. All the effort was worth the success.
> (6)

1. How is item 1 best written?
- **A.** Six students and a teacher were
- **B.** A teacher and six students was
- **C.** Six students or a teacher were
- **D.** Correct as is

2. What is the correct spelling in item 2?
- **A.** seens
- **B.** sceens
- **C.** scenes
- **D.** Correct as is

3. How is sentence 3 best written?
- **A.** asked the teacher
- **B.** asked to the teacher
- **C.** sought the teacher
- **D.** Correct as is

4. How is sentence 4 best written?
- **A.** She was open to the idea and greeted it with enthusiasm.
- **B.** She with enthusiasm was open to the idea and greeted it.
- **C.** With enthusiasm, she was open to the idea and greeted it.
- **D.** Correct as is

5. What is the correct spelling in sentence 5?
- **A.** there
- **B.** thier
- **C.** they're
- **D.** Correct as is

6. What is the correct spelling in sentence 6?
- **A.** sucess
- **B.** succes
- **C.** seccess
- **D.** Correct as is

Self-Assessment

Check your own answers in the **Grammar Handbook**

Prepositional Phrases, p. R84

Quick Reference: Capitalization, p. R70

Quick Reference: Punctuation, p. R68

Sentence Fragments, p. R71

Subject-Verb Agreement, p. R72

Transitive and Intransitive Verbs, p. R99

Key Standard
LC1.4 Use the mechanics of writing correctly; demonstrate correct language usage.
Other Standards LC1.3, LC1.6

The Literature You'll Read

The Concepts You'll Study

Vocabulary and Reading Comprehension
Vocabulary Focus: Understanding Synonyms and Antonyms
Drawing Conclusions
Making Judgments
Recognizing Text Organization

Writing and Language Conventions
Writing Workshop: Comparison-and-Contrast Essay
Appositives
Participial Phrases

Literary Analysis
Literary Focus: Character Development
First-Person Narrator
Unreliable Narrator
Irony

Speaking and Listening
Research Presentation
Dramatic Reading
Interview and Oral Report

Key Standard
R3.3 Analyze characters by examining what they think, say, and do, and by studying the words of the narrator and the reactions of other characters.

Character Development

> *I have discovered I cannot dream up characters as incredible as the ones I meet in the wilderness.*
> —Jean Craighead George

Your favorite character in a movie may be a lonesome wolf or a talking snake. Maybe it's a courageous young person about your age. Think about how you learned about this character. How is his or her personality revealed? What about likes and dislikes? Does your character take charge of a scene or remain in the background? By the end of the movie, has your character changed or remained the same?

Character development helps readers recognize which characters in a work are the most important. In literature, just as in movies, **main characters** are the ones who play a large role, while **minor characters** play a small one. Often, main characters undergo changes as the plot unfolds. Such characters are called **dynamic characters. Static characters** remain the same throughout the story. Writers help readers learn about characters by emphasizing their **traits,** or qualities, and their **motives,** or the reason they act the way they do. The process by which traits and motives are revealed is called **characterization.**

Characterization

Characterization is a process by which a writer reveals a character's **traits,** or qualities, and explains a character's **motives,** or what makes the character act the way he or she does. There are four main methods writers use: A writer may describe how a character looks; how a character thinks, speaks, and acts; or what others say or think about the character. The author may also comment directly on the character's behavior or personality. Read below and on the following page to learn more about the four ways characters are revealed.

- **The Character's Appearance** A person's appearance, or looks, conveys something about what kind of person he or she is. You can form an idea of what a fictional character is like by carefully reading descriptions of the character's face, clothing, and even how the character stands or moves.

- **The Character's Thoughts, Speech, and Actions** What a character thinks, says, and does tells a lot about him or her. The reader can get to know a character better when the writer reveals the character's thoughts or feelings. Notice also the words a character uses in a story. How the author uses speech and word choice can give the reader clues to a character's personality.

YOUR TURN Read the excerpt from Shirley Jackson's "One Ordinary Day, with Peanuts." What do Mr. Johnson's actions tell about him?

CHARACTER'S THOUGHTS, SPEECH, AND ACTIONS

When he had gone several blocks uptown, Mr. Johnson cut across the avenue and went along a side street, chosen at random; he did not follow the same route every morning, but preferred to pursue his eventful way in wide detours, more like a puppy than a man intent upon business. . . . Halfway down the block . . . a harassed woman, trying to watch a young child and the movers and the furniture all at the same time, gave the clear impression of endeavoring to shelter her private life from the people staring at her belongings. Mr. Johnson stopped, and for a moment joined the crowd, then he came forward and, touching his hat civilly, said, "Perhaps I can keep an eye on your little boy for you?"

—Shirley Jackson,
"One Ordinary Day, with Peanuts"

Details of *Autobiographical* (1954), Moses Soyer. Courtesy of ACA Galleries, New York. Copyright © Estate of Moses Soyer/Licensed by VAGA, New York.

- **What Others Say about the Character** As in real life, people in fiction talk about each other. When you are reading, notice what characters say about other characters. This will give you another perspective. For example, you might form one impression of a character based on his own thoughts. Then you might read what another character says about him and change your opinion. Note that the narrator of a story sometimes speaks directly about characters.

- **Direct Statements Made by the Writer about the Character** Often in literature, the narrator will make direct comments about a character. The narrator may report that a character is fearful, brave, generous, or stingy. The narrator may also comment on a character's motivations, behavior toward others, or secret longings.

YOUR TURN Read the excerpt on the right. What do Ben Price's words tell you about Jim Valentine?

WHAT OTHERS SAY ABOUT THE CHARACTER

"That's Dandy Jim Valentine's autograph. He's resumed business. Look at that combination knob—jerked out as easy as pulling up a radish in wet weather. He's got the only clamps that can do it. And look how clean those tumblers were punched out! Jimmy never has to drill but one hole. Yes, I guess I want Mr. Valentine. He'll do his bit next time without any short-time or clemency foolishness."

—O. Henry, "A Retrieved Reformation"

From "A Retrieved Reformation"

Dynamic and Static Characters

Think about a time in your life that changed you. Something happened, and as a result you were never the same. This is also true of characters in literature. Often, one or more of a story's main characters change as a result of the events or conflict in the story. A character might grow emotionally, learn a lesson, or change his or her behavior. Such a character is called a **dynamic character.** A **static character,** on the other hand, is one who doesn't change.

YOUR TURN In the model passage, do you think Henrietta is a dynamic or a static character? How do you know?

DYNAMIC AND STATIC CHARACTERS

Every once in a while I'd try to figure out what the thing was that made her so different now; and then one day, all of a sudden, I understood. . . . Everything else was the same—the drab white skin; the bony, yes, bony hands; the limp hair. But she had lost her waiting look. Henrietta didn't look as though she were waiting for anything at all anymore.

—Budge Wilson, "Waiting"

From "Waiting"

Drawing Conclusions

Key Standard
R3.2 Identify events that advance the plot and describe how they explain the past, present, and future.
Other Standards **R3.3, R3.4**

If you hear sirens outside your window and notice that smoke is coming from the building across the street, you might reasonably conclude that the building is on fire. You might **draw conclusions** by combining facts with your own knowledge and experience. An active reader can draw conclusions about a character's motives, or the events or theme of a story. As you read, use the strategies on this page to help you draw conclusions.

How to Apply the Skill

To **DRAW CONCLUSIONS**, an active reader will
- Look for facts and details
- Make logical inferences
- **Evaluate** information
- **Connect** to his or her own experience and knowledge
- Use a chart like this one to help draw conclusions

Try It Now!

Read and draw conclusions from the excerpt below.

I always wanted to be a writer and a teacher. With my heart and my soul I knew that I wanted to be around books all my life. . . . For four years I boarded with a couple [my mother] knew. I paid my rent in labor, and I ate vegetables I grew myself.

—Judith Ortiz Cofer, "An Hour with Abuelo"

	Inferences	Stated Facts
Character (or setting or plot)		
Conclusions:		

Here's how Rafael uses the strategies:

*"As I read the facts and details about Arturo's grandfather, I understand his hardships. I can logically guess that Arturo's grandfather was a very motivated person. I **evaluate** this information and conclude that he was very intelligent because he graduated first in his class."*

ACTIVE READER GUIDE

An Hour with Abuelo

by JUDITH ORTIZ COFER

 Key Standards
R3.5 Contrast points of view (first and third person, limited and omniscient) and explain how they affect the narrative.
R3.3 Analyze characters by examining what they think, say, and do, and by studying the words of the narrator and the reactions of other characters.
***Other Standards* W1.6, W2.3, W2.4, LC1.4, LC1.7, LS1.4, LS2.3**

Connect to Your Life

Do you know an elderly person, such as a grandparent, who likes to talk about life in the "old days"? With a classmate discuss why a very old person might want to tell a young person about his or her life. What might a young person get out of hearing the stories?

Build Background

HISTORY

In the story you are about to read, the narrator's grandfather talks about being drafted into the U.S. Army while he was a young man in Puerto Rico. Puerto Rico, an island about 1,000 miles southeast of Florida, was settled by Spaniards beginning in 1508. It remained under Spanish control for nearly four centuries.

At the end of the Spanish-American War, in 1898, Puerto Rico became a possession of the United States. In 1917 Puerto Ricans were granted U.S. citizenship. Thousands of Puerto Ricans have served in the U.S. armed forces since World War I. On July 25, 1952, Puerto Rico became a largely self-governing commonwealth where both Spanish and English are official languages.

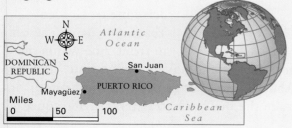

WORDS TO KNOW **Vocabulary Preview**
ammunition   orderly   suite
embroidered   parchment

Focus Your Reading

LITERARY ANALYSIS **FIRST-PERSON NARRATOR**

In a story told from a **first-person point of view,** the narrator is also a character. As the narrator tells the story, the words and phrases he or she uses are clues to his or her **character.** As you read "An Hour with Abuelo," try to form an idea of Arturo's character as it is revealed by what he says and how he says it. The way a character is revealed is called **characterization.**

ACTIVE READING **DRAWING CONCLUSIONS**

Active readers often need to **draw conclusions** about aspects of the works they read. To draw conclusions, combine information from what you have read with knowledge you have gathered from your own experience.

READER'S NOTEBOOK As you read the selection, write down characterization clues you find in the story and combine them with what you know from your own experience. Draw conclusions about Arturo and his grandfather.

Characterization Clues	My Experience	Conclusion
Arturo keeps a stack of school books beside his bed.	To read on your own means you are motivated.	Arturo is a motivated student.

AN HOUR with *Abuelo*

BY JUDITH ORTIZ COFER

Painting by Jan Wahlin.

"Just one hour, *una hora*,[1] is all I'm asking of you, son." My grandfather is in a nursing home in Brooklyn, and my mother wants me to spend some time with him, since the doctors say that he doesn't have too long to go now. *I don't have much time left of my summer vacation*, and there's a stack of books next to my bed I've got to read if I'm going to get into the AP English class I want. I'm going stupid in some of my classes, and Mr. Williams, the principal at Central, said that if I passed some reading tests, he'd let me move up.

Besides, I hate the place, the old people's home, especially the way it smells like industrial-strength ammonia and other stuff I won't mention, since it turns my stomach. And really the abuelo[2] always has a lot of relatives visiting him, so I've gotten out of going out there except at Christmas, when a whole vanload of grandchildren are herded over there

to give him gifts and a hug. We all make it quick and spend the rest of the time in the recreation area, where they play checkers and stuff with some of the old people's games, and I catch up on back issues of *Modern Maturity*.[3] I'm not picky, I'll read almost anything.

Anyway, after my mother nags me for about a week, I let her drive me to Golden Years. She drops me off in front. She wants me to go in alone and have a "good time" talking to Abuelo. I tell her to be back in one hour or I'll take the bus back to Paterson. She squeezes

> **ACTIVE READER**
>
> **MAKE INFERENCES** How is the narrator different from his cousins?

---

1. *una hora* (ōō'nä ō'rä) *Spanish.*
2. **abuelo** (ä-bwĕ'lō): the Spanish word for grandfather.
3. *Modern Maturity:* a magazine for retired people.

I was named after him.

my hand and says, *"Gracias, hijo,"*[4] in a choked-up voice like I'm doing her a big favor.

I get depressed the minute I walk into the place. They line up the old people in wheelchairs in the hallway as if they were about to be raced to the finish line by <u>orderlies</u> who don't even look at them when they push them here and there. I walk fast to room 10, Abuelo's "<u>suite</u>." He is sitting up in his bed writing with a pencil in one of those old-fashioned black hardback notebooks. It has the outline of the island of Puerto Rico on it. I slide into the hard vinyl chair by his bed. He sort of smiles and the lines on his face get deeper, but he doesn't say anything. Since I'm supposed to talk to him, I say, "What are you doing, Abuelo, writing the story of your life?"

It's supposed to be a joke, but he answers, "Sí,[5] how did you know, Arturo?"

His name is Arturo too. I was named after him. I don't really know my grandfather. His children, including my mother, came to New York and New Jersey (where I was born) and he stayed on the Island until my grandmother died. Then he got sick, and since nobody could leave their jobs to go take care of him, they brought him to this nursing home in Brooklyn. I see him a couple of times a year, but he's always surrounded by his sons and daughters. My mother tells me that Don[6] Arturo had once been a teacher back in Puerto Rico, but had lost his job after the war. Then he became a farmer. She's always saying in a sad voice, "Ay, bendito![7] What a waste of a fine mind." Then she usually shrugs her shoulders and says, "*Así*

es la vida."[8] That's the way life is. It sometimes makes me mad that the adults I know just accept whatever is thrown at them because "that's the way things are." Not for me. I go after what I want.

Anyway, Abuelo is looking at me like he was trying to see into my head, but he doesn't say anything. Since I like stories, I decide I may as well ask him if he'll read me what he wrote.

I look at my watch: I've already used up twenty minutes of the hour I promised my mother.

Abuelo starts talking in his slow way. He speaks what my mother calls book English. He taught himself from a dictionary, and his words sound stiff, like he's sounding them out in his head before he says them. With his children he speaks Spanish, and that funny book English with us grandchildren. I'm surprised that he's still so sharp, because his body is shrinking like a crumpled-up brown paper sack with some bones in it. But I can see from looking into his eyes that the light is still on in there.

"It is a short story, Arturo. The story of my life. It will not take very much time to read it."

"I have time, Abuelo." I'm a little embarrassed that he saw me looking at my watch.

"Yes, hijo. You have spoken the truth. La verdad. You have much time."

---

4. *Gracias, hijo* (grä′syäs ē′hō) *Spanish:* Thank you, son.
5. sí (sē) *Spanish:* yes.
6. **Don:** a Spanish title of respect, used before a man's name.
7. Ay, bendito! (ī bĕn-dē′tō) *Spanish:* Oh, goodness!
8. *Así es la vida* (ä-sē′ ĕs lä vē′dä) *Spanish.*

WORDS TO KNOW	**orderly** (ôr′dər-lē) *n.* an attendant who performs nonmedical tasks in a hospital or similar institution
	suite (swēt) *n.* a group of rooms used as a unit

593

Abuelo reads: "'I loved words from the beginning of my life. In the *campo*[9] where I was born one of seven sons, there were few books. My mother read them to us over and over: the Bible, the stories of Spanish conquistadors and of pirates that she had read as a child and brought with her from the city of Mayagüez;[10] that was before she married my father, a coffee bean farmer; and she taught us words from the newspaper that a boy on a horse brought every week to her. She taught each of us how to write on a slate with chalks that she ordered by mail every year. We used those chalks until they were so small that you lost them between your fingers.

"'I always wanted to be a writer and a teacher. With my heart and my soul I knew that I wanted to be around books all of my life. And so against the wishes of my father, who wanted all his sons to help him on the land, she sent me to high school in Mayagüez. For four years I boarded with a couple she knew. I paid my rent in labor, and I ate

ACTIVE READER

CLARIFY How does Arturo's grandfather feel about books and learning?

vegetables I grew myself. I wore my clothes until they were thin as <u>parchment</u>. But I graduated at the top of my class! My whole family came to see me that day. My mother brought me a beautiful *guayabera*,[11] a white shirt made of the finest cotton and <u>embroidered</u> by her own hands. I was a happy young man.

"'In those days you could teach in a country school with a high school diploma. So I went back to my mountain village and got a job teaching all grades in a little classroom built by the parents of my students.

"'I had books sent to me by the government. I felt like a rich man although the pay was very small. I had books. All the books I wanted! I taught my students how to read poetry and plays, and how to write them. We made up songs and put on shows for the parents. It was a beautiful time for me.

"'Then the war came, and the American President said that all Puerto Rican men would be drafted. I wrote to our governor and explained that I was the only teacher in the mountain village. I told him that the children would go back to the fields and grow up ignorant if I could not teach them their letters. I said that I thought I was a better teacher than a soldier. The governor did not answer my letter. I went into the U.S. Army.

"'I told my sergeant that I could be a teacher in the army. I could teach all the farm boys their letters so that they could read the instructions on the <u>ammunition</u> boxes and not blow themselves up. The sergeant said I was too smart for my own good, and gave me a job cleaning latrines. He said to me there is reading material for you there, scholar. Read the writing on the walls. I spent the war mopping floors and cleaning toilets.

"'When I came back to the Island, things had changed. You had to have a college degree to teach school, even the lower grades. My parents were sick, two of my brothers had been killed in the war, the others had stayed in Nueva York. I was the only one left to help the old people. I became a farmer. I married a

---

9. *campo* (käm′pō) *Spanish:* countryside.
10. **Mayagüez** (mī′ə-gwĕz′): a port city on the western coast of Puerto Rico.
11. *guayabera* (gwä-yä-bä′rä) *Spanish.*

WORDS
TO
KNOW

parchment (pärch′mənt) *n.* a paperlike writing material made from the skins of sheep or goats

embroidered (ĕm-broi′dərd) *adj.* ornamented with stitched designs **embroider** *v.*

ammunition (ăm′yə-nĭsh′ən) *n.* the explosive cartridges or shells designed to be used in guns

I loved words from the beginning of my life.

Letters (1992), Kim English. Oil, 17″ × 18″. Private Collection.

The Yellow Books (1887), Vincent Van Gogh. Oil on canvas, 73 cm × 93 cm. Private Collection, Switzerland/Giraudon, Paris/SuperStock.

good woman who gave me many good children. I taught them all how to read and write before they started school.'"

Abuelo then puts the notebook down on his lap and closes his eyes.

"*Así es la vida* is the title of my book," he says in a whisper, almost to himself. Maybe he's forgotten that I'm there.

For a long time he doesn't say anything else. I think that he's sleeping, but then I see that he's watching me through half-closed lids, maybe waiting for my opinion of his writing. I'm trying to think of something nice to say. I liked it and all, but not the title. And I think that he could've been a teacher if he had wanted to bad enough. Nobody is going to stop me from doing what I want with my life. I'm not going to let la vida get in my way. I want to discuss this with him, but the words are not coming into my head in Spanish just yet. I'm about to ask him why he didn't keep fighting to make his dream come true, when an old lady in hot-pink running shoes sort of appears at the door.

She is wearing a pink jogging outfit too. The world's oldest marathoner, I say to myself. She calls out to my grandfather in a flirty voice, "Yoo-hoo, Arturo, remember what day this is? It's poetry-reading day in the rec room! You promised us you'd read your new one today."

I see my abuelo perking up almost immediately. He points to his wheelchair, which is hanging like a huge metal bat in the open closet. He makes it obvious that he wants me to get it. I put it together, and with Mrs. Pink Running Shoes's help, we get him in it. Then he says in a strong deep voice I hardly recognize, "Arturo, get that notebook from the table, please."

I hand him another map-of-the-Island notebook—this one is red. On it in big letters it says, *POEMAS DE ARTURO*.[12]

I start to push him toward the rec room, but he shakes his finger at me.

"Arturo, look at your watch now. I believe your time is over." He gives me a wicked smile.

Then with her pushing the wheelchair—maybe a little too fast—they roll down the hall. He is already reading from his notebook, and she's making bird noises. I look at my watch and the hour is up, to the minute. I can't help but think that my abuelo has been timing me. It cracks me up. I walk slowly down the hall toward the exit sign. I want my mother to have to wait a little. I don't want her to think that I'm in a hurry or anything. ❖

ACTIVE READER

DRAW CONCLUSIONS
How do you think Arturo feels about visiting his grandfather now?

---

12. ***POEMAS DE ARTURO*** (pō-ā′mäs dā är-tōō′rō) *Spanish:* Arturo's poems.

THE OLD GRANDFATHER AND HIS LITTLE GRANDSON

by LEO TOLSTOY

Hermit (1888), Mikhail Vasilievich Nesterov. Oil on canvas, 91 cm × 84 cm. The State Russian Museum, St. Petersburg, Russia.

The grandfather had become very old. His legs would not carry him, his eyes could not see, his ears could not hear, and he was toothless. When he ate, bits of food sometimes dropped out of his mouth. His son and his son's wife no longer allowed him to eat with them at the table. He had to eat his meals in the corner near the stove.

One day they gave him his food in a bowl. He tried to move the bowl closer; it fell to the floor and broke. His daughter-in-law scolded him. She told him that he spoiled everything in the house and broke their dishes, and she said that from now on he would get his food in a wooden dish. The old man sighed and said nothing.

A few days later, the old man's son and his wife were sitting in their hut, resting and watching their little boy playing on the floor. They saw him putting together something out of small pieces of wood. His father asked him, "What are you making, Misha?"

The little grandson said, "I'm making a wooden bucket. When you and Mamma get old, I'll feed you out of this wooden dish."

The young peasant and his wife looked at each other, and tears filled their eyes. They were ashamed because they had treated the old grandfather so meanly, and from that day they again let the old man eat with them at the table and took better care of him. ❖

Connect to the Literature

1. **What Do You Think?** What especially do you remember after reading "An Hour with Abuelo"? Explain.

Comprehension Check
- When has Arturo visited his grandfather in the past?
- What were Arturo's grandfather's two ambitions?
- What does Abuelo say "with a wicked smile" to Arturo at the end of Arturo's visit?

Think Critically

2. How does Arturo's understanding of his grandfather change during his visit?

   Think About:
   - Arturo's plan to visit for exactly one hour
   - Arturo's usual feelings about adults
   - a surprise visit from "Mrs. Pink Running Shoes"

3. **ACTIVE READING** **DRAWING CONCLUSIONS** With a partner compare the notes you made in your **READER'S NOTEBOOK**. Did you draw similar conclusions? How did they differ?

4. Arturo's mother feels that her father's life has been "a waste of a fine mind." What do you think?

5. Arturo says, "I go after what I want." How does this attitude affect his relationship with his grandfather?

6. Why do you think the grandfather reads his life story to Arturo? What does Arturo gain from hearing it?

Extend Interpretations

7. **Different Perspectives** Imagine that "Mrs. Pink Running Shoes" had overheard Arturo's visit with his grandfather. How might she describe it to a friend? What kind of a person is the grandfather from her perspective? Contrast her point of view with Arturo's.

8. **Connect to Life** Many observers say that elderly people are no longer valued or respected in modern American life. What is your opinion?

Literary Analysis

FIRST-PERSON NARRATOR A **first-person narrator** tells the story directly to the reader, using pronouns like *I* and *me.* In "An Hour with Abuelo," the main character, Arturo, is the narrator. The reader learns a great deal about his **character** from the words and expressions he uses and the attitudes he displays. For example, early in the story Arturo mentions how he escapes to the recreation area during earlier visits with his grandfather:

I catch up on back issues of Modern Maturity. I'm not picky, I'll read almost anything.

The way readers learn about characters is through **characterization.** For example, Arturo's words reveal that he both likes to read and has a sense of humor, two things he shares with his grandfather.

Paired Activity With a partner create a web in which you note characteristics Arturo has in common with his grandfather. Find examples from the story that support your observations. When you are finished, draw conclusions about these two characters. Write those conclusions at the center of the web.

Arturo: "I'll read almost anything." Abuelo: "I had books. All the books I wanted."

Arturo: Abuelo "cracks me up." Abuelo gives Arturo "a wicked smile."

Conclusions?

Writing

Personal Essay What does the saying *"Así es la vida"* (That's the way life is) mean to you? Is it sad? Does it mean give up, or keep going? Could it be humorous? Write a personal essay in which you express your opinion. Draw on your own experiences or those of someone you know. Place your essay in your **Working Portfolio.**

Writing Handbook.
See p. R35: Drafting.

Speaking & Listening

Research Presentation Using the research assignment in Research & Technology on this page as a basis, prepare an oral report to give to the class. When organizing your oral presentation, keep in mind the background and interests of your audience. What points will be most interesting to them? You will also want your audience to know your perspectives on the subject, as well as the questions you developed that led to your discoveries. Have your list of sources ready in case your audience has questions about the origin of the facts you present.

Speaking and Listening Handbook
See p. R104: Research Presentations.

Research & Technology

Puerto Rico Use encyclopedias, magazines, and library databases to learn more about Puerto Rico. Identify a topic you would like to investigate. For example, you might want to find out more about Puerto Rico's history, involvement with America, what it means to be a self-governing commonwealth, or how the political transitions between 1898 and 1952 affected the people, culture, and customs. (See "History" p. 591.) Develop a list of questions that will lead you toward focused research. Using a word processing program, type up your findings. Present your report to the class (see Speaking & Listening, this page).

Research and Technology Handbook
See p. R112: Word Processing.

▶ **INTERNET** **Research Starter**
www.mcdougallittell.com

Vocabulary and Spelling

EXERCISE: RELATED WORDS On a sheet of paper, write the letter of the word that is not related in meaning to the other words in the set.

1. (a) hospital (b) theater (c) nurse (d) orderly
2. (a) suite (b) room (c) apartment (d) park
3. (a) galaxy (b) parchment (c) telescope (d) planet
4. (a) sewn (b) erased (c) knitted (d) embroidered
5. (a) war (b) gun (c) ammunition (d) hammer

SPELLING STRATEGY: HOMOPHONES Remember to think about meaning when using **homophones,** words that sound alike but that have different spellings and meanings, such as *suite* and *sweet.*
On a sheet of paper, write the homophone that belongs with each set of words below.

1. boundary, rim, outline, (boarder, border)
2. troop, regiment, division, (corps, core)
3. major, general, captain, (kernel, colonel)
4. eggs, toast, juice, (serial, cereal)
5. sour, salty, bitter, (suite, sweet)

Spelling Handbook
See p. R30.

CHOICES and CHALLENGES

Grammar in Context: Appositives

In "An Hour with Abuelo," appositive phrases add information that make nouns or pronouns more specific and precise.

> . . . I hate the place, the old people's home. . . .

> I walk fast to room 10, Abuelo's "suite."

An **appositive** is a noun or phrase that explains one or more words in a sentence. It is usually placed after a noun or pronoun to explain it. Often the noun or pronoun appositive has modifiers. An appositive and its modifiers make up an **appositive phrase.** Appositives giving the Spanish equivalent of English words are a part of this story's style.

> "Just one hour, *una hora*, is all I'm asking of you, son."

WRITING EXERCISE Rewrite each sentence, adding an appositive phrase to explain the underlined word.

Example: *Original* <u>Arturo</u> is the son of farmers.

Rewritten <u>Arturo, my grandfather,</u> is the son of farmers.

1. In the recreation room they play <u>backgammon</u>.
2. Abuelo starts to read the <u>story</u>.
3. <u>Abuelo</u> was forced to leave his work and join the army.
4. I'm not going to let <u>*la vida*</u> stop me.

Connection to the Literature Reread the last sentence in the first paragraph of the story. What appositive phrase do you find there?

Grammar Handbook
See p. R85: Appositive Phrases.

Judith Ortiz Cofer
born 1952

"With the stories I tell, . . . I try to get my audience past the particulars of my skin color, my accent, or my clothes."

Living in Two Places Judith Ortiz Cofer was born in Hormigueros, Puerto Rico, and moved to Paterson, New Jersey, as a toddler. She traveled back and forth between Paterson and the island during her childhood. She says her island grandfather taught her poetry, and her island grandmother taught her survival.

Two Languages Ortiz Cofer's family spoke Spanish at home, and she learned English at school. When she was in third grade, a teacher once punished her because she did not understand English. After that she became a dedicated reader. "I had to learn the language of the place where I was living in order to survive."

Latina Wherever I Am Judith Ortiz Cofer describes herself as a Puerto Rican writer whose literary language is English. She writes about both the Puerto Rican and American parts of her experience and identity. She has won recognition for her poetry, essays, and fiction, including the O. Henry Award for her story "Nada" and the 1990 Pushcart Prize for Nonfiction. She teaches writing and literature at the University of Georgia.

Waiting
by BUDGE WILSON

Key Standards

R3.3 Analyze characters by examining what they think, say, and do, and by studying the words of the narrator and the reactions of other characters.

R3.5 Contrast points of view (first and third person, limited and omniscient) and explain how they affect the narrative.

***Other Standards* R1.1, W1.2, W1.6, W2.3, LC1.2, LS1.6**

Connect to Your Life

Best Friends What are the qualities that make somebody a good friend? Working with a partner, create a word web listing these qualities. Then share your web with other groups.

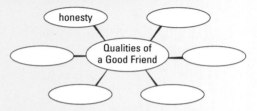

honesty / Qualities of a Good Friend

Build Background

SOCIAL STUDIES

"Waiting" is set in Nova Scotia, one of Canada's Atlantic provinces. The region's foggy, rocky countryside reminded 18th-century British settlers of Scotland, so they gave it the Latin name meaning "New Scotland." From the 1800s to the middle of the 20th century, Nova Scotia was an important center of shipbuilding.

"Waiting" takes place in the town of Shelburne during World War II, when the threat of German submarines in the waters offshore was real. Halifax, Nova Scotia's capital city, was the center for Allied naval operations in the western Atlantic during the war. Many sailors like those mentioned in the story were stationed in Nova Scotia.

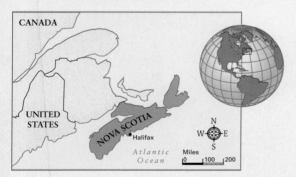

CANADA

UNITED STATES

NOVA SCOTIA · Halifax

Atlantic Ocean   Miles 0 100 200

N W E S

WORDS TO KNOW **Vocabulary Preview**

apathy	flamboyant	saunter	submissive
arresting	infuriatingly	stupefying	vigor
dominant	quarantine		

Focus Your Reading

LITERARY ANALYSIS | **UNRELIABLE NARRATOR**

The narrator of a work of fiction is the character or voice that tells the story. In life, one person's perspective on an event may be very different from another's. The same is true in fiction. A narrator who presents a biased or distorted version of events or of other characters is called an **unreliable narrator.** As you read "Waiting," look for clues that tell you that the main character and **first-person narrator,** Juliette, may be an unreliable narrator.

ACTIVE READING | **MAKING JUDGMENTS**

When you combine information from the work you are reading with what you already know from your own experience in order to evaluate some aspect of the work, you are **making judgments.** In "Waiting," you need to evaluate the things Juliette says, thinks, and does. Determine whether or not her characterization of Henrietta is accurate.

READER'S NOTEBOOK As you read "Waiting," jot down details and comments that will help you make a judgment as to whether Juliette is a reliable or unreliable narrator.

Is Juliette a Reliable Narrator?

What Juliette Says	Clues from the Story
Juliette says that Henrietta is her best friend.	Juliette yells at Henrietta and calls her "slowpoke."

Illustration by Meg Kelleher Aubrey.

Waiting

by Budge Wilson

"You must realize, of course, that Juliette is a very complex child." My mother was talking on the telephone. Shouting, to be more exact. She always spoke on the phone as though the wires had been disconnected, as though she were trying to be heard across the street through an open window. "She's so many-*sided,*" she continued. "Being cute, of course, is not enough, although heaven knows she could charm the legs off a table. But you have to have something more than personality."

I was not embarrassed by any of this. Lying on the living room floor on my stomach, I was pretending to read *The Bobbsey Twins at the Seashore.* But after a while I closed the book. Letting her words drop around me, I lay there like a plant enjoying the benefit of a drenching and beneficial rain. My sister sat nearby in the huge wingback chair, legs tucked up under her, reading the funnies.

"I hope you don't regard this as *boasting,* but she really is so very, *very* talented. Bright as a button in school—three prizes, can you believe it, at the last school closing—and an outstanding athlete, even at eight years old."

Resting my head on my folded arms, I smiled quietly. I could see myself eight years from now, receiving my gold medal, while our country's flag rose in front of the Olympic flame. The applause thundered as the flag reached its peak, standing straight out from the pole, firm and strong. As the band broke into a moving rendition of "O Canada," I wept softly. I stood wet and waterlogged from my last race, my tears melding with the chlorine and coursing slowly down my face. People were murmuring, "So young, so small, and so attractive."

"And such a leader!" My mother's voice hammered on. "Even at her age, she seems forever to be president of this and director of that. I feel very blessed indeed to be the mother of such a child." My sister stirred in her chair and coughed slightly, carefully turning a page.

It was true. I was president of grade 4 and manager of the Lower Slocum Elementary School Drama Club. I had already starred in two productions, one of them a musical. In an ornate crêpe paper costume composed of giant overlapping yellow petals, I had played Lead Buttercup to a full house. Even Miss Prescott's aggressive piano playing had failed to drown me out, had not prevented me from stealing the show from the Flower Queen. My mother kept the clipping from *The Shelburne Coast Guard* up on the kitchen notice board. It included a blurred newspaper picture of me with extended arms and open mouth. Below it, the caption read, "Juliette Westhaver was the surprise star of the production, with three solos and a most sprightly little dance, performed skillfully and with gusto. Broadway, look out!"

*M*ama was still talking. "Mm? Oh. Henrietta. Yes, well, she's fine, I guess, just fine. Such a serious, responsible little girl, and so fond of her sister." I looked up at Henrietta, who was surveying me over the top of her comics. There was no expression on her face at all.

But then Henrietta was not often given to expression of any kind. She was my twin, but apart from the accident of our birth, or the coincidence, we had almost nothing in common. It was incredible to me that we had been born to the same parents at almost the same moment, and that we had been reared in the same house.

But Henrietta was my friend and I hers. We were, in fact, best friends, as is so often the case with twins. And as with most close childhood friendships, there was one <u>dominant</u> member, one <u>submissive</u>. There was no doubt in this case as to who played the leading role.

Henrietta even looked submissive. She was thin and pale. She had enormous sky-blue eyes surrounded by a long fringe of totally colorless eyelashes. Her hair was a dim beige color without gradations of light or dark, and it hung straight and lifeless from two barrettes. Her fingers were long and bony, and she kept them folded in her lap, motionless, like a tired old lady. She had a straight little nose and a mouth that seldom smiled—it was serious and still and oddly serene. She often looked as though she were waiting for something.

Untidy and <u>flamboyant</u>, my personality and my person flamed hotly beside her cool <u>apathy</u>. My temper flared, my joys exploded. With fiery red cheeks and a broad snub nose, I grinned and hooted my way through childhood, dragging and pushing Henrietta along as I raced from one adventure to the next. I had a mop of wild black curls that no comb could tame. I was small, compact, sturdy, well-coordinated and extremely healthy. Henrietta had a lot of colds.

ACTIVE READER

CLARIFY In what ways are Juliette and Henrietta different?

When I start talking about Henrietta and me, I always feel like I'm right back there, a kid again. Sometimes, you know, I got fed up with her. If you have a lot of energy, for instance, it's no fun to go skiing with someone who's got lead in her boots. And for heaven's sake, she kept falling all the time. Scared to death to try the hills, and likely as not going down them on the seat of her pants. "Fraidy-cat! Fraidy-cat!" I'd yell at her from the bottom of the hill where I had landed right-side up, and she would start down the first part of the slope with straight and trembling knees, landing in a snow bank before the hill even got started. There were lots of fields and woods

---

WORDS TO KNOW

dominant (dŏm′ə-nənt) *adj.* ruling or controlling
submissive (səb-mĭs′ĭv) *adj.* willing to give in to or obey another
flamboyant (flăm-boi′ənt) *adj.* given to showy display; flashy
apathy (ăp′ə-thē) *n.* lack of strong feeling or interest

around our town, and good high hills if you were looking for thrills. You could see the sea from the top of some of them, and the wild wind up there made me feel like an explorer, a brave Micmac[1] hunter, the queen of the Maritime Provinces. Sometimes I would let out a yell just for the joy of it all—and there, panting and gasping and falling up the hill would be old Henrietta, complaining, forever complaining, about how tired she was, how cold.

But I guess I really loved Henrietta anyway, slowpoke though she was. I had lots and lots of other friends who were more interesting than she was. But it's a funny thing—she was nearly always my first choice for someone to play with.

There was a small woodlot to the east of the village, on land owned by my father. We called it The Grove. It had little natural paths in it, and there were open spaces under the trees like rooms or houses or castles, or whatever you wanted them to be that day. The grove of trees was on the edge of a cliff overhanging some big rocks, and at high tide the sea down there was never still, even when it was flat oil calm. So it could be a spooky kind of place to play in, too. I loved to go there when it was foggy and play spy. It was 1940 and wartime, and by then we were ten, going on eleven. From The Grove we could sometimes see destroyers, and once even a big aircraft carrier. In the fog, it wasn't hard to believe that the Nazis were coming, and that we were going to be blown to bits any minute.

We never told Mama or Papa about going to the cliff when the mist was thick. Henrietta hardly ever wanted to go on those foggy days. She was afraid of falling off the cliff onto the rocks, sure she would drown in the churned-up water, nervous about the ghostly shapes in the thick gray-white air. But she always went. I used to blackmail her. "If you don't go, I'll tell Mama about the time you pretended to be sick and stayed home from school because you didn't

have your homework done and were scared of Miss Garrison." Or I would just plain order her around. "I'm *going,* Henrietta, so get a move on and *hurry!*" She'd come padding out of the house in her stupid yellow raincoat, so that she wouldn't get a cold in the wet wind, and off we'd go—me fast and complaining about her slowness, and her slow and complaining about my speed. But she'd be there and we'd be together and we'd have fun. I'd be the spy, and she'd be the poor agonized prisoner of war, tied up to a tree by a bunch of Nazis. Sometimes I'd leave her tethered good and long, so she'd look *really* scared instead of pretend scared, while I prowled around and killed Nazis and searched for hidden weapons. Or we'd play Ghost, and I'd be the ghost—floating along on the edge of the cliff and shrieking in my special death shriek that I saved for ghost games. It started out low like a groan and then rose to a wail, ending in a scream so thin and high that it almost scared *me.* Sometimes, if she was especially wet and tired, Henrietta would start to cry, and that *really* made me mad. Even now, I can't stand crybabies. But you had to have a victim, and this was something she was extra good at. No point in wasting my death shriek on a person who wasn't afraid of ghosts. No fun to have the Nazis tying up someone who was big and strong and brave, particularly when the Nazis weren't actually there and you had to think them up and pretend the whole thing.

One time when we went there with a bunch of kids instead of just us two, I forgot all about her being tied to the tree and got nearly home before I raced back the whole half mile to untie her. She never said a word. It was snowing, and there were big fat snowflakes on those long white lashes of hers, and her eyes looked like they were going to pop right out of her head.

---

1. **Micmac:** a Native American people inhabiting Nova Scotia and other provinces of Canada.

I said I was real sorry, and next week I even bought her a couple of comic books out of my own allowance money, when she was home sick with bronchitis. Mama said she should have had the sense to wear a scarf and a warm hat, being as she was so prone to colds, and that's certainly true. She never told on me, and I don't know why. She sat up against the pillows and colored in her coloring book or read her funnies, or more often she just lay there on the bed, her hands lying limp on the quilt, with that patient, quiet, waiting look of hers.

ACTIVE READER

QUESTION Why doesn't Henrietta tell on her sister?

When the spring came, a gang of us would always start going out to The Grove on weekends to start practicing for our summer play. Year after year we did this, and it had nothing to do with those school plays in which I made such a hit. We'd all talk about what stories we liked, and then we'd pick one of them and make a play out of it. I would usually select the play because I was always the one who directed it, so it was only fair that I'd get to do the choosing. If there was a king or a queen, I'd usually be the queen. If you're the director, you can't be something like a page or a minor fairy, because then you don't seem important enough to be giving out instructions and bossing people around, and the kids maybe won't pay attention to all the orders. Besides, as my mother pointed out, I was smart and could learn my lines fast, and you couldn't expect some slow dummy to memorize all that stuff.

Henrietta's voice was so soft and quiet that no one could ever hear her unless they were almost sitting on her lap; so of course it would have been stupid to give her a part. She couldn't even be the king's horse or the queen's milk-white mule because she was so darn scrawny. You can't have the lead animal looking as though it should be picked up by the Humane Society and put in quarantine. But she was really useful to the production, and it must have been very satisfying for her. She got to find all the costume parts and rigged up the stage in the biggest cleared space among the trees, making it look like a ballroom or a throne room or whatever else we needed. She did a truly good job, and if it weren't for the fact that I can't stand conceited people, I probably would even have told her so. I liked Henrietta the way she was. I didn't want her strutting around looking proud of herself and putting on airs. One time one of the kids said, "Hey, Henrietta, that's a really great royal bedroom you made," and right away she started standing and moving around in a way that showed she thought she was a pretty smart stage manager.

I hate that kind of thing, and I knew the others wouldn't like it either. So I said, "Oh, sure! And the king must have just lost his kingdom in the wars. Who ever heard of a king sleeping on a pile of branches or having an old torn dishtowel at the window? Some king!" And everyone laughed. I always think that laughter is very important. It makes everyone happy right away and is a good way to ease tensions.

We had a lot of fun practicing for those plays. No one went away for the summer. No one needed to. The sea was right there alongside the village, with a big sandy beach only a quarter mile away. Some of the fishermen let us use their smaller flats for jigging,[2] and we could always swim or dig for clams or collect mussels. Besides, the war was on; people weren't spending money on cottages or trips. Seems to me that

2. **jigging:** fishing.

quarantine (kwôr′ən-tēn′) *n.* a place where a diseased animal is kept away from others

Staithes, Yorkshire (about 1900), Dame Laura Knight. Copyright ©
Dame Laura Knight, reproduced by permission of Curtis Brown
Group Ltd., London.

everyone just stuck around home and saved
paper and counted their ration stamps and
listened to the news on the radio. There was a
navy base nearby, and sometimes sailors came to
dinner. They'd tell us about life on the base and
all the dangers they were expecting and hoping
to experience when they started sailing to
Europe. I envied them like anything and couldn't
for the life of me see why you had to be eighteen
before you joined the navy, or why they
wouldn't let girls run the ships or use the guns.
Henrietta said she didn't want to be a sailor
anyway, because she'd be too scared, which of
course is only what you'd expect. Apart from
that, there wasn't much excitement. So the play
practices were our main entertainment during
those years. In the summer, we practiced on
most fine days, and in August we put on the
play in front of all our mothers and fathers and

uncles and aunts, and for the sisters and
brothers too young to take part.

The play we put on in 1942 was
about a rich nobleman called
Alphonse who falls in love with
an exquisitely beautiful but humble country
girl called Genevieve. I played the part of
Genevieve, and it was the nicest part I had
ever played. In the last scene, Genevieve and
the nobleman become engaged, and she gets to
dress up in a very gorgeous gown for a big
court ball. I had a real dress for this scene,
instead of the usual pieced-together scraps of
material dug out of old trunks from our attics.
My mother let me use one of her long dance
dresses from when she was young. It was
covered with sequins and even had some sort
of fluffy feather stuff around the hem; and it
was pale sapphire blue and very romantic
looking. I had trouble getting into it because I
was almost thirteen now and sort of big
through the middle. But my mother put in a
new zipper instead of the buttons, and I was
able to wear it after all. I had to move a little
carefully and not take very deep breaths, but I
was as tall as Mama now, and I felt like a real
woman, a true beauty. The neck was kind of
low, but I was pretty flat, so I didn't need to
worry about being indecent in front of Harold
Boutilier, who played the part of Alphonse.
Mama put a whole lot of makeup on me,
covering up the pimples I was starting to get,
and I thought I looked like a movie star, a
genuine leading lady. The zipper wasn't put
into the dress in time for the dress rehearsal,
but Harold wore a big bow at his neck and his
mother's velvet shorty coat, with a galvanized
chain around his waist that shone like real
silver. He had on his sister's black stockings
and a pair of high rubber boots, and he looked
very handsome. Up until this year he had just
seemed like an okay boy to me, as boys go,

but this summer I'd spent a lot of time watching him and thinking about him when I went to bed at night. I guess I had a big crush on him. And I was pretty sure that when he saw me in that blue dress, he'd have a crush on me right away, too.

ACTIVE READER

CLARIFY How does Juliette feel about wearing one of her mother's dresses?

On the day of the play, all our families started arriving at The Grove theater a full hour before we got started. It didn't rain, and there wasn't even one of those noisy Nova Scotian winds that shake the trees and keep you from hearing the lines. My mother was hustling around backstage helping with clothes and makeup. Mostly she was fussing with my face and my first costume and telling me how pretty I looked. We had rigged up eight bedspreads, some torn and holey, some beautiful, depending on the fear or the pride of the mothers who lent them; and behind this strung-out curtain, we prepared ourselves for the two o'clock production. Henrietta was moving quietly about on the stage, straightening furniture, moving props, standing back to look at the effect. Later on, just before the curtain went up, or rather was drawn aside, she went off and sat down against a tree, where she'd have a good view of the performance, but where she'd be out of sight. If any of us needed anything, she could get it for us without the audience seeing what she was doing.

In the first part of the play, the nobleman ignores the beautiful peasant girl, who comes on dressed in rags but heavily made up and therefore beautiful. He is of course looking for a wife, but no one even thinks of her as a possible candidate. She does a lot of sighing and weeping, and Alphonse rides around on his horse (George Cruikshank) looking handsome and tragic. Harold did this very well. Still, I could hardly wait for the last scene, in which I could get out of those rags and emerge as the radiant court butterfly. But I put all I had into this first scene, because when Alphonse turns down all the eligible and less beautiful women of the land and retires to a corner of the stage to brood (with George Cruikshank standing nearby, munching grass), Genevieve arrives on the scene to a roll of drums (our wooden spoon on Mrs. Eisner's pickling kettle). As Alphonse turns to look at her dazzling beauty, he recognizes her for what she is—not just a poor commoner, but a young woman of great charm and loveliness, worthy of his hand. At this point, she places her hand on her breast and does a deep and graceful curtsy. He stands up, bends to help her rise, and in a tender and significant gesture kisses her outstretched hand.

And that's exactly how we did it, right there on the foxberry patch, which looked like a rich green carpet with a red pattern, if you happened to have the kind of imagination to see it that way. I thought I would faint with the beauty of it all. Then the string of bedspreads was drawn across the scene, curtain hoops squeaking, and the applauding audience awaited the final scene.

I didn't waste any time getting into my other costume. Dressed in my blue gown, I peeked through the hole in Mrs. Powell's bedspread to assess the audience. I had not had time to look until now, but Mama had dressed me first, and she had six other girls to get ready for the ball scene. The crowd outside was large. There must have been forty-five or fifty people of various sizes and ages sitting on the cushions placed on top of the pine needles. The little kids were crawling and squirming around like they always do, and mothers were passing out pacifiers and bags of chips and jelly beans and suckers to keep them quiet during intermission. One little boy—Janet Morash's brother —was crying his head off, and I sure as fire

Illustration by Meg Kelleher Aubrey.

hoped he'd stop all that racket before the curtain went up. While I watched all this, I looked over to the left and saw three sailors coming through the woods. I knew them. They'd been to our house for supper a couple of times, but I never dreamt we'd be lucky enough to have the navy at our play. My big scene was going to be witnessed by more than just a bunch of parents and kids. There was even a little group of grade 12 boys in the back row.

We were almost ready to begin. Backstage, most of the makeup was done, and Mrs. Elliot was standing by the tree, making up Henrietta just for the heck of it. Henrietta had set up the stage and handed out the costumes, and she was putting in time like some of the rest of us. She just had on that old blue sweatshirt of hers and her dungarees, and it seemed to me that all that makeup was going to look pretty silly on someone who didn't have a costume on; but I didn't really care. If Henrietta wanted to make a fool of herself, it wasn't going to bother *me*.

In the last scene, all the courtiers and aristocrats are milling around in the ballroom, waiting for the nobleman to arrive with his betrothed. The orchestra is playing Strauss waltzes (on Mrs. Corkum's portable wind-up gramophone), and you can see that everyone is itchy footed and dying to dance, but they have to wait around until Alphonse arrives with Genevieve. It is a moment full of suspense, and I had to do a lot of smart and fierce directing to get that bunch of kids to look happy and excited and impatient all at the same time. But they did a really good job that afternoon. You could see that they thought they actually *were* lords and ladies and that it was a real live ball they had come to.

Suddenly there is a sound of trumpets (little Horace Miller's Halloween horn), and Alphonse comes in, very slowly and stately, with Genevieve on his arm. She is shy and enters with downcast eyes; but he turns around, bows to her, and she raises her head with new pride and confidence, lifting her arms to join him in the dance. We did all this beautifully, if I do say so myself, and as I started to raise my arms, I thought I would burst with the joy and splendor of that moment.

As it turned out, burst is just about exactly what I did. The waltz record was turned off during this intense scene, and there was total silence on the stage and in the audience. As my arms reached shoulder level, a sudden sound of ripping taffeta reached clear to the back of the audience. (Joannie Sherman was sitting in the last row, and she told me about it later.) I knew in one awful, <u>stupefying</u> moment that my dress had ripped up the back, the full length of that long zipper. I can remember standing there on the stage with my arms half raised, unable to think or feel anything beyond a paralyzed horror. After that day, whenever I heard that someone was in a state of shock, I never had to ask the meaning of that term. I knew. Joannie told me later that the whole stageful of people looked like they had been turned to stone and that it really had been a scream to see.

Suddenly, as quiet and quick as a cat, Henrietta glided onstage. She was draped in one of the classier bedspreads from the curtain, and no one would have known that she wasn't supposed to be there. I don't know how anyone as slow-moving as Henrietta could have done so much fast thinking. But she did. She was carrying the very best

ACTIVE READER

PREDICT What will happen to Juliette now that her dress has ripped?

bedspread—a lovely blue woven one that exactly matched my dress. She stopped in front of me, and lifting the spread with what I have to admit was a lot of ceremony and grace, she placed it gravely over my shoulders. Fastening it carefully with one of the large safety pins that she always kept attached to her sweatshirt during performances, she then moved backward two paces and bowed first to me and then to Harold before moving slowly and with great dignity toward the exit.

Emerging from my shock with the kind of presence of mind for which I was noted, I raised my arms and prepared to start the dance with Alphonse. But Harold, eyes full of amazement, was staring at Henrietta as she floated off the stage. From the back of the audience, I could hear two long, low whistles, followed by a deep male voice exclaiming, "Hubba, *hubba!*" to which I turned and bowed in graceful acknowledgement of what I felt to be a vulgar but nonetheless sincere tribute. The low voice, not familiar to me, spoke again. "Not *you,* pie-face!" he called, and then I saw three or four of the big boys from grade 12 leave the audience and run into the woods.

Somehow or other I got through that scene. Harold pulled his enchanted eyes back onstage, and the gramophone started the first few bars of "The Blue Danube" as we began to dance. Mercifully, the scene was short, and before long we were taking our curtain calls. "Stage manager! Stage manager!" shouted one of the sailors, and after a brief pause, old Henrietta came shyly forward, bedspread gone, dressed once more in her familiar blue sweatshirt and dungarees. The applause from the audience went on and on, and as we all bowed and curtsied, I stole a look at Henrietta. Slender, I thought, throat tight.

Slender, not skinny anymore. All in an instant I saw everything, right in the midst of all that clapping and bowing. It was like one of those long complicated dreams that start and finish within the space of five minutes, just before you wake up in the morning. Henrietta was standing serenely, quietly. As the clapping continued, while the actors and actresses feverishly bobbed up and down to acknowledge the applause, she just once, ever so slightly, inclined her head, gazing at the audience out of her astonishing eyes— enormous, <u>arresting</u>, fringed now with long dark lashes. Mrs. Elliot's makeup job had made us all see what must have been there all the time—a strikingly beautiful face. But there was something else there now that was new. As I continued to bow and smile, the word came to me to describe that strange new thing. *Power.* Henrietta had power. And what's more, she had it without having to *do* a single thing. All she needs to do, I thought, is *be.* The terrible injustice of it all stabbed me. There I was, the lead role, the director, the brains and <u>vigor</u> of our twinship, and suddenly, after all my years in first place, it was she who had the power. Afterwards I looked at them—the boys, the sailors, *Harold*—as they gazed at her. All she was doing was <u>sauntering</u> around the stage picking up props. But they were watching, and I knew, with a stunning accuracy, that there would always be watchers now, wherever she might be, whatever she wore, regardless of what she would be doing. And I also knew in that moment, with the same sureness, that I would never have that kind of power, not ever.

The next day, Mama stationed herself at the telephone, receiving all the tributes that came pouring in. A few moments per call were given over to a brief recognition of my acting talents

---

WORDS   **arresting** (ə-rĕs′tĭng) *adj.* striking
TO   **vigor** (vĭg′ər) *n.* physical or mental strength, energy, or force
KNOW   **saunter** (sôn′tər) *v.* to walk about slowly

Two Girls on a Cliff (about 1917), Dame Laura Knight. Oil on canvas, 23½″ × 28½″, courtesy of Sotheby's. Copyright © Dame Laura Knight, reproduced by permission of Curtis Brown Group Ltd., London.

and to an uneasy amusement over the split dress. The rest of the time was spent in shouted discussion of Henrietta's startling and surprising beauty. I lay face downward on my bed and let the words hail down upon me. "Yes, indeed. Yes. I quite agree. Simply beautiful. And a real bolt from the blue. She quite astonished all of us. Although of course I recognized this quality in her all along. I've often sat and contemplated her lovely eyes, her milky skin, her delicate

hands, and thought, 'Your time will come, my dear! Your time will come!' "

"Delicate hands!" I whispered fiercely into the mattress. "Bony! Bony!"

I suppose, in a way, that nothing changed too drastically for me after that play. I continued to lead groups, direct shows, spark activities with my ideas, my zeal. In school I did well in all my subjects and was good at sports, too. Henrietta's grades were mediocre, and she never even tried out for teams or anything, while I was on the swim team, the baseball team, the basketball team. She still moved slowly, languidly, as though her energy was in short supply, but there was a subtle difference in her that was hard to put your finger on. It wasn't as though she went around covered with all that highly flattering greasepaint that Mrs. Elliot had supplied. In fact, she didn't really start wearing makeup until she was fifteen or sixteen. Apparently she didn't need to. That one dramatic walk-on part with the blanket and the safety pin had done it all, although I'm sure I harbored a hope that we might return to the old Henrietta as soon as she washed her face. Even the sailors started coming to the house more often. They couldn't take her out, of course, or *do* anything with her. But they seemed to enjoy just looking at her, contemplating her. They would sit there on our big brown plush chesterfield under the stern picture of Great-great-grandmother Logan in the big gold frame, smoking cigarette after cigarette and watching Henrietta as she moved about with her <u>infuriatingly</u> slow, lazy grace, her grave confidence. Her serenity

soothed and excited them, all at the same time. Boys from grades 9 and 10 hung around our backyard, our verandah, the nearest street corner. They weren't mean to me. They simply didn't know I was there, not really.

I didn't spend much time with Henrietta anymore, or boss her, or make her go to The Grove in the fog or try to scare her. I just wasn't all that crazy about having her around the entire time, with those eyes looking out at me from under those long lashes, quiet, mysterious, full of power. And of course you had to trip over boys if you so much as wanted to ask her what time it was. Every once in a while I'd try to figure out what the thing was that made her so different now; and then, one day, all of a sudden, I understood. We were down at the beach, and she was just sitting on a rock or something, arms slack and resting on her knees, in a position I had often seen over the years. And in that moment I knew. Everything else was the same—the drab white skin; the bony, yes, bony hands; the limp hair. But she had lost her waiting look. Henrietta didn't look as though she were waiting for anything at all anymore. ❖

WORDS
TO
KNOW

infuriatingly (ĭn-fyŏŏr′ē-ā′tĭng-lē) *adv.* in a way that makes one very angry **infuriate** *v.*

Connect to the Literature

1. What Do You Think?
How did your impression of Juliette and Henrietta change as you neared the end of the story?

Comprehension Check
- At first, who is the more outgoing sister?
- Who rescues Juliette onstage?
- Who is the center of attention at the end of the story?

Think Critically

2. In the beginning, Juliette says that she and Henrietta were "best friends." What does friendship mean to Juliette at that point? Do you think Henrietta feels the same way? Explain.

3. How does the relationship between the two girls change after Henrietta's walk-on? Explain.

4. While Juliette takes her bow, she thinks, "Henrietta had power." What does Henrietta's power consist of?

5. At the end of the story, Juliette says that Henrietta had "lost her waiting look." What do you think she means?

> **Think About:**
> - the games they played in "The Grove"
> - the mother's statement that Henrietta was "a serious, responsible little girl."
> - Juliette's perception that Henrietta was no longer "skinny," but "slender."

6. ACTIVE READING | MAKING JUDGMENTS
Look over the notes you took in your 📖 READER'S NOTEBOOK. In your judgment, is Juliette reliable as a narrator? What clues from the story helped you decide? Explain.

Extend Interpretations

7. COMPARING TEXTS The sisters in "The White Umbrella" (page 522) have a much different relationship from that of Juliette and Henrietta. What differences can you mention? How are the two relationships similar? What statement could you make about the themes of these two stories?

8. Connect to Life Think about the people you like to do things with. Which person is a lot like you? How do the qualities you share affect your relationship?

Literary Analysis

UNRELIABLE NARRATOR Different people often have different perceptions of the same event. Likewise, a narrator of a story who is also a character in the story (called a **first-person narrator**) is likely to have biases or attitudes that can distort his or her presentation of the events. A first-person narrator who does not narrate events objectively is called an **unreliable narrator.** Throughout "Waiting," Juliette unintentionally drops hints that her perceptions are not objective.

Group Activity Does Juliette ever arrive at an understanding of herself and her relationship with her sister? In small groups, review the story, looking for details that help answer this question. Discuss your answer. Pay careful attention to the final scenes of the story.

REVIEW: FOIL A **foil** is a character who provides a contrast to another character. A writer can use a foil to draw attention to **characteristics** of the main character. In "Waiting" Juliette, the narrator, acknowledges that she and Henrietta are opposites. What qualities in Juliette, admirable and not so admirable, does Henrietta make apparent for the reader? How does the author make them apparent?

CHOICES and CHALLENGES

Writing

Compare and Contrast Characters Write an essay comparing and contrasting characteristics of the two sisters, Juliette and Henrietta. Organize your essay by first writing about one sister, and then writing about the other. Be sure to compare the qualities that are similar as well as different. Place your essay in your **Working Portfolio.**

Writing Handbook
See p. R47: Compare and Contrast Writing.

Speaking & Listening

Practice your speaking techniques by reading a section of "Waiting" out loud. As you read, picture what is happening as it happens. Raise and lower your voice when it seems natural, for example, when you are reading dialogue. Be sure to read slowly enough that listeners can follow along, and practice making eye contact with your audience periodically. Choosing a section in which something dramatic happens may make it more fun, and even easier, to read.

Speaking and Listening Handbook
See p. R102: Present.

Research & Technology

More Multiple Births? It has been reported that the number of multiple births (of twins and higher) has increased during the last decade. Consult the most recent edition of "The World Almanac and Book of Facts" in your school or public library to check this statement. Find statistics in the following 5 categories in the United States: total number of births in the country; number of twins; triplets; quadruplets; quintuplets and higher. Choose statistics from three different years in the last decade. Using spreadsheet software, label columns and insert data in the appropriate columns. Compare totals between years. (You can also calculate the number of single births and add that to your spreadsheet.) If your software allows it, create a chart or graph showing the percentages.

Research and Technology Handbook
See p. R115: Using Visuals.

Reading for INFORMATION
Begin your research by reading the magazine article "Face-to-Face with Twins" on page 617.

Vocabulary

STANDARDIZED TEST PRACTICE

An analogy contains two pairs of words that are related in the same way, as in the example TALL : SHORT :: old : young. This analogy is read as "*Tall* is to *short* as *old* is to *young*." In this example, both pairs contain words that are antonyms, that is, words that are opposites. An analogy may also use synonyms to express a relationship between words. For each item below, decide which Word to Know best completes the analogy.

1. LEAD : FOLLOW :: _____ : interest
2. GRACEFUL : CLUMSY :: enlivening : _____
3. HAPPY : GLAD :: confinement : _____
4. QUIET : LOUD :: _____ : overpowering
5. RELUCTANTLY: UNWILLINGLY :: strength : _____
6. HEALTH : ILLNESS :: _____ : pleasingly
7. MISLEAD : INFORM :: rush : _____
8. SAD : UNHAPPY :: _____ : striking
9. FALSIFY : LIE :: _____ : showy
10. LARGE : BIG :: _____ : controlling

Vocabulary Handbook
See p. R24.

WORDS TO KNOW				
apathy	dominant	infuriatingly	saunter	submissive
arresting	flamboyant	quarantine	stupefying	vigor

WAITING **615**

Grammar in Context: Participial Phrases

Descriptions of the characters in "Waiting" are often expressed in **participial phrases.**

> **Resting my head on my folded arms, I smiled quietly.**

> **Soaked to the skin, Henrietta waited patiently.**

Participles are verb forms ending in *–ing* or *–ed*. They function as adjectives to modify nouns or pronouns. Participles can also take objects. When they do, the participle, its object, and any words modifying the object are called a **participial phrase.**

WRITING EXERCISE Rewrite each incomplete sentence, adding a participial phrase that uses the participal in parentheses.

Example: *Original* I'd be the ghost, (floating).

Rewritten I'd be the ghost, floating along the edge of the cliff.

1. Henrietta was on the stage, (moving).
2. The zipper broke, (ripping).
3. (Attracted), the boys crowded around Henrietta.
4. I muttered to myself, (complaining).
5. (Having grown up), Henrietta changed my life forever.

Connect to the Literature Find another sentence with a participial phrase in the second paragraph of "Waiting."

Grammar Handbook
See p. R85: Participial Phrases.

Budge (Marjorie) Wilson
born 1927

"A person who loves to write is never lonely; within his or her own head a writer always has a safe and very interesting place to go."

Late Start Although Budge Wilson had wanted to be a writer ever since she was a child, she did not begin writing for publication until she was fifty. "It may seem odd for someone my age to be writing for and about children," she said. "But I remember my own youth very vividly, and I've watched my own children and their friends grow up. I don't find it very hard to enter the head of a fictional person who is much younger than I am."

Nova Scotia Writer Wilson, who makes her home in Nova Scotia, Canada, where she grew up, sets many of her stories in that province. These stories reflect her deep curiosity about people and her observations of them. Her fiction for young adults has won several awards. For example, *The Leaving,* a collection of short stories that includes "Waiting," won the Canadian Library Association's Young Adult Book Award for 1991.

AUTHOR ACTIVITY
Budge Wilson has commented on her reasons for writing "Waiting." "I have often been interested in bullies—adult bullies as well as ones who are children. Why do they behave the way they do?" Write a letter to Budge Wilson stating your ideas on bullies.

Key Standard
W1.3 Use such strategies as note-taking, outlining, and summarizing. . . .
Other Standards
R2.1, W2.5

rce: *National Geographic World*

Face-to-Face with Twins

by Judith E. Rinard

Reading for Information

Knowing which facts to record and how to organize them is a skill that you can use when you research any topic.

Taking Notes
Note taking is a way to collect information from sources. There are three basic techniques:

- **outlining:** arranging main ideas and supporting details in a logical order; using roman numerals for the main ideas, and capital letters and arabic numerals for the supporting ideas

- **paraphrasing:** using your own words to restate someone else's ideas

- **summarizing:** condensing the text to include the most important information

YOUR TURN *Use the questions and activities below to help you take notes on twins.*

❶ **Outlining Ideas** Use the format shown here to outline the article. It is not important to copy every word, just the key points.

I. Identical Twins	II. Fraternal Twins
A. one egg that splits in two	A.
B. identical genes	B.
1. two boys	
2. two girls	

Time to Split!

❶ IDENTICAL TWINS such as Elizabeth and Annie Frazee, 14, of Gettysburg, Pennsylvania, start out in their mother's womb as one egg that splits in two. Here Annie (in the red-flowered dress) and Elizabeth dramatize the split. A set of identical twins consists of either two girls or two boys. They develop with identical genes.

Fraternal, or nonidentical, twins start differently, growing from two separate eggs. Two boys, two girls, or a boy and a girl may make up a set of fraternal twins. They don't always look alike.

In the United States fraternal twins occur once in every 120 births. Identical twins occur only once in every 250 births.

Identical But Not the Same

ANNIE AND ELIZABETH say they're alike in many ways and different in others. That's common among identical twins. Annie and Elizabeth are both right handed. They both wear contact lenses. Their hair looks the same. They lost their baby teeth at about the same time. And they both got their only cavity in the same tooth when they were 9.

2 "But Annie wore braces and I didn't," says Elizabeth, left. "Annie has asthma and I don't. Plus Annie has more freckles." The twins' mother often got confused when the girls were babies. How could she tell them apart? One of Elizabeth's toes was more crooked than Annie's.

About 10 percent of identical twins are "mirror-image" twins: For example, one is right-handed, and the other is left-handed. But all twins have different fingerprints.

Annie and Elizabeth say they're best friends, yet competitive. "We fight over everything, but we do have different tastes in guys," says Annie.

Elizabeth adds, "Sometimes being a twin is so weird. It's also fun and kind of cool."

Annie agrees.

Not Identical... Yet Alike

We're the only two who know what we meant!

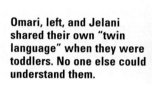

Omari, left, and Jelani shared their own "twin language" when they were toddlers. No one else could understand them.

3

SURE, OMARI AND JELANI look alike, but they're fraternal, not identical, twins. Like many twins, the boys share a strong bond. When they were very young they communicated with each other using words they invented and only they understood. About 40 percent of twins share such a personal language.

The boys seem to sense each other's thoughts or feelings, something many twins report. Says their mother, "Once at camp one twin was missing. The other twin didn't even know that but said, 'My brother's in trouble.'"

Twins have also told of feeling pain when their twin was hurt. Scientists do not understand how or why this happens.

Reading for Information *continued*

2 **Paraphrasing** In this section, the author uses quotations and dialogue to relate the similarities and differences between Annie and Elizabeth. Restate these similarities and differences in your own words.

3 Would you consider the detail about Omari's and Jelani's personal language a main idea or a supporting detail? Explain.

Lost (and Found) Twins

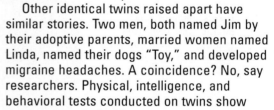

"I ALWAYS FELT THAT there was something missing," says Jerry Levey of Ocean, New Jersey. At age 32, Jerry (below, left) found out what it was. He had an identical twin brother, Mark in Paramus, New Jersey (below, right).

Separated at birth, the brothers had been adopted by different families. When Jerry and Mark were reunited as adults, seeing each other "was like looking in the mirror," Jerry says. They had the same nose, mustache, sideburns, and gestures. The brothers are both volunteer firefighters and bachelors, and both had worked as truckers in forestry.

Other identical twins raised apart have similar stories. Two men, both named Jim by their adoptive parents, married women named Linda, named their dogs "Toy," and developed migraine headaches. A coincidence? No, say researchers. Physical, intelligence, and behavioral tests conducted on twins show amazing similarities.

4

Reading for Information *continued*

4 Summarize in your own words the information provided about the Levey twins. What is the main idea? What are the supporting details?

Summarizing Using the notes that you have taken, write a short summary of this article. What is the main idea that relates to each set of twins?

Research & Technology
Activity Link: "Waiting," p. 615. Find another article about twins at the library. Use your note-taking skills to create an outline. How do the main ideas differ from those you found in "Face-to-Face with Twins"?

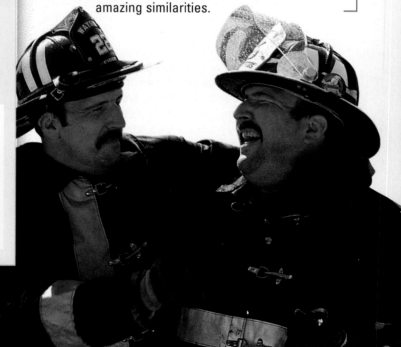

from **Growing Up**
by RUSSELL BAKER

Connect to Your Life

What have you heard about the Great Depression?

Build Background

Russell Baker grew up during the Great Depression of the 1930s. The stock market collapse in 1929 led to the closing of banks and to business failures. Overnight, people lost their jobs and their life savings. A drought turned farmland into a dust bowl. Economic insecurity threatened the majority of Americans and shaped the outlook of a generation.

People wait in relief lines for food and clothing in New York City.

An unemployed man sells apples on the street.

Drought turned farmland into barren deserts.

Focus Your Reading

LITERARY ANALYSIS | **IRONY**

Irony occurs when a writer says one thing but means another. **Exaggeration, understatement, and sarcasm** are techniques writers use to express irony. In the very first sentence in the selection you are about to read, the author establishes the ironic tone of his narration through exaggeration. "I began working in journalism when I was eight years old," turns out to mean something entirely different from what the reader expects.

WORDS TO KNOW **Vocabulary Preview**
gumption   maxim   stride   surly   zeal

ACTIVE READING | **RECOGNIZING TEXT ORGANIZATION**

One technique writers use to organize information is to **compare and contrast** two characters, events, situations, or other elements. In this selection from *Growing Up*, Russell Baker compares himself to his sister Doris. An active reader notes the **characterization** details that are being compared and contrasted. As you read, jot down in your 📖 **READER'S NOTEBOOK** the ways in which Russell and Doris differ from each other as well as the ways in which they are alike.

Key Standard
R3.3 Analyze characters by examining what they think, say, and do, and by studying the words of the narrator and the reactions of other characters.
Other Standards **R3.6, W1.2, W2.3, LS2.3**

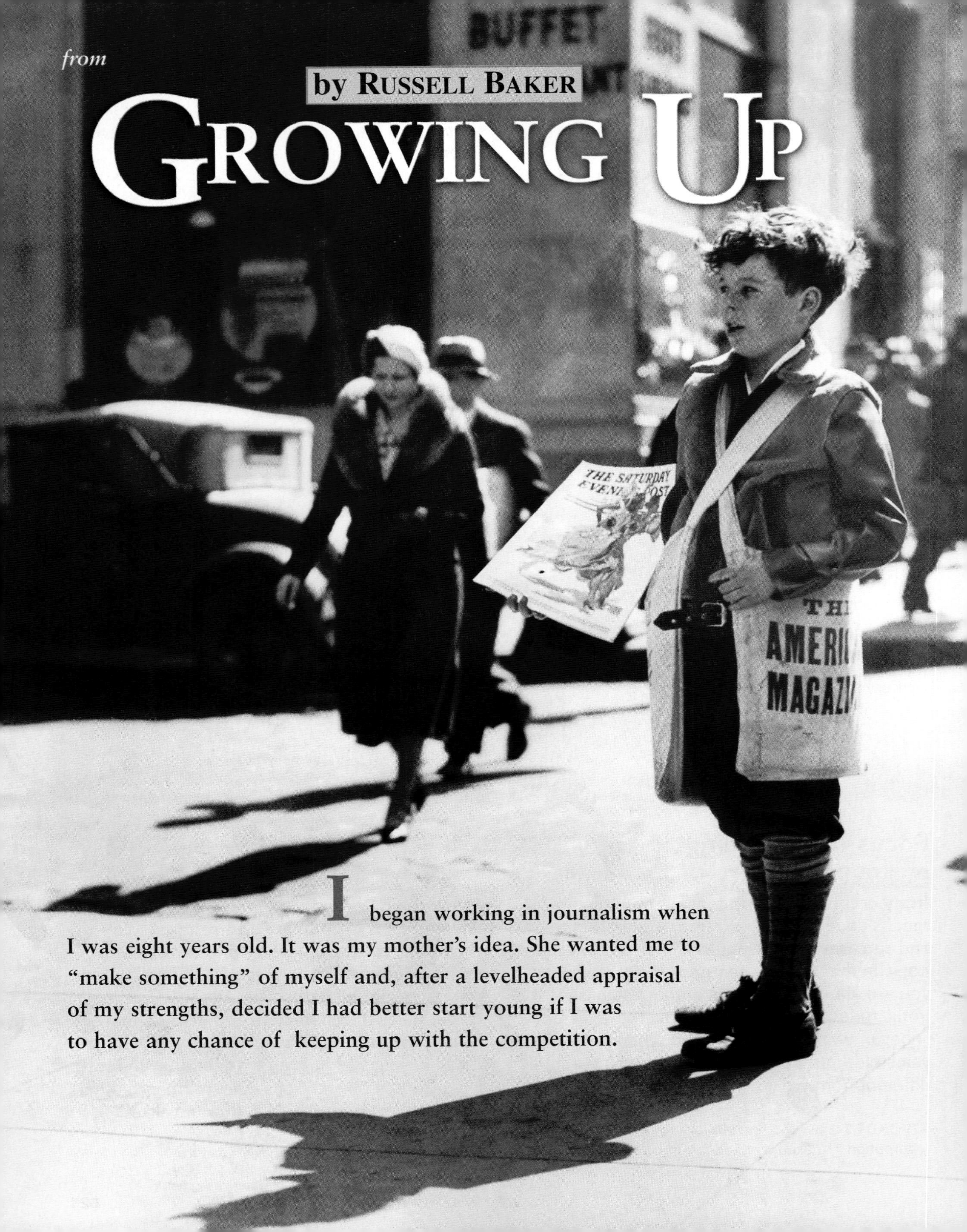

from

by RUSSELL BAKER

GROWING UP

I began working in journalism when I was eight years old. It was my mother's idea. She wanted me to "make something" of myself and, after a levelheaded appraisal of my strengths, decided I had better start young if I was to have any chance of keeping up with the competition.

The flaw in my character which she had already spotted was lack of "gumption." My idea of a perfect afternoon was lying in front of the radio rereading my favorite Big Little Book, *Dick Tracy Meets Stooge Viller.* My mother despised inactivity. Seeing me having a good time in repose, she was powerless to hide her disgust. "You've got no more gumption than a bump on a log," she said. "Get out in the kitchen and help Doris do those dirty dishes."

My sister Doris, though two years younger than I, had enough gumption for a dozen people. She positively enjoyed washing dishes, making beds, and cleaning the house. When she was only seven she could carry a piece of short-weighted cheese back to the A&P, threaten the manager with legal action, and come back triumphantly with the full quarter-pound we'd paid for and a few ounces extra thrown in for forgiveness. Doris could have made something of herself if she hadn't been a girl. Because of this defect, however, the best she could hope for was a career as a nurse or schoolteacher, the only work that capable females were considered up to in those days.

This must have saddened my mother, this twist of fate that had allocated all the gumption to the daughter and left her with a son who was content with Dick Tracy and Stooge Viller. If disappointed, though, she wasted no energy on self-pity. She would make me something of myself whether I wanted to or not. "The Lord helps those who help themselves," she said. That was the way her mind worked.

She was realistic about the difficulty. Having sized up the material the Lord had given her to mold, she didn't overestimate what she could do with it. She didn't insist that I grow up to be President of the United States.

Fifty years ago parents still asked boys if they wanted to grow up to be President, and asked it not jokingly but seriously. Many parents who were hardly more than paupers still believed their sons could do it. Abraham Lincoln had done it. We were only sixty-five years from Lincoln. Many a grandfather who walked among us could remember Lincoln's time. Men of grandfatherly age were the worst for asking if you wanted to grow up to be President. A surprising number of little boys said yes and meant it.

I was asked many times myself. No, I would say, I didn't want to grow up to be President. My mother was present during one of these interrogations. An elderly uncle, having posed the usual question and exposed my lack of interest in the Presidency, asked, "Well, what *do* you want to be when you grow up?"

I loved to pick through trash piles and collect empty bottles, tin cans with pretty labels, and discarded magazines. The most desirable job on earth sprang instantly to mind. "I want to be a garbage man," I said.

My uncle smiled, but my mother had seen the first distressing evidence of a bump budding on a log. "Have a little gumption, Russell," she said. Her calling me Russell was a signal of unhappiness. When she approved of me I was always "Buddy."

When I turned eight years old she decided that the job of starting me on the road toward making something of myself could no longer be safely delayed. "Buddy," she said one day, "I want you to come home right after school

> **"Have a little gumption, Russell."**

this afternoon. Somebody's coming and I want you to meet him."

When I burst in that afternoon she was in conference in the parlor with an executive of the Curtis Publishing Company. She introduced me. He bent low from the waist and shook my hand. Was it true as my mother had told him, he asked, that I longed for the opportunity to conquer the world of business?

My mother replied that I was blessed with a rare determination to make something of myself.

"That's right," I whispered.

"But have you got the grit, the character, the never-say-quit spirit it takes to succeed in business?"

My mother said I certainly did.

"That's right," I said.

He eyed me silently for a long pause, as though weighing whether I could be trusted to keep his confidence, then spoke man-to-man. Before taking a crucial step, he said, he wanted to advise me that working for the Curtis Publishing Company placed enormous responsibility on a young man. It was one of the great companies of America. Perhaps the greatest publishing house in the world. I had heard, no doubt, of the *Saturday Evening Post*?[1]

Heard of it? My mother said that everyone in our house had heard of the *Saturday Post* and that I, in fact, read it with religious devotion.

Then doubtless, he said, we were also familiar with those two monthly pillars of the magazine world, the *Ladies' Home Journal*[2] and the *Country Gentleman*.[3]

Indeed we were familiar with them, said my mother.

Representing the *Saturday Evening Post* was one of the weightiest honors that could be bestowed in the world of business, he said. He was personally proud of being a part of that great corporation.

My mother said he had every right to be.

Again he studied me as though debating whether I was worthy of a knighthood. Finally: "Are you trustworthy?"

My mother said I was the soul of honesty.

"That's right," I said.

The caller smiled for the first time. He told me I was a lucky young man. He admired my spunk. Too many young men thought life was all play. Those young men would not go far in this world. Only a young man willing to work and save and keep his face washed and his hair neatly combed could hope to come out on top in a world such as ours. Did I truly and sincerely believe that I was such a young man?

> It was 1932, the bleakest year of the Depression.

"He certainly does," said my mother.

"That's right," I said.

He said he had been so impressed by what he had seen of me that he was going to make me a representative of the Curtis Publishing Company. On the following Tuesday, he said, thirty freshly printed copies of the *Saturday Evening Post* would be delivered at our door. I would place these magazines, still damp with the ink of the presses, in a handsome canvas bag, sling it over my shoulder, and set forth through the streets to bring the best in

---

1. *Saturday Evening Post:* a magazine featuring illustrations, fiction, and essays.

2. *Ladies' Home Journal:* a popular women's magazine.

3. *Country Gentleman:* an agricultural and gardening magazine (not published since 1954).

journalism, fiction, and cartoons to the American public.

He had brought the canvas bag with him. He presented it with reverence fit for a chasuble.[4] He showed me how to drape the sling over my left shoulder and across the chest so that the pouch lay easily accessible to my right hand, allowing the best in journalism, fiction, and cartoons to be swiftly extracted and sold to a citizenry whose happiness and security depended upon us soldiers of the free press.

The following Tuesday I raced home from school, put the canvas bag over my shoulder, dumped the magazines in, and, tilting to the left to balance their weight on my right hip, embarked on the highway of journalism.

We lived in Belleville, New Jersey, a commuter town at the northern fringe of

Newark. It was 1932, the bleakest year of the Depression. My father had died two years before, leaving us with a few pieces of Sears, Roebuck furniture and not much else, and my mother had taken Doris and me to live with one of her younger brothers. This was my Uncle Allen. Uncle Allen had made something of himself by 1932. As salesman for a soft-drink bottler in Newark, he had an income of $30 a week; wore pearl-gray spats, detachable collars, and a three-piece suit; was happily married; and took in threadbare relatives.

With my load of magazines I headed toward Belleville Avenue. That's where the people were. There were two filling stations at the

4. **chasuble** (chăz′ə-bəl): a long, sleeveless garment worn by a priest during services.

intersection with Union Avenue, as well as an A&P, a fruit stand, a bakery, a barber shop, Zuccarelli's drugstore, and a diner shaped like a railroad car. For several hours I made myself highly visible, shifting position now and then from corner to corner, from shop window to shop window, to make sure everyone could see the heavy black lettering on the canvas bag that said *The Saturday Evening Post*. When the angle of the light indicated it was suppertime, I walked back to the house.

"How many did you sell, Buddy?" my mother asked.

"None."

"Where did you go?"

"The corner of Belleville and Union Avenues."

"What did you do?"

"Stood on the corner waiting for somebody to buy a *Saturday Evening Post*."

"You just stood there?"

"Didn't sell a single one."

"For goodness sake, Russell!"

Uncle Allen intervened. "I've been thinking about it for some time," he said, "and I've about decided to take the *Post* regularly. Put me down as a regular customer." I handed him a magazine and he paid me a nickel. It was the first nickel I earned.

Afterwards my mother instructed me in salesmanship. I would have to ring doorbells, address adults with charming self-confidence, and break down resistance with a sales talk pointing out that no one, no matter how poor, could afford to be without the *Saturday Evening Post* in the home.

I told my mother I'd changed my mind about wanting to succeed in the magazine business.

"If you think I'm going to raise a good-for-nothing," she replied, "you've got another think coming." She told me to hit the streets with the canvas bag and start ringing doorbells the instant school was out next day. When I objected that I didn't feel any aptitude for salesmanship, she asked how I'd like to lend her my leather belt so she could whack some sense into me. I bowed to superior will and entered journalism with a heavy heart.

My mother and I had fought this battle almost as long as I could remember. It probably started even before memory began, when I was a country child in northern Virginia and my mother, dissatisfied with my father's plain workman's life, determined that I would not grow up like him and his people, with calluses on their hands, overalls on their backs, and fourth-grade educations in their heads. She had fancier ideas of life's possibilities. Introducing me to the *Saturday Evening Post,* she was trying to wean me as early as possible from my father's world where men left with their lunch pails at sunup, worked with their hands until the grime ate into the pores, and died with a few sticks of mail-order furniture as their legacy. In my mother's vision of the better life there were desks and white collars, well-pressed suits, evenings of reading and lively talk, and perhaps—if a man were very, very lucky and hit the jackpot, really made something important of himself—perhaps there might be a fantastic salary of $5,000 a year to support a big house and a Buick with a rumble seat and a vacation in Atlantic City.

And so I set forth with my sack of magazines. I was afraid of the dogs that snarled behind the doors of potential buyers. I was timid about ringing the doorbells of strangers, relieved when no one came to the door, and scared when someone did. Despite my mother's instructions, I could not deliver an engaging sales pitch. When a door opened I simply asked, "Want to buy a *Saturday Evening Post?*" In Belleville few persons did. It was a town of 30,000 people, and most weeks I rang a fair majority of its doorbells. But I rarely sold my thirty copies. Some weeks I canvassed the entire town for six days and still had four or five unsold magazines on Monday evening; then I dreaded the coming of Tuesday morning, when a batch of thirty fresh *Saturday Evening Post*s was due at the front door.

"Better get out there and sell the rest of those magazines tonight," my mother would say.

I usually posted myself then at a busy intersection where a traffic light controlled commuter flow from Newark. When the light turned red I stood on the curb and shouted my sales pitch at the motorists.

"Want to buy a *Saturday Evening Post?*"

One rainy night when car windows were sealed against me I came back soaked and with not a single sale to report. My mother beckoned to Doris.

"Go back down there with Buddy and show him how to sell these magazines," she said.

Brimming with zest, Doris, who was then seven years old, returned with me to the corner.

She took a magazine from the bag, and when the light turned red she <u>strode</u> to the nearest car and banged her small fist against the closed window. The driver, probably startled at what he took to be a midget assaulting his car, lowered the window to stare, and Doris thrust a *Saturday Evening Post* at him.

"You need this magazine," she piped, "and it only costs a nickel."

Her salesmanship was irresistible. Before the light changed half a dozen times she disposed of the entire batch. I didn't feel humiliated. To the contrary. I was so happy I decided to give her a treat. Leading her to the vegetable store on Belleville Avenue, I bought three apples, which cost a nickel, and gave her one.

"You shouldn't waste money," she said.

"Eat your apple." I bit into mine.

"You shouldn't eat before supper," she said. "It'll spoil your appetite."

Back at the house that evening, she dutifully reported me for wasting a nickel. Instead of a scolding, I was rewarded with a pat on the back for having the good sense to buy fruit instead of candy. My mother reached into her bottomless supply of <u>maxims</u> and told Doris, "An apple a day keeps the doctor away."

By the time I was ten I had learned all my mother's maxims by heart. Asking to stay up past normal bedtime, I knew that a refusal would be explained with, "Early to bed and early to rise, makes a man healthy, wealthy, and wise." If I whimpered about having to get

WORDS
TO
KNOW

stride (strīd) *v.* to walk with long steps; *past tense*—**strode**
maxim (măk'sĭm) *n.* a short saying that expresses an accepted truth or rule; proverb

up early in the morning, I could depend on her to say, "The early bird gets the worm."

The one I most despised was, "If at first you don't succeed, try, try again." This was the battle cry with which she constantly sent me back into the hopeless struggle whenever I moaned that I had rung every doorbell in town and knew there wasn't a single potential buyer left in Belleville that week. After listening to my explanation, she handed me the canvas bag and said, "If at first you don't succeed . . ."

Three years in that job, which I would gladly have quit after the first day except for her insistence, produced at least one valuable result. My mother finally concluded that I would never make something of myself by pursuing a life in business and started considering careers that demanded less competitive <u>zeal</u>.

One evening when I was eleven I brought home a short "composition" on my summer vacation which the teacher had graded with an A. Reading it with her own schoolteacher's eye, my mother agreed that it was top-drawer seventh grade prose and complimented me. Nothing more was said

about it immediately, but a new idea had taken life in her mind. Halfway through supper she suddenly interrupted the conversation.

"Buddy," she said, "maybe you could be a writer."

I clasped the idea to my heart. I had never met a writer, had shown no previous urge to write, and hadn't a notion how to become a writer, but I loved stories and thought that making up stories must surely be almost as much fun as reading them. Best of all, though, and what really gladdened my heart, was the ease of the writer's life. Writers did not have to trudge through the town peddling from canvas bags, defending themselves against angry dogs, being rejected by <u>surly</u> strangers. Writers did not have to ring doorbells. So far as I could make out, what writers did couldn't even be classified as work.

I was enchanted. Writers didn't have to have any gumption at all. I did not dare tell anybody for fear of being laughed at in the schoolyard, but secretly I decided that what I'd like to be when I grew up was a writer. ❖

Connect to the Literature

1. What Do You Think?
What was your reaction when Russell's mother suggested he might be a writer?

Comprehension Check
- What did Russell's mother most want for him?
- How did Russell feel about selling magazines?
- What was Doris good at?

Think Critically

2. Why is Russell's mother so determined for him to "make something of himself"?

> **Think About:**
> - her personality
> - Russell's father's life
> - the times they lived in

3. When his mother says he might become a writer, Russell says, "I clasped the idea to my heart" and "I was enchanted." Why do you think Russell is so happy?

4. Russell is not successful when he tries to sell magazines but he doesn't quit. Why?

5. What do you think Russell's mother means by "gumption"? Explain.

6. | ACTIVE READING | RECOGNIZING TEXT ORGANIZATION |
Look back at the chart in your 📖 READER'S NOTEBOOK. Working with a partner, describe in your own words the differences and similarities between Doris and Russell. Which child has more "gumption"? Explain your answer.

Extend Interpretations

7. | COMPARING TEXTS | Think of the sisters in the story "Waiting" (p. 601). How is Juliette's attitude toward Henrietta similar to Russell's attitude toward Doris? How is it different? How do their attitudes change?

8. Connect to Life Do you think it is always possible to have a job that is "right" for you? Explain.

Literary Analysis

IRONY When a writer says one thing but means another, he or she is said to be using **irony.** Exaggeration, understatement, and sarcasm are techniques writers use to express irony. When using exaggeration, a writer depicts something as being somehow greater than it actually is. Understatement, by contrast, reduces the significance or full impact of something. Sarcasm can use either exaggeration or understatement but often with the intention of making fun of an issue, person, or group. All three techniques are present in the selection from *Growing Up.*

Paired Activity With a partner, go through the selection and identify examples of irony where the author uses exaggeration or its opposite, understatement.

REVIEW: CHARACTERIZATION
Characterization refers to the way writers describe the traits and motives of their characters. Writers of nonfiction use techniques of characterization just as writers of fiction do. Writers use direct description and the reaction of other characters to communicate traits and motives. Where do you find examples of characterization in "Growing Up"?

CHOICES and CHALLENGES

Writing

Character Sketch Write a character sketch of someone you know. Practice all the ways in which writers use characterization to describe a character to their readers. Think of the person's mannerisms, gestures, favorite sayings, physical qualities. Does the person have a distinctive walk? a certain way of talking? a dominant personality trait? You may want to add a second character to your sketch and write a bit of dialogue between the two. Read your sketch out loud to the class. Place your sketch in your **Working Portfolio**. 📁

Research & Technology

Works Progress Administration President Roosevelt's New Deal produced many government-administered relief agencies that created jobs for those left in need by the depression. Among these was the Works Progress Administration (WPA), which employed 2,100,000 annually. The WPA sponsored projects for writers, actors, artists, and musicians. These included Federal Writer's Projects, Federal Theater Projects, Federal Art Projects, and Federal Music Projects. Consult an encyclopedia, on-line or in your school library, or an almanac. Find the number of people employed by these four projects at each project's peak. Then, using spreadsheet software, label columns and enter this data, plus the total employed annually. Compare the total number of people employed in all four art programs to the annual employment rate for the entire WPA. You will find a percentage of people not employed by any of the four art-related projects. This number represents employment in other areas sponsored by the WPA. Create a chart of graph, and label each percentage.

Research and Technology Handbook
See Page R115: Using Visuals.

Russell Baker
born 1925

"'Buddy,' she said, 'maybe you could be a writer.' I clasped the idea to my heart."

Rural Infancy Russell Baker was born in Morrisonville, Virginia. His earliest memory is of waking in his crib and "staring into two huge eyes glaring at me from a monstrous skull." It was a cow that had poked its head into his window as it grazed next to the house.

Hard Times Baker's father died when Baker was five, and he and his sister and mother moved to New Jersey to live with an uncle. Baker's mother dominated his childhood. As he puts it, "I would make something of myself, and if I lacked the grit to do it, well, then she would make me make something of myself."

Famous Columnist Baker began as a newspaper reporter in 1947. From 1962 to 1998 he wrote a column called "The Observer" for the *New York Times*. His column was syndicated and appeared in hundreds of newspapers. He has won two Pulitzer prizes and many other awards and honorary degrees.

AUTHOR ACTIVITY
Writing a Column Russell Baker is known for his humorous columns as well as his political reporting and commentary. He has written about everyday events, such as stopping smoking, trimming a Christmas tree, and having a common cold. Read some of his columns and try writing a column of your own.

Building Vocabulary
Understanding Synonyms and Antonyms

Synonyms are words that have almost the same meaning. **Antonyms** have opposite meanings. Look at the pair of antonyms and the pair of synonyms in the excerpt.

Recognizing that *leading* is a synonym of *dominant* helps you guess the meaning of *submissive*, the antonym of *dominant*.

Standard R1.1

> We were, in fact, best friends, as is so often the case with twins. And as with most close childhood friendships, there was one dominant member, one submissive. There was no doubt in this case as to who played the leading role.
>
> —Budge Wilson, "Waiting"

Did you recognize that **dominant** and **leading** are **synonyms**?

And that **dominant** and **submissive** are **antonyms**?

Strategies for Building Vocabulary

You can use synonyms and antonyms to improve your vocabulary and add variety to your writing. You may also find synonym and antonym questions on tests.

❶ Collect Synonyms If you know many synonyms, you will be better able to choose the most appropriate words to use in your writing. Dictionaries and thesauruses are aids for finding and learning synonyms. In this thesaurus excerpt you can find synonyms for the word *harm*.

> **harm** To spoil the soundness or perfection of: [synonyms] — *blemish, damage, detract from, flaw, hurt, impair, injure, mar, tarnish.*

In synonym test questions you may be asked to indicate words that are similar in meaning. Antonym test questions may ask you to find words that are opposite in meaning.

1. Choose the word most similar in meaning to the underlined word.
a <u>tardy</u> worker
a. eager   **b.** late   **c.** punctual   **d.** restless

2. Choose the word opposite in meaning to the underlined word.
a <u>tense</u> environment
a. calm   **b.** angry   **c.** nervous   **d.** unhappy

❷ Learn Antonyms Use antonyms when you want to express contrasts. Dictionaries of synonyms and antonyms, as well as some thesauruses, can help you find antonyms of a word.

If you don't have a suitable reference book, try adding the prefixes *anti-, in-, un-,* and *ex-* to the word to explore opposites. Also, look up the word's definition in a standard dictionary and then guess what words might have opposite meanings. Check your guesses by looking them up in the dictionary.

EXERCISE Identify each pair as synonyms, antonyms, or unrelated words. Then write sentences using the antonym word pairs.

1. infuriate   pacify   _____
2. genuine   authentic   _____
3. abhor   cherish   _____
4. consolidate consequence   _____
5. prohibit   sanction   _____

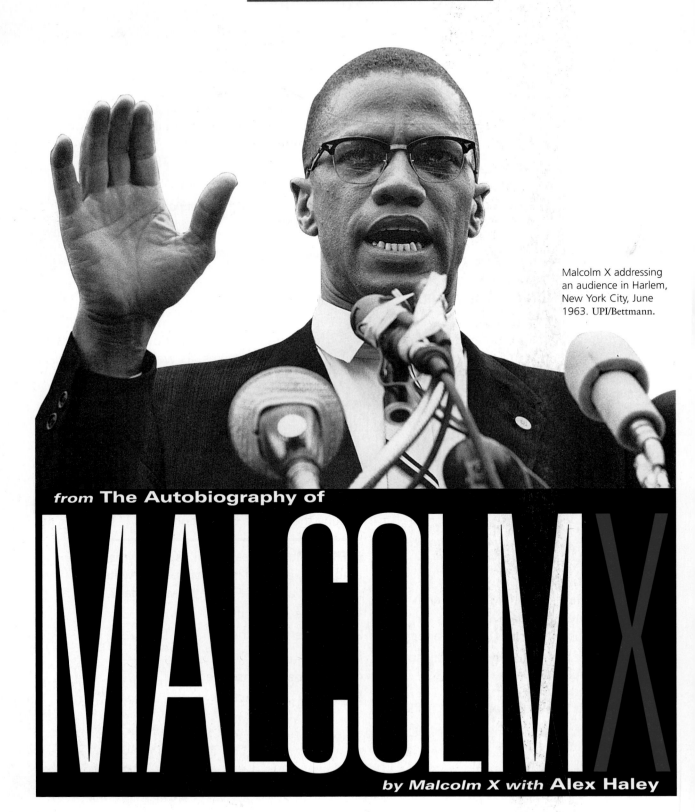

Malcolm X addressing an audience in Harlem, New York City, June 1963. UPI/Bettmann.

from **The Autobiography of**

MALCOLM X

by Malcolm X with **Alex Haley**

It was because of my letters that I happened to stumble upon starting to acquire some kind of a homemade education. I became increasingly frustrated at not being able to express what I wanted to convey in letters that I wrote, especially those to Mr. Elijah Muhammad.[1] In the street, I had been the most articulate hustler out there—I had commanded attention when I said something. But now, trying to write simple English, I not only wasn't articulate, I wasn't even functional. How would I sound writing in slang, the way I would *say* it, something such as, "Look, daddy, let me pull your coat about a cat, Elijah Muhammad—"

Many who today hear me somewhere in person or on television, or those who read something I've said, will think I went to school far beyond the eighth grade. This impression is due entirely to my prison studies.

It had really begun back in the Charlestown Prison, when Bimbi[2] first made me feel envy of his stock of knowledge. Bimbi had always taken charge of any conversations he was in, and I had tried to emulate him. But every book I picked up had few sentences which didn't contain anywhere from one to nearly all of the words that might as well have been in Chinese. When I just skipped those words, of course, I really ended up with little idea of what the book said. So I had come to the Norfolk Prison Colony still going through only book-reading motions. Pretty soon, I would have quit even these motions, unless I had received the motivation that I did.

I saw that the best thing I could do was get hold of a dictionary—to study, to learn some words. I was lucky enough to reason also that I should try to improve my penmanship. It was sad. I couldn't even write in a straight line. It was both ideas together that moved me to request a dictionary along with some tablets and pencils from the Norfolk Prison Colony school.

I spent two days just riffling uncertainly through the dictionary's pages. I'd never realized so many words existed! I didn't know *which* words I needed to learn. Finally, just to start some kind of action, I began copying.

In my slow, painstaking, ragged handwriting, I copied into my tablet everything printed on that first page, down to the punctuation marks.

I'd never realized so many words existed!

I believe it took me a day. Then, aloud, I read back, to myself, everything I'd written on the tablet. Over and over, aloud, to myself, I read my own handwriting.

I woke up the next morning, thinking about those words—immensely proud to realize that not only had I written so much at one time, but I'd written words that I never knew were in the world. Moreover, with a little effort, I also could remember what many of these words meant. I reviewed the words whose meanings I didn't remember. Funny thing, from the dictionary's first page right now, that *aardvark* springs to my mind. The dictionary had a picture of it, a long-tailed, long-eared, burrowing African mammal, which lives off termites caught by sticking out its tongue as an anteater does for ants.

I was so fascinated that I went on—I copied the dictionary's next page. And the same experience came when I studied that. With every succeeding page, I also learned of people and places and events from history. Actually

---

1. **Elijah Muhammad** (ē-lī′jə mōō-hăm′ĭd): 1897–1975; leader of the Black Muslim movement in the United States.
2. **Bimbi:** a fellow inmate.

the dictionary is like a miniature encyclopedia. Finally the dictionary's A section had filled a whole tablet—and I went on into the B's. That was the way I started copying what eventually became the entire dictionary. It went a lot faster after so much practice helped me to pick up handwriting speed. Between what I wrote in my tablet, and writing letters, during the rest of my time in prison I would guess I wrote a million words.

I never had been so truly free in my life.

I suppose it was inevitable that as my word base broadened, I could for the first time pick up a book and read and now begin to understand what the book was saying. Anyone who has read a great deal can imagine the new world that opened. Let me tell you something: from then until I left that prison, in every free moment I had, if I was not reading in the library, I was reading on my bunk. You couldn't have gotten me out of books with a wedge.[3] Between Mr. Muhammad's teachings, my correspondence, my visitors—usually Ella and Reginald[4]—and my reading of books, months passed without my even thinking about being imprisoned. In fact, up to then, I never had been so truly free in my life.

The Norfolk Prison Colony's library was in the school building. A variety of classes was taught there by instructors who came from such places as Harvard and Boston universities. The weekly debates between inmate teams were also held in the school building. You would be astonished to know how worked up convict debaters and audiences would get over subjects like "Should Babies Be Fed Milk?"

Available on the prison library's shelves were books on just about every general subject. Much of the big private collection that Parkhurst[5] had willed to the prison was still in crates and boxes in the back of the library—thousands of old books. Some of them looked ancient: covers faded, old-time parchment-looking binding. Parkhurst, I've mentioned, seemed to have been principally interested in history and religion. He had the money and the special interest to have a lot of books that you wouldn't have in general circulation. Any college library would have been lucky to get that collection.

As you can imagine, especially in a prison where there was heavy emphasis on rehabilitation, an inmate was smiled upon if he demonstrated an unusually intense interest in books. There was a sizable number of well-read inmates, especially the popular debaters. Some were said by many to be practically walking encyclopedias. They were almost celebrities. No university would ask any student to devour literature as I did when this new world opened to me, of being able to read and *understand*.

I read more in my room than in the library itself. An inmate who was known to read a lot could check out more than the permitted maximum number of books. I preferred reading in the total isolation of my own room.

When I had progressed to really serious reading, every night at about ten P.M. I would

---

3. **wedge:** a tapered piece of wood or metal used for splitting wood or rock.
4. **Ella and Reginald:** Malcolm's sister and brother.
5. **Parkhurst:** a millionaire interested in the education and training of prisoners.

be outraged with the "lights out." It always seemed to catch me right in the middle of something engrossing.

Fortunately, right outside my door was a corridor light that cast a glow into my room. The glow was enough to read by, once my eyes adjusted to it. So when "lights out" came, I would sit on the floor where I could continue reading in that glow.

At one-hour intervals the night guards paced past every room. Each time I heard the approaching footsteps, I jumped into bed and feigned sleep. And as soon as the guard passed, I got back out of bed onto the floor area of that light-glow, where I would read for another fifty-eight minutes—until the guard approached again. That went on until three or four every morning. Three or four hours of sleep a night was enough for me. Often in the years in the streets, I had slept less than that. ❖

RELATED READING

AARDVARK
by Julia Fields

Since
   Malcolm died
   That old aardvark
   has got a sort of fame
   for himself—
   I mean, of late, when I read
   The dictionary the first
   Thing I see
   Is that animal staring at me.
And then
   I think of Malcolm—
   How he read
   in the prisons
   And on the planes
   And everywhere
   And how he wrote
   About old Aardvark.
Looks like Malcolm X helped
Bring attention to a lot of things
We never thought about before.

Malcolm X
1925–1965

My whole life had been a chronology of—changes.

Preacher While Malcolm X was in prison he began to follow the teachings of Elijah Muhammad and the Nation of Islam, also known as the Black Muslims. Upon his release from prison, he became a Black Muslim minister and gained a wide reputation as a powerful speaker. Malcolm X preached in favor of black power and black nationalism, opposing white oppression and integration.

Pilgrim Because of a dispute within the faith, Malcolm X was expelled from the Black Muslims. After that, Malcolm X became a follower of traditional Islam. While on a pilgrimage to Mecca, the holy place of the Islamic faith, Malcolm X came to believe in the possibility of brotherhood among all peoples.

Author Upon his return to America Malcolm X began to work on his autobiography with Alex Haley, who later wrote *Roots.* On February 21, 1965, Malcolm X was assassinated. His autobiography was published after his death.

Key Standard
W1.1 Choose an appropriate type of organization, and use transitions to connect ideas effectively.
Other Standards **W1.2, W1.3, W1.4, W1.7, LC1.1, LC1.7**

Writing Workshop

Comparison-and-Contrast Essay

Showing differences and similarities . . .

From Reading to Writing Malcolm X and Russell Baker have different styles in relating their life stories and very different life experiences. If you look closely at their autobiographies, however, you can find similarities. For instance, both felt the need to make important changes in their lives. Comparing two characters—or two other related subjects—helps you to understand each of them better. One way to do this is by writing a **comparison-and-contrast essay.**

For Your Portfolio

WRITING PROMPT Write a comparison-and-contrast essay in which you explore the similarities and differences between two subjects of your choice.

Purpose: To inform, explain, or clarify
Audience: Anyone interested in your subjects

Basics in a Box

Comparison-and-Contrast Essay at a Glance

Introduction	Body	Conclusion
• introduces the **subjects** being compared • tells the **reason** for the comparison	explains similarities and differences Subject A only Both subjects Subject B only	• summarizes the comparison • explains new understanding

RUBRIC **STANDARDS FOR WRITING**

A successful comparison-and-contrast essay should

- introduce the subjects being compared
- state a clear purpose for the comparison
- include both similarities and differences and support each statement with examples and details
- follow a clear organizational pattern
- include transitional words and phrases to make similarities and differences clear
- summarize the comparison in the conclusion

Analyzing a Student Model

SPEAKING
See the Speaking and Listening Handbook, p. R100 for oral presentation tips.
OPPORTUNITY

M. De los Santos
Campbell Junior High

Juliette and Henrietta

When you hear the word *twins*, you probably think of two people who are exactly alike. However, in the story "Waiting" by Budge Wilson, the reader is introduced to Juliette and Henrietta, fraternal twins who seem to be very different. Juliette and Henrietta don't only differ in their physical appearance: their personalities seem to be complete opposites of each other. "She was my twin," Juliette says, "but apart from the accident of our birth, or the coincidence, we had almost nothing in common." Juliette is a brilliant leader, excelling in all of her activities. Henrietta is a follower who seems happiest when she is at home reading or coloring. Through Juliette's first-person point of view, the reader understands the deep differences between the sisters. The story also shows how growing up can reveal the swan that exists inside an ugly duckling.

The first way the twins differ is in their physical appearance. No one looking at Juliette and Henrietta could possibly confuse them. Juliette describes herself as having "fiery red cheeks and a broad snub nose." She has black hair that explodes in curls around her face and that cannot be tamed, like Juliette herself. She is "small, compact, sturdy, well-coordinated and extremely healthy." She is proud of her appearance. In contrast, Henrietta is pale. She is also very thin, with long fingers that Juliette calls bony. Although Henrietta has pretty sky-blue eyes, they are "surrounded by a long fringe of totally colorless eyelashes." According to Juliette, Henrietta's hair is also neutral in color and lifeless. She is serious and still, as if she is waiting for something. While Juliette is healthy, Henrietta is often sick.

Another way they differ is in their attitudes toward life. Juliette is fearless. Henrietta is afraid. Juliette is impossible to overlook. She is the athlete, the actress, the class president, the scholar, and an inventor of games. Juliette loves to ski down the hills and play games in the misty forest that leads to the edge of the cliffs. Juliette is always the hero or the daring spy in games. In the play that she and her friends perform for their parents, Juliette is the

---

RUBRIC
IN ACTION

❶ Introduction identifies the two subjects to be contrasted.

❷ Presents the features that will be compared

❸ Uses feature-by-feature organization (one feature per paragraph: Feature #1-physical appearance, #2-attitudes, #3-relationship with mother).

Another Option:
• Use subject-by-subject organization for overall structure.

❹ Transitional words signal differences.

❺ Provides specific examples to emphasize the contrast between sisters

leading lady and the director. What she says, the others do. "If you're the director, you can't be something like a page or a minor fairy, because then you don't seem important enough to be giving out instructions and bossing people around. . . ." Henrietta seems content to follow Juliette and let Juliette command the attention. She is afraid to ski, afraid of the cliffs, and afraid of the sea. Henrietta is a natural victim; she is always the prisoner of war left tied to a tree in the forest, sometimes for hours if Juliette forgets her. It is only when Henrietta is confined to bed with an illness that she can finally do what she likes best—color, or read her comics. Working behind the scenes for the annual play makes her happy, and even when Juliette takes praise away from her, she does not seem to resent it.

Another way they differ is in their relationship with their mother. Their mother seems to pay more attention to her talented and outgoing daughter. She tells a friend on the phone, "'I hope you don't regard this as *boasting,* but she really is so very, *very* talented. Bright as a button in school—three prizes, can you believe it, at the last school closing—and an outstanding athlete, even at eight years old.'" A newspaper clipping about Juliette has the place of honor on the kitchen bulletin board, and after Juliette's performances, her mother stations herself at the telephone to receive the complimentary calls. On the other hand, she describes Henrietta very differently. "She's fine, I guess, just fine. Such a serious, responsible little girl, and so fond of her sister."

Henrietta and Juliette are complete opposites in appearance, but it is their different personalities that really set them apart. By the end of the story, Juliette is able to recognize the beauty in her sister. "Henrietta had power," Juliette explains. "And what's more, she had it without having to *do* a single thing. All she needs to do, I thought, is *be.*" Juliette still gets good grades, acts as a leader in school, and shines in sports. However, by the end of the story, she respects Henrietta for the very different kind of person she is.

❻ Quotations support the writer's statements about character.

Another Option:
- Provide brief summaries of story events to support statements.

❼ Conclusion summarizes the contrast between the two subjects being compared.

❽ Explains the new understanding that both the reader and the character achieve

Writing Your Comparison-and-Contrast Essay

❶ Prewriting

Good writers are those who keep the language efficient.
—Ezra Pound, American poet and critic

To gather topics for your essay, **brainstorm** about reasons why you might compare two things. Do you want to see how two subjects are related? Do you want to prove that one idea is better than another? See the **Idea Bank** in the margin for more suggestions. After you choose two subjects to compare, follow the steps below.

Planning Your Comparison-and-Contrast Essay

► 1. **Explore similarities and differences.** Identify a few of the major features of each subject. For example, if you are comparing two story characters, look at appearance, age, attitude, behavior, and so on. Use a Venn diagram to show how they are similar and different.

► 2. **Focus on specific features.** What is the point of your essay? Choose the features that will help you make your point.

► 3. **Organize your thoughts.** There are two ways to organize your essay. You can discuss all the features of subject A before discussing the same features of subject B—this is the **subject-by-subject** pattern. Or, you can discuss how both A and B display one feature, then how A and B display the next feature, and so on—this is the **feature-by-feature** pattern. Choose the pattern that makes the most sense for your subjects.

Subject by Subject	Feature by Feature
Subject A	**Feature 1**
Feature 1	Subject A
Feature 2	Subject B
Subject B	**Feature 2**
Feature 1	Subject A
Feature 2	Subject B

---

❷ Drafting

It is important to get all your ideas down on paper before you begin to edit your work. You'll make adjustments and corrections later. As you write your first draft, keep the following ideas in mind:

• Make your **purpose** for the comparison clear in the introduction.

IDEA Bank

1. Your Working Portfolio 📁
Look for ideas in the **Writing** sections that you completed earlier in the unit.

2. Comparison Shopping
You make decisions about how to spend your money all the time. Think of two products you could compare and contrast, such as two skateboards, computers, pizzas, bicycles, pairs of jeans, or music CDs. Write a comparison-and-contrast essay to help you decide which is the best buy.

3. Critic's Corner
Brainstorm a list of movies or TV shows you have seen recently. Which ones did you especially like or dislike, and why? Pick two to compare and contrast.

Have a question?

See the **Writing Handbook**
Organizing Compare-and-Contrast Writing, p. R47
Paragraphs, p. R39
See **Language Network**
Prewriting, p. 312
Drafting, p. 315

Ask Your Peer Reader

• Why am I comparing and contrasting these two subjects?

• What is the strongest similarity between my subjects? What is the strongest difference?

• How could I improve the organization of my essay?

Need revising help?

Review the **Rubric,** p. 637.

Consider **peer reader** comments.

Check **Revising, Editing, and Proofreading,** p. R35.

Can't get a grip on dangling modifiers?

See the **Grammar Handbook,** p. R95.

SPELLING From Writing

As you revise your work, look back at the words you misspelled and determine why you made the errors you did. For additional help, refer to the strategies and generalizations in the **Spelling Handbook** on page R30.

SPEAKING Opportunity

Turn your essay into an oral presentation.

Publishing IDEAS

- Create an oversized chart to illustrate the similarities and differences between your two subjects. Hang your chart in the classroom.
- Videotape a commercial in which you compare and contrast your two items or subjects.

Publishing Options
www.mcdougallittell.com

- Stick to the same **organizational pattern** throughout your essay.
- Include **transitional words** that show similarities and differences between ideas.

❸ Revising

TARGET SKILL ▶ USING TRANSITIONS Transitional words and phrases show the relationship between ideas. To show similarities, use transitions such as *similarly, in the same way, also, like,* or *both.* To point out differences, use words like *however, in contrast, yet, but, on the other hand,* and *while.* Transitions weave your sentences together smoothly, and they show clearly which features are similar or different.

> *While*
> ∧ Juliette is very healthy, Henrietta is often sick.

❹ Editing and Proofreading

TARGET SKILL ▶ DANGLING MODIFIERS Few things are more confusing to readers than dangling or misplaced modifiers. Dangling modifiers have no word to modify: *Having studied for six hours, the test was easy.* (Who studied for six hours?) Instead, say: *Having studied for six hours, I found the test easy.* Now the reader knows to whom the sentence refers.

> *you* *think of*
> When you hear the word *twins,* ~~they are~~ probably ∧ two
> people who are exactly alike.

❺ Reflecting

FOR YOUR WORKING PORTFOLIO What did you learn about your subjects through writing your comparison-and-contrast essay? How well did your organization work? What was most difficult about writing this essay? Attach your reflections to your finished work. Save your comparison-and-contrast essay in your **Working Portfolio.**

Standardized Test Practice

Mixed Review

Before doing some investigating, all dogs seemed to make good
$\overline{\quad\quad}$
(1)
family pets. I was interested in many of the new breeds that have
$\overline{\quad}$
(2)
sprang up. However, my research showed that two breeds were suited
$\overline{\quad}$ $\overline{\quad}$
(3)
to my family. To decide between those types of dogs, I need to look at
$\overline{\quad}$
(4)
similarities and differences in their personalities, exercise demands,
and grooming needs. After charting my data, I found that making my
$\overline{\quad}$
(5)
decision was easier.

The Labrador retriever and the golden retriever has calm and
$\overline{\quad}$
(6)
friendly natures. They enjoy people of all ages; they play with children
and are gentle with the elderly.

Review Your Skills

Use the passage and the questions that follow it to check how well you remember the language conventions you've learned in previous years.

1. How is sentence 1 best written?
- **A.** All dogs, before doing some investigating, seemed
- **B.** All dogs seemed, before doing some investigating,
- **C.** Before doing some investigating, I thought all dogs seemed
- **D.** Correct as is

2. What is the correct verb form in sentence 2?
- **A.** had sprang
- **B.** had springed
- **C.** had sprung
- **D.** Correct as is

3. What is the correct spelling in sentence 3?
- **A.** too
- **B.** to
- **C.** tew
- **D.** Correct as is

4. What is the correct verb tense in sentence 4?
- **A.** I had needed
- **B.** I was needing
- **C.** I needed
- **D.** Correct as is

5. What is the correct spelling in sentence 5?
- **A.** datum
- **B.** datas
- **C.** datae
- **D.** Correct as is

6. What is the correct verb in sentence 6?
- **A.** have
- **B.** having
- **C.** had
- **D.** Correct as is

Key Standard
LC1.4 Use the mechanics of writing correctly; demonstrate correct language usage.
Other Standards **LC1.1, LC1.3, LC1.6**

Self-Assessment

Check your own answers in the **Grammar Handbook**

Quick Reference: Capitalization, p. R70

Quick Reference: Punctuation, p. R68

Dangling Modifiers, p. R95

Verb Tense, p. R80

Run-On Sentences, p. R71

Nothing Stays the Same

Do you agree with the idea that nothing stays the same? Do you think that the universe, and everything in it, is forever changing? Look in a mirror. You may look the same as you did yesterday, but in fact you're changing all the time. Each day you grow physically and emotionally. The characters in this unit undergo many changes—the changes of growing up—and learn many lessons.

Reflecting on Theme

OPTION 1

Act It Out Many of the characters in Unit Four learn from their experiences. With a group of classmates, choose three or more of those characters and prepare, and afterward present, a skit in which the characters discuss the expression "Learning the Hard Way."

THINK ABOUT
- the lesson each character learns
- how the lessons change the characters
- why the lessons are important

OPTION 2

Character Change Which of the characters in Unit Four do you think changes the most as a result of his or her choices? Which of the characters changes little or not at all? Discuss these questions with a small group of classmates, supporting your views with examples from the selections and insights from your own experience.

OPTION 3

Writing a Dialogue Choose a character from a selection in Part 2, and imagine that character in the situation of one of the characters in Part 1. How do you think the character from Part 2 would respond to the situation? What do you think he or she might say about learning the hard way? Write a dialogue between the character from Part 1 and the character from Part 2 to explore your ideas.

Self ASSESSMENT

READER'S NOTEBOOK

Which of the selections in this unit made you think most deeply about how nothing stays the same? Write a short paragraph in which you explain how the selection has influenced your thinking.

REVIEWING YOUR PERSONAL
WORDList

Vocabulary Review the new words you learned in this unit. If necessary, use a dictionary to check the meaning of each word.

Spelling Review your list of spelling words. If you're not sure of the correct spelling, use a dictionary or refer to the **Spelling Handbook** on page R30.

Key Standard
R3.3 Analyze characters by examining what they think, say, and do, and by studying the words of the narrator and the reactions of other characters.
***Other Standards* R3.4, R3.6, W2.1**

Reviewing Literary Concepts

Identifying Mood Mood is the feeling or atmosphere that a literary work conveys to readers, for example, horror, fright, happiness, or tension. Pick a story in this unit other than "The White Umbrella" and describe the mood that it conveys. What details in the story enable you to determine the mood?

Examining Characterization Characterization includes the techniques that writers use to create and develop characters. Make a chart, listing at the top each main character in the stories you have read. Then rate each technique according to its importance in making the character come alive for you. Use a scale from 1 to 5, with 5 being the most important.

	Steve Brand			
Presenting character's words and actions				
Showing character's thoughts				
Describing character's appearance				
Telling what others think about the character				

Self ASSESSMENT

READER'S NOTEBOOK

Copy the following literary terms covered in this unit. Next to each term, jot down a brief definition. If you have trouble explaining a particular concept, refer to the **Glossary of Literary and Reading Terms** on page R120.

mood	characterization
tone	point of view
dialect	character development
foil	
rhythm	farce
plot complications	word choice

Portfolio Building

- **Choices and Challenges—Writing** Several of the writing assignments in this unit asked you to develop and present your research. From your responses, choose the one that you think expresses your ideas most effectively. Explain the reasons for your evaluation in a cover note, attach it to the assignment, and place them together in your **Presentation Portfolio.**

- **Writing Workshops** In your comparison-and-contrast essay, you had the chance to examine and evaluate two different characters. Reread your essay. Then write a note listing several careers in which the skills you learned in writing this essay might be useful. Attach the note to your comparison-and-contrast essay.

- **Additional Activities** Review everything you created in your work for this unit, including any pieces you did on your own. Select one piece of writing or one activity that you consider your best work. Write a note explaining how it influenced your ideas about stepping forward. Add the note and the piece of writing to your **Presentation Portfolio.**

Self ASSESSMENT

Your **Presentation Portfolio** probably contains both old and recent pieces of writing. Write a note comparing a recent piece with an earlier one. Identify one strength that only the recent piece reflects.

Setting GOALS

As you completed the activities in this unit, you probably noticed strengths in certain skills but not in others. Look back through your **READER'S NOTEBOOK.** List one or two skills that you intend to develop in the next unit.

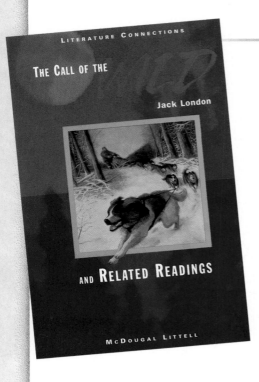

LITERATURE CONNECTIONS
The Call of the Wild

BY JACK LONDON

When the dog Buck is forced into battle for control of his destiny, he responds by following the call of the wild. The story of Buck explores the role environment plays in shaping character. A privileged, dignified dog from southern California is shipped to Alaska during the 1890s Gold Rush. Mistreated, he learns to survive as a member of a dogsled team, where "the law of club and fang" overrides the rules of civilized society.

These thematically related readings are provided along with *The Call of the Wild*:

The Wolf and the Dog
BY MARIE DE FRANCE

from **The Hidden Life of Dogs**
BY ELIZABETH MARSHALL THOMAS

Long Duel
BY ROBERT MURPHY

The Wolf Said to Francis
BY A. G. ROCHELLE

The Man Who Was a Horse
BY JULIUS LESTER

Unsentimental Mother
BY SALLY CARRIGHAR

More Choices

Dicey's Song
BY CYNTHIA VOIGT
Dicey achieves her goals while learning the hard way that nothing stays the same.

Family Farm
BY THOMAS LOCKER
Mike and Sarah are upset when their family faces problems. When they decide to raise pumpkins and flowers, however, their attitudes change.

The Goats
BY BROCK COLE
A boy and a girl learn how to survive after they are marooned on Goat Island.

Izzy, Willy-Nilly
BY CYNTHIA VOIGT
After Izzy loses her leg in a drunk-driving accident, she learns a difficult lesson about friendship, life, and coping with being different.

Lady Ellen Grae
BY VERA AND BILL CLEAVER
Eleven-year-old Ellen listens to an old man's confession about his cruel parents and must decide how to help.

Nothing but the Truth
BY AVI
Philip, a high school goof-off, gets caught up in a battle involving patriotism, school policy, the national media, and a struggle for justice.

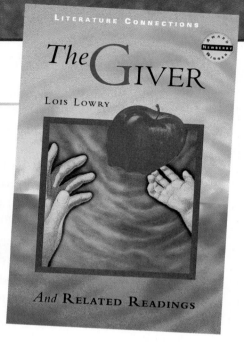

LITERATURE CONNECTIONS

The Giver

BY LOIS LOWRY

The Giver is a science fiction story about 12-year-old Jonas, who must choose between a "perfect" world devoid of strife or conflict and one filled with the joys and pains of a life of choices. Jonas begins to realize that his seemingly perfect world has many flaws and must decide where true integrity and loyalty lie.

These thematically related readings are provided along with *The Giver:*

Newbery Award Acceptance Speech
BY LOIS LOWRY

The Role of the Griot
BY D'JIMO KOUYATE

Jeremiah's Song
BY WALTER DEAN MYERS

The Pedestrian
BY RAY BRADBURY

The Forecast
BY DAN JAFFE

Old Glory
BY BRUCE COVILLE

Drawing by Ronnie C., Grade One
BY RUTH LECHLITNER

from **The Landscape of Memory**
BY MILTON MELTZER

Social Studies Connection

Tales from Shakespeare
BY CHARLES AND MARY LAMB
A retelling of Shakespeare's most popular plays, including *Romeo and Juliet, Macbeth,* and *Hamlet.*

Michelangelo's World
BY PIETRO VENTURA
In this story, Michelangelo recounts his own life and experiences.

A Murder for Her Majesty
BY BETH HILGARTNER
An English girl investigates her father's murder in Elizabethan England.

The Prince and the Pauper
BY MARK TWAIN
When the boy king Edward VI meets a pauper who looks just like him, they decide to switch places.

King Arthur and the Legends of Camelot
RETOLD BY MOLLY PERHAM
This retelling of the Arthurian legends recounts the adventures of King Arthur, Merlin, and the Knights of the Round Table.

Standardized Test Practice

Reading and Writing for Assessment

When you studied the test-taking strategies on pages 334–339, you learned helpful new techniques. The following pages will give you practice using these strategies and more.

PART 1 How to Read the Test Selection

Listed below are some basic reading strategies. By applying these strategies, and by taking notes, you can identify the information you need in answering test questions.

STRATEGIES FOR READING A TEST SELECTION

- **Before you begin reading, skim the questions that follow the passage.** These can help focus your reading.

- **Think about the title and message.** What does the title suggest about the overall message or theme of the selection?

- **Use active reading strategies such as analyzing, predicting, and questioning.** If the test directions allow you to mark on the test itself, make notes in the margin as you read.

- **Look for main ideas.** These are often stated at the beginning or end of paragraphs. Sometimes they are implied, not stated. After reading each paragraph, ask, "What was this passage about?"

- **Note the literary elements and techniques used by the writer.** Consider the effects of word choice, figurative language, and mood.

- **Evaluate the organization.** For a comparison-and-contrast essay, how well does the use of feature-by-feature or subject-by-subject organization work in the piece?

- **Look for expert testimony.** What supporting evidence or sources of information does the writer use? Why are these sources appropriate to the subject?

- **Make judgments about the writer's purpose.** Does the writer have a bias or use a particular tone? How does this affect the message and presentation of information?

Key Standard
R2.6 Evaluate the strength and accuracy of the evidence an author uses to support a claim. Recognize bias and stereotyping.
Other Standards **R1.3, R2.3, R3.4, W1.3, LC1.3, LC1.4, LC1.7**

Reading Selection

❶ A Land of Staggering Proportions
by Brad Darrach and Steve Petranek

1   **❷** Oh, what a fascinating walk you could take near the Martian equator next December, in the middle of a summer day. The weather would be perfect—high 60s and a bright orange Creamsicle-colored sky—but shirtsleeves would be out. You'd be wearing a light space suit to keep your blood from boiling because the "air" on Mars is so thin, about the same density as Earth's at twenty miles above sea level. The space suit would help with two other problems—the deadly ultraviolet light from the Sun, and the unbreathable Martian atmosphere, which is ninety-five percent carbon dioxide, with traces of nitrogen and argon.

2   The physical act of walking would seem effortless; you could endlessly hop, skip, or jump along because gravity is only about a third of what it is on Earth. A hundred-pound woman would feel as if she weighed thirty-eight pounds, and a world-class athlete could run a hundred meters in less than five seconds.

3   The **❸** vista would remind you of the Arizona and California deserts—fine sand littered with rocks and boulders. But the sand would be pink and reddish-brown, turned to rust. Of course, there wouldn't be any cacti or scrub plants like tumbleweed, any darting lizards or rabbits. The terrain would be much drier than any desert on Earth, so dry that an ice cube placed on the ground would quickly disappear, evaporating before it could melt, going straight from solid to vapor. You could walk just about anywhere you wanted on Mars, because the entire surface is land; there are no lakes, rivers, or oceans. Almost all of the water is underground or frozen.

4   **❹** There's as much land on Mars as there is on Earth, even though Mars is only half as big as Earth and weighs only a tenth as much. Because of its weaker gravity, Mars is not as dense as Earth; it's puffed up. If you dig a thousand feet below the surface of Earth, you would probably hit solid rock, but a thousand feet

❶ Think about the title.
One Student's Thoughts
"I wonder what kind of land has staggering proportions."

❷ Make judgments about the writers' purpose.
One Student's Thoughts
"The subject of the essay is scientific but the tone is conversational. The reader is asked to imagine a familiar scene (a walk) in an unfamiliar setting (Mars)."
YOUR TURN
Why do you think the writers use this tone?

❸ Use context clues to understand vocabulary.
One Student's Thoughts
"It seems that *vista* has something to do with the appearance of the land or terrain."

❹ Read actively—analyze.
One Student's Thoughts
"If there is as much land on Mars as on Earth, why does Mars weigh only a tenth as much?"
YOUR TURN
Look for evidence to answer this question.

below the crust of Mars you would find porous material, perhaps even a gravely slurry of rock and ice.

5   ❺ A day's walk on Mars would offer about as much Sun time as on Earth; Mars rotates once every 24 hours, 37 minutes. But the summer would last twice as long because Mars takes 687 Earth days to orbit the Sun.

6   ❻ A trek to any of Earth's natural wonders would pale by comparison to what can be seen on Mars. Mount Everest, at just over 29,000 feet, would seem a foothill compared to the Tharsis bulge, a broad, raised equatorial plain the size of the United States. On Tharsis sit extraordinary volcanoes, among them Olympus Mons, at almost 90,000 feet the highest known elevation in the solar system. The mighty Colorado River's cut through the Grand Canyon would seem a drainage ditch next to Valles Marineris, a gorge that would stretch from Seattle to Miami. . . .

7   You could spend a lifetime on the surface of Mars and never run out of new formations to see. . . . Just one thing, though. You would want to get back to base before dark. Most nights, even in summer, the temperature drops to about ⁻125°F.

❺ Evaluate the writers' use of comparison and contrast.

One Student's Thoughts
"The writers compare one feature in this paragraph, which is the amount of sun time on both planets."

YOUR TURN
How well does feature-by-feature organization work in the essay?

❻ Skim the questions that follow the passage.

One Student's Thoughts
"There's a question about natural wonders on both planets. The writers seem to think more highly of Mars, but I wonder how anything could make the Grand Canyon look like a drainage ditch!"

Use the strategies in the box and notes in the side column to help you answer the questions below and on the following pages.

Based on the selection you have just read, choose the best answer for each of the following questions.

1. Why do you think the essay is titled "A Land of Staggering Proportions"?
   A. People stagger when they walk on Mars.
   B. Mars has the biggest land mass known to humans.
   C. Everything on Mars is in proportion.
   D. Mars has many extreme aspects to it.

2. Why do the writers use a conversational tone?
   A. They don't care about the subject.
   B. They are trying to make the subject seem familiar.
   C. They like to take walks.
   D. Scientific papers should always be casually written.

3. What main idea do the writers support by mentioning that a world-class athlete could run 100 meters in less than five seconds?
   A. It is harder to run on Mars.
   B. There is less gravity on Mars.
   C. Physical movement is easier on Mars and Venus.
   D. There is less gravity on Earth.

4. What do the writers mean when they say that Earth's natural wonders would "pale in comparison" to what can be seen on Mars?
   A. The color of Earth's natural wonders are lighter.
   B. Earth's natural wonders are superior.
   C. Mars's natural wonders are superior.
   D. All of the above.

5. Why do you think the writers include information about how humans would react on Mars?
   A. They think humans will eventually live there.
   B. By putting the information in human terms, they hope to help the reader understand it.
   C. The writers want to show that humans could never live there.
   D. The writers want to show that humans should appreciate Earth.

STRATEGIES FOR ANSWERING MULTIPLE-CHOICE QUESTIONS

▶ **Ask questions** that help you eliminate some of the choices.

▶ **Pay attention to choices** such as "all of the above" or "none of the above." To eliminate them, all you need to find is one answer that doesn't fit the choice.

▶ **Choose the one best answer.** More than one choice may be true, but only one will be true and answer the question completely.

STRATEGIES IN ACTION

Choose the one best answer.

One Student's Thoughts
"This essay doesn't deal with other planets, *so I can eliminate choice C.*"

YOUR TURN
What other choices can you eliminate?

Pay attention to choices such as "all of the above."

One Student's Thoughts
"I don't think the writers are referring to the color of the planets when they use the word *pale*. So I can eliminate choice A. That means that choice D—all of the above— can't be right either."

YOUR TURN
Which of the remaining choices makes the most sense?

PART 3

How to Respond in Writing

You may be asked to write answers to questions about a reading passage. **Short-answer questions** often ask you to answer in a sentence or two. **Essay questions** require a fully developed piece of writing.

Short-Answer Questions

STRATEGIES FOR RESPONDING TO SHORT-ANSWER QUESTIONS

▸ **Identify key words** in the writing prompt that tell you the ideas to discuss. Make sure you know what each word means.
▸ **State your response directly** and to the point.
▸ **Support your ideas** by using evidence from the selection.
▸ **Use correct grammar.**

> **Sample Question**
> Answer the following question in one or two sentences.
>
> Explain what you think the writer's purpose was in comparing and contrasting Mars and Earth.

STRATEGIES
IN ACTION

Identify key words.

One Student's Thoughts
"The key words are *explain* and *purpose*. This means that I'll have to decide why the writer wrote the article and tell why I think that way."

YOUR TURN
What clues to the writer's purpose can you find in the selection?

Essay Questions

STRATEGIES FOR ANSWERING ESSAY QUESTIONS

▸ **Look for direction words** in the writing prompt that tell you what to write and what to do, such as *essay, analyze, describe,* or *compare and contrast.*
▸ **List the points** you want to make before beginning to write.
▸ **Write a strong introduction** that presents your main point.
▸ **Develop your ideas** by supporting your statements with evidence from the selection. Present the ideas in a logical order.
▸ **Write a conclusion** that summarizes your points.
▸ **Check your work for correct grammar.**

> **Sample Prompt**
> The writer of this selection sees Mars as having many outstanding features that make it different from Earth. Write an essay in which you summarize these features.

Identify direction words.

One Student's Thoughts
"The key direction words are *essay* and *summarize*. This means that I'll have to discuss the key features of Mars in a fully developed piece of writing."

YOUR TURN
What important points will you have to include in your essay?

Here is a student's first draft in response to the writing prompt at the bottom of page 650. Read it and answer the multiple-choice questions that follow.

1	Mars is half as big as Earth: weighing a tenth as much.
2	On Mars, there is less gravity and the air is thinner.
3	Mars is exposed to deadly ultraviolet light and summers
4	twice as long. The terrain is desert-like, containing
5	boulders and rocks littered on sand which varies in color
6	from reddish brown to pink. Mars has huge mountains and
7	gorges, but they have no plants, animals, lakes, rivers, or
8	other bodies of water. All the water is frozen underground.

STRATEGIES FOR REVISING, EDITING, AND PROOFREADING

▶ **Read the passage carefully.**
▶ **Notice the parts that are confusing.** What types of errors might cause that confusion?
▶ **Look for errors** in grammar, usage, spelling, and capitalization. Common errors include
  • sentence fragments
  • lack of subject-verb agreement
  • pronoun-antecedent problems
  • lack of transition words

1. What is the BEST way to revise the sentence in line 1 (Mars is half . . . tenth as much.)?

  A. Mars is half as big as Earth but weighs a tenth as much.

  B. Earth, half as big, weighs a tenth as much as Mars.

  C. Mars is half as big and weighing a tenth as much.

  D. Half as big as Mars, Earth weighs a tenth as much.

2. What is the BEST way to revise the sentence in lines 3–4 (Mars is exposed . . . twice as long.)?

  A. Mars is exposed to deadly ultraviolet light: summers last twice as long as on Earth.

  B. Mars is exposed to deadly ultraviolet light with summers last twice as long as on Earth.

  C. Mars is exposed to deadly ultraviolet light summers last twice as long as on Earth.

  D. Mars is exposed to deadly ultraviolet light; summers last twice as long as on Earth.

3. What is the BEST way to revise the sentence in lines 6–8 (Mars has huge . . . water.)?

  A. Mars has huge mountains and gorges, but no plants, animals, lakes, rivers, or other bodies of water.

  B. Mars has huge mountains and gorges; they have no plants, animals, lakes, rivers, or other bodies of water.

  C. There are huge mountains and gorges; but Mars has no plants, animals, lakes, rivers, or other bodies of water.

  D. Mars has huge mountains and gorges. There is no plants, animals, lakes, rivers, or other bodies of water.

Personal Challenges

taking that powerful energy that you have inside of you and

putting it into something real positive or creative, or something with love . . . .

Quincy Jones

Meeting Standards

The Literature You'll Read

The Concepts You'll Study

Vocabulary and Reading Comprehension
Vocabulary Focus: Multiple-Meaning Words and Homonyms
Fact and Opinion
Visualizing

Writing and Language Conventions
Writing Workshop: Opinion Statement
Independent Clauses and Compound Sentences
Adverb Clauses

Literary Analysis
Literary Focus: Setting
Setting and Sources
Setting

Speaking and Listening
Film Review
Reader's Theater

Key Standard
R3.1 Be able to describe the purposes and characteristics of different forms of prose, such as the short story, novel, or essay.

Setting in Fiction and Nonfiction

> *Setting . . . offers an arena for fantastic adventures, enchantments, heroic exploits, heart-stopping dangers, or comfort, peace, and contentment.*
>
> —Barbara H. Baskin

What would it be like to discover the skeleton of an ancient sailor? How would it feel to sail across the ocean in the dark, crowded belly of a ship? Can you imagine stalking a wild animal through the woods in springtime? Writers of fiction and nonfiction alike try to capture experiences like these by describing the setting in which they occurred. **Setting** is the time and place of the action in any piece of writing.

Setting can also include details about location, historical period, time of year, weather, or time of day. Anything in a story that helps readers picture what the writer is telling about can be part of the setting.

The *Titanic* had two grand staircases, each five stories high and covered by a glass dome. The staircase shown was named Olympic. Joseph A. Carvalho Collection.

Historical Period

Another aspect of setting is the **historical period** or era during which the action takes place. Works of historical fiction and informative nonfiction about history are set in the past. Much contemporary fiction—fiction written recently—is set in the present.

Short fiction usually takes place in a single time period, as do some novels. Novels, because they are longer, may also cover years, decades, or even centuries.

YOUR TURN The passage on the right is from *Immigrant Kids*, an informative nonfiction story about immigrating to America between 1880 and 1920. What details about the setting suggest that this piece of writing takes place in the past?

Source Material

Good nonfiction writers strive to retell history through vivid depictions of setting. Sometimes authors include **source material** in their writing. Photographs, diagrams, quotes, fine art, newspaper and magazine articles are used to support details in the story being told. Use of these kinds of sources helps the reader understand what happened, to whom, when, and under what conditions.

There are two types of sources. A **primary source** means the information comes from someone's firsthand experience or observation. Diaries, autobiographies, interviews, and letters are examples of primary sources. A **secondary source** is information based on the experience of someone other than the person who wrote it. Newspaper articles, literary nonfiction, and biographies, like the one in Unit Two about Eleanor Roosevelt, are types of secondary sources.

YOUR TURN What do you learn from this quote from an eyewitness, or primary source, about the setting of the night the *Titanic* sank? Writers also use photographs, like the ones on pages 655 and 656, as primary sources.

SETTING IN HISTORICAL PERIODS

Men, women, and children were packed into dark, foul-smelling compartments. They slept in narrow bunks stacked three high. They had no showers, no lounges, and no dining rooms. . . . Because the steerage conditions were crowded and uncomfortable, passengers spent as much time as possible up on deck.

—Russell Freeman, *Immigrant Kids*

FIRST HAND OBSERVATION

"It had become very much colder," [Jack Thayer] said later. "It was a brilliant, starry night. There was no moon, and I have never seen the stars shine brighter . . . sparkling like diamonds. . . . It was the kind of night that made one feel glad to be alive."

—Robert Ballard, *Exploring the* Titanic

The Active Reader: Skills and Strategies

Distinguishing Fact from Opinion

Suppose your teacher says, "The years during World War II were the most difficult in United States history." Should you record this as a fact in your notebook or should you wait for your teacher to support her opinion with facts?

A statement of fact can be proved. An opinion is a belief or feeling a person accepts as true, but that is not supported with proof or evidence. As you read, use the strategies on this page to help you distinguish fact from opinion.

How to Apply the Skill

To **distinguish fact from opinion,** an active reader will
- **Clarify** statements of fact as true or false
- Look for words or phrases that signal opinions
- **Evaluate** the writer's ideas and reasoning
- Look for supporting evidence

Try It Now!

Read and distinguish fact from opinion in the excerpt below.

On May 31, 1911, the hull of the *Titanic* was launched at the Harland & Wolff shipyards in Belfast, Ireland, before a cheering crowd of 100,000. Bands played, and people came from miles around to see the great wonder of the sea. Twenty-two tons of soap, grease, and train oil were used to slide her into the water. In the words of one eyewitness, she had "a rudder as big as an elm tree . . . propellers as big as a windmill. Everything was on a nightmare scale."

—Robert D. Ballard, *Exploring the* Titanic

Here's how Erlin uses the strategies:

"As I read, I identify whether something can be proved true or false. The first statement is a **fact** *and can be proved by verifying the date, time, and place where the* Titanic *was launched. I look for words or phrases that help me recognize* **opinions:** always, *or* never *and* I believe, *and* it seems. *The second sentence contains an opinion because the word* great *and the phrase* wonder of the sea *indicate a judgment and can't be proved."*

Key Standard
R2.6 Evaluate the strength and accuracy of the evidence an author uses to support a claim. Recognize bias and stereotyping.
Other Standard **R2.4**

from **Exploring the *Titanic***

by ROBERT BALLARD

Connect to Your Life

What do you know about exploration beneath the surface of the oceans?

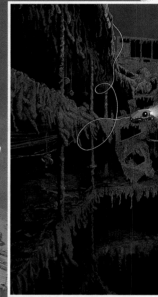

The robot *Jason Junior* explores the interior of the *Titanic*.

Build Background

Underwater exploration has expanded dramatically since the creation in the 1960s of mini-submarines called submersibles. Submersibles have mapped the ocean floors, discovered ecosystems that exist in total darkness, and explored shipwrecks. In these paintings, the submersible *Alvin* and its attached underwater robot *Jason Junior* explore the wreck of the *Titanic*.

Focus Your Reading

LITERARY ANALYSIS | **SETTING AND SOURCES**

The time and place in which a literary work occurs is its **setting.** Sources refer to the places the writer looks for factual information about the time and place. A **primary source** is a firsthand account of an event. A **secondary source** is a description based on an account from a primary source.

WORDS TO KNOW Vocabulary Preview

accommodations	feverishly	novelty	toll
dazzled	indefinitely	prophecy	tribute
eerie	list		

ACTIVE READING | **FACT AND OPINION**

A fact is a statement that can be proved. An opinion offers personal feelings or beliefs.

Fact: At 7:30 P.M., April 14, 1912, the steamer *Californian* warned the *Titanic* about icebergs. **Opinion:** The *Titanic*'s crew should have taken those warnings more seriously.

As you read the selection, jot down examples of fact and opinion in your 📖 **READER'S NOTEBOOK.**

Key Standard
R2.4 Identify an author's argument and point of view in a text.
***Other Standards* R1.3, R2.6, R3.1, W1.2, W2.3, LC1.3, LC1.4, LS1.8**

WHITE STAR LINE

ROYAL & UNITED STATES MAIL STEAMERS

FIRST SAILING OF THE LATEST ADDITION TO THE WHITE STAR FLEET

The Queen of the Ocean

TITANIC

LENGTH 882½ FT. OVER 45,000 TONS TRIPLE-SCREWS BEAM 92½ FT.

This, the Latest, Largest and Finest Steamer Afloat, will sail from

WHITE STAR LINE, PIER 10, SOUTHAMPTON

WEDNESDAY, APRIL 10TH

AT 12 NOON

calling at Cherbourg & Queenstown, Co. Cork

en route to NEW YORK

FROM · EXPLORING

THE TITANIC

BY ROBERT D. BALLARD

The story of the *Titanic* began before anyone had even thought about building the great ship. In 1898, fourteen years before the *Titanic* sank, an American writer named Morgan Robertson wrote a book called *The Wreck of the Titan*.[1] In his story, the *Titan*, a passenger ship almost identical to the *Titanic*, and labeled "unsinkable," sails from England headed for New York. With many rich and famous passengers on board, the *Titan* hits an iceberg in the North Atlantic and sinks. Because there are not enough lifeboats, many lives are lost.

The story of the *Titan* predicted exactly what would happen to the *Titanic* fourteen years later. It was an <u>eerie</u> <u>prophecy</u> of terrible things to come.

In 1907, nearly ten years after *The Wreck of the Titan* was written, two men began making plans to build a real titanic ship. At a London dinner party, as they relaxed over coffee and cigars, J. Bruce Ismay, president of the White Star Line of passenger ships, and Lord Pirrie, chairman of Harland & Wolff shipbuilders, discussed a plan to build three enormous ocean liners. Their goal was to give the White Star Line a competitive edge in the Atlantic passenger trade with several gigantic ships whose <u>accommodations</u> would be the last word in comfort and elegance.

The two men certainly dreamed on a grand scale. When these floating palaces were finally

AS HER NAME BOASTED, THE *TITANIC* WAS INDEED THE BIGGEST SHIP IN THE WORLD.

built, they were so much bigger than other ships that new docks had to be built on each side of the Atlantic to service them. Four years after that London dinner party, the first of these huge liners, the *Olympic*, safely completed her maiden voyage.[2]

On May 31, 1911, the hull of the *Titanic* was launched at the Harland & Wolff shipyards in Belfast, Ireland, before a cheering crowd of 100,000. Bands played, and people came from miles around to see this great wonder of the sea. Twenty-two tons of soap, grease, and train oil were used to slide her into the water. In the words of one eyewitness, she had "a rudder as big as an elm tree . . . propellers as big as a windmill. Everything was on a nightmare scale."

For the next ten months the *Titanic* was outfitted and carefully prepared down to the last detail. The final size and richness of this new ship was astounding. She was 882 feet long, almost the length of four city blocks. With nine decks, she was as high as an eleven-story building.

Among her gigantic features, she had four huge funnels, each one big enough to drive

---

1. **Titanic** (tī-tăn′ĭk) . . . **Titan** (tīt′n): In Greek mythology, the Titans were a race of giants. *Titanic* has come to be applied to any person or thing of great size or power.

2. **maiden voyage:** very first trip.

WORDS
TO
KNOW

eerie (îr′ē) *adj.* weird, especially in a frightening way
prophecy (prŏf′ĭ-sē) *n.* a prediction; foretelling of future events
accommodations (ə-kŏm′ə-dā′shənz) *n.* a room and food, especially in hotels or on ships or trains

660

two trains through. During construction an astonishing three million rivets had been hammered into her hull. Her three enormous anchors weighed a total of thirty-one tons—the weight of twenty cars. And for her maiden voyage, she carried enough food to feed a small town for several months.

As her name boasted, the *Titanic* was indeed the biggest ship in the world. Nicknamed "the Millionaires' Special," she was also called "the Wonder Ship," "the Unsinkable Ship," and "the Last Word in Luxury" by newspapers around the world.

The command of this great ocean liner was given to the senior captain of the White Star Line, Captain Edward J. Smith. This proud, white-bearded man was a natural leader and was popular with both crew members and passengers. Most important, after thirty-eight years' service with the White Star Line, he had an excellent safety record. At the age of fifty-nine, Captain Smith was going to retire after this last trip, a perfect final <u>tribute</u> to a long and successful career.

On Wednesday, April 10, 1912, the *Titanic*'s passengers began to arrive in Southampton for the trip to New York. Ruth Becker was <u>dazzled</u> as she boarded the ship with her mother, her younger sister, and two-year-old brother, Richard. Ruth's father was a missionary in India. The rest of the family was sailing to New York to find medical help for

The *Titanic* had two grand staircases, each five stories high and covered by a glass dome. The staircase shown was named Olympic. Joseph A. Carvalho Collection.

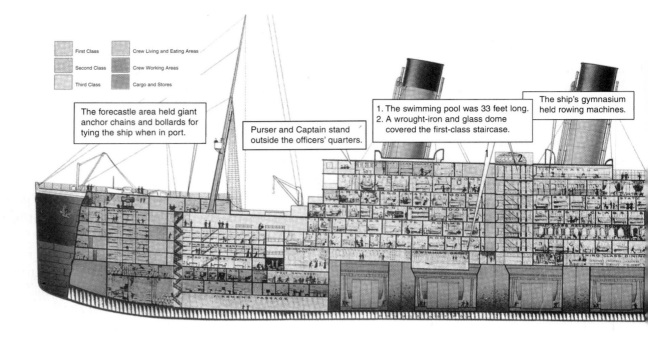

First Class
Second Class
Third Class
Crew Living and Eating Areas
Crew Working Areas
Cargo and Stores

The forecastle area held giant anchor chains and bollards for tying the ship when in port.

Purser and Captain stand outside the officers' quarters.

1. The swimming pool was 33 feet long.
2. A wrought-iron and glass dome covered the first-class staircase.

The ship's gymnasium held rowing machines.

young Richard, who had developed a serious illness in India. They had booked second-class tickets on the *Titanic*.

Twelve-year-old Ruth was delighted with the ship. As she pushed her little brother about the decks in a stroller, she was impressed with what she saw. "Everything was new. New!" she recalled. "Our cabin was just like a hotel room, it was so big. The dining room was beautiful—the linens, all the bright, polished silver you can imagine."

ACTIVE READER

FACT AND OPINION
Is this statement about the dining room a fact or an opinion?

Meanwhile, seventeen-year-old Jack Thayer from Philadelphia was trying out the soft mattress on the large bed in his cabin. The first-class rooms his family had reserved for themselves and their maid had thick carpets, carved wooden panels on the walls, and marble sinks. As his parents were getting settled in their adjoining stateroom,[3] Jack decided to explore this fantastic ship.

On A Deck, he stepped into the Verandah and Palm Court and admired the white wicker furniture and the ivy growing up the trellised

walls. On the lower decks, Jack discovered the squash court,[4] the swimming pool, and the Turkish bath[5] decorated like a room in a sultan's palace. In the gymnasium, the instructor was showing passengers the latest in exercise equipment, which included a mechanical camel you could ride on, stationary bicycles, and rowing machines.

Daylight shone through the huge glass dome over the Grand Staircase as Jack went down to join his parents in the first-class reception room.

There, with the ship's band playing in the background, his father pointed out some of the other first-class passengers. "He's supposed to be the world's richest man," said his father of Colonel John Jacob Astor, who was escorting the young Mrs. Astor. He also identified Mr. and Mrs. Straus, founders of Macy's of New York, the world's largest department store. Millionaire Benjamin Guggenheim was aboard, as were Jack's parents' friends from Philadel-

---

3. **stateroom:** a private cabin on a ship.
4. **squash court:** a walled court or room for playing squash, in which a rubber ball is hit off the walls.
5. **Turkish bath:** a steam bath.

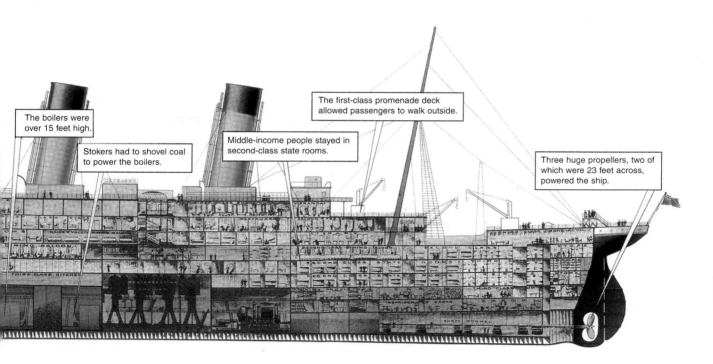

The boilers were over 15 feet high.

Stokers had to shovel coal to power the boilers.

Middle-income people stayed in second-class state rooms.

The first-class promenade deck allowed passengers to walk outside.

Three huge propellers, two of which were 23 feet across, powered the ship.

phia, Mr. and Mrs. George Widener and their son, Harry. Mr. Widener had made a fortune building streetcars. Mr. and Mrs. William Carter were also friends of the Thayers. Stowed in one of the holds below was a new Renault car that they were bringing back from England.

J. Bruce Ismay, president of the White Star Line, moved about the room saying hello to people. He wanted to make sure that his wealthy passengers were comfortable, that they would feel relaxed and safe aboard his floating palace.

Indeed, when Ruth Becker's mother had asked one of the second-class staff about the safety of the ship, she had been told that there was absolutely nothing to worry about. The ship had watertight compartments that would allow her to float indefinitely. There was much talk among the passengers about the *Titanic* being unsinkable.

In 1912, people were divided into social classes according to background, wealth, and education. Because of these class lines, the

Titanic was rather like a big floating layer cake. The bottom layer consisted of the lowly manual workers sweating away in the heat and grime of the boiler rooms and engine rooms. The next layer was the third-class passengers, people of many nationalities hoping to make a new start in America. After that came the second class—teachers, merchants, and professionals of moderate means like Ruth's family. Then, finally, there was the icing on the cake in first class: the rich and the aristocratic. The differences between these groups were enormous. While the wealthy brought their maids and valets[6] and mountains of luggage, most members of the crew earned such tiny salaries that it would have taken them years to save the money for a single first-class ticket.

At noon on Wednesday, April 10, the *Titanic* cast off. The whistles on her huge funnels were the biggest ever made. As she began her journey to the sea, they were heard for miles around.

6. **valets** (vă-lāz'): gentlemen's personal servants.

Moving majestically down the River Test, and watched by a crowd that had turned out for the occasion, the *Titanic* slowly passed two ships tied up to a dock. All of a sudden, the mooring ropes holding the passenger liner *New York* snapped with a series of sharp cracks like fireworks going off. The enormous pull created by the *Titanic* moving past her had broken the *New York*'s ropes and was now drawing her stern toward the *Titanic*. Jack Thayer watched in horror as the two ships came closer and closer. "It looked as though there surely would be a collision," he later wrote. "Her stern could not have been more than a yard or two from our side. It almost hit us." At the last moment, some quick action by Captain Smith and a tugboat captain nearby allowed the *Titanic* to slide past with only inches to spare.

It was not a good sign. Did it mean that the *Titanic* might be too big a ship to handle safely? Those who knew about the sea thought that such a close call at the beginning of a maiden voyage was a very bad omen.

Jack Phillips, the first wireless operator on the *Titanic,* quickly jotted down the message coming in over his headphones. "It's another iceberg warning," he said wearily to his young assistant, Harold Bride. "You'd better take it up to the bridge." Both men had been at work for hours in the *Titanic*'s radio room, trying to get caught up in sending out a large number of personal messages. In 1912, passengers on

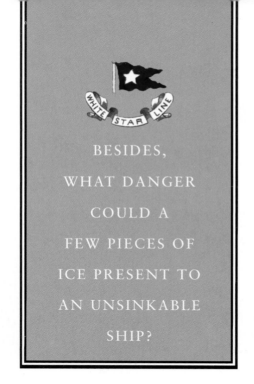

BESIDES, WHAT DANGER COULD A FEW PIECES OF ICE PRESENT TO AN UNSINKABLE SHIP?

ocean liners thought it was a real novelty to send postcard-style messages to friends at home from the middle of the Atlantic.

Bride picked up the iceberg message and stepped out onto the boat deck. It was a sunny but cold Sunday morning, the fourth day of the *Titanic*'s maiden voyage. The ship was steaming at full speed across a calm sea. Harold Bride was quite pleased with himself at having landed a job on such a magnificent new ship. After all, he was only twenty-two years old and had just nine months' experience at operating a "wireless set," as a ship's radio was then called. As he entered the bridge area, he could see one of the crewmen standing behind the ship's wheel steering her course toward New York.

Captain Smith was on duty in the bridge, so Bride handed the message to him. "It's from the *Caronia,* sir. She's reporting icebergs and pack ice ahead." The captain thanked him, read the message, and then posted it on the bulletin board for other officers on watch to read. On his way back to the radio room, Bride thought the captain had seemed quite unconcerned by the message. But then again, he had been told that it was not unusual to have ice floating in the sea lanes during an April crossing. Besides, what danger could a few pieces of ice present to an unsinkable ship?

Elsewhere on board, passengers relaxed on deck chairs, reading or taking naps. Some played cards, some wrote letters, while others chatted with friends. As it was Sunday, church services had been held in the morning, the first-class service led by Captain Smith. Jack Thayer spent most of the day walking about the decks getting some fresh air with his parents.

Two more ice warnings were received from nearby ships around lunch time. In the chaos of the radio room, Harold Bride only had time to take one of them to the bridge. The rest of the day passed quietly. Then, in the late afternoon, the temperature began to drop rapidly. Darkness approached as the bugle call announced dinner.

Jack Thayer's parents had been invited to a special dinner for Captain Smith, so Jack ate alone in the first-class dining room. After dinner, as he was having a cup of coffee, he was joined by Milton Long, another passenger going home to the States. Long was older than Jack, but in the easy-going atmosphere of shipboard travel, they struck up a conversation and talked together for an hour or so.

At 7:30 P.M., the radio room received three more warnings of ice about fifty miles ahead. One of them was from the steamer *Californian* reporting three large icebergs. Harold Bride took this message up to the bridge, and it was again politely received. Captain Smith was attending the dinner party being held for him when the warning was delivered. He never got to see it. Then, around 9:00 P.M., the captain excused himself and went up to the bridge. He and his officers talked about how difficult it was to spot icebergs on a calm, clear, moonless night like this with no wind to kick up white surf around them. Before going to bed, the captain ordered the lookouts to keep a sharp watch for ice.

After trading travel stories with Milton Long, Jack Thayer put on his coat and walked around the deck. "It had become very much colder," he said later. "It was a brilliant, starry night. There was no moon, and I have never seen the stars shine brighter . . . sparkling like diamonds. . . . It was the kind of night that made one feel glad to be alive." At eleven o'clock, he went below to his cabin, put on his pajamas, and got ready for bed.

In the radio room, Harold Bride was exhausted. The two operators were expected to keep the radio working twenty-four hours a day, and Bride lay down to take a much-needed nap. Phillips was so busy with the passenger messages that he actually brushed off the final ice warning of the night. It was from the *Californian*. Trapped in a field of ice, she had stopped for the night about nineteen miles north of the *Titanic*. She was so close that the message literally blasted in Phillips's ears. Annoyed by the loud interruption, he cut off the *Californian*'s radio operator with the words, "Shut up, shut up. I'm busy."

ACTIVE READER

QUESTION What warning did the *Californian* send the *Titanic*?

The radio room had received a total of seven ice warning messages in one day. It was quite clear that floating icebergs lay ahead of the *Titanic*.

High up in the crow's nest on the forward mast, Fred Fleet had passed a quiet watch. It was now 11:40 P.M., and he and his fellow lookout were waiting to be relieved so they could head below, perhaps for a hot drink before hopping into their warm bunks. The sea was dead calm. The air was bitterly cold.

Suddenly, Fleet saw something. A huge, dark shape loomed out of the night directly ahead of the *Titanic*. An iceberg! He quickly sounded the alarm bell three times and picked up the telephone.

"What did you see?" asked the duty officer.

"Iceberg right ahead," replied Fleet.

Immediately, the officer on the bridge

ordered the wheel turned as far as it would go. The engine room was told to reverse the engines, while a button was pushed to close the doors to the watertight compartments in the bottom of the ship.

The lookouts in the crow's nest braced themselves for a collision. Slowly the ship started to turn. It looked as though they would miss it. But it was too late. They had avoided a head-on crash, but the iceberg had struck a glancing blow along the *Titanic*'s starboard bow. Several tons of ice fell on the ship's decks

ACTIVE READER

CLARIFY Why had the *Titanic* come to a stop?

as the iceberg brushed along the side of the ship and passed into the night. A few minutes later, the *Titanic* came to a stop.

Many of the passengers didn't know the ship had hit anything. Because it was so cold, almost everyone was inside, and most people had already gone to bed. Ruth Becker and her mother were awakened by the dead silence.

Illustration by Ken Marschall, from *Inside the Titanic*, a Loewe/Madison Press Book. Copyright © 1997 Ken Marschall.

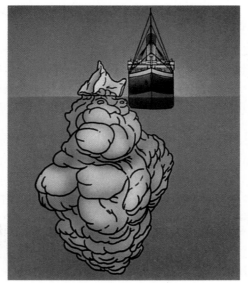

They could no longer hear the soothing hum of the vibrating engines from below. Jack Thayer was about to step into bed when he felt himself sway ever so slightly. The engines stopped. He was startled by the sudden quiet.

Sensing trouble, Ruth's mother looked out of the door of their second-class cabin and asked a steward[7] what had happened. He told her that nothing was the matter, so Mrs. Becker went back to bed. But as she lay there, she couldn't help feeling that something was very wrong.

Jack heard running feet and voices in the hallway outside his first-class cabin. "I hurried into my heavy overcoat and drew on my slippers. All excited, but not thinking anything serious had occurred, I called in to my father and mother that I was going up on deck to see the fun."

On deck, Jack watched some third-class passengers playing with the ice that had landed on the forward deck as the iceberg had brushed by. Some people were throwing chunks at each other, while a few skidded about playing football with pieces of ice.

Down in the very bottom of the ship, things were very different. When the iceberg had struck, there had been a noise like a big gun going off in one of the boiler rooms. A couple of stokers[8] had been immediately hit by a jet of icy water. The noise and the shock of cold water had sent them running for safety.

Twenty minutes after the crash, things looked very bad indeed to Captain Smith. He and the ship's builder, Thomas Andrews, had made a rapid tour below decks to inspect the damage. The mail room was filling up with water, and sacks of mail were floating about. Water was also pouring into some of the

---

7. **steward:** a worker on a ship who attends to the needs of the passengers.
8. **stokers:** workers who tended the boilers that powered steamships.

forward holds and two of the boiler rooms.

Captain Smith knew that the *Titanic*'s hull was divided into a number of watertight compartments. She had been designed so that she could still float if only the first four compartments were flooded, but not any more than that. But water was pouring into the first five compartments. And when the water filled them, it would spill over into the next compartment. One by one all the remaining compartments would flood, and the ship would eventually sink. Andrews told the captain that the ship could last an hour, an hour and a half at the most.

Harold Bride had just awakened in the radio room when Captain Smith stuck his head in the door. "Send the call for assistance," he ordered.

"What call should I send?" Phillips asked.

"The regulation international call for help. Just that." Then the captain was gone. Phillips began to send the Morse code "CQD" distress call, flashing away and joking as he did it. After all, they knew the ship was unsinkable.

Five minutes later, the captain was back. "What are you sending?" he asked.

"CQD," Phillips answered. Then Bride cut in and suggested that they try the new SOS signal that was just coming into use. They began to send out the new international call for help—it was one of the first SOS calls ever sent out from a ship in distress.

Ruth and her family had stayed in their bunks for a good fifteen minutes or so after the room steward had told them nothing was wrong. But Ruth's mother couldn't stop

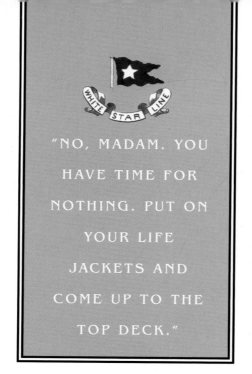

"NO, MADAM. YOU HAVE TIME FOR NOTHING. PUT ON YOUR LIFE JACKETS AND COME UP TO THE TOP DECK."

worrying as she heard the sound of running feet and shouting voices in the hallway. Poking her head out of the cabin, she found a steward and asked what the matter was.

"Put on your things and come at once," said the steward.

"Do we have time to dress?" she asked.

"No, madam. You have time for nothing. Put on your life jackets and come up to the top deck."

Ruth helped her mother dress the children quickly. But they only had time to throw their coats over their nightgowns and put on their shoes and stockings. In their rush, they forgot to put on their life jackets.

Just after midnight, Captain Smith ordered the lifeboats uncovered. The ship's squash court, which was thirty-two feet above the keel, was now completely flooded. Jack Thayer and his father came into the first-class lounge to try to find out exactly what the matter was. When Thomas Andrews, the ship's builder, passed by, Mr. Thayer asked him what was going on. He replied in a low voice that the ship had not much more than an hour to live. Jack and his father couldn't believe their ears.

From the bridge of the *Titanic*, a ship's lights were observed not far away, possibly the *Californian*'s. Captain Smith then ordered white distress rockets fired to get the attention of the nearby ship. They burst high in the air with a loud boom and a shower of stars. But the rockets made no difference. The mystery ship in the distance never answered.

In the radio room, Bride and Phillips now knew how serious the accident was and were

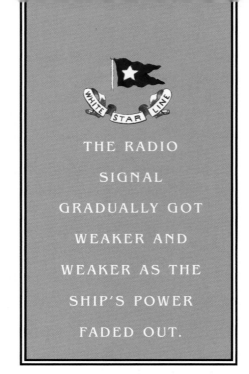

THE RADIO SIGNAL GRADUALLY GOT WEAKER AND WEAKER AS THE SHIP'S POWER FADED OUT.

feverishly sending out calls for help. A number of ships heard and responded to their calls, but most were too far away to come to the rescue in time. The closest ship they had been able to reach was the *Carpathia,* about fifty-eight miles away. Immediately, the *Carpathia* reported that she was racing full steam to the rescue. But could she get there in time?

Not far away, the radio operator of the *Californian* had gone to bed for the night and turned off his radio. Several officers and crewmen on the deck of the *Californian* saw rockets in the distance and reported them to their captain. The captain told them to try to contact the ship with a Morse lamp. But they received no answer to their flashed calls. No one thought to wake up the radio operator.

On board the *Titanic,* almost an hour after the crash, most of the passengers still did not realize the seriousness of the situation. But Captain Smith was a very worried man. He knew that the *Titanic* only carried lifeboats for barely half the estimated twenty-two hundred people on board. He would have to make sure his officers kept order to avoid any panic among the passengers. At 12:30 Captain Smith gave the orders to start loading the lifeboats—women and children first. Even though the *Titanic* was by now quite noticeably down at the bow and listing slightly to one side, many passengers still didn't want to leave the huge, brightly lit ship. The ship's band added to a kind of party feeling as the musicians played lively tunes.

About 12:45 the first lifeboat was lowered. It could carry sixty-five people, but left with only twenty-eight aboard. Indeed, many of the first boats to leave were half empty. Ruth Becker noticed that there was no panic among the crowds of passengers milling about on the decks. "Everything was calm, everybody was orderly." But the night air was now biting cold. Ruth's mother told her to go back to their cabin to get some blankets. Ruth hurried down to the cabin and came back with several blankets in her arms. The Beckers walked toward one of the lifeboats, and a sailor picked up Ruth's brother and sister and placed them in the boat.

"That's all for this boat," he called out. "Lower away!"

"Please, those are my children!" cried Ruth's mother. "Let me go with them!"

The sailor allowed Mrs. Becker to step into the lifeboat with her two children. She then called back to Ruth to get into another lifeboat. Ruth went to the next boat and asked the officer if she could get in. He said, "Sure," picked her up, and dumped her in.

Boat No. 13 was so crowded that Ruth had to stand up. Foot by foot it was lowered down the steep side of the massive ship. The new

ACTIVE READER

CLARIFY Why aren't any men getting in the lifeboats?

pulleys shrieked as the ropes passed through them, creaking under the weight of the boat and its load of sixty-four people. After landing in the water, Ruth's lifeboat began to drift. Suddenly Ruth saw another lifeboat coming down right on top of them! Fearing for their lives, the men in charge of her boat shouted, "Stop!" to the sailors up on the deck. But the noise was so great that nobody noticed. The second lifeboat kept coming down, so close that they could actually touch the bottom of it. All of a sudden, one of the men in Ruth's boat jumped up, pulled out a knife, and cut them free of their lowering ropes. Ruth's boat pushed away from the *Titanic* just as boat No. 15 hit the water inches away from them.

Below, in the third-class decks of the ship, there was much more confusion and alarm. Most of these passengers had not yet been able to get above decks. Some of those who did finally make it out had to break down the barriers between third and first class.

By 1:30 the bow was well down, and people were beginning to notice the slant of the decks. In the radio room, Bride and Phillips were still desperately sending out calls for help: "We are sinking fast . . . women and children in boats.

The last lifeboats pull away from the sinking *Titanic*, leaving approximately 1,500 people on board.
Illustration by Ken Marschall, from *Inside the Titanic*, a Loewe/Madison Press Book.
Copyright © 1997 Ken Marschall.

We cannot last much longer." The radio signal gradually got weaker and weaker as the ship's power faded out. Out on the decks, most passengers now began to move toward the stern area, which was slowly lifting out of the water.

By 2:05 there were still over 1,500 people left on the sinking ship. All the lifeboats were now away, and a strange stillness took hold. People stood quietly on the upper decks, bunching together for warmth, trying to keep away from the side of the tilting ship.

Captain Smith now made his way to the radio room and told Harold Bride and Jack Phillips to save themselves. "Men, you have done your full duty," he told them. "You can do no more. Abandon your cabin. Now it's every man for himself." Phillips kept working the radio, hanging on until the very last moment. Suddenly Bride heard water gurgling up the deck outside the radio room. Phillips heard it, too, and cried, "Come on, let's clear out."

Near the stern, Father Thomas Byles had heard confession and given absolution[9] to over one hundred passengers. Playing to the very end, the members of the ship's brave band finally had to put down their instruments and try to save themselves. In desperation, some of the passengers and crew began to jump overboard as the water crept up the slant of the deck.

A crowded lifeboat from the *Titanic* is hoisted aboard the *Carpathia*. UPI/Bettmann.

Jack Thayer stood with his friend Milton Long at the railing to keep away from the crowds. He had become separated from his father in the confusion on deck. Now Jack and his friend heard muffled thuds and explosions deep within the ship. Suddenly the *Titanic* began to slide into the water. The water rushed up at them. Thayer and Long quickly said goodbye and good luck to each other. Then they both jumped.

As he hit the water, Jack Thayer was sucked down. "The cold was terrific. The shock of the water took the breath out of my lungs. Down and down I went, spinning in all directions." When he finally surfaced, gasping for air and numbed by the water, the ship was about forty feet away from him. His friend Milton Long was nowhere to be seen. Jack would never see him again.

Jack Thayer was lucky. As he struggled in the water, his hand came to rest on an overturned lifeboat. He grabbed hold and hung on, barely managing to pull himself up out of the water. Harold Bride had been washed overboard and now also clung to this same boat.

Both Jack and Harold witnessed the mighty ship's last desperate moments. "We could see groups of . . . people aboard, clinging in clusters or bunches, like swarming bees; only to fall in masses, pairs, or singly, as the great part of the ship . . . rose into the sky. . . ." said Thayer. "I looked upwards—we were

9. **heard confession . . . absolution:** Father Byles has conducted a Roman Catholic religious practice in which a priest listens to people confess their sins and then declares them forgiven.

right under the three enormous propellers. For an instant, I thought they were sure to come right down on top of us. Then . . . she slid quietly away from us into the sea."

Out in the safety of her lifeboat, Ruth Becker also witnessed the end of the *Titanic*. "I could look back and see this ship, and the decks were just lined with people looking over. Finally, as the *Titanic* sank faster, the lights died out. You could just see the stern remaining in an upright position for a couple of minutes. Then . . . it disappeared."

Then, as Ruth recalled, "there fell upon the ear the most terrible noise that human beings ever listened to—the cries of hundreds of people struggling in the icy cold water, crying

Aboard the *Carpathia*, the only surviving honeymoon couple, Mr. and Mrs. George Harder, talk to Mrs. Hays, who lost her husband. The Illustrated London News Picture Library.

for help with a cry we knew could not be answered." In Thayer's words, they became "a long continuous wailing chant." Before long this ghastly wailing stopped, as the freezing water took its <u>toll</u>.

Jack Thayer and Harold Bride and a number of other survivors clung to their overturned lifeboat, inches away from an icy death in the North Atlantic. Numb from the cold and not daring to move in case the boat sank under their weight, they prayed and waited for help. Then, as the first light of dawn crept on the horizon, a rocket was seen in the distance. The *Carpathia* had come to their rescue. ❖

Connect to the Literature

1. **What Do You Think?** What was your reaction when you finished the selection?

Comprehension Check
- Why was Captain Smith given command of the *Titanic?*
- What kinds of accommodations did the ship have for wealthy passengers?
- How were the survivors of the *Titanic* finally rescued?

Think Critically

2. How would you describe the mood of the passengers and crew when the *Titanic* first set sail for New York on April 10, 1912?

   Think About:
   - "the Unsinkable Ship"
   - "Everything was new. New!"
   - the ship's band playing for the wealthiest people in the world

3. Did Captain Smith's response to the first reports of icebergs sent to the *Titanic* by the *California* seem appropriate? Explain.

4. What was your opinion of the behavior of the passengers and crew while the lifeboats were being loaded? Could more lives have been saved if evacuation efforts had been conducted differently?

5. **ACTIVE READING** | **FACT AND OPINION** Review the notes you took in your **READER'S NOTEBOOK.** How did Ballard's use of fact and opinion influence your reaction to his narration of the disaster?

Extend Interpretations

6. **What If?** *Exploring the* Titanic is a piece of literary nonfiction—that is, it provides factual information even though it reads like a piece of fiction. What if Ballard had chosen to write informative nonfiction, providing only the facts of the disaster without such devices as dialogue or characterization? Would the information have been more compelling for you, or not?

Literary Analysis

SETTING AND SOURCES Robert D. Ballard brings to life the setting of the early twentieth century by describing what was aboard the *Titanic*. In addition, the **primary sources** create an accurate picture of the *Titanic* in its last moments. Ballard uses photographs of the *Titanic* and quotations from eyewitness, like the following:

"We could see groups of . . . people aboard, clinging in clusters or bunches, like swarming bees; only to fall in masses, pairs, or singly, as the great part of the ship . . . rose into the sky."

The **secondary sources,** such as paintings and a newspaper article, lend credibility to the story. These sources also help readers follow the description of the crash and its devastating result.

Paired Activity After you have read the story, go back, with a partner, and find specific setting details. Look for primary and secondary sources such as photos, diagrams, newspaper articles, or pictures that help you see or better understand the setting.

Setting Detail	Primary Source	Secondary Source
"Daylight shone through the huge glass dome over the Grand Stair-case." (p. 662)	Photograph of the actual Olympic Staircase (p. 661)	
"The *Titanic* was like a big floating layer cake." (p. 663)		Cross-section diagram of the *Titanic* (p. 663)

CHOICES and CHALLENGES

Writing

Fact and Opinion Think of an event that actually happened and write a page or more of literary nonfiction describing it. You might write about a visit to a relative, a news item, or an everyday occurrence. Include both fact and opinion to make your writing believable and interesting. When finished, trade papers with a classmate. In pencil, circle the facts you find, and underline the opinions. Some other things to think about are: What made the writing believable? What made it interesting? Was there a definite setting? Place your work in your **Working Portfolio.**

Writing Handbook
See p. R45: Narrative Writing.

Speaking & Listening

Film Critic Watch the video clip from *A Night to Remember.* After you watch, analyze the effect the images and sound have on you as a viewer. What do you think the filmmakers were trying to achieve? In your opinion, did they succeed? With a group, discuss why or why not.

VIDEO: Literature in Performance

"A Night to Remember"

Research & Technology

SCIENCE

The exploration of the wreckage of the *Titanic* solved many mysteries about the ship's last hours. Use library and Internet resources to find out about other sunken ships that have been explored by archaeologists.

Reading for INFORMATION
Begin your research by reading "The Lives of *La Belle,*" page 675, about a sunken ship that is being excavated in Matagorda Bay on the Texas Gulf Coast.

Research and Technology Handbook
See p. R110: Getting Information Electronically.

Vocabulary

STANDARDIZED TEST PRACTICE

Choose the word or group of words that means the same, or nearly the same, as the underlined Word to Know.

1. Elegant <u>accommodations</u>
   - **A** clothes
   - **B** lodging
   - **C** manners
   - **D** accessories
2. <u>Eerie</u> sounds
   - **J** echoing
   - **K** deafening
   - **L** weird
   - **M** random
3. To work <u>feverishly</u>
   - **A** steadily
   - **B** carelessly
   - **C** frantically
   - **D** sickly
4. A disturbing <u>prophecy</u>
   - **J** prediction
   - **K** accident
   - **L** party
   - **M** performance
5. <u>Dazzled</u> spectators
   - **A** grumpy
   - **B** concerned
   - **C** desperate
   - **D** awestruck
6. To wait <u>indefinitely</u>
   - **J** patiently
   - **K** endlessly
   - **L** silently
   - **M** anxiously
7. A horrible <u>toll</u>
   - **A** loss
   - **B** collision
   - **C** explosion
   - **D** panic
8. A final <u>tribute</u>
   - **J** response
   - **K** honor
   - **L** triumph
   - **M** trial
9. To <u>list</u> to one side
   - **A** write
   - **B** slip
   - **C** show
   - **D** lean
10. An exciting <u>novelty</u>
    - **J** invention
    - **K** discussion
    - **L** solution
    - **M** occasion

Vocabulary Handbook
See p. R26: Synonyms.

Grammar in Context: Independent Clauses and Compound Sentences

To make the relationship between ideas clear, Robert D. Ballard often expresses two closely connected ideas in one compound sentence.

> The mail room was filling up with water, and sacks of mail were floating about.

A **compound sentence** contains two or more independent clauses. A **clause** is a group of words containing a **verb** and its **subject.** An independent clause is one that can stand by itself as a sentence. Independent clauses can be joined to form a compound sentence by using a comma and a **coordinating conjunction** (such as *and, but,* or *or*). When you combine sentences, be sure to choose the coordinating conjunction that expresses the correct relationship between the clauses.

> They had avoided a head-on crash, but the iceberg had struck a glancing blow along the *Titanic*'s starboard bow.

WRITING EXERCISE Rewrite each pair of sentences as a compound sentence.

Example: *Original* The first-class passengers had large cabins. The third-class passengers were packed into small ones.

Rewritten The first-class passengers had large cabins, <u>but</u> the third-class passengers were packed into small ones.

1. She was 882 feet long. Her funnels were enormous.
2. Jack heard explosions inside the ship. The *Titanic* began to slide into the water.
3. There was no moon. The stars shone brightly.

Connect to the Literature Find two other compound sentences in *Exploring the* Titanic. Why did the author link the ideas?

Grammar Handbook
See p. R84: Phrases and Clauses.

Robert D. Ballard
born 1942

"I want to recruit people to study science, just as a coach recruits basketball players."

To the Sea Robert Ballard has been fascinated by the sea since his childhood, when he explored beaches and read about famous sailors such as Captain Cook and Admiral Byrd. As an adult, Ballard helped pay for his education in oceanography by training dolphins at a marine park. Eventually, he joined the staff of the Woods Hole Oceanographic Institute in Massachusetts.

Exploring the *Titanic* Ballard began his search for the *Titanic* using remote-controlled underwater robots. On September 1, 1985, a robotic vessel recorded the first view of the *Titanic* in 73 years.

Recruiting Scientists Ballard, the explorer, has now set his sights on inspiring children to learn. "We need to declare war on ignorance, and the only way is through education," he says. "I want to recruit people to study science, just as a coach recruits basketball players." Ballard's other works include *Exploring Our Living Planet, Discovery of the* Titanic, *The Discovery of the* Bismarck, and *The Lost Wreck of the* Isis.

Source: *The Dallas Morning News*

Living·Arts

①

The Lives of La Belle

SPECIAL REPORT

by Bryan Woolley

*P*ALACIOS, Texas— He may have been C. Barange. That's the name engraved on the pewter bowl the archaeologists found beside his skeleton in November.

Near his skeleton the archaeologists found a small wooden cask that once contained wine or brandy, a pair of shoes, some buttons, a ring with a red gemstone setting and a leather wallet containing two wooden combs, one to groom his hair and the other, finer toothed one to remove lice from it.

The dead man and his tiny collection of belongings had lain in the mud since January 1686, when the small frigate they were on sank to the bottom of Matagorda Bay, a site about 80 miles east of what later became Corpus Christi, Texas. The ship was named *La Belle* and was owned by the French explorer René-Robert Cavelier, Sieur de La Salle.

The outline of *La Belle*'s hull begins to emerge from the floor of Matagorda Bay.

Excavating a 300-year-old shipwreck connects the explorers who sailed it and the scientists who found it.

Reading for Information

What does it take to start a town? Scientists are now studying what the French explorer La Salle brought to start a colony in America—thanks to the discovery of one of his ships, *La Belle*, which sank off the coast of Texas in the 17th century.

SQ3R

To read nonfiction and remember the information, use the study strategy SQ3R: Scan, Question, Read, Recite, Review.

YOUR TURN *Use SQ3R to answer the questions that follow.*

① **Scan** the article's text organizers. Note the title, subtitles, photos, and captions. What do you think the article is about?

Key Standard
R2.1 Understand differences between various categories of informational materials (such as textbooks, newspapers, and manuals).
Other Standards **R2.2, W2.3, W2.5**

The Expedition

2 In 1682, La Salle had explored the entire length of the Mississippi River and claimed its watershed—almost half the present United States—for King Louis XIV of France. He then convinced the king that a colony at the southern end of the great river would protect French lands from France's enemy, the Spanish, whose vast empire lay to the west and south.

King Louis gave La Salle four ships. According to the journal of Henri Joutel, a lieutenant of La Salle's who was eventually one of a handful of survivors, misfortune dogged the expedition from its beginning. First, Spanish pirates captured one of the ships in the Caribbean. Then, because of the primitive navigational methods of his time and even worse maps, La Salle overshot the mouth of the Mississippi, which is near present-day New Orleans. On February 18, 1685, he wound up in Matagorda Bay, halfway between present-day Galveston and Corpus Christi. He thought he had arrived where he wanted to go.

On February 29, *L'Amiable*, the largest of the three remaining ships, which carried many of the supplies needed to found the colony, ran aground and broke apart. Most of the supplies were lost. On March 12, one of the last two ships departed for France with a message to the king that La Salle had arrived at the mouth

Dolphin-shaped handles on a cannon.

of the Mississippi but needed more supplies. The king received La Salle's message but rejected it, complaining that he already had spent more on La Salle than Ferdinand and Isabella had on Columbus.

Meanwhile, back in Texas, the remaining 180 colonists were building a camp they called Fort St. Louis, and La Salle went roaming across the countryside, looking for the Mississippi. On March 15 of the next year, 1686, La Salle returned to learn that *La Belle*, his last ship, had run aground with the remainder of the colony's supplies and trade goods.

Realizing that he was cut off from France and that his dream of building a colony and making a fortune in the New World was doomed, La Salle continued in his searches for the Mississippi. He never found the river. On March 20, 1687, somewhere in East Texas, some of La Salle's own men murdered him.

In 1688, six ragged survivors of the expedition arrived in Canada and eventually returned to France, carrying their journals of the adventure. When they had left Fort St. Louis, only 20 of the colonists were still alive. Some of those died of smallpox. Native Americans killed the rest, except for a few children who were taken captive. They were rescued later by the Spanish.

The Project to Raise La Belle

Archaeologists from all over the country have made their way to the big blue warehouse on the Palacios waterfront on Matagorda Bay that serves as the project headquarters. The ground floor houses the Texas Historical Commission field office and a makeshift lab. There, the recovered artifacts are stabilized and prepared for shipment to Texas A&M, where they're cleaned and preserved for eventual public display.

At 6:30 each morning, about a dozen of the warehouse residents board the Texas Historical Commission's boat *Anomaly* for the hour-long ride to the cofferdam that surrounds the wrecked ship, 15 miles from shore. The cofferdam consists of two concentric circular walls of interlocking iron panels driven deep into the bay floor, 12 feet below the water's surface. The space between the two walls is filled with gravel. The water has been pumped out of the doughnut-shaped dam.

For eight hours a day, seven days a week, the archaeologists labor over the hulk on the muddy bay floor. With great care, they lift objects from

Reading for Information *continued*

❷ After scanning, **question** what you expect to find out when you read. Make a chart like the one below to begin recording your questions. Remember, no question is too simple. For example, you might ask, What else is La Salle known for?

Questions	Answers
What else is La Salle known for?	
What is watershed?	

❸ Make sure you understand a passage before moving to the next one. **Read** this section carefully. What is a cofferdam? You may need to consult a dictionary or reference source. As you read the entire selection, look for answers to questions you have formed.

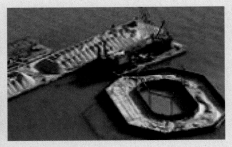

Stages in the construction of the cofferdam around the sunken remains of *La Belle*.

the casks in which they were packed more than three centuries ago, mark their location, label them and put them into containers for the trip to shore. About 4:30 P.M. they board the *Anomaly* again, motor back to their dock, and unload the day's finds.

In the lab, Kris Taylor, one of the scientists who have been excavating *La Belle*, shows off some of the rescued artifacts: navigator's dividers, used for plotting courses on charts; buckles from clothing, some of them intricately engraved; a wooden box containing a set of copper cauldrons,

a ladle, two candlesticks, a colander, and a pot; two seals for impressing wax images onto letters; chess and backgammon pieces; clay pipe stems; a brass writing implement with a screw top, amazingly similar to a modern fountain pen.

Besides such personal items, the archaeologists have recovered tons of lead shot and cannonballs and dozens of barrels and boxes still intact and neatly stacked inside the ship's hull, full of glass beads made in Venice, bronze hewn bells, brass straight pins, bronze finger rings, and iron ax heads, all apparently intended for trade with the Native Americans.

"This ship is a sort of colony kit," says Dr. Jim Bruseth, the project director. "Many colonies were established in the New World, but the stuff the people brought with them is gone. What we have on *La Belle* is a good inventory of what a country in Europe felt was important for establishing a colony in the New World. And the final pivot of LaSalle's dream, the straw that broke the camel's back, was the sinking of the ship which we've found." ❹

"People don't realize how important La Salle was," Dr. Bruseth adds. "If he had been successful, we might be speaking French today in Texas."

Reading for Information *continued*

❹ **Recite** the main ideas of the entire selection. Then write them down, using your own words. For example, what is the main idea in this paragraph? What are the supporting details?

Now review the whole article, checking to see how well you remembered the main ideas. You may be curious about something not included in the article. Suppose you want to know if the artifacts are still on display. How would you find the answer to that question?

Research & Technology
Activity Link: from *Exploring the* Titanic, p. 673. Research the discovery of a shipwreck other than *La Belle*. Use the study strategy SQ3R to read the articles you find. Then select one article, and write a summary of the main ideas.

Copper pots and a colander: supplies for the colony.

Last Cover

by PAUL ANNIXTER

Key Standard
W2.2 Write responses to literature that present interpretations that show careful reading and understanding of the text, and that support the interpretation with evidence from the selection. *Other Standards* R1.3, R3.1, R3.2, R3.6, W2.3, LC1.1, LC1.4, LS1.7

Connect to Your Life

Why do you think people develop strong ties with pets? What do pets offer their owners? What qualities does a good pet have? With a small group, make a word web listing them.

loyal

Qualities of a good pet

small

Build Background

SCIENCE

The red fox is the most common fox in the United States. Clever, quick, and gifted with keen hearing and a sharp sense of smell, a red fox makes an excellent hunter.

However, foxes are often hunted for their fur, for sport, or because their raids on chicken coops are a nuisance to farmers. In some fox hunts, like the one in this story, hunters on horseback use dogs to follow the scent of a fox. The dogs' barking reveals the fox's hiding place.

Fox Hunting, the Find, Currier & Ives. Scala/Art Resource, New York.

WORDS TO KNOW **Vocabulary Preview**

bleak	harried	predestined	wily
confound	invalid	sanction	
essence	passive	sanctuary	

Focus Your Reading

LITERARY ANALYSIS SETTING

The time and place in which a literary work occurs are called its **setting.** To understand place in a story, it is important to know such things as the region of the country; whether it is set in the city or a rural area; whether the geography is mountainous, swampy, or dry; and what kind of people live there (farmers, office workers, and so forth). Place is important to setting in fiction and nonfiction alike.

ACTIVE READING VISUALIZING

The process of forming a mental picture based on a written description is called **visualizing.** Good readers use the details writers supply to "see" the settings in their minds. As you read, use the details the author gives you to visualize the setting of "Last Cover."

📖 **READER'S NOTEBOOK.** Make two columns in your notebook. In the first, jot down some specific details from the story that describe setting. In the second, note the kind of mental picture you formed in your mind after reading these details.

Details From the Story	How I Picture Them
"The leafless woods were bleak and empty. . . ."	I picture a day with a gray sky and no leaves on the trees.

LAST COVER

by Paul Annixter

I'm not sure I can tell you what you want to know about my brother; but everything about the pet fox is important, so I'll tell all that from the beginning.

It goes back to a winter afternoon after I'd hunted the woods all day for a sign of our lost pet. I remember the way my mother looked up as I came into the kitchen. Without my speaking, she knew what had happened. For six hours I had walked, reading signs, looking for a delicate print in the damp soil or even a hair that might have told of a red fox passing that way—but I had found nothing.

"Did you go up in the foothills?" Mom asked.

I nodded. My face was stiff from held-back tears. My brother, Colin, who was going on twelve, got it all from one look at me and went into a heartbroken, almost silent, crying.

Three weeks before, Bandit, the pet fox Colin and I had raised from a tiny kit, had disappeared, and not even a rumor had been heard of him since.

Detail of illustration by Wendell Minor, from *Red Fox Running* by Eve Bunting. Illustration copyright ©1993 Wendell Minor. Reprinted by permission of Clarion Books/Houghton Mifflin Company. All rights reserved.

"He'd have had to go off soon anyway," Mom comforted. "A big, lolloping fellow like him, he's got to live his life same as us. But he may come back. That fox set a lot of store by you boys in spite of his wild ways."

"He set a lot of store by our food, anyway," Father said. He sat in a chair by the kitchen window mending a piece of harness. "We'll be seeing a lot more of that fellow, never fear. That fox learned to pine for table scraps and young chickens. He was getting to be an egg thief, too, and he's not likely to forget that."

"That was only pranking when he was little," Colin said desperately.

From the first, the tame fox had made tension in the family. It was Father who said we'd better name him Bandit, after he'd made away with his first young chicken.

"Maybe you know," Father said shortly. "But when an animal turns to egg sucking, he's usually incurable. He'd better not come pranking around my chicken run again."

It was late February, and I remember the <u>bleak</u>, dead cold that had set in, cold that was a rare thing for our Carolina hills. Flocks of sparrows and snowbirds had appeared, to peck hungrily at all that the pigs and chickens didn't eat.

"This one's a killer," Father would say of a morning, looking out at the whitened barn roof. "This one will make the shoats[1] squeal."

A fire snapped all day in our cookstove and another in the stone fireplace in the living room, but still the farmhouse was never warm. The leafless woods were bleak and empty, and I spoke of that to Father when I came back from my search.

"It's always a sad time in the woods when the seven sleepers are under cover," he said.

"What sleepers are they?" I asked. Father was full of woods lore.

"Why, all the animals that have got sense enough to hole up and stay hid in weather like this. Let's see, how was it the old rhyme named them?

Surly bear and sooty bat,
Brown chuck and masked coon,
Chippy-munk and sly skunk,
And all the mouses
'Cept in men's houses.

"And man would have joined them and made it eight, Granther Yeary always said, if he'd had a little more sense."

"I was wondering if the red fox mightn't make it eight," Mom said.

Father shook his head. "Late winter's a high time for foxes. Time when they're out deviling, not sleeping."

My chest felt hollow. I wanted to cry like Colin over our lost fox, but at fourteen a boy doesn't cry. Colin had squatted down on the floor and got out his small hammer and nails to start another new frame for a new picture. Maybe then he'd make a drawing for the frame and be able to forget his misery. It had been that way with him since he was five.

I thought of the new dress Mom had brought home a few days before in a heavy cardboard box. That box cover would be fine for Colin to draw on. I spoke of it, and Mom's glance thanked me as she went to get it. She and I worried a lot about Colin. He was small for his age, delicate and blond, his hair much lighter and softer than mine, his eyes deep and wide and blue. He was often sick, and I knew the fear Mom had that he might be

---

1. **shoats** (shōts): young pigs.

WORDS
TO
KNOW **bleak** (blēk) *adj.* harsh and dreary

predestined. I'm just ordinary, like Father. I'm the sort of stuff that can take it—tough and strong—but Colin was always sort of special.

Mom lighted the lamp. Colin began cutting his white cardboard carefully, fitting it into his frame. Father's sharp glance turned on him now and again.

"There goes the boy making another frame before there's a picture for it," he said. "It's too much like cutting out a man's suit for a fellow that's, say, twelve years old. Who knows whether he'll grow into it?"

Mom was into him then, quick. "Not a single frame of Colin's has ever gone to waste. The boy has real talent, Sumter, and it's time you realized it."

"Of course he has," Father said. "All kids have 'em. But they get over 'em."

"It isn't the pox[2] we're talking of," Mom sniffed.

"In a way it is. Ever since you started talking up Colin's art, I've had an invalid for help around the place."

Father wasn't as hard as he made out, I knew, but he had to hold a balance against all Mom's frothing.[3] For him the thing was the land and all that pertained to it. I was following in Father's footsteps, true to form, but Colin threatened to break the family tradition with his leaning toward art, with Mom "aiding and abetting[4] him," as Father liked to put it. For the past two years she had had dreams of my brother becoming a real artist and going away to the city to study.

It wasn't that Father had no understanding of such things. I could remember, through the years, Colin lying on his stomach in the front room making pencil sketches, and how a good drawing would catch Father's eye halfway across the room, and how he would sometimes gather up two or three of them to study, frowning and muttering, one hand in his beard, while a great pride rose in Colin, and in me too. Most of Colin's drawings were of the woods and wild things, and there Father was a master critic. He made out to scorn what seemed to him a passive, "white-livered" interpretation of nature through brush and pencil instead of rod and rifle.

At supper that night Colin could scarcely eat. Ever since he'd been able to walk, my brother had had a growing love of wild things, but Bandit had been like his very own, a gift of the woods. One afternoon a year and a half before, Father and Laban Small had been running a vixen through the hills with their dogs. With the last of her strength the she-fox had made for her den, not far from our house. The dogs had overtaken her and killed her just before she reached it. When Father and Laban came up, they'd found Colin crouched nearby, holding her cub in his arms.

Father had been for killing the cub, which was still too young to shift for itself, but Colin's grief had brought Mom into it. We'd taken the young fox into the kitchen, all of us, except Father, gone a bit silly over the little thing. Colin had held it in his arms and fed it warm milk from a spoon.

"Watch out with all your soft ways," Father had warned, standing in the doorway. "You'll make too much of him. Remember, you can't make a dog out of a fox. Half of that little critter has to love, but the other half is a wild hunter. You boys will mean a whole lot to him

---

2. **pox:** chickenpox, a contagious disease causing skin eruptions.

3. **frothing** (frôth′ĭng): light, meaningless talking.

4. **aiding and abetting:** helping and encouraging.

while he's a kit, but there'll come a day when you won't mean a thing to him and he'll leave you shorn."[5]

For two weeks after that Colin had nursed the cub, weaning it from milk to bits of meat. For a year they were always together. The cub grew fast. It was soon following Colin and me about the barnyard. It turned out to be a patch fox, with a saddle of darker fur across its shoulders.

I haven't the words to tell you what the fox meant to us. It was far more wonderful owning him than owning any dog. There was something rare and secret like the spirit of the woods about him, and back of his calm, straw-gold eyes was the sense of a brain the equal of a man's. The fox became Colin's whole life.

Each day, going and coming from school, Colin and I took long side trips through the woods, looking for Bandit. Wild things' memories were short, we knew; we'd have to find him soon, or the old bond would be broken.

Ever since I was ten, I'd been allowed to hunt with Father, so I was good at reading signs. But, in a way, Colin knew more about the woods and wild things than Father or me. What came to me from long observation Colin seemed to know by instinct.

It was Colin who felt out, like an Indian, the stretch of woods where Bandit had his den, who found the first slim, small fox-print in the damp earth. And then, on an afternoon in March, we saw him. I remember the day well, the racing clouds, the wind rattling the tops of the pine trees and swaying the Spanish moss. Bandit had just come out of a clump of laurel; in the maze of leaves behind him we caught a glimpse of a slim red vixen, so we knew he had found a mate. She melted from sight like a shadow, but Bandit turned to watch us, his mouth open, his tongue lolling as he smiled his old foxy smile. On his thin chops, I saw a telltale chicken feather.

Colin moved silently forward, his movements so quiet and casual he seemed to be standing still. He called Bandit's name, and the fox held his ground, drawn to us with all his senses. For a few moments he let Colin actually put an arm about him. It was then I knew that he loved us still, for all of Father's warnings. He really loved us back, with a fierce, secret love no tame thing ever gave. But the urge of his life just then was toward his new mate. Suddenly, he whirled about and disappeared in the laurels.

Colin looked at me with glowing eyes. "We haven't really lost him, Stan. When he gets through with his spring sparking,[6] he may come back. But we've got to show ourselves to him a lot, so he won't forget."

"It's a go," I said.

"Promise not to say a word to Father," Colin said, and I agreed. For I knew by the chicken feather that Bandit had been up to no good.

A week later the woods were budding, and the thickets were rustling with all manner of wild things scurrying on the love scent. Colin managed to get a glimpse of Bandit every few days. He couldn't get close though, for the spring running was a lot more important to a fox than any human beings were.

Every now and then Colin got out his framed box cover and looked at it, but he never drew anything on it; he never even picked up his pencil. I remember wondering if

---

5. **shorn:** cut off, like hair; forsaken.
6. **spring sparking:** the springtime mating period.

Albert's Son (1959), Andrew Wyeth. Tempera on panel, 74 cm × 61.5 cm, Copyright © Andrew Wyeth. The National Museum of Contemporary Art, Oslo, Norway. Photo by Jacques Lathion, Nasjonalgalleriet.

what Father had said about framing a picture before you had one had spoiled something for him.

I was helping Father with the planting now, but Colin managed to be in the woods every day. By degrees, he learned Bandit's range, where he drank and rested and where he was likely to be according to the time of day. One day he told me how he had petted Bandit again and how they had walked together a long way in the woods. All this time we had kept his secret from Father.

As summer came on, Bandit began to live up to the prediction Father had made. Accustomed to human beings, he moved without fear about the scattered farms of the region, raiding barns and hen runs that other foxes wouldn't have dared go near. And he taught his wild mate to do the same. Almost every night they got into some poultry house, and by late June Bandit was not only killing chickens and ducks but feeding on eggs and young chicks whenever he got the chance.

Stories of his doings came to us from many sources, for he was still easily recognized by the dark patch on his shoulders. Many a farmer took a shot at him as he fled, and some of them set out on his trail with dogs, but they always returned home without even sighting him. Bandit was familiar with all the dogs in the region, and he knew a hundred tricks to confound them. He got a reputation that year beyond that of any fox our hills had known. His confidence grew, and he gave up wild hunting altogether and lived entirely off the poultry farmers. By September, the hill farmers banded together to hunt him down.

It was Father who brought home that news one night. All time-honored rules of the fox chase were to be broken in this hunt; if the dogs couldn't bring Bandit down, he was to be shot on sight. I was stricken and furious. I remember the misery of Colin's face in the lamplight. Father, who took pride in all the ritual of the hunt, had refused to be a party to such an affair, though in justice he could do nothing but sanction any sort of hunt, for Bandit, as old Sam Wetherwax put it, had been "purely getting in the Lord's hair."

The hunt began next morning, and it was the biggest turnout our hills had known. There were at least twenty mounted men in the party and as many dogs. Father and I were working in the lower field as they passed along the river road. Most of the hunters carried rifles, and they looked ugly.

Twice during the morning I went up to the house to find Colin, but he was nowhere around. As we worked, Father and I could follow the progress of the hunt by the distant hound music on the breeze. We could tell just where the hunters first caught sight of the fox and where Bandit was leading the dogs during the first hour. We knew as well as if we'd seen it how Bandit roused another fox along Turkey Branch and forced it to run for him and how the dogs swept after it for twenty minutes before they sensed their mistake.

Noon came, and Colin had not come in to eat. After dinner Father didn't go back to the

WORDS TO KNOW

confound (kən-found′) v. to bewilder; confuse
sanction (săngk′shən) v. to give approval for

field. He moped about, listening to the hound talk. He didn't like what was on any more than I did, and now and again I caught his smile of satisfaction when we heard the broken, angry notes of the hunting horn, telling that the dogs had lost the trail or had run another fox.

I was restless, and I went up into the hills in midafternoon. I ranged the woods for miles, thinking all the time of Colin. Time lost all meaning for me, and the short day was nearing an end when I heard the horn talking again, telling that the fox had put over another trick. All day he had deviled the dogs and mocked the hunters. This new trick and the coming night would work to save him. I was wildly glad as I moved down toward Turkey Branch and stood listening for a time by the deep, shaded pool where for years we boys had gone swimming, sailed boats, and dreamed summer dreams.

Suddenly, out of the corner of my eye, I saw the sharp ears and thin, pointed mask of a fox—in the water almost beneath me. It was Bandit, craftily submerged there, all but his head resting in the cool water of the pool and the shadow of the two big beeches that spread above it. He must have run forty miles or more since morning. And he must have hidden in this place before. His knowing, crafty mask blended perfectly with the shadows and a mass of drift and branches that had collected by the bank of the pool. He was so still that a pair of thrushes flew up from the spot as I came up, not knowing he was there.

The fox had put over another trick.

Bandit's bright, <u>harried</u> eyes were looking right at me. But I did not look at him direct. Some woods instinct, swifter than thought, kept me from it. So he and I met as in another world, indirectly, with feeling but without sign or greeting.

Suddenly I saw that Colin was standing almost beside me. Silently as a water snake, he had come out of the bushes and stood there. Our eyes met, and a quick and secret smile passed between us. It was a rare moment in which I really "met" my brother, when something of his <u>essence</u> flowed into me and I knew all of him. I've never lost it since. My eyes still turned from the fox, my heart pounding. I moved quietly away, and Colin moved with me. We whistled softly as we went, pretending to busy ourselves along the bank of the stream. There was magic in it, as if by will we wove a web of protection about the fox, a ring-pass-not that none might penetrate. It was so, too, we felt, in the brain of Bandit, and that doubled the charm. To us he was still our little pet that we had carried about in our arms on countless summer afternoons.

Two hundred yards upstream, we stopped beside slim, fresh tracks in the mud where Bandit had entered the branch. The tracks angled upstream. But in the water the <u>wily</u> creature had turned down.

We climbed the far bank to wait, and Colin told me how Bandit's secret had been his secret ever since an afternoon three months before,

WORDS
TO
KNOW

harried (hăr′ēd) *adj.* worried; distressed **harry** *v.*
essence (ĕs′əns) *n.* basic nature or spirit
wily (wī′lē) *adj.* crafty; sly

Beech Trees (1903), Gustav Klimt. Österreichische Galerie, Vienna, Austria. Erich Lessing/Art Resource, New York.

when he'd watched the fox swim downstream to hide in the deep pool. Today he'd waited on the bank, feeling that Bandit, hard pressed by the dogs, might again seek the pool for sanctuary.

We looked back once as we turned homeward. He still had not moved. We didn't know until later that he was killed that same night by a chance hunter, as he crept out from his hiding place.

That evening Colin worked a long time on his framed box cover that had lain about the house untouched all summer. He kept at it all the next day too. I had never seen him work so hard. I seemed to sense in the air the feeling he was putting into it, how he was believing his picture into being. It was evening before he finished it. Without a word he handed it to Father. Mom and I went and looked over his shoulder.

It was a delicate and intricate pencil drawing of the deep branch pool, and there was Bandit's head and watching, fear-filled eyes hiding there amid the leaves and shadows, woven craftily into the maze of twigs and branches, as if by nature's art itself. Hardly a fox there at all, but the place where he was— or should have been. I recognized it instantly, but Mom gave a sort of incredulous sniff.

"I'll declare," she said, "it's mazy as a puzzle. It just looks like a lot of sticks and leaves to me."

Long minutes of study passed before Father's eye picked out the picture's secret, as few men's could have done. I laid that to Father's being a born hunter. That was a picture that might have been done especially for him. In fact, I guess it was.

Finally he turned to Colin with his deep, slow smile. "So that's how Bandit fooled them all," he said. He sat holding the picture with a sort of tenderness for a long time, while we glowed in the warmth of the shared secret. That was Colin's moment. Colin's art stopped being a pox to Father right there. And later, when the time came for Colin to go to art school, it was Father who was his solid backer. ❖

THINKING *through* the LITERATURE

Connect to the Literature

1. What Do You Think? How do you feel about the ending of the story? Share your reaction with a partner.

Comprehension Check
- Why does Father disapprove of keeping Bandit as a pet?
- How does Bandit let Colin know that the fox trusts him?
- What picture does Colin draw at the end?

Think Critically

2. ACTIVE READING VISUALIZING

As you read "Last Cover," how did you visualize the setting? Review the notes you took in your ⬛ READER'S NOTEBOOK and compare them with those of a partner.

3. How would you account for Colin's strong attachment to Bandit?

> **Think About:**
> - Colin's first experiences with Bandit
> - how Colin feels about nature
> - how Colin relates to his family

4. Why do you think Colin leaves the framed box cover blank for the entire summer?

5. Why do you think Father doesn't participate in the hunt?

6. What do you think Stan has learned about Colin by the end of the story? What do you think Stan has learned about himself?

7. What do you think the title of this story means?

Extend Interpretations

8. Critic's Corner According to Tai Ling Bloomfield, a seventh-grade member of the student board, "It didn't seem fair that Bandit had to die." Do you agree? Explain.

9. COMPARING TEXTS How would you compare Colin and the painter lady in "The War of the Wall"? After you've read both stories, think about ways in which the stories are similar, and ways in which they are different.

Literary Analysis

SETTING The time and place a story occurs are its **setting.** Place refers to the geographical area, as well as to the customs, values, and beliefs of the people who live in the area. "Last Cover" is set in the woods and hills of the western Carolinas. It is a rural area, and all of the characters in the story live on small farms.

The place where a story is set can have an important influence on its **plot** and **characters.** Look at how Paul Annixter's description of nature helps to describe how Stan is feeling when Bandit is lost.

It was late February, and I remember the bleak, dead cold that had set in, cold that was a rare thing for our Carolina hills.

FLASHBACK An interruption in the action of a story to present a scene that took place at an earlier time is called a flashback. On page 683 there is a flashback, beginning with the words, "One afternoon a year and a half before. . . ." This narrates how Colin found Bandit. How does this flashback help you understand Colin and Stan's relationship to Bandit throughout the rest of the story?

Writing

Response to Literature People are touched by stories in different ways. Explaining what a story means to you is called your response, or interpretation. Write a response to the story "Last Cover." Think about things like Colin's effort to track Bandit, and how Colin's father reacted to his art. What was their relationship like and how did it change? Use examples from the text to help explain why you feel the way you do about the story. Place your interpretation in your **Working Portfolio.**

Writing Workshop
See p. 75: Basics in a Box.

Speaking & Listening

Readers Theater With a small group, rehearse a Readers Theater presentation of key episodes from this story. Select background music that is appropriate to the mood of each episode. Present your reading to the class. Ask the audience for feedback on your group's delivery of the scene. How did it impact your audience? Did it represent the story and characters the way your audience had envisioned?

Art Connection

Look at the painting *Albert's Son* by Andrew Wyeth on page 685. What does Wyeth want you to think about Albert's son? What details give you clues about the boy's personality? Does Albert's son look like your image of either Colin or Stan? Explain your interpretation.

Research & Technology

Red Fox Facts With a small group, create a visual display of pictures of red foxes and interesting facts about them. One member of the group might do library research. Another might visit a zoo or interview a wildlife conservationist. A third might search the Internet for information. A fourth might design and assemble the display.

INTERNET Research Starter
www.mcdougallittell.com

Vocabulary

EXERCISE: SYNONYMS Write the Word to Know that is most closely related in meaning to the underlined word or phrase in each sentence below.

1. Bandit found <u>protection</u> in his hiding place.
2. The boys' father did not <u>support</u> the idea of raising a fox as a pet.
3. Bandit proved himself to be a <u>clever</u> trickster.
4. The winter was <u>cheerless</u> and bitterly cold.
5. Colin's avoidance of chores led his father to compare him to a <u>sick, bedridden person</u>.
6. His mother thought that Colin might be fated, or <u>expected</u>, to die at an early age.
7. The fox was able to <u>confuse</u> the dogs during the hunt.
8. A person who was <u>lacking in spirit and force</u> would not have pleased Colin's father.
9. To understand Colin's <u>true character</u>, his father needed to understand his art.
10. The farmers were <u>irritated</u> by Bandit's constant attacks on their chickens.

WORDS TO KNOW				
bleak	essence	invalid	predestined	sanctuary
confound	harried	passive	sanction	wily

Grammar in Context: Adverb Clauses

Paul Annixter makes the sequence of events in "Last Cover" clear by using adverb clauses that express time.

> It was Father who said we'd better name him Bandit, after he'd made away with his first young chickens.

> Ever since he had been able to walk, my brother had had a growing love of wild things . . .

An **adverb clause** is a group of words that modifies a verb, adjective, or adverb. A special kind of adverb clause tells when an action occurs. These usually begin with a conjunction such as *after, as, as long as, as soon as, before, during, since, until, when, whenever,* and *while.*

Punctuation Tip: When the adverb clause comes at the beginning of the sentence, use a comma.

WRITING EXERCISE Combine each pair of sentences by making one of them an adverb clause that expresses time.

Example: *Original* Bandit disappeared. The trouble started.

Rewritten When Bandit disappeared, the trouble started.

1. We lost our pet fox. I wanted to cry.
2. Colin sketched pictures. Father would study two or three of them.
3. They brought the fox home. They crowded around it in the kitchen.
4. The woods were budding. Bandit found a mate.
5. Noon came. Colin had still not come in to eat.

Connect to the Literature Find another sentence with an adverb clause of time in "Last Cover."

Grammar Handbook
See p. R84: Phrases and Clauses.

Paul Annixter
1894–1985

"It was while proving up on the land that I began writing, mostly nature stories about the animals and elements I was up against."

Early Training Paul Annixter is the pen name of Howard A. Sturtzel. He was the author of more than 500 short stories. When he was 9, Sturtzel and his mother were left alone to care for themselves and Sturtzel's paralyzed grandmother. To support the family, Sturtzel sold newspapers and candy and later worked as a bellhop. When he was 16, he traveled across the United States and Canada, living the life of a hobo. Eventually, Sturtzel settled on a timber claim in northern Minnesota, where he lived alone for a year and a half and began to write.

Collaboration After attending college, Sturtzel married Jane Comfort, the daughter of his favorite writer and tutor, Will Livington Comfort. Using the pen names Paul and Jane Annixter, Sturtzel and his wife worked together to produce more than 20 novels for young people. "Where one may have a weakness," he said of himself and his wife, "the other is apt to have a strength."

AUTHOR ACTIVITY
Tales of Animals Check out one of Paul Annixter's collections of stories, such as *Pride of Lions,* from your library and read another of his stories. How do his descriptions of nature compare with those you read in "Last Cover"?

Building Vocabulary
Multiple-Meaning Words and Homonyms

Many English words have more than one meaning. **Multiple-meaning words** are ones that have the same origin but that have acquired additional meanings over time based on the original meaning.

Homonyms are words that are spelled and pronounced alike but that are different in origin and meaning.

Key Standard
R1.3 Use context clues (definition, example, restatement, contrast) to determine the meaning of unknown words.
Other Standard **R1.0**

> Three weeks before, Bandit, the pet fox Colin and I had raised from a tiny kit, had disappeared, and not even a rumor had been heard of him since.
> —Paul Annixter, "Last Cover"

Multiple-meaning word
- an animal kept as a companion
- to pat or caress

Homonym
- a young, furry animal
- a set of implements used for a specific purpose

Strategies for Building Vocabulary

Try the following strategies when you can't tell which meaning of a word is intended.

❶ Use Context Clues When you see a familiar word used in an unfamiliar way, look at the words around it to see if they offer clues to its meaning. What do you think is the meaning of *squash* in the following passage?

> On the lower decks, Jack discovered the squash court, the swimming pool, and the Turkish bath decorated like a room in a sultan's palace.
> —Robert D. Ballard, *Exploring the* Titanic

From the context, it is unlikely that *squash* has anything to do with food. Because a court is mentioned, it probably has to do with sports. *Squash* in this context means a game played with a racket and a rubber ball.

❷ Use a Dictionary If the familiar meaning of a word doesn't make sense and there are no helpful context clues, try looking up the word in a dictionary. Read through the definitions. Try each one in place of the word until you find one that makes sense. Read the following sentence: *They used the scales of the **bleak** to make artificial pearls.*

The usual meaning of *bleak* does not fit this sentence. From context, you could tell that *bleak* is something with scales. The dictionary shows two entries for *bleak,* the first with the expected meaning of "gloomy and somber." The second entry has the meaning "a small European freshwater fish." Because the words have different origins and two separate dictionary entries, we know that *bleak* is a homonym.

EXERCISE Use context clues or a dictionary to find the meaning of each underlined word.

1. The boys began to <u>pine</u> for the fox.
2. Their father did not take part in the hunt, but he did <u>sanction</u> it.
3. The hunters were going to get Bandit, no matter what, and they looked <u>ugly</u>.
4. The fox found <u>sanctuary</u> in a pond.
5. The *Titanic* came within a <u>yard</u> or two of another ship.
6. There were cars in the <u>hold</u>.
7. The lookout on the evening <u>watch</u> hadn't seen anything unusual.
8. As the *Titanic* took on more water, it began to <u>list</u>.
9. The ship's <u>stern</u> rose before the ship sank.
10. The death <u>toll</u> was extremely high.

from Barrio Boy

by Ernesto Galarza

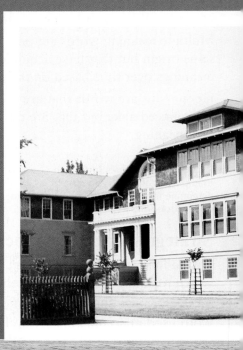

Right: Lincoln Grammar School, 4th and P Sts. Sacramento, 1909.
Far right: McKinley School, Miss Wilcox's class, circa 1914.

My mother and I walked south on Fifth Street one morning to the corner of Q Street and turned right. Half of the block was occupied by the Lincoln School. It was a three-story wooden building, with two wings that gave it the shape of a double-T connected by a central hall. It was a new building, painted yellow, with a shingled roof that was not like the red tile of the school in Mazatlán.[1] I noticed other differences, none of them very reassuring.

We walked up the wide staircase hand in hand and through the door, which closed by itself. A mechanical contraption screwed to the top shut it behind us quietly.

Up to this point the adventure of enrolling me in the school had been carefully rehearsed. Mrs. Dodson had told us how to find it and we had circled it several times on our walks. Friends in the *barrio*[2] explained that the director was called a principal, and that it was a lady and not a man. They assured us that there was always a person at the school who could speak Spanish.

Exactly as we had been told, there was a sign on the door in both Spanish and English: "Principal." We crossed the hall and entered the office of Miss Nettie Hopley.

Miss Hopley was at a roll-top desk to one side, sitting in a swivel chair that moved on wheels. There was a sofa against the opposite

---

1. **Mazatlán** (mä′ sət-län′): A seaport of western Mexico on the Pacific Ocean where Galarza had attended school.
2. **barrio** (bä′ rē-ō′): *Spanish,* an urban neighborhood, especially one where many Latinos live.

wall, flanked by two windows and a door that opened on a small balcony. Chairs were set around a table and framed pictures hung on the walls of a man with long white hair and another with a sad face and a black beard.

The principal half turned in the swivel chair to look at us over the pinch glasses crossed on the ridge of her nose. To do this she had to duck her head slightly as if she were about to step through a low doorway.

What Miss Hopley said to us we did not know but we saw in her eyes a warm welcome and when she took off her glasses and straightened up she smiled wholeheartedly, like Mrs. Dodson. We were, of course, saying nothing, only catching the friendliness of her voice and the sparkle in her eyes while she said words we did not understand. She signaled us

to the table. Almost tiptoeing across the office, I maneuvered myself to keep my mother between me and the gringo lady. In a matter of seconds I had to decide whether she was a possible friend or a menace. We sat down.

Then Miss Hopley did a formidable[3] thing. She stood up. Had she been standing when we entered she would have seemed tall. But rising from her chair she soared. And what she carried up and up with her was a buxom superstructure, firm shoulders, a straight sharp nose, full cheeks slightly molded by a curved line along the nostrils, thin lips that moved like steel springs, and a high forehead topped by hair gathered in a bun. Miss Hopley was

---

3. **formidable** (fôr′mĭ-də-bəl): inspiring admiration and wonder.

not a giant in body but when she mobilized it to a standing position she seemed a match for giants. I decided I liked her.

She strode to a door in the far corner of the office, opened it and called a name. A boy of about ten years appeared in the doorway. He sat down at one end of the table. He was brown like us, a plump kid with shiny black hair combed straight back, neat, cool, and faintly obnoxious.

Miss Hopley joined us with a large book and some papers in her hand. She, too, sat down and the questions and answers began by way of our interpreter. My name was Ernesto. My mother's name was Henriqueta. My birth certificate was in San Blas. Here was my last report card from the Escuela Municipal Numero 3 para Varones of Mazatlán, and so forth. Miss Hopley put things down in the book and my mother signed a card.

As long as the questions continued, Doña Henriqueta could stay and I was secure. Now that they were over, Miss Hopley saw her to the door, dismissed our interpreter and without further ado took me by the hand and strode down the hall to Miss Ryan's first grade.

Miss Ryan took me to a seat at the front of the room, into which I shrank—the better to survey her. She was, to skinny, somewhat runty me, of a withering[4] height when she patrolled the class. And when I least expected it, there she was, crouching by my desk, her blond radiant face level with mine, her voice patiently maneuvering me over the awful idiocies of the English language.

During the next few weeks,

Miss Ryan overcame my fears of tall, energetic teachers as she bent over my desk to help me with a word in the pre-primer. Step by step, she loosened me and my classmates from the safe anchorage of the desks for recitations at the blackboard and consultations at her desk. Frequently she burst into happy announcements to the whole class. "Ito can read a sentence," and small Japanese Ito, squint-eyed and shy, slowly read aloud while the class listened in wonder: "Come, Skipper, come. Come and run." The Korean, Portuguese, Italian, and Polish first graders had similar moments of glory, no less shining than mine the day I conquered "butterfly," which I had been persistently pronouncing in standard Spanish as boo-ter-flee. "Children," Miss Ryan called for attention. "Ernesto has learned how to pronounce butterfly!" And I proved it with a perfect imitation of Miss Ryan. From that celebrated success, I was soon able to match Ito's progress as a sentence reader with "Come, butterfly, come fly with me."

Like Ito and several other first graders who did not know English, I received private lessons from Miss Ryan in the closet, a narrow hall off the classroom with a door at each end. Next to one of these doors Miss Ryan placed a large chair for herself and a small one for me. Keeping an eye on the class through the open door she read with me about sheep in the meadow and a frightened chicken going to see the king, coaching me out of my phonetic ruts in words like *pasture, bow-wow-wow, hay,* and *pretty,* which to my Mexican ear and eye had so many unnecessary sounds and letters. She made me watch her lips and then close my eyes as she repeated words I found hard to read. When we came to know each other better, I tried interrupting to tell Miss Ryan how we said it in Spanish. It didn't work. She only said "oh" and went on with *pasture,*

---

4. **withering** (wĭth′ ər-ĭng): rendering speechless.

Miss Ryan called for attention. "Ernesto has learned how to pronounce butterfly!"

Classroom (1910).

bow-wow-wow, and *pretty.* It was as if in that closet we were both discovering together the secrets of the English language and grieving together over the tragedies of Bo-Peep. The main reason I was graduated with honors from the first grade was that I had fallen in love with Miss Ryan. Her radiant, no-nonsense character made us either afraid not to love her or love her so we would not be afraid, I am not sure which. It was not only that we sensed she was with it, but also that she was with us.

Like the first grade, the rest of the Lincoln School was a sampling of the lower part of town where many races made their home. My pals in the second grade were Kazushi, whose parents spoke only Japanese; Matti, a skinny Italian boy; and Manuel, a fat Portuguese who would never get into a fight but wrestled you to the ground and just sat on you. Our assortment of nationalities included Koreans, Yugoslavs, Poles, Irish, and home-grown Americans.

Miss Hopley and her teachers never let us forget why we were at Lincoln: for those who were alien, to become good Americans; for those who were so born, to accept the rest of us. Off the school grounds we traded the same insults we heard from our elders. On the playground we were sure to be marched up to the principal's office for calling someone a wop, a chink, a dago, or a greaser.[5] The school was not so much a melting pot as a griddle where Miss Hopley and her helpers warmed knowledge into us and roasted racial hatreds out of us.

At Lincoln, making us into Americans did not mean scrubbing away what made us originally foreign. The teachers called us as our parents did, or as close as they could pronounce our names in Spanish or Japanese. No one was ever scolded or punished for speaking in his native tongue on the playground. Matti told the class about his mother's down quilt, which she had made in Italy with the fine feathers of a thousand geese. Encarnación acted out how boys learned to fish in the Philippines. I astounded the third grade with the story of my travels on a stagecoach, which nobody else in the class had seen except in the museum at Sutter's Fort. After a visit to the Crocker Art Gallery and its collection of heroic paintings of the golden age of California, someone showed a silk scroll with a Chinese painting. Miss Hopley herself had a way of expressing wonder over these matters before a class, her eyes wide open until they popped slightly. It was easy for me to feel that becoming a proud American, as she said we should, did not mean feeling ashamed of being a Mexican. ❖

---

5. **wop,** etc.: offensive terms for Italians, Chinese, and Mexicans.

Ernesto Galarza
1905–1984

"What brought me and my family to the United States from Mexico also brought hundreds of thousands of others like us."

Planting and Harvesting Ernesto Galarza was born in a village in the mountains of the state of Nayarit, Mexico. Fleeing the upheavals of the Mexican Revolution, his family moved to Sacramento, California, where Galarza attended public school and worked alongside his family in the fields. Galarza, while still a school boy, became concerned about the Mexican agricultural workers' poor living conditions.

When a baby died and many people became sick from drinking polluted water, the workers asked Ernesto, who had learned English in school, to lead a protest. After graduation from high school Galarza continued his education, becoming the first Mexican American to earn a Ph.D. in Economics from Columbia University.

Teaching and Writing Galarza is the author of numerous books on social and economic topics geared toward the Mexican-American community. He became a labor organizer and, eventually, the executive secretary of the National Farm Labor Union.

In addition, Galarza was deeply committed to the education of young people. He and his wife, Mae, developed a bilingual education program that became a model for other programs. The scarcity of children's literature published in Spanish led Galarza to translate Mother Goose stories and write a series of children's stories called the *Colección Mini Libros. Barrio Boy*, published in 1971, grew out of stories he told his daughters. In 1976 Ernesto Galarza became the first Mexican American nominated for the Nobel Prize in literature.

Writing Workshop

Opinion Statement

Stating your beliefs . . .

From Reading to Writing Do you feel strongly about certain issues or events? Perhaps you think there should be better laws to protect wild animals like Bandit in "Last Cover." Or you might have your own ideas about how our natural environment should be preserved. From time to time, such issues will move you to speak out. Writing an **opinion statement** gives you a chance to express a clear position and back it up with reasons, facts, and other evidence.

For Your Portfolio

WRITING PROMPT Write an opinion statement about an issue that strongly interests you.

Purpose: To persuade or help others to understand an opinion

Audience: Your classmates and friends, members of your community

---

Basics in a Box

Opinion Statement at a Glance

Introduction	Presents the issue and states opinion
	Why I believe it
Body	Supporting Evidence · Supporting Evidence · Supporting Evidence
Conclusion	Summary of opinion

RUBRIC STANDARDS FOR WRITING

A successful opinion statement should

- clearly state the issue and your opinion of it in the introduction
- support your opinion with examples, facts, and statistics
- use language and details appropriate for your audience
- show clear reasoning
- sum up your opinion in the conclusion

Analyzing a Student Model

SPEAKING
See the Speaking and Listening Handbook, p. R100 for oral presentation tips.
OPPORTUNITY

Andrea Martinez
La Moille Middle School

Habitat Destruction

Did you know that over 140 animal species become extinct every day? It's true. In fact, in 1973 there were 109 species on the endangered list for America. As of 1999, that number jumped to 900. Why did this number jump so much in just 26 years? <u>The destruction of natural habitats by humans is one of the main causes of animal extinction. If we don't stop taking away the homes of our nonhuman neighbors, they will be gone.</u>

There are a few reasons why habitats are destroyed. <u>First, the human population has grown</u>. People are living longer, and more healthy children are being born. More people means more houses and apartments. This means more space is needed. People have moved into animal territory.

<u>Second, people move more often than they have in the past.</u> Different parts of the country attract large numbers of people because of good jobs or nice weather. When a large number of people move to the popular location, the city limits spread out, and animals' natural habitats are destroyed. Land is often gobbled up by developers who want to make money. Places that were peaceful are turned into huge resorts or condominium complexes. The building process and pollution hurt the ecology of the area. All creatures suffer as a result.

<u>Third, many businesses use natural resources such as trees and lakes.</u> This takes away habitats from animals. For many years, people didn't know the damaging effects of their actions. Now that we know how much harm we are doing, how can we let the problem continue?

RUBRIC
IN ACTION

❶ Dramatic statistics focus on the seriousness of the situation.
Another Option:
· Use a direct quotation.

❷ This sentence states the issue and the writer's position clearly.

❸ Within each of the first three paragraphs, the writer explains causes of the problem and then describes the effects of each.

Some people recognize that animal extinction is a problem, but they do nothing because they think it doesn't affect their own lives. They still have birds and squirrels in their back yards, so what's the difference? Well, the problem affects everyone. Imagine a future in which you can only see animals and insects in an encyclopedia. This is not the only negative effect. When a species becomes extinct, it affects the food chain. Several species that do damage to crops or harm other animals have increased in number because they no longer have predators. Eventually, these kinds of changes will affect everyone. Imagine not being able to buy fruit at the grocery store because fruit-eating insects have damaged all the crops.

Many people make the excuse that they don't need to help. They say they haven't done anything wrong. However, if people don't work to make changes, they are adding to the problem. People should get involved in saving the natural habitat of their environment so that animal species can continue to survive. There are many steps that a citizen can take, from contacting his or her senator or representative to joining a local conservation group. If people wait for others to do the job, it will be too late.

4 The writer anticipates and addresses opposing viewpoint.

5 Conclusion provides practical steps for taking action. It also restates the problem.

1. For Your Working Portfolio 🗁
Look for ideas in the **Writing** sections you completed earlier.

2. No Stereotypes
Think of groups that you feel are misjudged or treated unfairly. Defend one of them in your opinion statement.

3. Good Neighbors!
Think of a way to improve your neighborhood. Promote your plan in your opinion statement.

Have a question?

See the **Writing Handbook**
Persuasive Writing, p. R51
Elaboration, p. R41

See **Language Network,**
Proposal, p. 454.

Writing Your Opinion Statement

❶ Prewriting

Discover your opinions by **listing** your reactions to events in your school or community. **Write down** changes that you think need to be made or things that strike you as unfair. See the **Idea Bank** in the margin for more suggestions. After you have selected an issue, follow the steps below.

Planning Your Opinion Statement

▶ **1. Explore the issue.** Do you understand both sides of the issue completely? What questions do you have about the facts?

▶ **2. Focus your opinion.** Exactly how do you feel about the issue? Why do you feel that way? What facts support your opinion?

▶ **3. Identify your audience.** How much background do you need to give your audience? What do they already feel about the issue? How might you address their opposing views? Organize information accordingly.

▶ **4. Gather information.** What additional facts and other evidence do you need to support your opinion? Where will you find that evidence?

❷ Drafting

The most important part of drafting is getting your ideas down in writing. You can revise and polish your work later. Remember, though, that you will need to do each of the following:

- **State your opinion** clearly in your **introduction.**

- **Begin a new paragraph** for each of your **reasons** and include **evidence.** Examples, facts, and statistics will help you support your opinion.

- **Anticipate counter-arguments.** Address reader concerns.

- **Summarize your opinion** in the **conclusion.** Try to leave your audience with a memorable quote, question, or statement.

Ask Your Peer Reader

- How well did I explain my opinion?

- Did I support my statements with adequate evidence?

- Were my arguments organized in a logical and persuasive way?

❸ Revising

TARGET SKILL ▶ SUPPORTING YOUR OPINION Your essay should not only express your opinion, it should also persuade others to accept your view. Remember that simply stating your opinion is not enough to convince people. You must provide details, facts, and examples that strengthen your reasons. Revise with the idea of improving your organization and explain why your reasons are better than the counterpoints.

> Imagine a future in which you can only see animals and insects in an encyclopedia. This is not the only negative effect. *When a species becomes extinct, it affects the food chain. Several species that do damage to crops or harm other animals have increased in number because they no longer have predators.*

❹ Editing and Proofreading

TARGET SKILL ▶ PUNCTUATING CLAUSES To make your writing flow more smoothly, you might combine two or more clauses into one sentence. Keep your meaning clear by placing a comma after an introductory dependent (subordinate) clause, as shown below.

> When a large number of people move to the popular location, the city limits spread out, and animals' natural habitats are destroyed.

❺ Reflecting

FOR YOUR WORKING PORTFOLIO How did your opinion change or develop as you wrote your opinion statement? What did you enjoy most about writing your opinion statement? Attach your answers to your finished essay. Save your opinion statement in your **Working Portfolio.**

Need revising help?

Review the **Rubric,** p. 699.

Consider **peer reader** comments.

Check **Revision Guidelines,** p. R35.

SPELLING From Writing

 As you revise your work, look back at the words you misspelled and determine why you made the errors you did. For additional help, refer to the strategies and generalizations in the **Spelling Handbook** on page R30.

Concerned about punctuation?

See the **Grammar Handbook,** p. R90.

SPEAKING Opportunity

Turn your opinion statement into an oral presentation.

Publishing IDEAS

- Send your opinion statement as a letter to the editor of your local newspaper.

- Present your opinion statement to the class and form an action group to try to bring about a change.

Publishing Options
www.mcdougallittell.com

Standardized Test Practice

Mixed Review

> Even though, I don't in-line skate I believe city parks should have
> areas set aside for people who do. Having special areas set aside would
> (1)
> benifit everyone who uses the parks. If a person is taking a quiet stroll,
> (2)   (3)
> he or she doesn't want to be disturbed by in-line skaters going real fast.
>   (4)
> One false move by either person could result in one of them getting hurt
> bad. At the same time, in-line skating is an activity that many people   (5)
> enjoy. It was also healthy.
>   (6)

Review Your Skills

Use the passage and the questions that follow it to check how well you remember the language conventions you've learned in previous grades.

1. How is sentence 1 best written?
   A. Even though I don't, in-line skate, I believe
   B. Even though I don't in-line skate I, believe
   C. Even though I don't in-line skate, I believe
   D. Correct as is

2. What is the correct spelling in sentence 2?
   A. bennefit
   B. benefit
   C. bennifit
   D. Correct as is

3. How is item 3 best written?
   A. If a person is taking a quiet stroll he or she doesn't want
   B. If a person is taking, a quiet stroll, he or she doesn't want
   C. If a person, is taking a quiet stroll he or she doesn't want
   D. Correct as is

4. How is item 4 best written?
   A. in-line skaters going really quick
   B. in-line skaters going real quickly
   C. in-line skaters going really fast
   D. Correct as is

5. How is sentence 5 best written?
   A. getting hurt badly
   B. getting hurt really bad
   C. getting hurt very bad
   D. Correct as is

6. How is sentence 6 best written?
   A. It is also healthy.
   B. It would also be healthy.
   C. It will also be healthy.
   D. Correct as is

Key Standard
LC1.4 Use the mechanics of writing correctly; demonstrate correct language usage.
Other Standards **LC1.3, LC1.7**

Self-Assessment

Check your own answers in the **Grammar Handbook**

Quick Reference: Punctuation, p. R68

Spelling, p. R30

Adverbs, p. R82

The Literature You'll Read

The Concepts You'll Study

Vocabulary and Reading Comprehension
Vocabulary Focus: Researching Word Origins
Cause and Effect
Main Idea and Details
Paraphrasing
Monitoring
Summarizing

Writing and Language Conventions
Writing Workshop: Research Report
Using Adjective Clauses
Punctuating Dialogue

Literary Analysis
Genre Focus: Historical Fiction
Historical Fiction
Memoir
Imagery
Literary Nonfiction
Folk Tale

Speaking and Listening
Create an Insignia
Evaluate a Speech
Choral Reading
Adapt and Perform a Monologue

LEARNING the Language of *Literature*

Key Standard
R3.1 Be able to describe the purposes and characteristics of different forms of prose, such as the short story, novel, or essay.
Other Standards **R1.3, R3.2, R3.3**

Historical Fiction

> *I realized when I started doing research for my first book that history wasn't what I'd been taught in school. History is full of gossip; it's real people and emotion.*
>
> —Jean Fritz

Have you ever tried to imagine what it was like to live during the American Revolution, or in London at the time Shakespeare was writing his plays? Historical fiction can help make the past come alive.

Historical fiction is fiction set in the past. It contains a rich mixture of fact and fiction. Through novels and short stories, an author may combine factual information about the time, place, events, and real people of the period with fictional characters, dialogue, and details. All of these help you experience what it was like to live during the era when the story takes place.

Characters: Real and Imaginary

Historical fiction often includes a mix of real people from history as well as invented characters. They may be main characters or they may play only minor roles. The story will contain accurate historical details about them, but it may also include fictional elements such as conversations, thoughts, or feelings that the author creates. This blend of truth and fiction works to make each character come alive.

YOUR TURN "A Crown of Wild Olive" is set at the Olympic Games that took place every four years in Ancient Greece. What details describe the main character, Amyntas?

Setting

Setting is a particularly important element of historical fiction. Writers of historical fiction need to describe a place and time about which a reader may know very little. Before putting the first word on the page, writers do research and become experts on the era in which they set their stories. Some of these details will be real, such as descriptions of the houses people lived in or the kinds of clothes that they wore. Other details will be invented, such as the kind of weather or what people ate for dinner on a particular day.

YOUR TURN Read the passage to the right and think about how the writer created this scene. When and where is the story set?

Plot

In historical fiction, the plot may revolve around an event in history such as a war, a natural disaster, or a famous celebration. As the writer weaves his or her tale, the reader is able to imagine what it was like to participate in or witness that great event. In some cases, the events of the plot are completely made up by the writer, yet the characters and setting may still reflect the time period.

CHARACTER

This was the day of the Sacred Procession; the Priests and Officials, the beasts garlanded for sacrifice, the athletes marching into the waiting Stadium, while the Herald proclaimed the name and state of each one as he passed the rostrum. Amyntas, marching in with the Athenians, heard his own name called, and Leon's, among the names from Samos and Cyrene, Crete and Corinth, and Argos and Megara. And he smelled the incense on the morning air and felt for the first time, under his swelling pride in being Athenian, the thread of his own Greekness interwoven with the Greekness of all those others.

—Rosemary Sutcliff, "A Crown of Wild Olive"

SETTING

Half of Athens, it seemed, had crowded down to the port to watch the *Paralos*, the State Galley, sail for the Isthmus, taking their finest athletes on the first stage on their journey to Olympia.

Every fourth summer it happened; every fourth summer for more than three hundred years. Nothing was allowed to stand in the way, earthquake or pestilence or even war— even the long and weary war which, after a while of uneasy peace, had broken out again last year between Athens and Sparta.

—Rosemary Sutcliff, "A Crown of Wild Olive"

*R*ecognizing Cause and Effect

Key Standard
R2.3 Analyze text that uses cause-and-effect organization.

What happens when you stay up too late studying or watching television? You're tired the next morning, right? That's an example of a simple **cause-and-effect** relationship. Your life is full of them. Events in a story are often related to each other as cause and effect. That is, the first event in time—the cause—is a reason why a later event—the effect—happens. Examining cause-and-effect relationships enables readers to better understand how events are connected.

How to Apply the Skill

To understand **cause and effect,** an active reader will
- Identify signal, or transition, words that indicate cause and effect such as *because, therefore, since,* and *so*
- **Question** what happened and why
- **Clarify** the action by making a cause-effect chart
- Use prior knowledge

Try It Now!

Read the excerpt below. Look for cause and effect.

> Back in the spring the Herald had come, proclaiming the Truce of the Games; safe conduct through all lands and across all seas, both for athletes and for those who went to watch them compete. And now, from every Greek state, and from colonies and settlements all around the Mediterranean, the athletes would be gathering. . . .
>
> —Rosemary Sutcliff, "A Crown of Wild Olive"

Here's how Lindsay uses the skill:

"Reading 'A Crown of Wild Olive,' I made a cause-and-effect chart to clarify the plot."

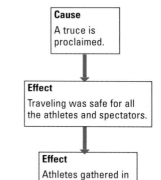

Cause
A truce is proclaimed.

↓

Effect
Traveling was safe for all the athletes and spectators.

↓

Effect
Athletes gathered in Olympia to compete.

A Crown of Wild Olive

by ROSEMARY SUTCLIFF

Connect to Your Life

Friendly Competition What are things that can bring together people from conflicting countries, cultures, or groups and help them respect each other? With a small group, make a word map of your ideas.

athletic competition

situations that bring people together

Build Background

SOCIAL STUDIES

Ancient Greece was not a united country but a collection of separate city-states. The two principal city-states were Athens and Sparta. While Athens valued culture, Sparta valued military strength. In 431 B.C., a war that would last on and off for many years broke out between Athens and Sparta.

The Olympic Games provided a truce between the city-states and took place every four years without interruption between 776 B.C. and about A.D. 393. Events included footraces for men and boys, chariot races, and the pentathlon, a five-part event that consisted of the broad jump, discus hurling, javelin throwing, the 200-yard dash, and wrestling. Each victor's prize was a crown of wild olive taken from a tree that grew within the precinct of the temple of Zeus.

> WORDS TO KNOW **Vocabulary Preview**
> angular reel   unaccountably
> dappled substance

Key Standard
R2.3 Analyze text that uses cause-and-effect organization.
Other Standards **R3.1, W2.1, W2.3, LS1.6**

Focus Your Reading

LITERARY ANALYSIS HISTORICAL FICTION

Fiction that is based on fact and takes place in the past is called **historical fiction.** Historical fiction combines facts along with details that come from the author's imagination. Writers of historical fiction sometimes use actual historical figures as characters, but usually the characters are the writer's creations. As you read, notice how the author makes the story come alive for you through factual as well as imaginative details.

ACTIVE READING CAUSE AND EFFECT

Two events are related as **cause and effect** when one event brings about the other. The event that happens first in time is the cause; the one that follows is the effect.

Cause	Effect
The offshore wind blew across the water.	It blurs the reflection of the galleys lying at anchor.

📖 READER'S NOTEBOOK

In your Reader's Notebook list the examples of cause and effect that you find as you read the story.

A Crown of Wild Olive

Detail of black-figure amphora
(ca 540 B.C.), Greek, Tampa (Florida)
Museum of Art, Joseph Veach Noble
Collection, 86.24.

by *Rosemary Sutcliff*

I t was still early in the day, but already it was growing hot,
the white dry heat of the Greek summer; and the faint offshore wind that made it bearable had begun to feather the
water, breaking and blurring the reflections of the galleys lying
at anchor in Pireaus Harbor.

Half of Athens, it seemed, had crowded down to the port
to watch the *Paralos*, the State Galley, sail for the Isthmus,
taking their finest athletes on the first stage of their journey
to Olympia.

Every fourth summer it happened; every fourth summer for
more than three hundred years. Nothing was allowed to stand
in the way, earthquake or pestilence or even war—even the long
and weary war which, after a while of uneasy peace, had
broken out again last year between Athens and Sparta.

Back in the spring the Herald[1] had come, proclaiming the
Truce of the Games; safe conduct through all lands and across

---

1. **herald:** a person who announces important news.

all seas, both for athletes and for those who went to watch them compete. And now, from every Greek state, and from colonies and settlements all around the Mediterranean, the athletes would be gathering. . . .

Aboard the *Paralos* was all the ordered bustle of departure, ropes being cast off, rowers in their places at the oars. The Athenian athletes and their trainers with them had gathered on the afterdeck. Amyntas, son of Ariston, had drawn a little apart from the rest. He was the youngest there, still several months from his eighteenth birthday and somewhat conscious that he had not yet sacrificed his boy's long hair to Apollo, while the rest, even of those entered for the boys' events—you counted as a boy at Olympia until you were twenty—were already short-haired and doing their Military Service. A few of them even had scars gained in border clashes with the Spartans, to prove that their real place, whatever it might be on the race track or in the wrestling pit, was with the men. Amyntas envied them. He was proud that he had been picked so young to run for Athens in the Boys' Double Stade,[2] the Four Hundred Yards. But he was lonely. He was bound in with all the others by their shared training; but they were bound together by something else, by another kind of life, other loyalties and shared experiences and private jokes, from which he was still shut out.

The last ropes holding ship to shore were being cast off now. Fathers and brothers and friends on the jetty were calling last moment advice and good luck wishes. Nobody called to Amyntas, but he turned and looked back to where his father stood among the crowd. Ariston had been a runner too in his day, before a Spartan spear wound had stiffened his left knee and spoiled his own hopes of an Olympic Olive Crown. Everyone said that he and Amyntas were very alike, and looking

back now at the slight dark man who still held himself like a runner, Amyntas hoped with a warm rush of pride that they were right. He wished he had said so, before he came aboard. There were so many things he would have liked to have said, but he was even more tongue-tied with his father than he was with the rest of the world when it came to saying the things that mattered. Now as the last ropes fell away, he flung up his hand in salute and tried to put them all into one wordless message. "I'll run the best race that's in me, Father—and if the Gods let me win it, I'll remember that I'm winning for us both."

Among the waving crowd, his father flung up an answering hand, as though he had somehow received the message. The water was widening between ship and shore. The Bos'n struck up the rowing time on his flute, and the rowers bent to their oars, sending the *Paralos* through the water toward the harbor mouth. Soon the crowd on shore was only a shingle of dark and colored and white along the waterfront. But far off beyond the roofs of the warehouses and the covered docks, a flake of light showed where high over Athens the sunlight flashed back from the upraised spear-blade of the great Athene of the Citadel,[3] four miles away.

They were out around the mole now, the one sail broke out from the mast, and they headed for the open gulf.

That night they beached the *Paralos* and made camp on the easternmost point of the long island of Salamis; and not long past noon the next day they went ashore at the Isthmus and took horse for Corinth on the far side, where a second galley was waiting to take

---

2. **double stade** (dŭb'əl stād): a footrace twice the length of a stadium.

3. **Athene . . .** (ə-thē'nə): in Greek mythology, the goddess of wisdom and warfare; also spelled Athena.

them down the coast. At evening on the fifth day they rode down into the shallow valley where Olympian Zeus[4] the Father of Gods and men had his sanctuary and where the Sacred Games were celebrated in his honor.

What with the long journey and the strangeness of everything, Amyntas took in very little of that first evening. They were met and greeted by the Council of the Games, whose president made them a speech of welcome, after which the Chief Herald read them the rules. And afterward they ate the evening meal in the athletes' mess; food that seemed to have no more taste nor <u>substance</u> than the food one eats in a dream. Then the dream blended away into a dark nothingness of sleep that took Amyntas almost before he had lain down in the narrow stretcher bed in the athletes' lodging, which would be his for the next month.

He woke to the first <u>dappled</u> fingers of sunlight shafting in through the doorway of his cell. They wavered and danced a little, as though broken by the shadows of tree branches. Somewhere farther down the valley a cuckoo was calling, and the world was real again, and his, and new as though it had been born that morning. He rolled over and lay for a few moments, his hands behind his head, looking up at the bare rafters; then shot off the bed and through the doorway in one swallow-dive of movement, to sluice[5] his head and shoulders in the icy water trickling from the mouth of a stone bull into a basin just outside. He came up for air, spluttering and shaking the water out of his eyes. For a moment he saw the colonnaded[6] court and the plane tree arching over the basin through a splintered brightness of flying droplets. And then suddenly, in the brightness, there stood a boy of about his own age, who must have come out of the lodging close behind him. A boy with a lean <u>angular</u> body and a dark, bony face under a shock of hair like the crest of an ill-groomed pony. For a long moment they stood looking at each other. Then Amyntas moved aside to let the other come to the conduit.[7]

As the stranger ducked his head and shoulders under the falling water, Amyntas saw his back. From shoulder to flank it was criss-crossed with scars, past the purple stage but not yet faded to the silvery white that they would be in a few years' time; pinkish scars that looked as though the skin was still drawn uncomfortably tight over them.

He must have made some betraying sound or movement, because the other boy ducked out from under the water, thrusting the wet russet hair back out of his eyes, and demanded curtly, "Have you never seen a Spartan back before?"

So that was it. Amyntas, like everyone else, had heard dark stories of Spartan boys flogged, sometimes to death, in a ritual test of courage before the shrine of Artemis Orthia, the Lady of the Beasts.[8]

"No," he said, "I am Athenian." And did not add that he hoped to see plenty of Spartan backs when once he had started his Military Service. It was odd, the cheap jibe came neatly into his head, and yet he did not even want to

---

4. **Zeus** (zo͞os): in Greek mythology, the principal god, ruler of the heavens, and lord of Olympus, home of the gods.

5. **sluice** (slo͞os): to wash.

6. **colonnaded** (kŏl′ə-nād′ĕd): having a series of evenly spaced columns.

7. **conduit**: a pipe for transporting fluids.

8. **Artemis . . .** (är′tə-mĭs): in Greek mythology, the goddess of the hunt and the moon.

WORDS TO KNOW
substance (sŭb′stəns) *n.* material quality
dappled (dăp′əld) *adj.* spotted
angular (ăng′gyə-lər) *adj.* bony and lean

712

speak it. It was as though here at Olympia, the Truce of the Games was not just a rule of conduct, but something in one's heart. Instead, he added, "And my name is Amyntas."

They seemed to stand confronting each other for a long time. The Spartan boy had the look of a dog sniffing at a stranger's fist and taking his own time to make sure whether it was friendly. Then he smiled; a slow, rather grave smile, but unexpectedly warm. "And mine is Leon."

"And you're a runner." Amyntas was taking in his build and the way he stood.

"I am entered for the Double Stade."

"Then we race against each other."

Leon said in the same curt tone, "May we both run a good race."

"And meanwhile,—when did you arrive, Leon?"

"Last night, the same as you."

Amyntas, who usually found it nearly as difficult to talk to strangers as he did to his own father, was surprised to hear himself saying, "Then you'll have seen no more of Olympia than I have. Shall we go and get some clothes on and have a look around?"

But by that time more men and boys were coming out into the early sunshine, yawning and stretching the sleep out of their muscles. And Amyntas felt a hand clamp down on his shoulder and heard the voice of Hippias his trainer, "Oh no you don't, my lad! Five days' break in training is long enough, and I've work for you before you do any sightseeing!"

After that, they were kept hard at it, on the practice track and in the wrestling school that had the names of past Olympic victors carved on the colonnade walls. For the last month's training for the Games had to be done at Olympia itself; and the last month's training was hard, in the old style that did not allow for rest days in the modern fashion that most of the Athenian trainers favored. Everything at Olympia had to be done the old way, even to clearing the stadium of its four years' growth of grass and weeds and spreading it with fresh sand. At other Crown Games, the work was done by paid laborers, but here, the contending athletes must do it themselves, to the glory of the Gods, as they had done it in the far-off days when the Games were new. Some of them grumbled a good deal and thought it was time that the Priests of Zeus and the Council of the Games brought their ideas up to date; but to Amyntas there seemed to be a sort of rightness about the thing as it was.

Cloaked Spartan warrior, (sixth century B.C.), Greek. Bronze, red marble base. Wadsworth Atheneum, Hartford (Connecticut). Gift of J. Pierpont Morgan.

His training time was passed among boys from Corinth and Epidauros, Rhodes and Samos and Macedon. At first they were just figures in outline, like people seen too far off to have faces, whom he watched with interest at track work, at javelin or discus throwing or in the wrestling pit, trying to judge their form as he knew they were trying to judge his and each other's. But gradually as the early days went by, they changed into people with faces, with personal habits, and likes and dislikes, suffering from all the strains and stresses of the last weeks before the Games. But even before those first few days were over, he and the Spartan boy had drifted into a companionable pattern of doing things together. They would sluice each other down, squatting in the stone hip-baths in the washing room after practice, and scrape the mess of rubbing oil and sand off each other's backs—it took Amyntas a little while to learn to scrape the bronze blade of the strigil[9] straight over the scars on Leon's back as though they were not there—and when they took their turn at scraping up the four years' growth of grass and sun-dried herbs from the stadium, they generally worked together, sharing one of the big rush carrying-baskets between them. And in the evenings, after the day's training was over, or in the hot noonday break when most people stretched themselves out in the shade of the plane trees for sleep or quiet talk, they seemed, more often than not, to drift into each other's company.

Once or twice they went to have a look at the town of tents and booths that was beginning to spring up all around the Sacred Enclosure and the Gymnasium buildings—for a Games Festival drew many people besides those who came to compete or to watch: merchants and wine sellers and fortune tellers, poets determined to get poems heard, horse dealers from Corinth and Cyrene, goldsmiths and leather-workers, philosophers gathering for the pleasure of arguing with each other, sword and fire swallowers, and acrobats who could dance on their hands to the soft notes of Phrygian pipes. But Leon did not much like the crowded noisy tent-ground; and most often they wandered down to the river that flung its loop about the south side of Olympia. It had shrunk now in the summer heat, to little more than a chain of pools in the middle of its pale dried-out pebbly bed; but there was shade under the oleander trees, and generally a whisper of moving air. And lying on the bank in the shade was free. It had dawned on Amyntas quite early that the reason Leon did not like the fairground was that he had no money. The Spartans did not use money, or at least, having decided that it was a bad thing, they had no coinage but iron bars so big and heavy that nobody could carry them about or

9. **strigil** (strĭj′əl): an instrument used for scraping the skin after a bath.

Detail of black-figure amphora (about 540–530 B.C.), Swing Painter, Greek. Attic, Tampa (Florida) Museum of Art, Joseph Veach Noble Collection, 86.26. Purchased in part with funds donated by Mr. Frank Duckwall.

Horsemen from the west frieze of the Parthenon. British Museum, London.

even keep a store at home that was worth enough to be any use. They were very proud of their freedom from wealth, but it made life difficult at a gathering such as this, when they had to mix with people from other states. Leon covered up by being extremely scornful of the foolish things for sale in the merchants' booths and the acrobats who passed the bowl around for contributions after their performance; but he was just that shade too scornful to be convincing. And anyway, Amyntas had none too much money himself, to get him through the month.

So they went to the river. They were down there one hot noontide something over a week after they had first arrived at Olympia; Amyntas lying on his back, his hands behind his head, squinting up into the dark shadow-shapes of the oleander branches against the sky; Leon sitting beside him with his arms around his updrawn knees, staring out into the dazzle of sunlight over the open riverbed. They had been talking runners' talk, and suddenly Amyntas said, "I was watching the Corinthian making

his practice run this morning. I don't *think* we have either of us much to fear from him."

"The Rhodian runs well," said Leon, not bringing back his gaze from the white dance of sunlight beyond the oleanders.

"But he uses himself up too quickly. He's the kind that makes all the front running at first and has nothing left for the home stretch. Myself, I'd say that red-headed barbarian[10] from Macedon had the better chance."

"He's well enough for speed; and he knows how and when to use it. . . . What do you give for Nikomedes' chances?"

"Nikomedes?—The boy from Megara? It's hard to say. Not much, from the form he's shown so far; but we've only seen him at practice, and he's the sort that sometimes catches fire when it comes to the real thing. . . ."

There was a long silence between them, and they heard the churring of the grasshoppers,

---

10. **barbarian:** here, a member of a non-Greek people.

like the heat-shimmer turned to sound. And then Amyntas said, "I think you are the one I have most to fear."

And Leon turned his head slowly and looked down at him, and said, "Have you only just woken to that? I knew the same thing of *you*, three days ago."

And they were both silent again and suddenly a little shocked. You might think that kind of thing, but it was best not to put it into words.

Leon made a quick sign with his fingers to avert ill luck; and Amyntas scrambled to his feet. "Come on, it's time we were getting back." They were both laughing, but a little breathlessly. Leon dived to his feet also and shot ahead as they went up through the riverside scrub. But the next instant, between one flying leap and the next, he stumbled slightly and checked, then turned back, stooping to search for something among the dusty root-tangle of dry grass and camomile. Amyntas, swerving just in time to avoid him, checked also.

"What is it?"

"Something sharp. . . ." Leon pulled out from where it had lain half-buried, the broken end of a sickle blade that looked as though it might have lain there since the last Games. "Seems it's not only the Stadium that needs clearing up." He began to walk on, carrying the jagged fragment in his hand. But Amyntas saw the blood on the dry ground where he had been standing.

"You have cut your foot."

"I know," Leon said, and went on walking.

"Yes, I *know* you know. Let me look at it."

"It's only a scratch."

"All the same—show me."

Leon stood on one leg, steadying himself with a hand on Amyntas's shoulder, and turned up the sole of his foot. "Look then. You can hardly see it."

There was a cut on the hard brown sole, not long, but deep, with the blood welling slowly. Amyntas said in sudden exasperation, "Haven't you *any* sense? Oh we all know about the Spartan boy with the fox under his cloak, and nobody but you Spartans think it's a particularly clever or praiseworthy story; but if you get dirt into that cut, you'll like enough have to scratch from the race!"

Leon suddenly grinned. "Nobody but we Spartans understand that story. But about the dirt, you could be right."

"I could. And that bit of iron is dirty enough for a start. Best get the wound cleaned up, in the river before we go back to the Gymnasium. Then your trainer can take over."

So with Leon sitting on a boulder at the edge of the shrunken river, Amyntas set to work with ruthless thoroughness to clean the cut. He pulled it open, the cool water running over his hands, and a thin thread of crimson fronded away downstream. It would help clean the wound to let it bleed a little; but after a few moments the bleeding almost stopped. No harm in making sure; he ducked his head to the place, sucked hard and spat crimson into the water. Then he tore a strip from the skirt of his tunic.[11] He would have commandeered Leon's own—after all it was Leon's foot—but he knew that the Spartan boys were allowed to own only one tunic at a time. If he did that, Leon would be left without a respectable tunic to wear at the Sacrifices. He lashed the thin brown foot tightly. "Now—put your arm over my shoulder and try to keep your weight off the cut as much as you can."

"Cluck, cluck, cluck!" said Leon, but he did as Amyntas said.

As they skirted the great open space of the Hippodrome, where the chariot races would be held on the second day of the Games, they

---

11. **tunic:** a loose-fitting garment extending to the knees.

came up with a couple of the Athenian contingent, strolling under the plane trees. Eudorus the wrestler looked around and his face quickened with concern, "Run into trouble?"

"Ran into the remains of a sickle blade someone left in the long grass," Amyntas said, touching the rusty bit of metal he had taken from Leon and stuck in his own belt. "It's near the tendon, but it's all right, so long as there's no dirt left in it."

"Near the tendon, eh? Then we'd best be taking no chances." Eudorus looked at Leon. "You are Spartan, I think?—Amyntas, go and find the Spartan trainer. I'll take over here." And then to Leon again, "Will you allow me to carry you up to the lodging? It seems the simplest way."

Amyntas caught one parting glimpse of Leon's rigid face as Eudorus lifted him, lightly as a ten-year-old, and set off toward the gymnasium buildings; and laughter caught at his stomach; but mixed with the laughter was sympathy. He knew he would have been just as furious in Leon's place. All this fuss and to-do over a cut that would have been nothing in itself—if the Games had not been only three weeks off.

He set off in search of the trainer.

In the middle of that night, Amyntas woke up with a thought already shaped and complete in his mind. It was an ugly thought, and it sat on his chest and mouthed at him slyly. "Leon is the one you have most to fear. If Leon is out of the race. . . ."

Minoan bull's head with gold horns, from Knossos, 1600 B.C., Archaeological Museum of Heraklion, Crete, Greece/Ancient Arts and Architecture Collection Ltd/Bridgeman Art Library.

He looked at it in the darkness, feeling a little sick. Then he pushed it away and rolled over on to his face with his head in his arms, and after a while he managed to go back to sleep again.

Next day, as soon as he could slip away between training sessions, he went out into the growing town of tents and booths, and found a seller of images and votive offerings, and bought a little bronze bull with silvered horns. It cost nearly all the money that he had to spare, so that he would not now be able to buy the hunting knife with silver inlay on the hilt that had caught his fancy a day or two since. With the little figure in his hand, he went to the Sacred Enclosure, where, among altars shaded by plane trees and statues of Gods and Olympic heroes, the great Temple of Zeus faced the older and darker house of Hera[12] his wife.

Before the Temple of Zeus, the ancient wild olive trees from which the victors' crowns were made cast dapple-shade across the lower steps of the vast portico. He spoke to the attendant priest in the deep threshold shadows beyond.

"I ask leave to enter and make an offering."

"Enter then, and make the offering," the man said.

And he went through into the vastness of the Temple itself, where the sunlight sifting through under the acanthus roof tiles made a honeycomb glow that hung high in the upper

---

12. **Hera** (hîr´ə): in Greek mythology, the wife of Zeus and goddess of the home.

spaces and flowed down the gigantic columns but scarcely touched the pavement under foot, so that he seemed to wade in cool shadows. At the far end, sheathed in gold and ivory, his feet half lost in shadows, his head gloried with the dim radiance of the upper air, stern and serene above the affairs of mortal men, stood the mighty statue of the God himself. Olympian Zeus, in whose honor the Sacred Games had been held for more than three hundred years. Three hundred years, such a little while; looking up at the heart-stilling face above him, Amyntas wondered if the God had even noticed yet, that they were begun. Everything in the God's House was so huge, even time. . . . For a moment his head swam, and he had no means of judging the size of anything, even himself, here where all the known landmarks of the world of men were left behind. Only one thing, when he looked down at it, remained constant in size; the tiny bronze bull with the silvered horns that he held in his hand.

He went forward to the first of the Offering Tables before the feet of the gigantic statue and set it down. Now, the tables were empty and waiting, but by the end of the festival, they would be piled with offerings; small humble ones like his own and silver cups

and tripods of gilded bronze to be taken away and housed in the Temple treasury. On the eve of the Games they would begin to fill up, with votive offerings made for the most part by the athletes themselves, for their own victory or the victory of a friend taking part in a different event. Amyntas was not making the offering for his own victory, nor for Leon's. He was not quite sure why he was making it, but it was for something much more complicated than victory in the Double Stade. With one finger still resting on the back of the little bronze bull, he sent up the best prayer he could sort out from the tangle of thoughts and feelings within himself. "Father of all things, Lord of these Sacred Games, let me keep a clean heart in this; let me run the best race that is in me and think of nothing more."

Outside again, beyond the dapple-shade of the olive trees, the white sunlight fell dazzling across his eyes, and the world of men, in which things had returned to their normal size, received him back; and he knew that Hippias was going to be loudly angry with him for having missed a training session. But unaccountably, everything, including Hippias's anger, seemed surprisingly small.

Bronze figure of Zeus, (ca first century B.C.), Roman. Christie's Images Ltd., 1999.

WORDS
TO
KNOW

unaccountably (ŭn'ə-koun'tə-blē) *adv.* without apparent explanation

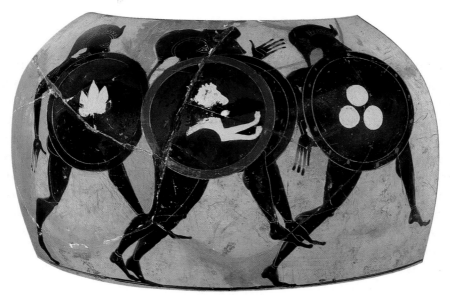

Detail of black-figure amphora (sixth century B.C.). A prize for the winner of the hoplite race.
Musée Vivenal, Compiegne, France. Erich Lessing/Art Resource, New York.

Leon had to break training for three days, at least so far as track-work was concerned; and it was several more before he could get back into full training; so for a while it was doubtful whether he would be able to take his place in the race. But with still more than a week to go, both his trainer and the Doctor-Priest of Asklepius[13] declared him fit, and his name remained on the list of entrants for the Double Stade.

And then it was the first day of the Festival; the day of solemn dedication, when each competitor must go before the Council to be looked over and identified and take the Oath of the Games before the great bronze statue of Zeus of the Thunderbolts.

The day passed. And next morning before it was light, Amyntas woke to hear the unmistakable, unforgettable voice of the crowds gathering in the Stadium. A shapeless surf of sound, pricked by the sharper cries of the jugglers and acrobats, and the sellers of water and honeycakes, myrtle and victors' ribbons calling their wares.

This was the day of the Sacred Procession; the Priests and Officials, the beasts garlanded for sacrifice, the athletes marching into the waiting Stadium, while the Herald proclaimed the name and state of each one as he passed the rostrum. Amyntas, marching in with the Athenians, heard his own name called, and Leon's, among names from Samos and Cyrene, Crete and Corinth, and Argos and Megara. And he smelled the incense on the morning air and felt for the first time, under his swelling pride in being Athenian, the thread of his own Greekness interwoven with the Greekness of all those others. This must have been, a little, the thing their Great-Grandfathers had felt when they stood together, shield to shield, to hurl back the whole strength of invading Persia so that they might remain free. That had been in a Games year, too. . . .

The rest of that day was given over to the chariot and horse races; and that night Amyntas went to his sleeping cell with the thunder of hooves and wheels still sounding somewhere behind his ears. He seemed to hear

---

13. **Asklepius** (ə-sklē′pē-əs): in Greek mythology, the god of medicine; also spelled Asclepius.

it in his dreams all night, but when he woke in the morning, it had turned into the sound that he had woken to yesterday, the surf-sound of the gathering crowd. But this morning it had a new note for him, for this was the Day, and the crowd that was gathering out there around the Stadium was his crowd, and his belly tightened and the skin prickled at the back of his neck as he heard it.

He lay for a few moments, listening, then got up and went out to the conduit. Leon came out after him as he had done that first morning of all, and they sluiced down as best they could. The water barely dribbled from the mouth of the stone bull now, for with the vast gathering of people and the usual end-of-summer drought, the water shortage was getting desperate, as it always did by the time the Festival days arrived.

"How is the foot?" Amyntas asked.

"I can't remember where the cut was, unless I look for it."

They stood looking at each other, the friendship that they had never put into words trying to find some way to reach across from one to the other.

"We cannot even wish each other luck," Amyntas said at last, helplessly.

And Leon said, almost exactly as he had said it at their first meeting, "May both of us run a good race."

They reached out and touched hands quickly and went their separate ways.

The next time they saw each other, they were waiting oiled and naked for the track, with the rest of the Double Stade boys just outside the arched way into the Stadium. The Dolichus, the long distance race, and the Stade had been run, each with its boys' race immediately after. Now the trumpet was sounding to start the Double Stade. Amyntas's eyes went to meet Leon's, and found the Spartan boy's slightly frowning gaze waiting for him. He heard the sudden roar of the crowd, and his belly lifted and tightened. A little stir ran through the waiting boys; the next time the starting trumpet sounded, the next time the crowd gave that roar, it would be for them. Hippias was murmuring last-minute advice into Amyntas's ear, but he did not hear a word of it. . . . He was going out there before all those thousands upon thousands of staring eyes and yelling mouths, and he was going to fail. Not just fail to win the race, but *fail*. His belly was churning now, his heart banging away right up in his throat so that it almost choked him. His mouth was dry and the palms of his hands were wet, and the beginnings of panic were whimpering up in him. He looked again at Leon and saw him run the tip of his tongue over his lips as though they were suddenly dry. It was the first time he had ever known the Spartan boy to betray anything of what was going on inside him, and the sight gave him a sense of companionship that somehow steadied him. He began to take deep quiet breaths, as he had been taught, and the rising panic quieted and sank away.

The voice of the crowd was rising, rising to a great roar; the Men's Double Stade was over. He heard the Herald crying the name of the winner and another roar from the crowd; and then the runners were coming out through the arched entrance; and the boys pressed back to let them past, filthy with sweat and sand and oil. Amyntas looked at the face of the man with the victor's ribbons knotted around his head and arms and saw that it was grey and spent and oddly peaceful.

"Now it's us!" someone said; and the boys were sprinting down the covered way, out into the open sun-drenched space of the Stadium.

The turf banks on either side of the broad track and the lower slopes of the Kronon Hill that looked down upon it were packed with a vast multitude of onlookers. Half-way down on the right-hand side, raised above the tawny grass on which everybody else sat, were the benches for the Council, looking across to the white marble seat opposite, where the Priestess of Demeter, the only woman allowed at the Games, sat as still as though she herself were carved from marble, among all the jostling, swaying, noisy throng. Men were raking over the silver sand on the track. The trumpeter stood ready.

They had taken their places now behind the long white limestone curbs of the starting line. The Umpire was calling: "Runners! Feet to the lines!"

Amyntas felt the scorching heat of the limestone as he braced the ball of his right foot into the shaped groove. All the panic of a while back had left him; he felt light, and clearheaded, and master of himself. He had drawn the sixth place, with Leon on his left and the boy from Megara on his right. Before him the track stretched white in the sunlight, an infinity of emptiness and distance.

The starting trumpet yelped, and the line of runners sprang forward like a wave of hunting dogs slipped from the leash.

Amyntas was running smoothly and without hurry. Let the green front-runners push on ahead. In this heat they would have burned themselves out before they reached the turning post. He and Leon were running neck and neck with the red-headed Macedonian. The Rhodian had gone ahead now after the front-runners; the rest were still bunched. Then the Corinthian made a sprint and passed the boy from Rhodes, but fell back almost at once. The white track was <u>reeling</u> back underfoot, the

Detail of black-figure stamnos (ca 525–500 B.C.), Group of Louvre, Greek. Tampa (Florida) Museum of Art, Joseph Veach Noble Collection, 86.34.

WORDS
TO
KNOW

reel (rēl) v. to go round and round

721

turning post racing toward them. The bunch had thinned out, the front-runners beginning to drop back already; and as they came up toward the turning post, the first boy from Macedon, and then Nikomedes catching fire at last, slid into the lead, with Amyntas and Leon close behind them. Rounding the post, Amyntas skidded on the loose sand and Leon went ahead; and it was then, seeing the lean scarred back ahead of him, that Amyntas lengthened his stride, knowing that the time had come to run. They were a quarter of the way down the home lap when they passed Nikomedes; the Megaran boy had taken fire too late. They were beginning to overhaul the redhead; and Amyntas knew in his bursting heart that unless something unexpected happened, the race must be between himself and Leon. Spartan and Macedonian were going neck and neck now; the position held for a few paces, and then the redhead gradually fell behind. Amyntas was going all out. There was pain in his breast and belly and in the backs of his legs, and he did not know where his next breath was coming from; but still the thin scarred back was just ahead. And then suddenly Amyntas knew that something was wrong; Leon was laboring a little, beginning to lose the first keen edge of his speed. Snatching a glance downward, he saw a fleck of crimson in the sand. The cut had reopened.

His body went on running, but for a sort of splinter of time his head seemed quite apart from the rest of him and filled with an unmanageable swirl of thoughts and feelings. Leon might have passed the top of his speed anyway; it might be nothing to do with his foot—But the cut *had* reopened. . . . To lose the race because of a cut foot. . . . It would be so easy not to make that final desperate effort that his whole body was

crying out against. Then Leon would keep his lead. . . . And at the same time another part of himself was remembering his father standing on the quayside at Piraeus as the *Paralos* drew away—crying out that he was not running only for himself but for Athens, his City and his people. . . . A crown of wild olive would be the greatest thing that anyone could give to his friend. . . . It would insult Leon to let him win . . . you could not do that to your friend. . . . And then, like a clean cold sword of light cutting through the swirling tangle of his thoughts, came the knowledge that greater than any of these things were the Gods. These were the Sacred Games, not some mere struggle between boys in the gymnasium. For one fleeting instant of time, he remembered himself standing in the Temple before the great statue of Zeus, holding the tiny bronze bull with the silvered horns. "Let me run the best race that is in me and think of nothing more."

He drove himself forward in one last agonizing burst of speed. He was breathing against knives, and the roar of the blood in his ears drowned the roar of the crowd. He was level with Leon—and then there was nothing ahead of him but the winning post.

The onlookers had crowded right down toward it; even above the howl of the blood in his head he heard them now, roar on solid roar of sound, shouting him in to victory. And then Hippias had caught him as he plunged past the post; and he was bending over the trainer's arm, bending over the pain in his belly, snatching at his breath and trying not to be sick. People were throwing sprigs of myrtle; he felt them flicking and falling on his head and shoulders. The sickness eased a little and his head was clearing; he began to hear friendly voices congratulating him; and Eudorus came shouldering through the crowd with a colored ribbon to tie around his head. But when he looked around for Leon, the Spartan boy had been swept away by his trainer. And a desolation rose in Amyntas and robbed his moment of its glory.

Afterward in the changing room, some of the other boys came up to congratulate him. Leon did not come; but when they had cleaned off the sand and oil and sweat and sluiced down with the little water that was allowed them, Amyntas hung about, sitting on the well curb outside while the trainer finished seeing to his friend's foot. And when Leon came out at last, he came straight across to the well, as though they had arranged to meet there. His face was as unreadable as usual.

"You will have cooled off enough by now. Do you want to drink?" Amyntas said, mainly because somebody had to say something, and dipped the bronze cup that always stood on the well curb in the pail that he had drawn.

Leon took the cup from him and drank and sat down on the well curb beside him. As Amyntas dipped the cup again and bent his head to drink in his turn, the ends of the victor's ribbon fell forward against his cheek, and he pulled it off impatiently and dropped it beside the well.

"Why did you do that?" Leon said.

"I shall never be sure whether I won that race."

"The judges are not often mistaken, and I never heard yet of folk tying victors' ribbons on the wrong man."

Amyntas flicked a thumb at Leon's bandaged foot. "You know well enough what I mean. I'll never be sure whether I'd have come first past the post, if that hadn't opened up again."

Leon looked at him a moment in silence, then flung up his head and laughed. "Do you really think that could make any difference? It would take more than a cut foot to slow me up, Athenian!—You ran the better race, that's all."

It was said on such a harsh, bragging note that in the first moment Amyntas felt as though he had been struck in the face. Then he wondered if it was the overwhelming Spartan pride talking or simply Leon, hurt and angry and speaking the truth. Either way, he was too tired to be angry back again. And whichever it was it seemed that Leon had shaken it off already. The noon break was over, and the trumpets were sounding for the Pentathlon.

"Up!" Leon said, when Amyntas did not move at once. "Are you going to let it be said that your own event is the only one that interests you?"

They went, quickly and together, while the trainer's eye was off them, for Leon was under orders to keep off his foot. And the people cheered them both when they appeared in the Stadium. They seldom cared much for a good loser, but Leon had come in a close second, and they had seen the blood in the sand.

The next day the heavyweight events were held; and then it was the last day of all, the Crowning Day. Ever after, Amyntas remembered that day as a quietness after great stress and turmoil. It was not, in truth, much less noisy than the days that had gone before. The roaring of the Stadium crowds was gone, but in the town of tents the crowds milled to and fro. The jugglers with knives and the eaters of fire shouted for an audience and the merchants cried their wares, and within the Sacred Enclosure where the winners received their crowns and made their sacrifices before the Temples of Zeus and Hera, there were the flutes and the songs in praise of the victors and the deep-voiced invocations to the Gods.

But in Amyntas himself, there was the quiet. He remembered the Herald crying his name and the light springy coolness of the wild olive crown as it was pressed down on his head; and later, the spitting light of pine torches under the plane trees, where the officials and athletes were feasting. And he remembered most, looking up out of the torchlight, and seeing, high and remote above it all, the winged tripods on the roof of the great Temple, outlined against the light of a moon two days past the full.

The boys left before the feasting was over; and in his sleeping cell Amyntas heard the poets sing in praise of some chariot team and the applause, while he gathered his few belongings together, ready for tomorrow's early start, and stowed his olive crown among them. Already the leaves were beginning to wilt after the heat of the day. The room that had seemed so strange the first night was familiar now, part of himself; and after tonight it would not know him anymore.

Next morning in all the hustle of departure, he and Leon contrived to meet and slip off for a little on their own.

The whole valley of Olympia was a chaos of tents and booths being taken down, merchants as well as athletes and onlookers making ready for the road. But the Sacred Enclosure itself was quiet, and the gates stood open. They went through, into the shade of the olive trees before the Temple of Zeus. A priest making the morning offering at a side altar looked at them; but they seemed to be doing no harm and to want nothing, so he let them alone. There was a smell of frankincense[14] in the air and the early morning smell of last night's heavy dew on parched ground. They stood among the twisted trunks and low-hanging branches and looked at each other and did not know what to say. Already they were remembering that there was war between Athens and Sparta, that the Truce of the Games would last them back to their own

states, but no further; and the longer the silence lasted, the more they remembered.

From beyond the quiet of the Enclosure came all the sounds of the great concourse breaking up; voices calling, the stamping of impatient horses. "By this time tomorrow everyone will be gone," Amyntas said at last. "It will be just as it was before we came, for another four years."

"The Corinthians are off already."

"Catching the cool of the morning for those fine chariot horses," Amyntas said, and thought, There's so little time, why do we have to waste it like this?

"One of the charioteers had that hunting knife with the silver inlay. The one you took a fancy to. Why didn't you buy it after all?"

"I spent the money on something else." For a moment Amyntas was afraid that Leon would ask what. But the other boy only nodded and let it go.

He wished suddenly that he could give Leon something, but there was nothing among his few belongings that would make sense in the Spartan's world. It was a world so far off from his own. Too far to reach out, too far to call. Already they seemed to be drifting away from each other, drifting back to a month ago, before they had even met. He put out a hand quickly, as though to hold the other boy back for one more moment, and Leon's hand came to meet it.

"It has been good. All this month it has been good," Leon said.

"It has been good," Amyntas agreed. He wanted to say, "Until the next Games, then." But manhood and Military Service were only a few months away for both of them. If they did meet at another Games, there would be the faces of dead comrades, Spartan or Athenian,

---

14. **frankincense** (frăng′kĭn-sĕns): a sweet-scented resin used as incense.

between them; and like enough, for one of them or both, there might be no other Games. Far more likely, if they ever saw each other again, it would be over the tops of their shields.

He had noticed before how, despite their different worlds, he and Leon sometimes thought the same thing at the same time and answered each other as though the thought had been spoken. Leon said in his abrupt, dead-level voice, "The Gods be with you, Amyntas, and grant that we never meet again."

They put their arms around each other's necks and strained fiercely close for a moment, hard cheekbone against hard cheekbone.

"The Gods be with you, Leon."

And then Eudorus was calling, "Amyntas! Amyntas! We're all waiting!"

And Amyntas turned and ran—out through the gateway of the Sacred Enclosure, toward where the Athenian party were ready to start, and Eudorus was already coming back to look for him.

As they rode up from the Valley of Olympia and took the tracks toward the coast, Amyntas did not look back. The horses' legs brushed the dry dust-grey scrub beside the track and loosed the hot aromatic scents of wild lavender and camomile and lentisk upon the air. A yellow butterfly hovered past, and watching it out of sight, it came to him suddenly that he and Leon had exchanged gifts of a sort, after all. It was hard to give them a name, but they were real enough. And the outward and visible sign of his gift to Leon was in the little bronze bull with the silvered horns that he had left on the Offering Table before the feet of Olympian Zeus. And Leon's gift to him. . . . That had been made with the Spartan's boast that it would take more than a cut foot to slow him up. He had thought at the time that it was either the harsh Spartan pride or the truth spoken in anger. But he understood now, quite suddenly, that it had been Leon giving up his own private and inward claim to the olive crown, so that he, Amyntas, might believe that he had rightfully won it. Amyntas knew that he would never be sure of that, never in all his life. But it made no difference to the gift.

The track had begun to run downhill, and the pale dust-cloud was rising behind them. He knew that if he looked back now, there would be nothing to see. ❖

Eastern colonnade of the Palaestra, once a public building for athletic training and practice at Olympia.

Connect to the Literature

1. What Do You Think?
What is your reaction to Amyntas's thoughts as he leaves the valley of Olympia after the games? Explain.

Comprehension Check
- What is Leon's reaction to Amyntas when they first meet?
- How does Leon cut his foot?
- What prayer does Amyntas make to Zeus?

Think Critically

2. As Amyntas sets off for the Games, what do you think winning means to him?

> **Think About:**
> - his father's injury
> - being the youngest athlete from Athens
> - his talk with his father before leaving

3. As they prepare for the Games together, how does Leon become both friend and opponent to Amyntas? How does Leon's injury add to this tension?

4. What do you think Amyntas gains from making his prayer to Zeus? Does he get what he prays for?

5. As Amyntas returns to Athens, how is he different than when he first set sail for the Games? Explain.

6. ACTIVE READING | CAUSE AND EFFECT
Review the examples of **cause and effect** you wrote in your ⬛ READER'S NOTEBOOK. How did the examples you found help you to better understand the story?

Extend Interpretations

7. COMPARING TEXTS Think of Felix and Antonio from "Amigo Brothers." (page 361) Compare and contrast their situation, friendship, and competition with those of Amyntas and Leon. How are they similar? How do they differ?

8. Connect to Life Who are the people who inspire you to do your best? Share some examples with a partner.

Literary Analysis

HISTORICAL FICTION Historical fiction differs from other types of fiction in that its setting and characters have a strong basis in historical fact. **Historical fiction** is always set in a past historical period and may include actual historical figures as characters. "A Crown of Wild Olive" includes details based in the author's research into ancient Greek history. Though there are no actual historical characters in the story, there are many historical details that bring the period to life, such as those describing the wars between Athens and Sparta, the method of raising Spartan boys, and the religious, social, and athletic significance of the Olympic Games.

Activity When you read historical fiction, it is important to distinguish between details based in historical fact and those invented by the author. Divide the class into two groups and have one group chart factual details and imaginative details about Amyntas and the other group do the same regarding Leon. Afterward, as a class, discuss what you learned about ancient Athens and Sparta by reading this story.

AMYNTAS		LEON	
Historical Detail	Imaginative Detail	Historical Detail	Imaginative Detail
Amyntas will cut his hair to mark his entrance into manhood.	He promises his father that he will win the race for both of them.	Leon was beaten to test his courage.	He has a "slow, rather grave" smile.

Writing

Dramatic Dialogue Write a dialogue that might have taken place between Amyntas and his father upon Amyntas's return to Athens. Keep in mind the conversation Amyntas and his father had at the beginning of the story as well as other key events.

Speaking & Listening

Olympic Insignia Although medals weren't a part of the ancient Olympics, work with a partner to create a gold medal design for the Games the story describes.

Remember that part of the significance of the Games was that they created a truce between two warring city-states, a truce especially represented by the friendship between Amyntas and Leon. Present your design to the class and explain its significance.

Art Connection

Look at the bronze statue of the Spartan warrior on page 713. What impression of Spartans does it and the behavior of the Spartans in "A Crown of Wild Olive" give you? Explain your interpretation.

Research & Technology

The Modern Olympics Choose an Olympics of the past century to research. How were the uniforms different from ones worn today? How were the opening ceremonies different? What country captured the most medals?

Reading for INFORMATION

Before you begin, read "Passing on the Flame," p. 728, to learn more about the origin and meaning of an important Olympic tradition.

Rosemary Sutcliff
1920–1992

"To me half the fun of writing a book is the research entailed."

Research and Writing British author Rosemary Sutcliff wrote fiction that enables her readers to imagine the lives of people of long ago. Sutcliff liked to immerse herself in the historical period she depicted in a story. "To me half the fun of writing a book is the research entailed," she said.

Painful Childhood As a child Sutcliff suffered from a form of rheumatoid arthritis and, until the age of ten, was educated at home by her mother, who read to her extensively. Sutcliff said that her mother's reading aloud to her provided examples of good writing that helped her later when she created her own stories.

AUTHOR ACTIVITY
Other Stories "A Crown of Wild Olive" is one of three stories in Sutcliff's *Heather, Oak, and Olive*. Read one of the other stories in the collection. Report back to the class.

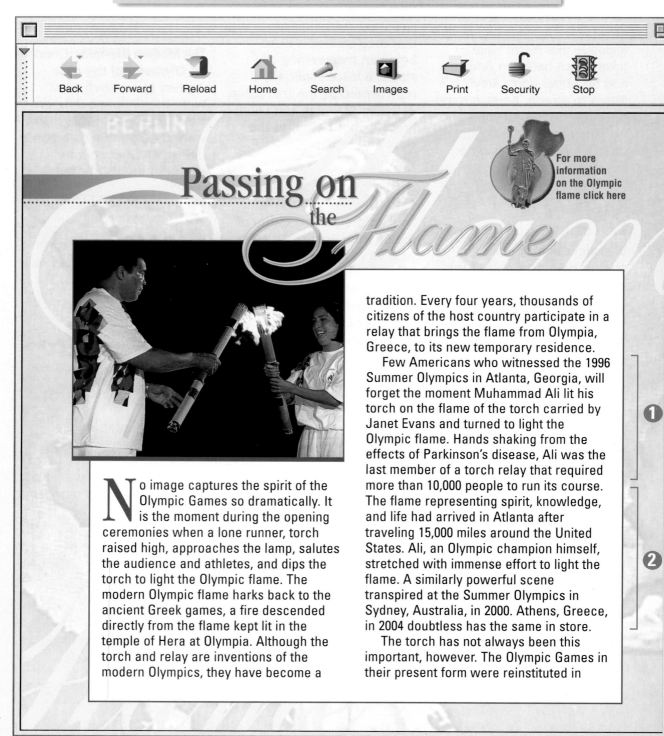

Back Forward Reload Home Search Images Print Security Stop

Passing on the *Flame*

For more information on the Olympic flame click here

N o image captures the spirit of the Olympic Games so dramatically. It is the moment during the opening ceremonies when a lone runner, torch raised high, approaches the lamp, salutes the audience and athletes, and dips the torch to light the Olympic flame. The modern Olympic flame harks back to the ancient Greek games, a fire descended directly from the flame kept lit in the temple of Hera at Olympia. Although the torch and relay are inventions of the modern Olympics, they have become a

tradition. Every four years, thousands of citizens of the host country participate in a relay that brings the flame from Olympia, Greece, to its new temporary residence.

Few Americans who witnessed the 1996 Summer Olympics in Atlanta, Georgia, will forget the moment Muhammad Ali lit his torch on the flame of the torch carried by Janet Evans and turned to light the Olympic flame. Hands shaking from the effects of Parkinson's disease, Ali was the last member of a torch relay that required more than 10,000 people to run its course. The flame representing spirit, knowledge, and life had arrived in Atlanta after traveling 15,000 miles around the United States. Ali, an Olympic champion himself, stretched with immense effort to light the flame. A similarly powerful scene transpired at the Summer Olympics in Sydney, Australia, in 2000. Athens, Greece, in 2004 doubtless has the same in store.

The torch has not always been this important, however. The Olympic Games in their present form were reinstituted in

❶

❷

Key Standard

R2.1 Understand differences between various categories of informational materials (such as textbooks, newspapers, and manuals).

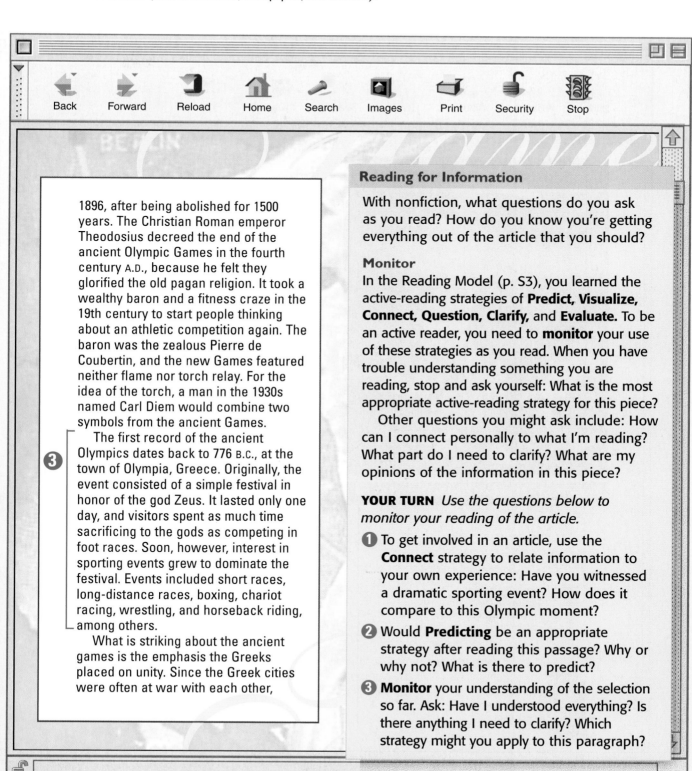

Back   Forward   Reload   Home   Search   Images   Print   Security   Stop

1896, after being abolished for 1500 years. The Christian Roman emperor Theodosius decreed the end of the ancient Olympic Games in the fourth century A.D., because he felt they glorified the old pagan religion. It took a wealthy baron and a fitness craze in the 19th century to start people thinking about an athletic competition again. The baron was the zealous Pierre de Coubertin, and the new Games featured neither flame nor torch relay. For the idea of the torch, a man in the 1930s named Carl Diem would combine two symbols from the ancient Games.

3 The first record of the ancient Olympics dates back to 776 B.C., at the town of Olympia, Greece. Originally, the event consisted of a simple festival in honor of the god Zeus. It lasted only one day, and visitors spent as much time sacrificing to the gods as competing in foot races. Soon, however, interest in sporting events grew to dominate the festival. Events included short races, long-distance races, boxing, chariot racing, wrestling, and horseback riding, among others.

What is striking about the ancient games is the emphasis the Greeks placed on unity. Since the Greek cities were often at war with each other,

Reading for Information

With nonfiction, what questions do you ask as you read? How do you know you're getting everything out of the article that you should?

Monitor

In the Reading Model (p. S3), you learned the active-reading strategies of **Predict, Visualize, Connect, Question, Clarify,** and **Evaluate.** To be an active reader, you need to **monitor** your use of these strategies as you read. When you have trouble understanding something you are reading, stop and ask yourself: What is the most appropriate active-reading strategy for this piece?

Other questions you might ask include: How can I connect personally to what I'm reading? What part do I need to clarify? What are my opinions of the information in this piece?

YOUR TURN *Use the questions below to monitor your reading of the article.*

1 To get involved in an article, use the **Connect** strategy to relate information to your own experience: Have you witnessed a dramatic sporting event? How does it compare to this Olympic moment?

2 Would **Predicting** be an appropriate strategy after reading this passage? Why or why not? What is there to predict?

3 **Monitor** your understanding of the selection so far. Ask: Have I understood everything? Is there anything I need to clarify? Which strategy might you apply to this paragraph?

Back Forward Reload Home Search Images Print Security Stop

FACKELSTAFFELLAUF OLYMPIA·BERLIN

A German postcard commemorating the first torch relay (1936).

For more on the history of the Olympic Games click here

For more on ancient Greece click here

athletes could not always travel safely to and from Olympia. The Greeks solved this problem by declaring a truce for the period of the Games, thus assuring everyone safe passage. To announce the truce, runners swept through the country to herald the time of Olympic peace. The people looked forward to these messengers who ushered in a spirit of unity and a short period of peace.

In addition to the heralds, another symbol associated with the ancient games at Olympia was a flame kept lit in the temple that was dedicated to Hera, the wife of Zeus. For the 1928 Amsterdam Games, Theodore Lewald revived this idea in order to establish a visible connection between the ancient and modern Olympiads. However, it was Carl Diem, a renowned Olympic historian, who brought together both the symbol of the flame and the symbol of the runners when he suggested a modern torch relay for the 1936 Olympics.

In 1936, when the torch relay debuted, 3,075 torchbearers carried the flame from Olympia, Greece, to Berlin, Germany—the site of the Tenth Summer Olympics. For the first time, a flame ignited by the sun in Olympia was faithfully carried by each runner at least a half mile before it was passed to the next. The whole event was carefully choreographed so that the last runner would enter Berlin's 100,000 seat stadium at the scheduled time to commence the Games.

Back   Forward   Reload   Home   Search   Images   Print   Security   Stop

American gold-medalist Jesse Owens (1936).

It was fitting that the birth of the torch relay coincided with African-American runner Jesse Owens's famous Olympic performance. As the German crowd cheered him on, Owens won four gold medals and shattered Hitler's claims that the Aryan race was physically superior. Owens's experience at the Games embodied the spirit of friendly but intense competition that the Olympics were supposed to

represent. When he had trouble qualifying in the long-jump competition, fouling in the first two of his attempts, a German champion long-jumper named Luz Long helped him out. Since Owens had stepped past the official takeoff line on each of his two jumps, Long advised Owens to mark a line several inches before the takeoff mark and jump there—just to be safe. Owens did and qualified for the event; later that day he jumped farther than his German friend and won the gold medal.

As Muhammad Ali took his torch and turned to light the flame, perhaps he paused for a moment, thinking of the tradition of unity and cooperation that Jesse Owens helped to establish.

4

Reading for Information *continued*

4 Pause to **evaluate:** What is your opinion of the use of the Olympic torch relay? What else should you evaluate about the article?

Research & Technology
Activity Link: "A Crown of Wild Olive" p. 727. Now that you have learned about the tradition of the torch, find out about the Olympic mascot or another Olympic tradition. With a partner, prepare a fact sheet about the tradition that you choose.

from Long Walk to Freedom

by NELSON MANDELA

Connect to Your Life

What do you know about the struggle against apartheid?

Build Background

In 1948 the white-controlled government of South Africa established apartheid, or racial segregation. The purpose was to maintain white control. Black South Africans had no political rights. The struggle against apartheid intensified in the 1980s. In 1990–1991 apartheid was repealed. In 1994, Nelson Mandela was elected president. In 1999, Thabo Mbeke became the next president.

NON-WHITE SHOP
THIS NOTICE IS DISPLAYED IN ACCORDANCE WITH THE PROVISIONS OF THE SHOP HOURS ORDINANCE. 1959.

NIE-BLANKE WINKEL
HIERDIE KENNISGEWING IS VERTOON OOREENKOMSTIG DIE BEPALINGS VAN DIE ORDONANSIE OP WINKELURE.1959

Background: South Africans wait to vote in April 1994. *Above left:* Apartheid was enforced by military and police power. *Above right:* Apartheid-era sign indicating a store where blacks were allowed to shop.

Focus Your Reading

LITERARY ANALYSIS **MEMOIR**

A **memoir** is a type of autobiography. In a memoir the author narrates events in his or her own life but also usually describes important events happening in the world. As you read the selection from *Long Walk to Freedom*, notice how Mandela's own story is connected to events in his country.

WORDS TO KNOW **Vocabulary Preview**
curtailed   indivisible   transitory
incomprehensible   resiliency

ACTIVE READING **MAIN IDEA AND DETAILS**

A writer's principle message is called the main idea. The main idea may be the central idea of an entire work or of one paragraph. Details such as facts or additional thoughts clarify, or support, the main idea. As you read this selection, choose a paragraph and jot down the main idea and supporting details in your 📖 **READER'S NOTEBOOK**.

Key Standard
R3.1 Be able to describe the purposes and characteristics of different forms of prose, such as the short story, novel, or essay.
Other Standards **R1.3, R2.6, W2.3, LC1.1, LC1.3, LC1.4, LC1.7, LS1.2**

Freedom to Walk Long

by Nelson Mandela

The policy of apartheid created a deep and lasting wound in my country and my people. All of us will spend many years, if not generations, recovering from that profound hurt. But the decades of oppression and brutality had another, unintended effect, and that was that it produced the Oliver Tambos,[1] the Walter Sisulus, the Chief Luthulis, the Yusuf Dadoos, the Bram Fischers, the Robert Sobukwes of our time—men of such extraordinary courage, wisdom, and generosity that their like may never be known

1. **Oliver Tambos . . . :** South Africans who, like Mandela, had fought against apartheid.

© Gideon Mendel/Magnum

733

> # I learned that courage was not the absence of fear, but the triumph over it.

again. Perhaps it requires such depth of oppression to create such heights of character. My country is rich in the minerals and gems that lie beneath its soil, but I have always known that its greatest wealth is its people, finer and truer than the purest diamonds.

It is from these comrades in the struggle that I learned the meaning of courage. Time and again, I have seen men and women risk and give their lives for an idea. I have seen men stand up to attacks and torture without breaking, showing a strength and resiliency that defies the imagination. I learned that courage was not the absence of fear, but the triumph over it. I felt fear myself more times than I can remember, but I hid it behind a mask of boldness. The brave man is not he who does not feel afraid, but he who conquers that fear.

I never lost hope that this great transformation would occur. Not only because of the great heroes I have already cited, but because of the courage of the ordinary men and women of my country. I always knew that deep down in every human heart, there is mercy and generosity. No one is born hating another person because of the color of his skin, or his background, or his religion. People must learn to hate, and if they can learn to hate, they can be taught to love, for love comes more naturally to the human heart than its opposite. Even in the grimmest times in prison, when my comrades and I were pushed to our limits, I would see a glimmer of humanity in one of the guards, perhaps just for a second, but it was enough to reassure me and keep me going. Man's goodness is a flame that can be hidden but never extinguished.

We took up the struggle with our eyes wide open, under no illusion that the path would be an easy one. As a young man, when I joined the African National Congress,[2] I saw the price my comrades paid for their beliefs, and it was high. For myself, I have never regretted my commitment to the struggle, and I was always prepared to face the hardships that affected me personally. But my family paid a terrible price, perhaps too dear a price for my commitment.

In life, every man has twin obligations—obligations to his family, to his parents, to his wife and children; and he has an obligation to his people, his community, his country. In a civil and humane society, each man is able to fulfill those obligations according to his own inclinations and abilities. But in a country like

---

2. **African National Congress:** the political party opposed to apartheid that Mandela helped found.

WORDS TO KNOW

resiliency (rĭ-zĭl′ yən-sē) *n.* the ability to recover quickly from illness, change, or misfortune

South Africa, it was almost impossible for a man of my birth and color to fulfill both of those obligations. In South Africa, a man of color who attempted to live as a human being was punished and isolated. In South Africa, a man who tried to fulfill his duty to his people was inevitably ripped from his family and his home and was forced to live a life apart, a twilight existence of secrecy and rebellion. I did not in the beginning choose to place my people above my family, but in attempting to serve my people, I found that I was prevented from fulfilling my obligations as a son, a brother, a father, and a husband.

In that way, my commitment to my people, to the millions of South Africans I would never know or meet, was at the expense of the people I knew best and loved most. It was as simple and yet as <u>incomprehensible</u> as the moment a small child asks her father, "Why can you not be with us?" And the father must utter the terrible words: "There are other children like you, a great many of them . . ." and then one's voice trails off.

I was not born with a hunger to be free. I was born free—free in every way that I could know. Free to run in the fields near my mother's hut, free to swim in the clear stream that ran through my village, free to roast mealies[3] under the stars and ride the broad backs of slow-moving bulls. As long as I obeyed my father and abided by the customs of my tribe, I was not troubled by the laws of man or God.

It was only when I began to learn that my boyhood freedom was an illusion, when I discovered as a young man that my freedom had already been taken from me, that I began to hunger for it. At first, as a student, I wanted freedom only for myself, the <u>transitory</u> freedoms of being able to stay out at night, read what I pleased, and go where I chose. Later, as a young man in Johannesburg, I yearned for the basic and honorable freedoms of achieving my potential, of earning my keep, of marrying and having a family—the freedom not to be obstructed in a lawful life.

But then I slowly saw that not only was I not free, but my brothers and sisters were not free. I saw that it was not just my freedom that was <u>curtailed</u>, but the freedom of everyone who looked like I did. That is when I joined the African National Congress, and that is when the hunger for my own freedom became the greater hunger for the freedom of my people. It was this desire for the freedom of my people to live their lives with dignity and self-respect that animated my life, that transformed a frightened young man into a bold one, that drove a law-abiding attorney to become a criminal, that turned a family-loving husband into a man without a home, that forced a life-loving man to live like a monk. I am no more virtuous or self-sacrificing than the next man, but I found that I could not even enjoy the poor and limited freedoms I was allowed when I knew my people were not free. Freedom is <u>indivisible</u>; the chains on any one of my people were the chains on all of them, the chains on all of my people were the chains on me.

It was during those long and lonely years that my hunger for the freedom of my own people became a hunger for the freedom of all

---

3. **mealies** *South African:* corn.

WORDS
TO
KNOW

incomprehensible (ĭn'kŏm-prĭ-hĕn'sə-bəl) *adj.* not understandable
transitory (trăn'sĭ-tôr'ē) *adj.* lasting only a short time; temporary
curtailed (kər-tāld') *adj.* cut short **curtail** *v.*
indivisible (ĭn'də-vĭz'ə-bəl) *adj.* incapable of being divided

735

people, white and black. I knew as well as I knew anything that the oppressor must be liberated just as surely as the oppressed. A man who takes away another man's freedom is a prisoner of hatred, he is locked behind the bars of prejudice and narrow-mindedness. I am not truly free if I am taking away someone else's freedom, just as surely as I am not free when my freedom is taken from me. The oppressed and the oppressor alike are robbed of their humanity.

When I walked out of prison, that was my mission, to liberate the oppressed and the oppressor both. Some say that has now been achieved. But I know that that is not the case. The truth is that we are not yet free; we have merely achieved the freedom to be free, the right not to be oppressed. We have not taken the final step of our journey, but the first step on a longer and even more difficult road. For to be free is not merely to cast off one's chains, but to live in a way that respects and enhances the freedom of others. The true test of our devotion to freedom is just beginning.

I have walked that long road to freedom. I have tried not to falter; I have made missteps along the way. But I have discovered the secret that after climbing a great hill, one only finds that there are many more hills to climb. I have taken a moment here to rest, to steal a view of the glorious vista that surrounds me, to look back on the distance I have come. But I can rest only for a moment, for with freedom come responsibilities, and I dare not linger, for my long walk is not yet ended. ❖

THINKING through the LITERATURE

Connect to the Literature

1. **What Do You Think?** What were your thoughts and emotions at the end of this piece?

   Comprehension Check
   - What does Mandela say are one's "twin obligations"?
   - What did Mandela realize that he had to do when he walked out of prison?

Think Critically

2. How does Mandela's understanding of freedom change over the course of the selection?

   Think About:
   - his memories of childhood
   - how his thoughts about freedom changed when he saw the oppression of others "who looked like I did"
   - his mission "to liberate the oppressed and the oppressor both"

3. How would you describe Mandela's goals for himself as a young man in Johannesburg? How do you think he feels about them, looking back over his life?

4. What is your reaction to Mandela's notion of the "twin obligations" of every citizen?

5. What does Mandela mean by "we are not yet free; we have merely achieved the freedom to be free"?

6. **ACTIVE READING** **MAIN IDEA AND DETAILS** With a small group, share the notes you took in your READER'S NOTEBOOK identifying the main idea and details. Can you observe one idea that runs through all of the paragraphs your group discussed?

Extend Interpretations

7. **Style** Mandela's writing style is very much like a sermon or inspirational speech. With a partner, take turns reading aloud passages from *Long Walk to Freedom.* What makes this piece effective when read aloud? Before you begin, see the Speaking & Listening exercise, page 738. You may want to combine these two activities.

8. **Connect to Life** From dictators that you might have read about in the newspaper to bullies in the playground, can you think of an example that supports Mandela's notion that the oppressor is as trapped as the oppressed? Explain.

Literary Analysis

MEMOIR In a **memoir** the author recalls significant events in his or her own life. Memoirs are usually told from the first-person point of view and are accounts of real occurrences. The author often establishes connections between his or her life and world events. Besides facts, a memoir may include feelings and opinions that give an idea of the impact of history on people's lives.

Activity As a class, make a chart that lists key events in Mandela's life and what he learned from them. Afterward, discuss how these events, as well as the insights he gained from them, linked Mandela more and more to his country and humanity in general.

Experiences in Mandela's Life	What He Learned from Them
As a child, Mandela likes to swim and roast mealies under the stars.	Looking back, he realizes that he was truly born free.
Mandela experiences hardships in prison.	He learns that even in the guards he can still see a "glimmer of humanity."

CHOICES and CHALLENGES

Writing

Personal Essay Mandela says, "The brave man is not he who does not feel afraid, but he who conquers that fear." Write an essay in which you discuss fear and courage and describe a time when you or someone you know acted courageously. Place the essay in your **Working Portfolio.**

Writing Handbook
See p. R47: Explanatory Writing.

Speaking & Listening

In the Extend Interpretations section on page 737, you were asked to read aloud passages from *Long Walk to Freedom.* While a partner is reading passages aloud, listen as if you were in the audience hearing a speech. Evaluate the text based on the following questions:

- What is the speaker's attitude toward the subject?
- What evidence is there to support the speaker's claims?
- What is the overall impact of the message?
- What is the speaker's particular purpose?

Take turns reading passages, evaluating as you listen.

Research & Technology

SOCIAL STUDIES

Use library resources and the Internet to find out about apartheid. What was it? How was it enforced? Who opposed it, and how did apartheid finally end? Write a brief report on your findings and present it to the class.

Research and Technology Handbook
See p. R110: Getting Information Electronically.

INTERNET **Research Starter**
www.mcdougallittell.com

Vocabulary and Spelling

EXERCISE A: ANTONYMS On your paper, write the letter of the word that is most opposite in meaning to each boldfaced word.

1. **resiliency:** (a) brittleness (b) strength (c) flexibility
2. **transitory:** (a) lively (b) lasting (c) short
3. **incomprehensible:** (a) companionable (b) spoken (c) understandable
4. **curtailed:** (a) enlarged (b) worried (c) abandoned
5. **indivisible:** (a) invisible (b) understandable (c) divisible

EXERCISE B: SUFFIXES *-ABLE* AND *-IBLE* Study the spelling words. Then, on a sheet of paper, answer the questions.

adapt + able = adaptable	vis + ible = visible
forget + able = forgettable	divis + ible = divisible
control + able = controllable	indivis + ible = indivisible
advise + able = advisable	cred + ible = credible
excite + able = excitable	tang + ible = tangible
change + able = changeable	ed + ible = edible

1. Is the suffix *-able* added to complete words or to roots?
2. How do the two words ending with a single vowel plus a single consonant in a stressed syllable change when *-able* is added?
3. Three of the base words end with a silent e. What happens to the e in the first two examples?
4. Is the suffix *-ible* added to complete words or to roots?

Spelling Handbook See p. R30.

Grammar in Context: Using Adjective Clauses

A writer can add important information to nouns with adjective clauses.

> In South Africa, a man of color who attempted to live as a human being was punished and isolated.

An **adjective clause** modifies a noun or pronoun and usually follows the word it modifies. Often it begins with a relative pronoun, such as *that, what, which, who, whom,* or *whose.*

Apply to Your Writing Adjective clauses let you make nouns more precise and help you avoid a series of short, choppy sentences. Compare:

The National Assembly adopted a new constitution. The constitution guarantees equal rights to all.

The National Assembly adopted a new constitution that guarantees equal rights to all.

WRITING EXERCISE Combine these sentences by turning one of them into an adjective clause.

Example: Original I was free to swim in the clear stream. The stream ran through my village.

Rewritten I was free to swim in the clear stream that ran through my village.

1. I never lost my hope. I hoped a great transformation would occur.
2. A father must say no to the child. A father loves the child dearly.
3. I have known men and women. They risked their lives for an idea.
4. Mandela started his walk on the long road. The road led to freedom.
5. The policy of apartheid created a deep wound in my country. The policy ended in 1991.

Grammar Handbook
See p. 84: Phrases and Clauses.

Nelson Mandela
born 1918

"My long walk is not yet ended."

Early Years Nelson Rolihlahla Mandela was born in an African village, the son of a tribal chief. "Rolihlahla" means "pulling the branch of a tree" or "troublemaker." As a boy he herded sheep and cattle and played hunting games with his friends.

Imprisonment After earning a law degree, Mandela and a friend opened the first black law office in South Africa. He joined the African National Congress (ANC) in 1944 and later became its president. The ANC was outlawed by the white government in 1960 because it resisted apartheid, but Mandela continued to lead protests. He was arrested in 1962, convicted of sabotage and treason, and sentenced to life in prison on Robben Island. He spent 27 years in prison and became an international symbol of the fight for racial justice.

Justice Achieved In 1990 Mandela was finally freed to international acclaim. He then worked with white government leaders to end apartheid and give black Africans the right to vote. For their work to end apartheid, Mandela and then-South African president F. W. de Klerk won the Nobel Prize for peace in 1993. In 1994, South Africa held its first election in which all citizens could vote. The ANC party won a majority, and Nelson Mandela became the first black president of South Africa.

The Elephant

by RUDYARD KIPLING

The Turtle

by MARY OLIVER

Connect to Your Life

No Choice We don't always have a choice about what happens in life. With a small group of classmates, talk about an experience when you or someone you know had to do something or endure something and had no choice about it. Was it a positive or negative experience?

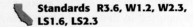

Standards R3.6, W1.2, W2.3, LS1.6, LS2.3

Build Background

SCIENCE

Rudyard Kipling was born and lived in India, where elephants were used as work animals. Elephants are still used today in the logging industry in some Asian countries. An elephant can carry a heavy load on its back and can carry a log as heavy as 600 pounds with its trunk.

Mary Oliver's poem describes the egg-laying behavior of a pond turtle. All turtles, even species that live in water, lay their eggs on land. The female crawls to a nesting site, digs a hole with her back feet, and lays her eggs. She covers them with sand or plant material, leaves the nest, and does not return. Baby turtles must dig their way out, find food, and survive entirely on their own.

Focus Your Reading

LITERARY ANALYSIS **IMAGERY**

Words and phrases that create vivid sensory experiences for the reader are called **images** or **sensory details.** For example, Pablo Neruda's description of the artichoke as a soldier in "Ode to an Artichoke" is an example of a visual image.

> *The soft-hearted*
> *artichoke*
> *put on armor,*
> *stood at attention . . .*

Many images appeal to the sense of sight, but images may also appeal to hearing, smell, taste, and touch. As you read the poems, pay attention to the imagery.

ACTIVE READING **PARAPHRASING**

When you paraphrase something, you restate it in your own words. Paraphrasing can often help you better understand a poem. A paraphrase often uses simpler language than the original, but it is not necessarily shorter, since it is not a summary. A paraphrase is a reshaping of information. To paraphrase, you need to
- find the **main idea** the writer conveys
- notice **details** that indicate what the writer feels or sees
- if possible, think of simpler or more familiar ways of saying what the writer has written

READER'S NOTEBOOK As you read these poems, think of ways you might paraphrase them. This is difficult with poetry; a paraphrase will lack the power and subtlety of the original, but look for main ideas that you could state in your own words and jot them down.

The Elephant

by
RUDYARD
KIPLING

I will remember what I was. I am sick of rope and chain—
 I will remember my old strength and all my forest-affairs.
I will not sell my back to man for a bundle of sugar-cane.
 I will go out to my own kind, and the wood-folk in their lairs.

I will go out until the day, until the morning break,
 Out to the winds' untainted kiss, the waters' clean caress.
I will forget my ankle-ring and snap my picket-stake.
 I will revisit my lost loves, and playmates masterless!

National Museum of Khmer Art,
Phnom Penh, Cambodia.

THINKING *through the* LITERATURE

- Why does the elephant yearn for its "past life"?
- The elephant says, "I will go out until the day." What does the elephant mean?
- What is the contrast between the elephant's "lost loves, and playmates" and itself?

The Turtle

by

MARY

OLIVER

breaks from the blue-black
skin of the water, dragging her shell
with its mossy scutes[1]
across the shallows and through the rushes
and over the mudflats, to the uprise,
to the yellow sand,
to dig with her ungainly[2] feet
a nest, and hunker there spewing
her white eggs down
into the darkness, and you think

of her patience, her fortitude,[3]
her determination to complete
what she was born to do—
and then you realize a greater thing—
she doesn't consider
what she was born to do.
She's only filled
with an old blind wish.
It isn't even hers but came to her
in the rain or the soft wind,
which is a gate through which her life keeps walking.

She can't see
herself apart from the rest of the world
or the world from what she must do
every spring.
Crawling up the high hill,
luminous[4] under the sand that has packed against her skin.
she doesn't dream
she knows
she is a part of the pond she lives in,
the tall trees are her children,
the birds that swim above her
are tied to her by an unbreakable string.

Soup tureen in the form of a
turtle (1790s). Sheffield City
Museum, South Yorkshire,
U.K./Bridgeman Art Library,
London/New York.

---

1. **scutes** (sküts): the bottom of the turtle's shell.
2. **ungainly**: clumsy.
3. **fortitude**: strength.
4. **luminous**: glowing.

Connect to the Literature

1. **What Do You Think?** What emotions or thoughts did the last lines of "The Turtle" evoke in you?

   Comprehension Check
   • What qualities does the turtle need to "complete / what she was born to do"?
   • What does the turtle "know" about her relationship to nature?

Think Critically

2. In the first stanza, what would you say impresses the speaker about the turtle's egg laying?

3. In the second stanza, the speaker realizes a "greater thing," namely, that the turtle is filled "with an old blind wish." What do you think this means?

   Think About:
   • "she doesn't consider / what she was born to do"
   • "She can't see / herself apart from the rest of the world"
   • "she knows / she is a part of the pond she lives in"

4. Both the elephant and the turtle have strong relationships to nature. How would you compare and contrast those relationships?

5. **ACTIVE READING** **PARAPHRASING**
   Select one of the two poems and rewrite it, or a portion of it, in your own words. Look at the notes you took in your **READER'S NOTEBOOK** for ideas. Your paraphrase should include the important elements of the poem you choose. Share your paraphrase with the class. Compare it with the paraphrases your classmates wrote.

Extend Interpretations

6. **Writer's Style** Mary Oliver says when reading poetry a reader should "look for verbs of muscle." How might this apply to each poem?

7. **Connect to Life** Do you think enough attention is paid to wild animals' need for their environment?

Literary Analysis

IMAGERY Words or phrases that appeal to a reader's senses are called images or sensory details. **Imagery** helps the reader imagine the sights, sounds, tastes, smells, or feelings the poet is describing. For example, Mary Oliver writes that the turtle is "luminous under the sand that has packed against her skin." This imagery appealing to the reader's senses of sight and touch makes the description mean more than "the turtle was covered with sand." Similarly, when the elephant says, "I will not sell my back to man for a bundle of sugar-cane," the imagery creates a more powerful picture than saying, "I don't like carrying heavy objects."

Activity With a partner, go back through both poems and use a chart to note images that strike you and their effect in the poems. Then, in a small group, discuss the images you have chosen.

"The Elephant"	"The Turtle"
Image: rope and chain	**Image:** breaking through "the blue-black skin" of the water
Effect: It helped me to imagine how the elephant is being held captive.	**Effect:** It helped me to see the stillness of the water.

CHOICES and CHALLENGES

Writing

Animal Poem or Description
Think of an animal that has made a lasting impression on you. What is unique about this animal? Write a poem or a descriptive paragraph about the animal. Place the description in your **Working Portfolio.**

Writing Handbook
See p. R43: Descriptive Writing.

Speaking & Listening

Choral Reading With a small group, practice a choral reading of both poems. Practice reading so that the meaning will be clear to a listener. Present your choral reading to the class.

Speaking and Listening Handbook
See p. R102: Present.

Research & Technology

Elephants Like People
Observers have commented on the many "human" qualities elephants seem to have. For example, elephants have long memories, and female elephants will care for each other's young. Use the library or other resources to investigate elephant behavior and how it resembles human behavior. Present your report to the rest of the class.

Research and Technology Handbook
See p. R111: Library Computer Services.

Mary Oliver
born 1935

"The poem was made not just to exist, but to speak—to be company."

Solitary Childhood Mary Oliver is known for highly descriptive poems about nature. She grew up in a small Ohio town and knew early on she wanted to write poetry. Her "friends" were the poets she read in books.

Student of Nature As a high school student, Oliver was happier rambling around in the woods than she was in the classroom. She always carried a knapsack filled with books and notebooks in which she recorded her thoughts and observations of nature. The poetry of Walt Whitman was always among the books she carried with her. She later described Whitman as "the brother I did not have."

Writing Poetry Oliver attended Ohio State University and Vassar College. Her first book of poems appeared in 1963. Mary Oliver has written more than 10 books of poetry and won many prizes. Her collection entitled *American Primitive* won the Pulitzer Prize and her *New and Selected Poems* won the National Book Award. She lives in Provincetown, Massachusetts.

AUTHOR ACTIVITY
"What blazes the trail is not necessarily pretty."
Oliver's poem "Skunk Cabbage" ends with this line. Read some of her other poems. Does this thought apply to them? What would you say about Oliver's view of nature?

Rudyard Kipling
For a biography, see page 137.

Building Vocabulary
Researching Word Origins

English has absorbed many words from other languages over the centuries. Understanding a word's **etymology**—its history and origin—can help you to make sense of a word you don't know and to recognize family relationships between words.

Most English words can be traced back to Old English (the earliest form of the language), Latin, or Greek, but English has borrowed words from other languages as well.

Key Standard
R1.2 Use knowledge of roots and affixes to understand vocabulary in different content areas.

> As they skirted the great open space of the **Hippodrome, where the chariot races would be held on the second day of the Games, they** came up with a couple of the Athenian contingent, strolling under the plane trees.
>
> —Rosemary Sutcliff, "A Crown of Wild Olive"

Greek *hippos:* horse
and *dromos:* racecourse

Latin *carrus:* cart

Old English *trēow:* tree

Strategies for Building Vocabulary

Learning about a word's origins will give you deeper knowledge of the word and will help you remember its meaning. It can also help you understand the meanings of related words. Use the following strategies to figure out etymology.

❶ **Use a Dictionary** An easy way to find a word's etymology is to use a dictionary. This information will usually appear at the beginning or end of the entry. Look at this dictionary entry for *contradict:*

con•tra•dict (kŏn'trə-dĭkt') *v.* **-dict•ed, -dict•ing, -dicts.** —*tr.* **1.** To assert or express the opposite of (a statement). **2.** To deny the statement of. See synonyms at **deny. 3.** To be contrary to; be inconsistent with. —*intr.* To utter a contradictory statement. [Lat. *contrādīcere, contrādict-,* to speak against : *contrā-,* contra- + *dīcere,* to speak] —**con'tra•dict'a•ble** *adj.* —**con'tra•dict'er, con'tra•dict'or** *n.*

This entry shows that *contradict* came from Latin, with the prefix *contra-,* "against," and *dicere,* "to speak." Its meaning hasn't changed much over time. Some words have gone through a variety of stages. In this situation the first word listed is the most recent, and the list moves backward in time from there.

❷ **Recognize Word Families** Words with the same origin usually have related meanings. The words in the following chart all come from the Latin word *sistere,* which means "to place, set, stop, or stand." As you can see, all of the words listed have something to do with firmness.

Words Derived from Latin *sistere*	
insist	to be firm in a demand
persist	to be stubbornly insistent or repetitious
resist	to try to fend off

EXERCISE Look up each word in a dictionary. Trace the derivation back to the oldest word listed and its meaning.

1. transitory
2. illustrious
3. resilient
4. seize
5. allege
6. frankfurter
7. footpath
8. honor
9. bottle
10. Olympics

Author Study VIRGINIA HAMILTON

Writer of Past and Present

"The past moves me and with me, although I remove myself from it. Its light often shines on this night traveler: and when it does, I scribble it down."

born 1936

"EXCEPTIONALLY FINE STORYTELLERS"

Virginia Hamilton grew up with stories. The youngest of five children, she was raised on a 12-acre farm near Yellow Springs, Ohio. In the quiet country evenings, sitting by the fire or on the porch, she loved listening to her parents, aunts, and uncles, who were all storytellers. They were "exceptionally fine storytellers," Hamilton has noted, "and realized, although I don't know how consciously, that they were passing along heritage and culture and a pride in their *history.*"

Virginia (*right*) with her uncle and cousin.

Her **LIFE** and **TIMES**

1936 Born March 12 in Yellow Springs, Ohio

1952 Receives scholarship to Antioch College

1958 Moves to New York City

1960 Marries Arnold Adoff

1930   1940   1950   1960

1941 United States enters World War II.

1942 Congress of Racial Equality (CORE) founded

1950–1953 Korean War Gen. MacArthur leads UN forces, 1950–1951.

Fascinated by the stories she heard, Hamilton began to keep a journal in which she wrote things that she thought were interesting or exciting. She loved to read and won prizes in school for reading the most books. At school in the 1940s, Hamilton was the only black child in her class until the seventh grade. Very little was taught in school about black history or accomplishment, but the lively talk and family stories in the Hamilton's home—such as how her maternal grandfather, Levi Perry, escaped from slavery by the Underground Railroad—gave her a deep and lasting pride in her African-American heritage.

"I WANTED WITH ALL MY SOUL TO GET TO MANHATTAN"

After she graduated from high school, Hamilton accepted a scholarship to nearby Antioch College, where she majored in writing. But she yearned for new surroundings. Of that period in her life, Hamilton has written: "I wanted with all my soul to get to Manhattan, but it seemed I was trapped forever." Finally, she found a summer job as a bookkeeper in New York City. Captivated by city life, she left college and moved to New York City.

Virginia Hamilton in New York City.

Did You Know?

- Virginia Hamilton once worked as a nightclub singer.
- She was named after her grandfather's home state.
- She is the first African-American woman to have won the Newbery Medal.
- She collects frog jokes and images of frogs.

1968
Publishes
The House of Dies Drear

1975
Wins Newbery Medal and National Book Award

1995
Receives Laura Ingalls Wilder Medal for lasting contributions to children's literature

1999
Publishes
Bluish

1970   1980   1990   2000

1964
Civil Rights Act passed.

1965–1973
U.S. ground troops in Vietnam War

1968
Martin Luther King, Jr., is assassinated.

1986
The space shuttle *Challenger* explodes.

1991
Soviet Union breaks up.

VIRGINIA HAMILTON

In the 1950s, the East Village, the section of New York City where Hamilton lived, was an exciting place to be. It was an active, integrated community of writers, artists, and musicians. The place inspired Hamilton to continue her reading and writing. Among other works of literature, she read the classics and works by Mexican writers. She also worked at different jobs while she continued her study of writing at The New School for Social Research. In 1960 she married Arnold Adoff, a young poet. And, remembering the stories she had heard as a child, Hamilton began to keep a scrapbook about Africa.

"WHAT I SEE IS ANOTHER TIME"

Hamilton's interest in Africa inspired her first published novel, *Zeely* (1967), the story of a young girl who imagines that a woman in her town is an African queen. Soon after the publication of *Zeely,* Hamilton moved back to Yellow Springs, Ohio. Memories of the stories Hamilton heard as a child continue to nourish her writing. "I choose what I see, and what I see is another time," Hamilton has said. She explains:

Memories of all those years, of summer days, winter nights, storms and sunshine, have given ample food to my imagination all of my life. So has living here in my hometown of Yellow Springs, Ohio. My husband and I built our house on the last few acres of my family's farm.

Virginia Hamilton and her husband, Arnold Adoff, at home in Ohio.

Today, Hamilton and her husband still live and work in Yellow Springs. She continues to write for young people in several genres—including fiction, folk tales, fantasy, and nonfiction. Hamilton spends time traveling and making speeches, but her first love is writing. She has published more than 34 books and collected many awards.

TALKING WITH VIRGINIA HAMILTON

In the following interview, Hamilton responds to questions about her life and her writing.

Q: Do you use a computer or word processor to do your writing?

A: When I'm writing, I use a computer with a word processing program.

Q: How do you start writing a novel?

A: That's a funny question. You just start, until a paragraph becomes a page and then you keep going page by page.

Q: Who influenced you to be a writer?

A: I started writing when I was in grade school, so I don't know who influenced me. I heard lots of stories from family.

Q: How do you find a good illustrator for your books?

A: I choose illustrators with my editor. We decide who would be good for a particular book.

Q: Besides yourself, what other authors do you enjoy reading?

A: I read many in my field and other adult writers: Cynthia Voigt, for one. I read extensively in my field.

Q: Do you have any advice for young writers?

A: Young writers should read as much as they can and write for at least 15 minutes a day, and keep a journal.

Q: Would there be any other occupation that you would be interested [in] other than being an author?

A: In my younger days I was a singer. I used to sing in clubs, and I have a daughter who is an opera singer and a son who is a song writer with his own band. So if I weren't a writer, I would be a singer.

Q: Do you visit classrooms and talk with students?

A: I don't do it anymore. I get so many requests, I can't go to schools and get my work done. I do answer a lot of fan mail and email.

Q: What was your favorite book as a child?

A: I loved the Nancy Drew books, because that's what was available. She had her own car and was very independent and solved mysteries.

Q: Did you keep a journal as a young child?

A: I kept a notebook and put everything in it that I thought was exciting. Unfortunately, I lost it when I was 13.

Q: Do you think that books are the future for kids?

A: I think reading is the future for kids whether they read from a computer or books. I think reading leads to books—I think books will continue READING!

INTERNET Author Link
www.mcdougallittell.com

NetActivities: Author Exploration

from Anthony Burns: The Defeat and Triumph of a Fugitive Slave

by VIRGINIA HAMILTON

Key Standard
R3.1 Be able to describe the purposes and characteristics of different forms of prose, such as the short story, novel, or essay.
Other Standard R3.2

What I Know About Slavery and Abolition	What I Want to Know	What I Learned

Connect to Your Life

Slavery and the Abolitionists What do you know about the institution of slavery in the United States and the abolitionist movement? Make a chart like this one and fill in the first two columns. Complete the third after you read the selection.

Build Background

HISTORY

In 1850 Congress enacted the Fugitive Slave Law in an attempt to prevent disputes between the Southern slaveholding states and the free states in the North. Under this law, the federal government claimed jurisdiction over the return of fugitives to slaveholders. Federal marshals were made responsible for helping recapture escaped slaves. Those who helped slaves to escape would be subject to fines and prison sentences. Some antislavery states—such as Massachusetts—resisted. They stood by their personal liberty laws and refused to accept the federal government's jurisdiction in these matters. Abolitionists, those who fought to abolish slavery, considered the practice of slave-catching to be kidnapping. When Anthony Burns, a fugitive from Virginia, was captured on the streets of Boston in 1854, the abolitionist community stood ready to fight for his freedom.

WORDS TO KNOW
Vocabulary Preview

agitate   mobilize
alleged   peer
compliance   petty
contradict   throb
illustrious   wretched

Focus Your Reading

LITERARY ANALYSIS   LITERARY NONFICTION

Writing that tells about actual people, places, and events is called nonfiction. Informative nonfiction provides information in a straightforward manner. **Literary nonfiction** also conveys information, but it does so by telling a story. Literary nonfiction includes literary elements like setting, character, and conflict. As you read this selection from *Anthony Burns,* notice the literary devices.

ACTIVE READING   MONITOR

Good readers actively **monitor** their reading strategies as they read. They stop now and then to review what they've learned and decide whether they need to adjust the reading strategies they are using in order to better understand what they're reading. Monitoring involves questions like: Do I need to ask more questions about what is going on in the selection? Do I need to clarify more in order to better understand the roles of key characters? Do I need to take more notes to remember key details of the selection?

READER'S NOTEBOOK As you read, use a chart to list the key characters involved in the capture, trial, and defense of Anthony Burns. In a column beside the names, jot down whether that person was trying to free Burns or return him to slavery.

ANTHONY BURNS:
THE DEFEAT AND
TRIUMPH OF A
FUGITIVE SLAVE

BY
VIRGINIA
HAMILTON

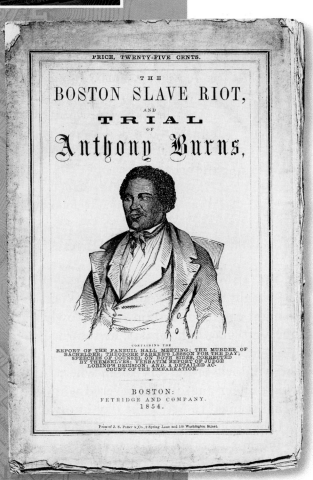

PRICE, TWENTY-FIVE CENTS.

THE
BOSTON SLAVE RIOT,
AND
TRIAL
OF
Anthony Burns,

CONTAINING THE
REPORT OF THE FANEUIL HALL MEETING; THE MURDER OF
BACHELDER; THEODORE PARKER'S LESSON FOR THE DAY;
SPEECHES OF COUNSEL ON BOTH SIDES, CORRECTED
BY THEMSELVES; VERBATIM REPORT OF JUDGE
LORING'S DECISION; AND, A DETAILED AC-
COUNT OF THE EMBARKATION.

BOSTON:
FETRIDGE AND COMPANY.
1854.

Price of J. S. Potter & Co., 2 Spring Lane and 130 Washington Street.

Cover of a pamphlet
describing the trial of
Anthony Burns and
resulting protests, 1854.

Anthony Burns: The Defeat and Triumph of a Fugitive Slave was inspired by real events that took place in Boston in the spring of 1854. Anthony Burns, an escaped slave from Virginia, was arrested on the streets of Boston on the evening of May 24, 1854, while on his way home from work. Under the provisions of the Fugitive Slave Law, a warrant had been issued for Burns's arrest by Colonel Charles F. Suttle, Burns's owner, who had journeyed north hoping to capture Burns and return him to slavery. Burns was brought before the U.S. Commissioner, Edward G. Loring, who, along with Suttle, U.S. District Attorney Benjamin Hallett, and other city officials, wanted to keep Burns's trial quiet. But acquaintances of Burns noticed his absence and by chance saw him being brought in chains into the courthouse, led by U.S. Marshal Freeman and his deputies, John Riley and Asa Butman. Butman was notoriously efficient in catching runaway slaves. Soon, the most prominent abolitionists in the area became involved in Burns's case: Theodore Parker, Richard Henry Dana Jr., and the Reverend Leonard Grimes. Both sides knew that the trial was not just about Anthony Burns; it was about slavery itself.

The excerpt you are about to read describes events on the first day of Burns's trial. It is a scene of internal and external struggle. Throughout his ordeal, Burns thinks back to figures from his childhood: "He Mars" John Suttle, father of Charles Suttle and Burns's owner when he was a child; "Mamaw," his mother; Janety, the sister who raised him; and "Big Walker," "driver," or foreman, of John Suttle's slaves who was rumored to have been Burns's father.

MAY 25, 1854

The weight of the past and the darkness of its night enclosed Anthony until slowly, with the growing light of day, he returned to the present.

The windows of the jury room where he was kept under guard were covered with iron bars that seemed to break the day into welts of pain. If he could somehow keep his eyes from those bright stripes, he might keep his suffering at bay. But it was no use.

Here I be! he despaired. Caught, I am, and no longer a man. Father, protect me!

He tried retreating again into the past, but all that would come to him was the time of sadness in Mamaw's cabin. With him these many years was the same question, born out of that night. "Who am I?" For the thousandth time he asked himself, "Be I the slave owner's own boy or the slave driver's son? He Mars John's or Big Walker's?"

Again, he lifted his good hand, as he had so many times before. Held it close to his eyes to see it better. There was no denying his skin was light brown. Big Walker had been a dark man, his mamaw a very black woman.

It had been whispered about the plantation that Big Walker Burns was once a freeman. That he had been tricked, caught, and brought down South. But Anthony never knew for certain if this was true, nor did any other of Mars John's black folks. Big Walker never said anything about it directly.

What matter any of it now? Anthony thought. Here I be, like a starved dog in his pen.

Anthony's stomach ached him, he was so hungry. He hadn't eaten since sometime in the dayclean before this. The room stank from the odor of stale ale and sweat. Anthony felt dizzy, then sick to his stomach from the stench. He would have to have something to eat and soon, or he would faint dead away.

Presently the heavy door to the jury room swung open. A man entered. He went over to Asa Butman. "Get him ready," he said. "We have to take him down now."

He came over to Anthony. "Deputy Marshal Riley," he said, introducing himself. "You are going to court now, Anthony. Go with Asa here. He will see that you fix yourself up a bit."

Anthony did as he was told. In a small room off to the side he washed his face and smoothed his hair. There was no comb or brush for him. He straightened his clothing. He took a tin cup of cold water that Asa offered him, but that was all he was given. When he and Butman came out again, Deputy Riley ordered irons closed around his wrists.

Anthony went numb into himself. He moved down the steps like a sleepwalker. When he entered the room set aside in this state Court House as a Federal courtroom, he made no response to seeing Colonel Suttle and William Brent there flanked by men he had never seen before—their lawyers. Also present was the one called Marshal Freeman. Some ten of his men, deputies, were with him.

Anthony took the prisoner's seat across from the judge's bench as he was directed by Asa.

"I'm makin' no promises, Tony," Colonel Suttle said to him calmly as he seated himself,

"and I'm makin' no threats."

Anthony heard what Suttle said but could give no answer. He was aware of all that went on around him, but it was hard now for him to keep his mind on any one thing for long. His head felt light. He wanted so much just to lie down. The wrist irons and the chain that connected them grew heavier by the minute. Anthony couldn't find the strength or will to lift a finger even to scratch his nose, which itched him. The itching became a dull aching. It in turn spread into a throbbing loneliness throughout his body. He felt miserably hot in his shoulders and deathly cold in his legs.

THE WRIST IRONS AND THE CHAIN THAT CONNECTED THEM GREW HEAVIER BY THE MINUTE.

Anthony bowed his head. For the rest of the time he sat as if hypnotized.

Asa Butman and one of his men took their seats on either side of Anthony. Also present and seated was the U.S. Attorney for the Federal Government, District of Massachusetts, Benjamin Hallett. Hallett was a politician who believed his position as U.S. District Attorney gave him the right to oversee the government's policy of rigidly executing the Fugitive Slave Act. He agreed with that policy, in fact. He and the other officials present hoped that the examination would be completed as soon as possible. There had been no inkling of a fugitive arrest in the morning papers. Reporters knew nothing yet about what was going on.

WORDS
TO   **throb** (thrŏb) *v.* to beat strongly (as though hurting)
KNOW

United States Commissioner Edward G. Loring.

Colonel Suttle and Mr. Brent intended to take the prisoner out of Boston and down South before the dreaded Boston "radicals"[1] knew about his capture. Ben Hallett hoped they would, too. For if the abolitionists found out, they had a hundred ways in which they might come to Burns's defense. They might try to mob Colonel Suttle or even have him prosecuted for kidnapping.

The prisoner was definitely the slave Anthony Burns. He had admitted as much when he had first faced the Colonel. It was a simple matter, then, of going through the proceeding according to law. Colonel Suttle had provided an affidavit[2] of ownership, and Commissioner Loring had issued a warrant for Burns's arrest. There would be a hearing as

soon as possible, it was hoped—all strictly according to provisions[3] of the Fugitive Slave Act. The Commissioner would then issue the Colonel a certificate allowing him to take the prisoner back to Virginia. But unknown to the Colonel or anyone else in the courtroom, the Boston abolitionists were already informed.

Coffin Pitts, Anthony's employer and landlord, had been looking for him all the previous night.

"Anthony? Anthony!" Coffin Pitts called. When he couldn't find him anywhere in his house, he went out at once in search of him. He looked everywhere in the fugitives' quarter he could think of, but Anthony seemed to have disappeared into thin air. Fearing the worst, he went straight to Exeter Place, the home of the abolitionist Reverend Theodore Parker.

Reverend Parker was the minister of the 28th Congregational Society. He believed, he always said, in an Almighty God and the equality and dignity of all who were God's children. He had gained national attention for the sermons he preached to thousands each Sunday in the enormous music hall called Tremont Temple.

"I know that men urge in argument," Theodore Parker preached, "that the Constitution of the United States is the supreme law of the land, and that it sanctions[4] slavery. There is no supreme law but that

---

1. **Boston "radicals":** local supporters of the abolition of slavery; abolitionists.
2. **affidavit** (ăf´ĭ-dā´vĭt): a written declaration made under oath before a notary public or other authorized officer.
3. **provisions:** stipulations of the law.
4. **sanctions:** permits.

made by God; if our laws <u>contradict</u> that, the sooner they end or the sooner they are broken, why, the better."

Almost every word that Parker uttered made Coffin Pitts smile in agreement. Yet he couldn't bring himself to awaken Reverend Parker when he got to his home. He waited, nodding and dozing, on Theodore Parker's front steps all night long.

Reverend Parker found him there Thursday morning when he opened the door to let in the morning air. "Good Lord, man, come in, come in!" he said, and ushered Deacon Pitts inside. "You must be chilled through. Here, let us have coffee." Parker proceeded to the kitchen and prepared coffee while Deacon Pitts told him of the missing Anthony Burns.

"I am sorry to have to tell you this," said Parker, "but there are Virginia slavers in town."

"Oh, no!" Deacon Pitts said.

"Yes, I'm afraid so," Parker answered. "Tuesday morning another colored man, a waiter from the Revere House, came to see me. Said he had waited on two Virginia slave hunters at breakfast.

"He gave me useful information," Parker continued. "The slavers are a Colonel Suttle and William Brent. But the man didn't know which slave it was they were after. So for two days I asked everyone I could think of, and nobody knew! Not even Reverend Grimes of your church—and he dared not question his congregation, lest they panic and run away north toward Canada."

Reverend Leonard Grimes had been born in Virginia of free parents who had bought their freedom from a sympathetic owner. As an adult there he ran a livery stable, and he used his horse-drawn carriages to transport fugitives farther north under cover of darkness. Once he went deep into Virginia and carried out an

entire slave family; three months later he was caught and sent to prison for two years for the crime of aiding runaways. After his release Reverend Grimes moved to Boston, where he continued his work as a minister and friend to all escaped slaves.

"The slavers have been among us, hunting, and we had no wind of it for two days!" exclaimed Deacon Pitts. "They caught us unawares."

"Yes, and I daresay the slavers are here after your Anthony," replied Reverend Parker. "Well. You may stay as long as you like, Deacon Pitts, but I must be off. Have yourself another of my brew. Get yourself warmed! I'm going to the Court House."

With that, Parker hurried out. He had not let Deacon Pitts see it, but he was seething with anger. That some men would even think to enslave other men made his blood boil. That was why, when the Fugitive Slave Act had become law in 1850, he had slapped a revolver down on his desk and left it there as clear warning to all slave hunters.

He knew that for the South, passage of the Fugitive Slave Act was a signal for an intensive manhunt in the North. And it was not long before Southern authorities sent people North to bring back fugitives and to spy on abolitionist groups. In response to this, Northern blacks and whites took direct action to head off <u>compliance</u> with the law. Theodore Parker found the rising tension and possibility of violence quite unpleasant. He was not a violent man himself. But if forced to, he would without question defend a fugitive with his life.

As he neared the Court House, Parker happened to meet Charles Mayo Ellis, a lawyer and member of the Boston Vigilance Committee. The Vigilance Committee was a large, secret body of abolitionists organized to

WORDS TO KNOW

contradict (kŏn′ trə-dĭkt′) v. to express the opposite of; to be contrary to
compliance (kəm-plī′ əns) n. the act of obeying a request or a command

755

operate on a moment's notice. Its main purpose was "to secure the fugitives and colored inhabitants of Boston and vicinity from any invasion of their rights."

Parker quickly explained the situation to Ellis. He then asked Ellis to go to the Court House to observe what was taking place and to keep watch over the fugitive. "I'll go find Richard Dana," Reverend Parker said. Richard Henry Dana was another member of the Vigilance Committee, a well-known novelist as well as an attorney.

But it was Reverend Leonard Grimes of the 12th Baptist Church who was the first of the Vigilance Committee to see Anthony Burns handcuffed in the prisoner's box. Passing by the Court House, he had noticed unusual activity and had gone inside, only to see Anthony surrounded by armed guards. Alarmed, Reverend Grimes approached Anthony.

"My son, are you all right?" he asked. "Please, tell me what I may do for you now."

Anthony made no reply, and looked through space at nothing. Sadness and fear, poor soul! the reverend thought. Anthony appeared to be in a trance, unmindful or unknowing of his situation. I can't leave him alone in his condition, the reverend decided.

One of the guards at Anthony's side stood up, menacing the reverend. He put his hand on his gun butt, and Reverend Grimes backed away from the prisoner's dock. He knew it was best to act timidly before such <u>petty</u> officials. Quickly, bowing his head slightly, he took a seat in the rear of the court to wait and see what would happen next.

The Reverend Theodore Parker.

The slave catchers watched him sit down. So did District Attorney Ben Hallett. Asa Butman whispered to Hallett, "Sir, might I throw that preacher out? He ain't got any business at all bein' in here."

"No, leave him alone," Hallett said. He knew Reverend Grimes to be a respected colored minister, able enough at fund-raising to have raised ten thousand dollars and built himself a church. "Better to have him in here where we can keep an eye on him than outside where he might make trouble," he explained.

"Yassir, as you wish, then," Asa said. "But give the word and he's out as quick as you please." He winked at Hallett as if they were conspirators.

WORDS
TO
KNOW

petty (pĕt′ ē) *adj.* of little importance, trivial

756

Ben Hallett looked pained. To think he must depend on the lowest life, such as Butman, to see that the Federal law was enforced! He turned away in distaste and busied himself with his court papers as Asa hurried back to his post beside Anthony.

MAY 25, 1854

Richard Henry Dana was not in his office when Theodore Parker went there looking for him. He had learned early that morning, as had Reverend Grimes, that a fugitive was about to appear in court before Commissioner Edward G. Loring. While passing the Court House on his way to work, Dana had been approached by a stranger and told the bad news.

"Good God!" he had said. "I need a runner!" He soon found a Negro youth he knew well, one of the many among the growing community of free persons and fugitives who lived in Boston.

Without further delay Dana sent the youth to find members of the Boston Vigilance Committee. For it was the Committee's sworn duty to defend, without fee, all black inhabitants of Boston and vicinity against slavers and bounty hunters.

Dana, one of the Committee's most <u>illustrious</u> members, had helped defend the fugitive slave Thomas Sims in court in 1851. As a young man he had withdrawn from Harvard when measles had weakened his eyesight, and had, in 1834, shipped out to California as a sailor to regain his health. After calling at California's ports loading cargo, his ship sailed around Cape Horn and returned home to Boston in 1835.

Dana's travel experiences cured him physically and also taught him sympathy for the less fortunate. He reentered Harvard and was admitted to the Massachusetts bar in 1840. That same year he published *Two Years Before the Mast*, a novel written from diaries he'd kept at sea about "the life of a common sailor as it really is." In it he revealed the awful abuses endured by his fellow seamen at the hands of their superiors. The book made him famous.

When the slavery question moved North with the fugitives, Dana put novel writing aside. His political party was Free Soil, which meant he did not oppose slavery in the South. But he vowed to fight against its spread into the western land tracts, such as Kansas and

> **ANTHONY MADE NO REPLY, AND LOOKED THROUGH SPACE AT NOTHING. SADNESS AND FEAR, POOR SOUL!**

Nebraska. He lost many of his wealthy, proslavery clients because of this "moderate" view, but he didn't care.

"I am against slavery in the North," he said again and again.

By 1854 Dana no longer put much faith in justice. He had defended two slaves already, Sims and another popularly known as Shadrach, and neither case had ended well. Sims had lost his case and was returned to Georgia, where he died. Shadrach had been "stolen," from the very Court House that now held Anthony Burns, by black abolitionists who managed to get him away to freedom.

Justice and law both had come out scarred and battered, Dana observed grimly at the time. But he believed that gentlemen must

WORDS TO KNOW

illustrious (ĭ-lŭs′ trē-əs) *adj.* well-known or distinguished

behave with justice. And if slave hunters wished to take back a slave, then they would have to proceed at every turn strictly according to the law.

Let them make a single wrong explanation, and I will have them! Richard Dana thought.

Now he braced himself and entered the courtroom.

Dana swiftly took in the scene, observing the armed guards around the prisoner. So that's Burns, he thought. And as pitiful-looking a fugitive as I've ever seen. Not the man Sims was, surely. This one looks lost witted.[5]

> ## "IT'S OF NO USE," ANTHONY RESPONDED, FINALLY. "THEY KNOW ME. MARS CHARLES, THE COLONEL, KNOWS ME. I WILL FARE WORSE IF I RESIST."

The slave had a small scar on his cheek—a brand of some kind, Dana supposed. One hand, his right, was hideously deformed, and Dana assumed at once that Burns had been awfully mistreated by his owner. He glanced over at the man within the bar—the railing that separated the public from the rest of the courtroom—who he rightly guessed was Colonel Charles Suttle, slave owner of Virginia, surrounded by his agent and lawyers.

So then, Dana thought, they mean to have it all their way, and quickly. But not so fast!

He walked over to Anthony, ignoring the guards and Marshal Freeman. "I'm a lawyer," he said to Anthony. "Richard Dana is my name.

Let me help you. And there will be no fee."

Anthony was shocked to hear the learned voice of a white man speaking to him. Who? . . . A buckra[6] again. Seems to care . . . kind voice. But the Colonel, he standing up. Glaring so at me.

Colonel Suttle, hearing what Dana had said, had risen to his feet. His face was red with fury.

Anthony dared not answer Richard Dana.

"Anthony," Dana persisted, "there are certain papers from Virginia that an owner must have in order. These might have mistakes. And you might get off if you have a lawyer."

There was a long silence. Anthony was thinking, Oh, I feel so ashamed. I should have said something to Reverend Grimes first, when Mr. Grimes come to talk to me. Should have said how sorry I was to have got myself captured. How I should've gone to the dedication of Reverend Grimes' church. Then maybe none of this would have happened.

Oh, so many shoulds!

The white man still stood there before him.

"I . . . I . . ." Anthony began.

"Yes?" Dana said quickly.

"I . . . don't know," Anthony finished, murmuring so low that Dana had to come even closer to hear.

Anthony didn't know what to do. He did know that Mars Charles would make his life miserable if it cost him extra time and money to get Anthony back down South.

"Anthony? Tell me what you want," Dana said.

"It's of no use," Anthony responded, finally. "They know me. Mars Charles, the Colonel, knows me. I will fare worse if I resist."

Dana straightened up. He reasoned that Anthony was frightened out of his wits by the

---

5. **lost witted:** completely bewildered.
6. **buckra:** *old slang,* a white person.

The Reverend Leonard Grimes.

numbers of hostile white men in the room—
a dozen guards, all armed, the Marshal, the
District Attorney, his owner, and the others.
Clearly, Anthony was threatened by them.

I can't defend him unless he wants me to,
Dana kept thinking. The fugitive must ask
to be represented. Dana could not otherwise
take his case. I need time! he was thinking.

At that instant four other abolitionist
lawyers, members of the Vigilance Committee,
entered the court: Charles Mayo Ellis,
Theodore Parker, Wendell Phillips, and a black
lawyer, Robert Morriss.

Not two minutes later the Commissioner,
Judge Edward Loring, walked briskly in.

Immediately, Marshal Freeman spoke loudly,
"The court. All rise."

Anthony was made to stand, as everyone in
the courtroom got to his feet. After the judge
sat down, Anthony and the rest sat.

Judge Loring looked askance at all the
guards in the room. He asked Marshal
Freeman why there were so many and
was told how difficult were the circumstances surrounding the capture of
Burns. Judge Loring then asked whether
the defendant was in the prisoner's dock.

"Yes, Your Honor," the Marshal
answered.

"Is the claimant[7] here, or his agent?"
Loring asked.

"Both of them are here, Judge,"
Marshal Freeman answered.

"Then we may begin," Judge
Loring said.

At that point Richard Dana asked to
speak to Loring privately.

Loring agreed, and Dana explained
how frightened the prisoner, Anthony
Burns, was. "He cannot act even in his
own behalf," Dana said. "I suggest that
you call him up to the bench instead of
addressing him in the prisoner's dock. He will
then be out of the way of the gaze of the
claimant, Colonel Suttle. And so we might
know what he wants to do."

"I intend to do that," Judge Loring said.
"But now I must proceed."

"Yes, of course," Dana said, "thank you,
Your Honor." And he sat down.

Judge Loring started the proceedings by
saying that he was presiding as a U.S.
Commissioner, that his duties were executive,
and that the hearing was an inquiry. The
question before the court, he said, was whether
he should award to Charles F. Suttle a certificate
authorizing him to take to Virginia the slave
Anthony Burns. The claim was that Anthony
Burns owed Mr. Suttle service and labor.

---

7. **claimant:** a person who makes a claim in court.

"There are three facts that are to be proved," Loring said. "And these are: that Anthony Burns escaped from slavery from the state of Virginia; that Anthony Burns was by the law of Virginia the slave of Charles F. Suttle; that the prisoner is indeed Anthony Burns.

"If counsel for Charles Suttle can prove these facts," the judge continued, "I am empowered to issue a certificate stating the proofs; this will allow the rendition of Anthony Burns."

Anthony listened now and understood. He knew what rendition was. Means me, he thought, taken back home by Mars Charles. Means me, a slave again.

He swallowed hard and felt himself retreat within. But there was no comfort now. His loneliness and fear, his <u>wretched</u> hunger, wouldn't permit him to bring the memory of Mamaw into this harsh place. Neither could he bring forth the child he had been. Where was that young Anthony now? he wondered, for he could not summon the image of the boy he had been.

The second counsel for Charles Suttle, Edward G. Parker, now rose, and read from the warrant for Anthony's arrest:

"In the name of the President of the United States of America, you are hereby commanded forthwith to apprehend Anthony Burns, a negro man, alleged now to be in your District, charged with being a fugitive from labor, and with having escaped from service in the State of Virginia, and have him forthwith before me, Edward G. Loring, one of the Commissioners of the Circuit Court of the United States, there to answer to the complaint of Charles F. Suttle, of Alexandria, alleging under oath that said Burns, on the twenty-fourth day of March last,

and for a long time prior thereto had owed service and labor to him in the State of Virginia and that, while held to service there by said Suttle, the said Burns escaped into the said State of Massachusetts. . . ."

He next read the record of the Virginia Court as required by the Fugitive Slave Act:

"In Alexandria Circuit Court, May 16, 1854. On the application of Charles F. Suttle, who this day appeared in Court and made satisfactory proof to the Court that Anthony Burns was held to service and labor by him in the State of Virginia, and service and labor are due to him from the said Anthony, and that the said Anthony has escaped. Anthony is a man of dark complexion, about six feet high, with a scar on one of his cheeks, and also a scar on the back of his right hand, and about twenty-three or four years of age—it is therefore ordered, in pursuance of an act of Congress, 'An Act respecting Fugitives from Justice and Persons escaping from the Service of their masters,' that the matter set forth be entered on the record of this Court."

The abolitionist lawyer Charles Mayo Ellis watched the proceedings closely. When he saw Richard Dana speak privately to Judge Loring, he supposed Dana meant to make himself the lawyer for Anthony Burns. But when this did not seem to be his purpose, Mr. Ellis made his way to Dana's side as quietly as he could.

As Edward Parker went on with the Alexandria Circuit Court record, Ellis spoke urgently to Richard Dana. "Loring is sitting as a *judge*, Richard. You must *do* something. Massachusetts law clearly forbids judges sitting on slave cases.

WORDS TO KNOW

wretched (rĕch′ ĭd) *adj.* miserable

"There's no jury," Ellis added. "The armed guards sitting illegally in the jury box are plainly petty thieves being used to terrify an already frightened man."

Richard Dana shrugged. "What can I do?" he said. "Anthony Burns would seem to want to go back without trouble to his master. He won't accept my aid."

Reverend Theodore Parker got to his feet. He could stand it no longer. It was clear to him that the poor fugitive was being tried without a lawyer. He marched angrily to the front of the courtroom just as Edward Parker was finishing and before Marshal Freeman could testify.

He strode up to the witness box and peered into it. On seeing that Anthony was handcuffed, he glared indignantly at Judge Loring. Next, he spoke to Anthony.

"I am Theodore Parker," he said. "I am a minister. Surely you want me to help you."

He could see that Anthony was frozen with fear. "Let us give you counsel," Parker said. "Richard Dana there is the best lawyer in Boston. He is on your side! The black man over there is Robert Morriss and a fine lawyer, too. Will you not let us defend you?"

Anthony began to shake all over. Lord, oh, Lord! Tell me what I must do! he thought.

But he couldn't help seeing that Mars Charles Suttle watched him, that Mars Brent watched him. Anthony commenced stammering, "Mars . . . Mars . . . Colonel . . . he know . . . he knows me . . . I shall have to go back. Mars Brent . . . know me."

Richard Henry Dana.

"But it can do you no harm to make a defense," urged Parker.

"I shall have to go back," Anthony said again. "If I must . . . go back, I want ter go back as easy as I can—but—do as you have a mind to."

Theodore Parker strode back to his seat. He was thinking that if Charles Suttle's lawyers put a nervous witness on the stand and the witness made a false statement, they might have a case. He gave a nod to Richard Dana, to say that Dana had the prisoner's permission to defend him.

Colonel Suttle's other lawyer, Seth Thomas, now rose. He was upset that Theodore Parker had interrupted, but he did not show it. He at once put William Brent upon the stand as a witness to prove the identity of the prisoner with the person named in the arrest warrant. Brent gave his testimony confidently.

He was a merchant from Richmond, Virginia, he said. And he was a close friend of Colonel Suttle.

"Do you know Anthony Burns?" Mr. Thomas asked.

"Yes, I know him well," he said. And he stated that Anthony Burns was the prisoner in the prisoner's box.

"Can you tell us something about Anthony Burns?" Thomas asked.

Brent began speaking as if reciting: "Anthony Burns was owned by the Colonel's mother. Colonel Suttle has owned him for some fourteen years. I paid the Colonel for the services of Anthony Burns in 1846, '47, and '48."

"Good. Now then," the lawyer said, "can you tell me what you know about his escape?"

"In March," said Brent, "Anthony was missing from Richmond. I didn't see him again until last day past, when he spoke to his master."

"Kindly repeat what was said then," said Thomas.

Theodore Parker rose to his feet again. Brent's statements concerning this conversation would be improper testimony. "You've got to defend him now," he told Richard Dana as he stood. "And if you won't, I will!"

Judge Loring struck with his gavel in an effort to quiet Reverend Parker. Before the Marshal and his deputies could think to restrain the pastor, Richard Dana rose to address the court. It was clear to him that the prisoner would have to have his aid at once. Under the Fugitive Slave Act, the testimony of the <u>alleged</u> fugitive could not be admitted as evidence.

Despite this, Anthony's testimony was about to be admitted. Dana had to prevent this.

He presented himself to Judge Loring as *amicus curiae*, or friend of the court—one who is called in to advise the court. "I urge Your Honor that there be a delay so that the prisoner can decide what would be his best course," he said.

"I oppose this motion, Your Honor," responded Seth Thomas. "The prisoner by his own statement has admitted that he is Charles Suttle's slave. He does not want a lawyer, nor does he want a defense."

"The prisoner is in no condition to determine whether he would have counsel or not!" Dana said heatedly. "He does not know what he is saying. He must be given time to recover himself and to talk with a lawyer."

Over the objections of both of Suttle's lawyers, Judge Loring had Anthony Burns brought before him. Marshal Freeman hurriedly unlocked Anthony's wrist irons before leading him to the judge.

Loring spoke to Anthony in a kindly manner, explaining what the claim against him was. "Anthony, do you wish to make a defense to this claim?" he asked. "If you do, you can have counsel to aid you, and you shall have time to make a defense. You have a right to a defense if you wish for one."

Anthony finally dared look around the room slowly. His gaze rested on Richard Dana and then on Robert Morriss, but he made no reply.

Dana thought it was all over then. But Judge Loring said to Anthony reassuringly. "Anthony, do you wish for time to think about this? Do you wish to go away and meet me here tomorrow or next day, and tell me what you will do?"

alleged (ə-lĕjd′) *adj.* supposed

All in the courtroom watched Anthony. He gave a slight twitching of his deformed hand, but no one knew whether he meant yes or no by the movement. He did not know himself.

I will have to go back, he was thinking. I will be whipped unto an inch of my life. I will die a slave.

Judge Loring looked doubtful, but at last he said to Anthony, "I understand you to say that you would."

Very faintly, Anthony said, "I would."

"Then you shall have it," Loring said.

Marshal Freeman whispered to the judge.

> ## HE GAVE A SLIGHT TWITCHING OF HIS DEFORMED HAND, BUT NO ONE KNEW WHETHER HE MEANT YES OR NO BY THE MOVEMENT.

Judge Loring replied out loud, "No sir, he must have the time necessary."

Again the Marshal whispered. Judge Loring replied sternly, "I can't help that, sir—he shall have the proper time."

The day was Thursday. "You shall have until Saturday morning," Judge Loring told Anthony and his defenders, and struck his gavel down.

Anthony was taken back to the jury room high up in the court building. There four men, including Deputy Asa Butman, guarded him.

"Tony, boy," Butman said to him, mimicking words spoken by Charles Suttle, "now we here are curious. Did the Colonel just *raise* you up or did he *buy* you from somebody?"

The other guards nodded encouragement. "Come on, lad, you know us here for your friends."

Anthony knew they thought him a fool. He had figured out that they hoped to get information from him for Mars Charles and Mars Brent. He knew there must be a reward for him. Every runaway slave had a price on his head.

Wonder how much Mars Charles think me worth?

Anthony played dumb; he acted confused, stared off into space, and told his jailers nothing.

THE COURT had emptied, and almost at once news of Anthony's arrest spread throughout Boston. The concerned public learned that slave hunters were in the city, hoping to force another wretched soul back into bondage.

All sympathetic citizens, and there were thousands, felt duty bound to disobey the Fugitive Slave act on behalf of the captured fugitive in their midst. But there was another factor that mobilized them: for months there had been a proposal before Congress that would allow slavery in the Great Plains lands of Kansas and Nebraska. The two tracts were to be territories within the Louisiana Purchase, the enormous parcel of land, stretching from the Gulf of Mexico to Canada, bought from France in 1803. The Missouri Compromise of 1820 had closed the Louisiana Purchase to slavery "forever." But people on the proslavery as well as the antislavery sides had been

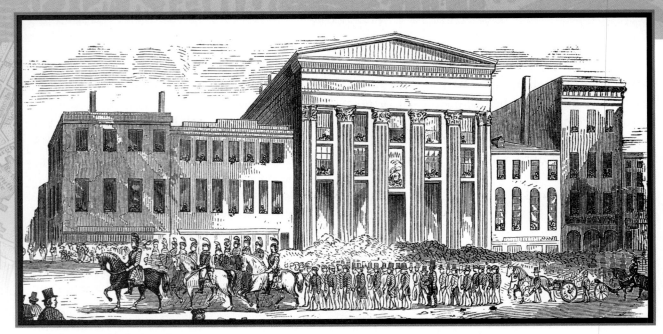

A marshal's posse with Anthony Burns.

sending their settlers into Kansas and Nebraska to agitate and to be in a position to vote for their sides once the territories were divided into states.

On May 25, 1854, the very same day that Anthony appeared in court, the Kansas-Nebraska Bill passed in the United States Senate. It permitted slavery in states that would be carved from the two territories if it was provided for in the state constitutions. So in effect it repealed the Missouri Compromise. After these victories for slavery, the jailing of a poor fugitive in a Boston court house at the bidding of a slave owner was the very last straw for those against slavery. Thus had the slavocracy rocked the cradle of liberty.

By evening the news that Anthony Burns had escaped from the South only to be captured in the free North moved from town to town and newspaper to newspaper across the country.

KIDNAPPING AGAIN! read the first leaflet out of Boston that told the tale:

A man was stolen Last Night
By the Fugitive Slave Bill Commissioner
He will have His

MOCK TRIAL

On Saturday, May 27, in the Kidnapper's Court
Before the Honorable Slave Bill Commissioner
At the Court House in Court Square
SHALL BOSTON STEAL ANOTHER MAN?

Thursday, May 25, 1854

Written by Reverend Parker, the leaflet was printed by the antislavery press and carried across Massachusetts by volunteers who worked on trains, stagecoaches, and trucks. As it was being distributed, Theodore Parker had time to fire off another leaflet:

**SEE TO IT THAT NO FREE CITIZEN
OF MASSACHUSETTS
IS DRAGGED INTO SLAVERY**

WORDS TO KNOW

agitate (ăj′ ĭ-tāt′) v. to stir up public interest in a cause

Overnight, without his ever knowing it, Anthony Burns became a symbol of freedom. But high up in the Court House he was a tired, miserable prisoner, alone save for his guard of petty criminals.

Anthony felt he had no one to turn to. He had no way of knowing that all through the night men watched the three massive doors of his granite prison Court House. It was a different time from 1851, when Thomas Sims was taken. The watchers made certain the authorities knew of their presence. Their message was clear: Anthony Burns was cared for.

Anthony was unaware that abolitionist ministers and lawyers argued fiercely hour upon hour over their next course of action on his behalf. There was no one to inform him that the slavers, Suttle and Brent, were followed everywhere by black men who never looked at them but were always in their sight. Suttle became so terrified that these blacks would try to lynch him, he and Brent moved to quarters in the Revere House attic and hired bodyguards.

In two short days Anthony had become a symbol to freedom lovers and a devilish token of danger to slavers like Suttle. But the courteous Reverend Leonard Grimes and his deacon, Coffin Pitts, never for an instant confused the man, the fugitive, with his cause. They agreed that Reverend Grimes must try to see Anthony the next morning.

Anthony knew none of this. He wished to shut out the prying questions of guards hoping to trick him. He did what he knew how to do best of all: He retreated within, taking comfort in his unchanging past. ❖

In the days that followed the initial hearing, several unsuccessful attempts were made to free Anthony Burns. Some of these attempts were peaceful, some of them were not. When the trial resumed, witnesses came forward to testify for both sides, but the final ruling was in the hands of Commissioner Loring. While pretending to be sympathetic to Anthony, Loring made decisions that troubled the defense. These decisions heightened tensions within the courtroom and the crowd that had gathered outside, as well as among a growing number of persons throughout Massachusetts and beyond who had learned of Anthony's plight. Could Anthony Burns resume his life as a free man or would he be returned to Charles Suttle as escaped "property," sure to face punishment and possibly death? The outcome of Loring's decision would prove that both cowardice and courage can be part of the human spirit.

One of the two checks used to purchase Anthony Burns.

Connect to the Literature

1. What Do You Think?
What were your feelings as you came to the end of this selection? Explain.

Comprehension Check
- Why is Anthony Burns brought before Judge Loring?
- How do the abolitionists find out about Burns's arrest?

Think Critically

2. **ACTIVE READING** | **MONITOR**
Review the notes you made in your 📖 READER'S NOTEBOOK. Compare them with those of a classmate to see if you agree on which characters were proslavery and which were antislavery. If you disagree, reread portions of the text and look for details to help you clarify the information.

3. How would you describe the change in the way Anthony Burns felt toward the abolitionists who were trying to help him? Why do you think Burns's feelings changed?

4. What were your feelings about Edward Loring, a judge sworn to uphold the Fugitive Slave Act yet a man who seems to act kindly toward Burns?

5. What do you think the author means when she says, "Anthony Burns became a symbol of freedom"?

> **Think About:**
> - efforts to keep Burns's arrest and trial a secret
> - the reaction of Grimes and Dana when they first see Burns
> - the pamphlets circulated by Parker

Extend Interpretations

6. What If? At one point, Anthony Burns thinks about what would have happened if he had gone to the dedication of Reverend Grimes's church. He thinks that he wouldn't have been arrested because he wouldn't have been on the street where the slave catchers found him. Do you agree? Why or why not?

7. Connect to Life Review the chart you created for Connect to Your Life on page 750. Do you have any questions the selection didn't answer? Discuss them with your classmates.

Literary Analysis

LITERARY NONFICTION Writers of both informative nonfiction and **literary nonfiction** describe actual people, places, and events in their works. In informative nonfiction this is done in a straightforward fashion. The writer of literary nonfiction, however, includes elements common to fiction, such as plot, setting, dialogue, and character development, for example, to present the information.

In the excerpt from *Anthony Burns,* Virginia Hamilton presents information about the actual events and participants in the capture and trial of Anthony Burns, but she dramatizes them with fictional elements that bring the events to life for the reader.

Activity With a partner, review the selection and jot down what literary elements, such as description or bits of dialogue, you discovered as you read the excerpt from *Anthony Burns.* Afterward, discuss how the selection's literary devices helped you to appreciate the real-life experiences of Anthony Burns.

Literary Elements

Description:
The author's description of the pain Burns felt from his wrist and ankle chains was really powerful.

The People Could Fly

from **The People Could Fly**
retold by VIRGINIA HAMILTON

Key Standard
R3.1 Be able to describe the purposes and characteristics of different forms of prose, such as the short story, novel, or essay.
Other Standards **R3.2, R3.6, W1.3, W1.4, W2.3, W2.5, LC1.4, LS2.1**

Connect to Your Life

Pass It On Can you think of an inspiring story that has been passed down to you? What did you learn from this story? Do you think that you could be like the hero or heroes who are a part of it? Share your responses with a partner.

Build Background

HISTORY

When Europeans colonized the Western Hemisphere, they brought with them the institution of slavery. A cheap labor supply was needed to support the large-scale farming the colonists established. People were kidnapped in Africa and sent to America to be sold as slaves. Between the 1500s and the 1800s, some 12 million Africans were sent to the Western Hemisphere.

Most slaves in the United States worked as field hands, planting and harvesting crops such as indigo, tobacco, rice, and cotton. Their work was long and tedious, usually beginning at sunrise and ending at sunset.

Laws in the Southern states prohibited slaves from owning property, getting an education, marrying, and buying their own freedom. Despite these laws, slaves managed to develop a sense of community, a means of communication, a culture, and a tradition. One part of that tradition is the body of stories, myths, and legends that the slaves told. Some of these stories had African origins; some were created in America. "The People Could Fly" is an example of one of these stories.

WORDS TO KNOW **Vocabulary Preview**
glinty   scorn   seize   shuffle   snag

Focus Your Reading

LITERARY ANALYSIS   FOLK TALE

African-American **folk tales** developed among Africans transported to America as slaves. Slaves were not allowed to speak their own language or learn how to read or write English, so they passed down their culture and experience orally. Tales such as "The People Could Fly" provided slaves comfort and hope and preserved their history.

ACTIVE READING   SUMMARIZING

You can check your understanding of what you read, and remember it better, if you **summarize** it. To summarize a story, retell only the **main ideas,** using your own words. Leave out unimportant details.

READER'S NOTEBOOK. A **story map** is one way to record and remember important details about a selection. A story map can also help you write a summary of a story. As you read, use a story map like this to record details from "The People Could Fly."

Characters: *Toby, Sarah, Driver,*
Conflict:
Time and Place:

Event 1:
Event 2:
Event 3:
Resolution:

[The People Could] *Fly*

retold by
Virginia Hamilton

Illustration by Leo and Diane Dillon, from *The People Could Fly* by
Virginia Hamilton. Illustration Copyright © 1985 Leo and Diane
Dillon. Reprinted by permission of Alfred A. Knopf, Inc.

They say the people could fly. Say that long ago in Africa, some of the people knew magic. And they would walk up on the air like climbin' up on a gate. And they flew like blackbirds over the fields. Black, shiny wings flappin' against the blue up there.

Then, many of the people were captured for Slavery. The ones that could fly shed their wings. They couldn't take their wings across the water on the slave ships. Too crowded, don't you know.

The folks were full of misery, then. Got sick with the up and down of the sea. So they forgot about flyin' when they could no longer breathe the sweet scent of Africa.

Say the people who could fly kept their power, although they shed their wings. They kept their secret magic in the land of slavery. They looked the same as the other people from Africa who had been coming over, who had dark skin. Say you couldn't tell anymore one who could fly from one who couldn't.

One such who could was an old man, call him Toby. And standin' tall, yet afraid, was a young woman who once had wings. Call her Sarah. Now Sarah carried a babe tied to her back. She trembled to be so hard worked and <u>scorned</u>.

The slaves labored in the fields from sunup to sundown. The owner of the slaves callin' himself their Master. Say he was a hard lump of clay. A hard, <u>glinty</u> coal. A hard rock pile,

wouldn't be moved. His Overseer[1] on horseback pointed out the slaves who were slowin' down. So the one called Driver cracked his whip over the slow ones to make them move faster. That whip was a slice-open cut of pain. So they did move faster. Had to.

Sarah hoed and chopped the row as the babe on her back slept.

Say the child grew hungry. That babe started up bawling too loud. Sarah couldn't stop to feed it. Couldn't stop to soothe and quiet it down. She let it cry. She didn't want to. She had no heart to croon[2] to it.

"Keep that thing quiet," called the Overseer. He pointed his finger at the babe. The woman scrunched low. The Driver cracked his whip across the babe anyhow. The babe hollered like any hurt child, and the woman fell to the earth.

The old man that was there, Toby, came and helped her to her feet.

"I must go soon," she told him.

"Soon," he said.

Sarah couldn't stand up straight any longer. She was too weak. The sun burned her face. The babe cried and cried, "Pity me, oh, pity me," say it sounded like. Sarah was so sad and starvin', she sat down in the row.

---

1. **Overseer:** a person who directs the work of others; a supervisor.
2. **croon:** to sing softly.

WORDS TO KNOW

scorn (skôrn) *v.* to treat with contempt
glinty (glĭn′ tē) *adj.* sparkling

> **There was a great outcryin'. The bent backs straighted up. Old and young who were called slaves and could fly joined hands.**

"Get up, you black cow," called the Overseer. He pointed his hand, and the Driver's whip snarled around Sarah's legs. Her sack dress tore into rags. Her legs bled onto the earth. She couldn't get up.

Toby was there where there was no one to help her and the babe.

"Now, before it's too late," panted Sarah. "Now, Father!"

"Yes, Daughter, the time is come," Toby answered. "Go, as you know how to go!"

He raised his arms, holding them out to her. *"Kum . . . yali, kum buba tambe,"* and more magic words, said so quickly, they sounded like whispers and sighs.

The young woman lifted one foot on the air. Then the other. She flew clumsily at first, with the child now held tightly in her arms. Then she felt the magic, the African mystery. Say she rose just as free as a bird. As light as a feather.

The Overseer rode after her, hollerin'. Sarah flew over the fences. She flew over the woods. Tall trees could not <u>snag</u> her. Nor could the Overseer. She flew like an eagle now, until she was gone from sight. No one dared speak about it. Couldn't believe it. But it was, because they that was there saw that it was.

Say the next day was dead hot in the fields. A young man slave fell from the heat. The Driver come and whipped him. Toby come over and spoke words to the fallen one. The words of ancient Africa once heard are never remembered completely. The young man forgot them as soon as he heard them. They went way inside him. He got up and rolled over on the air. He rode it awhile. And he flew away.

Another and another fell from the heat. Toby was there. He cried out to the fallen and reached his arms out to them. *"Kum kunka yali, kum . . . tambe!"* Whispers and sighs. And they too rose on the air. They rode the hot breezes. The ones flyin' were black and shinin' sticks, wheelin' above the head of the Overseer. They crossed the rows, the fields, the fences, the streams, and were away.

"<u>Seize</u> the old man!" cried the Overseer. "I heard him say the magic *words*. Seize him!"

WORDS
TO
KNOW

snag (snăg) *v.* to catch and tear
seize (sēz) *v.* to grab suddenly with force

Fly

The one callin' himself Master come runnin'. The Driver got his whip ready to curl around old Toby and tie him up. The slave owner took his hip gun from its place. He meant to kill old black Toby.

But Toby just laughed. Say he threw back his head and said, "Hee, hee! Don't you know who I am? Don't you know some of us in this field?" He said it to their faces. "We are ones who fly!"

And he sighed the ancient words that were a dark promise. He said them all around to the others in the field under the whip, ". . . *buba yali . . . buba tambe . . .*"

There was a great outcryin'. The bent backs straighted up. Old and young who were called slaves and could fly joined hands. Say like they would ring-sing. But they didn't <u>shuffle</u> in a circle. They didn't sing. They rose on the air. They flew in a flock that was black against the heavenly blue. Black crows or black shadows. It didn't matter, they went so high. Way above the plantation, way over the slavery land. Say they flew away to *Free-dom.*

And the old man, old Toby, flew behind them, takin' care of them. He wasn't cryin'. He wasn't laughin'. He was the seer. His gaze fell on the plantation where the slaves who could not fly waited.

"Take us with you!" Their looks spoke it, but they were afraid to shout it. Toby couldn't take them with him. Hadn't the time to teach them to fly. They must wait for a chance to run.

"Goodie-bye!" the old man called Toby spoke to them, poor souls! And he was flyin' gone.

So they say. The Overseer told it. The one called Master said it was a lie, a trick of the light. The Driver kept his mouth shut.

The slaves who could not fly told about the people who could fly to their children. When they were free. When they sat close before the fire in the free land, they told it. They did so love firelight and *Free-dom,* and tellin'.

They say that the children of the ones who could not fly told their children. And now, me, I have told it to you. ❖

WORDS
TO
KNOW

shuffle (shŭf′ əl) *v.* to slide the feet along the ground while walking

771

Connect to the Literature

1. **What Do You Think?**
   What emotion would you feel if you were one of the people left behind? Discuss your response with a partner.

   Comprehension Check
   - What special power did some of the people in Africa have?
   - What does the Driver do to Sarah and her baby?
   - Who went on to tell the story of the people who could fly?

Think Critically

2. **ACTIVE READING** **SUMMARIZING**
   Look at the notes that you took in the story map you put in your **READER'S NOTEBOOK**. Summarize the story in your own words. Make your summary as brief as possible, but be sure to include the main ideas. Compare your summary with that of a classmate and discuss how you might improve your summaries.

3. Since people really can't fly, what do you think this story meant to the people who heard it?

   Think About:
   - the way that enslaved people were treated
   - what the people wished for
   - how the people felt about themselves

4. How does Virginia Hamilton make this story and the characters come alive? How does she make it seem almost possible that the people could fly?

Extend Interpretations

5. **Writer's Style** The story retold as "The People Could Fly" was passed on by generations of storytellers before it was written down. In retelling it, Virginia Hamilton chose to have her narrator speak in dialect. The narrator's voice sounds as if it could be that of one of the characters in the story itself. How does this add to the story? How does it affect the reader?

6. **Connect to Life** What kind of power do words hold for you? Look through a book of quotations and choose two that express a feeling or an idea that you think is important. Explain why you think these quotations are powerful.

Literary Analysis

FOLK TALES Stories told by African-American slaves about their real and imaginary experiences are called African-American **folk tales.** These stories combine elements from Africa with American ones. Originally part of the oral tradition—stories told in family or community gatherings—many African-American folk tales were collected and written down by historians to preserve them. Virginia Hamilton wanted to bring them "out of the musty old manuscripts where nobody ever saw them" so that these stories could be read, retold, and understood by new generations. In "The People Could Fly," Hamilton skillfully brings one of these folk tales to life for her readers.

REVIEW: DIALECT Dialect is a form of language spoken in a certain place by a certain group of people. The spelling of words written in dialect can vary slightly from the correct spelling. Often, an apostrophe will take the place of a single letter. For example, with words like *cryin', callin',* and *runnin',* an apostrophe takes the place of the final "g," changing the pronunciation slightly.

Grammar in Context: Punctuating Dialogue

Hamilton uses dialogue to capture the unique voices of her characters.

> Toby was there where there was no one to help her and the babe.
> "Now, before it's too late," panted Sarah. "Now, Father!"
> "Yes, Daughter, the time is come," Toby answered. "Go, as you know how to go!"

To avoid confusing the reader, she places quotation marks at the beginning and end of direct speech and begins a new paragraph whenever the speaker changes.

Apply to Your Writing Capitalize the first word in a direct quotation if it is a complete sentence. At the end of a quotation, place periods and commas inside the quotation marks. Place question marks and exclamation points inside if they belong to the quotation; place them outside if they do not belong to the quotation.

WRITING EXERCISE Supply the missing punctuation marks in the sentences.

Example: _Original_ Keep that baby quiet, said the Overseer.

Rewritten "Keep that baby quiet," said the Overseer.

1. I can help you, the old man said to Sarah.
2. Sarah told him, I must go soon.
3. After a while, the Overseer said, Seize the old man!
4. Don't you know who we are? he said to their faces. We are ones who fly!
5. Take us with you! cried those who were left behind.
6. Good-bye, said the ones who could fly.

Grammar Handbook
See p. R93: Quotations.

Vocabulary

EXERCISE A: RELATED WORDS For each Word to Know, create and complete a diagram like the model below.

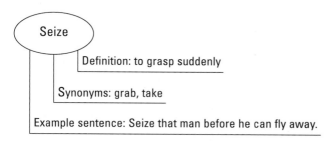

EXERCISE B: WORD ORIGINS Modern scholars believe that many of today's languages have their roots in one common language spoken around 7,000 years ago. English, a member of the Germanic family of languages, contains many words that come from other languages, particularly Greek and Latin. All of the vocabulary words in this selection are descended from Germanic words. Use a dictionary or encyclopedia to find some of the other modern languages in the Germanic family. How might words from a different language have entered English?

Vocabulary Handbook
See p. R26: Word Origins.

WORDS TO KNOW	glinty	scorn	seize	shuffle	snag

Looking for America

Speech by
Virginia Hamilton

PREPARING to *Read*

Build Background

In 1993, Virginia Hamilton gave a speech at a banquet in honor of the thirtieth anniversary of the Cooperative Children's Book Center. She spoke of the importance of memory, history, and the telling of stories: "We each have a story. We write it as we live it. We change it, we amend it, we revise it, but we continue telling our tales to ourselves, at least." In the portion of the speech reprinted here, Hamilton expresses how her work continues to grow out of her own life experiences.

I wonder, sometimes, there before the fire in a long winter, how I write certain of my own books. Take *The Planet of Junior Brown*. It's one of the few of my books I never tire of. It still reads well. It still makes me proud. If I could, I'd rewrite *M.C. Higgins, the Great*, but of course, I can't. I'd rewrite *W.E.B. DuBois* and *Paul Robeson*. I love *Anthony Burns* just the way it is—a very hard book to do, but it was good work and it pleases me. I don't know how I wrote the *Justice* trilogy. I like it a lot. I only remember that I was in a state of terror the whole time. There is really good stuff in *A Little Love*, things that I'm proud of—the way Grandmom and Pop talk, their fears, her forgetfulness. Grandmom and Pop seem very human to me. I didn't like Sheema's father when she finds him, but I thought I did a good job of presenting him. He came through as what he was. I think *A White Romance* and *Cousins* are very good books, although very different. They still seem true. *Plain City* seems the truest, but that may be because it's still so close to me. I enjoyed making its degree of difficulty read simply.

*T*his is the way I think about the work I do, and I think about it all the time. I have to do that because when a book is given out to the world, that is, when it is published, it becomes changed by the public who reads it. People have all kinds of ideas about what you have

done. So one needs to be very certain in oneself about what it is you have done.

The books I've mentioned and the rest of them, too, I suppose, come from who I am. I suspect they reflect how I was taught to see when I was very small.

When I was a child, I went looking for America. And looking, it was important that I notice every small thing, every sound, every sight. Things that I learned on our farm in the countryside then stay with me to this day, such as the fact that large birds, like hawks, crows, and owls, live at the tops of tall trees, while smaller birds, such as sparrows, robins, and jays, live lower down on low branches or in the brush trees. A very childish observation; yet, it seems to me I remember, then, that the big heavy birds should live below and the little lighter weight birdies should live atop things. Well, that wasn't the way things were, I observed.

I also noticed that country children like myself rode buses to school, while town children never had to. They could walk all the way, visiting the outdoors, the day, as they went. Sometimes, I wanted so much to be a town child. I often felt outside of things because I came from the countryside, except when it rained and thundered and lightninged, and the town children got caught and got wet.

We on the buses laughed and waved at them. Sometimes, the buses stopped to pick them up if the weather was particularly dangerous, and at those times, we were helpful as they came dripping inside with us.

Every spring, when the rain puddles turned warm from the sun, I would get out my red Elgin balloon-tire bike and pedal to school and back. There was nothing quite like that first day, with my books stacked securely in the wire basket in front, my bike shining from a fresh coat of paint. It's probably a given that I should become a storyteller. I remember vividly the sound of my bike tires over wet blacktop.

I think anyone who is taught to go looking for America will perhaps find it; or, if not, at least they will tell stories about how they went out looking.

THINKING *through the* LITERATURE

1. How do you think Virginia Hamilton's background prepared her to be a storyteller?

2. What do you think Hamilton means by the phrase "Looking for America"? Do you think she found it? Discuss.

3. **Connect to Life** Have you gone "Looking for America"? If you have, what have you seen? If you haven't, where would you go? Explain.

The Author's Style

Hamilton's Descriptive Style

Virginia Hamilton makes her stories come alive for the reader by the way she describes her characters and their experiences. Three elements of her descriptive style include simple language, realistic detail, and imagery.

Key Style Points

Word Choice Hamilton seldom chooses words that send her reader to the dictionary. Read the passage to the right and note how simply but accurately she describes the small details that lead up to Anthony Burns's being brought into the courtroom.

Realism Virginia Hamilton provides realistic descriptions of her characters, not only of how they look and act, but of how they feel and think as well. In this passage from "The People Could Fly," notice how she uses physical details to emphasize Sarah's thoughts and feelings.

Imagery In the excerpt to the right, notice the simple but powerful image that Hamilton uses to suggest Burns's feelings at his imprisonment.

Word Choice

Anthony did as he was told. In a small room off to the side he washed his face and smoothed his hair. There was no comb or brush for him. He straightened his clothing. He took a tin cup of cold water that Asa offered him, but that was all he was given.

—from *Anthony Burns*

Realism

The sun burned her face. The babe cried and cried, "Pity me, oh, pity me," say it sounded like. Sarah was so sad and starvin', she sat down in the row.

—from "The People Could Fly"

Imagery

The windows of the jury room where he was kept under guard were covered with iron bars that seemed to break the day into welts of pain.

—from *Anthony Burns*

Applications

1. **Active Reading** From either "The People Could Fly" or *Anthony Burns*, find another passage where Hamilton uses physical detail to emphasize a character's thoughts and feelings. Compare your choices with your classmates.

2. **Writing** Write a description of an event from your own experience. Try to include physical details that will help the reader understand how you felt such as, "The old abandoned house made me shiver inside."

3. **Viewing and Representing** Find a passage from either "The People Could Fly" or *Anthony Burns* that is rich in realistic detail and imagery and draw a sketch that illustrates it. Explain how the author's use of realistic details and imagery in that particular scene influenced your drawing.

Writing

700-Word Summary Write a 700-word summary of the excerpt from *Anthony Burns.* To summarize a work, retell the main ideas in your own words. Leave out unimportant ideas. Check your summary by asking yourself if someone who hasn't read the excerpt could use your summary to understand what happened. Put your summary in your **Working Portfolio.**

Writing Handbook
See p. R58: Summary.

Speaking & Listening

Dramatic Monologue Choose one of the passages from *Anthony Burns* in which Burns is thinking about his past or present condition. Expand the passage into a monologue. Perform your monologue for the class.

Speaking and Listening Handbook
See p. R102: Present.

Research & Technology

The Fugitive Slave Law Part of The Compromise of 1850, the Fugitive Slave Law was an attempt to settle the differences between North and South. Research the background of this law, who fought for it, who fought against it, and why it created such hardships for African Americans like Anthony Burns.

INTERNET Research Starter
www.mcdougallittell.com

Author Study Project

Storytelling

Events in history are themselves stories that invite us to get to know the people involved. Create a historical retelling of your own.

❶ Find Topics As a class, brainstorm a list of historical topics around which you could create stories. Write the topics on slips of paper. Then divide into groups and have a representative of each group draw a topic. As a group, follow the remaining steps and decide which group members will be responsible for research, retelling, and presentation.

❷ Gather Information Collect written information related to your topic. Find general historical accounts

from an encyclopedia to get the basic facts of the event: *what, where, when, who,* and *why.* Pay special attention to the *people* who were involved in this historical moment. If specific individuals played a key role, check to see if there are any biographies of them in your school library.

❸ Create the Retelling Choose a way of retelling the stories of the people you have learned about. A way of doing this could be a story; a dialogue or a monologue in which a character or characters describe a key incident; a poem; or even a ballad or song. One or two members of your group could create a poster to illustrate the retelling.

❹ Share the Retelling Present your retelling to the class. Videotape or audiotape your performance and evaluate its effectiveness.

Tasks for retelling
· Historical research· Everybody
· Prepare script· Kate
· Gather and make props·Danny
· Music
· Poster

Other Works by VIRGINIA HAMILTON

Creating stories, Virginia Hamilton says, enables her to explore "the known, the remembered, and the imagined, the literary triad of which all stories are made." While Hamilton's stories are set in a variety of times and places, her characters share similar challenges as they make important discoveries about places, people, and themselves.

The House of Dies Drear 1968
Edgar Allan Poe Award

Thomas has mixed feelings about the huge old house that his father has bought. The old house seems to hold a secret, and frightening things begin to happen. Danger and excitement build as Thomas tries to unravel the mystery.

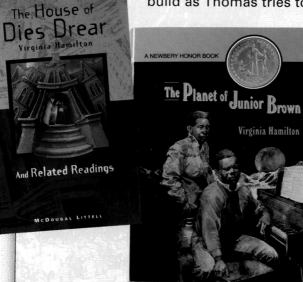

The Planet of Junior Brown 1971
Newbery Honor Book

Two unlikely friends in New York City play hooky from eighth grade for an entire semester. Junior Brown is a 300-pound neurotic musical prodigy who is befriended by Buddy, a tough, homeless, street kid.

M.C. Higgins, the Great 1974

Newbery Medal, Boston Globe-Horn Book Award,
National Book Award

Mayo Cornelius Higgins sits atop a 40-foot steel pole near his home on Sarah's Mountain, surveying the destruction caused by strip mining on the mountain. A huge pile of rubble will soon engulf the family's house, and Higgins is torn between the desire to escape from the destruction and the urge to fight for his home. Two strangers who enter his life may have the solution to his dilemma.

Justice and Her Brothers 1978

Justice has two brothers who are twins: Thomas is mean, and Levi is kind. One summer they discover that they have mysterious powers that allow them to mind-jump a million years into the future. What they find there is both frightening and fascinating. This is the first book of *The Justice Trilogy.* Other titles in the trilogy are *Dustland* and *The Gathering.*

Her Stories 1996

Coretta Scott King Award

Using a variety of voices, dialects, and styles, Hamilton retells trickster tales, folk tales, fairy tales, legends, and autobiographical stories that celebrate African-American women. The information Hamilton provides about the origins of the stories is as colorful and interesting as the stories themselves.

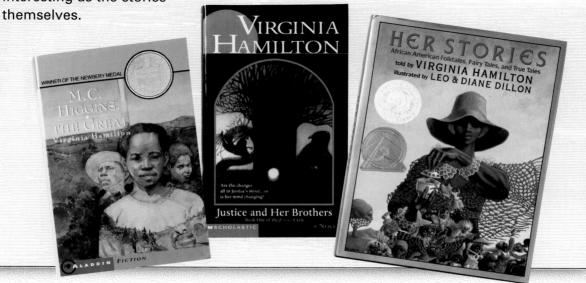

Key Standard
W2.3 Write research reports that contain a clear focus, include evidence gathered through a formal research process, and demonstrate documentation of sources.
Other Standards **R2.2, R2.6, W1.1, W1.2, W1.3, W1.4, W1.5, W1.7, LC1.3, LC1.7**

Writing Workshop

Research Report

Presenting facts about a topic . . .

From Reading to Writing What would it be like to live in a different place and in a different time period? Nonfiction history writers and writers of historical fiction such as "A Crown of Wild Olive" help readers understand people and societies of the past. They investigate several sources to build complete pictures of their subjects. Writing a **research report** can help you become familiar with sources of information and learn interesting facts about a subject.

For Your Portfolio

WRITING PROMPT Write a research report about a topic in American history or some other topic that interests you.

Purpose: To share information
Audience: Your classmates, your teacher, or anyone who shares your interest in the topic

---

Basics in a Box

Research Report at a Glance

| **Introduction** presents the thesis statement | → | **Body** presents evidence that supports the thesis statement | → | **Conclusion** restates the thesis | → | **Works Cited** lists the sources of information |

Research

RUBRIC STANDARDS FOR WRITING

A successful research report should

- include a strong introduction and thesis statement that clearly states the topic and the purpose
- use evidence from primary or secondary sources to develop and support ideas
- credit sources of information

- follow a logical pattern of organization, using transitions between ideas
- use information from multiple sources
- summarize ideas in the conclusion
- include a Works Cited list at the end of the report

Analyzing a Student Model

SPEAKING OPPORTUNITY

See the Speaking and Listening Handbook, p. R100 for oral presentation tips.

Sager 1

Weston Sager
English 701
Ms. Kilpatrick
May 8

Abe: A Biography

The penny and the five-dollar bill remind us of the 16th president of the United States—a strong, serious-looking man with a beard. President Lincoln didn't always have a beard, however. After he was elected president, a little girl wrote him a letter and suggested that he grow a beard. He followed her suggestion and even thanked her in person for the idea (Whitney 137). This shows his connection to the common people. In addition, the honorable 16th president of the United States abolished slavery, won the Civil War, and tried to hold the United States together during a terrible period in history. President Lincoln's achievements would have been a lot for any president, but they are even more amazing when you consider his background.

Abraham Lincoln's beginnings were humble. His father, Thomas Lincoln, was a farmer who frequently moved the family to different spots in Kentucky, Indiana, and Illinois. His mother, Nancy Hanks Lincoln, died when Abe was nine. However, he loved his stepmother, Sarah Bush Johnston, who encouraged him to try to better himself (Whitney 129). Although Abe was good with an ax and could build log cabins, make fence rails, and clear the forest for farmland, he preferred reading and telling stories to hard physical labor (Armbruster 174–175).

Abraham Lincoln held several jobs that taught him important lessons on his way to the presidency. He hauled cargo on a flatboat down the Mississippi River to New Orleans. This taught him about the horrors of slavery in the South (Whitney 129). He was a clerk and a postmaster general. He was also in the military, became a state legislator, and studied to be a lawyer (Whitney 130). In 1836 he was reelected to the state legislature and received his license to practice law (Whitney 131).

Politics continued to be important to him. In 1858 Abraham Lincoln ran for the Senate against a man named Stephen Douglas. In that

RUBRIC IN ACTION

1 Writer begins with an anecdote. The introduction makes the focus of the report clear.

2 Thesis statement is included here with the writer's perspective stated.

3 Writer chooses chronological order to present information. Specific dates are used.

Another Option:
· Organize by topic.

race, Lincoln had several debates with Douglas. These became known as the Lincoln-Douglas Debates. Big crowds came to listen. Abraham Lincoln was defeated, but the debates helped to make his name known all over the country. His major concern was the growing problem between the North and the South. The issue was whether slavery should be allowed in the land acquired in the Louisiana Purchase. Lincoln was strongly against the spread of slavery. He said, "A house divided against itself cannot stand" (Whitney 134).

By 1859, he was making public speaking appearances and impressed audiences everywhere he went (Whitney 136). In 1860 Abraham Lincoln won the presidential election. In 1864, his share of the votes increased and he won another term ("Lincoln"). His popularity in this election was due to his handling of the Civil War, which was the most important event of Lincoln's presidency. Although Lincoln had never wanted war, he acted shortly after the South broke from the Union and formed the Confederacy. He delivered the Emancipation Proclamation. He also appointed General Ulysses S. Grant to lead the Union soldiers (Armbruster 182). After many difficult battles, the Confederate General Robert E. Lee surrendered to the Union on April 9, 1865. The war ended soon after and the Union was preserved.

However, President Lincoln's leadership of the country was cut short by someone who did not share his opinions ("A. Lincoln"). On April 14, just days after the end of the war, John Wilkes Booth, a Confederate supporter, _____ 140). The nation

④ Credits source of each fact or quotation

⑤ Gives specific facts and other details to support main idea of each paragraph

Works Cited

"A. Lincoln." The History Place. 30 Apr. 2000
    <http://www.historyplace.com/lincoln/index.html>.
Armbruster, Maxim E. The Presidents of the United States. New
    York: Horizon, 1969.
"Lincoln, Abraham." Microsoft Encarta Encyclopedia. CD-ROM. 1998
    ed. Redmond: Microsoft, 1998.
Whitney, David C. The American Presidents. Pleasantville: Reader's
    Digest, 1996.

Works Cited
- Identifies sources of information used in a bibliography
- Presents the entries in alphabetical order
- Gives complete publication information
- Contains correctly punctuated entries
- Follows a preferred style

Need help with Works Cited?

See the **Writing Handbook,** Creating a Works Cited Page, p. R56.

Writing Your Research Report

❶ Prewriting and Exploring

Find a topic that really interests you by **listing** historical events or people that you want to know more about. Review the nonfiction and historical fiction selections in your book. **Ask** relevant questions about the real people or the cultures that are portrayed. See the **Idea Bank** in the margin for more suggestions. After you have chosen your subject, follow the steps below.

Planning Your Response to Literature

▷ 1. **Find your focus.** Create a cluster diagram of all of the ideas connected to your topic. If there is a lot of information, choose one or two cluster ideas to investigate.

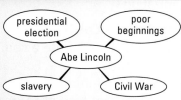

▷ 2. **Make a research plan.** Write down questions that you want answered about your topic. Which questions are related? Use your questions to guide your research.

▷ 3. **Identify your audience.** Who will read your report? How much background do you need to include about your subject? What will interest your readers most about your subject?

▷ 4. **Define your purpose.** What do you want your paper to accomplish? Try writing a **thesis statement**, one sentence that states your perspective and what you want to emphasize in your report.

---

❷ Researching

Use the questions that you have written about your topic to guide your research. Add other questions as you find facts that move your investigation farther along.

There are two types of sources—primary and secondary. **Primary sources** offer firsthand information. They include letters, diaries, journals, and historical documents. **Secondary sources** explain or comment on material from other sources. Encyclopedias, newspapers, magazines, and many books are examples of secondary sources.

Use library materials like the card catalog, a computer catalog, *Readers' Guide to Periodical Literature,* and other reference tools to compile research.

RESEARCH Tip

Check the index of the encyclopedia to find related subjects. Use the related subject headings to find other books in the library database.

INTERNET Tip

Try various search engines on the Internet to see if you can find more sources of information.

Evaluate Your Sources

You cannot believe everything that you read. Make sure that each source is reliable—accurate and up to date. Also, make sure the author presents an objective view before you begin to take notes. Check several sources to see if the accounts agree. Ask the following questions about sources found on the Internet.

What are the author's viewpoints and biases? Identify the author's gender, background, and political beliefs. How do they influence the presentation?

What are the qualifications of the author? Is the author from a respected institution? Is he or she a professional? Is the group a recognized organization?

Make Source Cards

Using index cards, create a source card for each source you use. For each, list the publication information in the correct form for that type of source. Then number the source cards sequentially. The cards will help you to create your Works Cited list and to find the source again if necessary. Follow the formats shown on the right.

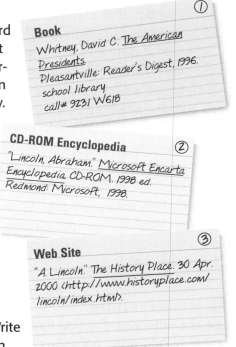

Book ①
Whitney, David C. _The American Presidents._
Pleasantville: Reader's Digest, 1996.
school library
call# 9231 W618

CD-ROM Encyclopedia ②
"Lincoln, Abraham." _Microsoft Encarta Encyclopedia_ CD-ROM. 1998 ed.
Redmond: Microsoft, 1998.

Web Site ③
"A. Lincoln." _The History Place._ 30 Apr. 2000 <http://www.historyplace.com/lincoln/index.html>.

Take Notes

Use index cards to record the information in your sources. Write the main idea of the note at the top of each card, along with the number that you assigned the source on the source card and the number of the page on which you found the fact. Write just one piece of information on each card. Paraphrase (rewrite in your own words) the fact or idea.

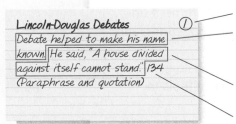

Lincoln-Douglas Debates ①
Debate helped to make his name known. He said, "A house divided against itself cannot stand." 134
(Paraphrase and quotation)

Source Number

Paraphrase or Summarize Restate ideas in your own words to avoid plagiarism. Plagiarism means using someone else's original words or ideas without giving credit.

Quotation Write the quotation exactly as it appears in the source and enclose it in quotation marks.

Page Number

Organize Your Material

Before writing your rough draft, it might be helpful to sort your note cards into groups of similar main ideas. Think about the order in which you want to discuss those main ideas. You might choose **chronological, cause-and-effect, comparison-and-contrast, problem-solution,** or some other method of organizing. Create an outline or a cluster diagram to help you decide on the order of the sections of your report.

Need help organizing your material?

See the **Writing Handbook,** p. R54

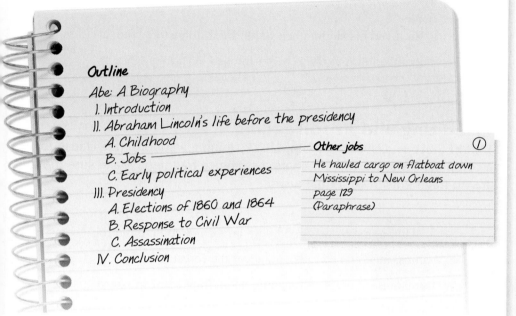

Outline

Abe: A Biography
 I. Introduction
 II. Abraham Lincoln's life before the presidency
   A. Childhood
   B. Jobs
   C. Early political experiences
 III. Presidency
   A. Elections of 1860 and 1864
   B. Response to Civil War
   C. Assassination
 IV. Conclusion

Other jobs ①
He hauled cargo on flatboat down Mississippi to New Orleans
page 129
(Paraphrase)

❸ Drafting

Using your outline as a guide, begin to write your first draft. Your goal is to get your ideas down on paper. You can revise later.

In your **introduction,** start with a question, a quotation, or an intriguing fact. Present your subject and the purpose of your paper in a strong statement of purpose. This will become your thesis statement.

Write a separate body paragraph for each of the main ideas in your outline, using transitions to connect one paragraph with the next. Begin with a topic sentence and follow it up with the facts and other details that you've researched. For every fact or idea taken from a source, write the author's name and page number in parentheses at the end of the sentence. Use the title of the source and the page number if no author is named.

Conclude by summarizing the importance of your topic or giving your own interpretation.

DRAFTING Tip

Consider drafting your paper on a computer. Revisions will be easier to make, and the computer's programs can help you in your proofreading.

Need help with word processing?

See the **Research and Technology Handbook,** p. R112.

Ask Your Peer Reader

- Did I support my statements with facts and examples?
- Was my organization clear and consistent?
- Did I cite sources wherever necessary?

As you revise your work, look back at the words you misspelled and determine why you made the errors you did. For additional help, refer to the strategies and generalizations in the **Spelling Handbook** on page R30.

**SPEAKING
Opportunity**

Turn your research report into an oral presentation.

**Publishing
IDEAS**

• Prepare a slide presentation about your subject. Generate slides on the computer or find them. Use your research report as a script and synchronize your words with the slides. Give your presentation to the class.

• Find a work of fiction or a movie that incorporates the subject of your research report. Develop a prologue for the work or the movie that will add to the reader's or audience's understanding.

Publishing Options
www.mcdougallittell.com

❹ Revising

TARGET SKILL ▶ **PRESENTING IDEAS IN A LOGICAL ORDER** Choose the order for your details that will make your paper most effective. Chronological order shows the relationship of time and events to each other; spatial order shows the physical location of places or things; and least to most important orders the details from weakest to strongest.

> *His mother, Nancy Hanks Lincoln, died when Abe was nine. However,*
> ∧ He loved his stepmother, Sarah Bush Johnston, who encouraged him to try to better himself (Whitney 129).

❺ Editing and Proofreading

TARGET SKILL ▶ **CLAUSES AS FRAGMENTS** Joining a subordinate clause to a complete sentence can eliminate a sentence fragment. Make sure there are no fragments in your final paper.

> Although Abe was good with an ax and could build log cabins, make fence rails, and clear the forest for farmland. He *of the* preferred reading and telling stories to hard physical labor (Armbruster 174–75).

❻ Making a Works Cited List

When you have finished revising and editing your report, make a **Works Cited** list and attach it to the end of your paper. See page R56 in the **Writing Handbook** for the correct format.

❼ Reflecting

FOR YOUR WORKING PORTFOLIO What were some problems you faced in doing your research report? What did you learn about doing a research report? Attach your answers to your finished report. Save your research report in your **Working Portfolio.**

Standardized Test Practice

Mixed Review

Many people take owning a book for granted. However, before 1450 and
(1)
the invention of the printing press. Only the very wealthy owned books.
Before that time, all books were copied by hand. This meant that books
were scarce and much expensiver than us modern readers can imagine.
(2)   (3)
After Johann Gutenberg invented the first movable-type printing press.
(4)
People could more easier afford books, and, as a result, more people learned
(5)
to read. A world without books isn't hardly believable today.
(6)

Review Your Skills

Use the passage and the questions that follow it to check how well you remember the language conventions you've learned in previous grades.

1. How is item 1 best written?

  A. However, before 1450 and the invention of the printing press: Only the very wealthy owned books.

  B. However, before 1450 and the invention of the printing press, only the very wealthy owned books.

  C. However, before 1450 and the invention of the printing press; only the very wealthy owned books.

  D. Correct as is

2. What is the correct comparative form in item 2?

  A. much more expensive

  B. much expensive

  C. more expensiver

  D. Correct as is

3. What is the correct pronoun case in item 3?

  A. than us

  B. than any of us modern readers

  C. than we modern readers

  D. Correct as is

4. How is item 4 best written?

  A. After Johann Gutenberg invented the first movable-type printing press, people

  B. After Johann Gutenberg invented. The first movable-type printing press, people

  C. After Johann Gutenberg invented the first movable-type printing press; people

  D. Correct as is

5. What is the correct comparative form in item 5?

  A. could more easy

  B. could more easily

  C. could easilier

  D. Correct as is

6. How is sentence 6 best written?

  A. A world without books is hardly unbelievable today.

  B. A world without books isn't scarcely believable today.

  C. A world without books is hardly believable today.

  D. Correct as is

Self-Assessment

Check your own answers in the **Grammar Handbook**

Quick Reference: Capitalization, p. R70

Quick Reference: Punctuation, p. R68

Double Negatives, p. R83

Sentence Fragments, p. R71

Comparative Adjectives and Adverbs, p. R82

Pronouns, p. R75

Key Standard
LC1.4 Use the mechanics of writing correctly; demonstrate correct language usage.
Other Standards LC1.3, LC1.6

Personal Challenges

In this unit, you read about characters and real people who have a special quality—the strength to stand up and meet challenges. How have your ideas about personal challenges changed or deepened now that you have read the selections in the unit? Use one or more of the options in each of the following sections to help assess the changes.

Key Standard
R3.1 Be able to describe the purposes and characteristics of different forms of prose, such as the short story, novel, or essay.
Other Standards **R3.2, R3.4, R3.6**

Reflecting on Theme

OPTION 1

Making Connections Review the selections in this unit and jot down the message or messages you got from each. Which messages do you think apply to situations encountered by young people? Discuss this question with a small group, supporting your views by relating the messages to situations from real life.

OPTION 2

Compare and Contrast Look back at the situations in selections from this unit that you found especially interesting. How well do the characters handle those situations? Would you react differently or similarly? Write a few paragraphs comparing and contrasting the characters' actions with what you think yours would be.

OPTION 3

Role-Playing Imagine that a friend needs more self-confidence to meet a new challenge. With a partner, role-play a conversation in which you attempt to inspire your friend with the will to overcome the challenge. Use examples from several selections to support your points.

Self ASSESSMENT

READER'S NOTEBOOK

Which of the characters in this unit reminds you the most of your personal heroes? Write a paragraph or two explaining your choice.

REVIEWING YOUR PERSONAL
WORDList

Vocabulary Review the new words you learned in this unit. If necessary, use a dictionary to check the meaning of each word.

Spelling Review your list of spelling words. If you're not sure of the correct spelling, use a dictionary or refer to the **Spelling Handbook** on page R30.

Reviewing Literary Concepts

OPTION 1

Examining Setting Setting is the time and place of the action of a literary work of fiction and nonfiction. Review the selections you have read in this unit. Which selection would be very different if the setting were changed? Which might be almost the same? Discuss these questions with a partner or with a small group of classmates.

OPTION 2

Literary Nonfiction and Historical Fiction How do these two kinds of writing differ? To remember the strengths and weaknesses of each, fill in a chart like the one shown. Then discuss with a partner your ideas about what information can be learned from each form that cannot be learned from the other.

Literary Nonfiction		Historical Fiction	
Strengths	Weaknesses	Strengths	Weaknesses

Portfolio Building

- **Choices and Challenges—Writing** Select the Writing assignment from this unit that you think expresses your ideas most effectively. Explain the reasons for your evaluation in a cover note, attach it to the assignment, and add both to your **Presentation Portfolio**.

- **Writing Workshops** In this unit, you wrote an Opinion Statement and a Research Report. Reread these two pieces and decide which you think is better in showing your strengths as a writer. Explain your choice on a cover page, attach it to the piece you have selected, and place it in your **Presentation Portfolio**.

- **Additional Activities** Think about the assignments you completed for **Speaking & Listening** and **Research & Technology**. Which did you find helpful? Which would you like to do more work on in the future? Keep a record of those assignments in your portfolio.

Self ASSESSMENT

READER'S NOTEBOOK

Copy the following literary terms onto a sheet of paper. Next to each term, jot down a brief definition. If you have trouble explaining a particular concept, refer to the **Glossary of Literary and Reading Terms** on page R120.

historical fiction	setting
literary nonfiction	memoir
folk tale	imagery
sensory detail	

Self ASSESSMENT

Look through your **Presentation Portfolio** to find an early draft that shows you learning something important about your subject or about yourself. How might you make it even better? List your suggestions and attach the list to the piece.

Setting GOALS

In the Reflect and Assess for Unit One, you were asked what kinds of writing you would like to become more skilled at. Look again at the list. Circle what you have learned so far. Make a list of the ones that remain and place it in your **READER'S NOTEBOOK.**

LITERATURE CONNECTIONS
Where the Red Fern Grows

BY WILSON RAWLS

Told in flashback, this story is about the close relationship between a boy and his hunting dogs on a poor farm in the Ozarks. The boy saves money to buy the dogs and is heartbroken when they die. Dreams, hard work and determination, success and disaster are all featured in the tale.

These thematically related readings are provided along with *Where the Red Fern Grows*:

Lob's Girl
BY JOAN AIKEN

Luke Baldwin's Vow
BY MORLEY CALLAGHAN

Old Dog
BY WILLIAM STAFFORD

The Grip
BY BRENDAN KENNELLY

Friends of the Hunted
BY RYLAND LOOS

Why They Quit: Thoughts from Ex-Hunters
BY DENA JONES JOLMA

Two Dreamers
BY GARY SOTO

More Choices

Good Night, Mr. Tom
BY MICHAEL MAGORIAN
This is the story of a kind old man who gives a young, abused boy the strength and courage to carry on.

The Miracle Worker
BY WILLIAM GIBSON
Anne Sullivan becomes a teacher to the blind and deaf Helen Keller, helping her to overcome tremendous odds to learn to communicate.
A McDougal Littell *Literature Connection*

Julie of the Wolves
BY JEAN CRAIGHEAD GEORGE
When Julie becomes lost in the woods, her chances of surviving are slim until she meets and is accepted by a pack of wolves.

Where the Lilies Bloom
BY VERA AND BILL CLEAVER
Fourteen-year-old Mary Call tells how her family found the strength to stay together after her father died.

So Far from the Bamboo Grove
BY YOKO KAWASHIMA WATKINS
A Japanese girl and her family make a daring escape to Japan, surviving despite incredible odds against them.
A McDougal Littell *Literature Connection*

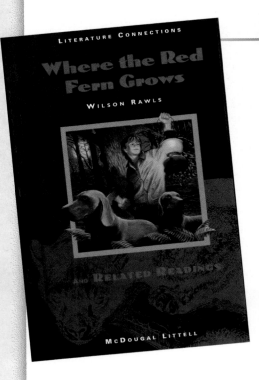

Roll of Thunder, Hear My Cry

BY MILDRED D. TAYLOR

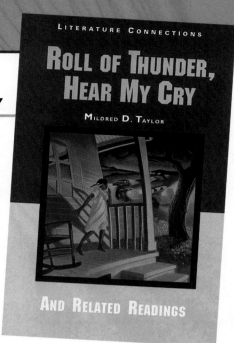

Set in Mississippi during the early years of the Great Depression, Mildred Taylor's novel describes the members of the African-American Logan family and their relationships with the land, their neighbors, and each other. The Logans must draw together in a fight to keep their 400-acre cotton farm.

These thematically related readings are provided along with *Roll of Thunder, Hear My Cry:*

from **Growing Up in the Great Depression**
BY RICHARD WORMSER

Depression
BY ISABEL JOSHLIN GLASER

The Stolen Party
BY LILIANA HECKER
TRANSLATED BY ALBERTO MANGUEL

Incident
BY COUNTEE CULLEN

Equal Opportunity
BY JIM WONG-CHU

from **Black Women in White America**
BY GERDA LERNER

The Clearing
BY JESSE STUART

The Five-Dollar Dive
BY YVONNE NELSON-PERRY

Social Studies Connection

The Fables of La Fontaine
TRANSLATED BY LISA COMMAGER
This is a collection of the French writer's most famous fables.

Perrault's Fairy Tales
BY CHARLES PERRAULT
A collection of the eighteenth-century French storyteller's fairy tales.

Robinson Crusoe
BY DANIEL DEFOE
Set in the seventeenth century, this is the story of one shipwrecked man's struggle to stay alive despite the odds.

Ferdinand Magellan
BY SCOTT BREWSTER
A biography of the courageous Portuguese explorer.

Tales from 1492
BY MARY ANN WHITTIER
A weekly news journal of the politics, people, and events of this very important year in exploration.

THE ORAL TRADITION

Tales from Around the World

"The greatest storyteller
in the world is in your
family because he's
telling the only story you
can truly recognize,
which is the story of you
and your family."

Tim Tingle

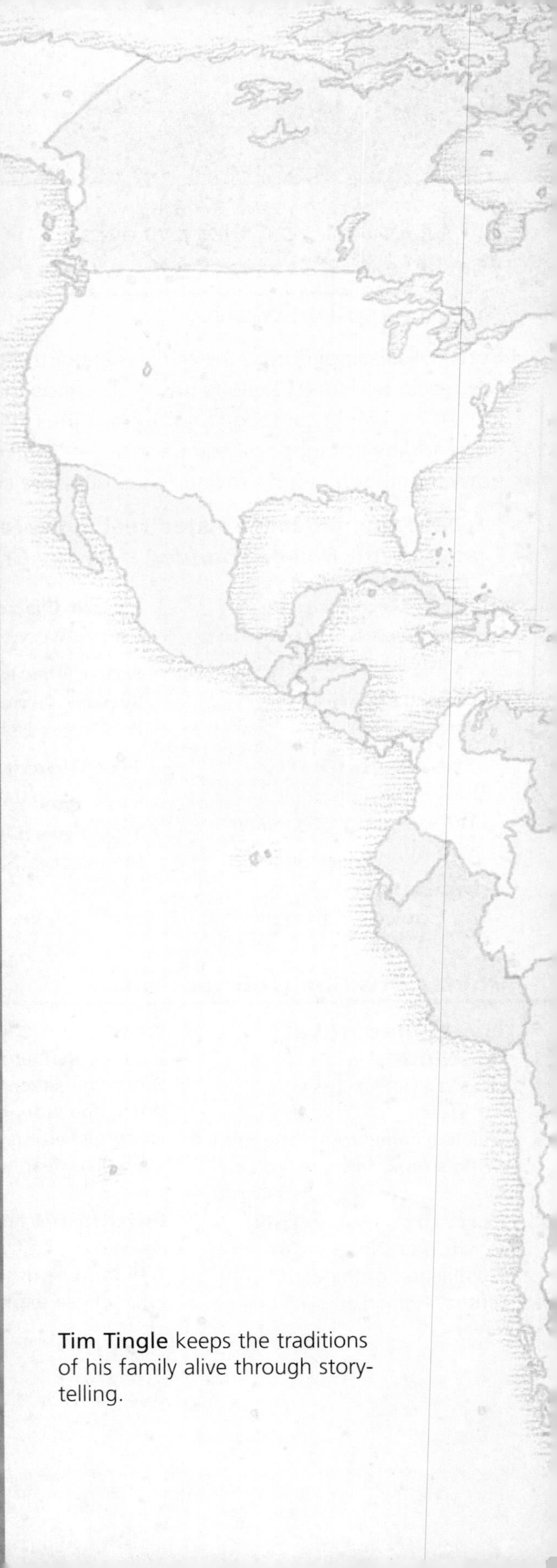

Tim Tingle keeps the traditions of his family alive through storytelling.

STORYTELLERS PAST AND PRESENT

Key Standard
R3.1 Be able to describe the purposes and characteristics of different forms of prose, such as the short story, novel, or essay.

TIM TINGLE

A Present-Day Storyteller Speaks

Tim Tingle is a storyteller whose stories are inspired by the rich cultural background of his family. The stories he admires most are those that celebrate "the specialness of simple people."

I was raised near the Gulf of Mexico, not far from Galveston Island. The house where I was raised was actually once a bunkhouse where cowboys slept. When my father came back from World War II, he purchased that old bunkhouse, put in indoor plumbing, and moved into it. That's where myself and my four brothers and sisters were raised.

We had a mixture of cultural backgrounds on my father's side. His granddad was Scottish-Irish—that's where the name Tingle comes from. My grandmother was a full-blooded Choctaw. The family moved from Choctaw territory in Oklahoma to Pasadena, Texas, for the jobs that were available there around 1910. I remember just sitting and listening to my dad and his brothers talk about people that they knew. My dad's anecdotes were always short, but they were always about the character of people. The single most important attribute of a good storyteller is to be a good listener and a keen observer.

I first started telling stories when I was in elementary school. Usually they were scary stories that I told around the campfire when I was camping with friends of mine. We'd keep each other up until one or two in the morning. I remember there was an old fellow who lived under a bridge not too far from our house, just kind of an old hermit, and we'd make up stories about how he lived, what prison he escaped from, just wild, imaginary stuff.

Now, I create my stories from several sources. I like to take historical events and put real characters in them. I love to visit places where I've never been before. I just listen and keep my mind open, and what I've found is that people with stories will seek me out. I have a little verse that I open one of my stories with. It goes like this:

I never go looking for stories to tell
But I walk the hallways
And the pathways
And the riverbanks
Where the stories dwell.

After I've performed a story at least a hundred times, then the characters become real to me. And when I tell a story that much, and I know the characters that well, then there will come a time in the telling of the story *when the story comes alive.* And then, before I know it, I look around and magically, the story's over with. We've all been a part of it, and we can all step back and applaud the magic of the story. And that to me is the special thing about live storytelling, that there comes a time, in the story, when the audience dissolves, the storyteller dissolves, and what is left is the *story.*

The key thing for young people of the 21st century is knowing and appreciating storytelling so that they can know *their* story. The films that are made about the lives that people go through in elementary and junior high and high school are never made by people who are experiencing that; they're always made by adults who strive to remember what it was like. The advance of technology doesn't mean that storytelling is dying, it means that it can reach more and more people—but it begins with *your* imagination.

VIDEO Literature in Performance

A Traditional Storyteller
Family elders, both men and women, are frequently the ones who are responsible for passing along family tales to their children and grandchildren.

Body language, including hand gestures, brings a tale to life.

Raising and lowering the voice can draw listeners into the dramatic tension of a story.

KEEPING THE PAST ALIVE

Storytellers like Tim Tingle represent a tradition that goes back to the dawn of history. In every culture, people told stories. Some of these stories took on a life of their own, outliving their storytellers and passing from one generation to the next. Through them, the past spoke to the present. Through them, the values of a culture stayed alive. These stories make up what is called the **oral tradition**. The chart below lists the types of stories in the oral tradition—**myths, folk tales, oral history,** and **fables**—together with their distinctive features and their common elements. The time line introduces each culture represented in this unit, listing one or more stories from its oral tradition and an interesting fact from its history.

. . .

*about **1000** B.C.
People from other
parts of Africa begin
to settle in Kenya.*

. . .

*about **500** B.C. The
philosopher
Confucius develops
a moral system
that focuses on
social order,
harmony, and
good
government.*

MYTHS

- *attempt to answer basic questions about the world*
- *are considered truthful by their originators*

FOLK TALES

- *are told primarily for entertainment*
- *feature humans or humanlike animals*

COMMON ELEMENTS

- **keep the past alive**
- **teach lessons about human behavior**
- **reveal the values of the society**

FABLES

- *are short tales that illustrate morals*
- *have characters that are animals*

ORAL HISTORY

- *is based on real events*
- *is considered factual by the teller*
- *passes along information*

INTERNET

Social Studies Connection
www.mcdougallittell.com

LINKS TO UNIT ONE

Learning from Experience

*You are making new discoveries all the time—and as you
experience new things, you learn more about yourself. You
also learn about other people, places, and things. In the
stories you are about to read, the main characters—
Birbal and Arap Sang—learn about themselves
and the worlds around them as they
encounter new situations. These themes
and characters link closely with
similar themes and characters
introduced in Unit One
selections.*

KENYA

Arap Sang and
the Cranes

retold by Humphrey Harman

"Before you give anything to anyone, you should first
carefully think out what your gift will mean to the
person. A gift is a great responsibility to the giver. . . ."
In this African folk tale, Arap Sang, a powerful chief,
gives a lavish gift to an animal who has helped him.
However, he learns through experience that his
generosity has unintended effects. Humphrey Harman
collected and retold folk tales from a number of
African peoples in Kenya and Zambia. This story, from
the Nyanza region of southwestern Kenya, is one of
his most popular.

The Foolish Men of Agra

retold by Rina Singh

Many stories describe someone seeking a wise person, but who ever heard of looking for a fool? This tale from northern India describes what happens when a king sends a wise man to look for the six most foolish men in the kingdom. You may be surprised at the "fools" the wise man finds and the conclusion he draws at the end of the story. The question of who is really wise—and who is really foolish—is one that can be learned only through experience.

AS YOU READ . . .

Determine the values and customs presented in these cultures.

Think about which decisions lead to positive results and which lead to negative results.

Consider what the characters learn about themselves and the world around them.

THE FOOLISH Men of Agra

retold by RINA SINGH

Although Akbar[1] admired Birbal's[2] wisdom, every now and then it gave him great pleasure to test it, hoping to outwit his friend.

One day he said, "I have met with the wisest men in my kingdom. Now I wish to meet the greatest fools. Birbal, find me the six most foolish men in Agra.[3] Bring them here tomorrow night."

"I will try, Jahanpanah,"[4] answered Birbal. "I will try."

The next morning, Birbal wandered through the streets of Agra, searching for fools. As he walked, he came upon a man lying on his back in a puddle of water, his arms stretched wide above his head, his legs waving in the air.

"What are you doing?" asked Birbal.

"I am trying to stand up. I slipped and fell in this puddle on my way to buy some fabric for my wife," said the man.

"Why not use your hands?" suggested Birbal.

"Oh no!" cried the man. "If I do that, I will lose the measurement of the fabric my wife wants."

"In that case, I will help you," said Birbal, yanking the man out of the puddle by his hair.

"Would you come with me, please?" asked Birbal.

"Of course!" agreed the man, too foolish to wonder why. As the two walked along, Birbal

Detail of Mughal portrait of Akbar and Prince Salim (19th century). The Newark Museum/Art Resource, New York.

saw a man riding a horse, with a bundle of straw on his head.

"Wouldn't you be more comfortable if you tied the straw to your saddle?" asked Birbal.

"I cannot do that, huzur,"[5] said the man. "My horse is so old and weak it might die from the extra burden. My own weight is enough for the poor creature."

"You are just the man I am looking for," said Birbal. "Please come with me."

"Of course!" agreed the man, too foolish to wonder why.

As the three walked along, they saw a man talking to himself. He was charging in their direction so fast that Birbal had no time to move out of his way, and they collided.

"Watch where you are going!" demanded Birbal.

"Watch where you are going!" retorted the man. "I was chasing the sound of my voice, and I was about to catch it when you got in my way!"

"Come with me," said Birbal. "I will help you find the sound of your voice."

As night fell, Birbal made his way toward the palace, with the three foolish men following him. Suddenly, near the palace gate, he noticed a man looking for something under a street light.

---

1. **Akbar** (ăk′bär).
2. **Birbal** (bîr′bäl).
3. **Agra** (ä′grə).
4. **Jahanpanah** (jə-hän′pə-nä′): a royal title meaning "Shelter of the World."
5. **huzur** (hə-zŏŏr′): a term of respect, like sir.

Mughal illustration of Akbar witnessing an extraordinary display of catching fish (1590). Victoria & Albert Museum, London/Art Resource, New York.

"What are you looking for?" Birbal asked.

"I have lost my gold ring in that patch of darkness," said the man, pointing to a spot some distance away.

"Then why are you looking for it under the light?" asked Birbal.

"How do you expect me to find it in the dark?" asked the man in return.

"Come along," said Birbal. "I will help you find your ring."

The man happily followed Birbal and the others through the palace gate.

"Jahanpanah!" said Birbal, as he lined up the men before Akbar. "I have brought you the four most foolish men of Agra."

"How did you decide they were the most foolish?" Akbar asked, amused by the strange group before him.

"By their actions, of course," said Birbal, and gave an account of each man.

"Well done, Birbal!" said Akbar, his eyes twinkling with mischief. "But I asked you to bring the six most foolish men. Here are only four."

"You have miscounted, Jahanpanah," said Birbal.

Akbar looked at Birbal very sternly.

"The other two foolish men are you and I." Birbal bowed respectfully. "You, Jahanpanah, because you set me such a foolish task. I, because I carried it out. That makes six, doesn't it?"

"It does, it does!" said Akbar, laughing until the tears rolled down his cheeks. ❖

Rina Singh
born 1955

From India to Canada Born in India, Rina Singh immigrated to Canada in 1980 and became a Canadian citizen. She earned a teaching degree from McGill University and a master's degree from Concordia University. After teaching creative writing for many years, she began teaching at an arts-based school. Singh lives in Toronto with her husband and two children, Amrita and Angad.

Foolish Men and Magic Braids In her books, Singh combines her love of stories with her knowledge of Indian culture. Many of her stories originated in northern India during the rule of the Moguls (also called Mughals), an empire that lasted from the early 1500s until the mid-1700s. "The Foolish Men of Agra" appears in her collection of retellings, *The Foolish Men of Agra and Other Tales of Mogul India*. (Agra was the capital city of Mogul India during part of the empire. It is best known as the site of a famous monument called the Taj Mahal.) Singh has written two other children's books, *The Magic Braid* and *Moon Tales*, and also published a collection of poetry translations called *Silences*.

Arap Sang and the Cranes

retold by Humphrey Harman

Some people of Africa believe that before you give anything to anyone, you should first carefully think out what your gift will mean to the person. A gift is a great responsibility to the giver, they say; and after they have said that they may tell you the story of Arap Sang and the Cranes.

Arap Sang was a great chief and more than half a god, for in the days when he lived great chiefs were always a little mixed up with the gods. One day he was walking on the plain, admiring the cattle.

It was hot. The rains had not yet come. The ground was almost bare of grass and as hard as stone. The thorn trees gave no shade; for they were just made of long spines and thin twigs and tiny leaves; and the sun went straight through them.

It was hot. Only the black ants didn't feel it, and they would be happy in a furnace.

The sun beat down on Arap Sang's bald head. (He was sensitive about this and didn't like it mentioned.) And he thought, "I'm feeling things more than I used to."

And then he came across a vulture sitting in the crook of a tree, his wings hanging down and his eyes on the lookout.

"Vulture," said Arap Sang, "I'm hot, and the sun is making my head ache. You have there a fine pair of broad wings. I'd be most grateful if

> *"Oh, go home, Baldy, and stop bothering people; it's hot."*

you'd spread them out and let me enjoy a patch of shade."

"Why?" croaked Vulture. He had indigestion. Vultures usually have indigestion; it's the things they eat.

"Why?" said Arap Sang mildly. "Now that's a question to which I'm not certain that I've got the answer. Why? Why, I suppose, because I ask you. Because it wouldn't be much trouble to you. Because it's pleasant and good to help people."

"Bah!" said Vulture.

"What's that?"

"Oh, go home, Baldy, and stop bothering people; it's hot."

Arap Sang straightened himself up, and his eyes flashed. He wasn't half a god for nothing; and when he was angry, he could be rather a terrifying person. And he was very angry now. It was that remark about his lack of hair.

The really terrifying thing was that when he spoke, he didn't shout. He spoke quietly, and the words were clear and cold and hard. And all separate like hailstones.

"Vulture . . ., you're cruel, and you're selfish. I shan't forget what you've said . . ."

"Vulture," he said, "you're cruel, and you're selfish. I shan't forget what you've said, and you won't either. Now get out!"

Arap Sang was so <u>impressive</u> that Vulture got up awkwardly and flapped off.

"Silly fool," Vulture said uncomfortably.

Presently Vulture met an acquaintance of his. (Vultures don't have friends; they just have acquaintances.) They perched together on the

---

WORDS TO KNOW **impressive** (ĭm-prĕs′ĭv) *adj.* grand; striking; majestic

same bough. Vulture took a close look at his companion, and then another, and what he saw was so funny that it cheered him up.

"He, he!" he giggled. "What's happened to you? Met with an accident? You're bald."

The other vulture looked sour, but at the same time you felt she might be pleased about something.

"That's good, coming from you," she said. "What have you been up to? You haven't got a feather on you above the shoulders."

Then they both felt their heads with <u>consternation</u>. It was quite true. They were bald, both of them; and so was every other vulture, the whole family, right down to this very day.

Which goes to show that if you can't be ordinarily pleasant to people, at least it's not wise to go insulting great chiefs who are half gods.

I said that he was rather a terrifying person.

Arap Sang walked on. He was feeling shaky. Losing his temper always upset him afterward. And doing the sort of magic that makes every vulture in the world bald in the wink of an eye, can take it out of you.

And he did want a bit of shade.

Presently he met an elephant. Elephant was panting across the plain in a tearing hurry and was most reluctant to stop when Arap Sang called to her.

"Elephant," said Arap Sang weakly. "I'm tired and I'm dizzy. I want to get to the forest and into a bit of shade, but it's a long way."

"It is hot, isn't it?" said Elephant. "I'm off to the forest myself."

"I'm sorry, . . . but you'd make my journey so slow. I must get to the forest."

"Would you spread out your great ears and let me walk along under them?" asked Arap Sang.

"I'm sorry," said Elephant, "but you'd make my journey so slow. I must get to the forest. I've got the most terrible headache."

"Well, I've got a headache too," protested the chief.

"I'm sure," said Elephant, "and no one could be sorrier about that than I am. Is it a very big headache?"

"Shocking big," said Arap Sang.

"There now," said Elephant. "Consider how big I am compared to you and what the size of my headache must be."

That's elephants all over, always so logical. Arap Sang felt that there was something wrong with this argument, but he couldn't just see where. Also, he had become a little uncomfortable about all those bald vultures, and he didn't want to lose his temper with anyone else. You have to be careful what you do when you're half a god. It's so dreadfully final.

"Oh, all right," he muttered.

"Knew you'd see it that way," said Elephant. "It's just what I was saying about you the other day. You can always rely on Arap Sang, I said, to behave reasonably. Well, goodbye and good luck."

And she hurried off in the direction of the distant forest and was soon out of sight.

Poor Arap Sang was now feeling very ill indeed. He sat on the ground, and he thought to himself, "I can't go another step unless I get some shade; and if I don't get some soon, I'm done for."

And there he was found by a flock of cranes.

They came dancing through the white grass, stamping their long, delicate legs so that the insects flew up in alarm and were at once snapped up in the cranes' beaks. They gathered around Arap Sang sitting on the ground; and he looked so distressed that they hopped up and down with embarrassment, first on one leg then the other. "Korong! Korong!" they called softly, and this happens to be their name as well.

"Good birds," whispered Arap Sang, "you must help me. If I don't reach shade soon, I'll die. Help me to the forest."

"But of course," said the cranes, and they spread their great, handsome black and white wings to shade him and helped him to his feet; and together, slowly, they all crossed the plain into the trees.

Then Arap Sang sat in the shade of a fine cotton tree and felt very much better. The birds gathered round him, and he looked at them and thought that he had never seen more beautiful creatures in the whole world.

"And kind. Kind as well as beautiful," he muttered. "The two don't always go together. I must reward them."

"I shan't forget your kindness," he said, "and I'll see that no one else does. Now I want each of you to come here."

Then the cranes came one after another and bowed before him, and Arap Sang stretched out his kindly hand and gently touched each beautiful sleek head. And where he did this, a golden crown appeared. And after the birds had gravely bowed their thanks, they all flew off to the lake, their new crowns glittering in the evening sun.

Arap Sang felt quite recovered. He was very pleased with his gift to the cranes.

Two months later, a crane dragged herself to the door of Arap Sang's house. She was a pitiful sight, thin with hunger, feathers broken and muddy from hiding in the reeds, eyes red with lack of sleep.

Arap Sang exclaimed in pity and horror. "Great Chief," said the crane, "we beg you to take back your gift. If you don't, there'll soon be not one crane left alive, for we are hunted day and night for the sake of our golden crowns." Arap Sang listened and nodded his head in sorrow.

"Great Chief, . . . we beg you to take back your gift."

"I'm foolish," he said, "and I harm my friends. I had forgotten that humans also were greedy and selfish and that they'll do anything for gold. Let me undo the wrong I have done by giving without thought. I'll make one more magic, but that'll be the last." Then he took their golden crowns, and in their place he put a wonderful halo of feathers which they have until this day.

But they still are called Crowned Cranes. ❖

Humphrey Harman

"I wrote down what I heard . . . an immense collection of stories."

An Englishman in Africa Humphrey Harman was born in England. He first traveled to Africa during World War II. After the war, he returned to Africa to become a teacher in Kenya. He later moved to Zambia and began training teachers at Chalimbana College.

Learning from Students Harman first learned African stories and legends from his students.

"I made them write and talk about their peoples as part of their work," he explained. He also stayed in students' homes during holidays and heard stories told by their relatives. "My interest in their stories intrigued them, and they would take great pains to see that I got something right, often calling in old men and women because it was known that such-and-such man 'had the best version.'" The storytellers were from many different ethnic groups, but the stories they told were often similar. Harman combined and edited these tales in books such as *Tales Told Near a Crocodile, African Samson,* and *Men of Masaba.*

PREPARING to *Read*

The Oral Tradition

LINKS TO UNIT TWO

Relationships

In Unit Two you read about characters who showed courage or who experienced changes within themselves. The characters had the courage to take risks and—despite their own hardships—succeed in teaching others about forgiveness, kindness, and respect. You are about to read about characters from different cultures who share similar motivations, attitudes, and values.

GERMANY

Ashputtle

retold by Jakob and Wilhelm Grimm

The Grimm brothers started collecting and retelling stories in the early 1800s. Many of their stories, including "Ashputtle," have been retold by other storytellers. You will almost certainly be familiar with at least one other version of "Ashputtle"–probably as "Cinderella." The story probably originated in China, but versions of it are found in many cultures.

The simple message of "Ashputtle" is that goodness is rewarded and evil is punished. In this version of the tale, the Grimm brothers challenge readers to think about what happens when people are forced to reexamine their relationships with others.

AS YOU READ . . .

Think about the lessons that the tales from different cultures teach.

Consider the risks the characters take.

Identify and analyze the recurring themes about human relationships that each tale conveys.

CHINA

Waters of Gold

retold by Laurence Yep

"Waters of Gold" is a folk tale created by Chinese people who immigrated to the United States. These tales helped Asian immigrants and their families remember their culture and values. Many of these tales concern human relationships and the capacity for change. Some stories, like "Waters of Gold," have elements of magic and reflect the belief that ordinary people may experience extraordinary things.

Waters of Gold

RETOLD BY LAURENCE YEP

A Spring Morning at Yen-ling-t'an (Chekiang) (Qing dynasty, China, 1642–1715), Wang Yuan-ch'i. Handscroll, ink and color on paper, 38 cm × 304.7 cm, courtesy of Museum of Fine Arts, Boston, Keith McLeod Fund (56.10). Photo Copyright © 1995 Museum of Fine Arts, Boston, all rights reserved.

Many years ago, there lived a woman whom everyone called Auntie Lily. She was Auntie by blood to half the county and Auntie to the other half by friendship. As she liked to say, "There's a bit of Heaven in each of us." As a result, she was always helping people out.

Because of her many kind acts, she knew so many people that she couldn't go ten steps without meeting someone who wanted to chat. So it would take her half the day to go to the village well and back to her home.

Eventually, though, she helped so many people that she had no more money. She had to sell her fields and even her house to her neighbor, a rich old woman. "If you'd helped yourself instead of others, you wouldn't have to do this," the neighbor said smugly. "Where are all those other people when you need them?"

"That isn't why I helped them," Auntie Lily said firmly. She wound up having to pay rent for the house she had once owned. She supported herself by her embroidery; but since her eyes were going bad, she could not do very much.

One day an old beggar entered the village. He was a ragbag of a man—a trash heap, a walking pig wallow. It was impossible to tell what color or what shape his clothes had once been, and his hair was as muddy and matted as a bird's nest. As he shuffled through the village gates, he called out, "Water for my feet. Please, water for my feet. One little bowl of water—that's all I ask."

Everyone ignored him, pretending to concentrate on their chores instead. One man went on replacing the shaft of his hoe. A woman swept her courtyard. Another woman fed her hens.

The beggar went to each in turn, but they all showed their backs to him.

After calling out a little while longer, the beggar went to the nearest home, which happened to belong to the rich old woman. When he banged at her door, he left the dirty outline of his knuckles on the clean wood. And when the rich woman opened her door, his smell nearly took her breath away.

Now it so happened that she had been chopping vegetables when the beggar had knocked. When the beggar repeated his request, she raised her cleaver menacingly. "What good would one bowl of water be? You'd need a whole river to wash you clean. Go away."

"A thousand pardons," the old beggar said, and shambled on to the next house.

Though Auntie Lily had to hold her nose, she asked politely, "Yes?"

"I'd like a bowl of water to wash my feet." And the beggar pointed one grimy finger toward them.

Her rich neighbor had stayed in her doorway to watch the beggar. She scolded Auntie Lily now. "It's all your fault those beggars come into the village. They know they can count on a free meal."

It was an old debate between them, so Auntie Lily simply said, "Any of us can have bad luck."

"Garbage," the rich old woman declared, "is garbage. They must have done something bad, or Heaven wouldn't have let them become beggars."

Auntie Lily turned to the beggar. "I may be joining you on the road someday. Wait here."

Much to the neighbor's distress, Auntie Lily went inside and poured water from a large jar in her kitchen into a bucket. Carrying it in both hands, she brought it outside to the beggar and set it down.

The beggar stood on one leg, just like a crane, while he washed one callused, leathery sole over the bucket. "You can put mud on any other part of me, but if my feet are clean, then I feel clean."

As he fussily continued to cleanse his feet, Auntie Lily asked kindly, "Are you hungry? I don't have much, but what I have I'm willing to share."

The beggar shook his head. "I've stayed longer in this village than I have in any other. Heaven is my roof, and the whole world my house."

Auntie Lily stared at him, wondering what she would look like after a few years on the

road. "Are you very tired? Have you been on the road for very long?"

"No, the road is on me," the beggar said, and held up his hands from his dirty sides. "But thank you. You're the first person to ask. And you're the first person to give me some water. So place the bucket of water by your bed tonight and do not look into it till tomorrow morning."

As the beggar shuffled out of the village again, Auntie Lily stared down doubtfully at the bucket of what was now muddy water. Then, even though she felt foolish, she picked it up again.

"You're not really going to take that scummy water inside?" laughed the rich neighbor. "It'll probably breed mosquitoes."

"It seemed important to him," she answered. "I'll humor him."

"Humoring people," snapped the neighbor, "has got you one step from begging yourself."

However, Auntie Lily carried the bucket inside anyway. Setting it down near her sleeping mat, she covered the mouth of the bucket with an old, cracked plate so she wouldn't peek into it by mistake, and then she got so caught up in embroidering a pair of slippers that she forgot all about the beggar and his bucket of water.

She sewed until twilight, when it was too dark to use her needle. Then, because she had no money for oil or candles, she went to sleep.

The next morning Auntie Lily rose and stretched the aches out of her back. She sighed. "The older I get, the harder it is to get up in the morning."

Detail of *Beggars and Street Characters* (1516), Zhou Chen. Album leaves; ink and colors on paper. Honolulu (Hawaii) Academy of Arts, gift of Mrs. Carter Galt, 1956 (2239.1).

She was always saying something like that, but she had never stayed on her sleeping mat—even when she was sick. Thinking of all that day's chores, she decided to water the herbs she had growing on one side of her house.

Her eyes fell upon the beggar's bucket with its covering plate. "No sense using fresh water when that will do as well. After all, dirt's dirt to a plant."

Squatting down, she picked up the bucket and was surprised at how heavy it was. "I must have filled it fuller than I thought," she grunted.

She staggered out of the house and over to the side where rows of little green herbs grew. "Here you go," she said to her plants. "Drink deep."

Taking off the plate, she upended the bucket; but instead of muddy brown water, there was a flash of reflected light and a clinking sound as gold coins rained down upon her plants.

Auntie Lily set the bucket down hastily and crouched, not trusting her weak eyes. However, where some of her herbs had been, there was now a small mound of gold coins. She squinted in disbelief and rubbed her aching eyes and stared again; but the gold was still there.

She turned to the bucket. There was even more gold inside. Scooping up coins by the handful, she freed her little plants and made sure that the stalks weren't too bent.

Then she sat gazing at her bucket full of gold until a farmer walked by. "Tell me I'm not dreaming," she called to him.

The farmer yawned and came over with his hoe over his shoulder. "I wish I were dreaming, because that would mean I'm still in bed instead of having to go off to work."

Auntie Lily gathered up a handful of gold coins and let it fall in a tinkling, golden shower back into the bucket. "And this is real?"

The farmer's jaw dropped. He picked up one coin with his free hand and bit into it. He flipped it back in with the other coins. "It's as real as me, Auntie. But where did you ever get that?"

So Auntie Lily told him. And as others woke up and stepped outside, Auntie told them as well, for she still could not believe her luck and wanted them to confirm that the gold was truly gold. In no time at all, there was a small crowd around her.

If the bucket had been filled with ordinary copper cash, that would have been more money than any of them had ever seen. In their wildest dreams, they had never expected to see that much gold. Auntie Lily stared at the bucket uncomfortably. "I keep thinking it's going to disappear the next moment."

The farmer, who had been standing there all this time, shook his head. "If it hasn't disappeared by now, I don't think it will. What are you going to do with it, Auntie?"

Auntie Lily stared at the bucket, and suddenly she came to a decision. Stretching out a hand, she picked up a gold coin. "I'm going to buy back my house, and I'm going to get back my land."

The farmer knew the fields. "Those old things? You could buy a valley full of prime land with half that bucket. And a palace with the other half."

"I want what I sweated for." Asking the farmer to guard her bucket, Auntie Lily closed her hand around the gold coin. Then, as the crowd parted before her, she made her way over to her neighbor.

Now the rich old woman liked to sleep late; but all the noise had woken her up, so she was just getting dressed when Auntie knocked. The old woman yanked her door open as she buttoned the last button of her coat. "Who started the riot? Can't a person get a good night's sleep?"

With some satisfaction, Auntie Lily held up the gold coin. "Will this buy back my house and land?"

"Where did you get that?" the old woman demanded.

"Will it buy them back?" Auntie Lily repeated.

The rich old woman snatched the coin out of Auntie Lily's hand and bit into it just as the farmer had. "It's real," the old woman said in astonishment.

"Will it?" Auntie asked again.

"Yes, yes, yes," the old woman said crabbily. "But where did you ever get that much gold?"

When Auntie Lily told her the story and showed her the bucket of gold, the rich old woman stood moving her mouth like a fish out of water. Clasping her hands together, she shut her eyes and moaned in genuine pain. "And I sent him away. What a fool I am. What a fool." And the old woman beat her head with her fists.

That very afternoon, the beggar—the ragbag, the trash heap, the walking pig wallow—shuffled once more through the village gates with feet as dirty as before. As he went, he croaked, "Water for my feet. Please, water for my feet. One little bowl of water— that's all I ask."

This time, people dropped whatever they were doing when they heard his plea. Hoes, brooms, and pots were flung down, hens and pigs were kicked out of the way as everyone hurried to fill a bucket with water. There was a small riot by the village well as everyone fought to get water at the same time. Still others rushed out with buckets filled from the jars in their houses.

"Here, use my water," one man shouted, holding up a tub.

A woman shoved in front of him with a bucket in her arms. "No, no, use mine. It's purer."

They surrounded the old beggar, pleading with him to use their water, and in the process of jostling one another, they splashed a good deal of water on one another and came perilously close to drowning the beggar. The rich old woman, Auntie Lily's neighbor, charged to the rescue.

"Out of the way, you vultures," the rich old woman roared. "You're going to trample him." Using her elbows, her feet, and in one case even her teeth, the old woman fought her way through the mob.

No longer caring if she soiled her hands, the old woman seized the beggar by the arm. "This way, you poor, misunderstood creature."

Fighting off her neighbors with one hand and keeping her grip on the beggar with the other, the old woman hauled him inside her house. Barring the door against the rest of the village, she ignored all the fists and feet thumping on her door and all the shouts.

"I really wasn't myself yesterday, because I had been up the night before tending a sick friend. This is what I meant to do." She fetched a fresh new towel and an even newer bucket and forced the beggar to wash his feet.

When he was done, he handed her the now filthy towel. "Dirt's dirt, and garbage is garbage," he said.

However, the greedy old woman didn't recognize her own words. She was too busy trying to remember what else Auntie Lily had done. "Won't you have something to eat? Have you traveled very far? Are you tired?" she asked, all in the same breath.

The old beggar went to the door and waited patiently while she unbarred it. As he shuffled

---

WORDS TO KNOW
jostling (jŏs'lĭng) *n.* roughly bumping, pushing, or shoving **jostle** *v.*
perilously (pĕr'ə-ləs-lē) *adv.* dangerously

outside, he instructed her to leave the bucket of water by her bed but not to look into it until the morning.

That night, the greedy old woman couldn't sleep as she imagined the heap of shiny gold that would be waiting for her tomorrow. She waited impatiently for the sun to rise and got up as soon as she heard the first rooster crow.

Hurrying to the bucket, she plunged her hands inside expecting to bring up handfuls of gold. Instead, she gave a cry as dozens of little things bit her, for the bucket was filled not with gold but with snakes, lizards, and ants.

The greedy old woman fell sick—some said from her bites, some claimed from sheer frustration. Auntie Lily herself came to nurse her neighbor. "Take this to heart: Kindness comes with no price."

The old woman was so ashamed that she did, indeed, take the lesson to heart. Though she remained sick, she was kind to whoever came to her door.

One day, a leper came into the village. Everyone hid for fear of the terrible disease. Doors slammed and shutters banged down over windows, and soon the village seemed deserted.

Only Auntie Lily and her neighbor stepped out of their houses. "Are you hungry?" Auntie Lily asked.

"Are you thirsty?" the neighbor asked. "I'll make you a cup of tea."

The leper thanked Auntie Lily and then turned to the neighbor as if to express his gratitude as well; but he stopped and studied her. "You're looking poorly, my dear woman. Can I help?"

With a tired smile, the rich old woman explained what had happened. When she was finished, the leper stood thoughtfully for a moment. "You're not the same woman as before: You're as kind as Auntie Lily, and you aren't greedy anymore. So take this humble gift from my brother, the old beggar."

With that, the leper limped out of the village; and as he left, the illness fell away from the old woman like an old, discarded cloak. But though the old woman was healthy again, she stayed as kind as Auntie Lily and used her own money as well and wisely as Auntie Lily used the waters of gold. ❖

Laurence Yep
born 1948

"I'm always pursuing the theme of being an outsider— an alien—and many teenagers feel they're aliens."

Young Writer When Laurence Yep was only 25, he published his first book. Two years later, his second book, *Dragonwings,* won a number of awards, including a Newbery Honor Award. Yep has written 2 plays and some 40 books, many of which reflect his cultural heritage.

Two Cultures Yep is a third-generation Chinese American. Some of his novels—such as *Child of the Owl* and *Sea Glass*—focus on Chinese-American characters who are caught between two cultures.

Ashputtle

retold by
JAKOB GRIMM AND WILHELM GRIMM

Portrait of a Young Woman, Sandro Botticelli. Städelsches Institute of Art, Frankfurt, Germany/SuperStock.

rich man's wife fell sick and, feeling that her end was near, she called her only daughter to her bedside and said: "Dear child, be good and say your prayers; God will help you, and I shall look down on you from heaven and always be with you." With that she closed her eyes and died. Every day the little girl went out to her mother's grave and wept, and she went on being good and saying her prayers. When winter came, the snow spread a white cloth over the grave, and when spring took it off, the man remarried.

His new wife brought two daughters into the house. Their faces were beautiful and lily-white, but their hearts were ugly and black. That was the beginning of a bad time for the poor stepchild. "Why should this silly goose sit in the parlor with us?" they said. "People who want to eat bread must earn it. Get into the kitchen where you belong!" They took away her fine clothes and gave her an old gray dress and wooden shoes to wear. "Look at the haughty princess in her finery!" they cried and, laughing, led her to the kitchen. From then on she had to do all the work, getting up before daybreak, carrying water, lighting fires, cooking and washing. In addition the sisters did everything they could to plague her. They jeered at her and poured peas and lentils into the ashes, so that she had to sit there picking them out. At night, when she was tired out with work, she had no bed to sleep in but had to lie in the ashes by the hearth. And they took to calling her Ashputtle because she always looked dusty and dirty.

One day when her father was going to the fair, he asked his two stepdaughters what he should bring them. "Beautiful dresses," said one. "Diamonds and pearls," said the other. "And you, Ashputtle. What would you like?" "Father," she said, "break off the first branch that brushes against your hat on your way home, and bring it to me." So he bought beautiful dresses, diamonds and pearls for his two stepdaughters, and on the way home, as he was riding through a copse,[1] a hazel branch brushed against him and knocked off his hat. So he broke off the branch and took it home with him. When he got home, he gave the stepdaughters what they had asked for, and gave Ashputtle the branch. After thanking him, she went to her mother's grave and planted the hazel sprig over it and cried so hard that her tears fell on the sprig and watered it. It grew and became a beautiful tree. Three times a day Ashputtle went and sat under it and wept and prayed. Each time a little white bird came and perched on the tree, and when Ashputtle made a wish the little bird threw down what she had wished for.

---

1. **copse** (kŏps): a patch of small trees or shrubs.

Now it so happened that the king arranged for a celebration. It was to go on for three days and all the beautiful girls in the kingdom were invited, in order that his son might choose a bride. When the two stepsisters heard they had been asked, they were delighted. They called Ashputtle and said: "Comb our hair, brush our shoes, and fasten our buckles. We're going to the wedding at the king's palace." Ashputtle obeyed, but she wept, for she too would have liked to go dancing, and she begged her stepmother to let her go. "You little sloven!"[2] said the stepmother. "How can you go to a wedding when you're all dusty and dirty? How can you go dancing when you have neither dress nor shoes?" But when Ashputtle begged and begged, the stepmother finally said: "Here, I've dumped a bowlful of lentils in the ashes. If you can pick them out in two hours, you may go." The girl went out the back door to the garden and cried out: "O tame little doves, O turtledoves, and all the birds under heaven, come and help me put

the good ones in the pot,
the bad ones in your crop."

Two little white doves came flying through the kitchen window, and then came the turtledoves, and finally all the birds under heaven came flapping and fluttering and settled down by the ashes. The doves nodded their little heads and started in, peck peck peck peck, and all the others started in, peck peck peck peck, and they sorted out all the good lentils and put them in the bowl. Hardly an hour had passed before they finished and flew away. Then the girl brought the bowl to her stepmother, and she was happy, for she thought she'd be allowed to go to the wedding. But the stepmother said: "No, Ashputtle. You have nothing to wear and you

don't know how to dance; the people would only laugh at you." When Ashputtle began to cry, the stepmother said: "If you can pick two bowlfuls of lentils out of the ashes in an hour, you may come." And she thought: "She'll never be able to do it." When she had dumped the two bowlfuls of lentils in the ashes, Ashputtle went out the back door to the garden and cried out: "O tame little doves, O turtledoves, and all the birds under heaven, come and help me put

the good ones in the pot,
the bad ones in your crop."

Then two little white doves came flying through the kitchen window, and then came the turtledoves, and finally all the birds under heaven came flapping and fluttering and settled down by the ashes. The doves nodded their little heads and started in, peck peck peck peck, and all the others started in, peck peck peck peck, and they sorted out all the good lentils and put them in the bowls. Before half an hour had passed, they had finished and they all flew away. Then the girl brought the bowls to her stepmother, and she was happy, for she thought she'd be allowed to go to the wedding. But her stepmother said: "It's no use. You can't come, because you have nothing to wear and you don't know how to dance. We'd only be ashamed of you." Then she turned her back and hurried away with her two proud daughters.

When they had all gone out, Ashputtle went to her mother's grave. She stood under the hazel tree and cried:

"Shake your branches, little tree,
Throw gold and silver down on me."

---

2. **sloven** (slŭv′ən): a person who is careless in appearance.

Whereupon the bird tossed down a gold and silver dress and slippers embroidered with silk and silver. Ashputtle slipped into the dress as fast as she could and went to the wedding. Her sisters and stepmother didn't recognize her. She was so beautiful in her golden dress that they thought she must be the daughter of some foreign king. They never dreamed it could be Ashputtle, for they thought she was sitting at home in her filthy rags, picking lentils out of the ashes. The king's son came up to her, took her by the hand and danced with her. He wouldn't dance with anyone else and he never let go her hand. When someone else asked for a dance, he said: "She is my partner."

She danced until evening, and then she wanted to go home. The king's son said: "I'll go with you, I'll see you home," for he wanted to find out whom the beautiful girl belonged to. But she got away from him and slipped into the dovecote.[3] The king's son waited until her father arrived, and told him the strange girl had slipped into the dovecote. The old man thought: "Could it be Ashputtle?" and he sent for an ax and a pick and broke into the dovecote, but there was no one inside. When they went indoors, Ashputtle was lying in the ashes in her filthy clothes and a dim oil lamp was burning on the chimney piece, for Ashputtle had slipped out the back end of the dovecote and run to the hazel tree. There she had taken off her fine clothes and put them on the grave, and the bird had taken them away. Then she had put her gray dress on again, crept into the kitchen and lain down in the ashes. Next day when the festivities started in again and her parents and stepsisters had gone, Ashputtle went to the hazel tree and said:

"Shake your branches, little tree,
Throw gold and silver down on me."

Whereupon the bird threw down a dress that was even more dazzling than the first one. And when she appeared at the wedding, everyone marveled at her beauty. The king's son was waiting for her. He took her by the hand and danced with no one but her. When others came and asked her for a dance, he said: "She is my partner." When evening came, she said she was going home. The king's son followed her, wishing to see which house she went into, but she ran away and disappeared into the garden behind the house, where there was a big beautiful tree with the most wonderful pears growing on it. She climbed among the branches as <u>nimbly</u> as a squirrel and the king's son didn't know what had become of her. He waited until her father arrived and said to him: "The strange girl has got away from me and I think she has climbed up in the pear tree." Her father thought: "Could it be Ashputtle?" He sent for an ax and chopped the tree down, but there was no one in it. When they went into the kitchen, Ashputtle was lying there in the ashes as usual, for she had jumped down on the other side of the tree, brought her fine clothes back to the bird in the hazel tree, and put on her filthy gray dress.

On the third day, after her parents and sisters had gone, Ashputtle went back to her mother's grave and said to the tree:

"Shake your branches, little tree,
Throw gold and silver down on me."

Whereupon the bird threw down a dress that was more radiant than either of the others, and the slippers were all gold. When she appeared at the wedding, the people were too

---

3. **dovecote** (dŭv′kōt′): a structure where tame pigeons are housed.

amazed to speak. The king's son danced with no one but her, and when someone else asked her for a dance, he said: "She is my partner."

When evening came, Ashputtle wanted to go home, and the king's son said he'd go with her, but she slipped away so quickly that he couldn't follow. But he had thought up a trick. He had arranged to have the whole staircase brushed with pitch, and as she was running down it the pitch pulled her left slipper off. The king's son picked it up, and it was tiny and delicate and all gold. Next morning he went to the father and said: "No girl shall be my wife but the one this golden shoe fits." The sisters were overjoyed, for they had beautiful feet. The eldest took the shoe to her room to try it on and her mother went with her. But the shoe was too small and she couldn't get her big toe in. So her mother handed her a knife and said: "Cut your toe off. Once you're queen you won't have to walk any more." The girl cut her toe off, forced her foot into the shoe, gritted her teeth against the pain, and went out to the king's son. He accepted her as his bride-to-be, lifted her up on his horse, and rode away with her. But they had to pass the grave. The two doves were sitting in the hazel tree and they cried out:

"Roocoo, roocoo,
There's blood in the shoe.
The foot's too long, the foot's too wide,
That's not the proper bride."

He looked down at her foot and saw the blood spurting. At that he turned his horse around and took the false bride home again. "No," he said, "this isn't the right girl; let her sister try the shoe on." The sister went to her room and managed to get her toes into the shoe, but her

heel was too big. So her mother handed her a knife and said: "Cut off a chunk of your heel. Once you're queen you won't have to walk any more." The girl cut off a chunk of her heel, forced her foot into the shoe, gritted her teeth against the pain, and went out to the king's son. He accepted her as his bride-to-be, lifted her up on his horse, and rode away with her. As they passed the hazel tree, the two doves were sitting there, and they cried out:

"Roocoo, roocoo,
There's blood in the shoe.
The foot's too long, the foot's too wide,
That's not the proper bride."

He looked down at her foot and saw that blood was spurting from her shoe and staining her white stocking all red. He turned his horse around and took the false bride home again. "This isn't the right girl either," he said. "Haven't you got another daughter?" "No," said the man, "there's only a puny little kitchen drudge that my dead wife left me. She couldn't possibly be the bride." "Send her up," said the king's son, but the mother said: "Oh no, she's much too dirty to be seen." But he insisted and they had to call her. First she washed her face and hands, and when they were clean, she went upstairs and <u>curtseyed</u> to the king's son. He handed her the golden slipper and sat down on a footstool, took her foot out of her heavy wooden shoe, and put it into the slipper. It fitted perfectly. And when she stood up and the king's son looked into her face, he recognized the beautiful girl he had danced with and cried out: "This is my true bride!" The stepmother and the two sisters went pale with fear and rage. But he

curtsey (kûrt'sē) v. to bend the knees and lower the body as a gesture of respect

Portrait of a Gentleman (16th century), Bartolomeo Veneto. Galleria Nazionale d'Arte Antica, Rome/Canali PhotoBank, Milan (Italy)/SuperStock.

lifted Ashputtle up on his horse and rode away with her. As they passed the hazel tree, the two white doves called out:

"Roocoo, roocoo,
No blood in the shoe.
Her foot is neither long nor wide,
This one is the proper bride."

Then they flew down and <u>alighted</u> on Ashputtle's shoulders, one on the right and one on the left, and there they sat.

On the day of Ashputtle's wedding, the two stepsisters came and tried to <u>ingratiate</u> themselves and share in her happiness. On the way to church the elder was on the right side of the bridal couple and the younger on the left. The doves came along and pecked out one of the elder sister's eyes and one of the younger sister's eyes. Afterward, on the way out, the elder was on the left side and the younger on the right, and the doves pecked out both the remaining eyes. So both sisters were punished with blindness to the end of their days for being so wicked and false. ❖

Jakob Grimm
1785–1863

Wilhelm Grimm
1786–1859

"Up to the very end, [Wilhelm and I] worked in two rooms next to each other, always under one roof." —Jakob Grimm

Reluctant Lawyers Jakob and Wilhelm Grimm were born in Hanau, Germany, and trained to be lawyers. Their widowed mother struggled to pay for their education. However, the brothers were much more interested in collecting local folk tales than they were in practicing law.

The Grimm Legacy Their first book together, *Kinder- und Hausmärchen* (Nursery and household tales), was published in 1812. The book was a scholarly collection of household tales, intended for adult readers, but young people read it anyway. Later editions of the book were made with young people in mind. Illustrations were added, and some of the grisly tales were removed. Today, Grimm fairy tales appear in more than 70 languages. The stories are known and loved throughout the world.

WORDS TO KNOW
alight (ə-līt′) *v.* to land lightly, as after flight
ingratiate (ĭn-grā′shē-āt′) *v.* to try to bring oneself into another's favor

LINKS TO UNIT THREE

Flights of Imagination

In the tales you are about to read, the contrast between appearance and reality is important. A greedy farmer, a jealous stepbrother, and an inexperienced boy learn that things are not always what people imagine them to be. A person or situation that appears one way at first glance may not live up to expectations. These characters and themes are closely linked to similar characters and themes in Unit Three.

PUERTO RICO

Lazy Peter and His Three-Cornered Hat

retold by Ricardo E. Alegría

"Lazy Peter and His Three-Cornered Hat" is a trickster tale that comes from Puerto Rico. The folklore of Puerto Rico has roots in the folklore of Spain, West Africa, and the Taino people of the Caribbean. Although trickster tales reflect an admiration for cleverness, the tricksters themselves are not depicted as heroic but as what they really are—con artists.

Young Arthur

retold by Robert D. San Souci

A helpless baby who is a king's son, a wizard who pretends to be a beggar, a young knight who may not be what he seems—the story of King Arthur is full of disguises and deceptions. This retelling of the classic medieval tale focuses on Arthur's belief "in his heart that he already was a knight, though no lord had dubbed him such." Can a sword in a stone prove who is the real king of England?

BRITAIN

AS YOU READ . . .

Pay attention to the theme of how things appear and how they really are in these tales from different cultures.

Decide what causes some characters to be deceived.

Consider the lessons the characters learn about appearances.

Young Arthur

retold by Robert D. San Souci

King Uther[1] heard the baby's wail and leaped to his feet. There was a sharp rap at the chamber door, and a servant entered grinning happily. "You have a son, " he told the king. Uther's joy knew no bounds. When he was ushered into Queen Igerna's bedchamber, Uther looked lovingly at mother and son. "The boy's name shall be Arthur," he declared, "and he shall be a great king. For Merlin [the magician] has foretold that he will one day rule the greatest kingdom under heaven."

But Uther's happiness did not last. His beloved queen died soon after Arthur's birth, and sadness sapped the king's spirit. He lost interest in ruling, and Merlin was unable to rouse him from his melancholy. "Unrest grows throughout the land," Merlin warned. "Your old foes are rising in rebellion. Give the babe into my keeping, for you have enemies even at court."

Anxious for his son's safety, Uther agreed. So Merlin, disguised as a beggar, took the infant Arthur to Sir Ector and his lady, who lived some distance from the court and all its dangers. He told them nothing about the child, save that his name was Arthur. The couple had recently lost their infant son and welcomed Arthur as their own. Soon rebellion divided the kingdom. Uther, reclaiming his old spirit, rallied his knights and barons. With Merlin always beside him, he drove back his enemies.

But as Uther celebrated his victory in the town of Verulum, traitors poisoned the town's wells. The king and his loyal followers were stricken. Merlin alone escaped. Though he tried his healing arts on Uther, he was forced to confess, "Sire, there is no remedy."

"Then," said the dying monarch, "I declare that my son shall be king of all this realm[3] after me. God's blessing and mine be upon him." With these words, Uther died.

When the rebels entered Verulum, only Merlin was alive.

"Tell us where Uther's son is hidden," they demanded, "so that we can slay him and end Uther's line."

But Merlin vanished before their eyes.

Young Arthur was raised as a son in Sir Ector's house. He learned to read and

---

1. **Uther** (yoo'thər).
2. **Igerna** (ē-gĕr'nə).
3. **realm:** kingdom.

WORDS TO KNOW

melancholy (mĕl'ən-kŏl'ē) *n.* sadness; depression
rebellion (rĭ-bĕl'yən) *n.* organized resistance to government or authority
reclaiming (rĭ-klā'mĭng) *adj.* getting back; recovering reclaim v.

write alongside his foster brother, Kay, who was four years older. By the time he was fifteen, Arthur was a tall, handsome, quick-witted lad. Though he had great strength, he also had a gentle manner.

Kay, who had recently been knighted, decided to train Arthur in the knightly arts himself. But Kay was vain and jealous of the favor Arthur found with their father, so he was a harsh taskmaster. Arthur came away from his lessons in swordsmanship with many bruises and cuts. When he complained, Kay replied, "A knight must be thick-skinned and ready to bear even <u>grievous</u> wounds without flinching." Yet if Arthur so much as pricked his brother, Kay would <u>bellow</u> loudly for the physician.

Eventually Kay appointed Arthur his apprentice.[4] This was an honor the younger boy would happily have forgone. However, seeing that Sir Ector wished it so, Arthur sighed and agreed. But he felt in his heart that he already was a knight, though no lord had dubbed him such.

Both Arthur and Kay knew it was vital to learn the arts of war. The kingdom was still at the mercy of upstart lords who ruled by fire and sword.

The story of Uther's lost son, the true heir to the throne, would have been forgotten but for Merlin. One Christmas Eve, the long-absent magician reappeared and summoned the bishops, lords, and common folk to London's square. There he drove a broadsword halfway into a huge stone. Written on the blade in blazing gold letters were the words: "Whoso pulleth out the

Young Knight (1893), Aubrey Beardsley. Pen and ink. Victoria & Albert Museum, London/Art Resource, New York.

sword from this stone is born the rightful King of England."

In the days that followed, knights and barons, cowherds and bakers, an endless parade of would-be kings eagerly pulled at the sword. But none could loosen it, let alone draw it forth.

When they accused Merlin of trickery, he said, "The rightful king has not yet come. God will make him known at the proper time."

Now it happened that a great tournament[5] was held in London. Among those who came were Sir Ector, Sir Kay, and young Arthur, who

---

4. **apprentice:** a person learning a trade.

5. **tournament:** a medieval sport in which groups of armored men fought against one another.

829

served Kay. So eager was the boy to see the jousts[6] that he forgot to pack Kay's sword. There was great upset when the mistake was discovered.

"Woe to you, boy," snarled Kay, "if your error costs me the victory I would otherwise win today!"

Even Sir Ector scolded Arthur and ordered, "Go back directly and fetch the missing sword."

Angry at his carelessness and impatient to see the contests, Arthur started homeward. Then he suddenly reined in his horse.

In the deserted city square was a massive stone with a sword plunged into its center. "Surely that sword is as good as the one left at home," he said. "I will borrow it. When Kay is finished, I will return it to this curious monument."

So saying, he <u>dismounted</u>, scrambled up the stone, took the sword handle, and tugged. The sword did not move. Impatient to return to the tournament, he pulled again. This time, the sword slid easily out of the stone. In his haste, he did not notice the words upon the blade. Shoving the weapon into his belt, he remounted and raced to where Sir Kay waited his turn upon the field.

The moment he saw the golden words upon the blade, Kay began to tremble with excitement. When Arthur asked what was

Merlin, Aubrey Beardsley.

amiss,[7] Kay shouted, "Go! Get away! You have caused enough trouble."

But Arthur was curious. So he followed as Kay ran to Sir Ector. "Look, Father!" cried Kay. "Here is the sword of the stone. Therefore, it is I who must be king of all this land!"

When Sir Ector and the others saw the sword and read the golden <u>inscription</u>, they began to shout, "The sword from the stone! The king's sword!"

Hearing only this much, Arthur thought that he had stolen a king's weapon. As people hurried excitedly toward Kay, Arthur spurred his horse away, certain he had committed a great crime.

Looking back, he saw Kay and Sir Ector ride off, surrounded by the greatest lords of the realm. Were they taking Kay to trial? he wondered. Had he brought ruin upon Sir Ector's household?

"A true knight would not run away," he said to himself, "and I am a true knight in my heart." Fearful, but determined to do what was right, the boy wheeled his horse around.

The great square was now filled with people. Just how terrible a crime had he committed?

---

6. **jousts:** combats between pairs of mounted knights.

7. **amiss:** wrong.

Upon the stone stood Kay, holding the sword. The crowd shouted each time he held the blade aloft. Then silence fell over the throng: Merlin had appeared at the edge of the square. People stood aside to let the magician approach the stone.

"Are you the one who pulled the sword from the stone?" Merlin asked.

"I am holding it, am I not?" Kay replied.

"The rightful king could pull it free a hundred times," said Merlin. "Slip the sword into the groove and pull it out again."

With a shrug, Kay reinserted the sword. But when he tried to jerk it free, it would not budge.

Suddenly all eyes turned toward Arthur, who was pushing his way through the crowd, bellowing at the top of his lungs. "It wasn't Kay's fault! I brought him the sword!"

Merlin peered closely at Arthur. Then he smiled and said, "Climb up and draw the sword from the stone." Uncertainly Arthur clambered up beside Kay. Grasping the pommel,[8] he easily pulled the sword out.

Then Merlin cried, "This is Arthur, son of Uther Pendragon, Britain's destined king."

An astonished Sir Ector knelt to pay the boy homage,[9] followed by Kay and many others. But all around, there was growing confusion and dispute. Some cried, "It is the will of heaven! Long live the king!" while others cried, "It is Merlin's plot to put a beardless boy, a puppet, on the throne, and so rule the land."

[But] The cries of "Long Live King Arthur!" soon carried the day. ❖

---

8. **pommel:** a knob on the hilt of a sword.
9. **homage:** a display of loyalty and respect.

Robert D. San Souci

born 1946

"I plan to continue writing for both children and adults, as long as I have stories to tell— and an audience that is willing to listen."

An Early Start Robert San Souci wanted to write books even before he could read them. "I always knew I wanted to be a writer. Before I knew how to read and write, I would listen carefully to stories that were read to me," he recalls. "Then I would retell them to my younger sister and brothers. But I would add a new twist or leave out parts I didn't find interesting—so the storytelling impulse was already at work in me."

Stories Across Cultures In 1978 San Souci published his first book, *The Legend of Scarface: A Blackfeet Indian Tale.* It won three awards, and he has been writing steadily ever since. Many of San Souci's books are retellings of folk tales from different cultures, including Chinese, French, African American, Creole, Russian, Japanese, and Armenian. Besides *Young Arthur*, he has written three other books about Arthurian legends: *Young Merlin*, *Young Guinevere*, and *Young Lancelot*.

Searching for New Ideas San Souci has published nearly 60 books—novels and nonfiction as well as folk tales. To find new ideas, he reads, researches, travels, and just listens to people talk. "I love to listen for the flow and rhythm of the language that different people use," he explains.

Lazy Peter and His

Carnival in Huejotzingo (1942), Diego Rivera. Watercolor on paper, 5 ¾" × 3 ¾",
Courtesy of Sotheby's, New York.

Three-Cornered Hat

RETOLD BY RICARDO E. ALEGRÍA

This is the story of Lazy Peter, a shameless rascal of a fellow who went from village to village making mischief.

One day Lazy Peter learned that a fair was being held in a certain village. He knew that a large crowd of country people would be there selling horses, cows, and other farm animals and that a large amount of money would change hands. Peter, as usual, needed money, but it was not his custom to work for it. So he set out for the village, wearing a red three-cornered hat.

The first thing he did was to stop at a stand and leave a big bag of money with the owner, asking him to keep it safely until he returned for it. Peter told the man that when he returned for the bag of money, one corner of his hat would be turned down, and that was how the owner of the stand would know him. The man promised to do this, and Peter thanked him. Then he went to the drugstore in the village and gave the druggist another bag of money, asking him to keep it until he returned with one corner of his hat turned up. The druggist agreed, and Peter left. He went to the church and asked the priest to keep another bag of money and to return it to him only when he came back with one corner of his hat twisted to the side. The priest said fine, he would do this.

Having disposed of three bags of money, Peter went to the edge of the village where the farmers were buying and selling horses and cattle. He stood and watched for a while until he decided that one of the farmers must be very rich indeed, for he had sold all of his horses and cows. Moreover, the man seemed to be a miser who was never satisfied but wanted always more and more money. This was Peter's man! He stopped beside him. It was raining; and instead of keeping his hat on to protect his head, he took it off and wrapped it carefully in his cape, as though it were very valuable. It puzzled the farmer to see Peter stand there with the rain falling on his head and his hat wrapped in his cape.

After a while he asked, "Why do you take better care of your hat than of your head?"

Peter saw that the farmer had swallowed the bait, and smiling to himself, he said that the hat was the most valuable thing in all the world and that was why he took care to protect it from the rain. The farmer's curiosity increased at this reply, and he asked Peter what was so valuable about a red three-cornered hat. Peter told him that the hat worked for him; thanks to it, he never had to work for a living because whenever he put the hat on with one of the corners turned over, people just handed him any money he asked for.

The farmer was amazed and very interested in what Peter said. As money-getting was his greatest ambition, he told Peter that he couldn't believe a word of it until he saw the hat work with his own eyes. Peter assured him that he could do this, for he, Peter, was hungry, and the hat was about to start working, since he had no money with which to buy food.

With this, Peter took out his three-cornered hat, turned one corner down, put it on his head, and told the farmer to come along and watch the hat work. Peter took the farmer to the stand. The minute the owner looked up, he handed over the bag of money Peter had left with him. The farmer stood with his mouth open in astonishment. He didn't know what to make of it. But of one thing he was sure—he had to have that hat!

 Peter smiled and asked if he was satisfied, and the farmer said yes, he was. Then he asked Peter if he would sell the hat. This was just what Lazy Peter wanted, but he said no, he was not interested in selling the hat because with it, he never had to work and he always had money. The farmer said he thought that was <u>unsound</u> reasoning because thieves could easily steal a hat, and wouldn't it be safer to invest in a farm with cattle? So they talked, and Peter pretended to be impressed with the farmer's arguments. Finally he said yes, that he saw the point, and if the farmer would make him a good offer, he would sell the hat. The farmer, who had made up his mind to have the hat at any price, offered a thousand pesos. Peter laughed aloud and said he could make as much as that by just putting his hat on two or three times.

As they continued <u>haggling</u> over the price, the farmer grew more and more determined to have that hat, until, finally, he offered all he had realized from the sale of his horses and cows—ten thousand pesos in gold. Peter still pretended not to be interested, but he chuckled to himself, thinking of the trick he was about to play on the farmer. All right, he said, it was a deal. Then the farmer grew cautious and told Peter that before he handed over the ten thousand pesos, he would like to see the hat work again. Peter said that was fair enough. He put on the hat with one of the corners turned up and went with the farmer to the drugstore. The moment the druggist saw the turned-up corner, he handed over the money Peter had left with him. At this the farmer was convinced and very eager to set the hat to work for himself. He took out a bag containing ten thousand pesos in gold and was about to hand it to Peter when he had a change of heart and thought better of it. He asked Peter please to excuse him, but he had to see the hat work just once more before he could part with his gold. Peter said that that was fair enough, but now he would have to ask the farmer to give him the fine horse he was riding as well as the ten thousand pesos in gold. The farmer's interest in the hat revived, and he said it was a bargain!

Lazy Peter put on his hat again, doubled over one of the corners, and told the farmer that since he still seemed to have doubts, this time he could watch the hat work in the church. The farmer was delighted with this, his doubts were stilled, and he fairly beamed thinking of all the money he was going to make once that hat was his.

They entered the church. The priest was hearing confession, but when he saw Peter

---

1. **sacristy** (săk′rĭ-stē): in a church, a room where sacred objects are stored. (page 845)

WORDS TO KNOW

unsound (ŭn-sound′) *adj.* not free from fault or weakness; not sensible; inaccurate
haggle (hăg′əl) *v.* to argue about terms or price; bargain
priceless (prīs′lĭs) *adj.* too valuable to be measured by price (page 845)

with his hat, he said, "Wait here, my son," and he went to the sacristy[1] and returned with the bag of money Peter had left with him. Peter thanked the priest, then knelt and asked for a blessing before he left. The farmer had seen everything and was fully convinced of the hat's magic powers. As soon as they left the church, he gave Peter the ten thousand pesos in gold and told him to take the horse also. Peter tied the bag of pesos to the saddle, gave the hat to the farmer, begging him to take good care of it, spurred his horse, and galloped out of town.

 As soon as he was alone, the farmer burst out laughing at the thought of the trick he had played on Lazy Peter. A hat such as this was priceless! He couldn't wait to try it. He put it on with one corner turned up and entered the butcher shop. The butcher looked at the hat, which was very handsome indeed, but said nothing. The farmer turned around, then walked up and down until the butcher asked him what he wanted. The farmer said he was waiting for the bag of money. The butcher laughed aloud and asked if he was crazy. The farmer thought that there must be something wrong with the way he had folded the hat. He took it off and doubled another corner down. But this had no effect on the butcher. So he decided to try it out some other place. He went to the mayor of the town.

The mayor, to be sure, looked at the hat but did nothing. The farmer grew desperate and decided to go to the druggist who had given Peter a bag of money. He entered and stood with the hat on. The druggist looked at him but did nothing.

The farmer became very nervous. He began to suspect that there was something very wrong. He shouted at the druggist, "Stop looking at me and hand over the bag of money!"

The druggist said he owed him nothing, and what bag of money was he talking about, anyway? As the farmer continued to shout about a bag of money and a magic hat, the druggist called the police. When they arrived, he told them that the farmer had gone out of his mind and kept demanding a bag of money. The police questioned the farmer, and he told them about the magic hat he had bought from Lazy Peter. When he heard the story, the druggist explained that Peter had left a bag of money, asking that it be returned when he appeared with a corner of his hat turned up. The owner of the stand and the priest told the same story. And I am telling you the farmer was so angry that he tore the hat to shreds and walked home. ❖

Ricardo E. Alegría
born 1921

"Culture is the way mankind expresses itself to live and live collectively . . . and it is manifested through popular art . . ."

Puerto Rican Patriot Ricardo Enrique Alegría is a leading proponent of Puerto Rican history and culture. He led the movement to save and revitalize Old San Juan—the historic neighborhood of the capital of Puerto Rico. Alegría is director of the Center for Advanced Studies of Puerto Rico and the Caribbean.

Collector of Folk tales Alegría is not only an anthropologist and historian but also an avid collector of folk tales. He has written many books and articles on the history and folklore of Puerto Rico.

PREPARING to Read

The Oral Tradition

LINKS TO UNIT FOUR

Nothing Stays the Same

Everything changes. For some people change is difficult; others take it as it comes. The tales you are about to read show that change is part of life, and we respond to it—whether we like it or not. The themes and characters link closely to similar themes and characters in Unit Four.

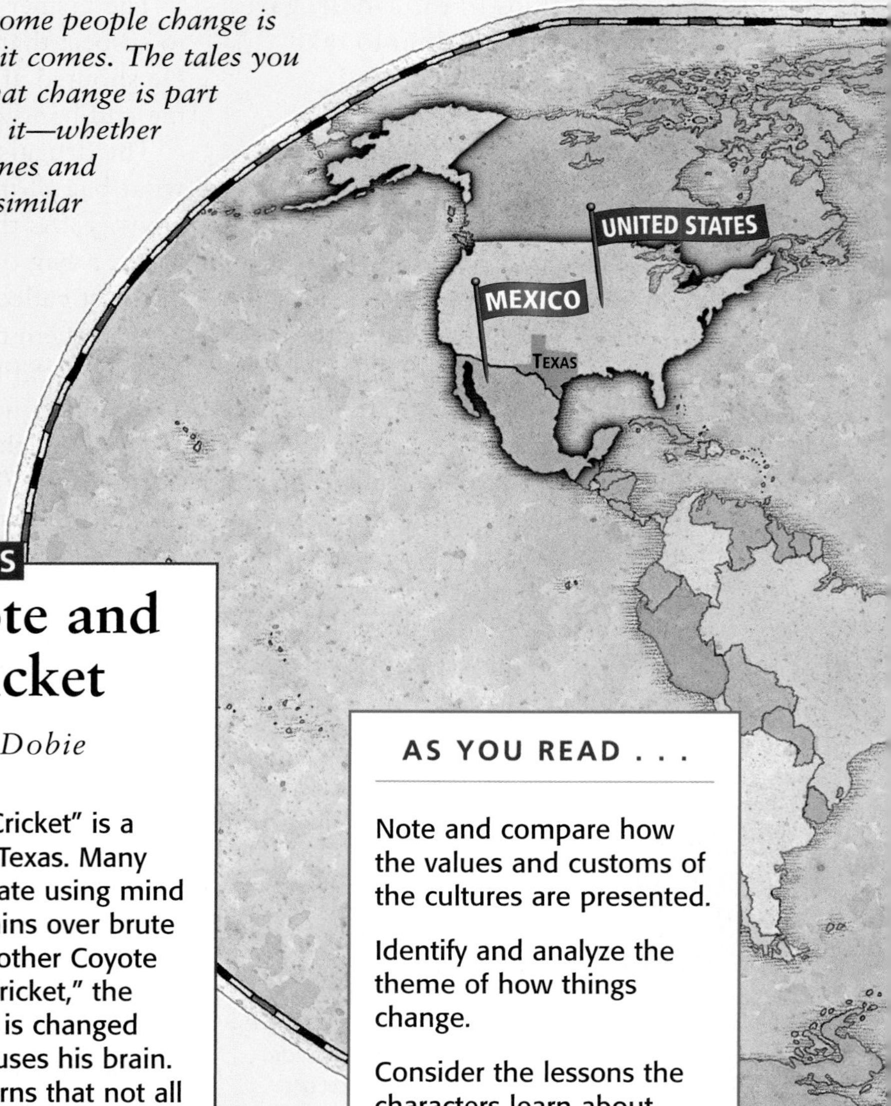

UNITED STATES

Brother Coyote and Brother Cricket

retold by J. Frank Dobie

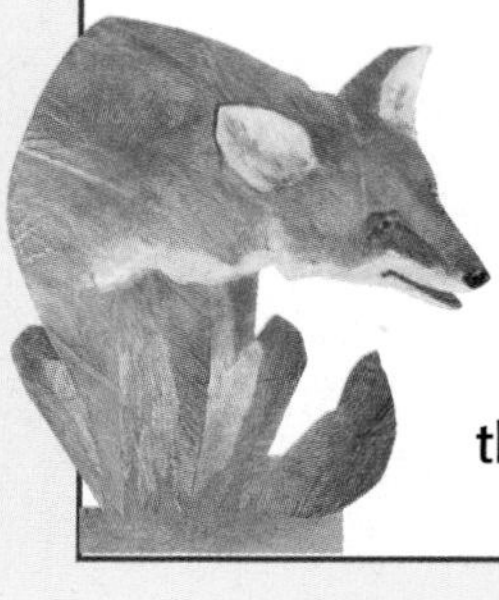

"Brother Coyote and Brother Cricket" is a trickster tale that comes from Texas. Many American folk tales celebrate using mind over might, brains over brute strength. In "Brother Coyote and Brother Cricket," the cricket's fate is changed because he uses his brain. The coyote learns that not all things change in one's favor.

AS YOU READ . . .

Note and compare how the values and customs of the cultures are presented.

Identify and analyze the theme of how things change.

Consider the lessons the characters learn about change.

Sundiata, Lion King of Mali

retold by David Wisniewski

Can a boy who is unable to walk or speak become ruler of a mighty empire? "How small the seed from which a great tree springs, and what storms the first sprout endures!" the king's adviser says in this dramatic tale of war and treachery. This oral history is based on the life of a man named Sundiata. He founded the ancient kingdom of Mali, for which the modern country of Mali is named.

MALI

MEXICO

The Force of Luck

retold by Rudolfo A. Anaya

"The Force of Luck" comes from an area of the U.S. Southwest that formerly belonged to Mexico. This area reflects a mixture of cultures that includes Spanish, Mexican, and Native American. In many Hispanic tales, including this one, people explain change as God's will.

◆ SUNDIATA, LION KING OF MALI ◆

retold by David Wisniewski

Listen to me, children of the Bright Country, and hear the great deeds of ages past. The words I speak are those of my father and his father before him, pure and full of truth. For we are *griots*. Centuries of law and learning reside within our minds. Thus we serve kings with the wisdom of history, bringing to life the lessons of the past so that the future may flourish.

Listen, then, to the story of Sundiata, the Lion King, who overcame all things to walk with greatness.

As the lion rules the savannah, with power and grace, so did Maghan Kon Fatta[1] rule Mali. One day two hunters approached his throne. Between them walked a maiden, hunchbacked and ill-favored. King Maghan caught his breath, for such a visit had been foretold.

"Great King," said the hunters, "we come from the land of Do,[2] where a terrible buffalo ravaged the countryside. We slew it, and in gratitude the king of Do bade us bring this damsel to you. Her name is Sogolon Kedjou.[3] Though homely, she is said to possess the very spirit of that buffalo, strong and courageous."

"Of such spirits great kings are born," whispered Maghan's *griot*.[4] "The son of lion and buffalo will be mighty indeed!"

So advised, the king wed Sogolon and grew to love her.

The next year, Sogolon gave birth to a boy. All rejoiced except Sassouma Bérété,[5] the first wife of the king. "Maghan already has my fine son as his heir," she muttered bitterly. "What need has he of another, especially from this hideous woman?"

But the new prince, Sundiata, though blessed by the spirits of buffalo and lion, proved unable to speak or walk. At this, Sassouma Bérété rejoiced.

For seven years Sogolon tried in vain to heal her son with potions and herbs. Sundiata dragged himself through the palace, ignored by some, ridiculed by others. His mother was heartbroken and his father despaired.

"How small the seed from which a great tree springs," counseled the king's *griot*, "and what storms the first sprout endures! Sundiata will grow in his own time, not yours, Great King."

The next day Maghan ordered his son brought before him. "My time grows short, Sundiata," he said, "so now I must present the gift that each king gives his heir."

A young man stepped forward. "This is Balla Fasséké,"[6] the king continued. "As his father has been my *griot*, so will he be yours. From him you will learn the history of your ancestors and the laws of this life. May your destiny be fulfilled, my son."

Sundiata sat up slowly, motioned Balla Fasséké to his side, and spoke his first words: "Balla, you are my *griot*."

Maghan's doubts disappeared, and he prepared Sundiata to rule.

But when Maghan Kon Fatta died, the council of elders paid no attention to his wishes. Instead, they allowed the son of Sassouma Bérété to ascend the throne.

Filled with pride, Sassouma lost no time in taunting Sundiata's mother: "It would seem that a walking boy is better than a crawling lion."

> "THE SON OF LION AND BUFFALO WILL BE MIGHTY INDEED!"

---

1. **Maghan Kon Fatta** (mä′gän kôn fä′tä).
2. **Do** (dō).
3. **Sogolon Kedjou** (sō′gō-lôn′ kä′jōō).
4. **griot** (grē-ō′): in West Africa, a storyteller who keeps alive the traditions of a people.
5. **Sassouma Bérété** (sä′sōō-mä bā-rā-tä′).
6. **Balla Fasséké** (bä′lä fä-sā-kä′).

WORDS TO KNOW

ravage (răv′ĭj) *v.* to destroy
ridiculed (rĭd′ĭ-kyōōld′) *adj.* made fun of ridicule v.

Seeing Sogolon's tears, Sundiata summoned Balla Fasséké. "Go to the master smith," he ordered, "and fetch me an iron rod!"

When Balla returned, Sundiata seized the rod with both hands, thrust it into the ground, and raised himself to his knees. Then, with a mighty effort, he pulled himself to his feet. The iron rod fell away, bent with strain, and Sundiata stood alone.

A crowd gathered in amazement as Sundiata took a step, then another and another. "Make way! Make way!" cried Balla Fasséké. "The lion is walking!"

When Sassouma Bérété heard of Sundiata's new strength, she feared he would challenge her son for the throne. Late one night, she called the nine great witches of Mali to her bedside. "You must use your powers to kill Sundiata," she commanded.

"Our magic is useless without his anger," said the witches.

"Go to his mother's garden and pick her spices," hissed Sassouma. "That will surely make him angry enough!"

But when Sundiata found the witches in his mother's garden, he greeted them courteously and helped them gather the spices.

"Alas, queen," the witches reported, "our magic cannot hurt a heart full of kindness. You can do nothing against him."

So Sassouma Bérété bided her time. When Sundiata was ten years old, she had Balla Fasséké sent away to the court of Sosso.[7] This evil land was ruled by Sumanguru,[8] a sorcerer king, whose huge armies and powerful magic

were greatly feared. Impressed by the young *griot's* skill, Sumanguru resolved to keep him in Sosso forever.

Sundiata was angered and saddened by the loss of his friend, and Sogolon's wise words brought new pain. "We must leave Mali," she said, "before our kin[9] fall victim to the queen's hatred. When you are a man, you will return and set all things right." Sundiata reluctantly agreed.

That evening, Sogolon and her children left all that they knew and loved.

For seven years, the family traveled the harsh road of <u>exile</u>, journeying through forest

---

7. **Sosso** (sō′sō).

8. **Sumanguru** (sōō′mäng-gōō′rōō).

9. **kin**: relatives.

and plain, from kingdom to kingdom. Rulers fearful of the queen's displeasure denied them shelter, and some gates were closed against them. Yet Sundiata grew in mind and spirit, even as his body grew in stature and strength.

In all these trials, Sundiata never forgot Balla Fasséké. At every court and caravan, he heard of the growing power of Sumanguru and of the unhappy lands under his control.

The family ended their travels in the city of Mema.[10] Weary and ill, Sogolon rested by the banks of the Niger. Sundiata found favor with the king of Mema, who took him on campaigns against the mountain tribes that troubled his kingdom. Observing Sundiata's courage and leadership, he decided to make the young prince his heir. He taught Sundiata the ways of war and government, and looked upon him as a son.

One day, frantic messengers pleaded to speak with Sundiata. "Son of lion and buffalo," they implored, "return to your homeland! Whatever honors you hold in Mema, leave them, and deliver your land from fire and sword."

"What has happened?" asked Sundiata.

"Sumanguru has invaded Mali," they said. "The king and his mother have fled. Our people have taken to the bush to fight, but they are leaderless. We have consulted the seers,[11] and they say that only you can save Mali. The throne of your father awaits you."

"The moment has come, my son," whispered Sogolon. "Your destiny is about to be fulfilled."

Sundiata lost no time. The king of Mema gave him half his army, rank upon rank of armored horsemen carrying great iron spears. Riding at the head of this column, Sundiata stopped at every kingdom that had aided him during his long exile, and gathered more troops. Soon a mighty host covered the savannah, and the thunder of hooves could be heard many miles away. The two armies clashed on the plain of Kirina.[12] All day the battle raged. Astride his gray charger, Sundiata galloped through the fray, searching for Sumanguru.

THE ARROW FLEW STRAIGHT AND TRUE, CUTTING THROUGH SUMANGURU'S CAPE . . .

Suddenly, Balla Fasséké was at Sundiata's side. The two friends embraced. "I escaped from the palace and followed Sumanguru's army, hoping to find you," said Balla. "For these seven years I have pretended <u>allegiance</u> to the sorcerer, and I have managed to discover his weakness." He pulled a wooden arrow from his robe. It was tipped with the spur[13] of a white rooster. "This is the *tana* of Sumanguru," Balla continued, "the charm he believes will erase his power. The slightest touch will defeat him utterly!"

Sundiata took the arrow and spurred his horse back into battle. He made his way through the dust and confusion to the hill where the sorcerer stood. Notching the arrow, he drew his mighty bow and let it fly.

The arrow flew straight and true, cutting through Sumanguru's cape and grazing his shoulder. At the sight of the *tana*, the sorcerer let out a harsh cry and galloped from the field.

---

10. **Mema** (mā′mä).

11. **seers**: prophets.

12. **Kirina** (kē-rē′nä).

13. **spur**: a sharp projection on the leg of certain kinds of birds.

Pursued by Sundiata and Balla Fasséké, Sumanguru fled to the slopes of Mount Koulikoro[14] and staggered into a dark cave. "Powers of night," he cried, "do not let me fall into the hands of Sundiata!"

IT IS SAID THAT SUMANGURU THEN BECAME ONE WITH THE STONE OF THE CAVE, FOR HE WAS NEVER SEEN AGAIN.

It is said that Sumanguru then became one with the stone of the cave, for he was never seen again. Disheartened by his flight, the sorcerer's army went down to defeat.

Sundiata returned in glory to Mali. Crowds lined the road the entire journey, shouting his praise. The twelve kings who had aided him in exile and in battle waited at his throne. As Sundiata sat, they drove their spears into the ground before him, swearing allegiance forever.

Sundiata spoke softly and Balla Fasséké conveyed his words to the multitude. "Hatred drove me from this land," he said, "because of what I seemed to be: a crawling child, unworthy of respect and unfit

---

14. **Koulikoro** (kōō′lē-kō′rō).

to rule. Mali has suffered great hardship as a result.

"Now I return as your king. Henceforth, none shall interfere with another's destiny. You, your children, and your children's children shall find their appointed place within this land forever."

This came to pass, and Sundiata, the Lion King, ruled the Bright Country for many golden years. ❖

David Wisniewski
born 1953

"A good story must have emotional content. It must pull at readers' hearts as well as their minds."

Clowning Around Before David Wisniewski was an author and an illustrator, he was a circus clown, a special-effects designer for theater and opera companies, and a puppeteer. The years he spent clowning and designing taught him that he wanted to entertain both children and adults. "My interest in reading folklore developed when my wife and I had our shadow puppet theater," he explains. "We used folk tales for our puppet presentations."

Cutting-Edge Art Wisniewski illustrates his books by cutting layers of paper with an extremely sharp knife. "It takes about three months to complete the intricate cutting and layering of the pieces. These eventually become three-dimensional pictures that are photographed and used as illustrations in my books," he says. The illustrations are so complicated that Wisniewski uses nearly 1,000 knife blades to create enough pictures for just one of his books. He enjoys the process because it involves "taking something that begins purely as an idea and turning it into something that can be appreciated by the mind and the senses."

The Force of
LUCK

Roadside Conference (1953), Archibald Motley Jr. Collection of Clark Atlanta University Art Galleries, Gift of the Estate of Irvin C. Mollison.

retold by Rudolfo A. Anaya

Once two wealthy friends got into a heated argument. One said that it was money which made a man prosperous, and the other maintained that it wasn't money, but luck, which made the man. They argued for some time and finally decided that if only they could find an honorable man, then perhaps they could prove their respective points of view.

One day while they were passing through a small village they came upon a miller who was grinding corn and wheat. They paused to ask the man how he ran his business. The miller replied that he worked for a master and that he earned only four bits[1] a day, and with that he had to support a family of five.

The friends were surprised. "Do you mean to tell us you can maintain a family of five on only fifteen dollars a month?" one asked.

"I live modestly to make ends meet," the humble miller replied.

The two friends privately agreed that if they put this man to a test, perhaps they could resolve their argument.

"I am going to make you an offer," one of them said to the miller. "I will give you two hundred dollars, and you may do whatever you want with the money."

"But why would you give me this money when you've just met me?" the miller asked.

"Well, my good man, my friend and I have a long-standing argument. He <u>contends</u> that it is luck which elevates a man to high position, and I say it is money. By giving you this money, perhaps we can settle our argument. Here, take it, and do with it what you want!"

So the poor miller took the money and spent the rest of the day thinking about the strange meeting which had presented him with more money than he had ever seen. What could he possibly do with all this money? Be that as it

may, he had the money in his pocket, and he could do with it whatever he wanted.

When the day's work was done, the miller decided the first thing he would do would be to buy food for his family. He took out ten dollars and wrapped the rest of the money in a cloth and put the bundle in his bag. Then he went to the market and bought supplies and a good piece of meat to take home.

On the way home he was attacked by a hawk that had smelled the meat which the miller carried. The miller fought off the bird, but in the struggle he lost the bundle of money. Before the miller knew what was happening the hawk grabbed the bag and flew away with it. When he realized what had happened he fell into deep thought.

"Ah," he moaned, "wouldn't it have been better to let that hungry bird have the meat! I could have bought a lot more meat with the money he took. Alas, now I'm in the same poverty as before! And worse, because now those two men will say I am a thief! I should have thought carefully and bought nothing. Yes, I should have gone straight home, and this wouldn't have happened!"

So he gathered what was left of his provisions and continued home, and when he arrived he told his family the entire story.

When he was finished telling his story his wife said, "It has been our lot to be poor, but have faith in God and maybe someday our luck will change."

The next day the miller got up and went to work as usual. He wondered what the two men would say about his story. But since he had never been a man of money he soon forgot the entire matter.

Three months after he had lost the money to

---

1. **four bits:** a slang term for fifty cents.

WORDS
TO   **contend** (kən-tĕnd') *v.* to argue
KNOW

the hawk, it happened that the two wealthy men returned to the village. As soon as they saw the miller they approached him to ask if his luck had changed. When the miller saw them he felt ashamed and afraid that they would think that he had squandered the money on worthless things. But he decided to tell them the truth, and as soon as they had greeted each other he told his story. The men believed him. In fact, the one who insisted that it was money and not luck which made a man prosper took out another two hundred dollars and gave it to the miller.

"Let's try again," he said, "and let's see what happens this time."

The miller didn't know what to think. "Kind sir, maybe it would be better if you put this money in the hands of another man," he said.

"No," the man insisted, "I want to give it to you because you are an honest man, and if we are going to settle our argument you have to take the money!"

The miller thanked them and promised to do his best. Then as soon as the two men left he began to think what to do with the money so that it wouldn't disappear as it had the first time. The thing to do was to take the money straight home. He took out ten dollars, wrapped the rest in a cloth, and headed home.

When he arrived his wife wasn't at home. At first he didn't know what to do with the money. He went to the pantry, where he had stored a large earthenware jar filled with bran. That was as safe a place as any to hide the money, he thought, so he emptied out the grain and put the bundle of money at the bottom of the jar, then covered it up with the grain. Satisfied that the money was safe, he returned to work.

That afternoon when he arrived home from work he was greeted by his wife.

"Look, my husband, today I bought some good clay with which to whitewash[2] the entire house."

"And how did you buy the clay if we don't have any money?" he asked.

"Well, the man who was selling the clay was willing to trade for jewelry, money, or anything of value," she said. "The only thing we had of value was the jar full of bran, so I traded it for the clay. Isn't it wonderful? I think we have enough clay to whitewash these two rooms!"

The man groaned and pulled his hair.

"Oh, you crazy woman! What have you done? We're ruined again!"

"But why?" she asked, unable to understand his anguish.

"Today I met the same two friends who gave me the two hundred dollars three months ago," he explained. "And after I told them how I lost the money they gave me another two hundred. And I, to make sure the money was safe, came home and hid it inside the jar of bran—the same jar you have traded for dirt! Now we're as poor as we were before! And what am I going to tell the two men? They'll think I'm a liar and a thief for sure!"

"Let them think what they want," his wife said calmly. "We will only have in our lives what the good Lord wants us to have. It is our lot to be poor until God wills it otherwise."

So the miller was consoled, and the next day he went to work as usual. Time came and went, and one day the two wealthy friends returned to ask the miller how he had done with the second two hundred dollars. When the poor miller saw them he was afraid they would accuse him of being a liar and a

---

2. **whitewash:** to paint something white.

WORDS TO KNOW

squander (skwŏn′dər) *v.* to spend carelessly
anguish (ăng′gwĭsh) *n.* great physical or mental suffering, as from grief or pain

847

spendthrift.[3] But he decided to be truthful, and as soon as they had greeted each other he told them what had happened to the money.

"That is why poor men remain honest," the man who had given him the money said. "Because they don't have money they can't get into trouble. But I find your stories hard to believe. I think you gambled and lost the money. That's why you're telling us these wild stories."

"Either way," he continued, "I still believe that it is money and not luck which makes a man prosper."

"Well, you certainly didn't prove your point by giving the money to this poor miller," his friend reminded him. "Good evening, you luckless man," he said to the miller.

"Thank you, friends," the miller said.

"Oh, by the way, here is a worthless piece of lead I've been carrying around. Maybe you can use it for something," said the man who believed in luck. Then the two men left, still debating their points of view on life.

Since the lead was practically worthless, the miller thought nothing of it and put it in his jacket pocket. He forgot all about it until he arrived home. When he threw his jacket on a chair he heard a thump, and he remembered the piece of lead. He took it out of the pocket and threw it under the table. Later that night after the family had eaten and gone to bed, they heard a knock at the door.

"Who is it? What do you want?" the miller asked.

"It's me, your neighbor," a voice answered. The miller recognized the fisherman's wife. "My husband sent me to ask you if you have any lead you can spare. He is going fishing tomorrow, and he needs the lead to weight down the nets."

The miller remembered the lead he had thrown under the table. He got up, found it, and gave it to the woman.

"Thank you very much, neighbor," the woman said. "I promise you the first fish my husband catches will be yours."

"Think nothing of it," the miller said and returned to bed. The next day he got up and went to work without thinking any more of the incident. But in the afternoon when he returned home he found his wife cooking a big fish for dinner.

"Since when are we so well off we can afford fish for supper?" he asked his wife.

"Don't you remember that our neighbor promised us the first fish her husband caught?" his wife reminded him. "Well, this was the fish he caught the first time he threw his net. So it's ours, and it's a beauty. But you should have been here when I gutted him! I found a large piece of glass in his stomach!"

"And what did you do with it?"

"Oh, I gave it to the children to play with," she shrugged.

When the miller saw the piece of glass he noticed it shone so brightly it appeared to illuminate the room, but because he knew nothing about jewels he didn't realize its value and left it to the children. But the bright glass was such a novelty that the children were soon fighting over it and raising a terrible fuss.

Now it so happened that the miller and his wife had other neighbors who were jewelers. The following morning when the miller had gone to work, the jeweler's wife visited the miller's wife to complain about all the noise her children had made.

"We couldn't get any sleep last night," she moaned.

---

3. **spendthrift:** a person who wastes money.

Detail of *Mujer con pescados* [Woman with fish] (1980), Francisco Zúñiga. Lithograph, 21⅞″ × 29½″, edition of 135. Courtesy of Brewster Gallery, New York.

"I know, and I'm sorry, but you know how it is with a large family," the miller's wife explained. "Yesterday we found a beautiful piece of glass, and I gave it to my youngest one to play with, and when the others tried to take it from him he raised a storm."

The jeweler's wife took interest. "Won't you show me that piece of glass?" she asked.

"But of course. Here it is."

"Ah, yes, it's a pretty piece of glass. Where did you find it?"

"Our neighbor gave us a fish yesterday, and when I was cleaning it I found the glass in its stomach."

"Why don't you let me take it home for just a moment. You see, I have one just like it, and I want to compare them."

"Yes, why not? Take it," answered the miller's wife.

So the jeweler's wife ran off with the glass to show it to her husband. When the jeweler saw the glass, he instantly knew it was one of the finest diamonds he had ever seen.

"It's a diamond!" he exclaimed.

"I thought so," his wife nodded eagerly. "What shall we do?"

"Go tell the neighbor we'll give her fifty dollars for it, but don't tell her it's a diamond!"

"No, no," his wife chuckled, "of course not." She ran to her neighbor's house. "Ah, yes, we have one exactly like this," she told the miller's wife. "My husband is willing to buy it for fifty dollars—only so we can have a pair, you understand."

"I can't sell it," the miller's wife answered. "You will have to wait until my husband returns from work."

That evening when the miller came home from work his wife told him about the offer the jeweler had made for the piece of glass.

"But why would they offer fifty dollars for a worthless piece of glass?" the miller wondered aloud. Before his wife could answer, they were interrupted by the jeweler's wife.

"What do you say, neighbor, will you take fifty dollars for the glass?" she asked.

"No, that's not enough," the miller said cautiously. "Offer more."

"I'll give you fifty thousand!" the jeweler's wife blurted out.

"A little bit more," the miller replied.

"Impossible!" the jeweler's wife cried. "I can't offer any more without consulting my husband." She ran off to tell her husband how the bartering was going, and he told her he was prepared to pay a hundred thousand dollars to acquire the diamond.

He handed her seventy-five thousand dollars and said, "Take this and tell him that tomorrow, as soon as I open my shop, he'll have the rest."

When the miller heard the offer and saw the money he couldn't believe his eyes. He imagined the jeweler's wife was jesting with him, but it was a true offer, and he received the hundred thousand dollars for the diamond. The miller had never seen so much money, but he still didn't quite trust the jeweler.

"I don't know about this money," he confided to his wife. "Maybe the jeweler plans to accuse us of robbing him and thus get it back."

"Oh no," his wife assured him, "the money is ours. We sold the diamond fair and square—we didn't rob anyone."

"I think I'll still go to work tomorrow," the miller said. "Who knows, something might happen and the money will disappear, then we would be without money and work. Then how would we live?"

So he went to work the next day, and all day he thought about how he could use the money. When he returned home that afternoon, his wife asked him what he had decided to do with their new fortune.

"I think I will start my own mill," he answered, "like the one I operate for my master. Once I set up my business we'll see how our luck changes."

The next day he set about buying everything he needed to establish his mill and to build a new home. Soon he had everything going.

Six months had passed, more or less, since he had seen the two men who had given him the four hundred dollars and the piece of lead. He was eager to see them again and to tell them how the piece of lead had changed his luck and made him wealthy.

Time passed and the miller prospered. His business grew, and he even built a summer cottage where he could take his family on vacation. He had many employees who worked for him. One day while he was at his store he saw his two benefactors riding by. He rushed out into the street to greet them and ask them to come in. He was overjoyed to see them, and he was happy to see that they admired his store.

"Tell us the truth," the man who had given him the four hundred dollars said. "You used that money to set up this business."

WORDS TO KNOW
bartering (bär′tər-ĭng) *n.* arguing over a price; bargaining **barter** *v.*
benefactor (běn′e-făk′tər) *n.* a person who provides money or help

The miller swore he hadn't, and he told them how he had given the piece of lead to his neighbor and how the fisherman had in return given him a fish with a very large diamond in its stomach. And he told them how he had sold the diamond.

"And that's how I acquired this business and many other things I want to show you," he said. "But it's time to eat. Let's eat first, then I'll show you everything I have now."

The men agreed, but one of them still doubted the miller's story. So they ate, and then the miller had three horses saddled, and they rode out to see his summer home. The cabin was on the other side of the river, where the mountains were cool and beautiful. When they arrived the men admired the place very much. It was such a peaceful place that they rode all afternoon through the forest. During their ride they came upon a tall pine tree.

"What is that on top of the tree?" one of them asked.

"That's the nest of a hawk," the miller replied.

"I have never seen one; I would like to take a closer look at it!"

"Of course," the miller said, and he ordered a servant to climb the tree and bring down the nest so his friend could see how it was built. When the hawk's nest was on the ground they examined it carefully. They noticed that there

Cargador al pie de la escalera [Porter at the foot of the stairway] (1956), Diego Rivera. Watercolor on rice paper, 15¼" × 10¾". Photo courtesy of Christie's, New York.

was a cloth bag at the bottom of the nest. When the miller saw the bag he immediately knew that it was the very same bag he had lost to the hawk which fought him for the piece of meat years ago.

"You won't believe me, friends, but this is the very same bag in which I put the first two hundred dollars you gave me," he told them.

"If it's the same bag," the man who had doubted him said, "then the money you said the hawk took should be there."

"No doubt about that," the miller said. "Let's see what we find."

The three of them examined the old, weather-beaten bag. Although it was full of holes and crumbling, when they tore it apart they found the money intact. The two men remembered what the miller had told them, and they agreed he was an honest and honorable man. Still, the man who had given him the money wasn't satisfied. He wondered what had really happened to the second two hundred he had given the miller.

They spent the rest of the day riding in the mountains and returned very late to the house.

As he unsaddled their horses, the servant in charge of grooming and feeding the horses suddenly realized that he had no grain for them. He ran to the barn and checked, but there was no grain for the hungry horses. So he ran to the neighbor's granary, and there he was able to buy a large clay jar of bran. He carried the jar home and emptied the bran into a bucket to wet it before he fed it to the horses. When he got to the bottom of the jar he noticed a large lump which turned out to be a rag-covered package. He examined it and felt something inside. He immediately went to give it to his master, who had been eating dinner.

"Master," he said, "look at this package which I found in an earthenware jar of grain which I just bought from our neighbor!"

The three men carefully unraveled the cloth and found the other one hundred and ninety dollars which the miller had told them he had lost. That is how the miller proved to his friends that he was truly an honest man.

And they had to decide for themselves whether it had been luck or money which had made the miller a wealthy man! ❖

Rudolfo A. Anaya
born 1937

"I am an oral storyteller, but now I do it on the printed page."

Rich Cultural Heritage Rudolfo Anaya was born in New Mexico where his family has lived for several generations. He grew up in a Mexican-American community noted for its storytellers. He became fascinated with the oral tradition of Spanish folk tales as well as his own cross-cultural background.

Drawn to the Past Anaya is now professor emeritus of English and creative writing at the University of New Mexico. His writings draw on New Mexico's Hispanic past, and he has won many awards for both fiction and nonfiction. The *New York Times* once claimed that Anaya is the most widely read writer in Hispanic communities.

Brother Coyote
and
Brother Cricket

by J. Frank Dobie

One summer evening about sundown a coyote trotting across the plain put his foot down on a tuft of grass wherein a cricket was singing *"Sereno en aquellos campos"*—"Serene in those fields."

The cricket jumped out and cried, "But, Brother Coyote, why are you destroying my palace?"

Illustration by Byron Gin.

"I really did not know you lived here until you exposed yourself," the coyote said.

"You are <u>crude</u> and you insult me," the cricket said. He was ready to spring away.

"Insult you!" the coyote jeered. "Why, you dwarf, I am merely seeking my living, and now that I have you, I am going to eat you up. I had rather have a red watermelon or a fat kid, but I eat a cricket or a grasshopper when it's handy. Maybe you will fill the hollow in one of my molars."

"But, Brother Coyote," the cricket said, now in his soothing way, "it is not fair."

The coyote sat down on the carpet of grass. "Brother Cricket," he said, "you know that when nature offers itself, it is fair for nature to accept."

"But, Brother Coyote, you haven't given me a chance."

"Chance?" exclaimed the coyote. "Why, what sort of chance do you expect?"

"I want to fight a duel."

"You fight a duel with me?" And the coyote laughed.

"Yes, fight a duel with you," the cricket said. "If I win, then my song will go on. If you win, then I'll fill the hollow in one of your respectable teeth."

The coyote looked away off across the plain, and saw a crow flying down in play at the waving tail of a striped skunk. "Well," he said, "perhaps the people need a comedy. All right, we'll have your duel, Brother Cricket."

"Oh, thank you very much, Brother Coyote."

"Now I sit here trembling at the sight of your armor and weapons," the coyote said. "But go on and name your terms."

"It is agreed," said the cricket. "You go and get your army together, and I will go and get my army together. Tomorrow when the sun is straight overhead, you have your army on the prairie just above the water called the Tank of the Seven Coons, and I will have my army in the thicket in the draw just below the dam to this tank. On the hour we shall engage in mortal combat."

"That is clear, General Cricket," said the coyote. "Until tomorrow at high noon, *adiós*."

"*Adiós*, General Coyote."

That night General Coyote went east and west, north and south, summoning in high voice his forces to gather on the prairie above the Tank of the Seven Coons. He summoned the lobo, the badger, the tiger of the deep canyon, the panther of the rimrock, the wildcat of the chaparral, the coon, the possum, the sharp fox, and all the other people with claws and teeth.

And in a singsong General Cricket summoned his forces—the horseflies, the mosquitoes, the honey bees, the bumblebees, the yellow jackets, the black hornets, and even a colony of red ants—all the people that have stingers and can stick. He told them to gather in the thicket in the draw below the Tank of the Seven Coons.

Long before high noon, the people of fang and claw were assembling on the prairie above the water tank. General Coyote was trotting about, looking this way and that way, smelling and listening. The sun stood straight up, and still he could not see one sign of General Cricket's army.

Finally he called the fox and ordered him to scout out the position of the enemy. With his long nose pointed ahead, his ears alert and his eyes peeled, the fox went trotting down the draw. General Coyote was watching him. When he came to the edge of the thicket, the

WORDS
TO
KNOW   **crude** (kro͞od) *adj.* lacking tact or good manners

fox flattened to the ground and began twisting into the brush. Just as he was poking his keen snout into a clump of whitebrush to see and smell more closely, General Cricket ordered a battalion[1] of black hornets to <u>assault</u> him.

They did, all at once. They stuck their stingers into his ears, into the corners of his eyes, into his nostrils, into his flanks, into every spot of his body where hair is short and skin is tender. He snapped and pitched, but only for a minute. He turned seventeen somersaults on the ground, and the black hornets came thicker. Then he streaked for the tank of water. He dived to escape his assaulters, and went to the bottom.

But in a minute he had to come back up for air. Then, sticking his long, long mouth out of the water, he cried at the top of his voice, "General Coyote, retreat! The enemy are upon us!"

General Cricket had already ordered the yellow jackets to attack the army of giants on the prairie, and the war cries of the bumblebees were in the air.

"Retreat!" the fox shrieked again.

General Coyote tucked his tail between his legs and retreated and every soldier in the army tucked his tail and retreated also—all except the bobcat. He retreated without tucking his tail. That is how General Cricket won the duel with General Coyote.

Thus a person should avoid being <u>vainglorious</u> and considering himself shrewder than he is. He may be outwitted by his own vanity. ❖

---

1. **battalion:** a large body of organized troops.

J. Frank Dobie
1888–1964

"One day it came to me that I would collect and tell the legendary tales of Texas . . . "

Texan by Birth J[ames] Frank Dobie was born on a ranch in Live Oak County, Texas, and lived in his native state most of his life. In college, Dobie planned to study law but instead developed a passion for literature and the classics. Dobie was in his forties when his first major novel, *A Vaquero of the Brush Country,* was published in 1929. His second work, *Coronado's Children,* gained him popular attention.

Texan by Choice Much of Dobie's writing focuses on the folklore of the Southwest, and was inspired by his friendships with cowboys, miners, and other talespinners. In 1939 he began a weekly newspaper column, originally called "My Texas," which ran until his death. He wrote over 25 books—including *A Texan in England,* which was inspired by the year he spent lecturing at Cambridge University. Dobie won numerous awards, including the Boys Club of America Junior Book Award.

WORDS TO KNOW — **assault** (ə-sôlt') *v.* to attack
vainglorious (vān-glôr'ē-əs) *adj.* vain and boastful

PREPARING to *Read*

The Oral Tradition

LINKS TO UNIT FIVE

Personal Challenges

Often when a personal challenge is great, so too are the rewards for success and the penalties for failure. In the tales you are about to read, characters face personal challenges that test their inner strength. These characters and the challenges they face relate closely to similar characters and challenges in Unit Five.

KENYA

Kelfala's Secret Something

retold by Adjai Robinson

The Kikuyu are the largest ethnic group in Kenya, a nation in east-central Africa. The Kikuyu are predominantly farmers who have a strong work ethic. Among the Kikuyu, the traditions and instructions of parents and elders are binding, almost like laws. Arranged marriages are the custom in this society that forms the backdrop of "Kelfala's Secret Something."

SCANDINAVIA

How Odin Lost His Eye

retold by Catharine F. Sellew

Scandinavia is the name given to a group of countries in northern Europe that includes Norway, Sweden, and Denmark. In these countries much of the land away from the seas is covered with snow. According to Norse (Scandinavian) mythology, the giant tree that supports all creation has three roots. One of the roots extends to a misty underworld. Another goes to Asgard (ăs'gärd), the heavenly realm where the gods dwell. The third root reaches Jötunheim (yō'tən-hīm'), the icy realm of the frost giants. From his throne in Asgard, Odin, the mightiest Norse god, keeps watch on all the lands of creation.

SCANDINAVIA

NORWAY

SWEDEN

DENMARK

LAOS

SOUTHEAST ASIA

VIETNAM

THAILAND

KENYA

AS YOU READ . . .

Note which behaviors are viewed as virtuous in each culture and how they are rewarded.

Note which behaviors are viewed as negative.

Identify the message or theme about love that each culture conveys.

Determine how the events in the stories foreshadow future actions.

SOUTHEAST ASIA

Pumpkin Seed and the Snake

retold by Norma J. Livo and Dia Cha

The Hmong (hmông) people live in the mountains of Vietnam, Thailand, and Laos. Since they did not develop a written language until the 1950s, they relied on strong oral and artistic traditions—such as pieces of cloth with elaborate needlework—to pass their cultural traditions from generation to generation. After the Vietnam War, many Hmong emigrated to the United States.

HOW ODIN LOST HIS EYE

RETOLD BY CATHARINE F. SELLEW

Odin astride Sleipnir. Illumination from *Poetic Edda* in a
13th-century Icelandic manuscript, The Granger Collection,
New York.

Once when the world was still very young, Odin sat on his throne in the most beautiful palace in Asgard. His throne was so high that he could see over all three parts of the world from where he sat. On his head he wore a helmet shaped like an eagle. On his shoulders perched two black ravens called Memory and Thought. And at his feet crouched two snarling wolves.

The great king gazed thoughtfully down on the earth below him. He had made the green land that stretched out before his eyes. With the help of the other gods he had made men and women who lived on that earth. And he felt truly like the All-father he was called.

The fair elves had promised they would help his children of the earth. The elves were the tiny people who lived between heaven and earth. They were so small that they could flit about doing their work unseen. Odin knew that they were the artists who painted the flowers and made the beds for the streams. They took care of all the bees and the butterflies. And it was the elves who brought the gentle rain and sunshine to the earth.

Even the ugly dwarfs, who lived in the heart of the mountains, agreed to help. They <u>forged</u> iron and metals, made tools and weapons. They dug gold and silver and beautiful jewels out of the earth. Sometimes they even cut the grain and ground the flour for the farmers on the earth.

All seemed to be going well. Odin found it hard to think of evil times. But he knew that the frost giants were only waiting for a chance to bring trouble to his children. They were the ones who brought cold and ice to the world and shook the earth in anger. They hated Odin and all the work of the gods.

And from high on his throne Odin looked down beyond the earth deep into the gloomy land of his enemies. He saw dark figures of huge men moving about. They looked like evil shadows. He, the king of the gods, must have more wisdom. It was not enough just to see his enemies. He must know more about them.

So Odin wrapped his tall figure in a blue cloak. Down from his throne he climbed. Down the broad rainbow bridge he strode and across the green earth till he came to one of the roots of the great evergreen tree. There, close by the tree, was a well full of clear water. Its surface was so still it was like a mirror. In it one could see pictures of things that had happened and things that were going to happen.

But beside the well sat an old man. His face was lined with the troubles of the world. His name was Mimir, which means "memory." No one, not even the great Odin, could see the pictures in the well unless he first drank some of its water. Only Mimir could give the magic drink.

"Aged Mimir," Odin said to the old man, "you who hold the knowledge of the past and future in your magic waters, let me have but one sip. Then I can know enough to protect the men and women of the earth from the hate of the giants."

Mimir looked kindly at Odin, but he did not smile. Although he spoke softly, his voice was so deep it reminded Odin of the distant roar of the ocean.

"The price of one drink from this well is not cheap," Mimir said. "And once you have drunk and gazed into the mirror of life, you may wish you had not. For sorrow and death as well as joy are pictured there. Think again before you ask to drink."

But once the king of the gods had made up his mind, nothing could change it. He was not afraid to look upon sorrow and death.

"What is your price, aged Mimir?" Odin asked.

"You are great and good, Odin," answered Mimir. "You have worked hard to make the world. Only those who know hard work may drink from my well. However, that is not enough. What have you given up that is very dear to you? What have you <u>sacrificed</u>? The price of a drink must be a great sacrifice. Are you still willing to pay the price?"

What could the king of the gods sacrifice? What was most dear to him? Odin thought of his handsome son, Balder, whom he loved most in the world. To give up his son would be like giving up life and all that was

WORDS
TO
KNOW

forge (fôrj) *v.* to shape metal by heating it and pounding on it with a hammer

sacrifice (săk′rə-fīs′) *v.* to give up something highly valued for the sake of something or someone more valued

859

wonderful around him. Odin stood silent before Mimir. Indeed that would be a high price!

Then Mimir spoke again. He had read Odin's thoughts.

"No, I am not asking for your dear son. The Fates[1] say his life must be short, but he has time yet to live and bring happiness to the gods and the world. I ask for one of your eyes."

 din put his hands up to his bright blue eyes. Those two eyes had gazed across the world from his high throne in the shining city of the gods. His eyes had taught him what was good and beautiful, what was evil and ugly. But those eyes had also seen his children, the men and women of the earth, struggling against the hate of the giants. One eye was a small sacrifice to win knowledge of how to help them. And without another

thought, Odin plucked out one of his blue eyes and handed it to Mimir.

Then Mimir smiled and gave Odin a horn full of the waters of his well.

"Drink deeply, brave king, so you may see all that you wish in the mirror of life."

Odin lifted the horn to his lips and drank. Then he knelt by the edge of the well and watched the pictures passing across its still and silent surface. When he stood up again, he sighed, for it was as Mimir had said. He had seen sorrow and death as well as joy. It was only the glorious promise at the end that gave him courage to go on.

So Odin, the great king of the gods, became one-eyed. If you can find Mimir's well, you will see Odin's blue eye resting on the bottom. It is there to remind men and women of the great sacrifice he made for them. ❖

---

1. **Fates:** goddesses who decide the course of people's lives.

Catharine F. Sellew
1922–1982

Myth Lover As a child, Catharine Sellew loved to listen as her mother read myths. Sellew later studied mythology and published a collection of Greek myths, *Adventures with the Gods*. She also retold Norse myths in *Adventures with the Giants* and *Adventures with the Heroes*.

A Skilled Writer Sellew also retold stories from the Old Testament and wrote a novel for teenagers, entitled Torchlight.

PUMPKIN
SEED
AND THE
SNAKE

RETOLD BY NORMA J. LIVO AND DIA CHA

"IF SOMEONE COULD REMOVE THIS ROCK FROM THE MIDDLE OF MY GARDEN I WOULD LET HIM MARRY ONE OF MY DAUGHTERS."

Once long ago, in another time and place, in a small village, there lived a widow and her two daughters. The older daughter was named Pumpkin Vine and the younger one was named Pumpkin Seed.

The family had a garden near the river. They had to work hard to prepare the field for the coming growing season. But they had a problem, because in the middle of the garden was a huge boulder. One day as she was working around the rock, the widow said to herself, "If someone could remove this rock from the middle of my garden I would let him marry one of my daughters."

At the end of the day, the family went home. The next day, the three women went back to work in the garden and found that the rock was gone! The widow started to laugh and said out loud, "I was only joking. I wouldn't allow either of my daughters to marry whoever removed that rock." The widow thought that was the last of the giant rock. But the next day when the widow and her daughters went back to the field to work, there was the rock, in its original place in the middle of the garden.

Once more the widow said to herself, "If someone would take this rock from the middle of the field I would let him marry one of my daughters."

The next day the rock was gone again, but the widow said, "I did not mean it. I wouldn't allow either of my daughters to marry whoever removed that rock," as she laughed.

The next morning the rock was back in its spot, and the widow again promised one of her daughters in marriage to the person who could remove the rock.

Just like the other times, the rock disappeared from the field and the widow again teased, "I did not mean it. I wouldn't allow either of my daughters to marry the person who moved the rock."

The next morning the widow went to the field alone and found the rock back in its place. Giggling a little, the widow whispered, "If someone would take this rock from the middle of the field I would let him marry one of my daughters."

This time, a snake that was nearby said, "If you promise not to lie anymore I will remove the rock."

The widow was so startled that she promised not to lie anymore. The snake slithered from the edge of the garden, laced his tail around the rock, and threw it into the river. Since the widow's two daughters hadn't come to the field with her, the snake followed the widow home.

When they got home the widow called from outside to her daughters. She told them what had happened and said that one of them would

IT WAS NOT AN UGLY SNAKE SLEEPING BESIDE PUMPKIN SEED, BUT THE MOST HANDSOME YOUNG MAN THAT SHE HAD EVER SEEN.

have to marry the snake. Pumpkin Vine and Pumpkin Seed didn't want to marry the snake. They refused to open the door and let the snake into the house.

The snake and the widow waited and waited until it was dark, but the girls wouldn't open the door. Then the mother whispered through the door to her daughters, "I will kill the snake when he falls asleep." Even though her mother had said this would work, Pumpkin Vine, being the older one, still refused to open the door. It was very dark outside by this time. Pumpkin Seed, on the other hand, thought that things would go as easily as her mother said, so she opened the door.

When the snake got into the house, Pumpkin Vine and Pumpkin Seed were frightened by its huge size and ugly shininess. Pumpkin Vine protested bitterly when her mother asked her to marry the snake. The widow finally convinced Pumpkin Seed to marry the snake. The snake followed Pumpkin Seed wherever she went. It curled up beside her feet when she sat down. When she went to

bed, the snake slid into her bed and coiled up beside her.

That night, with a sharp knife in one hand and a candle in the other, the widow crept into Pumpkin Seed's bedroom to kill the snake. But she discovered it was not an ugly snake sleeping beside Pumpkin Seed, but the most handsome young man that she had ever seen. She couldn't kill him.

The next day when Pumpkin Seed woke up, the snake was still alive. She cried and demanded to know why her mother hadn't kept her promise and killed it. "I'll kill the snake tonight, Pumpkin Seed. Please trust me," begged the widow.

That night, the snake again slid into Pumpkin Seed's bed and coiled up beside her. The widow came into the room with her sharp knife and the candle and crept up to the bed to kill the snake. Again, though, instead of an ugly snake sleeping beside Pumpkin Seed, it was the handsome young man. Once more, she just couldn't kill him.

The next morning Pumpkin Seed woke up and there the snake was in her bed, still alive. She cried and cried and demanded to know

"WHY SHOULDN'T I HAVE SOME OF THE GREEN BUBBLES?"

why her mother hadn't killed it. "I'll kill the snake tonight, Pumpkin Seed. Please give me one more chance. Please trust me," pleaded the widow.

When the sun rose the next morning bright and warm, Pumpkin Seed woke up and there was the snake—still alive. Now Pumpkin Seed had no choice. She had to go with the snake to his home. On the way they came to a lovely clear stream. "Pumpkin Seed, I will go take a bath over behind the rocks. You wait here while I am gone." "All right," Pumpkin Seed agreed.

"When I am gone, you will see lots of colorful bubbles pouring down the stream. You must not touch the green bubbles. You can play with the white and yellow ones, but do not touch the green bubbles," warned the snake. Pumpkin Seed nodded in agreement.

The snake had been gone for a while when, sure enough, Pumpkin Seed noticed a variety of colored bubbles floating down the stream. She stood in delighted amazement as the bright, glittering bubbles traveled smoothly down the clear water. She eagerly pulled out some of the yellow bubbles. To her surprise the bubbles turned into gold jewels in her hands. Then she gathered some white bubbles, and they turned into silver jewels. Pumpkin Seed was so happy. She had never had such beautiful riches. She gaily put them on her neck, her wrists, her ears, and her fingers.

As she was admiring them, she thought, "Why shouldn't I have some of the green bubbles?" So she reached down and scooped up some green bubbles, and before her startled eyes they turned into twisting snakes in her hands. They even stuck all over her hands. She frantically tried to remove the snakes, but they wouldn't come off.

A moment later a young, handsome man came toward her, and she quickly hid her wriggling hands behind her back. "Why are you hiding your hands?" asked the man.

Her voice quivered as she told him, "Oh, my husband is a snake. He went up the stream to bathe and he told me to keep my hands like this."

The young man smiled and said, "I am your husband. . . ." Pumpkin Seed interrupted him. "No, you can't be!"

The man smiled and said, "Look at this!" He raised his arm and showed her the remaining snakeskin in his armpit. She believed him when she saw the skin and felt ashamed when she showed him her hands. But he simply blew on her hands and the snakes fell off and disappeared like magic. Then they went home and lived happily for the rest of their lives. ❖

"Pumpkin Seed and the Snake" by Norma J. Livo and Dia Cha;
Libraries Unlimited, 800-237-6124; Englewood, CO.
Reprinted with permission.

Norma J. Livo
born 1929

"No matter what side of the family got together, music and storytelling were important."

Family Traditions Raised in Appalachia, Norma Livo says she grew up with her mother's "folklorish" stories and her father's "tall tales, music, and ballads full of mischief." When one of Livo's sons was diagnosed as having a learning disability, she returned to school to learn how to help him. She earned a doctorate in education and began using her own stories to teach her son to read.

Storytelling Scholar Livo introduced storytelling into elementary and secondary classrooms and designed storytelling courses for the University of Colorado, Denver—from which she retired as professor of education in 1992. Livo has also written many books on storytelling and folklore. She worked with Dia Cha, a Hmong immigrant, to retell "Pumpkin Seed and the Snake" and other tales collected in *Folk Stories of the Hmong: People of Laos, Thailand, and Vietnam.*

KELFALA'S SECRET SOMETHING

From *Samburu* by Nigel Pavitt.
Copyright © 1992 Nigel Pavitt,
reprinted by permission of
Henry Holt and Co., Inc.

RETOLD BY ADJAI ROBINSON

LISTEN, CHILDREN,

DO YOU KNOW THE

GITUYU? IT IS SUCH

AN ANIMAL THAT IN

KENYA IT IS SAID

THAT EVEN THE DOGS

WILL NOT EAT ITS

MEAT FOR SUPPER,

NOR THE HYENA, NOR

EVEN THE WILDCAT—

AND NEVER THE

POOREST OF PEOPLE.

THAT IS TRADITION.

THIS YOU MUST KNOW.

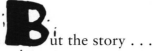

ut the story . . .

On the steep slopes of the Kilimanjaro[1] stood a tiny village of very <u>hardy</u> people. Mountain climbers were they all, and their gardens of tea and pyrethrum[2] and coffee were as dear to their hearts as the cap of snow shielding the head of their father mountain. The men and women had strong hands and great mountain strides. They were a happy people with warm hearts. And they were a people faithful to their traditions.

The young fellow, Kelfala, was one of these. Kelfala, the clown. People used to say that he was funny from the time he entered his mother's womb. He could make a thousand and one faces with his one fleshy face. His lips, he could twist and curl, and even if you wanted to hiss, your hissing would turn to laughing. If you listened to Kelfala's stories, I tell you, you would see and hear all the animals in the forest in this one Kelfala. And he sprang surprises as fast as he spinned yarns, on everything around.

Kelfala, the clown, was like his grandfather before him. He was funny. He was clever. Oh, he was a charming darling. It seemed that nothing or no one could resist Kelfala.

No one, except the beautiful Wambuna. She would not even turn his way.

Before, as children, these two had played together, laughed together, teased together. But Wambuna had gone into the girl's society, as all girls of the village do. There, the old women had taught her how to wash and care

---

1. **Kilimanjaro** (kĭl´ə-mən-jär´ō): the highest mountain in Africa.
2. **pyrethrum** (pī-rē´thrəm): a showy flowering plant.

for babies, how to prepare leaves and herbs for simple cures, how to sing the village songs, how to cook meats and yams and vegetables. Her roasted peanuts were always brown and tasty. And, if you ate her sauces, you would lick your fingers as if you were going to bite them, too. Her graces were admired even by other young girls. And when she came out,[3] she was given the oath: that from that time on, if she talked to any man outside her family, she was bound to marry him. That was tradition.

Kelfala would sit in the bush and watch this darling Wambuna. Her skin was as smooth as a mirror. Her mahogany-brown arms swayed gracefully by her sides, keeping time with her swaying hips. When she laughed, she showed ivory-white teeth. And just a smile from Wambuna sent warm thrills through clownish Kelfala. Her head, she carried erect, and the rings sat on her neck like rows of diamonds on a crown. The more Kelfala watched, the more he wanted Wambuna for his own.

But she had an endless stream of suitors. (If you could have seen her, you would not mind even being last, as long as you were in line.) Some of these young men went to her father to ask for Wambuna. That was tradition. But many had heard his loud "No-No" and tried to trick Wambuna, instead. But do you think she talked to the young men around? Well! You wait and see.

Always, they paid their visits to her at the garden, always when the elders were having their rest from the hot midday sun.

"Wambuna, let me get you water from the stream."

"Ay'ee, Wambuna, I hit my toe against a stone. It is gushing out blood!"

"Wambuna, your plants are not growing at all. You are so lazy. Yambuyi's plants are better than yours, lazy you!"

"Wambuna, hear your father? He is snoring

From *Samburu* by Nigel Pavitt. Copyright © 1992 Nigel Pavitt, reprinted by permission of Henry Holt and Co., Inc.

so hard under this hot sun, he has driven all the animals away!"

But Wambuna's lips were sealed, and all this teasing and coaxing only kept her lips tighter. She would not even raise her head to smile. She worked in silence, and if she talked at all, she only whispered kind things to her plants.

Now, Kelfala joined the line, too. And—tradition or not—he would not risk the father's "No-No." Why? He, Kelfala, the clown? Kelfala, who could coax words and

---

3. **when . . . out:** when she was officially regarded as having reached adulthood.

laughter out of trees? He would get Wambuna to speak!

He tried his hippopotamus face, to get her to shout in fear. He turned into a leopard, springing into Wambuna's path when she was alone, so she would cry for help. He hid behind a clump of trees and became Wambuna's mother, asking questions and questions and questions that needed answers.

But Wambuna's lips were sealed.

The stream of suitors grew smaller, like the village stream itself, shrinking and shrinking in the dry season when the rains have stopped. But Kelfala did not give up. Finally, he confided in two friends that he had a something that would win Wambuna for him. A secret something. (He did not tell them what.)

For two weeks Kelfala and his two friends, Shortie Bumpie and Longie Tallie, trailed Wambuna and her family as they went to the farm. Then Kelfala's day came. They spied Wambuna going alone to the farm with her basket balanced on her head. He and Shortie Bumpie and Longie Tallie set out behind her, *kunye, kunye, kunye* as if they were <u>treading</u> on hot coals. They stood behind the trees and bushes, unseen by anyone but themselves, and waited.

On this day, Kelfala had put on his best dress. But if you had seen him, you would think that he was the most unlikely suitor for a young girl. His dress was rags and tatters. He had rubbed grease all over his body, mud on his head, and funny chalk marks on his face. He also had painted his front teeth with red-black clay.

The birds were twitting happily as they caught worms on the dewy grass. Nearby the stream was flowing by, its waters dazzling in the early morning sunlight. From time to time Kelfala opened his sack, touched his something, and smiled to himself.

Wambuna started working hard and fast. Indeed, she was racing the sun. By the time the sun got halfway on its journey, she hoped to have gotten to the end of hers. She only stopped her work for a moment, went to the stream with her calabash[4] for water, then returned and kindled a fire. She took some yams from her little basket, put them on the hot coals, and returned to her plants. She was weeding the new grasses on her tea beds.

Kelfala's opportunity had come. Soon, Kelfala, the clown, Kelfala, the funny one, would be married to the most beautiful, the most gentle, the mildest lady on Kilimanjaro. At least, that is what Kelfala thought.

Kelfala spied here, there, and everywhere from his hiding, stepped out into the open, and hopped and skipped to the fireplace. Out of his sack he pulled his something and placed it on the hot coals beside Wambuna's yams. Then he squatted on the largest firestone and poled the red-hot coals. Shoving Wambuna's yams aside, he uttered a throaty chuckle, which he quickly trapped with his hands. He glanced again at the fireplace, and like a cock ready to peck at the yams, he tittered quietly to himself. But again he quickly stopped himself.

---

4. **calabash** (kăl′ə-băsh′): the dried, hollowed-out shell of a gourd, used as a bowl.

But only for a moment, for suddenly more chuckles escaped, and Kelfala howled like a ruffled owl. He hooted the monkeys out of the treetops. He rolled himself into a ball as he rolled and rolled with laughter. Kelfala, the laughing clown. He laughed and he laughed and he laughed.

Now, the bush came alive. Shortie Bumpie and Longie Tallie poked their heads out to see what was happening. At first they twitched their faces and cocked their ears. But as Kelfala rolled on and on, and the laughter rolled on and on, it dragged the two young men with it.

Wambuna—who had to poke her fire—tried to sneak past the hooting trio, but the loud roars quickly sank into *her* bones. Oh, how silly those three idle friends! Kelfala, that clown Kelfala! But as she watched them, her grin turned into a broad smile, *her* smile turned into a shy laugh, and without realizing it, she became one of the howling trio. She was all fits of laughter. Oh! How the tears ran down Wambuna's eyes.

All four laughed and laughed, laughed and laughed and laughed.

When all at once Kelfala stood, with arms akimbo⁵ and stomach shot forward, and pointed to Wambuna's fireplace.

"A beautiful girl like you," he laughed, "proud as the cotton tree and the greatest cook in the village, you, you roast a Gituyu with your yams!"

Wambuna turned around.

There by the giant firestone, on the ashes, was Kelfala's something. A shrunken, old, burnt Gituyu!

Wambuna caught her breath, looked from Kelfala to his friends, and cried out between tears and laughter. "A Gituyu! It cannot be. It cannot . . ."

> AS SHE WATCHED THEM, HER GRIN TURNED INTO A BROAD SMILE, *HER* SMILE TURNED INTO A SHY LAUGH, AND WITHOUT REALIZING IT, SHE BECAME ONE OF THE HOWLING TRIO.

But, at that Kelfala threw up his arms. "Aha! You have spoken to Kelfala. Kelfala, the great, Kelfala, the clown! Kelfala, the cunning one. Kelfala, the proud husband of a proud wife!"

"Wait a minute, Kelfala," one of his friends said. "Kelfala, I tell you now, she doesn't belong to you."

---

5. **akimbo** (ə-kĭm′bō): with hands on hips, and elbows bent outward.

"Oh, no, you Shortie Bumpie? The trick was mine, see?" and with that, Kelfala hopped.

"The plan was mine, see?" and with that, Kelfala skipped.

"The secret was mine, see?" and with that, he jumped.

"The Gituyu was mine, see? My secret something! And the laughter was mine, see, I started it." And with that, he laughed and laughed and laughed . . .

Wambuna stood, amazed, but she soon found support in Shortie Bumpie and Longie Tallie.

"I know that a man has had three wives, but never on this whole mountain has ever a woman shared three husbands," retorted Shortie Bumpie.

"Yes, Kelfala, this girl either belongs to all of us . . . or none of us," cried the other friend.

You could see Kelfala's heart heaving. "What did you say? You, Longie Tallie?" Wambuna lifted her eyes.

"Yes," Longie Tallie went on. "Wambuna laughed at you. She cried at you. She mumbled, she grumbled at you. She laughed-cried. She laughed-mumbled-cried at you. But she talked to all three of us!"

Wambuna pressed her lips together in a quiet, sly smile and looked into Kelfala's eyes. Then she walked back to her plants with her head raised up like a large pink rose in early spring.

Kelfala just looked, his head bowed like a weeping willow. But then, he tapped his bag and grinned. "Today is only for today. There is still tomorrow. There will always be another secret."

That was tradition, too. ❖

Adjai Robinson
born 1932

"Each book that I have written for boys and girls is also a book I have written for myself."

Folk Heritage Adjai Robinson was born in Sierra Leone, in West Africa. He grew up listening to local storytellers recount wonderful tales. Years later, Robinson continued the tradition by becoming a storyteller for radio and retelling African folk tales.

Back to Africa Robinson came to the United States to lead workshops about African folklore and to attend Columbia University in New York. In 1975, he returned to Africa, where he became the principal education officer at the Nigeria Teachers Institute. Robinson has published a number of children's books.

WORDS TO KNOW **retort** (rĭ-tôrt) v. respond to a comment, such as an insult or argument, with a reply of the same type, often quick, sharp, or witty

Interdisciplinary Projects

Key Standard
LS2.1 Deliver narrative presentations that contain a standard plot line, complex major and minor characters, and a definite setting.
Other Standards **R3.3, W2.3**

LITERATURE CONNECTION

Produce a Talk Show As a class, produce a talk show on "The Human Experience."

Step 1: Character List First, list the main characters in the selections you have read, the experiences each character has with others, and the lessons each character learns from experience.

Step 2: Volunteers Ask for volunteers to role-play the talk show host and the characters who will appear as guests on the show.

Step 3: Performance During the talk show, each character should express his or her opinion on what makes up the human experience. Students

serving as guests on the talk show should use voice inflection, good enunciation, and eye contact. The rest of the class can direct probing questions to the character and to the host or hostess.

Dramatize a Tale Perform as a play one of the tales you have read in this unit. Begin by listing the characters, dividing the tale into scenes, and choosing parts. To involve many students, choose a different cast for each scene. Then form small groups to be in charge of the script, props, costumes, music, sets, and publicity.

SOCIAL STUDIES CONNECTION

Make a Sequence Chart Review "Waters of Gold" or "The Force of Luck." Research either the Chinese immigration to the U.S. or the events of the Mexican-American War. Whichever topic you select, brainstorm questions about the topic and make a sequence chart like the one shown. Use books, encyclopedias, and computer databases to find out details. Then display your chart to the class.

Create an Oral Traditions Map Draw a map of the world. Then look at each of the stories presented in The Oral Tradition: Tales from Around the World. Identify the countries that are represented in these stories, and locate them on your map. Add the story titles to the map in the areas where they originated.

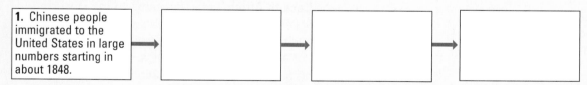

1. Chinese people immigrated to the United States in large numbers starting in about 1848.

ART CONNECTION

Create Your Own Pa ndau The Hmong have depicted their history, folk tales, and culture on pa ndau (pǎn-dou'), pieces of cloth with elaborate needlework. Pa ndau art can include appliqué, reverse appliqué, cross-stitches, chain stitches, batik, and embroidery. The stitching or appliqué is traditionally done on a blue background.

Step 1: Research Find pictures of Hmong pa ndau art in reference books in your library.

Step 2: Story Choose a story from Unit Six and create a pa ndau story cloth for it.

Step 3: Sketches Working with your classmates, sketch scenes from the story on paper.

Step 4: Cloth Then use fabric paint or one of the techniques mentioned to make the characters, actions, and scenery come to life on the cloth.

Step 5: Finished Pa ndau Display the pa ndau and use it to retell the story to a younger class.

Across Cultures

Compare Characters Select two stories from The Oral Tradition: Tales from Around the World. and identify the main characters in each. Compare and contrast the characters' personal qualities, their reactions to their situations, and their motivations for the way they behave. Draw a Venn diagram like the one shown. In the overlapping area, list the qualities that the characters have in common. Outside the overlap, list the qualities that are unique to each character.

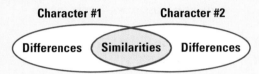

Character #1   Character #2

Differences   Similarities   Differences

Tell a Story Most folk tales come from the oral tradition. Tell a story to your class that you've heard told before. It could be a traditional tale or a recent tale from your family's history. You may want to wear a costume to suggest the story's particular time or place. Does your story have elements in common with your classmates' stories? What are they? What are the differences? How do the differences reflect different cultures?

Find the Number Three Events often happen in "threes" in folk tales—three tricks, three gifts, three wishes, or three visits. Use the diagram to record the events in threes in "Lazy Peter and His Three-Cornered Hat." Then add examples from stories from other cultures—such as "The Three Little Pigs" or "Goldilocks and the Three Bears"—that involve the use of the number three. Share your chart with the rest of the class.

	1st event	2nd event	3rd event
Lazy Peter			
Other tale			
Other tale			

Write a Persuasive Essay In "The Force of Luck" two friends have an argument. One friend thinks that it is luck that elevates a person to a high position. The other believes that it is money that moves a person to higher status. What do you think? Write a persuasive essay with examples that support your opinion.

INTERNET **Research Starter**
www.mcdougallittell.com

*Communication*Workshop

Bringing your subject to life with media . . .

From Reading to Writing What makes certain characters in literature good subjects for a presentation? Characters such as the clever Brother Cricket ("Brother Coyote and Brother Cricket") or Kelfala, the village clown ("Kelfala's Secret Something"), have human characteristics that make them entertaining. But how a character or a story is presented is equally as important. Creating a **multimedia presentation** is one way to grab an audience's attention. You can bring a character to life through a combination of sounds, visual elements, and text.

Basics in a Box

GUIDELINES AND STANDARDS	MULTIMEDIA PRESENTATION
Content	**Delivery**
A successful multimedia presentation should	**An effective presenter should**
• use media appropriate to the content	• have good posture and maintain eye contact with the audience
• use media from different sources	• vary pacing as well as the pitch, tone, and volume of voice
• capture the audience's attention with a strong beginning	• use gestures and body language to get the point across
• clearly, directly, and logically present information	• use visual aids effectively to help the audience understand the topic
• end by summarizing the topic and the points made	

Analyzing a Multimedia Presentation

SPEAKING
See the
Speaking and
Listening Handbook,
p. R100 for oral
presentation
tips.
OPPORTUNITY

<show first visual: clip of Cinderella movie>

Does everyone here know the story of Cinderella? OK, but how many of you have heard of Yeh-Shen or Cendrillon? These are Cinderella tales from China and the Caribbean. In each story a poor, mistreated girl is magically given a chance to appear in public wearing beautiful clothes. However, each story emphasizes a different aspect of the main character's personality.

<show second visual: picture of Yeh-Shen>

Yeh-Shen lives in southern China. Her only friend is the spirit that lives in the bones of her pet fish, which her cruel stepmother killed. This spirit gives her fancy clothes so that she can go to a festival. When Yeh-Shen loses one of her golden slippers, however, the fish bones no longer speak to her. Yeh-Shen is heartbroken and tries to get the slipper back, hoping that the spirit will return. Instead she is discovered by a king, who falls in love with her and marries her. The ending of the story is familiar, but Yeh-Shen is unique because she highly values her friendship with the fish.

<show third visual: picture of Cendrillon w/map of Carribean>

Cendrillon lives on a Caribbean island. Despite cruel treatment by her stepmother, she is a generous person. One day her godmother helps her attend a dance where she can meet Paul Thibault, a man who is very wealthy and kind. Cendrillon loses a slipper while leaving. When Paul comes to her house to find the owner of the slipper, the godmother wants to dress Cendrillon in beautiful clothes again.

<play audiotape of story from "She drew a shawl" to "in his eyes">

Cendrillon insists that Paul see her just as she really is.

<show fourth visual: Venn diagram>

Both Yeh-Shen and Cendrillon, like the heroines of most Cinderella tales, are humble and kind. However, each version of the story emphasizes different parts of the main character's personality. Yeh-Shen is memorable for her devoted friendship with the fish spirit, and Cendrillon is special because she insists on honesty in her relationships.

GUIDELINES IN ACTION

❶ Captures viewer's attention with video clip

❷ Introduction asks questions to involve audience; includes a thesis statement.
Another Option:
• Begin with music.

❸ Visual provides concrete image of the subject.

❹ Information is logically arranged in a subject-by-subject order. (First Yeh-Shen, then Cendrillon)
Another Option:
• Use feature-by-feature order.

❺ Audiotape varies the mode of presenting the material.

❻ Sums up similarities and differences between characters

❼ Conclusion reinforces the main idea.

IDEA Bank

1. Around the World
Explore the fairy tales of a particular country. Pick the character that appears most frequently, the one that reveals some aspect of the culture, or the one you find most interesting.

2. Admirable Aspects
Choose a legendary figure that reveals positive qualities in his or her adventures. Focus on one or two of those qualities in presenting the character.

Have a question?

See the **Research and Technology Handbook**
Using Visuals, p. R115
Sound, p. R117

Creating Your Multimedia Presentation

❶ Planning Your Presentation

List the titles of tales that you have read. **Brainstorm** names of characters with supernatural powers, characters that take the form of animals, and characters that resemble real people. See the **Idea Bank** in the margin for more suggestions. After you have chosen your character, follow the steps below.

Steps for Planning Your Multimedia Presentation

▶ 1. **Find out everything you can about your character.** Reread the story in which he or she appears and do research to find other information about him or her.

▶ 2. **Decide on your focus.** Your presentation can't include everything about your character. Will you show the character through a retelling of a story? Or will you put together ideas from different sources?

▶ 3. **Think about your audience.** How much background information do you need to give your audience? How much do they already know about the character?

▶ 4. **Organize your information.** What is the best order for presenting your ideas? At what points will media elements be effective?

▶ 5. **Plan your media elements.** Choose the best types of media for your presentation. Investigate where to obtain the materials and equipment you'll need. Consider the following options:

- **Audiotapes and compact discs** add sound effects, music, and voices.
- **Charts, posters, photos, slides,** and **graphs** provide visual representations of facts and information.
- **Videos** combine sound and visual effects.
- **Computers** can be used to generate visual aids or to create and project slides.

❷ Developing Your Presentation

You have gathered all the information that you want to include. Now it is time to put together your script and to insert media elements in the best places.

Steps for Developing Your Multimedia Presentation

▶ **1. Write a script.** You want your presentation to go well. Writing out what you want to say will help you be organized. Clearly show where you will use media elements in your script. Introduce and explain the elements if necessary.

▶ **2. Create a strong introduction and conclusion.** Begin your presentation with a vivid visual, a question, or an anecdote. Be sure to finish your presentation in a way that leaves your audience with a strong impression of your subject.

▶ **3. Collect and prepare your media elements.** Are your visuals big enough to be seen from the back of the room? Can your audio and video elements be heard? Have you practiced with the equipment so that you can use it easily?

▶ **4. Think about your media choices.** Are they effective? Do they accomplish what you want them to? Do they support the important points in your presentation? Lists, charts, and graphs will help give key facts and other data.

TECH Tool

A CD-ROM can provide both sound effects and visual images. You might be able to find your tale or legend on a CD-ROM. The text of the story might be accompanied by graphics that would be effective in your presentation. If you need help finding CD-ROMs or using them in a multimedia presentation, ask your school's technology adviser.

See **Language Network**
Using Media in Your Presentations, p. 561

❸ Practicing and Presenting

You must practice your entire presentation several times so that you can smoothly incorporate the media elements as you speak. Work on the following areas in your rehearsals:

• **Eye contact.** Know your script well enough that you can look at your audience from time to time during your presentation.

• **Facial expressions and gestures.** Practice appropriate expressions in front of a mirror and use gestures to emphasize important points.

• **Voice volume, tone, and pace.** Your voice must reach the back of the room. Vary the tone in which you speak to keep your audience interested. Speak slowly. Remember your audience is hearing your material for the first time.

• **Use of equipment.** Practice using the equipment. Ask for a rehearsal audience after you have practiced on your own. Work on their suggestions.

After rehearsing on your own, invite family and friends to view your presentation. Use their feedback to help you revise your organization or choice of words.

Ask Your Peer Reader

• Where do I need to give more background? information?

• How can I build a stronger introduction and conclusion?

• Which media elements were effective? Which elements were distracting? Why?

❹ Refining Your Presentation

TARGET SKILL ▷ **CREATING A STRONG OPENING** When you're surfing the channels on television, a program must grab your attention very quickly. The same is true for the first few seconds of a multimedia presentation. Start off with something that will immediately grab your audience's attention. Elements that work well include questions, humor, audio or video clips, and interesting anecdotes.

> *Does everyone here*
>
> *? OK, but how many of you have heard of*
>
> ~~Many people~~ know the story of Cinderella, ~~but not~~ Yeh-Shen or
>
> Cendrillon. These are Cinderella tales from China and the Caribbean.

❺ Editing and Proofreading

TARGET SKILL ▷ **CONSISTENT FORM** A great deal of information is packed into the visuals of a typical presentation. It is important that each visual be easy to read and understand. Remember to use correct and consistent capitalization. Also, always be sure that language is clear, consistent, and to the point.

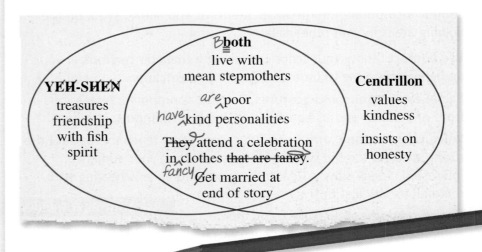

YEH-SHEN
treasures
friendship
with fish
spirit

both
live with
mean stepmothers
are poor
have kind personalities
They attend a celebration
in clothes ~~that are fancy~~.
fancy Get married at
end of story

Cendrillon
values
kindness

insists on
honesty

**SPELLING
From Writing**

As you revise your work, look back at the words you misspelled and determine why you made the errors you did. For additional help, refer to the strategies and generalizations in the **Spelling Handbook** on page R30.

**Publishing
IDEAS**

• Invite another class to watch your presentation.

• Host a family night and do your multimedia presentation.

Publishing Options
www.mcdougallittell.com

❻ Reflecting

FOR YOUR WORKING PORTFOLIO What did you learn about your character through doing your multimedia presentation? What did you learn about media while creating your presentation? What ideas do you have for another multimedia presentation? Attach your answers to your presentation script. Save your script in your **Working Portfolio.**

Standardized Test Practice

Mixed Review

"Cinderella" a classic fairy tale has been told and retold through the
(1)
years. Fairy tales were interesting because they tell a great deal about
(2)
basic human nature. Most cultures have fairy tales that have been read,
spoken, or sang throughout the years. One of the most famous
(3)
collections of fairy tales was published in the early 1800s by the Grimm
brothers, two brothers from Germany. This collection is still popular
(4)
today and includes "The Frog Prince," "Rapunzel," and "Hansel and
(5)
Gretel." Themes in these famous stories include the following: Things
people fear, Ideas people value, and Dreams people have.
(6)

Review Your Skills

Use the passage and the questions that follow it to check how well you remember the language conventions you've learned in previous grades.

1. How is sentence 1 best written?
   A. "Cinderella," a classic fairy tale has been told
   B. "Cinderella" a classic fairy tale, has been told
   C. "Cinderella," a classic fairy tale, has been told
   D. Correct as is

2. How is sentence 2 best written?
   A. Fairy tales are interesting
   B. Fairy tales had been interesting
   C. Fairy tales will be interesting
   D. Correct as is

3. How is sentence 3 best written?
   A. that have been read, spoke, or sung throughout the years.
   B. that have been read, spoke, or sang throughout the years.
   C. that have been read, spoken, or sung throughout the years.
   D. Correct as is

Key Standard
LC1.4 Use the mechanics of writing correctly; demonstrate correct language usage.
Other Standards **LC1.3, LC1.6**

4. How is sentence 4 best written?
   A. the Grimm brothers two brothers from, Germany.
   B. the Grimm brothers two brothers, from Germany.
   C. the Grimm brothers two brothers from Germany.
   D. Correct as is

5. How is sentence 5 best written?
   A. was still popular today
   B. were still popular today
   C. will still be popular today
   D. Correct as is

6. How is sentence 6 best written?
   A. things people fear, ideas people value, and dreams people have.
   B. Things people fear, ideas people value, and dreams people have.
   C. Things People Fear, Ideas People Value, and Dreams People Have.
   D. Correct as is

Self-Assessment

Check your own answers in the **Grammar Handbook**

Quick Reference Capitalization, p. R70

Quick Reference Punctuation, p. R90

Commonly Confused Verbs, p. R81

The Oral Tradition: Tales from Around the World

Key Standard
R3.4 Identify and analyze themes that appear across works.

In this unit you read stories that reflect many cultures. How have you grown as a reader and a writer because of reading them? Choose one or both of the options below to help assess how your thinking has developed.

Reflecting on Theme

OPTION 1

Examining Legends Work with a partner to review the legends you have read in this unit. Then in a chart like the one shown, list

Myth	Cultural Values
"King Arthur"	courage, self-confidence

each legend and one or more cultural values it reveals to you. Which legend do you think conveys the most important values?

OPTION 2

Evaluating Folk Tales Folk tales teach important lessons about human behavior. Review the folk tales you read in this unit and jot down a sentence or two about each, describing the lesson the tale teaches. Then decide which tales have the most to say to young people today. Share your evaluations with a group of classmates.

Portfolio Building

- **Personal Choice** Review the projects you completed during this unit. Select the one that helped you experience a culture most deeply. Write a note explaining what you gained from that project. Attach the note to the finished product, and add both to your **Presentation Portfolio.**

- **Setting Goals** Think about the goals you set for yourself this year. How have you improved as a reader and as a writer? Write a paragraph evaluating your progress over the course of the year and set three more goals for the next year.

LITERATURE CONNECTIONS

Introduction to Mythology

The warriors and heroes, and gods and goddesses of world mythology appear and reappear in literature and films. Here are their origins—presented by scholars and storytellers, from Bulfinch to San Souci. This collection offers an engaging introduction to the characters and stories of classical and world mythology. Maps, diagrams, and time lines add context. Part of the *NexText* series from McDougal Littell, the book comes with online activities at **www.nextext.com**.

LINKS WITH UNIT 1:
Learning from Experience

African Folktales
PAUL RADIN

Beat the Story-Drum, Pum-Pum
ASHLEY BRYAN

Folktales from India
A. K. RAMANUJAN

"Paradise on Earth: When the Moguls Ruled India"
MIKE EDWARDS
(*National Geographic,* April 1985)

LINKS WITH UNIT 2:
Relationships

Tongues of Jade
LAURENCE YEP

Grimm's Tales for Young and Old: The Complete Stories
RALPH MANHEIM (TRANSLATOR)

LINKS WITH UNIT 3:
Flights of Imagination

The Middle Ages
JOHN BRIQUEBEC

Knights in Armor
JOHN D. CLARE

Puerto Rico Mío: Four Decades of Change
JACK DELANO (PHOTOGRAPHER)

Puerto Rico: An Unfinished Story
DENIS J. HAUPTLY

LINKS WITH UNIT 4:
Nothing Stays the Same

Abubakari: The Explorer King of Mali
(VIDEOCASSETTE)

Cuentos: Tales from the Hispanic Southwest
JOSE GRIEGO Y MAESTAS AND RUDOLFO A. ANAYA

I'll Tell You a Tale: An Anthology
J. FRANK DOBIE

LINKS WITH UNIT 5:
Personal Challenges

Myths of the Norsemen: Retold from Old Norse Poems and Tales
ROGER LANCELYN GREEN

Anansi the Spider: A Tale of the Ashanti
FILMS INCORPORATED (VIDEOCASSETTE)

Folk Stories of the Hmong: Peoples of Laos, Thailand, and Vietnam
NORMA J. LIVO AND DIA CHA
LIBRARIES UNLIMITED (AUDIOCASSETTE)

The Language of Literature
Student Resource Bank

Reading for Different Purposes

Having a clear purpose can help you better remember and understand what you read. You may be reading for relaxation and pleasure. Perhaps you need information so you can pass a test. Maybe you need to follow directions to program your VCR or to fill out a form. Perhaps you need to analyze an argument to make sure it makes sense. You will need specific reading strategies for every type of reading you do. This Reading Handbook will help you become a better reader of all kinds of materials.

Reading Literature

Forms: stories, plays, poems, memoirs, biographies, some nonfiction

Purpose for reading: for pleasure, for increased understanding

Strategies for Reading

- **Predict**
- **Visualize**
- **Connect**
- **Question**
- **Clarify**
- **Evaluate**

See page S3 for details about each strategy.

Reading for Information

Forms: newspapers, magazines, reference works, on-line information, textbooks

Purpose for reading: to be informed

Strategies for Reading

- **Look for text organizers such as titles, subheads, graphics, and other devices.**
- **Notice the organization of the text.**
- **Look for connections to something you already know.**
- **Read, reread, and answer questions to increase your understanding.**

See pages R4–R11 for help with these strategies.

Critical Reading

On the second Monday in October, Americans celebrate Columbus Day. We honor the Italian explorer who has been credited with discovering the Americas in 1492. Some people, however, think that we need to look more closely at what Christopher Columbus actually did and at his place in history. I am one of those people.

First of all, although we honor Columbus as the first European to set foot in the Americas, he may not have been the first. Archaeologists have found Norse ruins in Greenland and what is now Newfoundland dating from around A.D. 1000. This evidence seems to prove that Vikings actually reached the North American continent nearly 500 years before Columbus ever left the shores of Spain.

Forms: newspaper editorials, advertisements, political ads, letters, opinion statements

Purpose for reading: to be informed, to make a decision

Strategies for Reading

- **Find the main ideas.**
- **Evaluate the supporting details.**
- **Determine the author's purpose.**
- **Decide how well the author achieved that purpose.**

See pages R12–R17 for detailed examples.

Functional Reading

Setting the Sleep Timer

1. Press the MENU key. The Setup menu will appear on your television.
2. Select the Timer Setup on your screen by using the UP/DOWN arrows on your remote control.
3. Now press the RIGHT/LEFT arrows. A menu of the Timer Setup will appear on the screen.
4. Sleep Timer: Use the RIGHT/LEFT arrows to program the length of time until the TV shuts down. You can select any time from ten minutes to four hours. Press ENTER to return to TV viewing.

Setting On/Off Timer

5. Follow steps 1 and 2 above to get to the Timer Setup menu. Using the UP/DOWN arrows on the remote control, select On Time on your screen.
6. Press the RIGHT or LEFT arrow to adjust the time your television will turn on automatically.
7. Press the TIMER button to choose either A.M. or P.M.
8. Repeat steps 5 through 7 to set Off Time. Use the UP/DOWN arrows to select the On/Off Timer and activate the timer by pressing a RIGHT/LEFT arrow.

WARNING: The On/Off timer will not work until the clock on your television has been set.

Forms: instruction manuals, applications, workplace documents, product information, technical directions, public notices

Purpose for reading: to make decisions and solve problems

Strategies for Reading

- **Skim the whole piece.**
- **Read the information in the order presented.**
- **Look carefully at any drawings or pictures.**
- **Reread when the meaning is unclear.**

See pages R18–R23 for examples.

Methods of Reading

When you read something for the first time, review material for a test, or search for specific information, you use different methods of reading. The following techniques are useful with all kinds of reading materials.

Skimming When you run your eyes quickly over a text, looking at headings, graphic features, and highlighted words, you are skimming. Skimming is useful in previewing textbook material that you must read for an assignment.

Scanning In a text, to find a specific piece of information, such as the date of a battle, use scanning. Place a card under the first line of a page and move it down slowly. Look for key words and phrases.

In-Depth Reading In-depth reading involves asking questions, taking notes, looking for main ideas, and drawing conclusions as you read slowly and carefully. Use this type of reading for literary works and textbooks.

Reading for Information

When you read informational materials such as textbooks, magazines, newspapers, and on-line text, you need to use specific strategies. It is important to study text organizers, such as headings and special type, that tell you what the main ideas, facts, and terms are on the page. It is also important to recognize patterns of organization in the text and to map them in a graphic organizer. Using these strategies will help you read and understand any kind of informational text.

Text Organizers

Writers use special features such as headings, large or dark type, pictures, or drawings to show you the most important information on the page. You can use these special features to help you understand and remember what you read.

Strategies for Reading

A First, look at the **title** and any **subheads**. These will tell you the main ideas of the lesson.

B Many textbooks have one or more **objectives** or **key terms** at the beginning of each lesson. Keep these in mind as you read. This will help you identify the most important details. You may also want to read any **questions** at the end of the section to find out what you'll need to learn.

C Look at the **visuals**— photographs, illustrations, time lines, or other graphics—and read their **captions**. These will help you understand what you are about to read.

B.C.	A.D.					
250		500	750	1000	1250	1500
	27	476				

LESSON 1

The Fall of the Roman Empire **A**

The world has grown old and lost its former vigor. . . . Winter no longer gives rain enough to swell the seed, nor summer enough to toast the harvest . . . the mountains are gutted and give less marble, the mines are exhausted and give less silver and gold . . . the fields lack farmers, the seas sailors, the encampments soldiers . . . there is no justice in judgments, competence in trades, discipline in daily life.

B

THINKING FOCUS

B *What led to the collapse of the Western Roman Empire?*

E Key Terms

* province
* barbarian

C ➤ *Roman emperors were often depicted in military dress. The carved figures on the breastplate of Augustus's armor represent a Roman victory over a Persian army.*

26

Chapter 2

This description, written in about A.D. 250 by one of the Roman Empire's church leaders, foretells the fate of that mighty empire. Within 200 years of the writing of this description, the Roman Empire would suffer great military and economic crises, weaken, and eventually collapse.

The Empire in Prosperity **A**

From 27 B.C. to A.D. 14, Julius Caesar's adopted son Octavian ruled as Rome's first emperor. Octavian was given the name Augustus, which means the revered or exalted one. As emperor, Augustus put an end to the chaos and power struggles that had occurred within the Roman Empire after Julius Caesar's assassination. Caesar and Augustus also expanded the empire by conquering the territory that ran along the Rhine and Danube rivers.

D Watch for **pulled-out text**—quotations or other materials that are placed in a box or in different type. Such text often includes especially surprising, important, or memorable information.

E Don't forget about the **key terms**. These are often boldfaced or underlined where they first appear in the text. Be sure you understand what they mean.

F Examine **maps**. Read their **titles**, **captions**, and **legends.** Make certain you know what the map shows and how it relates to the text.

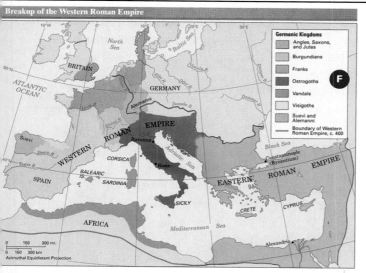

Breakup of the Western Roman Empire

Germanic Kingdoms
- Angles, Saxons, and Jutes
- Burgundians
- Franks
- Ostrogoths
- Vandals
- Visigoths
- Suevi and Alemanni
- Boundary of Western Roman Empire, c. 400

F

Expanding the Empire

Roman conquests of new territory continued under the emperors after Augustus. By A.D. 117, the Roman Empire had reached its greatest size. It extended from Britain in the north to Africa in the south and from Spain in the west to Syria in the east.

The lands and peoples captured by the empire were organized into **provinces,** or territories, of Rome. Rome maintained peace in its provinces by allowing individuals to continue living and working as usual. However, Roman officials did institute Roman laws in these territories. In addition, they appointed governors to rule the provinces and make sure that Roman law was enforced here.

E

Profiting from the Provinces

Rome benefited from its empire in many ways. Since enemies could reach Rome only by crossing the provinces, these territories pro-

tected Rome by acting as a buffer zone. They also produced food and other goods for the city of Rome. For example, Egypt and North Africa supplied Rome with most of

▲ *As powerful as it was, the Roman Empire did not last. How did its boundaries change as it weakened?*

▲ *Here Egyptian grain is loaded on a barge for shipment to Rome.*

C

27

Empires of the Ancient World

More Examples

To examine the structural features of other kinds of informational materials, see the pages listed below.

For examples of **newspaper articles**, see pages 219, 305, 470, and 675.

For examples of **magazine articles**, see pages 65, 138, 396, and 617.

For an example of **Internet articles**, see pages 549 and 728.

Patterns of Organization

Reading any type of writing is easier if you understand how it is organized. A writer organizes ideas in a sequence, or structure, that helps the reader see how the ideas are related. Four important structures are the following:

- main idea and supporting details
- chronological order
- comparison and contrast
- cause and effect

This page contains an overview of the four structures, which you will learn about in more detail on pages R7–R11. Each type has been drawn as a map or graphic organizer to help you see how the ideas are related.

Main Idea and Supporting Details

The main idea of a paragraph or a longer piece of writing is its most important point. Supporting details give more information or evidence about the statements made in the main idea.

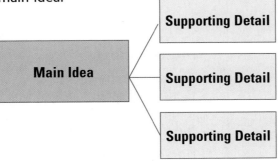

Chronological Order

Writing that is organized in chronological order presents events in the order in which they occur.

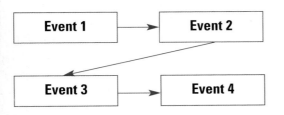

Comparison and Contrast

Comparison-and-contrast writing explains how two or more subjects are similar and how they are different.

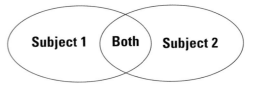

Cause and Effect

Cause-and-effect writing explains the relationship between events. The cause is the first event. The effect happens as a result of the cause. A cause may have more than one effect, and an effect may have more than one cause.

Single Cause with Multiple Effects

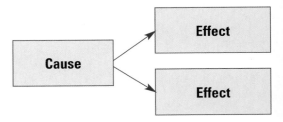

Multiple Causes with Single Effect

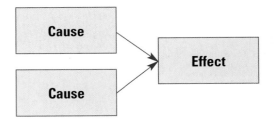

Cause-and-Effect Chain

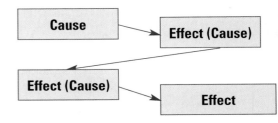

Main Idea and Supporting Details

The **main idea** of a paragraph is the basic point you should remember from your reading. The **supporting details** give you additional information about the main idea. A main idea can be stated directly, or it can be implied. If it is stated, it can appear anywhere in the paragraph. Often, it will be the first or the last sentence. An implied main idea is suggested by the details that are provided.

Strategies for Reading

- To find the **main idea,** ask, "What is this paragraph about?"
- To find **supporting details,** ask, "What else do I learn about the main idea?"

MODEL
Main Idea as the First Sentence

Main Idea

When the nomads of Africa began using camels in the third century A.D., trade across the Sahara became easier. The donkeys, horses, and oxen that had been used previously could not travel far without stopping for food and water. Camels, on the other hand, could cover 60 miles in a day and go for up to ten days without water.

Supporting Details

MODEL
Main Idea as the Last Sentence

Supporting Details

The new trade routes passed through lands occupied by the Soninke people. These farming people referred to their chief as ghana. Soon the land came to be known as the kingdom of Ghana. The tribal chiefs taxed the goods that traveled across their territory. By the eighth century, trade had made Ghana a rich kingdom.

Main Idea

MODEL
Implied Main Idea

Implied main idea: Gold and salt were two important items that were traded in West Africa.

The West African savannas and forests south of the savanna were rich in gold. No salt was available there, though. In the Sahara, on the other hand, there was abundant salt but no gold. Traders brought salt south through the desert and traded it for gold mined from the forests.

PRACTICE AND APPLY

MODEL

Gold and salt made the king of Ghana a powerful man. The king controlled the trade in these important items and collected gold nuggets and salt blocks from his people. He was not only the richest man in the kingdom but also its religious leader, military commander, and chief judge. Because Ghana had such a strong economy and army, the king could force the rulers of neighboring lands to give him gifts and pay taxes. If the rulers did so, the king of Ghana would treat them well.

Read the model above and then do the following activities.

1. Identify the main idea of the paragraph. Is it stated or implied? If it is stated, where does it appear in the paragraph?

2. List three details that support or give evidence for the main idea.

Chronological Order

Chronological, or time, order presents ideas in the order that they happened. Historical events are usually presented in chronological order. The steps of a process may also be presented in time order.

Strategies for Reading
- Look for the individual **steps or events in the sequence.**
- Look for words and phrases that identify **time,** such as *in a year*, *two hours earlier*, *in A.D. 1066*, and *later*.
- Look for words that signal **order,** such as *first, afterward, then, before, finally*, and *next*.

MODEL

| Event | Muhammad, the prophet and founder of Islam, died in A.D. 632. That same year, the Muslim |
| Time phrases | |

community chose a friend of Muhammad, Abu-Bakr, as its spiritual leader, or caliph.

After Muhammad's death, many Muslim people stopped following Islamic beliefs. Then Abu-Bakr used his strong army to control the people. By the time he died in 634, all of the Arabian Peninsula was under Muslim rule.

The next caliph, Umar, conquered Syria and parts of Egypt and Persia. The next leaders, Uthman and Ali, continued conquering lands. In just over 100 years, the land of Islam had grown so much that it covered 4,000 miles from the Indus River to the Atlantic Ocean.

The armies of Uthman and Ali did not make the caliphs safe, however. In 656, Uthman was assassinated. And in 661, so was Ali.

After Ali's death, a family called the Umayyads came to power. They moved the capital of the empire to Damascus, in the Syrian territory. They also became wealthy and gave up the simple lifestyle of the caliphs.

The actions of the Umayyads caused a split in the Muslim community. Groups against the Umayyads were formed. This division led to the overthrow of the Umayyads in 750 by a group called the Abbasids. In 762, the Muslim capital was moved again. This time it was set up, by the Abbasids, in Baghdad, in present-day Iraq.

Abbasid rule lasted for over 500 years, until 1258. By that time, the Muslim Empire had become a major sea power. It traded widely with countries in Europe, Africa, and Asia. The vision of one man, the prophet Muhammad, led to the growth of a vast melting pot of religions, cultures, and peoples.

PRACTICE AND APPLY

Reread the model and then do the following activities.
1. Create a time line on your paper extending from the death of Muhammad in 632 to the end of Abbasid rule in 1258.
2. List three words or phrases in the model that signal time and three that signal order. Find words and phrases in addition to the ones already done for you.
3. Although the model is organized in chronological order, it also includes other types of organization. The fourth paragraph, for example, is organized by **main idea**—the leaders' lack of safety—and **supporting details**. Find an example of **cause-and-effect** order in the model, and list the cause(s) and effect(s) on your paper.

Comparison and Contrast

Comparison-and-contrast writing explains how two different subjects are alike and different. This type of writing is usually organized by subject or by feature. In **subject organization,** the writer discusses subject 1, then discusses subject 2. In **feature organization**, the writer compares a feature of subject 1 with a feature of subject 2, then compares another feature of both, and so on.

Strategies for Reading

- Look for words and phrases that signal **comparison,** such as *like, similarly, both, also,* and *in the same way.*

- Look for words and phrases that signal **contrast,** such as *unlike, on the other hand, in contrast,* and *however.*

MODEL

Subjects

Comparison word

Contrast words

Two stories, "Kelfala's Secret Something" and "Pumpkin Seed and the Snake," are both folk tales that were told aloud long before they were written down. They are from very different cultures, however, and have differences as well as similarities.

"Kelfala's Secret Something" is a tale of the Kikuyu people of Kenya, in East Africa. "Pumpkin Seed and the Snake," on the other hand, is from the Hmong people of Southeast Asia. The subjects and morals of the two tales are similar. Both stories are about young people and marriage. Both have something to say about trickery.

A main character in each story is a young man. In "Pumpkin Seed and the Snake," however, the young man sometimes takes the form of a snake. Although both main characters have to perform a task to win their brides, their tasks differ. Kelfala must get the young girl Wambuna to talk to him. The snake, in contrast, must move a rock for Pumpkin Seed's mother.

Both main characters use some kind of trickery to accomplish their goals. Kelfala's whole plan to win Wambuna is based on a trick involving an imaginary animal. The snake, on the other hand, is basically honest and direct. He does what the mother asks and expects her to fulfill her promise. He only uses the trick of changing into a man and back to a snake to avoid being killed.

The snake's tale ends happily. He marries Pumpkin Seed and becomes a full-time man. Unlike the snake, however, Kelfala does not win his bride. He is so sure of himself that he brings two friends along to watch his success with Wambuna. His trick backfires, though. Since she talks to all three friends, she can't marry just Kelfala.

The moral of both "Pumpkin Seed and the Snake" and "Kelfala's Secret Something" seems to be that honesty is the best policy but that trickiness has its place. The snake proves that a little trickery can save your life. However, as Kelfala learned, if you get too tricky, you may end up getting tricked yourself.

PRACTICE AND APPLY

Reread the model and then do the following activities.

1. List all the words and phrases that signal comparisons and contrasts. Find words in addition to the ones already done for you.

2. This model compares the two folk tales feature by feature. One feature is what culture each tale is from; another is what the tales are about. List at least four other features the writer discusses.

3. Create a Venn diagram and fill in the similarities and the differences between "Kelfala's Secret Something" and "Pumpkin Seed and the Snake."

Cause and Effect

Cause-and-effect writing explains the relationship between events. A **cause** is an event that brings about another event. An **effect** is something that happens as a result of the first event. Cause-and-effect writing is usually organized in one of three ways:

1. Starting with cause(s) and explaining effect(s).
2. Starting with effects and explaining cause(s).
3. Describing a chain of causes and effects.

Strategies for Reading

- To find the **effect** or **effects,** ask "What happened?"
- To find the **cause** or **causes,** ask "Why did it happen?"
- Look for **signal words** and **phrases** such as *because, as a result, for that reason, so, consequently,* and *since.*

MODEL

Cause — **One of the worst diseases ever recorded was the bubonic plague, or Black Death. It broke out in China in the 1330s. Before it disappeared, 60 million people had died.**

Effect

The bubonic plague is a disease that is carried by rats. Fleas carry the plague from one rat to another. The fleas can also carry the disease to people. Sick people can pass the disease to other people very quickly.

In the Middle Ages, people **Signal Words** rarely took baths. **As a result,** most people had fleas and lice living on their bodies. The plague was probably spread when Mongol horsemen carrying infected fleas invaded China in the 14th century. Because China was an important trading center, many people from all over the world came there. Those people

were exposed to the disease and took it back to their home countries.

The Mongols kept moving westward, and in 1345, they attacked a port on the Black Sea where many Italian traders lived. When these traders returned to Italy, they infected their countrymen. The disease subsequently spread throughout Europe. In the five years between 1347 and 1352, 25 million Europeans died.

Why did the Black Death claim so many victims? Part of the reason is that people in medieval times did not understand that the disease was caused by infected fleas. They did things that caused the disease to spread. They didn't often take baths, and so they had fleas living on their bodies. They also dumped their garbage and sewage into the streets. The consequence was a perfect breeding ground for rats and fleas. Maybe the real question is not why so many people got the plague but how anyone managed to survive.

PRACTICE AND APPLY

A. Reread the model on this page and then do the following activities.

1. List one effect that happened because people in medieval times didn't often take baths.
2. Identify three words or phrases in the passage that signal causes and effects.
3. The bubonic plague spread by a series of causes and effects. Make a cause-and-effect graphic in which you show what happened (the effects) when people didn't take baths. In another graphic show the effects of throwing garbage and sewage into the streets. Look on page R6 for examples of graphic organizers.

B. Read the model below and then do the activities that follow.

MODEL

Tsunami is a word that brings fear to people who live near the sea. Also known in English as a tidal wave, a tsunami is a huge ocean wave caused by an underwater volcanic eruption or earthquake.

An earthquake or the explosion of a volcano on the ocean floor creates massive waves of energy. These energy waves spread out in widening circles, like waves from a pebble dropped into a pond. The waves are extremely long but not very high. For this reason, a ship out on the ocean may feel only a slight rise and fall of the water as a tsunami passes.

As the tsunami nears the shore, it begins to scrape along the ocean bottom. This friction causes the waves in the front to slow down. As a result, the waves traveling behind begin piling up and growing higher. This increase in height can happen very quickly—by as much as 90 feet in 10 or 15 minutes.

The effects of a tsunami can include the death of many people and the destruction of ships, buildings, and land along the shore. An especially dangerous situation may occur when the first part of a tsunami to hit the shore is the trough, or low point, rather than the crest of a wave. This trough sucks all the water away from the shore and may attract curious people on the beach. Within a few minutes, however, the crest of the wave will hit and may drown the onlookers. The most destructive tsunami ever recorded struck Awa, Japan, in 1703. It left more than 100,000 people dead.

1. List two events that can cause a tsunami to form.
2. List what happens when a tsunami nears the shore.
3. Fill in a cause-and-effect chart that shows the cause of a tsunami and its multiple effects.

C. After reading the model, do the activities that follow.

MODEL

In the Middle Ages, people believed that the earth was the center of the universe—that the moon, the sun, and the other planets moved in circles around the earth. This belief came not only from deeply held religious beliefs but from common sense. Everyone could see that the sun seemed to move around the earth from morning to evening. Because both religion and common sense agreed, the idea of an earth-centered universe was hard to change.

The idea did change, however. After studying the movement of the planets for 25 years, the astronomer Nicolaus Copernicus concluded that the sun was actually at the center of the universe. The earth, the other planets, and the stars revolved around the sun. Copernicus knew that people would not like his idea because it contradicted their religious beliefs, so he did not publish it until just before he died in 1543.

About 60 years later, the Italian astronomer Galileo Galilei built a telescope and used it to study the sky. Galileo then published his findings, which showed that Copernicus had been right. These findings seemed to go against the teaching of the Catholic Church. For this reason, Galileo became an enemy of the church. When he refused to stop working and publishing his ideas, he was put on trial. As a result of the trial, he was forced to sign a statement saying that the sun was not the center of the universe. Another consequence of the trial was that Galileo spent the rest of his life under arrest. Even so, his books and his ideas eventually spread throughout Europe.

1. List the causes of the following events:
   a. the strong belief in an earth-centered universe
   b. Copernicus's fear of publishing his ideas
2. List two effects of Galileo's trial.

Critical Reading: Persuasion

Every day you encounter writing whose purpose is to inform and persuade you. This writing can take many forms, including speeches, newspaper editorials, advertisements, and billboards. Good readers read critically, or question what they read. They make sure the details presented are accurate and truly support the author's main ideas.

What Is an Argument?

Much of the information you read is designed to persuade you to think a certain way. This type of writing presents an **argument** for believing or doing something.

An effective argument clearly makes a claim or states a position on an issue and supports it with good evidence and logical reasoning. It also presents opposing views and explains their weaknesses.

Strategies for Reading

- Look for a **statement of the main issue or problem** and the author's **position** on it.
- Evaluate the **evidence**—facts, statistics, and opinions—that **supports** the author's position.
- Evaluate the **evidence**—facts, statistics, and opinions—that **opposes** the author's position.

MODEL

On the second Monday in October, Americans celebrate Columbus Day. We honor the Italian explorer who has been credited with discovering the Americas in 1492. **Some people, however, think that we need to look more closely at what Christopher Columbus actually did and at his place in our history. I am one of those people.**

Author's position

First of all, although we honor Columbus as the first European to set foot in the Americas, he may not have been the first. Archaeologists have found Norse ruins in Greenland and what is now Newfoundland dating from around A.D. 1000. This evidence seems to prove that Vikings actually reached the North American continent nearly 500 years before Columbus ever left the shores of Spain.

Evidence supporting the author's position

Second, although Columbus did reach the Americas, he did not discover them. Nearly 100 million people were already living there when he arrived.

Defenders of Columbus argue that, in a way, he *did* discover the Americas. Even if he wasn't the first person, or even the first European, to set foot on the land, his voyages made the rest of the world aware of the Americas. In the years following Columbus's voyages, Europeans came to establish colonies and to explore the land.

Opposing view

I argue that this spread of cultures brought great harm as well as great good to the Americas. The Europeans who came to the Americas brought deadly diseases with them. The native people had no immunity to such diseases as mumps, measles, smallpox, and typhus. As a result, hundreds of thousands of them died.

Author's response

In conclusion, I don't suggest that people should boycott their local Columbus Day parades. I do think, though, that we should create a more balanced picture of the man we're honoring.

Restatement of the author's position

Tracing an Author's Argument

Mapping the structure of an argument can help you read the argument critically and decide if it is convincing.

Shown here is an example of a graphic that maps the argument presented in the model on the previous page. You can create any type of graphic that helps you organize the information presented in an argument. Be sure, however, to include the following elements:
• the main issue
• the author's position on the issue

• statements that support the author's position
• evidence given to support those statements
• statements against the author's position
• evidence given to support those statements
• author's conclusion

Issue: Honoring Columbus on Columbus Day

Author's position	We need to look more closely at what Christopher Columbus really did. **Support:** Columbus was not the first European to reach the Americas. **Evidence:** Norse ruins in Greenland and Newfoundland date from 500 years before Columbus's voyage. **Support:** Columbus did not discover the Americas. **Evidence:** 100 million people were already living there when Columbus arrived.
Opposing view	Columbus *did* discover the Americas in a sense. **Support:** He brought the area to the attention of the rest of the world and opened it to settlement. **Evidence:** Europeans came to establish colonies.
Author's response	Settlement had negative effects. **Support:** Colonists brought diseases that killed the native people. **Evidence:** Hundreds of thousands died.
Restatement of the author's position	It's fine to honor Columbus as long as we know whom and what we're honoring.

Evaluating Reasoning

In a good argument, the author uses evidence and sound reasoning to support his or her position. The conclusions the author makes follow clearly from the information presented.

Four types of faulty, or bad, reasoning to watch out for are **overgeneralization,** the **either-or fallacy,** the **cause-and-effect fallacy,** and **circular reasoning.**

Overgeneralization

An overgeneralization is a broad statement that says something is true for every case, with no exceptions. In fact, very few statements have no exceptions.

Overgeneralizations often include the words *all, none, everyone, no one, any,* and *anyone.*

> **Overgeneralization:**
> No one believes anymore that Christopher Columbus discovered America.
>
> **Reasonable statement:**
> Many people now believe that Christopher Columbus was not the first European to set foot in the Americas.

Either-Or Fallacy

The either-or fallacy states that there are only two possible ways to view a situation or only two options to choose from. In most situations, there are actually a number of views and options. Either-or fallacies often include the words *either . . . or.*

> **Either-or fallacy:**
> We must decide that Columbus's voyage to America was either good or bad.
>
> **Reasonable statement:**
> Columbus's voyage to America had both good and bad effects.

Cause-and-Effect Fallacy

In the cause-and-effect fallacy, the author makes the assumption that because one event follows another, the second event was caused by the first one. As you read, think carefully about the evidence that one event actually caused another.

> **Cause-and-effect fallacy:**
> Columbus gave gifts to the Taino people. The Taino greeted Columbus and his men warmly and generously.
>
> **Logical statement:**
> Columbus gave gifts to the Taino people to show his friendly intentions. The Taino were a peaceful people who responded warmly to their visitors.

Circular Reasoning

Circular reasoning is an attempt to support a statement by simply repeating it in other words. If a statement does not include any supporting facts and leaves you thinking "So?" it may be circular reasoning.

> **Circular reasoning:**
> Columbus liked the Taino people because he felt warmly about them.
>
> **Logical statement:**
> Columbus liked the Taino people because they welcomed him warmly and, some say, actually saved his life.

Evaluating Evidence

In addition to evaluating the reasoning of an argument, you must carefully examine the evidence the author presents to support his or her statements. First, you must know the difference between **facts** and **opinions.** Then you should assess the **adequacy, accuracy,** and **appropriateness** of the evidence.

There should be **adequate,** or enough, evidence to support what the author is saying. To increase **accuracy,** or correctness, evidence needs to come from reliable sources. To be **appropriate,** the evidence needs to apply to the topic and to be free of **stereotyping, bias and propaganda,** and **emotional appeals.**

Fact and Opinion

A fact is a statement that can be proved. An opinion is a statement of personal belief that cannot be proved.

> **Opinion Statement:**
> Columbus was the cause of much misery in the Americas.
>
> **Factual Statement:**
> The explorers and settlers who came after Columbus brought diseases that caused thousands of deaths among the native peoples.

Stereotyping

Stereotyping is a broad statement about a group of people that doesn't take individual differences into account.

> **Stereotyping:**
> The native Taino people treated Columbus well because, like all natives, they were warm and friendly.
>
> **Balanced statement:**
> Columbus said about the Taino people he met: "They are friendly and well-dispositioned people who . . . gave everything they had with good will."

Bias

Bias is a preference for one side of an argument.

> **Bias:**
> Columbus caused more harm than good to the world.
>
> **Unbiased statement:**
> Columbus's discovery had both good and bad effects on the world.

Propaganda

Propaganda is a form of communication that may use distorted, false, or misleading information.

> **Propaganda:**
> Columbus did great harm to the world and shouldn't be honored—even for a day.
>
> **Balanced statement:**
> Some people think that we need to look more closely at what Christopher Columbus did and at his effects on history.

Emotional Appeals

Emotional appeals are statements that create strong feelings rather than using fact and evidence to make a point. Be alert for statements that make you feel angry, sad, or even very happy. Because emotional appeals are directed at feelings rather than thoughts, they are also sometimes called **unreasonable persuasion.**

> **Emotional appeal:**
> Columbus is a fraud and anyone who honors him on Columbus Day is an idiot.
>
> **Balanced statement:**
> I don't suggest that people should boycott their local Columbus Day parades. I do think, though, that we should see a more balanced picture of the man we're honoring.

PRACTICE AND APPLY

A. Read the model on this page and do the activities that follow.

MODEL

What would you do if you brought home the hottest new CD by your favorite group, Spice C, and your father made you take it back because of its "disgusting lyrics"? You may think that an issue like that should stay in the family. I believe, though, that the issue of certain song lyrics affects us all.

I think that young people should be able to make their own decisions about what to listen to. Most other kids would probably agree with me. If we are not allowed to make our own decisions about what we read, see, and hear, how will we ever learn to think for ourselves? If we make a bad decision, we will learn from it and not make the same mistake again. I also believe that adults need to look beyond just the language of these songs and listen to their message. Nobody in his or her right mind could truly listen and not realize that these songs tell it just like it is.

Most parents, on the other hand, would say that the rough language and the violence in these songs are a bad influence on children. Parents see too much violence and offensive language in the world as it is, and they feel it is their duty to protect their children.

Most kids, and the musicians themselves, however, don't think the language is harmful. They believe that young people are exposed to that kind of language in many situations. If parents and other adults start censoring song lyrics, they won't stop until everything that's printed, shown on television, or heard on the radio is banned.

In conclusion, I think that kids must be allowed to make their own decisions about the music they listen to. Parents need to trust their children and give them the chance to act responsibly.

1. Map the structure of the argument in the model, using a graphic organizer like the one on page R6 or one that you create yourself. Be sure to include the issue, the author's position on the issue, support for the author's position, statements against the author's position, evidence to support the opposing position, and the author's conclusion.

2. The sentence, "Nobody in his or her right mind . . . " is an overgeneralization. Rewrite the statement to remove the overgeneralization.

3. Find another example of an overgeneralization in the model and write it on your paper. Then rewrite it to eliminate the problem.

4. If the author of the model was a member of Spice C, do you think he or she might have a preference for one side of the argument? Look at the examples of evidence on p. R15. What is a preference for one side of an argument called?

5. **On Your Own** With a partner, decide on an issue you would like to argue for or against. Then use the graphic on page R13 to map out your argument. Perhaps you want to write in favor of restricting song lyrics or about another issue that strongly interests you. Be sure to include the elements listed in activity 1 above and on page R13.

B. After reading the model, do the activities that follow.

MODEL

According to veterinarian and animal rights advocate Dr. Michael W. Fox, more than 100 million animals are used each year in laboratory tests. These animals are used to study such things as the causes and effects of illnesses or to test drugs. This unnecessary and cruel animal testing must be stopped.

The most important reason to stop this testing is that it's wrong to make living creatures suffer. Even though they can't talk or use tools like people do, animals have feelings. Zoologist Ann Speirs says that animals may suffer even more than people do, because they can't understand what's happening to them.

People who favor animal research argue that the medical advances gained justify animal experimentation. They also say that the suffering experienced by the animals is minor. People like that are dumber than any guinea pig or rat.

Another important reason to stop this testing is that everybody knows it isn't reliable. Many drugs that help animals are harmful to people. One example is the drug thalidomide. After it was tested in animals in the 1960s, it was given to pregnant women. Dr. Fox says that more than 10,000 of these women gave birth to handicapped babies. The process works the other way, too. Many drugs that help people kill animals. Two common examples are penicillin and aspirin.

Animal testing also affects the environment. The Animal Protection Service says that a quarter of a million chimpanzees, monkeys, and baboons are taken from their natural homes and used in laboratory experiments every year. Those animals will never be able to reproduce, and the whole species may become extinct.

A final reason for not using animals in experiments is that there are other research methods available. Two examples are using bits of animal tissue or cells and using computer models.

In conclusion, animal testing has to stop because it just can't go on.

1. State the author's position on the subject.
2. List two pieces of evidence the author uses to support the argument.
3. The sentence, "People like that are dumber than any guinea pig or rat" is an example of an emotional appeal. Rewrite the statement to make it more reasonable.
4. List two other examples of faulty evidence or two examples of faulty reasoning that you find. Rewrite them to correct the errors.
5. **On Your Own** The author of the model has a bias against animal testing. Find some examples of bias in newspapers or magazines and bring them to class. Good sources are newspaper editorial pages or personal essays in magazines.

Functional Reading

It takes special strategies to read the many different kinds of materials that help you function effectively in your everyday life. After studying the real-life examples in this section, you will be better able to fill out an application; understand product labels, public notices, and workplace documents; and follow various kinds of instructions. Look at each example as you read the strategies.

Product Information: Medicine Label

Strategies for Reading

Ⓐ Read the **list of conditions or illnesses** the medicine can be used to treat.

Ⓑ Pay attention to the **directions** that tell **who may take the medicine and who should not.** Also note the **recommended daily dose:** how much of the medicine can be taken and how often.

Ⓒ Read the **warnings section** carefully. This section tells users how long the medicine can safely be taken and explains what to do if the condition continues or new symptoms appear. It also contains a warning for new mothers and mothers-to-be.

Ⓓ **Always note this sentence,** which appears on many medicines. It serves as a reminder that the medicine can be dangerous in the wrong hands.

Extra-Strength Non-Aspirin Pain Reliever

Ⓐ **INDICATIONS:** For the temporary relief of minor aches and pains associated with the common cold, headache, toothache, muscular aches, backache, and arthritis, and for the reduction of fever.

Ⓑ **DIRECTIONS:** Adults and children 12 years of age and older: Take 2 tablets every 4 to 6 hours as needed. Take no more than a total of 8 tablets in any 24-hour period, or as directed by a physician. Not for use by children under 12 years of age.

Ⓒ **WARNINGS:** Do not take for pain for more than 10 days or for fever for more than 3 days unless directed by a physician. If pain or fever persists or gets worse, if new symptoms occur, or if redness or swelling is present, consult a physician. If you are pregnant or nursing a baby, seek the advice of a health professional before using this product.

Ⓓ **KEEP THIS AND ALL MEDICINES OUT OF CHILDREN'S REACH.** In case of accidental overdose, contact a physician or poison control center immediately.

 Mtd. for Aspirin Laboratories
Chicago, IL 60601

0 18946 65238

PRACTICE AND APPLY

Reread the sample label and answer the following questions.

1. List the conditions or illnesses this medicine can be used to treat.

2. How many tablets can safely be taken in one day?

3. Who should not take these tablets?

4. How often may these tablets be taken?

Public Notice

Strategies for Reading

A Look for information that answers the question, **"Whom is this notice for?"**

B Look for **instructions**—what the notice is asking or telling you to do.

C See if there is any information about **who created the notice.**

D Look for information about **how you can find out more** about the topic.

E Check out any **special features** designed to make the notice easier to understand.

UNITED STATES DEPARTMENT OF COMMERCE
Bureau of the Census
Washington, DC 20233-2000 **C**

OFFICE OF THE DIRECTOR

March 6, 2000

17031-0484706-88-110-421-12

159487366 AUTO ********** 5-DIGIT 60202

A TO RESIDENT AT   01087

11120 ELMWOOD AVE
EVANSTON, IL 60202-1203

About one week from now, you will receive a U.S. Census 2000 form in the mail.

B When you receive your form, please fill it out and mail it in promptly. Your response is very important. The United States Constitution requires a census of the United States every 10 years. Everyone living in the United States on April 1, 2000, must be counted. By completing your census form, you will make sure that you and members of your household are included in the official census count.

Official census counts are used to distribute government funds to communities and states for highways, schools, health facilities, and many other programs you and your neighbors need. Without a complete, accurate census, your community may not receive its fair share.

D You can help in another way too. We are now hiring temporary workers throughout the United States to help complete the census. Call the Local Census Office near you for more information. The phone number is available from directory assistance or the Internet at www.census.gov/jobs2000.

With your help, the census can count everyone. Please do your part. Thank you.

Sincerely,

Kenneth Prewitt

Kenneth Prewitt **C**
Director
Bureau of the Census

Enclosure

Por favor, vea el otro lado de esta página.
請翻到此頁背面。
본 페이지 뒷면을 보십시오. **E**
Xin xem mặt sau của trang này.
Basahin ang nasa likod ng pahinang ito.

United States
Census
2000

D-5(L)

PRACTICE AND APPLY

Reread the notice from the Bureau of the Census and answer the following questions.

1. Whom is the notice for?

2. What does the notice ask people to do?

3. Who must be counted in the census?

Workplace Document

Strategies for Reading

A **Read the title** to get an idea of what the document is about. Titles are usually at the top.

B **Ask yourself who needs to read the document.** Look for clues about whether it applies to you.

C **Notice any subheads or categories.** These may be underlined, in bold type, or set off in some other way. This document covers staffing, emergencies, and cleanup.

D **Look for instructions** on what jobs should be done and how to do them. Pay attention to sequence words such as *first*, *next*, *then*, *before*, and *after*.

PRACTICE AND APPLY

Reread the sample document and answer the questions.

1. What organization created the document?
2. Who needs to read the document?
3. Who should accompany children onto the playground?
4. If there is a fire, what should you do before opening a door?
5. What three things should you do before leaving for the day?

"Little Folks" Play Group **A**

Notice to Volunteers **B**

Safety Guidelines

We're glad you have volunteered to help with our Saturday morning play group for children ages 2–5. To keep our space clean and safe and our children happy, we all must follow these safety rules.

Staffing **C**
- An adult must be in the playroom at all times.
- Children who go outside to the playground must be accompanied by an adult.

Emergencies
- In case of emergency, dial 911 on the phone in the kitchen.
- In case of fire, evacuate children through the main door or the emergency exit. Before opening a door, **D** touch it to see if it is hot. A fire extinguisher is located next to the emergency exit.

Cleanup
- Make sure the playroom is clean at the end of the day. Put all toys in the toy chests. Wipe tabletops clean with a damp sponge.
- Turn off lights as you leave.

Technical Directions

Strategies for Reading

(A) Read all the steps carefully at least once before you begin.

(B) Look for numbers or letters that show the order in which to follow the steps.

(C) Match the numbers or letters to a picture if there is one.

(D) Look for words that tell you what to do, such as *press, select,* or *set.*

(E) Pay close attention to warnings or notes with more information.

(A) Setting the Sleep Timer

1. Press the MENU key. The Setup menu will appear on your television.

2. Select the Timer Setup on your screen by using the UP/DOWN arrows on your remote control.

(B) 3. Now press the RIGHT/LEFT arrows. A menu of the Timer Setup will appear on the screen.

4. Sleep Timer: Use the RIGHT/LEFT arrows to program the length of time until the TV shuts down. You can select any time from ten minutes to four hours. Press ENTER to return **(C)** to TV viewing.

Setting On/Off Timer

5. Follow steps 1 and 2 above to get to the Timer Setup menu. Using the UP/DOWN arrows on the remote control, select On Time on your screen.

6. Press the RIGHT or LEFT arrow to adjust the time your **(D)** television will turn on automatically.

7. Press the TIMER button to choose either A.M. or P.M.

8. Repeat steps 5 through 7 to set Off Time. Use the UP/DOWN arrows to select the On/Off Timer, and activate the timer by pressing a RIGHT/LEFT arrow.

WARNING: The On/Off timer will not work until the clock on **(E)** your television has been set.

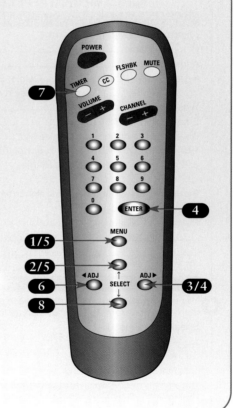

PRACTICE AND APPLY

Reread the sample directions and answer the questions.

1. What happens when you press the ENTER button?

2. Explain the steps for getting to the Timer Setup menu.

3. What does the warning tell you?

Application

Strategies for Reading

(A) Begin at the top. Skim the application to see what the different sections are.

(B) Look for **instructions about other materials** to be included with the application.

(C) Look for **difficult words or abbreviations,** such as *NA* (not applicable), *Ph.* (phone number), or *Y/N* (yes or no).

(D) Read **directions** carefully. Sometimes you must make specific choices.

(E) Watch for **sections you don't have to fill in** or **questions you don't have to answer.**

(A) CAMP CHILI PEPPER • DAY CAMP APPLICATION

CAMPER INFORMATION

Please print neatly.

Camper's Name _____ Today's Date _____

Address _____ City/State _____ Zip _____

Home Phone _____ Date of Birth _____ Male/Female (circle one)

YMCA Member? _____ **If so, enclose a copy of your membership card. (B)**

What school do you attend? _____ Grade _____

Emergency Contact _____ Home Phone _____ Work Ph. _____ **(C)**

Do you have a sibling attending camp? _____ If so, name _____

HEALTH INFORMATION: Check any of the following health problems that affect you:

___ asthma   ___ bee sting allergy   ___ food allergy   ___ diabetes

___ other (_____)   ___ NA

Please enclose a doctor's note describing any special care or medications you need.

Can you swim? _____

Please write a brief paragraph explaining why you want to attend Camp Chili Pepper.

_____

_____

_____

SESSION INFORMATION

(D) You may sign up for two activities in each session. You may sign up for the same activity more than once (for example, you may sign up for Music & Art in both Session 1 and Session 2).

Session 1 (June 17–21)

___ Activity A: Music & Art

___ Activity B: Soccer

___ Activity C: Nature Hiking

Session 2 (June 25–30)

___ Activity A: Music & Art

___ Activity B: Soccer

___ Activity C: Nature Hiking

FOR OFFICE USE ONLY

(E) Date _____   Session _____   Wait List _____   Siblings _____

PRACTICE AND APPLY

Reread the application and answer the questions.

1. List the three different sections on this application.

2. What materials might have to be submitted with the application?

3. Which section of the application should you leave blank?

4. What date should you write on the application?

Instruction Manual

Strategies for Reading

(A) **Read the title** to find out for what tasks the manual gives instructions.

(B) Notice any **subheads** or **categories**. Many manuals are divided into sections. You may not need to read the entire manual to get the information you need.

(C) Look for **instructions** on what steps to take and in what order.

(D) Pay attention to **hints, tips,** and **examples.** Hints and tips can help you avoid common mistakes. Examples give you a clearer understanding of the material.

(A) **Searching the Web**

(B) **1. Simple Searches**

(C) Your Internet connection is equipped with a search engine. Simply enter a term that you would like to find out about, and the engine will search more than one billion pages for that term.

(D) *Examples of search terms:* Shakespeare, typhoons, spiders

Hint: Make sure your search term is spelled correctly.

2. Advanced Searches

Sometimes you may need to use more than one term to perform a precise search. Here are some tips that can help you.

- Using **AND** tells the engine to search for documents that contain both terms.

  Examples: Galileo AND telescope, dogs AND training, science AND fiction

- Using **OR** tells the engine to search for documents that contain either term.

  Examples: movie OR film, car OR automobile, Kwanza OR Kwanzaa

- Using **NOT** tells the engine to search for documents that contain one item but not the other.

  Examples: Apollo NOT rocket, Titanic NOT movie, amazon NOT river

---

PRACTICE AND APPLY

Reread the sample manual and answer the questions.

1. What task does this manual explain?

2. What two types of searches does the manual explain how to perform?

3. Name the three types of advanced searches.

4. You type in "Lincoln" to search for Web pages about the city of Lincoln, Nebraska, but you keep finding information about Abraham Lincoln. What are some ways you could refine your search?

Vocabulary Handbook

❶ Context Clues

One way to figure out the meaning of a word you don't know is by using context clues. The context of a word is made up of the punctuation marks, words, sentences, and paragraphs that surround it.

1.1 *General Context* Sometimes you need to infer the meaning of an unfamiliar word by reading all the information in the sentence or paragraph.

> Kevin set out the broom, a dustpan, dusting rag, vacuum cleaner, and three trash bags before beginning the **monumental** task of cleaning his room.

1.2 *Definition Clue* Often a difficult word will be followed by a definition of its meaning. Commas, dashes, or other punctuation marks can signal a definition.

> Sometimes the explorers encountered **leads**—open channels of water—and were forced to wait until the ice formed before going on.

1.3 *Restatement Clues* Sometimes a writer restates a word or term in easier language. Commas, dashes, or other punctuation can signal restatement clues, as can expressions such as *that is, in other words,* and *or.*

> The boy put together a **hand-collated** set of trading cards; in other words, he put together a set of trading cards by hand.

1.4 *Example Clues* Sometimes a writer suggests the meanings of words with one or two examples.

> The cabin had several **annoyances**, including a leak in the roof, mildew in the shower, and a family of mice.

1.5 *Comparison Clues* Sometimes a word's meaning is suggested by a comparison to something similar. *Like* and *as* are words that signal comparison clues.

> The twins **barreled** through the living room like a tornado.

1.6 *Contrast Clues* Sometimes writers point out differences between things or ideas. Contrast clues are signaled by words like *although, but, however, unlike,* and *in contrast to.*

> The student was usually **bold,** but he became **hesitant** when he had to present a report to the class.

1.7 *Idiom and Slang* An idiom is an expression whose overall meaning is different from the meanings of the individual words. Slang is informal language containing made-up words and ordinary words used to mean something different from their meaning in formal English. Use context clues to figure out the meaning of idioms and slang.

> The mosquitoes **drove us crazy** on our hike through the woods. (idiom)

> That's a really **cool** backpack that you are wearing. (slang)

TIP One way to clarify your understanding of a word is to write a sentence using that word. Use one of the context-clue strategies in your sentence. For example, use restatement or definition clues in a sentence where understanding a word's precise meaning is important.

For more about context clues, see page 67; about idioms and slang, see page 142.

❷ Word Parts

If you know roots, base words, and affixes, you can figure out the meanings of many new words.

2.1 *Base Words* A base word is a complete word that can stand alone. Other words or word parts can be added to base words to form new words.

2.2 *Roots* Many English words contain roots that come from older languages, such as Latin, Greek, or Old English. A root is a word part that conveys the core meaning of a word. Knowing the meaning of a word's root can help you determine the word's meaning.

root	meanings	example
alt	high	altitude
vert	to turn	divert
grad	step, degree	graduate

2.3 *Prefixes* A prefix is a word part that appears at the beginning of a root or base word to form a new word. A prefix usually changes the meaning of a root or a base word.

prefix	meanings	example
ex-	out, from	export
in-	in, into, not	incite
pre-	before	preface
pro-	forward, favoring	propose
re-	again, back	rebound
un-	not, opposite	unhappy

2.4 *Suffixes* A suffix is a word part that appears at the end of a root or base word to form a new word. Some suffixes do not change word meaning.

These suffixes are
- added to nouns to change the number
- added to verbs to change the tense
- added to adjectives to change the degree of comparison
- added to adverbs to show how

suffix	meanings	example
-s, -es	to change the number of a noun	snack + -s, snacks
-ed, -ing	to change verb tense	walk + -ed, walked walk + -ing, walking
-er, -est	to change the degree of comparison in modifiers	wild + -er, wilder wild + -est, wildest

Other suffixes are added to a root or base word to change the word's meaning. These suffixes can also be used to change the word's part of speech.

suffix	meanings	example
noun -age	action or process	pilgrim + -age, pilgrimage
adjective -able	ability	remark + -able, remarkable
verb -ize	to make	public + -ize, publicize

To find the meaning of an unfamiliar word, divide the word into parts. Think about the meaning of the prefix, the suffix, and the root or base word. Use what you know to figure out the meaning of the word. Then check to see if the word makes sense in context.

For more about base words, see page 233; about prefixes and suffixes, see page 309.

❸ Word Origins

When you study a word's history and origin, you find out when, where, and how the word came to be. A complete dictionary entry includes each word's history.

> **dra•ma** (drä′mə) *n.* **1.** A work that is meant to be performed by actors. **2.** Theatrical works of a certain type or period in history. [Late Latin *drama, dramat-,* from Greek *dran,* to do or perform.]

This entry shows you that the earliest known ancestor of the word *drama* is the Greek word *dran.*

3.1 *Word Families* Words that have the same root make up a word family and have related meanings. The charts below show two common Greek and Latin roots. Notice how the meanings of the example words are related to the meanings of their roots.

Latin Root: *sens,* to sense or feel

English: **sensory** perceived through one of the senses

sensitive responds to senses or feelings

sensation a perception or feeling

Greek Root: *ast(e)r,* star

English: **asteroid** a small object in outer space

asterisk a star-shaped punctuation mark

astronomy the study of outer space

TIP Once you recognize a root in one English word, you will notice the same root in other words. Because these words developed from the same root, all of them share a core meaning.

3.2 *Foreign Words* Some words come into the English language and stay the way they were in their original language.

French	Spanish	Italian
beret	taco	alto
ballet	tornado	macaroni
vague	rodeo	cupola
mirage	bronco	

For more about word families, see page 233; about researching word origins, see page 742.

❹ Synonyms and Antonyms

When you read, pay attention to the precise words a writer uses.

4.1 *Synonyms* A synonym is a word that has the same or almost the same meaning as another word. Read each set of synonyms listed below.

occasionally/sometimes parcel/package

pledge/vow satisfy/please

rob/steal schedule/agenda

TIP You can find synonyms in a thesaurus or dictionary. In a dictionary, synonyms are often given as part of the definition of a word. Although synonyms have similar meanings, the words do not necessarily mean exactly the same thing.

4.2 *Antonyms* An antonym is a word with a meaning opposite of that of another word. Read each set of antonyms listed below.

accurate/incorrect   similar/different

reveal/conceal   rigid/flexible

fresh/stale   unusual/ordinary

Sometimes an antonym is formed by adding the negative prefix *anti-, in-,* or *un-* to a word as in the chart below.

word	prefix	antonym
climax	*anti-*	anticlimax
kind	*un-*	unkind
capable	*in-*	incapable

TIP Dictionaries of synonyms and antonyms, as well as some thesauri, can help you find antonyms.

TIP Some dictionary entries are followed by notes that discuss synonyms and antonyms. These notes often include sentences that illustrate the words' shades of meaning.

For more about synonyms and antonyms, see page 631.

⑤ Connotative and Denotative Meaning

Good writers choose just the right word to communicate specific meaning.

5.1 *Denotative Meaning* A word's dictionary meaning is called its denotation. For example, the denotative meaning of the word *thin* is "having little flesh; spare; lean."

5.2 *Connotative Meaning* The images or feelings you connect to a word give it finer **shades of meaning,** called connotation. Connotative meaning stretches beyond a word's most basic dictionary definition. Writers use connotations of words to communicate positive or negative feelings. Some examples are listed below.

Positive Connotations	Negative Connotations
thin	scrawny
careful	cowardly
fast	hasty
thrifty	cheap
young	immature

TIP A dictionary entry may be followed by a note that discusses connotative meanings of the entry word and other related words.

For more information about denotative and connotative meanings, see page 572.

6 Homonyms, Homophones, and Words with Multiple Meaning

Homonyms, multiple-meaning words, and homophones can be confusing to readers and can plague writers.

6.1 *Homonyms* Words that have the same spelling and pronunciation but different meanings and (usually) origins are called homonyms. Consider this example:

> The boy had to **stoop** to find his ball under the **stoop.**

Stoop can mean "a small porch," but an identically spelled word means "to bend down." Because the words have different origins, each word has its own dictionary entry.

6.2 *Words with Multiple Meanings* Multiple-meaning words are ones that have acquired additional meanings over time based on the original meaning. Consider these examples:

> Thinking of the horror movie made my skin **creep.**

> I saw my little brother **creep** around the corner.

These two uses of *creep* have different meanings, but both of them have developed from an original meaning. You will find all the meanings of *creep* listed in one entry in the dictionary.

6.3 *Homophones* Words that sound alike but have different meanings and spellings are called homophones. Consider this example:

> Paul heard his mother say on the phone, "I **hear** you as well as I would if you were **here** talking to me."

Homophones don't usually cause problems for readers, but they can be problems for writers. Many common words with Old English origins (*there, their; write, right*) have homophones. Be sure to check your writing for misspelled homophones.

For more about homonyms and multiple-meaning words, see page 693.

7 Analogies

7.1 *Analogy* An analogy is a statement that compares two pairs of words. The relationship between the first pair of words is the same as the relationship between the second pair of words. In the example below, each pair of words shows a relationship of an item to a category.

> TRACTOR : VEHICLE :: wrench : tool

A tractor is a type of vehicle, just as a wrench is a type of tool.

The sign : stands for "is to." The sign :: stands for "as." The analogy is read like this:

> "*Tractor* is to *vehicle* as *wrench* is to *tool*."

7.2 *Types of Analogies* Here are some common word relationships.

type of analogy	example	relationship
Part to whole	STAGE : THEATER	is a part of
Synonyms	SWEET : THOUGHTFUL	is similar in meaning
Antonyms	FANTASTIC : AWFUL	is different in meaning
Degree of intensity	SATISFACTORY : EXCELLENT	is less (or more) intense than
Characteristic to object	ROUGHNESS : SANDPAPER	is a quality of
Item to category	ANT : INSECT	is a type of

For more about analogies, see page 398.

⑧ Specialized Vocabulary

Professionals who work in fields such as law, science, or sports use their own technical or specialized vocabulary. Use these strategies to help you figure out the meanings of specialized vocabulary.

8.1 *Use Context Clues* Often the surrounding text gives clues that help you infer the meaning of an unfamiliar term.

8.2 *Use Reference Tools* Textbooks often define special terms when they are first introduced. Look for definitions or restatement clues in parentheses. Also you can try to find definitions in footnotes, a glossary, or a dictionary. If you need more information, refer to a specialized reference, such as

• an encyclopedia

• a field guide

• an atlas

• a user's manual

• a technical dictionary

⑨ Decoding Multisyllabic Words

Many words are familiar to you when you speak them or hear them. Sometimes these same words may be unfamiliar to you when you see them in print. When you come across a word unfamiliar in print, first try to pronounce it to see if you might recognize it. Use these syllabication generalizations to help you figure out a word's pronunciation.

Generalization 1: VCCV

When there are two consonants between two vowels, divide between the two consonants unless they are a blend or a digraph.

  pic/ture   a/brupt   feath/er

Generalization 2: VCCCV

When there are three consonants between two vowels, divide between the blend or the digraph and the other consonant.

  an/gler   mer/chant   tum/bler

Generalization 3: VCCV

When there are two consonants between two vowels, divide between the consonants, unless they are a blend or a digraph. The first syllable is a closed syllable, and the vowel is short.

  lath/er   ush/er   ten/der

Generalization 4: Common Vowel Clusters

Do not split common vowel clusters, such as long vowel digraphs, r-controlled vowels, and vowel diphthongs.

  par/ty   poi/son   fea/ture

Generalization 5: VCV

When you see a VCV pattern in the middle of a word, divide the word either before or after the consonant. Divide the word after the consonant if the first vowel sound is short. Divide the word before the consonant if the first vowel sound is long.

  mod/el   ro/bot   cra/zy

Generalization 6: Compound Words

Divide compound words between the individual words.

  grape/vine   life/guard

Generalization 7: Affixes

When a word includes an affix, divide between the base word and the affix.

  re/bound   rest/less

Spelling Handbook

1 Improving Your Spelling

Good spelling is important in all writing, from personal letters to research reports. You can improve your spelling by practicing a few good habits. Read and write as frequently as you can. Keep a personal spelling list of words you are not sure how to spell and review this list regularly. The following tips may also be helpful.

Ways to Improve Your Spelling

1. **Identify your spelling demons and conquer them.** Keep a list of the words you have misspelled in written assignments.

2. **Pronounce words carefully.** Pronouncing words correctly will help you spell them correctly. For example, if you pronounce the word *probably* correctly, you will not misspell it as *probly*.

3. **Get into the habit of seeing the letters in a word.** Look carefully at new or difficult words. For example, look at a word like *picnic*, close your eyes and picture the word in your mind, and spell it to yourself: p–i–c–n–i–c.

4. **Create a memory device for a tricky word.** Notice the following examples of memory devices.

bus**i**ness (i)	**I** was involved in a big bus**i**ness.
princi**pal** (pal)	The princi**pal** is my **pal**.
princi**ple** (ple)	Follow this princi**ple**, **ple**ase.
station**er**y (er)	Station**er**y is fine pap**er**.

How to Master the Spelling of Difficult Words

1. Look at the word and say it one syllable at a time.
2. Look at the letters and say each one.
3. Write the word without looking at it.
4. Check to see whether you spelled the word correctly. If you made a mistake, repeat steps 1–3.

One of the best ways to improve your spelling is to learn the following rules.

Words Ending in a Silent e
When a suffix beginning with a vowel is added to a word ending in a silent *e*, the *e* is usually dropped.

relate + -ion = relation
create + -ive = creative
amaze + -ing = amazing
fame + -ous = famous

When a suffix beginning with a consonant is added to a word ending in a silent *e*, the *e* is usually retained.

hope + -ful = hopeful
noise + -less = noiseless
state + -ment = statement
wide + -ly = widely

The following words are exceptions: *truly, argument, ninth, wholly.*

Words Ending in y
When a suffix is added to a word ending in *y* preceded by a consonant, the *y* usually is changed to *i*.

easy + -ly = easily
sixty + -eth = sixtieth

When *-ing* is added, however, the *y* does not change.

hurry + -ed = hurried
but hurry + -ing = hurrying
study + -ed = studied
but study + -ing = studying

When a suffix is added to a word ending in _y_ preceded by a vowel, the _y_ usually does not change.

employ + -er = employer
play + -ing = playing

Words Ending in a Consonant

In words of _one_ syllable that end in _one_ consonant preceded by one vowel, double the final consonant before adding an ending that begins with a vowel, such as _-ing, -ed,_ or _-er._ These are sometimes called 1 + 1 + 1 words.

bat + -ed = batted
bed + -ing = bedding
run + -er = runner
grab + -ed = grabbed

The rule does not apply to words of one syllable that end in one consonant preceded by two vowels.

treat + -ing = treating
loot + -ed = looted
near + -er = nearer
feel + -ing = feeling

The Suffixes -ness and -ly

When the suffix _-ly_ is added to a word ending in _l,_ both _l_'s are retained. When _-ness_ is added to a word ending in _n,_ retain both of the _n_'s.

actual + -ly = actually
thin + -ness = thinness

Prefixes

When a prefix is added to a word, do not drop a letter from either the prefix or the base word.

mis- + spell = misspell
re- + place = replace
il- + legal = illegal
im- + perfect = imperfect
un- + even = uneven
dis- + approve = disapprove
pre- + view = preview
ir- + regular = irregular

Words with the Seed Sound

Only one English word ends in _–sede: supersede._ Three words end in _–ceed: exceed, proceed,_ and _succeed._ All other verbs ending in the sound _seed_ are spelled with _–cede._

concede   precede   recede   secede

Words with ie and ei

When the sound is long _e_ (ē), the word is spelled _ie_ except after _c._

_i_ before _e_		except after _c_	
believe	shield	ceiling	deceive
yield	field	receive	conceive
niece	brief	conceit	receipt

The following words are exceptions: _either, weird, species, neither, seize, leisure._

❷ Using the Right Word

Like good musicians or good athletes, good writers do the little things well. One of these little things is the correct use of words. It is actually one of the keys to good writing. As you look at the following groups of words, notice how the words' meanings differ. Be careful when you spell those easily confused words.

accept, except   _Accept_ means "to agree to something" or "to receive something." _Except_ usually means "not including."

Kay did _accept_ the invitation to go camping.

Everyone _except_ the reporters dashed onto the field.

all ready, already   _All ready_ means "all are ready" or "completely prepared." _Already_ means "previously."

The astronauts were _all ready_ for the landing.

The other team has _already_ started practicing.

all right   *All right* is the correct spelling. *Alright* is nonstandard English and should not be used.

a lot   *A lot* is informal. It should not be used in formal writing. *Alot* is always incorrect.

borrow, lend   *Borrow* means "to receive something on loan." *Lend* means "to give out temporarily."

> Some students *borrow* money to pay for a college education.

> Please *lend* me a pencil.

capital, capitol, the Capitol   *Capital* means "excellent," "most serious," or "most important"; it also means "seat of government." *Capitol* means a "building in which a state legislature meets." The Capitol is the building in Washington, D.C., in which the U.S. Congress meets.

> Murder is a *capital* crime.

> The state senate held hearings at the *capitol.*

> In 1814 British soldiers burned the White House and *the Capitol.*

desert, dessert   *Des´ert* means "a wilderness" or "a dry sandy, barren region." *Desert´* means "to abandon." A *dessert* is a sweet food, such as a cake or pie, served at the end of a meal.

> The Gobi *Desert* is in eastern Asia.

> The soldiers *deserted* their position.

> Strawberry pie is a delicious *dessert.*

good, well   *Good* is always an adjective. *Well* is usually an adverb. *Well* can be an adjective meaning "in good health."

> Juan felt *good* about finishing the marathon.

> Julio plays the drums *well.*

> Marco was not *well* enough to play.

hear, here   *Hear* means "to listen to." *Here* means "in this place."

> Because of the noisy crowd, we couldn't *hear* the candidate.

> After leaving Italy, my grandparents settled *here* in Dallas.

its, it's   *Its* is a possessive pronoun. *It's* is a contraction of *it is* or *it has.*

> The city lost *its* electricity.

> *It's* almost time for summer vacation.

Lay, lie   *Lay* is a verb that means "to place." It takes a direct object. *Lie* is a verb that means "to be in a certain place" or "to be in a horizontal position." *Lie* never takes a direct object.

> *Lay* the books on the desk.

> Our land *lies* near the river.

lead, led   *Lead* can be a noun that means "a heavy metal" or a verb that means "to show the way." *Led* is the verb's past-tense form.

> A plumb is a weight made of *lead.*

> Maria *leads* the league in home runs.

> She *led* a discussion on ways to help homeless people.

learn, teach   *Learn* means "to gain knowledge." *Teach* means "to instruct."

> Raul is *learning* how to play chess.

> Alicia is *teaching* Spanish.

like, as, as if   Use *as* or *as if,* not *like,* to introduce a clause.

> He walks *as if* his ankle were sore.

loose, lose   *Loose* means "free" or "not fastened." *Lose* means "to mislay or suffer the loss of something."

> The door hinges are *loose.*

> The plane began to *lose* altitude.

of   Use *have,* not *of,* in phrases such as *could have, should have,* and *must have.*

> We could *have* won if our leading scorer had not fouled out.

passed, past   *Passed* is the past tense of pass and means "went by." *Past* is an adjective that means "of a former time." *Past* is also a noun that means "the time gone by."

We *passed* through the Grand Tetons during our vacation.

We have learned from our *past* experiences.

Ebenezer Scrooge relives his *past.*

peace, piece   *Peace* means "calm or quiet." *Piece* means "a part of something."

Music can bring a sense of *peace.*

We cut the pizza into *pieces.*

principal, principle   *Principal* means "of chief or central importance" or "the head of a school." *Principle* means "basic truth," "standard," or "rule of behavior."

The *principal* cities of France include Paris and Marseilles.

The school *principal* presented awards.

In social studies we discussed the *principles* of government.

raise, rise   *Raise* means "to lift" or "to make something go up." It takes a direct object. *Rise* means "to go upward." It does not take a direct object.

Dr. King's speeches *raised* hopes for a more just society.

The sun *rises* in the east.

set, sit   *Set* means "to place." It takes a direct object. *Sit* means "to occupy a seat or a place." It does not take a direct object.

He *set* the papers on the desk.

Let's *sit* here.

stationary, stationery   *Stationary* means "fixed or unmoving." *Stationery* means "fine paper for writing letters."

A *stationary* clock glowed on the wall.

I received a letter written on White House *stationery.*

than, then   *Than* is used to introduce the second part of a comparison. *Then* means "next in order."

The pen is mightier *than* the sword.

The air grew still, and *then* raindrops pattered on the roof.

their, there, they're   *Their* means "belonging to them." *There* means "in that place." *They're* is a contraction of *they are.*

In 1804, Lewis and Clark led *their* expedition from St. Louis.

The explorers built a fort in what is now North Dakota, and they spent the winter *there.*

Lewis and Clark collected valuable information about the geography of the Pacific Northwest; *they're* remembered for their wilderness travels.

to, too, two   *To* means "toward" or "in the direction of." *Too* means "also" or "very." *Two* is the number 2.

We went *to* the Library of Congress in Washington, D.C.

It was *too* cold to play baseball.

Two newspapers sent critics to review the new play.

weather, whether   *Weather* refers to conditions such as temperature or cloudiness. *Whether* expresses a choice.

Meteorologists use computers to forecast the *weather.*

We must decide *whether* to speak out or remain silent.

whose, who's   *Whose* is the possessive form of *who. Who's* is a contraction of *who is* or *who has.*

Whose arguments seem more convincing?

Who's going to volunteer to work at the hospital?

your, you're   *Your* is the possessive form of *you. You're* is a contraction of *you are.*

Please take *your* places at the starting line.

You're going to the library after school, aren't you?

① The Writing Process

The writing process consists of four stages: prewriting, drafting, revising and editing, and publishing and reflecting. As the graphic below shows, these stages are not steps that you must complete in a set order. Rather, you may return to any one at any time in your writing process, using feedback from your readers along the way.

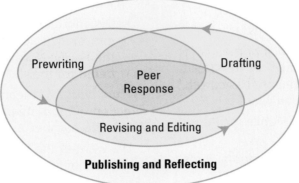

Prewriting · Drafting · Peer Response · Revising and Editing · **Publishing and Reflecting**

⑴ Prewriting

In the prewriting stage, you explore your ideas and discover what you want to write about.

Finding Ideas for Writing
Try one or more of the following techniques to help you find a writing topic.

Personal Techniques
- Practice imaging, or trying to remember mainly sensory details about a subject—its look, sound, feel, taste, and smell.
- Complete a knowledge inventory to discover what you already know about a subject.
- Browse through magazines, newspapers, and on-line bulletin boards for ideas.
- Start a clip file of articles that you want to save for future reference. Be sure to label each clip with source information.

Sharing Techniques
- With a group, brainstorm a topic by trying to come up with as many ideas as you can without stopping to critique or examine them.
- Interview someone who knows a great deal about your topic.

Writing Techniques
- After freewriting on a topic, try looping, or choosing your best idea for more freewriting. Repeat the loop at least once.
- Make a list to help you organize ideas, examine them, or identify areas for further research.

Graphic Techniques
- Create a pro-and-con chart to compare the positive and negative aspects of an idea or a course of action.
- Use a cluster map or tree diagram to explore subordinate ideas that relate to your general topic or central idea.

Determining Your Purpose
Your purpose for writing may be to express yourself, to entertain, to describe, to explain, to analyze, or to persuade. To clarify it, ask questions like these:

- Why did I choose to write about my topic?
- What aspects of the topic mean the most to me?
- What do I want others to think or feel after they read my writing?

Identifying Your Audience

Knowing who will read your writing can help you focus your topic and choose relevant details. As you think about your readers, ask yourself questions like these:

- What does my audience already know about my topic?
- What will they be most interested in?
- What language is most appropriate for this audience?

LINK TO LITERATURE Roald Dahl—the author of *Boy: Tales of Childhood,* on page 533—understood the importance of identifying his audience. According to Dahl, "Children are a great discipline because they are highly critical. . . . And if you think a child is getting bored, you must think up something that jolts [the child] back. Something that tickles."

Drafting

In the drafting stage, you put your ideas on paper and allow them to develop and change as you write.

Two broad approaches in this stage are discovery drafting and planned drafting.

Discovery drafting is a good approach when you are not quite sure what you think about your subject. You just plunge into your draft and let your feelings and ideas lead you where they will. After finishing a discovery draft, you may decide to start another draft, do more prewriting, or revise your first draft.

Planned drafting may work better for research reports, critical reviews, and other kinds of formal writing. Try making a writing plan or a scratch outline before you begin drafting. Then, as you write, you can fill in the details.
The changes you make in your writing during this stage usually fall into three categories: revising for content, revising for structure, and proofreading to correct mistakes in mechanics.

Use the questions that follow to assess problems and determine what changes would improve your work.

Revising, Editing, and Proofreading

Revising for Content

- Does my writing have a main idea or central focus? Is my thesis clear?
- Have I incorporated adequate detail? Where might I include a telling detail, revealing statistic, or vivid example?
- Is any material unnecessary, irrelevant, or confusing?

WRITING TIP Be sure to consider the needs of your audience as you answer the questions under Revising for Content and Revising for Structure. For example, before you can determine whether any of your material is unnecessary or irrelevant, you need to identify what your audience already knows.

Revising for Structure

- Is my writing unified? Do all ideas and supporting details pertain to my main idea or advance my thesis?
- Is my writing clear and coherent? Is the flow of sentences and paragraphs smooth and logical?
- Do I need to add transitional words, phrases, or sentences to make the relationships among ideas clearer?
- Are my sentences well constructed? What sentences might I combine to improve the grace and rhythm of my writing?

Proofreading to Correct Mistakes in Grammar, Usage, and Mechanics

When you are satisfied with your revision, proofread your paper, looking for mistakes in grammar, usage, and mechanics. You may want to do this several times, looking for different types of mistakes each time. The following checklist may help.

Sentence Structure and Agreement
- Are there any run-on sentences or sentence fragments?
- Do all verbs agree with their subjects?

- Do all pronouns agree with their antecedents?
- Are verb tenses correct and consistent?

Forms of Words
- Do adverbs and adjectives modify the appropriate words?
- Are all forms of *be* and other irregular verbs used correctly?
- Are pronouns used correctly?
- Are comparative and superlative forms of adjectives correct?

Capitalization, Punctuation, and Spelling
- Is any punctuation mark missing or not needed?
- Are all words spelled correctly?
- Are all proper nouns and all proper adjectives capitalized?

WRITING TIP For help identifying and correcting problems that are listed in the Proofreading Checklist, see the Grammar Handbook, pages R66–R99.

You might wish to mark changes on your paper by using the proofreading symbols shown in the chart below.

Proofreading Symbols

Symbol	Meaning	Symbol	Meaning
∧	Add letters or words.	/	Make a capital letter lowercase.
⊙	Add a period.	¶	Begin a new paragraph.
≡	Capitalize a letter.	ℊ	Delete letters or words.
⌣	Close up a space.	∿	Switch the positions of letters or words.
∧	Add a comma.		

1.4 Publishing and Reflecting

Always consider sharing your finished writing with a wider audience. Reflecting on your writing is another good way to bring closure to a project.

Creative Publishing Ideas
Following are some ideas for publishing and sharing your writing.

- Post your writing on an electronic bulletin board or send it to others via email.
- Create a multimedia presentation and share it with classmates.
- Publish your writing in a school newspaper or literary magazine.
- Present your work orally in a report, a speech, a reading, or a dramatic performance.
- Submit your writing to a local newspaper or a magazine that publishes student writing.
- Form a writing exchange group with other students.

WRITING TIP You might work with other students to publish an anthology of class writing. Then exchange your anthology with another class or another school. Reading the work of other student writers will help you get ideas for new writing projects and find ways to improve your work.

Reflecting on Your Writing
Think about your writing process and whether you would like to add what you have written to your portfolio. You might attach a note in which you answer questions like these:

- What did I learn about myself and my subject through this writing project?
- Which parts of the writing process did I most enjoy and which did I least enjoy?
- As I wrote, what was my biggest problem? How did I solve it?
- What did I learn that I can use the next time I write?

1.5 Using Peer Response

Peer response consists of the suggestions and comments your peers or classmates make about your writing.

You can ask a peer reader for help at any point in the writing process. For example, your peers can help you develop a topic, narrow your focus, discover confusing passages, or organize your writing.

Questions for Your Peer Readers

You can help your peer readers provide you with the most useful kinds of feedback by following these guidelines:

- Tell readers where you are in the writing process. Are you still trying out ideas, or have you completed a draft?

- Ask questions that will help you get specific information about your writing. Open-ended questions that require more than yes-or-no answers are more likely to give you information you can use as you revise.

- Give your readers plenty of time to respond thoughtfully to your writing.

- Encourage your readers to be honest when they respond to your work. It's OK if you don't agree with them—you always get to decide which changes to make.

Tips for Being a Peer Reader

Follow these guidelines when you respond to someone else's work:

- Respect the writer's feelings.

- Make sure you understand what kind of feedback the writer is looking for, and then respond accordingly.

- Use "I" statements, such as "I like . . . ," "I think . . . ," or "It would help me if . . . ." Remember that your impressions and opinions may not be the same as someone else's.

WRITING TIP Writers are better able to absorb criticism of their work if they first receive positive feedback. When you act as a peer reader, try to start your review by telling something you like about the piece. The chart below explains different peer-response techniques to use when you are ready to share your work.

Peer-Response Techniques

Sharing Use this when you are just exploring ideas or when you want to celebrate the completion of a piece of writing.

- *Will you please read or listen to my writing without criticizing or making suggestions afterward?*

Summarizing Use this when you want to know if your main idea or goals are clear.

- *What do you think I'm saying? What's my main idea or message?*

Replying Use this strategy when you want to make your writing richer by adding new ideas.

- *What are your ideas about my topic? What do you think about what I have said in my piece?*

Responding to Specific Features Use this when you want a quick overview of the strengths and weaknesses of your writing.

- *Are the ideas supported with enough examples? Did I persuade you? Is the organization clear enough for you to follow the ideas?*

Telling Use this to find out which parts of your writing are affecting readers the way you want and which parts are confusing.

- *What did you think or feel as you read my words? Would you show me which passage you were reading when you had that response?*

② Building Blocks of Good Writing

Whatever your purpose in writing, you need to capture your readers' interest, organize your ideas well, and present your thoughts clearly. Giving special attention to some particular parts of a story or an essay can make your writing more enjoyable and more effective.

2.1 Introductions

When you flip through a magazine trying to decide which articles to read, the opening paragraph is often critical. If it does not grab your attention, you are likely to turn the page.

Kinds of Introductions
Here are some introduction techniques that can capture a reader's interest.

- Make a surprising statement.
- Provide a description.
- Pose a question.
- Relate an anecdote.
- Address the reader directly.
- Begin with a thesis statement.

Make a Surprising Statement Beginning with a startling statement or an interesting fact can capture your reader's curiosity about the subject, as in the model below.

> MODEL
> Bats may seem like a nuisance, but not as much as the 99 pounds of insects a colony of bats can eat in one night. Despite their ugly faces and all the scary stories about them, bats are very important and useful animals.

Provide a Description A vivid description sets a mood and brings a scene to life for your reader. Here, details about wild geese swimming in an unfrozen river during the winter set the tone for an essay about water pollution.

> MODEL
> The temperature is 15 degrees. Drifts of snow hide picnic tables and swings. In the middle of the park, however, steam rises from a lake where Canada geese swim. It sounds beautiful, but the water is warm because it has been heated by a chemical plant upriver. In fact, the geese should have migrated south by now.

Ask a Question Beginning with a question can make your reader want to read on to find out the answer. The following introduction asks what two seemingly different things have in common.

> MODEL
> What do billiard balls and movie film have in common? It was in an effort to find a substitute for ivory billiard balls that John Hyatt created celluloid. This plastic substance was also used to make the first movies.

Relate an Anecdote Beginning with a brief anecdote, or story, can hook readers and help you make a point in a dramatic way. The anecdote below introduces a humorous essay about a childhood experience.

> MODEL
> When I was younger, my friends and I would rub balloons in our hair and make them stick to our clothes. Someone once said, "I get a charge out of this," not knowing that we were really generating static electricity.

Address the Reader Directly Speaking directly to readers establishes a friendly, informal tone and involves them in your topic.

> MODEL
>
> **Find out how to maintain your cardio-vascular system while enjoying yourself. Come to a free demonstration of Fit for Life at the Community Center Friday night at 7:00 P.M.**

Begin with a Thesis Statement A thesis statement expressing a paper's main idea may be woven into both the beginning and the end of nonfiction writing. The following is a thesis statement that introduces a literary analysis.

> MODEL
>
> **In "The Great Taos Bank Robbery," Tony Hillerman presents eccentric characters with loving detail. It is clear that he has affection for the hapless criminals as well as for the fascinated, easygoing townspeople.**

WRITING TIP In order to write the best introduction for your paper, you may want to try more than one of the methods and then decide which is the most effective for your purpose and audience.

2.2 Paragraphs

A paragraph is made up of sentences that work together to develop an idea or accomplish a purpose. Whether or not it contains a topic sentence stating the main idea, a good paragraph must have unity and coherence.

Unity

A paragraph has unity when all the sentences support and develop one stated or implied idea. Use the following techniques to create unity in your paragraphs.

Write a Topic Sentence A topic sentence states the main idea of the paragraph; all other sentences in the paragraph provide supporting details. A topic sentence is often the first sentence in a paragraph. However, it may also appear later in the paragraph or at the end, to summarize or reinforce the main idea.

> MODEL
>
> **Flying a hot-air balloon looks fun, but it requires a good mathematician to fly one safely. Since a balloon is controlled by heating and cooling the air inside the balloon, the pilot must know the temperature of the air outside it and how high he or she plans to fly in order to calculate the maximum weight the balloon can carry. It the pilot doesn't do the math correctly, the balloon could crash.**

LINK TO LITERATURE Notice the use of strong topic sentences in "The Noble Experiment" by Jackie Robinson, as told to Alfred Duckett. For example, on page 290 the first paragraph begins, "Winning his directors' approval was almost insignificant in contrast to the task which now lay ahead of the Dodger president." The rest of the paragraph then explains that task in detail.

Coherence

A paragraph is coherent when all its sentences are related to one another and flow logically from one to the next. The following techniques will help you achieve coherence in paragraphs.

- Present your ideas in the most logical order.
- Use pronouns, synonyms, and repeated words to connect ideas.
- Use transitional devices to show the relationships among ideas.

In the model below, the writer used some of these techniques to create a unified paragraph.

> MODEL
>
> **Just the name "alligator snapping turtle" brings to mind a ferocious, frightening creature. But this fascinating creature is protected by law. The alligator snapping turtle can grow to more than 200 pounds. In fact, whereas common snapping turtles rarely weigh 30 pounds, alligator snappers have been recorded with weights up to 300 pounds.**

2.3 Transitions

Transitions are words and phrases that show the connections between details. Clear transitions help show how your ideas relate to each other.

Kinds of Transitions

Transitions can help readers understand several kinds of relationships:

- Time or sequence
- Spatial order
- Degree of importance
- Compare and contrast
- Cause and effect

Time or Sequence Some transitions help to clarify the sequence of events over time. When you are telling a story or describing a process, you can connect ideas with such transitional words as *first, second, always, then, next, later, soon, before, finally, after, earlier, afterward,* and *tomorrow.*

> MODEL
> Long *before* mountain bikes were made, bicycles were much less comfortable. The *first* cycle, which actually had four wheels, was made in 1645 and had to be walked. *Later,* two-wheeled cycles with pedals were called boneshakers because of their bumpy ride.

Spatial Order Transitional words and phrases such as *in front, behind, next to, along, nearest, lowest, above, below, underneath, on the left,* and *in the middle* can help readers visualize a scene.

> MODEL
> The audience entered the theater *from the back.* The stage was *in front,* and fire exits were located *to the right and left* of the stage.

Degree of Importance Transitional words such as *mainly, strongest, weakest, first, second, most important, least important, worst,* and *best* may be used to rank ideas or to show degree of importance.

> MODEL
> At *best*, the canoeing trip would mean not hearing my little brother and sister squabbling over the TV. *At the very worst,* I could expect to be living in wet clothes for two weeks.

Compare and Contrast Words and phrases such as *similarly, likewise, also, like, as, neither . . . nor,* and *either . . . or* show similarity between details. However, *by contrast, yet, but, than, unlike, instead, whereas,* and *while* show difference. Note the use of both types of transitions in the model below.

> MODEL
> *While* my local public library is a quieter place to study *than* home, I don't always get much done in the library. I'm so used to the cheerful chatter of my baby brother that, *by contrast,* the stillness of the library makes me sleepy.

WRITING TIP When you begin a sentence with a transition such as *most important, therefore, nevertheless, still,* or *instead,* set the transition off with a comma.

Cause and Effect When you are writing about a cause-and-effect relationship, use transitional words and phrases such as *since, because, thus, therefore, so, due to, for this reason,* and *as a result* to help clarify that relationship and to make your writing coherent.

> MODEL
> *Because* we missed seven days of school as a result of snowstorms, the school year will be extended. *Therefore,* we will be in school until June 17.

Conclusions

A conclusion should leave readers with a strong final impression. Try any of these approaches.

Kinds of Conclusions

Here are some effective methods for bringing your writing to a conclusion:

• Restate your thesis.
• Ask a question.
• Make a recommendation.
• End with the last event.

Restate Your Thesis A good way to conclude an essay is by restating your thesis, or main idea, in different words. If possible, link the beginning of your conclusion with the information you have presented, as the model below shows.

> MODEL
> **As these arguments show, planting a tree on Arbor Day is more than just a pleasant symbolic act. It also makes your neighborhood a more attractive place and sets an example for others to follow. Planting one tree will make a difference in the environment that goes well beyond this one day.**

Ask a Question Try asking a question that sums up what you have said and gives readers something new to think about. The question below concludes a piece of persuasive writing and suggests a course of action.

> MODEL
> **If tutoring a younger student in writing, reading, or math can help you do better in these subjects yourself, shouldn't you take advantage of the opportunities to tutor at Western Elementary School?**

Make a Recommendation When you are persuading your audience to take a position on an issue, you can conclude by recommending a specific course of action.

> MODEL
> **Since learning a foreign language gives you a chance to expand your world view and make new friends, register for one of the introductory courses that start next fall.**

End with the Last Event If you're telling a story, you may end with the last thing that happens. Here, the ending includes an important moment for the narrator.

> MODEL
> **As I raced down the basketball court in the final seconds of the game, I felt as alone as I did on all those nights practicing by myself in the driveway. My perfect lay-up drew yells from the crowd, but I was cheering for myself on the inside.**

 Elaboration

Elaboration is the process of developing a writing idea by providing specific supporting details so your readers aren't left with unanswered questions.

• **Facts and Statistics** A fact is a statement that can be proved, while a statistic is a fact stated in numbers. Make sure the facts and statistics you supply are from a reliable, up-to-date source. As in the model below, the facts and statistics you use should strongly support the statements you make.

> MODEL
> **The Statue of Liberty, one of the most popular monuments in the United States, is expensive to maintain. From 1983 to 1986, it cost $66 million to renovate the copper-covered 151-foot-tall statue.**

WRITING TIP Facts and statistics are especially useful in supporting opinions. Be sure that you double-check in your original sources the accuracy of all facts and statistics you cite.

- **Sensory Details** Details that show how something looks, sounds, tastes, smells, or feels can enliven a description, making readers feel they are actually experiencing what you are describing. Which senses does the writer appeal to in this paragraph?

> MODEL
>
> **I was nervous during my math test last week. Chewing on my pencil left my mouth feeling dry and flaky. My palms were sweating so much, they left stains on the pages. The ticking of the clock seemed like the beating of a drum inside my head.**

- **Incidents** From our earliest years, we are interested in hearing stories. One way to illustrate a point powerfully is to relate an incident or tell a story, as shown in the example below.

> MODEL
>
> **People who are afraid of heights tend to panic even in perfectly safe situations. When my friend Jill and I rode to the top floor of a shopping mall, I enjoyed the view from the glass-enclosed elevator, but Jill's face was pale and her hands trembled.**

- **Examples** The model below shows how using an example can help support or clarify an idea. A well-chosen example often can be more effective than a lengthy explanation.

> MODEL
>
> **The origins of today's professional sporting events can be traced to ancient games from countries all over the world. For example, hockey is believed to have come from an old Dutch game called *kolf*, played on the ice with a ball and crooked sticks.**

LINK TO LITERATURE Notice on page 225 the use of examples in the selection from Russell Freedman's *Immigrant Kids.* When the writer states that none of the immigrants forgot his or her first glimpse of the Statue of Liberty, he elaborates by using the example of immigrant Edward Corsi's first impression.

- **Quotations** Choose quotations that clearly support your points and be sure that you copy each quotation word for word. Remember always to credit the source.

> MODEL
>
> **Usually, the reader is left to infer the theme of a work, but sometimes the author actually states the theme of his or her work. After the tragic events that come to pass in Rod Serling's teleplay *The Monsters Are Due on Maple Street*, the narrator says to the audience, "The tools of conquest do not necessarily come with bombs and explosions and fallout. There are weapons that are simply thoughts, attitudes, prejudices—to be found only in the minds of men. For the record, prejudices can kill and suspicion can destroy."**

2.6 Using Language Effectively

Effective use of language can help readers to recognize the significance of an issue, to visualize a scene, or to understand a character.

- **Specific Nouns** Nouns are specific when they refer to individual or particular things. If you refer to a city, you are being general. If you refer to Dallas, you are being specific. Specific nouns help readers identify the *who, what,* and *where* of your message.

- **Specific Verbs** Verbs are the most powerful words in sentences. They convey the action, the movement, and sometimes the drama of thoughts and observations. Verbs such as *trudged, skipped,* and *sauntered* provide a more vivid picture of the action than the verb *walked.*

- **Specific Modifiers** Use modifiers sparingly, but when you use them, make them count. Is the building *big* or *towering*? Are your poodle's paws *small* or *petite*? Once again, it is the more specific word that carries the greater impact.

③ Descriptive Writing

Descriptive writing appears almost everywhere, from cookbooks to poems. You might use a description to introduce a character in a narrative or to create a strong closing to a persuasive essay. Whatever your purpose and wherever you use description, the following guidelines for good descriptive writing will help you.

③.1 Key Techniques

Consider Your Goals What do you want to accomplish in writing your description? Do you want to show why something is important to you? Do you want to make a person or scene more memorable? Do you want to explain an event?

Identify Your Audience Who will read your description? How familiar are they with your subject? What background information will they need? Which details will they find most interesting?

Gather Sensory Details Which sights, smells, tastes, sounds, and textures make your subject come alive? Which details stick in your mind when you observe or recall your subject? Which senses does it most strongly affect?

> MODEL
> **Red and gold pennants welcomed us to the fairgrounds, where the delicious aroma of popcorn mingled with the pungent odor of the animals. Food vendors hawked their wares, and the tinny music of the carousel filled the air. Munching on roasted peanuts, we took our seats on the rough benches of the judging arena.**

You might want to use a chart like the one shown here to collect sensory details about your subject.

Sights	Sounds	Textures	Smells	Tastes

Organize Your Details Details that are presented in a logical order help the reader form a mental picture of the subject. Descriptive details may be organized chronologically, spatially, by order of importance, or by order of impression.

> MODEL
> **As I stepped into my grandmother's front hall, a whirl of sweet and salty odors overwhelmed me. Peeking around the corner, I witnessed a parade of pies, breads, and salads stretching across every inch of counter space.**

LINK TO LITERATURE Note on page 440 the organization of details describing Miss Pride's shop in Joan Aiken's "The Serial Garden." The narrator begins with the shop window as seen from the outside, then describes the interior of the store, and finally shows the reader Miss Pride herself.

Show, Don't Tell Instead of just telling about a subject in a general way, provide details and quotations that expand and support what you want to say and that enable your readers to share your experience. The following sentence, for example, just tells and doesn't show: *I was proud of myself when the local paper published my article.* The model below uses descriptive details to show how proud the writer felt:

> MODEL
> **I've delivered newspapers since I was eight, but last Thursday, for the first time, the newspaper printed an article I had written for a contest. I bought a pad of sticky notes and left messages for my customers: "Check out page B7. Enjoy the paper today." I thought about signing the article, but I decided that would be too much.**

3.2 Options for Organization

Spatial Order Choose one of these options to show the spatial order of a scene.

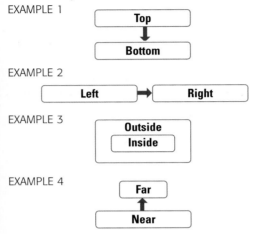

EXAMPLE 1 Top → Bottom

EXAMPLE 2 Left → Right

EXAMPLE 3 Outside / Inside

EXAMPLE 4 Far ← Near

MODEL
The room was quiet—too quiet. To my left loomed the big white refrigerator. To my right squatted the gas stove, blue pilots glowing. Straight ahead sat the huge island. Cutting board, knife, and half-chopped carrot lay abandoned upon it now. Stepping cautiously to the right of the island, I came in view of the oven. That's where I froze. The oven door was open. A faint, white light pulsed and flickered high in one corner.

WRITING TIP Some useful transitions for showing spatial relationships are *behind, below, here, in the distance, on the left, over,* and *on top.*

Order of Impression Order of impression is how you notice details.

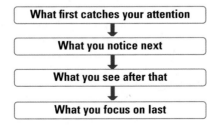

What first catches your attention → What you notice next → What you see after that → What you focus on last

MODEL
As she lost her balance on the slippery pebbles, her first thought was that she was going to sprain her ankle and be swept away by the surf. Her heart beat rapidly, but before she knew it, she was sitting in the sand while the warm surf rolled in, almost covering her. She realized that the water was not going to reach beyond her shoulders and that she was safe. Then, as suddenly, she felt the tug of the water in the other direction as the undertow flowed back, sweeping the sand from under her as it went. As soon as the water had receded she scrambled to her feet.

WRITING TIP Use transitions that help readers understand the order of the impressions you are describing. Some useful transitions are *after, next, during, first, before, finally,* and *then.*

Order of Importance You might use order of importance to organize your description.

Least Important → More Important → Most Important

MODEL
I think our school should offer karate as part of the gym program. There are several reasons this is a good idea. First, karate is fun, and anyone can learn to do it. Many students who want to learn martial arts can't afford to because private lessons are so expensive. Karate is also a great form of exercise. It improves strength, coordination, and grace. The most important reason, though, is that learning karate makes students more confident and gives them skills that can help them throughout life.

WRITING TIP Use transitions that help the reader understand the order of importance. Some useful transitions are *first, second, mainly, more important, less important,* and *least important.*

Narrative Writing

4

Narrative writing tells a story. If you write a story from your imagination, it is a fictional narrative. A true story about actual events is a nonfictional narrative. Narrative writing can be found in short stories, novels, news articles, and biographies.

RUBRIC STANDARDS FOR WRITING

A successful narrative should

- include descriptive details and dialogue to develop the characters, setting, and plot
- have a clear beginning, middle, and end
- have a logical organization with clues and transitions to help the reader understand the order of events
- maintain a consistent tone and point of view
- use language that is appropriate for the audience
- demonstrate the significance of events or ideas

4.1 Key Techniques

Identify the Main Events What are the most important events in your narrative? Is each event part of the chain of events needed to tell the story? In a fictional narrative, this series of events is the story's plot.

MODEL

Event 1	A kind stranger gives Roger money he doesn't really deserve.
Event 2	Roger goes to buy a fancy new bike with the money.
Event 3	A salesperson accuses him of not having the money to buy the bike.
Event 4	Roger decides not to buy the bike and leaves to find the stranger.

Define the Conflict What is the main problem the character faces? Is the conflict an internal one or an external one?

MODEL

The bikes were lined up in a row, beautiful, shiny, and bright. He ran his hand over the handlebars and felt his face flush with embarrassment. How could he spend all the stranger's money on a fancy bike that he didn't really need?

Depict Characters Vividly What do your characters look like? What do they think and say? How do they act? What vivid details can show readers what the characters are like?

MODEL

The salesperson strolled the show-room carpet like a rich prince walking the halls of his castle. He said nothing, but his pacing made the boy slightly nervous.

WRITING TIP Dialogue is an effective way of developing characters in a narrative. As you write dialogue, choose words that express your characters' personalities and show how the characters feel about one another and about the events in the plot.

MODEL

"Can I help you?" a voice from behind him asked.

Roger turned to see the salesperson looking down at him.

"I was just looking at this 12-speed, super-lightweight bike," Roger said, swallowing.

"That's a pretty expensive bike you're touching, young man," the salesperson replied skeptically.

4.2 Options for Organization

Option 1: Chronological Order One way to organize a piece of narrative writing is to arrange the events in chronological order, as shown below.

Introduction characters and setting	MODEL Roger walked into the store where he had seen the fancy new bikes.
Event 1	"Can I help you?" the salesperson asked, his voice showing interest in a sale. Roger mumbled and pointed toward the bikes against a wall.
Event 2	As his hand glided over the handlebars on the bike, he barely heard the salesperson ask if he even had the money for the new bike.
End perhaps show the significance of the events	Roger's hand flashed dollar bills, but he let go of the bike. He ran for the door, knowing he had to find the old woman who had given him the money.

WRITING TIP Try hooking your reader's interest by opening a story with an exciting event or some attention-grabbing dialogue. After your introduction, you may need to go back in time and relate the incidents that led up to the opening event.

Option 2: Character Chronological order is the most common way to organize a narrative. However, you may wish to focus more directly on character.

Introduce the main character.

↓

Describe the conflict the character faces.

↓

Relate the events and the changes the character goes through as a result of the conflict.

↓

Present the final change or new understanding.

Option 3: Focus on Conflict When the telling of a fictional narrative focuses on a central conflict, the story's plot may follow the model shown below.

Describe the main characters and setting	MODEL The brothers arrive at the high school gym long before the rest of the basketball team. Although the twins are physically identical, their personalities couldn't be more different. Mark is outgoing and impulsive, while Matt is thoughtful and shy.
Present the conflict	Matt realizes his brother is missing shots on purpose and believes they will lose the championship.
Relate the events that make the conflict complex and cause the characters to change	• Matt has a chance at a basketball scholarship if they win the championship. • Mark needs money to buy a car. • Matt and Mark have stood by each other no matter what.
Present the resolution or outcome of the conflict	Matt retells a family story in which their grandfather chose honor and integrity over easy money. Mark plays to win.

5 Explanatory Writing

Explanatory, or expository, writing informs and explains. For example, you can use it to explain how to cook spaghetti or to compare two pieces of literature. The rubric on the left shows you the basics of successful expository writing.

RUBRIC STANDARDS FOR WRITING

Successful explanatory writing should

• engage the interest of the reader

• state a clear purpose

• develop the topic with supporting details

• create a visual image for the reader by using precise verbs, nouns, and adjectives

• conclude with a detailed summary linked to the purpose of the composition

---

5.1 Types of Explanatory Writing

There are many types of explanatory writing. Select the type that presents your topic most clearly.

Compare and Contrast How are two or more subjects alike? How are they different?

MODEL
While the domestic honeybee has been bred for good honey production and gentleness, the Africanized bee is a "wild" bee that is quick-tempered and uncomfortable around animals and people.

Cause and Effect How does one event cause something else to happen? What are the results of an action or a condition?

MODEL
If the Africanized bees drive out or breed into domesticated honeybee colonies, commercial beekeepers in the United States could be forced out of business.

Analysis/Classification How does something work? How can it be defined? What are its parts? How can it be classified into categories?

MODEL
The Africanized honeybee is a new insect nuisance that could affect agriculture, recreation, and the environment.

Problem-Solution How can you identify, state and analyze a problem? How can it be solved?

MODEL
The best way to protect yourself against the stings of the Africanized bee is to understand how it behaves.

5.2 Compare and Contrast

Compare-and-contrast writing examines the similarities and differences between two or more subjects.

RUBRIC STANDARDS FOR WRITING

Successful compare-and-contrast writing should

• clearly state the subjects that are being compared and contrasted.

• include specific, relevant details.

• be easy to follow, using either feature-by-feature or subject-by-subject organization.

• use transitional words and phrases to signal similarities and differences.

• end with a conclusion that explains the decision made or creates a new understanding of the subjects compared.

Options for Organization

Compare-and-contrast writing can be organized in different ways. The examples that follow demonstrate feature-by-feature organization and subject-by-subject organization.

Option 1: Feature-by-Feature Organization

MODEL

Feature 1 I. **Similarities in Appearance**

Subject A. **Domestic honeybees are about five-eighths of an inch long.**

Subject B. **Africanized bees, contrary to rumor, are about the same size.**

Feature 2 II. **Differences in Temperament**

Subject A. **Domestic honeybees are bred to be gentle.**

Subject B. **The Africanized bee is a "wild" bee that is quick-tempered around animals and people.**

Option 2: Subject-by-Subject Organization

MODEL

Subject A I. **Domestic Honeybees**

Feature 1. **Domestic honeybees are about five-eighths of an inch long.**

Feature 2. **Domestic honeybees are bred to be gentle.**

Subject B II. **Africanized Bees**

Feature 1. **Africanized bees are about five-eighths of an inch long.**

Feature 2. **The Africanized bee is a "wild" bee that is quick-tempered around animals and people.**

WRITING TIP Remember your purpose for comparing and contrasting your subjects, and support your purpose with expressive language and specific details.

5.3 Cause and Effect

Cause-and-effect writing explains why something happened, why conditions exist, or what resulted from an action or condition.

RUBRIC STANDARDS FOR WRITING

Successful cause-and-effect writing should

- clearly state the cause-and-effect relationship being examined.
- show clear connections between causes and effects.
- present causes and effects in a logical order and use transitions effectively.
- use facts, examples, and other details to illustrate each cause and effect.
- use language and details appropriate to the audience.

Options for Organization

Your organization will depend on your topic and purpose for writing.

- If you want to explain the causes of an event, such as the threat of Africanized bees to commercial beekeeping, you might first state the effect and then examine its causes.

Option 1: Effect-to-Cause Organization

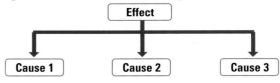

- If your focus is on explaining the effects of an event, such as the appearance of Africanized bees in the United States, you might first state the cause and then explain the effects.

Option 2: Cause-to-Effect Organization

- Sometimes you'll want to describe a chain of cause-and-effect relationships to explore a topic such as the myths about the Africanized honeybee.

Option 3: Cause-and-Effect Chain Organization

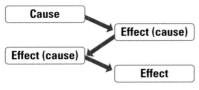

WRITING TIP You must test cause-and-effect relationships as you work. First, be sure that the first event you mention comes before the second event in time. Next, be sure that the effect you state could not have happened without the cause you state.

Problem-Solution

Problem-solution writing clearly states a problem, analyzes the problem, and proposes a solution to the problem. It can be used to identify and solve a conflict between characters, analyze a chemistry experiment, or explain why the home team keeps losing.

RUBRIC STANDARDS FOR WRITING

Successful problem-solution writing should

- give a clear and concise explanation of the problem and its significance.
- present a workable solution and include details that explain and support it.
- conclude by restating the problem.
- use language, tone, and details appropriate to the audience.

Options for Organization

Your organization will depend on the goal of your problem-solution piece, your intended audience, and the specific problem you choose to address. The organizational methods that follow are effective for different kinds of problem-solution writing.

Option 1: Simple Problem-Solution

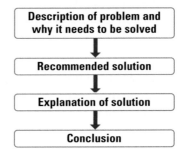

Option 2: Deciding Between Solutions

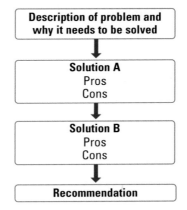

WRITING TIP Have a classmate read and respond to your problem-solution writing. Ask your peer reader: Is the problem clearly stated? Is the organization easy to follow? Do the proposed solutions seem logical?

Analysis/Classification

In writing an analysis, you explain how something works, how it is defined, or what its parts are. The details you include will depend upon the kind of analysis you write.

Process Analysis What are the major steps or stages in a process? What background information does the reader need to know—such as definitions of terms or a list of needed equipment—to understand the analysis? You might use process analysis to explain how to program a VCR or prepare for a test, or to explain how to replace a window pane.

Definition Analysis What are the most important characteristics of a subject? You might use definition analysis to explain a quality such as proficiency, the characteristics of a sonnet, or the features of a lever.

Parts Analysis What are the parts, groups, or types that make up a subject? Parts analysis could be used to explain the makeup of an organization or the anatomy of an insect.

Options for Organization

Organize your details in a logical order appropriate to the kind of analysis you're writing.

Option 1: Process Analysis A process analysis is usually organized chronologically, with steps or stages in the order they occur.

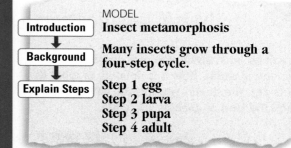

MODEL

Introduction → **Insect metamorphosis**

Background → **Many insects grow through a four-step cycle.**

Explain Steps → Step 1 egg
Step 2 larva
Step 3 pupa
Step 4 adult

Option 2: Definition Analysis You can organize the details in a definition or parts analysis in order of importance or impression.

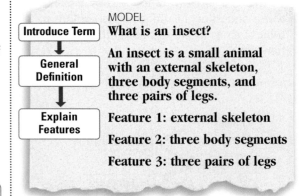

MODEL

Introduce Term → **What is an insect?**

General Definition → **An insect is a small animal with an external skeleton, three body segments, and three pairs of legs.**

Explain Features → **Feature 1: external skeleton**

Feature 2: three body segments

Feature 3: three pairs of legs

Option 3: Parts Analysis The following parts analysis explains the parts of an insect's body.

MODEL

Introduce Subject → **An insect's body is divided into three main parts.**

Explain Parts → **Part 1: The head includes eyes, mouth, and antennae.**

Part 2: The thorax has the legs and wings attached to it.

Part 3: The abdomen contains organs for digesting food, eliminating waste, and reproducing.

Option 4: Classification/Division The following classification divides things into groups or categories based on certain characteristics.

MODEL

One way that scientists classify insects is into species that are social insects and those that are not. The vast majority of insects are not social insects. The parents get together simply to mate. The female lays her eggs near a food source and then abandons them. Social insects, on the other hand, live in organized communities in which members depend on one another. Individual insects have specific roles within the community. All termites and ants are social insects. Many bees and some wasps are also social insects.

⑥ Persuasive Writing

Persuasive writing allows you to use the power of language to inform and influence others. It can take many forms, including speeches, newspaper editorials, billboards, advertisements, and critical reviews.

RUBRIC | **STANDARDS FOR WRITING**

Successful persuasion should

- have a strong introduction
- clearly state the issue and the writer's position
- present ideas logically
- answer opposing viewpoints
- end with a strong argument or summary or a call for action

---

⑥.1 Key Techniques

State Your Opinion Taking a stand on an issue and clearly stating your opinion are essential to every piece of persuasive writing you do.

> MODEL
> **Everyone should read "Waters of Gold." It teaches the importance of helping others and not expecting a reward for your kindness.**

Know Your Audience Who will read your writing? What do they already know and believe about the issue? What objections to your position might they have? What additional information might they need? What tone and approach would be most effective?

> MODEL
> **Do you ever feel that you could do more to help others? I just read a Chinese folktale about a woman who shared all that she had in order to help others in need.**

Support Your Opinion Why do you feel the way you do about the issue? What facts, statistics, examples, quotations, anecdotes, or opinions of authorities support your view? What reasons will convince your readers? What evidence can answer their objections?

> MODEL
> **We should all do what we can to help others. Knowing that we have done something worthwhile makes us feel good. Kind deeds are their own reward.**

Ways to Support Your Argument	
Statistics	Facts that are stated in numbers
Examples	Specific instances that explain your point
Observations	Events or situations you yourself have seen
Anecdotes	Brief stories that illustrate your point
Quotations	Direct statements from authorities

Begin and End with a Bang How can you hook your readers and make a lasting impression? What memorable quotation, anecdote, or statistic will catch their attention at the beginning or stick in their minds at the end? What strong summary or call to action can you conclude with?

> INTRODUCTION
> **If you want to spend an enjoyable evening with your neighbors seeing a live performance, shopping for handmade crafts, or enjoying good food, will you go to the Community Center? Probably not. It's just too hot!**

CONCLUSION
Many people have put their time into providing our town with entertainment. Many more have participated in events planned by others. But those numbers are decreasing because the Community Center is uncomfortable on hot summer evenings. Let's purchase an air-conditioning system so people can enjoy the Community Center.

6.2 Options for Organization

In persuasive writing, you need to gather information to support your opinions. Here are some ways you can organize material to convince your audience.

Option 1: Reasons for Your Opinion

MODEL

Your Opinion
Everyone should read "Waters of Gold." It teaches the importance of helping others and not expecting a reward in return.

Reason 1
It offers a model of behavior in Auntie Lily, who expects nothing for her kindness but is rewarded with a pail full of gold.

Reason 2
It makes an important moral point when a character is punished for pretending to be kind when she is actually greedy.

Reason 3
In real life, you probably won't be given gold for doing something kind, but reading the story will remind you of the value of good deeds.

WRITING TIP Effective support for your opinion is often organized from the weakest argument to the strongest.

Depending on the purpose and form of your writing, you may want to show the weaknesses of other opinions as you explain the strength of your own. Two options for organizing writing that includes more than just your side of the issue are shown below.

Option 2: Why Your Opinion Is Stronger

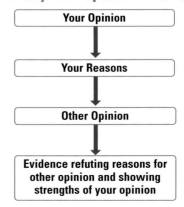

Option 3: Why Another Opinion Is Weaker

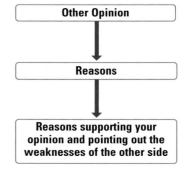

WRITING TIP Start a persuasive piece with a question, a surprising fact, or an anecdote to capture your readers' interest and make them want to keep reading. The ending of a persuasive piece is often the part that sticks in a reader's mind. Your conclusion might summarize the two sides of an issue, restate your position, invite readers to make up their own minds, or call for some action.

7 **Research Report Writing**

In research report writing, you can find answers to questions about a topic. You may find new, unanswered questions. Your writing organizes your ideas, questions, and information from various sources and presents it to your readers as a unified and coherent whole.

RUBRIC STANDARDS FOR WRITING

A successful research report should

- clearly state the purpose of the report in a thesis statement
- use evidence and details from a variety of sources to support the thesis
- contain only accurate and relevant information
- document sources correctly
- develop the topic logically and include appropriate transitions
- include a properly formatted Works Cited list

7.1 **Key Techniques**

Formulate Relevant, Interesting, and Researchable Questions Asking thoughtful questions will help you find an interesting, specific topic that you can develop in a research report. Begin by jotting down a list of basic questions about your general topic. Focus on the *who, what, where, when,* and *why* of your topic. If you were researching Eleanor Roosevelt, you might develop questions like these.

MODEL
What were Eleanor Roosevelt's most important accomplishments?

What difficulties did she overcome?

When did she live? What were the most important events of that time?

As you become familiar with your topic, narrow your questions down to a single question that will provide a sharp focus and make your readers think. Your answer to this question will become the thesis statement of your research report.

MODEL
How did Eleanor Roosevelt's activities change the perception of women's roles in society?

Make sure that there are research sources available that can provide you information to answer your question. If you cannot find sources, you need to revise your question.

Clarify Your Thesis A thesis statement is one or two sentences clearly stating the main idea that you will develop in your report. A thesis may also indicate the organizational pattern you will follow and reflect your tone and point of view.

MODEL
Eleanor Roosevelt's active participation in political and social issues changed the role of future first ladies and offered a new vision for the roles of women in general.

Document Your Sources You need to document, or credit, the sources where you find your evidence. In the example below, the writer uses and documents information from a magazine article.

MODEL
Eleanor Roosevelt was tireless in her work. A joke in Washington was that President Roosevelt prayed every night, "Dear God, please make Eleanor a little tired" (Goodwin 41).

Support Your Ideas You should support your ideas with relevant evidence—facts, anecdotes, and statistics—from reliable sources. In the example below, the writer includes a fact about how Eleanor Roosevelt helped women journalists.

> MODEL
> **To encourage newspapers to hire women, Eleanor Roosevelt did not allow men at her White House press conferences (Toor 63).**

7.2 Finding and Evaluating Sources

Begin your research by looking for information about your topic in books, magazines, newspapers, and computer databases. In addition to using your library's card or computer catalog, look up your subject in indexes, such as the *Readers' Guide to Periodical Literature* or the *New York Times Index*. The bibliographies in books that you find during your research may also lead to additional sources. The following checklist will help you evaluate the reliability of the sources you find.

Checklist for Evaluating Your Sources	
Authoritative	Someone who has written several books or articles on your subject or whose work has been published in a well-respected newspaper or journal may be considered an authority.
Up-to-date	Check the publication date to see if the source reflects the most current research on your subject.
Respected	In general, tabloid newspapers and popular-interest magazines are not reliable sources. If you have questions about whether you are using a respected source, ask your librarian.

7.3 Making Source Cards

For each source you find, record the bibliographic information on a separate index card. You will need this information to give credit to the sources in your paper. The samples at the right show how to make source cards for encyclopedia entries, magazine articles, and books. You will use the source number on each card to identify the notes you take during your research.

Encyclopedia Entry

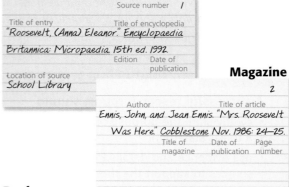

Magazine

Book

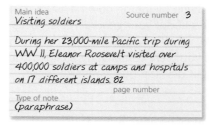

7.4 Taking Notes

As you find material that suits the purpose of your report, record each piece of information on a separate note card. You will probably use all three of the note-taking methods listed below.

- **Paraphrase,** or restate in your own words, the main ideas and supporting details of the passage.

- **Summarize,** or rephrase in fewer words, the original materials, trying to capture the key ideas.

- **Quote,** or copy word for word, the original text, if you think the author's own words best clarify a particular point. Use quotation marks to signal the beginning and the end of the quotation.

For more details on making source cards and taking notes, see the Research Report Workshop on pages 780–786.

7.5 Writing a Thesis Statement

A thesis statement in a research report defines the main idea, or overall purpose, of your report. A clear, one-sentence answer to your main question will result in a good thesis statement.

Question What did Eleanor Roosevelt do that made her such an important first lady in American history?

Thesis Statement Eleanor Roosevelt's active participation in political and social issues changed the role of future first ladies and offered a new vision for the roles of women in general.

7.6 Making an Outline

To organize your report, group your note cards by main ideas and arrange them in a logical order. Using your notes, make a topic outline, beginning with a shortened version of your thesis statement. Key ideas are listed after Roman numerals, and subpoints are listed after capital letters and Arabic numerals.

MODEL

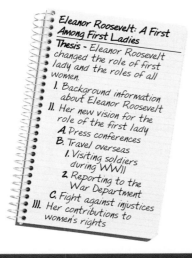

Eleanor Roosevelt: A First
Among First Ladies
Thesis - Eleanor Roosevelt
changed the role of first
lady and the roles of all
women.
I. Background information
about Eleanor Roosevelt
II. Her new vision for the
role of the first lady
A. Press conferences
B. Travel overseas
1. Visiting soldiers
during WWII
2. Reporting to the
War Department
C. Fight against injustices
III. Her contributions to
women's rights

7.7 Documenting Your Sources

When you quote one of your sources or rewrite in your own words information you have found in a source, you need to credit that source, using parenthetical documentation.

Guidelines for Parenthetical Documentation	
Work by One Author	Put the author's last name and, if appropriate, the page reference in parentheses: **(Toor 29)**. If you mention the author's name in the sentence, put only the page reference in parentheses: **(29)**.
Work by Two or Three Authors	Put the last names of the authors and the page reference in parentheses: **(Ennis and Ennis 24)**.
No Author Given	Give the title or a shortened version and the page reference: **("Roosevelt" 172)**.
Works by Same Author	Give the author's last name, the title or a shortened version, and the page reference: **(Roosevelt, <u>This I Remember!</u> 59)**.

WRITING TIP Presenting someone else's writing or ideas as your own is plagiarism. To avoid plagiarism, you need to credit sources as noted. However, if a piece of information is common knowledge—available in several sources—you do not need to credit the source. To see an example of parenthetical documentation, see the report on page 781.

7.8 Creating a Works Cited List

Print Sources

At the end of your research report, you need to include a Works Cited list. Any source that you have cited in your report needs to be listed alphabetically by the author's last name. If no author is given, use the editor's name or the title of the work. Note the guidelines for spacing and punctuation in the model list.

Electronic Sources

As well as print sources, you need to identify electronic sources, such as CD-ROMs or Internet databases, in your Works Cited list. If you read or print out an article on the Internet, document it as shown here. Electronic sources

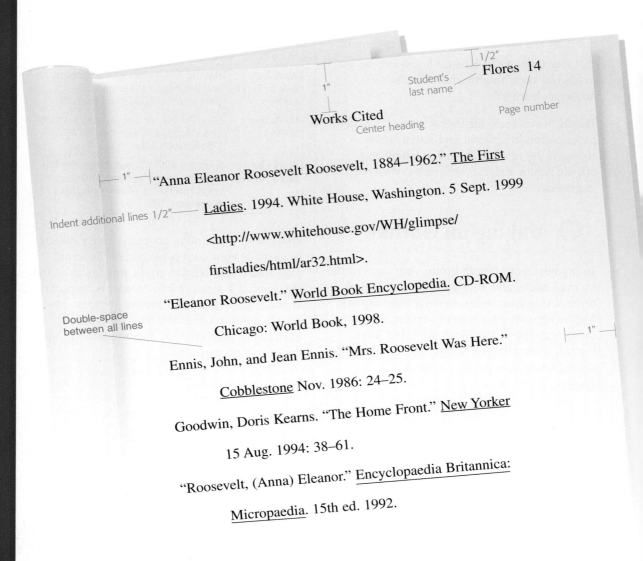

1/2"

Student's last name   Flores 14

1"   Page number

Works Cited
Center heading

1"   "Anna Eleanor Roosevelt Roosevelt, 1884–1962." The First

Indent additional lines 1/2"——— Ladies. 1994. White House, Washington. 5 Sept. 1999

<http://www.whitehouse.gov/WH/glimpse/

firstladies/html/ar32.html>.

"Eleanor Roosevelt." World Book Encyclopedia. CD-ROM.

Double-space between all lines   Chicago: World Book, 1998.

1"

Ennis, John, and Jean Ennis. "Mrs. Roosevelt Was Here."

Cobblestone Nov. 1986: 24–25.

Goodwin, Doris Kearns. "The Home Front." New Yorker

15 Aug. 1994: 38–61.

"Roosevelt, (Anna) Eleanor." Encyclopaedia Britannica:

Micropaedia. 15th ed. 1992.

should be included in the Works Cited list with print sources.

Internet Databases Works Cited entries for Internet databases include the same kind of information as entries for print sources. Additionally, you need to include the date you accessed the information and the electronic address of the source. Some of the information about the source may be unavailable. Include as much as you can. For more information on how to write Works Cited entries for Internet sources, see the MLA guidelines posted on the McDougal Littell Web site.

INTERNET Style Guidelines
www.mcdougallittell.com

CD-ROMs Entries for CD-ROMs include the publication medium (CD-ROM), the distributor, and the date of publication. Some of the information shown may not always be available. Include as much as you can.

Flores 15

Roosevelt, Eleanor. The Autobiography of Eleanor Roosevelt.

New York: De Capo, 1992.

Roosevelt, Mrs. Franklin D. (Eleanor). "My Mail." Dear Mrs.

Roosevelt. Franklin and Eleanor Roosevelt Institute. 7

Feb. 1933 <http://newdeal.feri.org/eleanor/mymail.htm>.

⑧ Model Bank

⑧.⒈ Summary

BASICS IN A BOX

A successful summary should

❶ accurately restate in your own words the main ideas of the work you are summarizing

❷ begin with your restatement of the main idea of the whole work

❸ contain restatements of the main supporting ideas of the work

❹ omit all unimportant details, no matter how interesting

❺ be shorter than the original work

Model 1: Summary

700-Word Summary of *A Christmas Carol* by Richard Marsden

A Christmas Carol is a play about the change of the wealthy Ebenezer Scrooge from stinginess to generosity. The play begins on the day of Christmas Eve in Victorian London, England, where there is much poverty. Scrooge, however, has no mercy for others and dislikes Christmas. Bob Cratchit, an underpaid clerk working for Scrooge, knows better than to expect any kindness from his employer. Fred, Scrooge's nephew, comes by to give his uncle some Christmas cheer, but Scrooge responds to him with bitterness. He responds the same way when a visitor arrives seeking Christmas donations.

Scrooge continues to complain about Christmas when he returns home that evening. After he goes into his bedroom, he is visited by the spirit of Jacob Marley. Marley was Scrooge's business partner. He died seven years earlier on Christmas Eve. His ghost returns to show Scrooge the heavy chains he must carry. They are the result of the mean ways in which he acted toward people while he was alive. Marley's spirit warns Scrooge that he will have to carry heavier chains than these if he does not change his life.

In order for Scrooge to change, however, he needs more persuasion. After the ghost of Jacob Marley, three more spirits visit Scrooge: the Spirit of Christmas Past, the Spirit of Christmas Present, and the Spirit of Christmas Yet to Come.

The Spirit of Christmas Past arrives as the clock strikes one. He takes Scrooge to a scene at a boarding school, where one by one the boys are leaving for Christmas break. Scrooge sees himself there at an early age, playing with a stuffed bear. The other boys are happy to be going home and celebrating Christmas. But Scrooge is not going home for Christmas. It is possible that this sadness he felt as a young boy is one of the reasons Scrooge grew to hate Christmas.

The spirit then takes Scrooge to a scene where he is a young adult. It is the time that Scrooge rejected his sweetheart because she did not have any money to bring to their marriage. The Spirit of Christmas Past makes it plain that Scrooge might have had a much different and happier life if he hadn't been so worried about money.

The Spirit of Christmas Present arrives next, and takes Scrooge to the Cratchit household. Scrooge thinks their house is not far away, but the spirit informs him that it is an entire world away from Scrooge's house. A funeral procession passes as they descend into the poor section of the city. At the Cratchit's, Scrooge sees Tiny Tim. The boy is his parents' joy. Scrooge also sees that the boy is deathly ill. Scrooge wants to help Tiny Tim, but the spirit repeats the cold, heartless words that Scrooge spoke that afternoon about the deaths decreasing the surplus population. He reminds Scrooge of his opinion that the poor have more than enough help. They can fend for themselves.

When the Spirit of Christmas Yet to Come arrives, Scrooge is not ready for what he sees. He expects this spirit to talk to him like the others did. But the dark form is silent, cloaked, and hidden. His behavior creates a sense of death. First, the spirit takes Scrooge to a time immediately after his own death. Scrooge is shocked at the behavior of his servants. They show no loyalty to him as they plunder his house, stealing anything of value. They never liked their employer and don't respect him after he has died.

Next the spirit takes him to the Cratchit house, where another death has occurred—the death of Tiny Tim. Scrooge watches the Cratchit family struggle to cope with their grief. He is surprised to learn that his nephew, Fred, has offered them his services. It is an act that Scrooge secretly wishes he had done before it was too late.

The four spirits teach Scrooge a hard lesson about charity. He knows that if he does not change his ways, people will not be sorry when he dies. Terrified by that prospect, and now genuinely concerned for others, Scrooge wakes up the next day overjoyed that he still has time to change his life. He realizes that he has another chance to become a better person. Immediately, he begins improving his ways. After buying a Christmas goose for the Cratchits, he sets out to Fred's house brimming with Christmas cheer. Scrooge has changed completely, providing a merry holiday for the Cratchits and everyone else, including himself.

8.2 Book Review

BASICS IN A BOX

A successful book review should

❶ have an introduction that gives the title of the work, its author, and perhaps some information about the author

❷ summarize the work without giving away the ending

❸ if the work is fiction, discuss the plot, setting, and important characters

❹ explain why you admire or dislike the work, supporting your reactions with examples from the work

❺ conclude with a restatement of your opinion of the book or a recommendation to other readers

Model 2: Book Review

The True Confessions of Charlotte Doyle
Reviewed by Sheila Ashford

Have you ever taken a trip by yourself? Were you excited? Scared? *The True Confessions of Charlotte Doyle* by Avi tells the story of a thirteen-year-old girl who sails aboard a ship called the *Seahawk* from Liverpool, England, to Providence, Rhode Island, in the summer of 1832. As she prepares for the trip, Charlotte looks forward to what she thinks will be a great adventure. But the adventure turns out to be far more exciting—and far more dangerous—than Charlotte ever imagined. *The True Confessions of Charlotte Doyle* tells the gripping story of how a young girl must face mutiny, murder, and the possibility of her own death. ❶ ❷

Almost as soon as she boards the *Seahawk*, Charlotte senses that something is wrong. She is befriended by an old, black sailor named Zacharia who tells her that the captain of the *Seahawk*, Captain Jaggery, is a particularly cruel man and not to be trusted. Charlotte goes to Captain Jaggery and tells him that she wants to return to England but the captain flatters Charlotte by telling her that she will be a positive influence on the crew. ❸

As the story continues, the reader learns a lot about what it was like to sail in the early 1800s. The novel describes how the sailors worked, what they ate, as well as what was involved in operating the ship, keeping watch, and making repairs. Charlotte is fascinated by the crew's work and especially impressed with how Captain Jaggery runs things. So impressed, that when she finds out about a plot against him, she tells the captain. Angered by what Charlotte tells him, the captain orders all hands on deck.

From that moment on, Charlotte discovers more and more the true, cruel nature of Captain Jaggery. As an "example," he orders the flogging of Charlotte's friend Zacharia. Shortly thereafter, Charlotte sees a canvas bag that was used to bury sailors in the sea being dumped overboard and she is told that it contains the body of her old friend. Blaming herself, Charlotte joins the crew, asking for no special treatment because she is a girl. Instead, she receives especially cruel treatment from the captain.

Captain Jaggery sails the ship into a hurricane. Avi describes the storm with lots of convincing detail, especially when he shows what the crew had to go through to save the ship. Jaggery drives the crew mercilessly but he saves the worst treatment for Charlotte. When the ship's second in command, a man who helped the captain beat Zacharia, is found dead, Jaggery accuses Charlotte of murder, orders her trial, and finds her guilty. It is only through some unexpected help that Charlotte's story does not end here.

The True Confessions of Charlotte Doyle is a great adventure novel that held my interest from first page to last. It shows how cruel people can be, but it shows how brave people can be too. We might not want to take the kind of trip that Charlotte Doyle did, but we can read her story and feel like we are right on board!

8.3 Friendly Letter

Model 3: Friendly Letter

BASICS IN A BOX

A successful friendly letter should

❶ begin with a heading that contains your street address, town or city, state and ZIP code, and the date you write the letter

❷ have a salutation that begins with a capital letter and is followed by a comma

❸ have a body that is written in an informal, conversational tone

❹ have a closing that begins with a capital letter and is followed by a comma

❺ end with your signature under the closing

> 603 Pine Street ❶
> Alton, Pennsylvania 18406
> August 7, 2000
>
> Dear José, ❷
> I enjoyed your last letter so much that I had to hurry and answer it. How did you learn to ride a horse so quickly? In the photo you sent me, you look very impressive up there in the saddle. Do you ride in shows or just for fun? Wish me luck when I learn to ride! ❸
> Write and tell me more about your wilderness ride. Say "hi" to your family for me.
>
> Your friend, ❹
> Beth ❺

8.4 Email

Model 4: Friendly Email

BASICS IN A BOX

A successful email should

❶ have the exact email address of the person you are writing to in the "To:" line

❷ state the subject of the email in the "Subject" line

❸ have a body that is written in an informal, conversational tone

❹ close with your name

❺ end with your exact email address after your name

Tips on "Netiquette"

- Always end your messages with your name and email address.
- Always include a subject heading.
- Take as much care with spelling and punctuation as you would in a friendly letter.
- Don't write in all capitals because it looks as if you are shouting.

To: Beth_Baldwin@Oneworld.net ❶
cc:
bcc:
Subject: Wilderness Rides ❷

I'm back from my wilderness ride and it was great. I rode with a guide, seven other kids about my age, and two pack horses. The ride lasted one week. Except for the one afternoon when it rained, the weather was nice. I had such a great time, I would recommend the wilderness ride to anybody who likes to see nature close up. ❸

José Salazar ❹
joses@infoarrow.net ❺

Writing Handbook

8.5 Persuasive Essay

BASICS IN A BOX

A successful persuasive essay should

❶ open with a dramatic statement of the issue and your opinion

❷ address the audience you are trying to persuade

❸ provide facts, examples, and reasons to support your opinion

❹ answer opposing views

❺ show clear reasoning

❻ include strategies such as summaries to help readers remember your message

❼ end with a strong position statement or call to action

See page R100 for tips on delivering your persuasive presentation orally.

Model 5: Persuasive Essay

Important Hours
by Gina Maraini

❷ "The Golden Years." That is what some people call old age. They think it is a time of peace and relaxation. But many old people spend time alone. Some cannot get out of their homes because of illness. "What can I do?" you ask. More than you think. Even spending an hour a week can mean a lot to an older person who lives alone. ❶

Some kids might say that they can only do good for an older person if they have lots of time and lots of patience. It's easy to talk yourself out of volunteering your time by saying, "I only have an hour a week. What good would that do?" Never underestimate just how much good you can do even in a little bit of time. ❹

Sometimes things happen that seem unimportant to a kid but can really be a problem to an old person. If a small object like a pen or pencil slides under furniture, an older person often is not able to stoop down and pick it up. But they feel embarrassed to ask for help. So, the pen stays there. Sometimes it gets forgotten about and becomes lost. You can help that older person find these things. And by helping, you are reminding that person that he or she is not forgotten about either. ❸

R64   WRITING HANDBOOK

Persuasive Essay at a Glance

Introduction		Body		Conclusion

Introduction

present the issue dramatically

→

Body

address target audience
- facts
- examples
- reasons

→

Conclusion

summary and call to action

Sometimes it is hard for an older person to reach up high. Putting things away, like groceries, becomes a problem. Often the older person gets tired and gives up. You can help to put groceries and other heavy objects away. And by doing that, you are helping that older person feel like he or she can still keep up with life's challenges.

❷ One of the most important things you can do for a senior citizen who lives alone is to give that person someone to talk to. Old people, who have lived long lives and had many experiences, have stories to tell that you can learn a lot from. And it is important for you to say so, too. That way, you can show the older person that he or she is contributing to your life.

❼ But you can make a real contribution to an older person's life, too. Even if you only have an hour to spend, you can help an older person feel cared about and important. Find ways to reach out, whether through volunteer organizations or just by being aware of who is alone in your neighborhood. And always remember: as much as you give, you get back so much more, simply by knowing the difference that you have made. **❺** **❻**

Grammar Handbook

❶ Quick Reference: Parts of Speech

Part of Speech	Definition	Examples
Noun	Names a person, place, thing, idea, quality, or action.	Theseus, Greece, boat, freedom, joy, sailing
Pronoun	Takes the place of a noun or another pronoun.	
Personal	Refers to the one speaking, spoken to, or spoken about.	I, me, my, mine, we, us, our, ours, you your, yours, she, he, it, her, him, hers, his, its, they, them, their, theirs
Reflexive	Follows a verb or preposition and refers to a preceding noun or pronoun.	myself, yourself, herself, himself, itself, ourselves, yourselves, themselves
Intensive	Emphasizes a noun or another pronoun.	(Same as reflexives)
Demonstrative	Points to specific persons or things.	this, that, these, those
Interrogative	Signals questions.	who, whom, whose, which, what
Indefinite	Refers to person(s) or thing(s) not specifically mentioned.	both, all, most, many, anyone, everybody, several, none, some
Relative	Introduces subordinate clauses and relates them to words in the main clause.	who, whom, whose, which, that
Verb	Expresses action, condition, or state of being.	
Action	Tells what the subject does or did, physically or mentally.	run, reaches, listened, consider, decides, dreamt
Linking	Connects subjects to that which identifies or describes them.	am, is, are, was, were, sound, taste, appear, feel, become, remain, seem
Auxiliary	Precedes and introduces main verbs.	be, have, do, can, could, will, would, may, might
Adjective	Modifies nouns or pronouns.	**strong** women, **two** epics, **enough** time
Adverb	Modifies verbs, adjectives, or other adverbs.	walked **out**, **really** funny, **far** away
Preposition	Relates one word to another (following) word.	at, by, for, from, in, of, on, to, with
Conjunction	Joins words or word groups.	
Coordinating	Joins words or word groups used the same way.	and, but, or, for, so, yet, nor
Correlative	Join words or word groups used the same way and are used in pairs.	both . . . and, either . . . or, neither . . . nor
Subordinating	Joins word groups not used the same way.	although, after, as, before, because, when, if, unless
Interjection	Expresses emotion.	wow, ouch, hurrah

➋ Quick Reference: The Sentence and Its Parts

The diagrams that follow will give you a brief review of the essentials of the sentence—subjects and predicates—and of some of its parts.

The speaker's **pockets** **bulged** with oranges.

The **complete subject** includes all the words that identify the person, place, thing, or idea that the sentence is about.

The **complete predicate** includes all the words that tell or ask something about the subject.

pockets

The **simple subject** tells exactly whom or what the sentence is about. It may be one word or a group of words, but it does not include modifiers.

bulged

The **simple predicate**, or **verb**, tells what the subject does or is. It may be one word or several, but it does not include modifiers.

At the drug store, an understanding clerk **had given** the speaker **a chocolate bar.**

A **prepositional phrase** consists of a preposition, its object, and any modifiers of the object. In this phrase, *at* is the preposition and *drug store* is its object.

subject

A **direct object** is a word or group of words that tells who or what receives the action of the verb in the sentence.

Verbs often have more than one part. They may be made up of a **main verb,** like *given,* and one or more **auxiliary,** or **helping verbs,** like *had.*

An **indirect object** is a word or group of words that tells *to whom* or *for whom* or *to what* or *for what* about the verb. A sentence can have an indirect object only if it has a direct object. The indirect object always comes before the direct object in a sentence.

❸ Quick Reference: Punctuation

Punctuation	Function	Examples
End Marks period, question mark, exclamation point	to end sentences	We can start now. When would you like to leave? What a fantastic hit!
	initials and other abbreviations	Mrs. Dorothy Parker, C. P. Cavafy, McDougal Littell Inc., P.M., A.D., lbs., oz., Blvd., Dr.

	items in outlines	I. Volcanoes
		    A. Central-vent
		        1. Shield

	exception: post-office abbreviations	NE (Nebraska), NV (Nevada)
Commas	before conjunction in compound sentence	I have never disliked poetry, but now I really love it.
	items in a series	She is brave, loyal, and kind. The slow, easy route is best.
	words of address	Maria, how can I help you? You must do something, soldier.
	parenthetical expressions	Well, just suppose that we can't? Hard workers, as you know, don't quit. I'm not a quitter, believe me.
	introductory phrases and dependent clauses	In the beginning of the day, I feel fresh. Having finished my chores, I went out. While she was out, I was here.
	nonessential phrases and clauses	Ed Pawn, captain of the chess team, won. Ed Pawn, who is the captain, won. The two leading runners, sprinting toward the finish line, finished in a tie.
	in dates and addresses	September 21, 2001. Mail it by May 14, 2000, to Hauptman Company, 321 Market Street, Memphis, Tennessee.
	in letter parts	Dear Jim, Sincerely yours,
	for clarity or to avoid confusion	By noon, time had run out. What the minister does, does matter. While cooking, Jim burned his hand.
Semicolons	in compound sentences that are not joined by coordinators *and*, etc.	The last shall be first; the first shall be last. I read the Bible; however, I have not memorized it.
	with items in series that contain commas	We invited my sister, Jan; her friend, Don; my uncle Jack; and Mary Dodd.
	in compound sentences that contain commas	After I ran out of money, I called my parents; but only my sister was home, unfortunately.

Punctuation	Function	Examples
Colons	to introduce lists	**Correct:** Those we wrote were the following: Dana, John, and Will. **Incorrect:** Those we wrote were: Dana, John, and Will.
	before a long quotation	Abraham Lincoln wrote: "Four score and seven years ago, our fathers brought forth on this continent a new nation. . . ."
	after the salutation of a business letter	To Whom It May Concern: Dear Leonard Atole:
	with certain numbers	1:28 P.M., Genesis: 2–5
Dashes	to indicate an abrupt break in thought	I was thinking of my mother—who is arriving tomorrow—just as you walked in.
Parentheses	to enclose less important material	It was so unlike him (John is always on time) that I began to worry.
Brackets	to enclose editorial explanation in quoted material	"They [the Glenview Cardinals] came to play, but we were prepared."
Hyphens	with a compound adjective before nouns	The not-so-rich taxpayer won't stand for this!
	in compounds with *all-, ex-, self-, -elect*	The ex-firefighter helped rescue him. Our president-elect is self-conscious.
	in compound numbers (to ninety-nine)	Today, I turn twenty-one.
	in fractions used as adjectives	My cup is one-third full.
	between prefixes and words beginning with capital letters	Which pre-Raphaelite painter do you like best? It snowed in mid-October.
	when dividing words at the end of a line	How could you have any reasonable expectations of getting a new computer?
Apostrophes	to form possessives of nouns and indefinite pronouns	my friend's book, my friends' book, anyone's guess, somebody else's problem
	for omitted letters in numbers/contractions	don't (omitted **o**); he'd (omitted **woul**) the class of '99 (omitted **19**)
	to form plurals of letters and numbers	I had two A's and no 2's on my report card.
Quotation Marks	to set off a speaker's exact words	Sara said, "I'm finally ready." "I'm ready," Sara said, "finally." Did Sara say, "I'm ready"? Sara said, "I'm ready!"
	for titles of stories, short poems, essays, songs, book chapters	I liked Paulsen's "Dirk the Protector" and Roethke's "The Bat." I like Joplin's "Me and Bobby McGee."
Ellipses	for material omitted from a quotation	"When in the course of human events . . . and to assume among the powers of the earth. . . ."
Italics	for titles of books, plays, magazines, long poems, operas, films, TV series, names of ships	*The House on Mango Street, Hamlet, Newsweek, The Odyssey, Madama Butterfly, Gone with the Wind, Seinfeld, Titanic*

4 Quick Reference: Capitalization

Category/Rule	Examples
People and Titles	
Names and initials of people	Gish Jen, J. Frank Dobie
Titles with names	Professor Holmes, Senator Long
Deities and members of religious groups	Jesus, Allah, the Buddha, Zeus, Baptists, Roman Catholics
Names of ethnic and national groups	Hispanics, Jews, African Americans
Geographical Names	
Cities, states, countries, continents	Philadelphia, Kansas, Japan, Europe
Regions, bodies of water, mountains	the South, Lake Baykal, Mount McKinley
Geographic features, parks	Great Basin, Yellowstone National Park
Streets and roads, planets	318 East Sutton Drive, Charles Court, Jupiter, Pluto
Organizations and Events	
Companies, organizations, teams	Ford Motor Company, Boy Scouts of America, St. Louis Cardinals
Buildings, bridges, monuments	Empire State Building, Eads Bridge, Washington Monument
Documents, awards	the Declaration of Independence, Stanley Cup
Special named events	Mardi Gras, World Series
Governmental bodies, historical periods and events	U.S. Senate, House of Representatives, Middle Ages, Vietnam War
Days and months, holidays	Thursday, March, Thanksgiving, Labor Day
Specific cars, boats, trains, planes	Porsche, *Mississippi Queen*, Orient Express, Concorde
Proper Adjectives	
Adjectives formed from proper nouns	French cooking, Freudian psychology, Edwardian age, Atlantic coast
First Words and the Pronoun *I*	
The first word in a sentence or quotation	This is it. He said, "Let's go."
Complete sentence in parentheses	(Consult the previous chapter.)
Salutation and closing of letters	Dear Madam, Very truly yours,
First lines of most poetry	Then am I
The personal pronoun *I*	A happy fly / If I live / Or if I die.
First, last, and all important words in titles	*A Tale of Two Cities*, "The World Is Not a Pleasant Place to Be"

⑤ Writing Complete Sentences

5.1 *Sentence Fragments* A sentence fragment is a group of words that does not express a complete thought. It may be missing a subject, a predicate, or both. A sentence fragment makes you wonder What is this about? or What happened?

Missing Subject or Predicate You can correct a sentence fragment by adding the missing subject or predicate to complete the thought.

> **INCORRECT:** The Monsters Are Due on Maple Street *is a spooky tale. Tells about ordinary neighbors turning into a mob. Fearful people.*
>
> **CORRECT***:* The Monsters Are Due on Maple Street *is a spooky tale* that *tells about ordinary neighbors turning into a mob* of *fearful people.*

Phrase and Subordinate-Clause Fragments When the fragment is a phrase or a subordinate clause, you may join the fragment to an existing sentence.

> **INCORRECT:** *Under normal circumstances. The conflicts neighbors have with one another are easy to ignore. However, these unresolved problems can suddenly become huge. When a crisis threatens.*
>
> **CORRECT:** *Under normal circumstances, the conflicts neighbors have are easy to ignore. However, these unresolved problems can suddenly become huge* when *a crisis threatens.*

GRAMMAR PRACTICE

Rewrite this paragraph, correcting the sentence fragments.

(1) In *The Monsters Are Due on Maple Street.* **(2)** Normal social bonds were broken. **(3)** The small amount of community feeling that existed on Maple Street. **(4)** Was quickly destroyed. **(5)** A sense of community is necessary. **(6)** If people are to live together safely and happily.

(7) The earliest human communities came into being. **(8)** When the need for safety arose. **(9)** Neighbors in a community. **(10)** Give one another practical and emotional support. **(11)** They work to resolve. **(12)** Problems among members rather than ignoring conflict. **(13)** Even neighbors who live close together. **(14)** Do not necessarily share similar values. **(15)** Is essential in building a strong, stable community. **(16)** A true community. **(17)** Might have been able to stand up to the outside threat posed in this teleplay. **(18)** Without community Maple Street.

5.2 *Run-on Sentences* A run-on sentence consists of two or more sentences written incorrectly as one. A run-on sentence occurs because the writer either used no end mark or used a comma instead of a period to end the first complete thought. A run-on sentence may confuse readers because it does not show where one thought ends and the next begins.

Forming Separate Sentences One way to correct a run-on sentence is to form two separate sentences. Use a period or other end punctuation after the first sentence, and capitalize the first letter of the next sentence.

> **INCORRECT:** *In "A Crown of Wild Olive," Amyntas and Leon meet at the Olympic Games they are suspicious of each other because their countries are at war their rooms at Olympia are near each other.*
>
> **CORRECT:** *In "A Crown of Wild Olive," Amyntas and Leon meet at the Olympic Games. They are suspicious of each other because their countries are at war. Their rooms at Olympia are near each other.*

Forming Compound Sentences You can also correct a run-on sentence by rewriting it to form a compound sentence. One way to do this is by using a comma and a coordinating conjunction.

Never join simple sentences with a comma alone, or a run-on sentence will result. You need a comma followed by a conjunction such as *and, but,* or *or* to hold the sentences together.

> **INCORRECT:** *Leon cut his foot on the sickle, Amyntas helped clean the wound.*
> **CORRECT:** *Leon cut his foot on the sickle, and Amyntas helped clean the wound.*

You may use a semicolon to join two ideas that are closely related.

In addition, you can correct a run-on sentence by using a semicolon and a conjunctive adverb. Commonly used conjunctive adverbs are *however, therefore, nevertheless,* and *besides.*

> **INCORRECT:** *Amyntas spent his money on the bronze bull he left it as an offering. He did not want to be happy that Leon was hurt he still wanted to win.*
> **CORRECT:** *Amyntas spent his money on the bronze bull; he left it as an offering. He did not want to be happy that Leon was hurt; however, he still wanted to win.*

GRAMMAR PRACTICE

Rewrite this paragraph, correcting the run-on sentences.

(1) In "A Crown of Wild Olive" Athens and Sparta agree to a truce so they can take part in the Olympic Games many ships from all over Greece sail safely to Olympia. **(2)** This story reflects an actual tradition from those times. **(3)** All wars had to stop for many reasons, first, the people wanted the games to be a time of unity. **(4)** Often there were battles between the different cities, wars lasted many years. **(5)** Second, Olympia was a religious center the games had religious importance. **(6)** The Greeks worshiped Zeus there people visited from all over the ancient world. **(7)** In the story, Amyntas spends time in the temple of Zeus he leaves the bronze bull as an offering. **(8)** Afterward, the Athenians and the Spartans leave Olympia everyone begins thinking about war again.

❻ Making Subjects and Verbs Agree

6.1 *Simple and Compound Subjects* A verb must agree in number with its subject. **Number** refers to whether a word is singular or plural. When a word refers to one thing, it is singular. When a word refers to more than one thing, it is plural.

Agreement with Simple Subjects Use a singular verb with a singular subject.

When the subject is a singular noun, you use the singular form of the verb. The present-tense singular form of a regular verb usually ends in *-s* or *-es.*

> **INCORRECT:** *In "Seventh Grade" Victor sign up for French class on the first day of school. A girl he like enrolls in the same class.*
> **CORRECT:** *In "Seventh Grade" Victor <u>signs</u> up for French class on the first day of school. A girl he <u>likes</u> enrolls in the same class.*

USAGE TIP To find the subject of a sentence, first find the verb. Then ask *who* or *what* performs the action of the verb. Say the subject and the verb together to see if they agree.

Use a plural verb with a plural subject.

> **INCORRECT:** *Girls pays attention when Victor's friend Michael scowls at them.*
> **CORRECT:** *Girls <u>pay</u> attention when Victor's friend Michael scowls at them.*

Agreement with Compound Subjects Use a plural verb with a compound subject whose parts are joined by *and,* regardless of the number of each part.

> **EXAMPLE:** *Victor and Teresa <u>talk</u> after their French class with Mr. Bueller.*

When the parts of a compound subject are joined by *or* or *nor,* make the verb agree in number with the part that is closer to it.

Usually *or* and *nor* appear with their correlatives *either* and *neither.*

INCORRECT: *Mr. Bueller asks whether Victor or the other students speaks any French. Neither Victor nor Teresa respond at first.*
CORRECT: *Mr. Bueller asks whether Victor or the other students* <u>speak</u> *any French. Neither Victor nor Teresa* <u>responds</u> *at first.*

GRAMMAR PRACTICE

Write the correct form of the verb given in parentheses.

1. In the story "Seventh Grade," Gary Soto (describe, describes) Victor's first day of school.

2. Victor (selects, select) French as his one elective.

3. According to a fashion magazine Michael read, men should (scowls, scowl).

4. Michael's upper lip (quivers, quiver) as he walks down the halls.

5. Neither the girls nor Victor (think, thinks) that Michael's scowl will really work.

6. Fashion magazines (consists, consist) of many advertisements with models in them.

7. In homeroom, Victor and Teresa (sits, sit) two rows away from each other.

8. Some girls (laugh, laughs) when he answers in English class.

9. The math problems in his book (scare, scares) him.

10. In French class, only the teacher (know, knows) that Victor's answer is gibberish.

6.2 *Pronoun Subjects* When a pronoun is used as a subject, the verb must agree with it in number.

Agreement with Personal Pronouns
When the subject is a singular personal pronoun, use a singular verb. When the subject is a plural personal pronoun, use a plural verb.

Even though *I* and *you* are singular, they take the plural form of the verb.

INCORRECT: *In "Zebra" Adam watches as the others play at recess. He are not able to play because of his accident.*
CORRECT: *In "Zebra" Adam watches as the others play at recess. He* <u>is</u> *not able to play because of his accident.*

When *he, she,* or *it* is the part of the subject closer to the verb in a compound subject containing *or* or *nor*, use a singular verb. When a pronoun is a part of a compound subject containing *and*, use a plural verb.

INCORRECT: *When Adam and the other students takes the summer art class, neither they nor he ignore John Wilson as he begins to teach them about art.*
CORRECT: *When Adam and the other students* <u>take</u> *the summer art class, neither they nor he* <u>ignores</u> *John Wilson as he begins to teach them about art.*

Agreement with Indefinite Pronouns
When the subject is a singular indefinite pronoun, use the singular form of the verb.

The following are singular indefinite pronouns: *another, either, nobody, anybody, everybody, somebody, no one, anyone, everyone, someone, one, nothing, anything, everything, something, each,* and *neither.*

EXAMPLE: *In Adam's class with Mrs. English, everybody* <u>listens</u> *to the stories.*

When the subject is a plural indefinite pronoun (*both, few, many,* or *several*), use the plural form of the verb.

EXAMPLES: *Few* <u>draw</u> *well at first. Many* <u>need</u> *a lot of practice.*

The indefinite pronouns *some, all, any, none,* and *most* can be either singular or plural. When the pronoun refers to one thing, use a singular verb.

When the pronoun refers to several things, use a plural verb.

EXAMPLES: *Some* <u>believe</u> *that the United States should not have gone to Vietnam, but John Wilson does not give his opinion in the story. All of his energy* <u>goes</u> *into making art.*

GRAMMAR PRACTICE

Write the correct form of the verb given in parentheses.

1. In "Zebra" one (learn, learns) how John Wilson and Adam become friends.
2. John (tell, tells) Adam that he has an idea for a summer art class.
3. Many of Adam's classmates (think, thinks) that the summer art class will be fun.
4. Some (go, goes) to camp during the summer months, while others just (hang, hangs) around.
5. Anybody can learn how to draw, although some (have, has) a special talent for it.
6. Among psychologists, many (believe, believes) that making art is good therapy.
7. Andrea and Adam wonder if anybody else (want, wants) to take the class.
8. Both (take, takes) the summer art class.
9. A broken umbrella, an empty can, a doll—anything (qualify, qualifies) as material for making sculptures.
10. All (are, is) able to be transformed into beautiful objects.
11. In many ways, Adam (seem, seems) to bond with his teacher.
12. Each of the students (leave, leaves) the class having learned something special.

6.3 Common Agreement Problems

Several other situations can cause problems in subject-verb agreement.

Agreement with Irregular Verbs Use the singular forms of the irregular verbs *do, be,* and *have* with singular subjects. Use the plural forms of these verbs with plural subjects.

	Do	Be	Have
Singular Subjects	I do	I am/was	I have
	you do	you are/were	you have
	the dog does	Joe is/was	Pat hasn't
	it does	he isn't/wasn't	she has
	each doesn't	either is/was	anybody has
Plural Subjects	we do	we are/were	we have
	dogs do	boys are/were	girls have
	they do	they are/were	they haven't
	many don't	both are/were	few have

WATCH OUT! Look carefully at words that come before the subject. Remember that the subject may not be the noun or pronoun closest to the verb.

INCORRECT: *The selection "Eleanor Roosevelt" do much to show the struggle of a dynamic first lady, and it have some insights into her success. Eleanor are a splendid achiever; she have qualities that anyone can cultivate.*

CORRECT: *The selection "Eleanor Roosevelt" does much to show the struggle of a dynamic first lady, and it has some insights into her success. Eleanor is a splendid achiever; she has qualities that anyone can cultivate.*

Interrupting Words Be sure the verb agrees with its subject when a word or words come between them.

Sometimes one or more words come between the subject and the verb. The interrupter does not affect the number of the subject.

INCORRECT: *Eleanor, moreover, encourage the hiring of female reporters by closing her press conferences to men.*

CORRECT: *Eleanor, moreover, encourages the hiring of female reporters by closing her press conferences to men.*

Interrupting Phrases Be certain that the verb agrees with its subject when a phrase comes between them.

The subject of a verb is never found in a prepositional phrase, which may follow the subject and come before the verb.

INCORRECT: *Eleanor, in spite of several tragedies in her life, triumph over adversity. This woman of many talents rank high in the list of great Americans.*

CORRECT: *Eleanor, in spite of several tragedies in her life, <u>triumphs</u> over adversity. This woman of many talents <u>ranks</u> high in the list of great Americans.*

Phrases beginning with *including, as well as, along with,* and *in addition to* are not part of the subject.

> **EXAMPLE:** *Her mother's coldness, as well as her father's alcoholism, <u>creates</u> a challenging situation for a young child. Eleanor's strong will, along with her other outstanding qualities, <u>makes</u> her a wonderful role model.*

The subject of the verb is never found in an appositive, which may follow the subject and come before the verb.

> **EXAMPLE:** *Eleanor, one of several self-trained diplomats, <u>helps</u> create the United Nations after World War II. Her assistants, a dedicated group, still <u>sing</u> her praises.*

Inverted Sentences When the subject comes after the verb, be sure the verb agrees with the subject in number.

A sentence in which the subject follows the verb is called an inverted sentence. Questions are usually in inverted form, as are sentences beginning with *here, there,* and *where*. (*Where are the* **reporters**? *There is a* **press conference** *today*.)

> **EXAMPLE:** *Where <u>does</u> Eleanor find the courage to overcome her shyness? How <u>does</u> she grow during her life? <u>Do</u> other first ladies follow her example? There <u>are</u> many more questions we would like answered about the great lady, Eleanor Roosevelt.*

USAGE TIP To check subject-verb agreement in inverted sentences, place the subject before the verb. For example, to check agreement, change *There are many people* to *Many people are there.*

GRAMMAR PRACTICE

Write the correct form of each verb given in parentheses.

1. Readers, while examining "Eleanor Roosevelt," (learn, learns) about the powerful influence that a father can have on his daughter.

2. Eleanor's father, in spite of his faults, (seem, seems) to have helped her feel unconditionally loved.

3. However, Eleanor's mother, in addition to the rest of the family, (was, were) relatively cold to her and filled her with self-doubt.

4. There (was, were) a sort of second mother to Eleanor, who lived near London.

5. How (is, are) Eleanor's early years related to her later achievements?

6. Joseph Lash, one of her biographers, (note, notes) that her childhood loneliness helped her understand people who felt left out.

7. Her heredity, as far as Eleanor was concerned, (appear, appears) to explain her great energy.

8. Looking back, she calmly recalls, "I think I (have, has) a good deal of my uncle Theodore in me. . . ."

9. What do you think (was, were) her greatest achievement?

10. *Presidential Wives*, one of several books by Paul Boller, (remind, reminds) us of the vitality of women like Eleanor.

❼ Using Nouns and Pronouns

7.1 *Plural and Possessive Nouns* Nouns refer to people, places, things, and ideas. Nouns are plural when they refer to more than one person, place, thing, or idea. Possessive nouns show who or what owns something.

Plural Nouns Follow these guidelines to form noun plurals.

Nouns	To Form Plural	Examples
Most nouns	add -s	jaw—jaws
Most nouns that end in s, sh, ch, x, or z	add -es	fox—foxes flash—flashes
Most nouns that end in ay, ey, oy, or uy	add -s	delay—delays valley—valleys
Most nouns that end in a consonant and y	change y to i and add -es	cavalry—cavalries casualty—casualties
Most nouns that end in o	add -s	alto—altos arroyo—arroyos soprano—sopranos
Some nouns that end in a consonant and o	add -es	echo—echoes hero—heroes tomato—tomatoes
Most nouns that end in f or fe	change f to v, add -es or -s	sheaf—sheaves knife—knives but belief—beliefs

WATCH OUT! The plurals of many musical terms that end in o preceded by a consonant are formed by adding -s. These nouns include *tempos* and *concertos*.

Some nouns use the same spelling in both singular and plural: *series, fish, sheep, cannon*. Some noun plurals use a form that doesn't follow any rule: *teeth, geese*.

> **INCORRECT:** *In* Knotes in My Yo-yo String, *Jerry Spinelli writes about his fantasys of perfection. Baseball, yo-yoes, drawing within the lines, and cleaning his locker are a few of the activitys at which he tries to be perfect.*
>
> **CORRECT:** *In* <u>Knots</u> in My Yo-Yo String, *Jerry Spinelli writes about his* <u>fantasies</u> *of perfection. Baseball,* <u>yo-yos</u>, *drawing within the lines, and cleaning his locker are a few of the* <u>activities</u> *at which he tries to be perfect.*

Possessive Nouns Follow these guidelines to form possessive nouns.

Nouns	To Form Possessive	Examples
Singular nouns	add apostrophe and -s	league—league's
Plural nouns ending in s	add apostrophe	fields—fields' brigades—brigades'
Plural nouns not ending in s	add apostrophe and -s	children—children's oxen—oxen's

> **INCORRECT:** *Jerrys' drawing is never good enough to win the* Times Herald *contest, even though the other childrens' drawings are messier. Neatness, according to the newspapers' judges, isn't the only standard.*
>
> **CORRECT:** <u>Jerry's</u> *drawing is never good enough to win the* Times Herald *contest, even though the other* <u>children's</u> *drawings are messier. Neatness, according to the* <u>newspaper's</u> *judges, isn't the only standard.*

USAGE TIP The dictionary usually lists the plural form of a noun if the plural form is irregular or if there is more than one plural form. Dictionary listings are especially helpful for nouns that end in o, f, and, fe.

WATCH OUT! Be careful when placing apostrophes in possessive nouns. A misplaced apostrophe changes the meaning. For example, *boy's* refers to possession by one boy, but *boys'* refers to possession by two or more boys.

GRAMMAR PRACTICE

Write the correct noun given in parentheses.

(1) This story describes Jerry (Spinelli's, Spinellis') attempts at perfection. **(2)** He is a fanatic about making sure his (colores, colors) do not go outside the lines. **(3)** He takes few chances when playing (sports, sportes), because he does not want to make an error.

(4) After a game, he goes over the (plaies, plays) in his mind so he can do better next time. **(5)** I'll bet if his mom asked him to peel (potatos, potatoes), he would spend a week completing the task. **(6)** Fortunately, he realizes that his imagination has no (boundarys, boundaries).

7.2 *Pronoun Forms* A personal pronoun is a pronoun that can be used in the first, second, or third person. A personal pronoun has three forms: the subject form, the object form, and the possessive form.

Subject Pronouns Use the subject form when the pronoun is the subject of a sentence or clause. *I, you, he, she, it, we,* and *they* are subject pronouns.

Using the correct pronoun form is seldom a problem when the sentence has just one pronoun. Problems can arise, however, when a noun and a pronoun or two pronouns are used in a compound subject or compound object. To see if you are using the correct pronoun form, read the sentence, using only one pronoun.

> **INCORRECT:** A Christmas Carol *tells the familiar tale of Scrooge. Him and the three Spirits of Christmas are the main characters.*
> **CORRECT:** A Christmas Carol *tells the familiar tale of Scrooge.* He *and the three Spirits of Christmas are the main characters.*

Use the subject form when the pronoun follows a linking verb.

You often hear the object form used as a predicate pronoun ("It is him"). For this reason, the subject form may sound awkward to you, though it is preferred in more formal writing.

> **INCORRECT:** *The Spirits showed Scrooge his future, but it was him who decided to change.*
> **CORRECT:** *The Spirits showed Scrooge his future, but it was* he *who decided to change.*

USAGE TIP To check the form of a predicate pronoun, see if the sentence still makes

sense when the subject and the predicate pronoun are reversed. *(It was he. He was it.)*

Object Pronouns Use the object form when the pronoun is the object in a clause, sentence, or of a preposition. *Me, you, him, her, it, us,* and *them* are object pronouns.

> **EXAMPLE:** *Scrooge's Christmas Eve changed* him. *His new approach to the Cratchit family worked wonders for* them.

Possessive Pronouns Never use an apostrophe in a possessive pronoun. *My, mine, your, yours, his, her, hers, its, our, ours, their,* and *theirs* are possessive pronouns.

Writers may confuse the possessive pronouns *its, your,* and *their* with the contractions *it's, you're,* and *they're.* Remember that the pairs are spelled differently and have different meanings.

> **INCORRECT:** *Scrooge thanked the Spirits for they're help. On Christmas morning, he sent a turkey to the Cratchets. To him, it's price was small for the joy it gave.*
> **CORRECT:** *Scrooge thanked the Spirits for* their *help. On Christmas morning, he sent a turkey to the Cratchits. To him,* its *price was small for the joy it gave.*

GRAMMAR PRACTICE

Write the correct pronoun form given in parentheses.

(1) Charles Dickens wrote *A Christmas Carol* in 1843, when (he, him) was 31 years old. **(2)** This work of (him, his) was written in only a few weeks. **(3)** In 1836 he was a famous writer; that year (he, him) and Catherine Hogarth were married. **(4)** (He, Him) was famous enough to tour America in 1842. **(5)** Did you know that it was (him, he) who wrote other novels about Christmas? **(6)** All of (they're, their) dates of composition are from the 1840s. **(7)** (They, Them) include the rest of the books mentioned here, such as *The Chimes,* published in 1844. **(8)** The next year saw another Christmas book of (his, him), *The Cricket on the Hearth.* **(9)** The year following, *The Battle of Life* took (it's, its) place among his titles. **(10)** Finally, *The Haunted Man,* an 1848 effort, was (him, his). **(11)** These books are said to be part of the first phase of (his', his) works. **(12)** (Them, They) have rather serious themes mixed with some humor. **(13)** When Thackeray, a fellow writer, reviewed *A Christmas Carol,* he said that (its, it's) publication was a national benefit.

7.3 ***Pronoun Antecedents*** An antecedent is the noun or pronoun to which a personal pronoun refers. The antecedent usually precedes the pronoun.

Pronoun and Antecedent Agreement A pronoun must agree with its antecedent in
> NUMBER—*singular or plural*
> PERSON—*first, second, or third*
> GENDER—*male or female*

Use a singular pronoun to refer to a singular antecedent; use a plural pronoun to refer to a plural antecedent.

Do not allow interrupting words to determine the number of the personal pronoun.
> **INCORRECT:** *In "Dark They Were, and Golden-Eyed," Harry did not let his initial feeling of dread and panic influence him. Instead, he ignored them and settled with his family on Mars.*
> **CORRECT:** *In "Dark They Were, and Golden-Eyed" Harry did not let his initial feeling of dread and panic influence him. Instead, he ignored <u>it</u> and settled with his family on Mars.*

If the antecedent is a noun that could be either male or female, use *he or she (him or her, his or her)* or reword the sentence to avoid the need for a singular pronoun.
> **EXAMPLES:** *<u>Each</u> one of the colonists on Mars began to change, and <u>he or she</u> did not realize that anything odd was happening.*
> **OR**
> *<u>All</u> of the colonists on Mars began to change, and <u>they</u> did not realize that anything odd was happening.*

Be sure that the antecedent of a pronoun is clear.

In most cases, do not use a pronoun to refer to an entire idea or clause. Writing is much clearer when the exact reference is repeated.
> **INCORRECT:** *Harry's worries centered on his fear that he would change like the others. They are hard to ignore because everyone is beginning to look different.*
> **CORRECT:** *Harry's worries centered on his fear that he would change like the others. <u>His worries</u> are hard to ignore because everyone is beginning to look different.*
> **INCORRECT:** *As Sam is talking to Harry outside of the store, he learns that his eyes are turning yellow. This is a major turning point in the story. He realizes that he cannot resist change.*
> **CORRECT:** *As Sam is talking to Harry outside of the store, <u>Harry</u> learns that his eyes are turning yellow. This is a major turning point in the story. <u>Harry</u> realizes that he cannot resist change.*

USAGE TIP To avoid vague pronoun reference, do not use *this* or *that* alone to start a clause. Instead, include a word that clarifies what *this* or *that* refers to—*this experience, this situation, that concept.*

Indefinite Pronouns as Antecedents When a singular indefinite pronoun referring to a person is the antecedent, use *he or she (him or her, his or her)* or rewrite the sentence to avoid the need for a singular pronoun.
> **INCORRECT:** *Everyone on Mars was beginning to undergo changes in their appearance without realizing it.*
> **CORRECT:** *Everyone on Mars was beginning to undergo changes in <u>his or her</u> appearance without realizing it.*
> **OR**
> **CORRECT:** *<u>All the colonists</u> on Mars were beginning to undergo changes in <u>their</u> appearance without realizing it.*

Indefinite Pronouns

Singular

another	each	everybody	neither	somebody
anybody	either	everyone	nobody	someone
anyone		everything	no one	something
anything			nothing	
			one	

Plural

both	few	many	several

Singular or Plural

all	any	most	none	some

WATCH OUT! Avoid the indefinite use of *you* and *they*.

INCORRECT: *At home they used Martian words.*

CORRECT: *At home family members used Martian words.*

INCORRECT: *Joe thought you should always thank them.*

CORRECT: *Joe thought a person should always thank his or her friends.*

GRAMMAR PRACTICE

Rewrite this paragraph to make the pronoun reference clear.

(1) In "Dark They Were, and Golden-Eyed" a war on Earth eliminates their chance of returning home. **(2)** When they hear the news, they feel hopeless. **(3)** Nobody knows what they will do. **(4)** At first everything is fine, but it changes when Harry sees that the plants are growing differently. **(5)** People start speaking words they have never heard before, and they sound strange. **(6)** Each person is changing, but they don't worry about it. **(7)** It is something that only Harry worries about. **(8)** Also, the American names they gave to the land seem strange after a while. **(9)** They don't sound as natural as the old Martian names. **(10)** This shows how Mars slowly takes the Earth out of them and makes them its own.

7.4 **Pronoun Usage** The form that a pronoun takes is always determined by its function within its own clause or sentence.

Who and Whom Use *who* or *whoever* as the subject of a clause or sentence.

INCORRECT: *In "The Night the Bed Fell," whom started all the ruckus?*

CORRECT: *In "The Night the Bed Fell," who started all the ruckus?*

Use *whom* as the direct or indirect object of a verb or verbal and as the object of a preposition.

People often use *who* for *whom* when speaking. In written English the pronouns should be used correctly.

INCORRECT: *Mother wanted to rescue who? Who was she worrying about?*

CORRECT: *Mother wanted to rescue whom? Whom was she worrying about?*

In trying to determine the correct pronoun form, ignore interrupters that come between the subject and the verb.

INCORRECT: *Whom, in your estimation, was in the most danger during the ordeal?*

EXAMPLE: *Who, in your estimation, was in the most danger during the ordeal?*

Pronouns in Contractions Do not confuse the contractions *it's, they're, who's,* and *you're* with possessive pronouns that sound the same—*its, their, whose,* and *your*.

INCORRECT: *Briggs and the narrator have no idea who's fault the commotion is.*

CORRECT: *Briggs and the narrator have no idea whose fault the commotion is.*

Pronouns with Nouns Determine the correct form of the pronoun in phrases such as *we girls* and *us boys* by dropping the noun and saying the sentence without the noun that follows the pronoun.

INCORRECT: *I believe that a story is most interesting when us readers are confused along with the characters.*

CORRECT: *I believe that a story is most interesting when we readers are confused along with the characters.*

GRAMMAR PRACTICE

Write the correct pronoun given in parentheses.

(1) (Who, Whom) in "The Night the Bed Fell" remains the calmest? **(2)** Let (whomever, whoever) thinks he or she would not be scared think again. **(3)** Those (who, whom) have a lot of relatives will best understand this story. **(4)** To (who, whom) in the class has a similar experience happened? **(5)** Heather tells us about a misunderstanding she had with her cousins, (who, whom) she stays with in the summer. **(6)** But (their, they're) all still good friends. **(7)** What would you do if you heard a crash in the middle of the night in (your, you're) house? **(8)** After a scare like that (its, it's) hard to get back to sleep.

❽ Using Verbs Correctly

8.1 *Verb Tenses and Forms* Verb tense shows the time of an action or a condition. Writers sometimes cause confusion when they use different verb tenses in describing actions that occur at the same time.

Consistent Use of Tenses When two or more actions occur at the same time or in sequence, use the same verb tense to describe the actions.

> **INCORRECT:** *In "The Eternal Frontier" Louis L'Amour writes about outer space. He considered the effect of space-age technology on our daily lives.*
>
> **CORRECT:** *In "The Eternal Frontier" Louis L'Amour <u>writes</u> about outer space. He <u>considers</u> the effect of space-age technology on our daily lives.*

A shift in tense is necessary when two events occur at different times or out of sequence. The tenses of the verbs should clearly indicate that one action precedes the other.

> **INCORRECT:** *We once have found adventure in the discovery of new lands. Now we will receive transmissions from places that in the past we only imagine.*
>
> **CORRECT:** *We once <u>found</u> adventure in the discovery of new lands. Now we <u>receive</u> transmissions from places that in the past we only <u>imagined</u>.*

Tense	Verb Form
Present	open/opens
Past	opened
Future	will/shall open
Present perfect	have/has opened
Past perfect	had opened
Future perfect	will/shall have opened

Past Tense and the Past Participle The simple past form of a verb can always stand alone. The past participle of the following irregular verbs should always be used with a helping verb.

Present Tense	Past Tense	Past Participle
be (is/are)	was/were	(have, had) been
begin	began	(have, had) begun
break	broke	(have, had) broken
bring	brought	(have, had) brought
choose	chose	(have, had) chosen
come	came	(have, had) come
do	did	(have, had) done
drink	drank	(have, had) drunk
eat	ate	(have, had) eaten
fall	fell	(have, had) fallen
freeze	froze	(have, had) frozen
give	gave	(have, had) given
go	went	(have, had) gone
grow	grew	(have, had) grown
lose	lost	(have, had) lost

USAGE TIP Some writers use gradual shifts in verb tense (such as from the past to the past participle) to move from the past up through to the present. This can be used to show developments throughout a historical period as in the example above. When using this technique, be careful to use verb tenses that clearly convey your message.

GRAMMAR PRACTICE

Write the correct verb tense for each sentence.

(1) "The Eternal Frontier" (deals, dealt, will deal) with the opportunities that the space age offers. **(2)** Some medical developments (are beginning, began, begun) with the space age—for example, laparoscopy and robotics. **(3)** Both of these areas (grow, grew, have grown) to advance the field of surgery dramatically. **(4)** In 1993 a "robotic assistant" (begin, began, has begun) helping in surgery. **(5)** People also (come, have came, have come) to expect simpler procedures because of these new techniques. **(6)** Laser surgery (is, have been, will be) another procedure that avoids cutting into tissue. **(7)** Such techniques (spring, sprang, have sprung) from technology developed for space exploration.

8.2 *Commonly Confused Verbs* The following verb pairs are easily confused.

Let and Leave *Let* means "to allow or permit." *Leave* means "to depart" or "to allow something to remain where it is."

> **INCORRECT:** *Rudyard Kipling, the author of "Rikki-tikki-tavi," often leaves animal characters tell his stories.*
> **CORRECT:** *Rudyard Kipling, the author of "Rikki-tikki-tavi," often lets animal characters tell his stories.*

Lie and Lay *Lie* means "to rest in a flat position." *Lay* means "to put or place."

> **INCORRECT:** *Rikki-tikki was laying in the middle of the path.*
> **CORRECT:** *Rikki-tikki was lying in the middle of the path.*

Sit and Set *Sit* means "to be in a seated position." *Set* means "to put or place."

> **INCORRECT:** *The mongoose set on the shoulder of the boy who immediately sat a piece of meat before it.*
> **CORRECT:** *The mongoose sat on the shoulder of the boy who immediately set a piece of meat before it.*

Rise and Raise *Rise* means "to move upward." *Raise* means "to move something upward."

> **INCORRECT:** *Nag just raised up, rising his head threateningly.*
> **CORRECT:** *Nag just rose up, raising his head threateningly.*

Learn and Teach *Learn* means "to gain knowledge or skill." *Teach* means "to help someone learn."

> **INCORRECT:** *Rikki-tikki learned Nag to fear something.*
> **CORRECT:** *Rikki-tikki taught Nag to fear something.*

Here are the principal parts of these troublesome verb pairs.

Present Tense	Past Tense	Past Participle
let	let	(have, had) let
leave	left	(have, had) left
lie	lay	(have, had) lain
lay	laid	(have, had) laid
sit	sat	(have, had) sat
set	set	(have, had) set
rise	rose	(have, had) risen
raise	raised	(have, had) raised
learn	learned	(have, had) learned
teach	taught	(have, had) taught

GRAMMAR PRACTICE

Choose the correct verb from each pair of words.

(1) Rudyard Kipling's tale "Rikki-tikki-tavi" (learns, teaches) readers many facts about the cobra and its natural enemy, the mongoose. **(2)** Most snakes (lay, lie) hidden to avoid people and animals much of the time. **(3)** The cobra, however, (raises, rises) to seek out its victim. **(4)** (Letting, Leaving) a cobra alone is no protection either. **(5)** An unintentional disturbance can (set, sit) one against you. **(6)** Both male and female, while protecting their eggs, for example, will (raise, rise) up against any approaching intruder. **(7)** The venom of the cobra is a deadly nerve- and muscle-paralyzing substance that (lets, leaves) a human being dead within a few hours.

❾ Using Modifiers Effectively

9.1 *Adjective or Adverb?* Use an adjective to modify a noun or a pronoun. Use an adverb to modify a verb, an adjective, or another adverb.

> **INCORRECT:** *Traditional Chinese families do not regard a two-income household as high as American families do, so the family in "The White Umbrella" must be real desperate if the mother has to work outside the home.*
> **CORRECT:** *Traditional Chinese families do not regard the two-income household as <u>highly</u> as American families do, so the family in "The White Umbrella" must be <u>rather</u> desperate if the mother has to work outside the home.*

Use an adjective after a linking verb to describe the subject.

Remember that in addition to forms of the verb *be*, the following are linking verbs: *become, seem, appear, look, sound, feel, taste, grow,* and *smell*.

> **EXAMPLES:** *The narrator feels <u>bad</u> that her mother is working, although her sister thinks <u>differently</u>, not caring if anybody knows.*

GRAMMAR PRACTICE

Write the correct modifier in each pair.

(1) In "The White Umbrella" the two sisters listen as Eugenie Roberts plays the piano (real, really) well. **(2)** They wait (respectful, respectfully) for her lesson to finish. **(3)** People (usual, usually) begin piano lessons when they are young. **(4)** Children develop (valuable, valuably) skills at the piano, such as the ability to follow rhythm and read music. **(5)** Music is something that (deep, deeply) affects all people. **(6)** Although musicians come from many different countries, they are able to play together (perfect, perfectly). **(7)** Music is a (natural, naturally) human expression.

9.2 *Comparisons and Negatives*

Comparative and Superlative Adjectives
Use the comparative form of an adjective when comparing two things.

Comparative adjectives are formed by adding -er to short adjectives (small–smaller) or by using the word *more* with longer adjectives (horrible–more horrible).

> **INCORRECT:** *Traveling across the Atlantic Ocean in days past was uncomfortabler than flying is today.*
> **CORRECT:** *Traveling across the Atlantic Ocean in days past was much <u>more uncomfortable</u> than flying is today.*

Use the superlative form when comparing three or more things.

The superlative is formed by adding -est to short adjectives (tall–tallest) or by using the word *most* with longer adjectives (interesting–most interesting).

> **INCORRECT:** *Obtaining passage, traveling steerage, or passing through customs: which was difficultest?*
> **CORRECT:** *Obtaining passage, traveling steerage, or passing through customs: which was <u>most difficult</u>?*

The comparative and superlative forms of some adjectives are irregular.

Adjective	Comparative	Superlative
good	better	best
well	better	best
bad	worse	worst
ill	worse	worst
little	less *or* lesser	least
much	more	most
many	more	most
far	farther *or* further	farthest *or* furthest

Comparative and Superlative Adverbs
When comparing two actions, use the comparative form of an adverb, which is formed by adding -er or the word *more*.

> **INCORRECT**: *European immigrants, frequenter than not, entered the United States frightened and exhausted.*
> **CORRECT**: *European immigrants, <u>more frequently</u> than not, entered the United States frightened and exhausted.*

WATCH OUT! Do not use both -er and *more*. Do not use both -est and *most*. Remove *more* and *most* from the following sentence: *The ship was more faster than the most fastest winds.* Do you notice the improvement?

When comparing more than two actions, use the superlative form of an adverb, which is formed by adding -est or by using the word *most*.

> **EXAMPLE**: *Of the several ports of entry, European immigrants entered through Ellis Island most often.*

Double Negatives
To avoid double negatives, use only one negative word in a clause.

Besides *not* and *no,* the following are negative words: *never, nobody, none, no one, nothing,* and *nowhere.*

> **EXAMPLE**: *Most immigrants <u>didn't ever</u> regret moving to a new country.*

GRAMMAR PRACTICE

Write the correct modifier in each pair.

(1) More than 60 years after Ellis Island opened as the (larger, largest) port of entry to this country, it was abandoned. **(2)** In the 1980s the facilities underwent the (greatest, most greatest) restoration ever. **(3)** The National Park Service helped supervise but did not try to find (any, no) funding sources. **(4)** The Statue of Liberty-Ellis Island Restoration Project (activelier, more actively) solicited contributions. **(5)** In 1990 there was a (grand, grandly) reopening of the main building. **(6)** The museum and examination rooms remind us that our immigration process used to be (worse, worser). **(7)** Which films, objects, and oral histories (more vividly, most vividly) record our past?

9.3 Special Problems with Modifiers
The following terms are frequently misused in spoken English, but they should be used correctly in written English.

Them and Those *Them* is always a pronoun and never a modifier for a noun. *Those* is a pronoun when it stands alone. It is an adjective when followed by a noun.

> **INCORRECT**: *In "Growing Up" Baker describes them experiences that led him to become a writer.*
> **CORRECT**: *In "Growing Up" Baker describes <u>those</u> experiences that led him to become a writer.*

Bad and Badly Always use *bad* as an adjective, whether before a noun or after a linking verb. *Badly* should generally be used to modify an action verb.

> **EXAMPLES**: *Knowing that he had done <u>badly</u>, he returned to the house defeated. He felt <u>bad</u> because he did not sell any papers.*

WATCH OUT! Avoid the use of *here* after *this* or *these*. Similarly, avoid using *there* after *that* or *those*. Notice the improvement when *here* and *there* are removed from the following sentence:

>**INCORRECT:** *I was amused by this here story. Russell's attempt to sell that there Saturday Evening Post was funny.*
>**CORRECT:** *I was amused by this story. Russell's attempt to sell that Saturday Evening Post was funny.*

This, That, These, and Those Whether used as adjectives or pronouns, *this* and *these* refer to people and things that are nearby, and *that* and *those* refer to people and things that are farther away.

>**EXAMPLES:** *After deciding to concentrate on writing, Baker found this work more satisfying than that tiresome routine of selling papers.*

Good and Well *Good* is always an adjective, never an adverb. Use *well* as either an adjective or an adverb, depending on the sentence.

When used as an adjective, *well* usually refers to a person's health. As an adverb, *well* modifies an action verb. In the expression "feeling good," *good* refers to being happy or pleased.

>**EXAMPLES:** *Baker's little sister sold papers well. Baker felt good about her success and bought her an apple.*

Few and Little, Fewer and Less *Few* refers to numbers of things that can be counted; *little* refers to amounts or quantities. *Fewer* is used when comparing numbers of things; *less* is used when comparing amounts or quantities.

>**INCORRECT:** *As a writer, Baker would encounter less angry dogs. He would have few sense of rejection and fewer hardship than he would if he continued trying to sell the Saturday Evening Post.*
>**CORRECT:** *As a writer, Baker would encounter fewer angry dogs. He would have less sense of rejection and less hardship than he would if he continued trying to sell the Saturday Evening Post.*

Write the modifier from each pair that fits the meaning of the sentence.

(1) In "Growing Up," Russell Baker's mother is one of (them, those) mothers who works hard to guide her children. **(2)** Times were hard during the Depression and (few, less) people lived in luxury. **(3)** Naturally, she was concerned that Russell grow up to have a (good, well) profession. **(4)** (This, That) concern motivated her to teach him about character and gumption. **(5)** She was disappointed when he sold papers (bad, badly). **(6)** Russell had (few, little) interest in selling papers; however, the experience taught him about himself. **(7)** He learned that such a profession would give him (few, less) satisfaction than a job collecting garbage. **(8)** He needed a job that would accommodate (good, well) his lack of gumption.

⑩ Phrases and Clauses

A phrase is a group of related words that does not have a subject and predicate and that functions in a sentence as a single part of speech. Phrases may appear anywhere in a sentence. If a phrase appears at the beginning of a sentence, it is called an introductory phrase. Because phrases can act as a single part of speech, they are classified as prepositional phrases, appositive phrases, infinitive phrases, participial phrases, and gerund phrases.

10.1 *Prepositional Phrases* When a phrase consists of a preposition, its object, and any modifiers of the object, it is called a prepositional phrase. Prepositional phrases that modify nouns or pronouns are called adjective phrases. Prepositional phrases that modify a verb, an adjective, or another adverb are adverb phrases.

>**ADJECTIVE PHRASE:** *In the excerpt from I Never Had It Made, Jackie Robinson tells the story of his integration of the Brooklyn Dodgers.*

ADVERB PHRASE: *Jackie Robinson had played <u>for the Montreal Royals</u>.*

10.2 *Appositive Phrases* An appositive phrase is a group of words that identifies or provides further information about a noun or pronoun that directly precedes the phrase.

> **EXAMPLE:** *Jackie Robinson, <u>an exceptional athlete</u>, was Branch Rickey's pick to be the first African-American player to join the Dodgers.*

10.3 *Infinitive Phrases* An infinitive phrase consists of an infinitive (*to* + a verb) along with its modifiers and objects.

> **EXAMPLE:** *Branch Rickey wanted <u>to integrate major-league baseball</u>.*

10.4 *Participial Phrases* A participial phrase is a group of words that includes a participle. There are two kinds of participles: past and present. The past participle is usually formed by adding *-d* or *-ed* to the present tense; however, irregular verbs do not follow this rule. The present participle is formed by adding *-ing* to the present tense of any verb. A participle with its objects and modifiers is called a participial phrase. Participial phrases act as adjectives, modifying a noun or a pronoun.

> **EXAMPLE:** *<u>Having read Robinson's autobiography</u>, I can better imagine the difficulties he faced.*

10.5 *Gerund Phrases* A gerund is a verb form ending in *-ing* that functions as a noun. A gerund phrase is a group of words that includes a gerund and its modifiers and objects.

> **EXAMPLE:** *<u>Maintaining his self-control</u> was one of Robinson's best defenses.*

GRAMMAR PRACTICE

Identify each underlined phrase as a prepositional phrase, an appositive phrase, an infinitive phrase, a participial phrase, or a gerund phrase.

(1) After reading Jackie Robinson's autobiography, I wanted <u>to find out more about</u> Robinson. **(2)** <u>Searching through the library</u>, I came across several books and articles on the subject. **(3)** Opposition to Robinson died down after his first year with the Dodgers. **(4)** <u>Voted the most valuable player in the league in 1949</u>, Robinson went on to be one of the most popular Dodger players. **(5)** Robinson played his entire major-league career with the same team, <u>the Brooklyn Dodgers</u>. **(6)** <u>Reading about this period in American sports history</u> was sometimes a painful experience. **(7)** In 1962 Robinson became the first African American <u>to enter the National Baseball Hall of Fame</u>.

10.6 *Independent (Main) and Dependent (Subordinate) Clauses* A clause is a group of words that contains a subject and a verb. There are two kinds of clauses: main (independent) clauses and subordinate (dependent) clauses. A main clause can stand alone as a complete sentence. A dependent clause cannot stand alone as a sentence and must be attached to a main clause to form a complex sentence. If a dependent clause is not attached to a main clause, it is considered a sentence fragment.

> **INDEPENDENT CLAUSE:** *I read "Amigo Brothers."*
> **DEPENDENT CLAUSE:** *After I finished dinner*
> **COMPLEX SENTENCE:** *After I finished dinner, I read "Amigo Brothers."*

10.7 *Adjective and Adverb Clauses* An adjective clause is a dependent clause used as an adjective. Adjective clauses are usually introduced by the relative pronouns *who, whom, whose, which,* and *that.* An adverb clause is a dependent clause that is used as an adverb to modify a verb, an adjective, or another adverb.

> **ADJECTIVE CLAUSE:** *Felix and Antonio are the names of the boys <u>who are the main characters in "Amigo Brothers."</u>*
> **ADVERB CLAUSE:** *The boys had to make a decision <u>before they met in the division final match in August.</u>*

10.8 *Noun Clauses* A noun clause is a dependent clause that is used in a sentence as a noun. A noun clause may be used as a subject, a direct object, an indirect object, a predicate noun, or an object of a preposition.

EXAMPLE: *The division final match would determine* who would represent the Boys Club in the Golden Gloves Tournament.

GRAMMAR PRACTICE

Identify each underlined clause as a main or dependent clause. If the clause is dependent, identify it as an adjective clause, an adverb clause, or a noun clause.

(1) Antonio and Felix promised each other not to pull their punches. **(2)** Each boy wondered what would happen to their friendship after the fight. **(3)** Felix went to a movie called *The Champion* when he wanted to psych himself for the fight. **(4)** Antonio went up to the rooftop, where he did some heavy thinking. **(5)** In the end, Felix and Antonio didn't care which of them won the division final match.

⑪ The Structure of Sentences

The structure of a sentence is determined by the number and kind of clauses it contains. Sentences are classified as simple, compound, complex, and compound-complex.

11.1 *Simple Sentences* A simple sentence is made up of one independent clause and no dependent (or subordinate) clauses.

INDEPENDENT CLAUSE
Sam ran to the theater.

INDEPENDENT CLAUSE
Max waited in front of the theater.

A simple sentence may contain a compound subject or a compound verb.

SIMPLE SENTENCE WITH A COMPOUND SUBJECT: *Sam and Max went to the movie.*
SIMPLE SENTENCE WITH A COMPOUND VERB: *They clapped and whistled at their favorite parts.*

11.2 *Compound Sentences* A compound sentence is made up of two or more independent clauses joined together.

INDEPENDENT CLAUSES
Sam likes action movies, but **Max prefers comedies.**

Independent clauses can be joined with a comma and a coordinating conjunction, a semicolon, or a conjunctive adverb preceded by a semicolon and followed by a comma.

COMPOUND SENTENCE WITH A COMMA AND A COORDINATING CONJUNCTION: *I have not seen the movie yet, **but** I heard it is terrific.*
COMPOUND SENTENCE WITH A SEMICOLON: *The actor jumped from one building to another; he barely made the final leap.*
COMPOUND SENTENCE WITH A CONJUNCTIVE ADVERB:
*The actor knew all the lines; **however,** he didn't play the part very well.*

WATCH OUT! Do not confuse a compound sentence with a simple sentence that has compound parts.

GRAMMAR PRACTICE

Identify the subject and verb in each part of the compound sentence; identify the conjunction or semicolon.

(1) Yellowstone Park was crowded, and most of the campgrounds were full. **(2)** A family of bears approached our car, but the mother bear led her cubs away. **(3)** We took our new video camera with us, and my sister taped some of our adventures. **(4)** My brother and I went for a hike, but we got lost. **(5)** My brother was in a hurry to get back, so I feared being left behind.

11.3 *Complex Sentences* A complex sentence is made up of one independent clause and one or more dependent clauses.

INDEPENDENT CLAUSE
I would like to be an actor, although **I've never been on stage before.**
DEPENDENT CLAUSE

An independent clause can stand alone as a sentence. A dependent clause also has a subject and a predicate, but cannot stand alone. It is often introduced by a subordinating conjunction, such as *when, if, because, although,* or *until.*

GRAMMAR PRACTICE

In each of the following complex sentences, identify each clause as either independent or dependent.

(1) Although Florence Nightingale came from a wealthy English family, she was known for her wit and beauty. **(2)** She could speak and read many languages before she turned 16. **(3)** Before she was 30, she decided on her true mission in life; she would care for sick people. **(4)** Since her family did not approve of her plans, she secretly read books on health and nursing. **(5)** Florence became an expert on hospitals and public health because she worked so hard. **(6)** While the Crimean War was raging, she cared for wounded soldiers in Turkey and reorganized the military hospitals. **(7)** Because she was so diligent, the soldiers called Nightingale the Lady with the Lamp.

GRAMMAR PRACTICE: MIXED REVIEW

Identify each sentence as **Simple, Compound,** or **Complex.**

(1) When the ancient Egyptians were at their strongest, they used hieroglyphics, a kind of picture writing. **(2)** Few Egyptians wrote in hieroglyphics after A.D. 394. **(3)** It was forgotten after a few centuries because no one used it. **(4)** Later, people studied the ancient Egyptian civilization, and they wanted to read the hieroglyphics. **(5)** They tried to interpret it, but no one knew how. **(6)** Then in 1799, a French soldier found the clue to hieroglyphics. **(7)** While the French army was building a fort near the town of Rosetta in Egypt, the soldier found a black stone. **(8)** A message was carved on the Rosetta stone in hieroglyphics, in another ancient Egyptian language, and in ancient Greek. **(9)** People could read Greek, and they compared it with hieroglyphics. **(10)** It took 23 years before scholars translated hieroglyphics.

11.4 *Compound-Complex Sentences* A compound-complex sentence is made up of two or more independent clauses and one or more dependent clauses. If you start with a compound sentence, all you need to do to form a compound-complex sentence is add a dependent clause.

COMPOUND SENTENCE:

INDEPENDENT CLAUSES
All the students wanted to be in the play, but many were too shy to audition.

COMPOUND-COMPLEX SENTENCE:

INDEPENDENT CLAUSES
All the students wanted to be in the play, but many were too shy to audition, although some finally found the courage to do so.
DEPENDENT CLAUSE

GRAMMAR PRACTICE

In each of the following compound-complex sentences, identify each clause as independent or dependent.

(1) The *Titanic* was the second of three sister ships; the other two were named *Olympic* and *Gigantic,* which was later renamed *Britannic.* **(2)** While it was on its maiden voyage in April 1912, the *Titanic* hit an iceberg, and the ship sank in 2 hours 40 minutes. **(3)** While *Titanic* foundered in its last moments, the ship split in two, and each half plunged two and half miles to the bottom of the ocean. **(4)** The ship's bow slammed into the ocean floor, and the stern landed almost a half-mile away, as people struggled to survive at the ocean's surface. **(5)** The ship had 2,200 people on board, and although *Titanic* had lifeboat capacity for 1,178, only 705 survived.

GRAMMAR PRACTICE: MIXED REVIEW

Identify each sentence with **S** for simple, **CD** for compound, **CX** for complex, and **CC** for compound-complex.

(1) In Greek mythology, Daedalus tried to escape from Crete. **(2)** After he made wings out of feathers, he flew to the island of Santorini. **(3)** A plane, the *Daedalus,* made the same journey in 1988; it was powered solely by human muscle. **(4)** Although people had wanted to power planes by human muscle for many years, the existing planes were too heavy. **(5)** When lightweight material was invented in the 1970s, people used the material to make the *Daedalus,* and finally planes were light enough. **(6)** Its wingspan was 112 feet, but it weighed only 68.5 pounds. **(7)** Although the plane had huge wings and weighed very little, the pilot required great strength. **(8)** The plane had a bicycle mechanism, and it was pedaled by an Olympic cyclist from Greece. **(9)** The cyclist trained hard for the flight; it was a test of endurance. **(10)** The flight was 74 miles long and took 3 hours and 54 minutes.

⑫ Correcting Capitalization

12.1 *Proper Nouns and Adjectives*

A common noun names a whole class of persons, places, things, or ideas. A proper noun names a particular person, place, thing, or idea. A proper adjective is an adjective formed from a proper noun. All proper nouns and proper adjectives are capitalized.

Names and Personal Titles Capitalize the name and title of a person.

Also capitalize the initials and abbreviations of titles that stand for those names. *Thomas Alva Edison, T. A. Edison, Governor James Thompson,* and *Mr. Aaron Copland* are capitalized correctly.

EXAMPLES: *In* The Autobiography of Malcolm X, *Malcolm X tells how his desire to write letters—to Elijah Muhammad, for example—inspired him to study.*

Capitalize a word referring to a family relationship when it is used as someone's name (Uncle Al) but not when it is used to identify a person (Jill's uncle).

EXAMPLES: *If the people he mentions—Ella and Reginald—had been aunt and uncle instead of sister and brother, he might have called them Aunt Ella and Uncle Reginald.*

WATCH OUT! Do not capitalize personal titles used as common nouns. *(We met the **m**ayor.)*

Languages, Nationalities, Religious Terms Capitalize the names of languages and nationalities as well as religious names and terms.

Capitalize languages and nationalities, such as *French, Gaelic, Chinese,* and *Tagalog.* Capitalize religious names and terms, such as *Allah, Jehovah, Bible,* and *Koran.*

EXAMPLES: *This famous African American was a Muslim, so he must have read the Koran.*

School Subjects Capitalize the name of a specific school course *(Civics 101, General Science).* Do not capitalize a general reference to a school subject *(social studies, algebra, art).*

EXAMPLES: *Malcolm X read about history and religion, but at first he could have used courses such as Penmanship 101 or Beginning English.*

WATCH OUT! Do not capitalize minor words in a proper noun that is made up of several words *(Field Museum **of** Natural History).*

Organizations, Institutions Capitalize the important words in the official names of organizations and institutions *(Congress, University of Texas).*

Do not capitalize words that refer to kinds of organizations or institutions (*college, hospital, museums*) or words that refer to specific organizations but are not their official names (*to the museum*).

> **EXAMPLES:** *He began reading in <u>Charlestown Prison</u> but really explored in depth the <u>library</u> at <u>Norfolk Prison Colony</u>.*

Geographical Names, Events, Time Periods
Capitalize geographical names, as well as the names of events, historical periods and documents, holidays, and months and days, but not the names of seasons or directions.

WATCH OUT! Do not capitalize a reference that does not use the full name of a place, event, or period. (*The Empire State Building was once the tallest **building** in the world.*)

> **EXAMPLES:** *As Malcolm X studied the dictionary, he learned about the aardvark, a termite-eating mammal from Africa. He read constantly—<u>summer</u>, <u>winter</u>, <u>spring</u>, and <u>fall</u>—in the library and in his cell.*

Names	Examples
Continents	Africa, South America
Bodies of water	Pacific Ocean, Lake Charles, Amazon River
Political units	Maine, Japan, Brasília
Sections of a country	the South, Middle Atlantic States
Public areas	the Loop, the Boston Common
Roads and structures	Park Avenue, Hoover Dam, Chrysler Building
Historical events	the War of 1812, the Emancipation Proclamation
Documents	Magna Carta, the Treaty of Paris
Periods of history	the Middle Ages, Reconstruction
Holidays	Arbor Day, New Year's Day
Months and days	May, Sunday
Seasons	summer, autumn
Directions	north, south

GRAMMAR PRACTICE

Write the correct forms of the words given in parentheses.

(1) Like (malcolm X, Malcolm X), Jawaharlal Nehru, first (prime minister, Prime Minister) of India, used prison for serious reading and writing. **(2)** While imprisoned, (nehru, Nehru), too, used letter writing to improve his communication skills. **(3)** His letters to his daughter, Indira, later (prime minister, Prime Minister) Ghandi, were the basis for a book on (world history, World History). **(4)** In prison, too, Nehru completed his (autobiography, Autobiography). **(5)** A Brahmin from (kashmir, Kashmir), he was educated at (harrow school, Harrow School) and (cambridge university, Cambridge University) in England. **(6)** He was as eloquent in (hindi, Hindi) as in (english, English).

12.2 *Titles of Created Works* Titles need to follow certain capitalization rules.

Poems, Stories, Articles Capitalize the first word, the last word, and all other important words in the title of a poem, a story, or an article. Enclose the title in quotation marks.

> **EXAMPLE:** Walt Whitman's poem "Song of Myself" celebrates his humanity and the joy of living in a glorious world.

Books, Plays, Magazines, Newspapers, Films Capitalize the first word, the last word, and all other important words in the title of a book, play or musical, magazine, newspaper, or film. Underline or italicize the title to set it off.

Within a title, don't capitalize articles, conjunctions, and prepositions of fewer than five letters.

> **EXAMPLE:** It appeared in his book *Leaves of Grass,* whose unconventional form and apparent immodesty shocked readers.

In cases where a title that is ordinarily italicized appears in a sentence that itself is in italics, the title should then appear in ordinary type to set it off from the rest of the sentence.

EXAMPLE: *Madeleine L'Engle's novel* A Wrinkle in Time *is an example of science fiction.*

GRAMMAR PRACTICE

Rewrite this paragraph, correcting punctuation and capitalization of titles.

(1) Some of Walt Whitman's first published poems appeared in the small book leaves of grass. **(2)** Others—such as those about the Civil War—beat! beat! drums!, when lilacs last in the dooryard bloom'd, and o captain! my captain!—appeared in the collection drum-taps. **(3)** Whitman was also a journalist: founder of the freeman, editor-printer of the long islander, editor of the Brooklyn daily eagle and the Brooklyn times, and reporter or writer for numerous other newspapers. **(4)** Some of his short stories were published in popular magazines such as the democratic review. **(5)** Others—for example, the half-breed—appeared in collections. **(6)** Whitman even wrote a novel: franklin evans. **(7)** Some collections of his works include the complete writings of walt whitman and the uncollected poetry and prose of walt whitman.

⓭ Correcting Punctuation

13.1 *Compound Sentences* Punctuation helps organize longer sentences that have several clauses.

Commas in Compound Sentences Use a comma before the conjunction that joins the clauses of a compound sentence.

EXAMPLE: *In* Boy: Tales of Childhood *Roald Dahl describes trips to the candy store with his friends, and he tells about the prank which got him into trouble.*

Semicolons in Compound Sentences Use a semicolon between the clauses of a compound sentence when no conjunction is used. Use a semicolon before, and a

comma after, a conjunctive adverb that joins the clauses of a compound sentence.

Conjunctive adverbs include *therefore, however, then, nevertheless, consequently,* and *besides.*

EXAMPLES: *The boys each received a weekly allowance; they enthusiastically spent their money at the local sweetshop. Licorice was one of their favorite types of candy; however, Thwaites's father told them it was made from rats' blood.*

USAGE TIP Even when clauses are connected by a coordinating conjunction, you should use a semicolon between them if one or both clauses contain a comma.

The Great Mouse Plot, a silly little prank, had painful consequences; but the five boys would still say it was fun.

GRAMMAR PRACTICE

Rewrite these sentences, adding commas and semicolons where necessary.

(1) The boys in the story like the sweetshop but they dislike Mrs. Pratchett because she is dirty all the time. **(2)** There were few health codes in 1923 so Mrs. Pratchett could get away with wearing dirty clothes and wrapping up candy in newspaper. **(3)** There are other reasons the boys don't like her for example, she often accuses them of stealing. **(4)** They never steal anything from the shop but Mrs. Pratchett always yells at them. **(5)** The mouse prank seems like a good idea and it is a way to get back at her. **(6)** The boys think that the prank might have killed Mrs. Pratchett they are relieved when they see that she is alive.

13.2 *Elements Set Off in a Sentence* Most elements that are not essential to a sentence are set off by commas to highlight the main idea of the sentence.

Introductory Words Use a comma to separate an introductory word from the rest of the sentence.

EXAMPLE: *Certainly, "The Old Grandfather and His Little Grandson," by Leo Tolstoy, teaches an important lesson.*

Use a comma to separate an introductory phrase from the rest of the sentence.

Use a comma to set off more than one introductory prepositional phrase but not for a single prepositional phrase in most cases.

> **EXAMPLE:** *In this tale of family life, we see the effect our conduct has. At home our actions are a powerful teacher.*

Interrupters Use commas to set off a word that interrupts the flow of a sentence.

> **INCORRECT:** *The parents fortunately were ashamed when they realized what they were teaching their son. They thought about their behavior therefore and decided to improve their conduct.*
>
> **CORRECT:** *The parents, fortunately, were ashamed when they realized what they were teaching their son. They thought about their behavior, therefore, and decided to improve their conduct.*

Use commas to set off a group of words that interrupts the flow of a sentence.

> **EXAMPLE:** *Misha noticed his parents treating his grandfather badly and, to his parents' surprise, started to make a wooden bucket for them.*

Nouns of Address Use commas to set off a noun in direct address at the beginning of a sentence.

> **EXAMPLE:** *"Father, your table manners are an embarrassment. Please eat in the corner," the father might have said.*

Use commas to set off a noun in direct address in the middle of a sentence.

> **EXAMPLE:** *The boy's mother asked, "What are you making, Misha, from those pieces of wood?"*

Appositives Set off with commas an appositive phrase that is not necessary to the meaning of the sentence.

The following sentence could be understood without the words set off by commas.

> **EXAMPLE:** *The father, the old man's son, scolded the grandfather.*

Do not set off with commas an appositive phrase that is necessary to the meaning of the sentence.

The following sentence could not be understood without the appositives following Misha:

> **EXAMPLE:** *Misha the child was showing what Misha the man would be like.*

USAGE TIP Sometimes if a comma is missing, a reader may group parts of a sentence in more than one way. A comma separates the parts so they can be read in only one way.

For Clarity Use a comma to prevent misreading or misunderstanding.

> **EXAMPLE:** *While the old man was eating, bits of food that would sometimes drop out of his mouth disgusted the couple.*

GRAMMAR PRACTICE

Rewrite these sentences. Add or delete commas where necessary.

(1) In our part of the world aged parents were once expected to live with their children. **(2)** Today a variety of lifestyles are available to senior citizens, and the variety is increasing. **(3)** Many however still live in familiar surroundings. **(4)** They may rent or own senior-citizen housing either houses or apartments. **(5)** In spite of these options according to the latest census more than 67 percent of seniors still live in family homes. **(6)** Some people of course are able to live independently. **(7)** These people can get help nursing or housekeeping care. **(8)** Would you believe Willard that not even 1 percent live in traditional nursing homes? **(9)** People may go in as couples or singly. **(10)** In 2000 4 million more elderly people lived in this country than did in 1990.

13.3 *Elements in a Series* Commas should be used to separate three or more items in a series and to separate adjectives preceding a noun.

Subjects, Predicates, and Other Elements

Use a comma after every item except the last in a series of three or more items.

Subjects or predicates may occur in series.

EXAMPLE: *In "The Highwayman" <u>the highwayman himself, the landlord's daughter, and the soldiers</u> are the main characters. The soldiers <u>come to the inn, lay a trap there, and tie up the robber's sweetheart.</u>*

Predicate adjectives often occur in series.

EXAMPLE: *The robber's sweetheart is <u>brave, faithful, and self-sacrificing</u>. The entire poem by Alfred Noyes is <u>romantic, atmospheric, and exciting.</u>*

USAGE TIP Note in the example that a comma followed by a conjunction precedes the last element in the series. That comma is always used.

Adverbs and prepositional phrases may also occur in series.

EXAMPLE: *The bold highwayman approaches the inn confidently, eagerly, but quietly. The highwayman came riding at midnight, in the silence, and by moonlight.*

Two or More Adjectives In most sentences, use a comma after each adjective except the last of two or more adjectives that precede a noun.

If you can reverse the order of adjectives without changing the meaning or if you can use *and* between them, separate the two adjectives with a comma.

EXAMPLE: *The beautiful, black-eyed daughter was braiding a dark red loveknot into her lovely long hair.*

GRAMMAR PRACTICE

Rewrite each sentence, inserting commas where they are needed.

(1) The poem "The Highwayman" speaks of a time when wagons stagecoaches and carriages were the main means of transportation. **(2)** The design of these vehicles had changed little from the Middle Ages

through the 17th 18th and 19th centuries. **(3)** Those who preyed on travelers could find wealthy unprotected victims by lying in wait on the roads. **(4)** The dashing daring dangerous highwaymen held great appeal for many. **(5)** We often find today's robbers less charming more frightening and often more dangerous. **(6)** Stagecoaches traveled in stages stopped at scheduled points and changed horses at each stop. **(7)** Can you visualize the highwayman's big powerful black charger?

13.4 *Dates, Addresses, and Letters*

Punctuation in dates, addresses, and letters makes information easy to understand.

Dates Use a comma between the day of the month and the year. If the date falls in the middle of a sentence, use another comma after the year.

EXAMPLES: *The sailing recorded in* Exploring the Titanic *took place on April 10, 1912, amidst great fanfare.*

Addresses Use a comma to separate the city and the state in an address or other location. If the city and state fall in the middle of a sentence, use a comma after the state too.

EXAMPLES: *The hull of the ship was launched in Belfast, Ireland, before thousands of spectators and several bands.*

Parts of a Letter Use a comma after the greeting and after the closing in a letter.

EXAMPLE:
Dear Mother,
You cannot imagine how gorgeous the Titanic *is. Our stateroom seems straight out of the Grand Hotel!*

Affectionately,
Millicent

GRAMMAR PRACTICE

Rewrite the following sentences, correcting the comma errors.

(1) Like the wreck of the *Titanic,* the *Hindenburg* disaster of May 6 1937 was the result of a simple accident. **(2)** The *Hindenburg* was a showpiece in its time, traveling back and forth between Germany and Lakehurst New Jersey for a year before it was destroyed. **(3)** Research at the library in Chicago Illinois revealed that the airship was named for Paul von Hindenburg, a German military leader and president. **(4)** The hydrogen-filled *Hindenburg* crashed in Lakehurst New Jersey when the gas caught fire. **(5)** On September 14 1996 I first read about the *Hindenburg* tragedy, in which 35 people met their doom.

13.5 *Quotations* Quotation marks let readers know exactly who said what. Incorrectly placed or missing quotation marks cause confusion.

Quotation Marks Use quotation marks at the beginning and the end of direct quotations and to set off titles of short works.

> **INCORRECT:** *In Langston Hughes's Thank You, M'am, Roger replies simply, Yes'm, to some of the woman's questions. He replies, No'm, to others.*
>
> **CORRECT:** *In Langston Hughes's "Thank You, M'am," Roger replies simply, "Yes'm," to some of the woman's questions. He replies, "No'm," to others.*

Capitalize the first word of a direct quotation, especially in a piece of dialogue.

> **EXAMPLE:** *The woman replies, "Um-hum," to Roger's apology.*

USAGE TIP If quoted words are from a written source and are not complete sentences, they can begin with a lowercase letter.

> **EXAMPLE:** *Mark Twain said that cauliflower was "nothing but cabbage with a college education."*

End Punctuation Place periods inside quotation marks. Place question marks and exclamation points inside quotation marks if they belong to the quotation; place them outside if they do not belong to the quotation. Place semicolons outside quotation marks.

> **INCORRECT:** *The boy asks, "You gonna take me to jail"?*
> *The woman replies, "Not with that face"!*
> *Offered food, he says, "That will be fine;" then he eats.*
>
> **CORRECT:** *The boy asks, "You gonna take me to jail?"*
> *The woman replies, "Not with that face!"*
> *Offered food, he says, "That will be fine"; then he eats.*

Use a comma to end a quotation that is a complete sentence but is followed by explanatory words.

> **EXAMPLE:** *"I wanted a pair of blue suede shoes," said the boy.*

Divided Quotations Capitalize the first word of the second part of a direct quotation if it begins a new sentence.

> **EXAMPLE:** *"Well, you didn't have to snatch my pocketbook," Mrs. Jones replied. "You could have asked me."*

Brackets in Quotations Use brackets to enclose an editorial explanation in quoted material.

> **EXAMPLE:** *"They [the Glenview Cardinals] came to play, but we were ready," said the quarterback.*

GRAMMAR PRACTICE

Rewrite this paragraph, inserting appropriate punctuation and capitalization.

(1) Langston Hughes once wrote children should be born without parents. **(2)** His difficult childhood may have been the inspiration for one of his best-loved poems, titled dreams. **(3)** It begins with the line hold fast to dreams; it is short, so I have memorized it. **(4)** You may know it the teacher said. I have seen the first stanza printed on T-shirts. **(5)** My soul has grown deep like the rivers Hughes says in The Negro Speaks of Rivers. **(6)** How happy he would have been at his memorial service to hear his favorite Ellington song, Do Nothing 'Til You Hear from Me! **(7)** Have you read any stories by Hughes other than Thank You, M'am?

Grammar Glossary

This glossary contains various terms you need to understand when you use the Grammar Handbook. Used as a reference source, this glossary will help you explore grammar concepts and the ways they relate to one another.

 A

Abbreviation An abbreviation is a shortened form of a word or word group; it is often made up of initials. (B.C., A.M., *Maj.*)

Active voice. *See* **Voice.**

Adjective An adjective modifies, or describes, a noun or pronoun. (*happy* camper, she is *small*)

A *predicate adjective* follows a linking verb and describes the subject. (The day seemed *long*.)

A *proper adjective* is formed from a proper noun. (*Jewish* temple, *Alaskan* husky)

The *comparative* form of an adjective compares two things. (*more alert, thicker*)

The *superlative* form of an adjective compares more than two things. (*most abundant, weakest*)

What Adjectives Tell	Examples
How many	*some* writers *much* joy
What kind	*grand* plans *wider* streets
Which one(s)	*these* flowers *that* star

Adjective phrase. *See* **Phrase.**

Adverb An adverb modifies a verb, an adjective, or another adverb. (Clare sang *loudly*.)

The *comparative* form of an adverb compares two actions. (*more generously, faster*)

The *superlative* form of an adverb compares more than two actions. (*most sharply, closest*)

What Adverbs Tell	Examples
How	climb *carefully* chuckle *merrily*
When	arrived *late* left *early*
Where	climbed *up* moved *away*
To what extent	*extremely* upset *hardly* visible

Adverb, conjunctive. *See* **Conjunctive adverb.**

Adverb phrase. *See* **Phrase.**

Agreement Sentence parts that correspond with one another are said to be in agreement.

In *pronoun-antecedent agreement*, a pronoun and the word it refers to are the same in number, gender, and person. (*Bill* mailed *his* application. The *students* ate *their* lunches.)

In *subject-verb agreement*, the subject and verb in a sentence are the same in number. (*A child cries* for help. *They cry* aloud.)

Ambiguous reference An ambiguous reference occurs when a pronoun may refer to more than one word. (Bud asked his brother if *he* had any mail.)

Antecedent An antecedent is the noun or pronoun to which a pronoun refers. (If *Adam* forgets *his* raincoat, *he* will be late for school. *She* learned *her* lesson.)

Appositive An appositive is a noun or phrase that explains one or more words in a sentence. (Cary Grant, *an Englishman*, spent most of his adult life in America.)

An *essential appositive* is needed to make the sense of a sentence complete. (A comic strip inspired the musical *Annie*.)

A *nonessential appositive* is one that adds information to a sentence but is not necessary to its sense. (O. Henry, *a short-story writer*, spent time in prison.)

Article Articles are the special adjectives *a, an,* and *the*. (*the* day, *a* fly)

The definite article (the word *the*) is one that refers to a particular thing. (*the* cabin)

An indefinite article is used with a noun that is not unique but refers to one of many of its kind. (*a* dish, *an* otter)

Auxiliary verb. *See* **Verb.**

 C

Clause A clause is a group of words that contains a verb and its subject. (*they slept*)

An *adjective clause* is a subordinate clause that modifies a noun or pronoun. (Hugh bought the sweater *that he had admired*.)

An **adverb clause** is a subordinate clause used to modify a verb, an adjective, or an adverb. (Ring the bell *when it is time for class to begin*.)

A **noun clause** is a subordinate clause that is used as a noun. (*Whatever you say* interests me.)

An **elliptical clause** is a clause from which a word or words have been omitted. (We are not as lucky as *they*.)

A **main (independent) clause** can stand by itself as a sentence. (*the flashlight flickered*)

A **dependent (subordinate) clause** does not express a complete thought and cannot stand by itself. (*while the nation watched*)

Clause	Example
Main (independent)	The hurricane struck
Subordinate (dependent)	while we were preparing to leave.

Collective noun. *See* **Noun.**

Comma splice A comma splice is an error caused when two sentences are separated with a comma instead of an end mark. (*The band played a medley of show tunes, everyone enjoyed the show.*)

Common noun. *See* **Noun.**

Comparative. *See* **Adjective; Adverb.**

Complement A complement is a word or group of words that completes the meaning of a verb. (The kitten finished the *milk*.) *See also* **Direct object; Indirect object.**

An **objective complement** is a word or a group of words that follows a direct object and renames or describes that object. (The parents of the rescued child declared Gus a *hero*.)

A **subject complement** follows a linking verb and renames or describes the subject. (The coach seemed *anxious*.) *See also* **Noun (predicate noun); Adjective (predicate adjective).**

Complete predicate The complete predicate of a sentence consists of the main verb plus any words that modify the verb or complete the verb's meaning. (The student *produces work of high caliber*.)

Complete subject The complete subject of a sentence consists of the simple subject plus any words that modify or describe the simple subject. (*Students of history* believe that wars can be avoided.)

Sentence Part	Example
Complete subject	The man in the ten-gallon hat
Complete predicate	wore a pair of silver spurs.

Compound sentence part A sentence element that consists of two or more subjects, verbs, objects, or other parts is compound. (*Lou* and *Jay* helped. Laura *makes* and *models* scarves. Jill sings *opera* and *popular music*.)

Conjunction A conjunction is a word that links other words or groups of words.

A **coordinating conjunction** connects related words, groups of words, or sentences. (*and, but, or*)

A **correlative conjunction** is one of a pair of conjunctions that work together to connect sentence parts. (*either . . . or, neither . . . nor, not only . . . but also, whether . . . or, both . . . and*)

A **subordinating conjunction** introduces a subordinate clause. (*after, although, as, as if, as long as, as though, because, before, if, in order that, since, so that, than, though, till, unless, until, whatever, when, where, while*)

Conjunctive adverb A conjunctive adverb joins the clauses of a compound sentence. (*however, therefore, yet*)

Contraction A contraction is formed by joining two words and substituting an apostrophe for a letter or letters left out of one of the words. (*didn't, we've*)

Coordinating conjunction. *See* **Conjunction.**

Correlative conjunction. *See* **Conjunction.**

 D

Dangling modifier A dangling modifier is one that does not clearly modify any word in the sentence. (*Dashing for the train, the barriers got in the way.*)

Demonstrative pronoun. *See* **Pronoun.**

Dependent clause. *See* **Clause.**

Direct object A direct object receives the action of a verb. Direct objects follow transitive verbs. (Jude planned the *party*.)

Direct quotation. *See* **Quotation.**

Divided quotation. *See* **Quotation.**

Double negative A double negative is the incorrect use of two negative words when only one is needed. (*Nobody* did*n't* care.)

End mark An end mark is one of several punctuation marks that can end a sentence. See the punctuation chart on page R68.

 Fragment. *See* **Sentence fragment.**

Future tense. *See* **Verb tense.**

 Gender The gender of a personal pronoun indicates whether the person or thing referred to is male, female, or neuter. (My cousin plays the tuba; *he* often performs in school concerts.)

Gerund A gerund is a verbal that ends in *-ing* and functions as a noun. (*Making* pottery takes patience.)

 Helping verb. *See* **Verb (auxiliary verb).**

Illogical comparison An illogical comparison is a comparison that does not make sense because words are missing or illogical. (My computer is *newer than Kay.*)

Indefinite pronoun. *See* **Pronoun.**

Indefinite reference Indefinite reference occurs when a pronoun is used without a clear antecedent. (My aunt hugged me in front of my friends, and *it* was embarrassing.)

Independent clause. *See* **Clause.**

Indirect object An indirect object tells to whom or for whom (sometimes to what or for what) something is done. (Arthur wrote *Kerry* a letter.)

Indirect question An indirect question tells what someone asked without using the person's exact words. (*My friend asked me if I could go with her to the dentist.*)

Indirect quotation. *See* **Quotation.**

Infinitive An infinitive is a verbal beginning with *to* that functions as a noun, an adjective, or an adverb. (He wanted *to go* to the play.)

Intensive pronoun. *See* **Pronoun.**

Interjection An interjection is a word or phrase used to express strong feeling. (*Wow! Good grief!*)

Interrogative pronoun. *See* **Pronoun.**

Intransitive verb. *See* **Verb.**

Inverted sentence An inverted sentence is one in which the subject comes after the verb. (*How was the movie? Here come the clowns.*)

Irregular verb. *See* **Verb.**

 Linking verb. *See* **Verb.**

 Main clause. *See* **Clause.**

Main verb. *See* **Verb.**

Modifier A modifier makes another word more precise. Modifiers most often are adjectives or adverbs; they may also be phrases, verbals, or clauses that function as adjectives or adverbs. (*small* box, smiled *broadly*, house *by the sea*, dog *barking loudly*)

An *essential modifier* is one that is necessary to the meaning of a sentence. (Everybody *who has a free pass* should enter now. None *of the passengers* got on the train.)

A *nonessential modifier* is one that merely adds more information to a sentence that is clear without the addition. (We will use the new dishes, *which are stored in the closet.*)

 Noun A noun names a person, a place, a thing, or an idea. (*auditor, shelf, book, goodness*)

An *abstract noun* names an idea, a quality, or a feeling. (*joy*)

A *collective noun* names a group of things. (*bevy*)

A *common noun* is a general name of a person, a place, a thing, or an idea. (*valet, hill, bread, amazement*)

A *compound noun* contains two or more words. (*hometown, self-control, screen test*)

A *noun of direct address* is the name of a person being directly spoken to. (*Lee*, do you have the package? No, *Suki*, your letter did not arrive.)

A *possessive noun* shows who or what owns or is associated with something. (*Lil's* ring, a *day's* pay)

A *predicate noun* follows a linking verb and renames the subject. (Karen is a *writer.*)

A *proper noun* names a particular person, place, or thing. (*John Smith, Ohio, Sears Tower, Congress*)

Number A word is singular in number if it refers to just one person, place, thing, idea, or action and plural in number if it refers to more than one person, place, thing, idea, or action. (The words *he, waiter,* and *is* are singular. The words *they, waiters,* and *are* are plural.)

 Object of a preposition The object of a preposition is the noun or pronoun that follows a preposition. (The athletes cycled along the *route.* Jane baked a cake for *her.*)

Object of a verb The object of a verb receives the action of the verb. (Sid told *stories*.)

Participle A participle is often used as part of a verb phrase. (had *written*) It can also be used as a verbal that functions as an adjective. (the *leaping* deer, the medicine *taken* for a fever)

The ***present participle*** is formed by adding *-ing* to the present form of a verb. (*Walking* rapidly, we reached the general store.)

The ***past participle*** of a regular verb is formed by adding *-d* or *-ed* to the present form. The past participles of irregular verbs do not follow this pattern. (*Startled*, they ran from the house. *Spun* glass is delicate. A *broken* cup lay there.)

Passive voice. *See* **Voice.**

Past tense. *See* **Verb tense.**

Perfect tenses. *See* **Verb tense.**

Person Person is a means of classifying pronouns.

A ***first-person*** pronoun refers to the person speaking. (*We* came.)

A ***second-person*** pronoun refers to the person spoken to. (*You* ask.)

A ***third-person*** pronoun refers to some other person(s) or thing(s) being spoken of. (*They* played.)

Personal pronoun. *See* **Pronoun.**

Phrase A phrase is a group of related words that does not contain a verb and its subject. (*noticing everything, under a chair*)

An **adjective phrase** modifies a noun or a pronoun. (The label *on the bottle* has faded.)

An **adverb phrase** modifies a verb, an adjective, or an adverb. (Come *to the fair*.)

An **appositive phrase** explains one or more words in a sentence. (Mary, *a champion gymnast,* won gold medals at the Olympics.)

A **gerund phrase** consists of a gerund and its modifiers and complements. (*Fixing the leak* will take only a few minutes.)

An **infinitive phrase** consists of an infinitive, its modifiers, and its complements. (*To prepare for a test,* study in a quiet place.)

A **participial phrase** consists of a participle and its modifiers and complements. (*Straggling to the finish line,* the last runners arrived.)

A **prepositional phrase** consists of a preposition, its object, and the object's modifiers. (The Saint Bernard does rescue work *in the Swiss Alps.*)

A **verb phrase** consists of a main verb and one or more helping verbs. (*might have ordered*)

Possessive A noun or pronoun that is possessive shows ownership or relationship. (*Dan's* story, *my* doctor)

Possessive noun. *See* **Noun.**

Possessive pronoun. *See* **Pronoun.**

Predicate The predicate of a sentence tells what the subject is or does. (The van *runs well even in winter*. The job seems *too complicated*.) *See also* **Complete predicate; Simple predicate.**

Predicate adjective. *See* **Adjective.**

Predicate nominative A predicate nominative is a noun or pronoun that follows a linking verb and renames or explains the subject. (Joan is a computer *operator*. The winner of the prize was *he*.)

Predicate pronoun. *See* **Pronoun.**

Preposition A preposition is a word that relates its object to another part of the sentence or to the sentence as a whole. (Alfredo leaped *onto* the stage.)

Prepositional phrase. *See* **Phrase.**

Present tense. *See* **Verb tense.**

Pronoun A pronoun replaces a noun or another pronoun. Some pronouns allow a writer or speaker to avoid repeating a proper noun. Other pronouns let a writer refer to an unknown or unidentified person or thing.

A **demonstrative pronoun** singles out one or more persons or things. (*This* is the letter.)

An **indefinite pronoun** refers to an unidentified person or thing. (*Everyone* stayed home. Will you hire *anybody*?)

An **intensive pronoun** emphasizes a noun or pronoun. (The teacher *himself* sold tickets.)

An **interrogative pronoun** asks a question. (*What* happened to you?)

A **personal pronoun** shows a distinction of person. (*I* came. *You* see. *He* knows.)

A **possessive pronoun** shows ownership. (*My* spaghetti is always good. Are *your* parents coming to the play?)

A **predicate pronoun** follows a linking verb and renames the subject. (The owners of the store were *they*.)

A *reflexive pronoun* reflects an action back on the subject of the sentence. (Joe helped *himself*.)

A *relative pronoun* relates a subordinate clause to the word it modifies. (The draperies, *which* had been made by hand, were ruined in the fire.)

Pronoun-antecedent agreement. *See* **Agreement.**

Pronoun forms

The *subject form* of a pronoun is used when the pronoun is the subject of a sentence or follows a linking verb as a predicate pronoun. (*She* fell. The star was *she*.)

The *object form* of a pronoun is used when the pronoun is the direct or indirect object of a verb or verbal or the object of a preposition. (We sent *him* the bill. We ordered food for *them*.)

Proper adjective. *See* **Adjective.**

Proper noun. *See* **Noun.**

Punctuation Punctuation clarifies the structure of sentences. See the punctuation chart on page R68.

 Q

Quotation A quotation consists of words from another speaker or writer.

A *direct quotation* is the exact words of a speaker or writer. (Martin said, "*The homecoming game has been postponed.*")

A *divided quotation* is a quotation separated by words that identify the speaker. ("*The homecoming game,*" said Martin, "*has been postponed.*")

An *indirect quotation* reports what a person said without giving the exact words. (*Martin said that the homecoming game had been postponed.*)

 R

Reflexive pronoun. *See* **Pronoun.**

Regular verb. *See* **Verb.**

Relative pronoun. *See* **Pronoun.**

Run-on sentence A run-on sentence consists of two or more sentences written incorrectly as one. (The sunset was beautiful its brilliant colors lasted only a short time.)

 S

Sentence A sentence expresses a complete thought. The chart below shows the four kinds of sentences.

A **compound-complex sentence** contains two or more independent clauses and one or more dependent clauses. (*I would like to be an archaeologist, but I have never visited an ancient site, although I have had opportunities.*)

A *complex sentence* contains one main clause and one or more subordinate clauses. (*Open the windows before you go to bed. If she falls, I'll help her up.*)

A *compound sentence* is made up of two or more independent clauses joined by a conjunction, a colon, or a semicolon. (*The ship finally docked, and the passengers quickly left.*)

A *simple sentence* consists of only one main clause. (*My friend volunteers at a nursing home.*)

Kind of Sentence	Example
Declarative (statement)	Our team won.
Exclamatory (strong feeling)	I had a great time!
Imperative (request, command)	Take the next exit.
Interrogative (question)	Who owns the car?

Sentence fragment A sentence fragment is a group of words that is only part of a sentence. (*When he arrived. Merrily yodeling.*)

Simple predicate A simple predicate is the verb in the predicate. (John *collects* foreign stamps.)

Simple subject A simple subject is the key noun or pronoun in the subject. (The new *house* is empty.)

Split infinitive A split infinitive occurs when a modifier is placed between the word *to* and the verb in an infinitive. (*to quickly speak*)

Subject The subject is the part of a sentence that tells whom or what the sentence is about. (*Lou* swam.) *See* **Complete subject; Simple subject.**

Subject-verb agreement. *See* **Agreement.**

Subordinate clause. *See* **Clause.**

Superlative. *See* **Adjective; Adverb.**

 T

Transitive verb. *See* **Verb.**

 U

Unidentified reference An unidentified reference usually occurs when the word *it, they, this, which,* or *that* is used. (In California *they* have good weather most of the time.)

 V

Verb A verb expresses an action, a condition, or a state of being.

An *action verb* tells what the subject does, has done, or will do. The action may be physical or mental. (Susan *trains* guide dogs.)

An *auxiliary verb* is added to a main verb to express tense, add emphasis, or otherwise affect the meaning of the verb. Together the auxiliary and main verb make up a verb phrase. (*will* intend, *could have* gone)

A *linking verb* expresses a state of being or connects the subject with a word or words that describe the subject. (The ice *feels* cold.) Linking verbs include *appear, be (am, are, is, was, were, been, being), become, feel, grow, look, remain, seem, smell, sound,* and *taste*.

A *main verb* expresses action or state of being; it appears with one or more auxiliary verbs. (will be *staying*)

The *progressive form* of a verb shows continuing action. (She *is knitting*.)

The past tense and past participle of a *regular verb* are formed by adding *-d* or *-ed*. (open, opened) An *irregular verb* does not follow this pattern. (*throw, threw, thrown; shrink, shrank, shrunk*)

The action of a *transitive verb* is directed toward someone or something, called the object of a verb. (Leo *washed* the windows.) An *intransitive verb* has no object. (The leaves *scattered*.)

Verb phrase. *See* **Phrase.**

Verb tense Verb tense shows the time of an action or the time of a state of being.

The *present tense* places an action or condition in the present. (Jan *takes* piano lessons.)

The *past tense* places an action or condition in the past. (We *came* to the party.)

The *future tense* places an action or condition in the future. (You *will understand*.)

The *present perfect tense* describes an action in an indefinite past time or an action that began in the past and continues in the present. (*has called, have known*)

The *past perfect tense* describes one action that happened before another action in the past. (*had scattered, had mentioned*)

The *future perfect tense* describes an event that will be finished before another future action begins. (*will have taught, shall have appeared*)

Verbal A verbal is formed from a verb and acts as another part of speech, such as a noun, an adjective, or an adverb.

Verbal	Example
Gerund (used as a noun)	Lamont enjoys *swimming*.
Infinitive (used as an adjective, an adverb, or a noun)	Everyone wants *to help*.
Participle (used as an adjective)	The leaves *covering the drive* made it slippery.

Voice The voice of a verb depends on whether the subject performs or receives the action of the verb.

In the *active voice* the subject of the sentence performs the verb's action. (We *knew* the answer.)

In the *passive voice* the subject of the sentence receives the action of the verb. (The team *has been eliminated*.)

Speaking and Listening Handbook

Good communicators do more than just talk. They use specific techniques to present their ideas effectively, and they are attentive and critical listeners.

Organization and Delivery

In school, in business, and in any community, one of the best ways to present information is to deliver it in person—speaking directly to a live audience.

Audience and Purpose

When preparing and presenting a speech, your goal is to deliver a focused, coherent presentation that both conveys your ideas clearly and also relates to the background and interests of your audience. By understanding your audience, you can tailor your speech to them appropriately and effectively.

- **Know your audience** What kind of group are you presenting to—fellow classmates? an entire school assembly? a group of teachers? What are their interests and backgrounds? Understanding their different points of view can help you address each group in the most appropriate way.

- **Understand your purpose** Keep in mind your purpose for speaking. Are you trying to persuade the audience to do something? Are you presenting the audience with some latest research? Perhaps you simply want to entertain them by sharing a story or experience.

- **Organize effectively** As you prepare your presentation, it's important to arrange the information—details, reasons, descriptions, and examples—effectively and persuasively. Think about your audience and the best way to organize the information so that they understand, absorb, and are interested by it.

Writing Your Speech

If you are writing your speech beforehand, rather than working from notes or memory, use the following guidelines to help you:

- **Create a unified speech** Do this first by organizing your speech into paragraphs, each of which develops a single main idea. Then make sure that just as all the sentences in a paragraph support the main idea of the paragraph, so all the paragraphs in your speech support the main idea of the speech.

- **Use appropriate language** The subject of your speech—and the way you choose to present it—should match both your audience and the occasion. Tailor your language accordingly. For example, if you were telling a funny story to a group of friends, your speech might be informal and lighthearted. However, if you were describing your science project to a panel of judges, your speech would probably be serious, formal, and well organized.

- **Provide evidence** Include relevant facts, statistics, and incidents; quote experts to support both your ideas and your opinions. Elaborate—or provide specific details, perhaps with visual or media displays—to clarify what you are saying.

- **Emphasize points** To help your audience in following the main ideas and concepts of your speech, be sure to draw attention to important points. You can do this with your voice, using effective volume, tempo, inflection, and pitch. You can also do this with nonverbal elements, such as eye contact, facial expressions, hand gestures, and props—all of which can help hold your audience's interest and attention.

- **Start strong, finish strong** As you begin your speech, consider using a "hook"—an interesting question or statement to capture your audience's attention. At the end of the speech, restate your main ideas simply and clearly. Perhaps conclude with a powerful example or anecdote to reinforce your message.

Prepare/Practice/Present

Confidence is the key to a successful presentation. Use these techniques to help you prepare and present your speech to your class.

Prepare

- **Review your information** Reread your written report and review your background research—you'll feel much more confident during your speech.

- **Organize your notes** Some people prefer to include only a minimum number of key points. Others prefer the entire script. Write each main point, or each paragraph, of your speech on a separate index card. Be sure to include your most important evidence and examples. It helps to number your cards.

- **Plan your visual aids** If you are planning on using visual aids, such as slides, posters, charts, graphs, video clips, overhead transparencies, or computer projections, now is the time to design them and decide how to work them into your speech.

Practice

- **Rehearse** Rehearse your speech several times, possibly in front of a practice audience. If you are using visual aids, practice handling them. Adapt your rate of speaking, pitch, and tone of voice to your audience and setting. Your style of performance should express the purpose of your speech. Use the following chart to help your style express your purpose.

Purpose	Pace	Pitch	Tone
to persuade	fast but clear	even	urgent
to inform	plenty of pauses	even	authoritative
to entertain	usually builds to a "punch"	varied to create characters or drama	funny or dramatic

TIP: It might also be helpful to time yourself during rehearsals, to ensure that your speech does not run too long.

- **Evaluate your performance** When you have finished each rehearsal, evaluate your performance. How did you do? Did you slow down for emphasis, pause to let an important point sink in, or use gestures for emphasis? Make a list of aspects of your presentation that you will try to perfect for your next rehearsal.

Present

- **Begin your speech** In order to break the tension of the opening moments, try to look relaxed and remember to smile!

- **Make eye contact** During your speech, try to make eye contact with audience members. This will not only establish the feeling of personal contact but will help you determine if the audience understands your speech.

- **Remember to pause** A slight pause after important points will provide emphasis and give your audience time to think about what you are saying.

- **Maintain good posture** Stand up straight and avoid nervous movements that may distract the audience's attention from what you are saying.

- **Use expressive body language** A good speaker captures the attention of an audience through body language as well as through words. In front of an audience, use your entire body to help express your meaning. Lean forward when you make an important point; move your hands and arms for emphasis. Your body language will show that you really believe in what you are saying.

Narrative Presentations

When you make a narrative presentation, you tell a story or present a subject using a story-type format. A good narrative keeps an audience both informed and entertained. It also allows you to deliver a message in a unique and creative way.

- **Establish a setting** Think about a definite setting for your story. Does the action take place in a home? a classroom? a neighborhood park? How does the story relate to things the audience already knows about past or current events? familiar places or people?

- **Create a plot** What happens in your story? Is it funny? tragic? suspenseful? How do you want the events to unfold? Over what period of time? A standard plot line includes exposition (to draw the audience in), a central conflict (the reason the story is told), rising action (to create tension), a climax (the height of action), and a denouement, or resolution (to show the final outcome).

- **Determine a point of view** Is a narrator telling the story from the third-person point of view? Who is the main character of the story? What is his or her point of view? If he or she is telling the story, make the audience believe that they are hearing the voice and opinions of a very particular person. In real life, people are complex and not easy to define in a word or two. Make an effort to give your main and minor characters real-life qualities.

- **Use effective language** Include sensory details and concrete language to develop the plot and the character. Think about the adjectives you use to describe something and the verbs you use to show an action. Let your audience touch, taste, hear, and smell what's happening in the story.

- **Employ narrative devices** Use a range of devices to keep your narrative interesting: snappy, believable dialogue; language that builds up tension in a scene; suspense to keep your audience members on the edge of their seats; characters' movements, gestures, and facial expressions to convey action and emotion.

- **Focus on the delivery** Once you've created your narrative, your next responsibility is to make the story come alive in presentation. Remember, it's not just what you say but how you say it. Speak clearly and confidently. Pace yourself and pause for emphasis. Use a range of voices, movements, gestures, and expressions to convey different emotions and moods.

GUIDELINES HOW TO ANALYZE YOUR NARRATIVE PRESENTATION

- Did you choose a setting that makes sense and contributes to a believable narrative?
- Does your plot flow well and create the right mood for your audience?
- Is your character—and his or her point of view—realistic and memorable?
- Did you use strong, sensory language that allows your audience to experience the story?
- Did you use a range of narrative devices to keep your audience interested?
- Did you deliver effectively and persuasively?

 Oral Summaries of Articles and Books

When you deliver an oral summary of an article or book, you do so to share your understanding of the main ideas and significant details of a piece with your audience.

- **Introduce the subject** Let your audience know right away what the article or book is about. Who is the author and why did he or she write the piece? What is the main idea behind the piece?

- **Provide supporting details** Discuss the significant details of the piece. What evidence was provided to support the main idea? Direct your audience to specific, relevant quotes from the text.

- **Use your own words** Deliver the information simply and clearly, expressed in your own words (unless quoting from the source). Present your material in a way that is easy for your audience to understand.

- **Convey comprehension** Show your audience that you really understand the piece. Don't simply repeat or rehash. Go beyond superficial details and offer to answer questions.

GUIDELINES HOW TO ANALYZE YOUR ORAL SUMMARY

- Did you introduce the subject clearly?
- Did you present the main idea(s) right away?
- Did you discuss the supporting details of the speech, using quotes when necessary?
- Did you summarize the information using your own clear and simplified words?
- Did you show your audience that you really understand the piece?

4 Research Presentations

A research presentation is an informative, investigative presentation based on your own research work. After you pose relevant questions to guide your research, you will organize your information and attempt to explain, teach, and enlighten an audience about a particular subject.

- **Target your audience** Think about what your audience may already know about the subject. Taking this information into consideration, develop a focused, organized presentation.

- **Introduce the topic** Grab your audience's attention by posing an interesting, relevant question or stating a fascinating fact.

- **Convey a clear and accurate perspective** Concisely explain to your audience the purpose of your presentation, what you hope they will get out of it, and how you went about collecting the information for it.

- **Present your research** Offer your audience the "meat" of your presentation: all the evidence, statistics, and details on the subject, gained from your research. A formal research process often includes using a card catalog, computer databases, magazines, newspapers, encyclopedias, and dictionaries. Consider using visual aids, and be sure to cite your reference sources. See The Writing Handbook, page R56, for information on creating a Works Cited List.

GUIDELINES HOW TO ANALYZE YOUR RESEARCH PRESENTATION

- Did you think about your audience's previous knowledge of the subject?
- Did you hook your audience with an interesting question or fact?
- Did you explain the purpose and framework of the presentation?
- Did you explain the process you used to collect information?
- Did you present your research clearly and concisely?
- Did you cite a variety of sources and use effective presentation aids?

5 Persuasive Presentations

When you deliver a persuasive presentation, you offer a clear statement on a subject, provide relevant evidence to support your position, and attempt to convince the audience to accept your point of view.

- **Determine your position** In order to develop a clear position on a subject, you need to know enough about it to make an informed, intelligent decision. Learn about all positions on the topic before deciding which is right for you.

- **State your position** Present your position on the subject clearly, confidently, and enthusiastically.

- **Support your position** Use strong, supportive evidence to back up your position. Arm yourself with relevant facts, statistics, and expert quotes.

- **Provide a strong defense** Consider your audience's own biases and opinions on the subject. What kind of questions or doubts might they have? Prepare for and address them before they are raised.

- **Deliver effectively** Engage your audience. Give them something to think about by posing challenging questions. Make them aware of a problem and how it might affect them or someone they know. Show them that you really believe in what you are saying by showing your own emotions. Make them believe it too.

GUIDELINES HOW TO ANALYZE YOUR PERSUASIVE PRESENTATION

- Did you present a clear statement or argument?
- Did you support your argument with convincing, well-articulated facts?
- Did you use sound logic in developing the argument?
- Did you use voice, facial expression, gestures, and posture effectively?
- Did you hold the audience's interest?

6 Active Listening for Information

Active listeners listen carefully and with purpose. They think about what they hear—before, during, and after any presentation—whether it's a speech, a class lecture, or even a television program.

Before Listening

- **Keep an open mind** Don't prejudge the speaker. Listen to what he or she has to say, and then evaluate the content critically but fairly.
- **Prepare yourself** Review what you already know about the speaker's topic.

Then think of some questions you'd like to ask or information you'd like to learn more about.

- **Listen with purpose** Try to match how you listen with why you are listening. For example, you may listen to a joke for entertainment, while you would listen to a lesson in order to gain information. Which would you want to pay more attention to?

Listening with a Purpose		
Situation	**Reason for Listening**	**How to Listen**
Your friend tells a funny story about her pet gerbil.	For enjoyment; to provide your friend with an audience	Maintain eye contact; show you understand; react to the story.
You're listening to a speech titled "Wolves of the Tundra."	For enjoyment; to learn something new	Think about what you already know; listen for ideas that add to your knowledge.
Your mother explains why you can't keep an alligator as a pet.	To understand her point of view; to find opportunities to share your own ideas	Listen carefully; respond positively to valid points; listen for opportunities to state your own reasons.
You and your friends are trying to arrange a trip to a concert.	To solve a problem	Identify goals and problems; listen closely to each other's ideas and build on them.
You are watching a television program about cooking or carpentry.	To follow directions	Listen for words such as *first*, *second*, *next*, and *finally*; take notes that you can refer to later.

While Listening

- **Block out distractions** Keep your eyes on the speaker, focus your mind, and ignore outside interference.
- **Look for signals** of main ideas. See the Guidelines box on the next page.

- **Take notes, if appropriate** Jot down phrases, main ideas, and questions that occur to you.
- **Look for relationships between ideas** Note comparisons and contrasts, causes and effects, and problems and solutions.
- **Identify tone, mood, and gesture** To aid in your comprehension, note how the speaker uses word choice, voice pitch, posture, and gesture to convey meaning.

  TIP: If you are listening to oral instructions or directions, be sure to take notes and clarify anything that is unclear. Consider restating the information to the speaker to make sure that you understand what was said.

GUIDELINES **HOW TO RECOGNIZE MAIN IDEAS**

- Did you listen for ideas presented first or last?
- Did you listen for ideas repeated several times for emphasis?
- Did you note statements that begin with phrases such as "My point is . . ." or "The important thing is . . ."?
- Did you pay attention to ideas presented in a loud voice or with forceful gestures?
- In a multimedia presentation, did you note points the speaker had reproduced on a chart or on any other visual aid?

After Listening
- **Review notes taken** Make sure you understand what was said.
- **Ask questions** Ask the speaker probing questions to elicit more information. Demand additional evidence to support claims and conclusions made. Clarify anything that was unclear or confusing.

- **Summarize, paraphrase and evaluate** Restate the speaker's ideas in your own words. Clarify your reasons for agreeing or disagreeing.
- **Respond to the speaker** Respond to persuasive statements with questions, challenges, or affirmations.

GUIDELINES **HOW TO EVALUATE WHAT YOU HEAR**

- What is the purpose of the talk and does the speaker achieve it?
- Does the information make sense? Does it contradict anything you already know?
- Are ideas presented in an interesting and logical way?
- Are points supported with facts and details?
- Do you still have any questions after hearing the talk?
- Do you agree with what the speaker said? Why or why not?

7 Critical Listening

As you listen to a speaker's ideas, you will want to analyze, evaluate, and critique those ideas. Use the following critical listening strategies as you listen to a public speaker:

- **Determine the speaker's purpose** Identify the speaker's purpose in giving the speech. Is the speaker trying to inform? to persuade? to express thoughts or feelings? to entertain?
- **Listen for the main idea** Figure out the speaker's main message before allowing yourself to be distracted by seemingly convincing facts and details of the speech.

- **Distinguish between fact and opinion** Know the difference between opinion statements such as "I think/I believe" vs. fact statements such as "Statistics show" or "It has been proven."

- **Recognize the use of rhetorical devices** Some speakers use special techniques to accomplish different purposes when they express their ideas. Noting these techniques as you listen will enable you to identify these purposes. For example, a speaker may use **repetition** of certain words or phrases, which allows him or her to emphasize ideas or draw your attention to something important. The speaker may also pose **rhetorical questions,** questions that you are not expected to respond to, to involve you in the topic. The speaker may use a third device such as an **allusion,** an indirect reference to something, for the purpose of pleasing and making a connection to a listener who recognizes the reference.

- **Provide feedback** Respond constructively to what the speaker says. Let the speaker know your questions and concerns regarding the speech's content and delivery. What was the speech's overall impact on you, the listener?

- **Analyze use of media** If the speech included a combination of images, text, and sound (such as electronic journalism), analyze the techniques and how effective they were in contributing to your understanding of what was said.

 Recognize Persuasive Devices

An important part of critical listening is the ability to recognize persuasive devices—techniques used to persuade you to accept a particular opinion. Persuasive devices may represent faulty reasoning and provide misleading information. They are often used in advertising and in propaganda. Some persuasive devices that you should learn to recognize:

- **Inaccurate generalization** A generalization is a broad statement about a number of people or things, such as "Maps are hard to read." Although some generalizations are true, other generalizations are too broad to be true. The statement "All teenagers like junk food" is an example of an inaccurate generalization.

- **Either/Or** A writer may try to convince an audience that there are only two choices, or ways of looking at something, when in fact there may be many. The statement "If you don't join the glee club, you have no school spirit" is an example of either/or reasoning.

- **Bandwagon** A bandwagon statement appeals to people's desires to belong to a group. For example, a statement like "Everyone at your school already has this hot new watch" is an example of a bandwagon device.

- **Snob appeal** This technique appeals to people's need to feel superior to other people. A statement like "You deserve the best, so buy this jacket" relies on snob appeal.

HOW TO LISTEN CRITICALLY

- Are you aware of the speaker's purpose in addressing you?
- Does the speaker seem confident in his or her knowledge of the subject?
- Does the speaker convince with concrete evidence rather than creative rhetoric?
- Are you able to distinguish between personal opinions and verifiable facts?
- Does the speaker use faulty or misleading persuasive devices?
- Did you clarify any information that seemed unclear or confusing?
- Did you respond constructively and analyze the effect of media supplements?

9 Group Communication

There are many reasons to have a group discussion, from just sharing your ideas to solving problems. Participating successfully in group communication requires all of your listening, speaking, and social skills.

Assigned Roles

A group discussion operates most effectively when each member plays a specific role. These roles may include

- **Chairperson** Responsible for introducing the topic for discussion, explaining the agenda or goals of the meeting, participating in and keeping discussion focused, and helping resolve conflict fairly.

- **Recorder** Responsible for taking notes during discussion, participating in discussion, and organizing/copying notes to distribute to entire group later.

- **Participants** Responsible for contributing facts or ideas to discussion, responding constructively to others' ideas, reaching agreement or voting on a final decision.

Guidelines for Discussions

Use these techniques to develop your group communication skills.

- **Listen attentively** Listen carefully and respectfully to each member. Pay attention to important ideas and details. Take notes about issues you want to discuss later.

- **Contribute to the discussion** Join in and share your ideas. Don't be afraid if your ideas are new or different. Share reasons for your ideas. Avoid sarcasm and contribute positive and helpful comments.

- **Be respectful** Take turns speaking. Don't interrupt someone else. Avoid using disrespectful language or dismissing other's ideas without evaluating them.

- **Stay on track** Stay focused on the subject at hand. Avoid straying off topic, and politely rein in those who do.

Conducting Interviews

Conducting a personal interview can be an effective way to get information.

Preparing for the Interview

- Select your interviewee carefully. Think about the information you want to learn. Identify who has the kind of knowledge and experience you are looking for.

- Research any information by or about the person you will interview. The background details will help you focus and get to the point during the interview.

- Prepare a list of questions. Create open-ended questions that can't be answered simply with a "yes" or "no." Arrange your questions in order of significance, from most important to least important.

Participating in the Interview

- Consider working with a partner. You might choose one note taker and one speaker.

- Ask your questions clearly and listen carefully. Give the person that you are interviewing plenty of time to answer.

- Listen interactively and flexibly. Be prepared to follow up on a response you find interesting, even if it was not on your initial list of questions.

- Avoid arguments. Be tactful and polite.

- Take notes even if you have a recording device. This will help in your write-up of the interview. Jot down main ideas or important statements that can be used as quotes.

Following up on the interview

- Summarize your notes while they are still fresh in your mind.

- Send a thank-you note to the interview subject.

TIP: Remember that as an interviewer, your role is to listen rather than to talk about yourself. Show that you are interested in the person you are interviewing.

① Getting Information Electronically

Electronic resources provide you with a convenient and efficient way to gather information.

⓫ Online Resources

When you use your computer to communicate with another computer or with another person using a computer, you are working "online." Online resources include commercial information services and information available on the Internet.

What You'll Need

• To access online resources, you need a computer with a modem to link you to the Internet. Your school computer lab or resource center may be linked to the Internet or to a commercial information service.

• To use CD-ROMs, you need a computer system with a CD-ROM reader.

Commercial Information Services

You can subscribe to various services that offer information such as the following:

• up-to-date news, weather, and sports reports

• access to encyclopedias, magazines, newspapers, dictionaries, almanacs, and databases (collections of information)

• electronic mail (email) to and from other users

• forums, or ongoing electronic conversations among users interested in a particular topic

Internet

The Internet is a vast network of computers. News services, libraries, universities, researchers, organizations, and government agencies use the Internet to communicate and to distribute information. The Internet includes two key features:

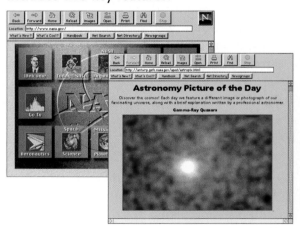

• **World Wide Web** provides you with information on particular subjects and links you to related topics and resources (such as the Web pages shown above).

• **Electronic mail** (email), allows you to communicate with other email users worldwide.

⓬ Navigating the Web

With access to the World Wide Web, you can find virtually any piece of information once you know how to look for it. Here are some tips to get you started.

Choose a Search Engine or a Directory

A **search engine** combs through Web sites looking for your topic. A **directory** allows you to search within groups of **databases**, or collections of information arranged for ease of retrieval, which are, in turn, grouped by subject, such as Reference, Sports, or Entertainment.

Enter Key Words

Once you've chosen a starting point, enter the **key word** or words that describe your topic. By using more than one word, you will narrow your search. For example, using the key word "baseball" will find sites with information on baseball. The key words "Dodgers baseball" will help you find sites with information on the specific team.

Investigate Your Options

Once you receive the results of your search, scan the site listings and their summaries to see which ones look promising. If you click on a site and it's not useful, back up and try again. Sites at the top of the list usually will be more relevant than those found farther down.

Tips for Getting the Most out of Your Search

- **Note the source** Because anyone can put information on the Web, it's wise to check where the information comes from. For example, sites produced by government agencies or educational institutions tend to be more reliable than the personal Web pages of individuals.
- **Refine your search** If you're not getting the results you want, search again, using more key words or different key words.
- **Explore other avenues** One search engine may produce different results than another, and the same goes for directories.

- **Link around** Many Web sites have links to other sites with related content that you might not find searching on your own.

 CD-ROM

A CD-ROM (compact–disc–read-only memory) stores data that may include text, sound, photographs, and video.

Almost any kind of information can be found on CD-ROMs, which you can use at the library or purchase, including

- encyclopedias, almanacs, and indexes
- other reference books
- news reports from newspapers, magazines, television, or radio
- museum art collections
- back issues of magazines

 Library Computer Services

Many libraries offer computerized catalogs and a variety of other electronic resources.

Computerized Catalogs

You may search for a book in a library by typing the title, author, subject, or key words into a computer terminal. If you enter the title of a book, the screen will display information such as the book's call number and whether it is on the shelf or checked out of the library.

Other Electronic Resources

In addition to computerized catalogs, many libraries offer electronic versions of books or other reference materials. They may also have a variety of indexes on CD-ROM, which allow you to search for magazine or newspaper articles on topics.

② Word Processing

Word-processing and publishing programs are a type of software that allow you to draft, revise, edit, and format your writing and to produce neat, professional-looking papers. They also allow you to share your writing with others.

② **Prewriting and Drafting**

A computer makes it easy to experiment with different ways of expressing and organizing your ideas. You can use it to keep an electronic journal or portfolio, to organize your notes in files, or to access templates for special writing formats. It also allows you to store multiple drafts and even to add graphics to clarify and enhance your message.

WRITING TIP Create a separate file to use as a writing notebook. Keep all of your story starters, ideas to research, and other writing ideas in this file.

② **Revising and Editing**

The programs that make computer hardware function are called **software**. One type of software is a word-processing program. Improving the quality of your writing becomes easier when you use a word-processing program to revise and edit.

What You'll Need
• Computer
• Word-processing program
• Printer

Revising a Document

Most word-processing programs allow you to make the following kinds of changes:
• add or delete words
• undo a change you have made in the text

• move text from one location in your document to another
• save a document with a new name, allowing you to keep old drafts for reference
• view more than one document at a time, so you can copy text from one document and add it to another

Editing a Document

Many word-processing and publishing programs have the following features to help you catch errors and polish your writing:

• The **spell checker** automatically finds misspelled words and suggests possible corrections.
• The **grammar checker** spots possible grammatical errors and suggests ways you might correct them.
• The **thesaurus** suggests synonyms for a word you want to replace.
• The **dictionary** will give you the definitions of words so you can be sure you have used words correctly.
• The **search and replace** feature searches your whole document and corrects every occurrence of something you want to change, such as a misspelled name.

WRITING TIP Even if you use a spell checker, you should still proofread your draft carefully to make sure you've used the right words. For example, you may have used *there* or *they're* when you should have used *their*. A spell checker will not be able to pick up this type of error.

2.3 # Formatting Your Work

Format is the layout and appearance of your writing on the page. You may choose your formatting options before or after you write.

Formatting Type

You may want to make changes in the typeface, type size, and type style of the words in your document. For each of these, your word-processing or publishing program will most likely have several options to choose from. These options allow you to

- **change the typeface** to create a different look for the words in your document
- **change the type size** of the entire document or of just the headings of sections in the paper
- **change the type style** when necessary; for example, use italics or underline for the titles of books and magazines

Typeface	Size	Style
Geneva	7-point Times	*Italic*
Times	10-point Times	**Bold**
Chicago	12-point Times	Underline
Courier	14-point Times	

Formatting Pages

Not only can you change the way individual words look; you can also change the way they are arranged on the page. Some of the formatting decisions you make will depend either on how you plan to use a printout of a draft or on the guidelines provided for an assignment.

- **Set the line spacing,** or the amount of space you need between lines of text. Double spacing is commonly used for final drafts. Double spacing also allows you room to write changes and corrections as you revise and edit drafts of your writing.

- **Set the margins,** or the amount of white space around the edges of your text. A one-inch margin on all sides is commonly used for final drafts.

- **Create a header** for the top of the page or a footer for the bottom if you want to include such information as your name, the date, or the page number on every page.

- **Determine the alignment** of your text. The screen below shows your options.

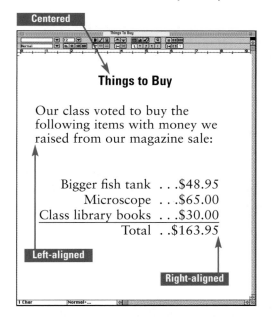

WRITING TIP Keep your format simple. Your goal is to create not only an attractive document but also one that is easy to read. Your readers will have difficulty if you change the type formatting frequently. Formatting that draws attention to itself also draws attention away from what you have to say.

TECHNOLOGY TIP Some word-processing and publishing programs or other software packages provide preset templates, or patterns, for writing outlines, memos, letters, newsletters, or invitations. If you use one of these templates, you will not need to adjust the formatting.

2.4 Working Collaboratively

Computers allow you to share your writing electronically. Send a copy of your work to someone via email or put it in someone's drop box if your computer is linked to other computers on a network. Then use the feedback of your peers to help you improve your writing.

Peer Editing on a Computer

The writer and the reader can both benefit from the convenience of peer editing on screen, or at the computer.

- Be sure to save your current draft. Then make a copy of it for each of your peer readers.

- You might have your peer readers enter their comments in a different typeface or type style from the one you used for your text, as shown in the the example below.

- Ask each of your readers to include his or her initials in the file name.

- If your computer allows you to open more than one file at a time, open each reviewer's file and refer to the files as you revise your draft.

TECHNOLOGY TIP Some word-processing programs allow you to leave notes for your peer readers in the side column or in a separate text box. If you wish, leave these areas blank so your readers can write comments or questions.

Peer Editing on a Printout

Some peer readers prefer to respond to a draft on paper rather than on the computer.

- Double-space or triple-space your document so that your peer editors can make suggestions between the lines.

- Leave extra-wide margins to give your readers room to note their reactions and questions as they read.

- Print out your draft. Photocopy it if you want to share it with more than one reader.

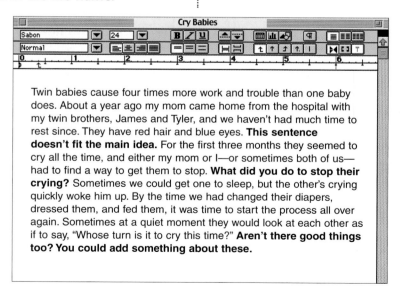

Cry Babies

Twin babies cause four times more work and trouble than one baby does. About a year ago my mom came home from the hospital with my twin brothers, James and Tyler, and we haven't had much time to rest since. They have red hair and blue eyes. **This sentence doesn't fit the main idea.** For the first three months they seemed to cry all the time, and either my mom or I—or sometimes both of us— had to find a way to get them to stop. **What did you do to stop their crying?** Sometimes we could get one to sleep, but the other's crying quickly woke him up. By the time we had changed their diapers, dressed them, and fed them, it was time to start the process all over again. Sometimes at a quiet moment they would look at each other as if to say, "Whose turn is it to cry this time?" **Aren't there good things too? You could add something about these.**

③ Using Visuals

Tables, graphs, diagrams, and pictures often communicate information more effectively than words alone do. Many word-processing and publishing programs allow you to create visuals to use with written text.

③.1 When to Use Visuals

Use visuals when you need a clear, easily understandable way to present complex concepts and processes or large amounts of numerical information such as those that appear in a **technical presentation**. Visuals can also help to make a presentation look more interesting.

Although you should not expect a visual to do all the work of written text, combining words and pictures or graphics can increase a reader's understanding and enjoyment of your writing.

What You'll Need

- A graphics program to create visuals
- Access to clip-art from a CD-ROM, a computer disk, or an online service

A Variety of Programs

Many word-processing and publishing programs allow you to create and insert graphs, tables, time lines, diagrams, and flow charts into your document.

An art program allows you to create border designs for a title page or to draw an unusual character or setting for narrative or descriptive writing.

You may also be able to add clip art, or pre-made pictures, to your document. Clip art can be used to illustrate an idea or concept in your writing or to make your writing more appealing for young readers.

③.2 Kinds of Visuals

Tables and Databases

Tables allow you to arrange facts or numbers into rows and columns so that your reader can compare information more easily. In many word-processing programs, you can create a table by choosing the number of vertical columns and horizontal rows you need and then entering information in each box, as the illustration shows. The kind of table shown below is often called a **database.** It organizes and stores information on a subject important to the creator. In this case the subject is babysitting. Table-formatting options allow you to change the appearance of your chart in several ways. These options allow you to

- choose the type of border
- vary the size and number of columns and rows
- pick a background color for the chart to set it off from the rest of the presentation

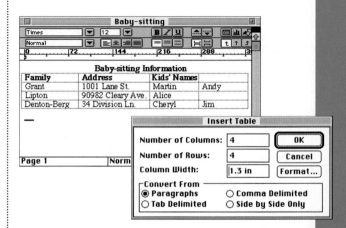

Spreadsheets

A spreadsheet program provides you with a preset table of rows and columns. The columns are identified by letters and the rows by numbers. The place where a column and row meet is called a **cell.** For example, the cell in the top left corner is A1. The program is set up to perform calculations automatically, based on formulas input by the user.

	A	B	C	D	E
1					
2					
3					

Spreadsheet programs allow you to present tabular information in graphs and/or charts, as shown below.

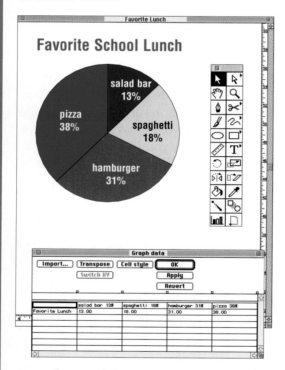

Graphs and Charts

Use a graph or chart to help communicate complex information in a clear visual image. For example, use a line graph to show how a trend changes over time, a bar graph to compare statistics, or a pie chart, like the one above, to compare percentages. Explore displaying data in

more than one visual format before deciding which will work best for you.

TECHNOLOGY TIP To help your readers easily understand the information, use a different color or shade of gray for each section.

Other Visuals

Art and design programs allow you to create visuals for your writing. Many word-processing and publishing programs include the following features:

- **drawing tools** that allow you to draw, color, and shade pictures

- **clip art** that you can copy or change with drawing tools

- **page borders** that you can use to decorate title pages, invitations, or brochures

- **text options** that allow you to combine words with your illustrations

- **tools for making geometric shapes** in flow charts, time lines, and diagrams that show a process or sequence of events

④ Creating a Multimedia Presentation

A multimedia presentation is a combination of text, sound, and visuals such as photographs, videos, and animation. Your audience reads, hears, and sees your presentation at a computer, following different "paths" you create to lead the user through the information you have gathered.

4.1 Features of Multimedia Programs

To start planning your multimedia presentation, you need to know what options are available to you. You can combine sound, photos, videos, and animation to enhance any text you write about your topic.

What You'll Need
- Individual programs to create and edit the text, graphics, sound, and videos you will use
- A multimedia authoring program that allows you to combine these elements and create links between screens

Sound
Including sound in your presentation can help your audience understand information in your written text. For example, the user may be able to listen and learn from
- the pronunciation of an unfamiliar or foreign word
- a speech
- a recorded news interview
- a musical selection
- a dramatic reading of a work of literature

Photos and Videos
Photographs and live-action videos can make your subject come alive for the user. Here are some examples:
- videotaped news coverage of a historical event
- videos of music, dance, or theater performances
- charts and diagrams
- photos of an artist's work
- photos or video of a geographical setting that is important to the written text

Mount Saint Helens A

16K/OK

Image remaining to be scanned: 48%

Cancel

TECHNOLOGY TIP You can download photos, sound, and video from Internet sources onto your computer. This process allows you to add elements to your multimedia presentation that would usually require complex editing equipment.

Animation

Many graphics programs allow you to add animation, or movement, to the visuals in your presentation. Animated figures add to the user's enjoyment and understanding of what you present. You can use animation to illustrate

- what happens in a story
- the steps in a process
- changes in a chart, graph, or diagram
- how your user can explore information in your presentation

TECHNOLOGY TIP You can now find CD-ROMs with videos of things like wildlife, weather, street scenes, and events, and other CD-ROMs with recordings of famous speeches, musical selections, and dramatic readings.

4.2 Planning Your Presentation

To create a multimedia presentation, first choose your topic and decide what you want to include. Then plan how you want your user to move through your presentation.

Imagine that you are creating a multimedia presentation about the 1980 volcanic eruption of Mount Saint Helens in the state of Washington. You know you want to include the following items:

- text describing the 1980 eruption of Mount Saint Helens
- animated diagram showing what happens when a volcano erupts
- photo of an eruption
- recorded interviews with people affected by the eruption
- video of rescue work and cleanup after the eruption
- photo of Mount Saint Helens today, showing how much vegetation has grown back
- text about current volcano research

You can choose one of the following ways to organize your presentation:

- **step by step** with only one path, or order, in which the user can see and hear the information
- **a branching path** that allows users to make some choices about what they will see and hear, and in what order

A flow chart can help you figure out the path a user can take through your presentation. Each box in the flow chart on the following page represents something about Mount Saint Helens for the user to read, see, or hear. The arrows on the flow chart show a branching path the user can follow.

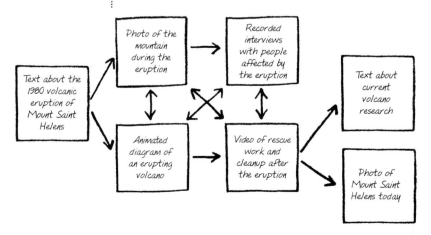

Whenever boxes branch in more than one direction, it means that the user can choose which item to see or hear first.

WRITING TIP You usually need permission from the person or organization that owns the copyright on materials if you want to copy them. You do not need permission, however, if you are not making money from your presentation, if you use it only for educational purposes, and if you use only a small percentage of the original material.

4.3 Guiding Your User

Your user will need directions to follow the path you have planned for your multimedia presentation.

Most multimedia authoring programs allow you to create screens that include text or audio directions that guide the user from one part of your presentation to the next. In the example below, the user can choose between several paths, and directions on the screen explain how to make the choice.

If you need help creating your multi-media presentation, ask your school's technology adviser. You may also be able to get help from your classmates or your software manual.

Navigational buttons take the user back and forth, one screen at a time.

The user clicks on a button to select any of these options.

This screen shows a picture of Mount Saint Helens.

Glossary of Literary and Reading Terms

Glossary of Literary and Reading Terms

Act An act is a major section of a play. Each act may be further divided into smaller sections, called scenes. *The Monsters Are Due on Maple Street* has two acts.

African-American Folk Tale African-American folk tales are examples of oral literature. They developed among Africans who had been transported to America as slaves and were passed down orally for generations. "The People Could Fly" is an example of a written retelling of an African-American folk tale.

See also **Oral Literature.**

Alliteration Alliteration is a repetition of a sound or letter at the beginning of words. Writers use alliteration to emphasize particular words and to give their writing a musical quality. Note the repetition of the c sound in this line:

> Over the cobbles he clattered and clashed . . .
>
> —Alfred Noyes, from "The Highwayman"

See pages 193, 461.

Allusion An allusion is a reference to a famous person, place, event, or work of literature. In "A Crown of Wild Olive," the author makes an allusion to the war that broke out between Athens and Sparta in 431 B.C., known by historians as the Peloponnesian War.

Analogy An analogy is a point-by-point comparison between two apparently dissimilar things made to clarify a certain point about one of them. In "Amigo Brothers" Felix draws an analogy between the boxing match he and his friend Antonio must fight and the match in the boxing movie *The Champion* in order to put himself into a competitive frame of mind.

> When Felix finally left the theater, he had figured out how to psyche himself for tomorrow's fight. It was Felix the Champion vs. Antonio the Challenger.
>
> —Piri Thomas, from "Amigo Brothers"

Analysis Analysis is a process of breaking something down into its elements so that they can be examined individually. When you analyze a literary work, you examine its parts in order to understand how they work together in the piece as a whole.

Anecdote An anecdote is a short, entertaining account about a person or an event. Anecdotes are often included in larger works to entertain or make a point. In the excerpt from *Growing Up*, Russell Baker tells an amusing anecdote about his sister, Doris, returning some cheese to a grocery store.

Antagonist In a story, an antagonist is a force working against the **protagonist,** or main character; an antagonist can be another character, society, or a force within the main character. In "The Scholarship Jacket," Mr. Boone, the math teacher, is an antagonist because he opposes Martha's right to the scholarship jacket.

See also **Protagonist.**

Author's Perspective An author's perspective is the author's beliefs or attitudes as expressed in his or her work. In "Eleanor Roosevelt," William Jay Jacobs's perspective is that Eleanor Roosevelt was a remarkable woman because she survived a painful childhood and went on to become a great humanitarian. An author usually expresses his or her perspective through voice and tone.

See also **Voice, Tone.**

Author's Purpose An author's purpose is his or her reason for creating a particular work. The purpose may be to entertain, to explain or inform, to express an opinion, or to persuade readers to do or believe something. An author may have more than one purpose for writing, but usually one is the most important.

See pages 101, 414, 415.

Autobiography An autobiography is a form of nonfiction in which a person tells the story of his or her own life. Jackie Robinson's *I Never Had It Made* is an example of autobiography.

See pages 83, 296.

Biographer *See* **Biography.**

Biography A biography is the story of a person's life, written by someone else. The subjects of biographies are often famous people, as in William Jay Jacobs's "Eleanor Roosevelt." A biographer is one who writes, composes, or produces a biography.

See pages 83, 98.

Cast of Characters In the script of a play, a cast of characters is a list of all the characters in the play, usually in order of appearance. This list is usually found at the beginning of the script.

Cause and Effect Two events are related as cause and effect when one event brings about the other. The event that happens first is the cause; the one that follows is the effect. This statement shows a cause-and-effect relationship:

> He pointed out that I couldn't play for a few days anyhow because of my bum arm.
>
> —Jackie Robinson, from "The Noble Experiment"

See pages 29, 109, 381, 708, 709.

Character A character is a person, an animal, or an imaginary creature that takes part in the action of a literary work. Generally, a work focuses on one or more **main characters** (also called **major** characters), but it may also include less important characters, called **minor characters.** Characters who change little, if at all, are called **static characters.** Characters who change significantly are called **dynamic characters.** Character **traits** are those aspects of a character's personality that are permanent and consistent, unlike feelings and emotions.

Character Motives *See* **Motivation.**

See pages 17, 62, 161, 216, 589.

Characterization Characterization includes all the techniques writers use to create and develop characters. There are four basic methods of developing a character: (1) presenting the character's words and actions, (2) presenting the character's thoughts, (3) describing the character's appearance, and (4) showing what others think about the character. In "An Hour with Abuelo," Arturo's description of his reading characterizes him as a motivated student.

> *I* don't have much time left of my summer vacation, and there's a stack of books next to my bed I've got to read if I'm going to get into the AP English class I want.
>
> —Judith Ortiz Cofer, from "An Hour with Abuelo"

See pages 62, 216, 586, 629.

Chronological Order Chronological order is the order in which events happen in time. In the biography "Eleanor Roosevelt," the events of Roosevelt's life are told in chronological order, beginning with her birth and ending with her death.

See pages 86, 87.

Clarifying The process of pausing while reading to review previous events in a work and to check one's understanding is called clarifying. Readers stop to reflect on what they know, to make inferences about what is happening, and to better understand what they are reading.

See pages 4, 391, 458.

Climax In the plot of a story or play, the climax (or **turning point**) is the point of maximum interest. At the climax, the conflict is resolved and the outcome of the plot becomes clear. The climax of "The War of the Wall," for example, occurs when the neighborhood kids return and see the finished mural for the first time.

See also **Conflict, Plot.**

Comedy A comedy is a dramatic work that is meant to be light, often humorous in tone, and usually ends happily with a peaceful resolution of the main conflict.

See also **Farce.**

Comparison The process of pointing out what two or more things have in common is called making a comparison. In the

excerpt from *Boy: Tales of Childhood,* Roald Dahl compares Mr. Coombes, the headmaster of Llandaff school, as he opens the school door to an avenging angel:

> Suddenly it swung open, and through it, like the angel of death, strode Mr. Coombes. . . .
>
> —Roald Dahl, from *Boy: Tales of Childhood*

See also **Metaphor, Simile.**

Conflict Conflict is a struggle between opposing forces. In an **external conflict,** such as the battle between Rikki and the cobras in "Rikki-tikki-tavi," a character struggles against another character or against some outside force. **Internal conflict**, on the other hand, is a struggle that is within a character. In "Eleanor Roosevelt," for example, the young Eleanor experiences internal conflict after her father's death.

> For many months after her father's death she pretended that he was still alive.
>
> —William Jay Jacobs, from "Eleanor Roosevelt"

See pages 34, 118.

Connecting A reader's process of relating the content of a literary work to his or her own knowledge and experience is called connecting. In "A Day's Wait," for example, Schatz's fever may lead readers to recall their own experiences of being ill.

See pages 19, 278, 533.

Connotation A word's connotations are the ideas and feelings associated with the word, as opposed to its dictionary definition. For example, the word *mother,* in addition to its basic meaning ("a female parent"), has connotations of love, warmth, and security.

Context Clues Unfamiliar words are often surrounded by words or phrases—called context clues—that help readers understand their meaning. A context clue may be a definition, a synonym, an example, a comparison or contrast, or any other expression that enables readers to infer the word's meaning.

Contrast The process of pointing out differences between things is called contrast. In "Last Cover," for example, the narrator contrasts himself with his brother, Colin, when he says,

> I was following in Father's footsteps, true to form, but Colin threatened to break the family tradition. . . .
>
> —Paul Annixter, from "Last Cover"

Couplet A couplet is a rhymed pair of lines in a poem. Shel Silverstein's "Sarah Cynthia Sylvia Stout Would Not Take the Garbage Out" is written almost completely in couplets.

> The garbage reached across the state,
> From New York to the Golden Gate.
>
> —Shel Silverstein, from "Sarah Cynthia Sylvia Stout Would Not Take the Garbage Out"

Deductive Reasoning In nonfiction the structure of a text may be organized using deductive reasoning. Deductive reasoning is the process of logical reasoning from principles to specific instances, or reasoning from whole to part.

See also **Inductive Reasoning, Structure.**

Denotation A word's denotation is its dictionary definition.

See also **Connotation.**

Denouement See **Plot.**

Description Description is the process by which a writer creates a picture in readers' imaginations. A good description includes details that enable readers to visualize a scene, a character, or an object.

Details, Sensory Words and phrases that help readers see, hear, taste, feel, even smell what an author is describing are called sensory details. Note the sensory details in this passage from "The Scholarship Jacket":

> There was a cool breeze blowing and a sweet smell of mesquite fruit in the air, but I didn't appreciate it. I kicked at a dirt clod. I wanted that jacket so much.
>
> —Marta Salinas, from "The Scholarship Jacket"

Dialect A dialect is a form of language that is spoken in a certain place or by a certain group of people. Dialects of a language may differ from one another in pronunciation, vocabulary, and grammar. In the excerpt Mrs. Pratchett speaks a dialect of the British working class:

> "Let's 'ave a look at some of them titchy ones."
>
> —Roald Dahl, from *Boy: Tales of Childhood*

See pages 26, 192, 546, 772.

Dialogue The words that characters speak aloud are called dialogue. In most literary works, dialogue is set off with quotation marks. In play scripts, however, each character's dialogue simply follows his or her name.

See page 248.

Drama A drama, or play, is a form of literature meant to be performed by actors before an audience. In drama, the characters' dialogue and actions tell the story. A playwright, or dramatist, is one who writes plays. Plays are generally performed live on a stage in a theater, or they may be filmed or broadcast.

See also **Prop, Scenery, Script, Stage.**

Drawing Conclusions Combining several pieces of information to make an inference is called drawing a conclusion. A reader's conclusions may be based on the details presented in a literary work, on his or her previous inferences, or on a combination of these.

See pages 206, 590, 591.

Dynamic Character *See* **Character.**

Essay An essay is a short work of nonfiction that deals with a single subject. One type of essay, such as "Homeless," emphasizes personal feelings and is called a **personal essay.** Another, such as "The Eternal Frontier," is written primarily to convey information and persuade the reader. This type is called a **persuasive essay.**

See pages 43, 101, 467.

Evaluating Evaluating is the process of judging the worth of something or someone. A work of literature, or any of its parts, may be evaluated in terms of its entertainment value, its believability, its originality, or its emotional power.

See page 463.

Exaggeration An extreme overstatement of an idea is called an exaggeration, and is often used for purposes of emphasis or humor. Exaggeration is used as a form of irony, along with understatement and sarcasm. In the excerpt from *Growing Up*, Russell Baker uses exaggeration to emphasize the irony in the reverence the representative from the *Saturday Evening Post* has for his product:

> He had brought the canvas bag with him. He presented it with reverence fit for a chasuble.
>
> —Russell Baker, from *Growing Up*

See also **Irony, Sarcasm, Understatement.**

Exposition Exposition, which is usually found at the beginning of a story or play, serves to introduce the main characters, to describe the setting, and sometimes to

establish the conflict. In "The War of the Wall," for example, the first three paragraphs provide most of the exposition.

See also **Plot.**

Extended Metaphor *See* **Metaphor.**

External Conflict *See* **Conflict.**

Fable A fable is a brief story that teaches a lesson about human nature. In many fables, animals act and speak, like human beings. Usually, a fable—"Ant and Grasshopper," for example—concludes with a **moral**.

See page 311, 315, 321, 796.

Fact and Opinion A fact is a statement that can be proved, such as "April has 30 days." An opinion, in contrast, is a statement that cannot be proved, such as "April is the nicest month of the year." Opinions usually reflect personal beliefs and are often debatable.

Falling Action *See* **Plot.**

Fantasy A fantasy is a story that takes place in an unreal, imaginary world, such as the garden in "The Serial Garden." Fantasies often involve magic or characters with superhuman powers.

See pages 412, 455.

Farce A farce is a type of exaggerated comedy that contains an absurd plot, ridiculous situations, and humorous dialogue. The main purpose of farce is to keep the audience laughing. Neil Simon's *A Defenseless Creature* is a farce.

> WOMAN. (*Pointing an evil finger at* KISTUNOV, *she jumps on the desk and punctuates each sentence by stepping on his desk bell.*) A curse! A curse on your bank! I put on a curse on you and your depositors! May the money in your vaults turn to potatoes!
>
> —Neil Simon, from *A Defenseless Creature*

Fiction Fiction is prose writing that tells an imaginary story. The writer of a fictional work may invent all the events and characters in it or may base parts of the story on real people or events.

Figurative Language Authors use figurative language to create fresh and original descriptions. Figurative expressions, while not literally true, help readers picture ordinary things in new ways. In many, one thing is described in terms of another—as when this speaker explains:

> an ocean would never laugh
> if clouds weren't there
> to kiss her tears
>
> —Nikki Giovanni, from "The World Is
> Not A Pleasant Place To Be"

See page 194.
See also **Metaphor, Personification, Simile.**

Flashback In a literary work, a flashback is an interruption of the action to present a scene that took place at an earlier time. In "Last Cover," for example, a flashback is used to show how Colin found Bandit.

> We'd taken the young fox into the kitchen, all of us, except Father, gone a bit silly over the little thing. Colin had held it in his arms and fed it warm milk from a spoon.
>
> —Paul Annixter, from "Last Cover"

Foil A character who provides a striking contrast to a main character is called a foil. The foil helps make the main character's qualities apparent to the reader. For example, Bess acts as a foil for Lottie in "The Richer, the Poorer."

Folklore The traditions, customs, and stories that are passed down within a culture are known as its folklore. Folklore includes various types of literature, such as legends, folk tales, myths, trickster tales, and fables.

Folk Tale A folk tale is a story that has been passed from generation to generation by word of mouth. Folk tales may be set in the distant past and involve supernatural events, and the characters in them may be animals, people, or superhuman beings. "The Force of Luck" is an example of a folk tale.

See page 796.

Foreshadowing Foreshadowing occurs when a writer provides hints that suggest future events in a story. For example, in "Amigo Brothers" the rivalry between the two friends anticipates elements in, and gives readers hints about, the boxing match.

> Felix watched his friend disappear from view, throwing rights and lefts.
>
> —Piri Thomas, from "Amigo Brothers"

Form A literary work's form is its structure or organization. The form of a poem includes the arrangement of words and lines on the page. Some poems follow predictable patterns, with the same number of syllables in each line and the same number of lines in each stanza. Other poems, like Langston Hughes's "To You," have irregular forms.

See page 192.

Free Verse Poetry without regular patterns of rhyme and rhythm is called free verse. Some poets use free verse to capture the sounds and rhythms of ordinary speech. "Mooses" is an example of a poem written in free verse.

> The goofy Moose, the walking house-frame,
> Is lost
> In the forest. He bumps, he blunders,
>   he stands.
>
> —Ted Hughes, from "Mooses"

See page 204.

Generalization A generalization is a broad statement about an entire group, such as "Novels take longer to read than short stories." Not all generalizations are true. Some are too broad or not supported by sufficient evidence, like the statement "All seventh graders are tall."

Genre A type or category of literature is called a genre. The main literary genres are fiction, nonfiction, poetry, and drama.

Haiku Haiku is a traditional form of Japanese poetry. A haiku normally has three lines and describes a single moment, feeling, or thing. In a traditional haiku, the first and third lines contain five syllables each, and the second line contains seven syllables.

Historical Fiction Historical fiction is fiction that is set in the past. It may contain references to actual people and events of the past. Though based in fact, it also contains fictional elements such as description and dialogue. "A Crown of Wild Olive" is an example of historical fiction.

See pages 706, 726.

Humor Humor is a quality that provokes laughter or amusement. Writers create humor through exaggeration, amusing descriptions, irony, and witty and insightful dialogue. Shel Silverstein's "Sarah Cynthia Sylvia Stout Would Not Take the Garbage Out" is an example of a humorous work.

See pages 394, 455.

Hyperbole An author's use of exaggeration or overstatement for emphasis is called hyperbole. A good example of hyperbole is Ernest Lawrence Thayer's description of the crowd's response to Casey:

> Then from the gladdened multitude went
>   up a joyous yell—
> It rumbled in the mountaintops, it rattled
>   in the dell;
> It struck upon the hillside and rebounded
>   on the flat;
> For Casey, mighty Casey, was advancing
>   to the bat.
>
> — Ernest Lawrence Thayer, from
> "Casey at the Bat"

Idiom An idiom is an expression that has a meaning different from the meaning of its individual words. For example, "go to the dogs" is an idiom meaning "go to ruin."

Imagery Imagery consists of words and phrases that appeal to readers' senses. Writers use sensory details to help readers imagine how things look, feel, smell, sound, and taste. Note the imagery in these lines:

> the fertile plants
> tangled,
> turned into
> tendrils, cattails,
> moving bulbs.
>
> —Pablo Neruda, from "Ode to an Artichoke"

See pages 194, 743.

Inductive Reasoning In nonfiction the structure of a text may be organized using inductive reasoning. Inductive reasoning is the process of determining principles, or generalizations, by logic or observation, or reasoning from part to whole.

See also **Deductive Reasoning, Structure.**

Inference An inference is a logical guess or conclusion based on evidence. For example, when Mr. Johnson hands out peanuts to strangers in "One Ordinary Day, with Peanuts," readers can infer that he wants to make new friends.

See pages 46, 347, 348.

Informative Nonfiction See **Nonfiction.**

Internal Conflict. See **Conflict.**

Interview An interview is a conversation, such as that conducted by a writer or reporter, in which facts or statements are drawn from another person, recorded, and then broadcast or published.

Irony Irony is a contrast between what is expected and what actually exists or happens. Exaggeration, sarcasm, and understatement are techniques writers use to express irony. The excerpt below turns out to be highly ironic given the kinds of expectations it raises about Russell Baker's early career in journalism and what actually happens:

> I began working in journalism when I was eight years old. It was my mother's idea. She wanted me to "make something" of myself and, after a level-headed appraisal of my strengths, decided I had better start young if I was to have any chance of keeping up with the competition.
>
> —Russell Baker, from *Growing Up*

See also **Exaggeration, Sarcasm, Understatement.**

See pages 358, 629.

Jargon Jargon is a specialized vocabulary used by members of a particular profession.

Legend A legend is a story handed down from the past about a specific person—usually someone of heroic accomplishments. Legends usually have some basis in historical fact.

Limerick A limerick is a short, humorous poem composed of five lines. It usually has the rhyme scheme *aabba*, created by two rhyming couplets followed by a fifth line that rhymes with the first couplet. A limerick typically has a sing-song rhythm.

Literary Nonfiction See **Nonfiction.**

Main Character See **Character**.

Main Idea A main idea is a writer's principal message. It may be the central idea of an entire work or a thought expressed in the topic sentence of a paragraph. (The term *main idea* is usually used in discussions of nonfiction.)

See pages 223, 732.

Memoir A memoir is a form of autobiographical writing in which a person recalls important events in his or her life. Although basically personal, a memoir may deal with events that have significance beyond the writer's individual life. Nelson Mandela's memoir, *Long Walk to Freedom*, for example, describes his growing awareness of the effects of racism in his native country, South Africa.

See page 737.

Metaphor A metaphor is a comparison of two things that have some quality in common. Unlike a simile, a metaphor does not contain the word *like* or *as*; instead, it says that one thing is another. The first lines of Alfred Noyes's "The Highwayman" contain a series of metaphors:

> The wind was a torrent of darkness among the gusty trees.
> The moon was a ghostly galleon tossed upon cloudy seas.
> The road was a ribbon of moonlight over the purple moor, . . .
>
> —Alfred Noyes, from "The Highwayman"

In an **extended metaphor**, two things are compared at some length and in several ways. The poem "Ode to an Artichoke" is based on an extended metaphor in which an artichoke is compared to a soldier.

See pages 194, 379, 564.

Meter In poetry, meter is the pattern of accented and unaccented syllables. The meter in a line of poetry creates its rhythm. Not all poems have regular meter. "The Pasture" is an example of a poem with regular meter.

> I'm going out to clean the pasture spring;
> I'll only stop to rake the leaves away
> (and wait to watch the water clear, I may):
> I shan't be gone long.—You come too.
>
> —Robert Frost, from "The Pasture"

Minor Character *See* **Character.**

Monitoring Good readers monitor their understanding of what they are reading by stopping occasionally and adjusting their use of the active-reading strategies of visualizing, predicting, clarifying, questioning, connecting, and evaluating.

Mood A mood, or atmosphere, is a feeling that a literary work conveys to readers. Writers use a variety of techniques— including word choice, dialogue, description, and plot complications—to establish moods. In *The Monsters Are Due on Maple Street,* for example, Rod Serling creates a mood of tension and anticipation.

> [Les] *stops suddenly as, behind him, the car engine starts up all by itself. Les whirls around to stare at the car. The car idles roughly, smoke coming from the exhaust, the frame shaking gently. Les's eyes go wide, and he runs over to the car. The people stare at the car.*
>
> —Rod Serling, from *The Monsters Are Due on Maple Street*

See pages 519, 520, 530.

Moral A moral is a lesson that a story teaches. Morals are often stated directly at the end of fables.

Motivation A character's motivation is the reason why he or she acts, feels, or thinks in a certain way. For example, in "Zebra," a desire to help Adam get well is part of John Wilson's motivation. Motivations may be stated directly, or they may be implied.

> She handed him a large brown envelope. It was addressed to Adam Zebrin, Eighth Grade, at the school. The sender was John Wilson with a return address in Virginia.
>
> —Chaim Potok, from "Zebra"

Myth A myth is a traditional story, usually of unknown authorship, that deals with basic questions about the universe. Gods and heroes often figure prominently in myths, which may attempt to explain such things as the origin of the world, mysteries of nature, or social customs. "How Odin Lost His Eye" is an example of a myth.

See page 796.

Narrative A narrative is writing that tells a story. The events in a narrative may be real, or they may be imaginary. Narratives that deal with real events include biographies and autobiographies. Fictional narratives include myths, short stories, novels, and narrative poems.

See pages 388.

Narrative Poetry Poetry that tells a story is called narrative poetry. Like fiction, narrative poetry contains characters, settings, plots, and themes. It may also contain such elements of poetry as rhyme, rhythm, imagery, and figurative language. "The Highwayman" is an example of a narrative poem.

Narrator The narrator is the teller of a story.

See page 614.
See also **Point of View.**

Nonfiction Writing that tells about real people, places, and events is called nonfiction. Writers of nonfiction often get their information from both **primary sources** (original, firsthand accounts) and **secondary sources** (descriptions based on primary sources). **Informative nonfiction** is written mainly to provide factual information. A work of **literary nonfiction,** on the other hand, reads like a work of fiction—although it too provides factual information.

See pages 82, 230, 766.
See also **Autobiography, Biography, Essay.**

Novel A novel is a work of fiction that is longer and more complex than a short story. A novel's setting, plot, characters, and theme are usually developed in greater detail than a short story's.

Onomatopoeia Onomatopoeia is the use of words whose sound suggests their meaning—like *whir, buzz, pop,* and *sizzle.* In "The Highwayman," the onomatopoeic *tlot-tlot* is used to imitate the clopping of a horse's hoofs on a road.

> *Tlot-tlot; tlot-tlot!* **Had they heard it?**
> **The horse hoofs ringing clear;**
> *Tlot-tlot, tlot-tlot,* **in the distance? Were they deaf that they did not hear?**
>
> —Alfred Noyes, from ''The Highwayman''

See pages 193, 461.

Oral History Oral histories are stories of people's lives that have been passed down by word of mouth. Oral histories include both factual information and imaginative interpretation. In recent times, many oral histories have been written down.

Oral Literature Oral literature includes different kinds of narratives of unknown authorship that have been passed down by word of mouth from generation to generation. Oral literature includes folk tales, legends, and myths. In recent times,

some oral narratives have been written down, but oral literature remains an important aspect of many cultures throughout the world.

See **African-American Folk Tale, Folk Tale, Myth.**

Parallelism Parallelism is the use of similar grammatical constructions to express ideas that are equal in importance. The parallel elements may be words, phrases, sentences, or paragraphs. Note in the example below how the parallel sentence structures help the reader to see that to Roald Dahl, feeling like a hero was the same as being one.

> **I felt like a hero. I *was* a hero. It was marvelous to be so popular.**
>
> —Roald Dahl, from *Boy: Tales of Childhood*

Paraphrasing Readers who paraphrase restate information in their own words. Paraphrasing helps readers to clarify meaning.

Personification The giving of human qualities to an animal, object, or idea is known as personification. In "Rikki-tikki-tavi," for example, the mongoose and the cobras are personified, conversing as if they were human.

> **Rikki-tikki licked his lips. "This is a splendid hunting ground," he said, and his tail grew bottlebrushy at the thought of it; . . .**
>
> —Rudyard Kipling, from "Rikki-tikki-tavi"

See pages 121,135.

Play *See* **Drama.**

Playwright *See* **Drama.**

Plot A story's plot is the sequence of related events that make up the story. In a typical plot, an **exposition** introduces the characters and establishes the main conflict. **Complications** arise as the characters try to resolve the conflict. Eventually, the plot builds toward a **climax,** the point of greatest interest or suspense. In the final stage of the plot, called the **resolution,** or the **denouement,** loose ends are tied up and the story is brought to a close. **Denouement** (dā′nōō-män′) is from a French word that means "untying"—in this stage, the tangles of the plot are often untied.

See pages 16, 171, 343, 561.

Poetry Poetry is a type of literature in which ideas and feelings are expressed in compact, imaginative, and musical language. Poets arrange words in ways intended to touch readers' senses, emotions, and minds. Most poems are written in lines, which may contain regular patterns of rhyme and rhythm. These lines may, in turn, be grouped in stanzas.

See page 191.

Point of View Every story is told from a particular point of view, or perspective. When a story is told from the **first-person point of view,** the narrator is a character in the story and uses first-person pronouns, such as *I, me, we,* and *us.* In a story told from a **third-person point of view,** on the other hand, the narrator is not a character; he or she uses third-person pronouns, such as *he, she, it, they,* and *them.*

The **third-person omniscient** (all-knowing) point of view allows the narrator to relate the thoughts and feelings of several, if not all, the story's characters. The narrator of "Rikki-tikki-tavi" for example reveals the thoughts and feelings of more than one character. If events are related from a **third-person limited point of view,** as in "Seventh Grade," the narrator tells us what one character thinks, feels, and observes.

See pages 83, 106, 135, 598.

Predicting Using what you know to draw a conclusion about what may happen is called predicting. Good readers gather information as they read and combine that information with prior knowledge to predict upcoming events in a story.

See pages 121, 361, 438, 521, 522.

Primary Sources See **Nonfiction.**

Prop The word *prop,* an abbreviation of *property,* refers to any physical object that is used in a drama. In the play based on Charles Dickens's *A Christmas Carol,* the props include a turkey and a dove.

See also **Drama, Scene, Scenery, Script, Stage.**

Propaganda Text that uses false or misleading information to present a certain point of view is called propaganda.

Prose Prose is the ordinary form of spoken and written language—that is, it is language that lacks the special features of poetry.

Protagonist The central character in a story, play, or novel is called the protagonist. The protagonist is involved in the main conflict of the plot and often changes during the course of the work. The character who opposes the protagonist is the **antagonist.** In "A Retrieved Reformation," Jimmy Valentine is the protagonist and his pursuer, Ben Price, is the antagonist.

> Ben Price knew Jimmy's habits. He had learned them while working up the Springfield case. Long jumps, quick getaways, no confederates, and a taste for good society—these ways had helped Mr. Valentine to become noted as a successful dodger of retribution. It was given out that Ben Price had taken up the trail of the elusive cracksman, and other people with burglar-proof safes felt more at ease.
>
> —O. Henry, from "A Retrieved Reformation"

See also **Antagonist.**

Questioning The process of raising questions while reading is called questioning. Good readers ask questions in an effort to understand characters and events, looking for answers as they continue to read.

See page 299.

Radio Play A radio play is a drama that is written specifically to be broadcast over the radio. Because the audience is not meant to see a radio play, sound effects are often used to help listeners imagine the setting and the action. The stage directions in the play's script indicate the sound effects.

Realism Realism involves the vivid description of characters and the world in which they live. A realistic description emphasizes a character's thoughts and feelings by describing how the character looks and acts. In "The People Could Fly," Virginia Hamilton provides a particularly realistic description of the character of Sarah.

> The sun burned her face. The babe cried and cried, "Pity me, oh, pity me," say it sounded like. Sarah was so sad and starvin', she sat down in the row.
>
> —Virginia Hamilton, from "The People Could Fly"

Repetition Repetition is a use of any element of language—a sound, a word, a phrase, a grammatical structure—more than once. Writers use repetition to stress ideas and to create memorable sound effects, as in these lines:

> He did not come in the dawning. He did not come at noon;
> And out of the tawny sunset, before the rise of the moon, . . .
>
> —Alfred Noyes, from "The Highwayman"

See also **Alliteration, Rhyme.**

Resolution *See* **Plot.**

Rhyme Rhyme is a repetition of sounds at the end of words. Words rhyme when their accented vowels and all the letters that follow have identical sounds. *Dog* and *log* rhyme, as do *letter* and *better.*

The most common form of rhyme in poetry is **end rhyme,** where the rhyming words occur at the end of lines. Rhyme that occurs within a line is called **internal rhyme.**

See pages 193, 199, 303, 461.

Rhyme Scheme A rhyme scheme is the pattern of rhymes in a poem. A rhyme scheme can be described by using letters to represent the rhyming sounds at the ends of lines. Lines that rhyme are given the same letter. For example, in the following poem, the rhyme scheme is *abab:*

> If I can stop one Heart from breaking *a*
> I shall not live in vain *b*
> If I can ease one Life the Aching *a*
> Or cool one Pain *b*
>
> —Emily Dickinson, from "If I Can Stop One Heart from Breaking"

Rhythm The rhythm of a line of poetry is the pattern of stressed and unstressed syllables in the line. When this pattern is repeated throughout a poem, the poem is said to have a regular beat. Note the rhythm in these lines (the mark ´ indicates a stressed syllable; the mark ˘, an unstressed syllable):

> The wínd wăs ă tórrĕnt ŏf dárknĕss ămóng thĕ gústy̆ treés.
> The moón wăs ă ghóstly̆ gálleŏn tóssed ŭpón clóudy̆ seás.
>
> —Alfred Noyes, from "The Highwayman"

See pages 193, 303, 458.

Rising Action *See* ***Plot.***

Sarcasm Sarcasm is a device writers use to express irony. Sarcasm may use either understatement or exaggeration, but with the purpose of upsetting or even offending someone. When Russell Baker's mother tells him that he has "no more gumption than a bump on a log," she is using exaggeration to the point of sarcasm.

See also **Exaggeration, Irony, Understatement.**

Glossary of Literary and Reading Terms

Scanning Scanning is the process of searching through writing for a particular fact or piece of information. When you scan, your eyes sweep across a page, looking for key words that may lead you to the information you want.

Scene In a play, a scene is a section presenting events that occur in one place at one time. Each scene presents an episode of the play's plot. For example, in *A Christmas Carol,* Scene 1 shows what occurs in Scrooge's shop, and Scene 2 shows what occurs at Scrooge's home.

Scenery The painted backdrop or other structures used to create the setting for a play.

See also **Drama, Stage.**

Science Fiction Science fiction is fiction based on real or imagined scientific developments. Science fiction stories are often set in imaginary places and in the future. Ray Bradbury's "Dark They Were, and Golden-Eyed" is an example of science fiction.

See pages 411, 436.

Script The text of a play, motion picture, or broadcast is called a script.

See also **Drama, Stage.**

Secondary Sources *See* **Nonfiction.**

Sensory Details *See* **Details.**

Sequence The order in which events occur or ideas are presented is called a sequence. In a narrative, events are usually presented in chronological order—the order in which they happened. A writer may use clue words and phrases—such as *then, until, after a while,* and *finally*—to help readers understand the sequence of events.

See also **Chronological Order.**

Setting The setting of a story, poem, or play is the time and place of the action. Elements of setting may include geographic location, historical period (past, present, or future), the season of the year, the time of day, and the beliefs, customs, and standards of a society. The influence of setting on characters' decisions and actions may vary from work to work.

See pages 18, 26, 43, 655, 672, 690.

Setting a Purpose The process of establishing specific reasons to read a literary work is called setting a purpose. Readers often come to a piece of writing with a purpose in mind, such as reading for entertainment, for information, or to analyze or evaluate a piece of writing. Readers can look at a work's title, headings and subheadings, and illustrations to preview the work and then set a purpose for their reading.

Short Story A short story is a brief work of fiction that can usually be read in a single sitting. A short story generally focuses on one or two main characters and on a single conflict.

Simile A simile is a comparison of two things that have some quality in common. In a simile, the comparison is conveyed by means of the word *like* or *as.* Note the simile in this sentence:

What is left looks rather like a gigantic, black pancake.

—Roald Dahl, from *Boy: Tales of Childhood*

See page 194, 564.

Skimming Skimming is the process of reading quickly to identify the main idea of, or to get an overview of, a work or passage. It involves reading the title, the headings, the words in special type, and the first sentence of each paragraph, as well as any charts, graphs, and time lines that accompany the writing.

Sound Effects. *See* **Alliteration, Onomatopoeia, Repetition, Rhyme, Rhythm.**

Speaker In a poem, the speaker is the voice that talks to the reader—like the narrator in a work of fiction. Frequently, recognizing the speaker's attitude is a key to understanding a poem's meaning. In some poems, such as "The Bat," by Theodore Roethke, the speaker expresses the feelings of the poet. In others, the speaker's attitude and the poet's may not be the same.

See page 192, 204.

Speech A speech is a prepared talk given in public. Sometimes, speeches are later published. Virginia Hamilton's "Looking For America" is an excerpt from a speech.

Stage The level and raised platform on which entertainers usually perform.

See also **Drama.**

Stage Directions In the script of a play, the instructions to the actors, director, and stage crew are called stage directions. They may suggest scenery, lighting, music, sound effects, and ways for actors to move and speak. In the plays in this book, stage directions appear in italic type and are enclosed in parentheses.

> **(The percussion thunders. Scrooge hurls himself through the descending snowflakes and sends the children scattering.)**
>
> —Frederick Gaines, from *A Christmas Carol*

See pages 246, 275.

Stanza A group of lines within a poem is called a stanza. A stanza is like a paragraph in a work of prose. "The Rider," by Naomi

Shihab Nye, for example, contains three stanzas.

See pages 192.

Static Character *See* **Character.**

Stereotype A stereotype is a generalization about a group of people, in which individual differences are disregarded. Stereotypes may lead to unfair judgments of individuals on the basis of race, ethnic background, or physical appearance.

Story Map A story map is a visual organizer that helps a reader understand a work of literature. A story map helps a reader to keep track of setting, characters, events, and conflicts.

Structure The structure of a work of literature is the way in which it is put together. In poetry, structure involves the arrangement of words and lines to produce a desired effect. One structural unit in poetry is the stanza. In prose, structure involves the arrangement of such elements as sentences, paragraphs, and events. "Dark They Were, and Golden-Eyed," for example, has the overall structure of a third-person fictional narrative. It has a circular structure in which the end mirrors the beginning.

See page 491.

Style A style is a manner of writing; it involves how something is said rather than what is said. The excerpt from *Boy: Tales of Childhood,* for example, has a playful style that relies on exaggeration, humor, and colorful words. Many elements contribute to style, including word choice, sentence length, tone, and figurative language.

> I lifted the heavy glass lid of the gobstopper jar and dropped the mouse in. Then I replaced the lid as silently as possible. My heart was thumping like mad, and my hands had gone all sweaty.
>
> —Roald Dahl, from *Boy: Tales of Childhood*

Summarizing Summarizing is telling the main ideas of a piece of writing briefly in one's own words, omitting unimportant details.

See pages 287, 767.

Surprise Ending An unexpected plot twist at the end of a story is called a surprise ending. "A Retrieved Reformation" is an example of a story with a surprise ending.

See page 372.

Suspense Suspense is a feeling of growing tension and excitement felt by a reader. Writers create suspense by raising questions in readers' minds about what might happen. For example, in "A Retrieved Reformation," a suspenseful moment occurs when Agatha is trapped inside the bank vault and readers wonder whether she will suffocate.

See pages 372.

Symbol A symbol is a person, a place, an object, or an action that stands for something beyond itself. In "The White Umbrella," for example, the umbrella mentioned in the story title symbolizes the ambivalence the main character feels toward her mother's having to take a job to help support the family. This ambivalence is resolved at the end of the story when the character throws the umbrella away.

See page 394.

Table of Contents In most nonfiction books or in books arranged by chapter or section, the contents of the book are shown in a table of contents. The table of contents usually appears at the beginning of the book and lists chapter and section titles and the page where each begins. Besides helping you to find specific parts of the book, the table of contents can give you an overview of the material covered by the book.

Tall Tale A tall tale is a humorously exaggerated story about impossible events, often relating the supernatural abilities of the main character. The tales about folk heroes such as Paul Bunyan, Pecos Bill, and Davy Crockett are tall tales.

Teleplay A play written for television is called a teleplay. In a teleplay, the stage directions usually include camera instructions. *The Monsters Are Due on Maple Street* is an example of a teleplay.

See page 429.

Text Organizers Text organizers include headings, tables of contents, and graphic elements such as charts, tables, time lines, boxes, bullets, and captions.

Theme A theme is the message about life or human nature that is conveyed by a literary work. A work may have more than one theme, and in many cases readers must infer the writer's message. One way to infer a fictional work's theme is to decide what general statement could be supported by the experiences of the main character. For example, a theme of "The Scholarship Jacket" is having to stand up for one's beliefs.

See pages 18, 284, 413, 429, 498.

Title The title of a piece of writing is the name that is attached to it. A title often refers to an important aspect of the work to which it is attached. For example, the title "The War of the Wall" refers to Lou and the narrator's conflict with the "painter lady."

See page 467.

Tone The tone of a work is the writer's attitude toward his or her subject. Words such as *amused, objective,* and *angry* can be used to describe different tones. The tone of "Winter Poem," for example, might be described as dreamy or escapist.

> once a snowflake fell
> on my brow and i loved
> it so much and i kissed
> it and it was happy and called its cousins
>
> —Nikki Giovanni, from "Winter Poem"

See pages 519, 520, 530.

Tragedy A tragedy is a dramatic work that presents the downfall of a dignified character or characters who are involved in historically or socially significant events. The events in a tragic plot are set in motion by a decision that is often an error in judgment. Succeeding events are linked in a cause-and-effect relationship and lead to a disastrous conclusion, often death.

Trickster Tale Trickster tales are folktales that reflect an admiration for cleverness. The tricksters themselves are not depicted as heroic but as what they really are—con artists. "Brother Coyote and Brother Cricket" is an example of a trickster tale from Texas.

Turning Point *See* **Plot.**

Understatement Writers use understatement as a means of expressing irony. Understatement de-emphasizes the significance of something. Writer Russell Baker uses understatement when he comments that, as a child, as far as he could tell, what writers did "couldn't be classified as work."

See also **Exaggeration, Irony, Sarcasm.**

Unreliable Narrator A narrator who does not narrate events objectively is called an unreliable narrator. An unreliable narrator is usually a character in the work whose biases or lack of self-awareness distorts his or her presentation of events. Juliette in "Waiting" is an example of an unreliable

narrator. Note in the quotation below the bias with which she imagines how others will comment about her.

> People were murmuring, "So young, so small, and so attractive."
>
> —Budge Wilson, from "Waiting"

Visualizing The process of forming a mental picture based on a written description is called visualizing. Good readers use the details supplied by writers to picture characters, settings, and events in their minds.

See pages 249, 250, 478, 553.

Voice A writer's or narrator's voice is his or her unique style of expression. Voice can reveal much about the author or narrator's personality, beliefs, and attitudes. The voice in "The Elephant" expresses the pain of imprisonment and longing for freedom.

> I will remember what I was. I am sick
> of rope and chain—
> I will remember my old strength and
> all my forest-affairs.
>
> —Rudyard Kipling, from "The Elephant"

See also **Author's Perspective, Tone.**

Word Choice Word choice is an important part of the writing process. Writers carefully select words to give precise descriptions, create a particular mood, and increase the impact of their writing. Notice how the words Gish Jen chooses help to create a mood in "The White Umbrella":

> The umbrella glowed like a scepter on the blue carpet while Mona, slumping over the keyboard, managed to eke out a fair rendition of a cat fight.
>
> —Gish Jen, from "The White Umbrella"

Glossary of Words to Know

In English and Spanish

A

abundance (ə-bŭn′dəns) *n.* wealth
 abundancia *n.* gran cantidad

accede (ăk-sēd′) *v.* to consent due to outside influences
 acceder *v.* consentir en lo que otro solicita o quiere

acclaimed (ə-klāmd′) *adj.* welcomed publicly with praise **acclaim** *v.*
 aclamado(a) *adj.* que recibe felicitaciones

accommodations (ə-kŏm′ə-dā′shənz) *n.* a room and food, especially in hotels or on ships or trains
 acomodaciones *n.* las facilidades disponibles para un viajero en hoteles, barcos o trenes

aggrievedly (ə-grē′vĭd-lē) *adv.* in a manner suggesting that one has been badly treated
 gravemente herido(a) *adv.* de una manera que sugiere que alguien ha sido seriamente lastimado

agile (ăj′əl) *adj.* quick and light in movement
 ágil *adj.* que puede moverse con facilidad

agitate (ăj′ĭ-tāt′) *v.* to stir up public interest in a cause
 agitar *v.* mover con frecuencia y violentamente

alight (ə-līt′) *v.* to land lightly, as after flight
 posarse *v.* despositarse

alleged (ə-lĕjd′) *adj.* supposed
 presunto *adj.* supuesto

allegiance (ə-lē′jəns) *n.* loyalty
 fidelidad *n.* lealtad

ambiguous (ăm-bĭg′yōō-əs) *adj.* can be understood in more than one way
 ambiguo(a) *adj.* incierto; confuso

amiss (ə-mĭs′) *adj.* out of proper order; wrong
 mal *adj.* extraño

ammunition (ăm′yə-nĭsh′ən) *n.* the explosive cartridges or shells designed to be used in guns
 municiones *n.* cargas de las armas

anguish (ăng′gwĭsh) *n.* great physical or mental suffering, as from grief or pain
 angustia *n.* aflicción

angular (ăng′gyə-lər) *adj.* bony and lean
 anguloso(a) *adj.* que tiene o forma ángulos

anonymous (ə-nŏn′ə-məs) *adj.* not having one's name known
 anónimo(a) *adj.* de nombre desconocido

antagonism (ăn-tăg′ə-nĭz′əm) *n.* hostility; unfriendliness
 antagonismo *n.* oposición

antidote (ăn′tĭ-dōt′) *n.* something that prevents the evil effects of something else; remedy
 remedio *n.* cualquier sustancia que sirve para prevenir o combatir una enfermedad

apathy (ăp′ə-thē) *n.* lack of strong feeling or interest
 apatía *n.* falta de interés

arresting (ə-rĕs′tĭng) *adj.* striking
 chocante *adj.* que sorprende; causa extrañeza

assault (ə-sôlt´) *v.* to attack
  atacar *v.* acometer

assiduously (ə-sĭj´ōō-əs-lē) *adv.* in a steady and hard-working way
  con dedicación *adv.* de una manera destinada

audible (ô´də-bəl) *adj.* able to be heard
  audible *adj.* que puede oírse

B

balk (bôk) *v.* to refuse to move or act
  resistirse *v.* no consentir

barrage (bə-räzh´) *n.* a rapid, heavy attack
  descarga *n.* una sucesión rápida de golpes o balas

barren (băr´ən) *adj.* empty; deserted
  estéril *adj.* vacío

bartering (bär´tər-ĭng) *n.* arguing over a price; bargaining **barter** *v.*
  trocar *v.* cambiar una cosa por otra; regatear

beckon (bĕk´ən) *v.* to summon or call, usually by a gesture or nod
  llamar *v.* atraer con un gesto

bedlam (bĕd´ləm) *n.* a noisy confusion
  pandemonio *n.* locura colectiva

bellow (bĕl´ō) *v.* to shout in a deep voice; roar
  bramar *v.* gritar con voz gruesa; rugir

benefactor (bĕn´ə-făk´tər) *n.* a person who provides money or help
  benefactor *n.* bienhechor; una persona que provee dinero o ayuda

bleak (blēk) *adj.* harsh and dreary
  sombrío *adj.* melancólico; triste

bluff (blŭf) *v.* to mislead or deceive; to fake
  engañar *v.* hacer creer algo que es falso

brooding (brōō´dĭng) *adj.* full of worry; troubled **brood** *v.*
  dar vueltas *v.* pensar mucho sobre un punto

C

chaos (kā´ŏs´) *n.* extreme confusion or disorder
  caos *n.* confusión; desorden

chaotic (kā-ŏt´ĭk) *adj.* confused; disordered
  caótico *adj.* confuso; desordenado

charitable (chăr´ĭ-tə-bəl) *adj.* generous in giving
  caritativo(a) *adj.* benéfico

circuit (sûr´kĭt) *n.* the path of an electric current; connected electronic elements
  circuito *n.* conjunto de conductores eléctricos

clench (klĕnch) *v.* to hold or grip tightly
  apretar *v.* sujetar firmemente

coincidence (kō-ĭn´sĭ-dəns) *n.* accidental sequence of events that seems planned
  coincidencia *n.* dos acciones independientes que suceden al mismo tiempo, resultando en una conexión inesperada

combatant (kəm-băt´nt) *n.* fighter
  luchador *n.* una persona que lucha o pelea

compassionate (kəm-păsh´ə-nĭt) *adj.* having sympathy for the sufferings of others
  compasivo(a) *adj.* que siente compasión

complex (kəm-plĕks´) *adj.* consisting of interconnected parts; intricate
  complejo(a) *adj.* formado por elementos diferentes

compliance (kəm-plī´əns) *n.* the act of obeying a request or a command
  acatamiento *n.* obediencia; conformidad

composure (kəm-pō′zhər) *n.* an undisturbed state of mind; calmness
compostura *n.* manera de comportarse

compulsory (kəm-pŭl′sə-rē) *adj.* that which must be done; required
compulsorio *adj.* obligatorio

confirm (kən-fûrm′) *v.* to make certain
confirmar *v.* corroborar la verdad o certeza de una cosa

confound (kən-found′) *v.* to bewilder; confuse
confundir *v.* mezclar cosas o personas; agobiar

consolation (kŏn′sə-lā′shən) *n.* something that comforts
consuelo *n.* algo que conforta

consternation (kŏn′stər-nā′shən) *n.* amazement and confusion; dismay
consternación *n.* asombro y confusión; estupefacción

contemplate (kŏn′təm-plāt′) *v.* to look at attentively and thoughtfully
contemplar *v.* mirar con atención

contend (kən-tĕnd′) *v.* to argue
porfiar *v.* disputar

contorted (kən-tôr′tĭd) *adj.* twisted or pulled out of shape **contort** *v.*
torcer *v.* desfigurarse; retorcer

contradict (kŏn′trə-dĭkt′) *v.* to express the opposite of; to be contrary to
contradecir *v.* decir lo contrario de lo que otro afirma

convalescing (kŏn′və-lĕs′ĭng) *adj.* recovering gradually from an illness **convalesce** *v.*
convalecer *v.* recobrar las fuerzas perdidas por una enfermedad

conviction (kən-vĭk′shən) *n.* a strong belief; assuredness
convicción *v.* convencimiento; ideas; creencias

convoluted (kŏn′və-lōō′tĭd) *adj.* difficult to understand; complicated
enrollado(a) *adj.* difícil de entender; complicado

cower (kou′ər) *v.* to crouch or shrink down in fear
meterse en un lugar *v.* esconderse

credibility (krĕd′ə-bĭl′ĭ-tē) *n.* believability
credibilidad *n.* calidad de creer

crude (krōōd) *adj.* lacking tact or good manners
tosco(a) *adj.* sin modales; grosero

crux (krŭks) *n.* the most important point or element
punto crítico *n.* elemento más importante

cunningly (kŭn′ĭng-lē) *adv.* in a clever way that is meant to trick or deceive
hábilmente *adv.* de una manera ingeniosa

currency (kûr′ən-sē) *n.* money
moneda *n.* dinero

curtailed (kər-tāld′) *adj.* cut short **curtail** *v.*
reducido *adj.* cortado

curtsey (kûrt′sē) *v.* to bend the knees and lower the body as a gesture of respect
hacer una reverencia *v.* hacer un gesto para demostrar respeto

cynical (sĭn′ĭ-kəl) *adj.* mistrustful of others' sincerity
cínico(a) *adj.* desvergonzado; impúdico

D

dappled (dăp′əld) *adj.* spotted
manchado *adj.* moteado

dazzled (dăz′əld) *adj.* amazed or overwhelmed by a spectacular display **dazzle** *v.*
deslumbrado(a) *adj.* estado de sentirse sobrecogido o maravillado por una vista espectacular

defiant (dǐ-fī´ənt) *adj.* willing to stand up to opposition; bold
desafiante *adj.* provocador

despair (dǐ-spâr´) *v.* to lose hope
desesperar *v.* perder la esperanza

destitute (dĕs´tǐ-tōot´) *n.* people lacking the necessities of life
indigente *n.* una persona que le falta lo necesario para vivir

devastating (dĕv´ə-stā´tǐng) *adj.* extremely destructive **devastate** *v.*
devastador(a) *adj.* asolador

diffidently (dǐf´ǐ-dənt-lē) *adv.* reserved or restrained in manner
tímidamente *adv.* de una manera que demuestra una falta de confianza

din (dǐn) *n.* a loud, confused mixture of noises
estrépito *n.* clamoreo; una mezcla de ruidos

disciplinarian (dǐs´ə-plə-nâr´ē-ən) *n.* someone who enforces strict discipline
ordenancista *n.* alguien que cree en las reglas de orden y disciplina

discreet (dǐ-skrēt´) *adj.* careful about what one says or does
discreto(a) *adj.* dotado de discreción

dismally (dǐz´məl-lē) *adv.* in a gloomy or depressed manner
triste *adj.* deprimente; terrible

dismay (dǐs-mā´) *n.* loss of courage in the face of trouble
desencanto *n.* tristeza honda que resulta cuando no se obtiene lo esperado

dismount (dǐs-mount´) *v.* to get down from a horse
desmontarse *v.* bajarse de un caballo

dispel (dǐ-spĕl´) *v.* to scatter; get rid of
disipar *v.* hacer que algo desaparezca de un lugar

diverted (dǐ-vûr´tǐd) *adj.* turned away **divert** *v.*
desviar *v.* distraer

dominant (dŏm´ə-nənt) *adj.* ruling or controlling
dominante *adj.* que quiere imponer su voluntad

drawl (drôl) *v.* to speak slowly, stretching the vowel sound
arrastrar las palabras *v.* hablar lentamente

dwindle (dwǐn´dl) *v.* to become less, until little remains
disminuir *v.* hacer menor

E

eerie (îr´ē) *adj.* weird, especially in a frightening way
escalofriante *adj.* que sorprende de una forma atemorizante

elaborate (ǐ-lăb´ə-rāt´) *v.* to state at greater length or in greater detail
elaborar *v.* expresar con más detalles

elective (ǐ-lĕk´tǐv) *n.* an optional academic course or subject
electivo *n.* opcional; un curso o materia opcional

eloquence (ĕl´ə-kwəns) *n.* forceful, convincing speech
elocuencia *n.* facultad de hablar bien

elusive (ǐ-lōo´sǐv) *adj.* escaping from capture as by daring, cleverness, or skill
evasivo *adj.* recurso para no comprometerse con una respuesta

embroidered (ĕm-broi´dərd) *adj.* ornamented with stitched designs **embroider** *v.*
bordado *adj.* adornado con aguja e hilo

emerge (ǐ-mûrj´) *v.* to come into sight
emerger *v.* surgir; aparecer

eminent (ĕm′ə-nənt) *adj.* better than most others; very famous
eminente *adj.* muy famoso

encrusted (ĕn-krŭst′əd) *adj.* covered as if with crusts **encrust** *v.*
incrustar *v.* cubierto con una capa de algo

endeavor (ĕn-dĕv′ər) *v.* to try
intentar *v.* esforzar; tratar

enfeebled (ĕn-fē′bəld) *adj.* deprived of strength; made weak **enfeeble** *v.*
debilitar *v.* quitar, perder fuerza

enhance (ĕn-hăns′) *v.* to increase the attractiveness of
acrecentar *v.* aumentar la belleza de

essence (ĕs′əns) *n.* basic nature or spirit
esencia *n.* ser propia de las cosas

ethnicity (ĕth-nĭs′ĭ-tē) *n.* a racial, national, or cultural heritage
etnia *n.* agrupación natural de individuos de la misma cultura

evading (ĭ-vā′dĭng) *adj.* avoiding; escaping **evade** *v.*
evitar *v.* protegerse de algo negativo

exile (ĕg′zīl′) *n.* a forced absence from one's native country
exilio *n.* una forzada ausencia del país de origen

exotic (ĭg-zŏt′ĭk) *adj.* unusual or different
exótico *adj.* procedente de lo diferente

exuberantly (ĭg-zōō′bər-ənt-lē) *adv.* full of enthusiasm or joy
exuberante *adj.* gran abundacia de felicidad

F

falsify (fôl′sə-fī′) *v.* to make false by adding to or changing
falsificar *v.* tratar de que un documento falso sea aceptado como verídico

feint (fānt) *v.* to make a pretended attack in order to draw attention away from one's real purpose or target
fingir *v.* disimular

ferocity (fə-rŏs′ĭ-tē) *n.* extreme fierceness; intensity
ferocidad *n.* fiereza; violencia

fervent (fûr′vənt) *adj.* having or expressing great warmth or depth of feeling
ferviente *adj.* ardiente

feverishly (fē′vər-ĭsh-lē) *adv.* in a highly emotional or nervous way
de una manera febril *adv.* de una manera muy emocional o nerviosa

fidget (fĭj′ t) *v.* to behave nervously or restlessly
jugar nerviosamente *v.* contener los nervios a través de una actividad inconsciente

finale (fə-năl′ē) *n.* the concluding part
final *n.* el último acto

flamboyant (flăm-boi′ənt) *adj.* given to showy display; flashy
rimborante *adj.* replandeciente; ornamentado

flimsy (flĭm′zē) *adj.* not solid or strong
ligero *adj.* insubstancial; débil

flourishing (flûr′ĭ-shĭng) *adj.* getting along well and successfully; thriving **flourish** *v.*
floreciente *adj.* que prospera

flustered (flŭs′tərd) *adj.* nervous or confused **fluster** *v.*
ponerse nervioso *v.* actuar de una manera confundida o ansiosa

forage (fôr′ĭj) *v.* to search for what one wants or needs, especially for food
hurgar *v.* buscar lo que se necesita, especialmente alimento

forge (fôrj) *v.* to shape metal by heating it and pounding on it with a hammer
forjar *v.* fraguar; dar la primera forma con el martillo o prensa a cualquier metal

forlorn (fôr-lôrn′) *adj.* a sense of alone-ness and sadness
acongojado(a) *adj.* melancólico

frail (frāl) *adj.* delicate; weak and fragile
frágil *adj.* delicado; débil

frugally (frōō′gə-lē) *adv.* in a thrifty way; economically
de una manera frugal *adv.* de una manera económica

G

game (gām) *adj.* ready and willing to proceed
seguir en la pelea *v.* estar en juego, no darse por vencido

gaudy (gô′dē) *adj.* excessively bright and showy
llamativo(a) *adj.* chillón

gaunt (gônt) *adj.* thin and bony
enjuto(a) *adj.* delgado

genial (jēn′yəl) *adj.* pleasant; friendly
simpático *adj.* afable; amistoso

glinty (glĭn′ tē) *adj.* sparkling
destello *n.* fulgor

grievous (grē′vəs) *adj.* painful; serious
penoso(a) *adj.* doloroso(a); serio(a)

gumption (gŭmp′shən) *n.* an ability to think and act without being urged; initiative
cacúmen *n.* iniciativa; la calidad de pensar y actuar por sí mismo

H

habitual (hə-bĭch′ōō-əl) *adj.* established by long use
habitual *adj.* establecido por uso largo

haggle (hăg′əl) *v.* to argue about terms or price; bargain
regatear *v.* discutir el precio

hardy (här′dē) *adj.* in robust good health
robusto(a) *adj.* resistente; de buena salud

harried (hăr′ēd) *adj.* worried; distressed
harry *v.*
preocupado *adj.* que teme algo

haughty (hô′tē) *adj.* condescendingly proud
altivo(a) *adj.* de demasiado orgullo

I

idiosyncrasy (ĭd′ē-ō-sĭng′krə-sē) *n.* a personal way of acting; odd mannerism
idiosincrasia *n.* índole de temperamento y carácter de cada persona

illuminate (ĭ-lōō′mə-nāt′) *v.* to light up
iluminar *v.* alumbrar

illustrious (ĭ-lŭs′ trē-əs) *adj.* well-known or distinguished
ilustre *adj.* de distinguida prosapia, casa, origen

impertinent (ĭm-pûr′tn-ənt) *adj.* not having good manners; rude
impertinente *adj.* que no viene al caso

impetus (ĭm′pĭ-təs) *n.* a force that produces motion or action; impulse
ímpetu *n.* movimiento acelerado y violento

impoverished (ĭm-pŏv′ər-ĭsht) *adj.* poor
empobrecer *v.* hacer que uno quede pobre

impressive (ĭm-prĕs′ĭv) *adj.* grand; striking; majestic
impresionante *adj.* grandioso(a); majestuoso(a)

improvise (ĭm′prə-vīz′) *v.* to speak or perform without preparation
improvisar *v.* inventar en el momento

incalculable (ĭn-kăl′kyə-lə-bəl) *adj.* too great to be measured or counted
incalculable *adj.* que no puede calcularse

incapacitated (ĭn′kə-păs′ĭ-tā′tĭd) *adj.* deprived of the ability to engage in normal activities; disabled
incapacitate *v.*
incapacitado(a) *adj.* que no tiene la habilidad de hacer ciertas cosas

incoherent (ĭn′kō-hîr′ənt) *adj.* without connection or harmony
incoherente *adj.* no coherente

incomprehensible (ĭn′kŏm-prĭ-hĕn′sə-bəl) *adj.* not understandable
incompresible *adj.* que no se comprende

incorporate (ĭn-kôr′pə-rāt′) *v.* to make part of another thing; merge
incorporar *v.* unir una o más cosas para que hagan un todo

incredulous (ĭn-krĕj′ə-ləs) *adj.* unable or unwilling to believe something
incrédulo(a) *adj.* que no cree

incriminate (ĭn-krĭm′ə-nāt′) *v.* to cause to appear guilty
incriminar *v.* acriminar

indefinitely (ĭn-dĕf′ə-nĭt-lē) *adv.* for an unlimited length of time
indefinidamente *adv.* que no llega al fin

indivisible (ĭn′də-vĭz′ə-bəl) *adj.* incapable of being divided
indivisible *adj.* que no puede ser dividido

indomitable (ĭn-dŏm′ĭ-tə-bəl) *adj.* unconquerable
indomable *adj.* que no se puede domar

inevitably (ĭn-ĕv′ĭ-tə-blē) *adv.* in a way that is impossible to avoid or prevent
inevitable *adj.* que no se puede evitar

infuriatingly (ĭn-fyŏŏr′ē-ā′tĭng-lē) *adv.* in a way that makes one very angry
enfurecido(a) *adj.* enojado

ingratiate (ĭn-grā′shē-āt′) *v.* to try to bring oneself into another's favor
congraciarse *v.* ganar el favor o respeto de otro

initial (ĭ-nĭsh′əl) *adj.* first
inicial *adj.* primero

insatiable (ĭn-sā′shə-bəl) *adj.* impossible to satisfy
insaciable *adj.* imposible de satisfacer

inscription (ĭn-skrĭp′shən) *n.* something written, carved, or engraved on a surface
inscripción *n.* acción de inscribir

insinuation (ĭn-sĭn′yōō-ā′shən) *n.* a suggestion or hint intended to insult
insinuación *n.* manera sutil de insultar

integrated (ĭn′tĭ-grā′tĭd) *adj.* open to people of all races or ethnic groups without restriction; desegregated
integrate *v.*
integrado(a) *adj.* abierto(a) a personas de todas razas o grupos étnicos sin restricciones; no segregado(a)

intense (ĭn-tĕns′) *adj.* showing great concentration or determination
intenso(a) *adj.* algo que muestra gran concentración o determinación

intently (ĭn-tĕnt′lē) *adv.* with fixed attention
atentamente *adv.* con atención fija

interval (ĭn′tər-vəl) *n.* the amount of time between two events
intervalo *n.* la cantidad de tiempo entre dos sucesos

intricate (ĭn′trĭ-kĭt) *adj.* arranged in a complex way
intrincado *adj.* presentado de una manera compleja

invalid (ĭn′və-lĭd) *n.* a sickly or disabled person
inválido *n.* persona enferma o sin habilidad

ironically (ī-rŏn′ĭk-lē) *adv.* in a way that is contrary to what is expected or intended
irónicamente *adv.* de una manera contraria a lo esperado o lo intentado

J

jauntily (jôn′tĭ-lē) *adv.* in a light and carefree way
gallardamente *adv.* de una manera ligera y despreocupada

jeer (jîr) *v.* to mock; to taunt
burlarse *v.* tratar con desprecio; ridiculizar

jostling (jŏs′lĭng) *n.* a rough bumping, pushing, or shoving **jostle** *v.*
entrada a empellones *n.* chocar o empujar con fuerza
entrar a empellones *v.*

L

legacy (lĕg′ə-sē) *n.* something handed down from an ancestor or from the past
herencia *n.* algo heredado de un antepasado o del pasado

legitimate (lə-jĭt′ə-mĭt) *adj.* in accordance with accepted practices; reasonable
legítimo(a) *adj.* según las prácticas aceptadas; razonable

liberation (lĭb′ə-rā′shən) *n.* a state of freedom reached after a struggle
liberación *n.* estado de libertad alcanzado después de una lucha

linger (lĭng′gər) *v.* to continue to stay; delay leaving
vacilar *v.* quedarse; tardar en partir

list (lĭst) *v.* to tilt; lean
escorar *v.* voltear, inclinar

loathsome (lōth′səm) *adj.* disgusting
repugnante *adj.* asqueroso(a)

M

macabre (mə-kä′brə) *adj.* suggesting the horror of death and decay
macabro(a) *adj.* que sugiere el horror de la muerte y la descomposición

malignant (mə-lĭg′nənt) *adj.* filled with evil; threatening
maligno(a) *adj.* malvado(a); amenazante

maneuver (mə-nōō′vər) *v.* to guide or direct through a series of movements
maniobrar *v.* guiar o dirigir a través de una serie de movimientos

maxim (măk′sĭm) *n.* a short saying that expresses an accepted truth or rule; proverb
máxima *n.* una frase corta que expresa una verdad o regla aceptada; refrán

melancholy (mĕl′ən-kŏl′ē) *n.* sadness; depression
melancolía *n.* tristeza; depresión

menacing (mĕn′ĭs-ĭng) *adj.* threatening **menace** *v.*
amenazante *adj.* que indica peligro

merge (mûrj) *v.* to blend together
combinarse *v.* unirse

migrant (mī′grənt) *adj.* moving from place to place
migratorio(a) *adj.* mudarse de un sitio a otro

mistrust (mĭs-trŭst′) *v.* to have no confidence in
desconfiar *v.* no tener confianza

mobilize (mō′bə-līz′) *v.* to assemble for a purpose
movilizar *v.* reunir para un propósito

mortal (môr′tl) *adj.* of the earth; not a spirit
mortal *adj.* de la Tierra; no un espíritu

multitude (mŭl′tĭ-tōōd′) *n.* a very great number
multitud *n.* un gran número

muster (mŭs′tər) *v.* to call forth; to summon up
poder valerse de uno mismo *v.* contar con un talento propio sin temor

N

neurotic (nŏŏ-rŏt′ĭk) *adj.* having excessive anxiety and emotional upset
neurótico(a) *adj.* tener ansiedad excesiva y malestar emocional

nimbly (nĭm′blē) *adv.* quickly and lightly
ágilmente *adv.* rápidamente y ligeramente

novelty (nŏv′əl-tē) *n.* something new, original, or unusual
novedad *n.* algo nuevo, original o inusual

nuisance (nōō′səns) *n.* someone or something that is annoying and bothersome
molestia *n.* alguien o algo irritante y fastidioso

O

odious (ō′dē-əs) *adj.* causing or deserving strong dislike
odioso(a) *adj.* causa o merece una fuerte antipatía

optimistic (ŏp′tə-mĭs′tĭk) *adj.* hopeful about the future; confident
optimista *adj.* lleno(a) de esperanza acerca del futuro; confiado(a)

orderly (ôr′dər-lē) *n.* an attendant who performs nonmedical tasks in a hospital or similar institution
enfermero *n.* una persona que cuida de un enfermo; camillero

P

pandemonium (păn′də-mō′nē-əm) *n.* a noisy upset; a wild uproar
pandemonio *n.* malestar ruidoso; tumulto turbulento

parchment (pärch′mənt) *n.* a paperlike writing material made from the skins of sheep or goats
pergamino *n.* papel muy fino

passive (păs′ĭv) *adj.* inactive; lacking in energy or willpower
pasivo(a) *adj.* inactivo(a); sin energía ni fuerza

peer (pîr) *v.* to look intently
escudriñar *v.* mirar intensivamente

pensively (pĕn′sĭv-lē) *adv.* in a way that suggests deep thought
pensativamente *adv.* pensando con tranquilidad

perilously (pĕr′ə-ləs-lē) *adv.* dangerously
arriesgadamente *adv.* peligrosamente

perpetual (pər-pĕch′ōō-əl) *adj.* continual; unending
perpetuo(a) *adj.* eterno(a), sin fin

persistent (pər-sĭs′tənt) *adj.* refusing to give up; continuing stubbornly
persistente *adj.* que rechaza el acto de abandonar; que sigue obstinadamente

petition (pə-tĭsh′ən) *n.* a formal request
solicitud *n.* pedido formal

petty (pĕt′ē) *adj.* of little importance, trivial
insignificante *adj.* sin importancia, trivial

plague (plāg) *v.* to annoy
plagar *v.* fastidiar

pledge (plĕj) *n.* something given to guarantee fulfillment of a promise
compromiso *n.* algo que se hace para garantizar una promesa

poised (poizd) *adj.* balanced or held in suspension
equilibrado(a) *adj.* balanceado(a) o suspendido(a)

portly (pôrt′lē) *adj.* stout or overweight
corpulento(a) *adj.* grueso o con demasiado peso

predestined (prē-dĕs′tĭnd) *adj.* having one's fate decided beforehand **predestine** *v.*
predestinado(a) *adj.* que tiene el destino determinado de antemano **predestinar** *v.*

presentable (prĭ-zĕn′tə-bəl) *adj.* fit to be seen by people
presentable *adj.* listo(a) para ser visto(a) por la gente

priceless (prīs′lĭs) *adj.* too valuable to be measured by price
inapreciable *adj.* que tiene demasiado valor para fijarse un precio

priority (prī-ôr′ĭ-tē) *n.* something that must receive attention first
prioridad *n.* algo que debe ser atendido primero

prominent (prŏm′ə-nənt) *adj.* well-known; widely recognized
prominente *adj.* bien conocido(a); reconocido(a) en muchas partes

prophecy (prŏf′ĭ-sē) *n.* a prediction; foretelling of future events
profecía *n.* una predicción inspirada de eventos futuros

provision (prə-vĭzh′ən) *n.* a supplying of needs
provisión *n.* la oferta de unas necesidades

provocation (prŏv′ə-kā′shən) *n.* something that produces an emotional or physical reaction
provocación *n.* algo que produce una reacción física o emocional

Q

quarantine (kwôr′ən-tēn′) *n.* a place where a diseased animal is kept away from others
cuarentena *n.* lugar donde se aparta un animal enfermo

quench (kwĕnch) *v.* to put out; to extinguish
aplacar *v.* apagar; extinguir

quiver (kwĭv′ər) *v.* to shake with a slight, rapid movement
temblar *v.* vibrar con un movimiento rápido y sutil

R

ravage (răv′ĭj) *v.* to destroy
devastar *v.* destruir

ravenous (răv′ə-nəs) *adj.* extremely hungry; greedy
voraz *adj.* que tiene mucha hambre; glotón

reassurance (rē′ə-shŏŏr′əns) *n.* a restoring of confidence
afirmación repetida *n.* una restauración de confianza

rebellion (rĭ-bĕl′yən) *n.* organized resistance to government or authority
rebelión *n.* resistencia organizada al gobierno o las autoridades

recede (rĭ-sēd′) *v.* to become fainter and more distant
retirarse *v.* llegar a ser débil y más lejano

reclaiming (rĭ-klā′mĭng) *adj.* getting back; recovering **reclaim** *v.*
recuperado(a) *adj.* obtenido(a) de nuevo; recobrado(a) **recuperar** *v.*

redundant (rĭ-dŭn′dənt) *adj.* more than what is necessary
redundante *adj.* más de lo necesario

reel (rēl) *v.* to go round and round
dar vueltas *v.* hacer girar

rehabilitate (rē′hə-bĭl′ĭ-tāt′) *v.* to restore to useful life, as through therapy and education
rehabilitar *v.* restaurar a una vida útil a través de la terapia y educación

repress (rĭ-prĕs′) *v.* to hold something back
reprimir *v.* retener algo

resign (rĭ-zīn′) *v.* to give up (a job or an award, for instance)
renunciar *v.* el acto de dejar un trabajo

resiliency (rĭ-zĭl′ yən-sē) *n.* the ability to recover quickly from illness, change, or misfortune
resiliencia *n.* la capacidad de recuperarse rápidamente de una enfermedad, un cambio o la desventura

resume (rǐ-zo̅o̅m′) *v.* to go on again; continue
resumir *v.* volver a empezar; seguir

retaliate (rǐ-tăl′ē-āt′) *v.* to get revenge; get even
vengarse *v.* ejercer represalias

retort (rǐ-tôrt′) *v.* respond to a comment, such as an insult or argument, with a reply of the same type, often quick, sharp, or witty
retorcer *v.* responder a un comentario, tal como un insulto o argumento, con una respuesta del mismo tipo, apenas rápida, penetrante o cómica

retribution (rĕt′rə-byo̅o̅′shən) *n.* punishment for bad behavior
punición *n.* castigo por actuar de una manera maleducada

revelation (rĕv′ə-lā′shən) *n.* something made known to others
revelación *n.* algo que se da a conocer otros

revert (rǐ-vûrt′) *v.* to return to a former condition
revertir *v.* regresar a una condición anterior

revive (rǐ-vīv′) *v.* to become conscious; wake up
meterse *v.* recobrar la consciencia; despertarse

ridiculed (rǐd′ǐ-kyo̅o̅ld′) *adj.* made fun of
ridicule *v.*
ridiculizado(a) *adj.* burlarse de
ridiculizar *v.*

righteous (rī′chəs) *adj.* caused by an insult to one's sense of right
honrado(a) *adj.* causado(a) por un insulto al sentido de lo apropiado

rummage (rŭm′ĭj) *v.* to search thoroughly by moving the contents about
revolver *v.* buscar moviendo los contenidos

S

sacrifice (săk′rə-fīs′) *v.* to give up something highly valued for the sake of something or someone more valued
sacrificar *v.* renunciar a algo de alto valor por consideración a algo o alguien de más valor

sanction (săngk′shən) *v.* to give approval for
sancionar *v.* aprobar

sanctuary (săngk′cho̅o̅-ĕr′ē) *n.* shelter; protection
santuario *n.* refugio; protección

saturated (săch′ə-rā′tǐd) *adj.* soaked with moisture; drenched
saturado(a) *adj.* empapado de humedad; remojado

saunter (sôn′tər) *v.* to walk about slowly
pasear *v.* caminar lentamente

scheme (skēm) *v.* to plot or plan in a secretive way
formar proyectos *v.* maquinar una intriga o planear de una manera secreta

scorn (skôrn) *v.* to treat with contempt
despreciar *v.* tratar con desdén

scowl (skoul) *v.* to look angry by drawing the eyebrows together and frowning
mirar ceñudamente *v.* parecer enojado(a) por fruncir el entrecejo

scuttle (skŭt′l) *v.* to run quickly, with hurried movements
correr tan aprisa como pueda *v.* correr con movimientos veloces

seize (sēz) *v.* to grab suddenly with force
asir *v.* agarrar de repente con fuerza

self-denial (sĕlf′dǐ-nī′əl) *n.* a giving up of one's own desires or interests
abnegación *n.* la devolución de los propios deseos o intereses de una persona

sentimental (sĕn′tə-mĕn′tl) *adj.* showing or characterized by tender emotions
sentimental *adj.* que muestra o se caracteriza por emociones tiernas

sheepishly (shē′pĭsh-lē) *adv.* with a bashful or embarrassed look
tímidamente *adv.* con una mirada tímida o avergonzada

shrewdly (shrōōd′lē) *adv.* wisely; in a clever way
astutamente *adv.* inteligentemente; de una manera lista

shuffle (shŭf′əl) *v.* to slide the feet along the ground while walking
arrastrar los pies *v.* mover los pies a través del suelo al caminar

simultaneously (sī′məl-tā′nē-əs-lē) *adv.* at the same time
simultáneamente *adv.* que pasa o se hace al mismo tiempo

smugly (smŭg′lē) *adv.* in a self-satisfied way
presumidamente *adv.* de una manera que tiene satisfacción vanidosa

snag (snăg) *v.* to catch and tear
rasgar con un gancho *v.* agarrarse y romperse

solitude (sŏl′ĭ-tōōd) *n.* the state of being alone
soledad *n.* el estado de estar solo(a)

specify (spĕs′ə-fī) *v.* to make known or identify
especificar *v.* revelarse o identificar

speculating (spĕk′yə-lā′tĭng) *adj.* thinking about different possibilities; guessing what might happen
speculate *v.*
especulativo(a) *adj.* que piensa en las posibilidades; que adivina lo que puede pasar **especular** *v.*

spherical (sfîr′ĭ-kəl) *adj.* having the shape of a round ball
esférico(a) *adj.* que tiene la forma de una pelota redonda

spurn (spûrn) *v.* to reject or turn down scornfully
desdeñar *v.* rechazar o rehusar con desdén

squander (skwŏn′dər) *v.* to spend carelessly
malgastar *v.* derrochar

staunchest (stônch′əst) *adj.* strongest; most determined; most firm
más sólido(a) *adj.* más fuerte; más determinado(a); más firme

stride (strīd) *v.* to walk with long steps; *past tense*—**strode**
caminar a zancadas *v.* andar con pasos largos

stupefying (stōō′pə-fī′ĭng) *adj.* stunning; shocking **stupefy** *v.*
estupefacto(a) *adj.* asombroso(a)

stupendous (stōō-pĕn′dəs) *adj.* tremendous; amazing
estupendo(a) *adj.* tremendo(a); impresionante

submissive (səb-mĭs′ĭv) *adj.* willing to give in to or obey another
sumiso(a) *adj.* con la voluntad de obedecer a otro

substance (sŭb′stəns) *n.* material quality
substancia *n.* calidad material

suede (swād) *n.* leather with a soft, fuzzy surface
gamuza *n.* piel con superficie suave y vellosa

suite (swēt) *n.* a group of rooms used as a unit
suite *n.* apartamento lujoso

summon (sŭm′ən) *v.* to call for or send for with authority or urgency; to order to come or appear
convocar *v.* llamar o mandar llamar con autoridad o urgencia; mandar a llegar y aparecer

surly (sûr′lē) *adj.* ill-tempered; gruff
áspero(a) *adj.* de mal humor; rudo(a)

surplus (sûr′pləs) *adj.* extra; more than is needed
sobrante *adj.* excedente; más de lo necesario

susceptible (sə-sĕp′tə-bəl) *adj.* easily affected or influenced
susceptible *adj.* afectado(a) o influido(a) fácilmente

T

tantalizing (tăn′tə-lī′zĭng) *adj.* arousing interest without satisfying it **tantalize** *v.*
tentador(a) *adj.* que inspira interés sin satisfacer **tentar** *v.*

taunt (tônt) *v.* to make fun of; jeer
burlar *v.* provocar con burlas; ridiculizar

teeming (tē′mĭng) *adj.* full of people or things **teem** *v.*
prolífico(a) *adj.* lleno(a) de gente o cosas **estar lleno(a)** *v.*

tensing (tĕns′ĭng) *n.* a tightening or becoming taut **tense** *v.*
tensión *n.* aplicación de fuerza para ajustar **tensar** *v.*

throb (thrŏb) *v.* to beat strongly (as though hurting)
pulsar *v.* latir fuertemente (como si doliera)

toll (tōl) *n.* the amount of loss or destruction caused by a disaster
número de muertos *n.* el número de personas que muere a causa de un desastre

transform (trăns-fôrm′) *v.* to change the form or appearance of
transformar *v.* cambiar la forma o aspecto de

transitory (trăn′sĭ-tôr′ē) *adj.* lasting only a short time; temporary
transitorio(a) *adj.* dura sólo un ratito; temporal

translucent (trăns-lōō′sənt) *adj.* allowing light to pass through
translúcido(a) *adj.* que deja pasar la luz

tread (trĕd) *v.* to walk on, in, or along
pisar *v.* caminar encima, en o a través

tribute (trĭb′yōōt) *n.* an action or gift that honors a deserving individual
tributo *n.* homenaje o celebración en nombre de una persona que lo merece

trudge (trŭj) *v.* to walk heavily; plod
caminar pesadamente *v.* andar con trabajo; andar pausadamente

U

ultimate (ŭl′tə-mĭt) *adj.* final; most important
último(a) *adj.* final; más importante

unaccountably (ŭn′ə-koun′tə-blē) *adv.* without apparent explanation
inexplicablemente *adv.* sin explicación aparente

unbridled (ŭn-brīd′ld) *adj.* lacking in restraint or control
sin brío *adj.* sin restricciones

unobtrusively (ŭn′əb-trōō′sĭv-lē) *adv.* in a way that attracts little or no attention
discretamente *adv.* de una manera que atrae poca atención

unperceived (ŭn′pər-sēvd′) *adj.* not seen
desapercibido(a) *adj.* no visto(a)

unsound (ŭn-sound′) *adj.* not free from fault or weakness; not sensible; inaccurate
defectuoso(a) *adj.* débil; falta de sentido; no preciso(a)

urgency (ûr′jən-sē) *n.* insistence; a condition of pressing importance
urgencia *n.* insistencia; condición de importancia emergente

usher (ŭsh′ər) *v.* to make known the presence or arrival of; to introduce
anunciar *v.* revelar la presencia o llegada; introducir

V

vainglorious (vān-glôr′ē-əs) *adj.* vain and boastful
vanaglorioso(a) *adj.* vano(a) y jactancioso(a)

valedictorian (văl′ĭ-dĭk-tôr′ē-ən) *n.* student with highest academic rank in a class
valedictorian *n.* la persona que saca las notas más altas de una clase

vicinity (vĭ-sĭn′ĭ-tē) *n.* neighborhood
vecindad *n.* barrio

vigil (vĭj′əl) *n.* a time of staying awake in order to keep watch or guard something
vigilia *n.* período de mantenerse despierto(a) para observar o cuidar algo

vigor (vĭg′ər) *n.* physical or mental strength, energy, or force
vigor *n.* fuerza o energía física o mental

vile (vīl) *adj.* disgusting, unpleasant
de sabor desagradable *adj.* tener sabor a bilis

virtuous (vûr′chōō-əs) *adj.* morally good; honorable
virtuoso(a) *adj.* de buen carácter moral; honorable

W

wan (wŏn) *adj.* sickly; pale
descolorido(a) *adj.* enfermizo(a); pálido(a)

welfare (wĕl′fâr′) *n.* well-being
bienestar *n.* comodidad

whim (hwĭm) *n.* a fanciful notion or impulse
capricho *n.* una idea o impulso fantástico

wily (wī′lē) *adj.* crafty; sly
artero(a) *adj.* hábil; travieso(a)

wince (wĭns) *v.* to shrink as in pain or distress
sobresaltarse *v.* recular como si se sintiera dolor

wretched (rĕch′ĭd) *adj.* miserable
lastimoso(a) *adj.* miserable

Z

zeal (zēl) *n.* eagerness; enthusiasm
fervor *n.* ardor; entusiasmo

Pronunciation Key

Symbol	Examples	Symbol	Examples	Symbol	Examples
ă	at, gas	m	man, seem	v	van, save
ā	ape, day	n	night, mitten	w	web, twice
ä	father, barn	ng	sing, anger	y	yard, lawyer
âr	fair, dare	ŏ	odd, not	z	zoo, reason
b	bell, table	ō	open, road, grow	zh	treasure, garage
ch	chin, lunch	ô	awful, bought, horse	ə	awake, even, pencil, pilot, focus
d	dig, bored	oi	coin, boy		
ĕ	egg, ten	ŏŏ	look, full	ər	perform, letter
ē	evil, see, meal	ōō	root, glue, through		
f	fall, laugh, phrase	ou	out, cow		**Sounds in Foreign Words**
g	gold, big	p	pig, cap	KH	*German* ich, auch; *Scottish* loch
h	hit, inhale	r	rose, star		
hw	white, everywhere	s	sit, face	N	*French* entre, bon, fin
ĭ	inch, fit	sh	she, mash	œ	*French* feu, cœur; *German* schön
ī	idle, my, tried	t	tap, hopped		
îr	dear, here	th	thing, with	ü	*French* utile, rue; *German* grün
j	jar, gem, badge	*th*	then, other		
k	keep, cat, luck	ŭ	up, nut		
l	load, rattle	ûr	fur, earn, bird, worm		

Stress Marks

′ This mark indicates that the preceding syllable receives the primary stress. For example, in the word *language,* the first syllable is stressed: lăng′gwĭj.

ˌ This mark is used only in words in which more than one syllable is stressed. It indicates that the preceding syllable is stressed, but somewhat more weakly than the syllable receiving the primary stress. In the word *literature,* for example, the first syllable receives the primary stress, and the last syllable receives a weaker stress: lĭt′ər-ə-chŏŏr′.

Adapted from *The American Heritage Dictionary of the English Language, Third Edition;* Copyright © 1992 by Houghton Mifflin Company. Used with the permission of Houghton Mifflin Company.

Index of Fine Art

Index of Skills

Literary Concepts

Reading and Critical Thinking Skills

Vocabulary Skills

Speaking and Listening

facial expression, 877, R101
gestures, 877, 874, R101
pacing, 571, 874, 877, R101
pause, R102
pitch, 571, 874, R101
posture, 874, R102
stress, R101
tone, 874, 877, R101, R134–R135
volume, 874, 877, R101
Directions, following, R103
Discussion, R108
Dramatic adaptation, 322
skit, 176
video, 176
Dramatic presentation, 579–583, R102. *See also* Reading aloud (oral reading); Storytelling.
author interview, 468, R127
dialogue, 35, 184, 437, 547, R123
dramatic reading, 407
monologue, 456, 777
play, 562
poetry performance, 200, 462
radio play, 136, R131
Reader's Theater, 691
recording, 182
scene, 176, 359, 615, R132
talk show, 328, 872
Group communication, R108
assigned roles, R108
Interviewing, 44, 85, 107, 231, 297, 373, 468, 599, R109, R127
Listening strategies, R102–R104
Multimedia. *See* Multimedia presentations *under* Viewing and Representing.
Music, 468, 615, 738, 872, 875, R117
Narrative presentation, R102–R103, R128. *See also* Storytelling.
Nonverbal cues. *See* Delivery.
Organization, R100–R102
Oral history, 630, 796, R129
Oral literature, R129. *See also* Oral tradition *under* Literary Concepts.
Oral summary, 874, R103, R134
Peer review, 583. *See also* Peer review *under* Assessment.
Persuasive devices, recognizing, R107
bandwagon, R107
either/or, R107
inaccurate generalization, R107, R126
snob appeal, R107
Persuasive presentations, R104–R105
Plot, R102, R129
Point of view, R102, R130

Practicing and presenting a speech, R101, R133. *See also* Delivery.
appropriate language, R100
evaluation, R101
organization, R101
visual aids, 874, 875, R101
Public speaking, R100–R102. *See also* Delivery; Reading aloud (oral reading).
classroom lesson, 242
debate, 217
oral report, 205, 231, 630
speech, 63, 119, R133
stress, R101
technical presentation, R115
trial argument, 462
victory speech, 373
Questioning, R103. *See also* Questioning *under* Reading and Critical Thinking Skills.
Reading aloud (oral reading), R102. *See also* Delivery; Public speaking.
drama, 249
poetry, 196, 199, 200, 205, 380, 389, R130
volume, R101
Radio script, 136, R132
Recordings, 571, 738
Rehearsal, 583, 877, R101
Research presentation, R104
Rhetorical devices, recognizing, R107
Role-playing, 244, 330, 788
Scripts, 580–581, R132
Setting, R102, R132
Speaker's purpose, R102–R103
Speaking and Listening Handbook, R100–R109
Speaking techniques, 583, R100–R104. *See also* Delivery.
Staging a scene, 579–583
Storytelling, 777, 794–795, 872–873. *See also* Narrative presentation; Oral tradition *under* Literary Concepts.
Summary, oral, 874, R103, R134
Visual aids, 874, 875, R101
Writing a speech, R100
appropriate language, R100
audience, R100
beginning, R100
clarity, R100
end, R100
evidence (research), R100
organization, R100
purpose, R100

Viewing and Representing

Assessment

Index of Titles and Authors

Page numbers that appear in italics refer to biographical information.

Acknowledgments (continued)

Susan Bergholz Literary Services: "Names/Nombres" by Julia Alvarez, first published in *Nuestro*, March 1985. Copyright © 1985 by Julia Alvarez. Reprinted by permission of Susan Bergholz Literary Services, New York. All rights reserved.

"Bums in the Attic," from *The House on Mango Street* by Sandra Cisneros, published by Alfred A. Knopf, a division of Random House, Inc., New York in 1994. Copyright © 1984 by Sandra Cisneros. Reprinted by permission of Susan Bergholz Literary Services, New York. All rights reserved

Alfred A. Knopf Children's Books: "Zebra," from *Zebra and Other Stories* by Chaim Potok. Copyright © 1998 by Chaim Potok. Reprinted by permission of Alfred A. Knopf Children's Books, a division of Random House, Inc.

Naomi Shihab Nye: "The Rider" by Naomi Shihab Nye, first published in *Invisible*. Reprinted by permission of the author.

Smithsonian Magazine: "Offerings at the Wall" by Don Moser, originally appeared in *Smithsonian*, May 1995. Reprinted with permission of the author.

Scholastic: "A Crush," from *A Couple of Kooks and Other Stories About Love* by Cynthia Rylant. Published by Orchard Books, an imprint of Scholastic Inc. Copyright © 1990 by Cynthia Rylant. Reprinted by permission of Scholastic Inc.

Atheneum Books For Young Readers: Excerpt from "Eleanor Roosevelt," from *Great Lives: Human Rights* by William Jay Jacobs. Copyright © 1990 by William Jay Jacobs. Reprinted with the permission of Atheneum Books for Young Readers, an imprint of Simon & Schuster Children's Publishing Division.

Simon & Schuster: Excerpt from *No Ordinary Time* by Doris Kearns Goodwin. Copyright © 1994 by Doris Kearns Goodwin. Reprinted with the permission of Simon & Schuster, Inc.

Random House: Excerpt from *Living Out Loud* by Anna Quindlen. Copyright © 1987 by Anna Quindlen. Reprinted by permission of Random House, Inc.

Pantheon Books: "The War of the Wall," from *Deep Sightings and Rescue Missions* by Toni Cade Bambara. Copyright © 1996 by The Estate of Toni Cade Bambara. Reprinted by permission of Pantheon Books, a division of Random House, Inc.

Life: "Primal Compassion" by Charles Hirshberg, *Life*, November 1996. Copyright © 1996 by Time Inc. Reprinted by permission.

Delacorte Press: Excerpt from *My Life in Dog Years* by Gary Paulsen. Copyright © 1998 by Gary Paulsen. Used by permission of Delacorte Press, a division of Random House, Inc.

Unit Two

Henry Holt and Company: "The Pasture," from *The Poetry of Robert Frost*, edited by Edward Connery Lathem. Copyright 1944, © 1958 by Robert Frost. Copyright © 1967 by Lesley Frost Ballantine. Copyright 1930, 1939, © 1969 by Henry Holt and Company. Reprinted by permission of Henry Holt and Company, Inc.

"A Time to Talk," from *The Poetry of Robert Frost*, edited by Edward Connery Lathem. Copyright 1944, © 1958 by Robert Frost. Copyright © 1967 by Lesley Frost Ballantine. Copyright 1930, 1939, © 1969 by Henry Holt and Company. Reprinted by permission of Henry Holt and Company, Inc.

HarperCollins Publishers: "The World Is Not a Pleasant Place to Be," from *My House* by Nikki Giovanni. Copyright © 1972 by Nikki Giovanni. Reprinted by permission of HarperCollins Publishers, Inc.

Alfred A. Knopf: "To You," from *Collected Poems* by Langston Hughes. Copyright © 1994 by the Estate of Langston Hughes. Reprinted by permission of Alfred A. Knopf, Inc.

Candlewick Press: "What Do Fish Have to Do with Anything?" from *What Do Fish Have to Do with Anything?: And Other Stories* by Avi. Copyright © 1997 by Avi Wortis. Reprinted by permission of Candlewick Press, Cambridge, MA.

The Boston Herald: Excerpt from "The Difference a City Year Makes" by Lauren Beckham, *The Boston Herald*, June 10, 1996. Copyright © 1996 by *The Boston Herald*. Reprinted with permission of *The Boston Herald*.

Dutton Children's Books: Excerpt from *Immigrant Kids* by Russell Freedman. Copyright © 1980 by Russell Freedman. Used by permission of Dutton Children's Books, a division of Penguin Putnam Inc.

Susan Bergholz Literary Services: "Good Hot Dogs" / "Buenos Hot Dogs" from *My Wicked, Wicked Ways* in English, published by Third Woman Press and in hardcover by Alfred A. Knopf, and from *Cool Salsa* in Spanish, published by Henry Holt. Copyright © 1987 by Sandra Cisneros in English. Copyright © 1994 by Sandra Cisneros in Spanish. Reprinted by permission of Susan Bergholz Literary Services, New York. All rights reserved.

Faber and Faber: "Scaffolding," from *Death of a Naturalist* by Seamus Heaney. Copyright © 1966 by Seamus Heaney. Reprinted by permission of Faber and Faber Limited.

University Of Minnesota Press: *A Christmas Carol* by Charles Dickens, adapted by Frederick Gaines, from *Five Plays from the Children's Theatre Company of Minneapolis*, published by the University of Minnesota Press. Copyright © 1975 by Frederick Gaines. All rights reserved.

Bilingual Press/Editorial Bilingüe: "The Scholarship Jacket" by Marta Salinas, from *Nosotras: Latina Literature Today* (1986), edited by María del Carmen Boza, Beverly Silva, and Carmen Valle. By permission of Bilingual Press/Editorial Bilingüe, Arizona State University, Tempe, AZ.

Arte Público Press: "Graduation Morning," from *Chants* by Pat Mora. Reprinted with permission from the publisher of *Chants*, Arte Público Press—University of Houston, 1985.

CMG Worldwide: Excerpt from *I Never Had It Made* by Jackie Robinson, as told to Alfred Duckett. By permission of CMG Worldwide Inc. on behalf of Rachel Robinson.

The James Reeves Estate: "Ant and Grasshopper," from *Fables from Aesop* retold by James Reeves, published by Blackie & Son Ltd. Copyright © 1961 by James Reeves. Reprinted by permission of the James Reeves Estate.

Ennis Rees: "The Ant and the Grasshopper," from *Fables from Aesop* by Ennis Rees. Copyright © 1964 by Ennis Rees. Reprinted by permission of the author.

Doubleday: "The Richer, the Poorer" by Dorothy West. Copyright © 1995 by Dorothy West. Used by permission of Doubleday, a division of Random House, Inc.

Unit Three

Bantam Books: "One Ordinary Day, with Peanuts," from *Just An Ordinary Day: The Uncollected Stories* by Shirley Jackson. Copyright © 1997 by The Estate of Shirley Jackson. Used by permission of Bantam Books, a division of Random House, Inc.

"The Eternal Frontier" from *Frontier* by Louis L'Amour. Copyright © 1984 by Louis L'Amour Enterprises, Inc. Used by permission of Bantam Books, a division of Random House, Inc.

Piri Thomas: Excerpt from *Stories from El Barrio* by Piri Thomas. Copyright © 1978 by Piri Thomas. Reprinted by permission of the author.

Simon & Schuster Books for Young Readers: "Ode to an Artichoke," translation of the Pablo Neruda poem "Oda a la Alcachofa," from *The Yellow Canary Whose Eye Is so Black* by Cheli Duran. Copyright © 1977 by Cheli Duran Ryan. Reprinted with permission of Simon & Schuster Books for Young Readers, an imprint of Simon & Schuster Children's Publishing Division.

Agencia Literaria: "Oda a la Alcachofa," from *Pablo Neruda Poesía I* by Pablo Neruda. Copyright © 1954 by Pablo Neruda. Reprinted by permission of Agencia Literaria Carmen Balcells.

HarperCollins Publishers: Excerpt from *An American Childhood* by Annie Dillard. Copyright © 1987 by Annie Dillard. Reprinted by permission of HarperCollins Publishers, Inc.

"Sarah Cynthia Sylvia Stout Would Not Take the Garbage Out" from *Where The Sidewalk Ends* by Shel Silverstein. Copyright © 1974 by Evil-Eye Music, Inc. Reprinted by permission of HarperCollins Publishers, Inc.

"Winter Poem," from *My House* by Nikki Giovanni. Copyright © 1972 by Nikki Giovanni. Reprinted by permission of HarperCollins Publishers, Inc.

Doubleday: "The Bat," from *The Collected Poems of Theodore Roethke* by Theodore Roethke. Copyright © 1938 by Theodore Roethke. Used by permission of Doubleday, a division of Random House, Inc.

"Key Item," from *Buy Jupiter and Other Stories* by Isaac Asimov. Copyright © 1975 by Isaac Asimov. Used by permission of Doubleday, a division of Random House, Inc.

Viking Penguin: "Mooses," from *Under the North Star* by Ted Hughes. Copyright © 1981 by Ted Hughes. Used by permission of Viking Penguin, a division of Penguin Putnam Inc.

National Wildlife: "They're Well-Suited for Studying Moose" by Steve Mirsky, *National Wildlife*, June/July 1997. Copyright © 1997 by the National Wildlife Federation. Reprinted with permission from *National Wildlife*.

Barbara Hogenson Agency: "The Night the Bed Fell," from *My Life and Hard Times* by James Thurber. Copyright © 1933 by James Thurber. Copyright © renewed 1961 by Helen Thurber and Rosemary A. Thurber. Reprinted by arrangement with Rosemary A. Thurber and the Barbara Hogenson Agency.

The Rod Serling Trust: "The Monsters Are Due on Maple Street" by Rod Serling. © 1960 by Rod Serling. © 1988 by Carolyn Serling, Jody Serling, and Anne Serling Sutton. Reprinted by permission of Writers & Artists and Carol Serling, on behalf of the Estate of Rod Serling.

Brandt & Brandt Literary Agents and A. M. Heath: "The Serial Garden," from *Armitage, Armitage, Fly Away Home* by Joan Aiken. Copyright © 1966 by Macmillan & Co., Ltd. Copyright © 1969 by Joan Aiken Enterprises, Ltd. Copyright renewed © 1994 by Joan Aiken Enterprises, Ltd. Reprinted by permission of Brandt & Brandt Literary Agents, Inc., and A. M. Heath & Co., Ltd., on behalf of the author.

The Boston Globe: "Four Decades in Space" by Richard Sanchez and Sean McNaughton, *The Boston Globe*, October 29, 1998. Copyright © 1998 by *The Boston Globe*. Reprinted courtesy of *The Boston Globe*.

Don Congdon Associates: "Dark They Were, and Golden-Eyed" as "The Naming of Names," from *Thrilling Wonder Stories* by Ray Bradbury. Copyright © 1949 by Standard Magazines, Inc., renewed 1976 by Ray Bradbury. Reprinted by permission of Don Congdon Associates, Inc.

"The Golden Kite, the Silver Wind" from *Classic Stories I* by Ray Bradbury. Copyright © 1953 by Epoch Associates, renewed 1981 by Ray Bradbury. Reprinted by permission of Don Congdon Associates, Inc.

The Charlotte Observer: Excerpt from "Ray Bradbury, Science Fiction Supernova, Has Little Use for the Internet" by Sandy Hill, *The Charlotte Observer*, October 12, 1997. Copyright © 1997 by *The Charlotte Observer*. Reprinted with permission of *The Charlotte Observer*.

Unit Four

Gish Jen: "The White Umbrella" by Gish Jen, first published in *The Yale Review*. Copyright © 1984 by Gish Jen. Reprinted by permission of the author.

Farrar, Straus & Giroux and David Higham Associates: "The Bicycle and the Sweetshop," "Mr. Coombs," and "The Great Mouse Plot," from *Boy: Tales of Childhood* by Roald Dahl. Copyright © 1984 by Roald Dahl. Reprinted by permission of Farrar, Straus & Giroux, Inc., and David Higham Associates.

CyberPalate: An adaptation of "A Chocolate Timeline," from CuisineNet Diner's Digest, www.cuisinenet.com. Copyright © 1999 by CyberPalate. Reprinted by permission of CyberPalate.

Neil Simon: "A Defenseless Creature," from *The Good Doctor* by Neil Simon. Copyright © 1974 by Neil Simon. Reprinted by permission of Neil Simon.

Hugh Noyes: "The Highwayman," by Alfred Noyes. Reprinted by permission of Hugh Noyes, for the Trustees of the Literary Estate of Alfred Noyes.

Alfred A. Knopf Children's Books: "Staying in the Lines," from *Knots in My Yo-Yo String: Autobiography of a Kid* by Jerry Spinelli. Text copyright © 1998 by Jerry Spinelli. Reprinted by permission of Alfred A. Knopf Children's Books, a division of Random House, Inc.

Scholastic: "An Hour with Abuelo," from *An Island Like You: Stories of the Barrio* by Judith Ortiz Cofer. Published by Orchard Books, an imprint of Scholastic Inc. Copyright © 1995 by Judith Ortiz Cofer. Reprinted by permission of Scholastic Inc.

Philomel Books and Stoddart Publishing Company: "Waiting," from *The Leaving and Other Stories* by Budge Wilson. Copyright © 1990 by Budge Wilson. Used by permission of Philomel Books, a division of Penguin Putnam, Inc., and by permission of Stoddart Publishing Company Ltd., Don Mills, Ontario, Canada.

National Geographic Society: "Face-to-Face with Twins" by Judith Rinard, *National Geographic World*, April 1998. Copyright © 1998 by National Geographic Society. Reprinted by permission of the National Geographic Society.

NTC/Contemporary Publishing, Inc.: Excerpt from *Growing Up* by Russell Baker. Copyright © 1982 by Russell Baker. Used with permission of NTC/Contemporary Publishing Group, Inc.

Random House: Excerpt from *The Autobiography of Malcolm X* by Malcolm X, with the assistance of Alex Haley. Copyright © 1964 by Alex Haley and Malcolm X, renewed © 1965 by Alex Haley and Betty Shabazz. Reprinted by permission of Random House, Inc.

Marian Reiner: "Aardvark," by Julia Fields from *Nine Black Poets*, edited by R. Baird Shuman. Copyright © 1968 by Julia Fields. Used by permission of Marian Reiner for the author.

Unit Five

Scholastic: Excerpt from *Exploring the Titanic* by Robert D. Ballard. Copyright © 1988 by The Madison Press Ltd. Text copyright © 1988 by Robert D. Ballard and Family. Reprinted by permission of Scholastic Inc.

The Dallas Morning News: "The Lives of LaBelle" by Bryan Woolley, *The Dallas Morning News*, February 9, 1997. Copyright © 1997 by *The Dallas Morning News*. Reprinted with permission of *The Dallas Morning News*.

Hill and Wang: "The Last Cover," from *The Pride of Lions and Other Stories* by Paul Annixter. Copyright © 1960 by Hill and Wang, renewed copyright 1988 by Hill and Wang. Reprinted by permission of Hill and Wang, a division of Farrar, Straus & Giroux, Inc.

University of Notre Dame Press: Excerpt from *Barrio Boy* by Ernesto Galarza. Copyright © 1971 by University of Notre Dame Press. Used by permission of Notre Dame Press.

David Higham Associates: "A Crown of Wild Olive," from *Heather, Oak, and Olive: Three Stories* by Rosemary Sutcliff. Copyright © 1971 by Rosemary Sutcliff. Reprinted by permission of David Higham Associates.

Little, Brown and Company: Excerpt from *Long Walk to Freedom* by Nelson Mandela. Copyright © 1994 by Nelson Rolihlahla Mandela. By permission of Little, Brown and Company.

Grove/Atlantic: "The Turtle," from *Dream Work* by Mary Oliver. Copyright © 1992 by Mary Oliver. Reprinted with permission of Grove/Atlantic, Inc.

The Read-In Foundation: Excerpt from "An Interview with Virginia Hamilton," from The Read-In Foundation, http://www.readin.org. Used by permission of The Read-In Foundation and Virginia Hamilton.

Alfred A. Knopf Children's Books: Excerpt from *Anthony Burns: The Defeat and Triumph of a Fugitive Slave* by Virginia Hamilton. Copyright © 1988 by Virginia Hamilton. Reprinted by permission of Alfred A. Knopf Children's Books, a division of Random House, Inc.

Excerpt from *The People Could Fly: American Black Folktales* by Virginia Hamilton. Text copyright © 1985 by Virginia Hamilton. Reprinted by permission of Alfred A. Knopf Children's Books, a division of Random House, Inc.

Virginia Hamilton: Excerpt from "Looking for America," a speech given by Virginia Hamilton, 23 October 1993. Originally published by the Friends of the CCBC, Inc. Copyright © 1993 by Virginia Hamilton. Reprinted by permission of Virginia Hamilton.

Unit Six

Key Porter Books Limited: "The Foolish Men of Agra," from *The Foolish Men of Agra and Other Tales of Mogul India* retold by Rina Singh. Copyright © 1998 by Rina Singh. Reprinted by permission of Key Porter Books Limited.

Random House UK: "Arap Sang and the Cranes," from *Tales Told Near a Crocodile* by Humphrey Harman. Copyright © 1962 by Humphrey Harman. Reprinted by permission of Random House UK, Ltd.

Curtis Brown, Ltd.: "Waters of Gold," from *Tongues of Jade* by Laurence Yep, published by HarperCollins. Text copyright © 1991 by Laurence Yep. Reprinted by permission of the author and Curtis Brown, Ltd.

Doubleday: "Ashputtle," from *Grimm's Tales for Young and Old* by Jakob & Wilhelm Grimm. Copyright © 1977 by Ralph Manheim. Used by permission of Doubleday, a division of Random House, Inc.

Random House Children's Books: Excerpts from *Young Arthur* by Robert D. San Souci. Copyright © 1997 by Robert D. San Souci. Used by permission of Random House Children's Books, a division of Random House, Inc.

Ricardo E. Alegría: "Lazy Peter and His Three-Cornered Hat," from *The Three Wishes* by Ricardo E. Alegría. Puerto Rican folktale collected and adapted by Ricardo E. Alegría, Ph.D. Reprinted by permission of the author.

Houghton Mifflin: *Sundiata, Lion King of Mali* by David Wisniewski. Copyright © 1992 by David Wisniewski. Reprinted by permission of Houghton Mifflin Company.

Museum of New Mexico Press: "La Suerte: The Force of Luck" by Rudolfo A. Anaya, from *Cuentos: Tales from the Hispanic Southwest* by José Griego y Maestas and Rudolfo Anaya. Copyright © 1980. Reprinted with the permission of the Museum of New Mexico Press.

Little, Brown and Company: "Brother Coyote and Brother Cricket," from *I'll Tell You a Tale* by J. Frank Dobie. Copyright 1928, 1930, 1931, 1935, 1936, 1938, 1939, 1941, 1947, 1949, 1950, 1951, 1952, 1955, © 1960 by J. Frank Dobie. Reprinted by permission of Little, Brown and Company.

"How Odin Lost His Eye," from *Adventures with the Giants* by Catherine Sellew. Copyright © 1950 by Catherine Sellew Hinchman. Reprinted by permission of Little, Brown and Company.

Library Unlimited: "Pumpkin Seed and the Snake," from *Folk Stories of the Hmong* by Norma J. Livo and Dia Cha. Copyright © 1991 by Libraries Unlimited, Inc. By permission of Libraries Unlimited, Inc. www.lu.com.

G. P. Putnam's Sons: "Kelfala's Secret Something," from *Three African Tales* by Adjai Robinson. Copyright © 1979 by Adjai Robinson. Reprinted by permission of G. P. Putnam's Sons, a division of Penguin Putnam Inc.

The editors have made every effort to trace the ownership of all copyrighted material found in this book and to make full acknowledgment for its use. Omissions brought to our attention will be corrected in a subsequent edition.

Art Credits

Cover

Illustration copyright © 1999 Gary Overacre.

Front Matter

ix School Division, Houghton Mifflin Company; **x** Painting copyright © 1999 Brad Holland; **xii** Illustration by Bernie Fuchs; **xiv** Copyright © Kamil Vojnar/Photonica; **xv** Copyright © Frank Capri/Saga Archive Photos; **xvi** Photography by Laurie Rubin; **xviii** Copyright © 1996 Ann Giordano/Photonica; **xix** Ron Rovtar; **xx, xxi** Larry Cameron; **S2–S3** Photos by Sharon Hoogstraten; **S6** Photo by Sharon Hoogstraten; **S8** Copyright © Richard T. Nowitz/Corbis; **S9** *Young Knight* (1893), Aubrey Beardsley. Victoria & Albert Museum, London/Art Resource; **S11** *top* Photo by Sharon Hoogstraten; *bottom* The Granger Collection, New York; **S12** The Granger Collection, New York; **S14** *background* Photo by Sharon Hoogstraten; *foreground* Copyright © Adam Woolfitt/Woodfin Camp/PictureQuest; **S16** The Granger Collection, New York; **S17** *left* King Arthur in Combat (14th century), Robert de Barron; *right* The Granger Collection, New York; **S19** Detail of *January's Shadows*, Robert Frank.

Unit One

12–13 *background* Copyright © PhotoDisc; **15** *bottom* Illustration by Robert Ingpen, courtesy of Viking Press; *right* Random House; **17** *bottom left* Illustration by Hugh Harrison; *bottom center, Mexican Morning* (1942). Private Collection/GG Kopilak/SuperStock; *bottom right, Ada & Vincent* (1967), Alex Katz. Oil on canvas, 94½" × 71½". Copyright © Alex Katz/Licensed by VAGA, New York/Marlborough Gallery, New York; **18** *January's Shadows*, Robert Frank; **19** RMIP/Richard Haynes; **25** Detail of illustration by Pamela Daly; **36** The Granger Collection, New York; **37** *top* Detail of illustration by Rosanne Kaloustian; *bottom* Kiwi Studios; **42** *bottom* Courtesy of Algonquin Books of Chapel Hill; **45** Copyright © Bill Eichner; **46** *background, inset top* UPI/Corbis-Bettmann; *center* DLF Group; *inset bottom* Copyright © Seny Norasingh/Light Sensitive; **49, 55** Details of *Silent Fall*, Nicholas Wilton. Acrylic on wood, 24" × 14½"; **53** *background* Pat O'Hara/Corbis; **56** Corbis-Bettmann; **63** AP/Wide World Photos; **64;** AP/Wide World Photos **65** AP/Wide World Photos; **74** Margaret Miller; **82** *left* Illustration by Ken Marschall, from *Exploring the Titanic* by Robert D. Ballard. Copyright © 1988 by Madison Publishing Inc. Used by permission of Scholastic Inc.; *bottom* The *Boston Globe*; *right* Grolier Publishing; **83** *top* Corbis-Bettmann; *bottom* Courtesy of the Franklin D. Roosevelt Library; **85** *left* Brown Brothers; *center* Lewis W. Hine Collection. Milstein Division of United States History, Local History & Genealogy, The New York Public Library, Astor Lenox and Tilden Foundations; **86** RMIP/Richard Haynes; **87** *left to right* Copyright © Archive Photos/PNI; The Granger Collection, New York; Copyright © Archive Photos/PNI; UPI/Corbis-Bettmann; Corbis-Bettmann; **108** Courtesy of The New York Times; **110** Gillian Darley/Corbis; **120** Schomberg Center for Research in Black Culture, The New York Public Library, Astor, Lenox and Tilden Foundations; **121** Copyright © Victoria McCormick/Animals Animals; **122** *montage* Copyright © Victoria McCormick/Animals Animals; Copyright © James H. Carmichael, Jr./The Image Bank; Copyright © Renee

Lynn/Photo Researchers, Inc.; **125** E. H. Rao/Photo Researchers, Inc.; **126** *montage* Copyright © Michael Fogden/DRK Photo; Copyright © Pat Anderson/Visuals Unlimited; **127** Copyright © Sudip D. Bhaumik/Dinodia Picture Agency; **129** *montage* Copyright © Ralph Reinhold/Animals Animals; Copyright © 1999 Ben Klaffke; **130–131** *montage* Copyright © Jim Merli/Visuals Unlimited; D. Cavagnaro/DRK Photo; **133** *montage* Paolo Koch/Photo Researchers, Inc.; Copyright © Marilyn Silverstone/Magnum Photos, Inc.; **137** Stock Montage; **138, 140** Copyright © 1996 Alon Reininger/Contact Press Images; **150** *center left* Austin History Center, Austin Public Library; *bottom, left to right* Austin History Center, Austin Public Library; The Granger Collection, New York; Smithsonian Institution; **151** *center right* Austin History Center, Austin Public Library; *bottom, left to right* Austin History Center, Austin Public Library; National Park Service: Statue of Liberty National Monument; Copyright © Henry Ford Museum & Greenfield Village; **152–153** *bottom* Museum of the City of New York; **152** *center right* O. Henry Memorial Museum; **153** *right* Montana Historical Society; **163** *top* Detail of *Portrait of Prince Eristoff* (1925), Tamara de Lempicka. Courtesy of Barry Frideman Ltd., New York. Copyright © 1996 Artists Rights Society (ARS), New York/SPADEM, Paris; *bottom* Austin History Center, Austin Public Library; **173** MGM, William Haines/The Everett Collection; **174** *top* 1935, Warner Brothers/The Kobal Collection; *center left, bottom left* The Everett Collection; **176** *top, Jimmy Valentine,* Learning Corp. of America. Distributed by Coronet/MTI Films, St. Louis, Missouri; *bottom* RMIP/Richard Haynes; **177** *top* Greensboro Historical Museum, Inc.; *center left* Modern Library/Random House; *bottom left* A Signet Classic/The Penguin Group; **184** Painting copyright © 1999 Brad Holland; **186, 187** School Division, Houghton Mifflin Company.

Unit Two

189 Illustration by Bernie Fuchs **191** *left to right* Little, Brown and Company; McFarland & Company, Inc. Publishers; *Robert Frost Among His Poems: A Literary Companion to the Poet's Own Biographical Contexts and Associations* © 1996 Jeffrey S. Cramer by permission of McFarland & Company, Inc., Publishers; Beacon Press; Penguin Putnam; **194** *Galena* (1988), Robert L. Barnum. Private Collection; **195** RMIP/Richard Haynes; **200** The Granger Collection, New York; **205** Copyright © Nancy Crampton; **218** Copyright © Coppelia Kahn; **220, 221** Copyright © City Year, Boston; **223** *top right* Corbis-Bettmann; *bottom left* AP/Wide World Photos; **224** Lewis W. Hine Collection. Milstein Division of United States History, Local History & Genealogy, The New York Public Library, Astor Lenox and Tilden Foundations; **232** Copyright © 1988 Chicago Tribune Co., all rights reserved; **234, 235** RMIP/Richard Haynes; **236** Copyright © Andrew Onyemere/Photonica; **237** *left* Manuelle Toussaint/Liaison Agency; *right* Georges Merillon/Liaison Agency; **245** *left to right* Heinemann Publishers; Copyright © Plays, Inc.; Movie Still Archives; Playbill® is a registered trademark of Playbill, Inc. All rights reserved. Used by permission; **247** Movie Still Archives; **248** Detail of *Rush Hour* (1983), George Segal. Courtesy Sidney Janis Gallery, New York. Copyright © George Segal/Licensed by VAGA, New York; **249** RMIP/Richard Haynes; **250** Photofest; **251** Movie Still Archives; **255** Photofest; **261** Movie Still Archives; **267, 271, 273** Photofest; **277** Culver Pictures; **279** Photo by Sharon Hoogstraten; **285** Detail of *Retrato de muchacha* [Portrait of a girl] (1929), Frida Kahlo. Oil on canvas, 46½″ × 31½″. Collection of the Dolores Olmedo Patiño Foundation, Museo Frida Kahlo, Mexico City; **287** *left* National Baseball Hall of Fame Library & Archive, Cooperstown, New York; *center, Wipe Out Discrimination* (1949), Milton Ackoff. Offset lithograph, printed in color, 43⅞″ × 32¾″. The Museum of Modern Art, New York, gift of the Congress of Industrial Organizations. Photography copyright © 1998 The

Museum of Modern Art, New York; *right* Archive Photos/PNI; **288–289** *background* Photo by Sharon Hoogstraten; **298** Courtesy of The Chicago Defender; **299** top Detail of *Baseball Scene of Batter, Catcher, and Umpire* (1915), Joseph Christian Leyendecker. Photo courtesy of the Archives of the American Illustrators Gallery, New York. Copyright © 1995 ARTShows and Products of Holderness 03245; **304** *left* Harvard University Archives; *right* Courtesy of C.T.I./GLAD Productions, Inc.; **305** Copyright © Peter Roger/Life Magazine; **306, 307, 308** AP/Wide World Photos; **310** *left, The Grasshopper and the Ant,* Charles Henry Bennett (1828–1867). Pen and ink drawing. The Granger Collection, New York; *right, Victorian Parlor II* (1945), Horace Pippin. Oil on canvas, 25¼″ × 30″. The Metropolitan Museum of Art, Arthur Hoppock Hearn Fund, 1958 (58.26); **311** Copyright © Tony Freeman/PhotoEdit; **314** The Granger Collection, New York; **320** Copyright © Alison Shaw; **322** RMIP International; **330** Illustration by Bernie Fuchs; **332, 333** School Division, Houghton Mifflin Company.

Unit Three

345 *Retrato de muchacha* [Portrait of a girl] (1929), Frida Kahlo. Oil on canvas, 46½″ × 31½″. Collection of the Dolores Olmedo Patiño Foundation, Museo Frida Kahlo, Mexico City; **346** *Idle Hands* (1935), Will Barnet. Oil on canvas, 36″ × 26″. Licensed by VAGA, New York; **347** RMIP/Richard Haynes; **348** *top* Detail of *Autobiographical* (1954), Moses Soyer. Courtesy of ACA Galleries, New York; **360** AP/Wide World Photos; **361, 362** Copyright © G. Biss/Masterfile; **368, 371** *background* Photos by Sharon Hoogstraten; **371** *inset* Copyright © G. Biss/Masterfile; **373** *El abrazo* [The hug] (1966), Fletcher Martin. Acrylic on paper, 22″ × 17″. Private collection; **374** Eugenio Castro; **375, 378** Artichoke. Copyright © Jeff Venier/Landry Design; Illustration copyright © Jeff Venier/Landry Design; **380** Archive France/Archive Photos; **390** Rollie McKenna; **392** Enzo and Paolo Ragazzi/Corbis; **395** *left* UPI/Bettmann; *right* AP/Wide World Photos; **396, 397** Copyright © Ted Wood Photography; **402** *right* The Granger Collection, New York; **409** Copyright © Frank Capri/Saga/Archive Photos; **410** *left, Skater* (1956), Giacomo Manzu. Bronze, 80″ × 23″ × 17⅝″. Hirshhorn Museum and Sculpture Garden, Smithsonian Institution, Washington, D.C. Gift of Joseph H. Hirshhorn, 1966. Photo by Lee Stalsworth; *bottom* Detail of illustration by Kam Mak; **411** Copyright © Archive Photos; **412** *left, Le jardin potager, Yerres* [The kitchen garden, Yerres] (1875–77), Gustave Caillebotte. Private collection; *right* Illustration by Ruth Sanderson; **413** Illustration by Paul Rátz de Tagyos; **414** RMIP/Richard Haynes; **415** *top, Rush Hour* (1983), George Segal. Courtesy Sidney Janis Gallery, New York. Copyright © George Segal/Licensed by VAGA, New York; **416** *top* Copyright © Archive Photos; **417, 424** Illustration by Paul Rátz de Tagyos; **428** Copyright © Archive Photos; **430** Detail of *Rush Hour* (1983), George Segal. Courtesy Sidney Janis Gallery, New York. Copyright © George Segal/Licensed by VAGA, New York; **431** UPI/Bettmann; **432** *top right* Copyright © 1995 Hank Morgan; *bottom left, bottom center, bottom right* Copyright © Sam Odgen; **437** AP/Wide World Photos; **438** *top* Detail of illustration by Ruth Sanderson; *bottom* Clay Perry/Corbis; **439, 441, 445, 452, 454** Photos by Sharon Hoogstraten; **460** Copyright © Shel Silverstein; **462** *left* Stock Montage; *right* AP/Wide World Photos; **463** NASA; **464–465** Copyright © John Lurner/Tony Stone Images; **466** Science Source/Photo Researchers, Inc./NASA; **469** AP/Wide World Photos; **470–471** Reprinted courtesy of the Boston Globe; **474–477** *top background* Kris Coppieters/SuperStock; **474** *top* Copyright © Frank Capri/Saga/Archive Photos; *center left* Copyright © 2002 by Universal City Studio, Inc. Courtesy of Universal Studios Publishing Rights, a division of Universal Studios Licensing, Inc. All rights reserved; *bottom middle* Reprinted by permission of Don Congdon Associates, Inc.; *bottom right* Corbis-Bettmann; **475** *center right* Reprinted by permission of Don Congdon Associates, Inc.; *bottom left* NASA; *bottom right* Courtesy of Alliance Atlantis Communications Inc.; **476–477** *bottom background* Archive Photos; **476** Everett Collection, Inc.; **477** *left* AP/Wide World Photos; *center right, left to right* From *1984* by George Orwell. Reprinted by permission of Penguin Books; From *Brave New World* by Aldous Huxley. Copyright © 1932 by Harper & Brothers. Used by permission of HarperCollins; From *Cat's Cradle* by Kurt Vonnegut, Jr. Reprinted by permission of Dell Publishing, a division of Bantam Doubleday Dell Publishing Group, Inc.; From *Fahrenheit 451* by Ray Bradbury. Reprinted by permission of Ballantine Books, a division of Random House, Inc.; **492** Detail of painting by Nancy Ekholm Burkert; **502–505** *top background* Kris Coppieters/SuperStock; **502** *inset* Copyright © Frank Capri/Saga/Archive Photos; **504** *top* AP/Wide World Photos; *left* From *The Martian Chronicles* by Ray Bradbury (Bantam ed: jacket cover) Used by permission of Bantam Books, a division of Random House, Inc.; *right* From *Fahrenheit 451* by Ray Bradbury. Reprinted by permission of Ballantine Books, a division of Random House, Inc.; **504-505** *background* Archive Photos; **505** *bottom, left to right* From *Something Wicked This Way Comes* by Ray Bradbury. Copyright © 1962, 1977 by Ray Bradbury. Used by permission of Avon Books, a division of The Hearst Corporation; From *A Medicine for Melancholy* by Ray Bradbury. Copyright © 1990 by Ray Bradbury. Cover illustration by Tim O'Brien. Used by permission of Avon Books, a division of The Hearst Corporation; From *Vintage Bradbury* by Ray Bradbury. Reprinted by permission of Vintage Books; From *The Toynbee Convector* by Ray Bradbury. Reprinted by permission of Ballantine Books, a division of Random House, Inc.; **512** Copyright © Kamil Vojnar/Photonica; **514, 515** School Division, Houghton Mifflin Company.

Unit Four

516 Photography by Laurie Rubin; **519** Illustration by Stephen Peringer; **521** RMIP/Richard Haynes; **522** Detail of *Girl at Piano* (1966), Will Barnet. Oil on canvas, 64″ × 39″. Private collection. Copyright © 1995 Will Barnet/Licensed by VAGA, New York; **523** Photo by Sharon Hoogstraten; **526** Copyright © Tony Stone Images; **532** Copyright © Jerry Bauer; **534, 535, 536–545** *top*, **539, 545** Photos by Sharon Hoogstraten; **548** Copyright © Sophie Baker; **549–552** *top* Copyright © PhotoDisc; **549** *center* Copyright © FoodPix; *bottom* Danny Lehman/Corbis; **550** *top left* North Carolina Museum of Art/Corbis; *center* Historical Picture Archive/Corbis; *bottom right* Alastair Shay, Papilio/Corbis; **551** *center* Gianni Dagli Orti/Corbis; *bottom left* Copyright © David Young-Wolfe/PhotoEdit; *bottom right* Mary Evans Picture Library; **552** *bottom right* Copyright © Richard Hutchings/PhotoEdit; **553** *top* Detail of lithograph with hand coloring, Honoré Daumier. Courtesy of the Boston Public Library, Print Department; *bottom* Sovfoto; **554–555** *border* Copyright © PhotoDisc; **562** Detail of lithograph with hand coloring, Honoré Daumier. Courtesy of the Boston Public Library, Print Department; **563** Bernard Gotfryd/Archive Photos; **564** *background* Copyright © Adam Jones/Natural Selection; *bottom left* From a collection of paste jewelry (18th century), French and English. Cameo Corner, London/Bridgeman Art Library, London/New York; *top right, Turpin's Flight Through Edmonton,* George Cruikshank. Private collection/Bridgeman Art Library, London/New York; *bottom right, The Escort,* Robert Alexander

Hillingford. John Noott Galleries, Broadway, Worcestershire, U.K./Bridgeman Art Library, London/New York; **565, 567, 569** *background* Photo by Sharon Hoogstraten; **571** *top* Detail of illustration by Charles Mikolaycak. Copyright © 1995 Carole Kismaric Mikolaycak; *bottom* The Granger Collection, New York; **573** Courtesy of the author; **575** *left* Photofest; *right* Movie Still Archives; **576–577** UPI/Corbis-Bettmann; **578** Courtesy of the author; **579–581** RMIP/Richard Haynes; **586** *left to right* Detail of painting by Jan Wahlin; Illustration by Hugh Harrison; *Hermit* (1888), Mikhail Vasilievich Nesterov. Oil on canvas, 91 cm × 84 cm. The State Russian Museum, St. Petersburg, Russia; RMIP/Richard Haynes; **588** Austin History Center, Austin Public Library; **589** Illustrations by Meg Kelleher Aubrey; **590** RMIP/Richard Haynes; **591** *top* Detail of *Letters* (1992), Kim English. Oil, 17″ × 18″. Private collection; *bottom* Kiwi Studios; **600** Courtesy of Arte Público Press; **601** *top* Detail of illustration by Meg Kelleher Aubrey; *bottom map* Robert Voights; **602** *background* Cupak/Martius/H. Armstrong Roberts; **616** Rick Janson; **617–619** Richard Nowitz/National Geographic Society Image Collection; **620** Photos Copyright © Bob Sacha; **621** *background* UPI/Corbis-Bettmann; *center right* Underwood & Underwood/Corbis; *bottom right* Corbis-Bettmann; **622** Corbis-Bettmann; **625** AP/Wide World Photos; **627** Reprinted by permission of Don Congdon and Associates, Inc. Copyright © 1982 by Russell Baker; **628** Copyright © Archive Photos/PNI; **630** Copyright © Yvonne Hemsey/Liaison Agency; **635** *bottom* The Granger Collection, New York; **642** Photography by Laurie Rubin; **644, 645** School Division, Houghton Mifflin Company.

Unit Five

652 Copyright © 1996 Ann Giordano/Photonica; **653–654** *background* MicroArt; **654** Frances King Collection/Sacramento (California) Archives and Museum Collection Center; **655** Joseph A. Carvalho Collection; **656** Brown Brothers; **657** RMIP/Richard Haynes; **658** Illustration by Ken Marschall copyright © 1997 from *Inside the Titanic*, a Loewe/Madison Press Book; **659** Courtesy of The Titanic Historical Society, Inc. Photo by Sharon Hoogstraten; **660** *top* Corbis-Bettmann; **662–663** Illustration by Ken Marschall copyright © 1997 from *Inside the Titanic*, a Loewe/Madison Press Book; **661** Joseph A. Carvalho Collection; **664** Corbis-Bettmann; **665** Photos by Sharon Hoogstraten; **667, 668** *top middle* Corbis-Bettman; **668** *top right, bottom left,* **669** *top,* **670** Photos by Sharon Hoogstraten; **673** From *A Night to Remember.* Courtesy of Carlton International Media Ltd.; **674** Barbara Nitke; **675–678** Photos courtesy of the Texas Historical Commission; **679** *top,* **686** Detail of illustration by Wendell Minor, from *Red Fox Running* by Eve Bunting. Illustration copyright © 1993 Wendell Minor. Reprinted by permission of Clarion Books/Houghton Mifflin Company. All rights reserved; **691** Detail of *Albert's Son* (1959), Andrew Wyeth. Tempera on board, 74 cm × 61.5 cm. The National Museum of Contemporary Art, Oslo, Norway. Photo by Jacques Lathion, Nasjonalgalleriet; **692** Farrar, Straus & Giroux; **694–695** *background* Stock Boston; *foreground* Ralph Shaw Collection/Sacramento (California) Archives and Museum Collection Center; **695** *foreground* Frances King Collection/Sacramento (California) Archives and Museum Collection Center; **697** *background* Stock Boston; *foreground* Brown Brothers; **698** University of Notre Dame Press; **705** Ron Rovtar; **706** *left* Oxford Book of Historical Stories, Oxford University Press; *bottom* From *I, Juan de Pareja.* Used by permission of HarperCollins Canada Ltd.; *right* From *Dragonwings.* Used by permission of Harper & Row; **708** RMIP/Richard Haynes; **710** *background* Photo by Sharon Hoogstraten; *foreground* Photos by Maria Daniels; **712**

Photos by Sharon Hoogstraten; 714 Photo by Maria Daniels; 717 *bottom left,* 719, 720 Photo by Sharon Hoogstraten; 721 Photo by Maria Daniels; 722–724 Photo by Sharon Hoogstraten; 725 Michael Bennett. Courtesy of the Perseus Project (www.perseus.tufts.edu); 728 AP/Wide World Photos; 731 Corbis-Bettmann; 732 *background* AP/Wide World Photos; *left* Copyright © Selwyn Tait/Black Star/PNI; *right* Copyright © A. Ramey/Stock Boston/PNI; 739 AP/Wide World Photos; 741 Kevin R. Morris/Corbis; 744 Barbara Savage Cheresh; 746–750 *border* North Wind Picture Archives; 746 *top, center left, bottom middle* Photos copyright © 1999. Used by permission of Virginia Hamilton; *bottom right* Corbis-Bettmann; 747 *center right* Photo copyright © 1999. Used by permission of Virginia Hamilton; *bottom left* Reprinted with the permission of Simon & Schuster Books for Young Readers, an imprint of Simon & Schuster Children's Publishing Division from *The House of Dies Drear* by Virginia Hamilton, illustrated by Eros Keith. Illustrations copyright © 1968 Macmillan Publishing Company; *bottom middle* UPI/Corbis-Bettmann; 748 Jim Callaway Photography; 751 *background* Courtesy of The Bostonian Society/Old State House; *foreground, The Boston Slave Riot, and Trial of Anthony Burns.* Boston: Fetridge and Company, 1854. This item is reproduced by permission of the Huntington Library, San Marino, California; 752 Stock Montage; 754 From *History of Harvard Law School, vol. 2,* by Charles Warren; 756 Corbis-Bettmann; 759 From *Men of Mark* by Rev. William J. Simmons; 761, 764 Corbis-Bettmann; 765 Courtesy of the Massachusetts Historical Society; 766–767 *border* North Wind Picture Archives; 772–773 *border* NorthWind Picture Archives; 774–775 *top background* Earth Scenes/Copyright © Peter Weimann; 774 Photo copyright © 1999. Used by permission of Virginia Hamilton; 775 Copyright © C. Bradley Simmons/Bruce Coleman, Inc.; 776–779 *border* North Wind Picture Archives; 776 Photos copyright © 1999. Used by permission of Virginia Hamilton; 777 RMIP/Richard Haynes; 778 *top* Photo copyright © 1999. Used by permission of Virginia Hamilton; *bottom left* School Division, Houghton Mifflin Company; *bottom right* From *The Planet of Junior Brown.* Used by permission of Simon & Schuster; 779 *bottom left* From *M. C. Higgins, the Great.* Used by permission of Simon & Schuster; *bottom middle* From *Justice and Her Brothers.* Used by permission of Scholastic Inc.; *bottom right* Illustraion by Leo & Diane Dillon from *Her Stories: African American Folktales, Fairy Tales, and True Tales* by Virginia Hamilton. Published by the Blue Sky Press, an imprint of Scholastic Inc. Illustration copyright © 1995 by Leo & Diane Dillon. Reprinted by permission; 788 Copyright © 1996 Ann Giordano/Photonica; 790, 791 School Division, Houghton Mifflin Company.

Unit Six

792–793 *background map* John Sandford; 793–795 Photos by Rolland Krueger; 796–799 *background maps* John Sandford; 796 *top* Photo by Carl Purcell; *bottom* The Granger Collection, New York; 797 *top left* Odyssey/Frerck/Chicago; *top center* The Bettmann Archive; *top right* Copyright © Earl & Nazima Kowall/Corbis; *middle left* Copyright © Tom Wagner/Odyssey/Chicago; *center* Copyright © 1992 by David Wisniewski. Reprinted by permission of Clarion Books/Houghton Mifflin Co. All rights reserved; *middle right* Copyright © Andre Jenny/Stock South/PNI; *bottom left* Copyright © Archivo Iconographico, S.A./Corbis; *bottom center* La Casa del Libro, San Juan, Puerto Rico; *bottom right* Copyright © Charlotte Kahler; 798 Copyright © James A. Sugar/Black Star Publishing/PictureQuest; 799 Detail of Mughal portrait of Akbar and Prince Salim (19th century), The Newark

Museum/Art Resource, New York; **800** Copyright © Corbis; **803** Courtesy of the author; **804** *background* Copyright © Ann Purcell; Carl Purcell/Words & Pictures/PictureQuest; *foreground* Copyright © Owen Franken/Stock, Boston/PictureQuest; **805** Copyright © Art Wolfe/Stone; **806** Copyright © Art Wolfe/Stone; **808** Copyright © James A. Sugar/Black Star Publishing/PictureQuest; **810–811** *background map* John Sandford; **810** Detail of *Portrait of a Gentleman* (16th century), Bartolomeo Veneto. Galleria Nazionale d'Arte Antica, Rome/Canali PhotoBank, Milan (Italy)/SuperStock; **811** Detail *of Beggars and Street Characters* (1516), Zhou Chen. Album leaves, ink and colors on paper. Honolulu (Hawaii) Academy of Arts, gift of Mrs. Carter Galt, 1956 (2239.1); **817** Photo by K. Yep; **825** Culver Pictures; **826–827** *background map* John Sandford; **827** Copyright © Richard T. Nowitz/Corbis; **828** Copyright © Richard T. Nowitz/Corbis; **831** Courtesy of the author; **832** *background* Copyright © Ron Watts/Corbis; **836–837** *background map* John Sandford; **836** Detail of an illustration by Byron Gin; **837** *top, right,* Copyright © 1992 by David Wisniewski. Reprinted by permission of Clarion Books/Houghton Mifflin Co. All rights reserved; *bottom* Detail of *Mujer con pescados* [Woman with fish] (1980), Francisco Zúñiga. Lithograph, 21⅞″ × 29½″, edition of 135. Courtesy of Brewster Gallery, New York; **839, 841, 843–844** Copyright © 1992 by David Wisniewski. Reprinted by permission of Clarion Books/Houghton Mifflin Co. All rights reserved; **844** Courtesy of Clarion Books; **852** Mario Longoria; **853** Illustration by Byron Gin; **855** Courtesy of the Barker Texas History Center, University of Texas; **856–857** *background map* John Sandford; **866** From *Samburu* by Nigel Pavitt. Copyright © 1992 Nigel Pavitt, reprinted by permission of Henry Holt and Co., Inc.; **857** *bottom,* **861, 863, 864** Courtesy of Adrienne McGrath. Photo by Sharon Hoogstraten; **865** Courtesy of Norma J. Livo; **875** RMIP/Richard Haynes.

End Matter

R2 *left* Illustration by Hugh Harrison; *right* The Granger Collection, New York; **R4** Art Resource, New York; **R4–R5** From *Across the Centuries* in *Houghton Mifflin Social Studies* by Armento, et al. Coyright © 1999 by Houghton Mifflin Company. Reprinted by permission of Houghton Mifflin Company. All rights reserved; **R5** Art Resource, New York.

Teacher Review Panels *(continued)*

Bonnie Garrett Davis Middle School, Compton School District

Sally Jackson Madrona Middle School, Torrance Unified School District

Sharon Kerson Los Angeles Center for Enriched Studies, Los Angeles Unified School District

Gail Kidd Center Middle School, Azusa School District

Myra LeBendig Foshay Learning Center, Los Angeles Unified School District

Dan Manske Elmhurst Middle School, Oakland Unified School District

Joe Olague Language Arts Department Chairperson, Alder Middle School, Fontana School District

Pat Salo Sixth-Grade Village Leader, Hidden Valley Middle School, Escondido Elementary School District

FLORIDA

Judi Briant English Department Chairperson, Armwood High School, Hillsborough County School District

Beth Johnson Polk County English Supervisor, Polk County School District

Sharon Johnston Learning Resource Specialist, Evans High School, Orange County School District

Eileen Jones English Department Chairperson, Spanish River High School, Palm Beach County School District

Jan McClure Winter Park High School, Orange County School District

Wanza Murray English Department Chairperson (retired), Vero Beach Senior High School, Indian River City School District

Shirley Nichols Language Arts Curriculum Specialist Supervisor, Marion County School District

Debbie Nostro Ocoee Middle School, Orange County School District

Barbara Quinaz Assistant Principal, Horace Mann Middle School, Dade County School District

OHIO

Joseph Bako English Department Chairperson, Carl Shuler Middle School, Cleveland City School District

Deb Delisle Language Arts Department Chairperson, Ballard Brady Middle School, Orange School District

Ellen Geisler English/Language Arts Department Chairperson, Mentor Senior High School, Mentor School District

Dr. Mary Gove English Department Chairperson, Shaw High School, East Cleveland School District

Loraine Hammack Executive Teacher of the English Department, Beachwood High School, Beachwood City School District

Sue Nelson Shaw High School, East Cleveland School District

Mary Jane Reed English Department Chairperson, Solon High School, Solon City School District

Nancy Strauch English Department Chairperson, Nordonia High School, Nordonia Hills City School District

Ruth Vukovich Hubbard High School, Hubbard Exempted Village School District

TEXAS

Gloria Anderson Language Arts Department Chairperson, Campbell Middle School, Cypress Fairbanks Independent School District

Gwen Ferguson Assistant Principal, Northwood Middle School, North Forest Independent School District

Rebecca Hadavi Parkland Middle School, Ysleta Independent School District

Patricia Jackson Pearce Middle School, Austin Independent School District

Sandy Mattox Coppell Middle School North, Coppell Independent School District

Adrienne C. Myers Foster Middle School, Longview Independent School District

Pam Potts Clute Intermediate School, Brazosport Independent School District

Frank Westermann Jackson Middle School, North East Independent School District

Bessie B. Wilson W.E. Greiner Middle School, Dallas Independent School District

Manuscript Reviewers *(continued)*

Shirley Herzog Reading Department Coordinator, Fairfield Middle School, Fairfield, Ohio

Ellen Kamimoto Ahwahnee Middle School, Fresno, California

Maryann Lyons Literacy Specialist and Mentor Teacher, San Francisco Unified School District, San Francisco, California

Karis MacDonnell Dario Middle School, Miami, Florida

Bonnie J. Mansell Downey Adult School, Downey, California

Martha Mitchell Memorial Middle School, Orlando, Florida

Ellen Moir GATE Coordinator and teacher, Twin Peaks Middle School, Poway, California

Nancy Nachman Landmark High School, Jacksonville, Florida

Katerine L. Noether Warren E. Hyde Middle School, Cupertino, California

Gloria Perry Bancroft Middle School, Long Beach, California

Karen Williams Perry English Department Chairperson, Kennedy Junior High School, Lisle, Illinois

Julia Pferdehirt Freelance writer; former Special Education Teacher, Middleton, Wisconsin

Phyllis Stewart Rude English Department Head, Mears Junior-Senior High School, Anchorage, Alaska

Leo Schubert Bettendorf Middle School, Bettendorf, Iowa

Lynn Thomas Borel Middle School, Burlingame, California

Gertrude H. Vannoy Curriculum Liaison Specialist and Gifted and Horizon Teacher, Meany Middle School, Seattle, Washington

Richard Wagner Language Arts Curriculum Coordinator, Paradise Valley School District, Phoenix, Arizona

Stevie Wheeler Humanities Department Chair, Rincon Middle School, San Diego, California

Stephen J. Zadravec Newmarket Junior-Senior High School, Newmarket, New Hampshire

STUDENT GUIDE TO THE CALIFORNIA STANDARDS

At the beginning of every lesson in this book, you will see a listing of Key Standards covered in the lesson. You will often see Other Standards as well that relate to the lesson. The standards are identified by combinations of letters and numbers (like R1.1). These combinations are codes that refer to standards from the Reading and Language Arts Framework for California Public Schools. The standards define the skills that you are expected to develop during 7th grade.

The following chart contains a simplified version of those standards. When you see a list of codes, you can use this chart to find out which skills you will be studying as you work through the selection. In this way, you will be able to keep track of what you learn throughout the year.

READING (R)

1.0 Word Study, Fluency, and Vocabulary Development

Use word origins, word relationships, and context clues to figure out the meaning of unfamiliar words.

Vocabulary and Concept Development

1.1 Identify idioms, analogies, metaphors, and similes in prose and poetry.

1.2 Use knowledge of roots and affixes to understand vocabulary in different content areas.

1.3 Use context clues (definition, example, restatement, contrast) to determine the meaning of unknown words.

2.0 Reading Comprehension (Informational Materials)

Read and understand purposes of and different types of reading materials. Restate and connect key ideas, arguments, and points of view. Use the structure and organization of a piece for help in understanding it.

Structural Features of Informational Materials

2.1 Understand differences between various categories of informational materials (such as textbooks, newspapers, and manuals).

2.2 Locate information by using different types of consumer, workplace, and public documents.

2.3 Analyze text that uses cause-and-effect organization.

Comprehension and Analysis of Text

2.4 Identify an author's argument and point of view in a text.

2.5 Understand and explain the use of a simple device by following technical directions.

Expository Critique

2.6 Evaluate the strength and accuracy of the evidence an author uses to support a claim. Recognize bias and stereotyping.

3.0 Literary Response and Analysis

Read and respond to important works of literature. Understand the meaning of the ideas presented and connect them to other pieces of literature.

Structural Features of Literature

3.1 Be able to describe the purposes and characteristics of different forms of prose, such as the short story, novel, or essay.

Analysis of Narrative Text

3.2 Identify events that advance the plot and describe how they explain the past, present, and future.

3.3 Analyze characters by examining what they think, say, and do, and by studying the words of the narrator and the reactions of other characters.

3.4 Identify and analyze themes that appear across works.

3.5 Contrast points of view (first and third person, limited and omniscient) and explain how they affect the narrative.

Literary Criticism

3.6 Analyze several responses to a literary work. Decide how different literary elements may have affected those responses.

WRITING (W)

1.0 Writing Strategies

Use the writing process to write clear, coherent, and focused essays. The writing should show an understanding of audience and purpose and contain an introduction, supporting details, and a conclusion.

Organization and Focus

1.1 Choose an appropriate type of organization, and use transitions to connect ideas effectively.

1.2 Support statements with such evidence as facts, statistics, examples, and anecdotes.

1.3 Use such strategies as notetaking, outlining, and summarizing to help determine a structure for composition drafts.

Research and Technology

1.4 Identify research topics, and develop questions and ideas to help guide investigation of the topic.

1.5 Use citations and a properly formatted bibliography to give credit to all sources used.

1.6 Create effective documents by using word-processing skills and publishing programs.

Evaluation and Revision

1.7 Revise writing to improve organization, word choice, and logic.

2.0 Types of Writing

Write narrative, expository, persuasive, and descriptive texts that show correct grammar, usage, punctuation, and spelling. Writing should also demonstrate understanding of all the skills mentioned in Writing Standard 1.0.

2.1 Write fictional or autobiographical narratives that contain a standard plot line, complex major and minor characters, and a definite setting.

2.2 Write responses to literature that present interpretations that show careful reading and understanding of the text, and that support the interpretation with evidence from the selection.

2.3 Write research reports that contain a clear focus, include evidence gathered through a formal research process, and demonstrate documentation of sources.

2.4 Write a persuasive composition that presents a clear proposition or proposal, supports that position with evidence, and addresses a reader's possible arguments.

2.5 Write summaries of reading materials that include the main idea and key supporting details, and that are written in the student's own words.

WRITTEN AND ORAL ENGLISH LANGUAGE CONVENTIONS (LC)

Show an understanding of sentence structure, grammar, punctuation, capitalization, and spelling.

1.0 English Language Conventions

1.1 Place modifiers correctly; use the active voice.

1.2 Identify and properly use infinitives and participles; have clear pronoun/antecedent references.

1.3 Identify all parts of speech and types of sentences.

1.4 Use the mechanics of writing correctly; demonstrate correct language usage.

1.5 Use hyphens, dashes, brackets, and semicolons correctly.

1.6 Use correct capitalization.

1.7 Correctly spell words when adding affixes to base words.

LISTENING AND SPEAKING (LS)

1.0 Listening and Speaking Strategies

Deliver oral presentations that present ideas clearly and show an awareness of audience. Evaluate the content of oral presentations.

Comprehension

1.1 Ask the speaker questions to gather information or evidence that supports the speaker's statements.

1.2 Determine the speaker's attitude.

1.3 Respond to persuasive messages by questioning, challenging, or agreeing with the statements.

Organization and Delivery of Oral Communication

1.4 Organize information to achieve a particular purpose, and to appeal to the audience.

1.5 Arrange supporting details, reasons, etc., in a way that will be most effective for the audience.

1.6 Use voice, gestures, and eye contact effectively to keep audience interested.

Evaluation of Oral and Media Communications

1.7 Provide helpful feedback to the speaker about both content and the effect on the listener.

1.8 Analyze the effect on the viewer of images, text, and sound in electronic journalism.

2.0 Types of Presentations and Their Characteristics

Deliver different types of well-organized formal presentations that show a command of standard American English and display the skills and strategies listed in Listening and Speaking Standard 1.0.

2.1 Deliver narrative presentations that contain a standard plot line, complex major and minor characters, and a definite setting.

2.2 Deliver oral summaries of articles and books that include the main idea and key supporting details, and that are written in the student's own words.

2.3 Deliver research presentations that contain a clear focus, include evidence gathered through a formal research process, and demonstrate documentation of sources.

2.4 Deliver persuasive presentations that present a clear proposition or proposal, support that position with evidence, and address a reader's possible arguments.